ENCYCLOPEDIA OF
DOGS

ENCYCLOPEDIA OF DOGS

TOM JACKSON

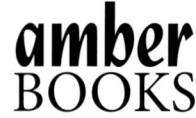

Copyright © 2024 Amber Books Ltd

All rights reserved. No part of this publication may be reproduced, stored in a retrieval system, or transmitted in any form or by any means, electronic, mechanical, photocopying, recording, or otherwise, without prior written permission of the copyright holder.

Published by
Amber Books Ltd
United House
North Road
London N7 9DP
United Kingdom
www.amberbooks.co.uk
Facebook: amberbooks
YouTube: amberbooksltd
Instagram: amberbooksltd
X(Twitter): @amberbooks

ISBN: 978-1-83886-447-7

Project Editor: Anna Brownbridge
Designer: Keren Harragan and Rick Fawcett
Picture Research: Adam Gnych and Terry Forshaw

Printed in China

Contents

Introduction	6
Companion Dogs	8
Hunting Dogs	166
Working Dogs	292
Index	446
Picture credits	448

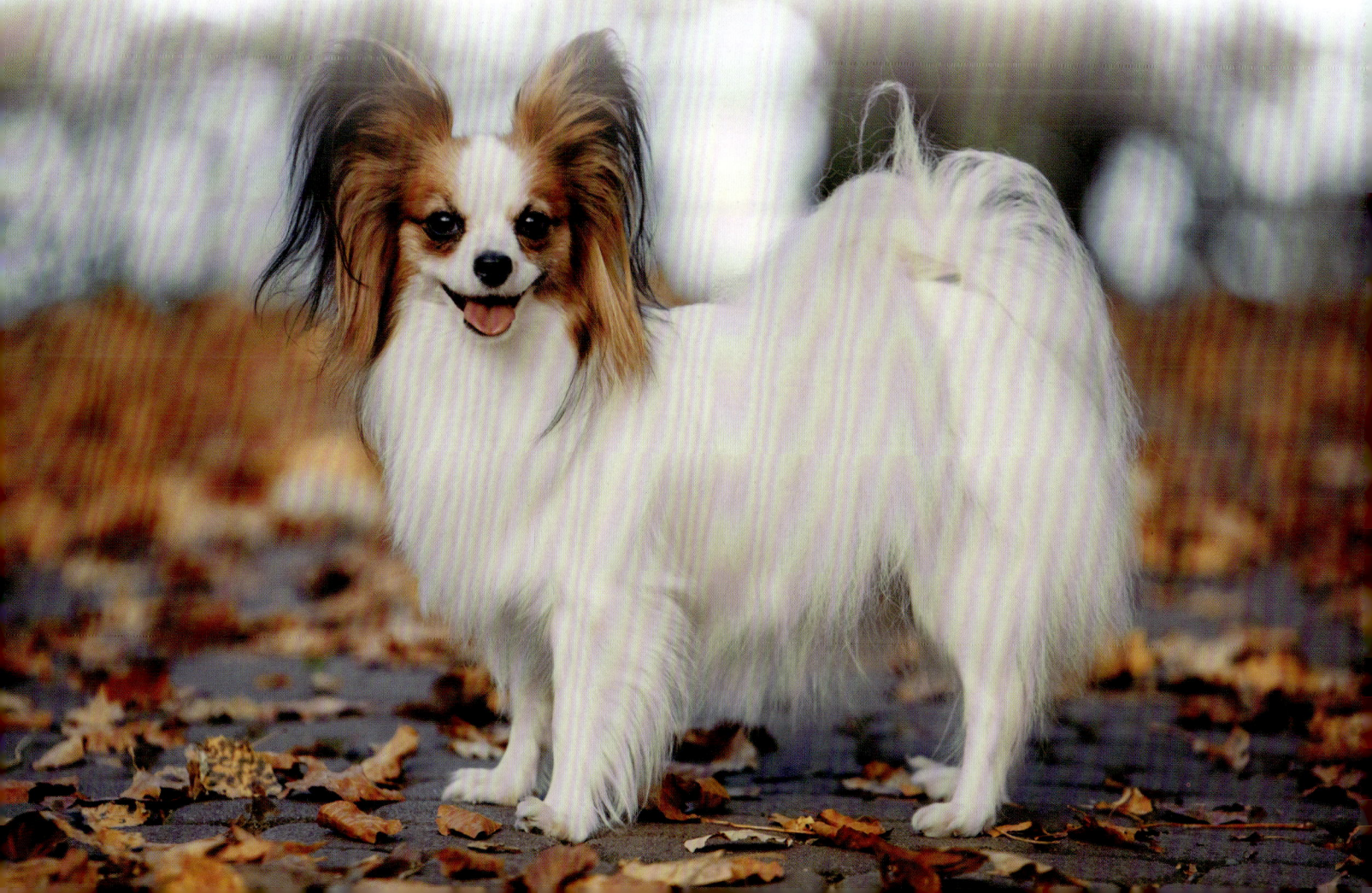

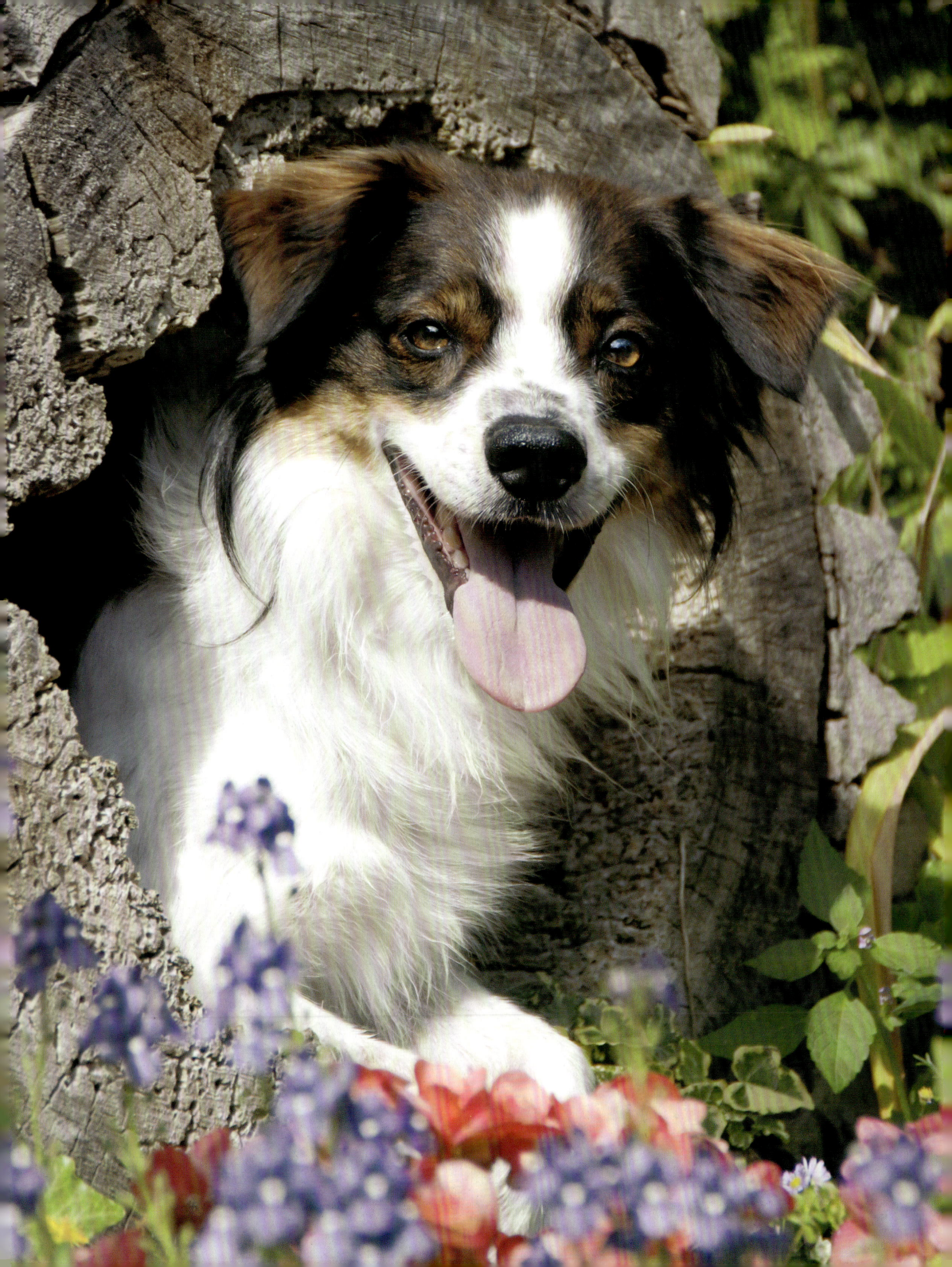

Introduction

No other animal has got so close to us as the dog. It has a place in homes, our workplaces and our hearts. These incredible animals have two sides, two opposites, and we are drawn to both. Firstly, the dog is a smart, athletic and independent animal that is just one step from life on the wild side. By contrast we have bred these amazing creatures into hundreds of breeds, each one with a distinct character and look and which was created for a very particular purpose.

This book casts an eye across the full expanse of dogkind, from the primitive breeds that have been unchanged for millennia to the hard-working farm dogs, many hunting breeds and "designer dogs" being developed today. We will learn something of the history of each, guidance on making a home for different breeds and tips on how to provide them with care. The dog breeds are drawn from all corners of the world and walks of life but nevertheless they have one true job, to be our friend, our unquestioning companion. They simply make life better. In the wise words of the esteemed dog lover, C.J. Frick:

"Be the person your dog thinks you are."

OPPOSITE:
Something to smile about
A kromfohrländer seems happy staying cool on a warm day inside this hollow log. It is typical of this chirpy German breed, which owes its very existence to just being so incredibly lovable during the country's darkest days.

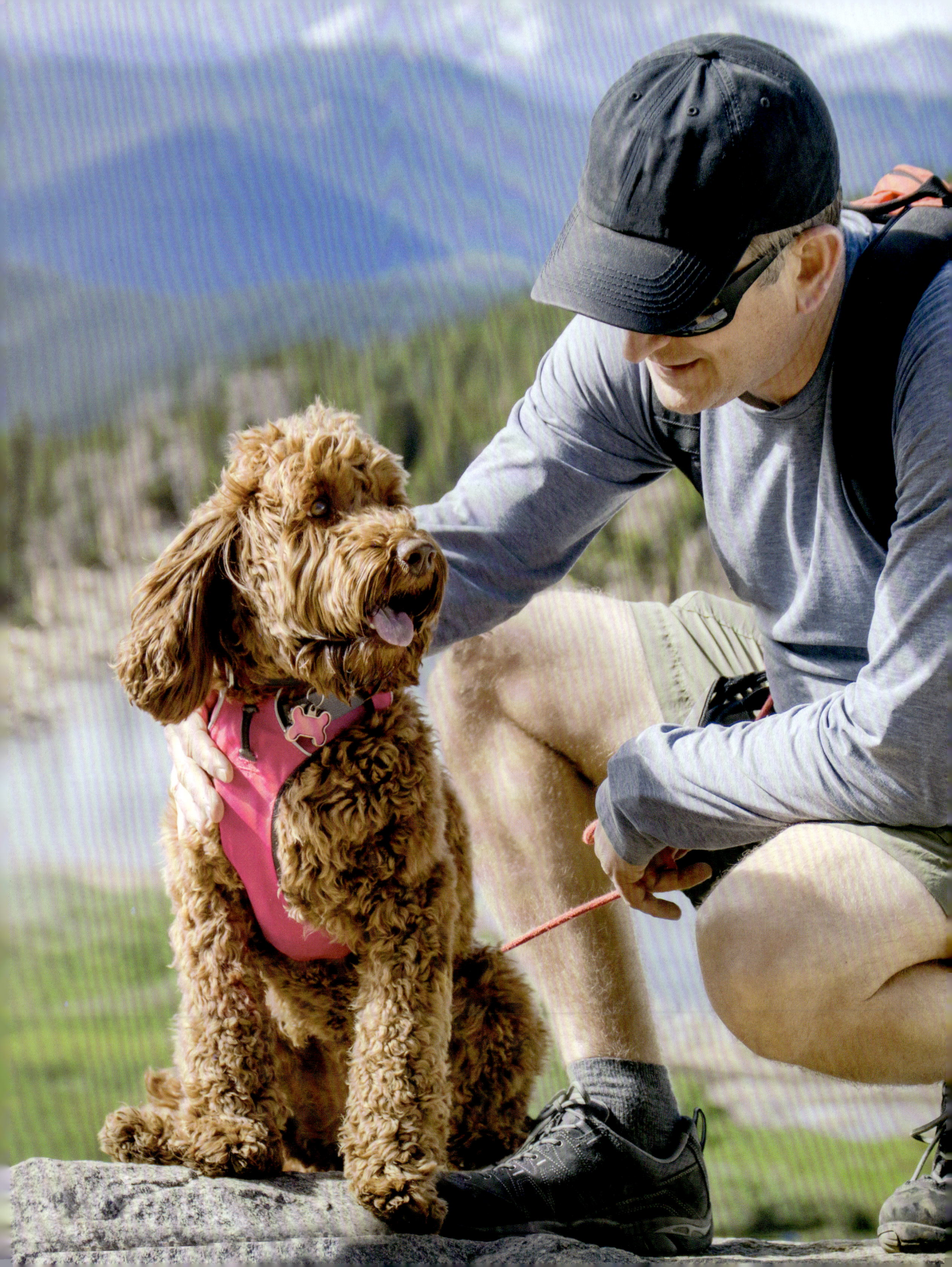

Companion Dogs

Today most dogs are kept as companions, and even those that work all day with the police, on sheep farms or as gundogs, are providing companionship to their handlers. Any dog breed can be a companion dog, including the dalmatian, which was bred to escort noblemen in their carriages, and Labradors, which swam in the icy waters of the North Atlantic to retrieve fish lost from nets. However, most often the small breeds that are cheaper to keep and easier to exercise make the best pets. Mostly these are small working dogs like terriers, which are ferocious little hunters small enough to fit into burrows in search of vermin, and spaniels that could wriggle into thickets to flush birds. However, there are also breeds created purely to give companionship and pleasure—and perhaps a bit of warmth, too—to their owners. They include everything from the fluffy Pekingese to the intriguing xolo or Mexican hairless. Which dog would you choose to share your life with?

OPPOSITE:
Good friends
This brown labradoodle appears to be enjoying a day out in the countryside as much as its companion. The healthy relationship between human and dog should always be a mutually beneficial one.

COMPANION DOGS

Affenpinscher

This lively little German dog's name means "ape terrier" or perhaps a better translation is monkey dog. The cute little dog is a fearless ball of energy and fun, and is one of the oldest toy companion breeds created in Europe. In the 1600s, the little dog was bred from terrier-like dogs as a stable dog given free reign to relentlessly persecute the rats and any other pests that were a constant problem. As a result the dog is a self-starter that sees itself as an equal member of the team. And that chutzpah embodied in such a little dog, endeared the breed to its masters. The affenpinscher was brought into households to tackle mice. By day the dog was a steadfast defender of the home, and at night the scruffy sentinel was welcomed into the beds of their owners to add a little warmth.

Thus, the stage was set for the affenpinscher to become an out and out companion, and it became a stock breed for miniaturising other dogs into toy breeds. Its owner will enjoy their dog's engaging confidence. Owners of affenpinschers often comment that they enjoy "being owned" by their cute little pets.

CHARACTERISTICS

Coat
A wiry coat that appears in various colours, although black is most common
Height
24–28cm (9–11in)
Weight
3–4kg (7–9lb)
Lifespan
10–12 years
Personality
Fearless and amusing
Origin
Germany

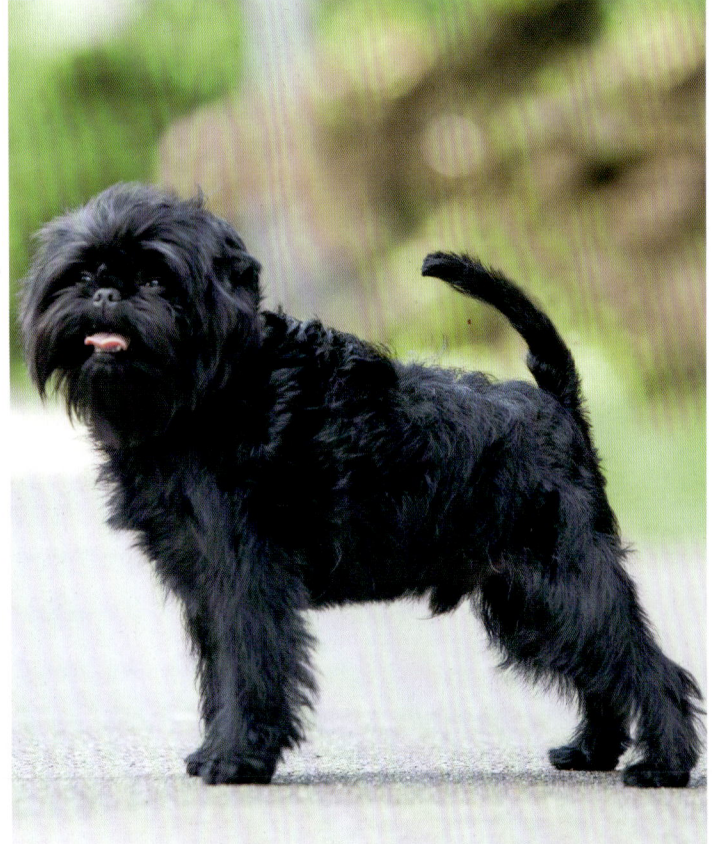

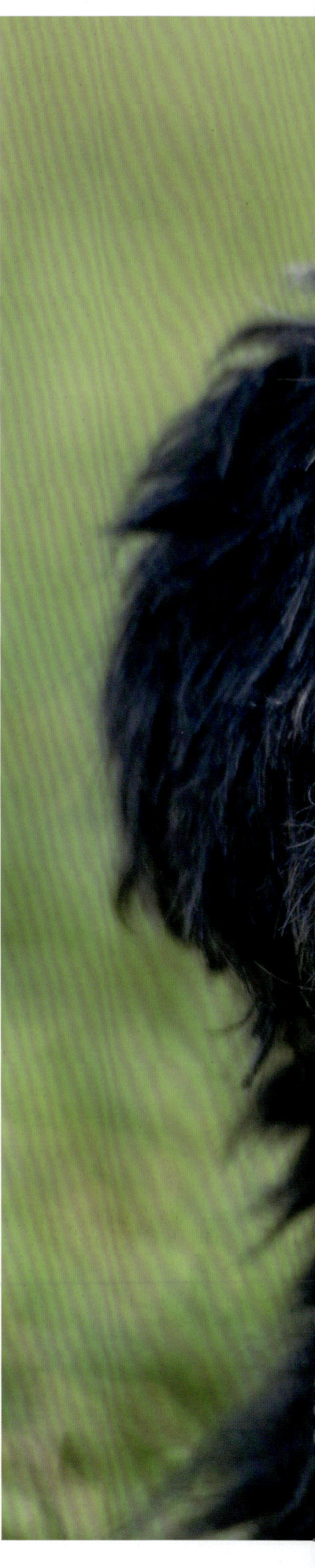

ABOVE:
Unusual dog
The affenpinscher is a rare breed. It is known for being spunky and curious.

RIGHT:
Easy going
An affenpinscher will fit into any home but needs regular grooming and moderate exercise.

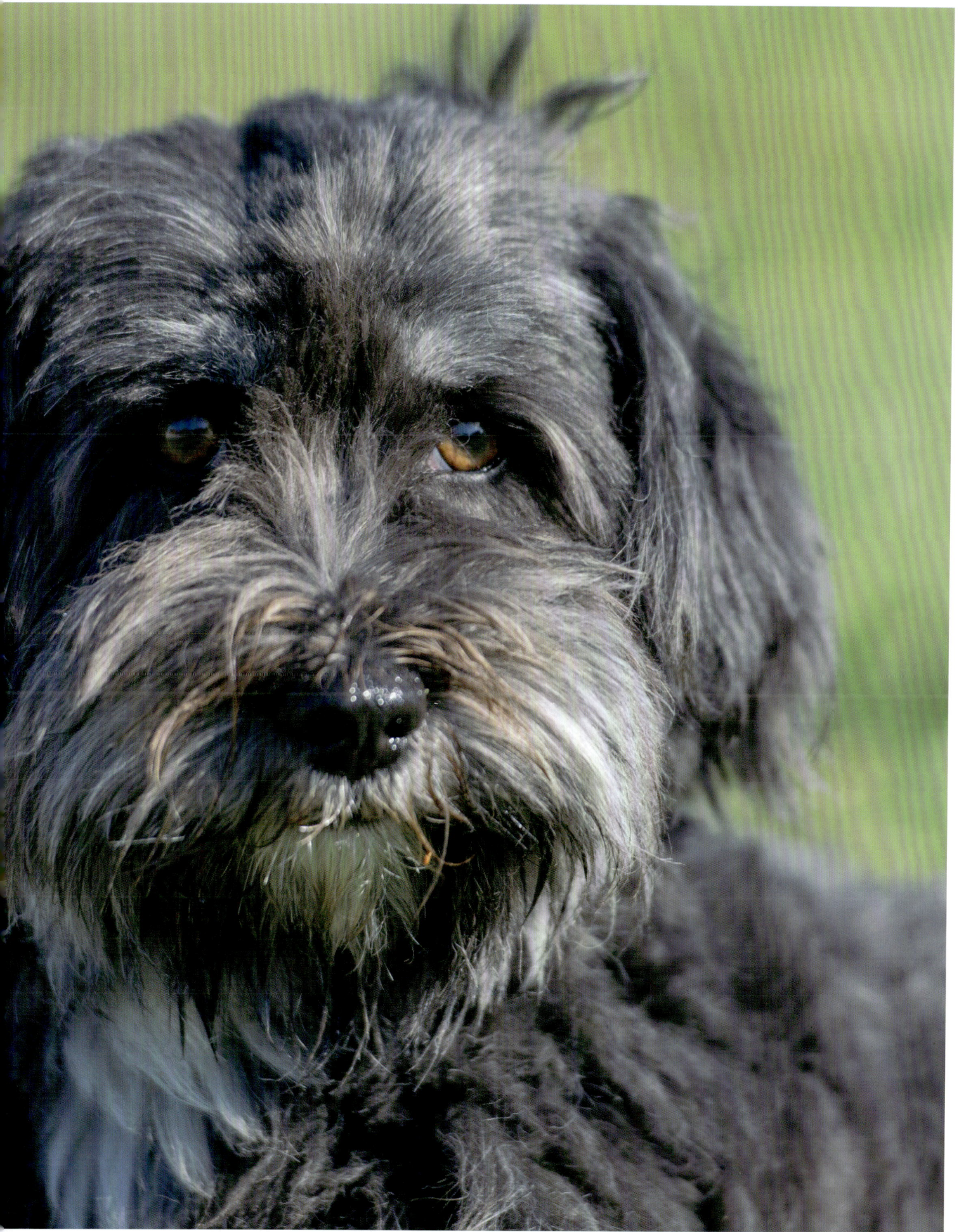

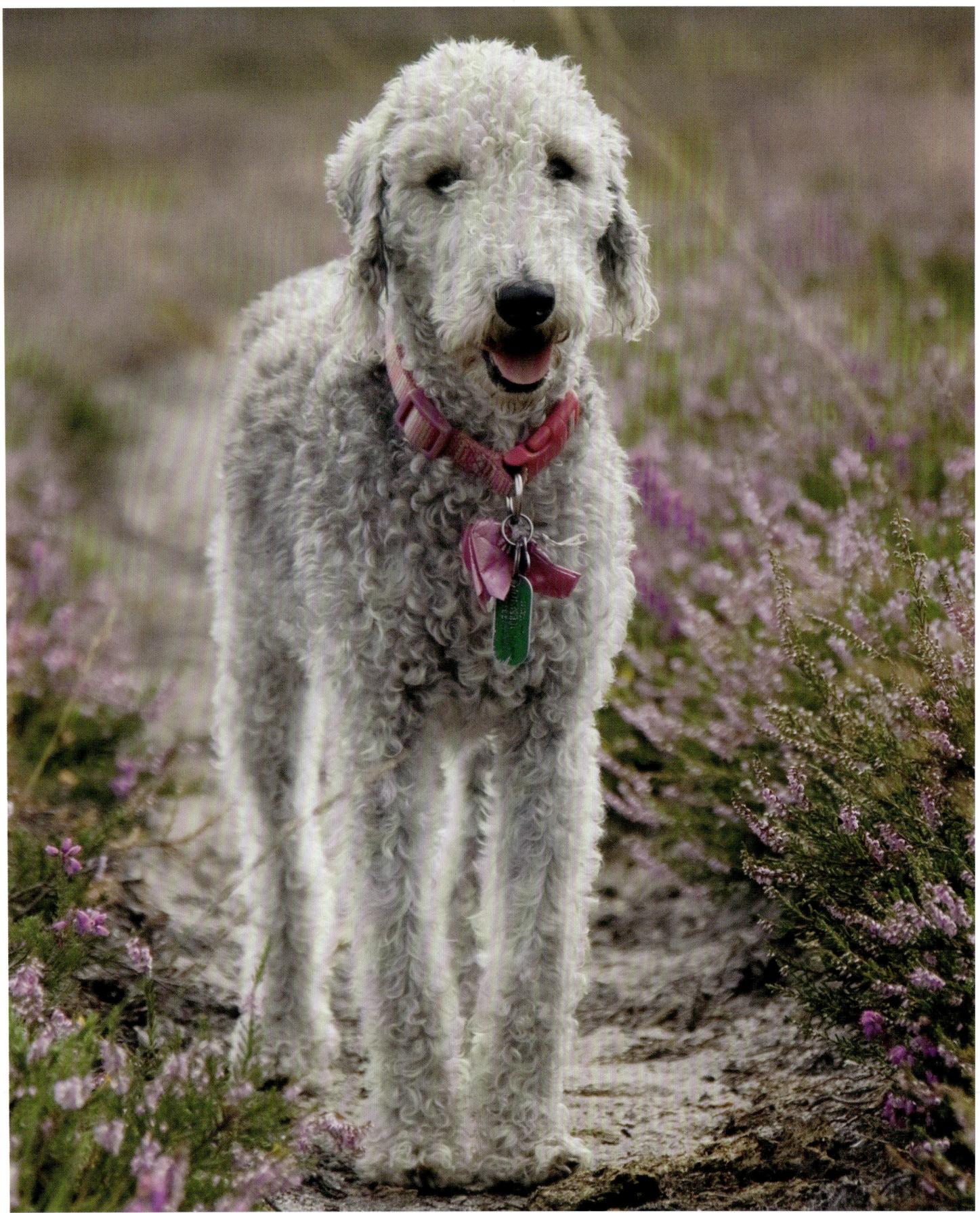

ABOVE:
Having fun
The Bedlington terrier is a versatile and adaptable dog that can fit into different lifestyles and environments.

Bedlington Terrier

CHARACTERISTICS

Coat
The thick coat can be blue, liver or sandy, with or without tan markings. It gets lighter as the dog ages

Height
40–43cm (16–17in)

Weight
8–10kg (18–22lb)

Lifespan
14–15 years

Personality
Charming and playful

Origin
England

Hailing from the town of Bedlington, Northumberland, in the far north of England, this small dog is often clipped to have the appearance of a lamb. The body is shorn of the close woolly curls to accentuate the spring-loaded arched back. The curls left on the legs give them a more chunky appearance. Most obviously Bedlington terrier owners often like to leave a topknot of curls on the top of the head that extends along the muzzle and gives a unique profile to their little dogs.

The terrier was created by crossing feisty terriers with the lithe whippet. The aim was to create a dog for tackling rats among the mud and soot of close-packed mining villages and industrial mill towns. The result was a dog that "looked like a lamb but had the heart of a lion". The terrier was also used on days off as a racing dog.

Today, Bedlingtons are a stylish and eye-catching member of a family, albeit one that can be wilful at times. The dog is small enough to fit into any home and does not shed much so is an easy companion for an active family.

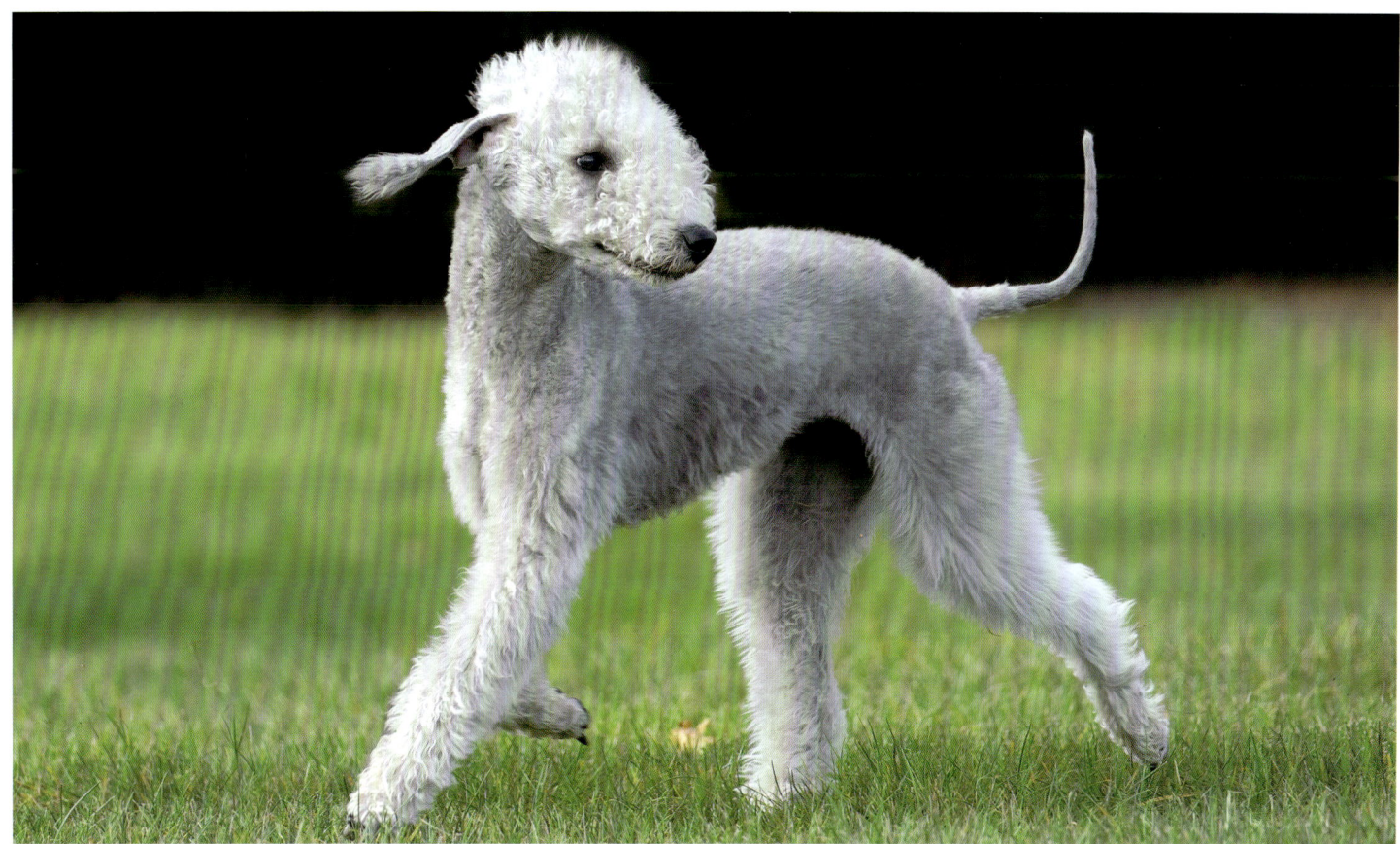

ABOVE:
On the go
The Bedlington terrier needs regular grooming to maintain its coat and prevent matting, as well as moderate exercise and mental stimulation.

COMPANION DOGS

Bichon Frise

CHARACTERISTICS

Coat
A white silky, medium-length coat. The coat is hypoallergenic, making it suitable for people with allergies

Height
23–28cm (9–11in)

Weight
5–7kg (11–15lb)

Lifespan
Around 12 years

Personality
Playful and curious

Origin
Tenerife

Small and fluffy, the bichon frise is the archetypal lap dog breed, with a long history of being loved and looked after. The breed's name is a French term that literally means "small dog with curly hair", but despite that this dog has its roots in the Canary Islands of Spain, specifically Tenerife. Even here we have a confusing term. These islands are not named after the birds but instead the Canary has its root in the Latin for "islands of dogs", which was a product of a long history of maritime traders and settlers coming and going from North Africa and the Mediterranean. The ancestors of the bichon frise were living on Tenerife in the 13th century around the time of the islands' Spanish conquest, and they became popular souvenirs for the European sailors that passed through the archipelago during the Age of Exploration. Inevitably the super-cute little dogs became a must-have for the elites of Europe, and became synonymous with aristocrats. From the 18th century, revolution across Europe shattered the nobility and their patronage of the bichon frise, but this breed would always find admirers. Its looks, good nature and trainability meant it became a circus dog, capturing the hearts of audiences far and wide—and the breed is still known as something of a performer that loves attention.

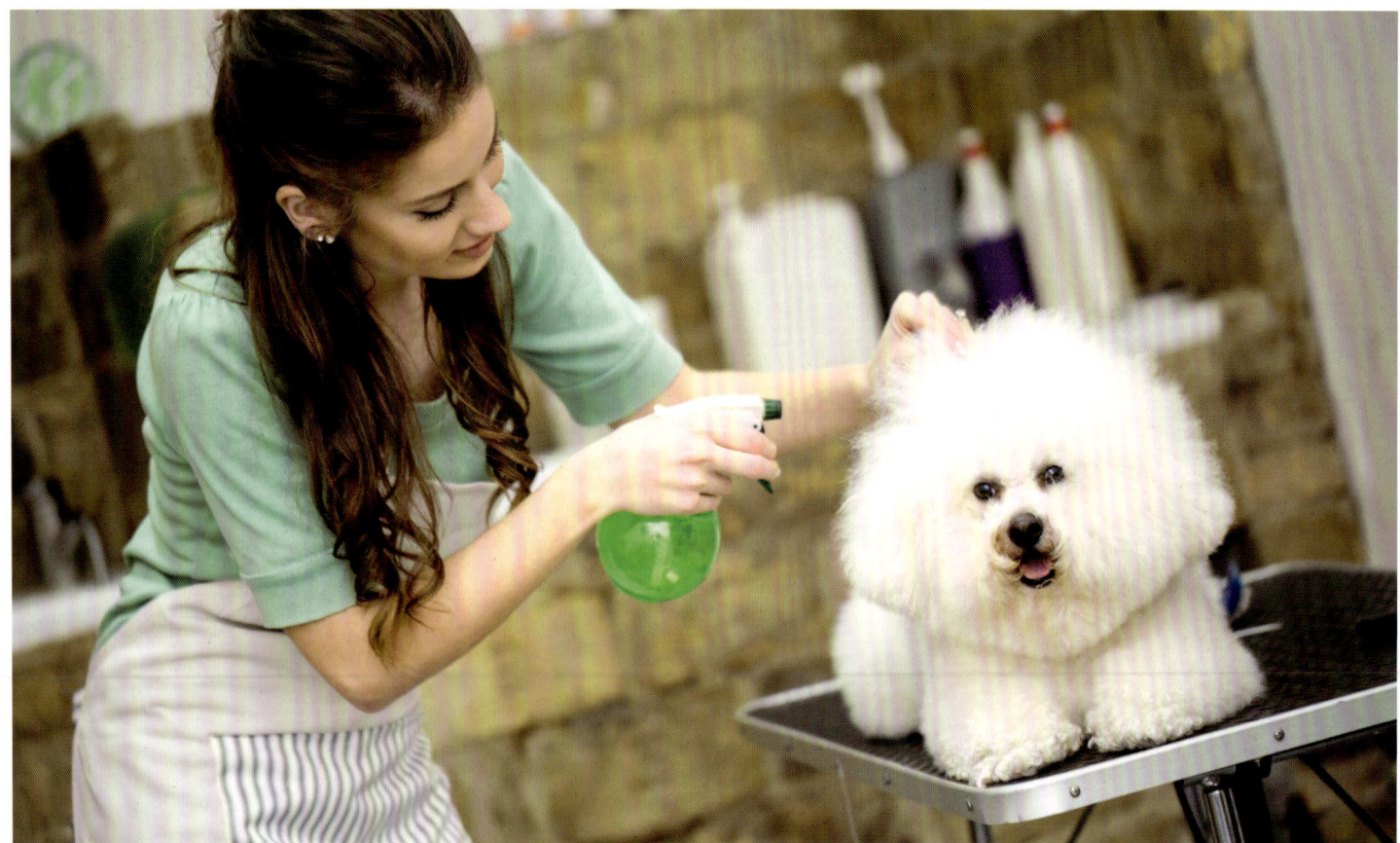

ABOVE:

High maintenance
The bichon frise has a low-shedding coat but it still needs brushing and trimming every four to six weeks.

COMPANION DOGS

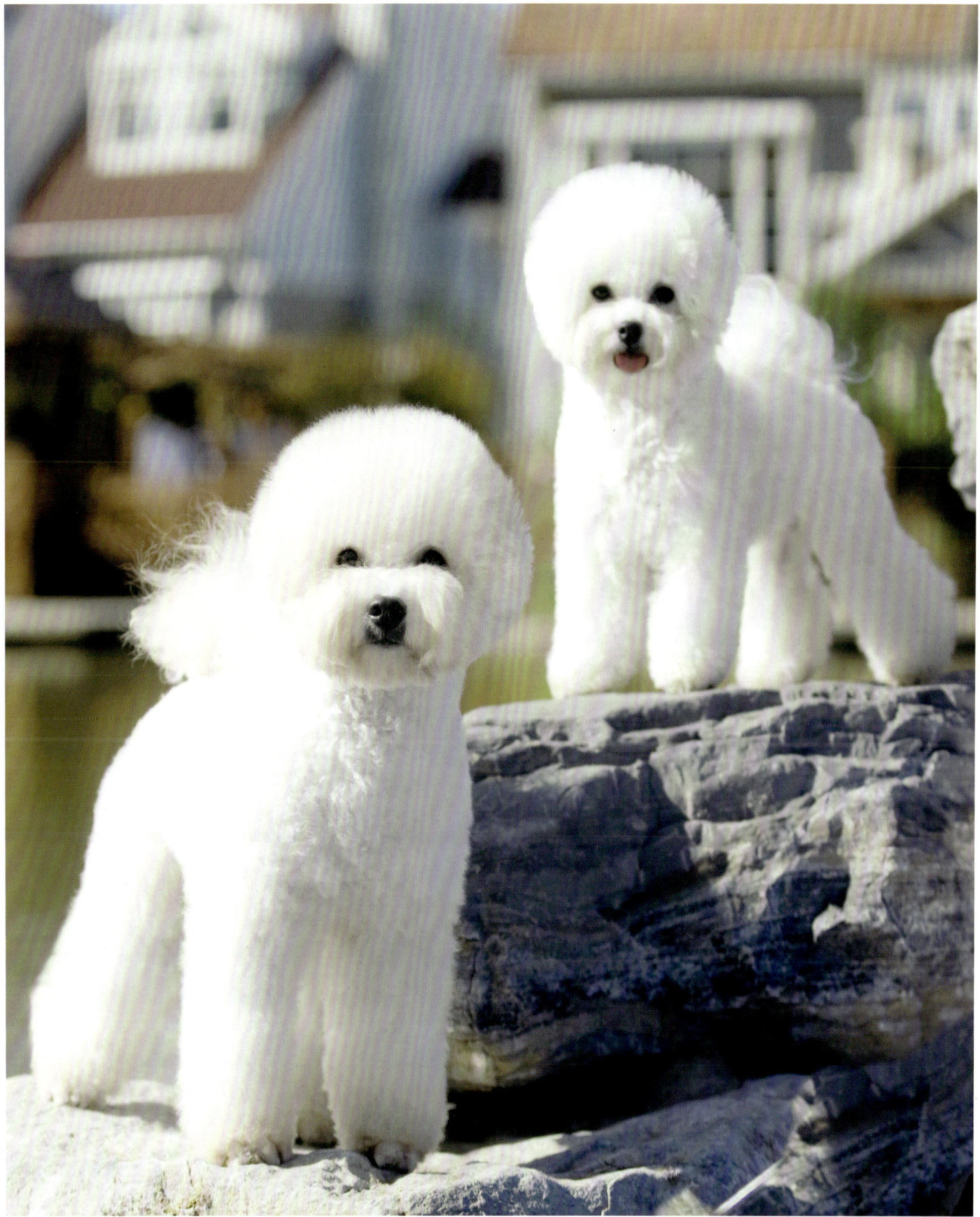

ABOVE:
In the city
The bichon frise is an ideal city dog with little need for extensive activities. However, the dogs suffer from separation anxiety if left alone for too long.

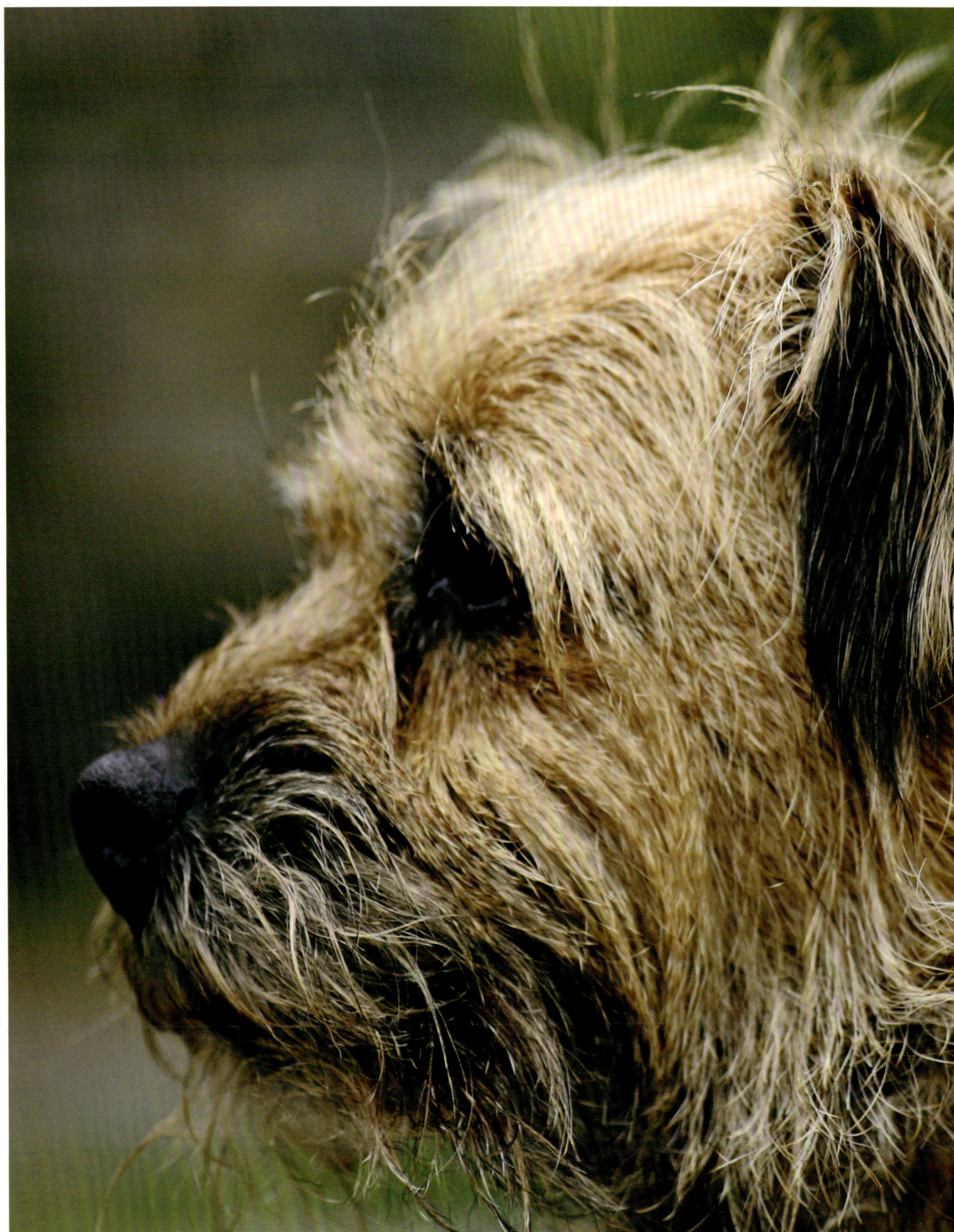

Border Terrier

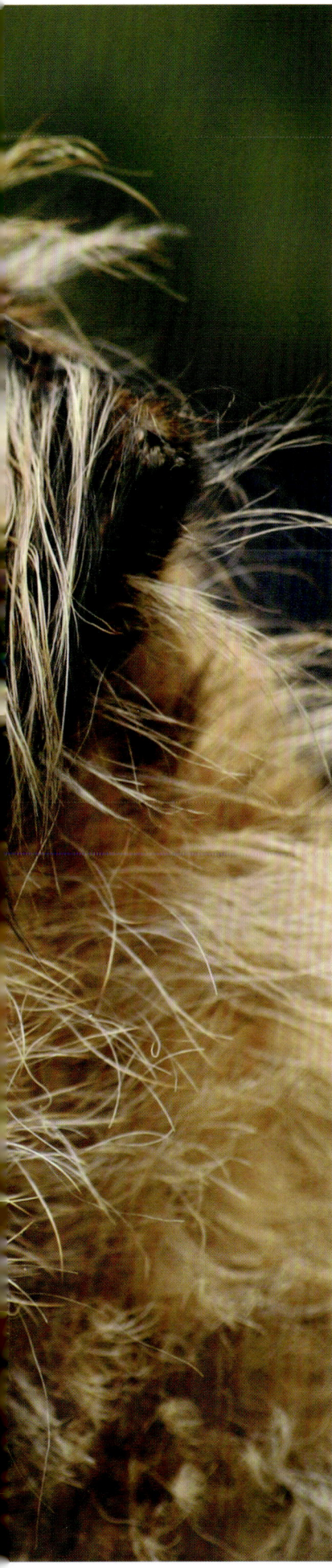

The border in question here is that between England and Scotland, more specifically the Cheviot Hills, an open region of rolling pastureland. The terrier was bred as a special forces operative deployed by hill farmers raising sheep here. The coat is wiry and weatherproof for the blustery and perennially wet conditions. The dog also has long legs for chasing foxes through the steep and rugged terrain, which is criss-crossed with stone walls. The terrier is also compact enough to dig its way into a den, flushing the sheep-killing predator out into the open.

This role is not so in demand today, but the border terrier retains the energy and sense of playful urgency that wins the hearts of owners today. The dog was developed by working people and so is very easy to keep, with its rough coat needing only minimal grooming. They are usually friendly with people and other dogs, but have a strong prey drive and so may give chase to cats. Eager to please, this breed responds best to positive training with plenty of praise and rewards of food.

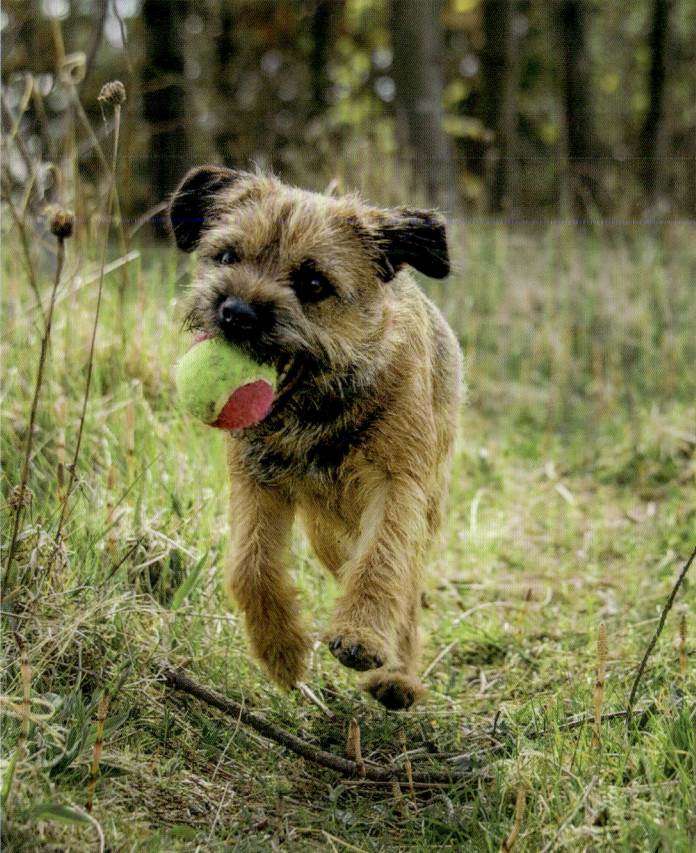

CHARACTERISTICS

Coat
A wiry coat that comes in various colours. It sheds moderately but is easy to groom
Height
25–28cm (10–11in)
Weight
5–7kg (11–15lb)
Lifespan
13–14 years
Personality
Brave and affectionate
Origin
Scotland and England

LEFT:
Otter-like
Border terriers have a distinctive otter-shaped head with sleek lines and a short, wide muzzle.

ABOVE:
All go
The terrier is an adaptable dog that can live in different environments.

COMPANION DOGS

Boundless energy
Border terriers need plenty of exercise and mental stimulation to prevent boredom and a descent into mischief.

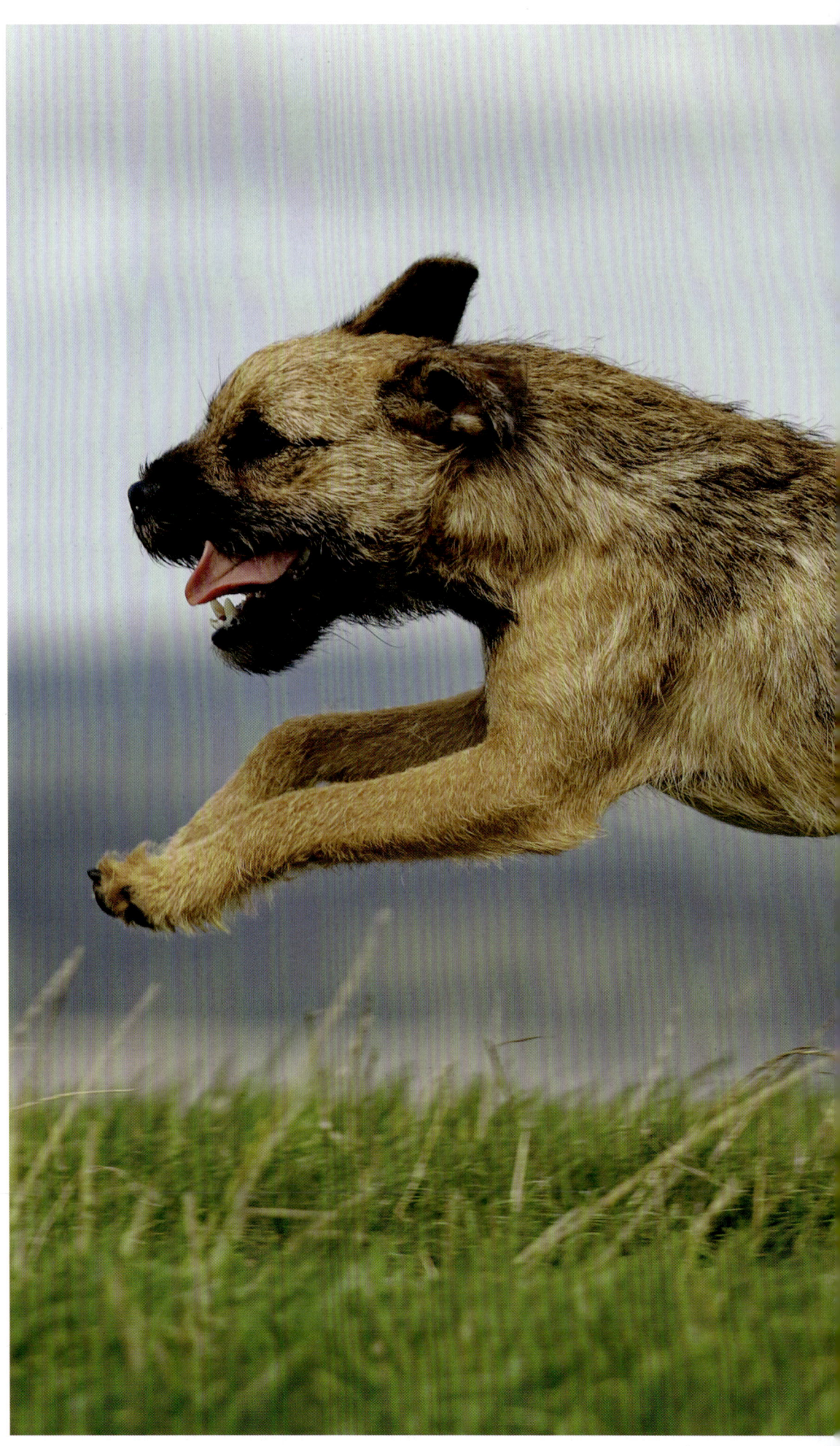

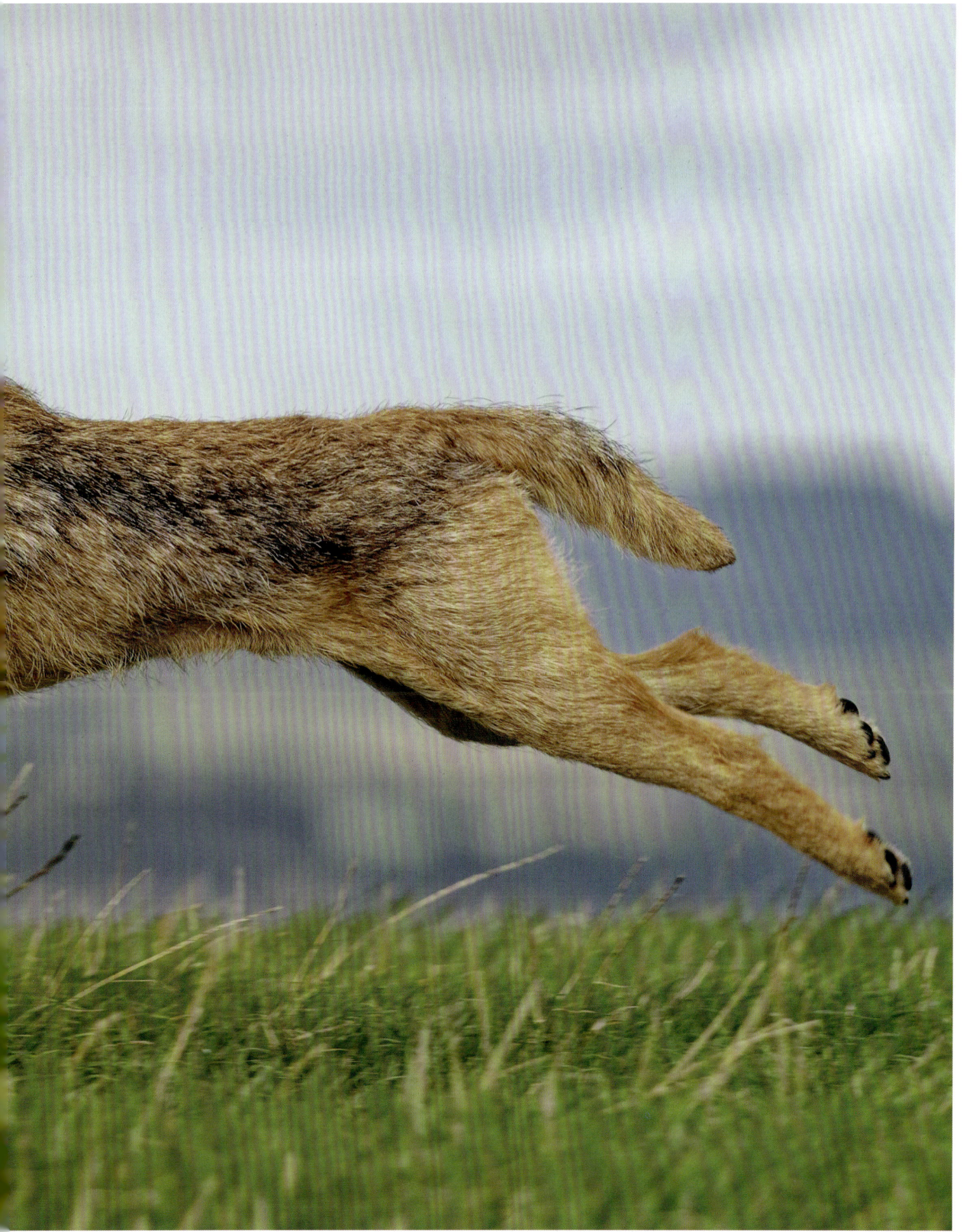

COMPANION DOGS

Brussels Griffon

CHARACTERISTICS

Coat
Has a smooth or rough coat that comes in red, black and tan, solid black, or belge (a mix of black and reddish-brown)

Height
23–28cm (9–11in)

Weight
3–5kg (7–11lb)

Lifespan
Around 12 years

Personality
Well-mannered and energetic

Origin
Belgium

The Arnolfini Portrait is a scene of domesticity painted in 1434 by the Flemish master Jan van Eyck. It shows a wealthy Italian merchant with his pregnant wife at home among their most significant and symbolic possessions. And one of them is a tiny little dog with a rough coat and big personality. This was a stable dog, bred to drive out the rats, that had found its way into the affections of this upwardly mobile Renaissance family, and the ancestor of today's Griffon Bruxellois, or the Brussels Griffon. The breed has a similar heritage to the affenpinscher, but in the 19th century it underwent a significant shift, being crossed with pugs and King Charles spaniel to give them a flat face with an upturned nose.

There are two varieties bred today. The short-haired griffon has a smooth coat, while the rough-haired griffon has a medium-length wiry coat and an elaborate moustache. This second type descends from street dogs that thrived in the Brussels of the 19th century, often taken in by cab drivers and the city's stableboys. With a heritage that combines hunting, companionship and an independent spirit, the Brussels griffon makes a lively and rewarding pet.

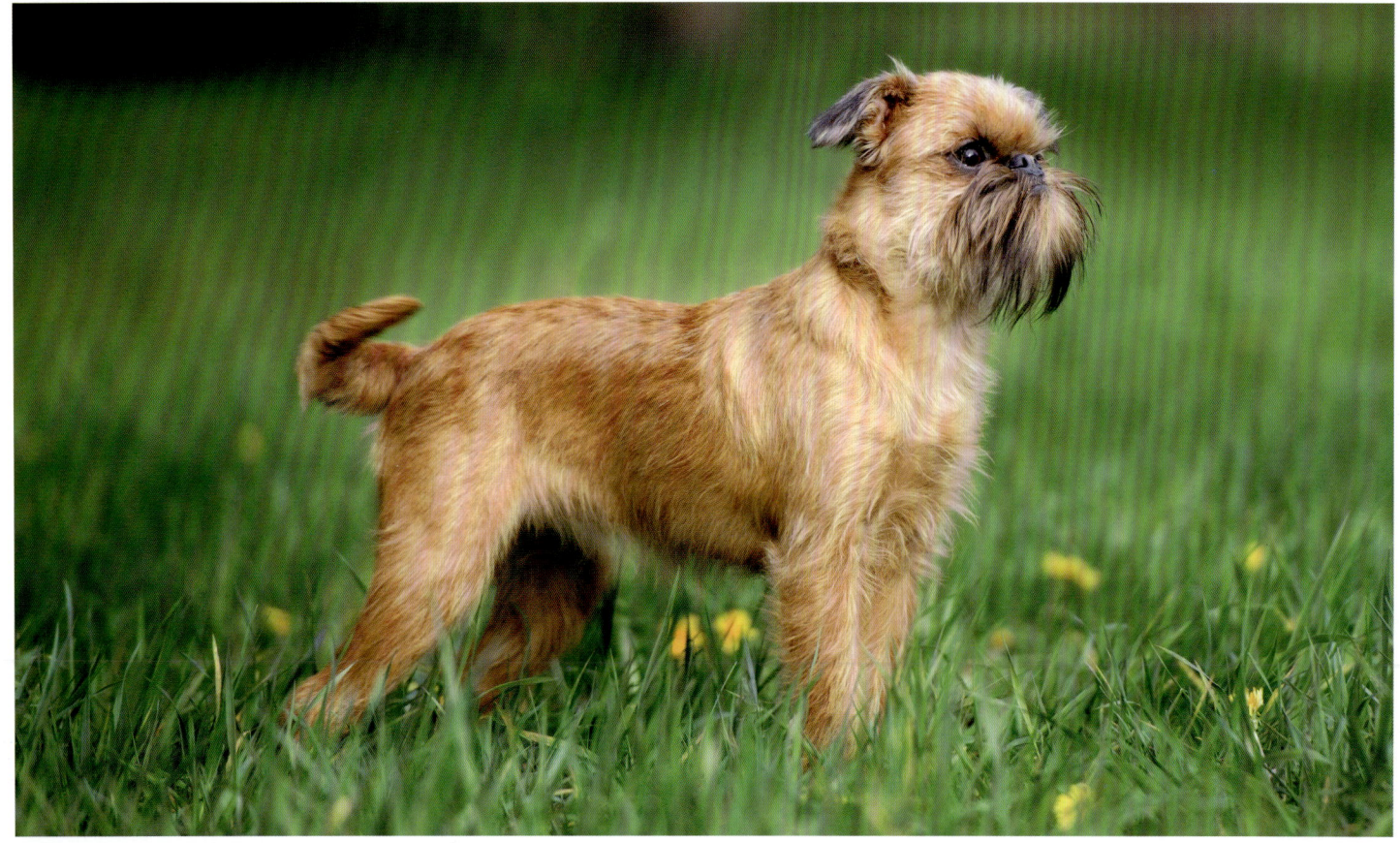

ABOVE:
Small guy
The Brussels griffon is the smallest griffon breed. It originated in what is now Belgium from a now-extinct breed called the smousje.

COMPANION DOGS

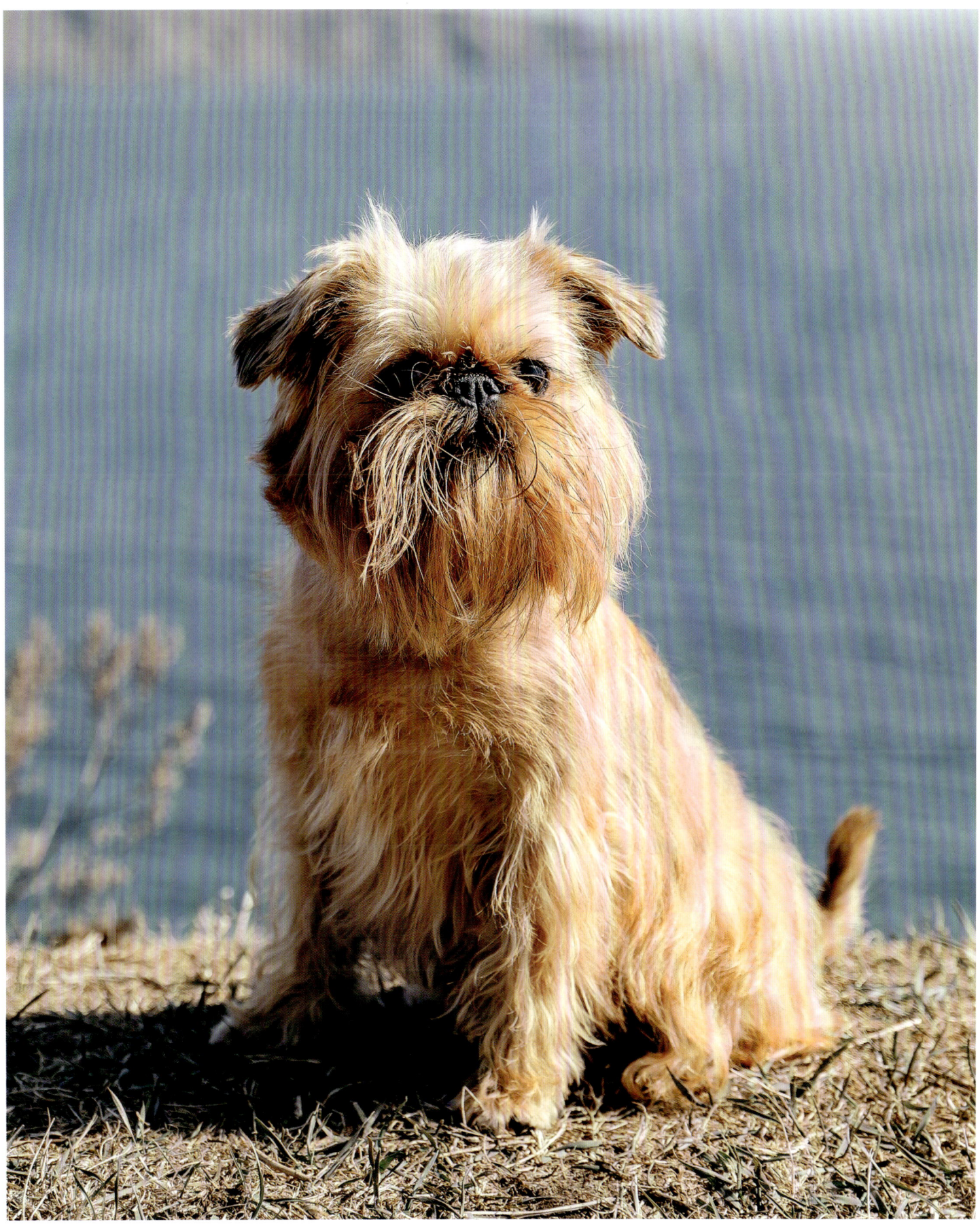

ABOVE:
Heads up
The Brussels griffon has a round head, large eyes and a distinct facial fur that almost gives it a human-like expression.

COMPANION DOGS

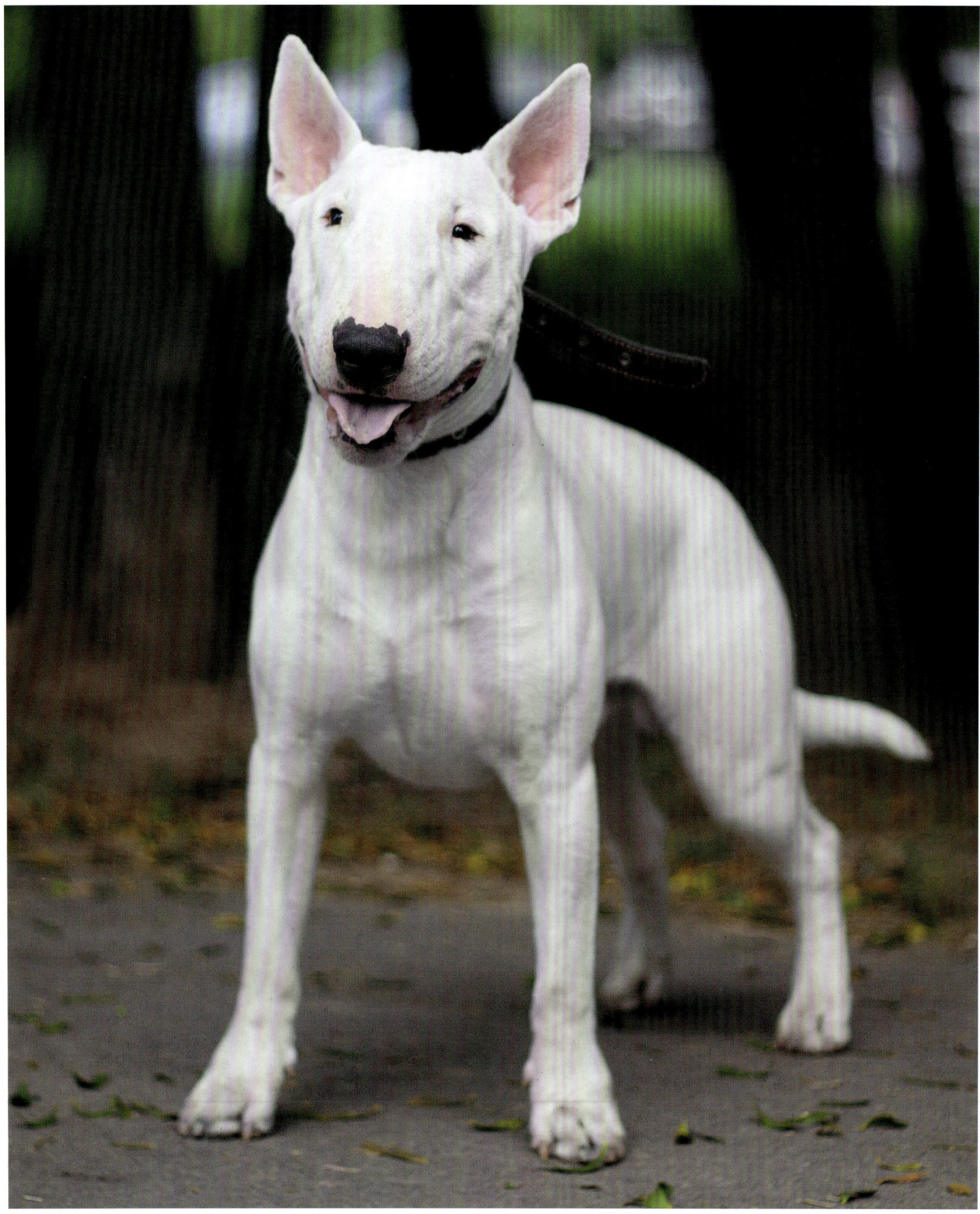

ABOVE:
Egg head
The breed has a distinctive egg-shaped head and small triangular eyes.

English Bull Terrier

CHARACTERISTICS

Coat
Smooth coat that can be white or coloured
Height
53–56cm (21–22in)
Weight
23–32kg (51–71lb)
Lifespan
10–12 years
Personality
Stubborn and loyal
Origin
England

This breed was created to not only look tough and menacing but to also be a prizefighting gladiator. At least that was the aim, but the results were perhaps a failure on both counts. The English bulldog was a breed created for bull baiting, a sport where a pack of burly dogs would torment a bull, and spectators would bet on the winner. This was outlawed in the mid 1800s, and so the illegal "sport" of dog fighting was born, where dogs were made to fight in pits secluded in cellars and remote barns.

Bulldogs had the temperament but not the physique for this sport, and so the bull terrier was conceived to combine the agility and stamina of the terrier with the bulk of the bulldog.

Dog fighting proved less popular than the dogs bred for it, and as fight pits were closed by the authorities the bull terrier became a favoured breed for wealthy young gentlemen as a well turned-out companion. Breeders retained the distinctive wide body and short coat but selected dogs with a more amiable temperament more suited to civilized society. Today, the bull terrier is a fun-loving, loyal and affectionate companion for owners who can provide enough exercise and attention. The breed may suffer from deafness and skin allergies so regular check-ups and care are recommended.

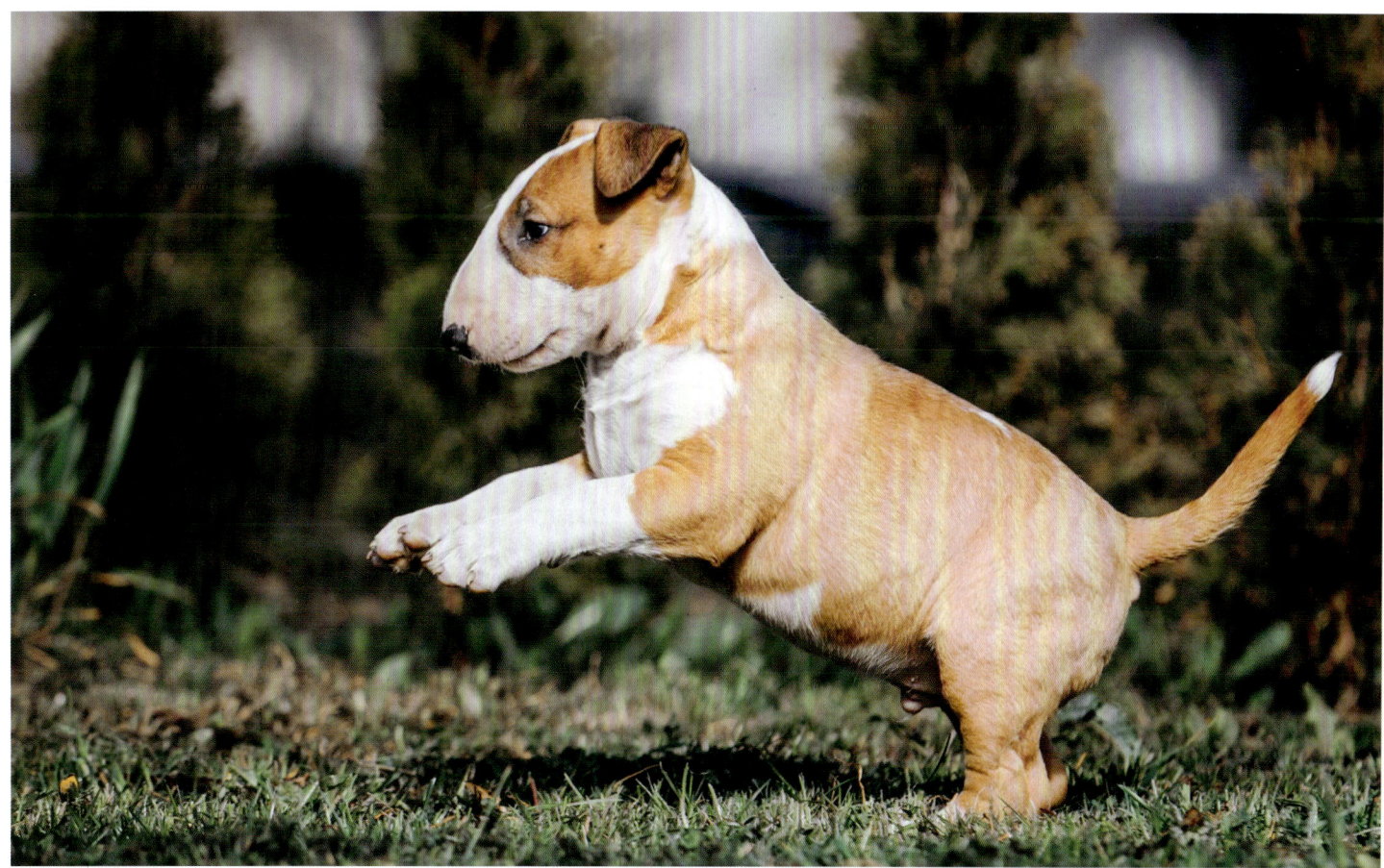

ABOVE:
Big dog energy
The bull terrier is a muscular, agile and courageous dog.

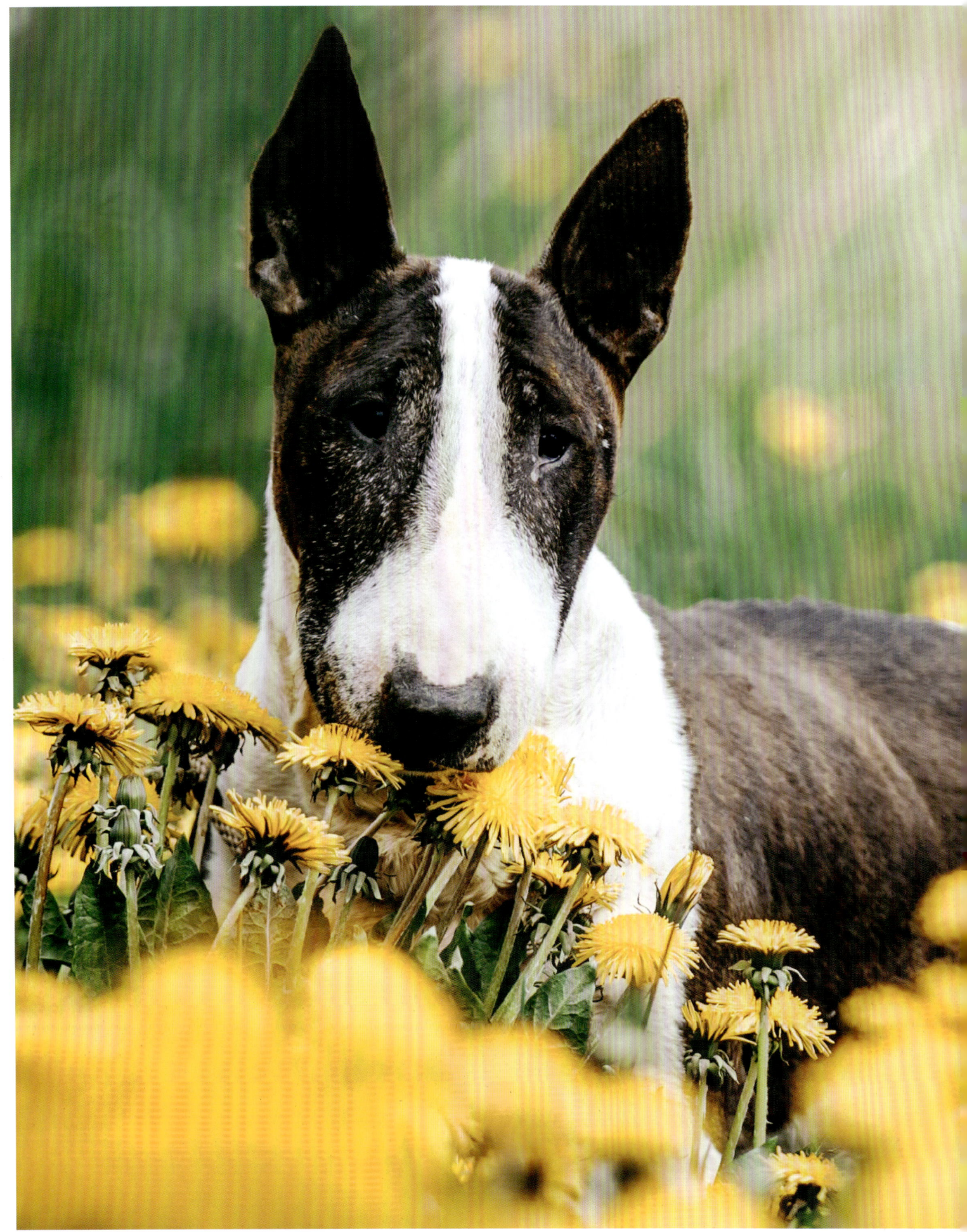

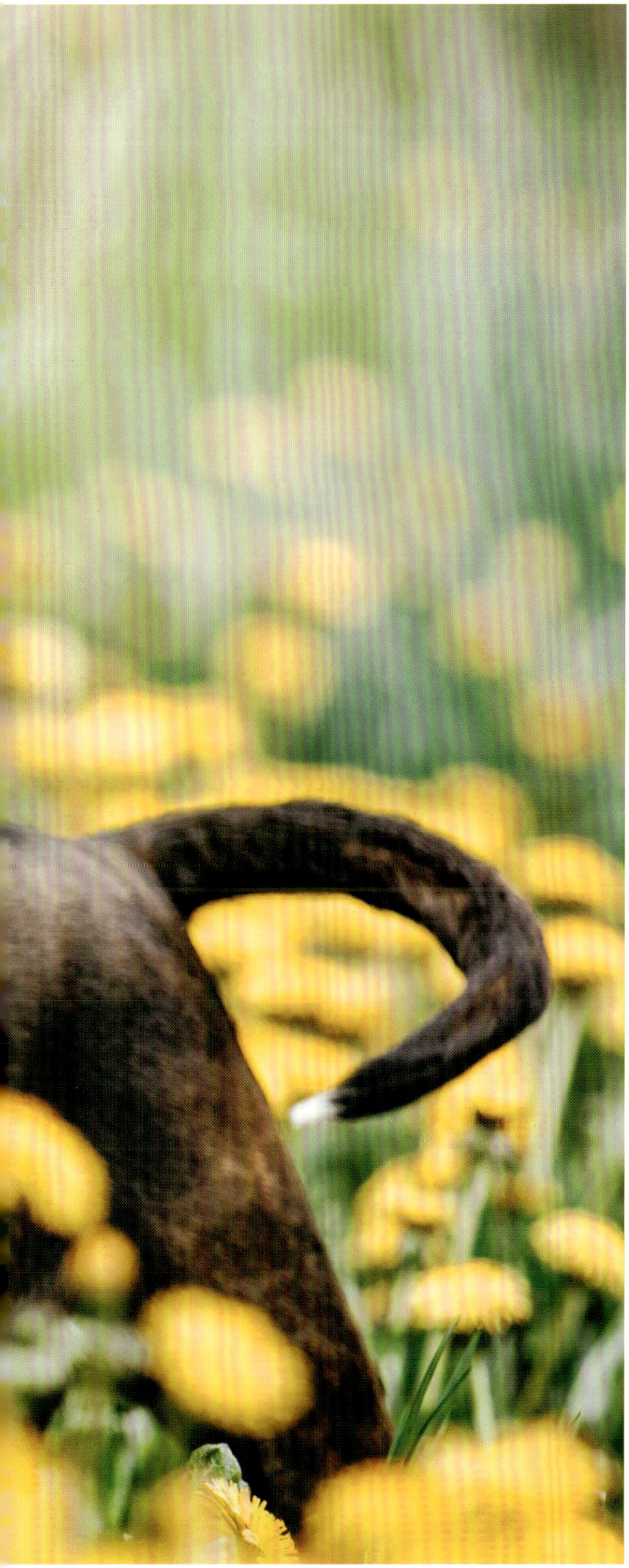

COMPANION DOGS

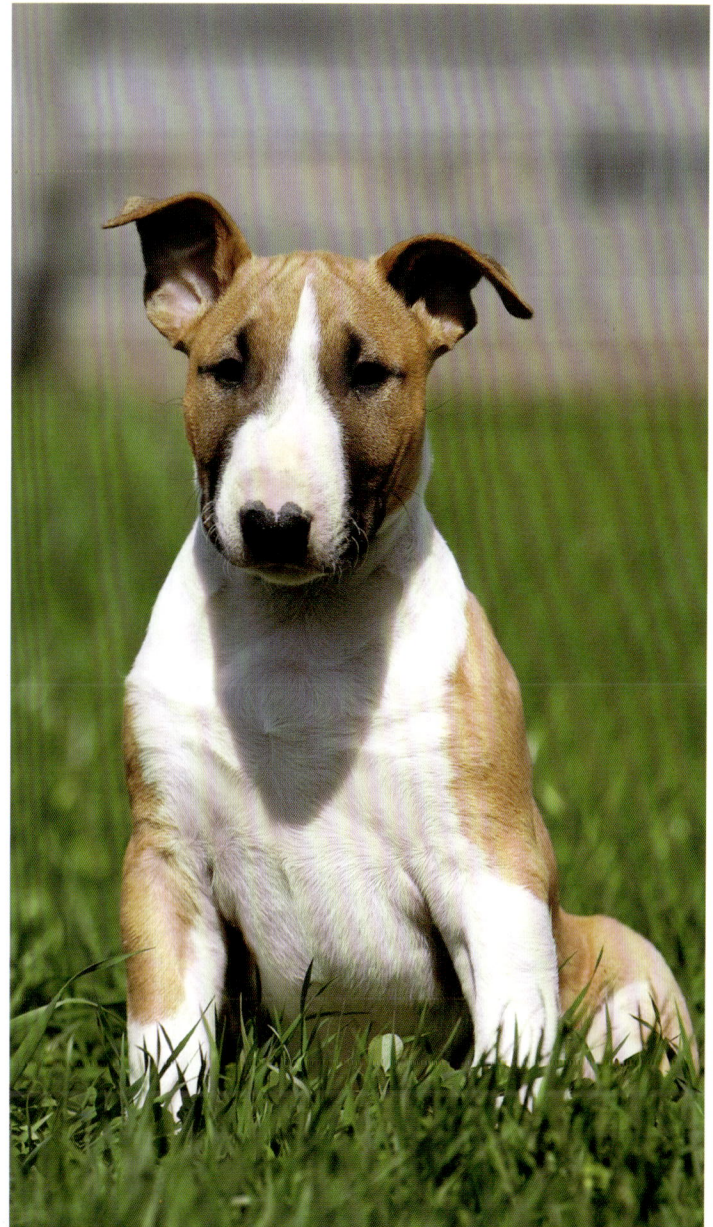

LEFT:
Personality problems
Bull terriers can be very stubborn and independent and so need consistent socialization when young to ensure they can get along with other dogs and animals in later life.

ABOVE:
Young terrier
Even though it's only young, this bull terrier pup cuts an impressive, muscular, figure.

Cavalier King Charles Spaniel

CHARACTERISTICS

Coat
The coat is smooth and silky with extensive feathering

Height
30–33cm (12–13in)

Weight
5–8kg (11–18lb)

Lifespan
Around 12 years

Personality
Gentle and graceful

Origin
England

The king in question here is actually two monarchs, Charles I and II of England, a father and son that lived through the civil wars that began to reshape the English state. Both Charleses were cavaliers in the styling of their times. They dressed in flamboyantly draped clothing and wide feathered hats and wore long curly wigs. Charles I enjoyed the company of toy spaniels, breeding his own, the King Charles spaniel, which was a cuddlesome comforter that kept him and his family warm in those draughty palaces. The cosy family life was interrupted somewhat in 1649 as Charles I was executed by the forces of the Parliament, and the new Charles II had already fled to France. Once Charles II was restored to the throne, the spaniels also returned. The ears and feathered coats of the royal dogs evoked the style of the royalist class. The British royals continued to develop the breed, crossing it with pugs and exotic Asian toy dogs. In the 1920s, breeders looked to revive the original King Charles spaniel, and created today's cavalier type with a longer snout and squarer skull. This modern breed has four colour types: Blenheim, or chestnut and white; a tricolour of black, white and tan; black and tan; and ruby.

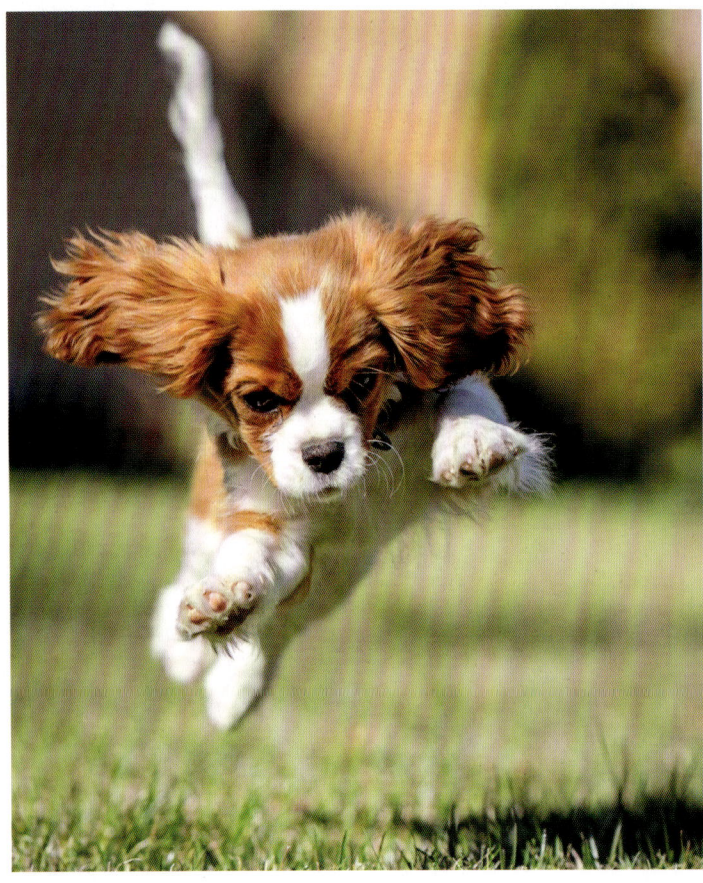

ABOVE:
Play time
The spaniel tends to be active and affectionate in temperament.

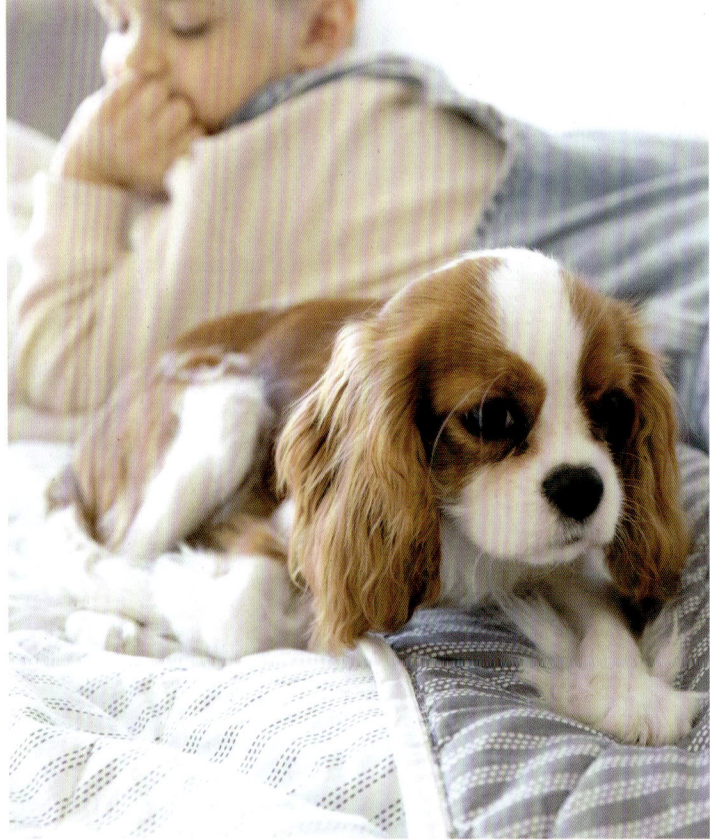

ABOVE:
Homebody
The cavalier King Charles spaniel can get a lot of its exercise around the house so is good for families that have limited space and cannot get out into open country easily.

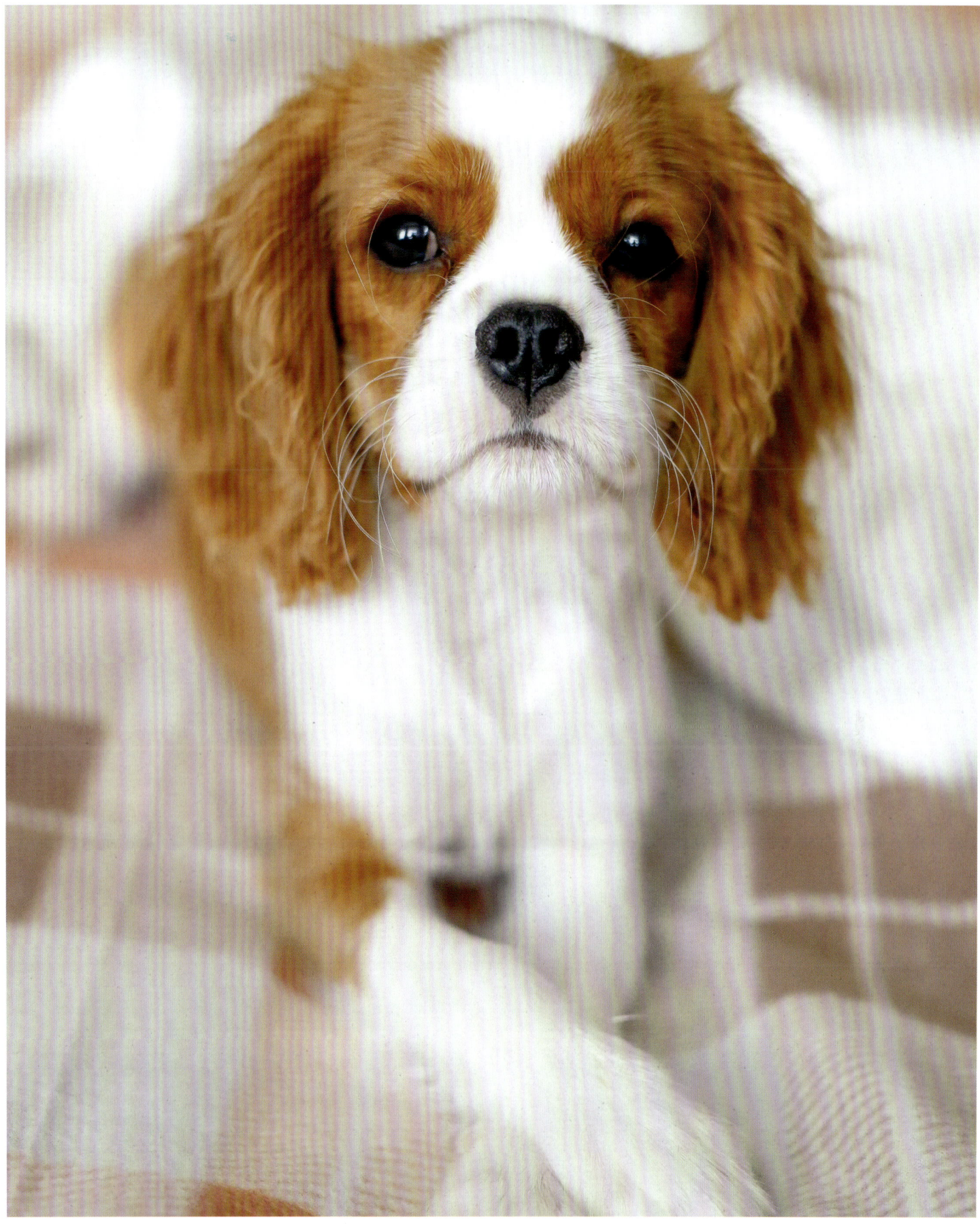

ABOVE:
Hair care
The spaniel's feathering on the ears, chest, legs and tail needs a good deal of brushing so the dog looks its best.

COMPANION DOGS

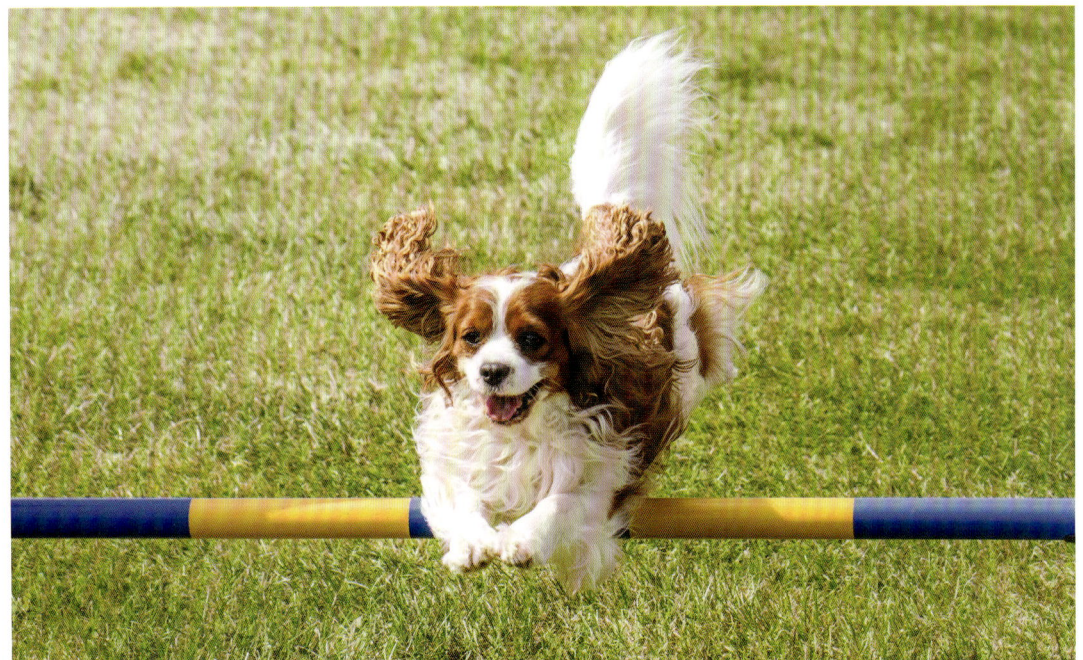

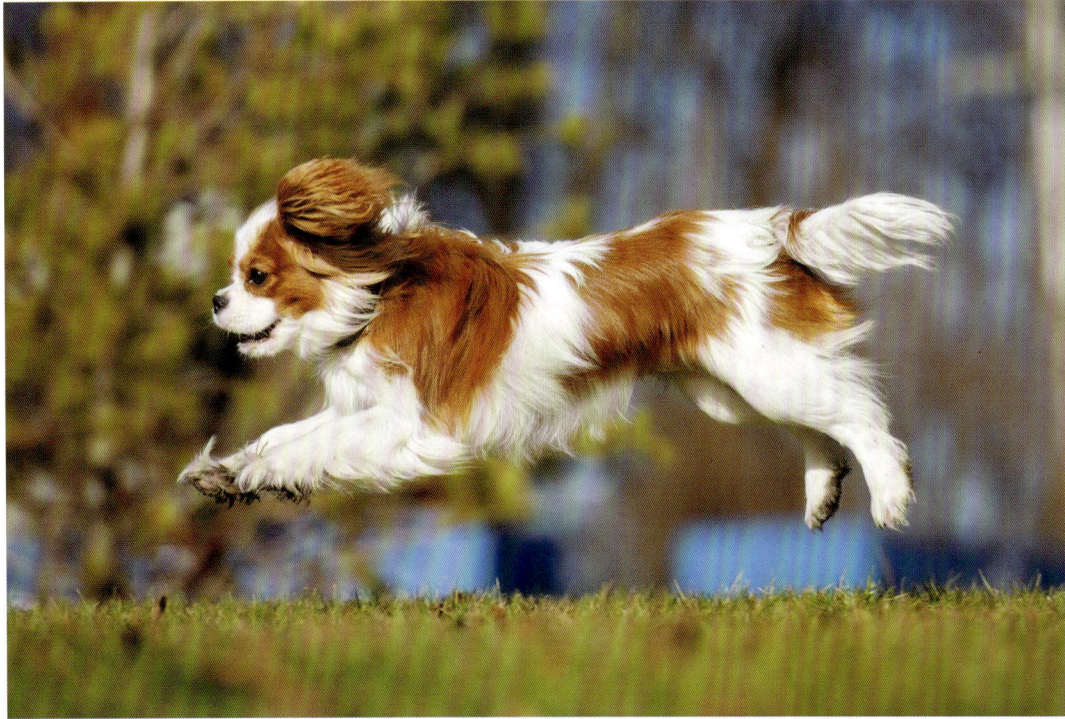

ALL PHOTOGRAPHS:
Happy to perform
The King Charles spaniel is very agile and is a family-friendly breed, making it an ideal lap dog and companion for all ages.

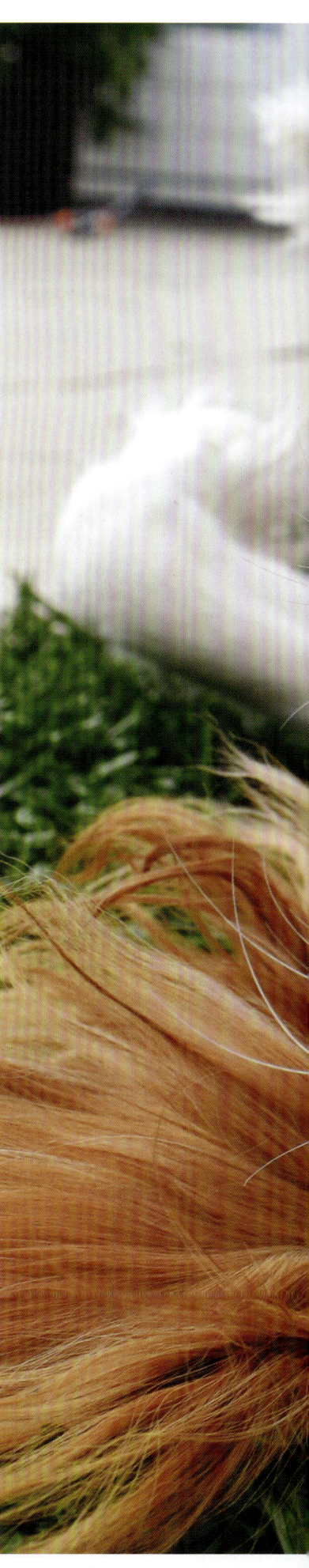

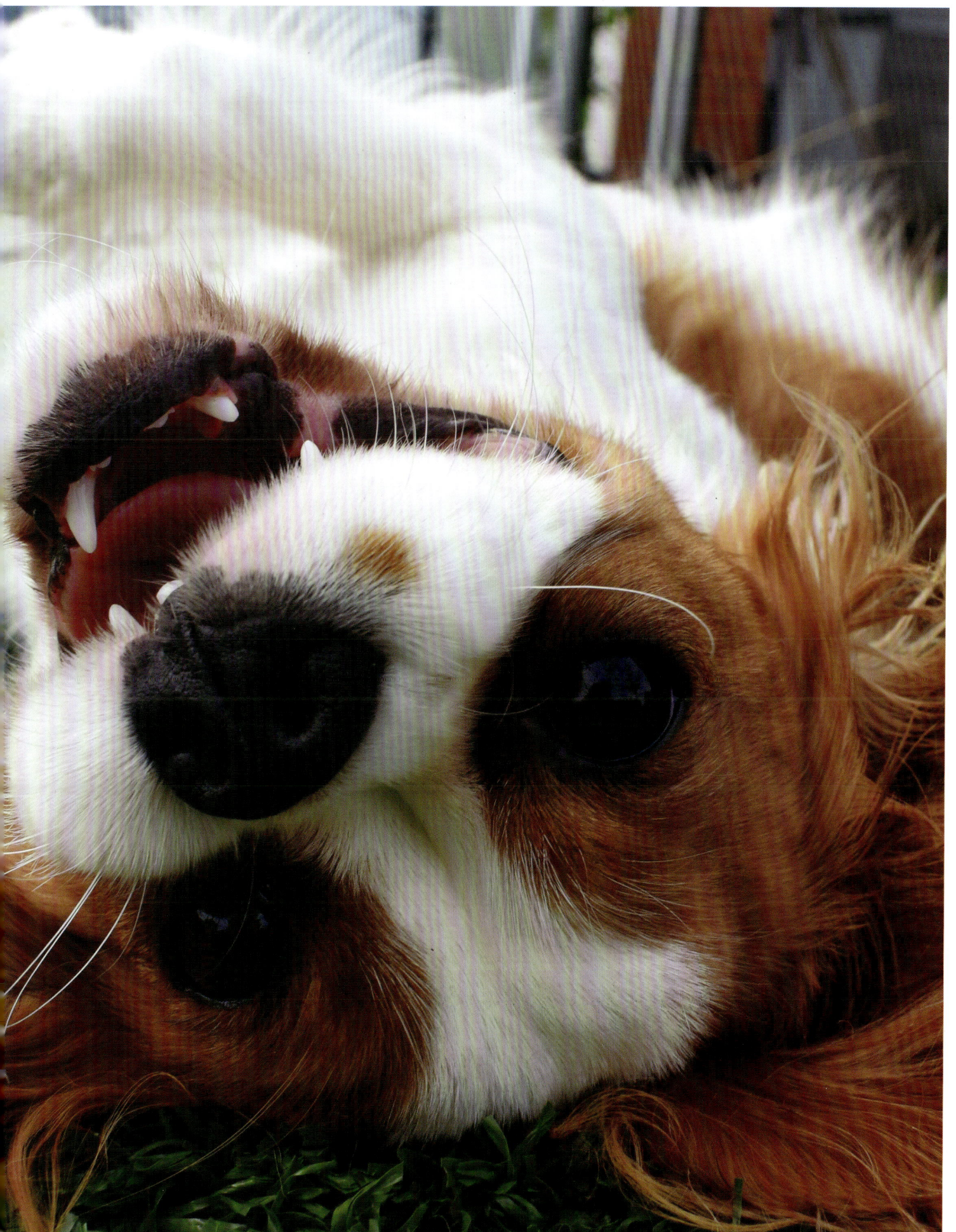

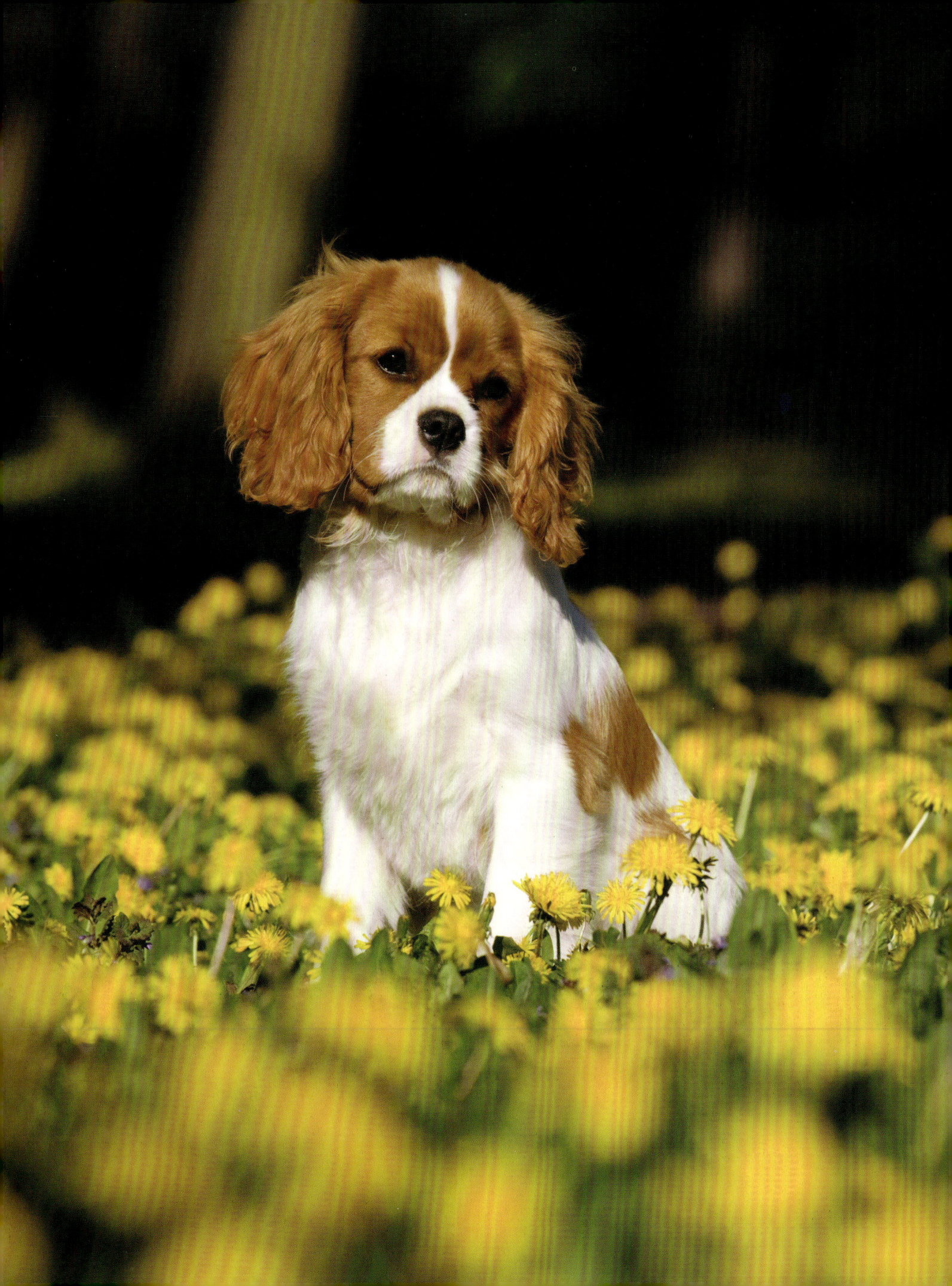

COMPANION DOGS

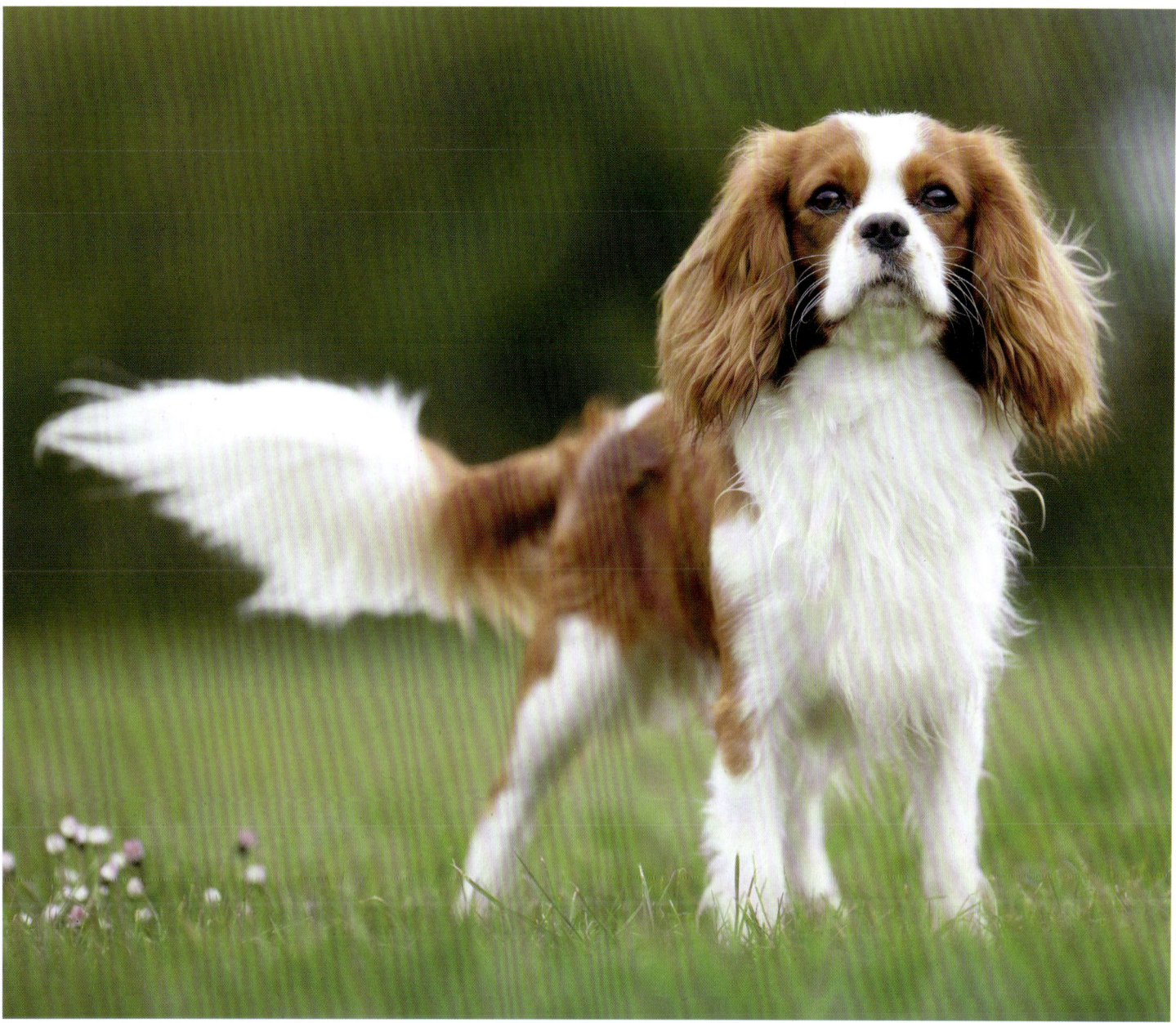

OPPOSITE:
Young pup
This little pup is already showing off the long, pendulous ears typical of this breed.

ABOVE:
Historic hair
This breed's long ears resemble the wig style of the royalist factions in the English Civil War from which England had recently emerged when Charles II was restored to the throne.

COMPANION DOGS

Cesky Terrier

This little terrier with a striking look was developed in the late 1940s in what is now Czechia. The Cesky is now the country's national dog. The breeder, František Horák, crossed existing terriers to produce a hunting dog that could work tracking ducks, foxes and rabbits in the forests of Bohemia as well as quell pests in and around the home. The Cesky terrier is a muscular little dog that has short legs and a somewhat rectangular body. The front feet are noticeably larger than the hind ones. The coat is often clipped so that the body hair is kept short, while both sets of legs have furry "boots" of longer hair. The belly hair is left long creating weather-proof insulation and protection when working in dense woodlands and thickets. The colour of the leg hairs matches that of the breed's very long, pointy beard, one of its defining features. The Cesky is gentle and loyal and has retained a wariness of strangers. It is protective, and makes a good watchdog but stays calm and does not overreact and bark at every disturbance.

CHARACTERISTICS

Coat
Wavy coat with silky hair that is blue-grey or platinum. The coat on the extremities blends to liver

Height
25–32cm (10–13in)

Weight
6–10kg (13–22lb)

Lifespan
12–14 years

Personality
Playful and intelligent

Origin
Czechia

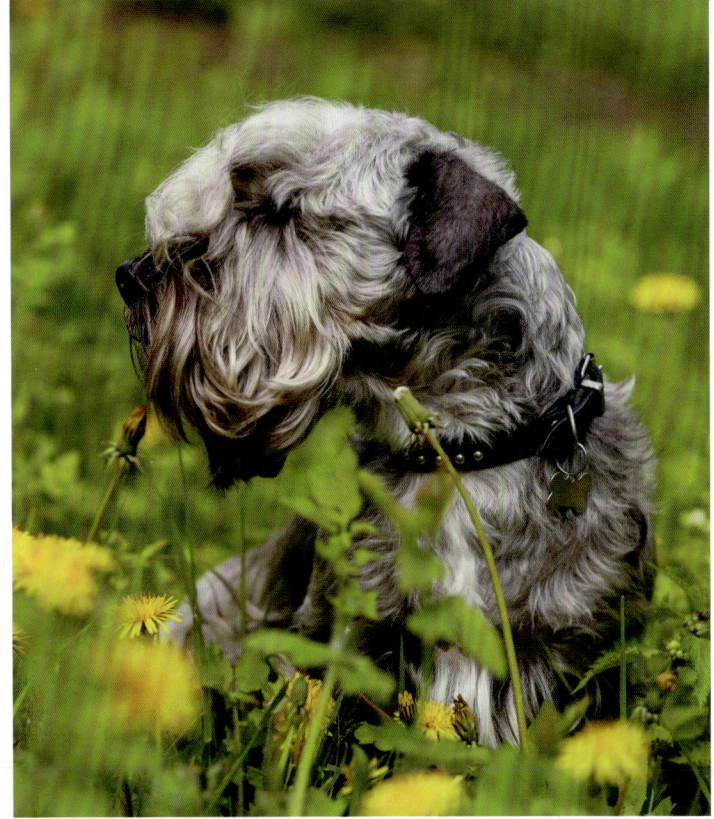

ABOVE:
Unusual breed
Outside of Czechia this terrier is a rare breed. It is thought that there are only about 600 living in North America, for example. Nevertheless it makes a wonderful family dog, if you're lucky enough to find one.

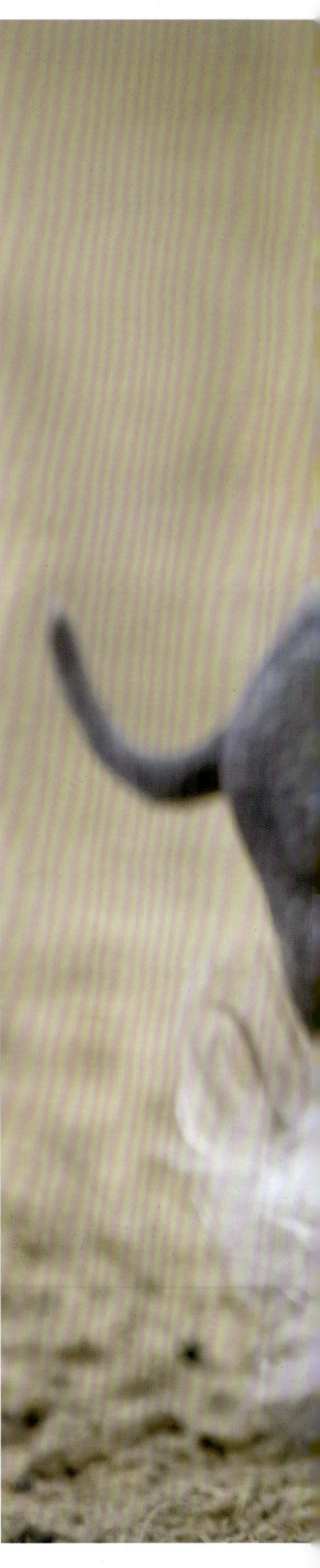

RIGHT:
Haircuts
The dog's head hair is often left long on the front. This adds to the overall look of elegance by helping to enhance the long neck.

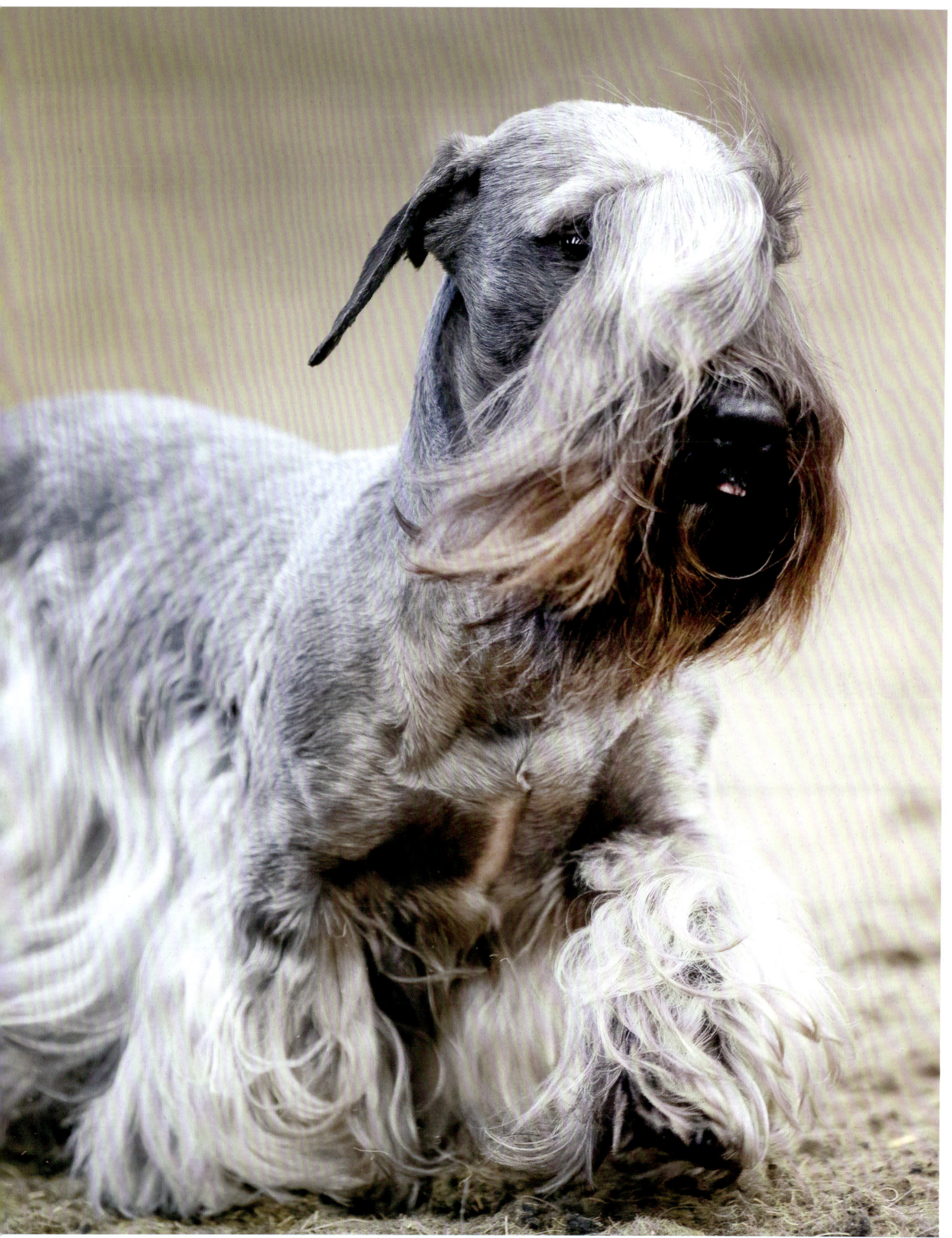

COMPANION DOGS

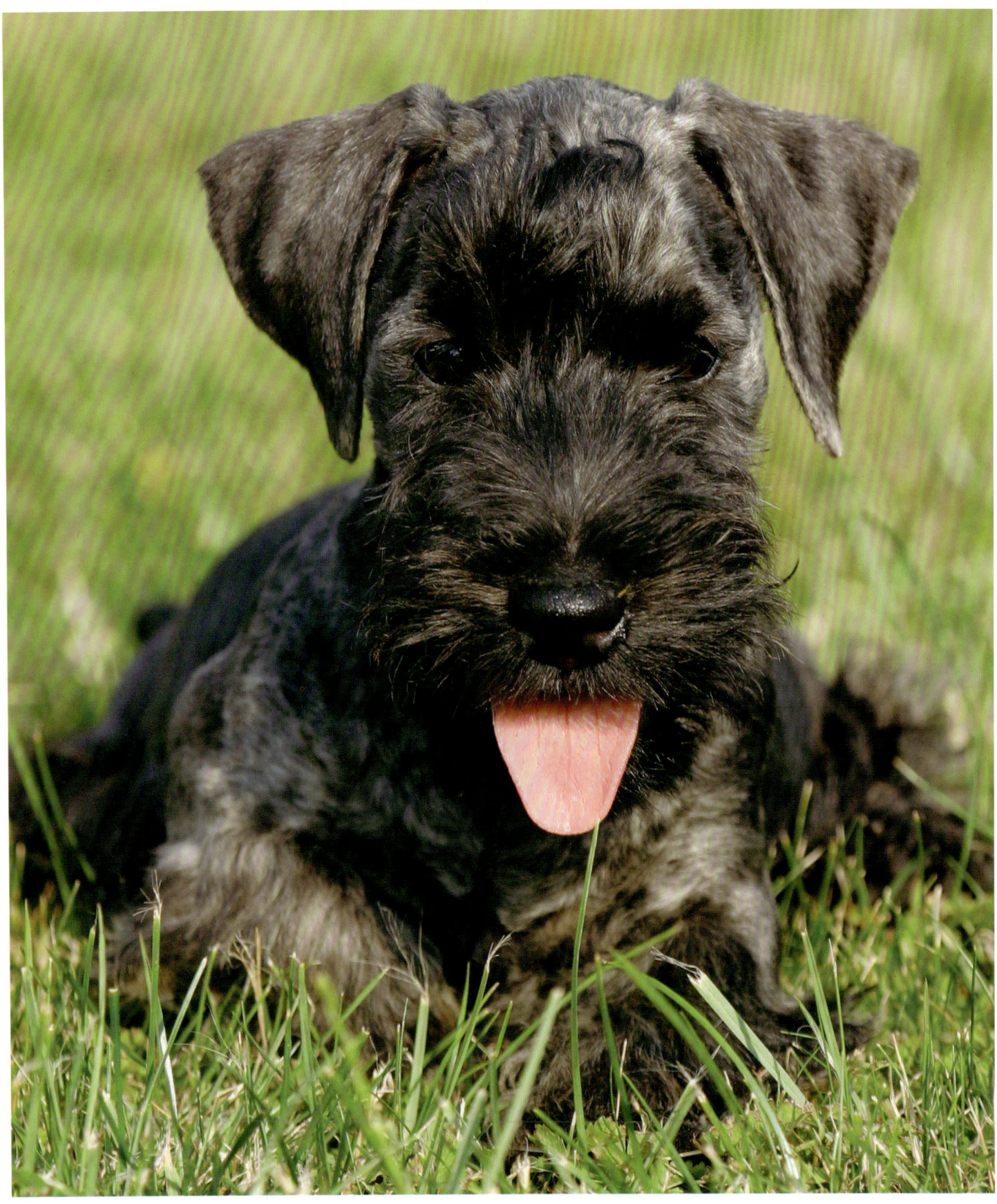

ABOVE:
Hair maintenance
This Czech dog needs a lot of combing and trimming to keep its soft coat in good condition.

OPPOSITE:
An ideal size
A Czech breed that was developed to be smaller than other terriers so it could fit into narrow burrows in pursuit of prey.

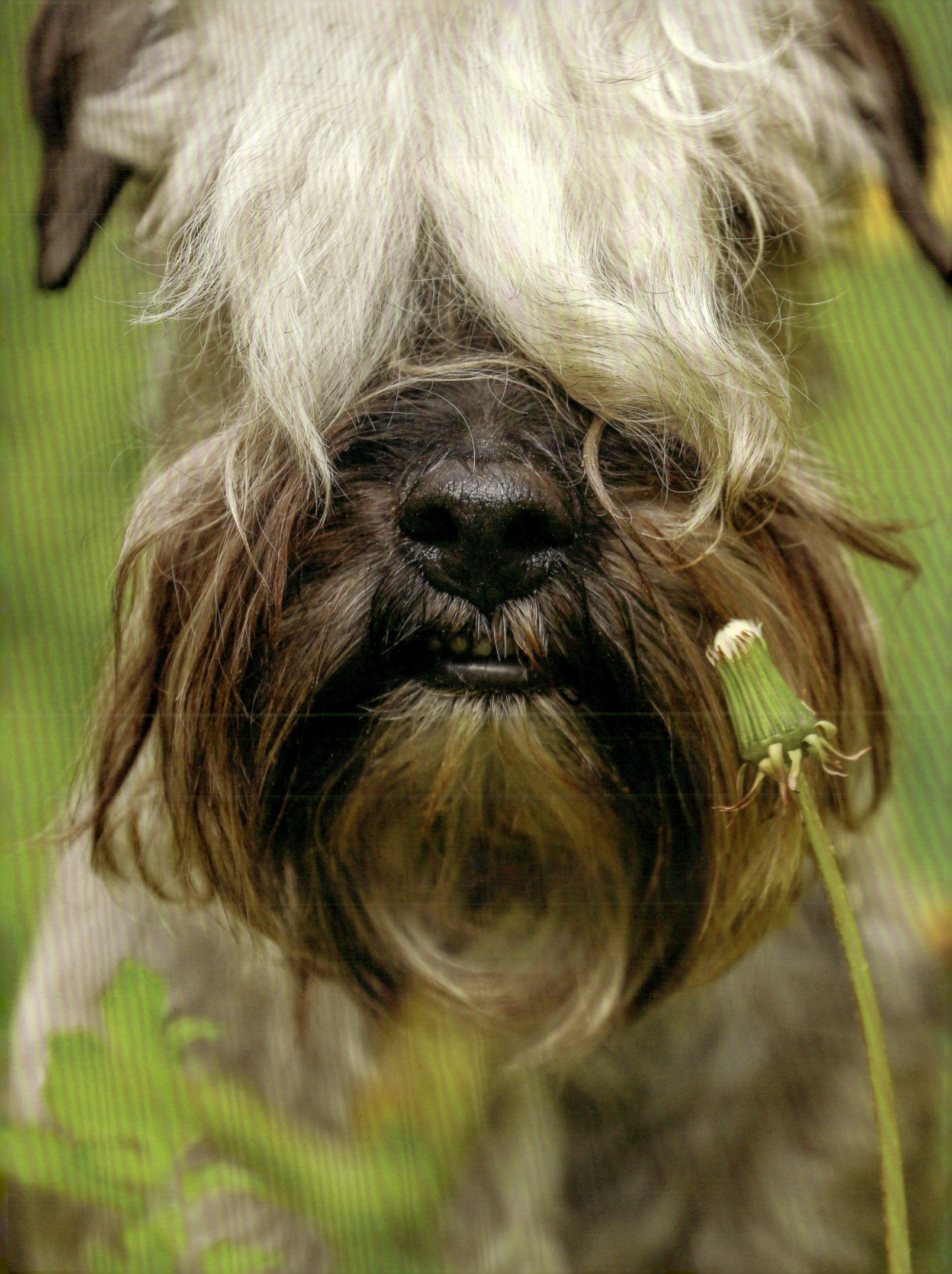

COMPANION DOGS

Chihuahua

Famously tiny enough to fit into a fashionable handbag, this Mexican breed includes the smallest dogs in the world. By way of comparison, they are not much larger than a squirrel. The chihuahua is named after the Mexican state Chihuahua, although this breed pre-dates the European conquest of the area. The dogs were created by the Aztecs, who ruled here prior to the arrival of Columbus and the Spanish in the 1500s. The Aztecs called their breed, a tiny dog that barely barked, the techichi. It was a source of food as well as being used in sacred rituals. After Cortez destroyed the Aztec empire the dogs were thought to have gone extinct. However, by the 1850s, survivors were discovered living in the remote villages of Chihuahua in northern Mexico, hence their common name.

The chihuahua is generally a feisty dog that is entirely devoted to its owner. Most will need a lot of careful socialization to draw out their better traits. Some are overly confident or timid and shy if not trained properly. Nevertheless, the chihuahua is quick-witted and can be trained easily with plenty of positive reinforcement and patience.

CHARACTERISTICS
Coat
Two coat varieties: smooth or long-coated. There are many colours, such as fawn, cream, gold, red, white, black, chocolate, silver, blue, bicolor, tricolour, brindle and merle
Height
15–23cm (6–9in)
Weight
2–3kg (5–7lb)
Lifespan
Around 12 years
Personality
Charming and devoted
Origin
Mexico

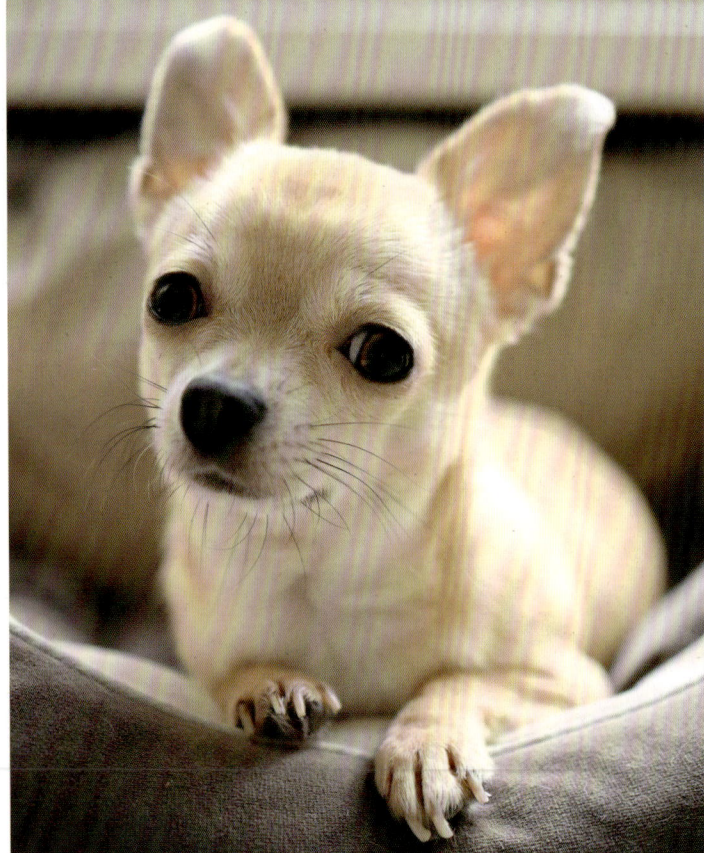

ABOVE:
Go anywhere
The chihuahua is a good choice for people who want a dog that can accompany them anywhere and everywhere.

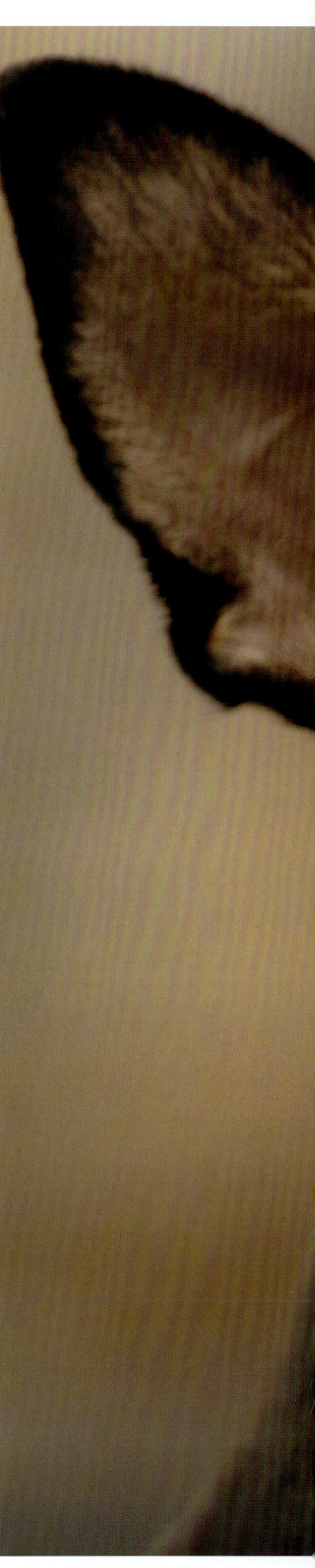

RIGHT:
Little charmer
The chihuahua is a charming dog that thrives on love and attention.

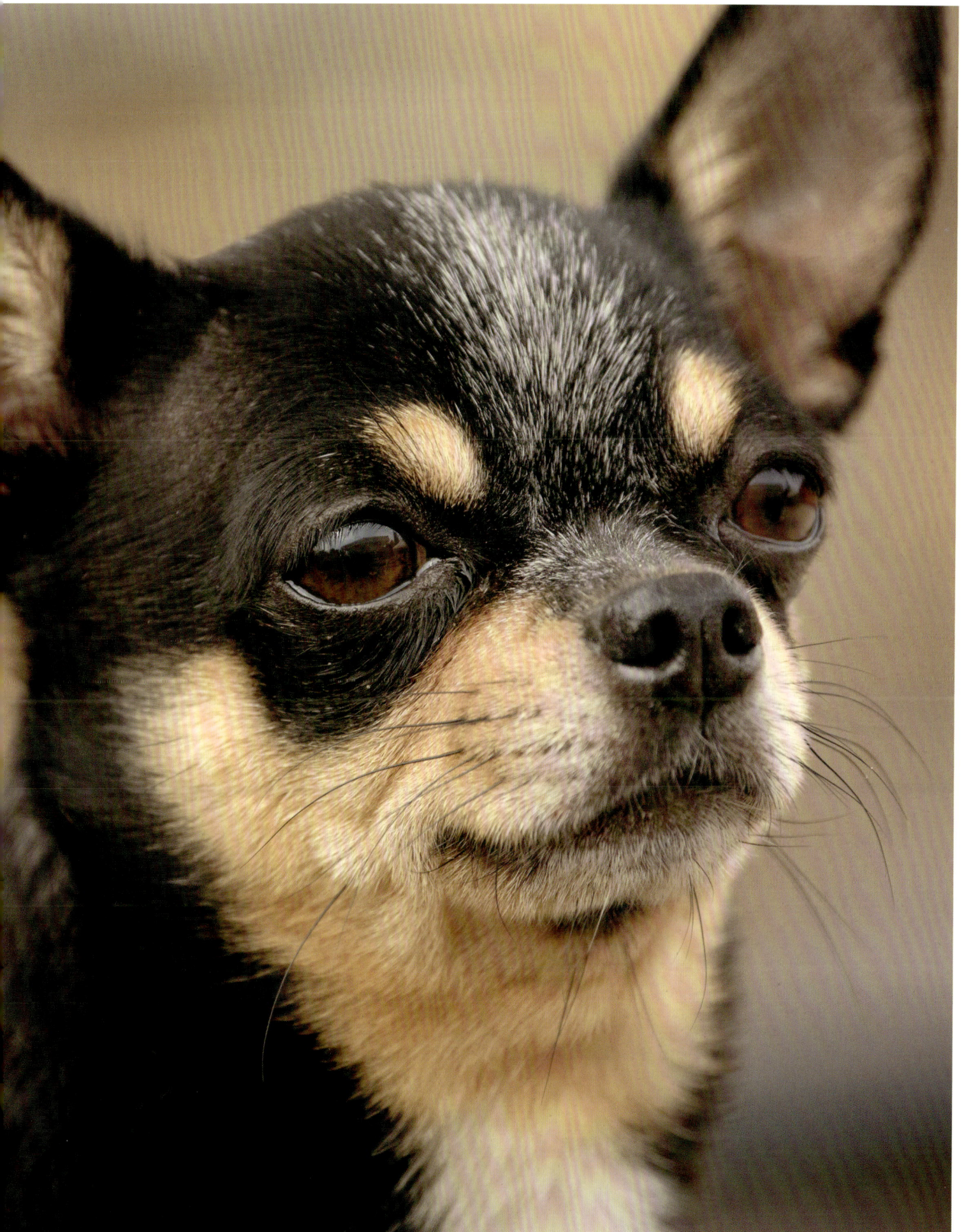

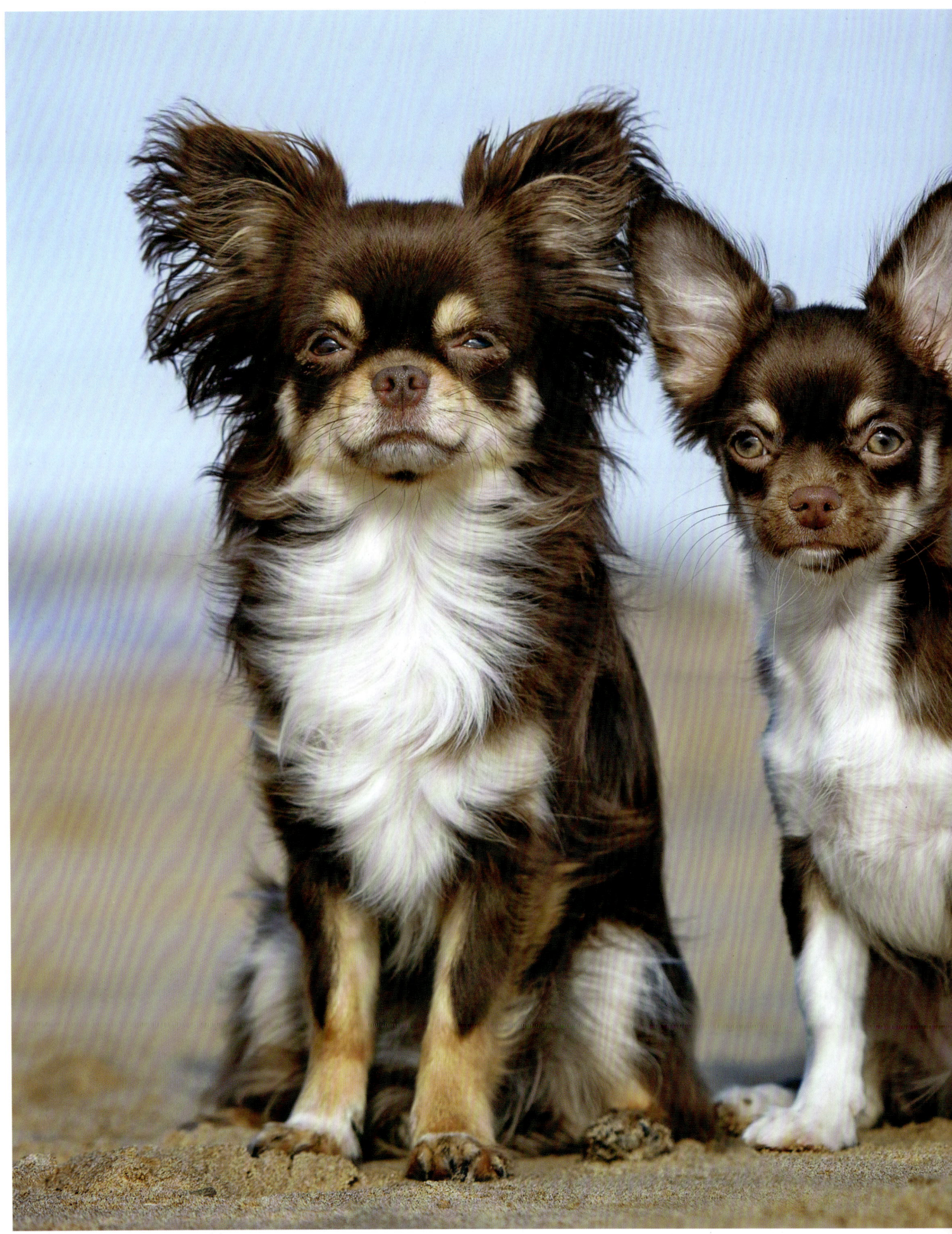

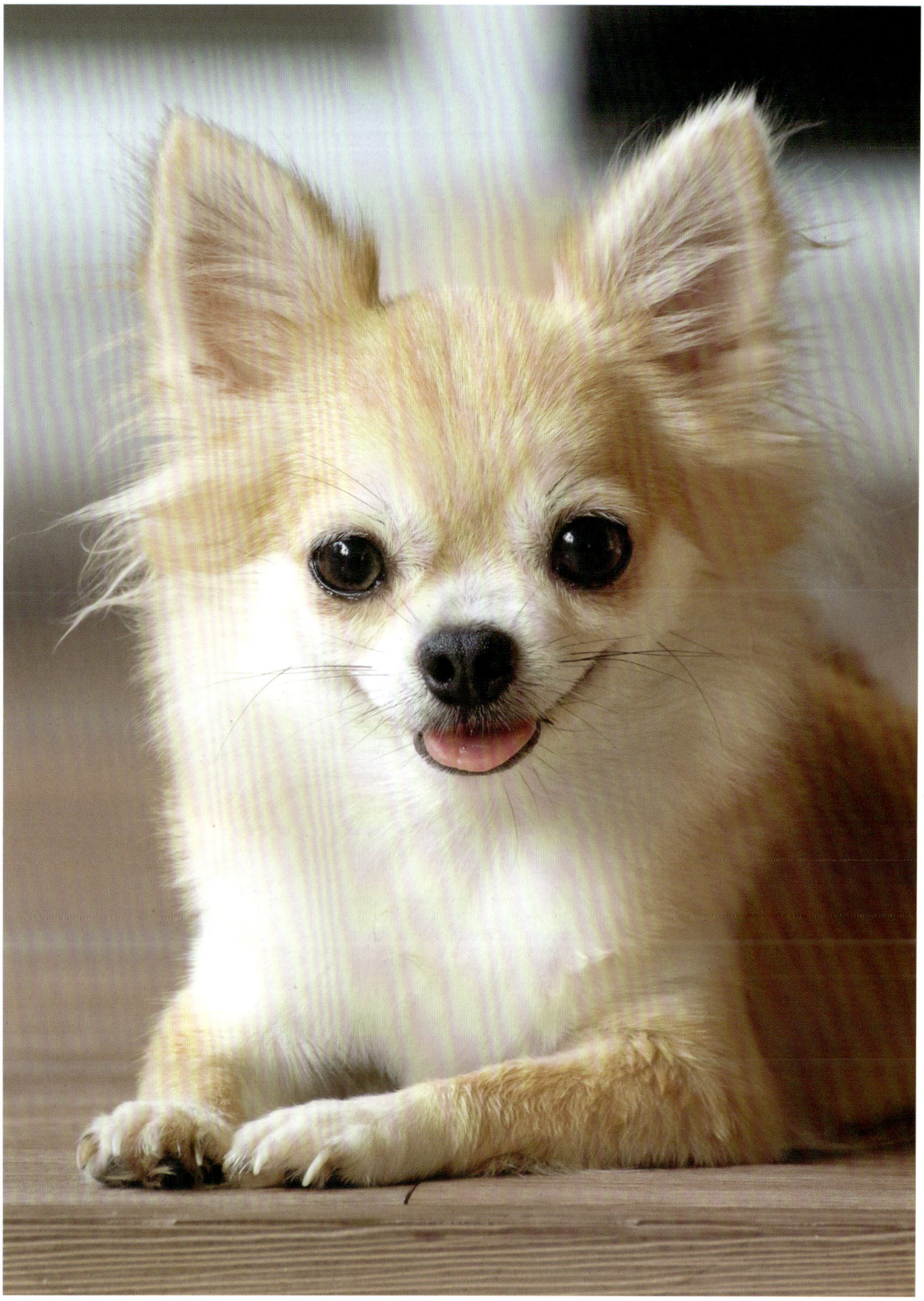

COMPANION DOGS

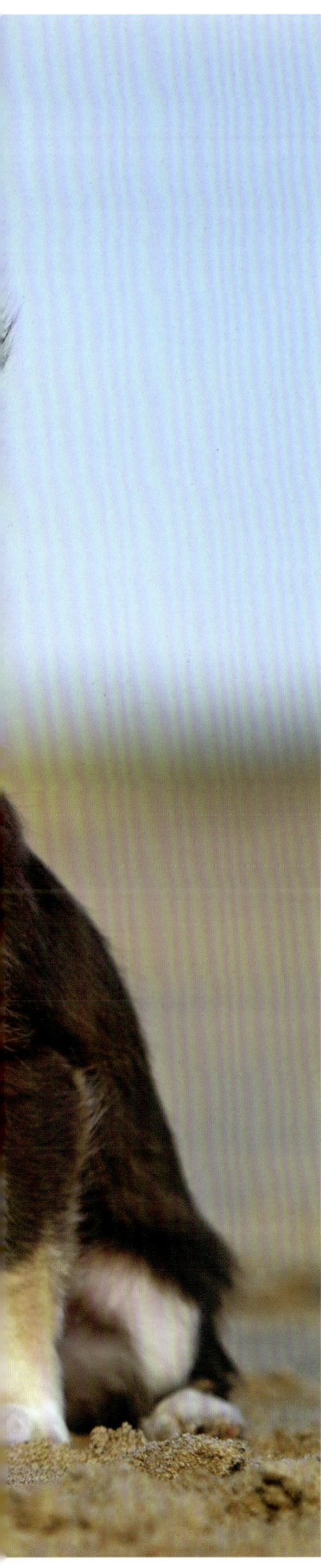

LEFT:
Perfect pets
Chihuahuas are suitable for first-time owners who are looking for a small and low-maintenance dog that can adapt to different environments.

ABOVE:
Keen for attention
This breed can be prone to separation anxiety if left alone for too long.

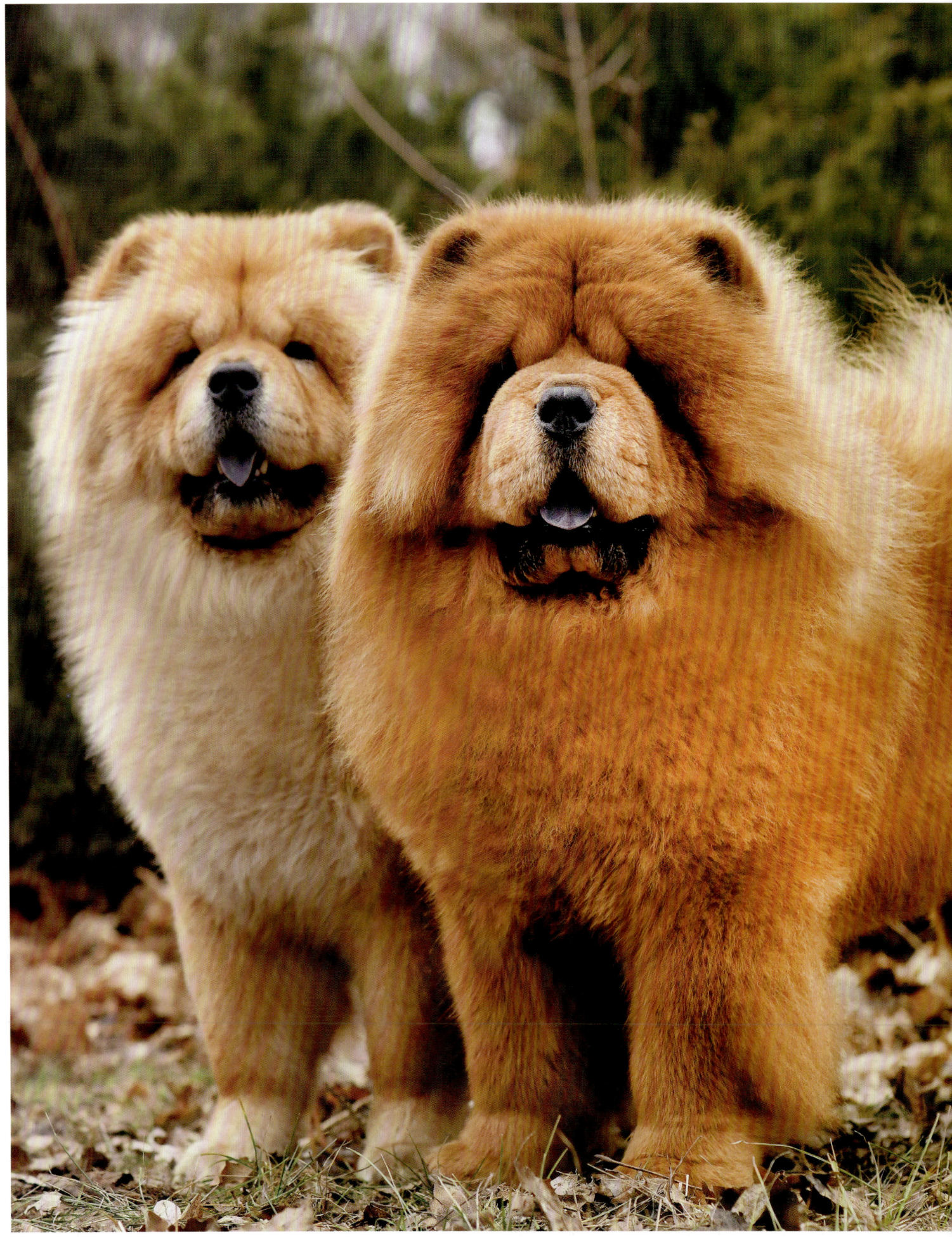

Chow Chow

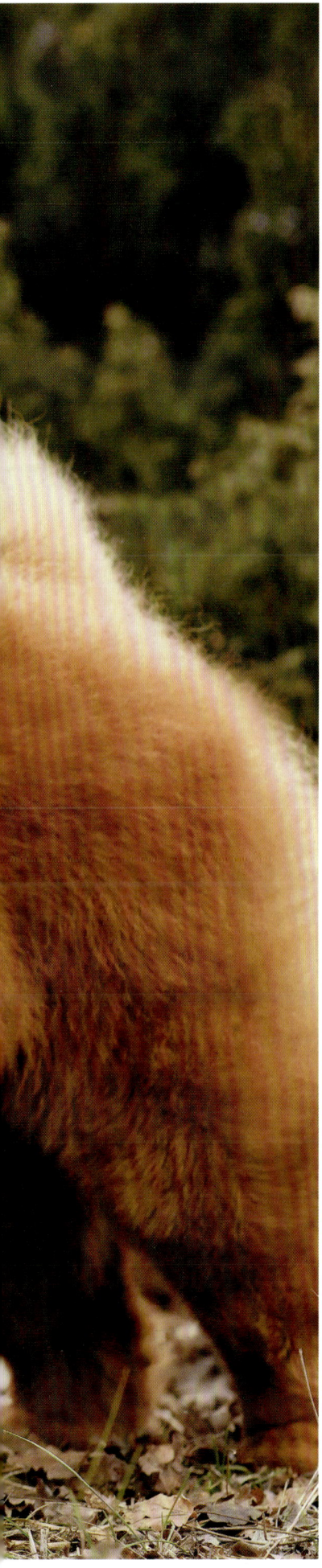

This distinctive Chinese dog with its teddy-bear looks and plush coat complete with a leonine mane is a very ancient breed. It dates back at least 2,200 years in the historical record. Chow chows appear on the hunt beside their masters in Han Dynasty wall carvings from the 3rd century BC. This dog, originating in wintery forests of northern China and beyond, is thought to be a close relative of the original common ancestor of the spitz-type dogs. The spitz-type dogs are all adapted to cold and include everything from the Alaskan malamute to the pomeranian and Norwegian elkhound.

Chow chows were bred to hulk loads, help with hunts and stand guard. They also won the hearts of their handlers and became well-kept pets. It is said that one Tang Dynasty emperor kept 5,000 of them! The Chinese call this breed the songshi quan, which means "puffy lion dog". The international name for the dogs is derived from a British slang term. In the 1820s, when the Chinese dogs were first put on show in London Zoo, they became known as chow chows, a term that previously referred to the collections of curious objects brought back by cargo ships as they returned from the far east.

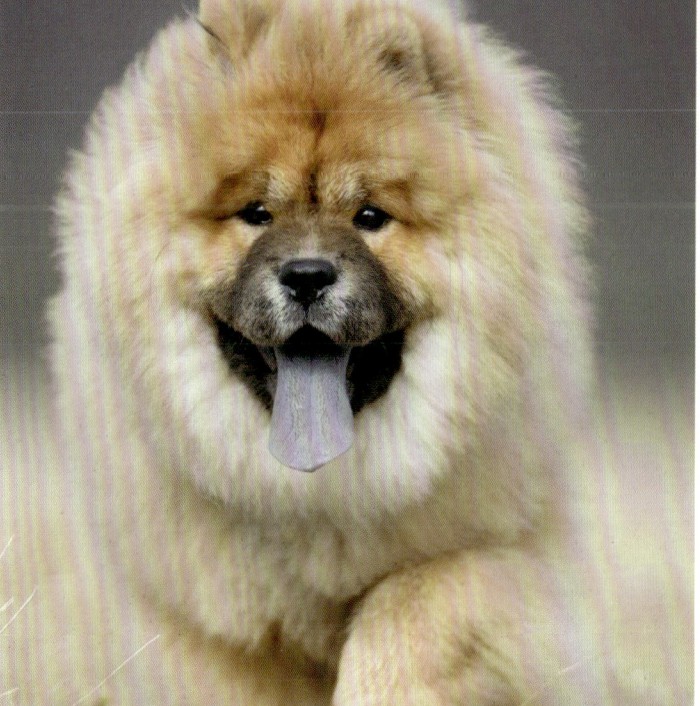

CHARACTERISTICS

Coat
Thick double coat that can be red, black, blue, cinnamon or cream in colour

Height
46–56cm (18–22in)

Weight
21–32kg (46–71lb)

Lifespan
8–12 years

Personality
Dignified and reserved

Origin
China

LEFT:
Boxy looks
The chow chow has a square profile and a lion-like mane. It needs regular grooming and a moderate amount of exercise. It can be wary of strangers and other dogs.

ABOVE:
Blue flash
The dog is well suited to the climates of northern China. It is also known for a distinctive blue-black tongue—and a seemingly scowling expression.

COMPANION DOGS

Clumber Spaniel

CHARACTERISTICS

Coat
A medium-length white coat with lemon or orange markings
Height
43–51cm (17–20in)
Weight
25–34kg (55–75lb)
Lifespan
10–12 years
Personality
Easy-going and slow-paced
Origin
England

This sturdy creature is among the largest and is certainly the heaviest of the spaniels, a group of breeds that are known for their eagerness and work ethic. The Clumber spaniel, named after the country estate of its creator, the Duke of Newcastle, has these qualities but dispenses them at a slower pace. This is due in part to the breed's level-headedness and also its cumbersome body and short legs.

The Clumber Spaniel was developed as a gundog that could push its way through the thick undergrowth that would thwart its more agile cousins. This was achieved in the late 18th century by crossing archaic spaniel breeds with basset hounds. The result was a dog with a powerful nose and relentless drive to track prey, and the body to muscle into the thickest recesses of a woodland to drive out quarry that had sought refuge there.

If that seems like hard work, then the Clumber spaniel would appear to agree. This slow-paced, low-energy breed loves to sleep a lot—and eat a lot in between. It is gentle and affectionate but aloof with strangers. The breed can suffer from some health problems, such as hip and spine disorders.

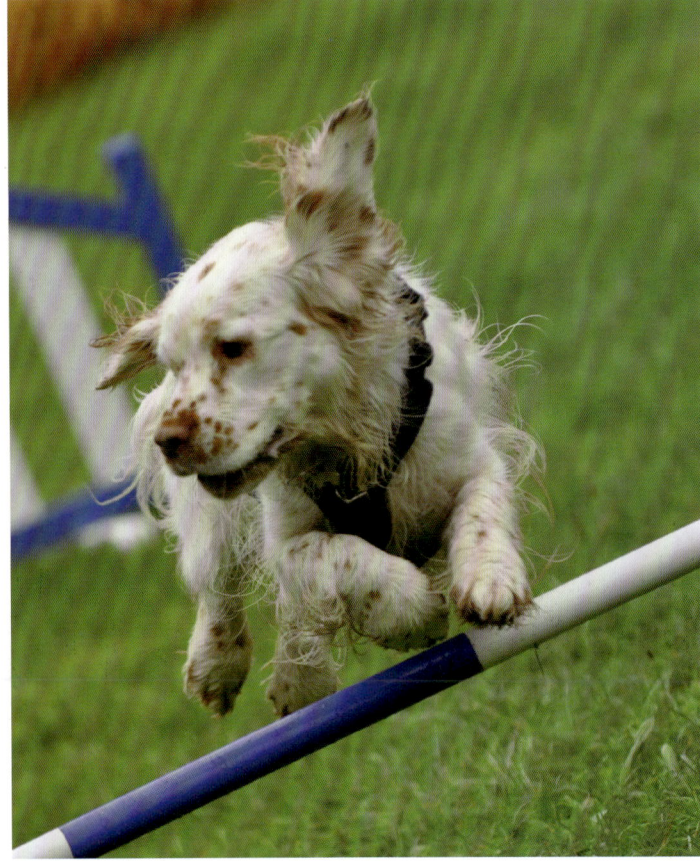

ABOVE:
Outdoor breeds
The Clumber spaniel is a good family pet that gets along well with children.

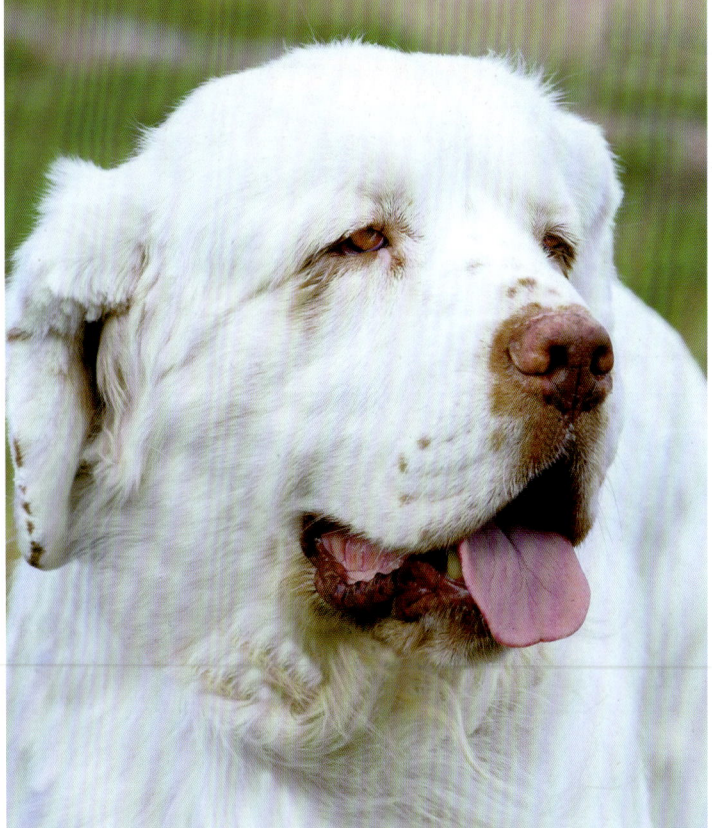

ABOVE:
Heat sensitive
The dogs find it hard to shed excess heat fast enough by panting, and so may become overheated on warm days.

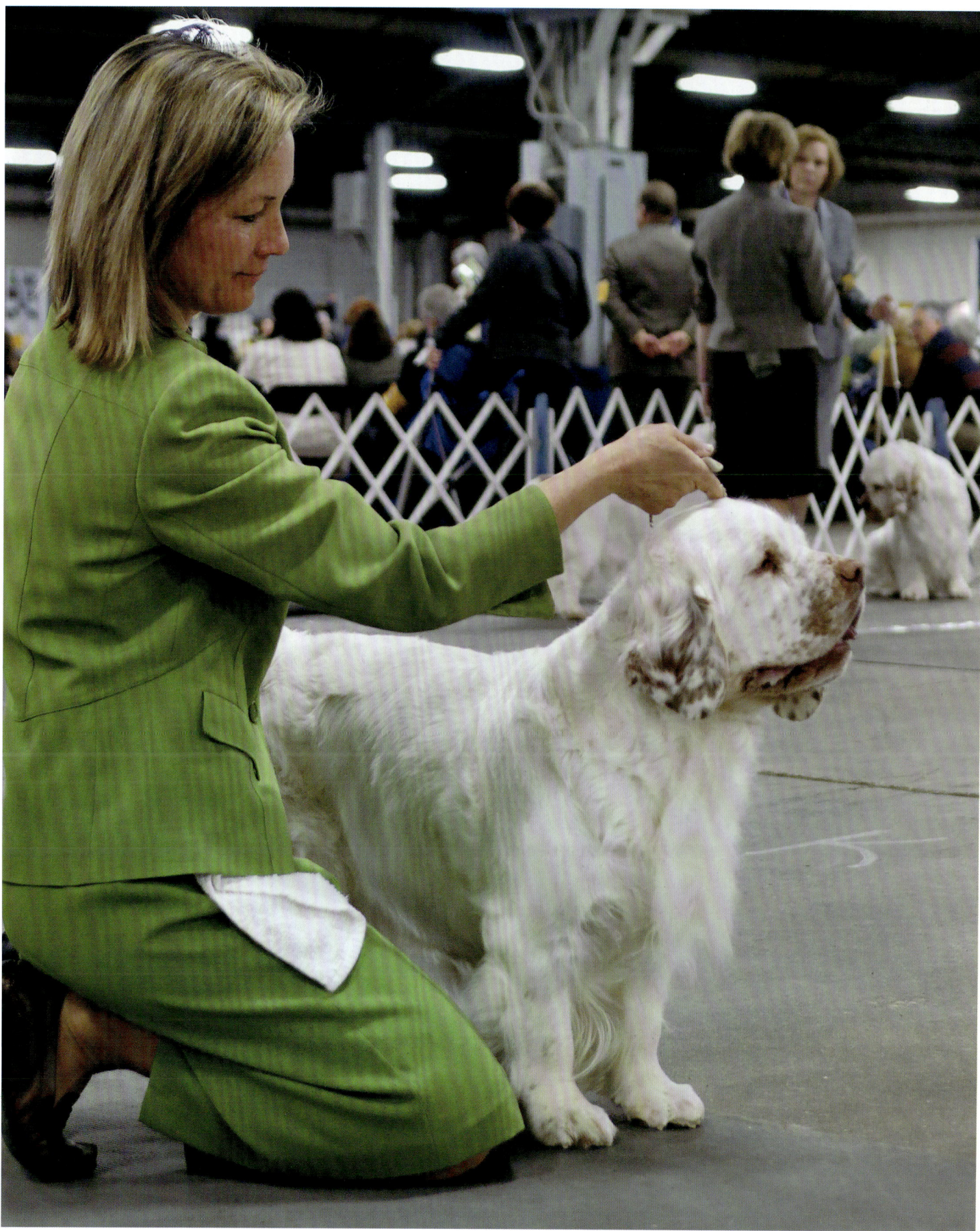

ABOVE:
Pros and cons
The good-looking spaniel has a lot going for it. However, it sheds a lot, has a tendency to drool and is a confirmed snorer.

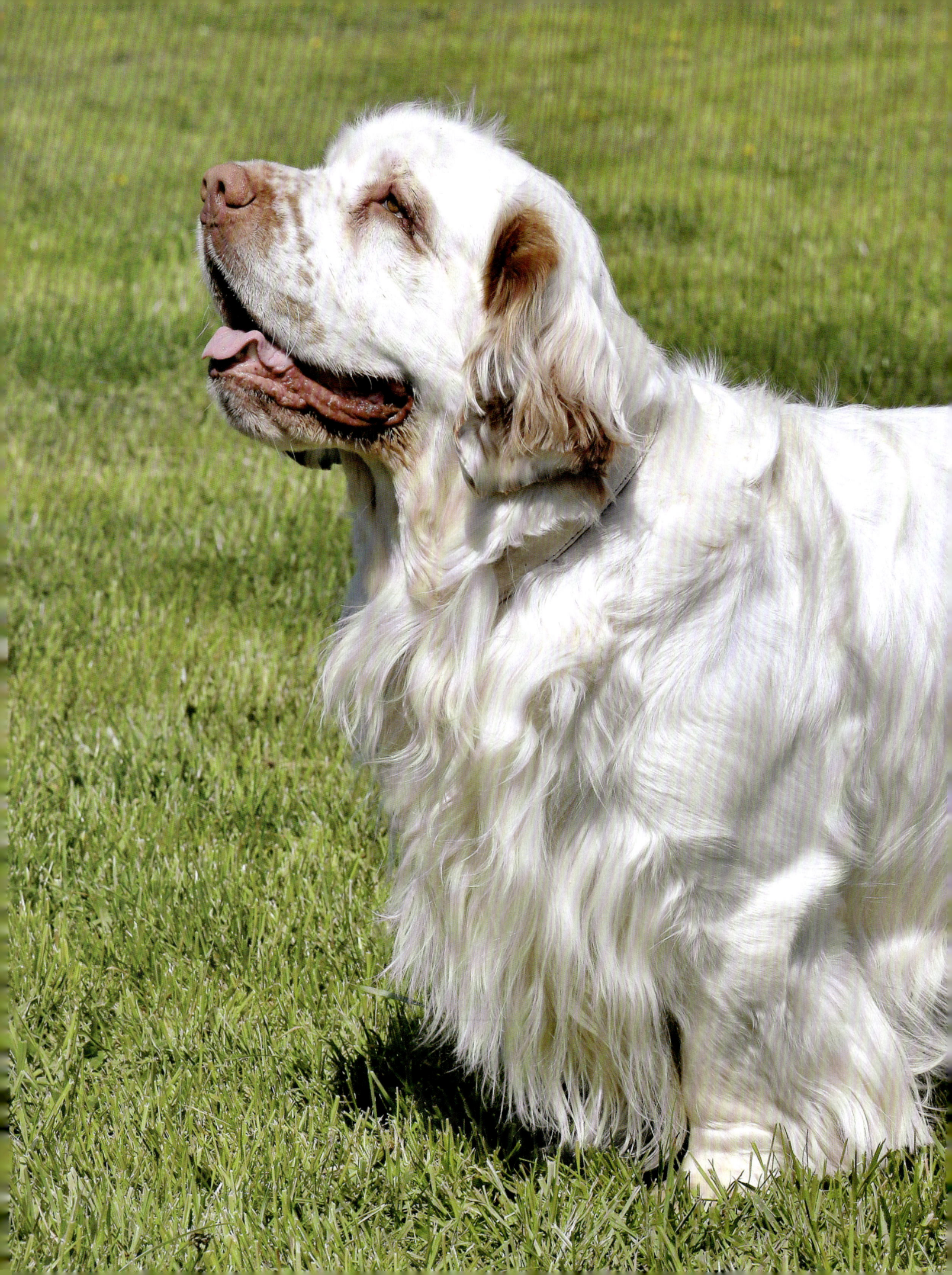

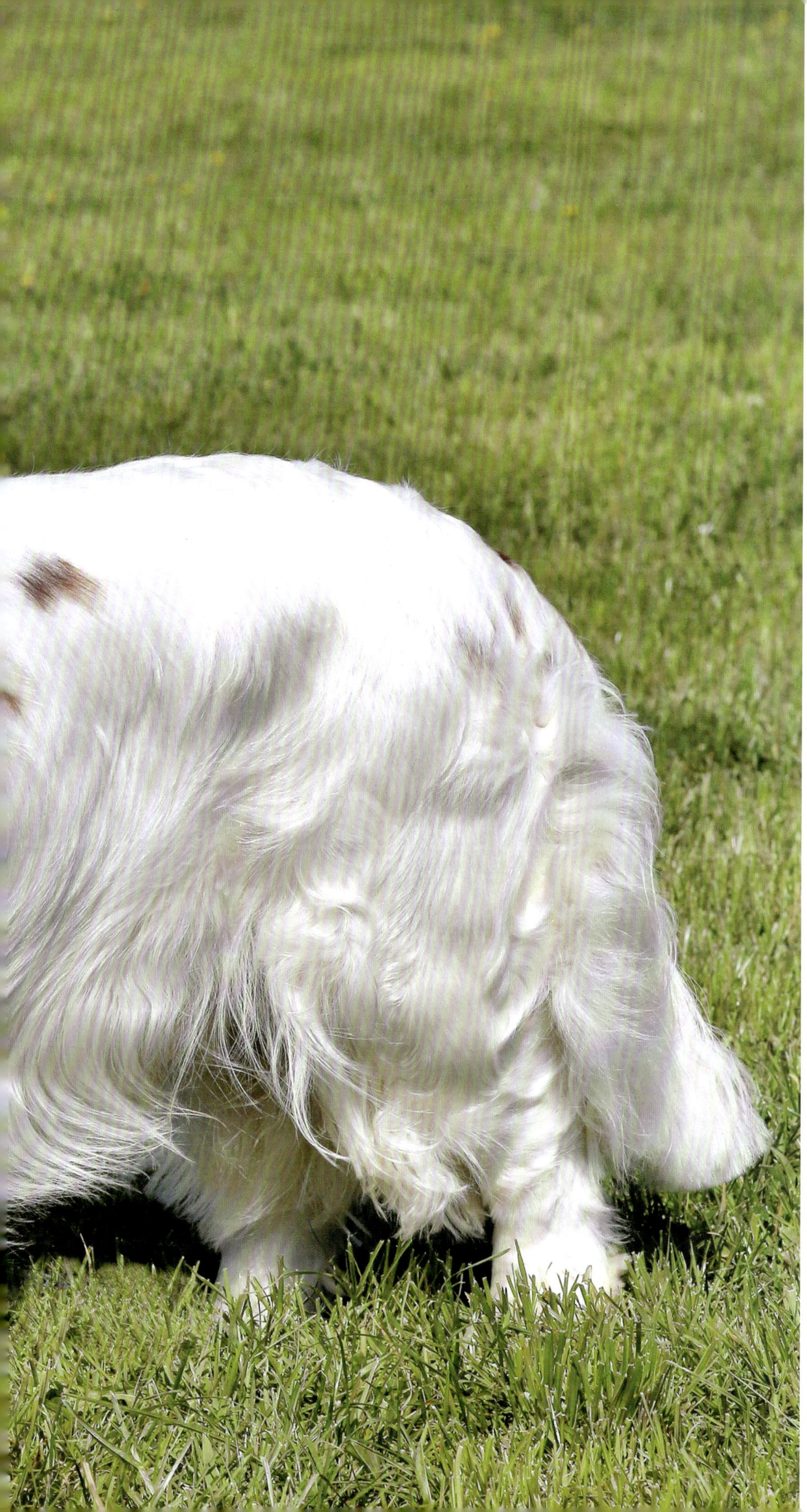

COMPANION DOGS

Out and about
This breed enjoys swimming and fetching but it can be stubborn and independent at times.

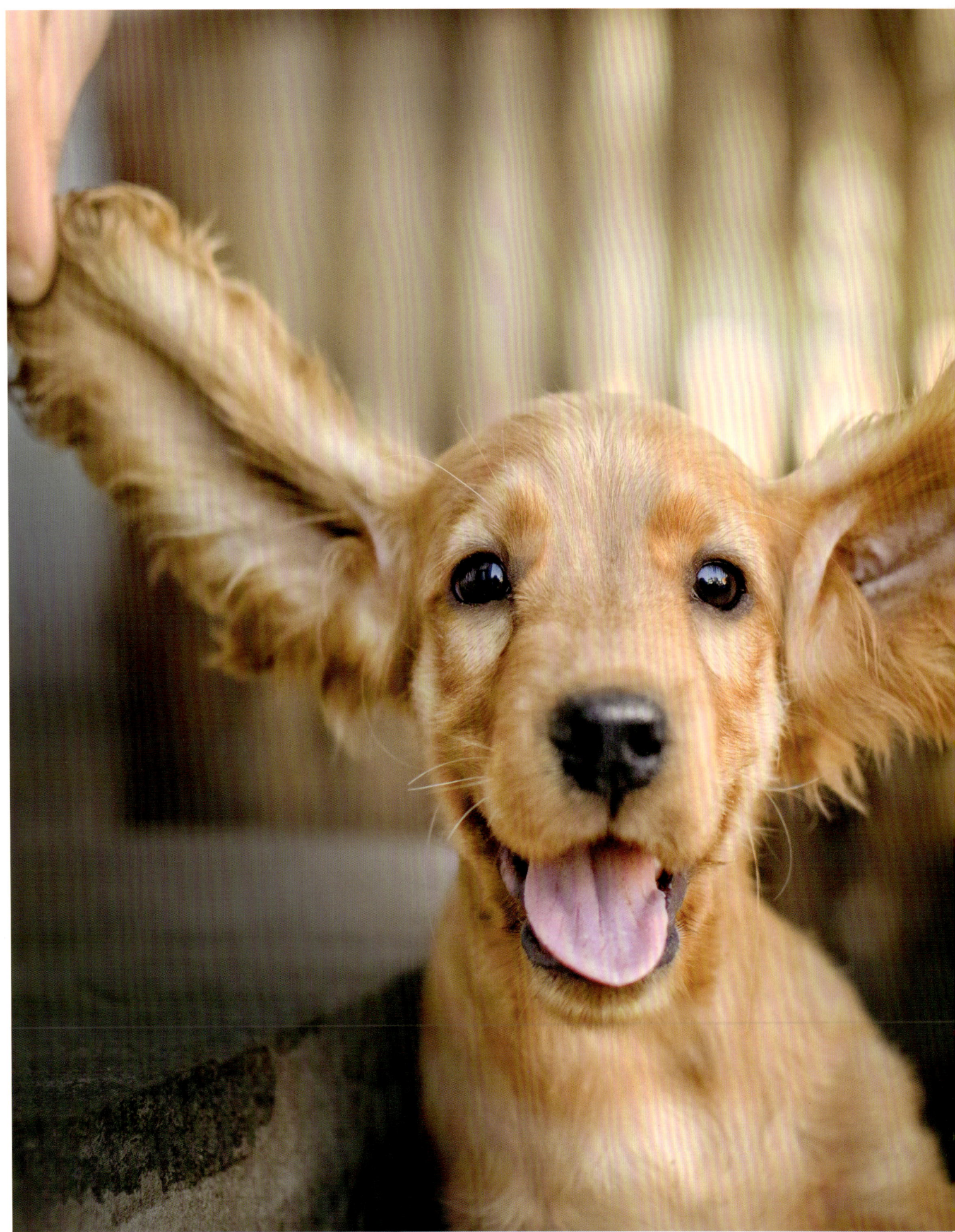

COMPANION DOGS

Cocker Spaniel

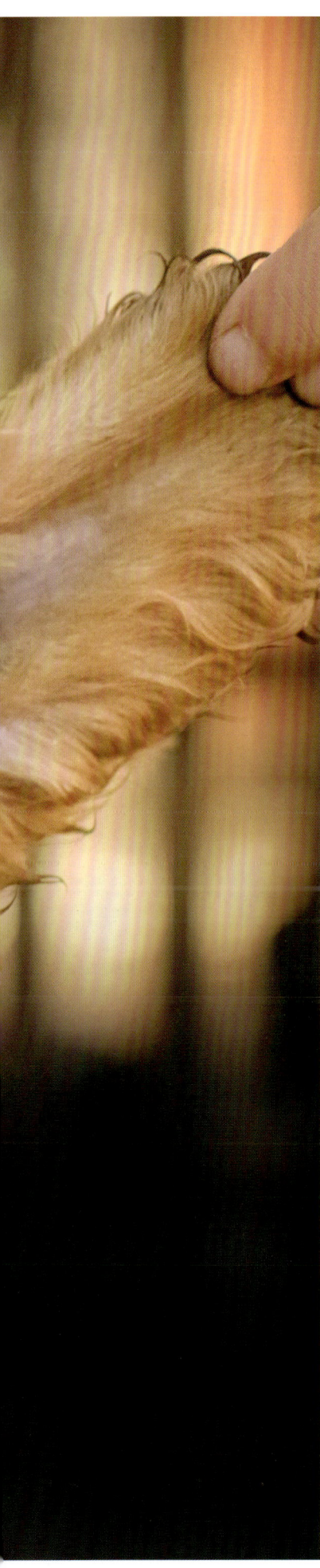

The original spaniel was a bird hunter, while later refinements led to a division between the land and water spaniels. The cocker spaniel is a small English land spaniel that was bred further still to be a specialist hunter of woodcock and grouse. These are small land-feeding birds that live among hedgerows and woodlands. They spend their days stalking among the foliage foraging for worms and grubs among the leaf litter and loose soil. When disturbed, the birds flap off the ground but do not head for the sky, but zig zag through the trees before dropping back out of sight. The cocker spaniel was bred to be small enough to track the birds through the dense undergrowth but have the power and tenacity to push on come what may so the birds were forced into the open.

As a result, the breed has that spaniel get-up-and-go but is easier to feed and house. This makes the cocker one of the most favoured spaniel pet breeds. There is an American version of the cocker that is bred for show. It is slightly smaller than the original English breed with a more profuse coat.

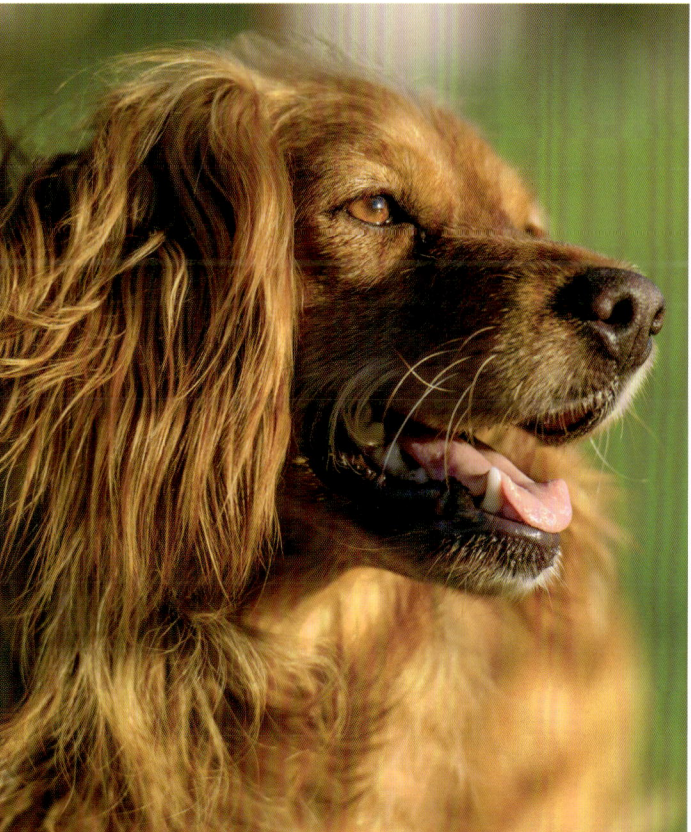

CHARACTERISTICS

Coat
Long and silky coat in various colours and patterns
Height
38–41cm (15–16in)
Weight
13–15kg (29–33lb)
Lifespan
12–15 years
Personality
Gentle and busy
Origin
England

LEFT:
Hairy features
The cocker spaniel has ears fringed with long, wavy hairs.

ABOVE:
Good dog
Small and energetic, these friendly dogs have a reputation for being easy to train, eager to please and always happy.

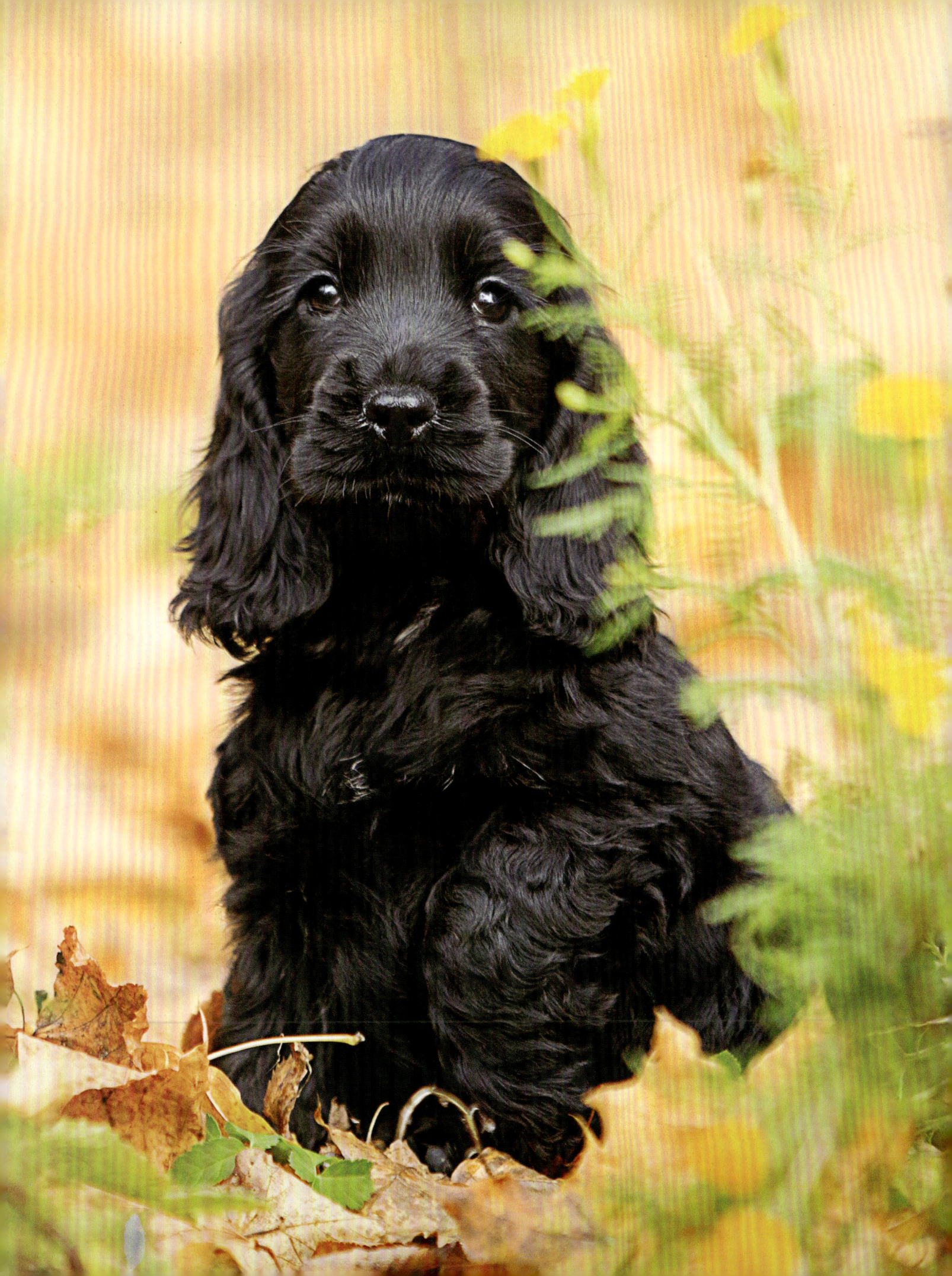

COMPANION DOGS

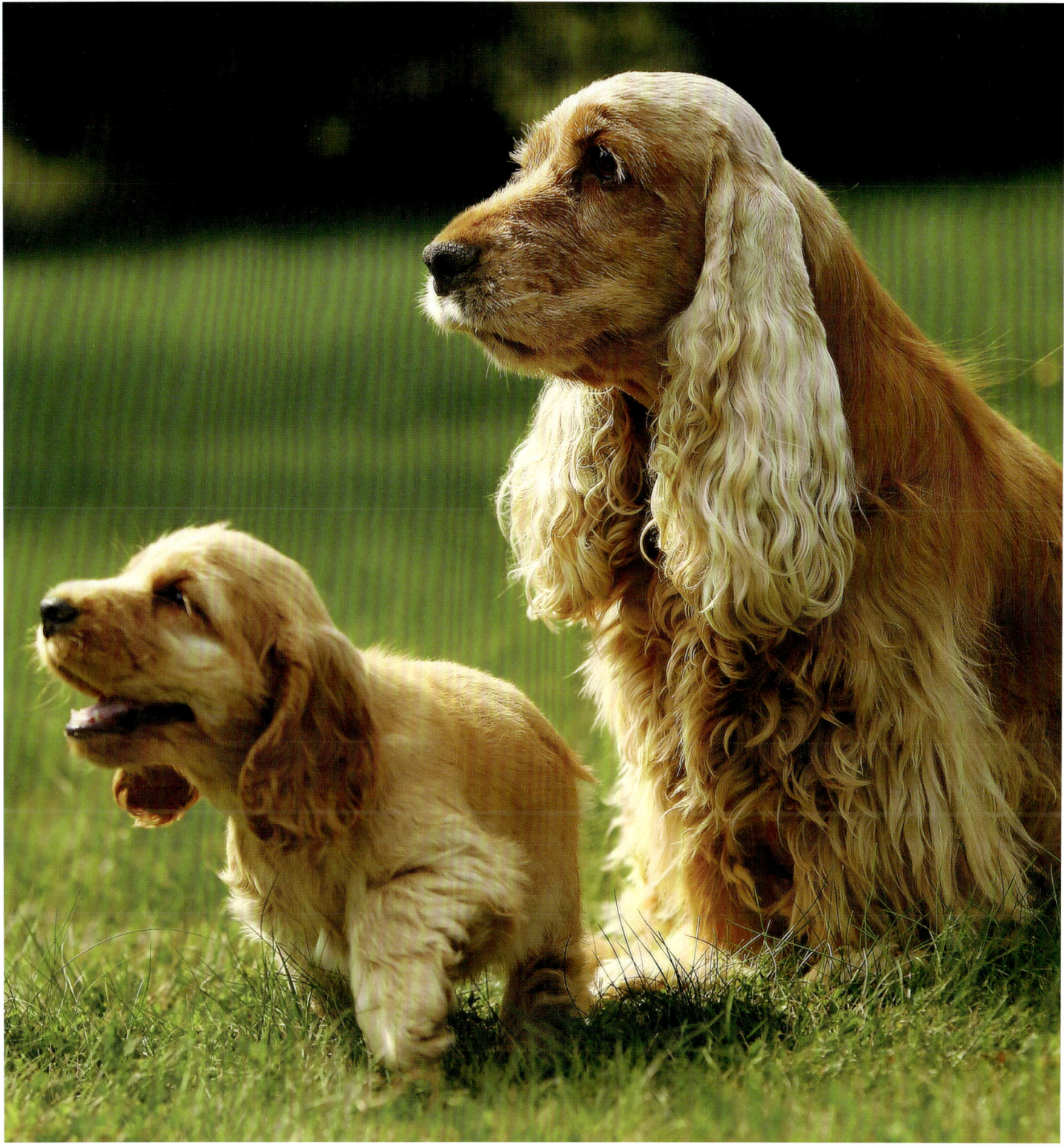

OPPOSITE:
Shiny coat
This breed of dogs needs regular grooming to keep their coats healthy.

ABOVE:
Puppies
Adult and young cocker spaniels alike are people-oriented and good with children.

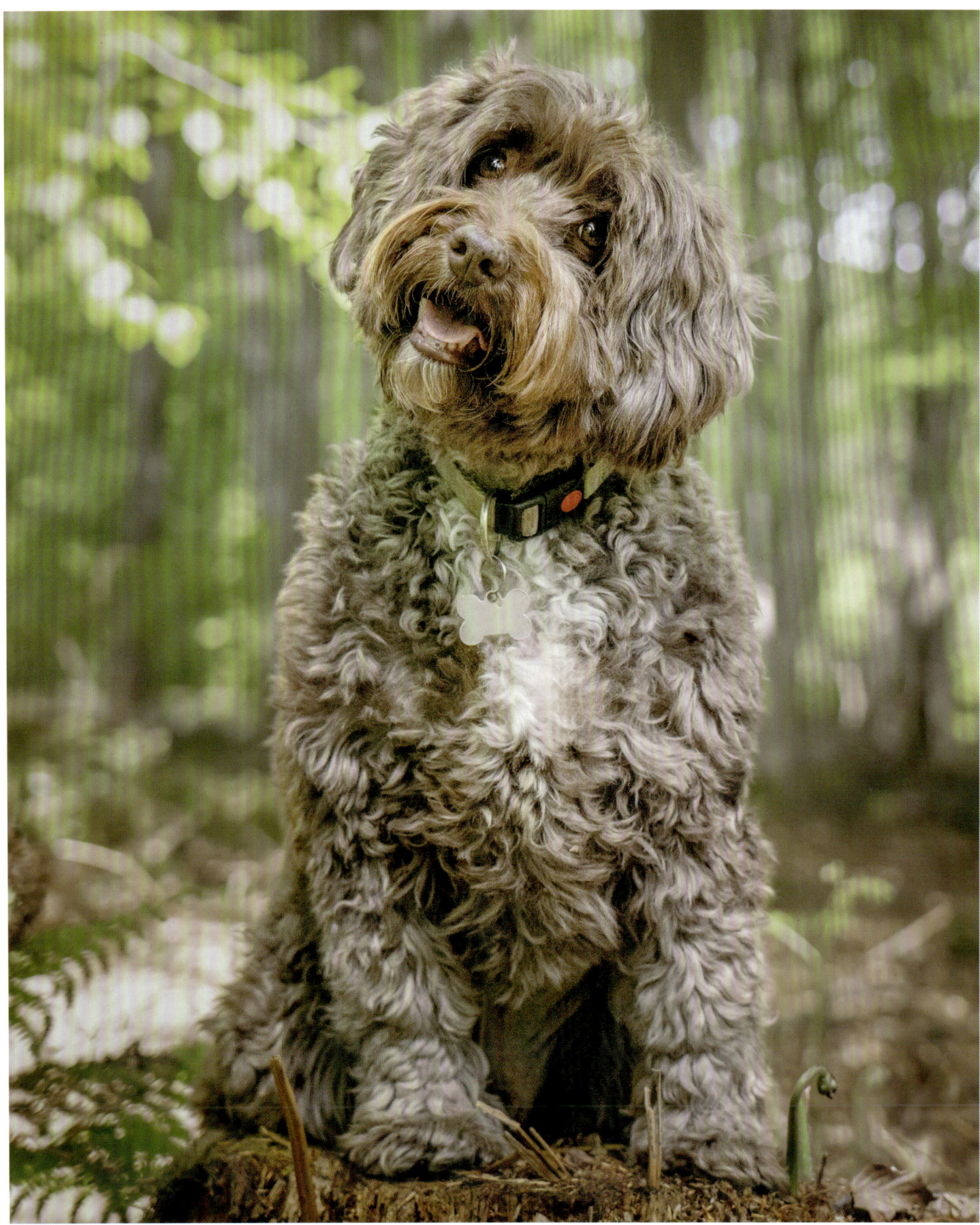

ABOVE:
Familiar features
The cockapoo has large round eyes and drooping ears. There is also long hair on the muzzle.

Cockerpoo

CHARACTERISTICS

Coat
Has varying lengths and has a range of waviness and colours
Height
25–38cm (10–15in)
Weight
5kg–10kg (11–22lb)
Lifespan
14–15 years
Personality
Affectionate and tractable
Origin
United States

Now very popular as a family pet, the cockerpoo is a crossbreed between a cocker spaniel and a poodle, mostly miniatures. They are also sometimes called cockapoos or spoodles. These crossbreedings were started in the United States in the 1960s, and today the cockerpoo is one of the most sought after types of dog. The original reasoning behind the hybridisation was to create an ideal pet dog that had the intelligence and fun-loving personality of a spaniel with the good looks of a low-shedding poodle coat. It is also claimed that this outbreeding helps to reduce the numerous congenital health problems that build up in dog breeds that have been interbred for centuries. Breeding organizations are now trying to consolidate the cockerpoo with hope of it achieving the status of a breed in its own right. As is common with crossbreeds the size of the dogs is variable and attempts are being made to classify the dogs by size as miniature and standard.

Cockerpoos are generally healthy, but breeding is more haphazard, and they are highly adaptable dogs that fit into many lifestyles. They are easily trained and affectionate to all members of the family.

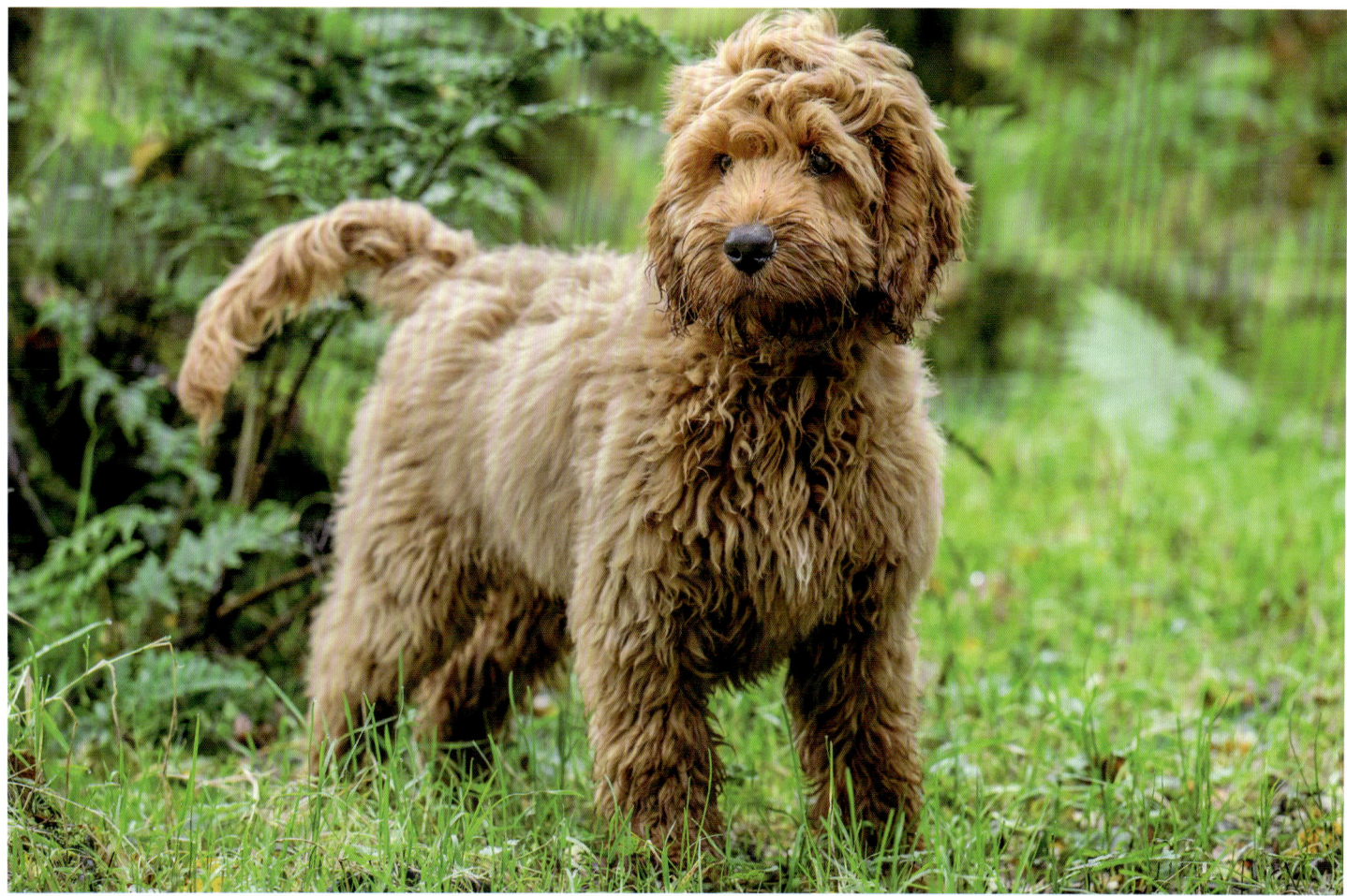

ABOVE:
Woolly and wavy
The coat of a cockapoo is always curly and the tail usually feathered. The body is squarer than either of its parental breeds.

COMPANION DOGS

Dalmatian

The origin of this most-distinctive of dogs is not clear. Historians say there is evidence that the dalmatian was first created everywhere from Britain to North Africa to the Middle East. However, there is no doubt that in the 1800s the dogs became closely associated with the eastern coast of the Adriatic Sea in what is now Croatia and Montenegro but was once better known as Dalmatia. Dalmatians were bred as hunting dogs and guardian dogs but became known as coach dogs. In this role dogs would run alongside horse-drawn carriages with the primary aim of fending off attack and standing guard over the horses during breaks in the journey. The dogs caught the attention of the nobility who were not only attracted to the utility of being accompanied by a phalanx of dalmatians but also because it looked so incredibly elegant. At the same time over in America, the breeds became fire-house dogs. They ran ahead of the firetruck helping to clear the path with their barking. And today, of course, the dalmatian is most famed as the leading characters in the novel and blockbuster cartoon *The Hundred and One Dalmatians*, where they need to be saved from a cruel villain who wants them only for their spotted coats.

CHARACTERISTICS

Coat
A short white coat with dark black, brown or liver; the spots begin to show at around four weeks
Height
56–61cm (22–24in)
Weight
18–27kg (40–60lb)
Lifespan
Around 10 years
Personality
Active and dignified
Origin
Croatia

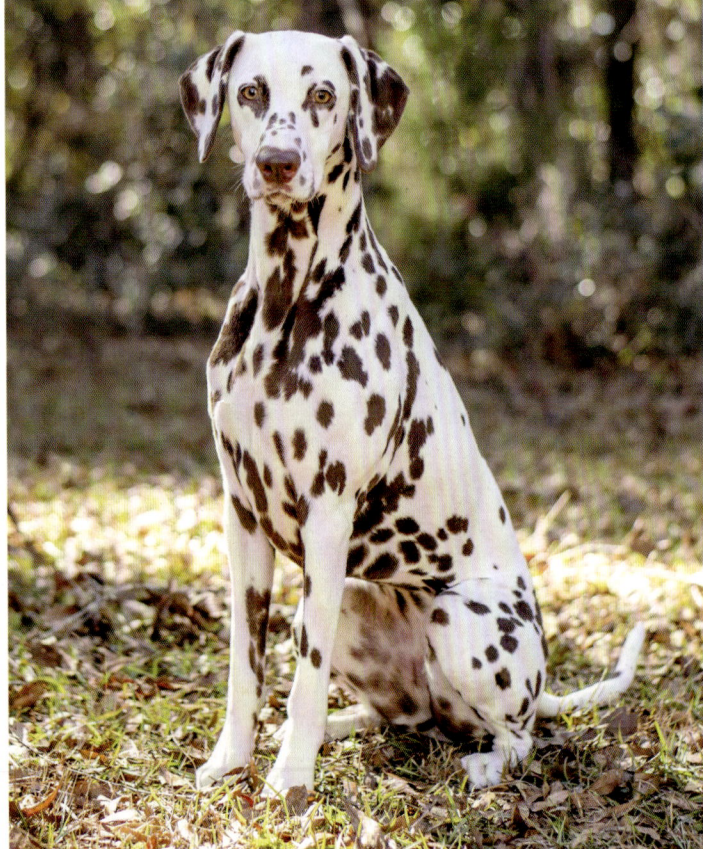

ABOVE:
Developing spots
The dog's famous dark spots appear once they are a few weeks old.

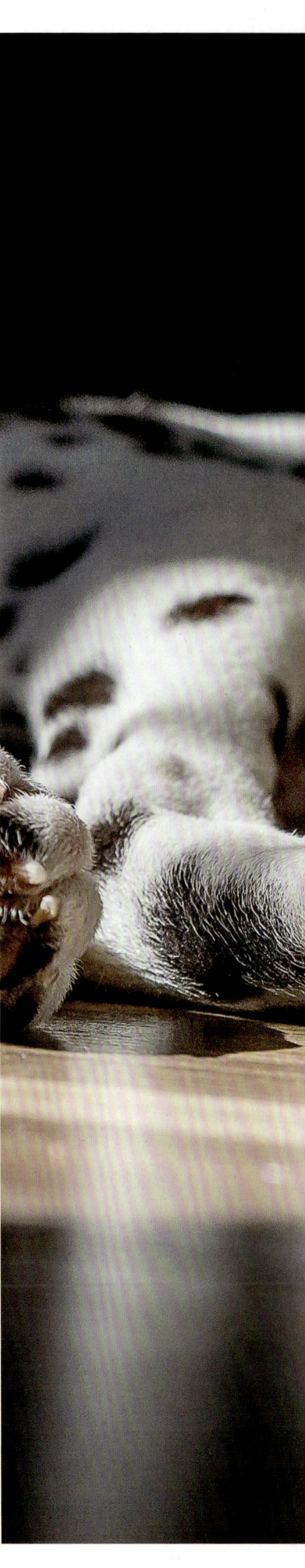

RIGHT:
Easy companion
The dalmatian is a low-maintenance dog in terms of grooming but it sheds a lot. The white coat sheds a lot more than the black parts.

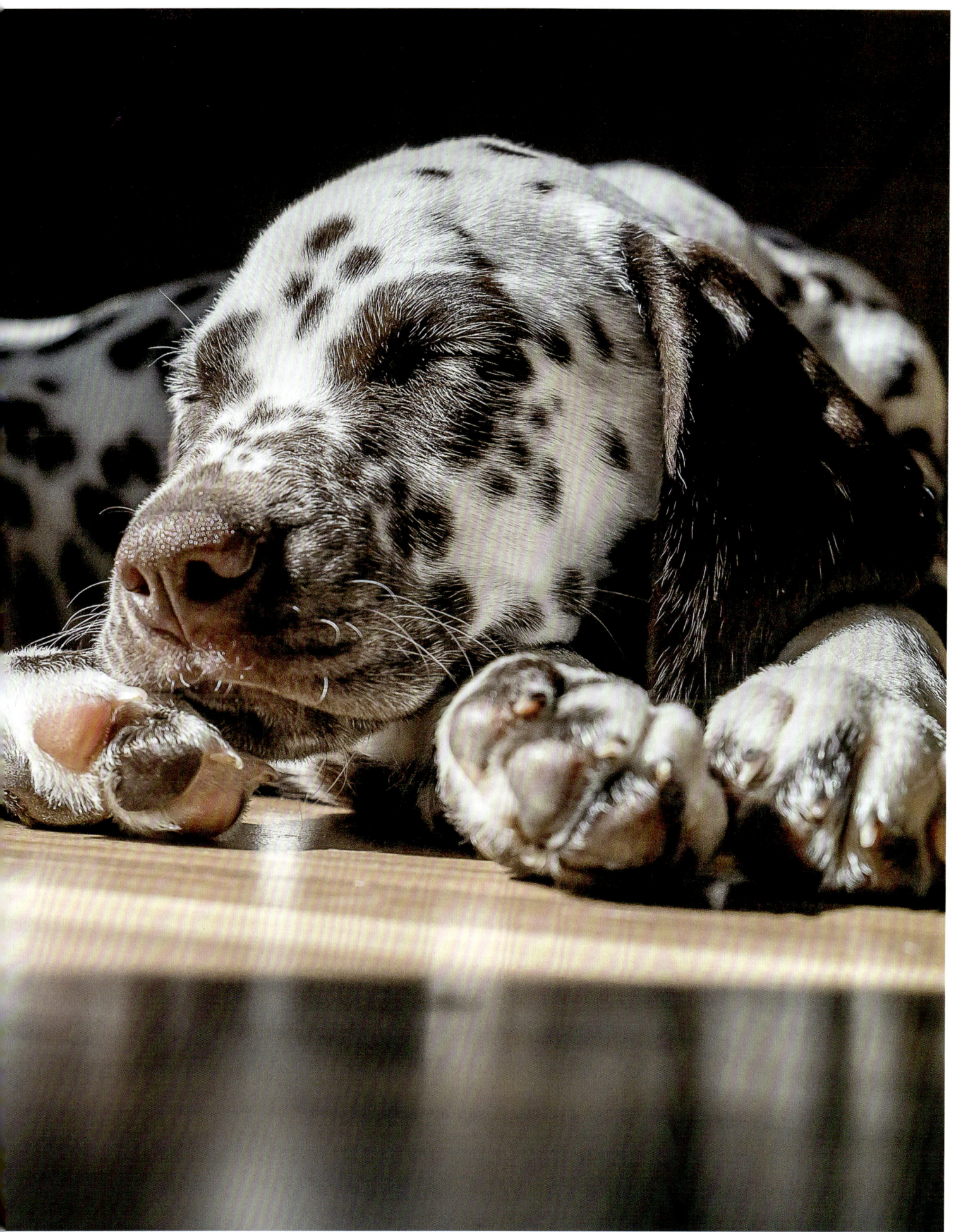

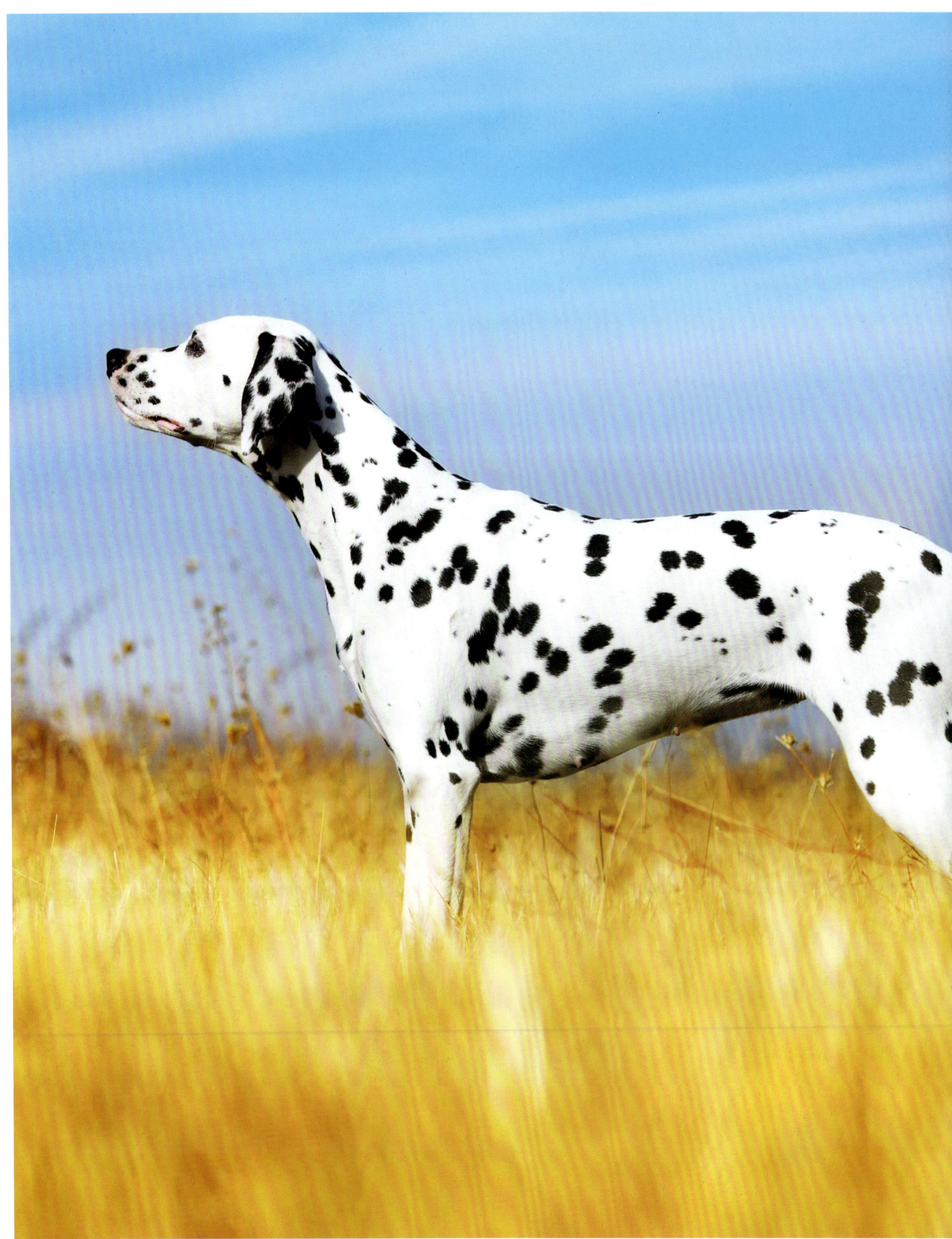

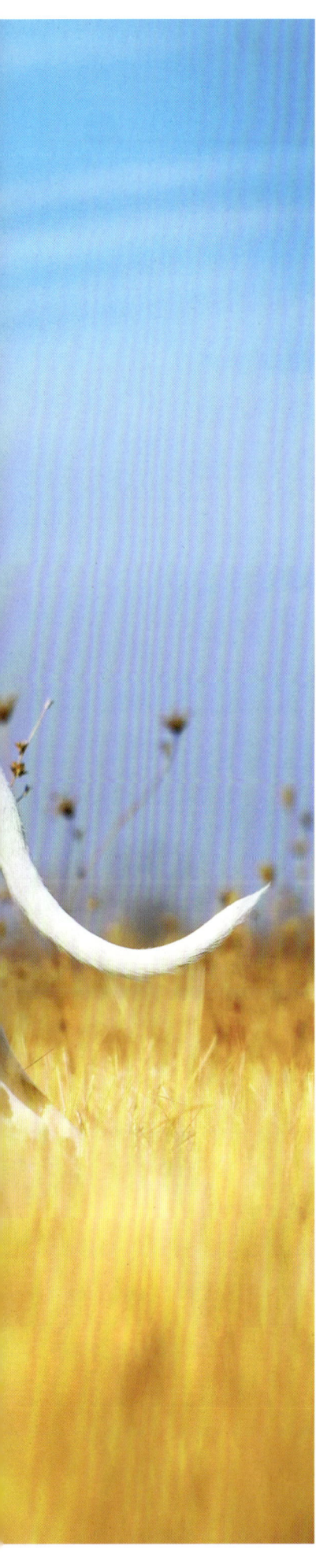

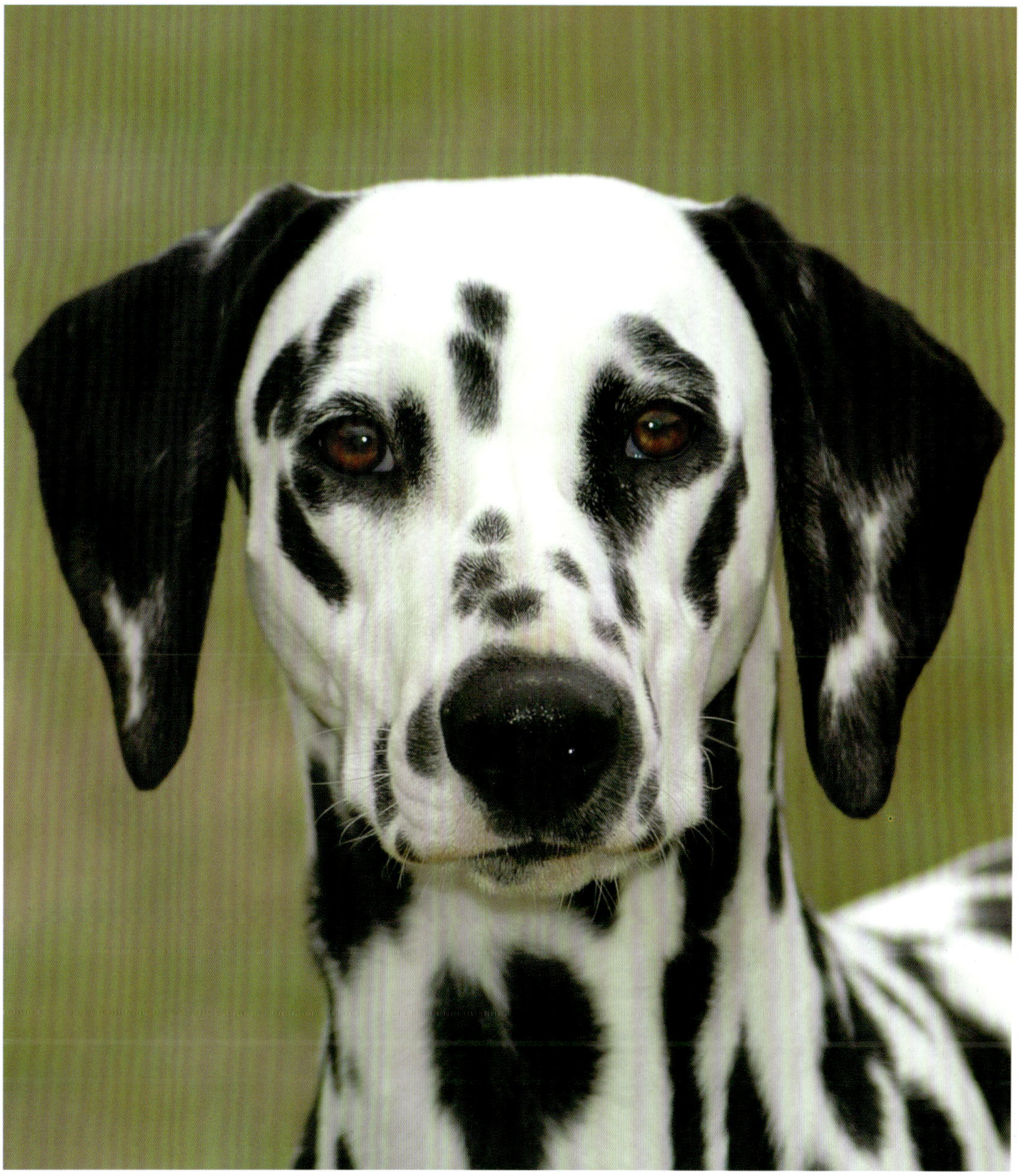

LEFT AND ABOVE:
Prestigious pooch
The Dalmatian ran alongside the conveyances as a symbol of the wealth and status of the passengers inside.

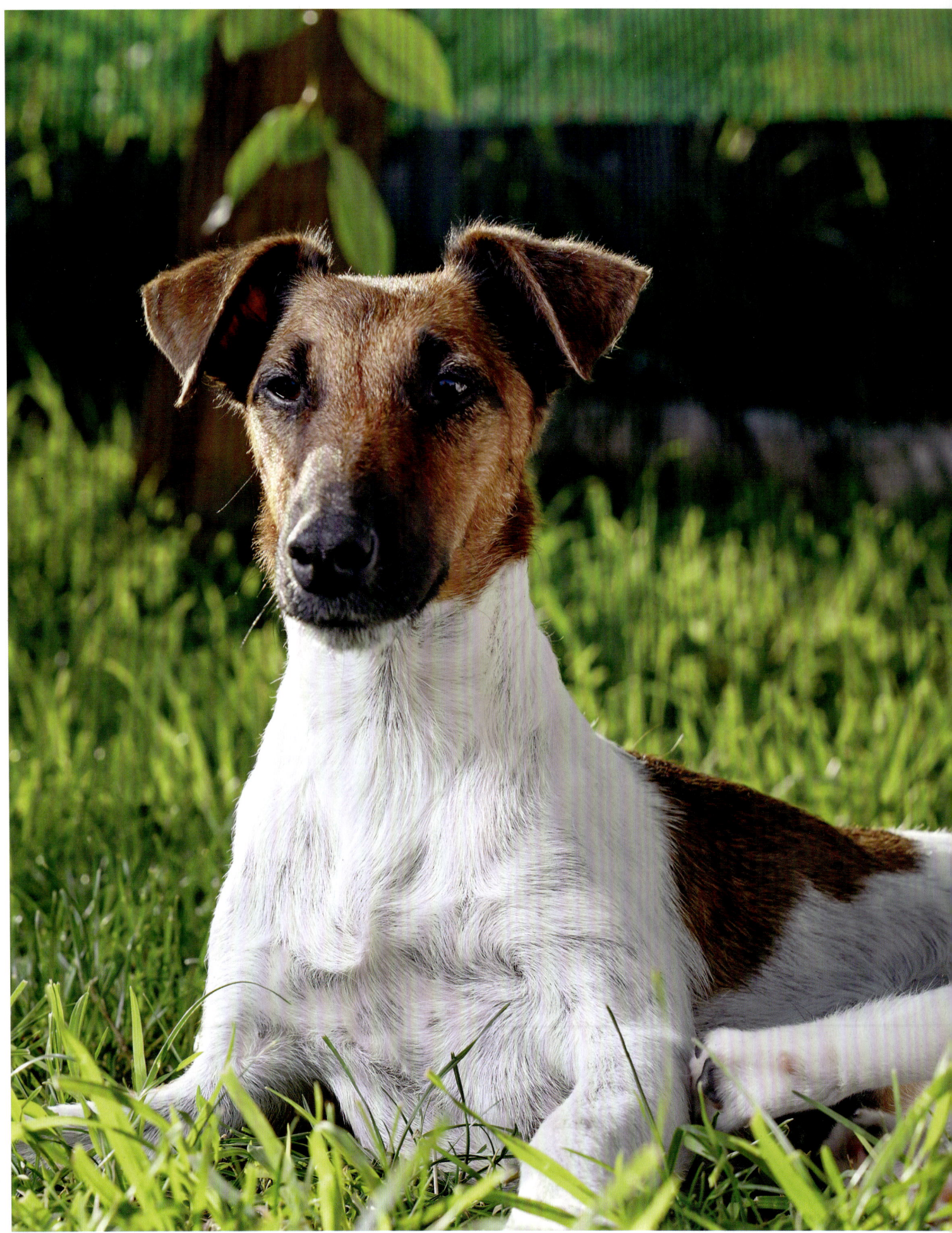

Smooth Fox Terrier

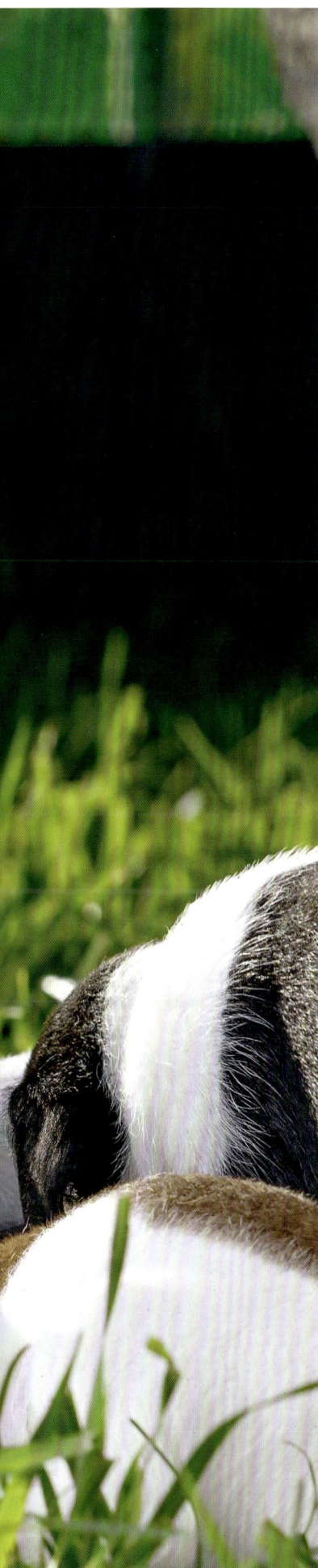

For many years, these tenacious little dogs were as much a part of a British fox hunt as the pack of foxhounds. The small terriers could not hope to keep up with the loping hounds and so were allowed to follow the pack stowed in the hunting master's saddlebag. They were called upon only if the fox had gone to ground. The terrier would be small enough to follow the fox underground, scrabbling with its feet to dig the quarry out. Once the fox was forced back out into the open, the hounds would take over, and the terrier would resume its position among the hunt followers.

The smooth fox terrier is a little smaller than its wire-haired cousin, and so could fit into smaller burrows. However, it found rough ground and thorny cover harder to handle.

Fox hunting with hounds is now forbidden in Britain, but the sociable smooth fox terrier has been adopted as a firm favourite as a family pet. Their shorter coat sheds less than that of the wire fox terrier, which adds to its appeal.

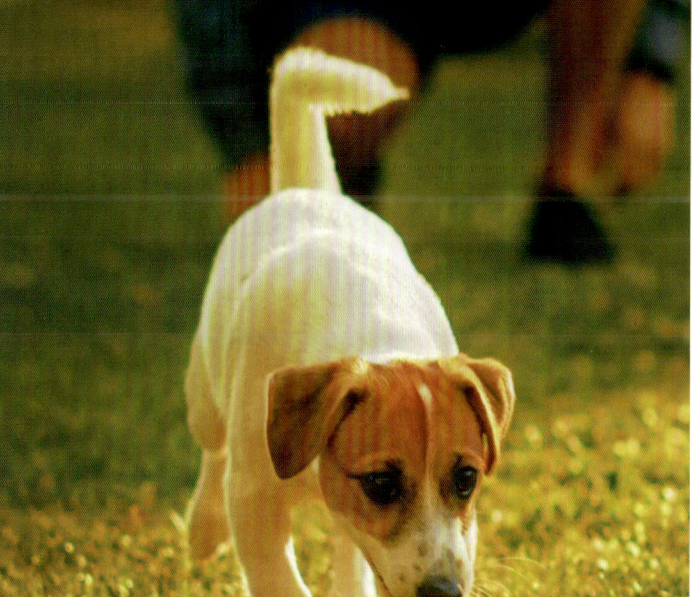

CHARACTERISTICS

Coat
A short and smooth coat that is mostly short; generally white with black or tan markings
Height
Up to 39cm (15in)
Weight
Up to 8kg (18lb)
Lifespan
Around 10 years
Personality
Gregarious and brave
Origin
Britain

LEFT:
Head shape
The dog has a distinctive V-shaped head.

ABOVE:
Certain profile
The fox terrier generally carries its tail erect.

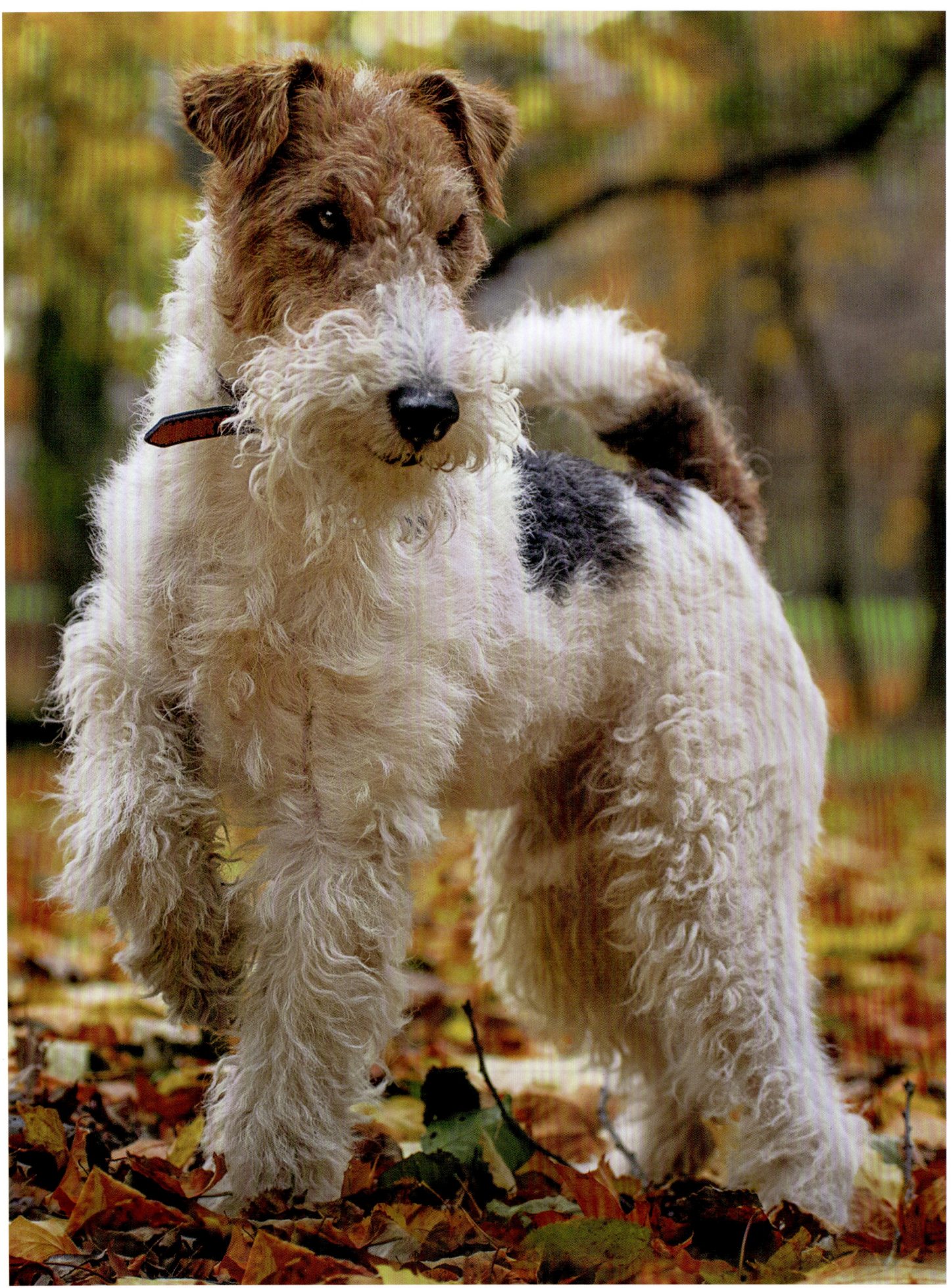

Wire Fox Terrier

CHARACTERISTICS

Coat
A wiry coat that is white with black and tan markings. Shed hair needs to be plucked regularly. The coat needs thorough stripping quarterly

Height
Up to 39cm (15in)

Weight
Up to 8kg (18lb)

Lifespan
Around 10 years

Personality
Clever and confident

Origin
Britain

The fox terriers have been an established breed since the end of the 18th century. The wire fox terrier, named after its coarse, wiry coat, is the bigger and chunkier of the two British breeds (the other being the smooth fox terrier). As its name suggests the breed is a tormentor of foxes, with the job of driving these wild canids from any hiding place that is too confined for baying hounds to get at. The wiry coat sheds a lot, which is a fact not lost on fox terrier owners, and is well suited to the rough and tumble of fox baiting in the mud and brambles. The breed is mostly white, and traditionally was not allowed to have any reddish markings in case it was mistaken for the fox. Today, this breed is permitted to have small tan markings. The hairs on the muzzle are traditionally kept long as a protective measure for a dog that has the job of poking its nose into fox holes.

Fox terriers are bold, intelligent and very athletic, which is perhaps why one of comic-book literature's most enduring dog heroes is a wire fox terrier. Hergé chose this breed for Tintin's sidekick and frequent saviour Snowy.

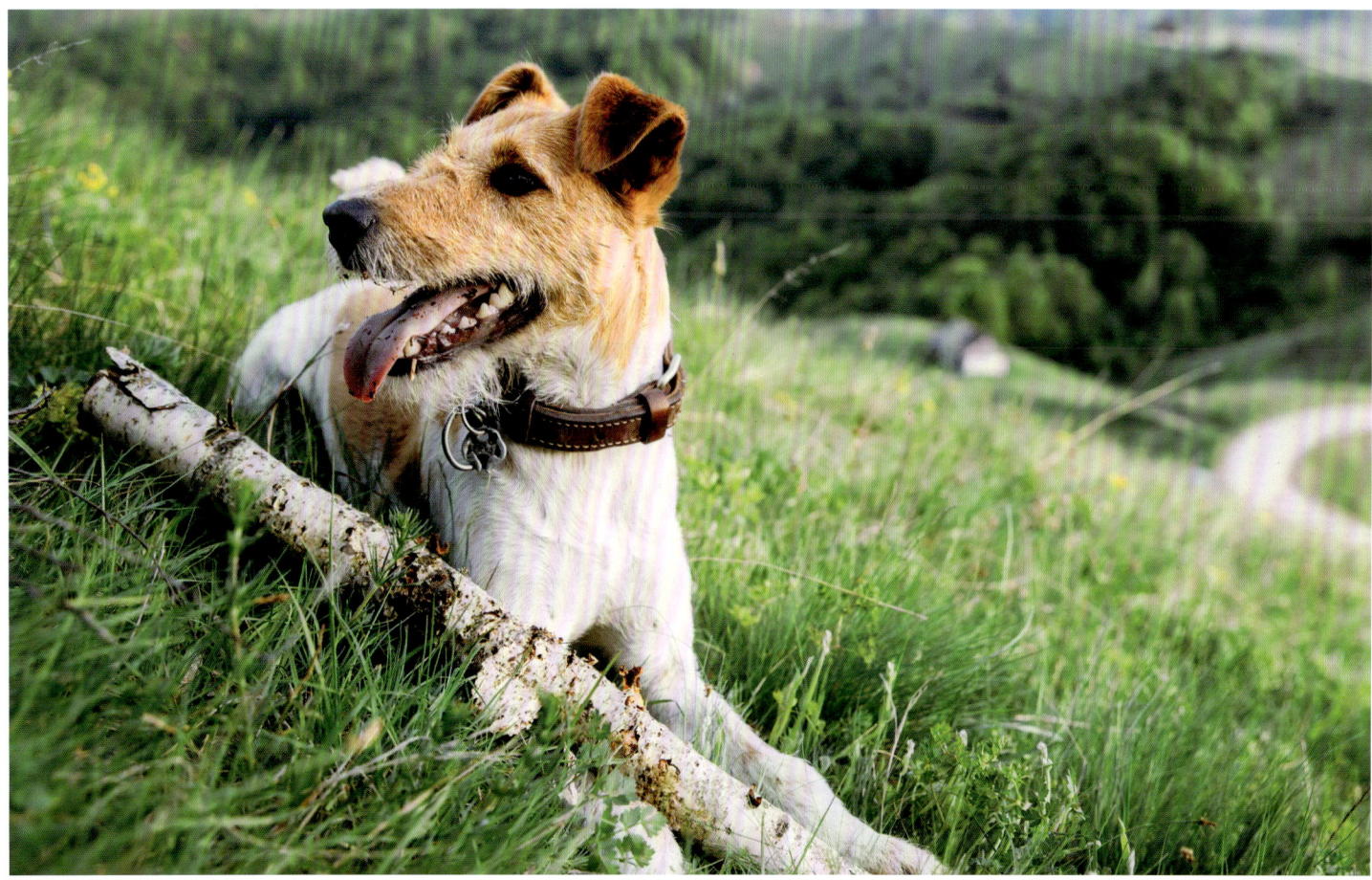

OPPOSITE:
Power supply
The fox terrier's back legs are noticeably longer than the front legs. This gives them the leg drive needed to stand firm when facing off a fox in a burrow.

ABOVE:
Care instructions
There is no need to clip the wiry coat. Instead they shed naturally.

COMPANION DOGS

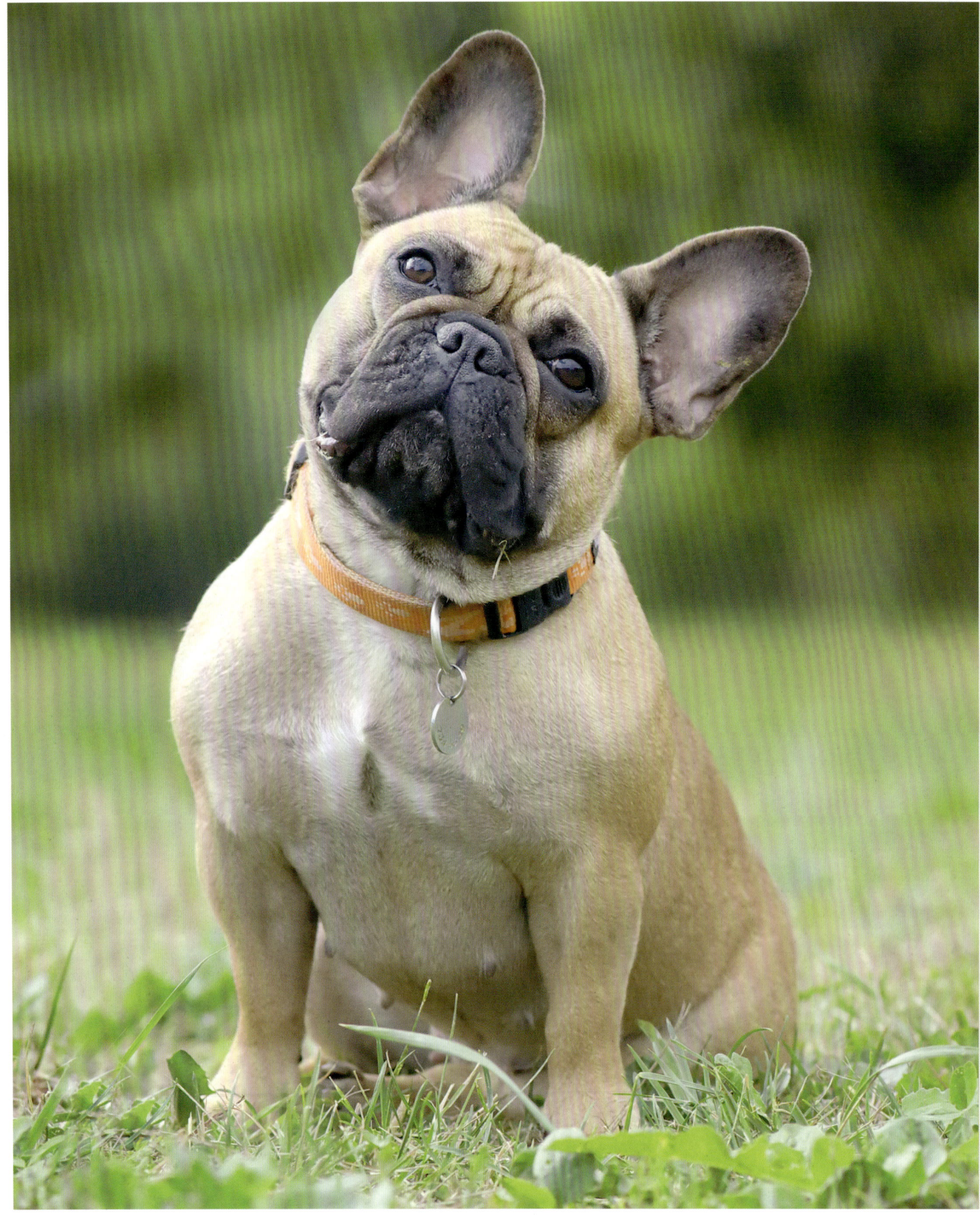

ABOVE:
Unusual looks
The French bulldog is well known for its large bat ears that go well with a clownish personality.

French Bulldog

CHARACTERISTICS

Coat
Short coat that is fawn, white, black or brindle

Height
28–33cm (11–13in)

Weight
11–13kg (24–29lb)

Lifespan
Over 10 years

Personality
Playful and alert

Origin
France

The French bulldog has the gross anatomy of other bulldog breeds only it is considerably smaller. The breed was developed in the 19th century from toy English bulldogs which were imported to France. These little dogs became more of a common sight in France due to the trade with the lacemakers of the English Midlands, where toy bulldogs were very popular. Some lacemakers moved to northern France and brought their dogs with them.

There is one obvious defining feature with this breed: those pointed bat ears high on the head. (Other bulldogs have semi-erect ears.) The curious ears are matched by the French bulldog's flat face and large imploring eyes, which melt the hearts of its owners. The ears and face are the result of crosses with other European short-faced breeds such as the pug. In France the dog has the name Bouledogue Français.

The cute looks and easy nature of the French bulldog soon endeared the breed to many, and it transitioned from being the pet of rural working people to the dog of choice for wealthy Parisians. The French bulldog has since become a popular pet worldwide, although meeting a little resistance in Britain, where the original breed is still a national symbol.

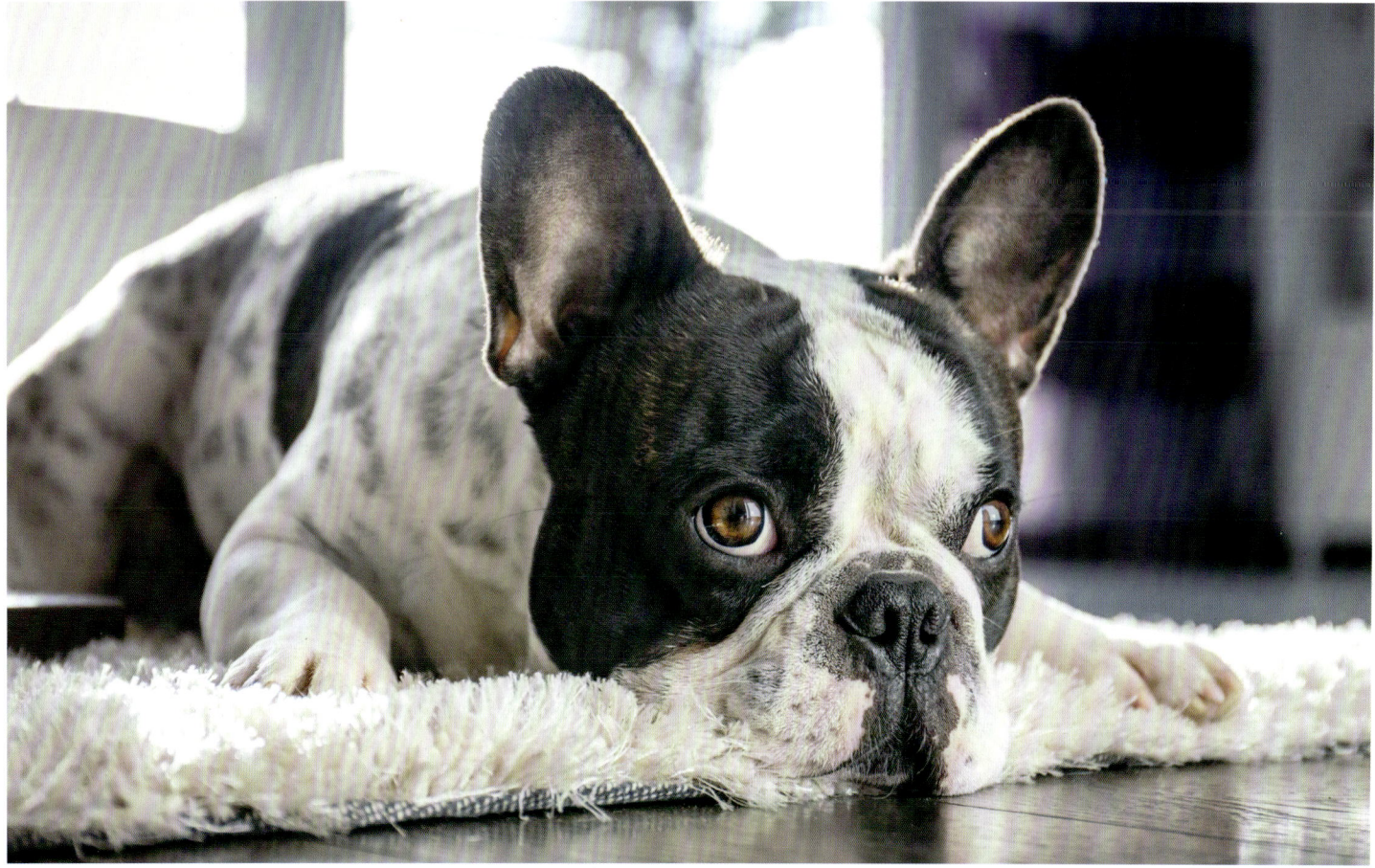

ABOVE:
Troubling features
The bulldog has lifelong health issues related to its flat face and short muzzle, which interfere with breathing and heat regulation.

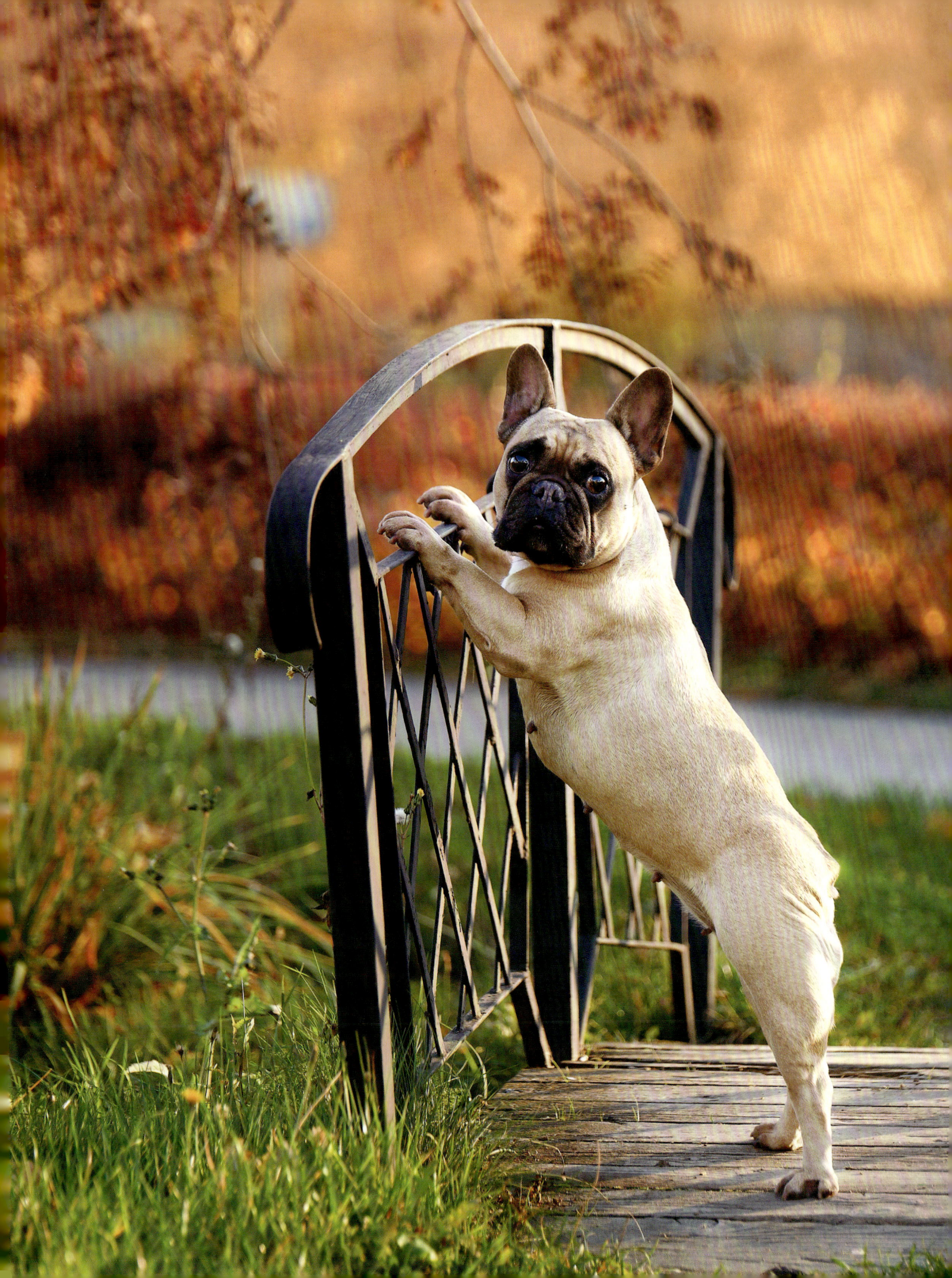

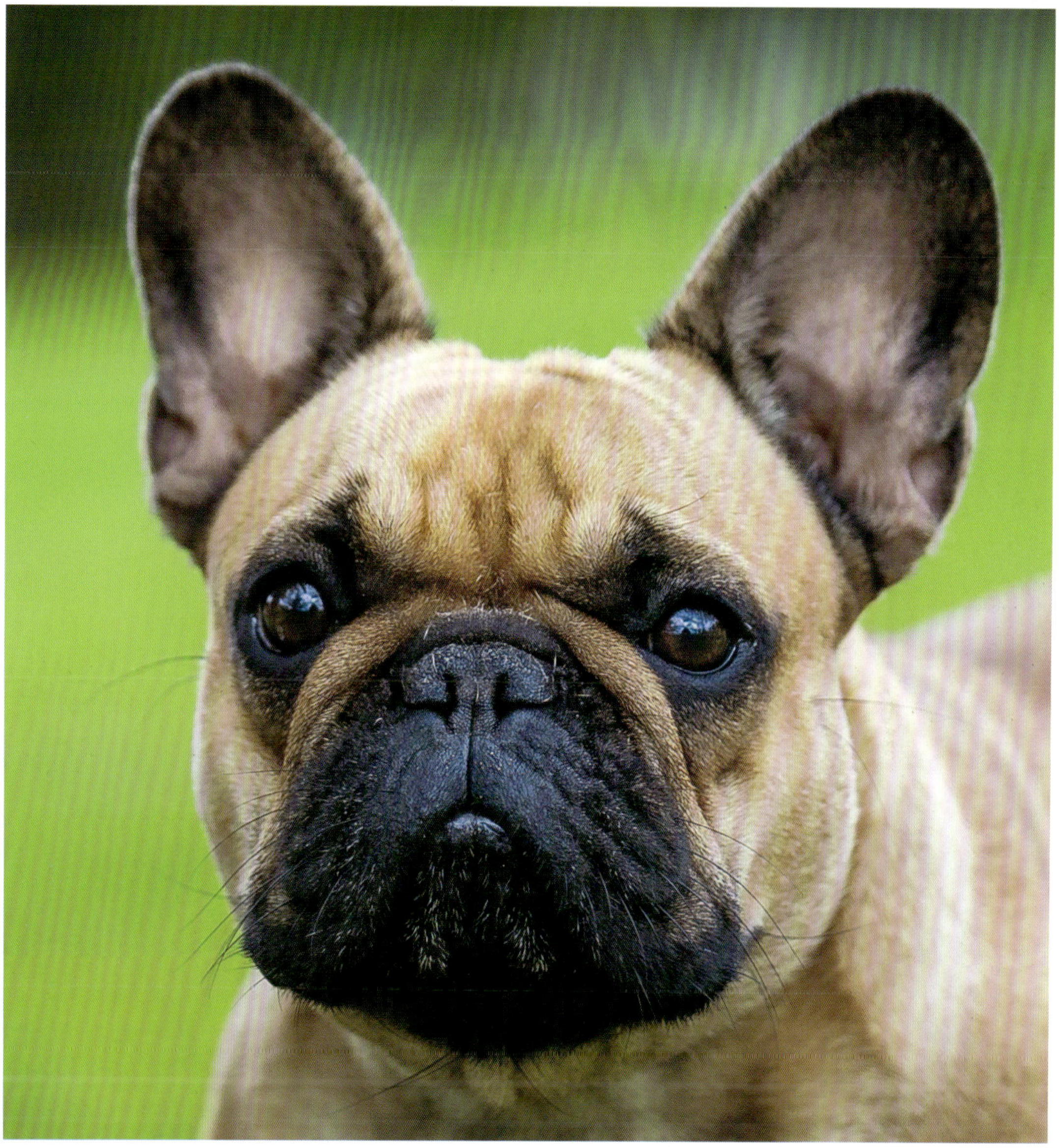

COMPANION DOGS

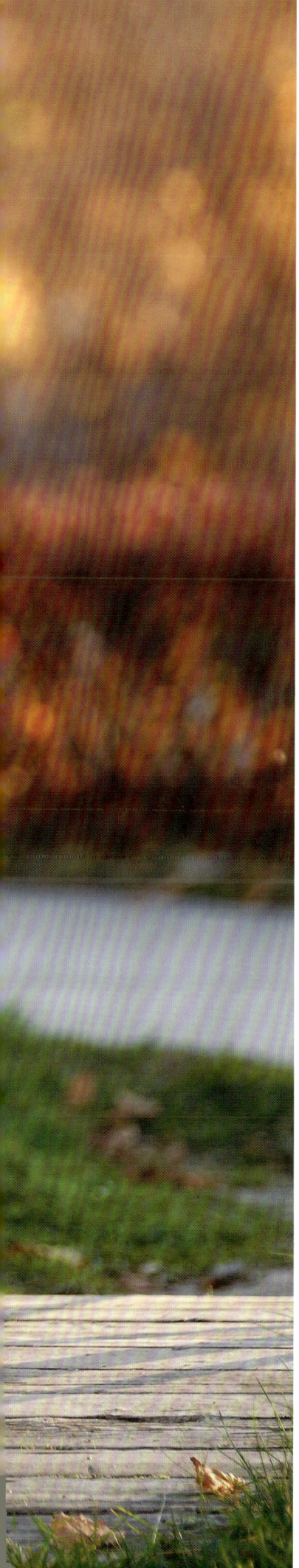

LEFT AND ABOVE:
Former job
Bulldogs were formerly bred for bull-baiting, a sport in which dogs were sent to attack a tethered bull. This activity has been banned for almost 200 years.

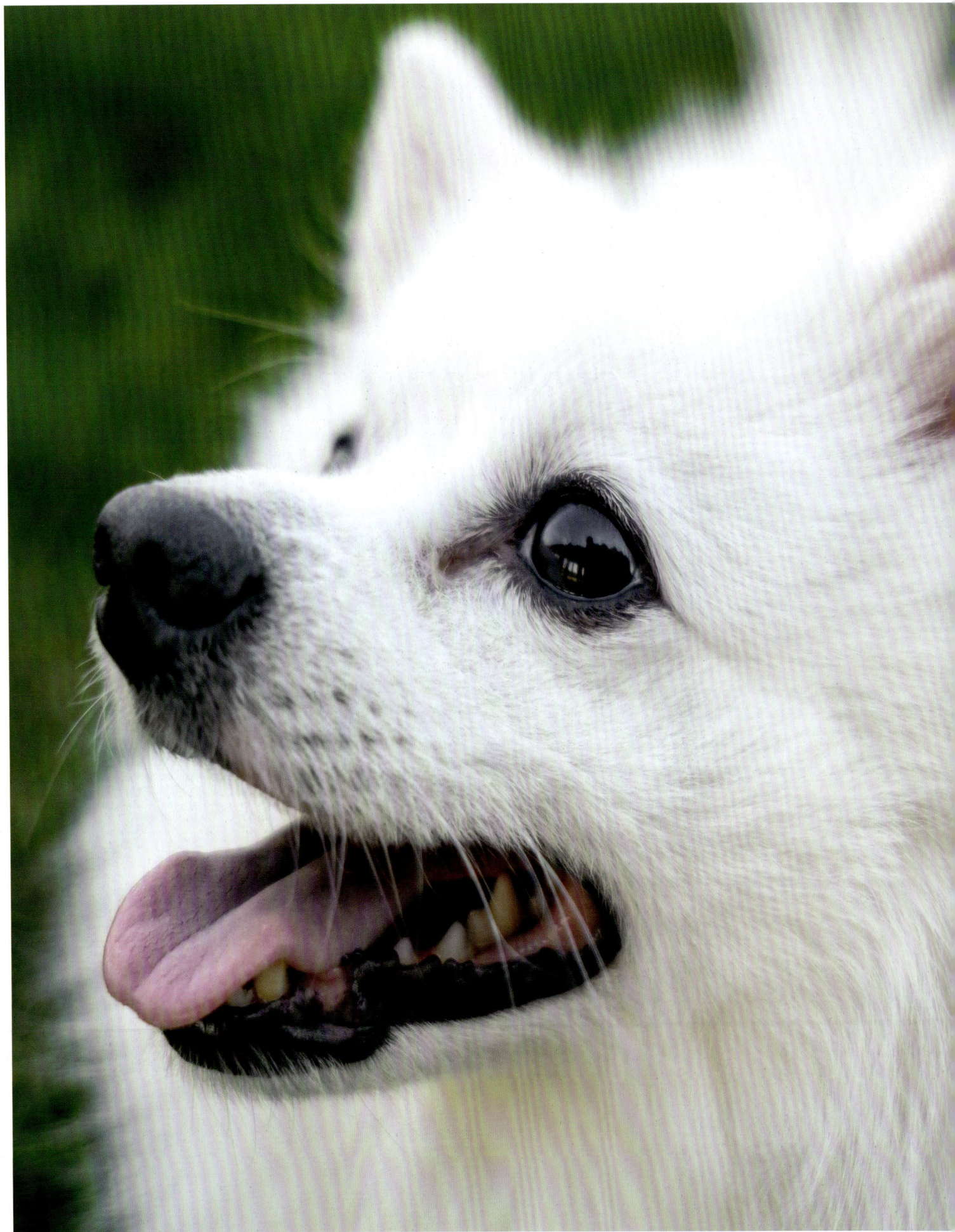

German Spitz

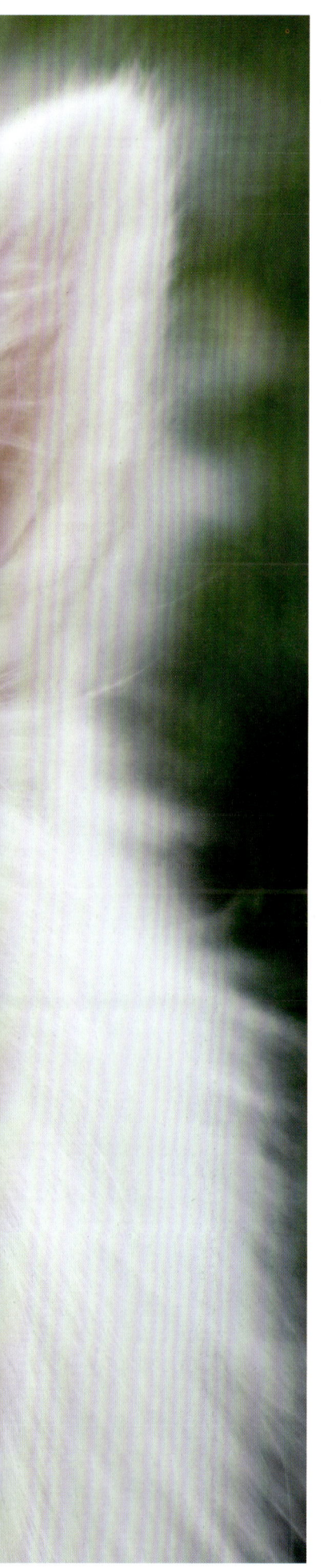

Expert analysis suggests that the German spitz is the oldest breed from Central Europe. It resembles the 6,000-year-old remains of dogs found in peat bogs. The lively breed is a descendant of the no-nonsense spitz-type herding dogs originally from the forests of East Asia but now spread across the Arctic. They include the elkhounds and huskies. The German spitz displays the same wedge-shaped heads, upright ears and curly tails of their kind, but have a very different role and demeanour. For a start, the German breed is smaller than most of its brethren. That said there are three sizes: Gross (giant), Mittel (medium, or miniature) and Klein (small, or toy). White Gross type dogs have been used as shepherd dogs in northern Germany, while in the south, black Gross dogs were used to guard vineyards at night. The smaller varieties came later as the breed had less use as a working dog and more appeal as a pet. The dogs are devoted to their owners and make entertaining companions. They are vocal dogs and will bark alerts when strangers are near.

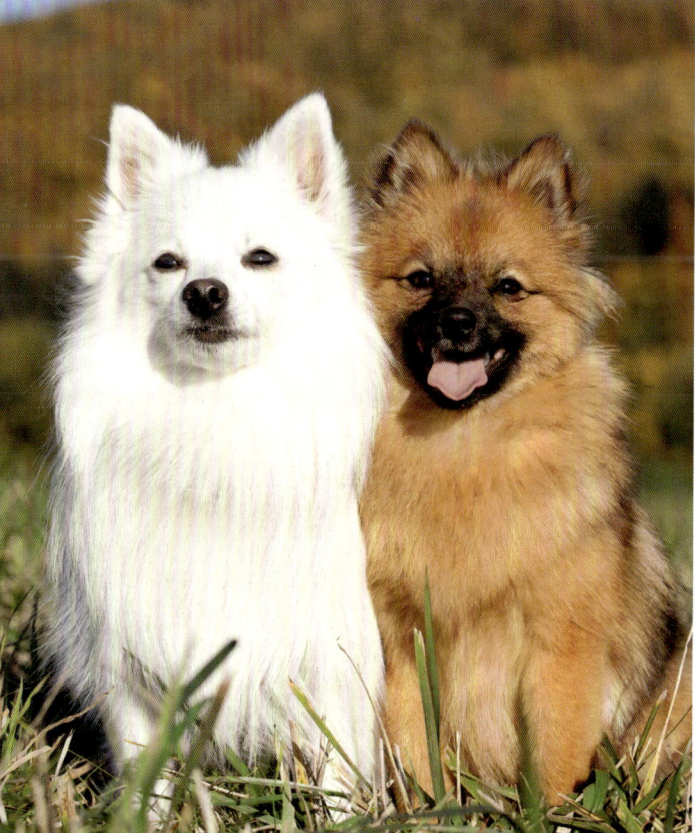

CHARACTERISTICS

Coat
A thick double coat in many colours
Height
23–50cm (9–20in)
Weight
8–18kg (18–40lb)
Lifespan
14–15 years
Personality
Clever and attentive
Origin
Germany

LEFT:
Smart story
There is a well-known national myth in Germany about how the spitz is very smart. In the story a spitz outwits a pug that is trying to steal its food.

ABOVE:
Neck hair
The German spitz has a warm mane which marks it out as an ancient breed that descended from Nordic herding dogs. The breed is rare outside of Germany.

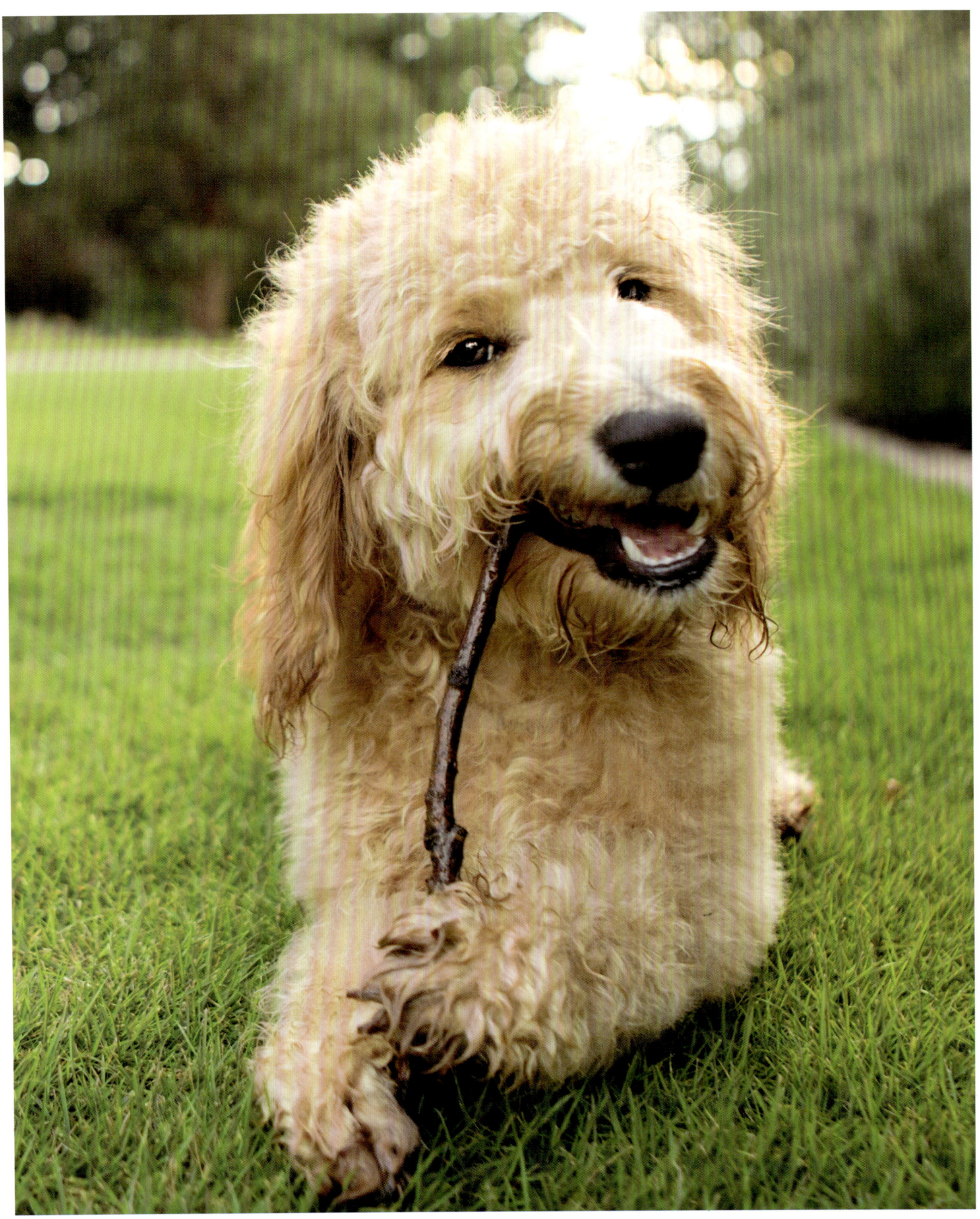

ABOVE:
Keeping busy
Goldendoodles are energetic and athletic dogs that need plenty of exercise and mental stimulation. They love to play fetch, swim and explore new places.

Goldendoodle

CHARACTERISTICS

Coat
Shaggy to curly and can have different colours such as cream, gold, red, chocolate or black
Height
Up to 61cm (24in)
Weight
23–41kg (51–90lb)
Lifespan
10–15 years
Personality
Sociable and compliant
Origin
United States and Australia

The goldendoodle is one of the new, so-called designer dogs, created by crossbreeding golden retrievers with poodles of all sizes. The result is a dog with great looks, smart wits and playfulness, in keeping with the traits of both its parents. As well as being an increasingly popular choice as a pet, it is also a good assistance and therapy dog.

Goldendoodles come in different sizes, depending on the size of the poodle parent. The goldendoodle can have three kinds of coat: straight like a retriever, curly like a poodle and a wavy form that is something in between. Having said that, the dogs all inherit the poodle's low shedding rate. This not only makes the dog an easier house companion but also reduces the problems with allergies to dog hair. They still need regular grooming to keep their coats healthy.

Goldendoodles are friendly and gentle dogs that get along with everyone and everything. They are not aggressive or territorial, and they rarely bark. They enjoy being around people and other animals, and they thrive on attention and affection. Goldendoodles are not suitable for being left alone for long periods of time, as they can suffer from separation anxiety and boredom.

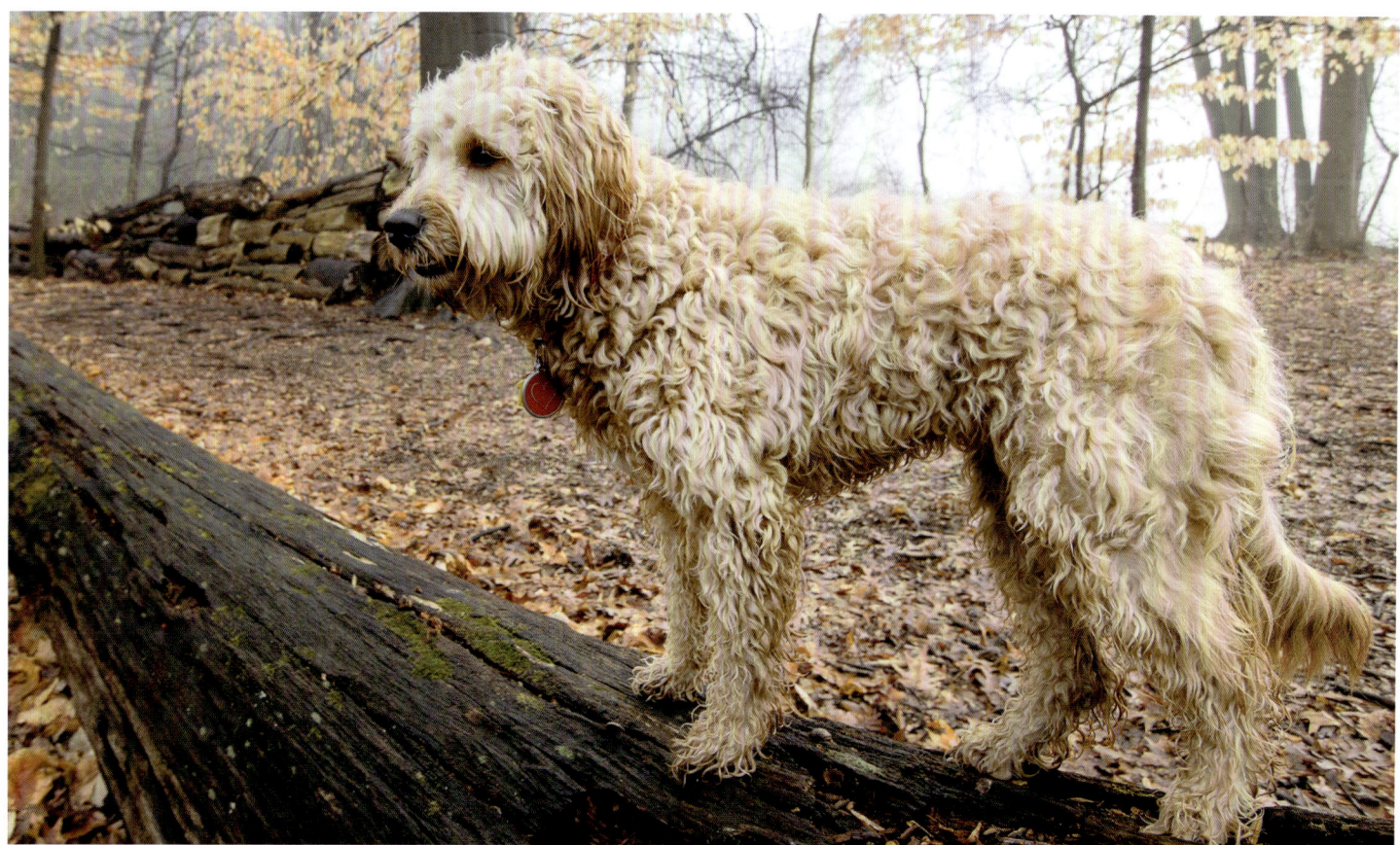

ABOVE:
An easy pet
The goldendoodle is easy to train. They can learn a variety of commands and tricks, and do well in agility and obedience competitions.

COMPANION DOGS

Golden Retriever

CHARACTERISTICS

Coat
Dense and water-resistant that ranges in colour from light to dark gold

Height
51–61cm (20–24in)

Weight
25–34kg (55–75lb)

Lifespan
12–13 years

Personality
Intelligent and gentle

Origin
Scotland

With a strong look and a strong brand, these dogs are known the world over as the intelligent, sensible and obedient dogs that are used to guide visually impaired people around bustling streets. The breed, however, was created in Scotland in the mid 19th century as an enhanced gundog by Lord Tweedmouth. The noble breeder built the breed on his favourite gundog, which he described as a yellow retriever. Then he crossed in Irish setter and bloodhound for a good sense of smell and prey drive, and water spaniels to give the dog a waterproof coat and a constitution to suit the rugged Highlands. It took about 50 years of careful breeding but the result was an exceptionally willing dog that retrieves game on land and water and makes a good companion in the meantime. The dogs move very well with a strong but smooth running style. It is medium sized and so can get involved in the rough and tumble of family life more than a small dog, but is more economical to keep than a giant dog.

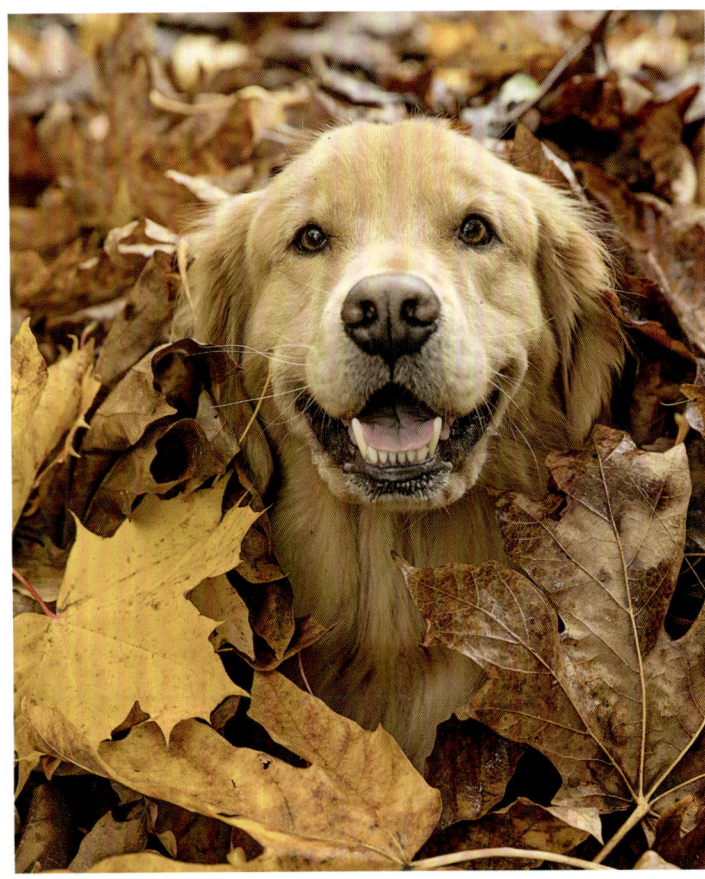

ABOVE:
Personable
This breed is known for its friendly, intelligent and playful personality.

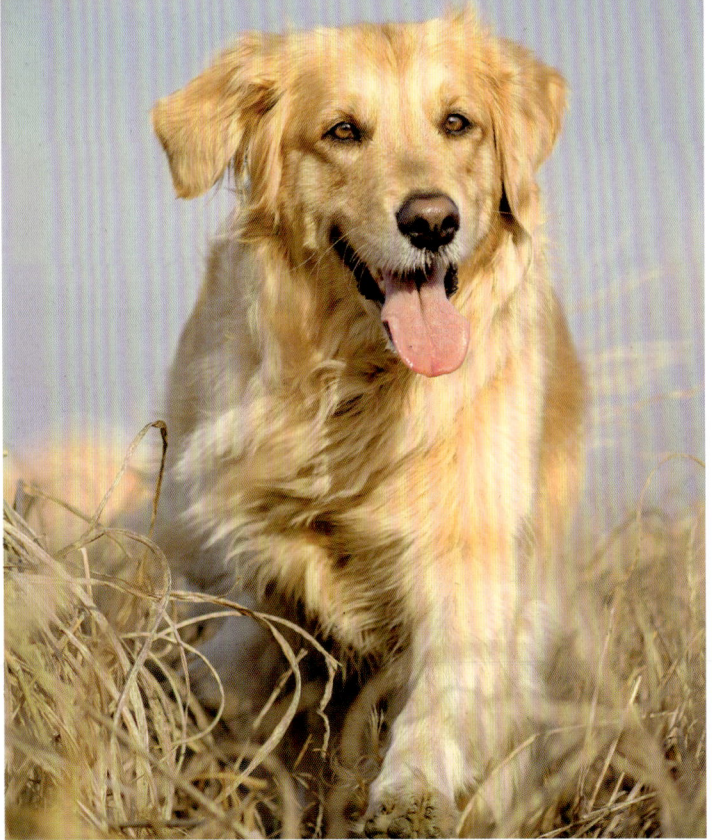

ABOVE:
Active and alert
Golden retrievers require regular exercise and grooming and plenty of mental stimulation.

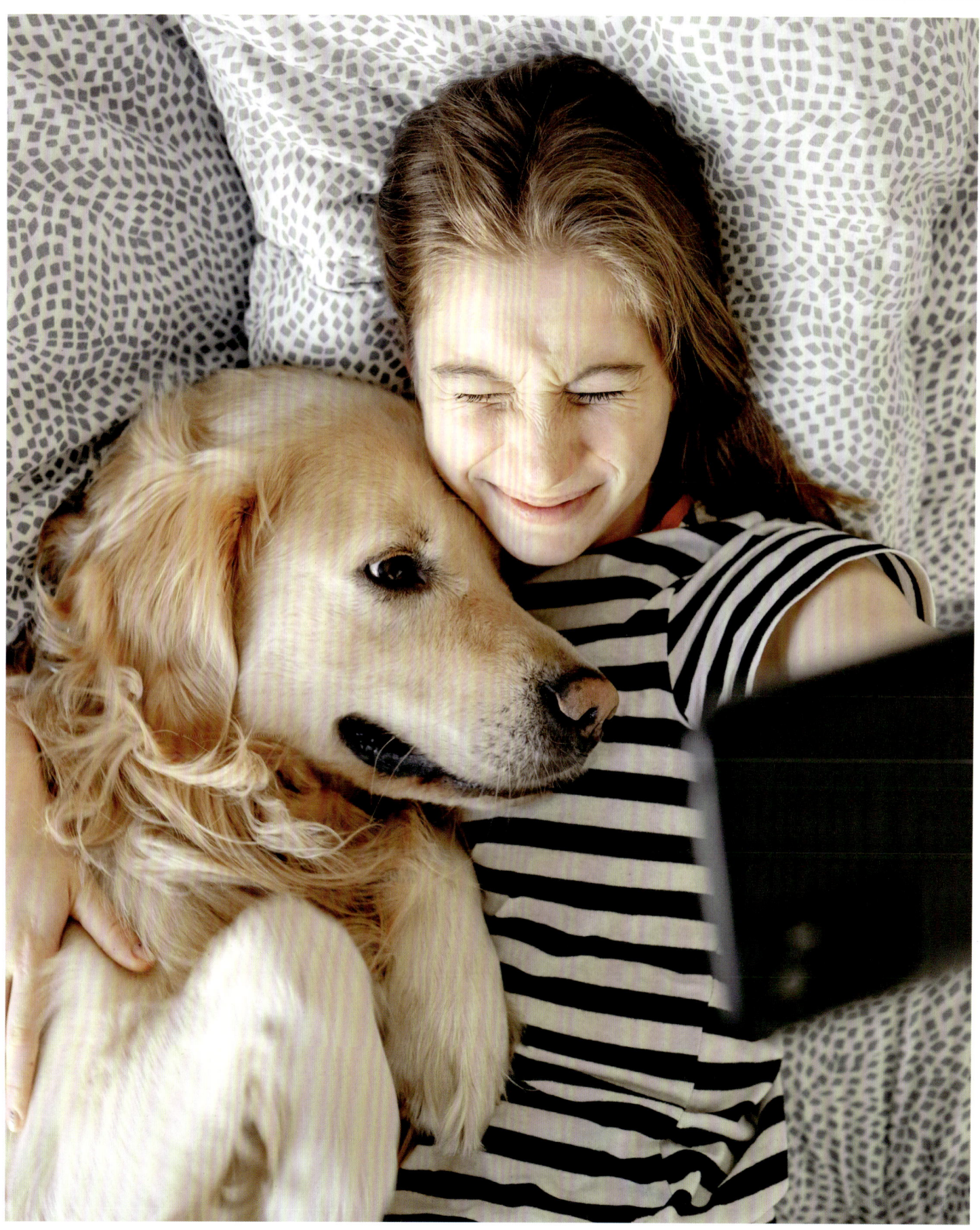

ABOVE:
Happy families
Golden retrievers are great family dogs, as they get along well with children and other pets.

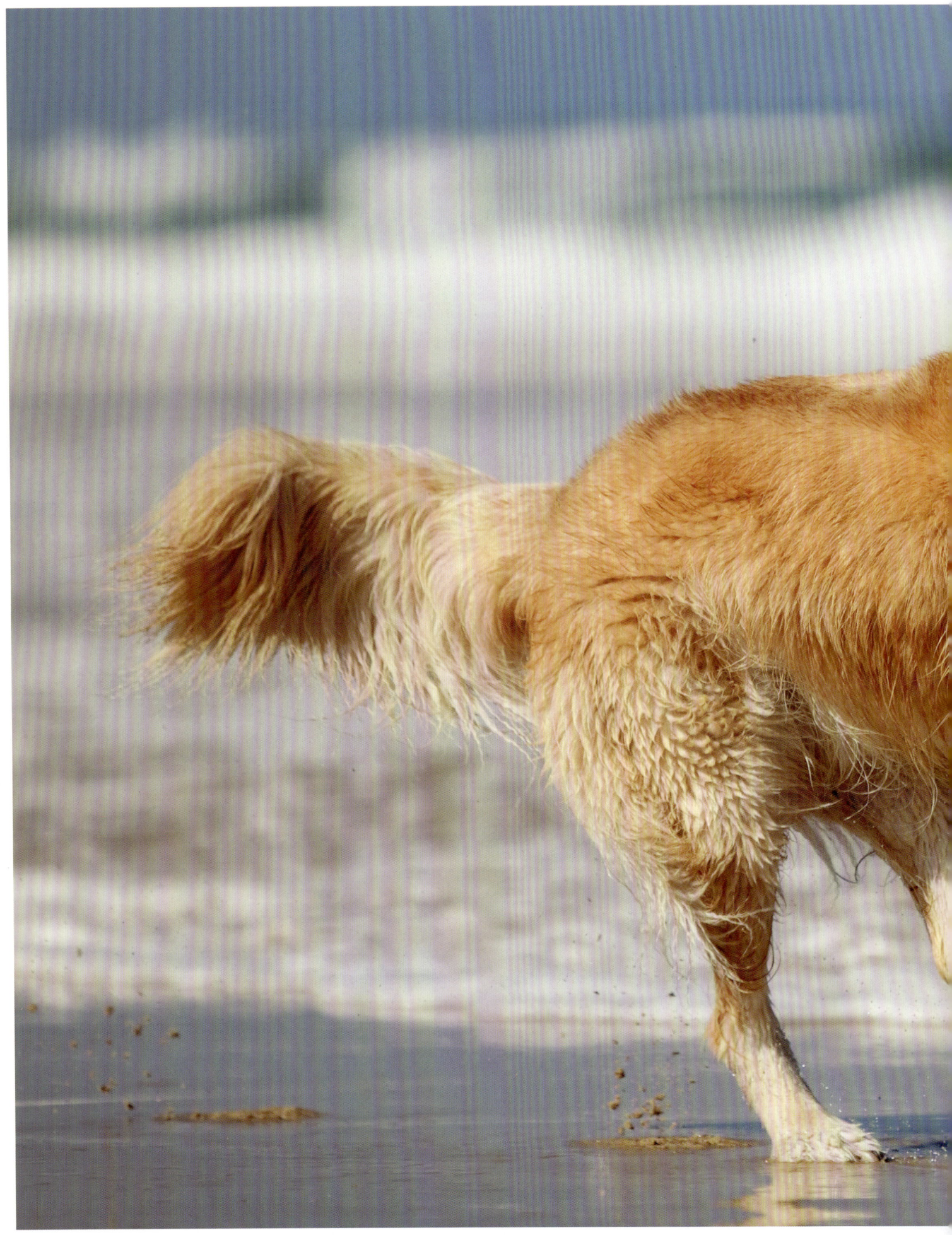

COMPANION DOGS

Sea and sand
Labradors are reknowned for their high trainability and adaptability.

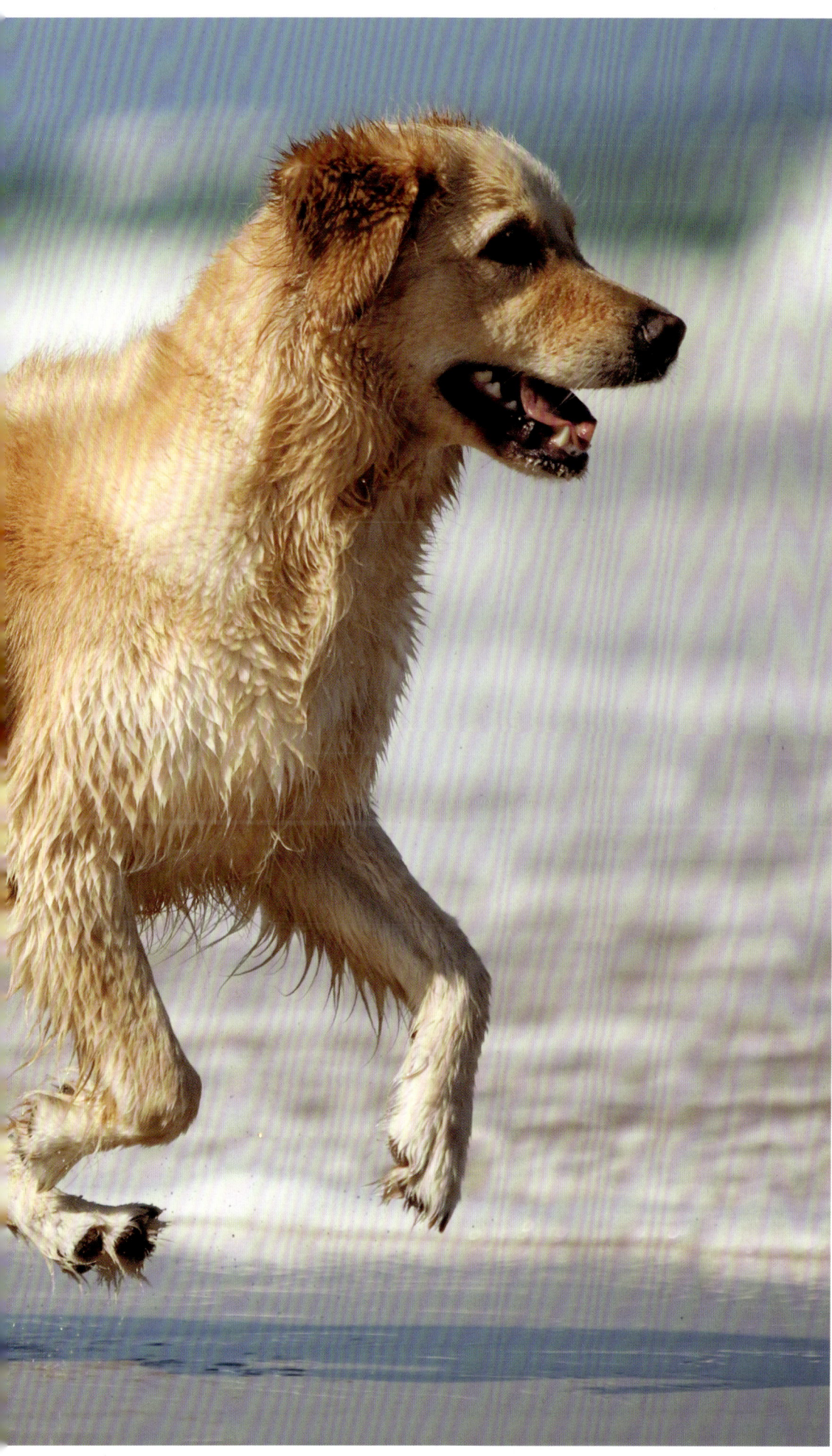

COMPANION DOGS

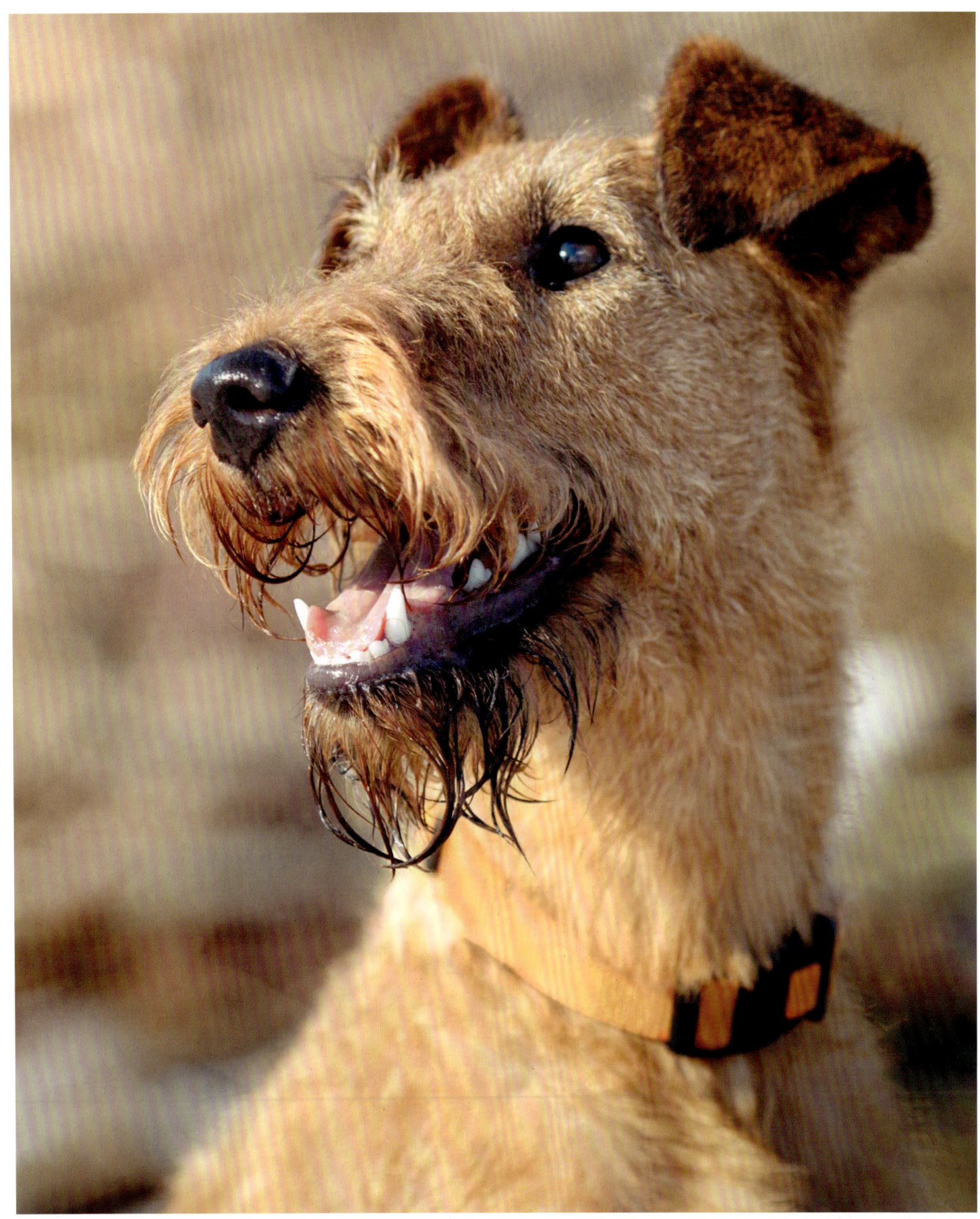

ABOVE:
Facial hair
The Irish terrier is famed for its bearded muzzle.

Irish Terrier

CHARACTERISTICS

Coat
Dense and wiry; coat comes in shades of red or wheaten
Height
46–48cm (18–19in)
Weight
11–12kg (24–26lb)
Lifespan
12–15 years
Personality
Bold and devoted
Origin
Ireland

This long-legged terrier was the all-purpose farm dog of County Cork in the rural southwest of Ireland. Its job was to keep the rats down, which it did with a characteristic eagerness and intelligence. It also made a good watchdog—and still does; this terrier makes a point of alerting its owners of any strangers. The Irish dog is undoubtedly one of the oldest terrier breeds, but its more distant history is largely unknown. Whatever happened back then, it led to one of the healthiest dog breeds. Irish terriers are able to outlive most dogs

The Irish terrier has a distinctive appearance, with a slender, elegant body, a long head, small ears that fold forward and a dense, wiry coat that comes in shades of red or a yellower wheaten. The dog enjoys companionship and outdoor activities. Being a farmyard breed, it needs a lot of exercise and mental stimulation. Without that boredom will take over, leading to some destructive behaviours. It can get along well with children and other dogs, but may chase or fight with smaller animals. The Irish terrier can be stubborn and independent, so it requires consistent training and socialization from an early age.

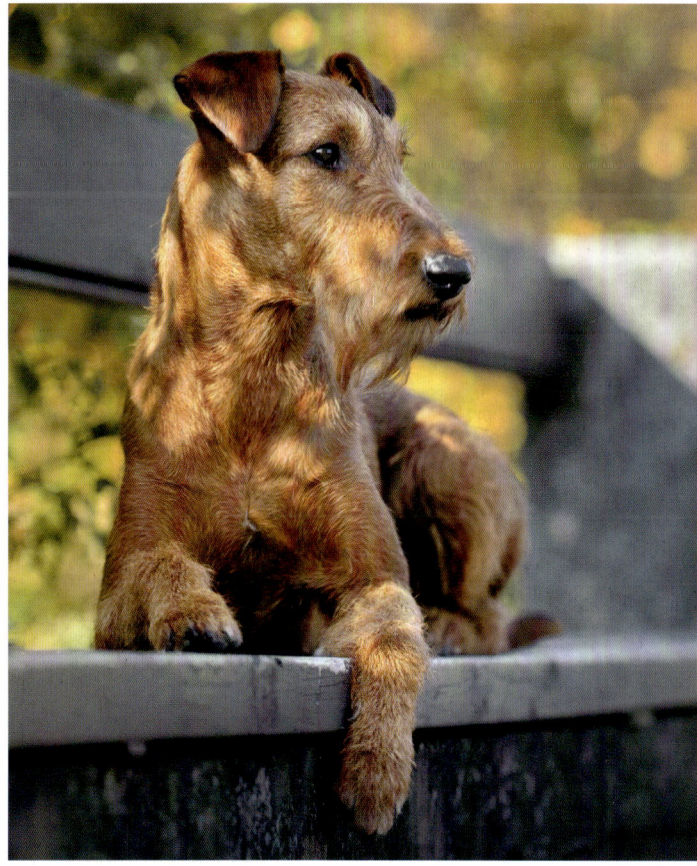

ABOVE:
Upkeep
The Irish terrier needs regular grooming to keep its coat in good condition.

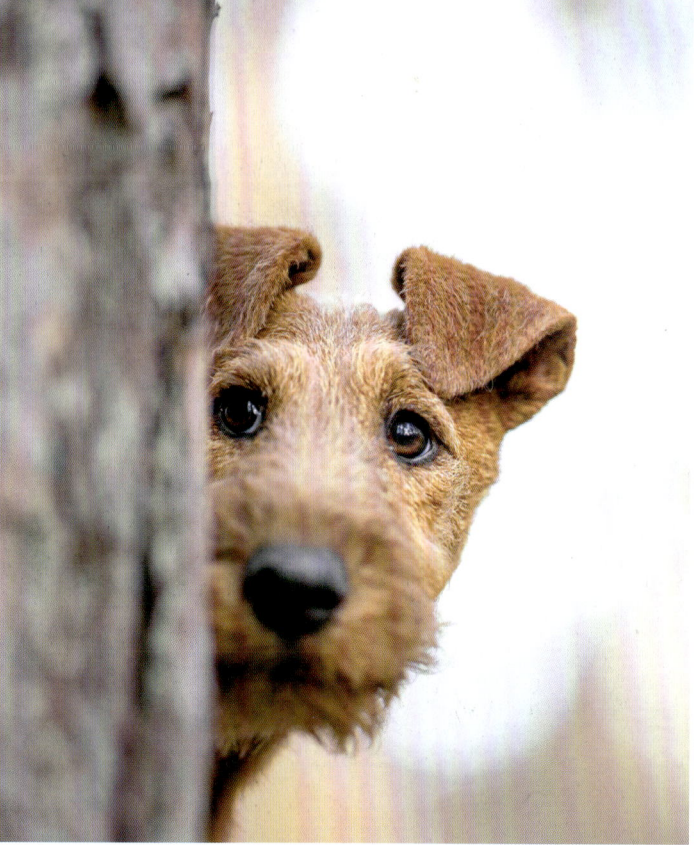

ABOVE:
On alert
The terrier is a vigilant breed ever ready to step in and protect its family.

COMPANION DOGS

Jack Russell Terrier

CHARACTERISTICS

Coat
Smooth or wiry and mostly white with patches of tan or black
Height
25–30cm (10–12in)
Weight
5–6kg (11–13lb)
Lifespan
13–14 years
Personality
Clever and eager
Origin
England

This spirited little dog makes a perfect companion breed. It has the right personality, being smart and loyal, and it has an eager stamina so is always up for some fun. However, its shorter coat is easy to keep and those little legs mean the dog cannot overwhelm its owner—of just about any age—with bursts of speed and strength.

The dogs began their existence as a fox terrier bred by the English clergyman Reverend John "Jack" Russell. Rev. Russell was known as the "Sporting Parson", and developed a dog that could run with the hounds but was small and compact enough to enter fox dens and flush them out. He aimed to produce a dog with the proportions of a vixen. Today, Russell terriers that fit this description are called Parson Russell Terriers. They are a bit more robust than Jack Russells, and have noticeably longer legs. The smaller and more amenable Jack Russell, with its short or wiry coat, is the breed that has persisted best to this day. Nevertheless, the dogs have a high prey drive and will bark unless well socialized. And despite the short legs, the dogs still need plenty of time devoted to exercise and stimulation.

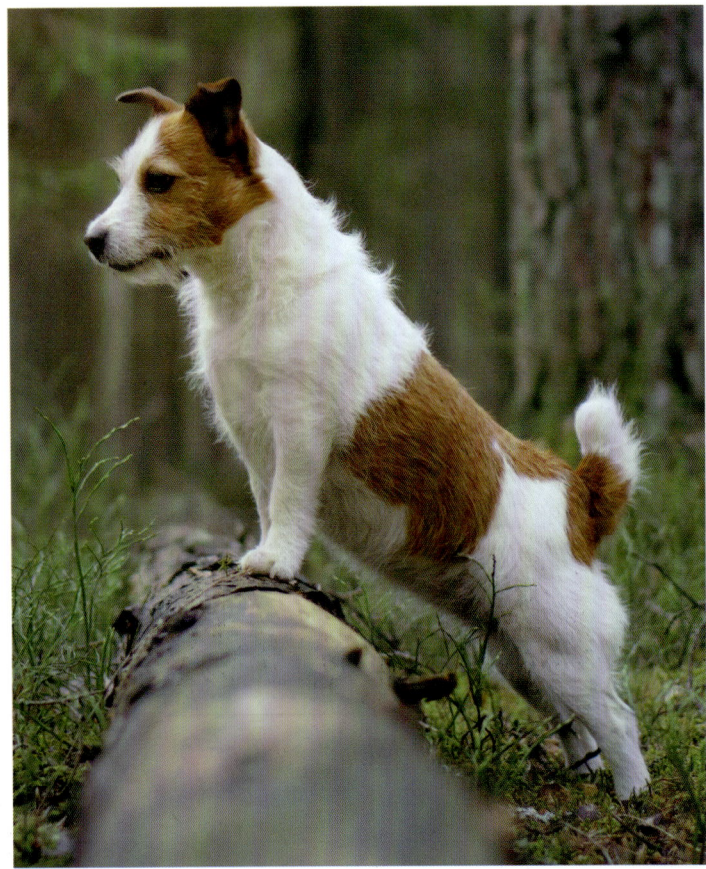

ABOVE:
Long body
The body length of a Jack Russell always exceeds the length of its legs.

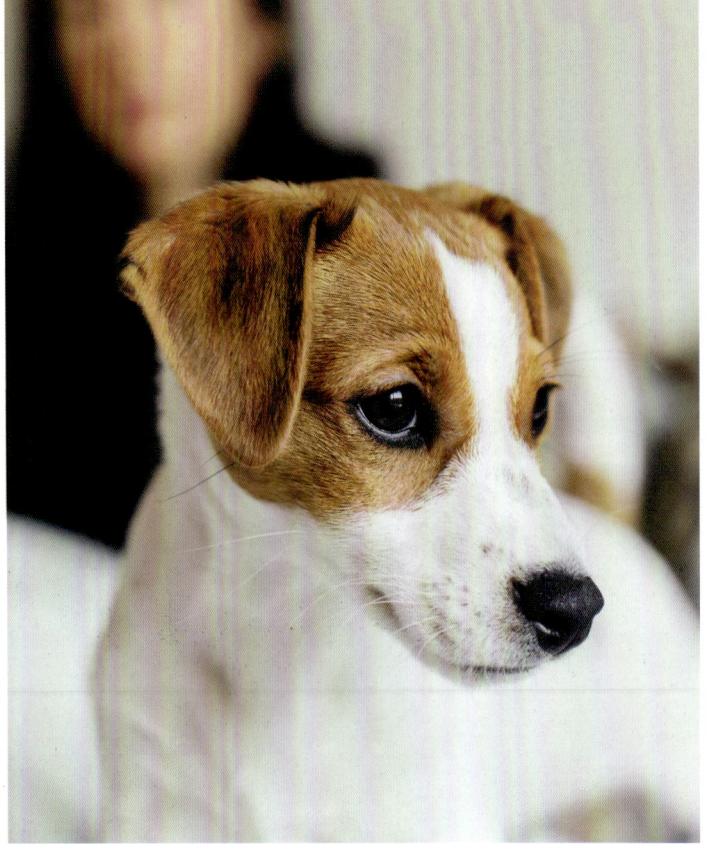

ABOVE:
Head shape
The Jack Russell has a flat head—flatter than the Parson Russell dogs—and it generally has markings on the head.

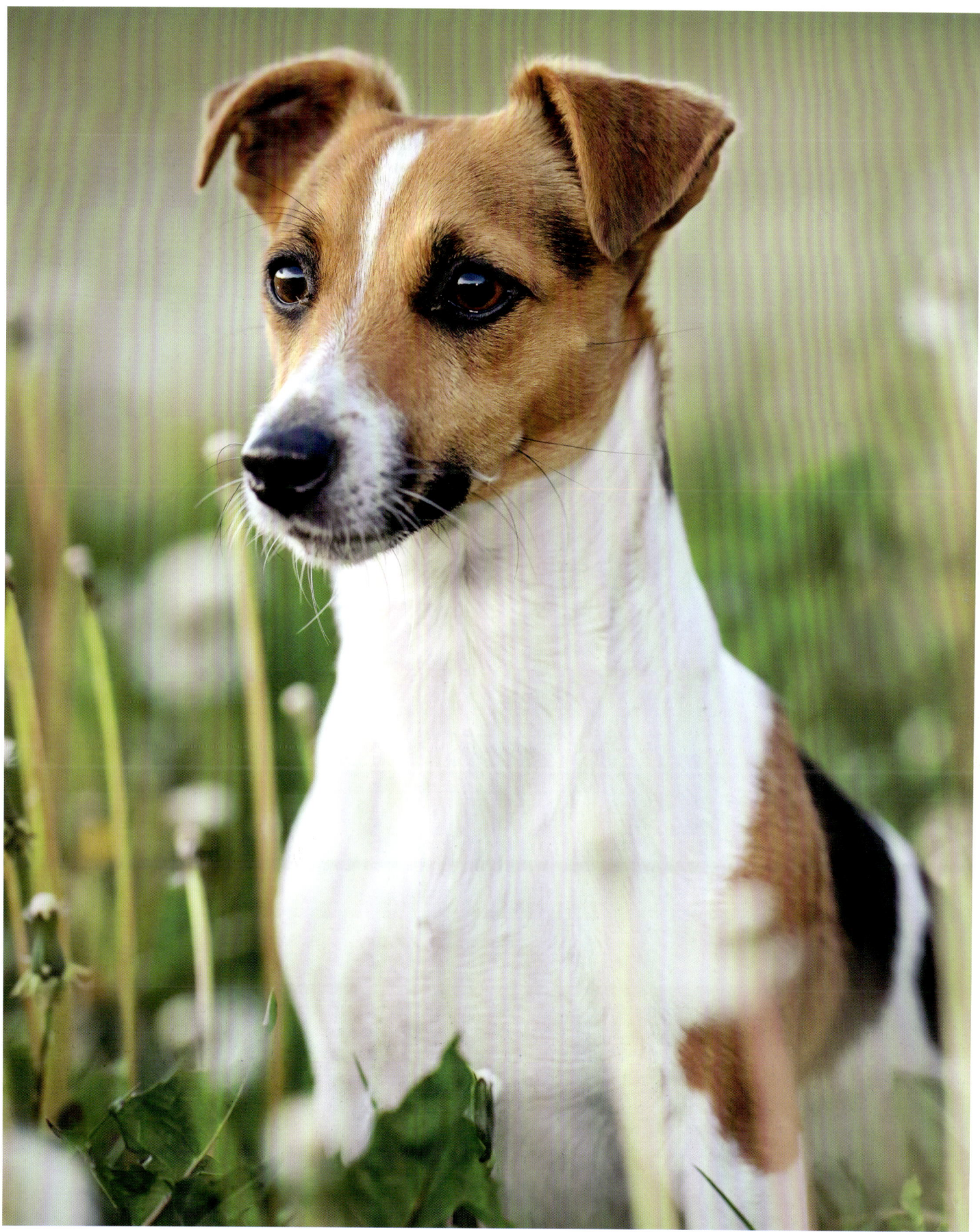

ABOVE:
Keen features
The dog has dark, almond-shaped eyes and mobile V-shaped ears.
These bring out the breed's intelligent expression.

COMPANION DOGS

RIGHT:
Wag the tail
The dog's tail is an important communicator. A relaxed dog wags its tail in a relaxed way. When it's nervous, the tail is held lower than usual. When the tail is held high, the dog is excited and stimulated by something.

OPPOSITE TOP AND BOTTOM:
Handful of joy
This breed are known for their intelligence, athleticism, and high energy levels.

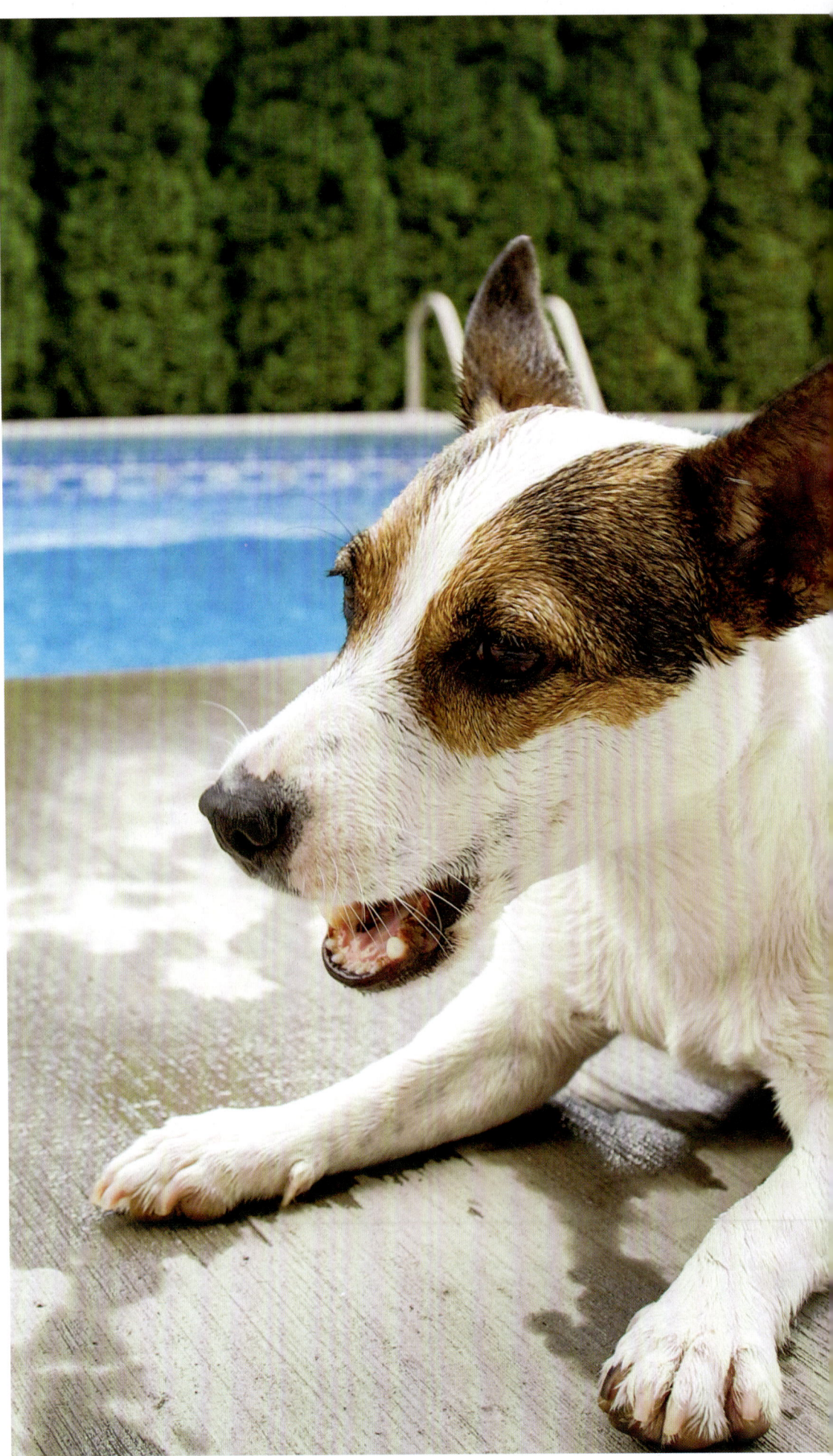

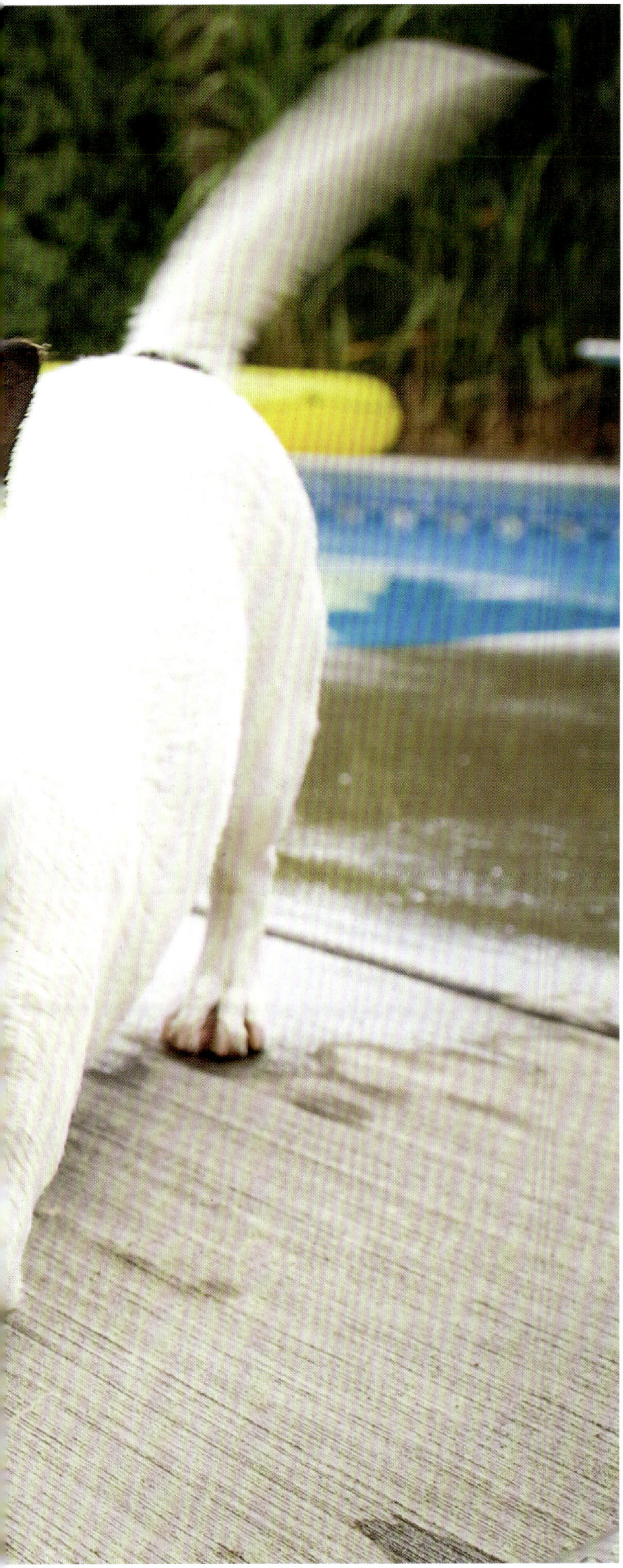

COMPANION DOGS

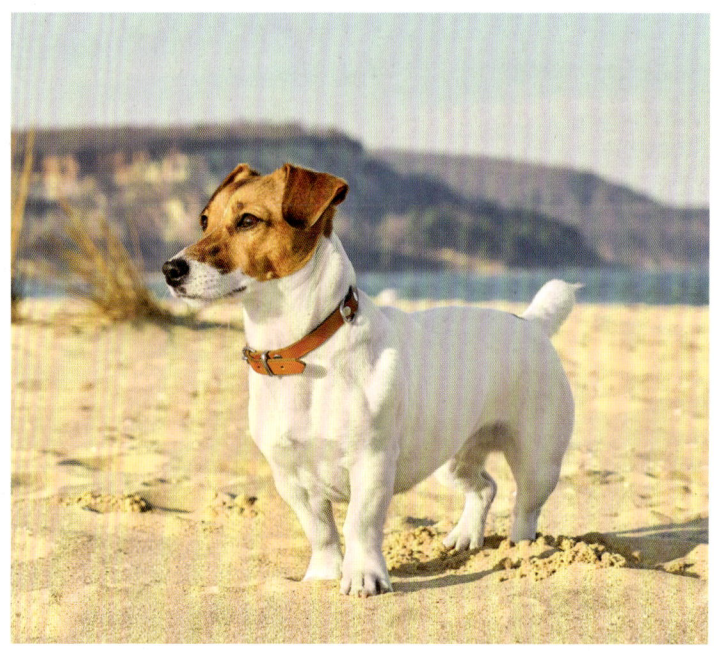
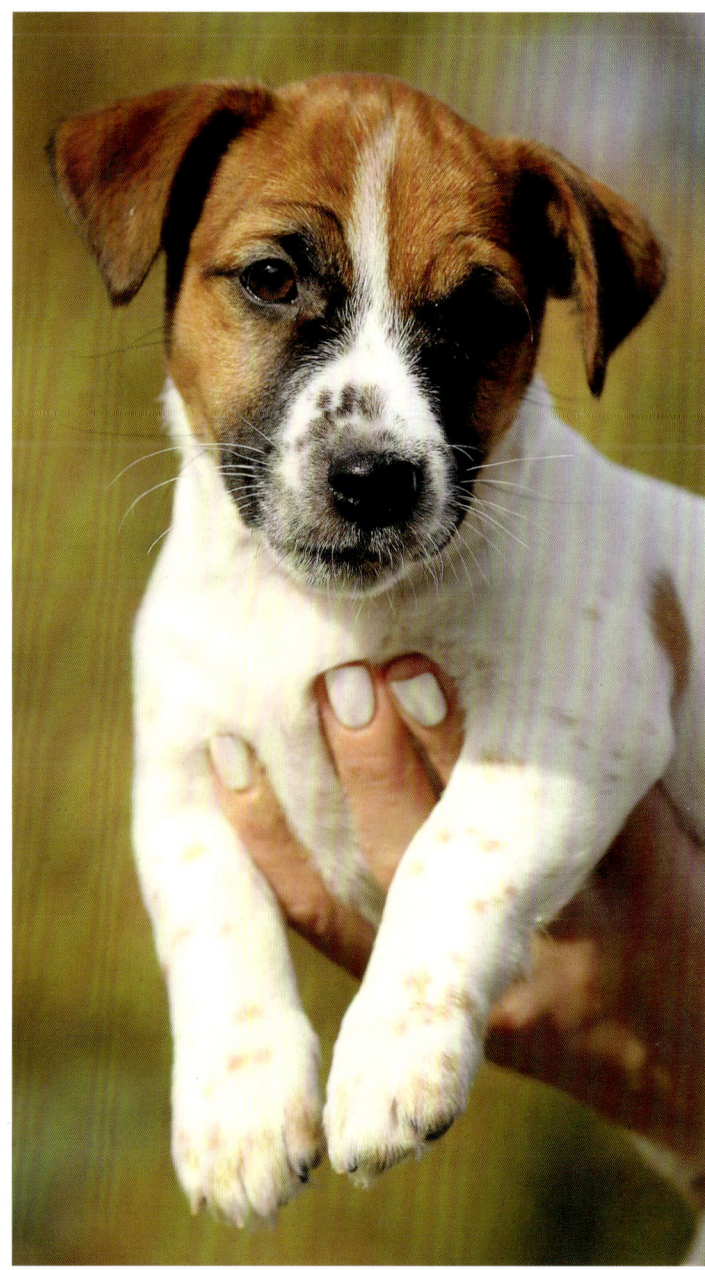

COMPANION DOGS

Japanese Chin

The origin of this most unusual of breeds is a matter of national pride. Some insist the breed was first developed in China, others say Korea, while the Japanese prefer that this is a breed created for the comfort and pleasure of their imperial family. It is probable that there is truth in all of these assertions. The dogs arrived in Japan in the last 1,000 years, presumably from the Asian mainland. Once in Japan, the dogs became gifts exchanged by the nobility. The cute face and big eyes make them a perky plaything, while just as importantly the long, flowing coat made them cosy hand and lap warmers.

The dog is small and nimble and can scamper around on furniture a bit like a cat would. (It also washes its face with its licked paws.) The Japanese chin has retained a high prey drive, and so will scamper after whatever catches its eye. As a result the dog does not need much exercise or stimulation and is at home in a small house or flat. However, its long coat does shed a lot.

CHARACTERISTICS

Coat
Long feathered coat that is black, red and white
Height
20–28cm (8–11in)
Weight
2–3kg (5–7lb)
Lifespan
Over 10 years
Personality
Noble and loving
Origin
Japan

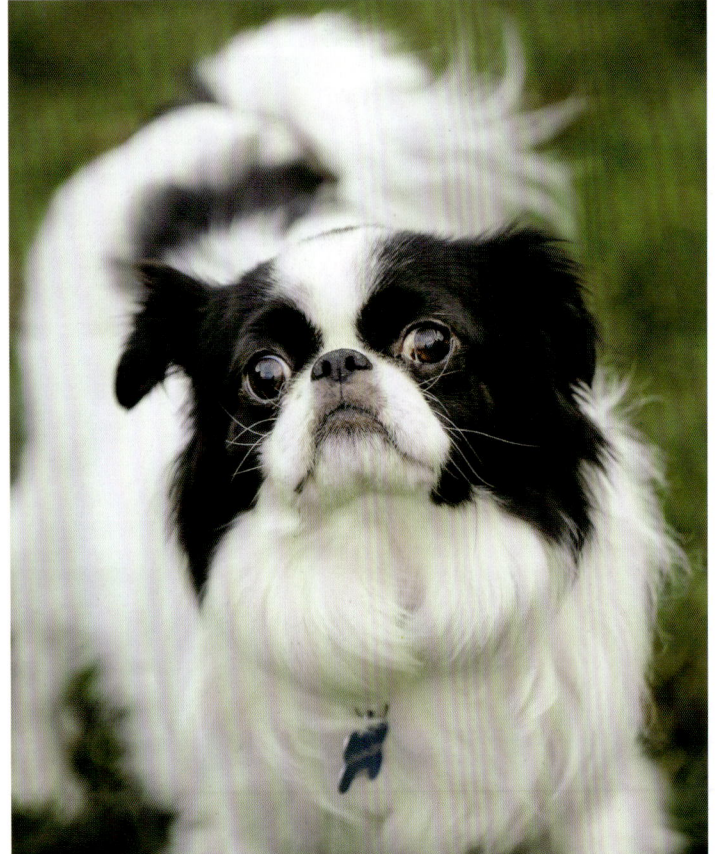

ABOVE:
Who are you?
The Japanese chin is loyal to its owner and needs a lot of companionship. It can become insecure and yappy if it is left alone for long periods.

RIGHT:
Snub-nosed
The chin can have health problems that are related to the unnaturally short face.

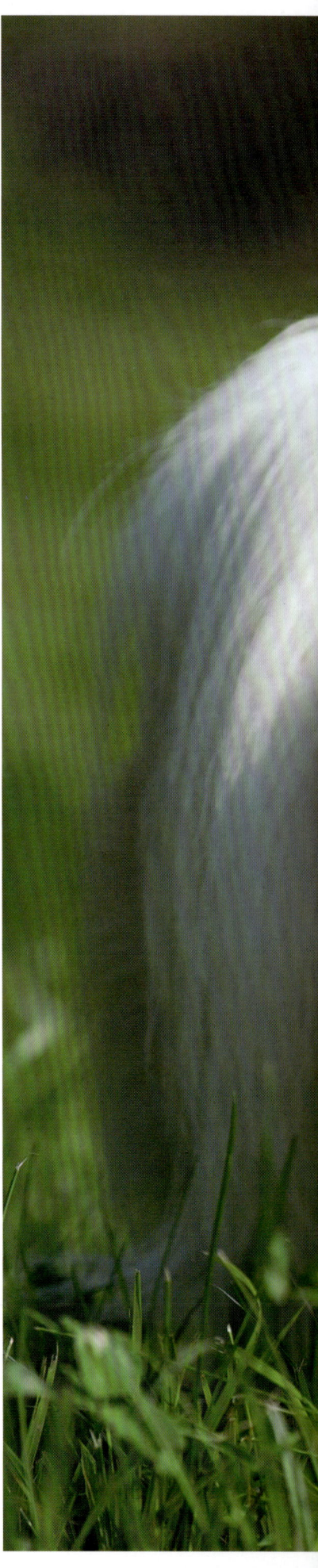

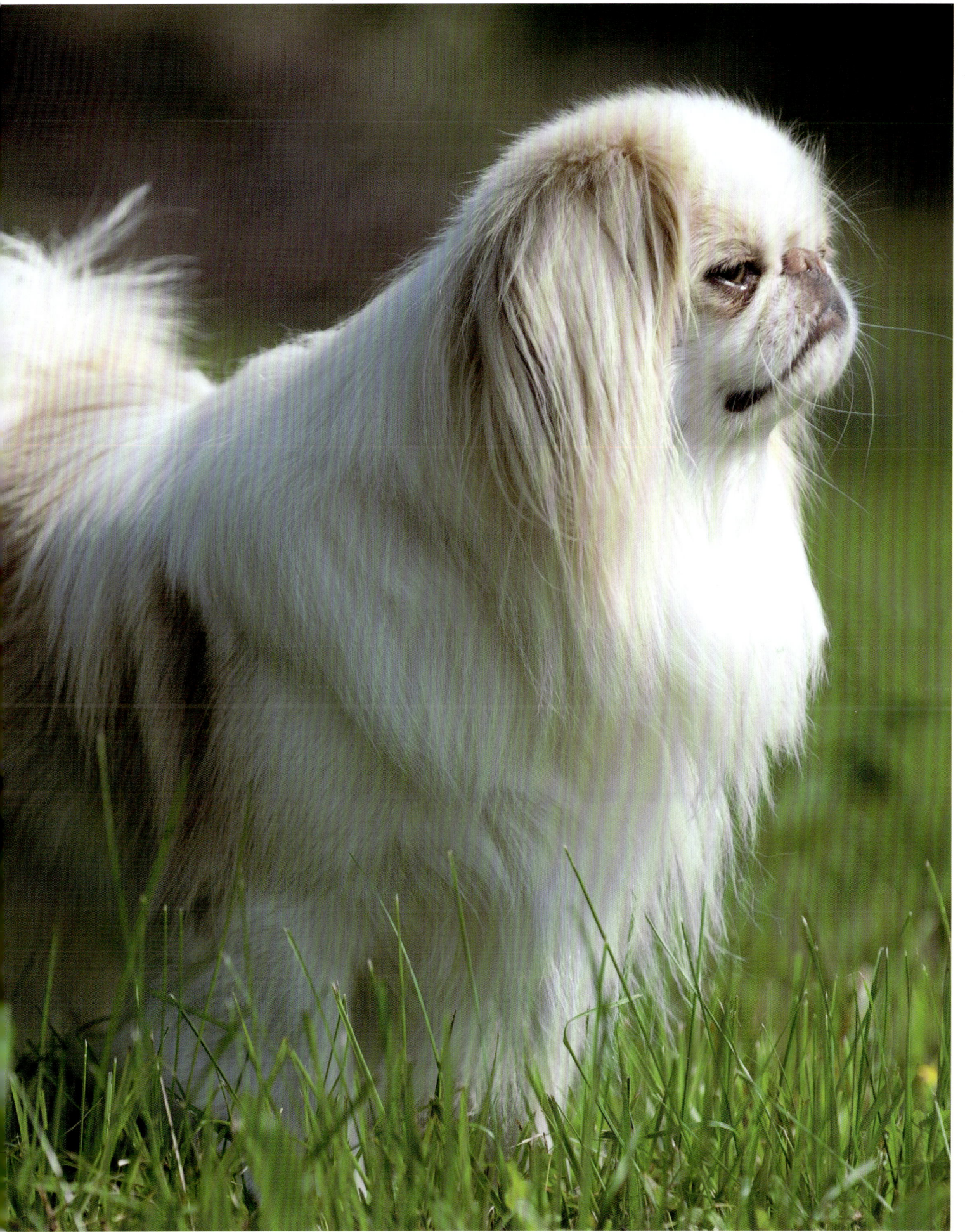

COMPANION DOGS

Kooikerhondje

This Dutch breed resembles a spaniel and its history extends into the Middle Ages, from before ducks and other waterfowl were routinely hunted with guns. The kooikerhondje were part of the team that operated the duck-trapping ponds that were common in the Low Countries. The artificial ponds were filled with flocks of tame ducks and wild ducks would join them for a dabble and a rest. The duck catcher and their dog worked as a team to force wild ducks along a certain path (always against the wind) and into wicker traps. The name kooikerhondje means "duck catcher's small dog" in Dutch. And what could be more Dutch than being included in the paintings of a Dutch master? The Kooikerhondje is depicted in many paintings from the 17th and 18th centuries by Rembrandt, Gerard ter Borch, and Jan Steen. William of Orange, a Dutch prince who would later become king of the United Kingdom, was reportedly saved from a Spanish assassin by his kooikerhondje, Kuntz.

CHARACTERISTICS

Coat
Sleek and wavy with distinctive orange-red and white colouring
Height
35–40cm (14–16in)
Weight
9–11kg (20–24lb)
Lifespan
12–13 years
Personality
Alert and kind
Origin
The Netherlands

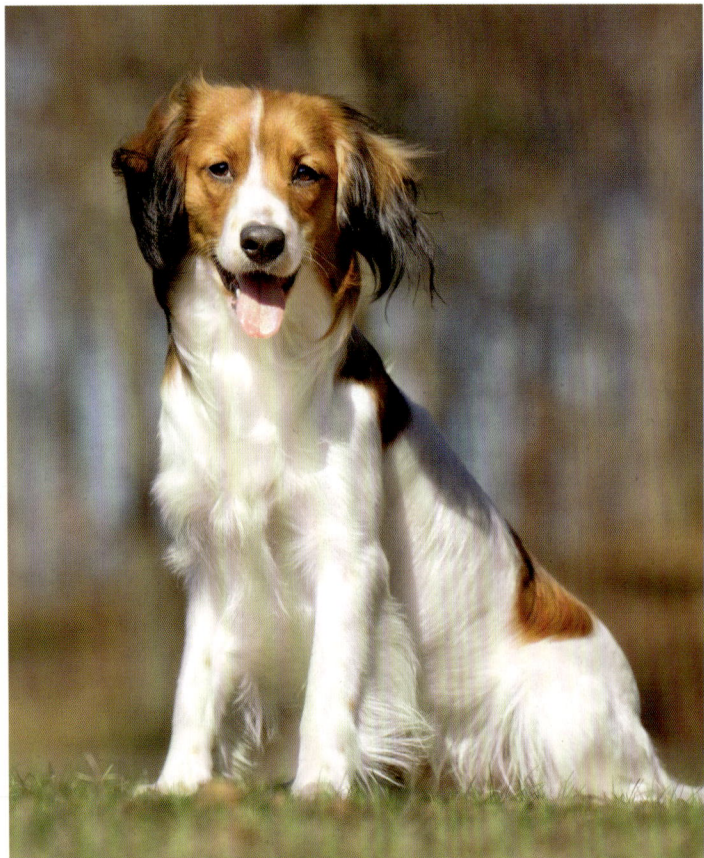

ABOVE:
Blazing eyes
The dog has bright, almond-shaped eyes that give a clear and friendly gaze.

RIGHT:
Let's be friends
The breed is friendly, alert, intelligent and eager to please, but can be wary of strangers and other dogs.

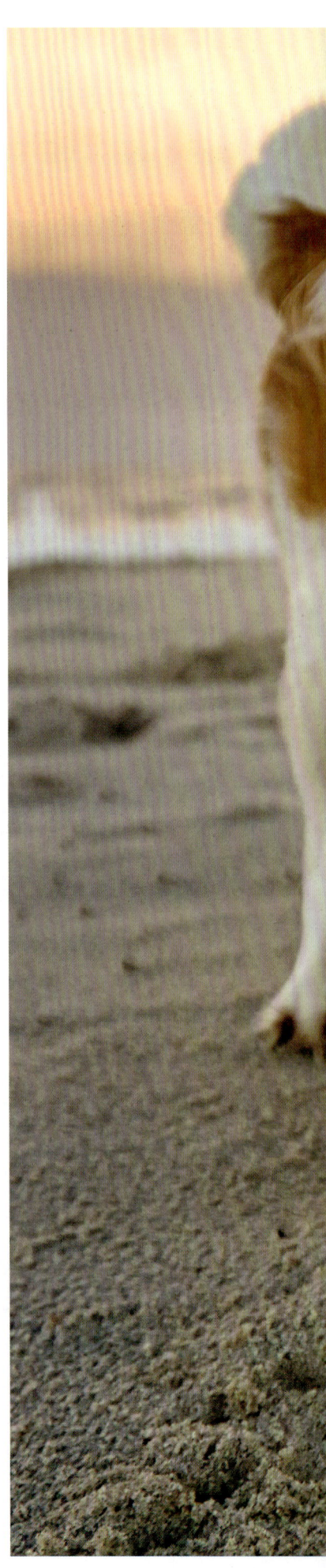

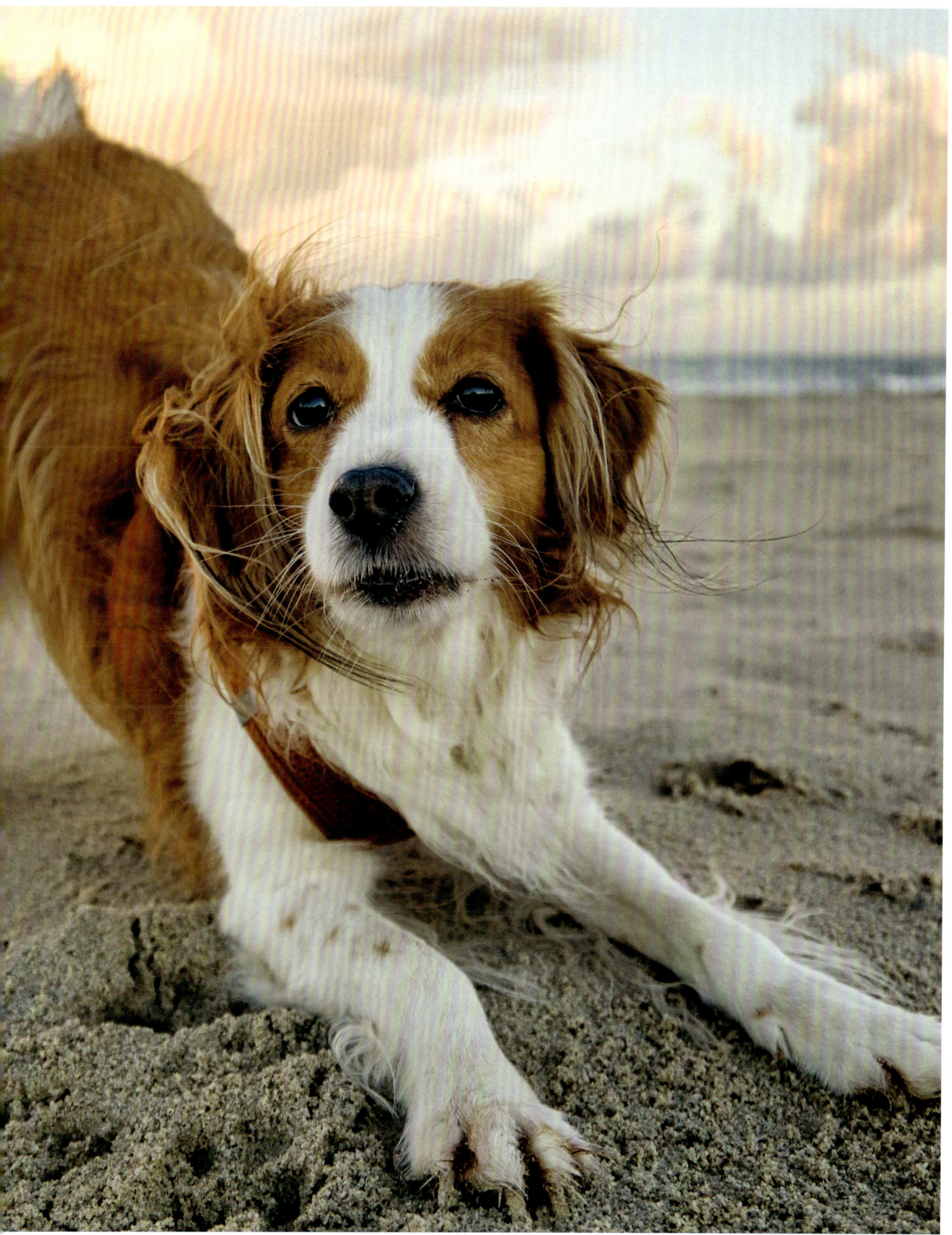

COMPANION DOGS

Kromfohrländer

CHARACTERISTICS

Coat
Two coat types, a smooth-haired and a rough-haired, both thick with white and brown markings
Height
38–46cm (15–18in)
Weight
9–16kg (20–35lb)
Lifespan
Up to 17 years
Personality
Loyal and charming
Origin
Germany

This German breed was developed in the years after the Second World War and is descended from a stray dog named Peter (Original Peter was his full name). Peter was a griffon-type dog found by American soldiers in France and brought to Germany in 1945. The squad lost Peter, who wound up living with Ilse Schleifenbaum in the Siegerland region of western Germany. Peter bred with a fox terrier (by the name of Fifi) and produced a litter that all looked like their father. Schleifenbaum decided she would use them as the founding stock of a new breed of faithful companion dogs—little friendly pets that appeared to smile at you. She named the breed after the local landscape of furrowed farmland, Krom Fohr. By 1955, the Kromfohrländer was an accepted breed. The dog was bred purely as a companion and has lost almost all of its terrier-like impulses. Kromfohrländers are very loyal to their owner, and tend to be somewhat indifferent to the affections of anyone else. The breed's hardy stock of descendants, survivors of the conflagration of Europe at war, means that this breed lives longer than most.

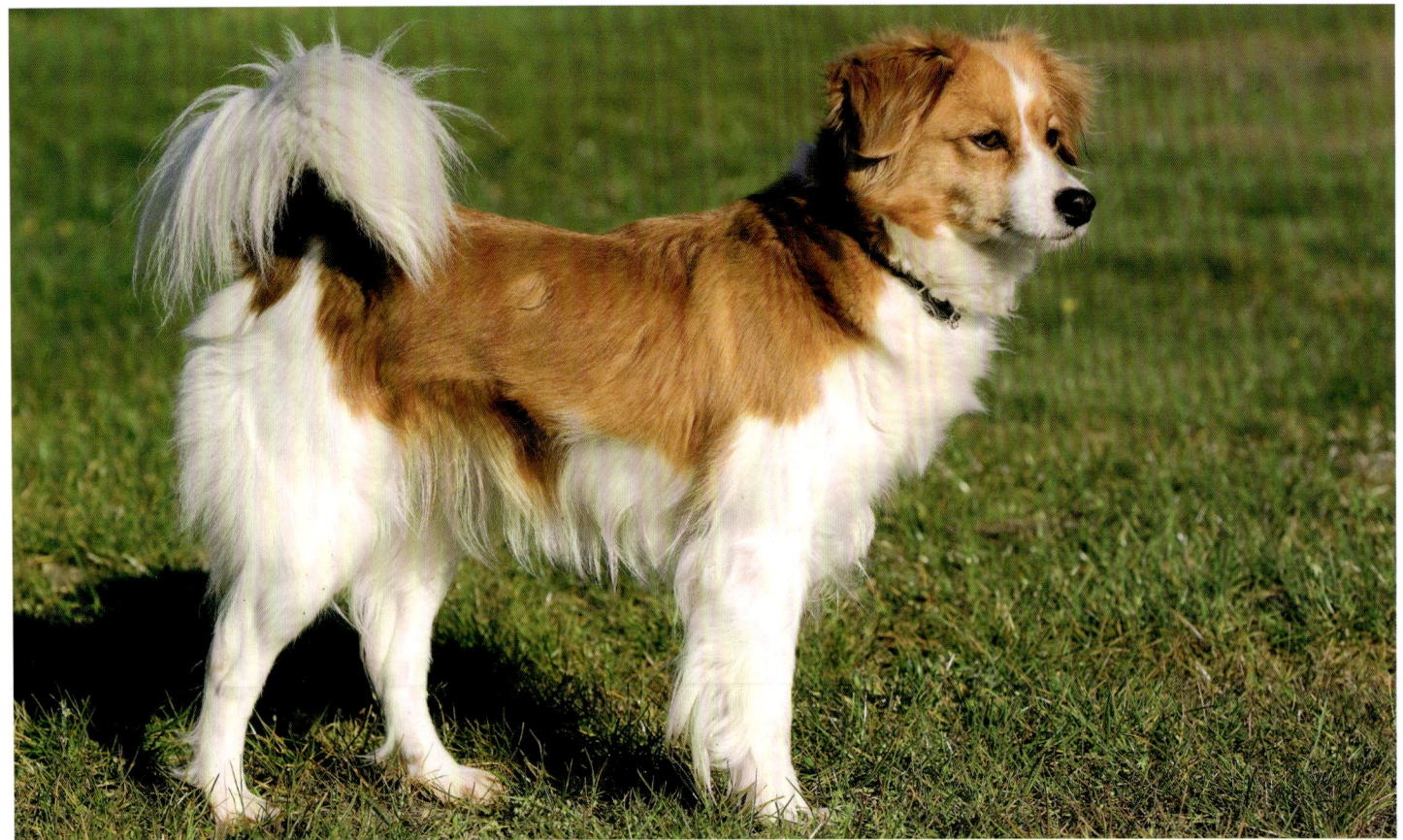

ABOVE:
Feathery features
The coat is wavy and luxuriant. The tail and upper thighs are heavily feathered.

COMPANION DOGS

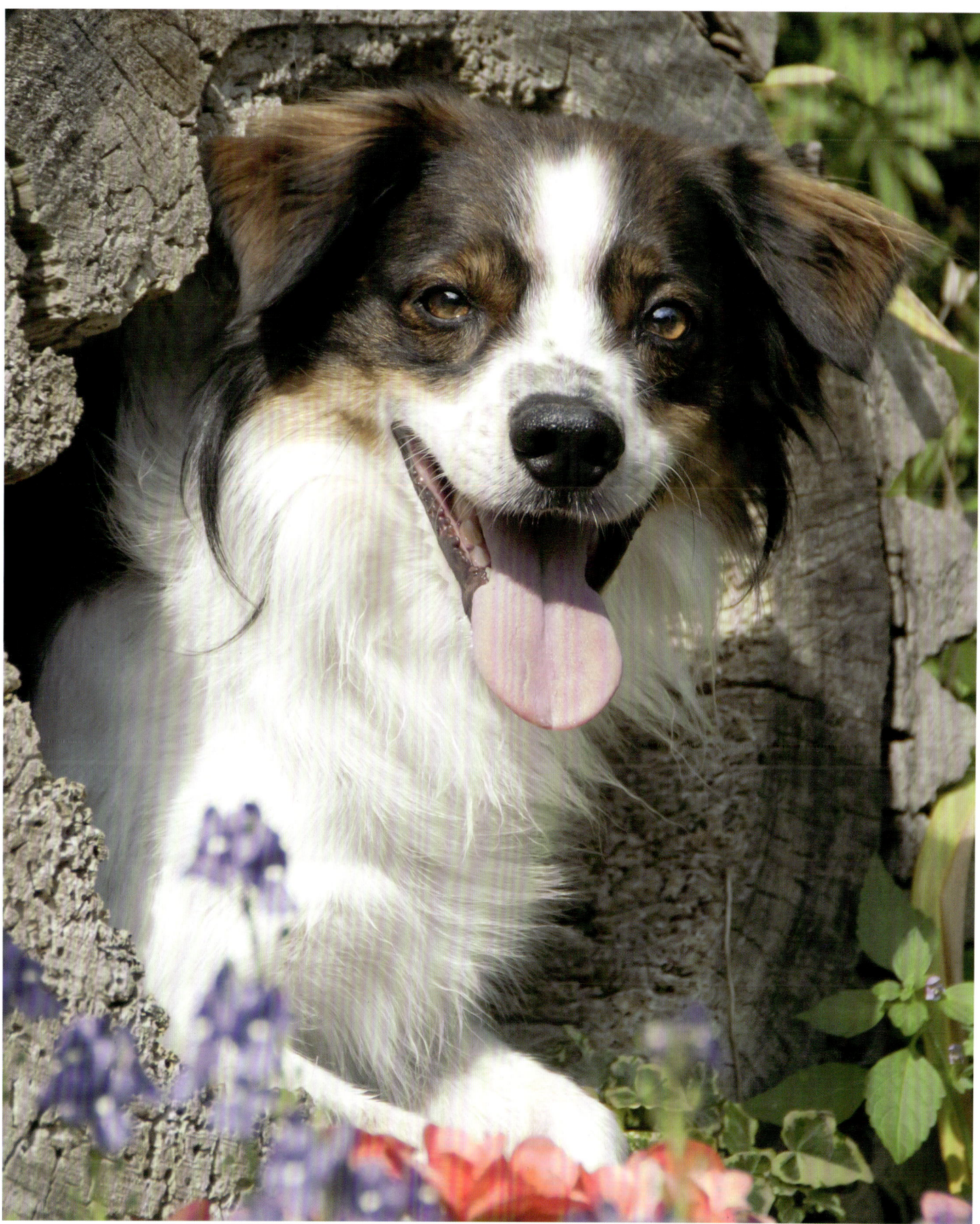

ABOVE:
Unusual breed
Despite its obvious attributes these German dogs remain rare. They are not widely recognized as a distinct breed outside of their home country.

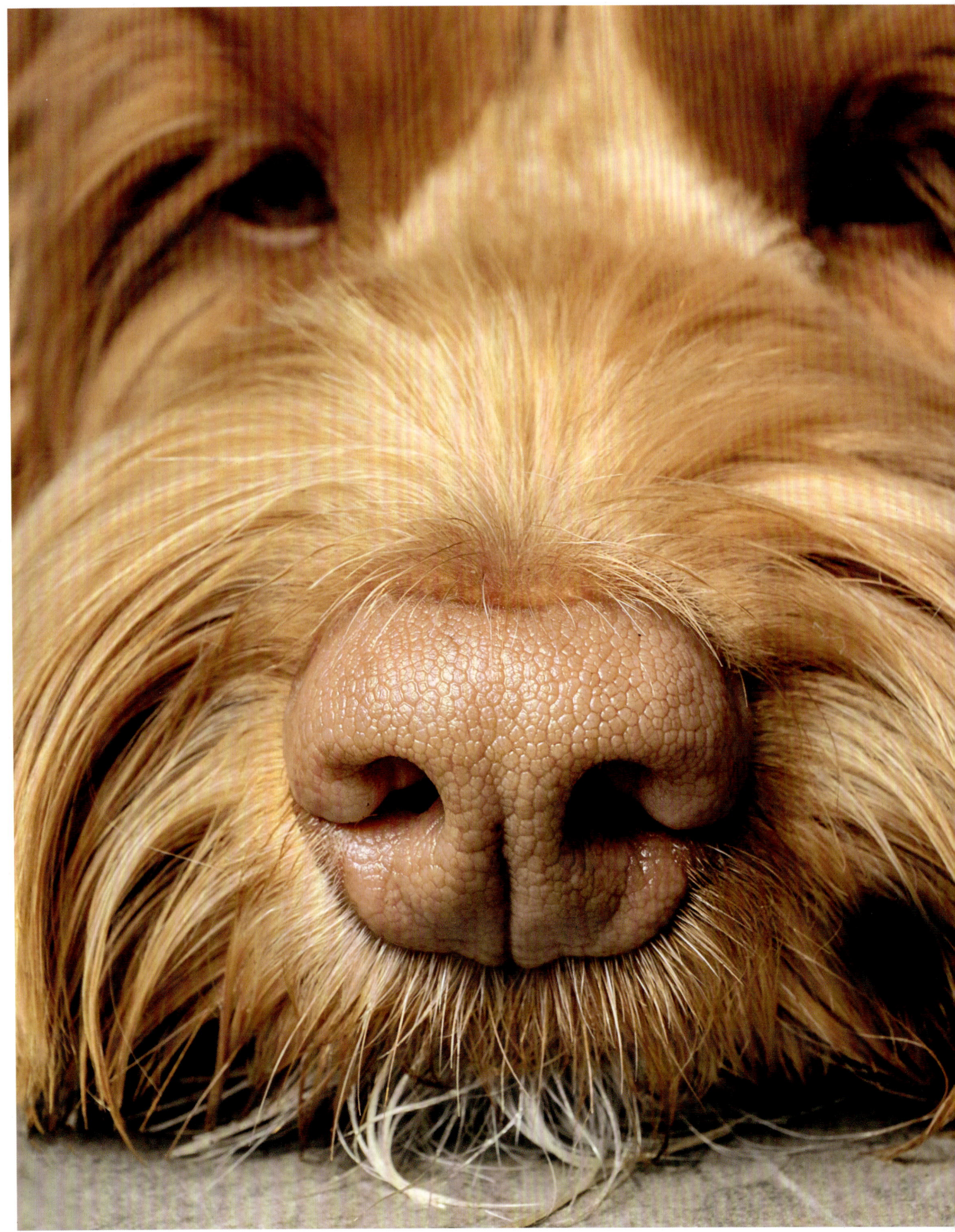

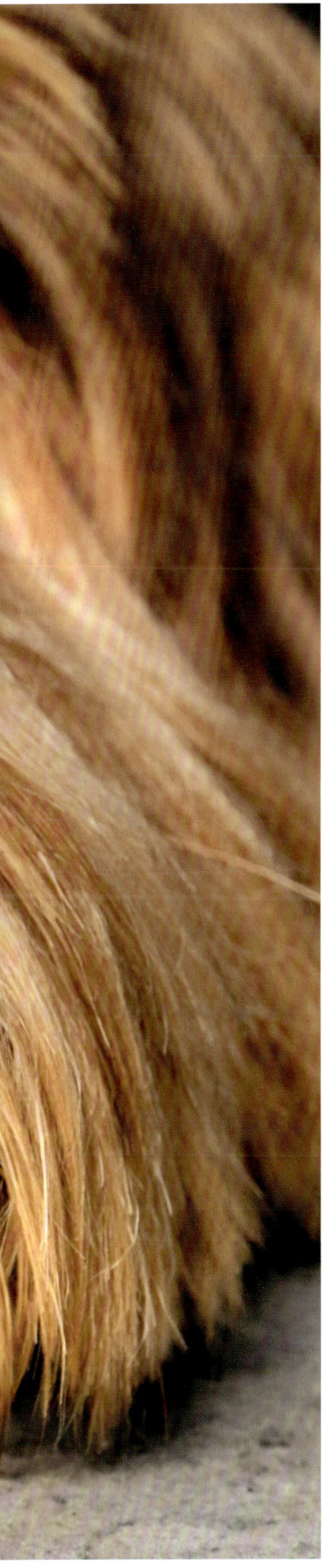

Labradoodle

The official story goes that the first labradoodle was created in the 1980s by the Australian breeder Wally Conron. He was responding to the request of a visually impaired woman for a guide dog that would not exacerbate her husband's virulent allergy to Labradors (a common choice of guide dog). Conron's solution was a crossbreed of a Labrador and a standard poodle. One of the pups was Sultan, who showed the docile temperament of a Labrador that suits assistance work and just as crucially had the curly, low-shedding coat of a poodle. Sultan became the first official labradoodle. Since then the popularity of the crossbreed has exploded. Families love their friendly and energetic personalities and are also attracted to the convenience of the low-shedding coat that still has a cuddlesome texture. Labradoodles are not currently recognized by the main kennel clubs, but it is likely that they have been bred since at least the 1950s. For example, Donald Campbell the adventurer who set land and speed records had a Labrador–poodle cross called Maxie back in 1949.

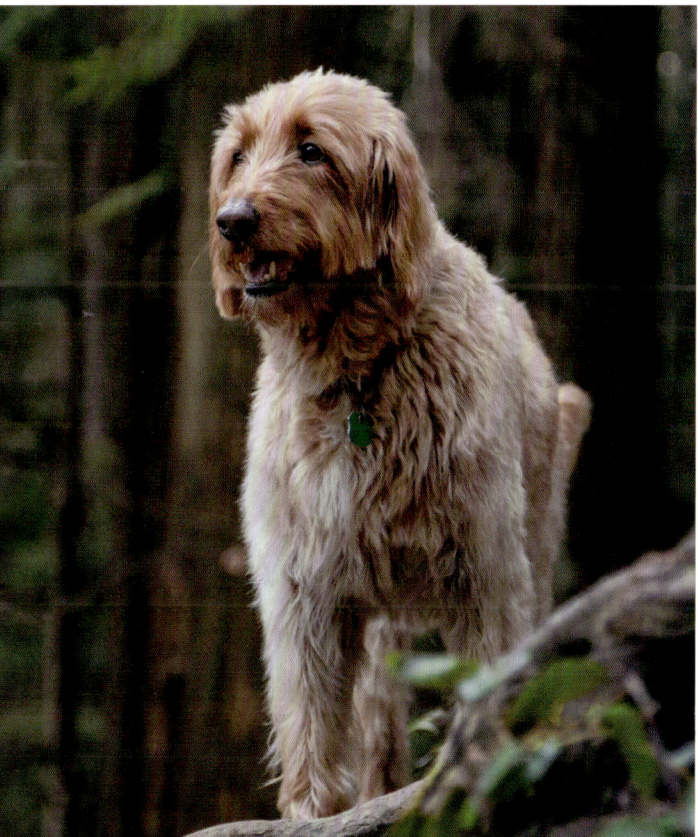

CHARACTERISTICS

Coat
Seen in any colour and can be woolly (tightly curled like a poodle's) or fleece coat (long and loosely curled like a Labrador's)

Height
36–61cm (14–24in)

Weight
7–29kg (15–65lb)

Lifespan
14–15 years

Personality
Clever and playful

Origin
Australia

LEFT:
Keeping active
The labradoodle is a very clever dog, and the crossbreed needs a lot of stimulation to prevent destructive behaviours.

ABOVE:
A varied crossbreed
The dog is a larger variety of labradoodle and has a fleece coat.

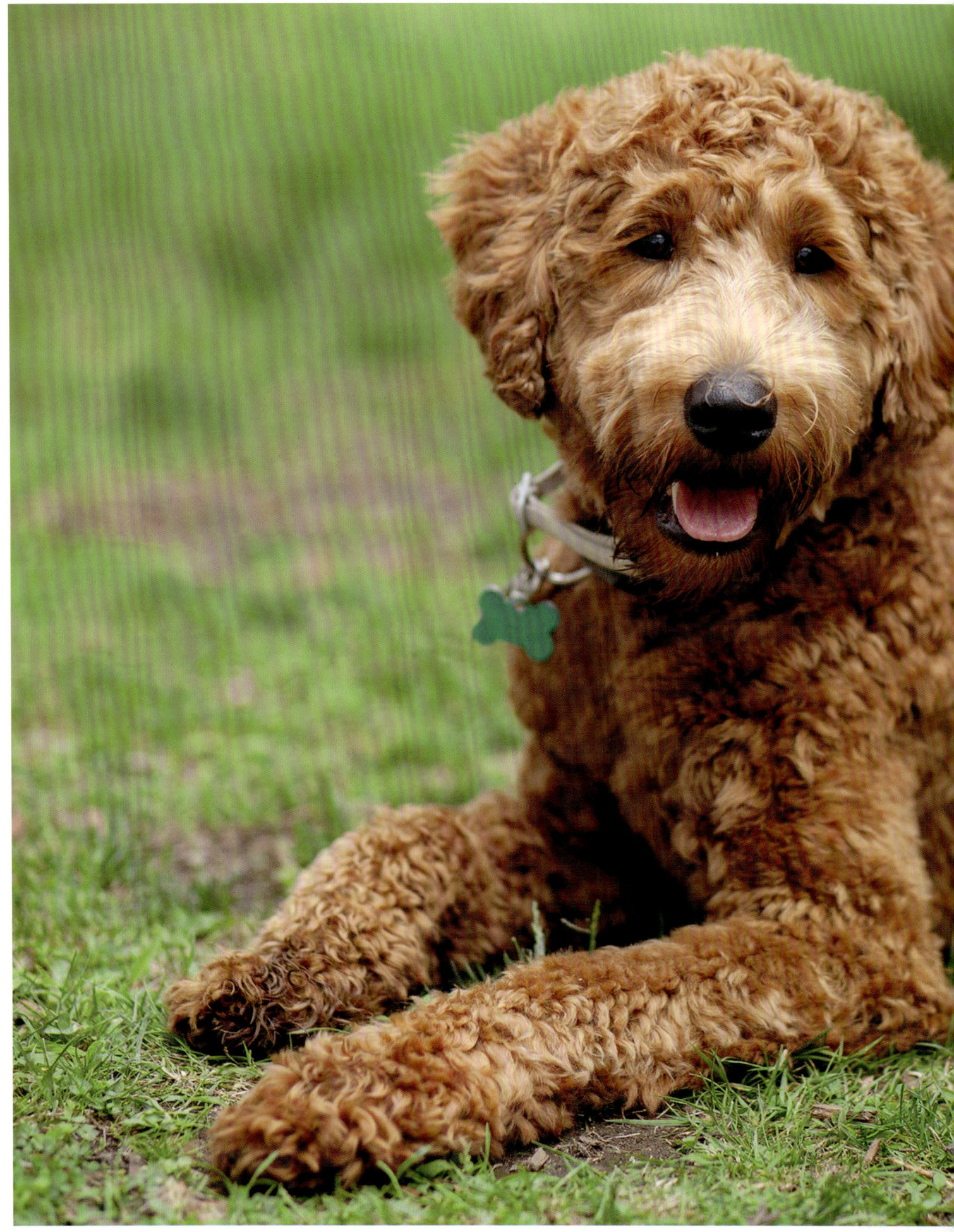

COMPANION DOGS

Outdoor dogs
Without plenty of physical exercise and games, this labradoodle can be prone to chewing of furniture.

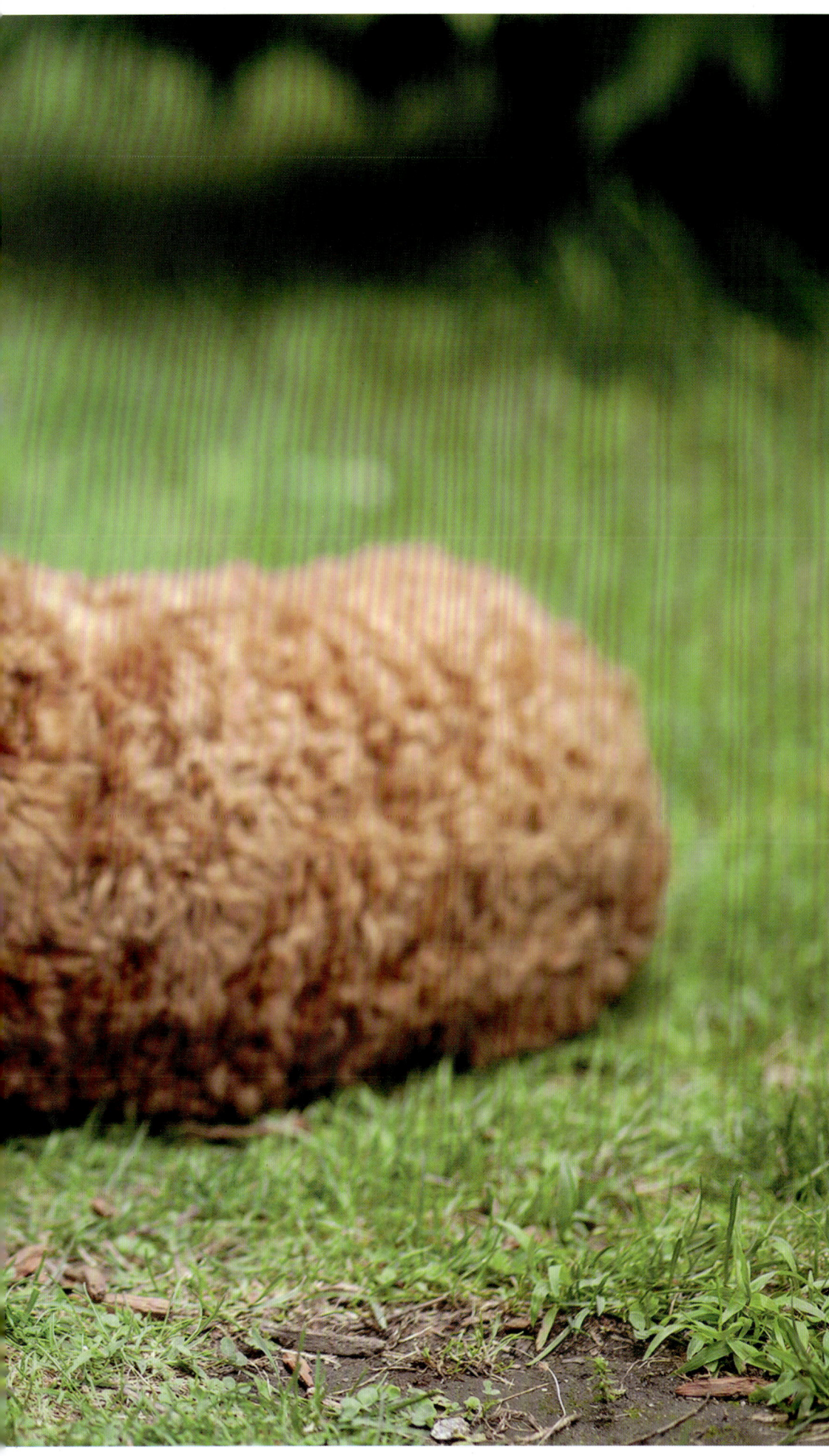

COMPANION DOGS

Labrador Retriever

The name Labrador does not begin with this dog, the world's most popular pet breed. In fact it belongs to the 15th century Portuguese explorer who put his name—since Anglicized—to the coastal region of eastern Canada. Today Labrador is teamed with Newfoundland as a Canadian province, and it is Newfoundland where this famous breed originated. The breed was developed as a gundog that would collect ducks from land and water, and as a fisher's dog that happily dived into the sea to collect any fish that had flopped out of the nets.

These hardy and capable dogs were taken to Britain in the last half of the 19th century (and it is at this point they were named Labrador dogs). British breeders refined the dogs into today's breed. The Canadian dogs' long hair, which allowed them to swim in near-freezing water, was replaced with shorter coats. The strong and wide "otter" tail that serves as a rudder in the water remained. In the English-speaking world at least, the Labrador is by far the most popular pet breed, with twice as many being registered by owners as the next nearest breeds.

CHARACTERISTICS
Coat
Short, dense and weatherproof, seen in black, chocolate brown or yellow
Height
55–57cm (22in)
Weight
25–37kg (55–82lb)
Lifespan
10–12 years
Personality
Friendly and active
Origin
Canada

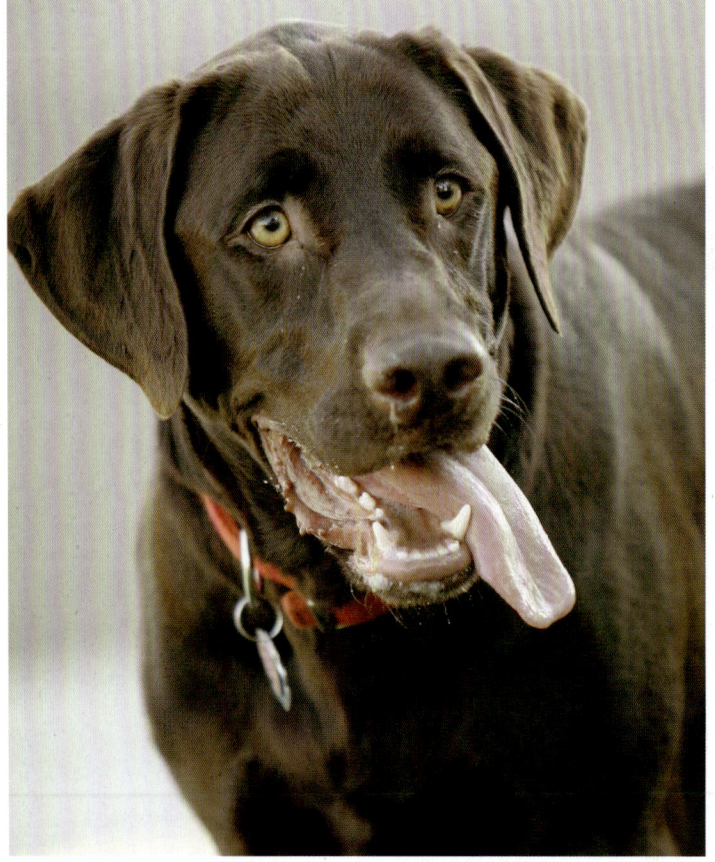

ABOVE:
Coat control
The Labrador retriever sheds throughout the year, especially the yellow ones.

RIGHT:
Popular pooch
The Labrador is one of the most popular and reliable family pets in the world.

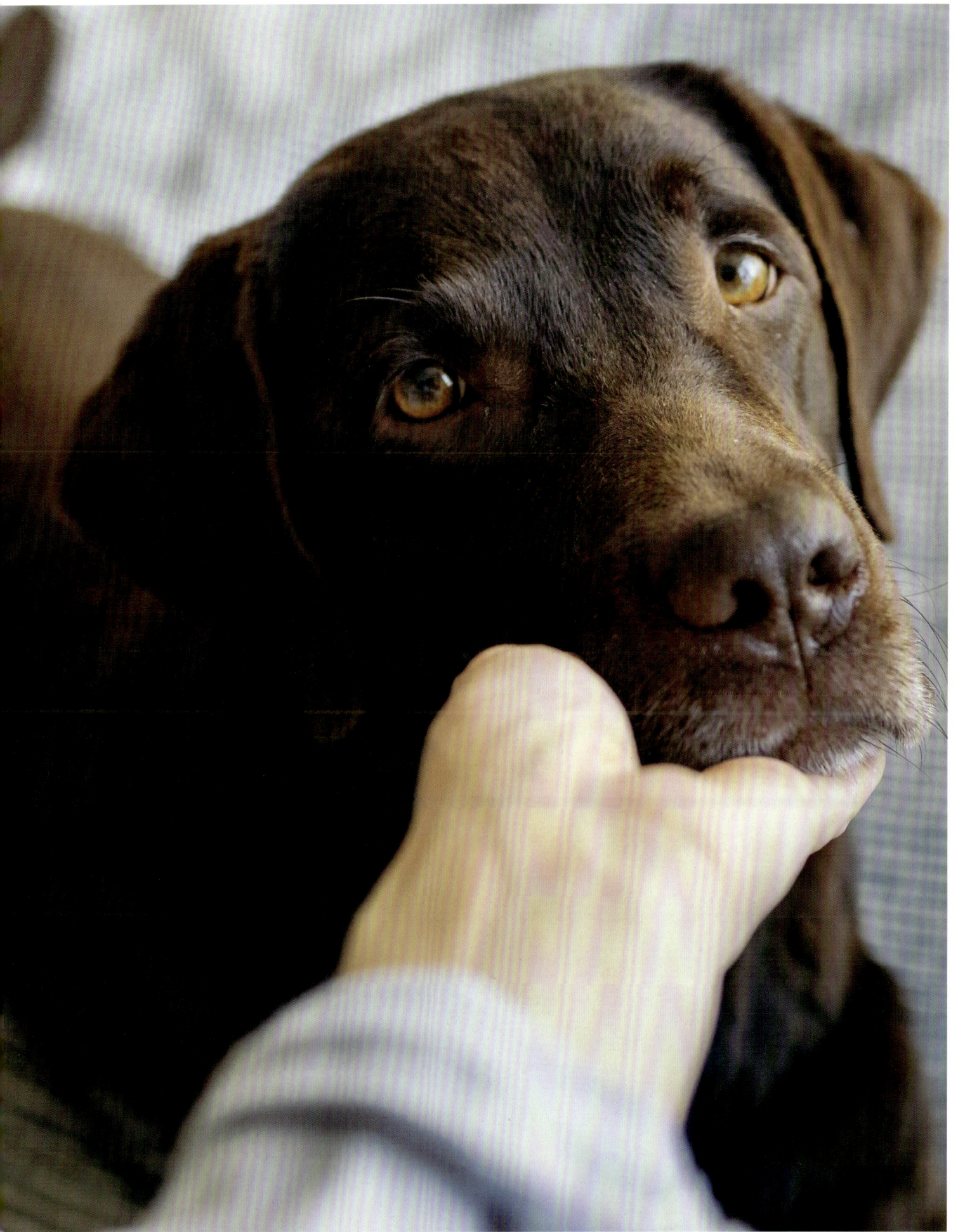

COMPANION DOGS

Lovely labrador
The popularity of this breed is thanks to its friendly, energetic and playful personality.

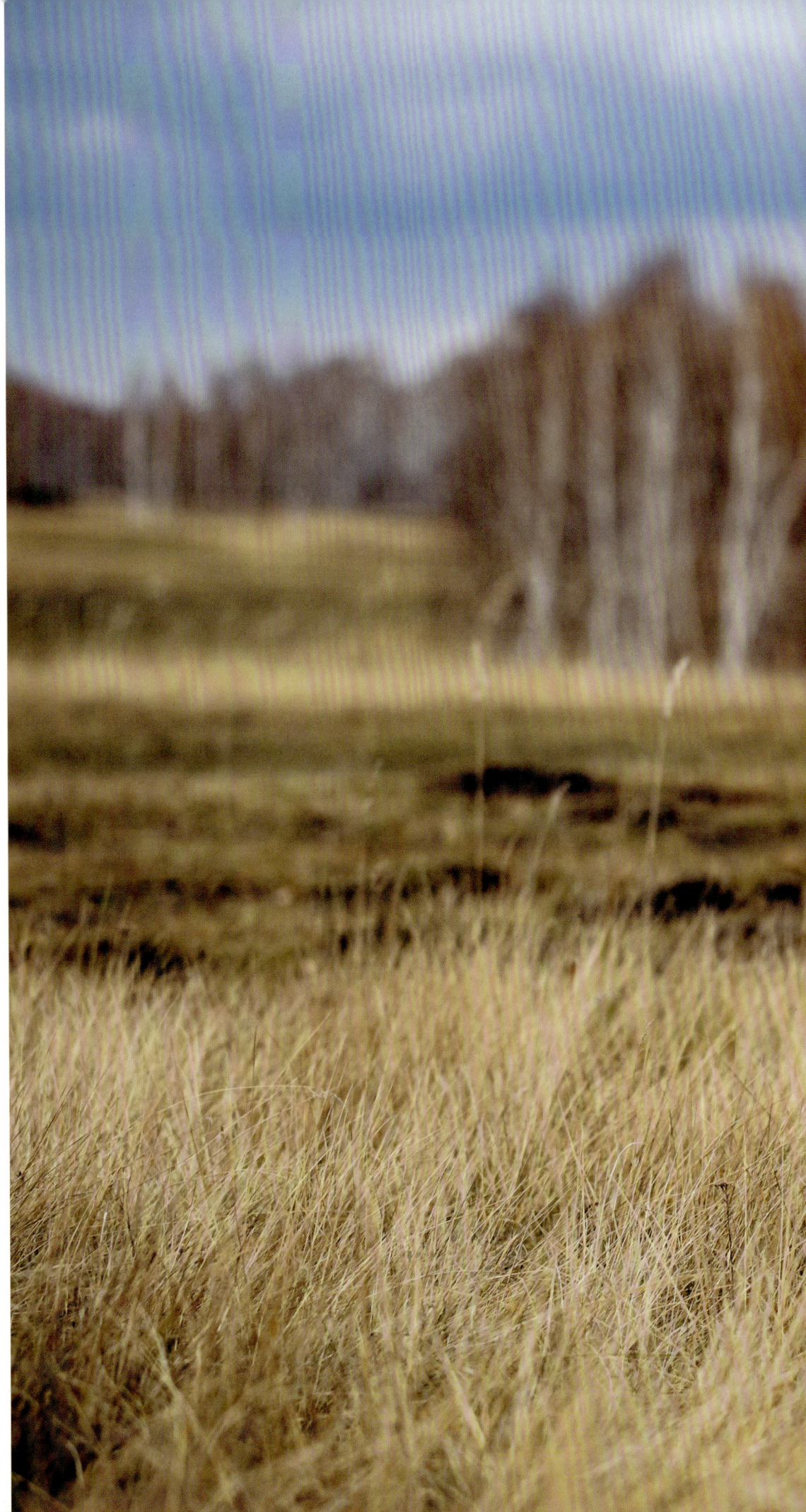

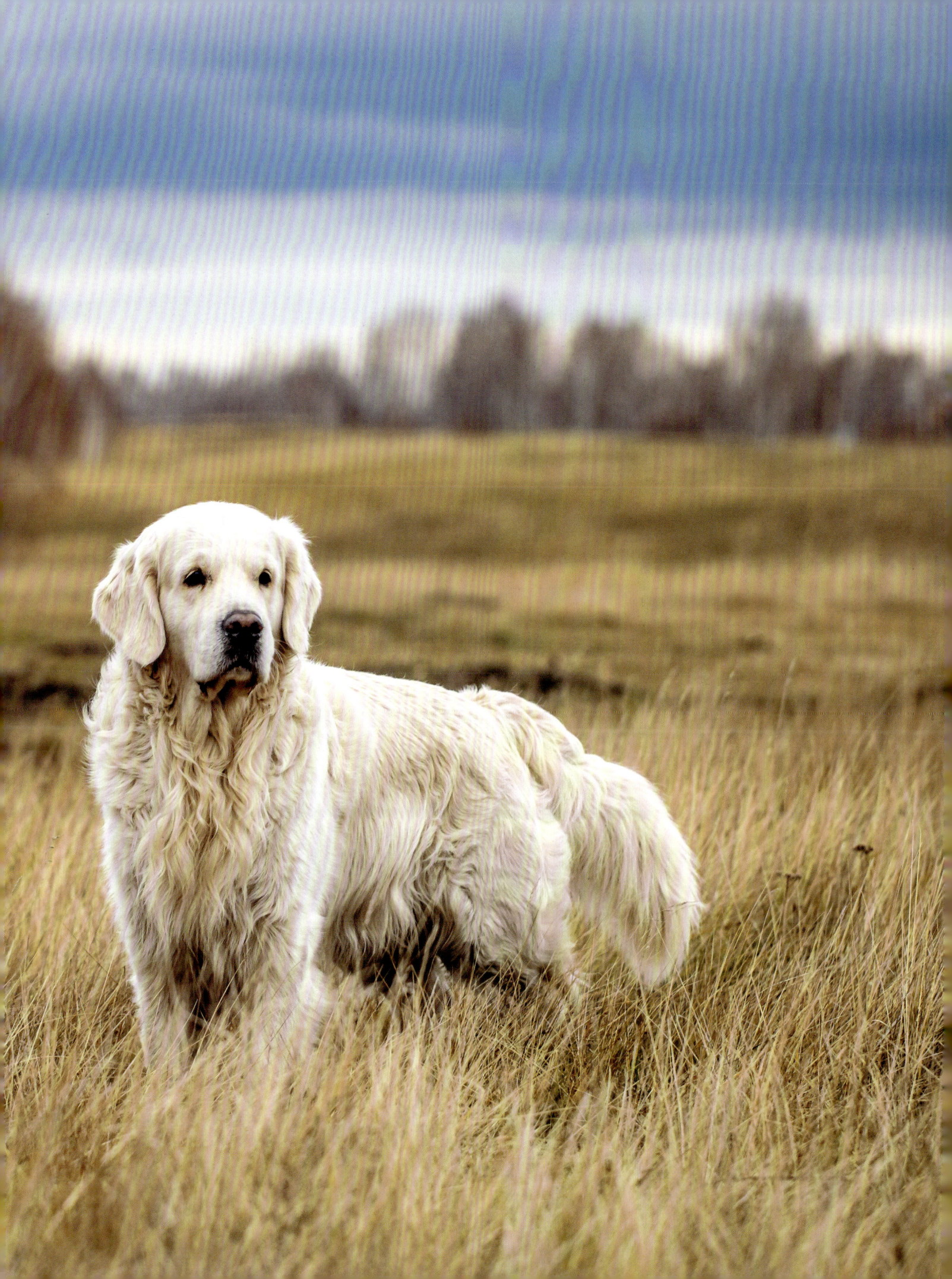

COMPANION DOGS

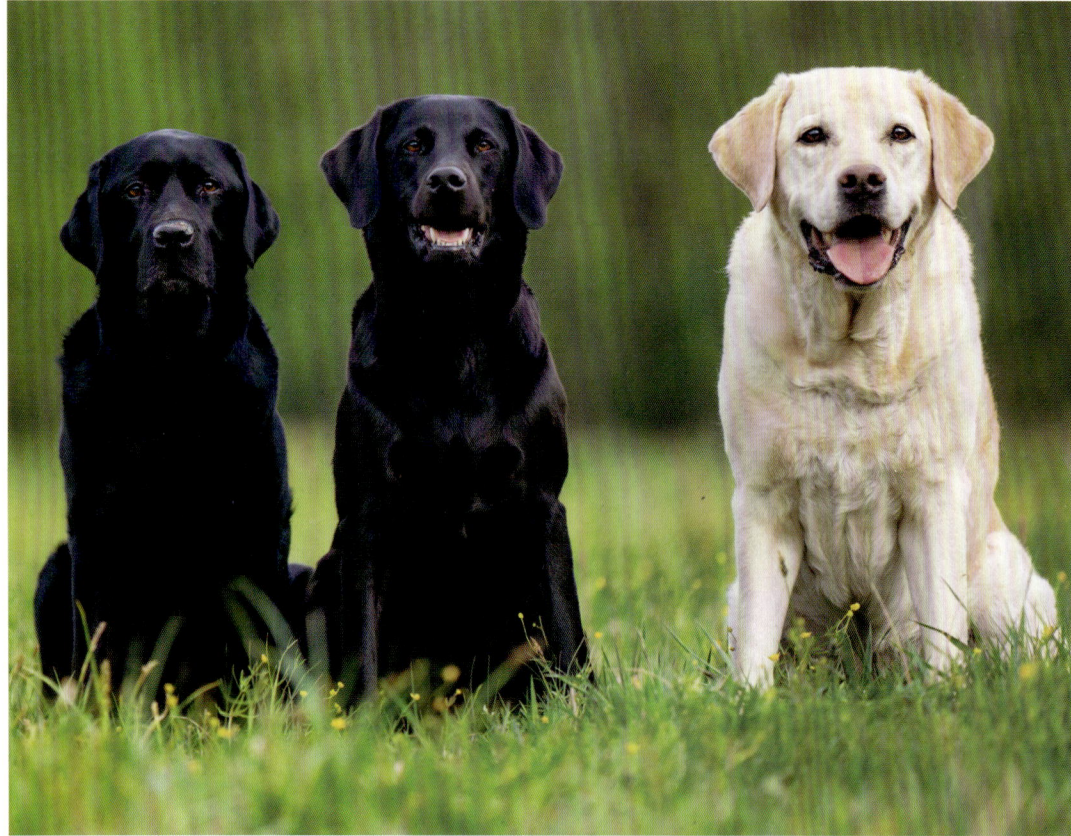

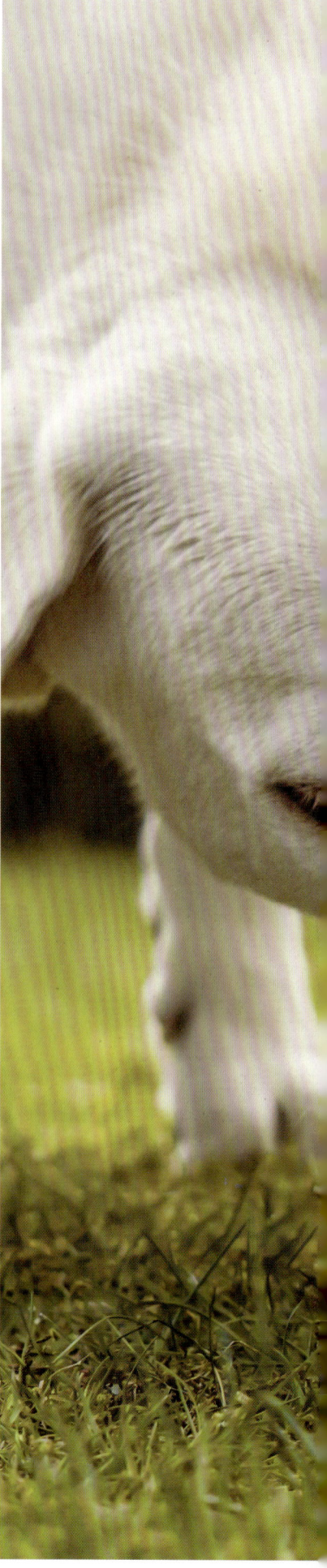

ABOVE:
Pet care
Despite their short coat, all labradors need regular grooming.

RIGHT:
Guide dog
A Labrador puppy out training to be a guide dog for a visually impaired person. The dog will keep its owner safe while crossing the road or navigating crowded streets.

OPPOSITE:
Eating
All dogs are carnivores and have a short gut that processes nutrient-rich meat in a few hours. Labradors can overeat and be overfed – easily and enjoy dry foods that are less packed with calories. A chew toy or bone will keep the teeth and gums in good condition.

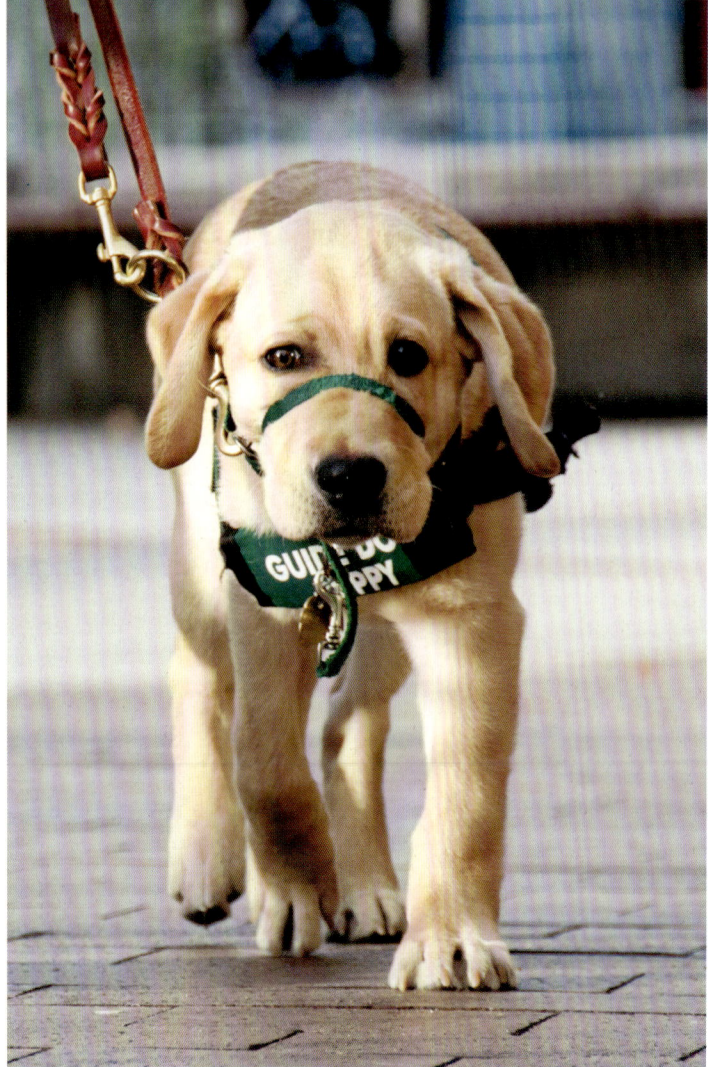

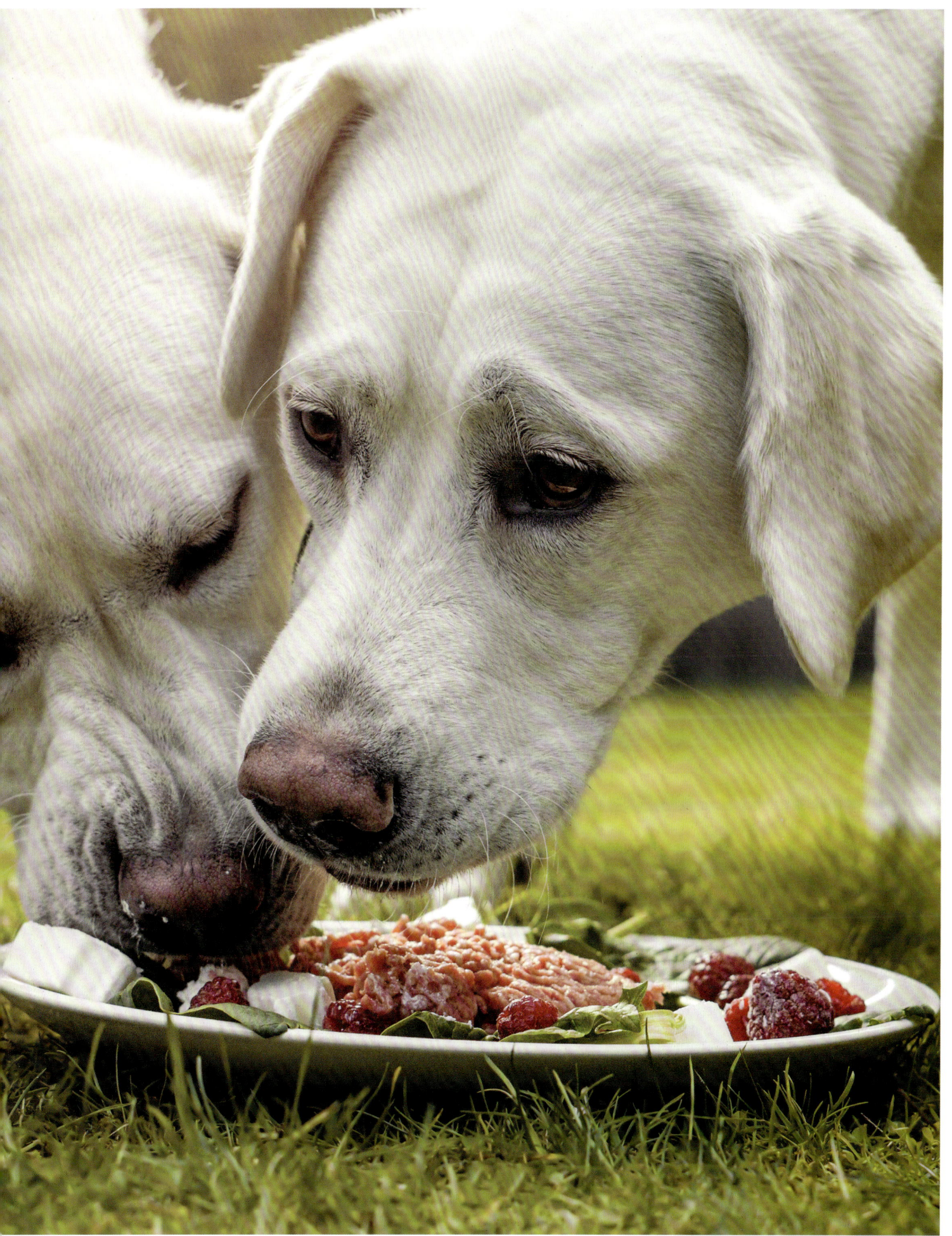

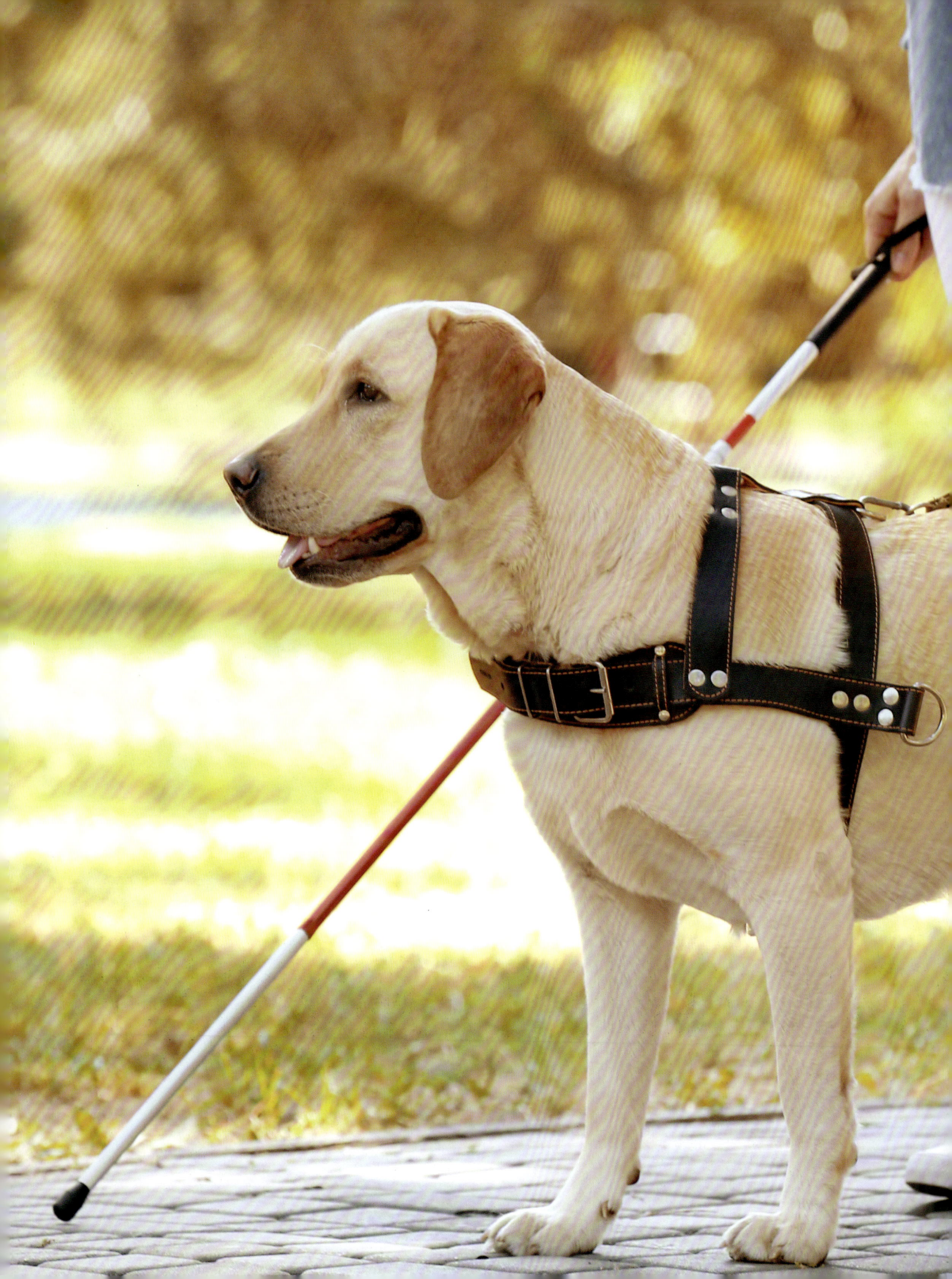

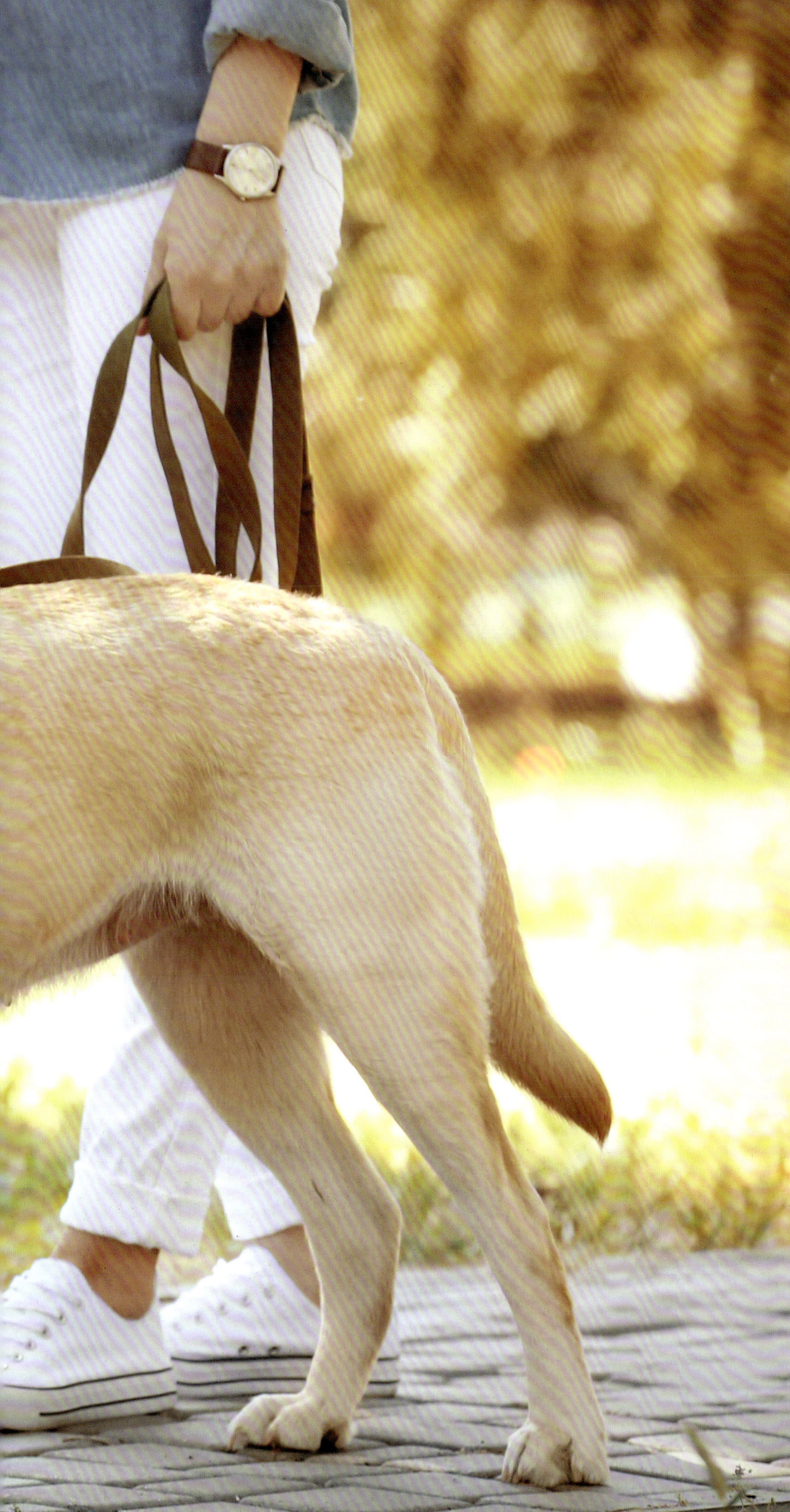

COMPANION DOGS

Guide dog
While the human dictates the direction, a guide dog is there to navigate obstacles and stop when danger appears.

COMPANION DOGS

Lagotto Romagnolo

CHARACTERISTICS

Coat
Woolly and curly that can be off-white, orange, brown or roan

Height
41–48cm (16–19in)

Weight
11–16kg (24–35lb)

Lifespan
12–14 years

Personality
Eager and easygoing

Origin
Italy

This dog breed originated in Italy, specifically in the marshlands around the delta of the River Po, which meets the Adriatic in northwestern Italy. This region is traditionally known as Romagna, and so the breed's name is Italian for the "lake dog of Romagna". The breed is thought to be the progenitor of all water dog breeds, with webbed feet to help when doggy paddling, and the shaggy, waterproof coat that suits plunging into shallow water to retrieve ducks or whatever else. The ancient dog is in less demand for its retrieving skills today. Many of the wetlands that were once frequented are now drained. Nevertheless the dog's nose has earned it a new role as a highly prized truffle dog. To this end the breed has been adjusted throughout the 20th century to boost its smelling skills, and there are none of the original lake dog left. Today the lagotto Romagnolo is considered the world's best truffle hound, and handlers hope their dog finds large quantities of these exclusive edible fungi. Aside from making money for the family, the lagotto Romagnolo is a loyal and friendly pet that enjoys playing games and learning new skills.

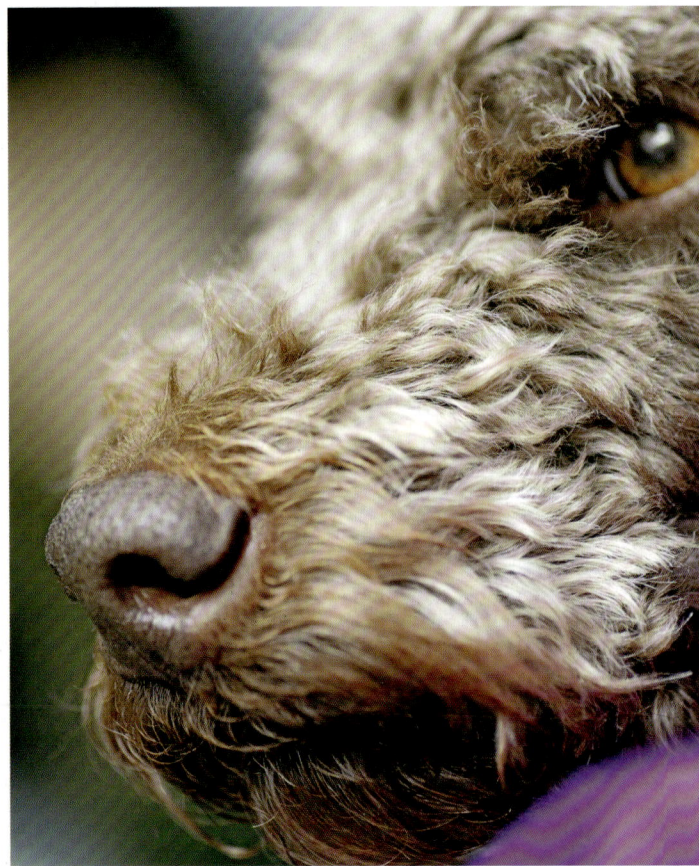

ABOVE:
Weekly brush
The characteristic curly coat of this needs weekly attention.

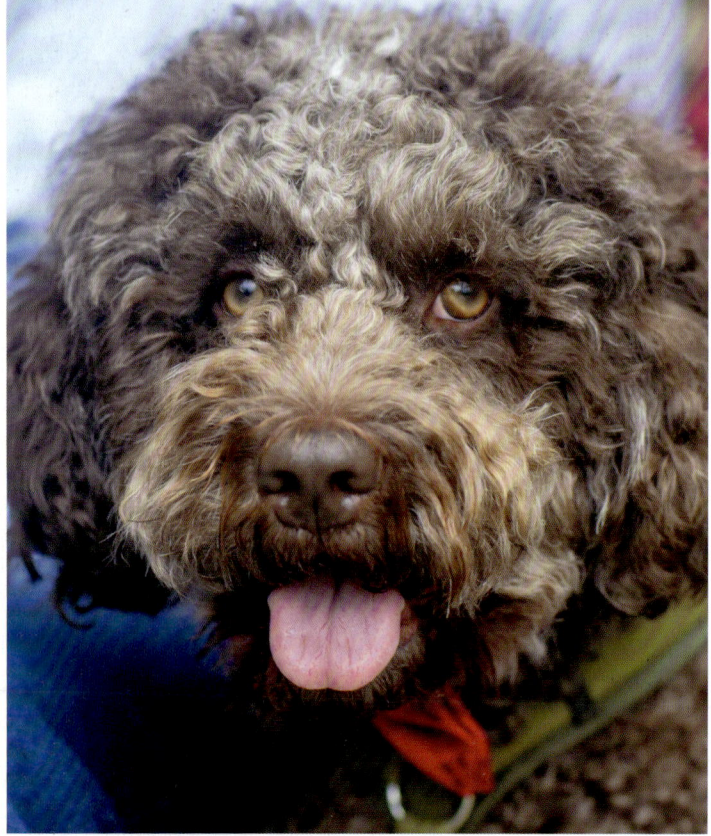

ABOVE:
Broad and bouncy
The lovable lagotto is a small to medium-sized dog with a square body and a broad head.

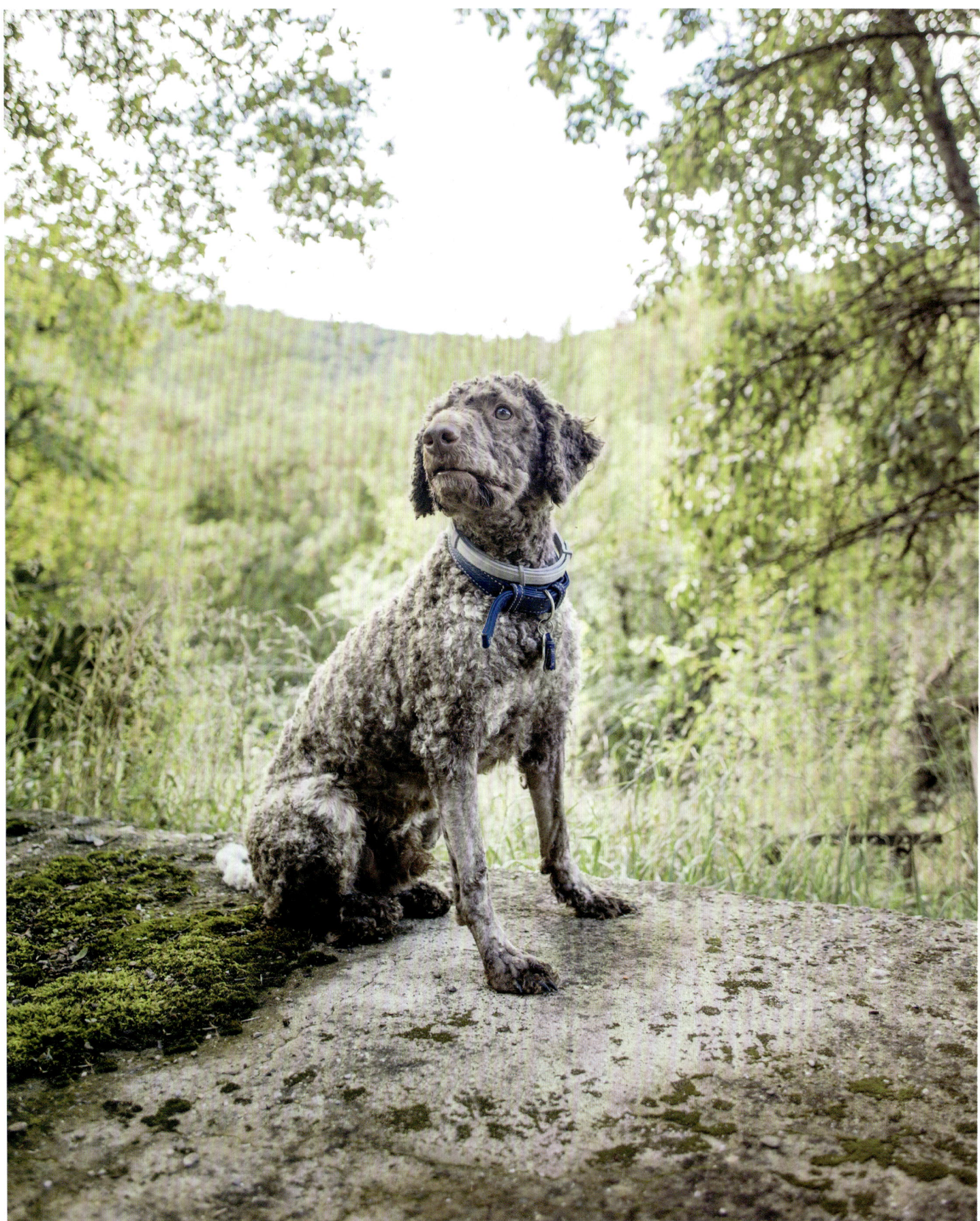

ABOVE:
Action packed
The Italian breed is a good companion for active families.

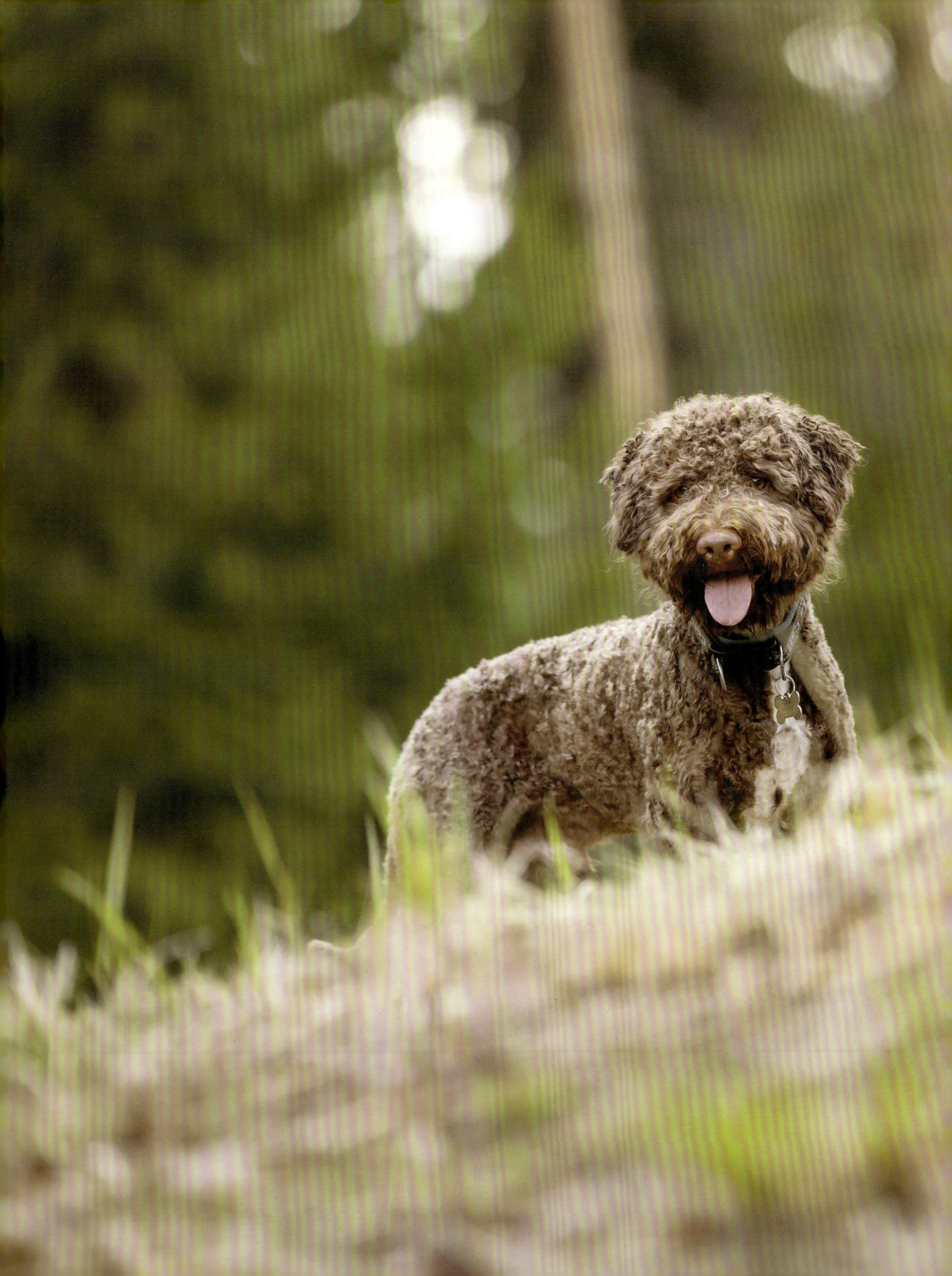

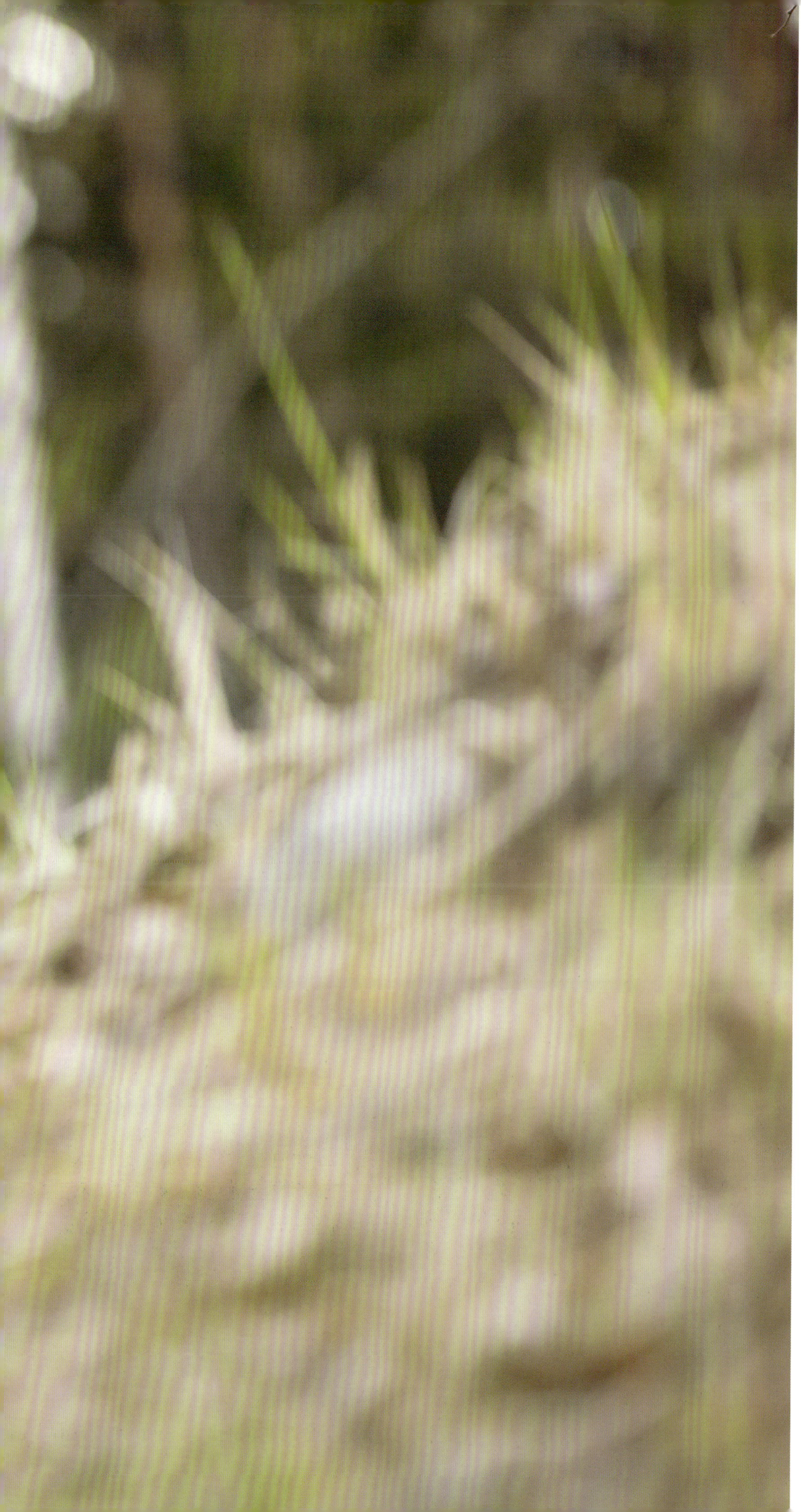

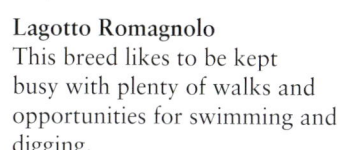

COMPANION DOGS

Lagotto Romagnolo
This breed likes to be kept busy with plenty of walks and opportunities for swimming and digging.

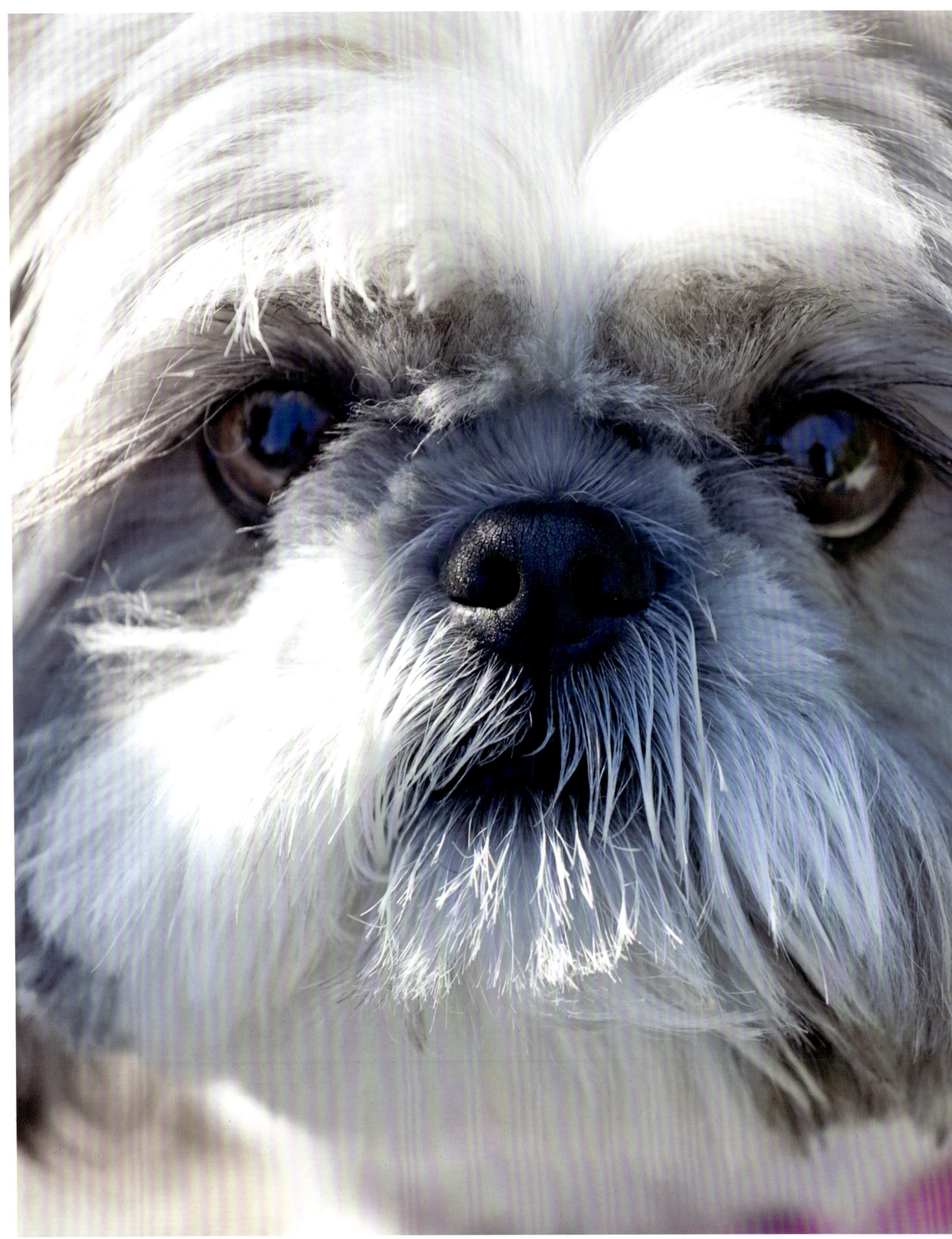

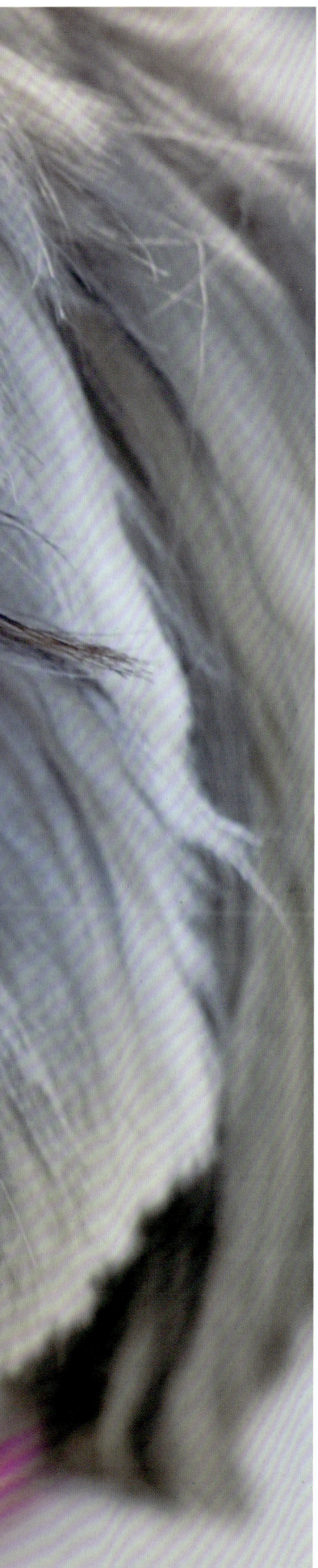

Lhasa Apso

This 1,000-year-old Tibetan breed traditionally stands guard at the entrances to temples, monasteries and palaces. The small but robust sentinels would yap at any intruders, alerting the monks inside. The dogs are still revered by monks as spiritual guardians and a bringer of good fortune. The name Lhasa apso means longhaired dog of Lhasa (Tibet's capital), but the breed is also known as the "bearded lion dog". This nickname speaks to the breed's perky courage as well as the mane-like coat. The flat coat is often left to grow long and parted in the middle to create a floor-length fringe. Tibetans believe that their land is watched over by the scared Snow Lion, and the Lhasa apso are this creature's representatives on earth.

The Lhasa apso's breeding gives it an independent and aloof personality. It has a very strong bond with its owners (and wider family) but the watchdog traits come to the fore when any strangers come near. This breed can make a rewarding companion for a loving family that admire its exotic looks and long history.

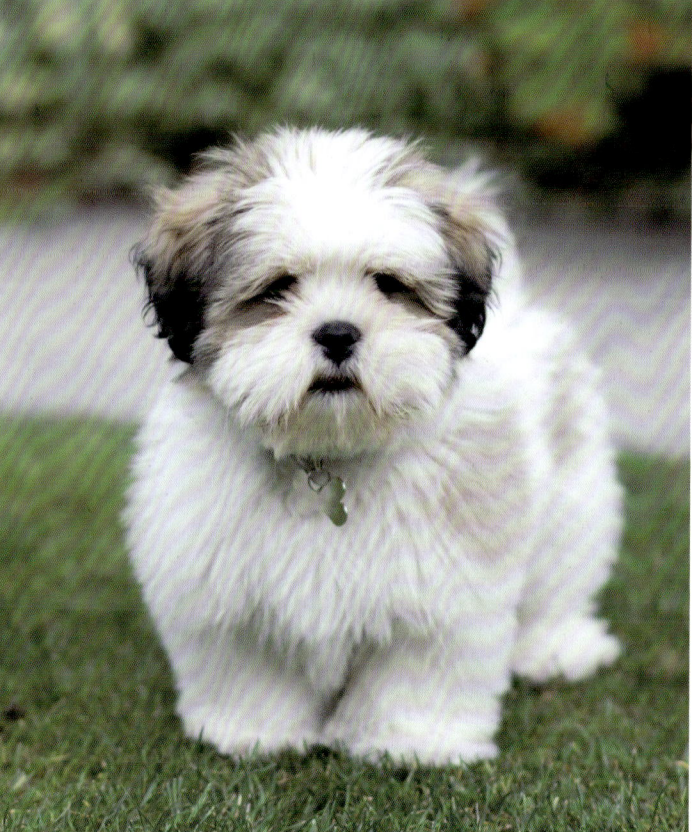

CHARACTERISTICS

Coat
Long and silky that comes in various colours and patterns
Height
Up to 25 cm (10in)
Weight
6–7kg (13–15lb)
Lifespan
15–18 years
Personality
Loyal and confident
Origin
Tibet

LEFT:
Long or short
The Lhasa apso's silky locks require a lot of grooming.

ABOVE:
Demanding love
The breed needs moderate exercise, and training helps it to ward off aggression and stubbornness.

COMPANION DOGS

Lhasa Apso
The breed typically has long silky locks. Domestically it is often kept clipped short for easier maintenance.

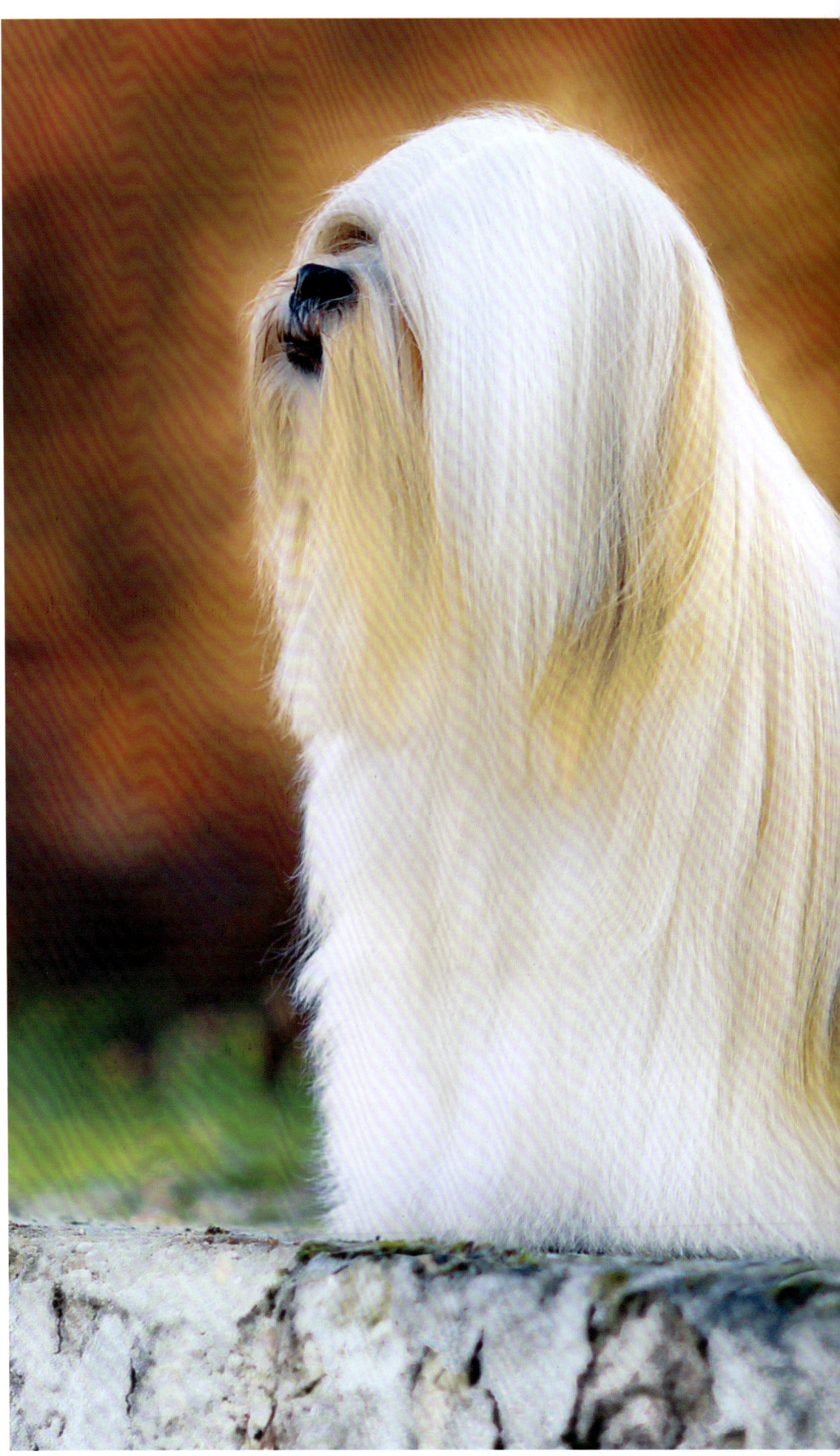

COMPANION DOGS

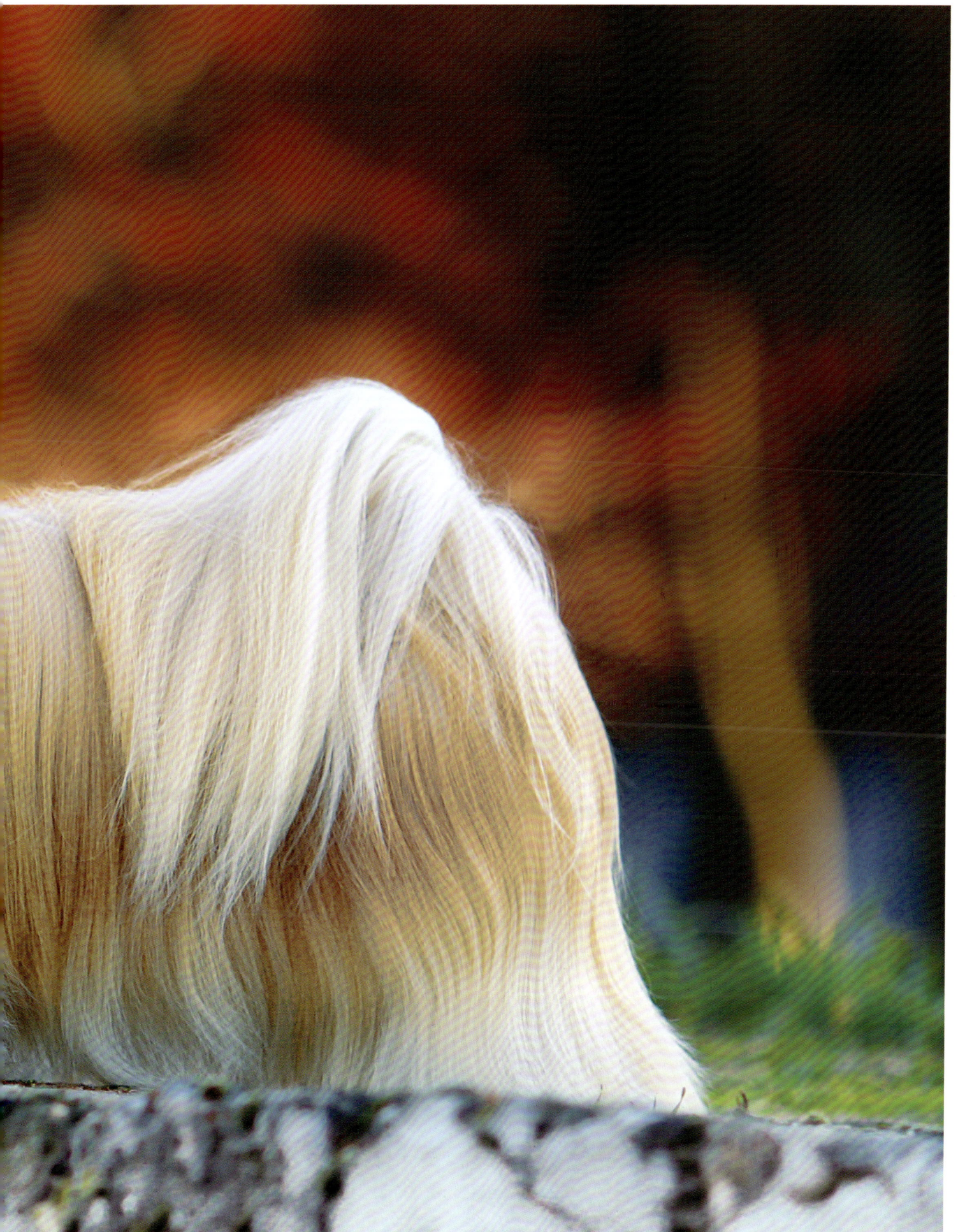

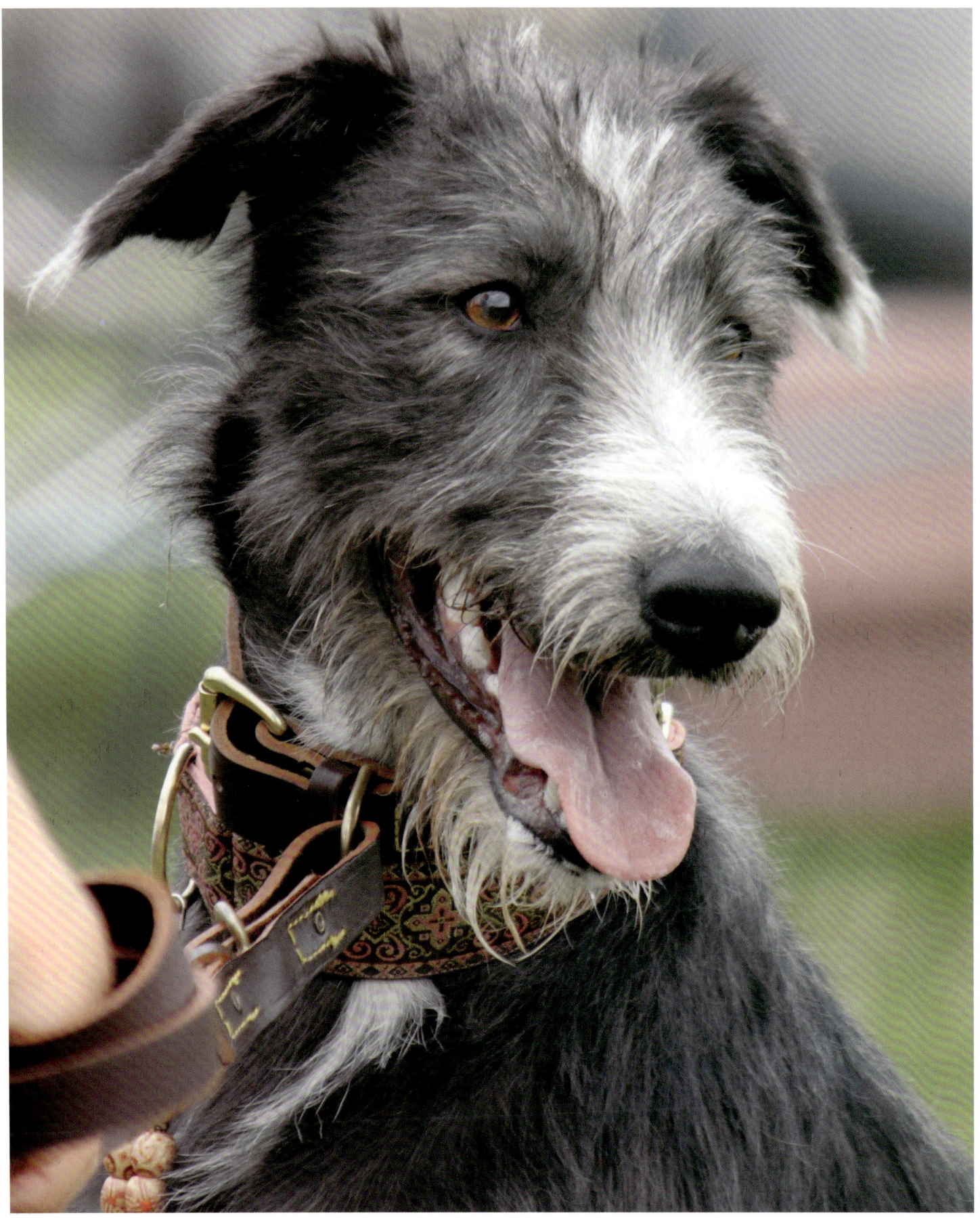

ABOVE:
Welcome wanted
Lurchers make good family pets for experienced owners who can provide them with enough physical and mental challenges.

Lurcher

CHARACTERISTICS

Coat
A variety of coat types and colours depending on the breeds involved in their ancestry

Height
55–71cm (22–28in)

Weight
27–32kg (60–71lb)

Lifespan
13–14 years

Personality
Loyal and tolerant

Origin
Britain and Ireland

A lurcher is a crossbreed created by mating a sighthound, such as a greyhound or less commonly Irish wolfhounds, with another breed, usually a terrier, but also sometimes a herding dog, such as a border collie. The name "lurcher" comes from an old English word meaning "to lurk" or "steal" and these dogs were often used by poachers because they combined speed and drive with intelligence and tenacity. That made lurchers ideal for hunting rabbits and hares with minimum fuss. Lurchers are popular in Britain and Ireland, where they have been a common dog for around 500 years. Back then only the gentry were allowed to own sighthounds, so a lurcher made a good alternative for common people who had the need for speed. Today lurchers remain a popular choice as a gangly yet calm and loyal companion dog. However, they are much less common beyond the British Isles and not recognised as a breed in their own right.

Lurchers are also easily trainable but will need a lot of exercise and stimulation to keep them happy and healthy. Some lurchers can live with cats and other small animals if raised with them from puppyhood, but others may not be able to resist their hunting instincts.

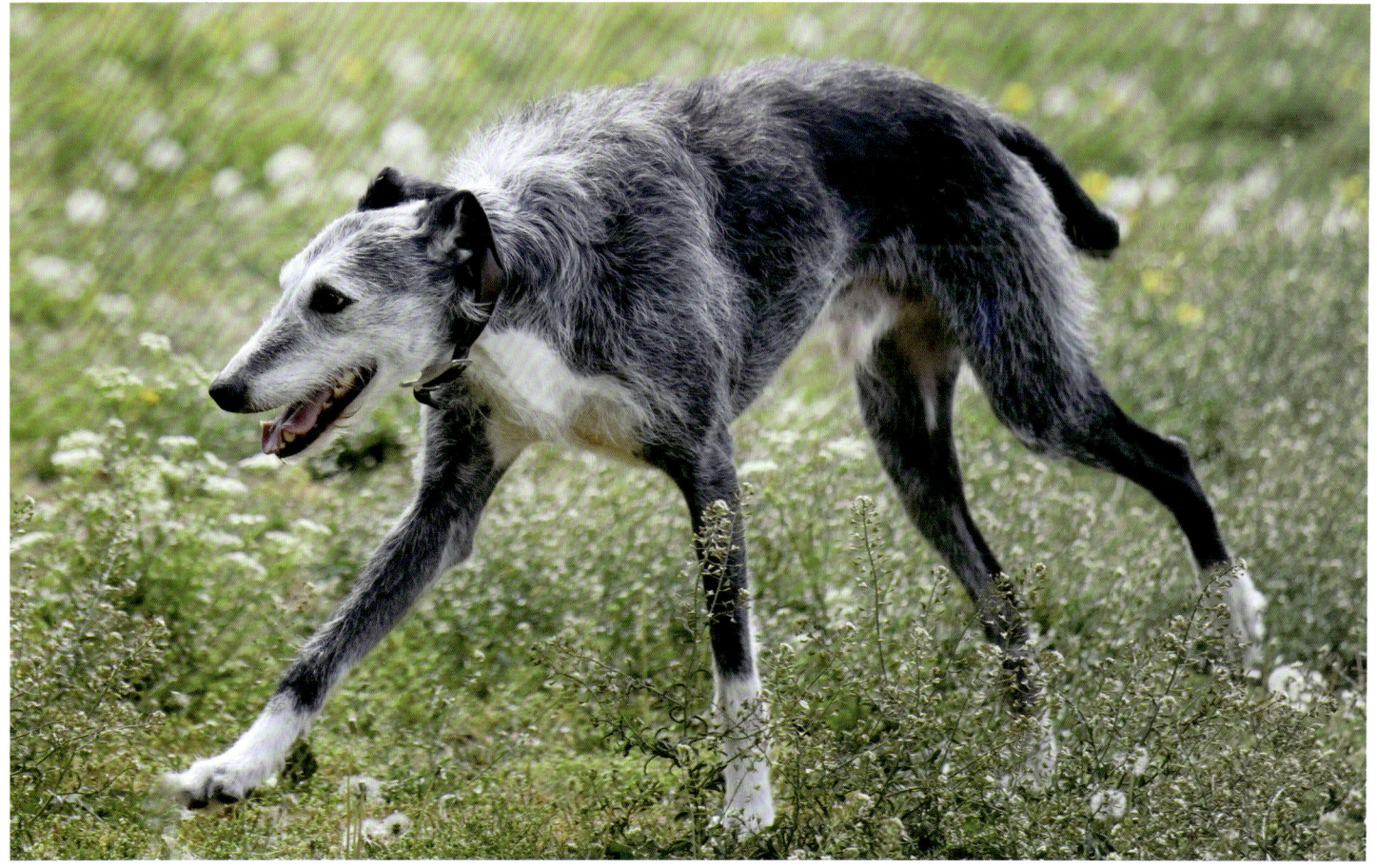

ABOVE:
Long and lean
Lurchers are generally tall, athletic and very fast.

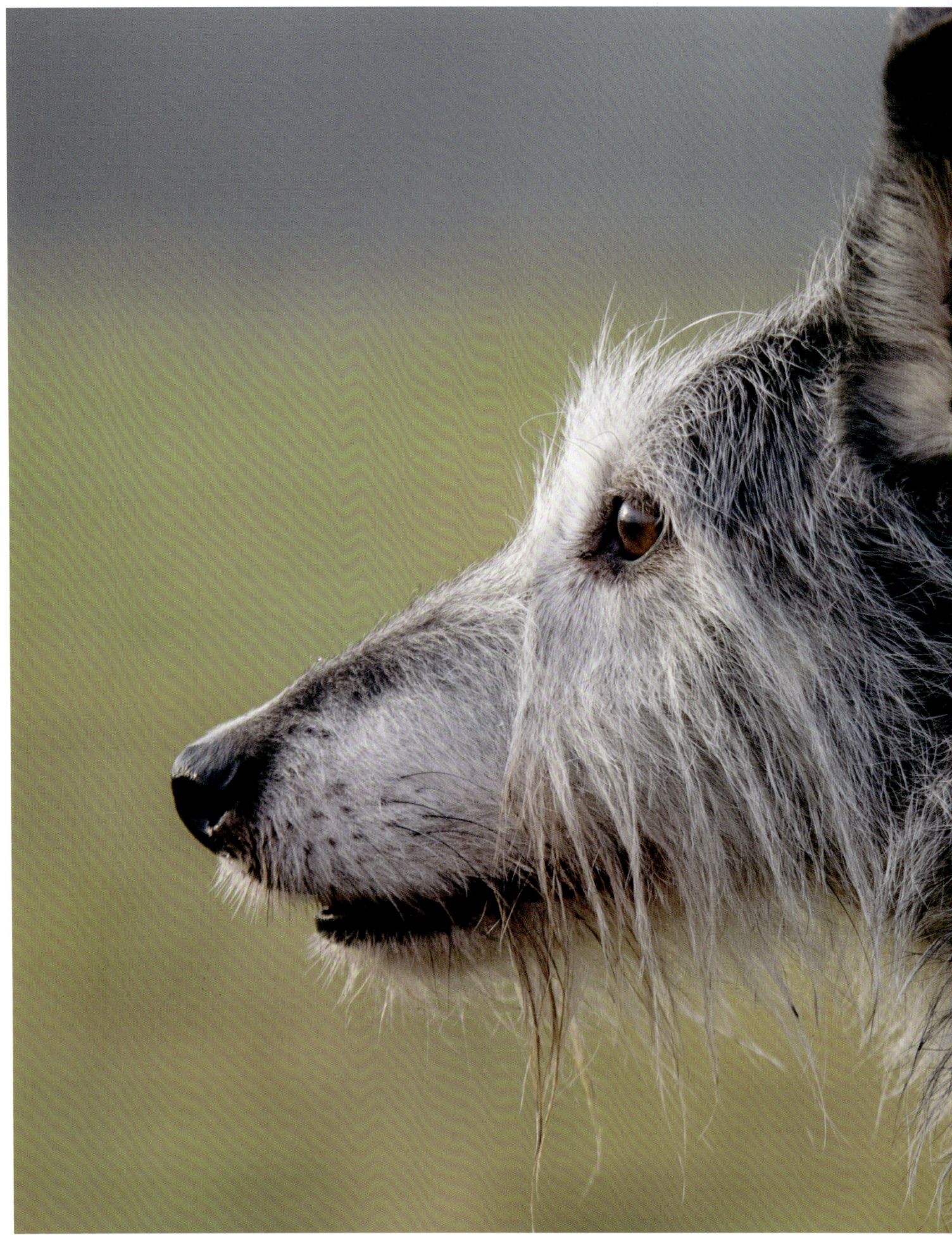

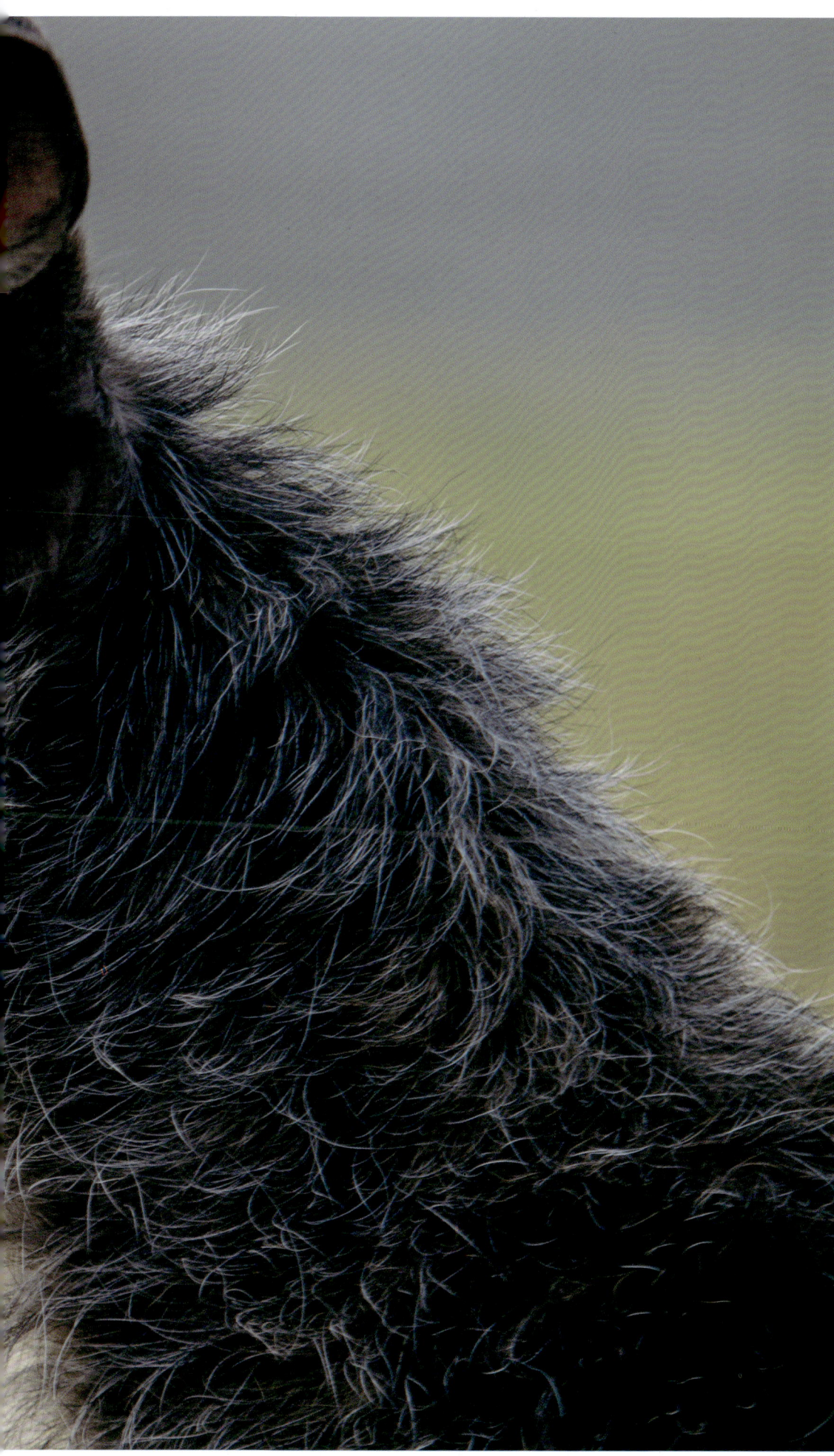

COMPANION DOGS

Eagle eyes
Lurchers have a keen sense of sight, and therefore are observant by nature.

COMPANION DOGS

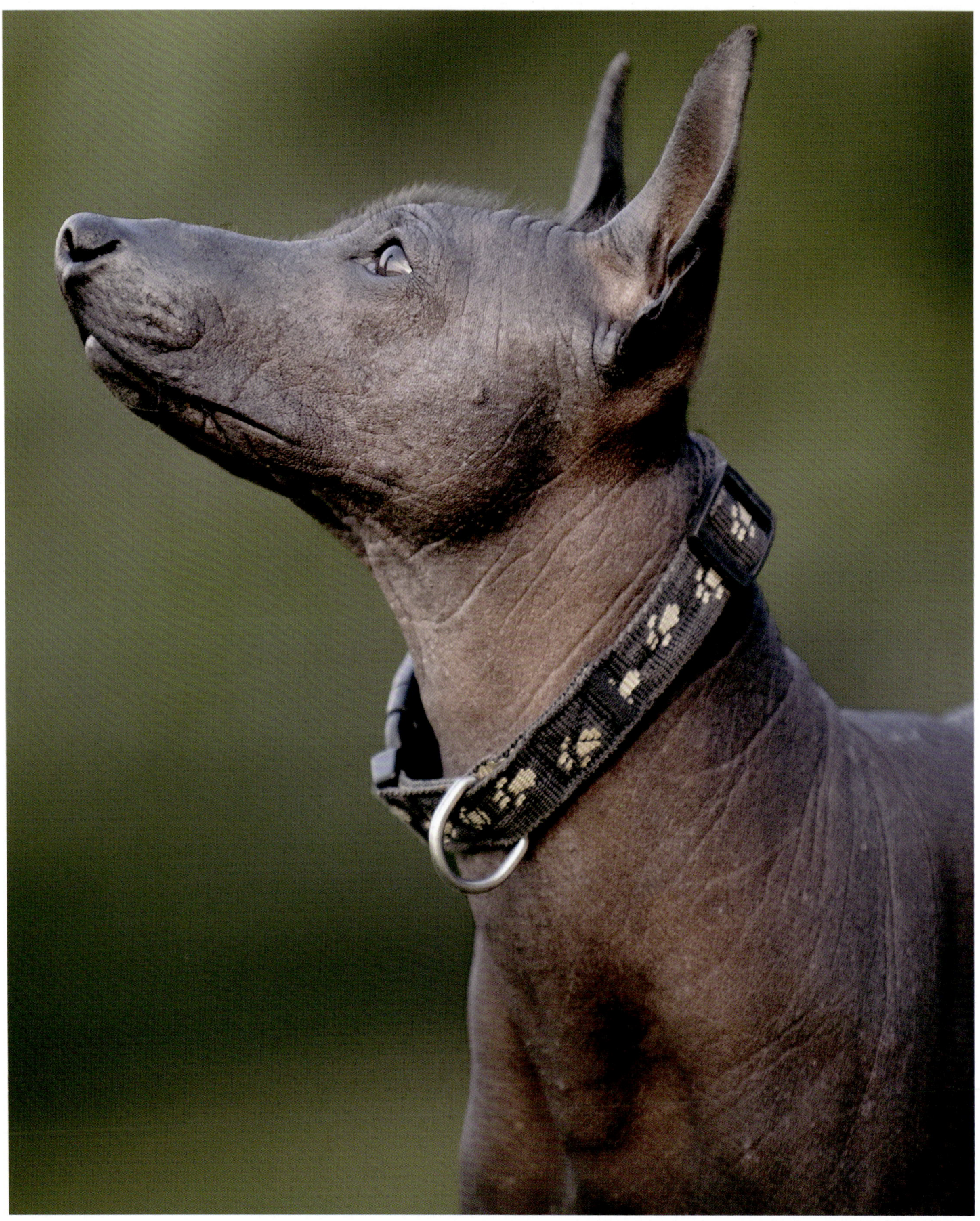

ABOVE:
Strange looks
The xolo is an active and intelligent breed that makes a good watchdog and loyal companion.

Mexican hairless

CHARACTERISTICS

Coat
Smooth variety has bare skin that may have some tufts of hair on the head, feet and tail. The coated variety has a short, smooth coat that covers the entire body and is red, black or bronze

Height
25–60cm (10–24in)

Weight
2–18kg (5–40lb)

Lifespan
Around 10 years

Personality
Calm and alert

Origin
Mexico

The Mexican hairless does what it says on the tin. This 3,000-year-old breed comes from Mexico and is largely devoid of hair, apart from a few tufts on the head, tail and feet. The breed also goes by the name xolo (pronounced show-low), which is short for the Nahuatl word xoloitzcuintli. Nuhautl was the language of several pre-Columbian civilizations, not least the Aztecs, who saw the Mexican hairless as the living embodiment of the dog of Xolotl, the dog of fire and monsters. In life the dogs protected people from evil spirits, and in death a pet Mexican hairless was buried with its owner to act as a guide through the underworld. The dogs were also sacrificed and eaten for ritual purposes. In a more quotidian role, the hairless dogs give out a lot of heat, and rural Aztec families would use them as bed-warmers. The coldest winter spells were referred to as "three-dog nights."

Today, the Mexican hairless comes in three sizes: standard, miniature and toy, and there are two coat varieties, a coated form as well as the eponymous hairless type. The hairless dogs are mostly toothless but the coated ones have a full set of gnashers.

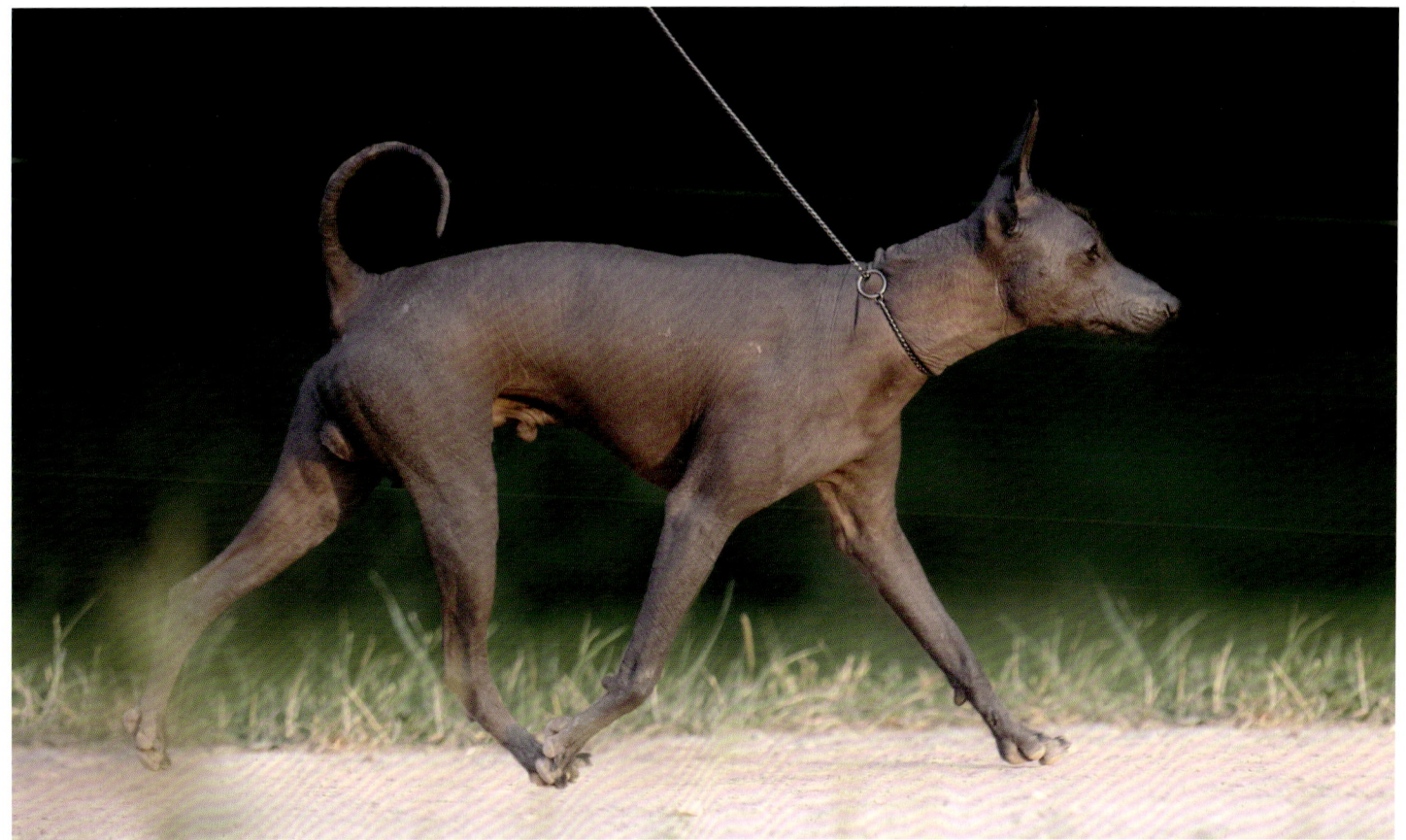

ABOVE:
Skin care
The skin of the hairless variety is tough and leathery but tight to the touch. It may need sunscreen and moisturiser to protect it from sun and wind.

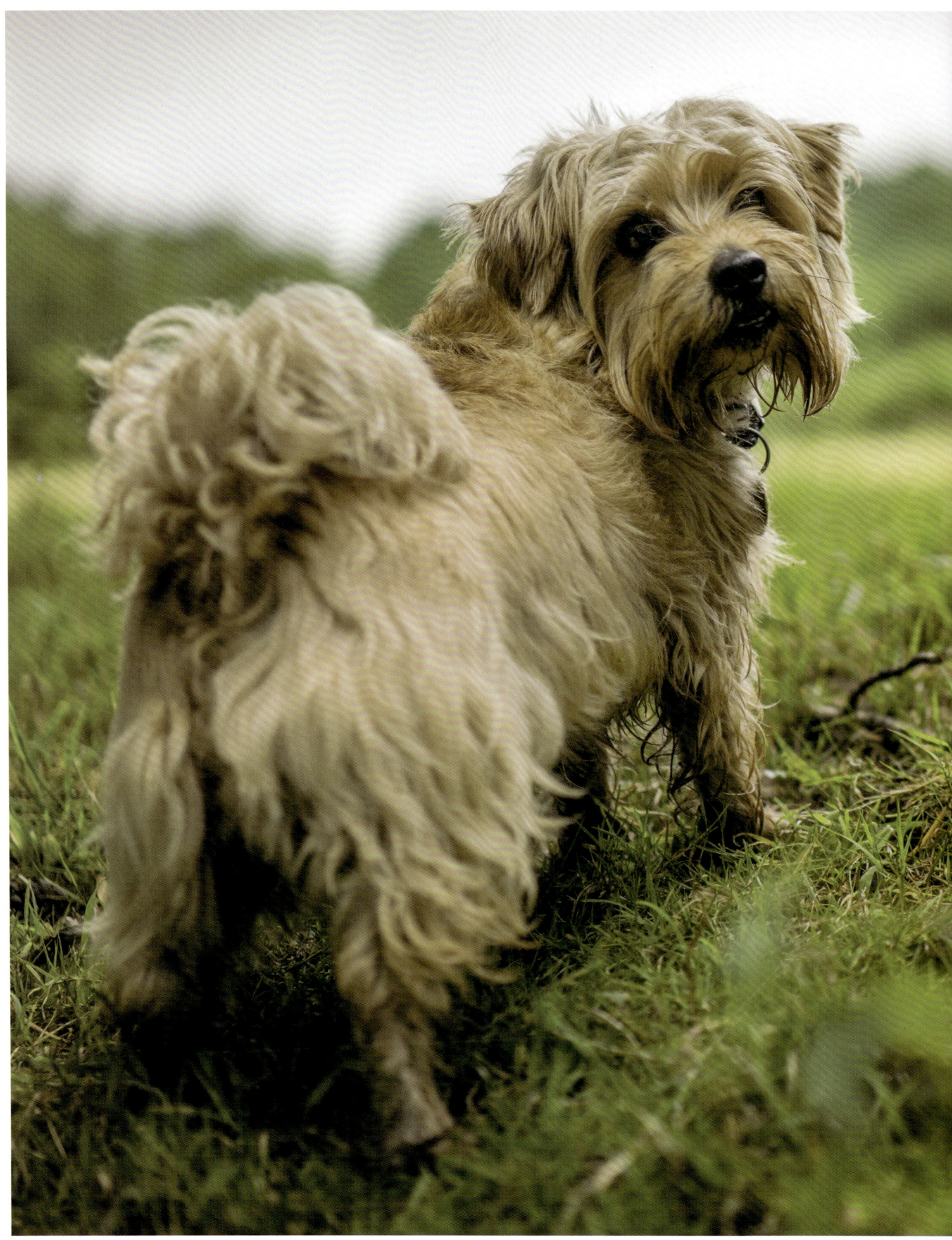

Norfolk Terrier

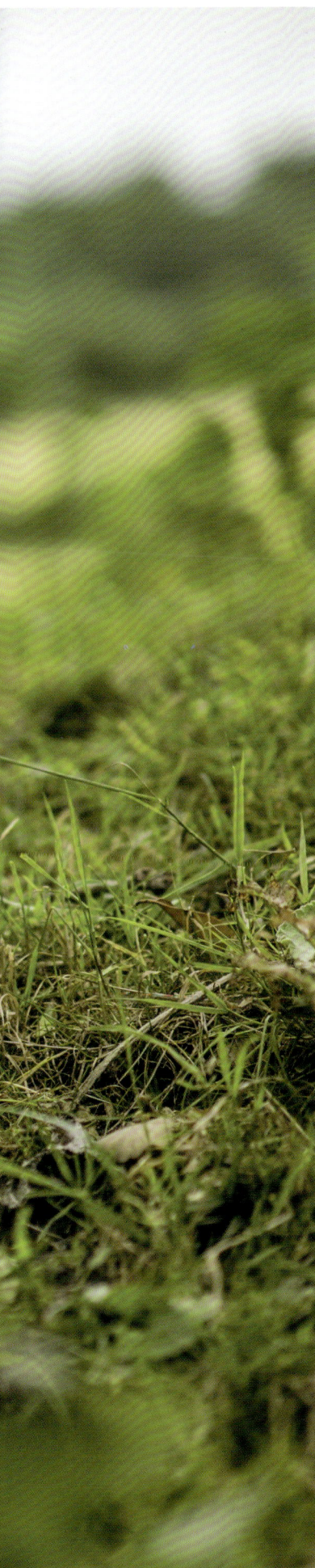

This feisty little breed is one of the newer kinds of terriers. It was developed in the early 20th century by Frank Jones, "Roughrider" to his friends, an East Anglian dog breeder and horseman. Jones's creation was a small, red-coated terrier that was ideal for catching rats around the stables and barns. The terriers worked in little packs, and that social aspect of the breed has helped it become a good choice as a family pet, especially for households that include other animals. However, the breed still has a strong prey drive and a tendency to dig and bark.

The Norfolk terrier was bred from a range of Scottish terriers, such as the border, cairn and Glen of Imaal breeds, which were crossed with the red terriers of eastern England. Until the 1960s, all terriers created by Jones were dubbed Norwich terriers, but then the two varieties were recognized as separate breeds. Today a Norwich terrier has ears pricked upright, while the Norfolk terrier has floppy dropped ears.

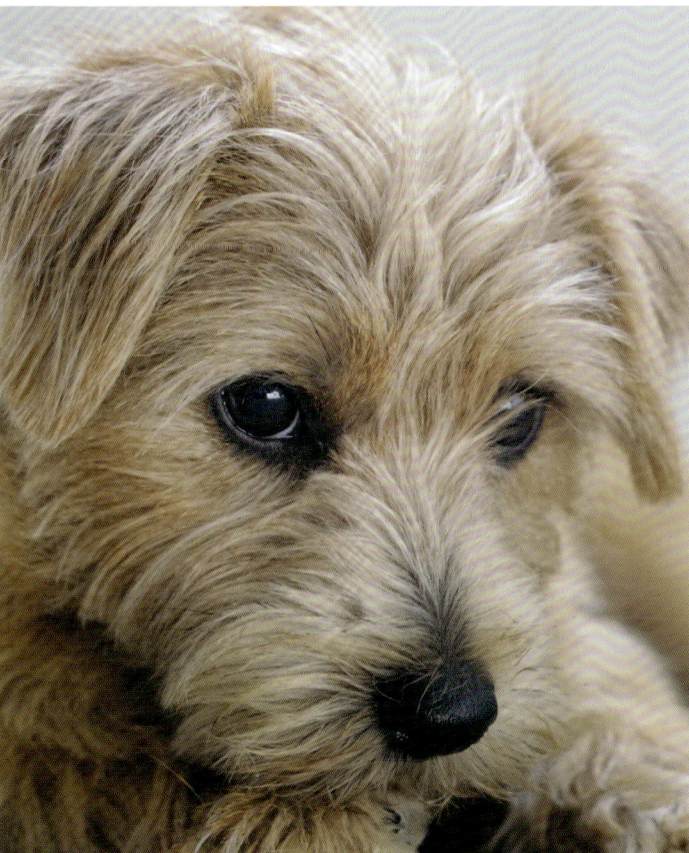

CHARACTERISTICS

Coat
A hard, wiry and straight coat that can be red, wheaten, black and tan, or grizzled

Height
22–25cm (9–10in)

Weight
5–6kg (11–13lb)

Lifespan
14–15 years

Personality
Fun-loving and tenacious

Origin
England

LEFT:
Keep on moving
The Norfolk terrier needs moderate exercise and regular grooming.

ABOVE:
Taking sides
Norfolks often bond very closely to their owners and are jealous of their other relationships.

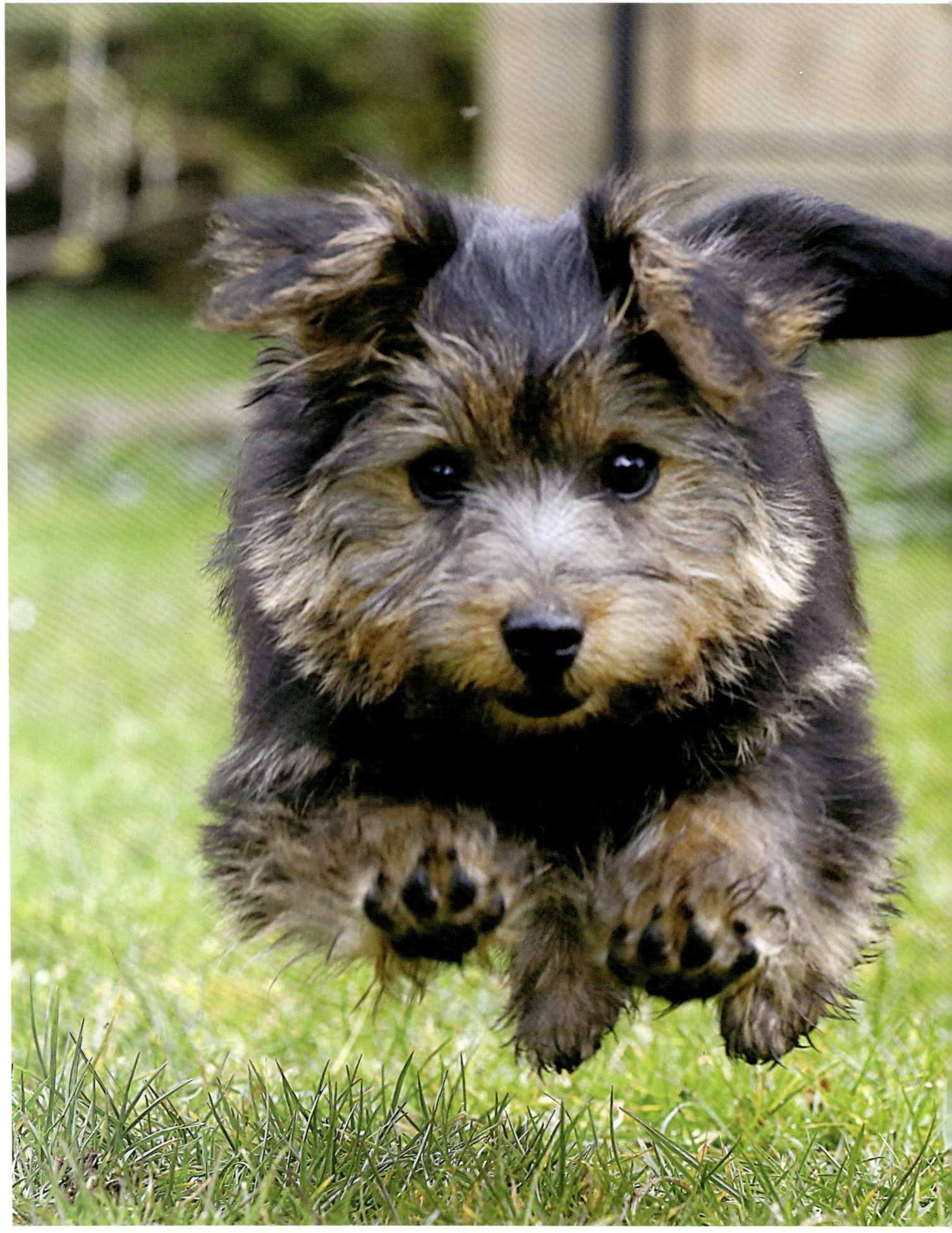

COMPANION DOGS

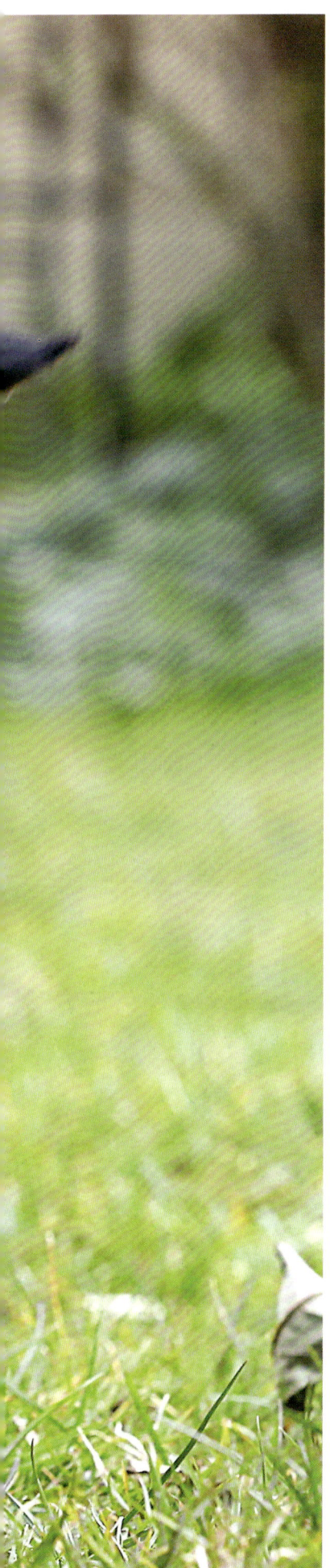
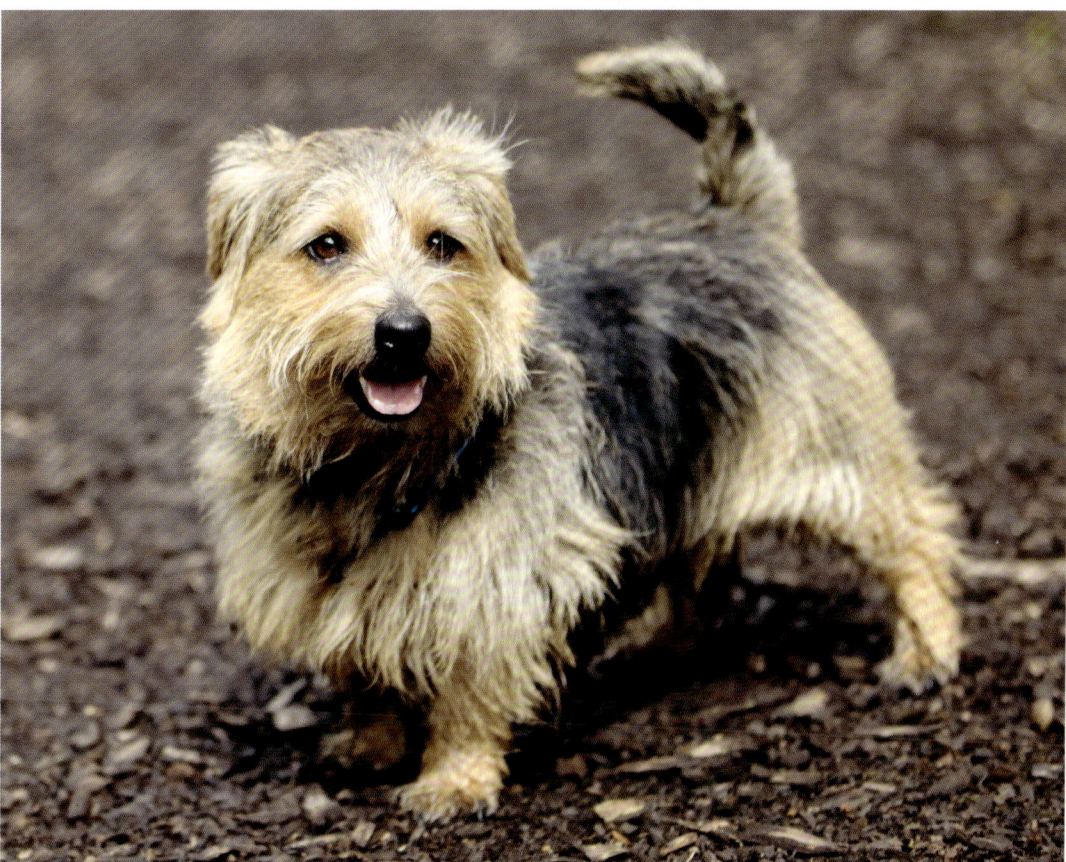
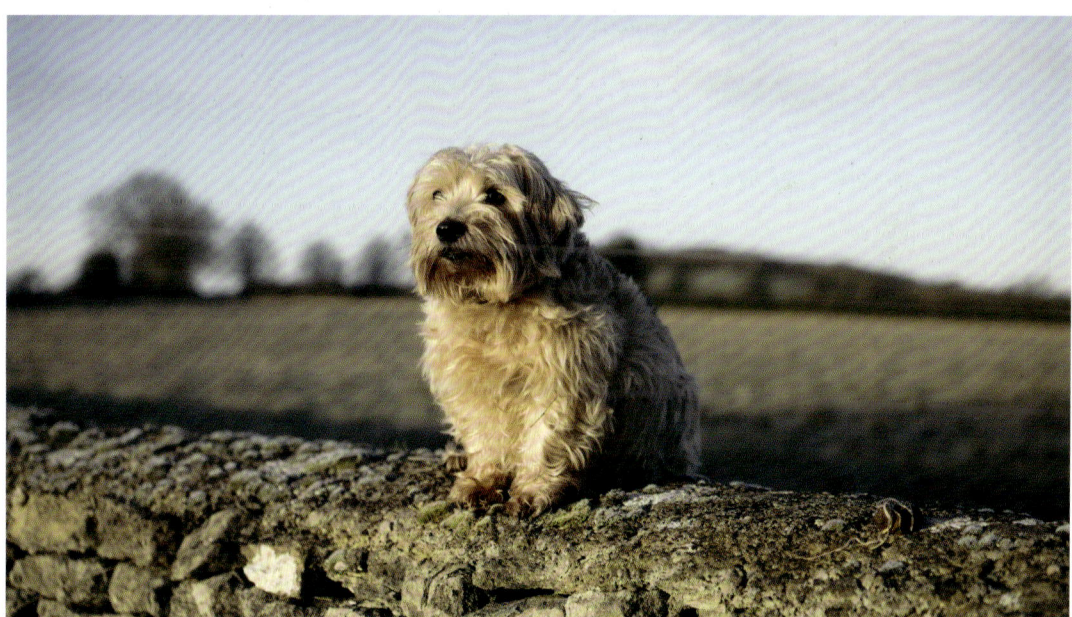

ALL PHOTOGRAPHS:
Jumping for joy
The Norfolk terrier has a reputation as a good traveller, being portable, adaptable and more or less up for anything.

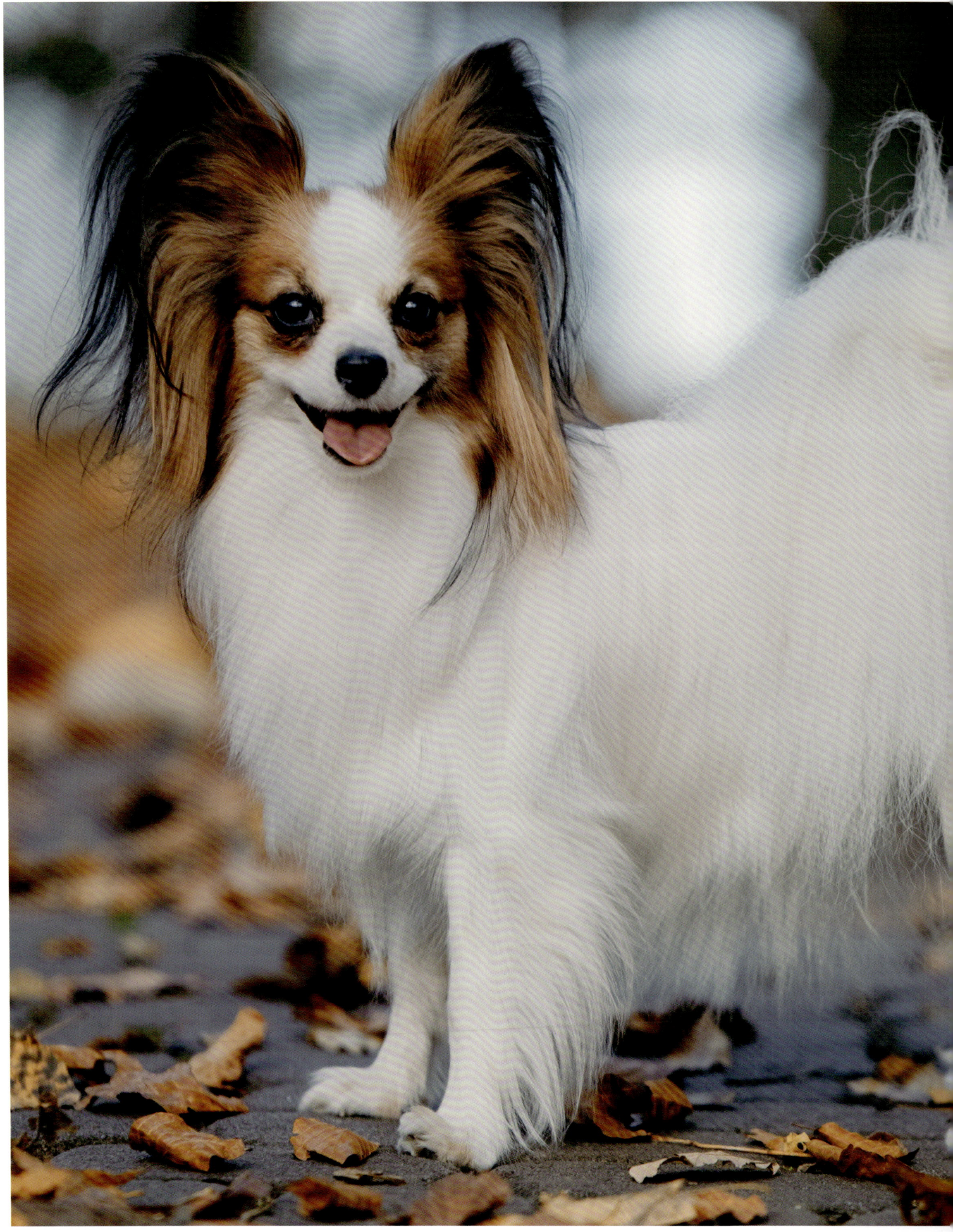

Papillon

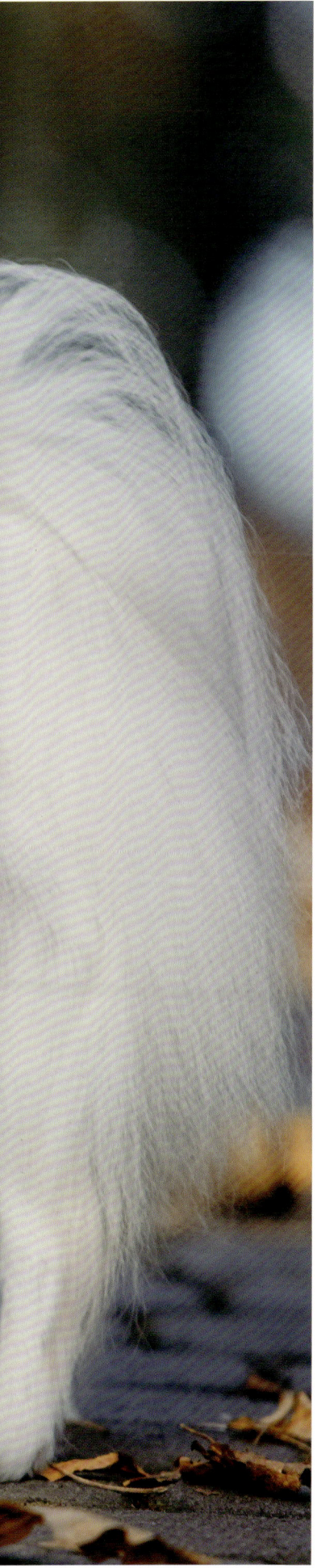

The French word for butterfly is "papillon", and his cute little dog earned that name from the long, elaborate fringes on the ears that give the dog's head the look of a swallowtail butterfly. Papillons are small, toy dogs that have their origins in France's ancien régime. Already a superstar breed after featuring in the work of Renaissance masters, such as Titian, the dogs caught the attention of the French royalty. The dogs were a favourite of Madame Pompadou, Louis XV's official mistress. And as the French Revolution loomed at the end of the 18th century, the reviled Marie Antoinette was known to lavishly pamper her papillons.

Papillons are good companions for people who live in small houses or flats. They do not need much space or exercise. These elegant and lively dogs get the stimulation they need by wandering around their home. They are an intelligent breed that is friendly and easy to train. The breed has few health problems, and lives several years longer than dogs ten times the size.

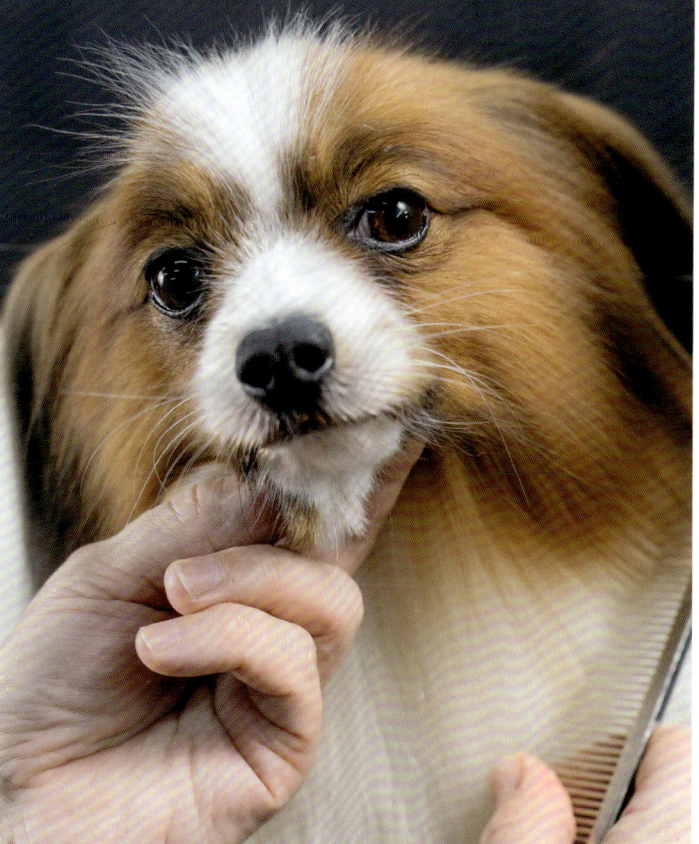

CHARACTERISTICS

Coat
A long, silky coat with several colour combinations. The base colour is white

Height
20–28cm (8–11in)

Weight
2–5kg (5–11lb)

Lifespan
Around 14 years

Personality
Happy and affectionate

Origin
France

LEFT:
Front and back
As well as the impressive ears, papillons have an eye-catching plumed tail.

ABOVE:
Moth eared
A papillon dog with dropped ears is known as a phalène type. The term "phalène" means "moth".

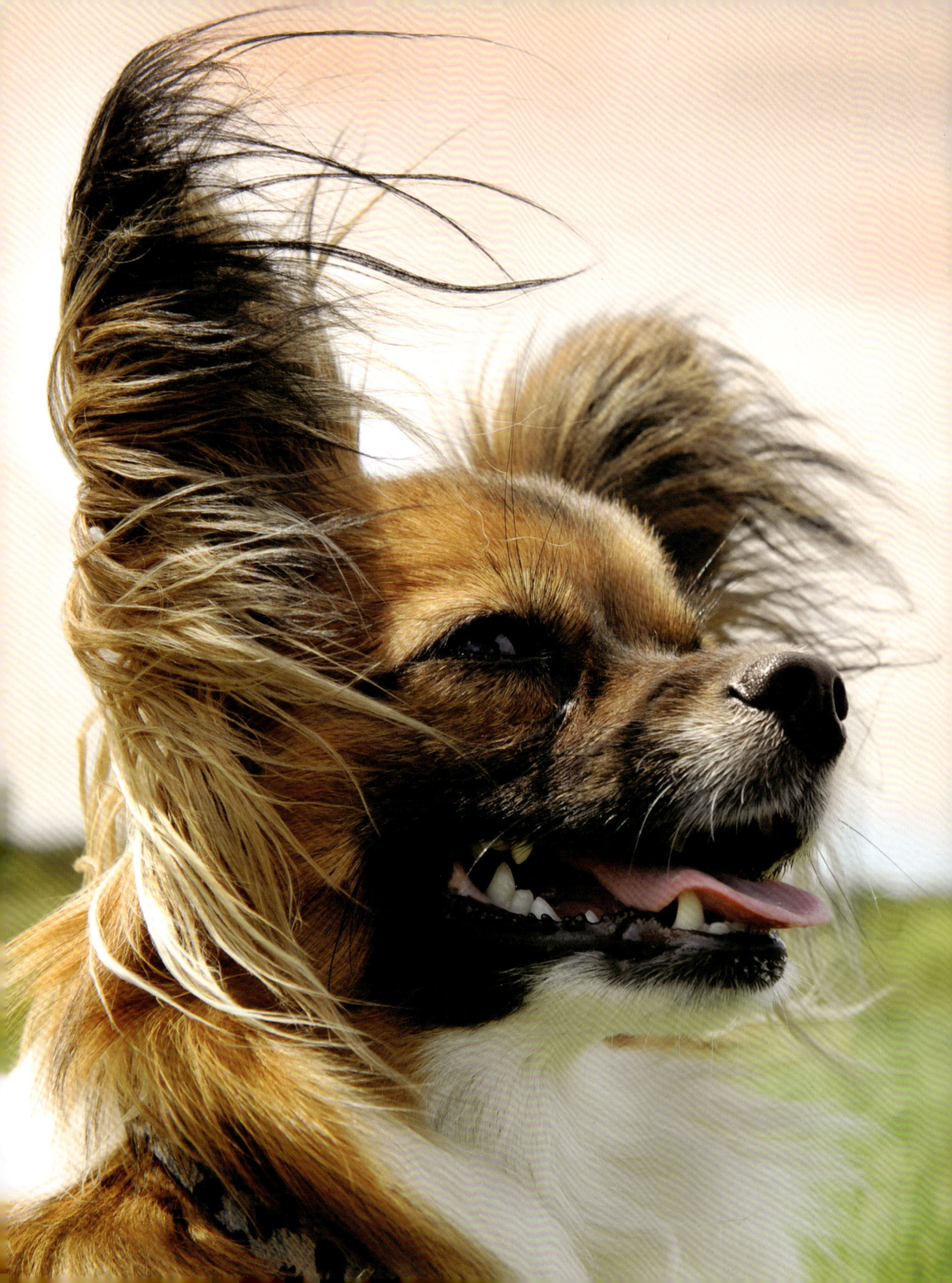

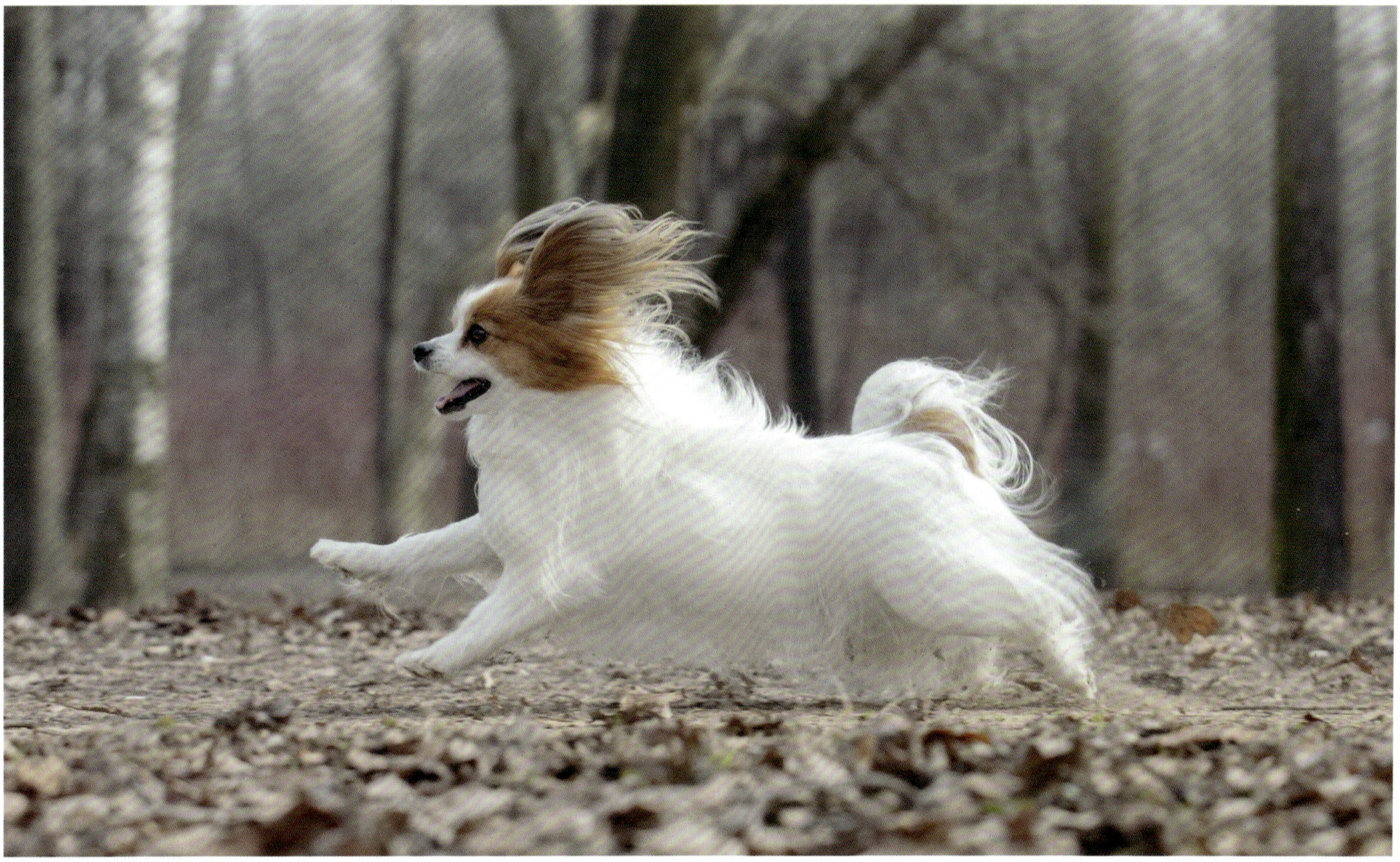

COMPANION DOGS

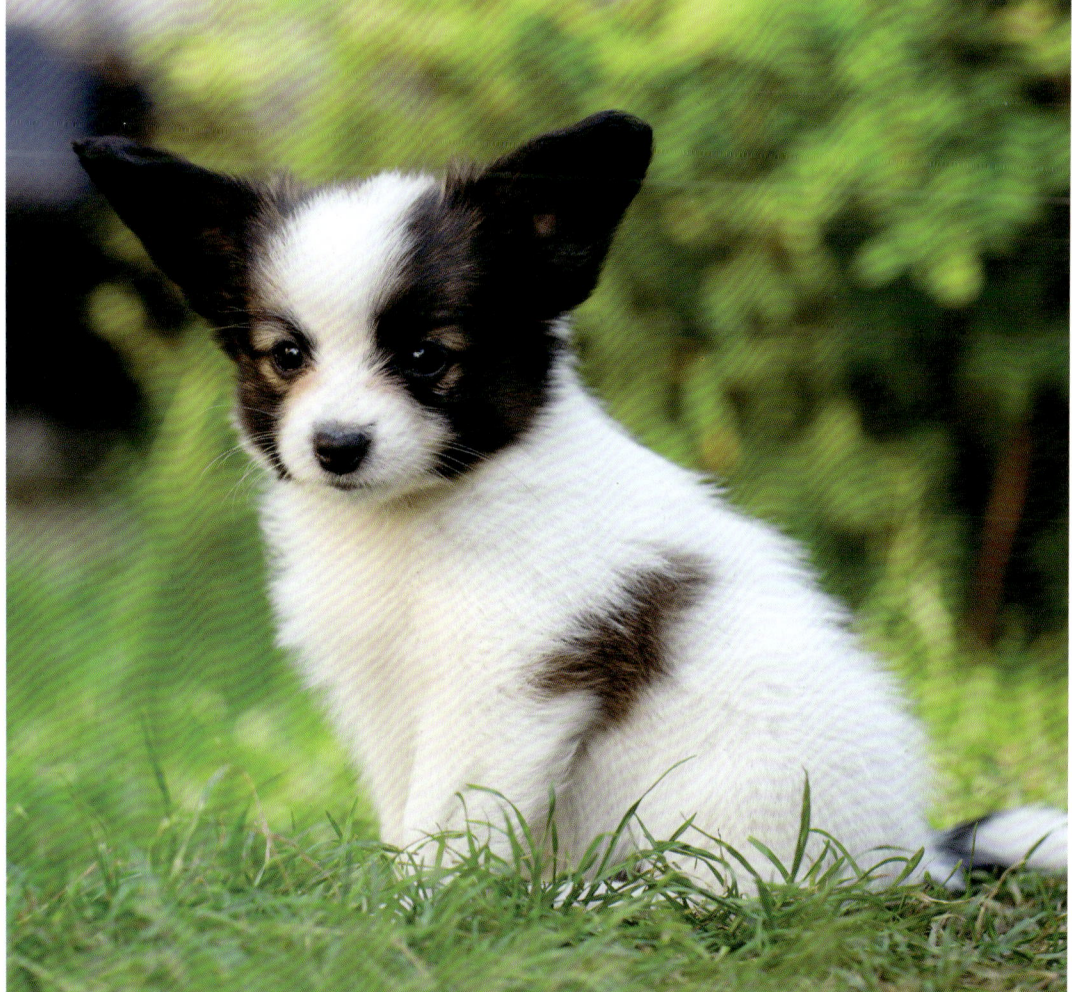

ALL PHOTOGRAPHS:
Energetic
The papillon is one of the brightest and most trainable of the toy breeds. Papillon dogs are a great choice for first time owners thanks to their sweet natures.

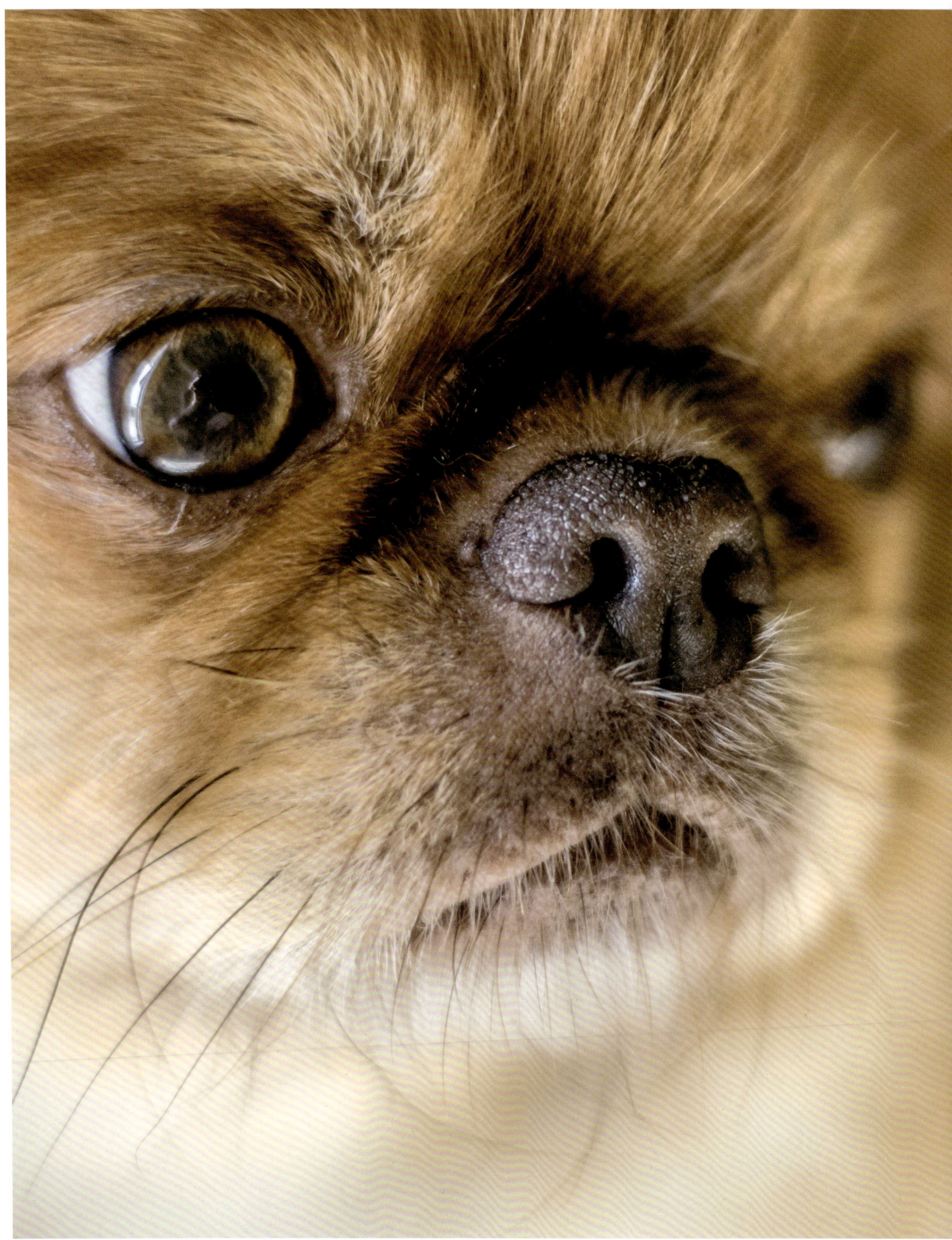

Pekingese

Legend has it that this distinctive little dog was created by none other than Buddha himself, who was able to shrink a lion—a powerful symbol in Chinese Buddhism—into a cute little dog. Behind all myths there is some truth, and in this case it is likely that the Pekingese is a miniature version of larger working dogs. The name Pekingese comes from the older, colonial name for Beijing. This is the location of the Forbidden City, the home of the Emperor and his large family. By tradition, the Pekingese was a companion dog only fit for a king. When British troops broke into this inner sanctum during the Opium Wars, the royal family killed their precious Pekingese rather than let it fall into the hands of the enemy. Nevertheless foreign breeders did get their hands on Pekingese, and by the turn of the 20th century, the unique breed was making a stir across the world.

This small, fluffy dog has a flat face and large eyes. Its long silky coat sheds a lot and needs a lot of regular grooming to prevent tangles and keep the Pekingese looking its best. It can be stubborn and difficult to train and does not get along well with other dogs or children.

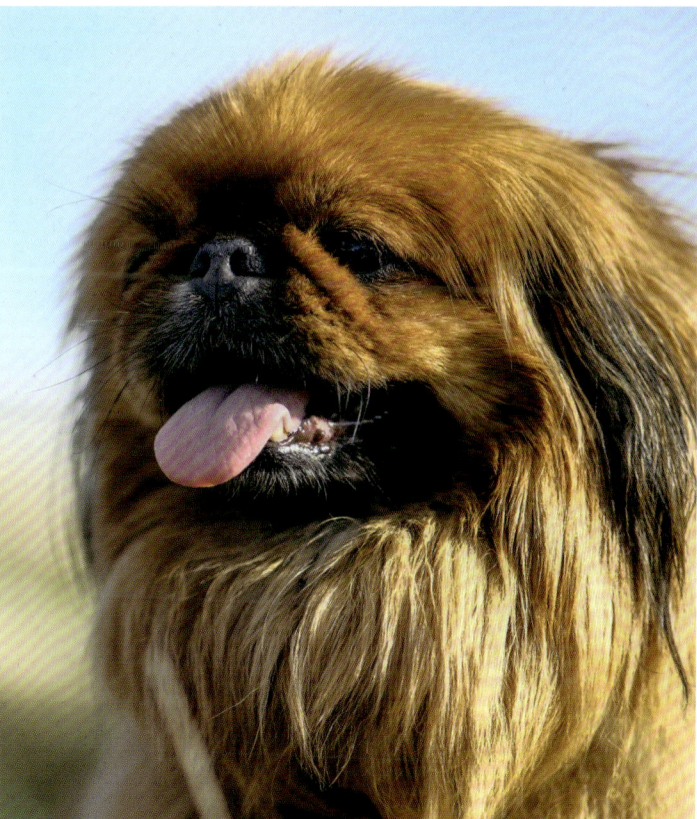

CHARACTERISTICS

Coat
A long and thick coat that comes in various colours and patterns
Height
15–23cm (6–9in)
Weight
Around 5kg (11lb)
Lifespan
Around 12 years
Personality
Noble and affectionate
Origin
China

LEFT:
Royal dog
For centuries, only Chinese royalty was allowed to own a Pekingese.

ABOVE:
Head and shoulders
The coat is longest at the neck and shoulders. This gives the Pekingese their famous "lion's mane".

COMPANION DOGS

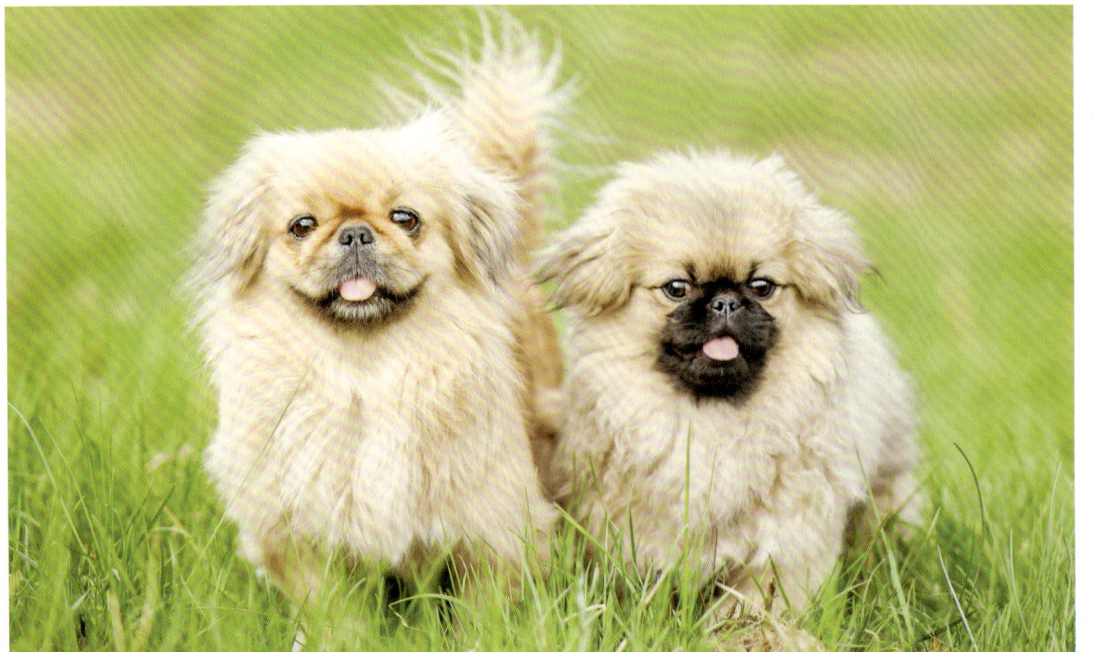

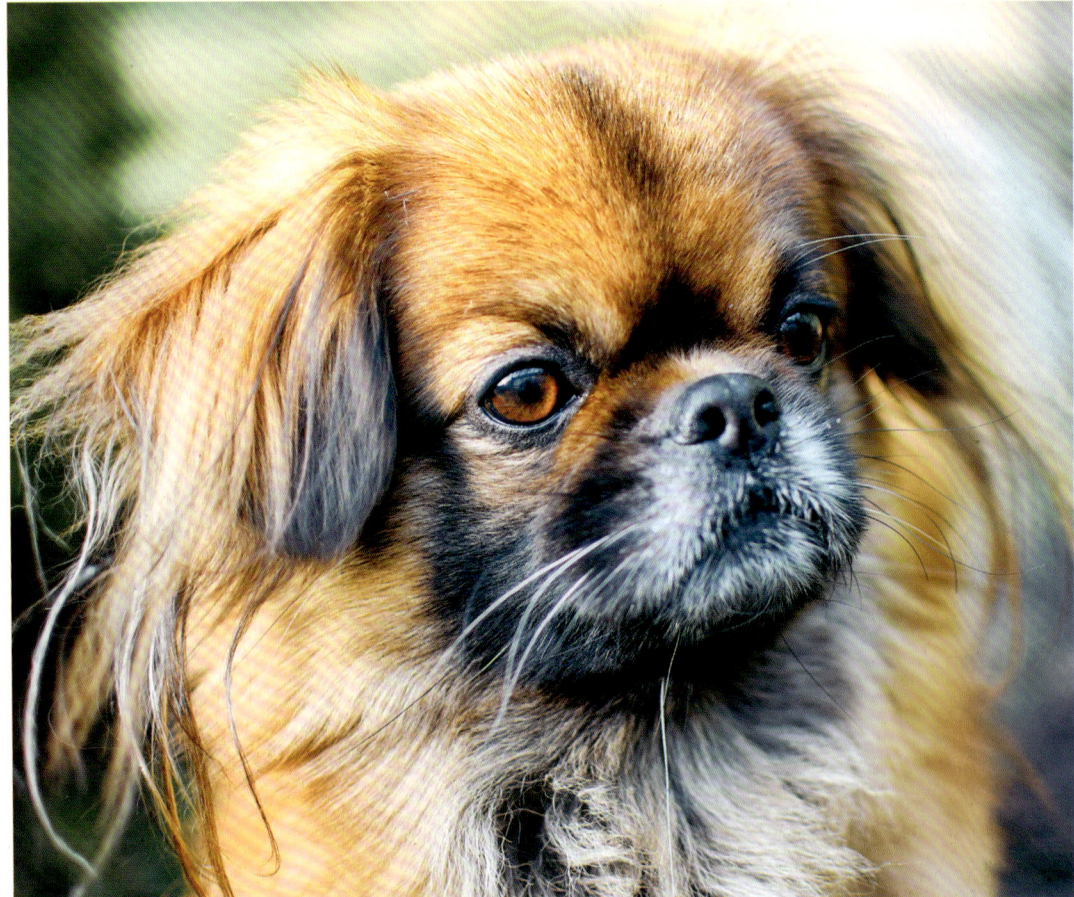

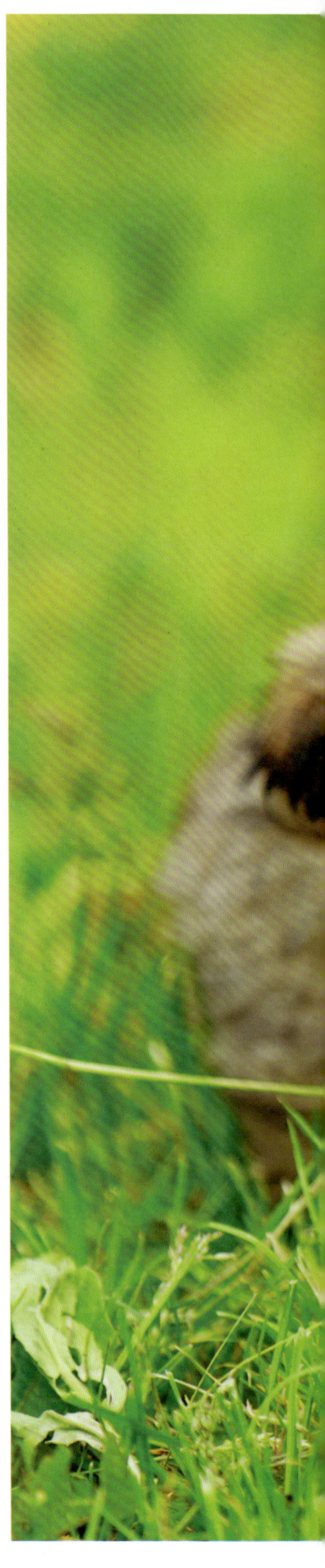

ABOVE TOP & BOTTOM:
Historic breed
DNA analysis suggests that this is one of the oldest distinctive dog breeds of all: it was recorded 1,400 years ago in the Chinese imperial court.

RIGHT:
Growing fast
Pekingese puppies develop quickly after birth. Within a couple of weeks, they start to do dog-like things, such as wagging the tail, barking and generally having fun.

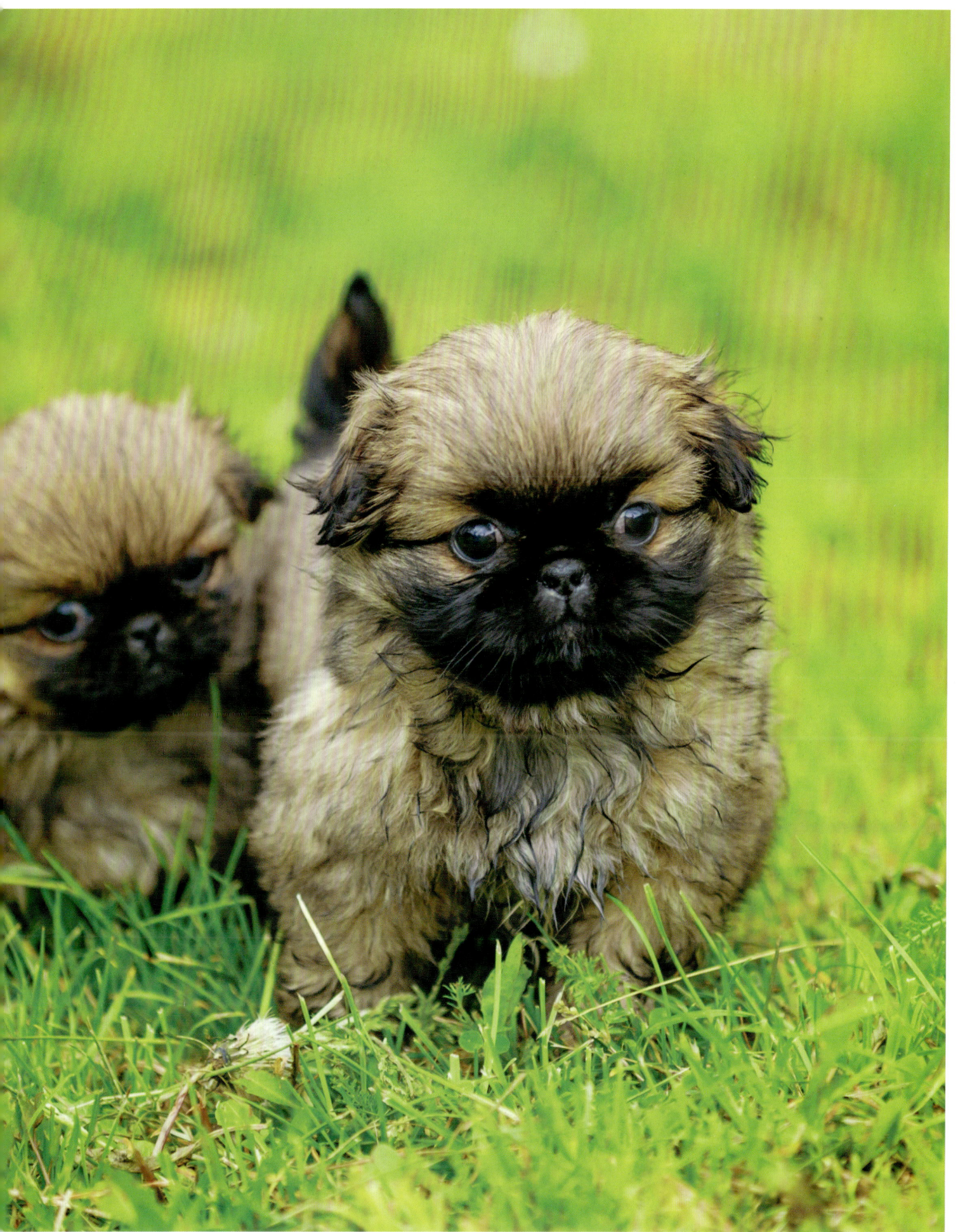

COMPANION DOGS

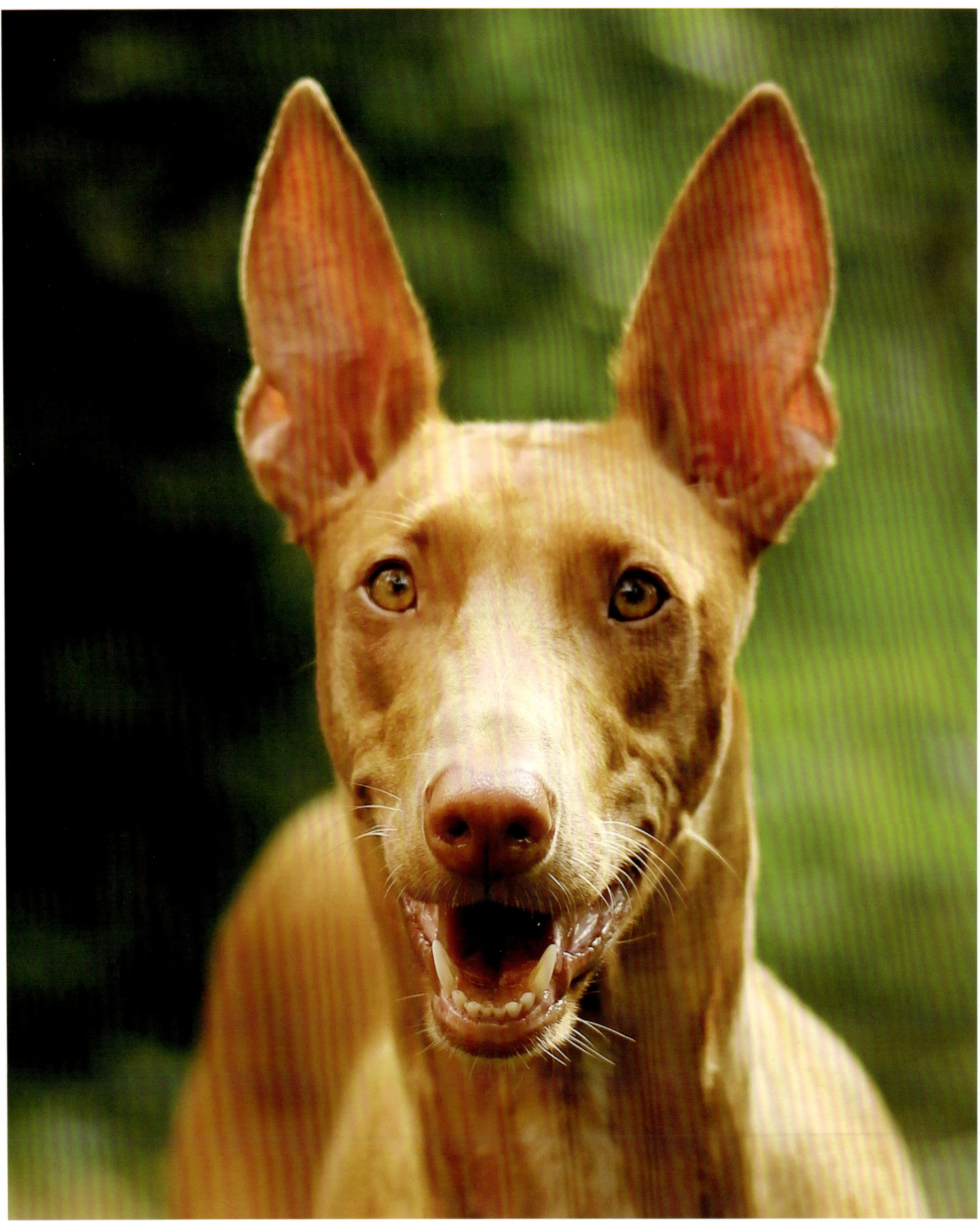

ABOVE:
Blushing dog
The breed is known for its ability to blush when excited or happy, turning its ears and nose pink.

Pharaoh Hound

CHARACTERISTICS

Coat
Short and glossy and can be chestnut or tan in colour
Height
53–63cm (21–25in)
Weight
20–25kg (44–55lb)
Lifespan
10 years
Personality
Smart and independent
Origin
Malta

Like other breeds from the Mediterranean, this tall hound resembles the dogs painted on murals in ancient Egyptian tombs and temples. As the name suggests, it is assumed that the breed came from Egypt at some point in the distant past, but the pharaoh hounds of today were established in Malta, a rocky island country halfway between North Africa and Italy. The dogs were brought here by Phoenician traders at least 2,500 years ago. On Malta the dogs are used to hunt rabbits, which it chases in short, graceful sprints. It runs with a graceful gait that allows it to pick its way through the rocky terrain.

The pharaoh hound is a loyal, intelligent and friendly dog that needs plenty of exercise and socialization. It needs to be on a leash when outdoors because its powerful prey drive means it is likely to dash off in any direction at any moment. This feature does not endear the pharaoh hound to other pets. However, the dog's ability to crack a smile does endear it to its owners, and this is a breed for an experienced owner with plenty of time to devote to their pet.

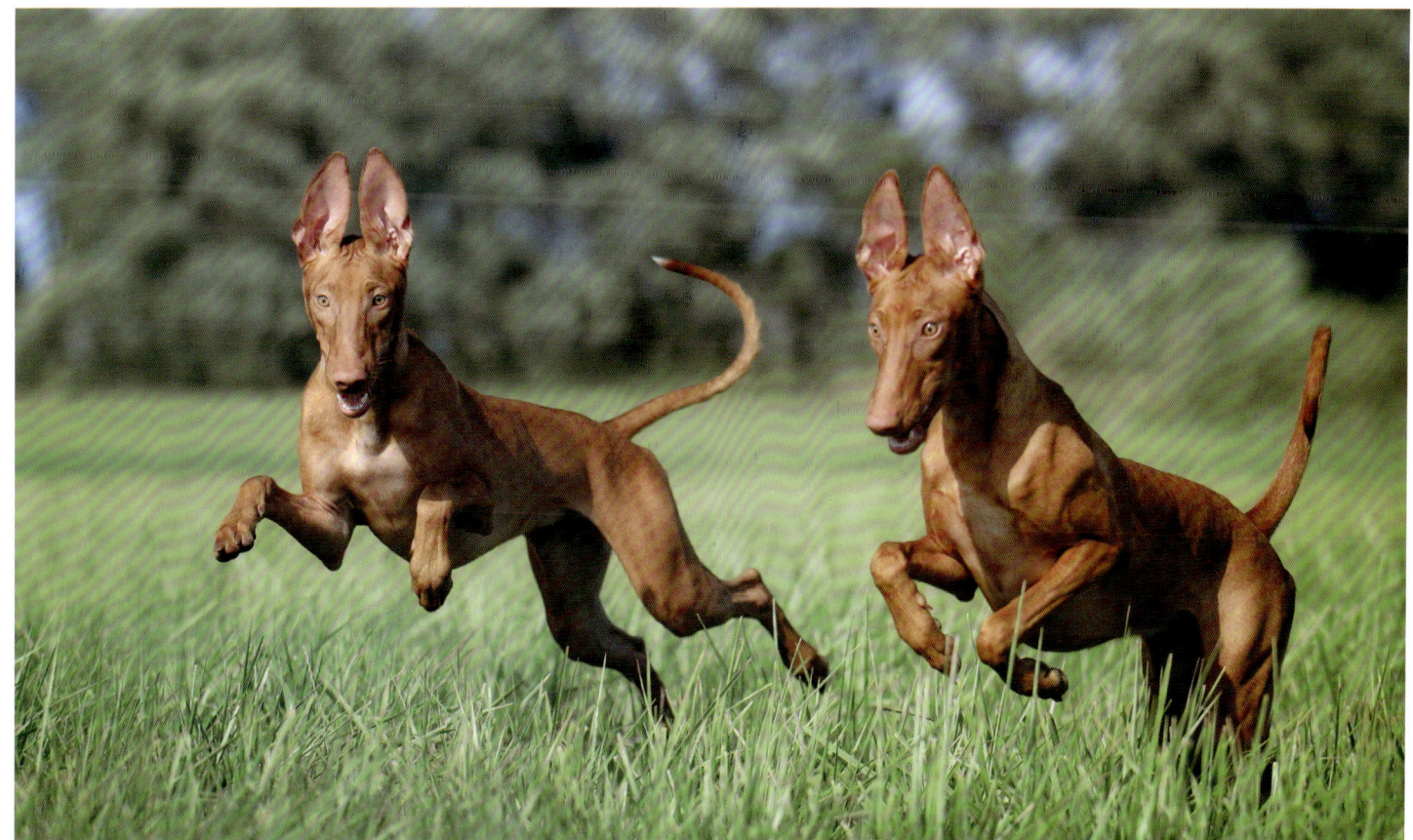

ABOVE:
Ancient heritage
The pharaoh hound has a slender and graceful body, a long and narrow head, large pointed ears and amber-coloured eyes.

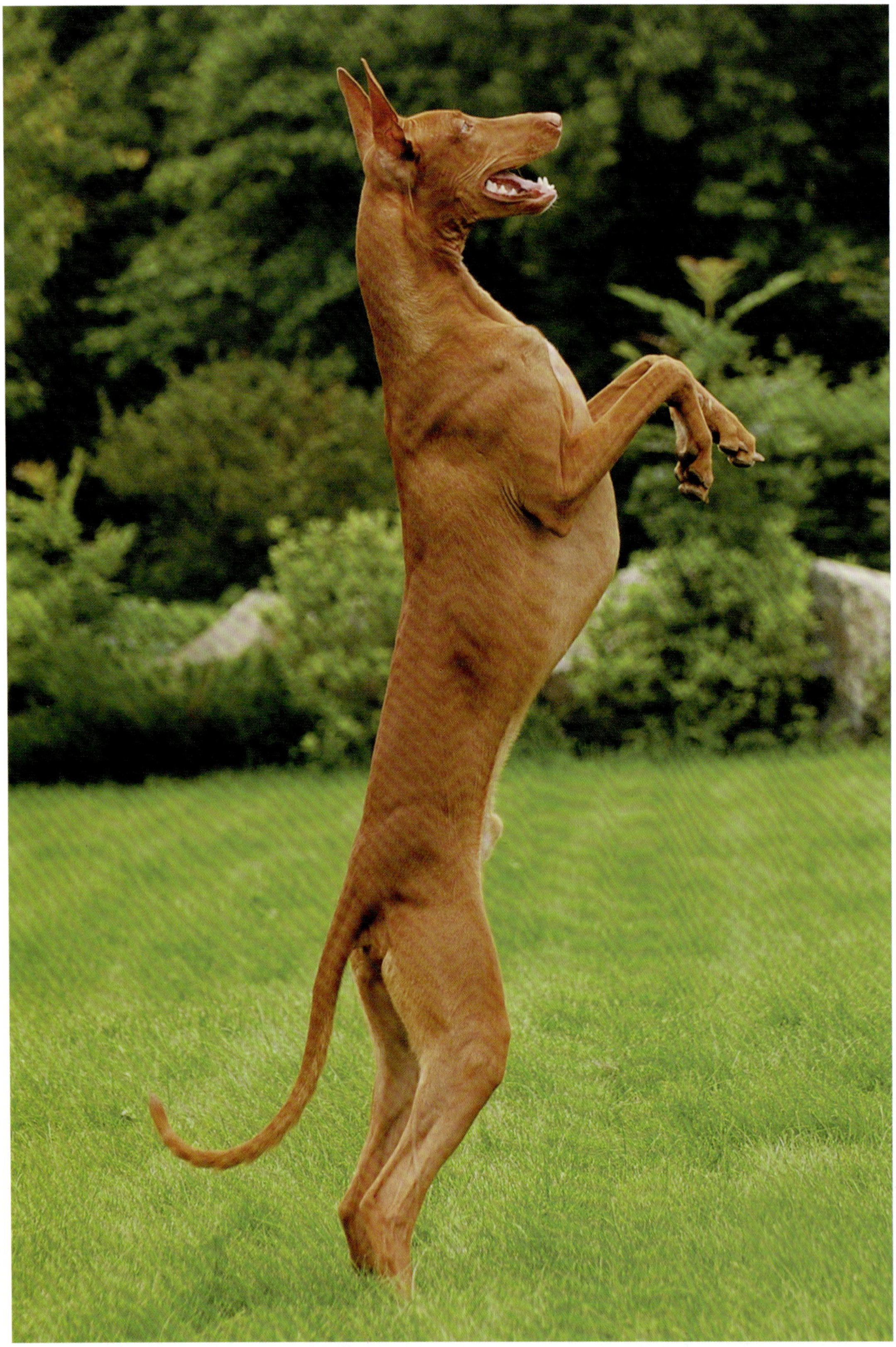

COMPANION DOGS

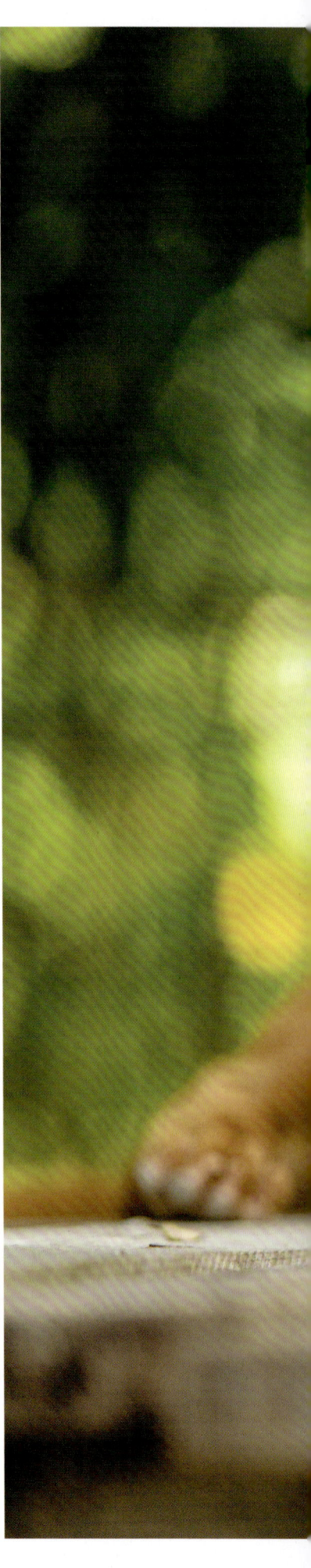

ABOVE:
Tricks and training
A pharaoh hound loves to show off. Dogs enjoy learning tricks. It keeps their minds occupied and earns them some praise.

RIGHT:
Born to run
The pharaoh hound needs appropriate outlets for their abundant energy. Provide daily running opportunities in a safely enclosed area, and include daily walks in your routine as well.

COMPANION DOGS

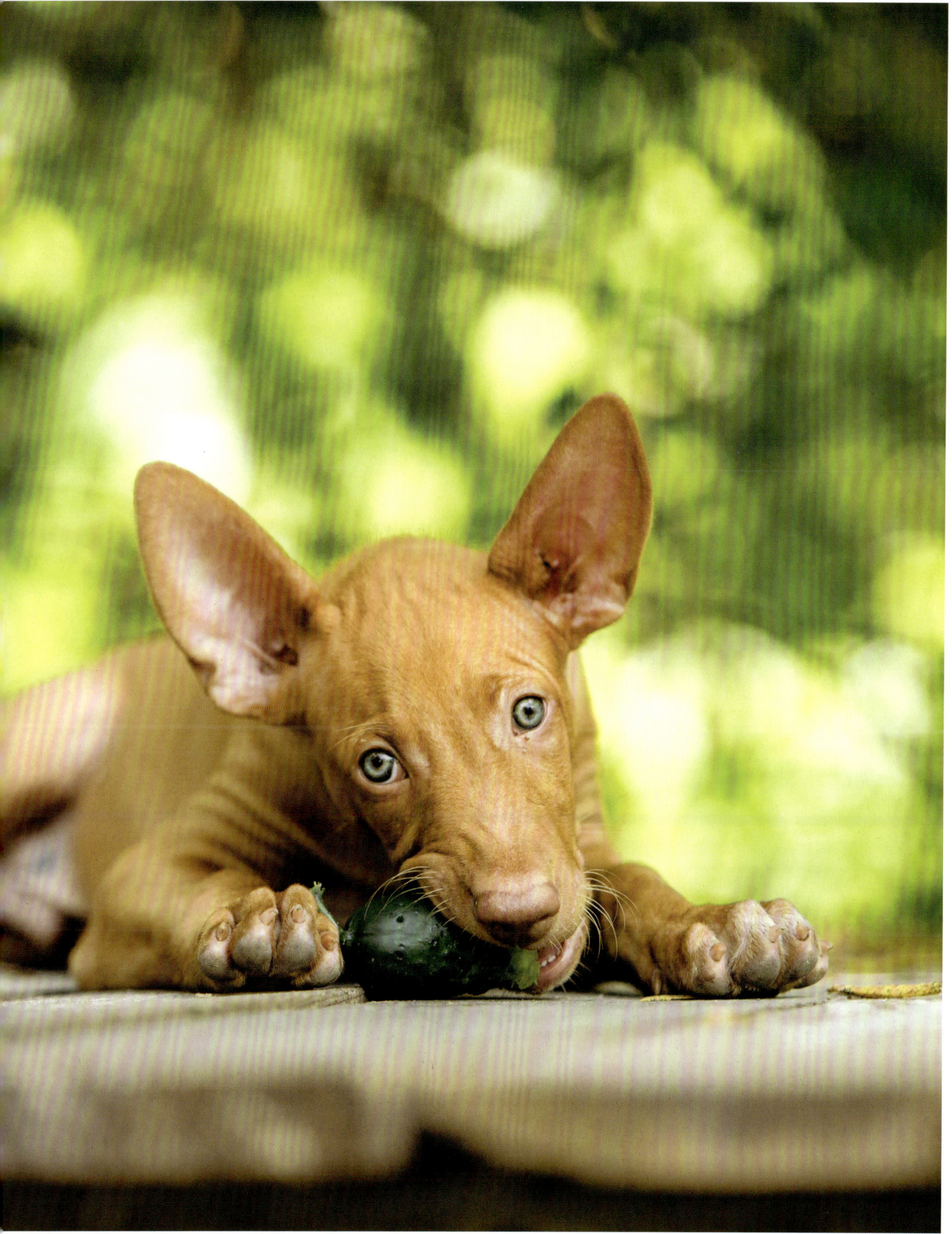

COMPANION DOGS

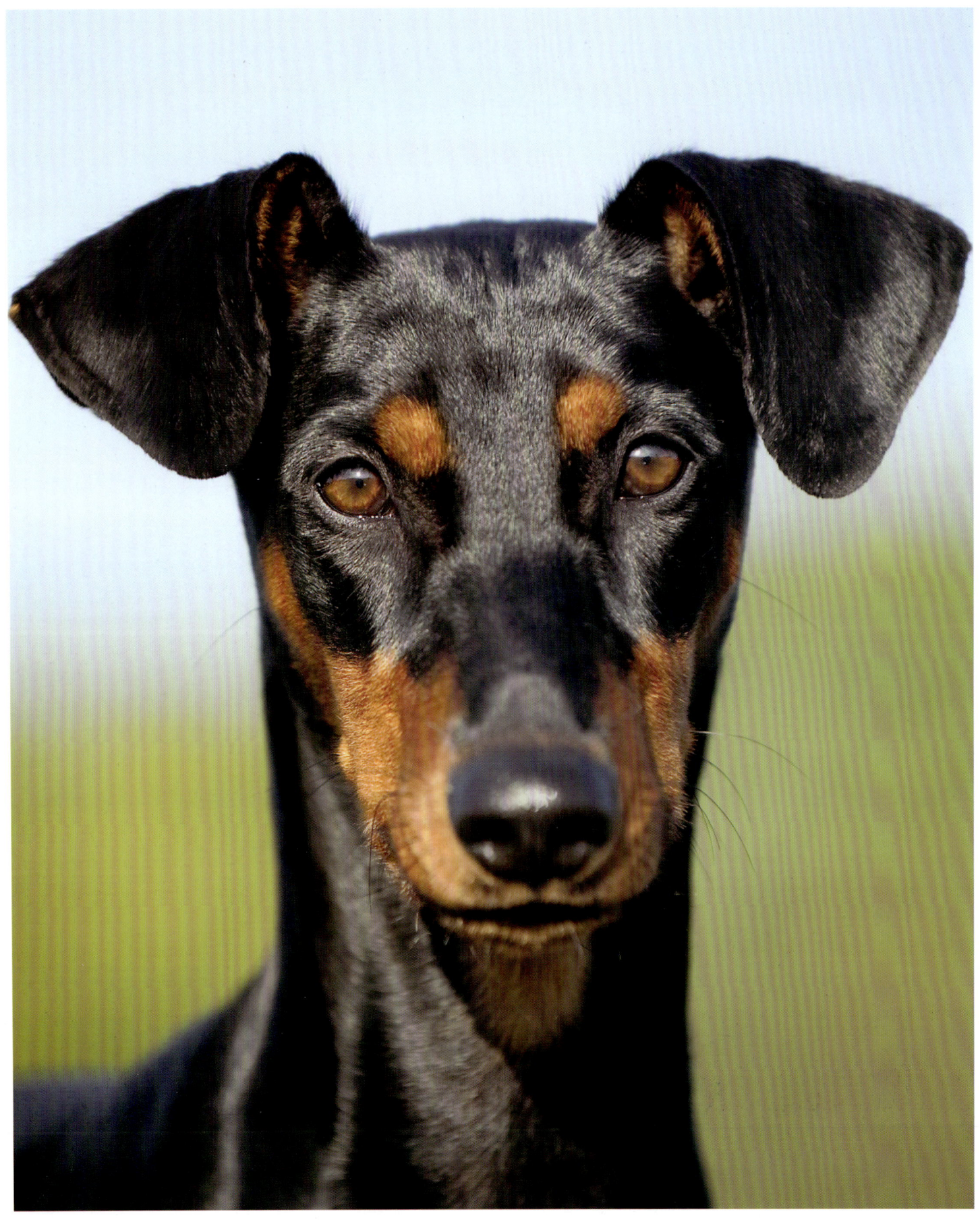

ABOVE:
Clear eyed
The pinscher has triangular, drop ears and a short, sleek but thick coat.

Pinscher

CHARACTERISTICS

Coat
Shimmering coat of red, black or often blue with red accents
Height
43–48cm (17–19in)
Weight
11–16kg (24–35lb)
Lifespan
12–14 years
Personality
Smart and adaptable
Origin
Germany

Among Germany's oldest breeds, the pinscher is an all-rounder dog: it is blessed with great intelligence, high energy, strength and stamina, all wrapped up in an elegant package. Nothing phases a pinscher and it can be put to work as a watchdog and protector—or rat killer extraordinaire. The name pinscher is derived from the same root as the English term pinch or pincer. All can give the wrong person a nasty nip. The pinscher makes a great guardian dog, but must be trained well to prevent it getting overly protective. Training is also needed to control barking episodes and to be sociable with other dogs.

The development of the pinscher goes all the way back to the 7th century with the development of farm dogs. Roll forward about 500 years and this farm dog is crossed with a hunting breed called the tanner. Next terrier blood is added to create the rattenfanger, a dog for killing vermin and standing guard, and this is the basis for the modern pinscher. Since then the pinscher has diversified into a very miniature variety as well as the Doberman, a more menacing form.

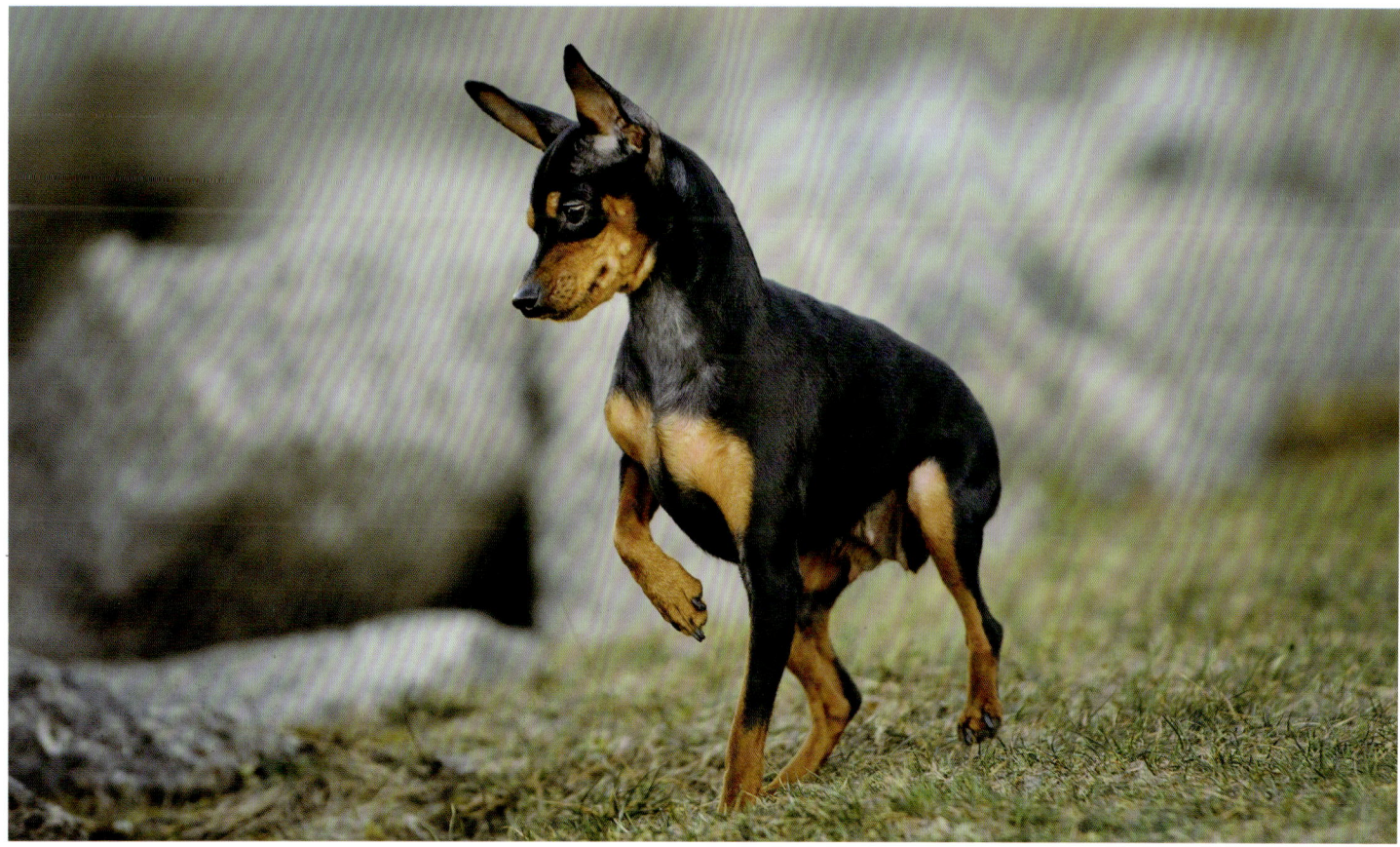

ABOVE:
Under instruction
The pinscher has a reputation for aggression, but with proper training it can be gentle and affectionate.

COMPANION DOGS

Pomeranian

CHARACTERISTICS

Coat
A thick, double coat that comes in many colours, such as white, black, brown, red, orange, cream, blue, sable, black and tan, brindle, and merle

Height
22–28cm (9–11in)

Weight
2–3kg (5–7lb)

Lifespan
12–15 years

Personality
Feisty and curious

Origin
Germany

The Pomeranian is named after the region of Pomerania, which is now split between northern Poland and Germany. It is the smallest of all the spitz-type dogs and is essentially a toy verson of the German spitz. In many countries it is known as the zwergspitz, or "dwarf spitz". The little dog looks like a mobile ball of fluff, and it carries itself like a dog that thinks it is much bigger. The coat forms a ruff around the neck and a plumed tail that curls over the back. The Pomeranian has a fox-like face with small, erect ears and dark, almond-shaped eyes. The breed certainly has its admirers. One Pomeranian fan was Queen Victoria, who kept several during her long years in mourning. It is reported her favourite Pomeranian, Turi, stood vigil over her death bed in 1901.

The Pomeranian is small enough to be exercised in doors. The little breed is a lively, intelligent and loyal dog that loves to be the centre of attention. It is friendly enough, especially if socialized well from an early age. However, it can be yappy and territorial, when other dogs and people enter its home. It may not be especially suitable for a family with very young children or other pets.

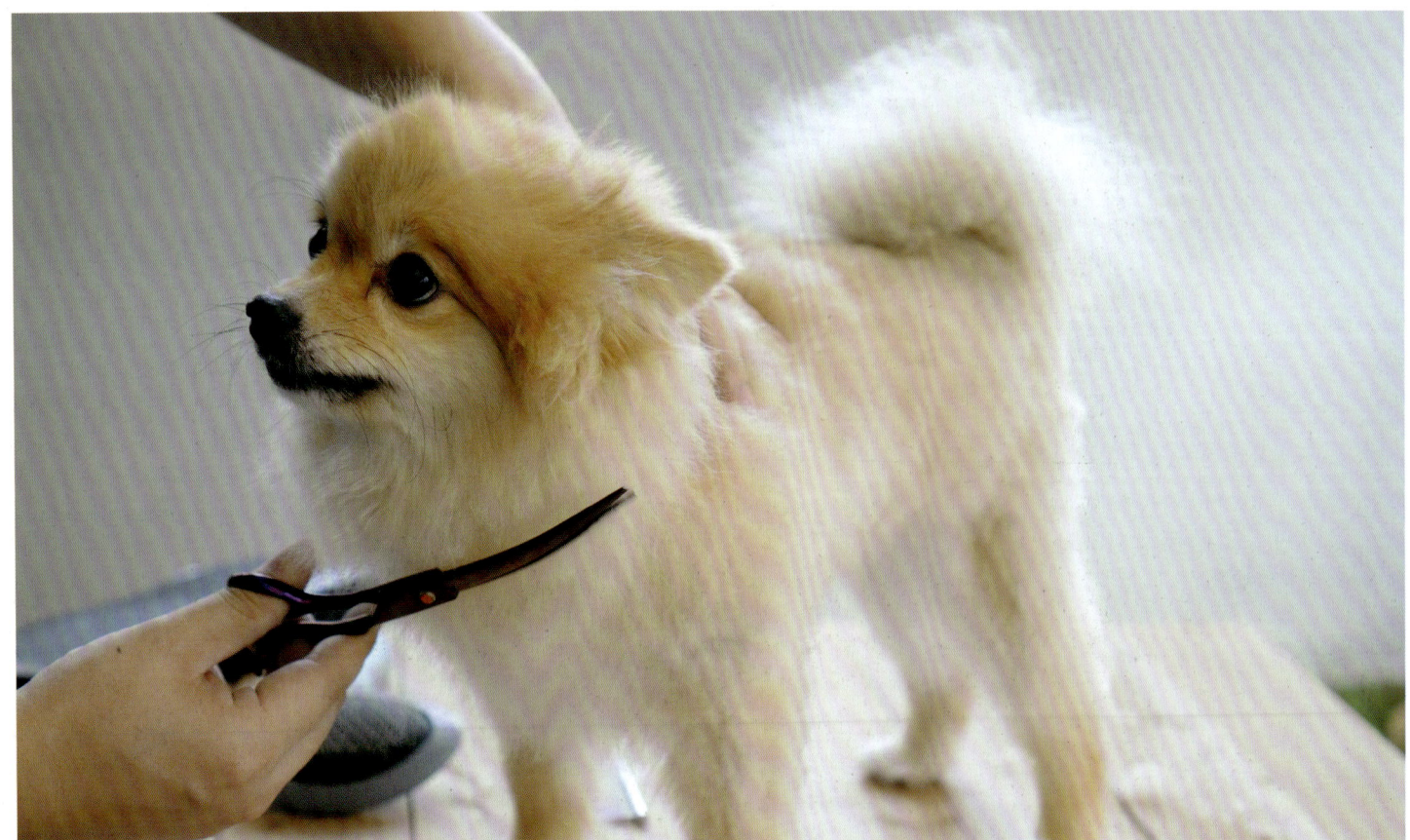

ABOVE:
Work in progress
The Pomeranian needs regular grooming to keep its coat in good condition, as well as daily exercise and mental stimulation to prevent boredom.

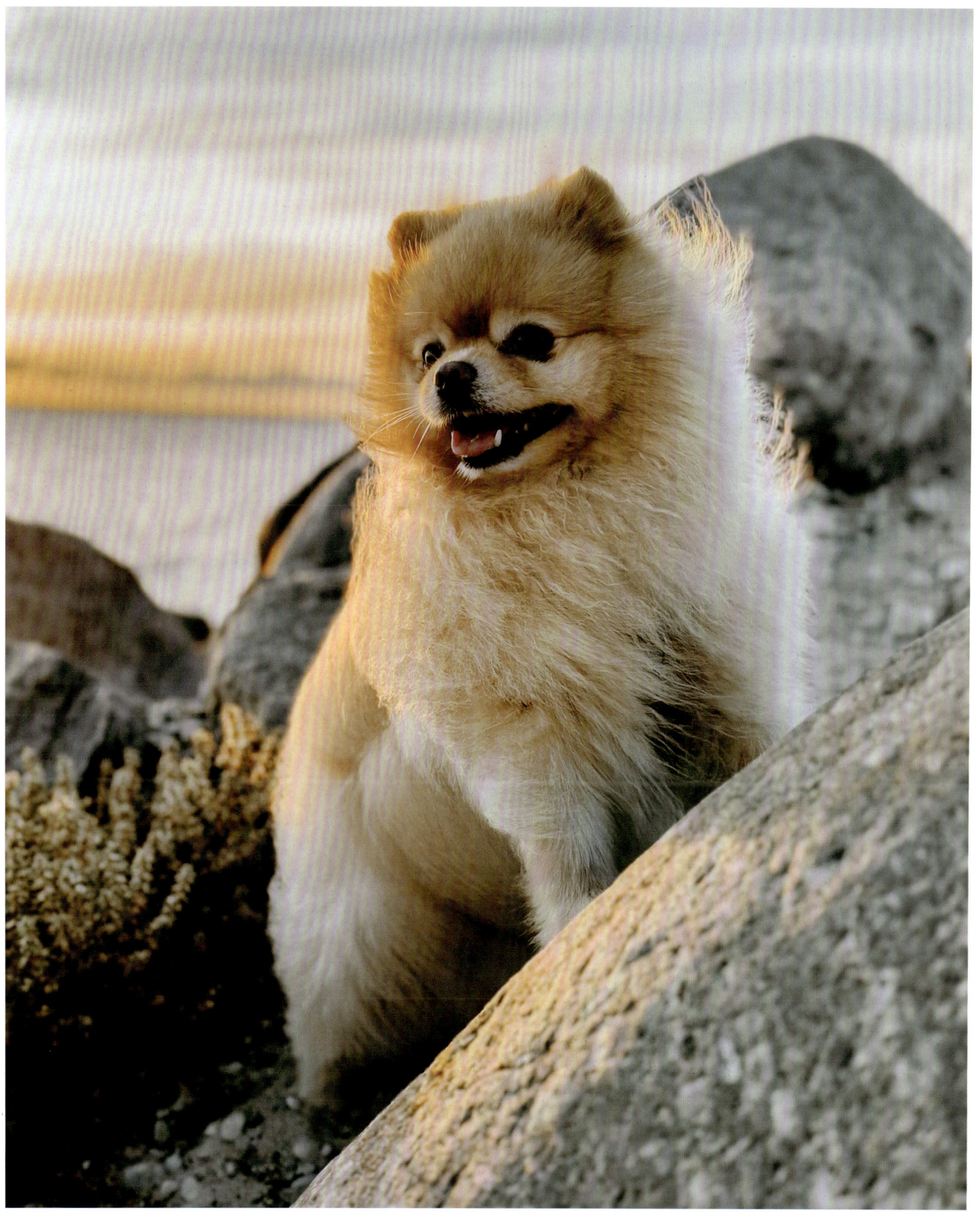

ABOVE:
Happy dog
The Pomeranian is known for the way its upturned mouth creates a smile-like expression.

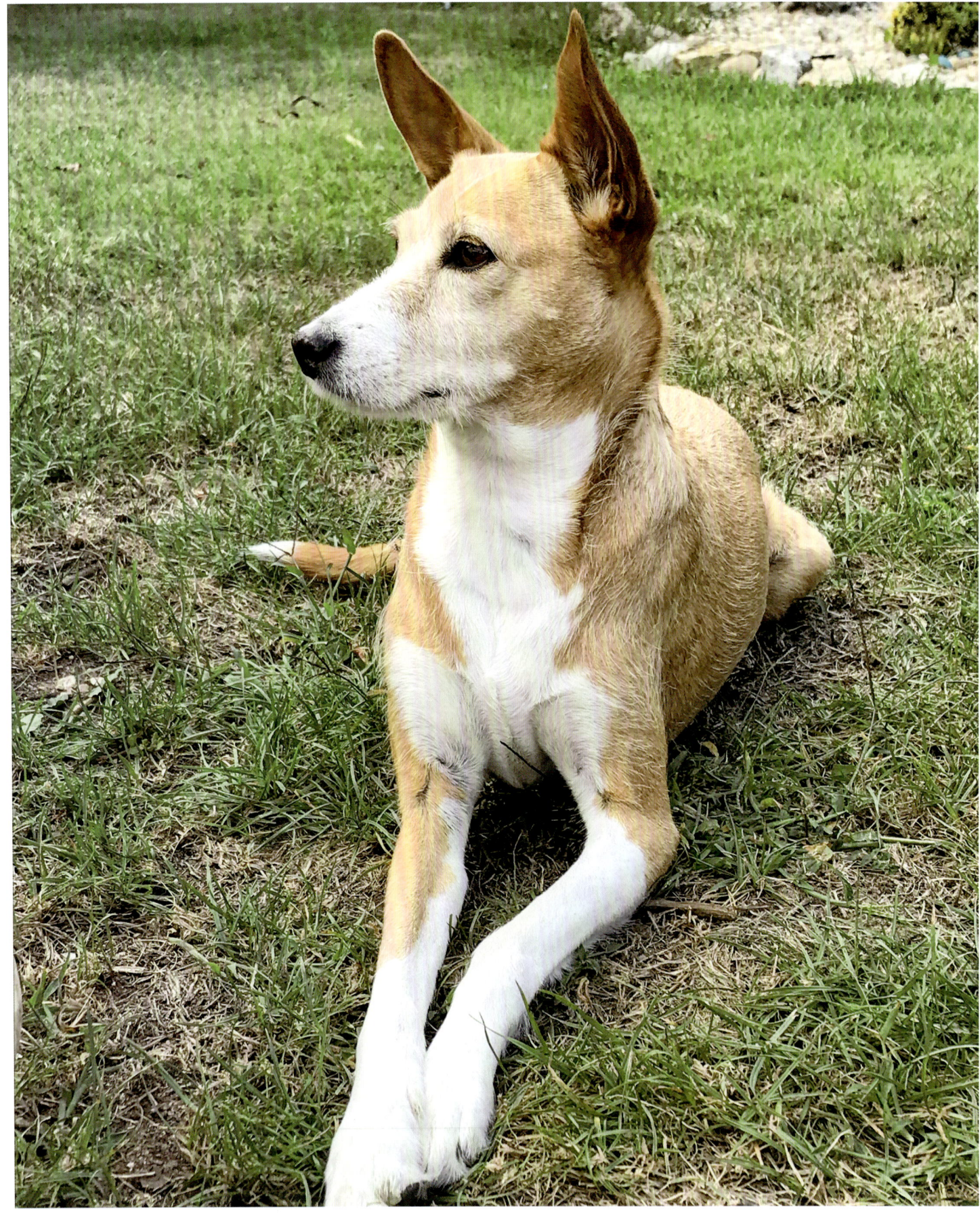

ABOVE:
The real deal
The medio variety embodies the authentic type of the Portuguese podengo.

Portuguese Podengo

CHARACTERISTICS

Coat
Two coat types, smooth and wirehaired, both coming in various colours, such as gold, red, white, grey, fawn and chestnut
Height
20–70cm (8–28in)
Weight
4–30kg (9–66lb)
Lifespan
Around 12 years
Personality
Independent and alert
Origin
Portugal

The podengo is another ancient breed said to be descended from dogs spread through the Mediterranean and along the maritime trade routes of the Phoenicians. Its name means simply "dog with pointed ears" and, in common with many of the Mediterranean breeds, the podengo has the slender, lithe elegance of the dogs represented in ancient carvings and paintings.

The podengo is a hunting dog at heart, with a strong sense of smell and good running ability. There are three varieties based on size. The larger dogs, the podengo grande, were once used to catch deer and boar. The middle variety, the podengo medio, was a rabbit hunter. The smaller variety, also known as podengo pequeno, was a rat catcher and found a calling aboard ship, controlling the vermin, as the human Portuguese crew set about pushing back the frontiers of the unknown as they led the exploration of the Atlantic in the 15th century. In this way the podengo was one of the first European breeds to make it to the Americas. The small podengo is the most popular as a pet today, and is a lively family member that needs firm leadership.

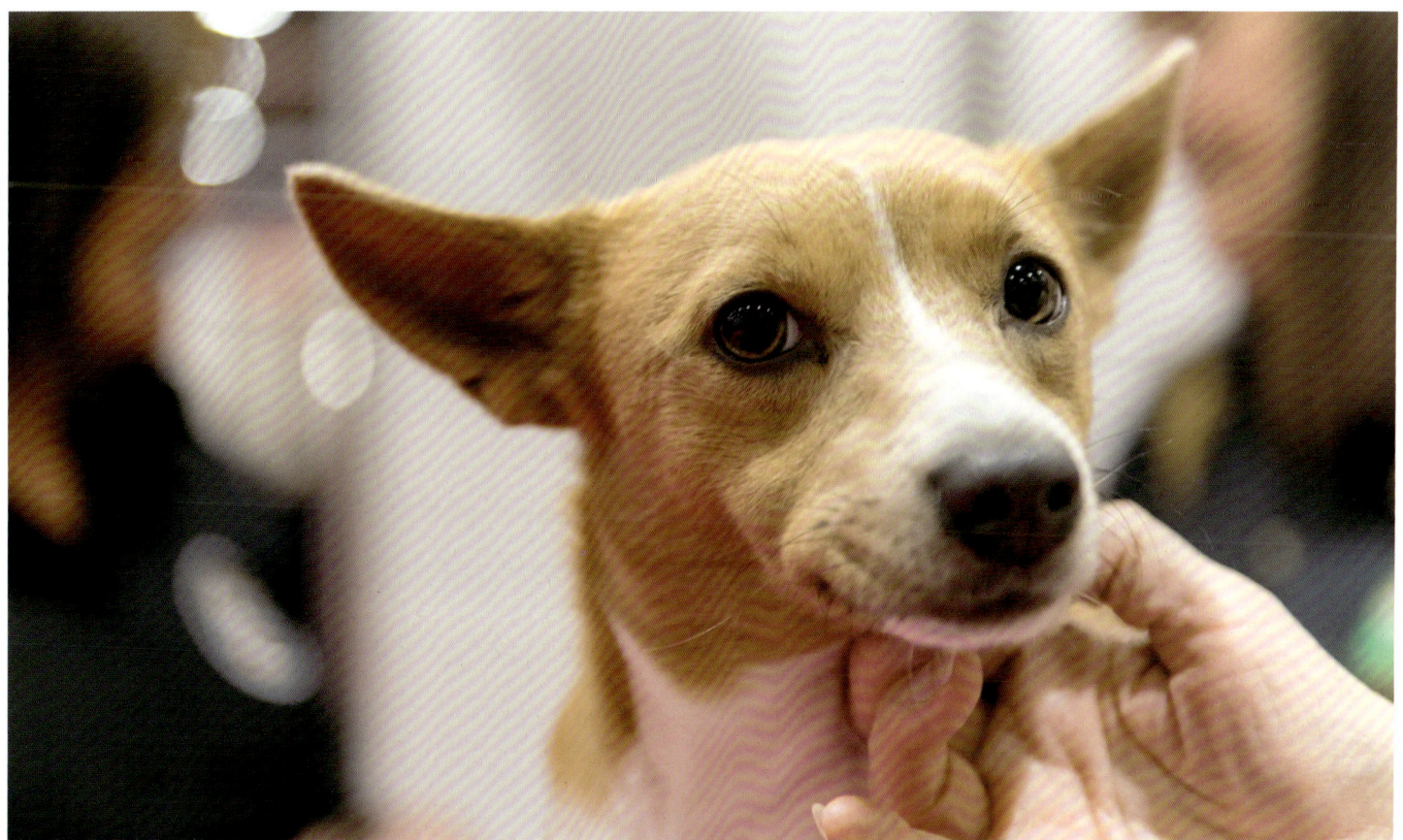

ABOVE:
Bundle of fun
The podengo is a lively, agile, playful, alert and intelligent dog that is loyal to its family but may be suspicious of strangers.

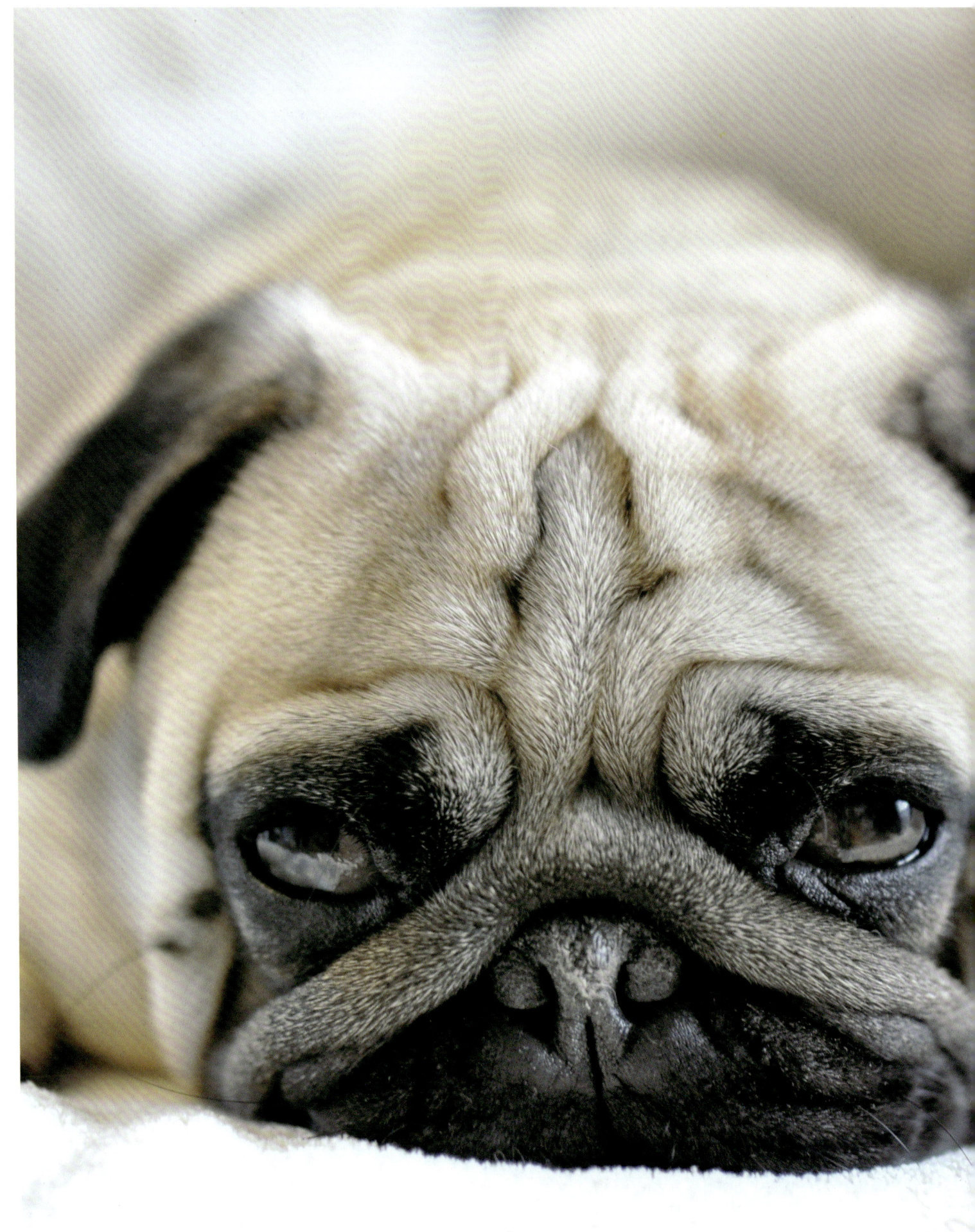

COMPANION DOGS

Pug

Small and sturdy with a wrinkled inquisitorial look, the pug is perhaps revealing what its owner is thinking. Are you friendly? If the answer is in the affirmative then the pug will be the first to confirm the acquaintance. The flat-faced dogs have the look of a bruiser—the name pug comes from the Latin for "fist"—but they are very sociable and love attention.

Like many brachycephalic breeds (with a stunted snout and nasal cavity) the pug breed originates in the palaces of China. Like its imperial kennel-mates the shih tzu and Pekingese, these original pugs were a protected breed steeped in status. One could only get one as a gift from the emperor. That all changed in the 16th century, when Dutch traders brought them back to Europe. The pug was given a European refinement, crossed with griffons and other toy breeds to reduce its size. The following century, the pug became the signature breed of the House of Orange. When William and Mary took the British throne in 1689, the pug became the must-have breed for British nobility.

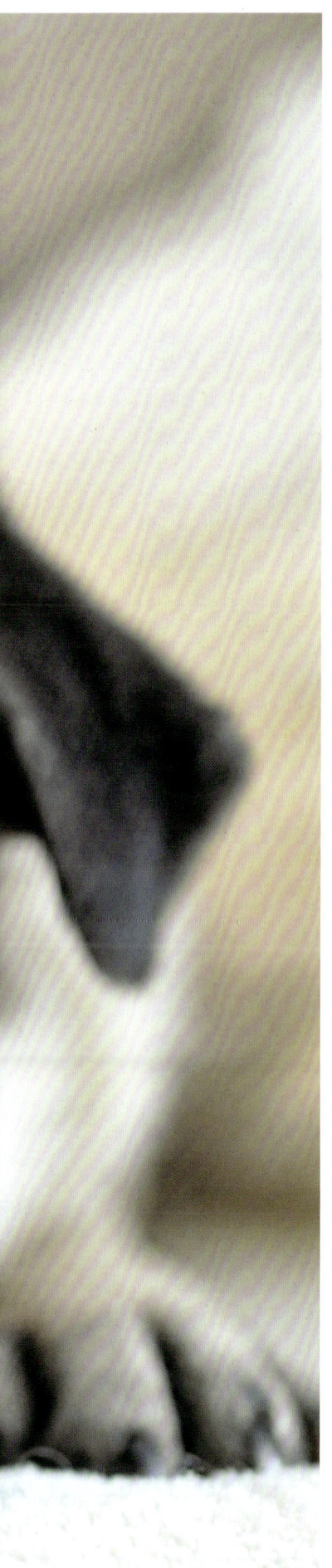

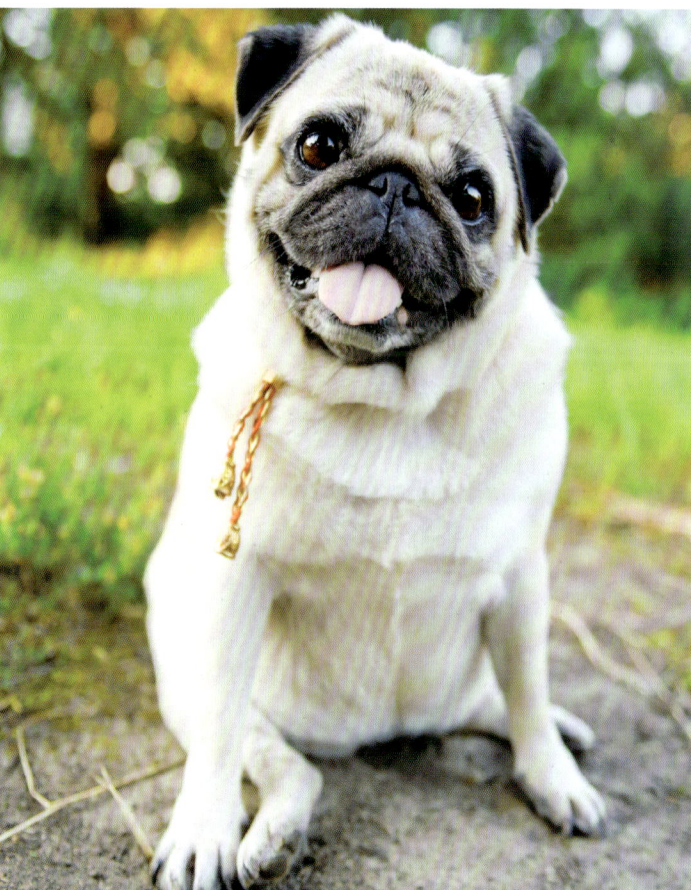

CHARACTERISTICS

Coat
A short, glossy coat that can be fawn, apricot, silver or black

Height
25–28 cm (10–11in)

Weight
6–8kg (13–18lb)

Lifespan
Around 10 years

Personality
Charming and loving

Origin
China and the Netherlands

LEFT:
Health issues
The pug's flat face can cause breathing problems and sensitivity to heat.

ABOVE:
Happy to be involved
Pugs love human companionship and can get along well with children and other pets.

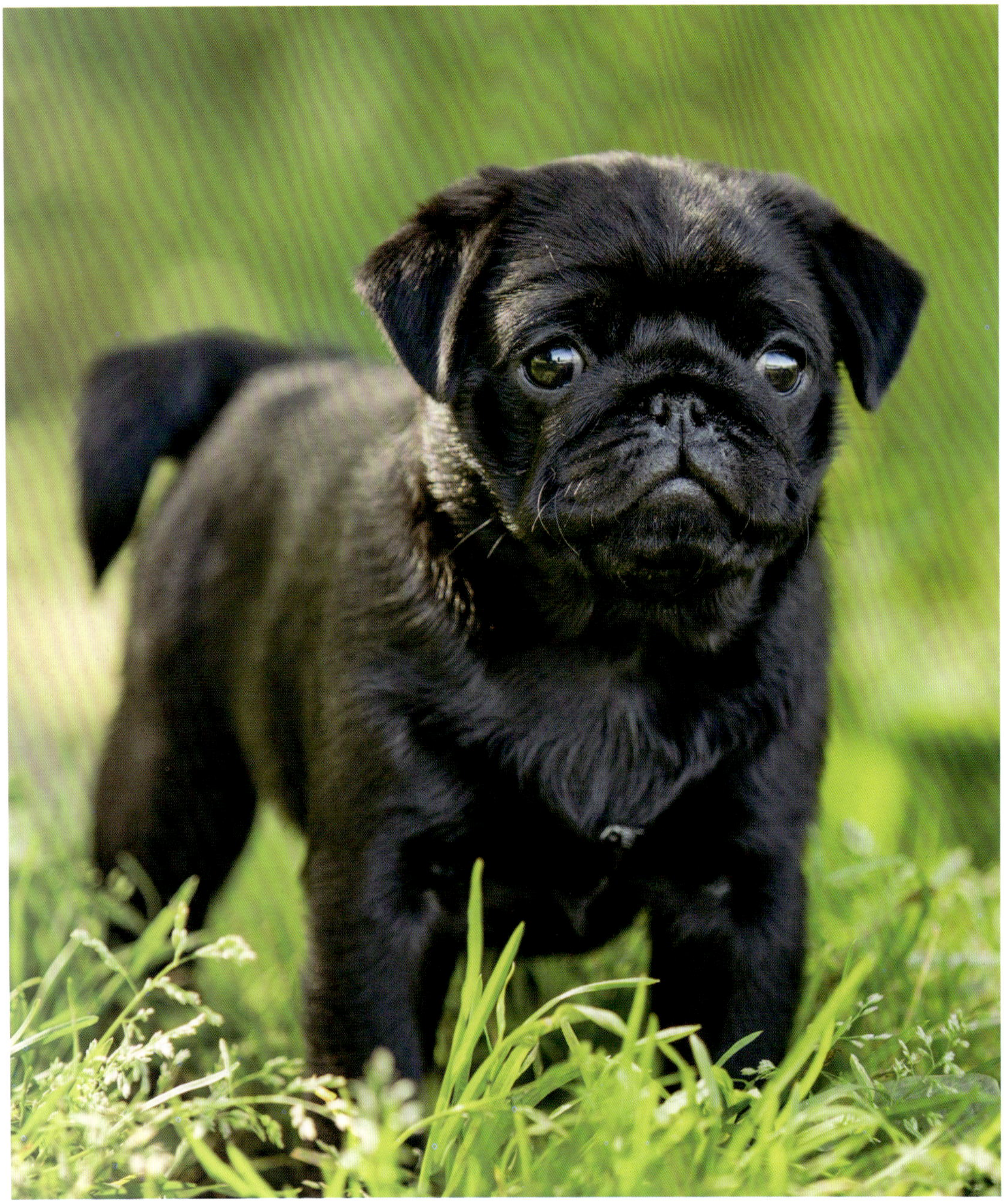

COMPANION DOGS

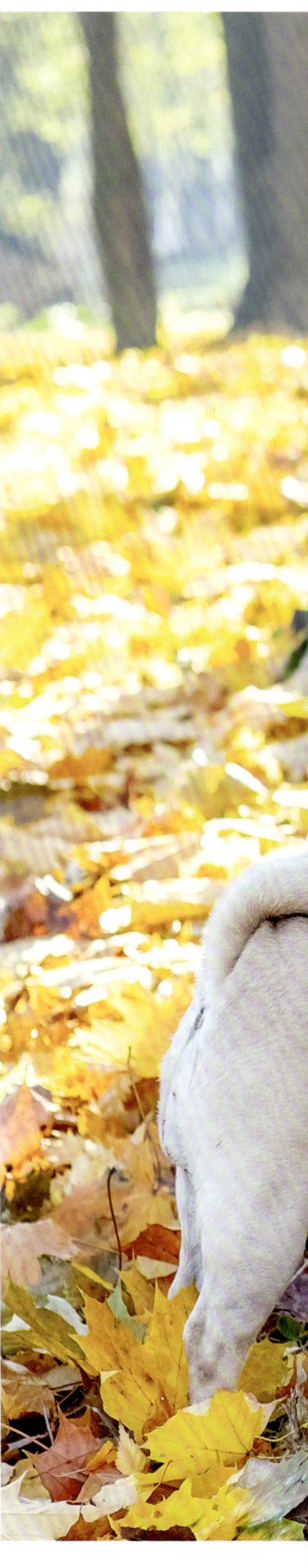

ABOVE:
Playful pets
Pugs are happy in almost all environments.

RIGHT:
Careful owners
Pugs need regular grooming and careful eye care.

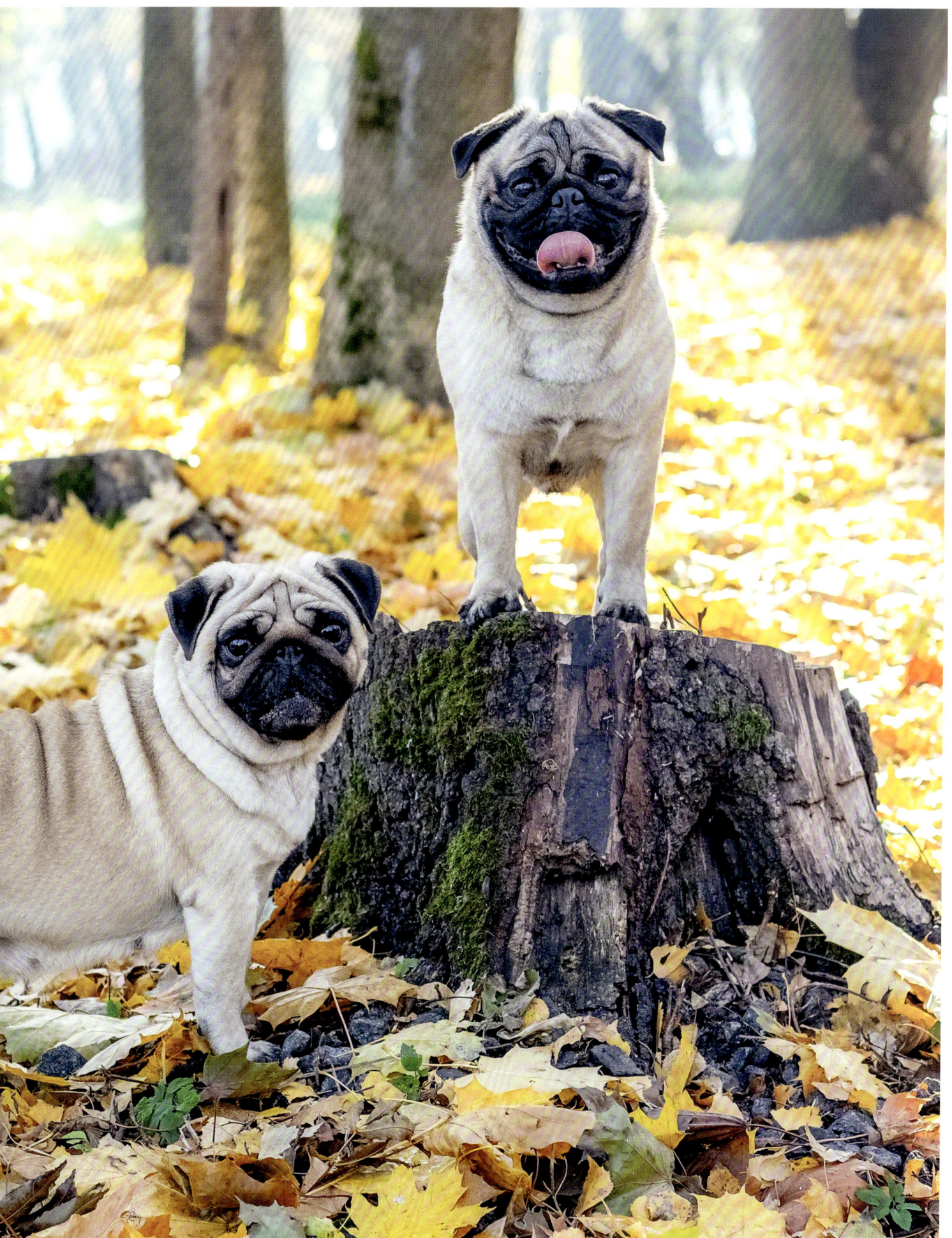

COMPANION DOGS

Puggle

CHARACTERISTICS

Coat
Short, smooth coat that comes in various colours, such as brown, black, white and brindle
Height
25–38cm (10–15in)
Weight
7–14kg (15–31lb)
Lifespan
10–13 years
Personality
Playful and clever
Origin
United States

A new arrival on the designer dog scene, the puggle is a crossbreed of two very small breeds, the pug and beagle, each of which bring a strong set of features. The pug is a tough-looking toy dog with a heart of gold, while the beagle is a playful and agile scenthound with brains to match. The puggle hybrid was first created in the 1980s and quickly won admirers, not least among Hollywood celebrities. It is a small to medium-sized dog, with a hint of the wrinkled snout of the pug coupled with the imploring twinkle of a beagle. It is small and soppy enough to sit on the lap but also athletic enough for plenty of fun and games in and out of the house.

The reason for the cross is to create a cute companion dog that does not have the health problems that have accumulated in the purebred varieties, the pug especially. However, as with all crossbreeds, the process is quite a gamble. The idea is that the pug's love of home will temper the beagle's drive to roam, but that is not always the result. Puggles are said to be easy to train but they can also be stubborn and independent nevertheless.

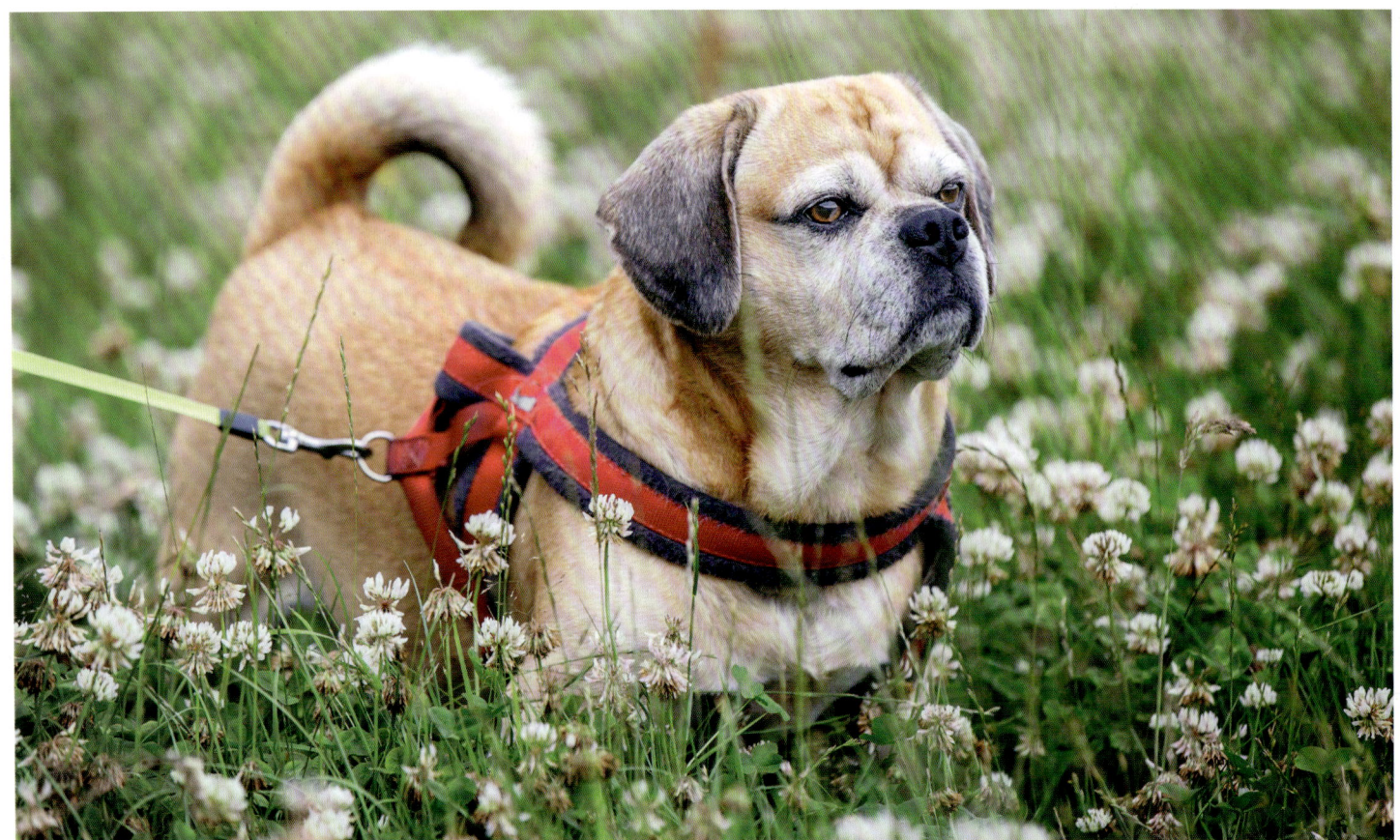

ABOVE:
Get moving
These dogs need at least 30 minutes of exercise per day. They need regular grooming, dental care and nail trimming.

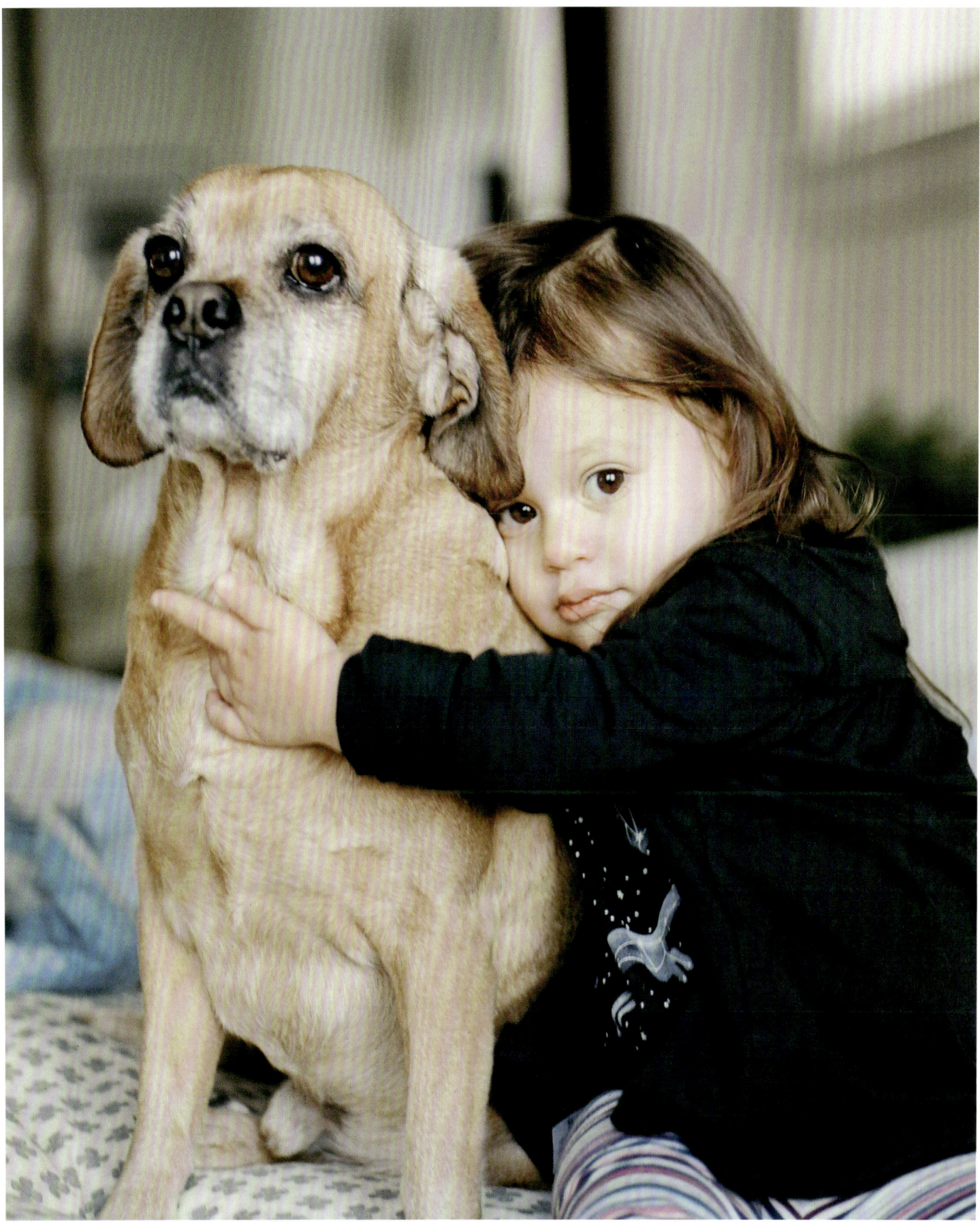

ABOVE:
Family friendly
Puggles are playful and outgoing dogs that make great family pets. They get along well with children.

COMPANION DOGS

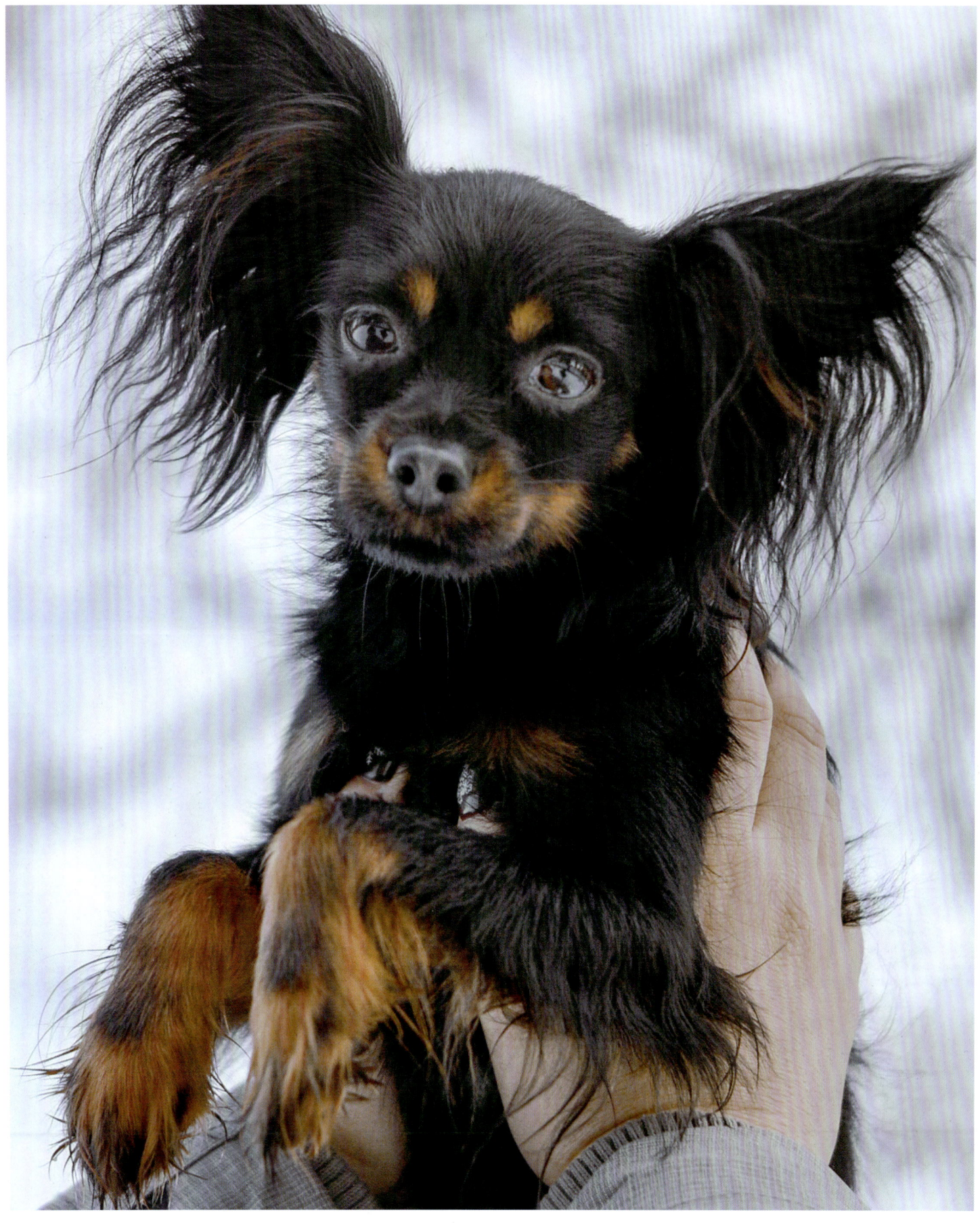

ABOVE:
Long-haired
The long-haired variety has a wavy coat with long fringes on the ears, tail and legs.

Russian Toy

CHARACTERISTICS

Coat
Either smooth or long-haired. The colours can be black and tan, blue and tan, or red with or without black or brown

Height
20–28cm (8–11in)

Weight
Up to 3kg (7lb)

Lifespan
Around 12 years

Personality
Friendly and loyal

Origin
Russia

The breed of little lap dogs was developed in the 18th century from miniature English terriers. The Russian nobility wanted a dog that emulated the fine-living of their fellow empire builders along the opposing edge of Europe. Peter the Great himself kept one named Lisetta. Two varieties were created—smooth and long-haired—although even the latter was not that shaggy. As a result the tiny Russian breed has a fragile doll-like quality but that belies the dogs' robustness in body and spirit. The original breeders had in mind that the dogs would act as low-cost watchdogs, so they are an alert breed that habitually challenges strangers.

In the upheaval that followed the Russian Revolution, the breed became very rare. Inevitably the restored breed of today has some significant differences from the original. Today's breed has a square body, a small head, large eyes and erect ears. It is very loyal to its family and has playful instincts. Energetic and alert, it needs moderate exercise and regular grooming. The Russian toy is a rare breed outside of Russia, but it has gained some popularity elsewhere since the 1990s.

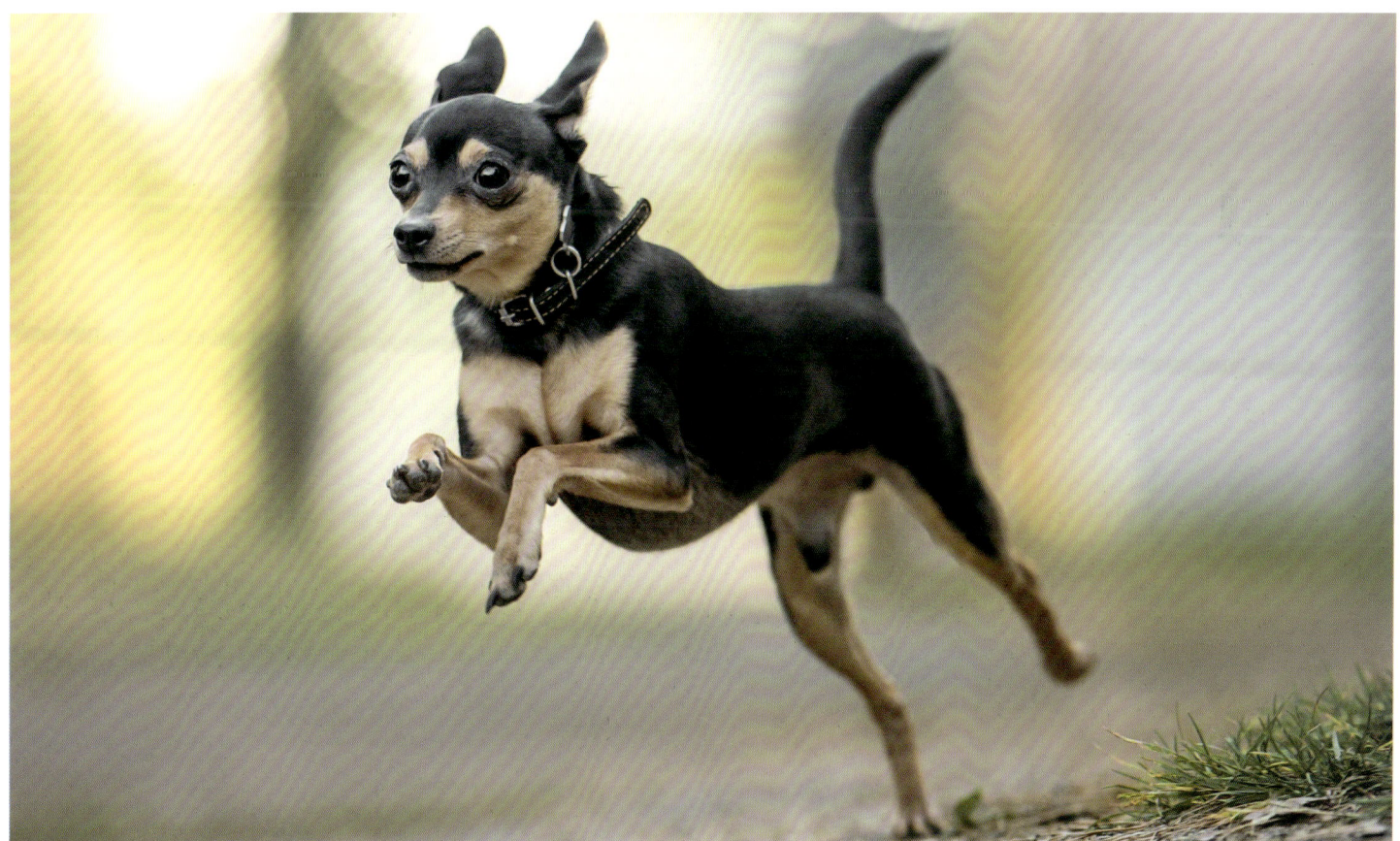

ABOVE:
Super smooth
The smooth variety has a short and shiny coat.

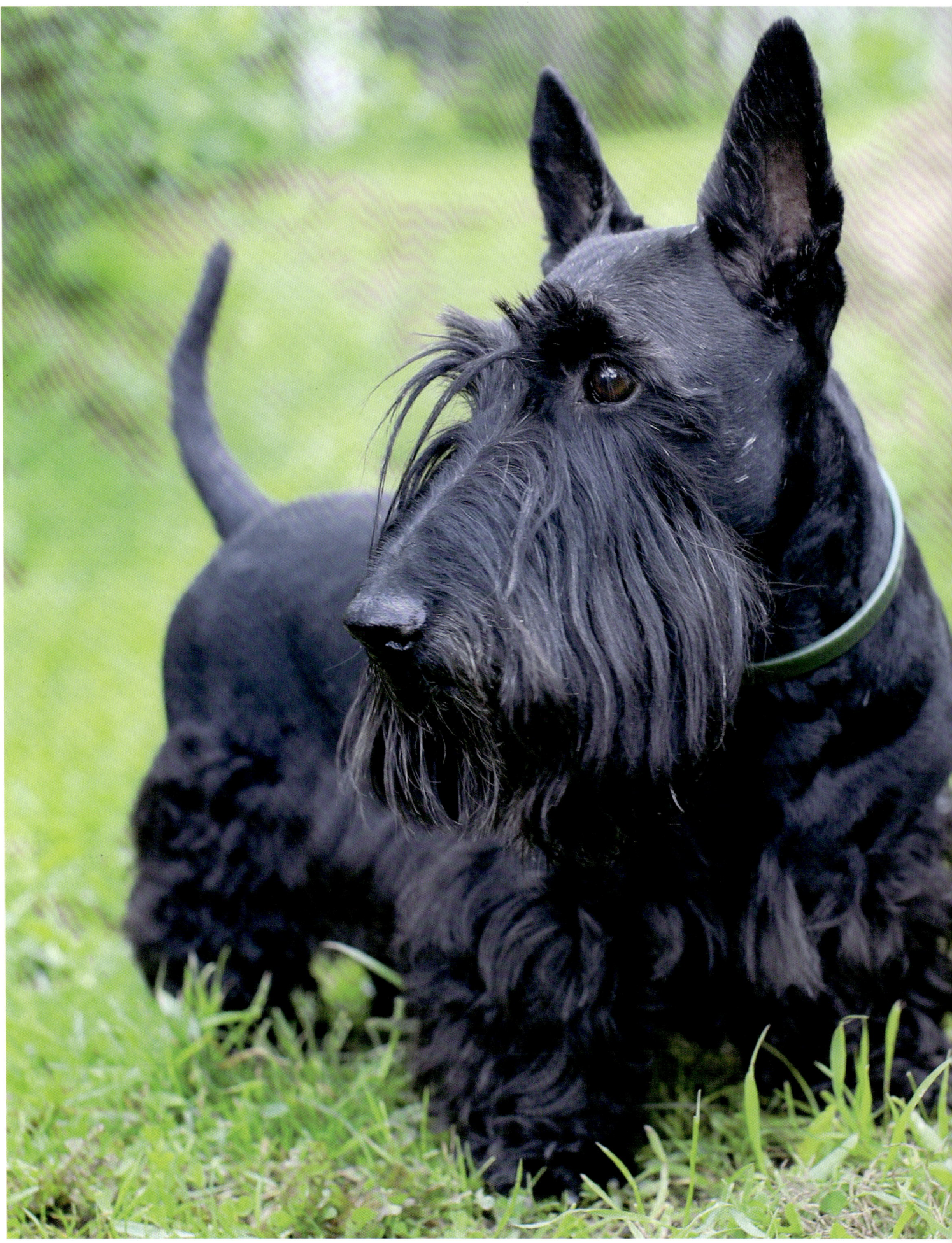

Scottish Terrier

The Scottish Terrier, also known as the Scottie, or less commonly the Aberdeen Terrier, is a small but sturdy dog breed that originated in Scotland. They have a distinctive appearance that begins with the noticeably long head which carries a pair of erect ears, some bushy eyebrows and a neat beard. They are the most familiar of four Highland terrier breeds: the others are the Skye, Cairn and West Highland white terriers. All were originally kept to suppress vermin on farms. As a result they still have a strong prey drive and retain a fearless attitude.

Scotties have been described as businesslike, so they perform their role with an aloof efficiency and a minimum of fuss. This applies if they are on rat patrol, standing sentinel as a watchdog or being a much loved pet. They can be stubborn and territorial, and they may not get along well with other dogs or animals. They are best suited for owners who can provide them with firm but gentle leadership.

CHARACTERISTICS

Coat
Wiry in black, brindle or wheaten
Height
25–28cm (10–11in)
Weight
9–11kg (20–24lb)
Lifespan
9–15 years
Personality
Confident and active
Origin
Scotland

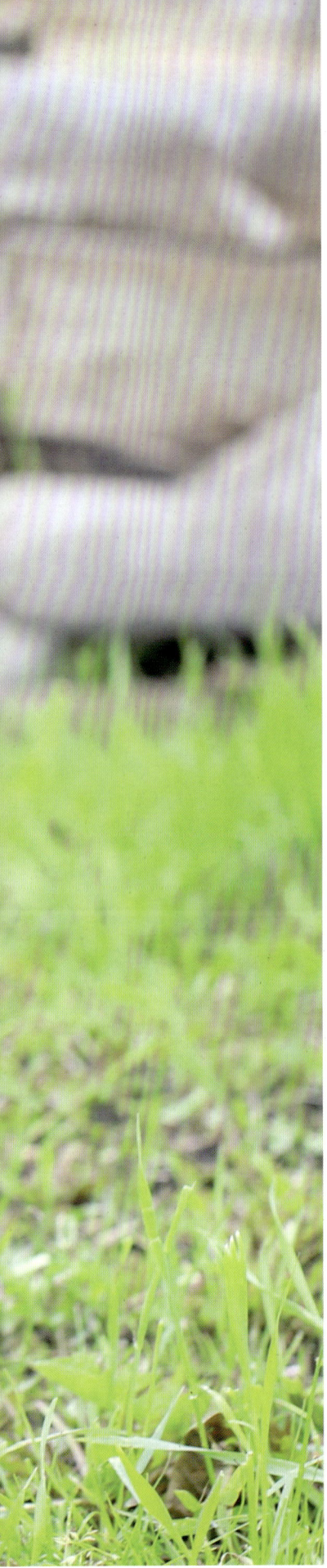

LEFT:
Shiny hair
Scotties need regular grooming to keep their coat in good condition.

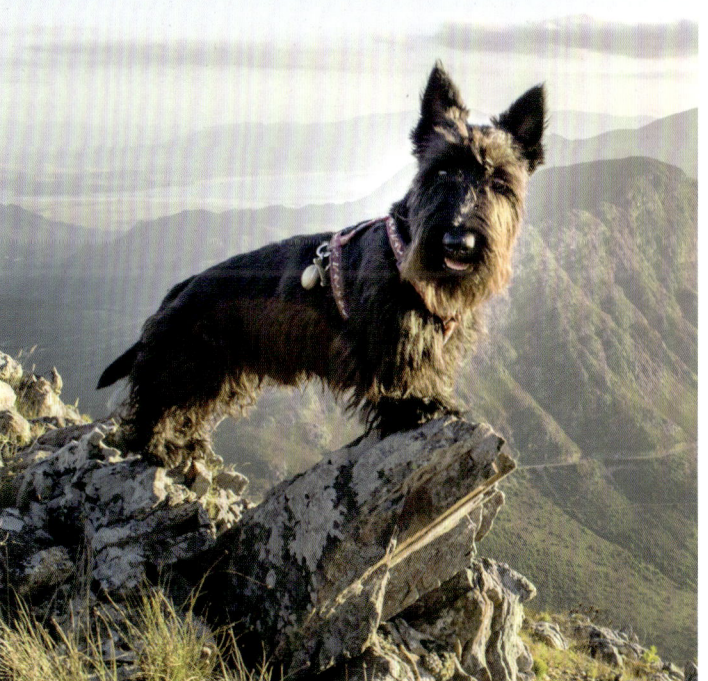

ABOVE:
Mountain home
Despite the Highland heritage Scottish terriers are not very active dogs and do not require a lot of exercise, but they do enjoy walks and playing games.

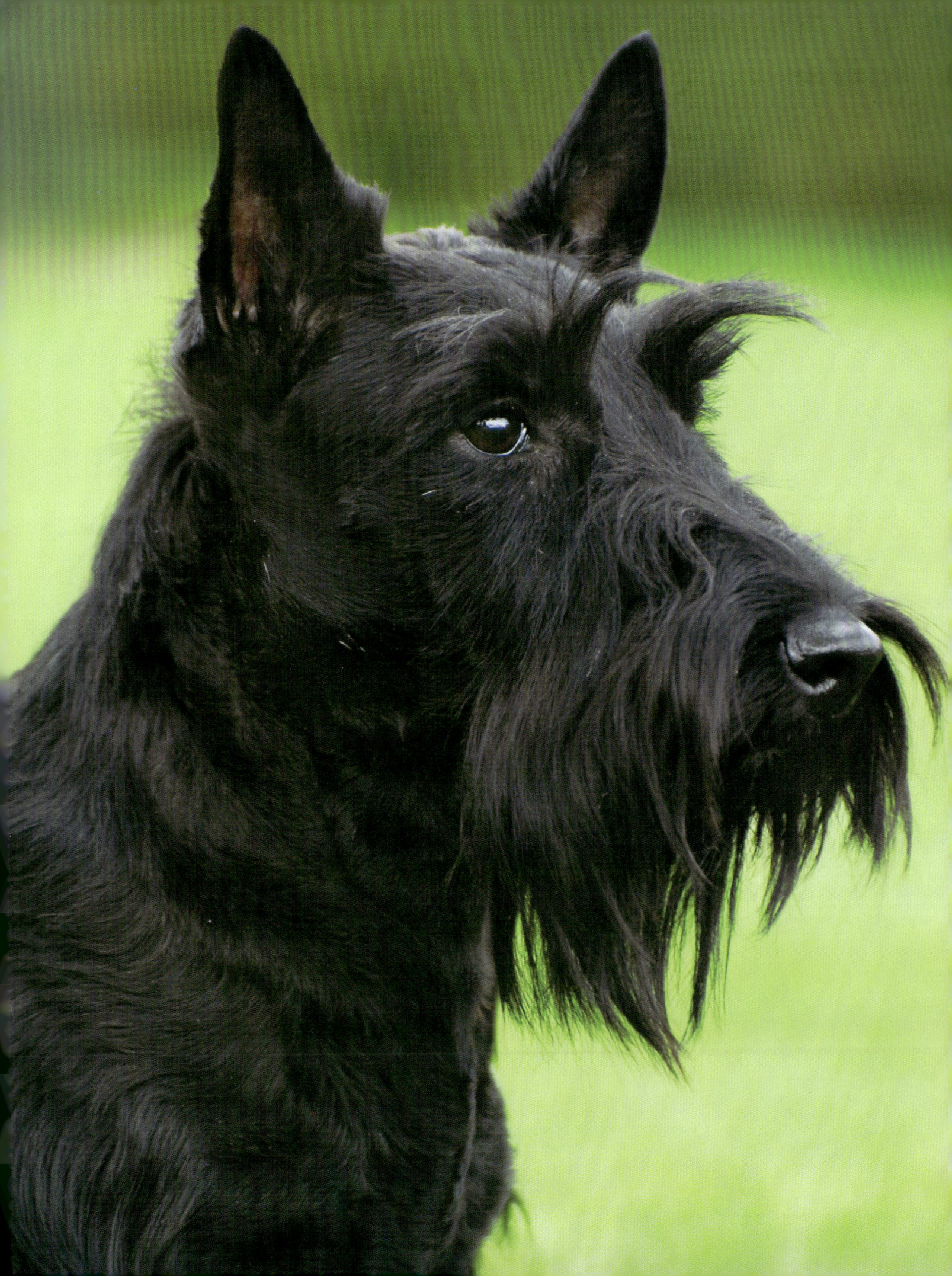

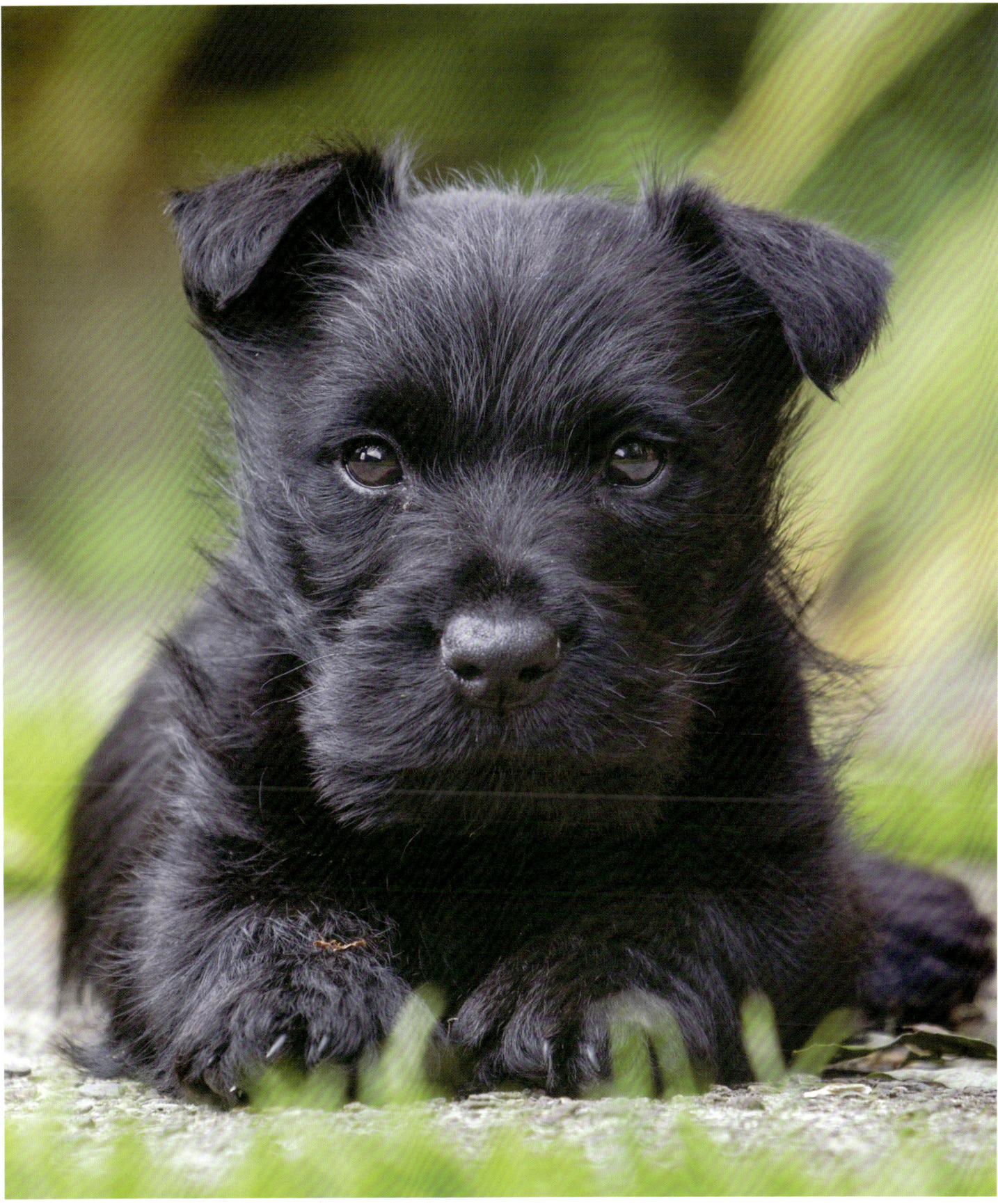

OPPOSITE AND ABOVE:
Scottie dog
Scottish terriers may be prone to some health issues such as bleeding disorders, joint problems, allergies and cancer.

COMPANION DOGS

Shih Tzu

This striking little breed is a Chinese derivative of the many Tibetan lion dog breeds, such as the Lhasa apso. As is the case with most of the Chinese companion breeds, the ones that thrived and then survived the tumult of revolution were those developed by the royal household. The imperial family would control the breed. They were not for sale and shih tzu owners of antiquity could only receive them as a gift from the emperor.

The name shih tzu translates as "lion dog", and they were bred to resemble the stylized lions seen in Chinese art. Neither resemblance is strong; real lions have never lived wild in China during recorded history. Shih tzus have long silky hairs that fall as a floor-length fringe. The dogs also have a distinctive face due to an underbite which gives them their cute expression. A shih tzu makes an easy pet that will be a loyal and affectionate companion for people of all ages.

CHARACTERISTICS
Coat
Long and silky and coming in various colours and patterns
Height
Up to 27cm (11in)
Weight
5–8kg (11–18lb)
Lifespan
Around 10 years
Personality
Playful and graceful
Origin
China

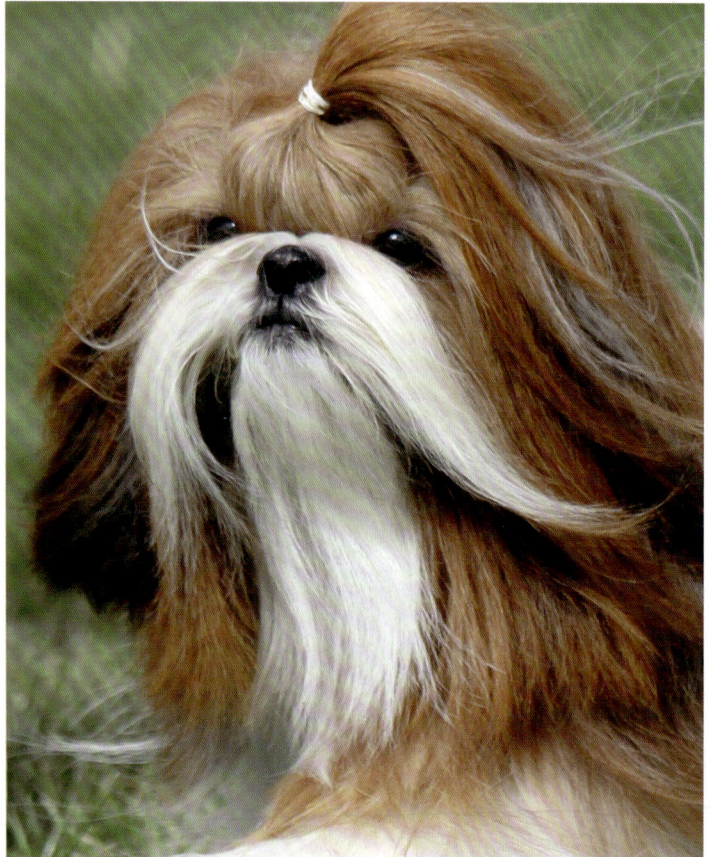

ABOVE:
Looking good
The shih tzu will need daily grooming to keep their coat looking great. Luckily it sheds only a little.

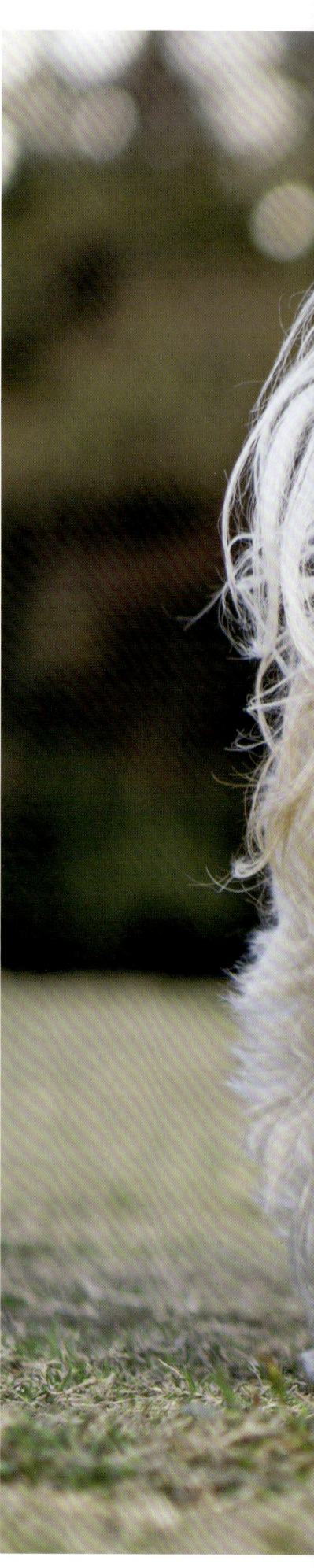

RIGHT:
Posing pooch
The shih tzu is a lively and affectionate dog that enjoys human company.

COMPANION DOGS

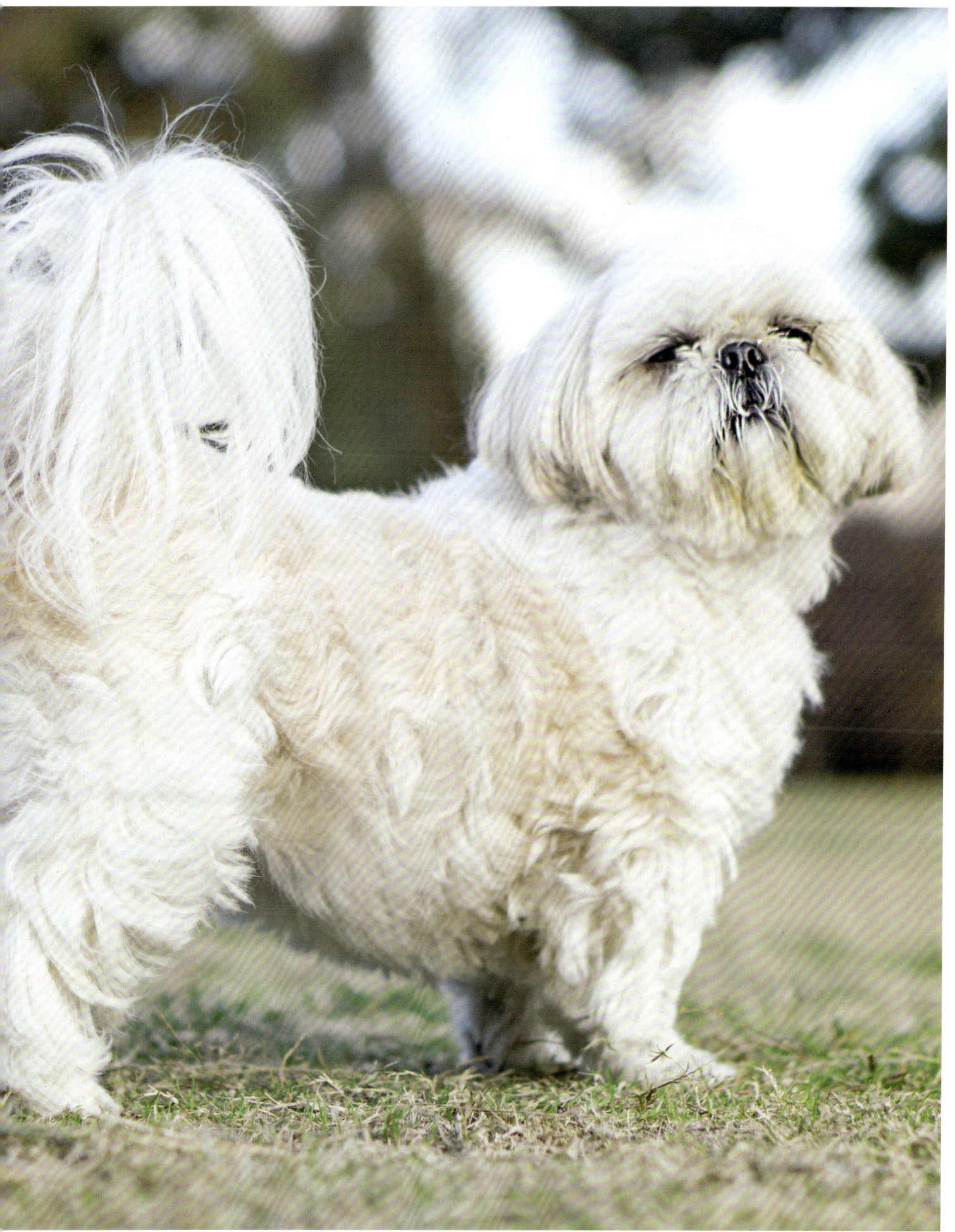

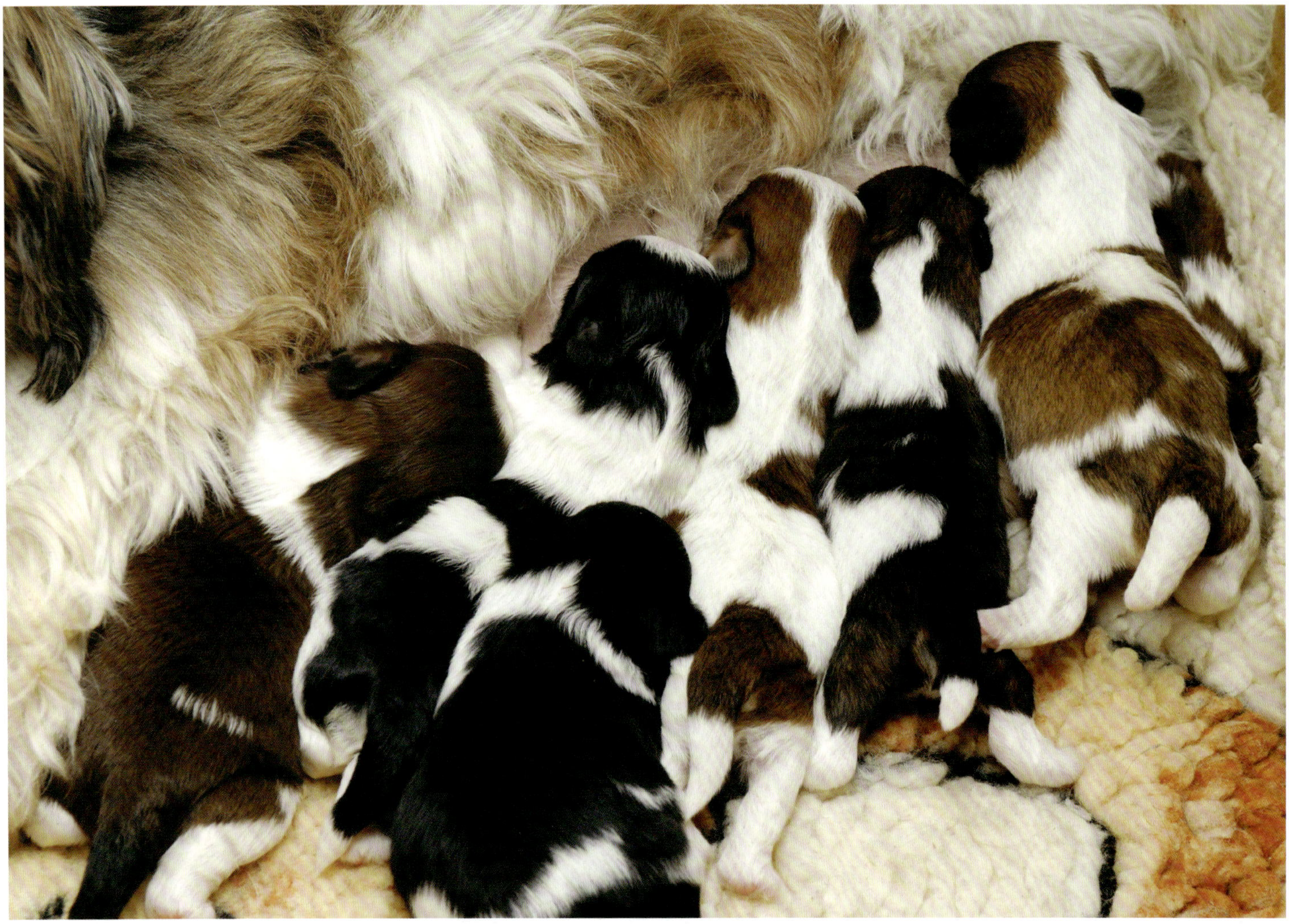

COMPANION DOGS

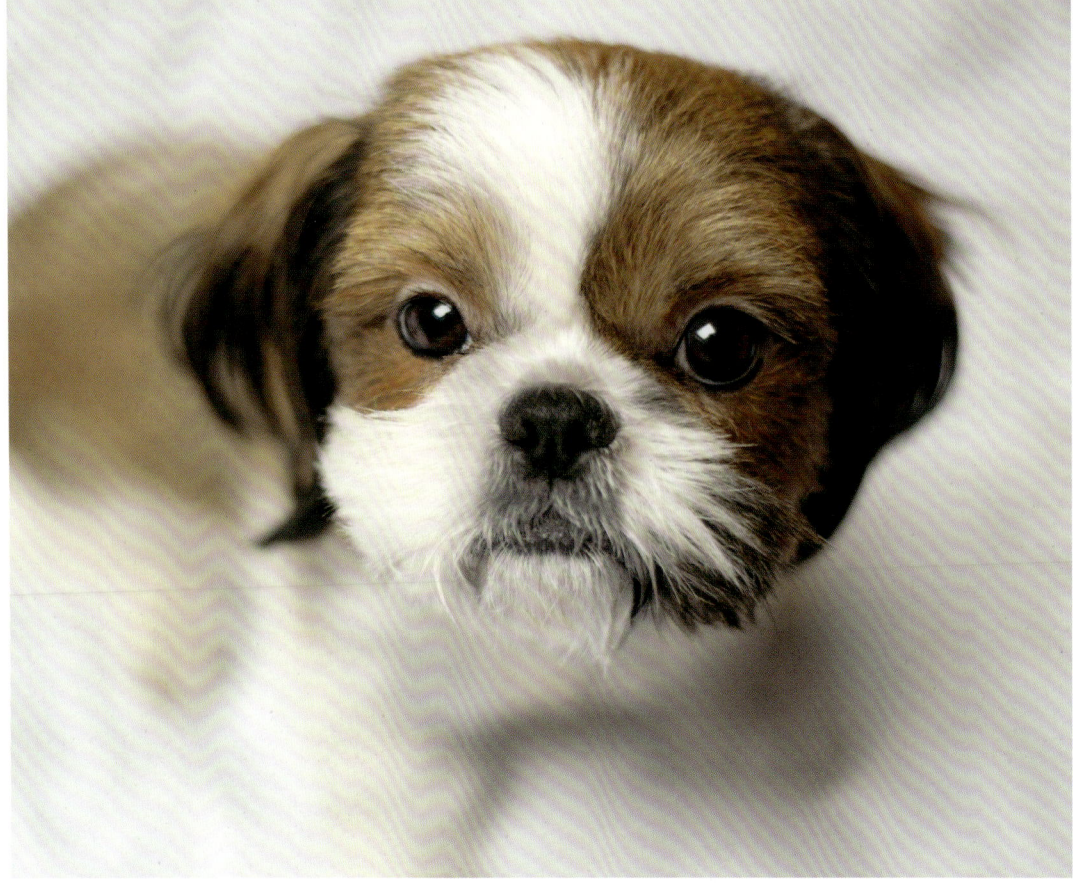

ABOVE:
Suckling
A litter of seven-day-old shih tzu puppies have a meal of their mother's milk.

OPPOSITE AND RIGHT:
On the run
Even when the coat is clipped, the tail and body hair still has an elaborate plume.

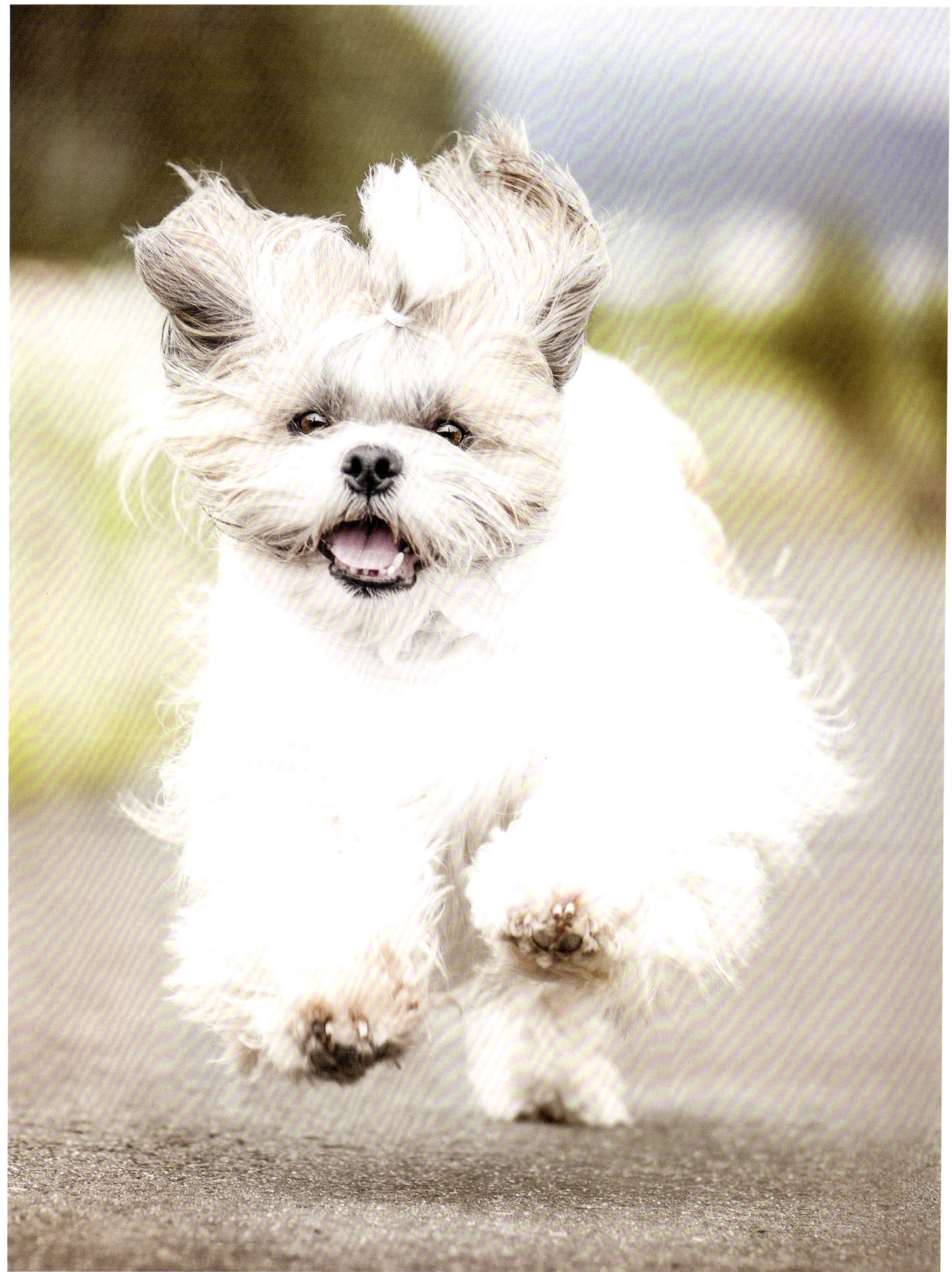

COMPANION DOGS

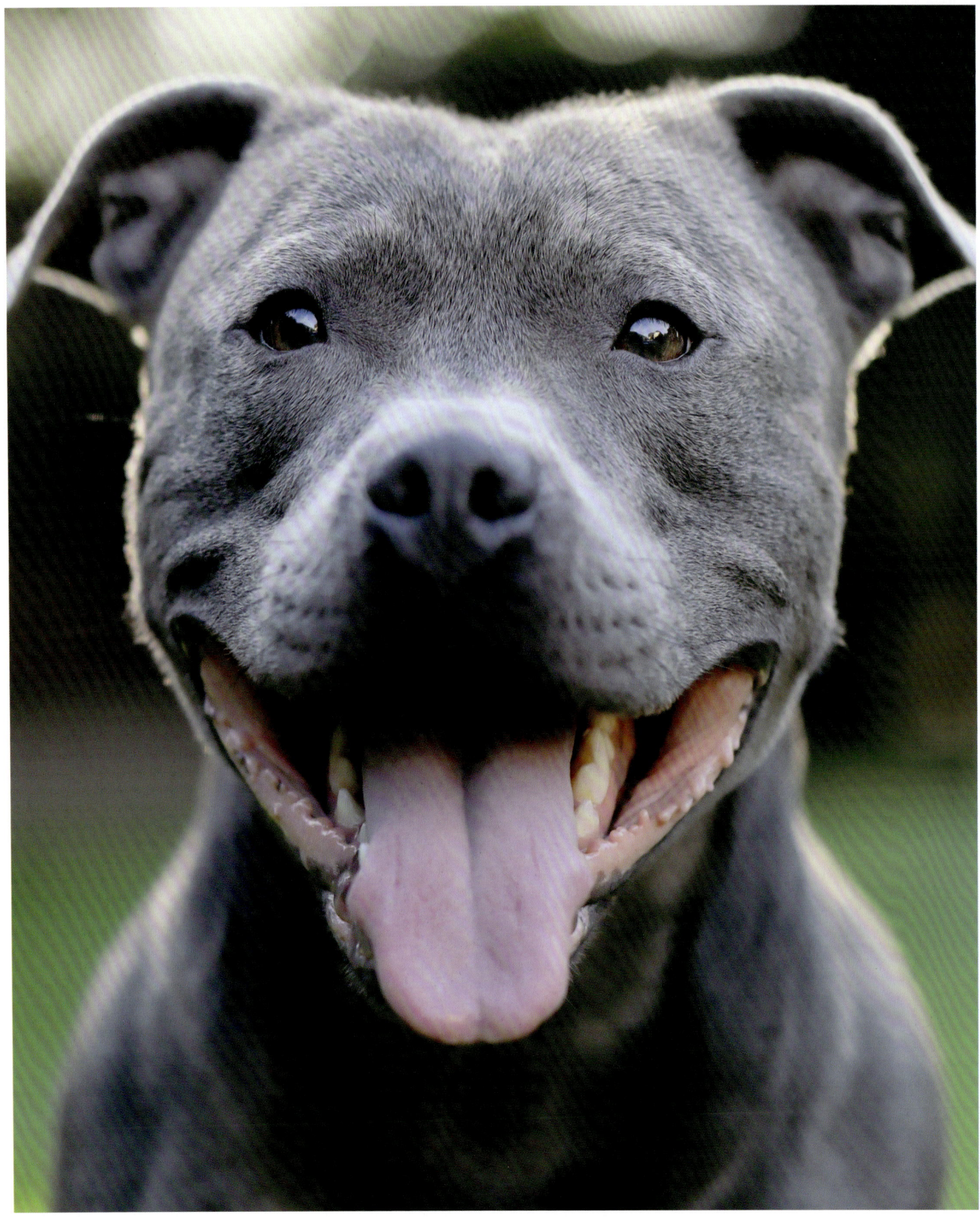

ABOVE:
Big bite
The breed has a broad head with a short muzzle and powerful jaws.

Staffordshire Bull Terrier

CHARACTERISTICS

Coat
Short and smooth and coming in various colours, such as white, black, blue, fawn, red or brindle, with or without white markings

Height
36–41cm (14–16in)

Weight
11–17kg (24–37lb)

Lifespan
10–16 years

Personality
Fearless and obedient

Origin
England

Also known as the staffy, the Staffordshire bull terrier is a fighting dog from the English Midlands. To that end it was more of a success than the more generic English bull terrier. The staffy was created in the same way by crossing bulldogs with local terriers, but more of the terrier's looks were retained. The staffy has the rotund bulk of a bulldog, which appeals to certain owners, but it also has the agility of a terrier and a longer muzzle (and nose) better suited for heavy exertions and lung-sapping athleticism. The breed has close links to the Boston terrier and the American pit bull terrier, but of course has its own distinctive appearance and temperament. The muscular and athletic dog has half-pricked ears and dark, round eyes.

In more recent years the dog became a burly companion and has the personality to fit into a family if given firm training. The Staffordshire bull terrier can live in an apartment or a house with a small garden, as long as it gets enough attention and activity. Nevertheless, hints of the fearlessness and tenacity required for the fighting pit can play out if the dog is not given careful correction.

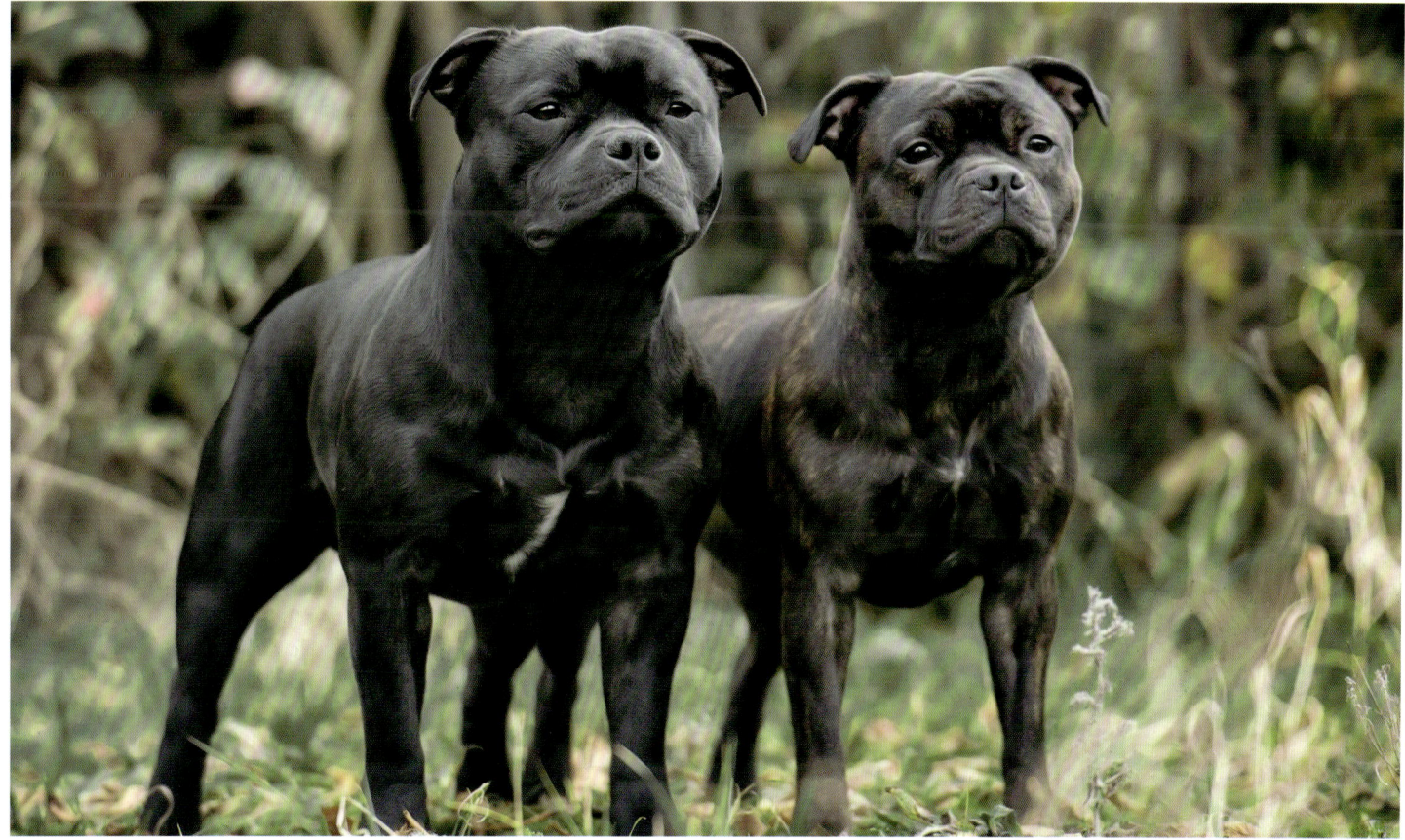

ABOVE:
Capable breed
The Staffordshire bull terrier is a highly intelligent and affectionate dog that is especially good with children if trained and socialized well. Each owner will know how far to trust their staffy.

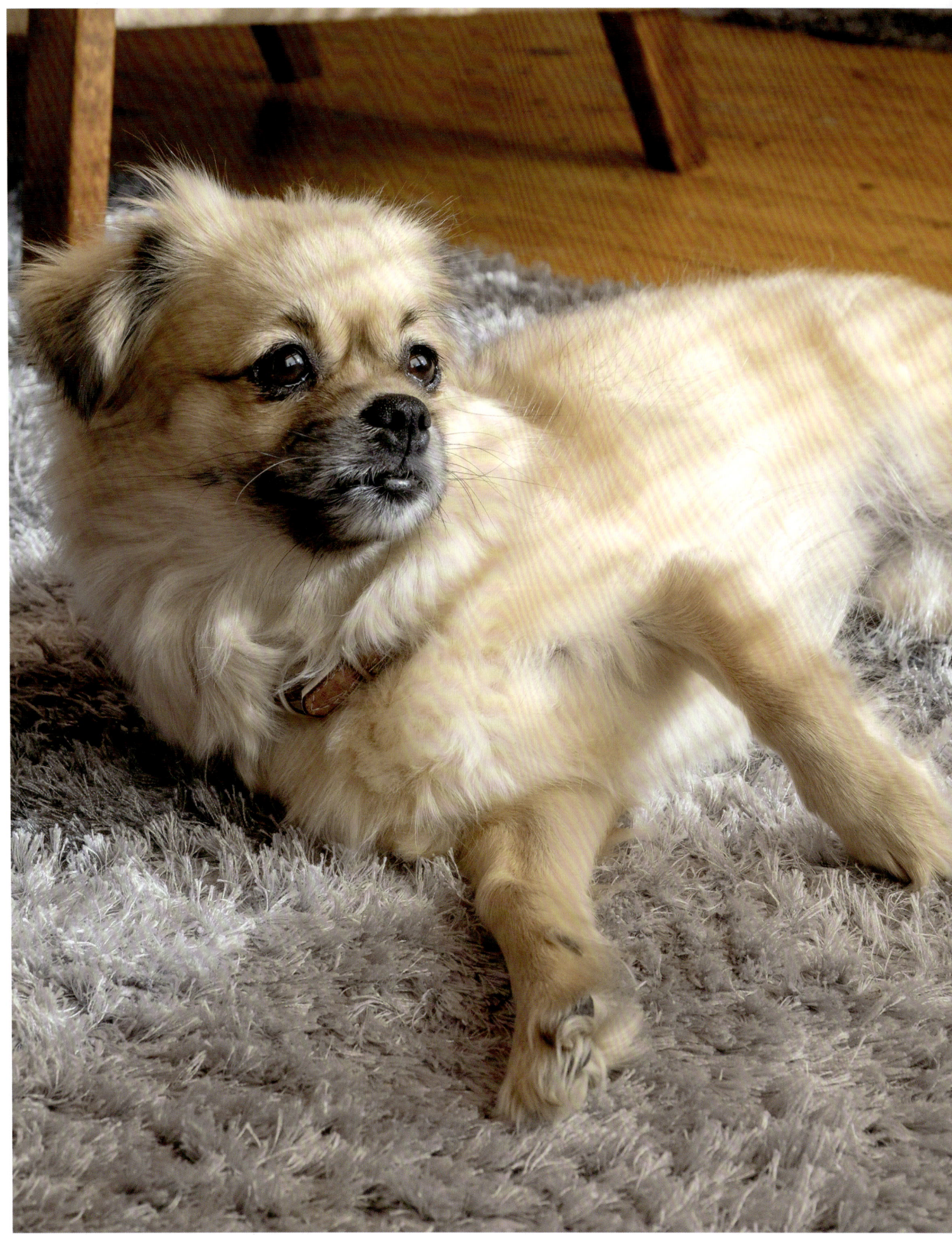

COMPANION DOGS

Tibetan Spaniel

The Tibetan spaniel is a small dog breed that was developed as a companion and watchdog by Buddhist monks. They worked alongside Tibetan mastiffs. The spaniels lounged on the walls of the monastery, able to see further than the bigger dogs standing guard on the ground. One bark was enough to bring the giant mastiffs to the alert. On cold nights, monks might redeploy a spaniel or two from guard duty to keep their beds warm.

Despite its name, it is not a true spaniel, but rather a unique breed with a short muzzle, large eyes, feathered ears and tail, and a mane of hair around its neck.

The dogs came to the attention of western breeders in the 1900s, when missionaries returning from the region brought back their new pet dogs. The breed is alert, independent and loyal to its family but can be wary of strangers and stubborn at times. The Tibetan spaniel needs moderate exercise and socialization, but is well able to adapt to different living environments as long as it has plenty of human engagement.

CHARACTERISTICS

Coat
Silky double coat that requires regular brushing and comes in various colours and patterns
Height
25cm (10in)
Weight
4–7kg (9 15lb)
Lifespan
Around 12 years
Personality
Alert and confident
Origin
Tibet

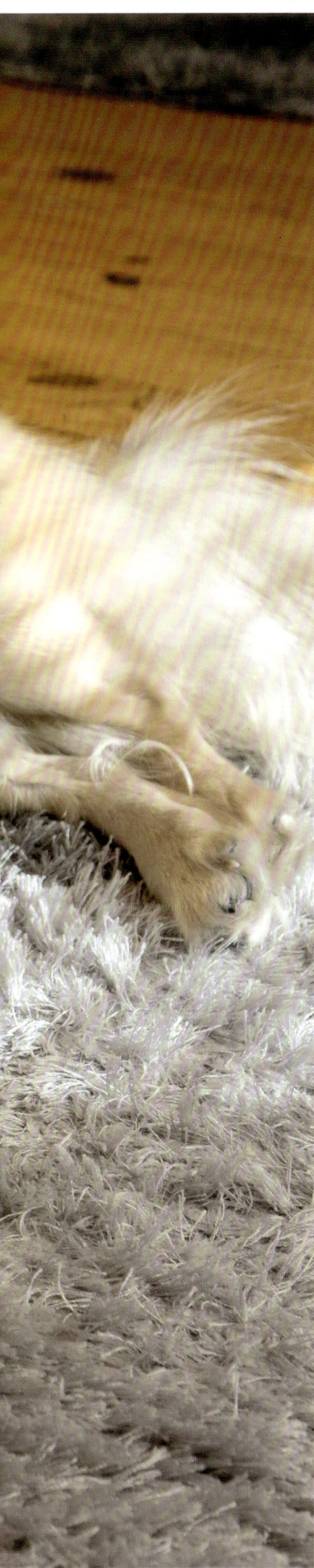

LEFT:
Happy at home
The small spaniel loves to laze around. It can get a lot of the exercise it needs around the house.

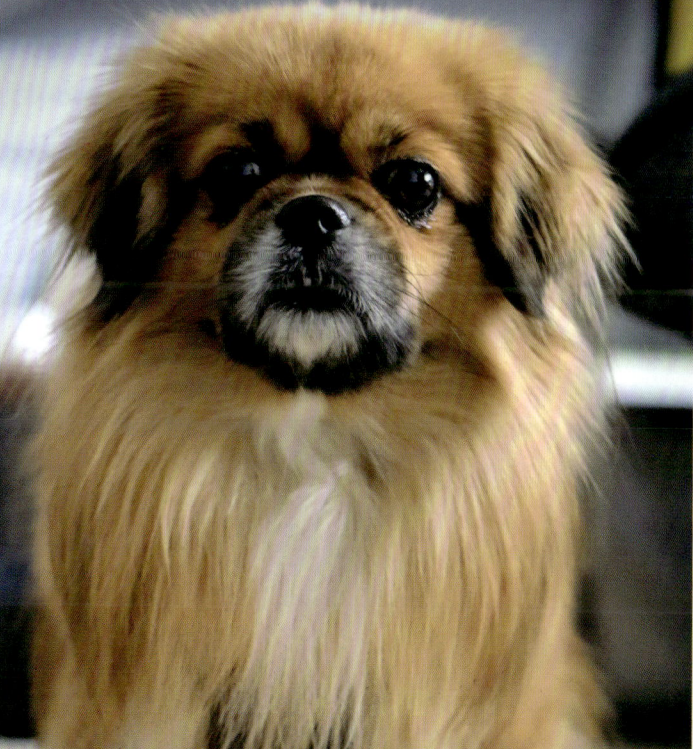

ABOVE:
What you looking at?
The Tibetan watchdog has a rather haughty expression.

COMPANION DOGS

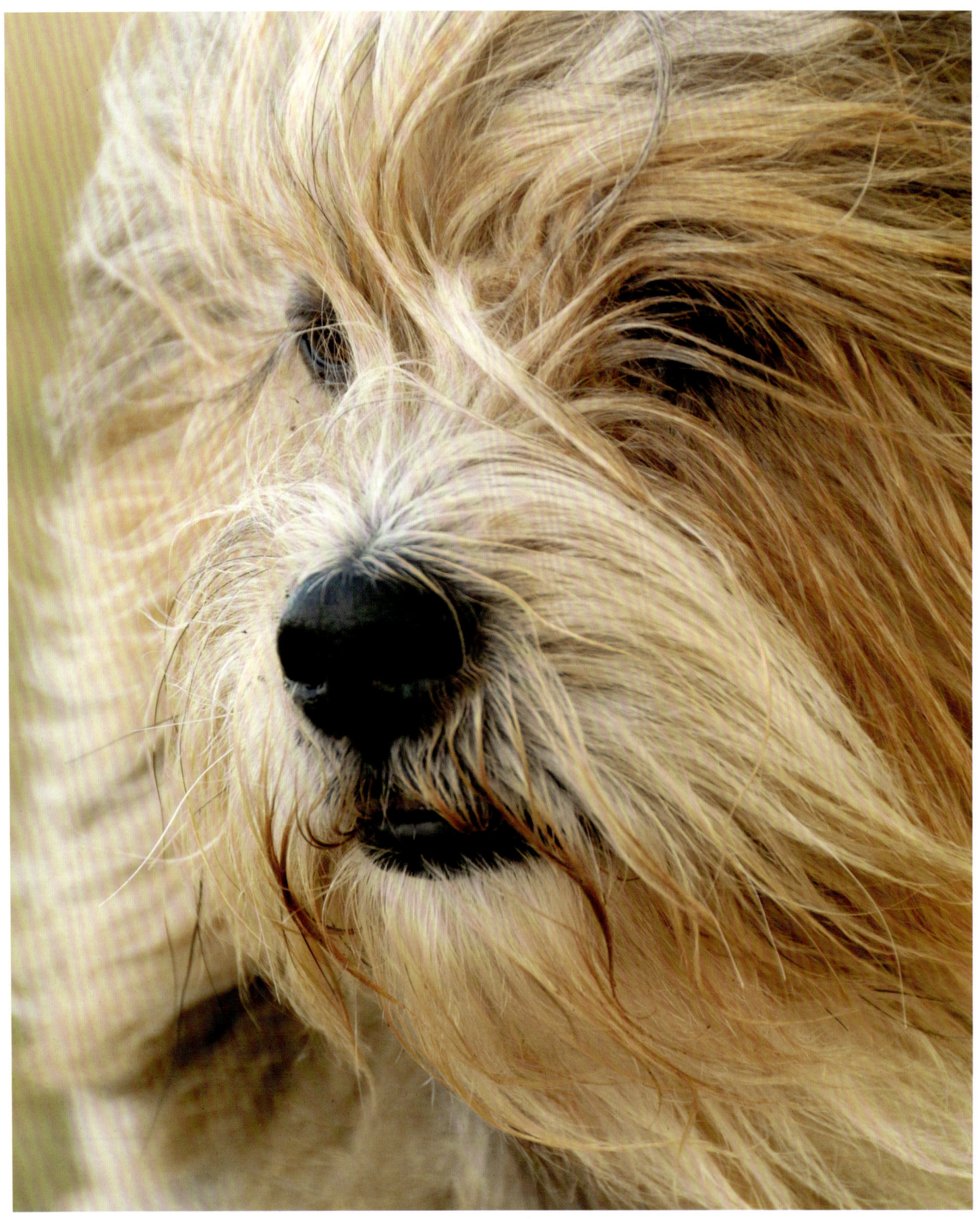

ABOVE:
Weather shield
The dog also has a long fringe of head hair that shields its eyes from snow, dust and the glare of the sun.

Tibetan Terrier

CHARACTERISTICS

Coat
Shaggy coat that comes in many colours and patterns
Height
36–41cm (14–16in)
Weight
8–14kg (18–31lb)
Lifespan
Around 10 years
Personality
Loving and active
Origin
Tibet

The name "terrier" is misleading here, as is this dog's superficial resemblance to Old English sheepdogs and other shaggy breeds. The Tibetan terrier was developed in isolation far up on the Tibetan Plateau and its closest relatives are the Tibetan spaniel (also not a spaniel) and the Lhasa apso lapdog. The Tibetan terrier was a herding dog used to watch over mountain goats, sheep and yaks. Its long, shaggy coat is there as a windbreak for the harsh Himalayan climate. The breed is also known for its large, flat feet that act like snowshoes that will not sink when padding over thick snow.

The Tibetan terrier is a lively, playful and affectionate dog that bonds strongly with its family. It was the breed of choice to accompany traders on long journeys away from Tibet. After the Chinese annexation of Tibet in 1951, the world centre of the Tibetan terrier shifted over the border into Nepal, where Tibetan culture was maintained in high isolated valleys. With that said, the Tibetan terrier is a rare breed that is hard to find but it makes a loving companion for the family that can make space for it.

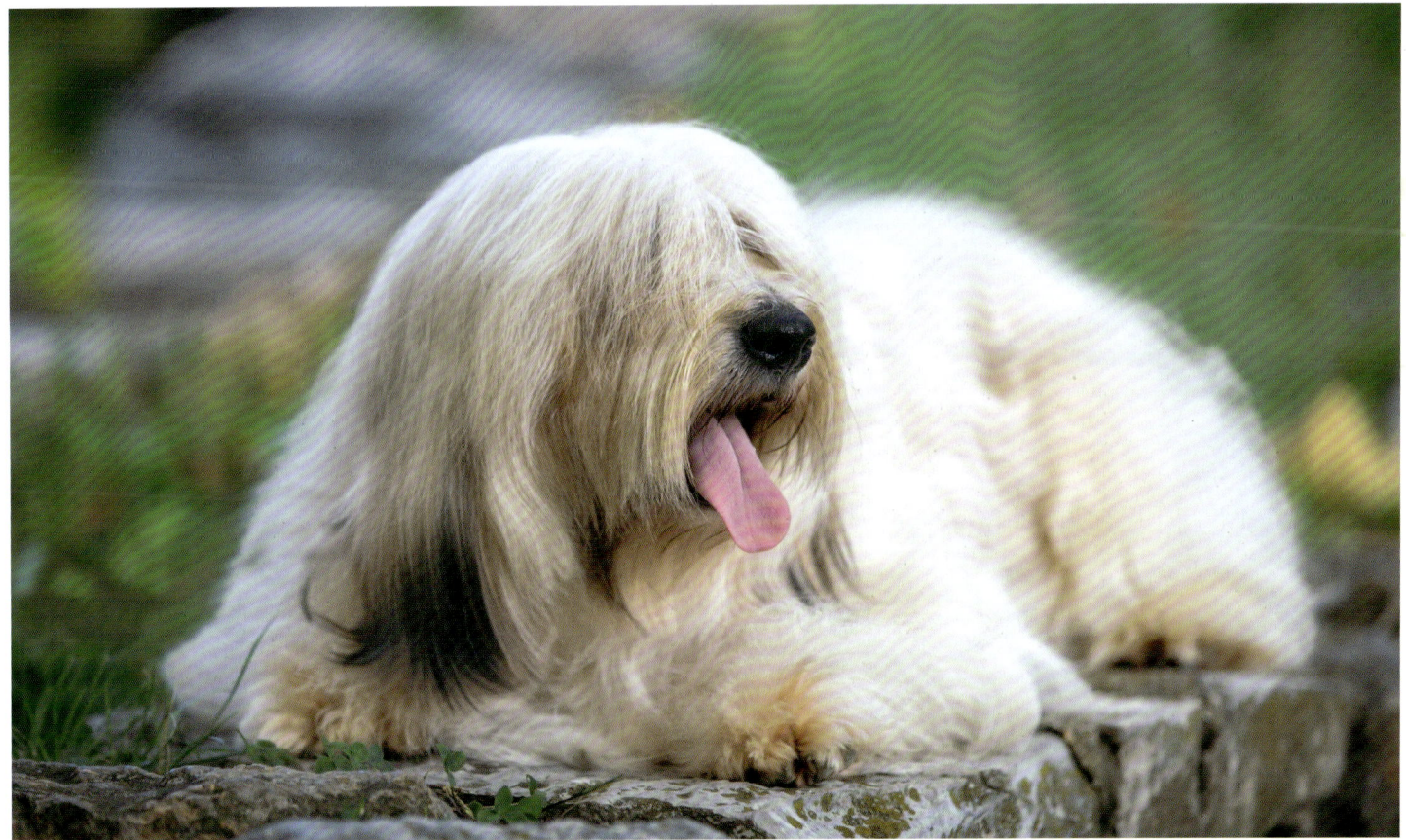

ABOVE:
Chilling out
The breed is intelligent and adaptable but is best suited to life in a cold climate.

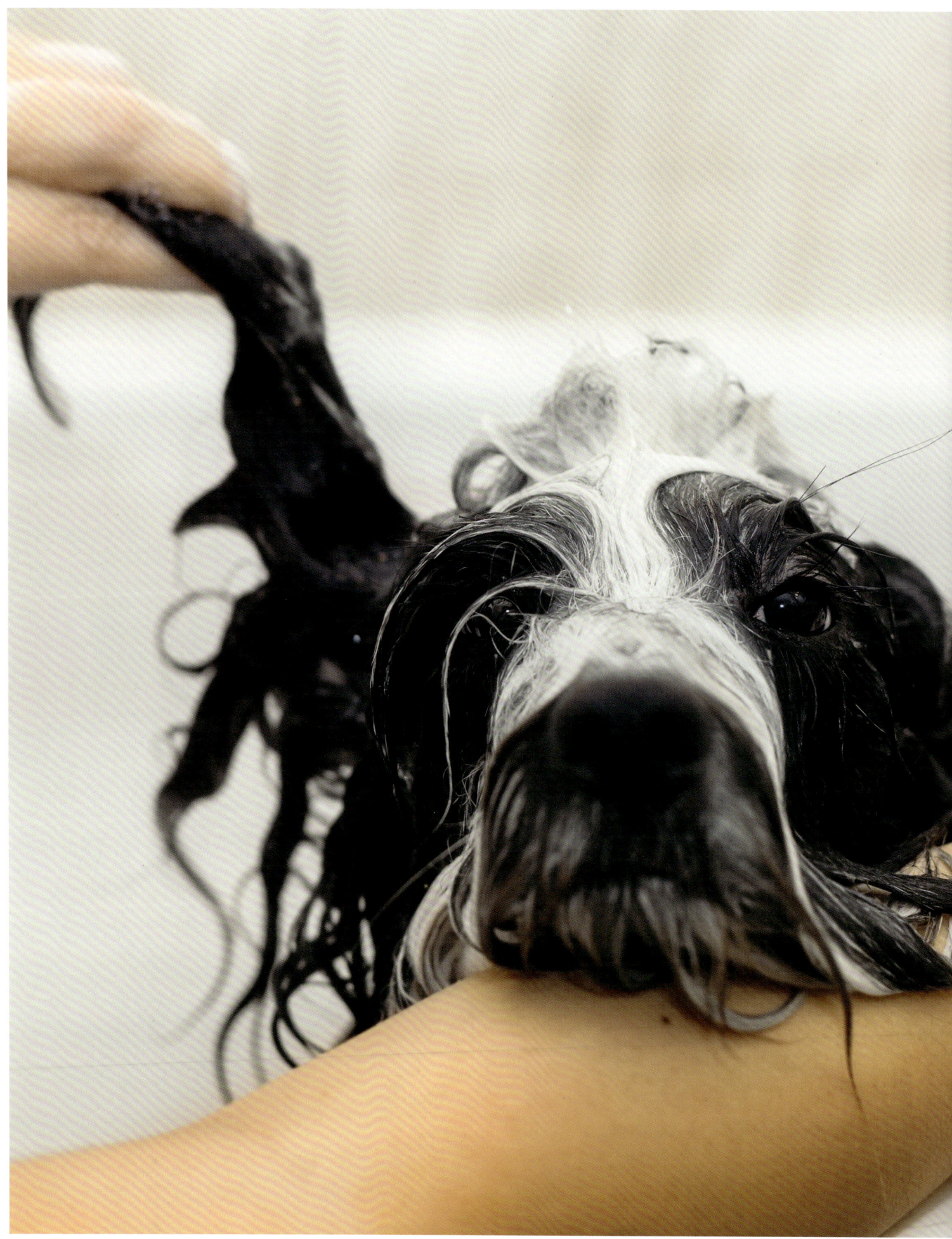

COMPANION DOGS

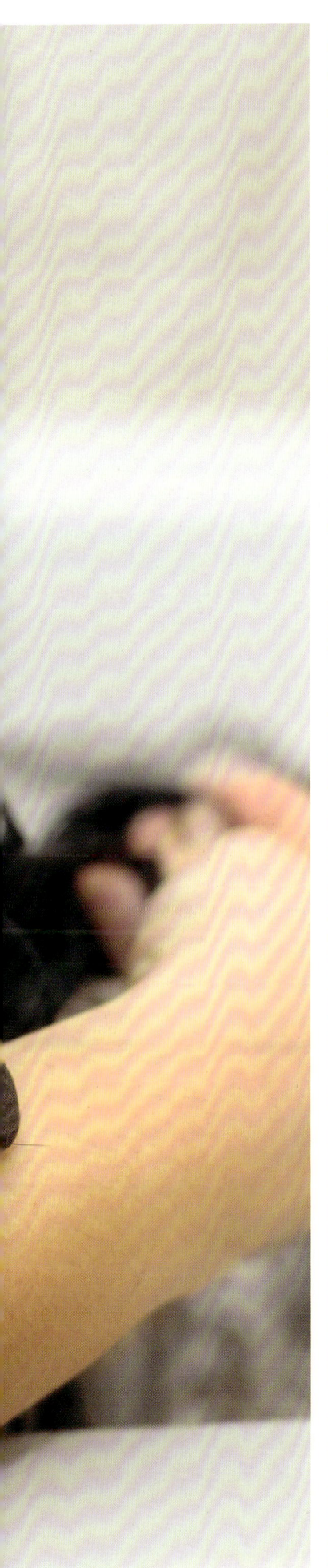
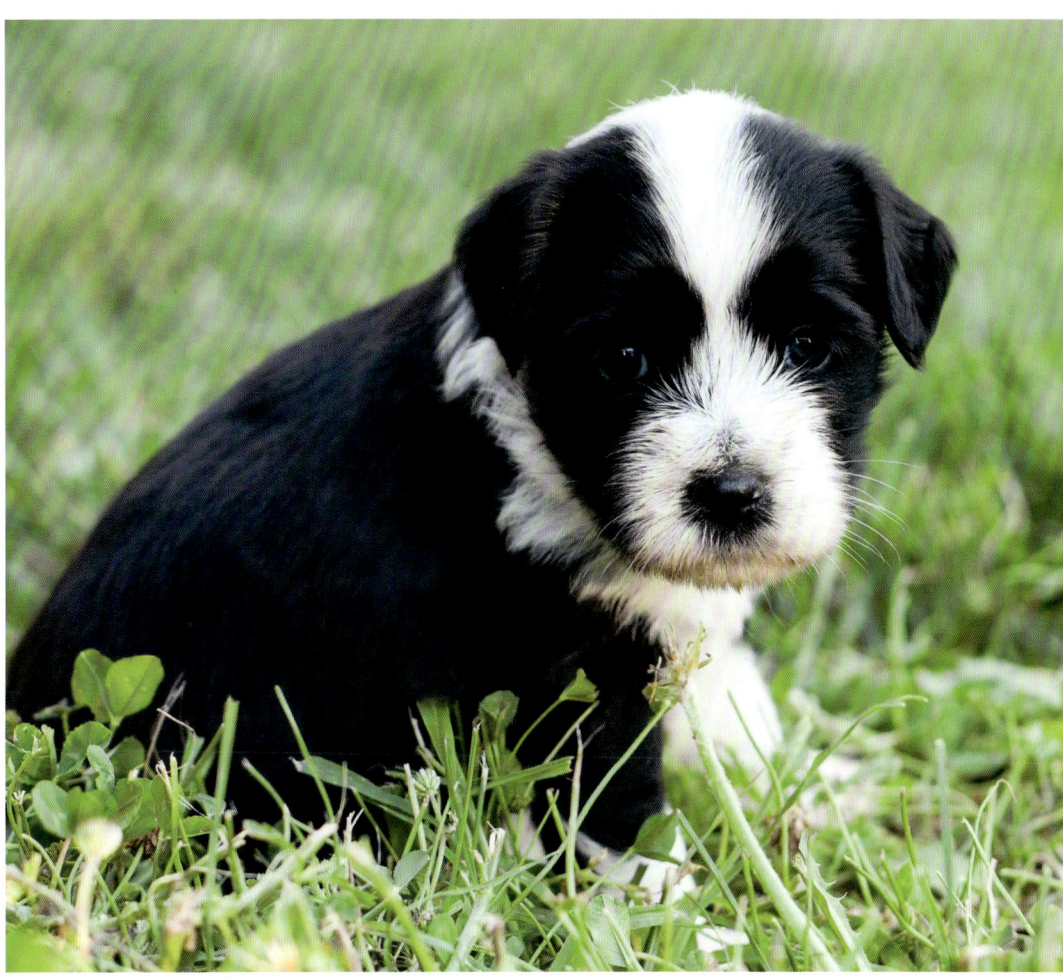
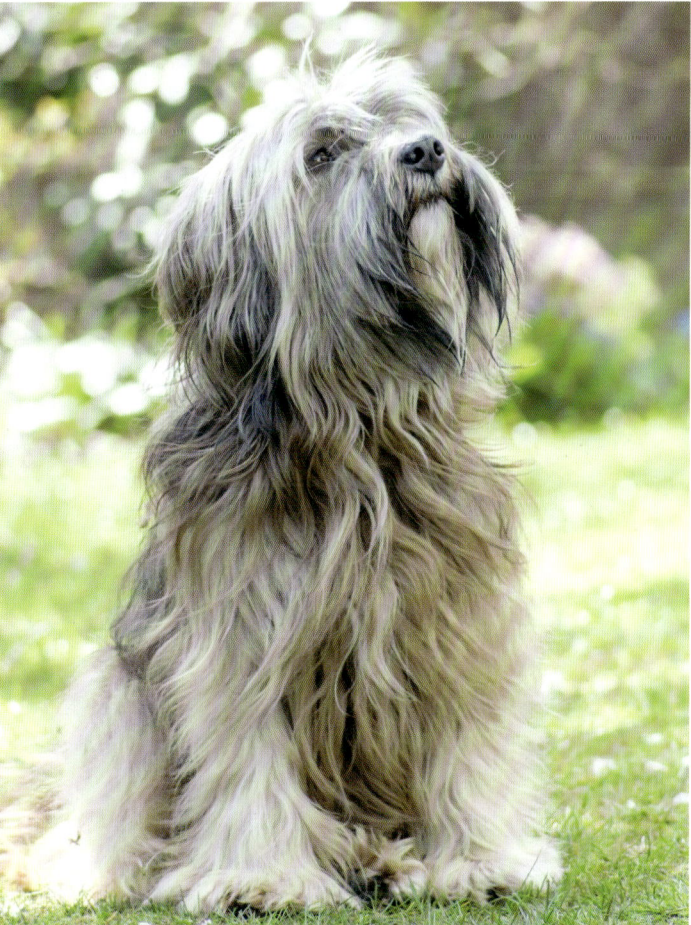

ALL PHOTOGRAPHS:
Happy pup
This breed are fun-loving outgoing dogs while at the same time being trustworthy and calm in a family environment.

COMPANION DOGS

Welsh Terrier

CHARACTERISTICS

Coat
Hard and wiry with a distinctive black and tan colouring
Height
Up to 39cm (15in)
Weight
9–10kg (20–22lb)
Lifespan
9–15 years
Personality
Friendly and smart
Origin
Wales

Larger than most terriers, the Welsh breed was developed to take on larger more dangerous enemies, such as badgers and otters. Both these predators would not be classed as vermin today by most of the residents of post-industrial Wales but they have some fighting ability that needed to be matched by the Welsh terrier. Only the Airedale terrier is consistently larger.

The Welsh terrier is one of the oldest and purest of the British terrier breeds, and it has a distinctive black and tan coat that is hard and wiry. The progenitor of the breed is thought to be the black and tan terrier, a vigorous ancient breed that was once widespread across Britain. The Welsh terrier is a lively and intelligent dog and so needs an outlet for being active and having fun. It is usually friendly with people and other dogs, but it has a strong prey drive and a stubborn streak so is best served by a fenced area that it can exercise in when not out, leashed, on a walk. If that is achieved then the breed makes a more winning and amenable house dog than the smaller more voluble terriers.

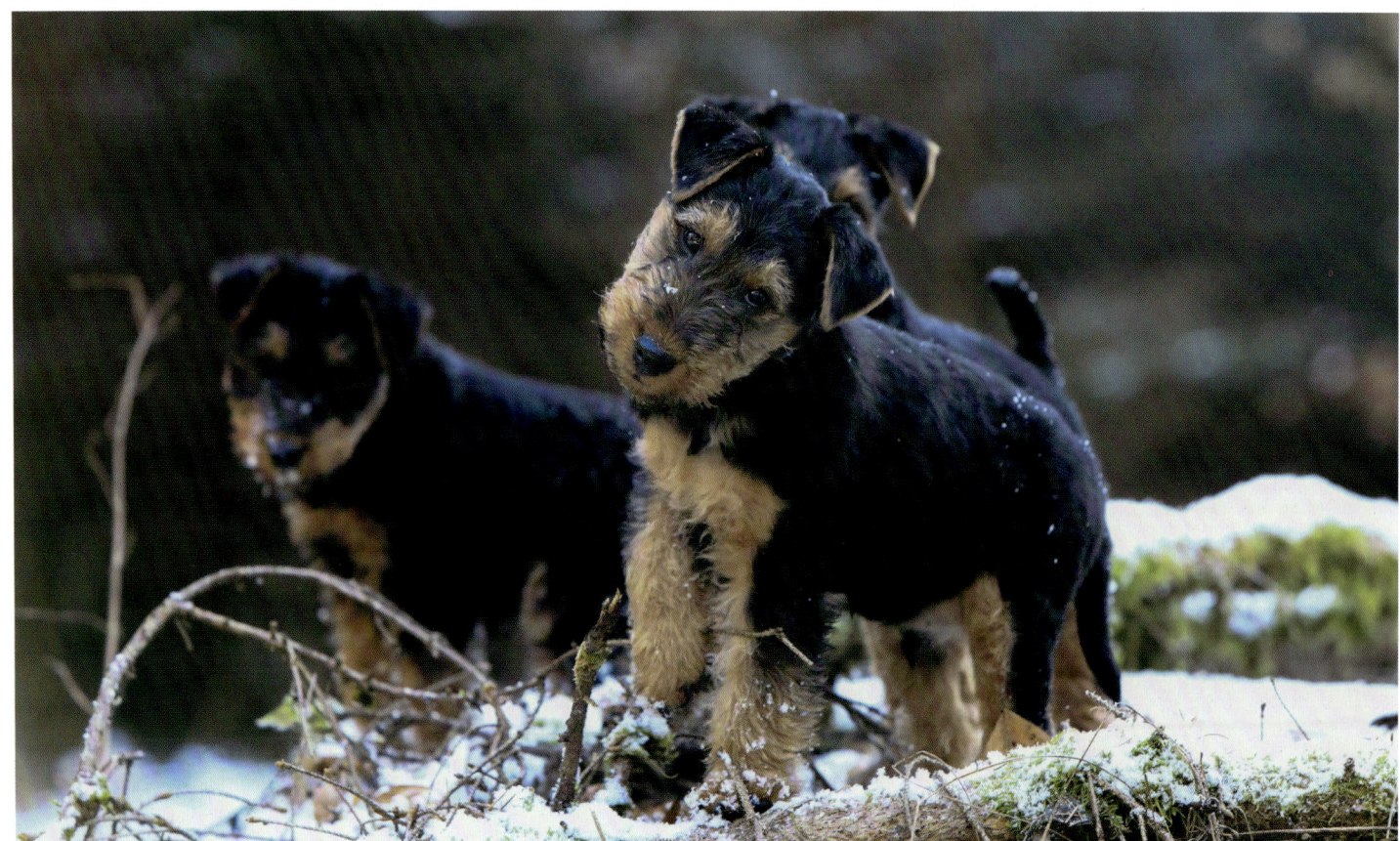

ABOVE:
Bright future
These puppies will grow up into good companions for active owners if given consistent training and supervision.

COMPANION DOGS

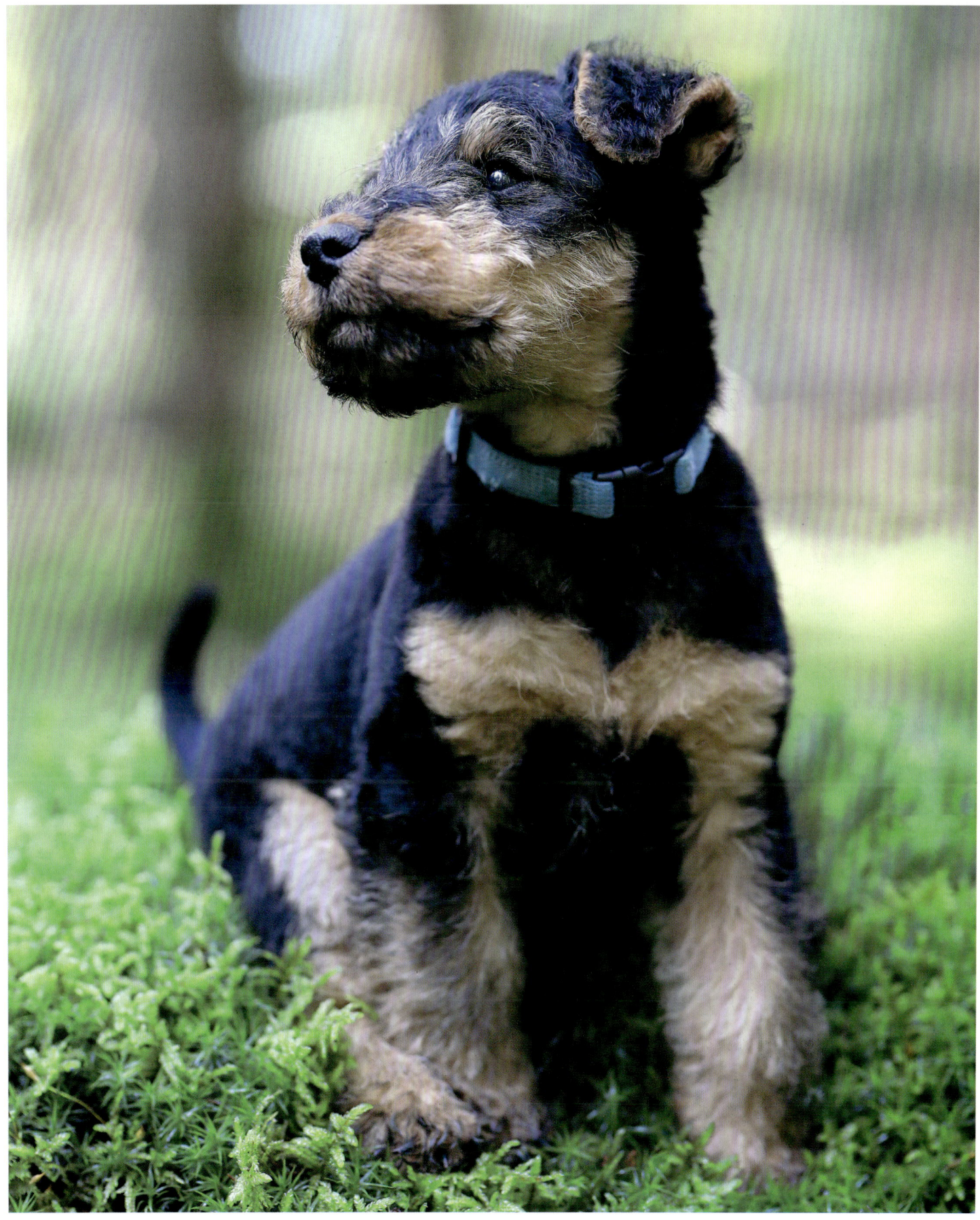

ABOVE:
What next?
The terrier needs plenty of exercise and mental stimulation to prevent boredom.

COMPANION DOGS

Care and attention
Without adequate attention and care from their owners, this breed has a tendancy for frustration which often results in an urge to dig.

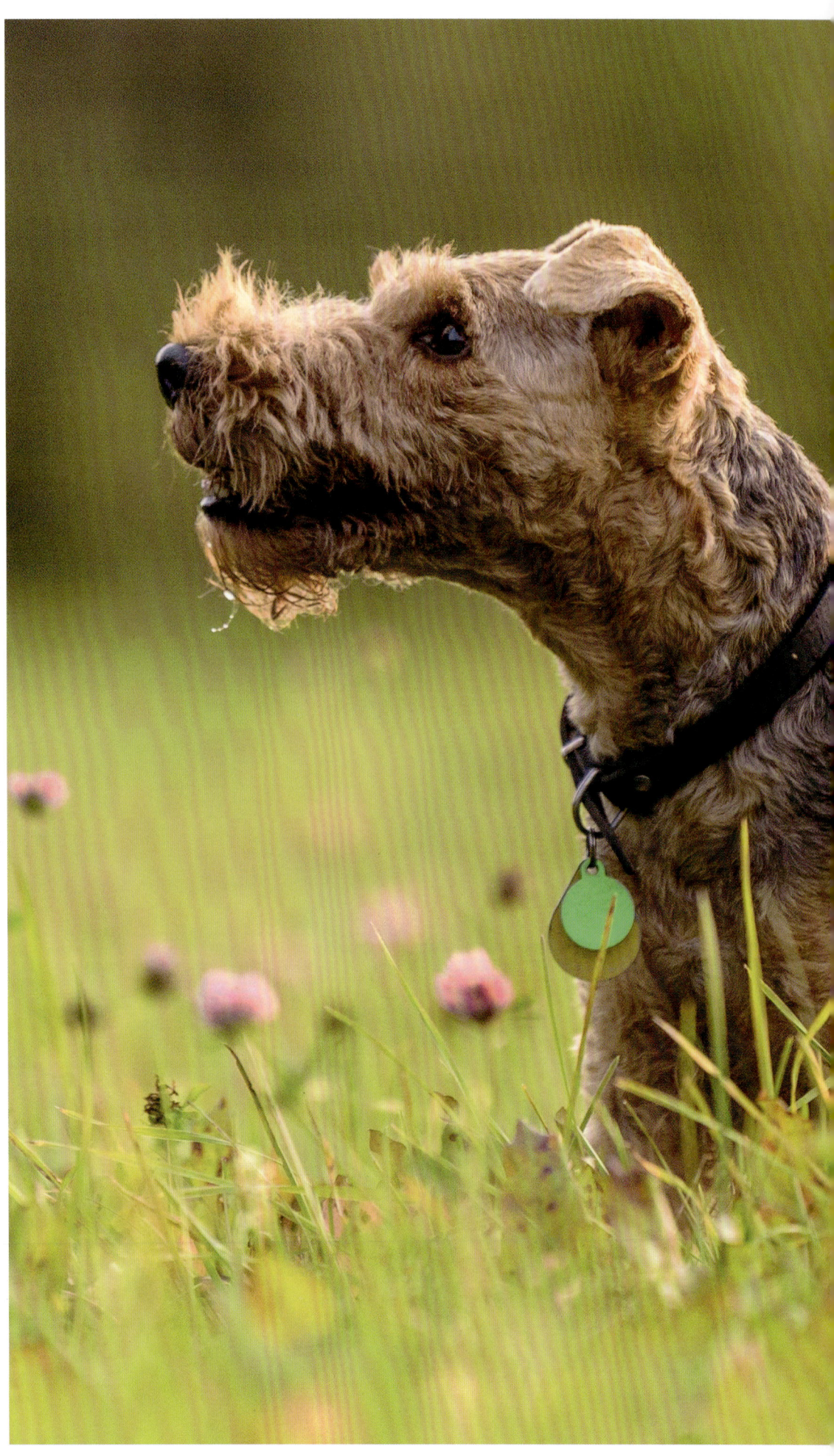

COMPANION DOGS

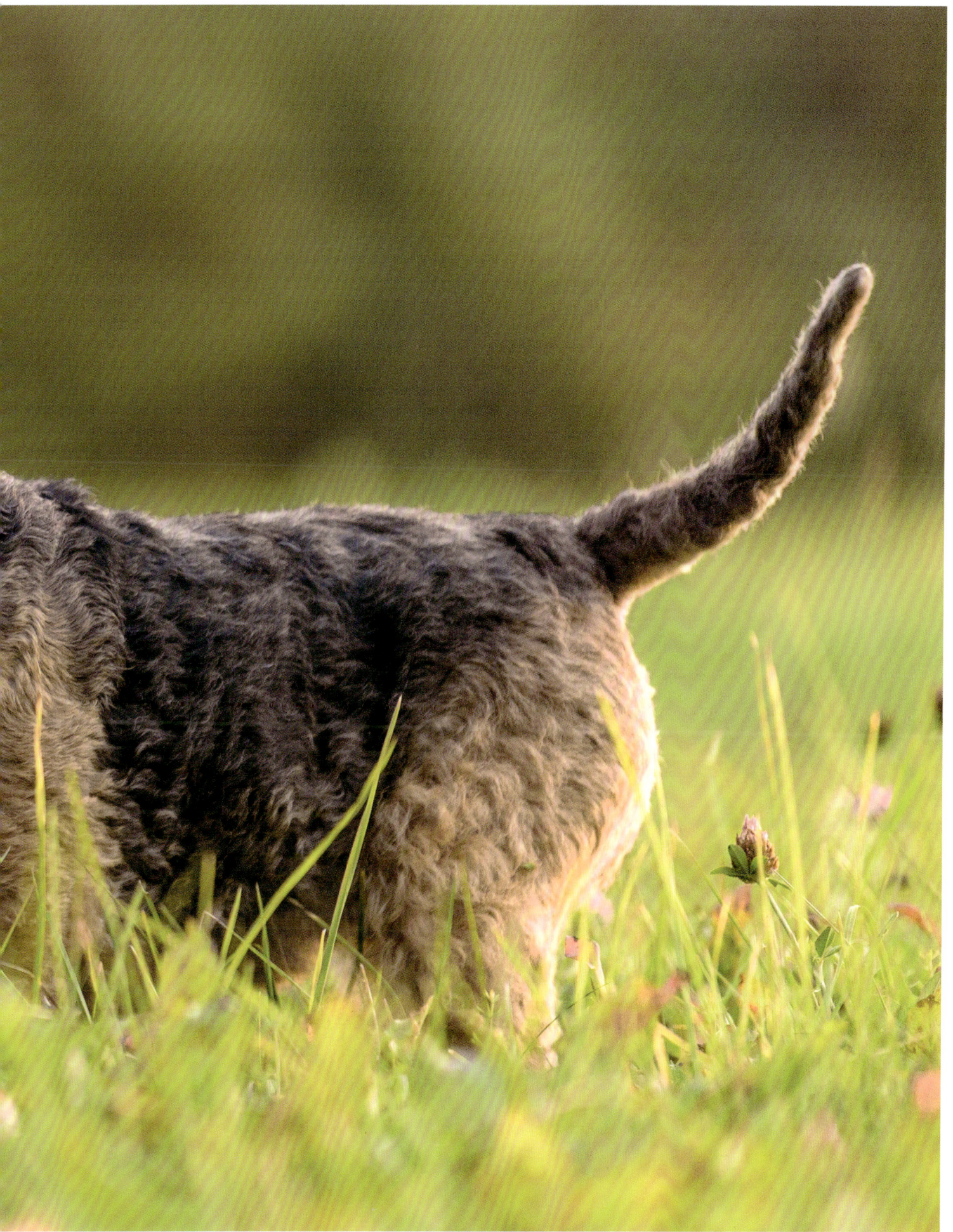

COMPANION DOGS

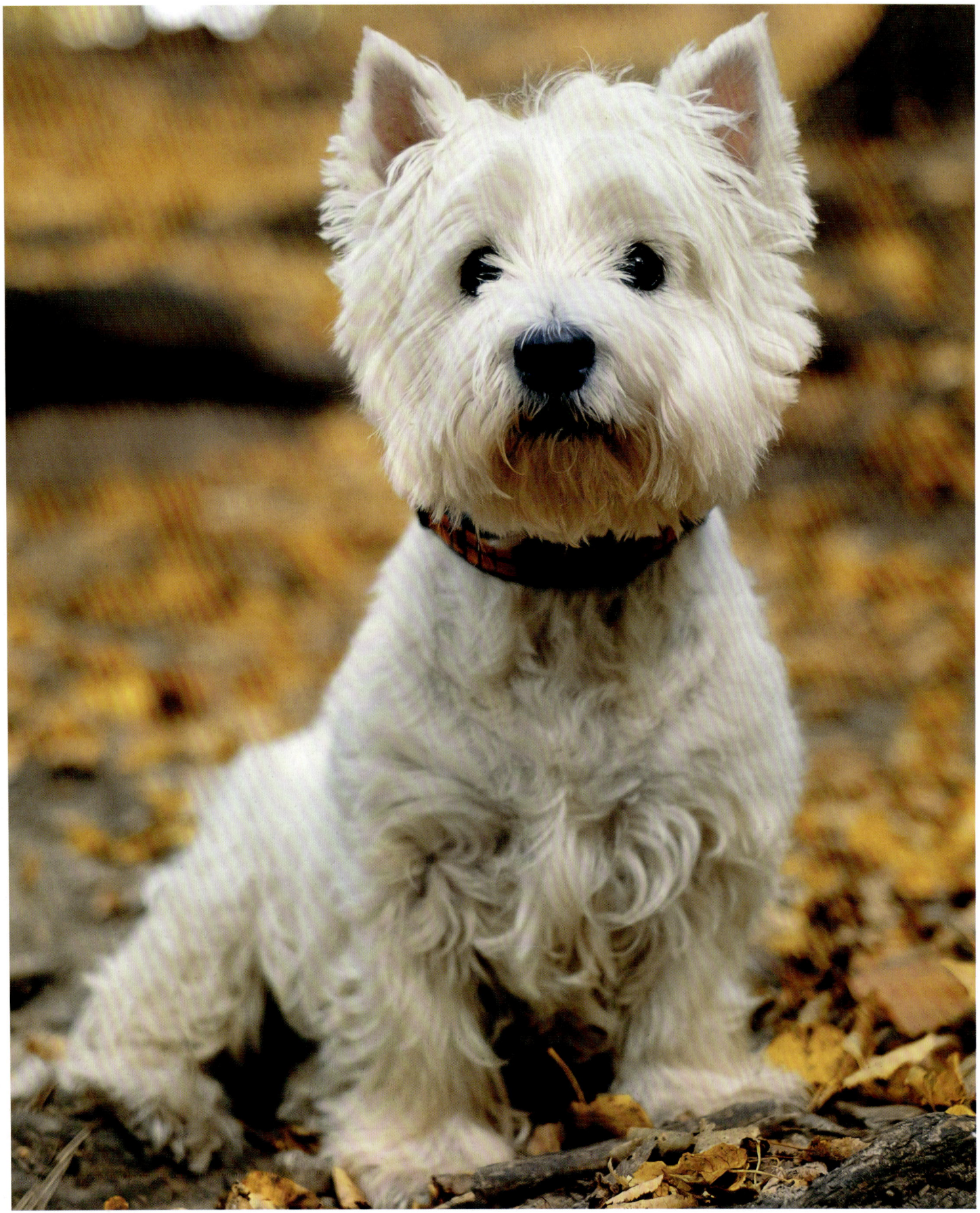

ABOVE:
Everyone's favourite
The West Highland white terrier, also known as the westie, has a winning temperament that suits most people.

West Highland White Terrier

CHARACTERISTICS

Coat
Double coat that is always white
Height
25–28cm (10–11in)
Weight
7–10kg (15–22lb)
Lifespan
9–15 years
Personality
Alert and sociable
Origin
Scotland

The term terrier means "earth dog". These little dogs were developed for working down and dirty among the fallen leaves and undergrowth to seek and destroy rats—even chasing them underground if necessary. The West Highland white terrier, or westie for short, is the chief exterminator of the rugged mountains of northwestern Scotland—a beautiful, denuded land so steeped in the national identity that it is frequently chosen to represent the rest of the country. The westie plays its part here as well.

The westie has longer legs than other Scottish terriers, and a distinctive, plush white harsh coat that makes it stand out among the rough and tough terrier breeds. The dog has a soft white undercoat that makes it ideal for cold and wet conditions. The westie is an active breed. It is very social because in its original pest control work it would often have been sent out to hunt in small packs. That trait is combined with a high prey drive so the alert little dog is best kept on a leash away from home. In common with other terriers, the westie might not fully appreciate its true size and so it will attempt to dominate larger dogs if not checked.

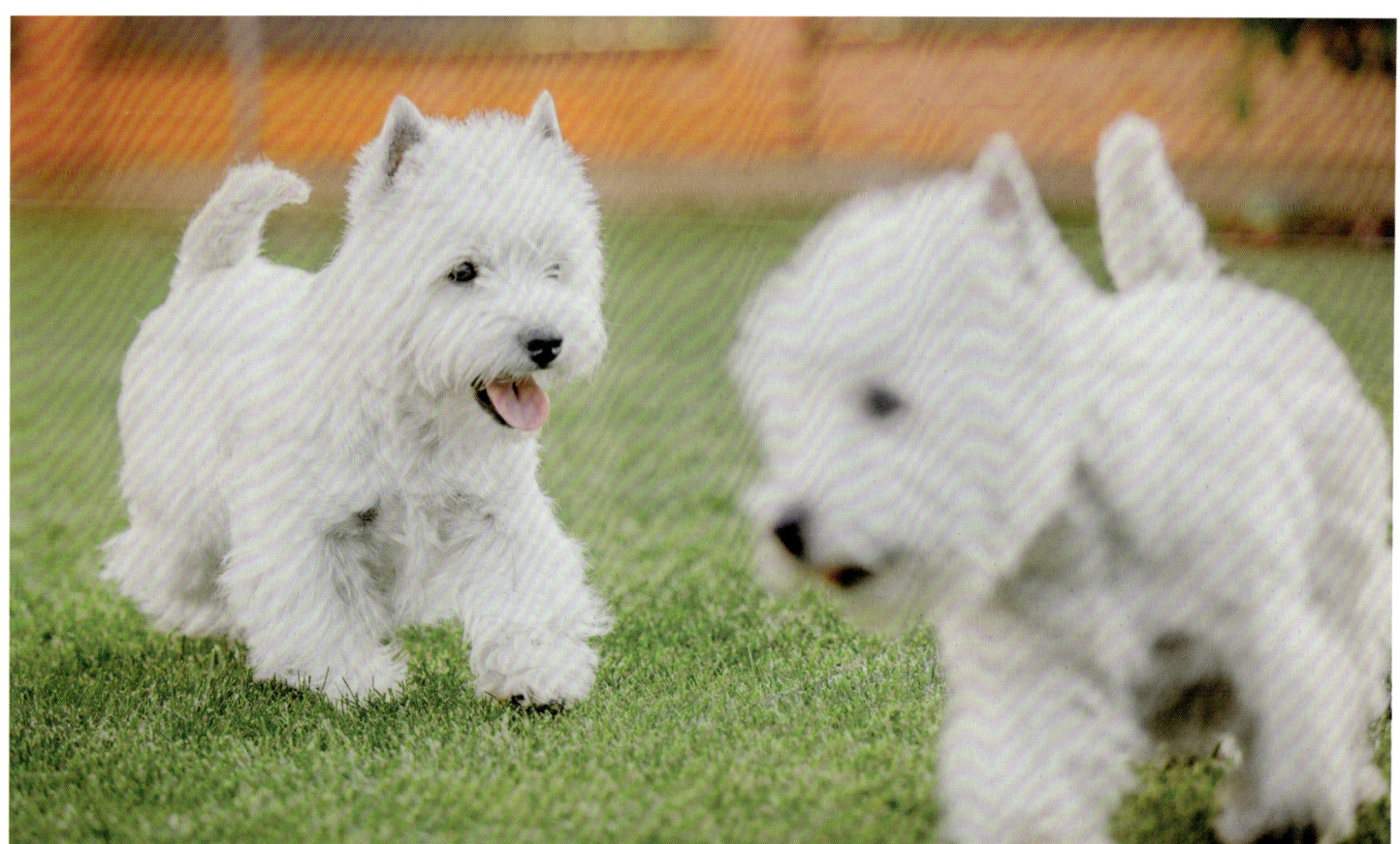

ABOVE:
Gently does it
The breed is intelligent, quick to learn and can be good with children. However, the dog does not always tolerate rough handling.

Yorkshire Terrier

Known as the yorkie, this tiny little dog is famed for having a big opinion of itself. Coupled with the good looks of a long, silky coat, the Yorkshire terrier has long been one of the more popular lapdog breeds. In Victorian England, elegant ladies of means would have a well-kept, elegant yorkie on their lap, but the breed's original inception was more working class, among the scraps of wool and cotton mills. Scottish weavers migrating into Yorkshire to work at the vast purpose-built factories of the early Industrial Revolution brought with them terriers to keep the rats down. Various breeds were used including Dandie Dinmont, a small border breed. The result was a tough little dog—some of the smallest of all breeds—that was well suited to its new life in Yorkshire, a land of tough people. It was a common joke that the weavers created their dogs' lush silken coats on their looms. The yorkie may not appear to get the joke. It can be frequently vocal and protective of its owners.

CHARACTERISTICS

Coat
Silky and long and usually black and tan, but other colours are possible

Height
20–23cm (8–9in)

Weight
Up to 3kg (7lb)

Lifespan
12–15 years

Personality
Feisty and fun

Origin
England

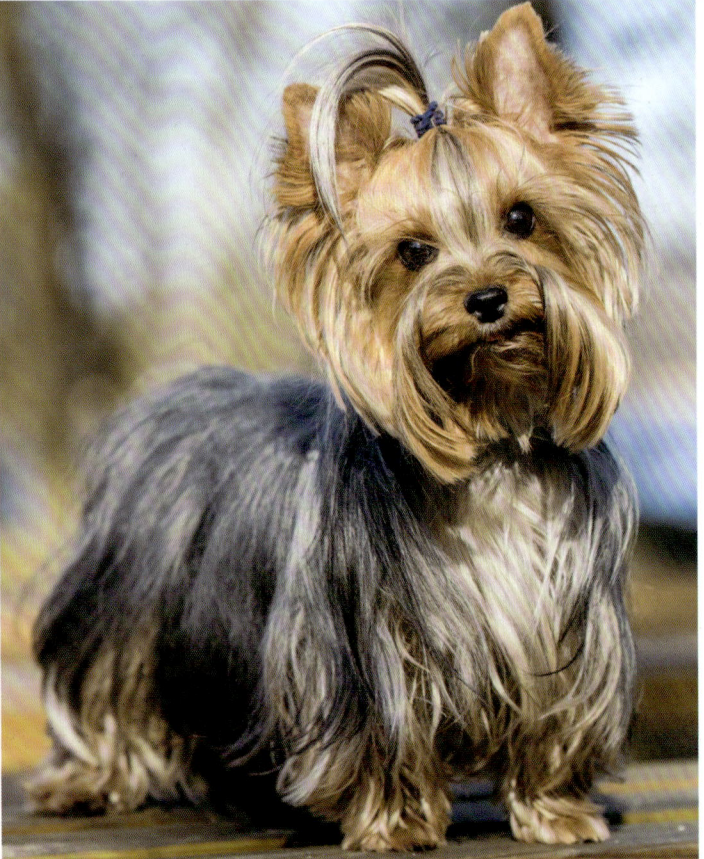

ABOVE:
Bright spark
A yorkie is a lively, confident and intelligent dog that loves to play and chase.

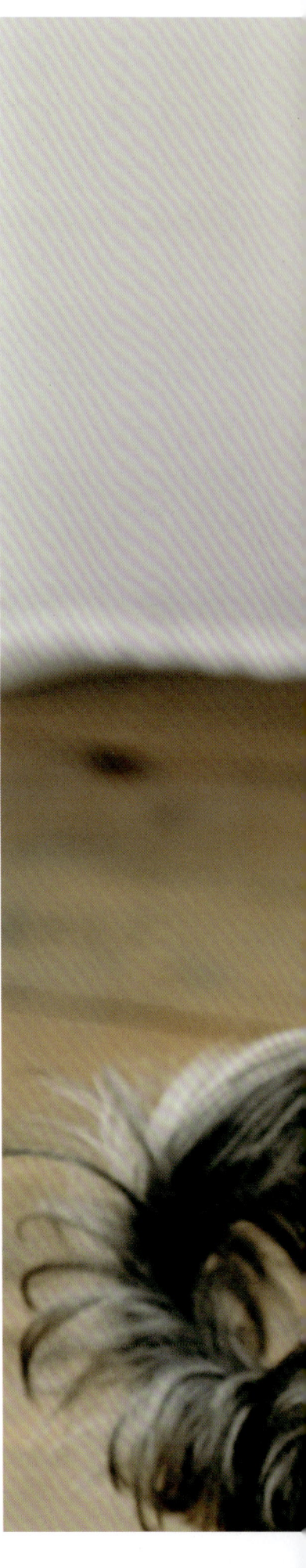

RIGHT:
Grooming
The Yorkshire terrier needs daily grooming and exercise to keep it healthy and happy.

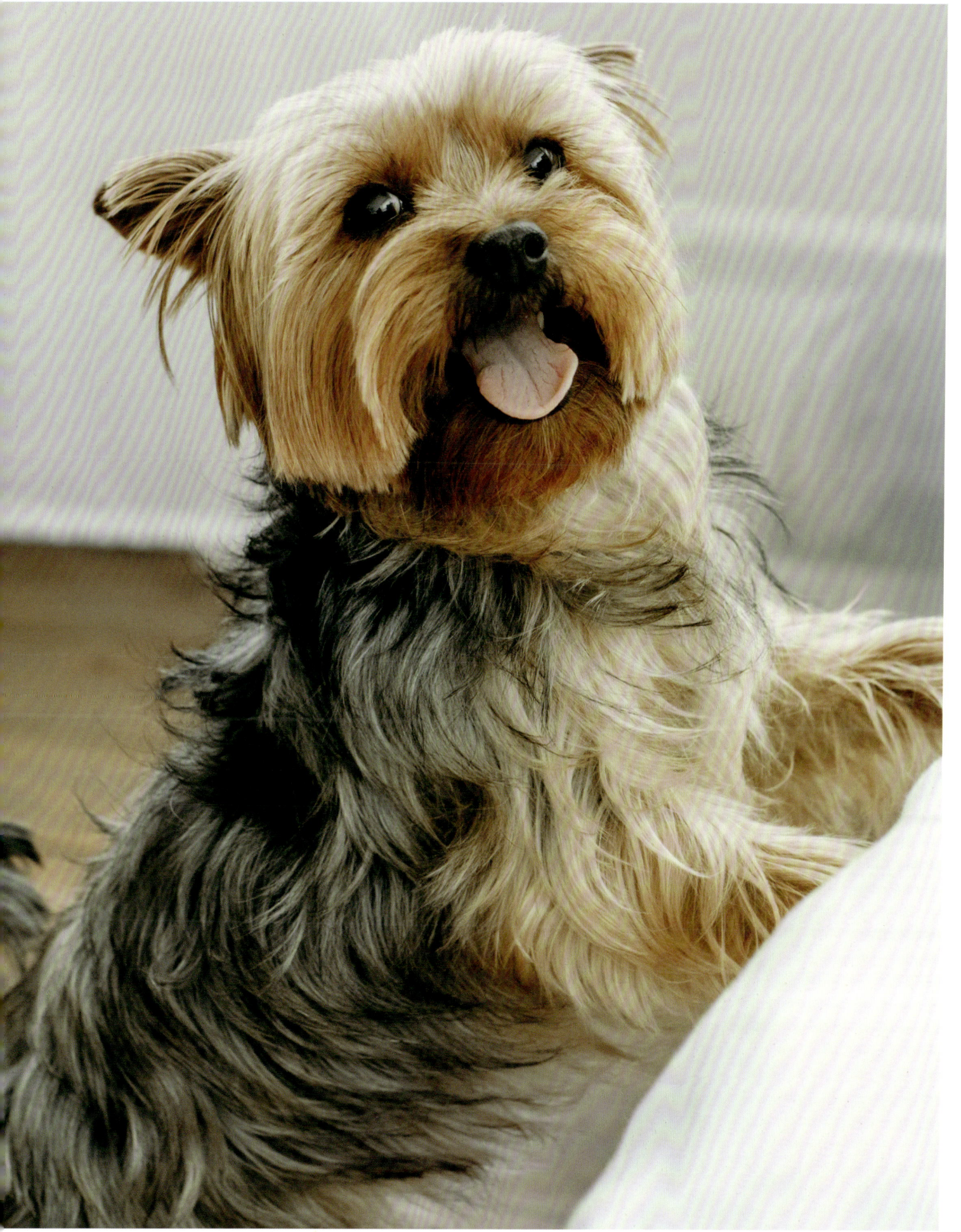

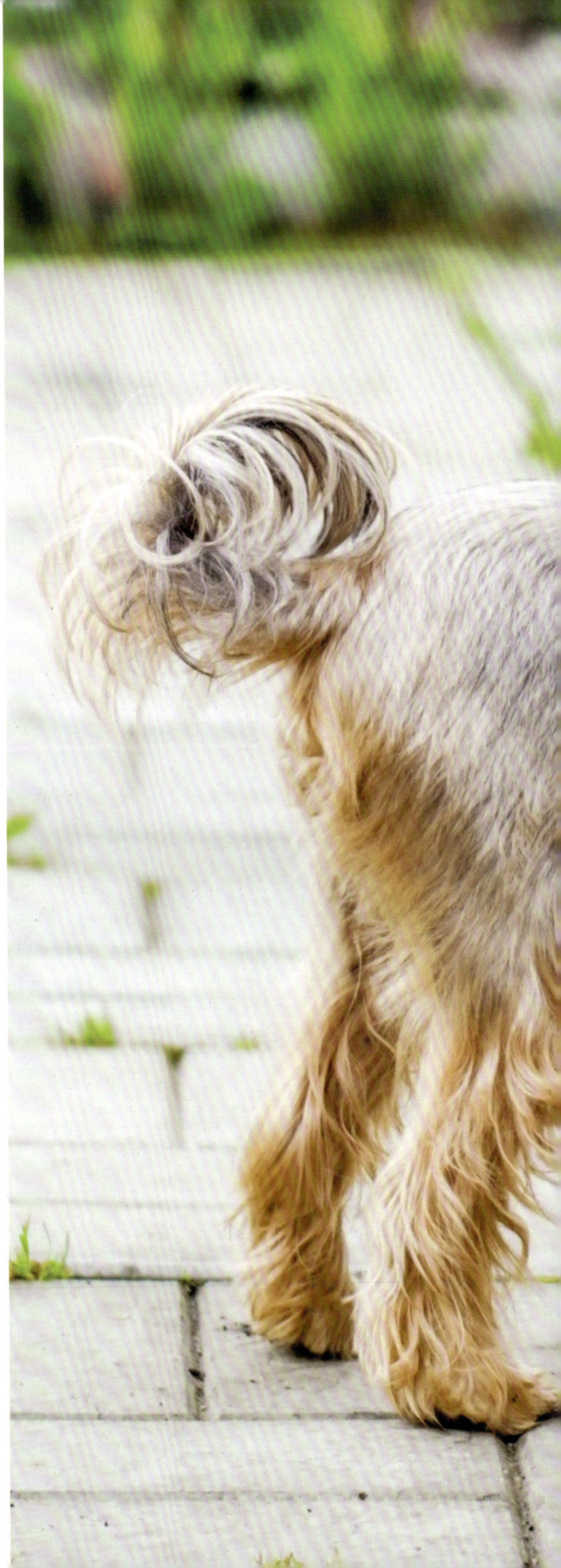

COMPANION DOGS

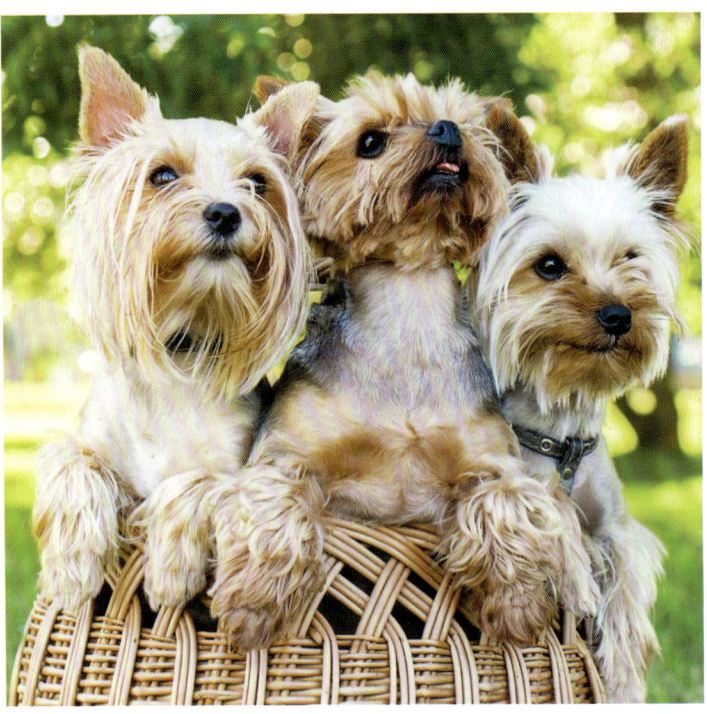

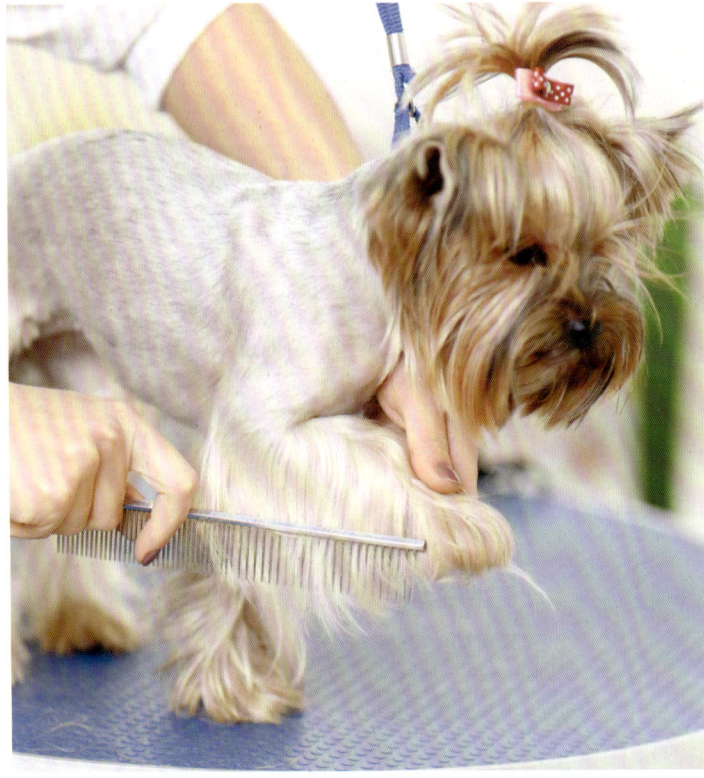

ALL PHOTOGRAPHS:
Yorkshire terrier
With plenty of valuable time and dedication, this loving breed will give back all that care and attention in love and affection.

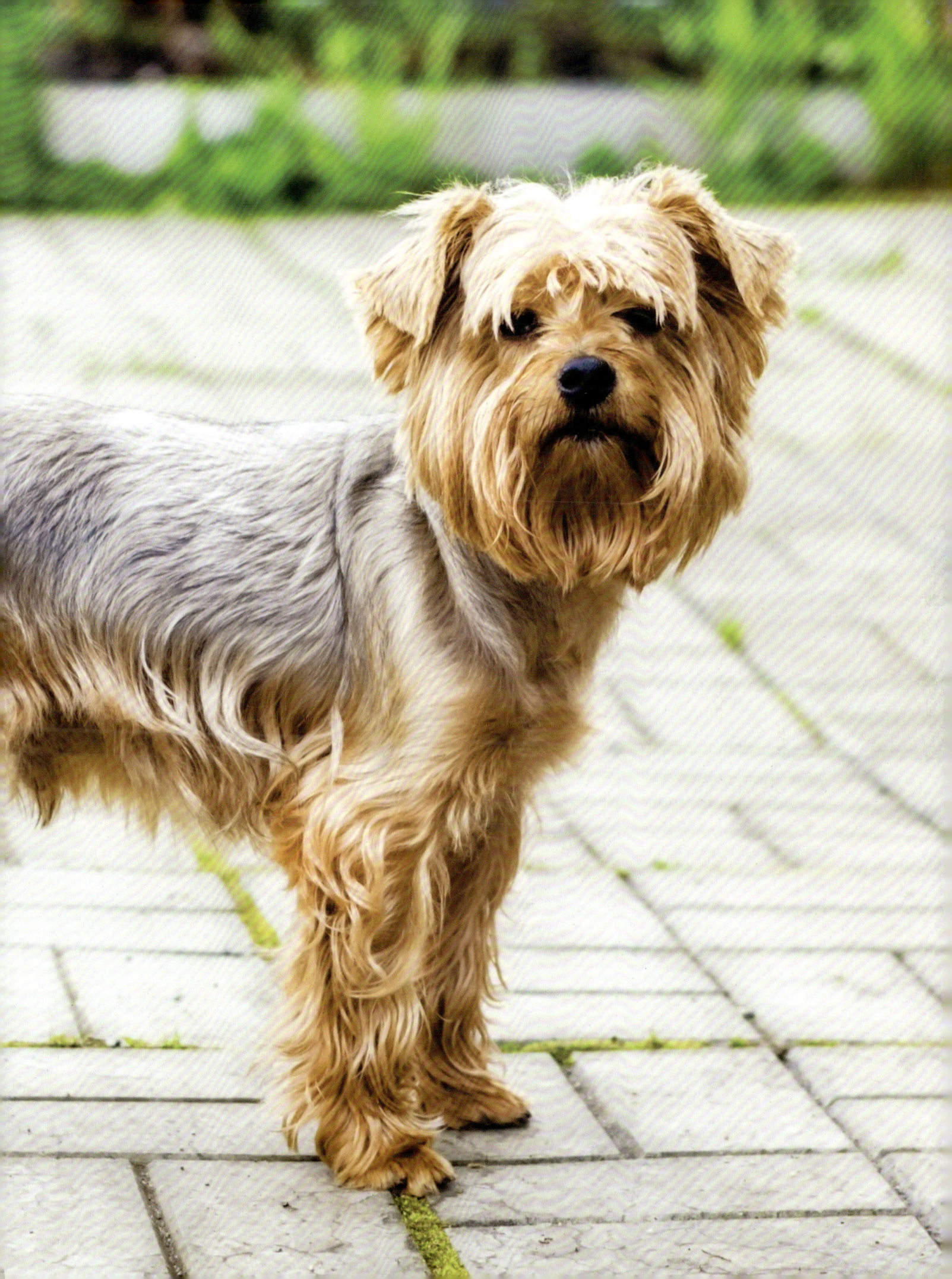

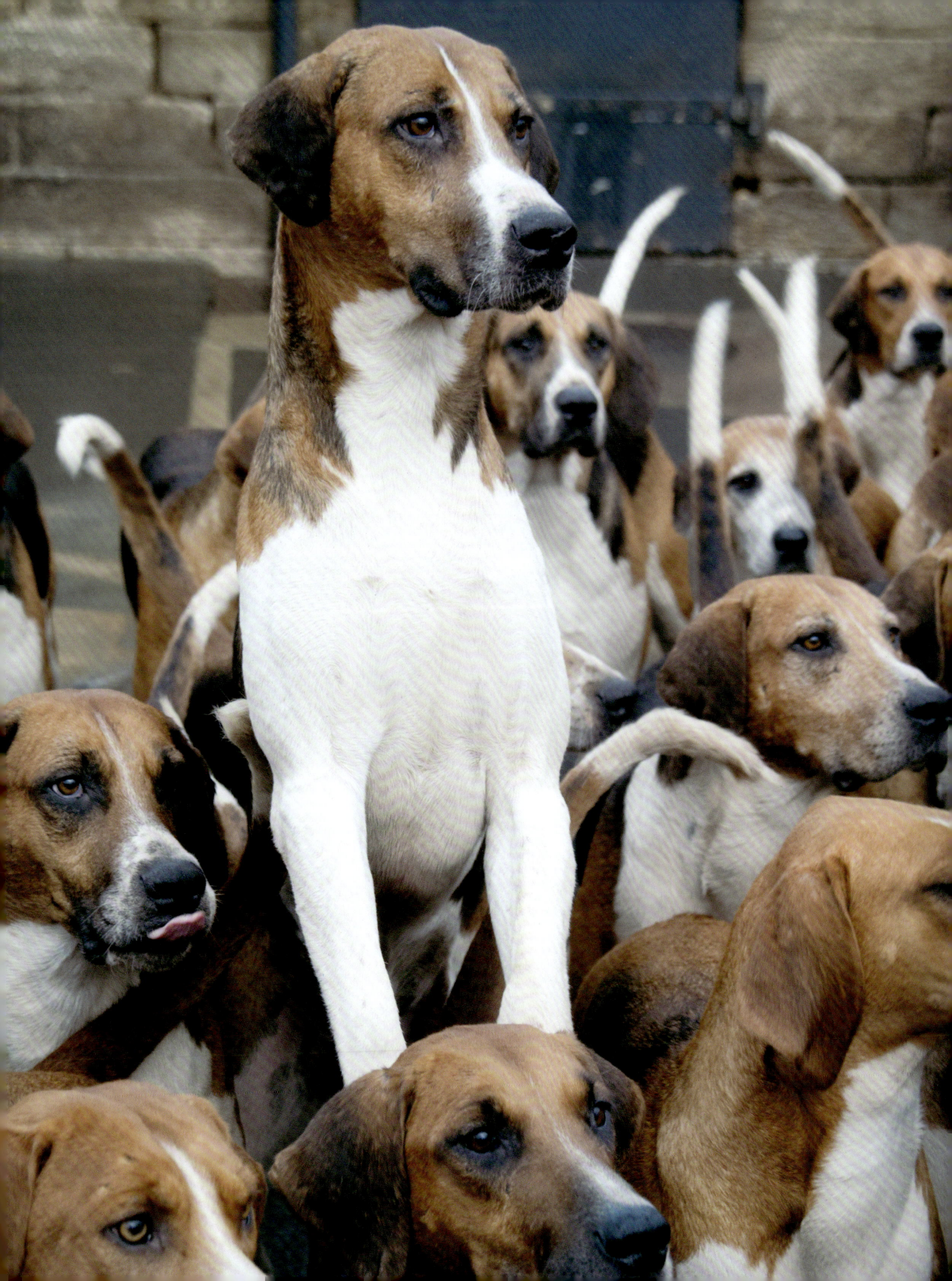

Hunting Dogs

We can never forget that dogs are hunters, descended from the most widespread, successful and adaptable hunting animal that has ever lived. Since we humans and dogs agreed to live together, we have exploited each other in the hunt for more food. The dog's skill is to track prey and pursue it for as long as it takes. The human's job is then to step in and kill the creature, and then all parties get their rewards. Over the centuries, hunting dogs have been divided into scenthounds that track quarry with a powerful sense of smell, and sighthounds that lock eyes on a target and run and run after them at great speed without let-up. Within those groups there are gundogs, which are bred as assistants that locate prey, flush it into the open and then retrieve any kills. All hunting dogs have been bred for intelligence, agility and obedience, and so can make the transition to family life very well.

OPPOSITE:
English foxhounds
A pack of hounds prepare for the pursuit of a hunt, just as their wolf descendants would have done. Hunting with hounds like this is a controversial activity. It is banned in some countries but embraced in others.

HUNTING DOGS

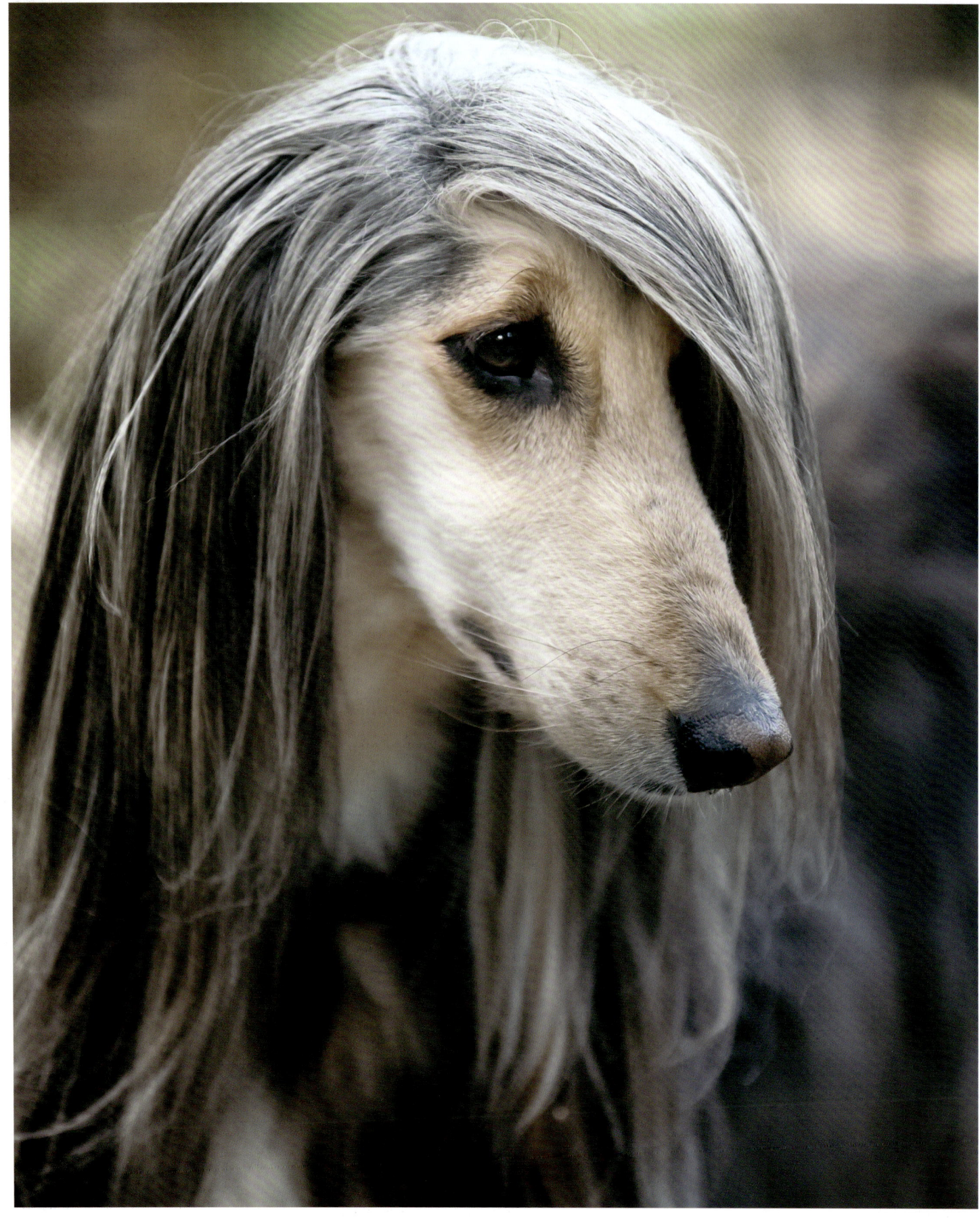

ABOVE:
Working it
As one might expect, good-looking hounds such as these require a lot of grooming to keep the coat tangle-free.

Afghan Hound

CHARACTERISTICS

Coat
A very long and silky coat and a tail with a ring curl at the tip. Can be any colour but tends to be tan, red or gold

Height
63–74cm (25–29in)

Weight
23–29kg (50–64lb)

Lifespan
12–14 years

Personality
Aloof and affectionate

Origin
Afghanistan

According to some authorities, the Afghan hound is the oldest dog breed of all, predating written history. (Legend has it that Noah loaded Afghans aboard the Ark!) Despite the name, this South Asian breed's origins are not clear, but are thought to be somewhere in the cold mountains of what is now India, Pakistan or Afghanistan.

The silken-coated dog is a fleet-footed sighthound. It was used to chase down prey such as deer and goats, and fight off the menace of wolves. The Afghan hound was the dog of choice among the tribal chieftains of its rugged homeland. This caught the eye of British military men scouting the farthest reaches of the Raj in the late 19th century, and the dogs soon became a favourite among the British aristocracy. After that the craze spread. Both Zeppo Marx and Pablo Picasso had eye-catching Afghans.

The hound is a loyal companion and can be playful. However, as is often the case for primitive breeds built for wild country, these dogs are not very easy to train and have a stubbornly independent streak. The dog loves to chase and must be kept on a leash when away from home, or left to exercise in a fenced area.

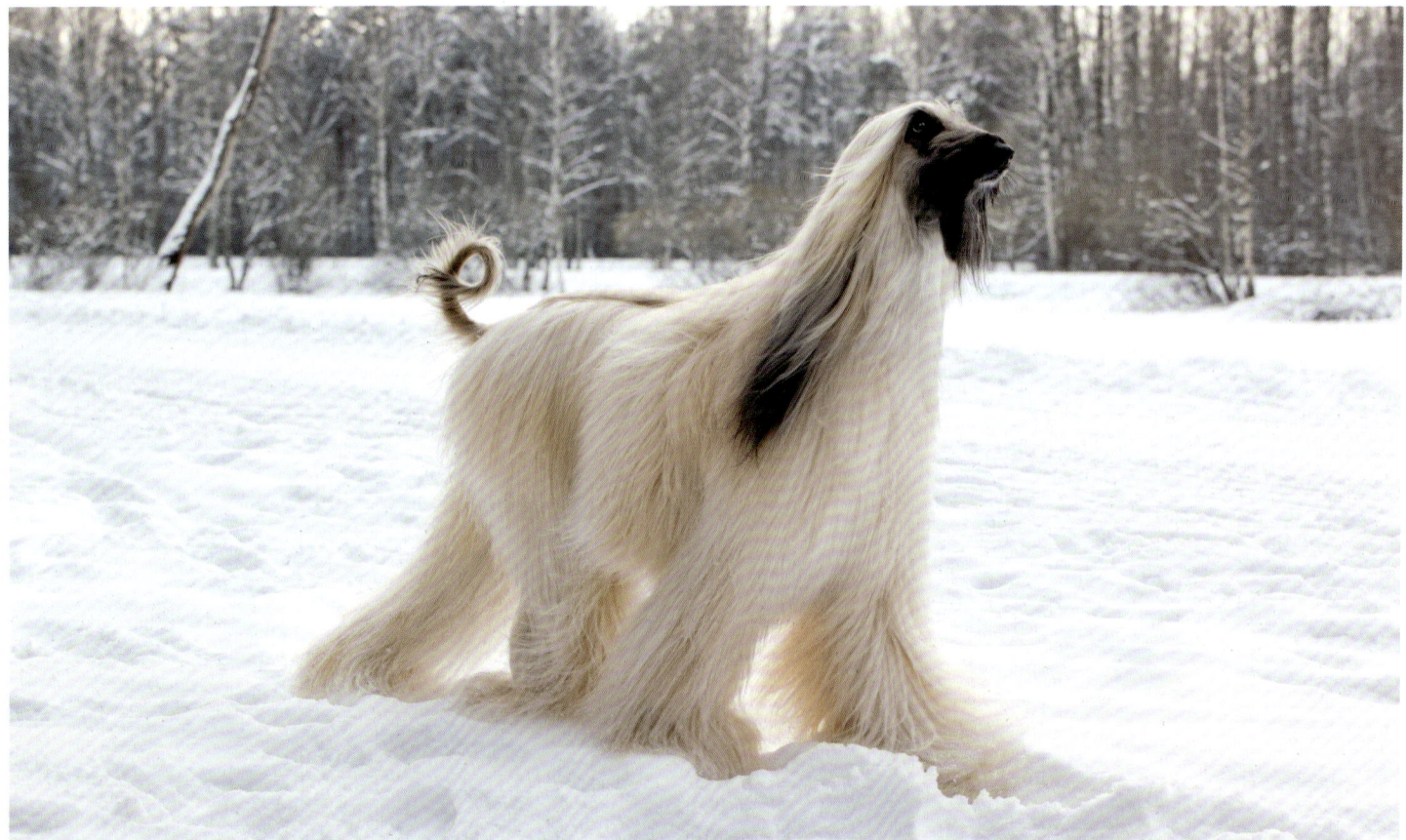

ABOVE:
Eye catching
The hound retains a noble appearance, tall and proud but moving well so its luxurious coat shimmies rhythmically.

HUNTING DOGS

Hunting dog
This dog is a sight hound breed that once caught hares and goats and saw off attacks from snow leopards and wolves.

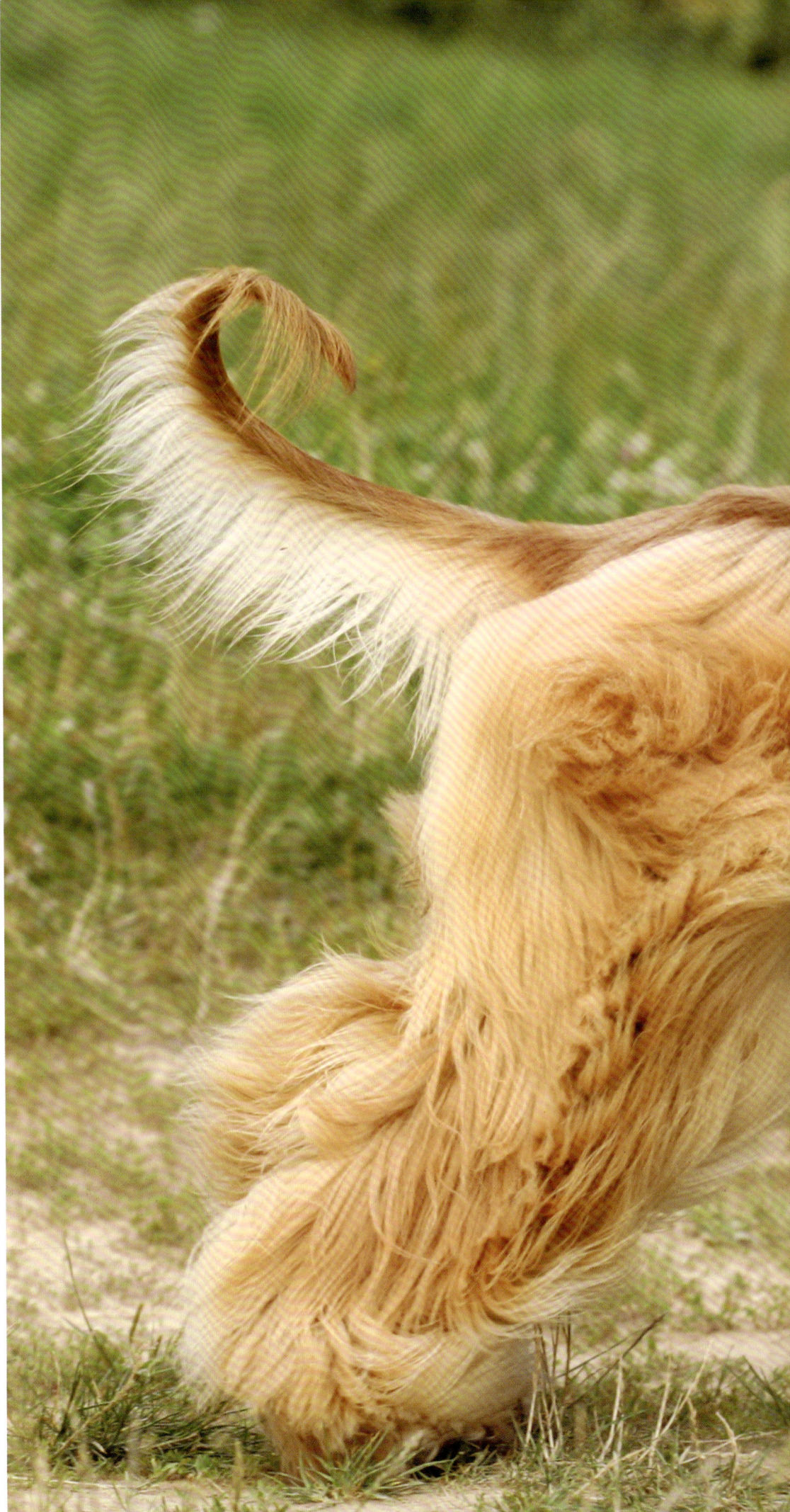

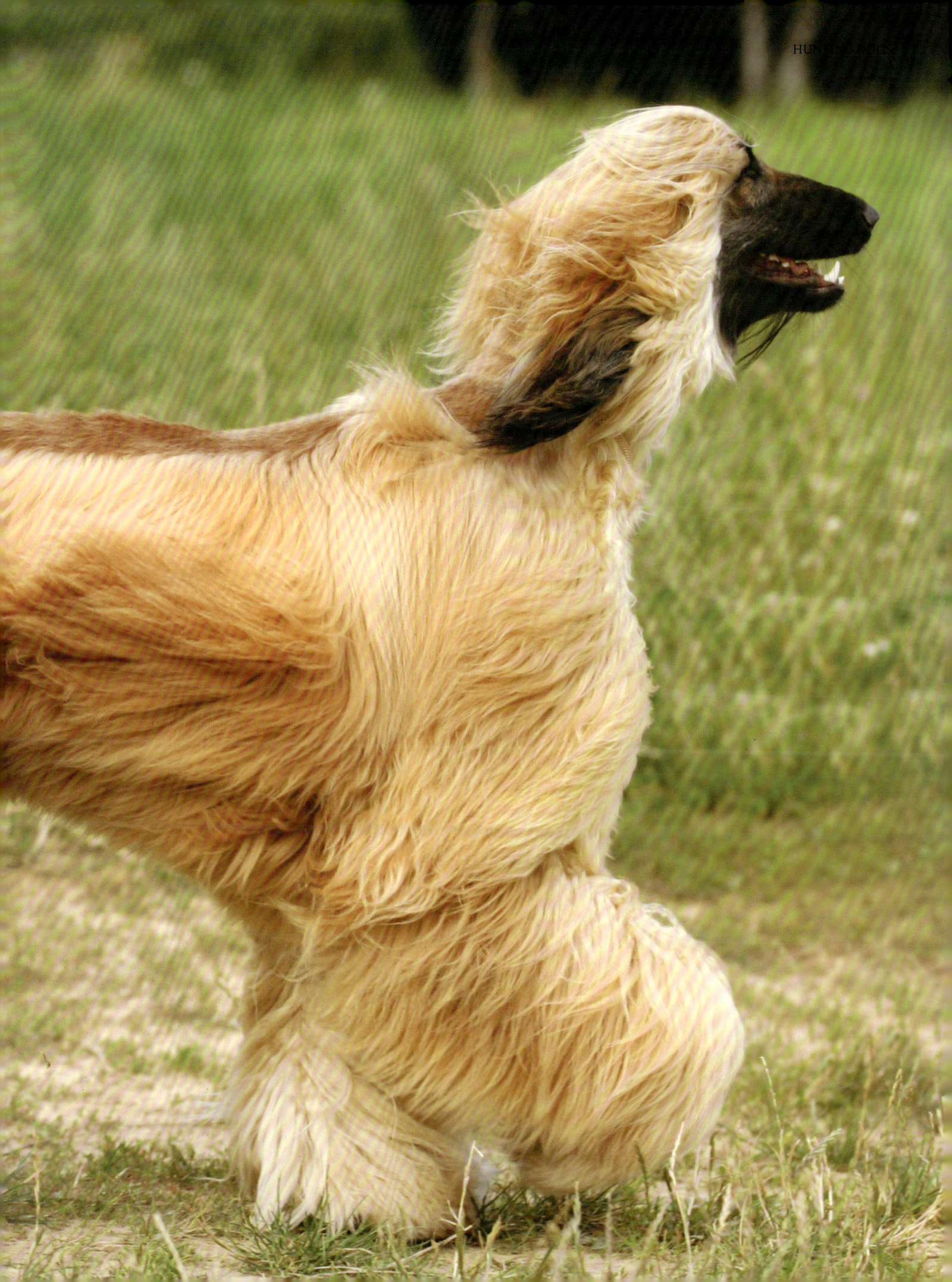

HUNTING DOGS

RIGHT:
Afghan pup
It will take several months for this puppy to grow the length of locks shown by its glamorous mother.

OPPOSITE TOP:
Show business
An Afghan hound – the most unruly of breeds – steals the show as Crufts, one of the world's most prestigious dog shows, which is held yearly in England. For some dogs, their job is to be put on show as prime specimens of their breed or pedigree. The prize winners will then become hugely valuable as breeding animals.

OPPOSITE BOTTOM:
Posing pups
The hound's long, flowing locks make it a spectacular breed that turns heads.

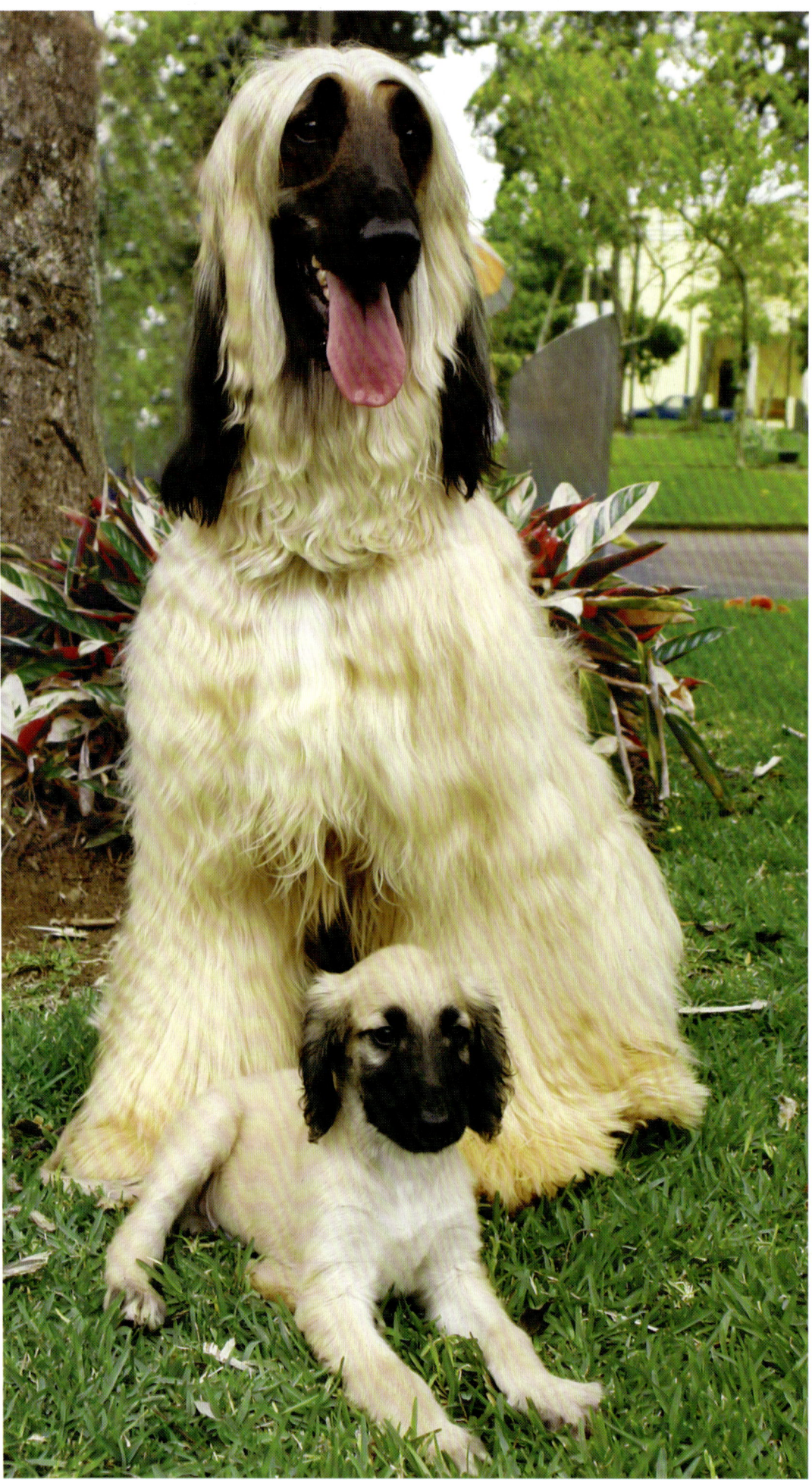

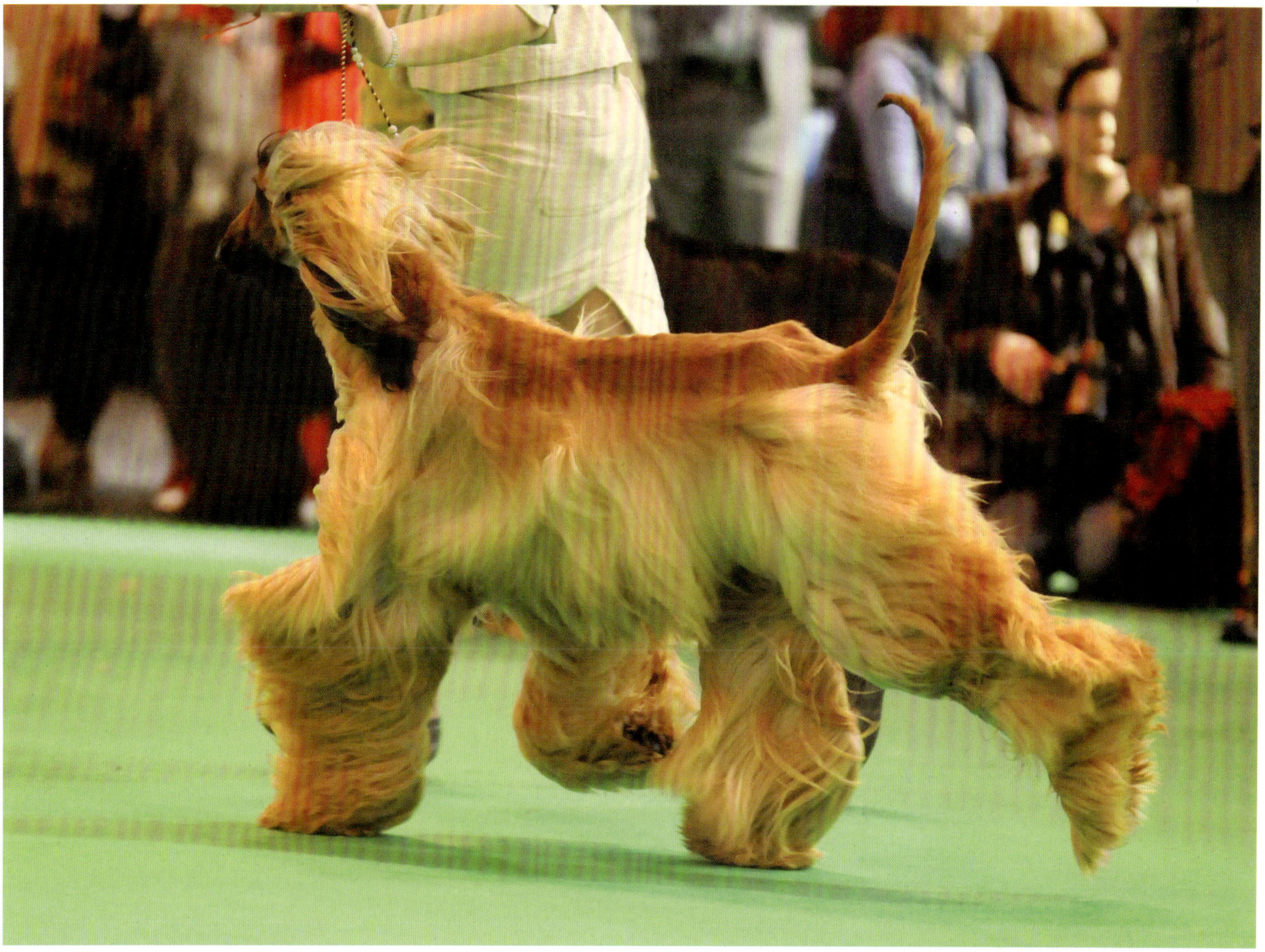

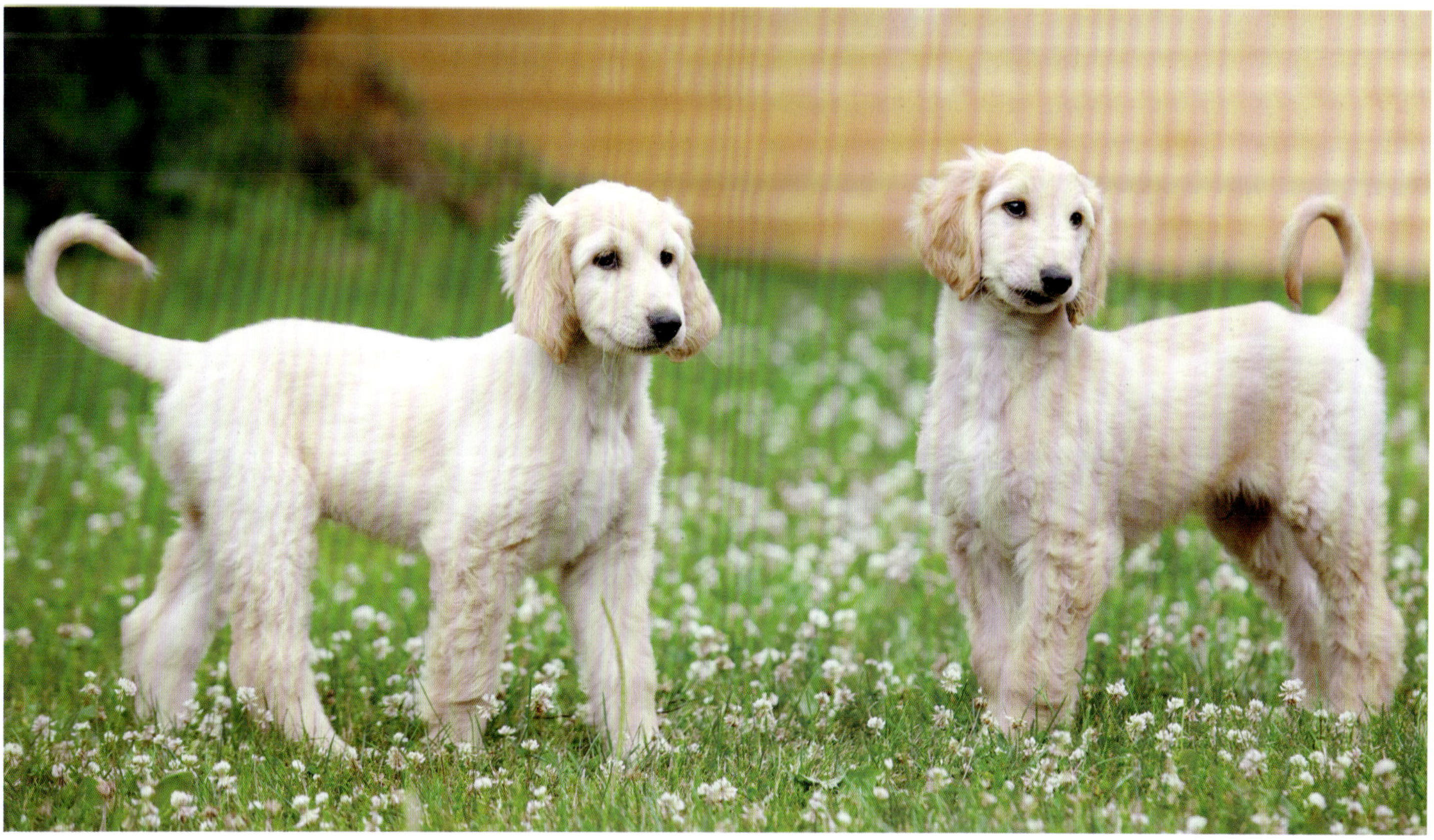

HUNTING DOGS

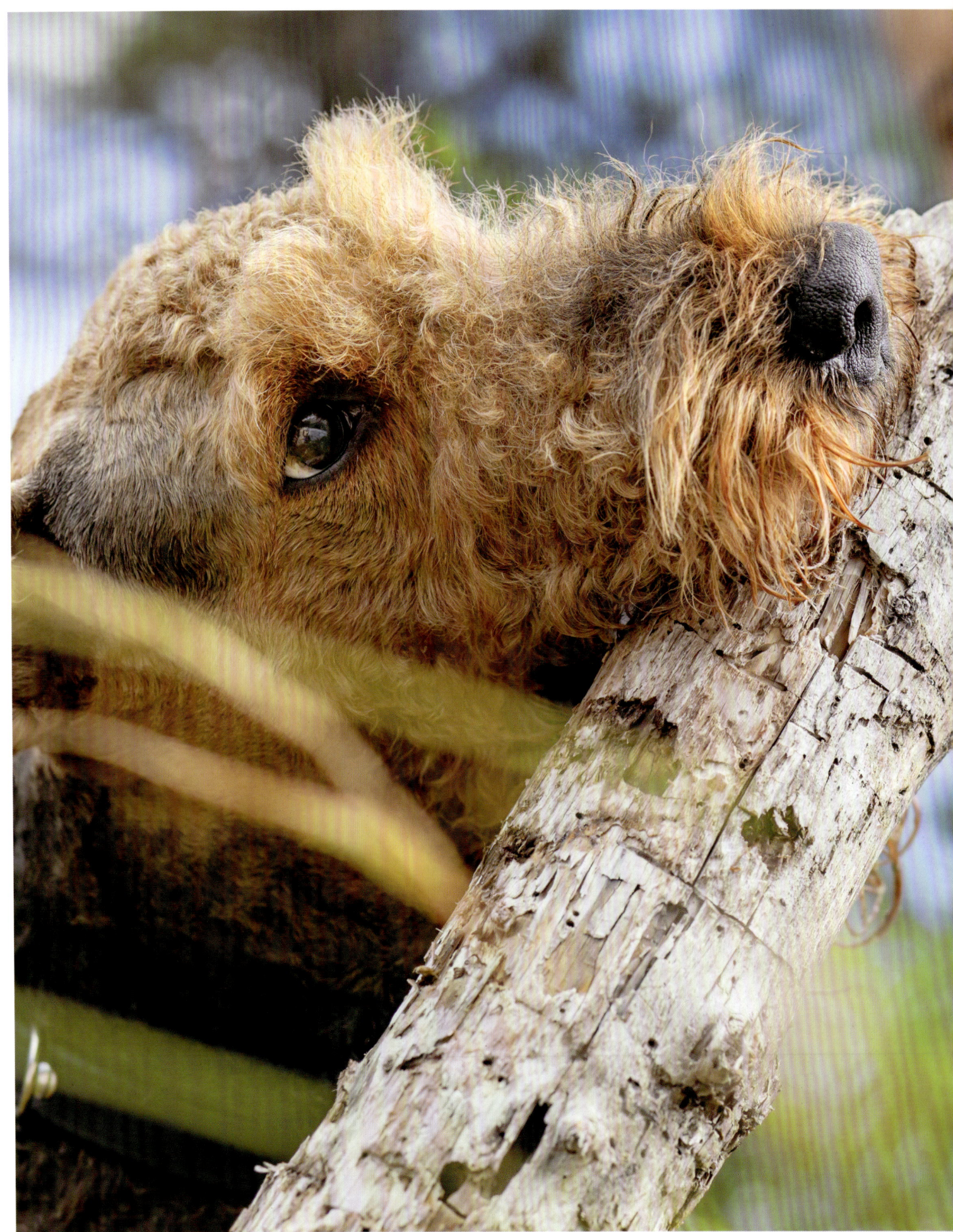

Airedale Terrier

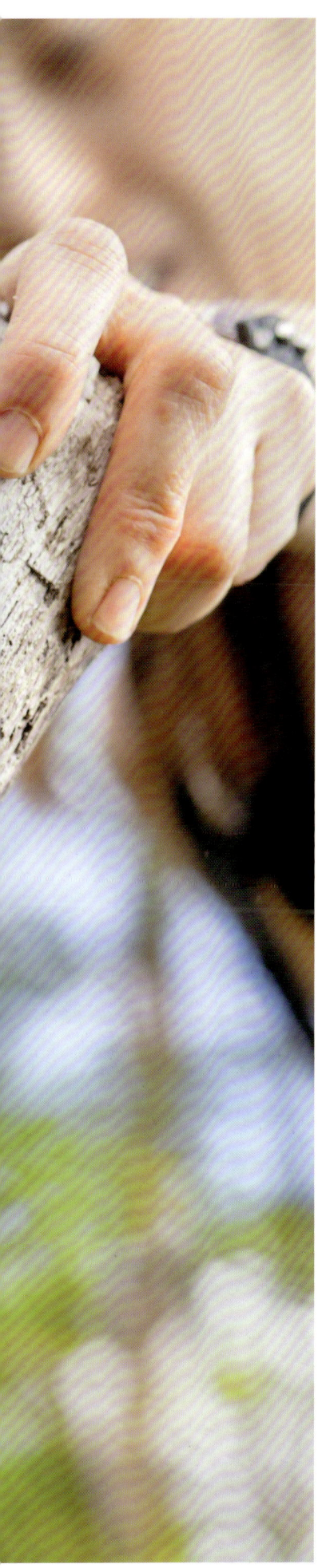

This English breed was created in the mid-19th century in Airedale, or the valley of the River Aire which flows through West Yorkshire, which was back then an industrial heartland. This working man's dog was bred to be the "King of Terriers". It is the tallest of the terriers, and the dog was developed to be a tough rat catcher working hard among the mills and factories. It was also used for hunting ducks, perhaps now and then working alongside a poacher getting something extra to feed the family.

The terrier was bred from a wide range of lines, including the otterhound and the now extinct black and tan terrier. There are also hints of Irish terrier, setters and some herding dogs in the bloodline as well.

The Airedale terrier rose to prominence in the First World War as a messenger and guard dog working for the British forces. The breed then became popular in North America as an all-round hunting dog that could catch waterfowl, gamebirds and small mammals.

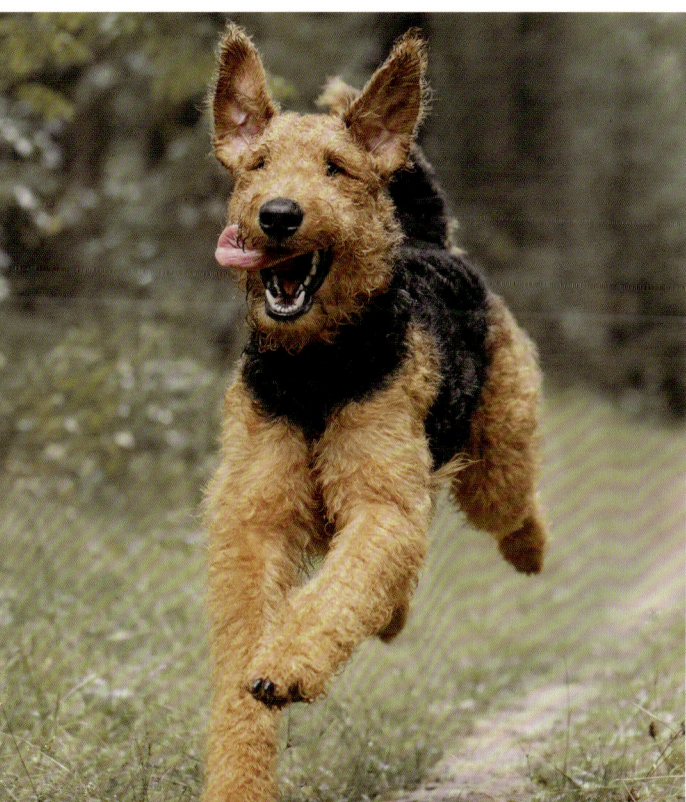

CHARACTERISTICS

Coat
The black and tan coat is hard and wiry on the outside while the underfur is much softer

Height
56–61cm (22–24in)

Weight
18–29kg (40–65lb)

Lifespan
10–12 years

Personality
Mischievous and devoted

Origin
England

LEFT:
Keeping busy
An energetic and intelligent dog like an Airedale needs a lot of exercise and stimulation to fend off boredom. Without this the dog will become aggressive and destroy property with its bites and chewing.

ABOVE:
Coat benefits
As a pet, one attraction of this breed is its hypoallergenic coat, which does not shed much.

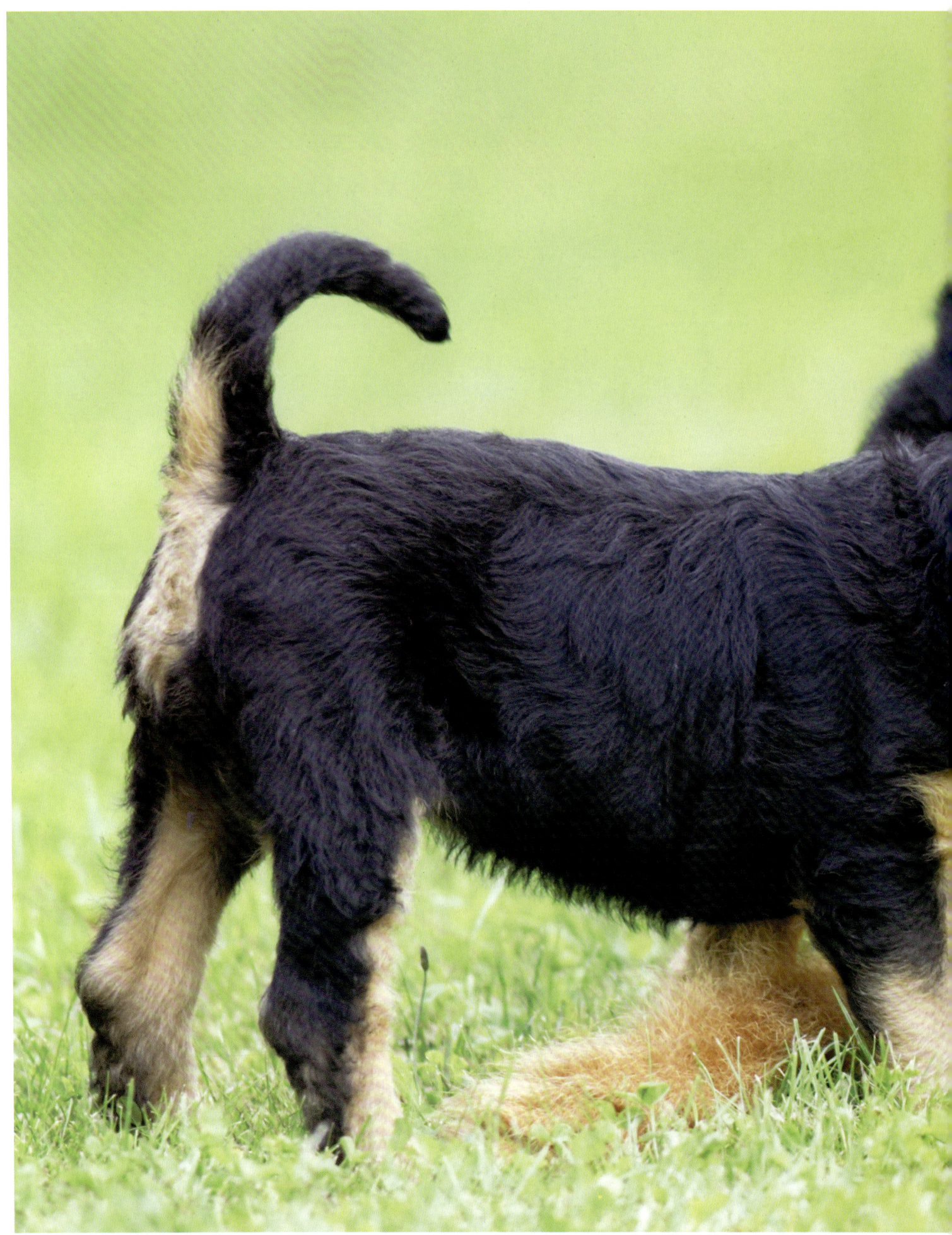

HUNTING DOGS

Airedale family
A mother shows her pups how to behave around other dogs – say hello and don't bite!

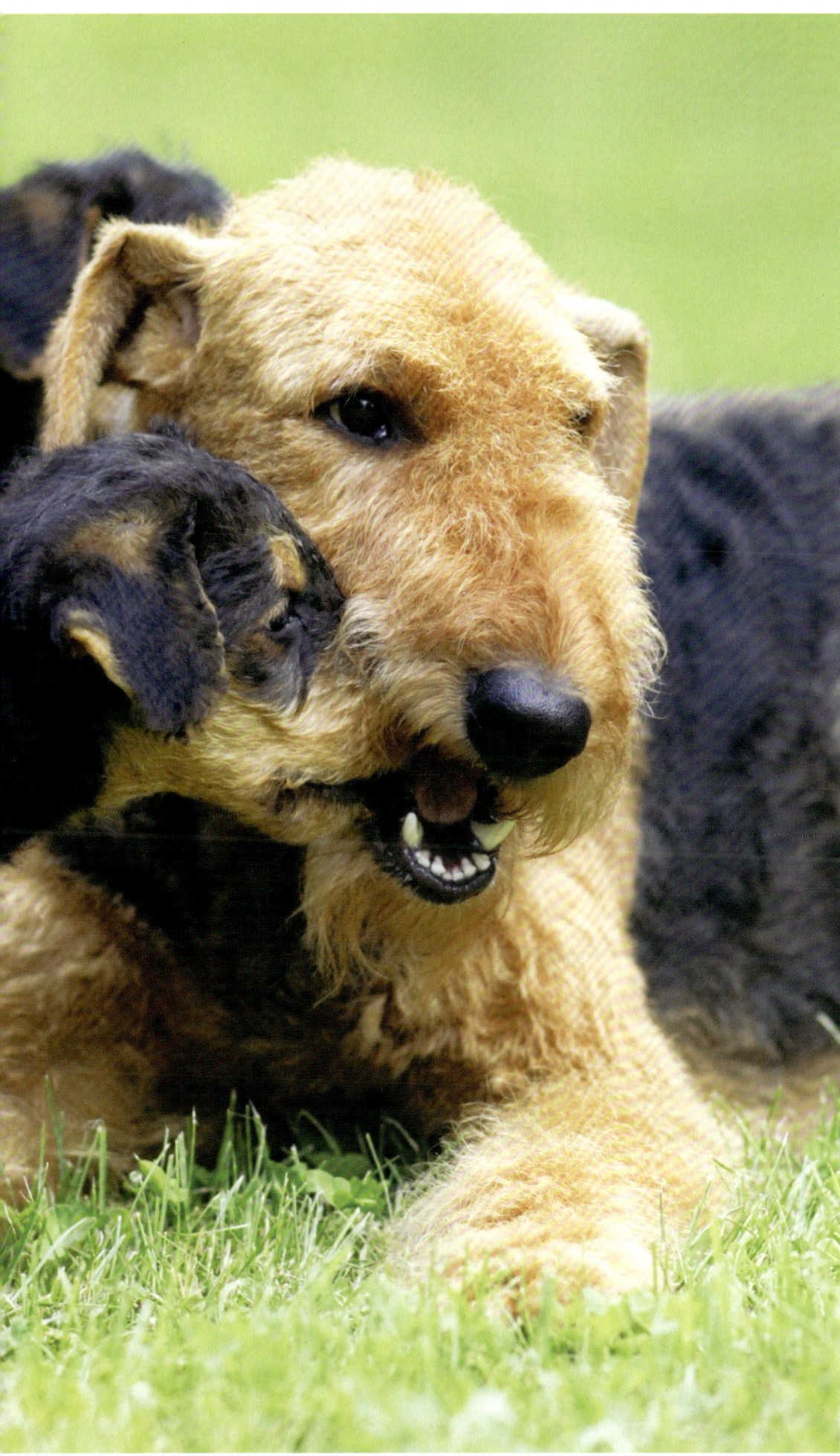

177

HUNTING DOGS

Majestic breedr
As with all terriers, the Airedale once worked killing rats and other vermin.

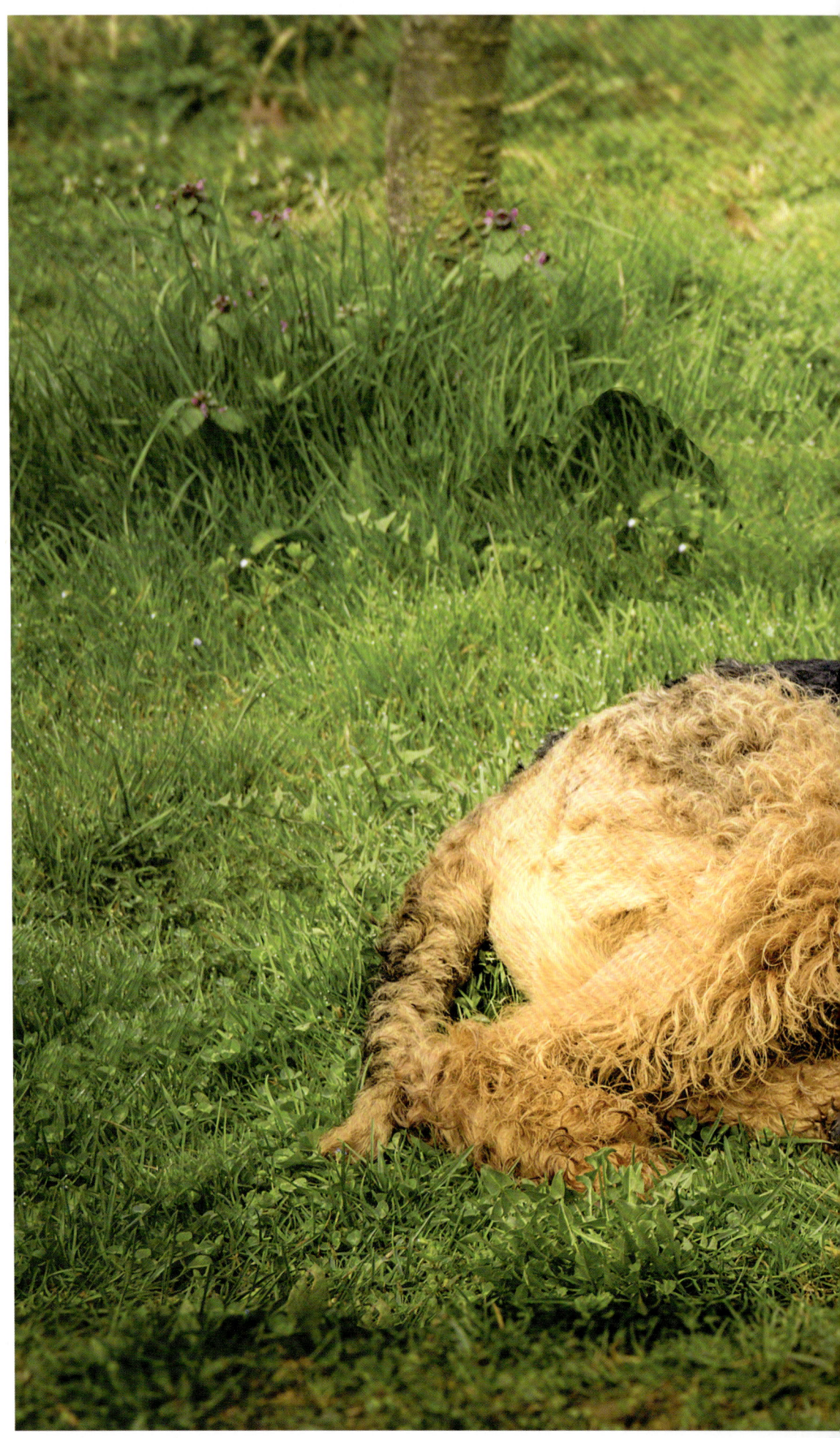

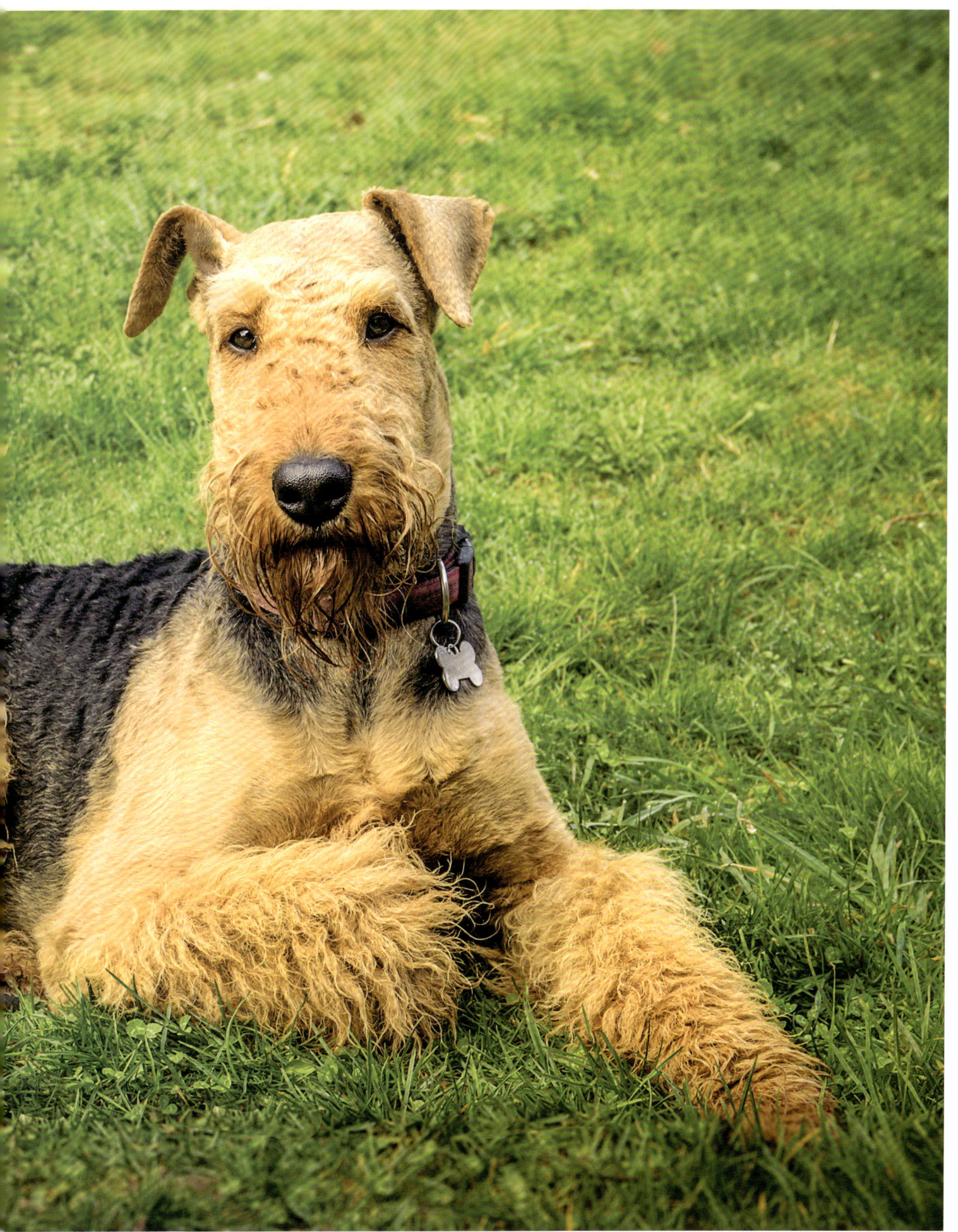

HUNTING DOGS
Akita Inu

This Japanese breed is named after the mountainous Akita Prefecture in Honshu, the country's largest island. In fact the full name means the "Japanese Akita" which distinguishes it from the American Akita breed that emerged in the 1950s. Many US servicemen returning home after the occupation of Japan brought these dogs with them.

The Akita is a large hunting dog breed developed for life in the wild outdoors, hunting for boars and bears. It is also a useful guard dog and at times in its long history the breed has been crossed with mastiffs from mainland Asia to create a bigger, tougher fighting dog. The breed was established in its current form in the 1920s, when the Japanese government set up a registry of pure-bred Akitas. However, after the Second World War the number of registered dogs dropped to only 16. Other dogs were crossed with German shepherd dogs brought in by the US military, and this is evident in the American Akita, which is slightly larger and heavier. The Japanese breed was meticulously restored from survivors found in remote parts of the country.

CHARACTERISTICS
Coat
A thick double coat that can be white, brindle or red, with white markings on the chest, belly and legs
Height
58–70cm (23–28in)
Weight
34–45kg (75–99lb)
Lifespan
10–12 years
Personality
Loyal and protective
Origin
Japan

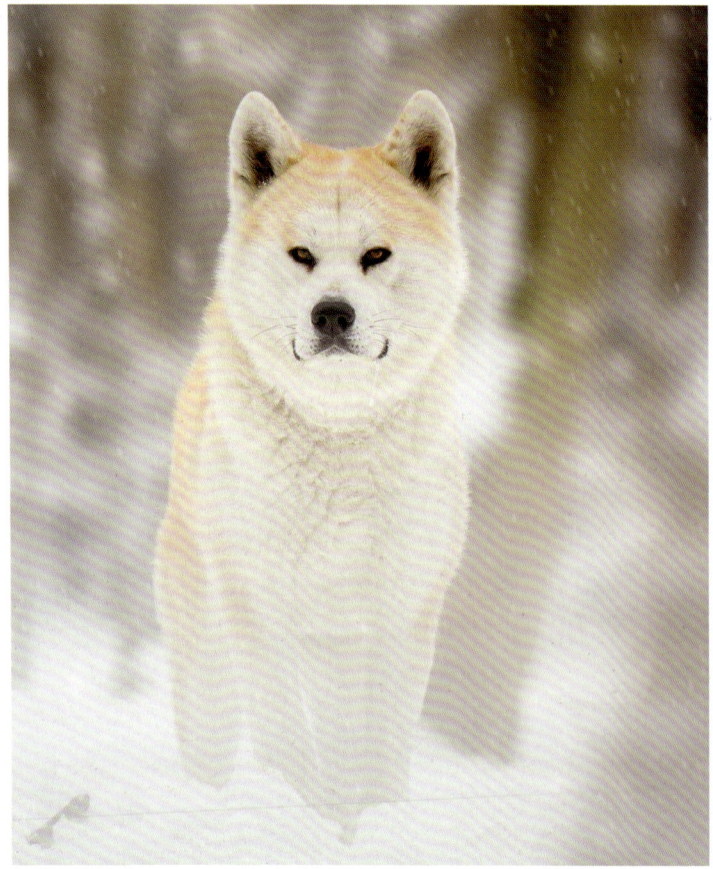

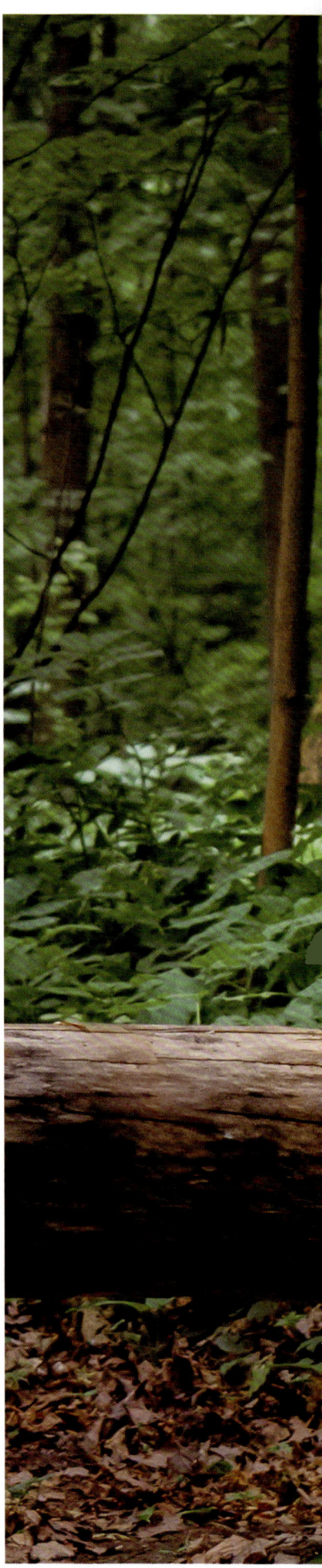

ABOVE:
National pride
In Japan, the Akita is a symbol of good luck. It is very devoted to its family and will protect them from any threat.

RIGHT:
Worldwide presence
Outside Japan, the Akita carries more sheepdog blood and tends to be larger than the native breed.

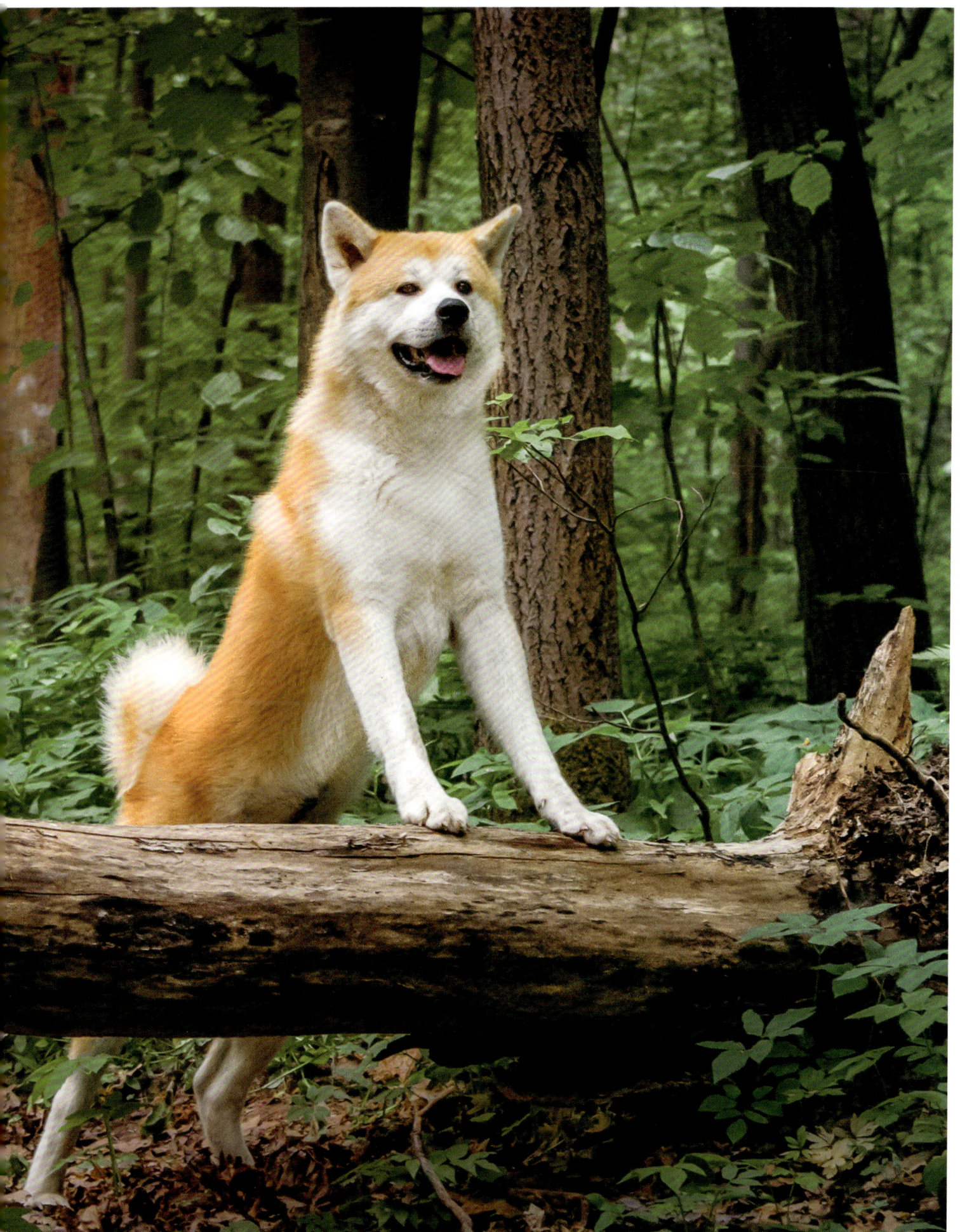

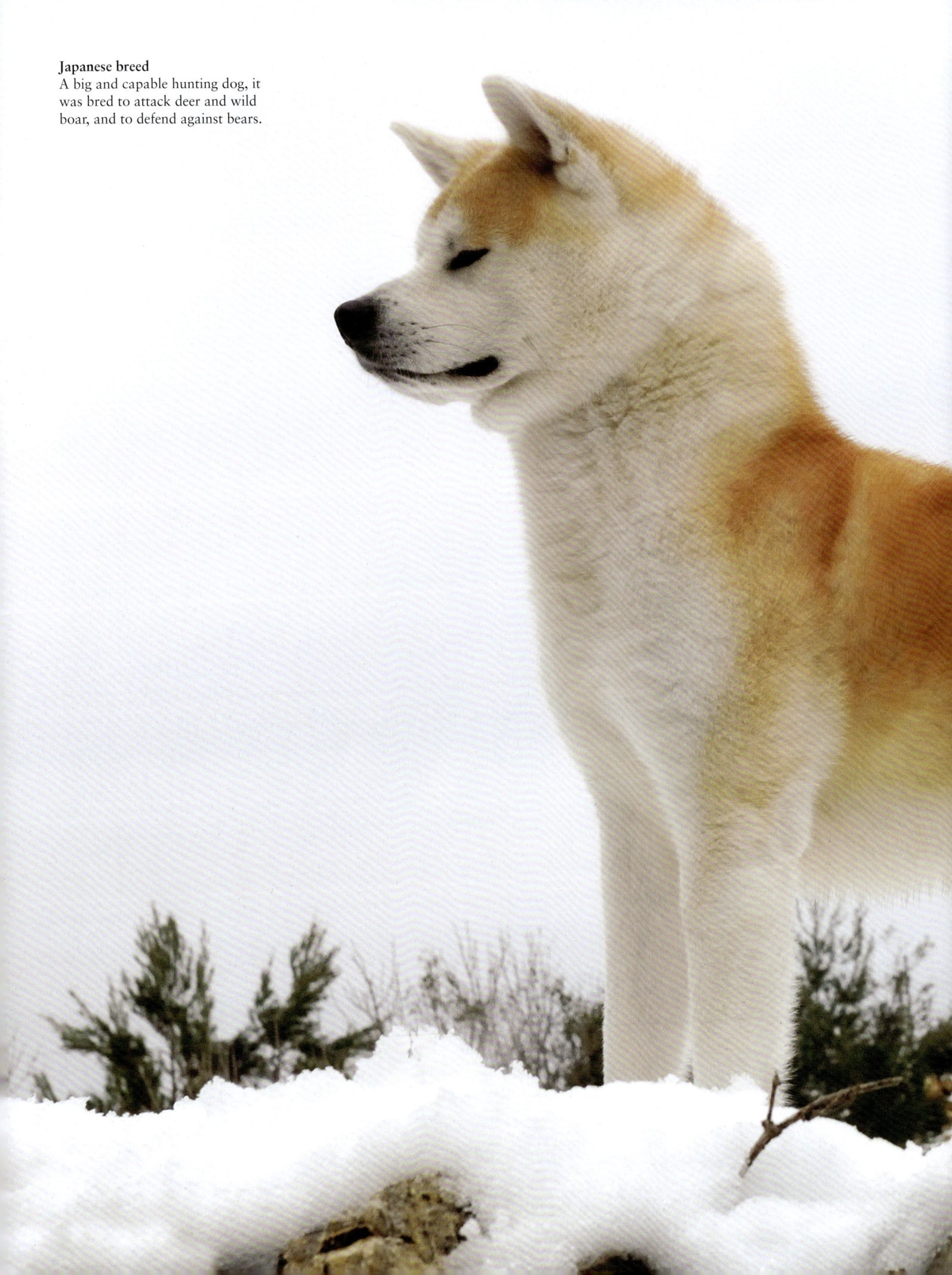

Japanese breed
A big and capable hunting dog, it was bred to attack deer and wild boar, and to defend against bears.

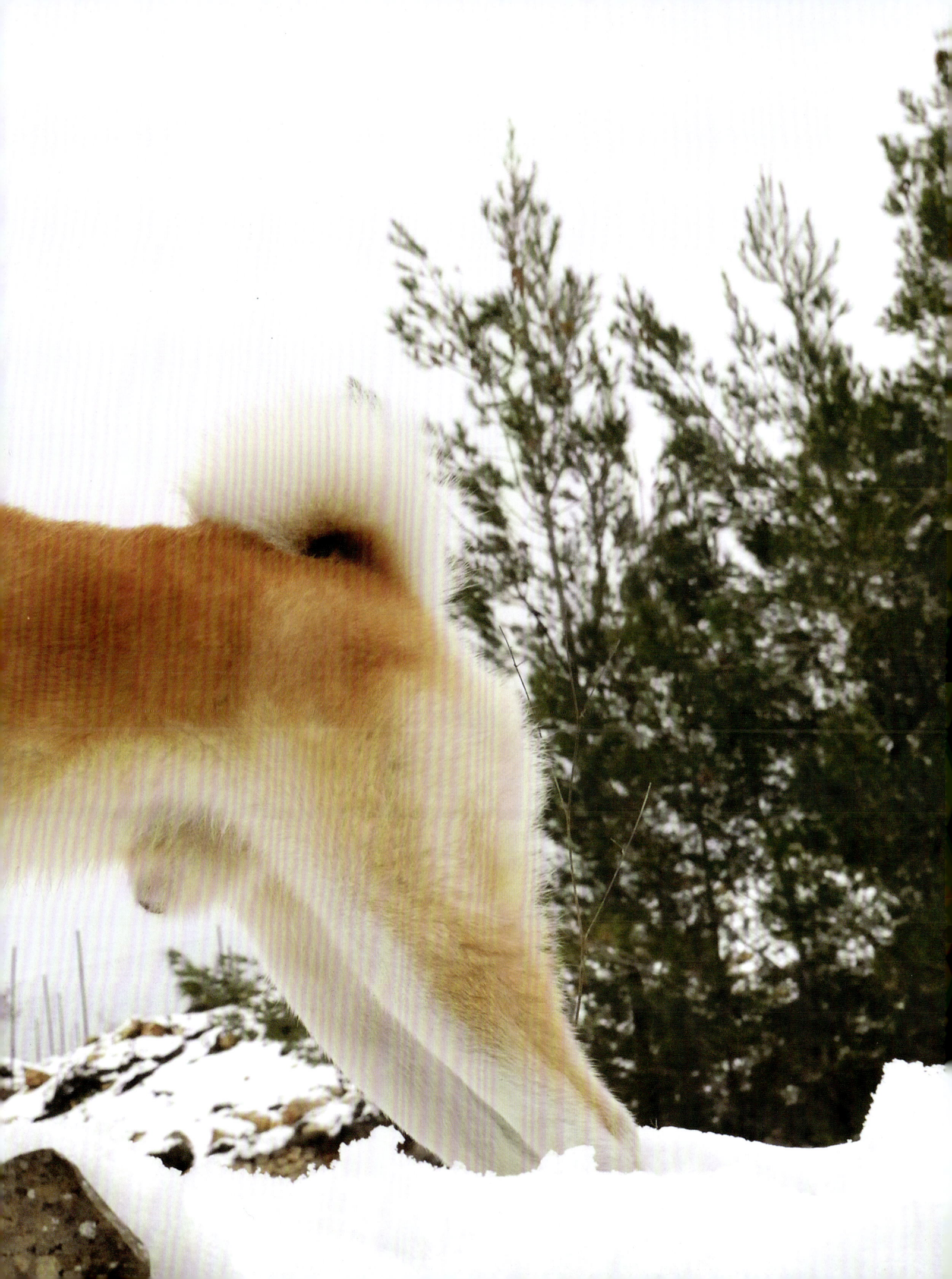

HUNTING DOGS

Happy families
A family of Akitas take the opportunity to rest in the warmth.

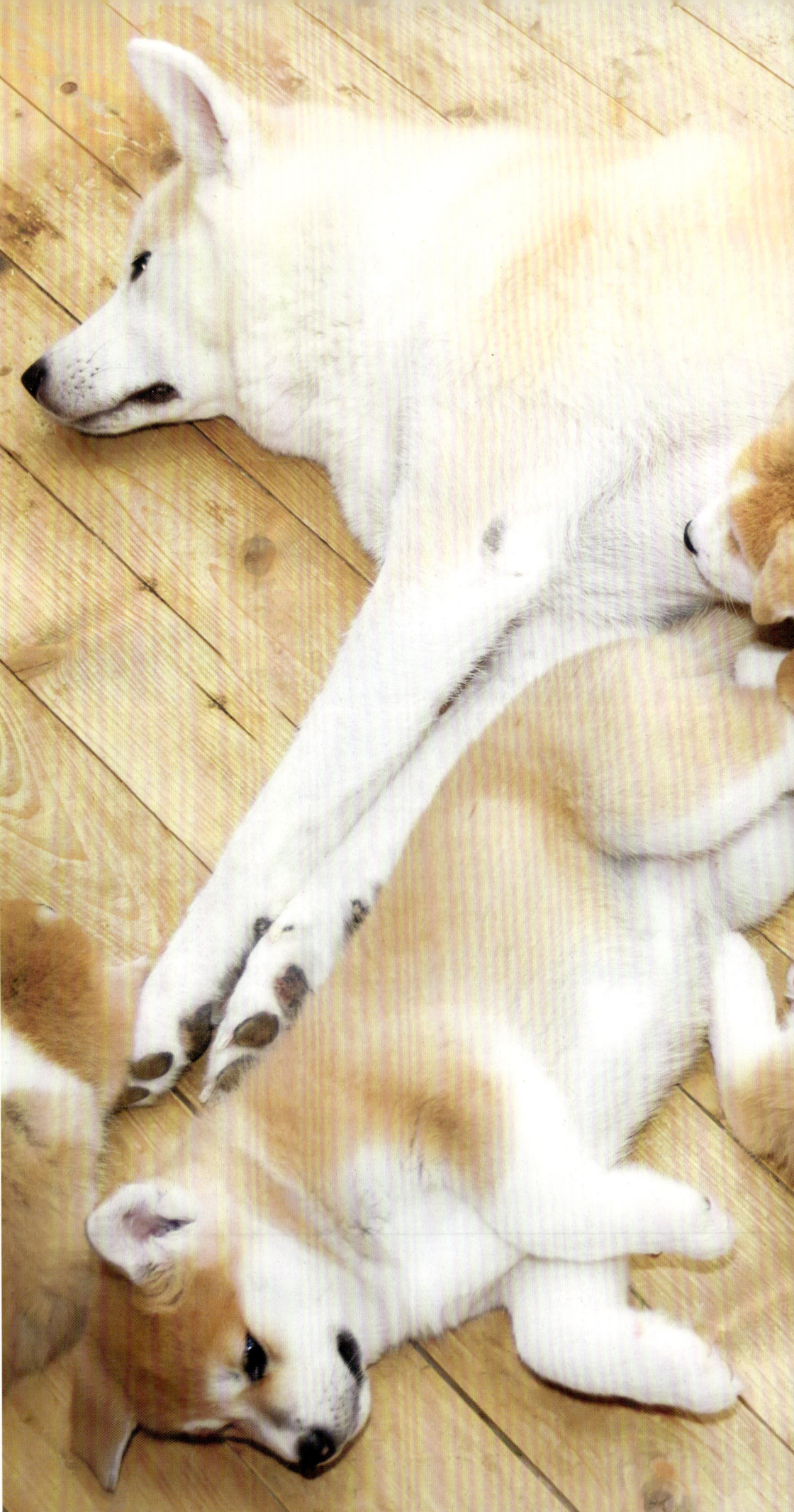

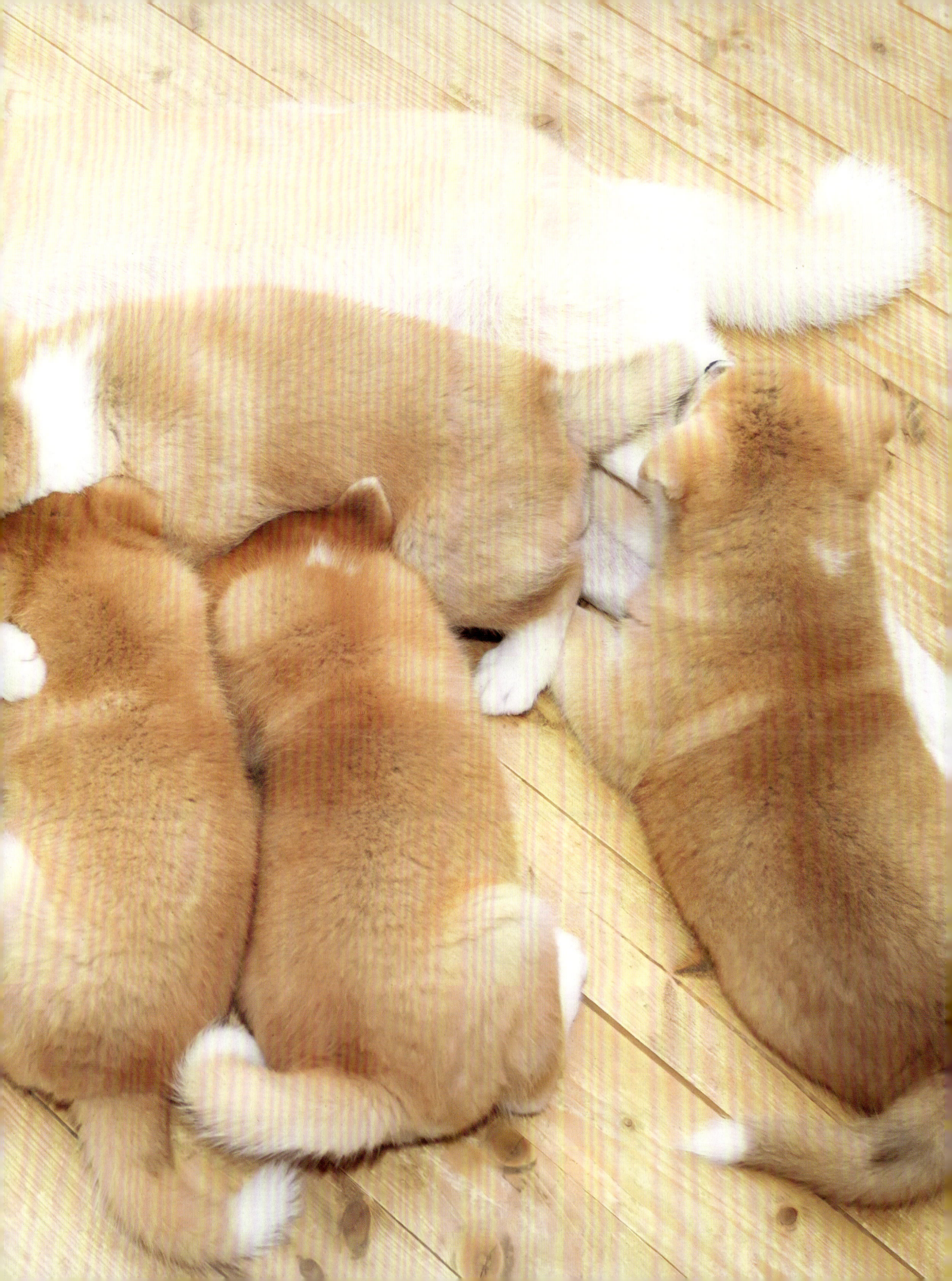

HUNTING DOGS

American English Coonhound

CHARACTERISTICS

Coat
This breed has a short, dense coat that is black and tan with white ticking on the legs, chest and face
Height
58–66cm (23–26in)
Weight
21–41kg (46–90lb)
Lifespan
10–11 years
Personality
Devoted and sociable
Origin
North America

This is one of six dog breeds developed in North America to hunt for raccoons, an abundant source of fur and food out on the frontier. This particular breed was developed from the English foxhound, while other coonhound breeds lean more towards the bloodhound and other European scenthound breeds.

The American English coonhound was officially recognized at the start of the 20th century, but it was already a common breed 100 years before that. The elites of the North American colonies, even George Washington, had maintained an interest in British bloodsports even after severing political ties with the old country. Packs of foxhounds had been introduced in the late 1600s, and they were crossbred with local dogs to create a fast and agile breed that could track its prey for hours. The phrase "barking up the wrong tree" is linked to this dog. The raccoon would habitually escape into the branches, and the dogs would bark loudly at its base—and keep barking even if the raccoon had made an escape.

The breed is friendly and sociable but has a strong prey drive and can become stubborn if it catches an intriguing scent. A pet American English will need a lot of attention and exercise to keep it happy and stimulated.

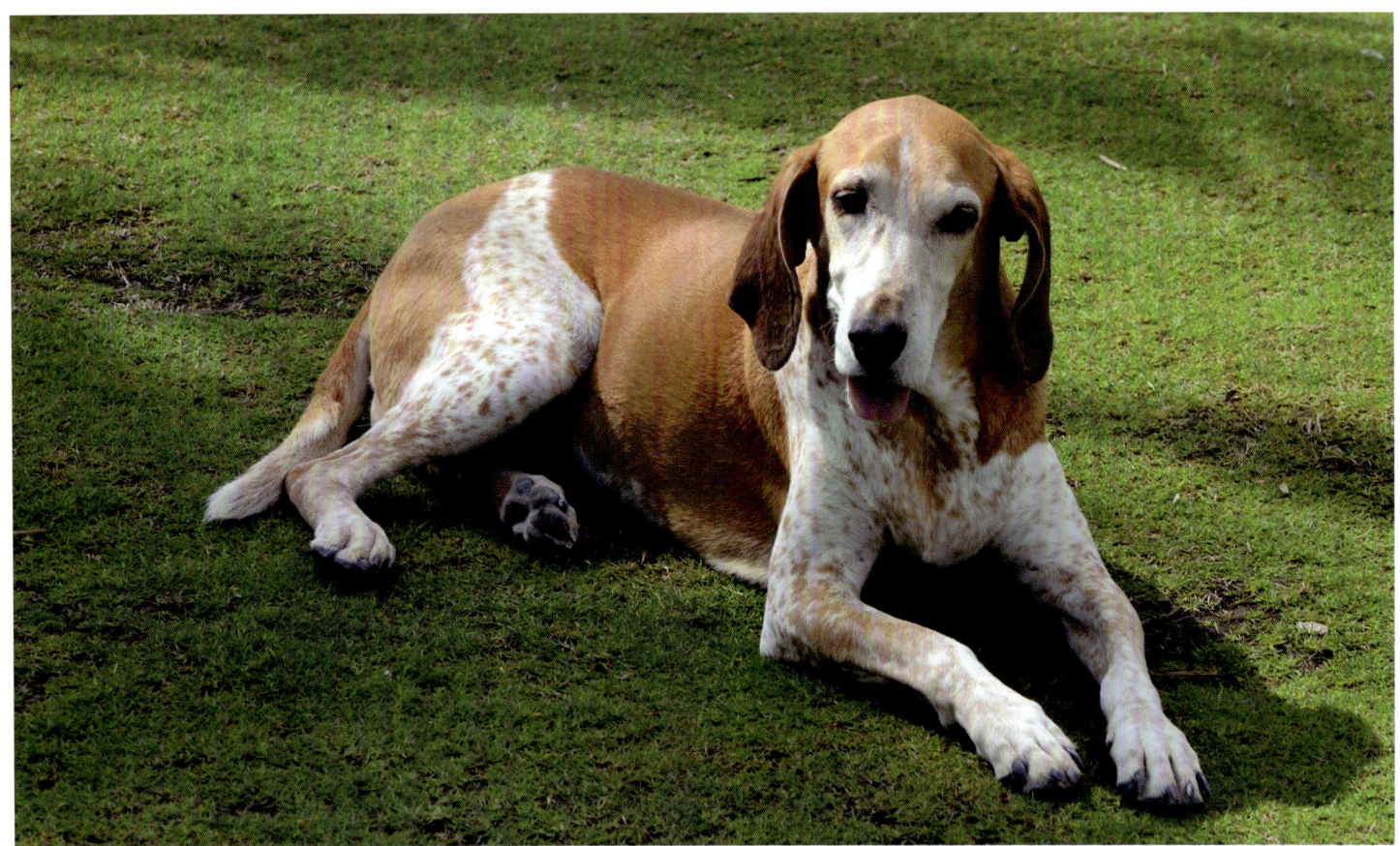

ABOVE:
Big head
The American English has a broad head, a domed skull, long ears and dark brown eyes that express kindness and intelligence. It is sometimes called the redtick coonhound.

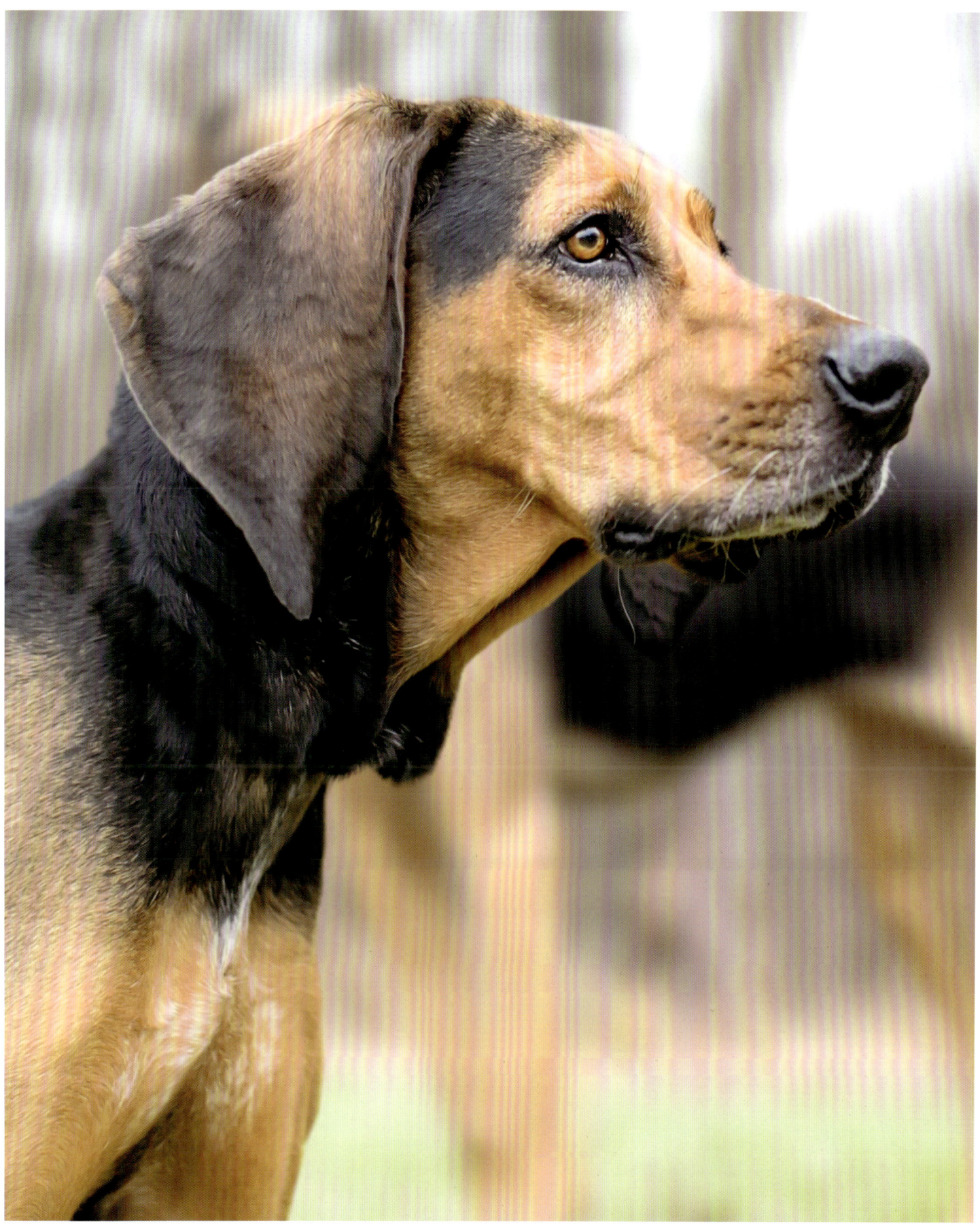

ABOVE:
Stay wild
Owners living in a densely populated area should think twice before choosing this breed as a companion, albeit a very devoted one. The dog has a particularly loud and resonating bark.

HUNTING DOGS

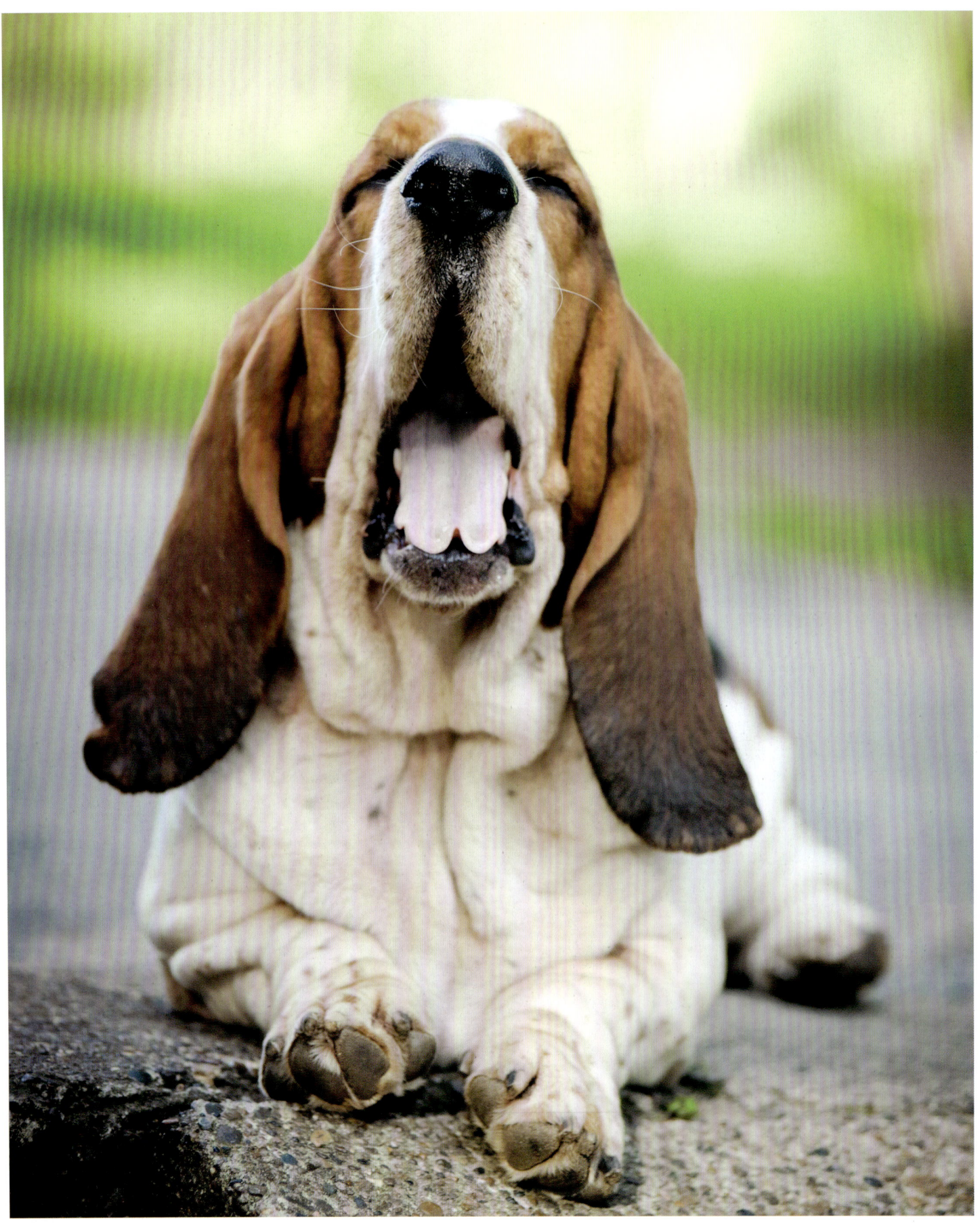

ABOVE:
Keeping clean
Basset hounds need frequent ear cleaning to avoid infections.

Basset Hound

CHARACTERISTICS

Coat
A short, smooth coat that is mostly tri-coloured black, white and tan or lemon and white (a bi-colour version), but several other colours are recognized

Height
33–38cm (13–15in)

Weight
18–27kg (40–60lb)

Lifespan
10–13 years

Personality
Charming and steadfast

Origin
France

This iconic and much-loved breed was originally developed as a scenthound for hunting hares, rabbits and deer. What was needed was not a fleet-footed dog that streaked after prey. Instead, the basset was bred to be low to the ground so it could plod steadily over rough ground as it tracked game. The breed has its origins in the fields of Flanders in Belgium and France, and the term "basset" comes from the French word bas, meaning "low". Today the low-slung but chunky dog complete with droopy ears gives the breed a certain scruffy appeal, and makes it a charming addition to the family.

The basset hound's long nose gives it an excellent sense of smell, second only to the bloodhound it is said. The long ears, known as leathers, help to trap the scent of prey around the head. The basset hound is not built for speed but is nevertheless a strong animal that requires regular exercise to stay healthy and keep its weight down. Although it can be stubborn at times, the basset is a devoted pet that is friendly and outgoing in a low-key fashion. It gets along well with children and other pets.

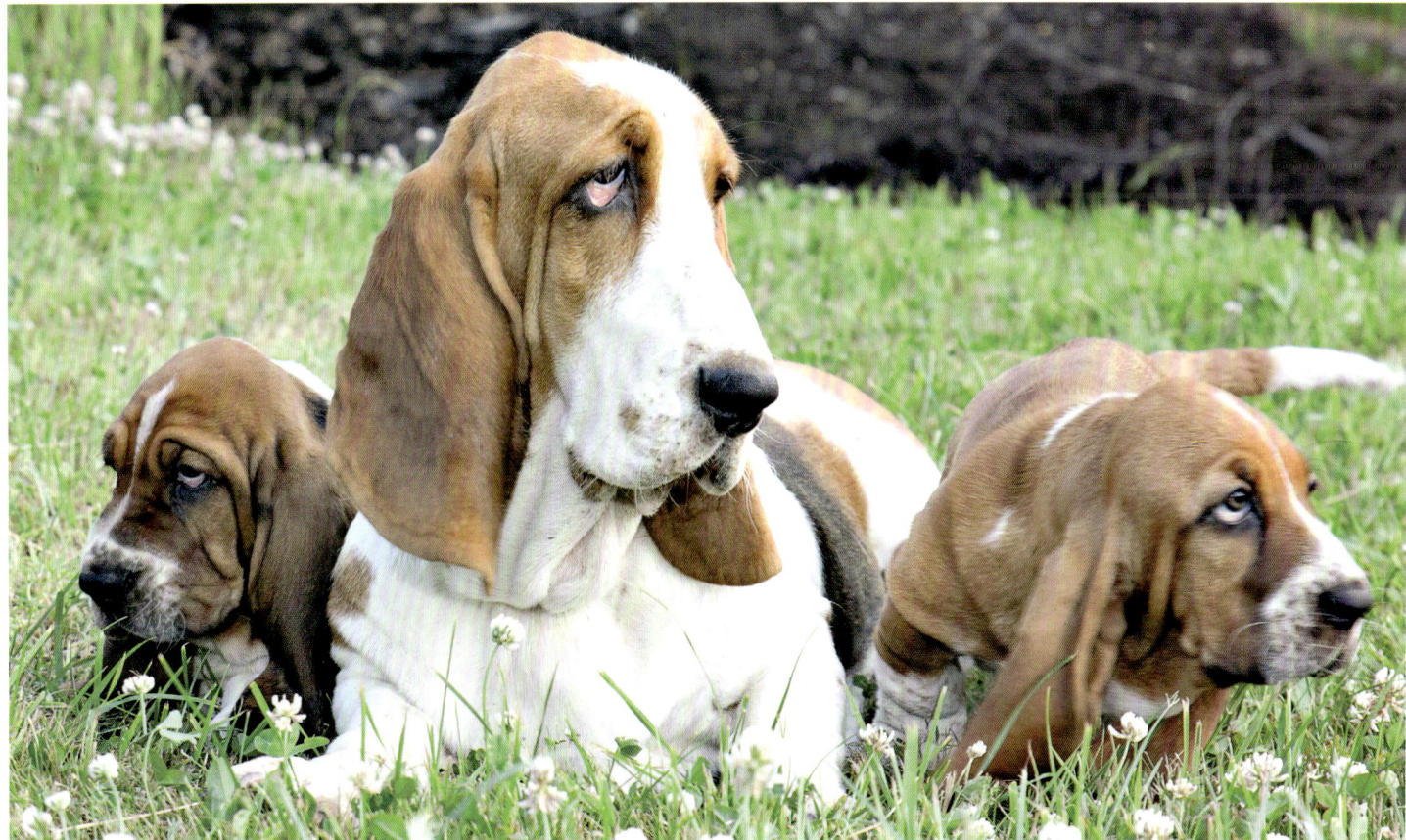

ABOVE:
Why the long face?
Bassets are known for their sunken eyes and gloomy, sagging visage but owners still know when their dogs are happy.

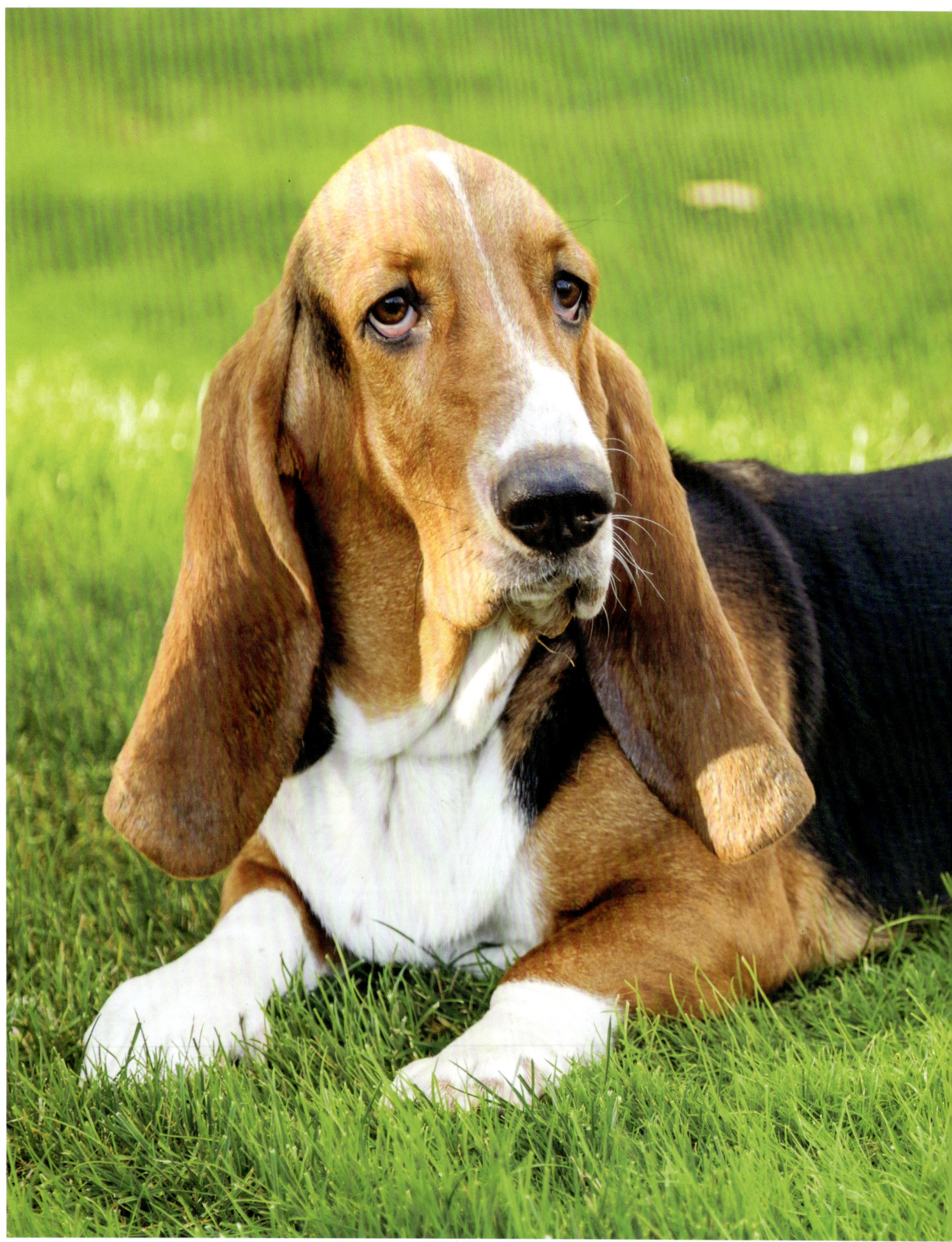

HUNTING DOGS

Basset hound
This breed tend to drool a good deal so be prepared for an occasional assault with some slobber.

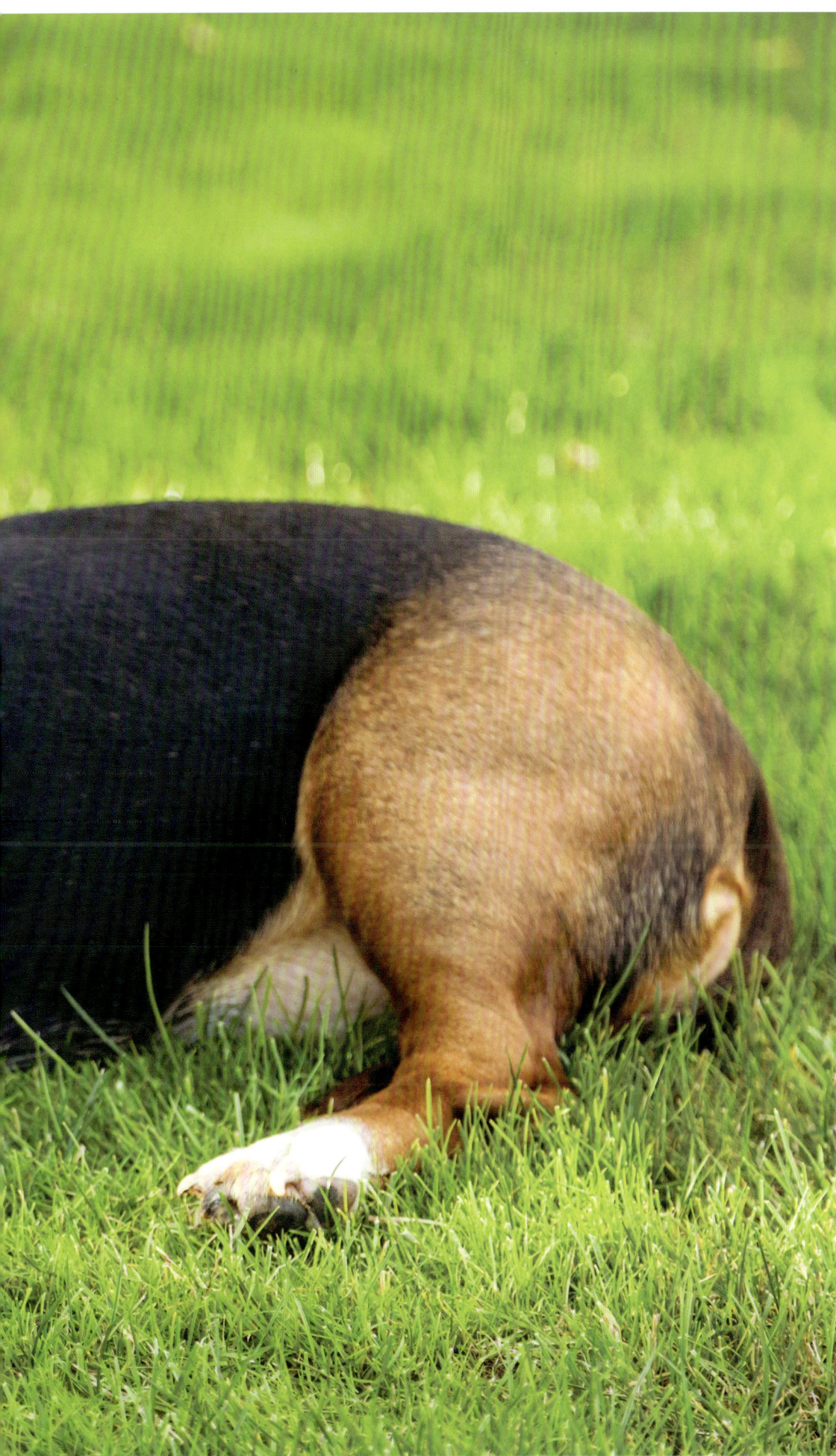

HUNTING DOGS
Beagle

CHARACTERISTICS

Coat
A short, easy-care coat that comes in various colours, usually with white, black and tan markings

Height
33–40cm (13–16in)

Weight
9–11kg (20–24lb)

Lifespan
13 years

Personality
Playful and tolerant

Origin
England

No one is quite sure when this breed originated or how it got its name. It was likely developed as a British pack hound for hunting hares and rabbits, and could date back as far as pre-Roman times. Its name is also something of a mystery. It is possible that it stems from the ancient British language—an early form of Welsh essentially—and meant "small". An alternative idea is that the name is derived from a later French term that mimics the dogs' calls as they hunt.

By the 16th century, the small dogs had become an essential feature of any self-respecting estate, along with packs of larger fox and deer hounds. While the foxhounds were followed on horseback, the beagles led the hunting party on foot. That made the "foot hound" breed a much less expensive dog for catching a meal, and this advantage made the beagle popular across Europe and North America. Even today, beaglers lead these little hunters to catch rabbits in the American woods.

Elsewhere beagles have found uses as detection dogs, sniffing out drugs and explosives. They make a playful companion but retain an independent spirit. This is illustrated best by perhaps the most famous beagle of all: Snoopy.

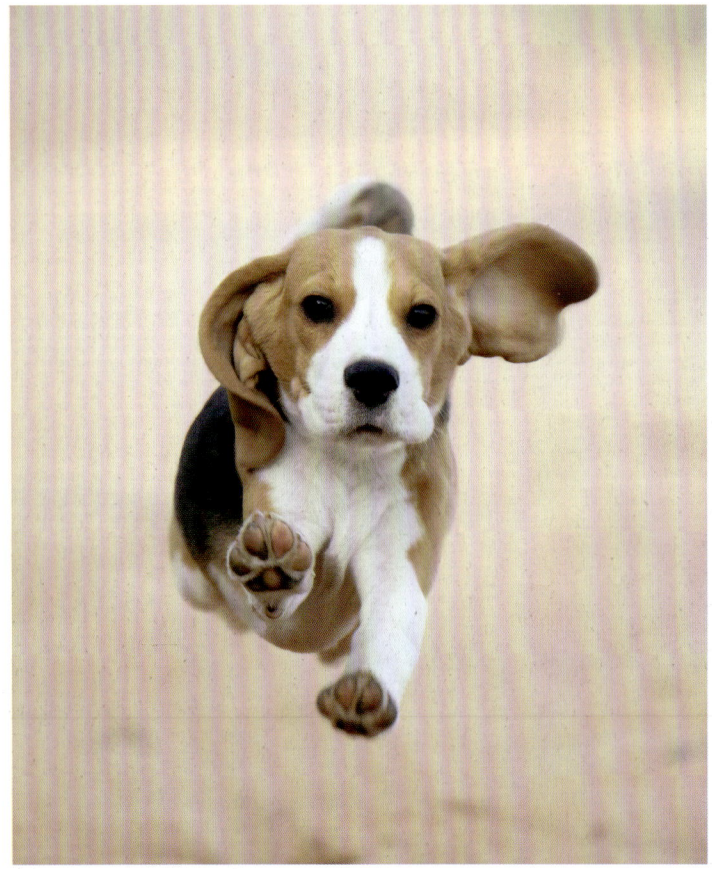

ABOVE:
Happy and lucky
The beagle has a friendly, curious and playful personality, but it can also be stubborn and independent.

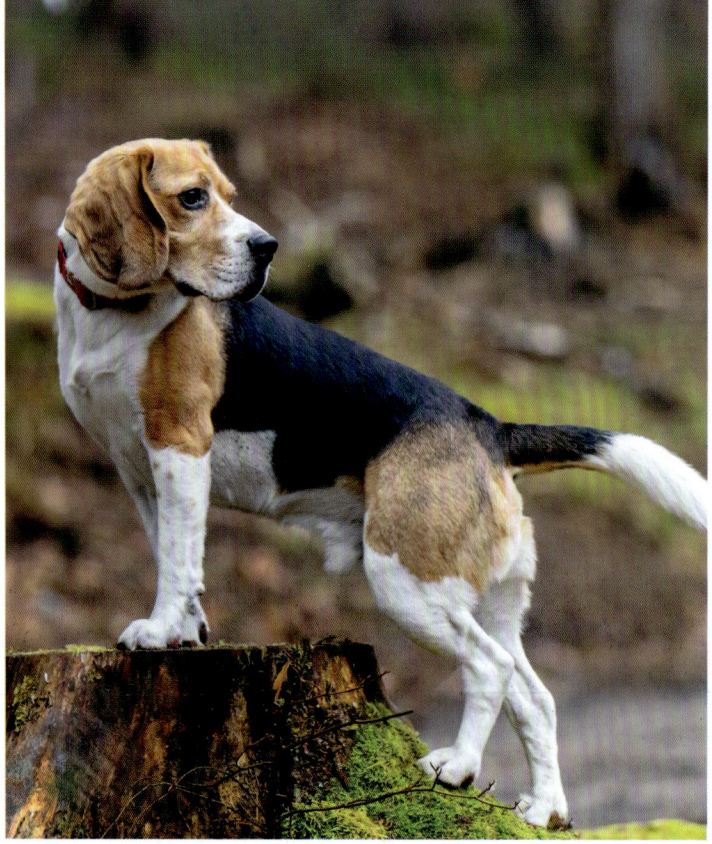

ABOVE:
A good specimen
The beagle is generally healthy, but it can be prone to some conditions such as epilepsy, ear infections, obesity and cherry eye.

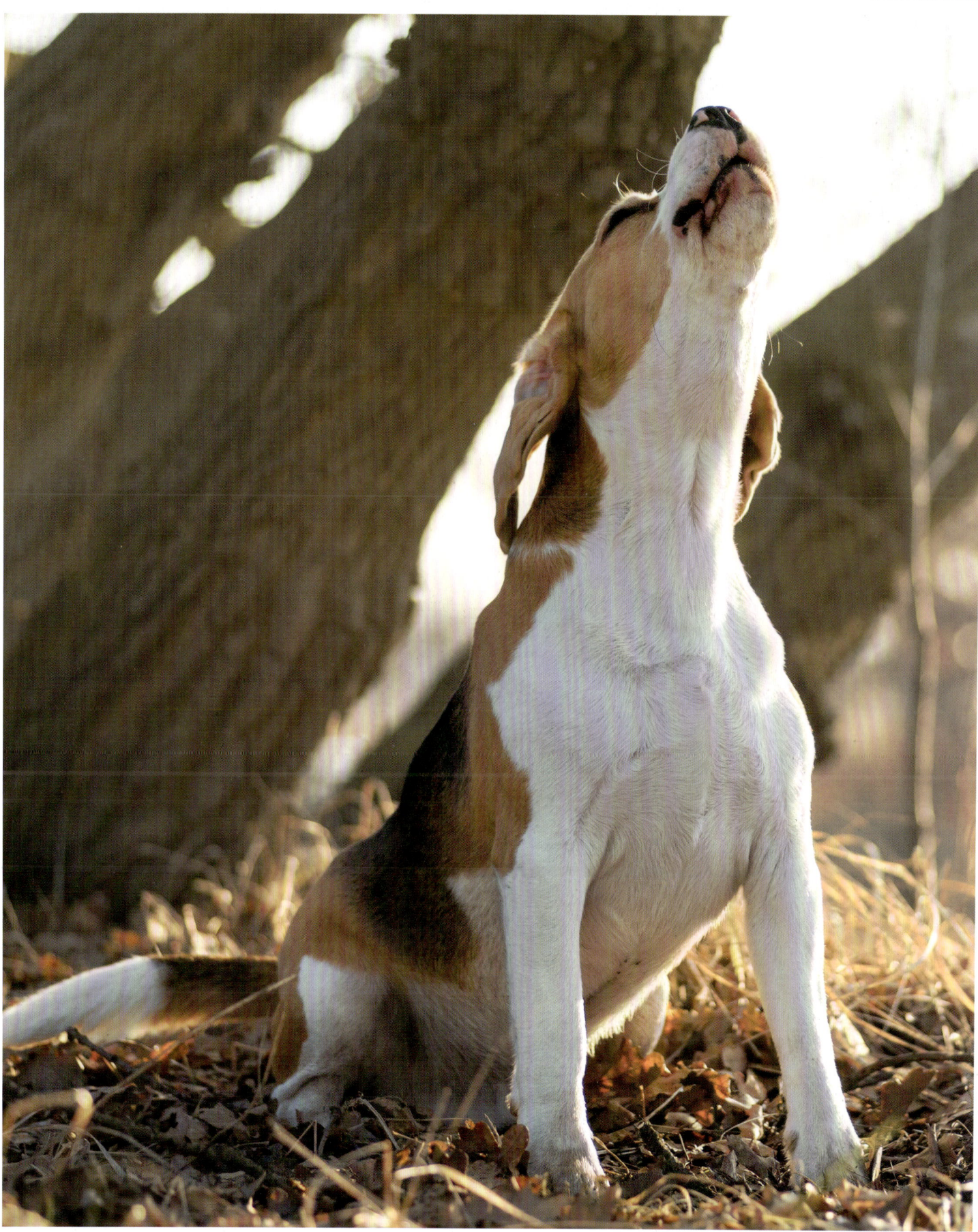

ABOVE:
Look at me
The beagle needs a lot of exercise and mental stimulation.

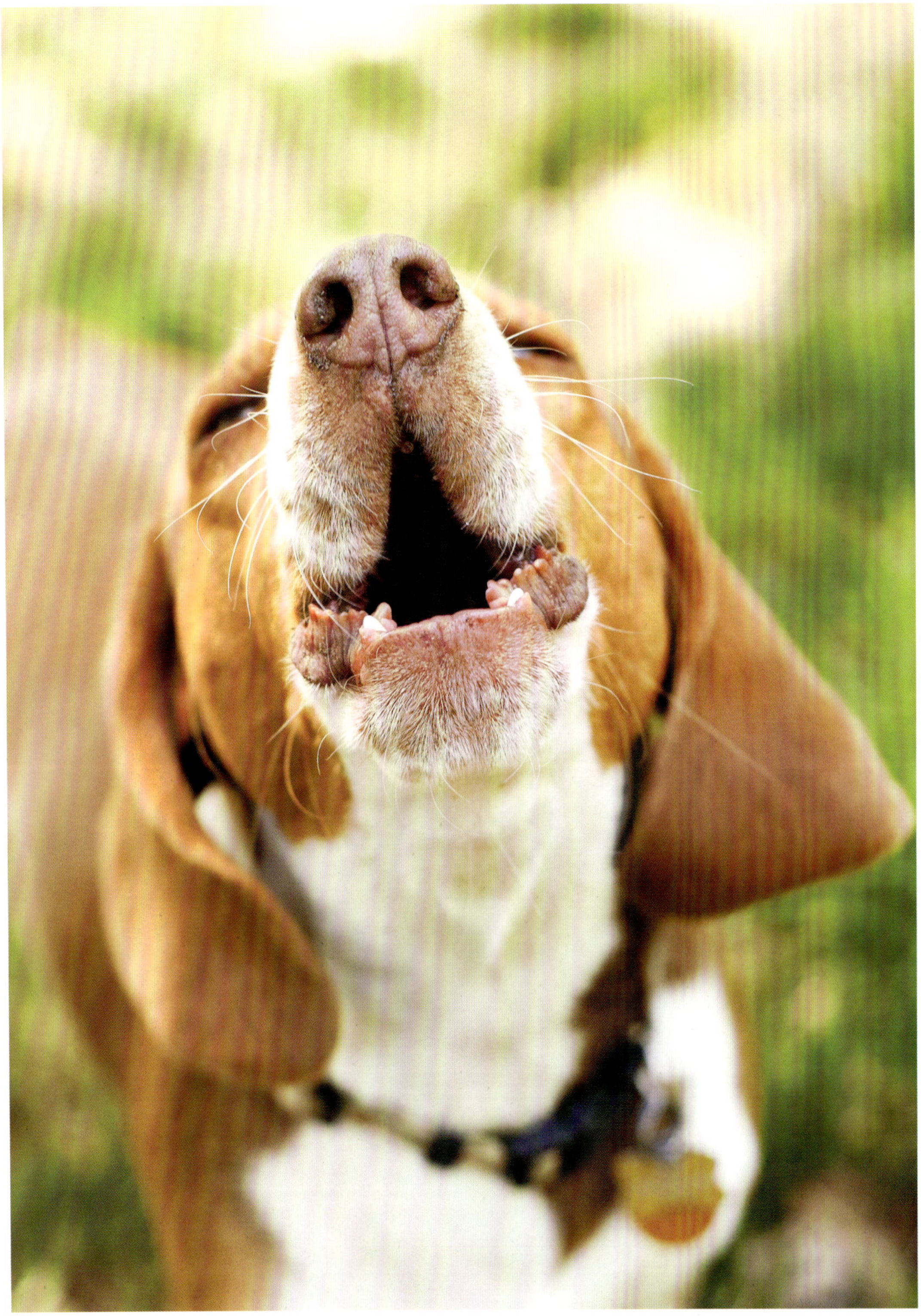

HUNTING DOGS

ABOVE AND RIGHT:
Curious hound
This breed needs a secure fence to prevent it from wandering off following its nose.

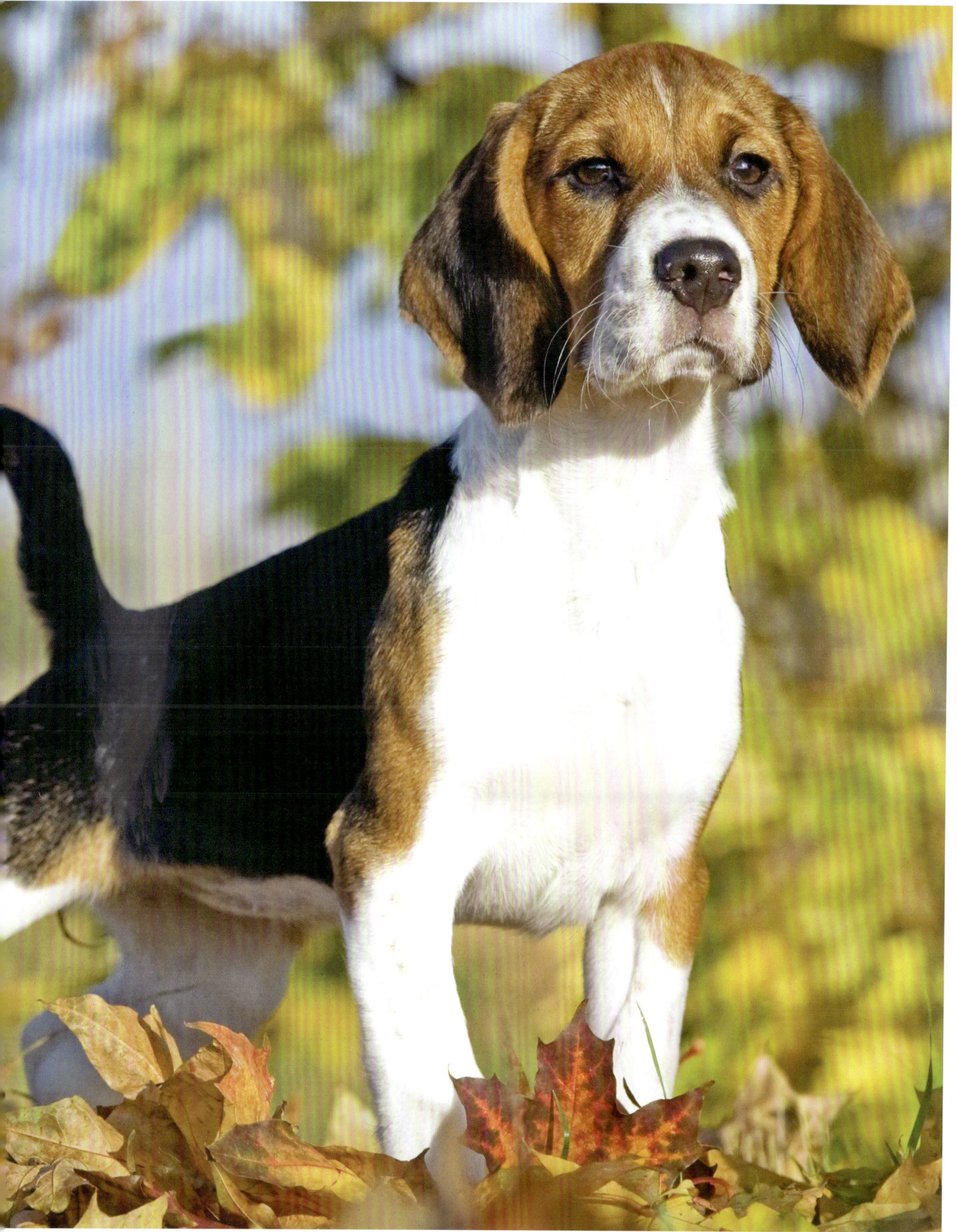

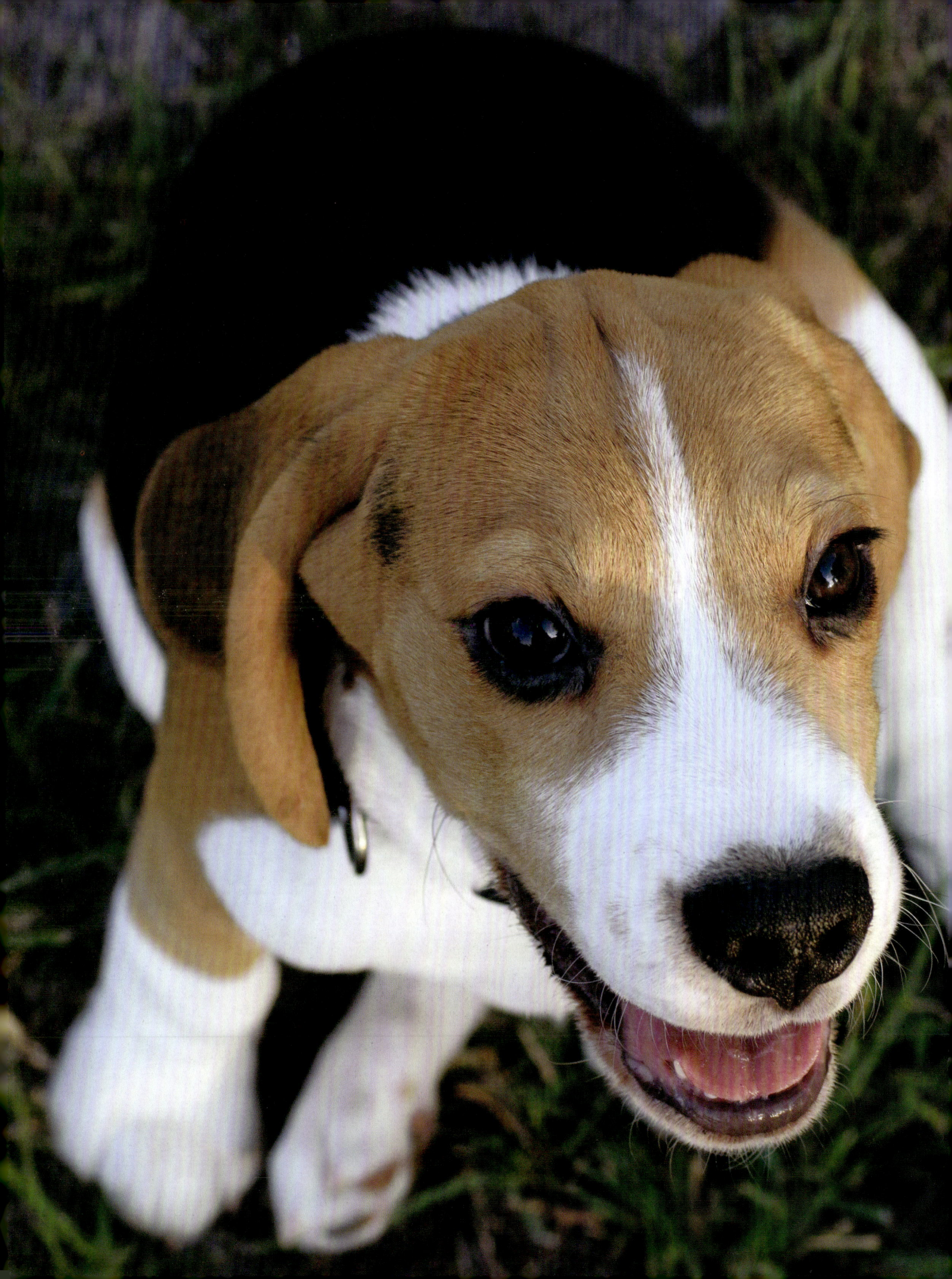

HUNTING DOGS

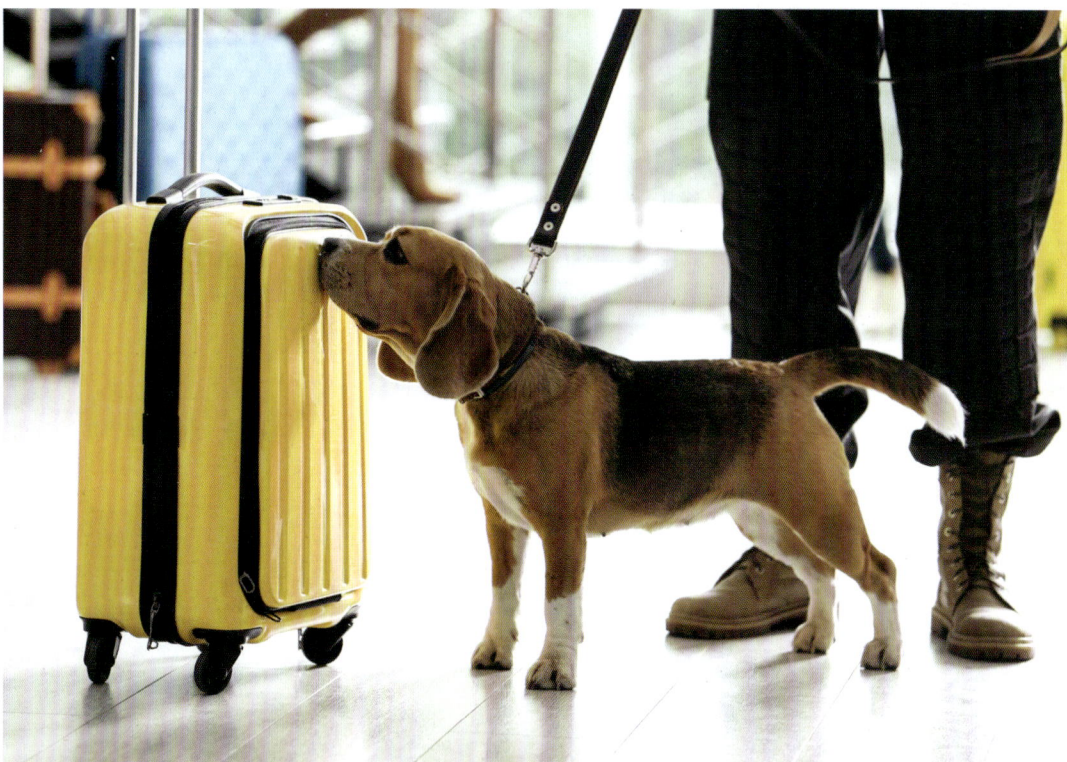

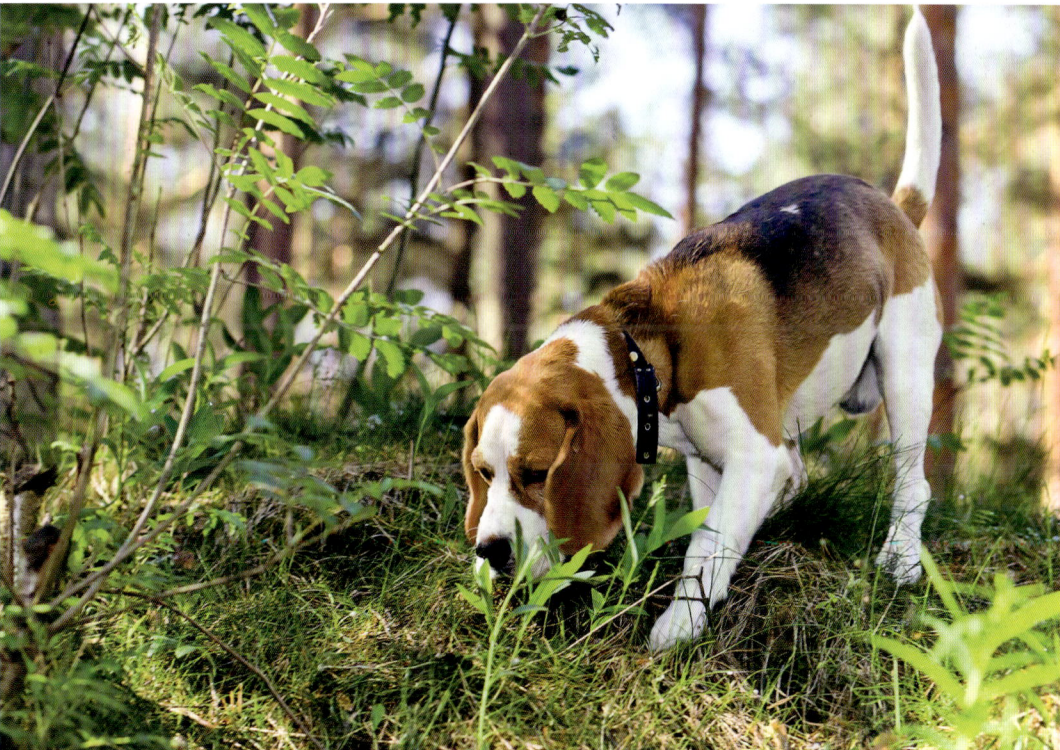

ALL PHOTOGRAPHS:
Out and about
This compact scent hound breed is an ideal candidate as a sniffer dog. Drug dogs are trained to recognize the scents of illegal substances. If it smells any of them in this luggage the dog will simply sit down next to the bag and await its human handler.

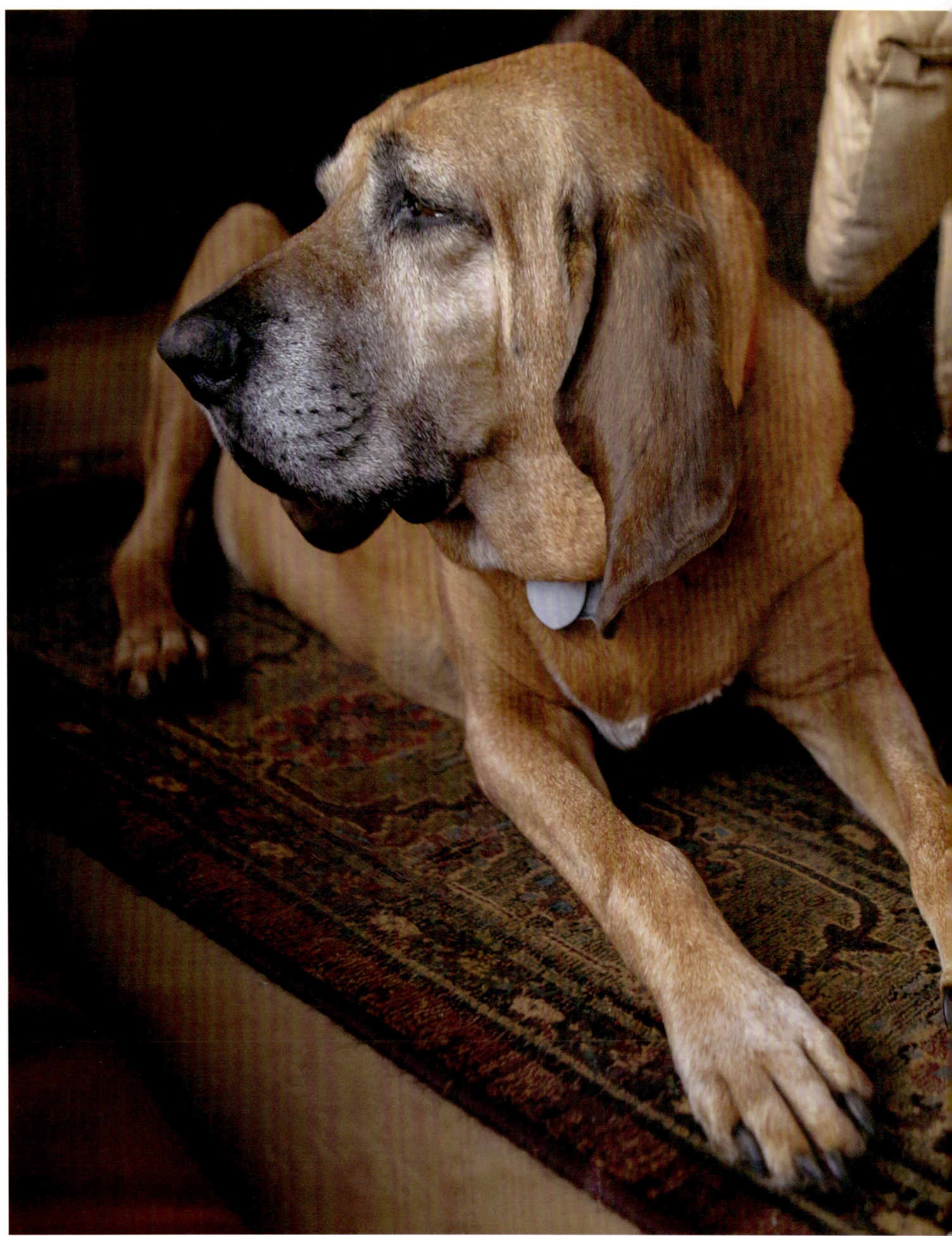

Bloodhound

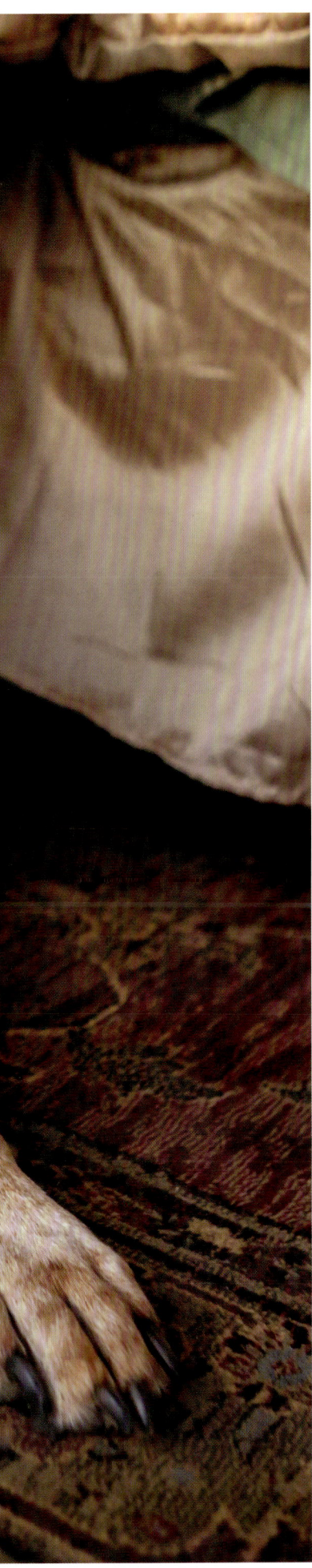

This substantial breed is known the world over for its superlative sense of smell. Its long nose houses a large and intensely folded olfactory cavity that is lined with 230 million odour-sensitive nerve cells. That is 45 times the number in the human nose, and the dog has a sense of smell at least 1,000 times stronger than ours. Coupled with the bloodhound's strong prey drive, the dog is able to track an animal (or person) that has left a scent trail more than 100 miles long!

The bloodhound is thought to have its origins in the ancient Mediterranean region. It is mentioned by Roman historians. That would make it the first scenthound breed. While the dogs are undemanding and gentle indoors, they become much more active outside where their scent world becomes much more crowded. They must be kept on the leash when away from home, so they can be stopped from their dogged pursuit of a beguiling scent. At home they need a fenced area to run in.

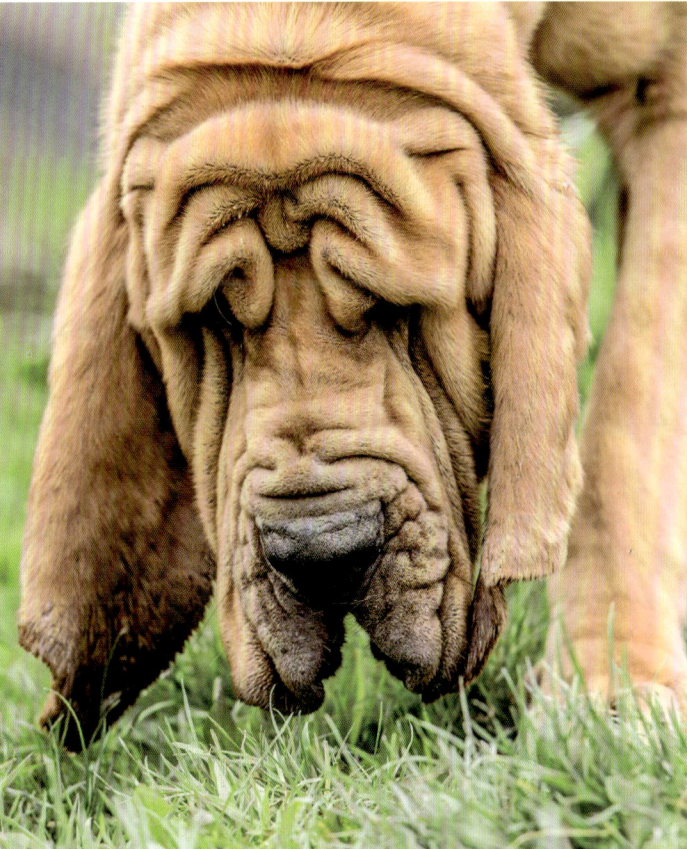

CHARACTERISTICS
Coat
The fur is usually tan, black or red in colour making a short and dense coat
Height
58–69cm (23–27in)
Weight
36–50kg (79–110lb)
Lifespan
10–12 years
Personality
Sociable and dogged
Origin
Mediterranean

LEFT:
Keeping healthy
Bloodhounds need regular grooming to keep their ears, eyes and skin clean and healthy.

ABOVE:
Sniffing machine
The breed is recognizable for the wrinkled skin around the eyes, jowls and floppy ears.

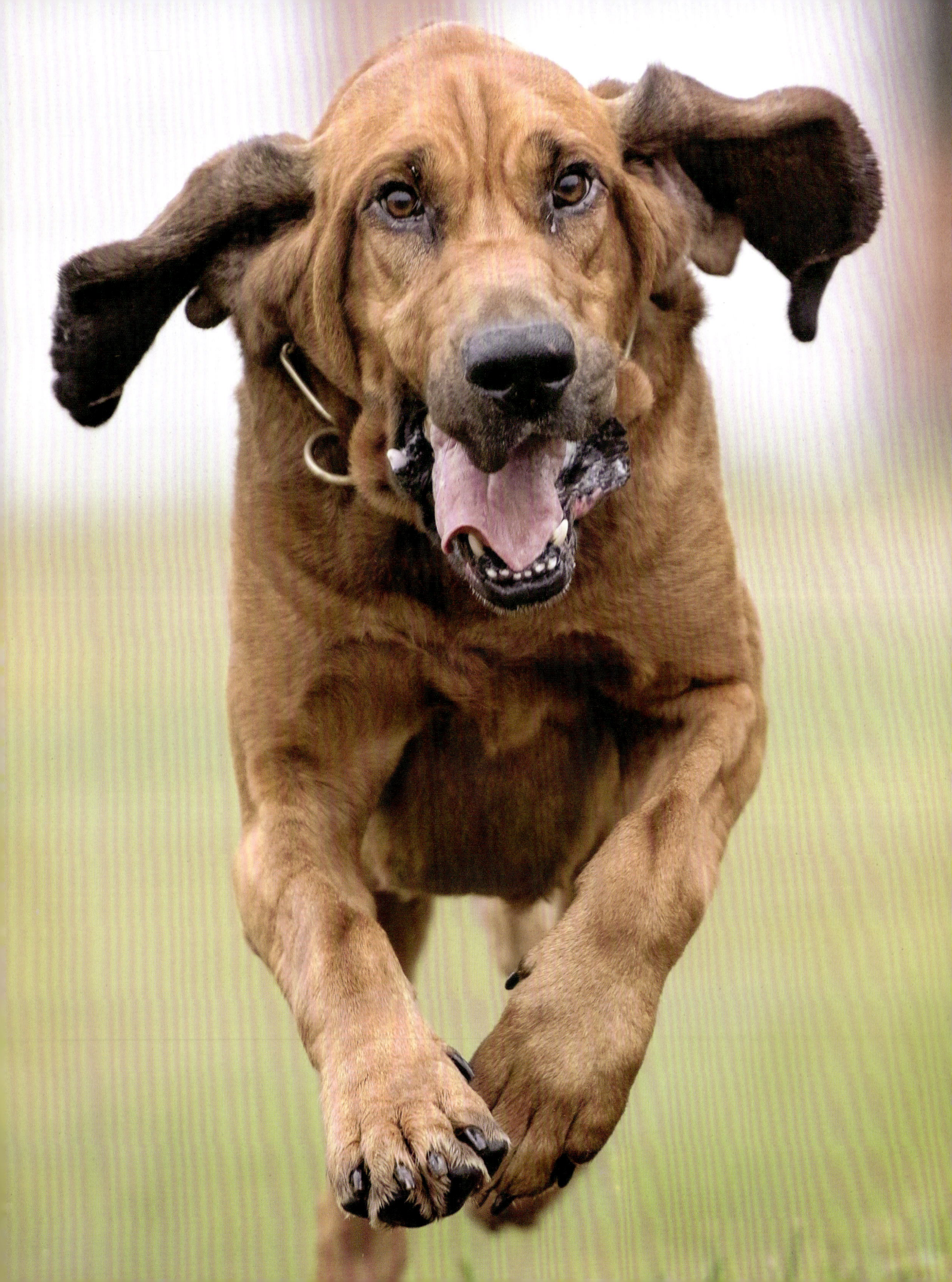

HUNTING DOGS

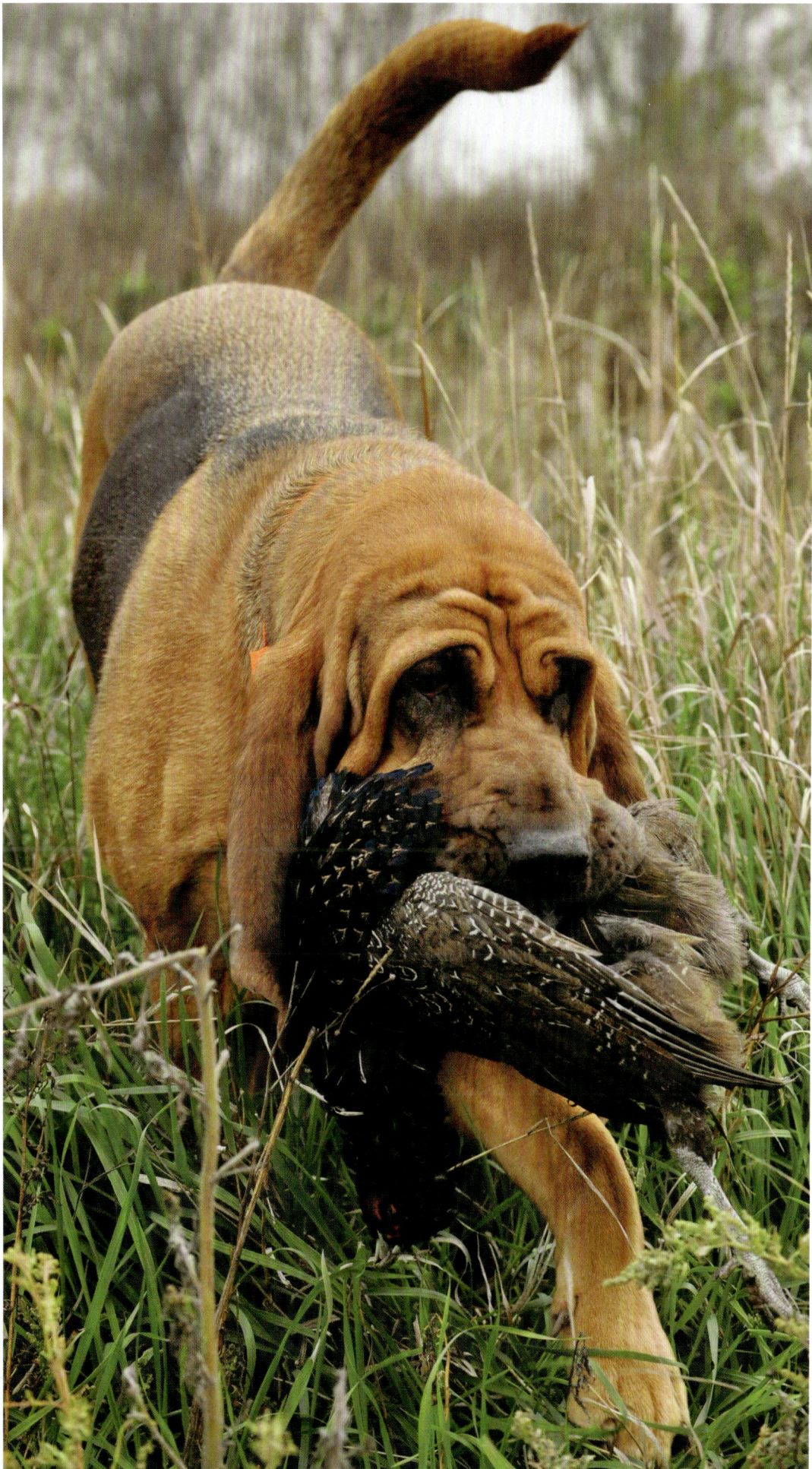

BOTH PHOTOGRAPHS:
Hunting desire
The bloodhound breed has a high motivation to find prey and is hard to stop once it has a scent. This is harnessed by people for all kinds of hunts – not least ones to find fugitives from the law in North America.

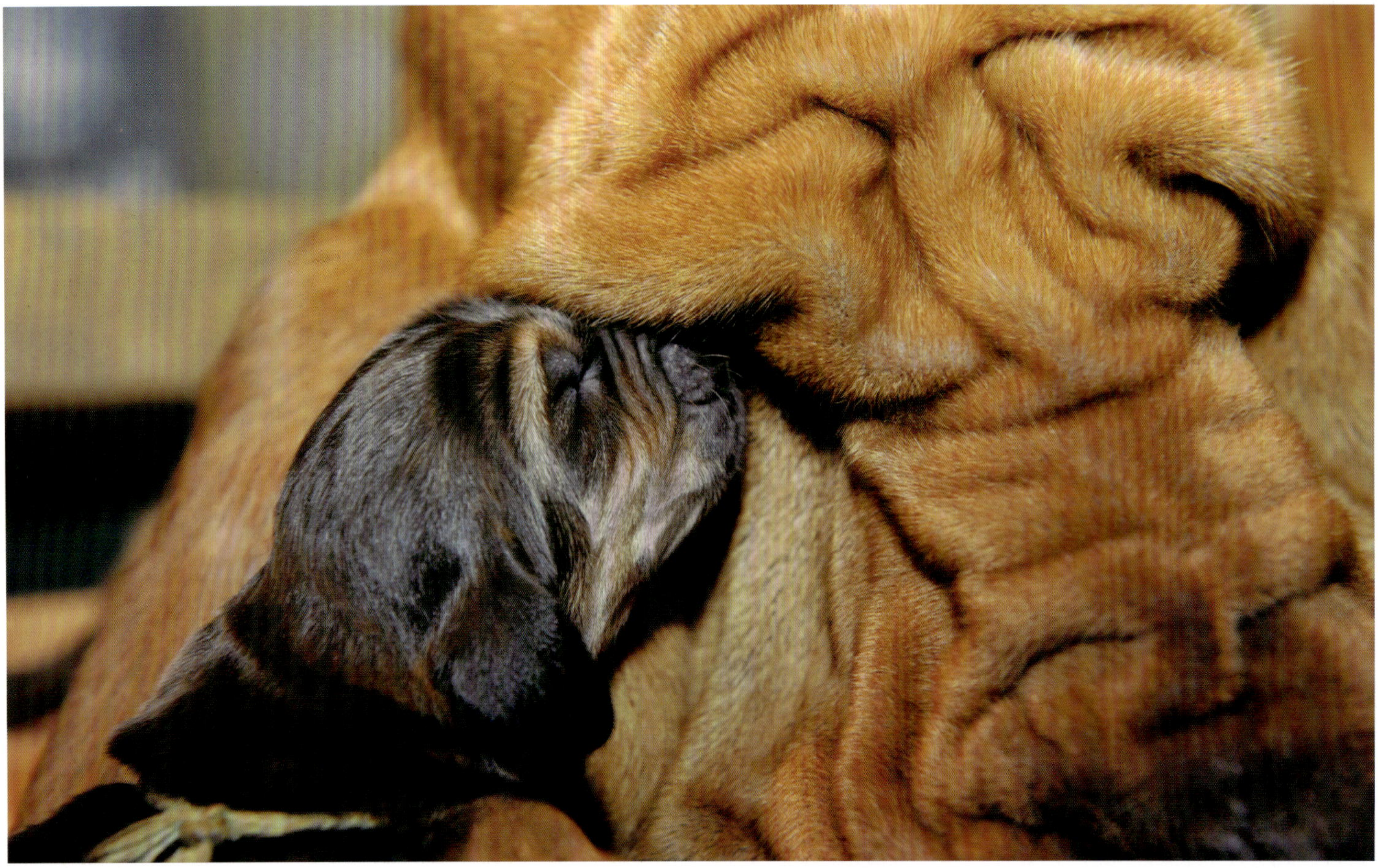

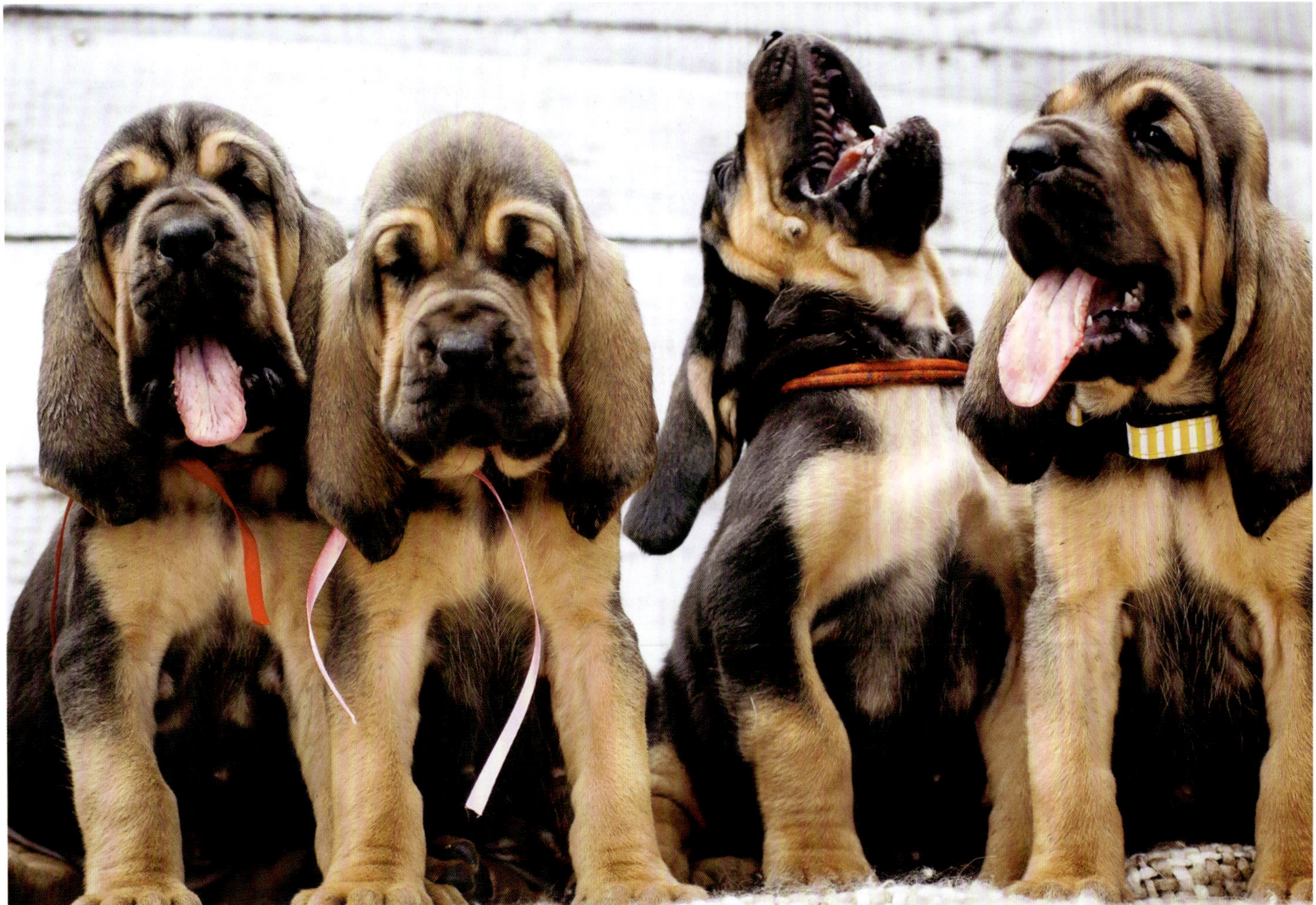

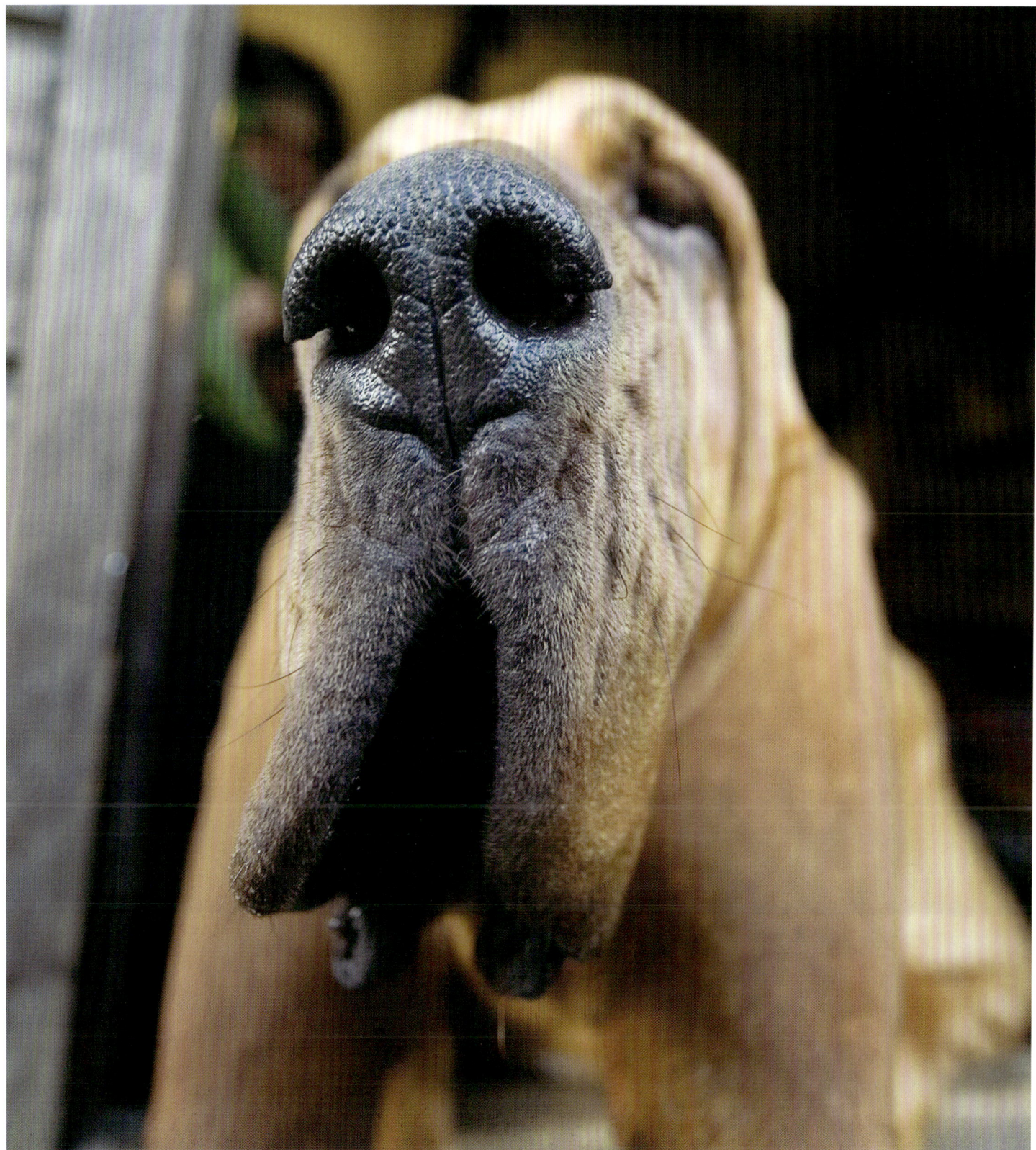

OPPOSITE TOP AND BOTTOM:
Bloodhound mother and puppy
Most puppies are entirely dependent on their mother for the first four weeks and then spend more time away from her.

ABOVE:
Jowls
The long, slobbering jowls of a scent hound keeps the lining of the nose moist and more sensitive to scents in the air.

HUNTING DOGS

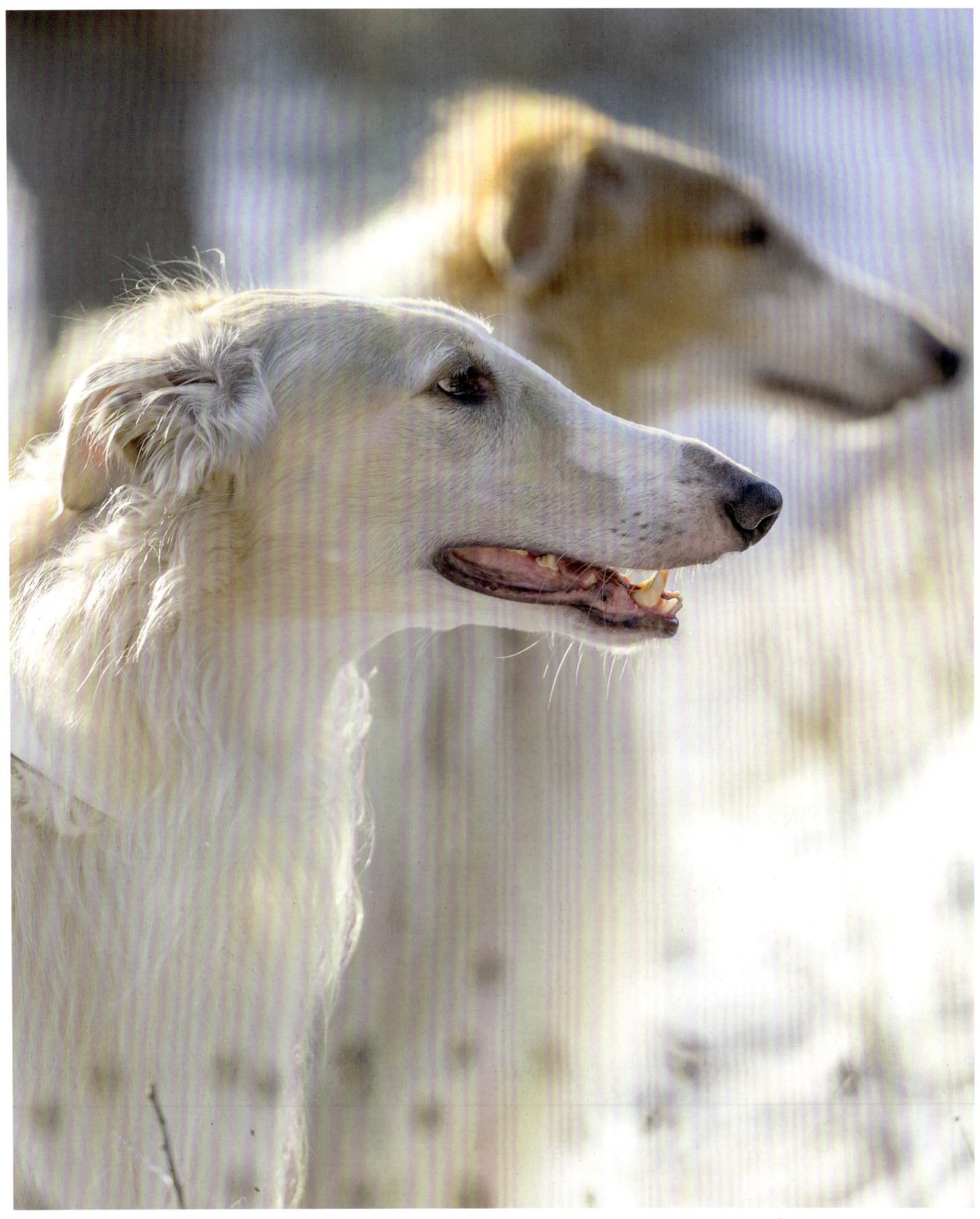

ABOVE:
Frilly neck
Borzois have a frill of long hairs on their slender necks and tassels around the ears.

Borzoi

CHARACTERISTICS

Coat
Long and silky coat that can be any colour
Height
68–74cm (27–29in)
Weight
27–48kg (60–106lb)
Lifespan
11–13 years
Personality
Eager and independent
Origin
Russia

The word borzoi means "fast" in Russian, and this sighthound breed from that country lives up to its name. In the days of imperial Russia, aristocratic hunting parties travelled far into the wilderness aboard specially equipped trains with several dozen borzoi aboard. One of these spectacular hunts was immortalized by Leo Tolstoy in his epic *War and Peace*. He describes how 130 borzoi under the control of 20 horsemen are unleashed to drive out and kill wolves.

The October Revolution of 1917 put an end to the Russian nobility, and the revolutionaries also slaughtered the borzoi, seen as a symbol of the aristocracy. The breed was saved from extinction by a few that had been taken to Britain and America, where the elegant breed was better known for a while as the Russian wolfhound.

Borzois are calm and dignified dogs but are reserved with strangers. Borzois are not suitable for homes that have other small animals and, for dogs that match up to wild wolves, it is no surprise that the breed needs a large amount of daily exercise with plenty of space to run. The strong prey drive means the dog is likely to chase other animals when it gets the chance. The long coat that does so much to give the breed its graceful look also needs careful grooming.

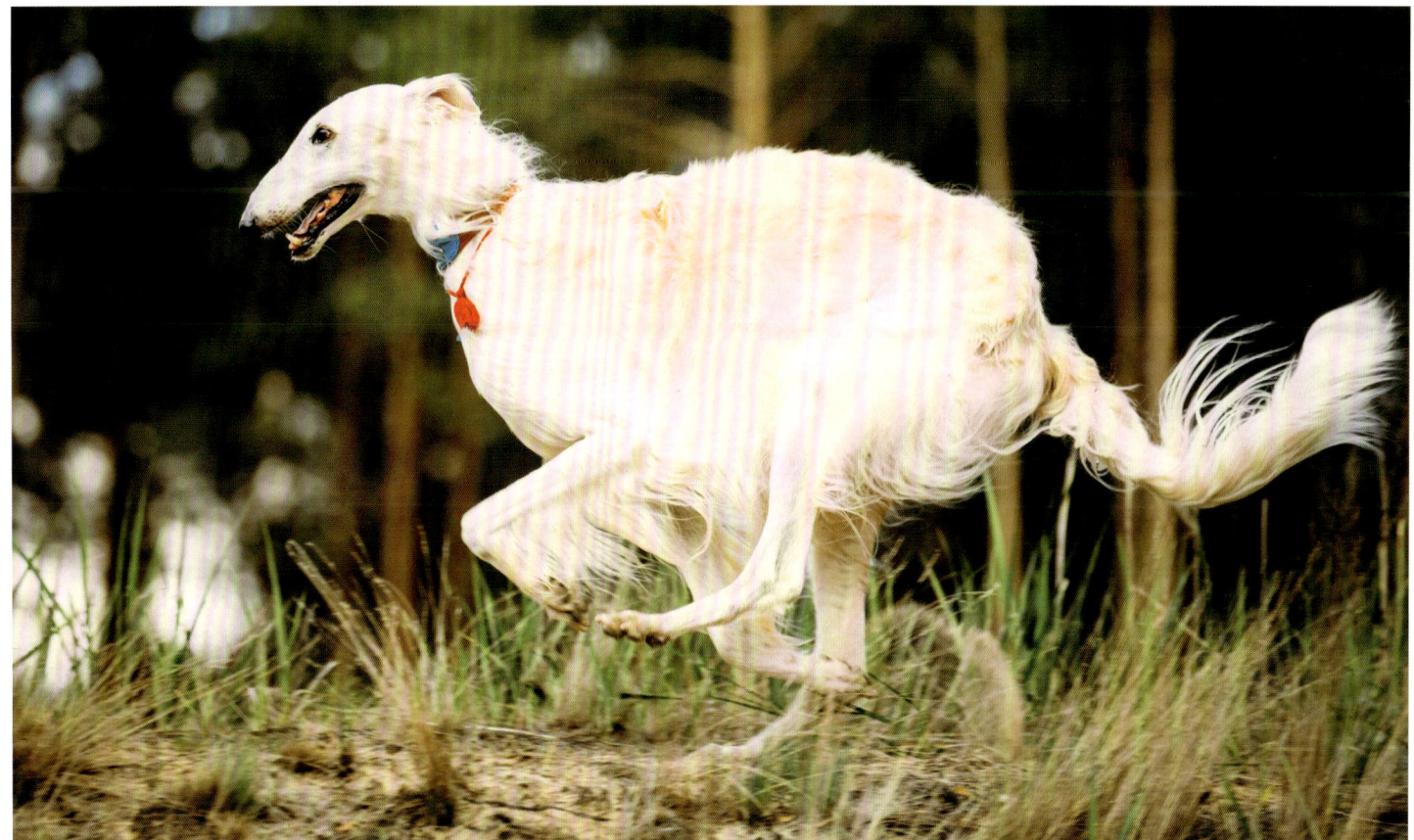

ABOVE:
Speed and style
Some borzois have highly feathered legs and long tasselled tails and this hair flows as the fast dogs gallop.

HUNTING DOGS

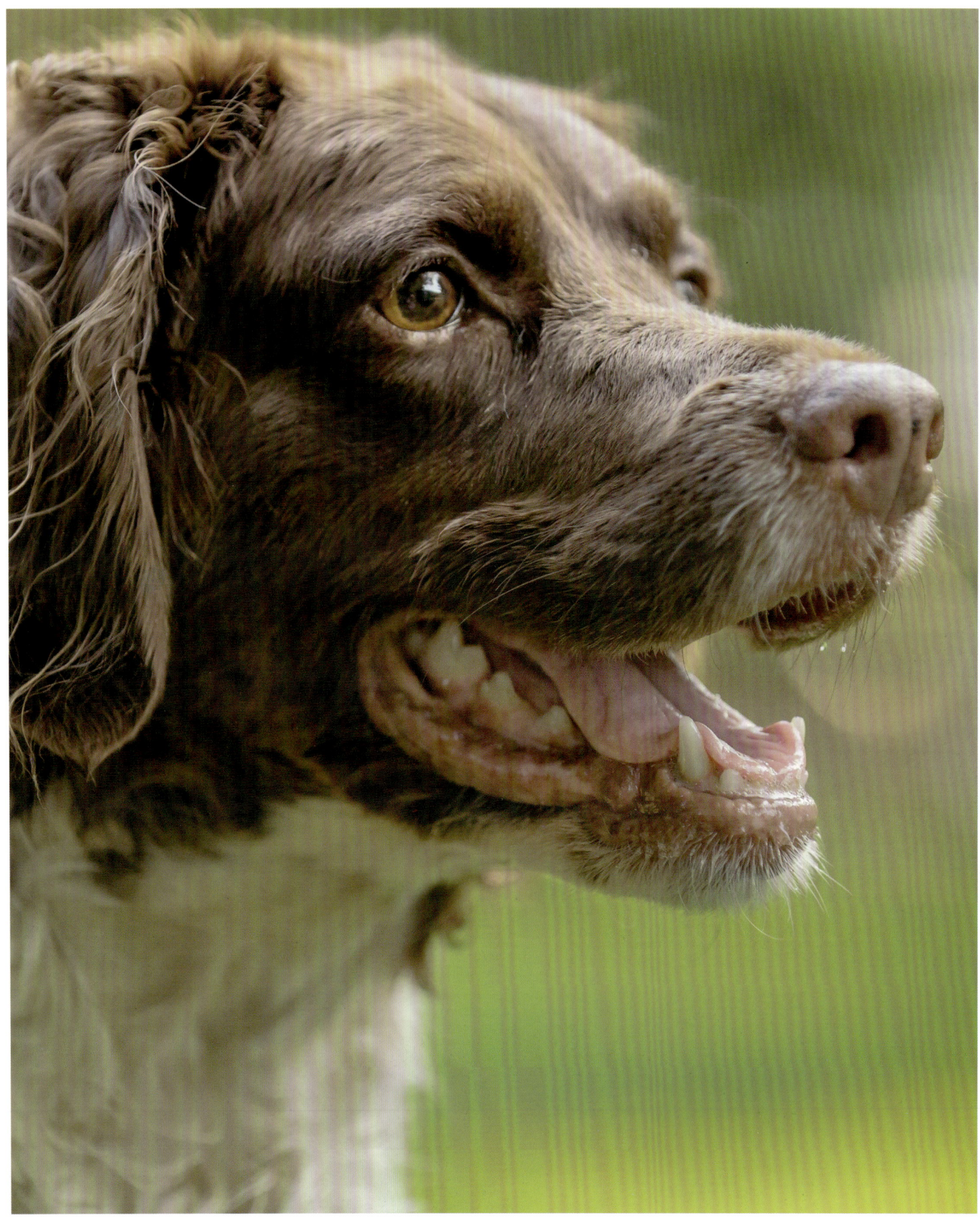

ABOVE:
Sharp eyes
The Brittany spaniel has oval eyes, flopped triangular ears and an inquisitive blunt muzzle.

Brittany Spaniel

CHARACTERISTICS

Coat
Medium-length and flowing hair that comes in various colours, such as orange and white, liver and white, or black and white

Height
47–51cm (19–20in)

Weight
14–18kg (31–40lb)

Lifespan
12–14 years

Personality
Reliable and friendly

Origin
France

This eager gundog is the top choice for many field sports enthusiasts. It has a gentle demeanour but is a fast and faithful bird dog that bounds into action whenever required. Despite the name it is not a spaniel but developed pointer. The longer length of leg is the giveaway here. The breed is smaller than a setter but taller than a true spaniel. It combines a certain hardiness with agility and clean movement.

The breed was developed in Brittany in northwestern France in the late Middle Ages, and it even adorns some 17th century tapestries. The dog was used by peasant folk (and poachers no doubt) as a hunter of duck as well as woodcock, pheasant and partridge, all of which were an important source of wild-caught food.

Brittany spaniels are very energetic dogs and will need a lot of exercise and mental stimulation to stay happy and healthy. They are usually friendly and gentle but can become timid and submissive. They need to be trained with plenty of positive reinforcement and they benefit from early and prolonged socialization. Away from blood sports, this breed are good candidates for other dog sports such as agility courses, obedience trials and flyball.

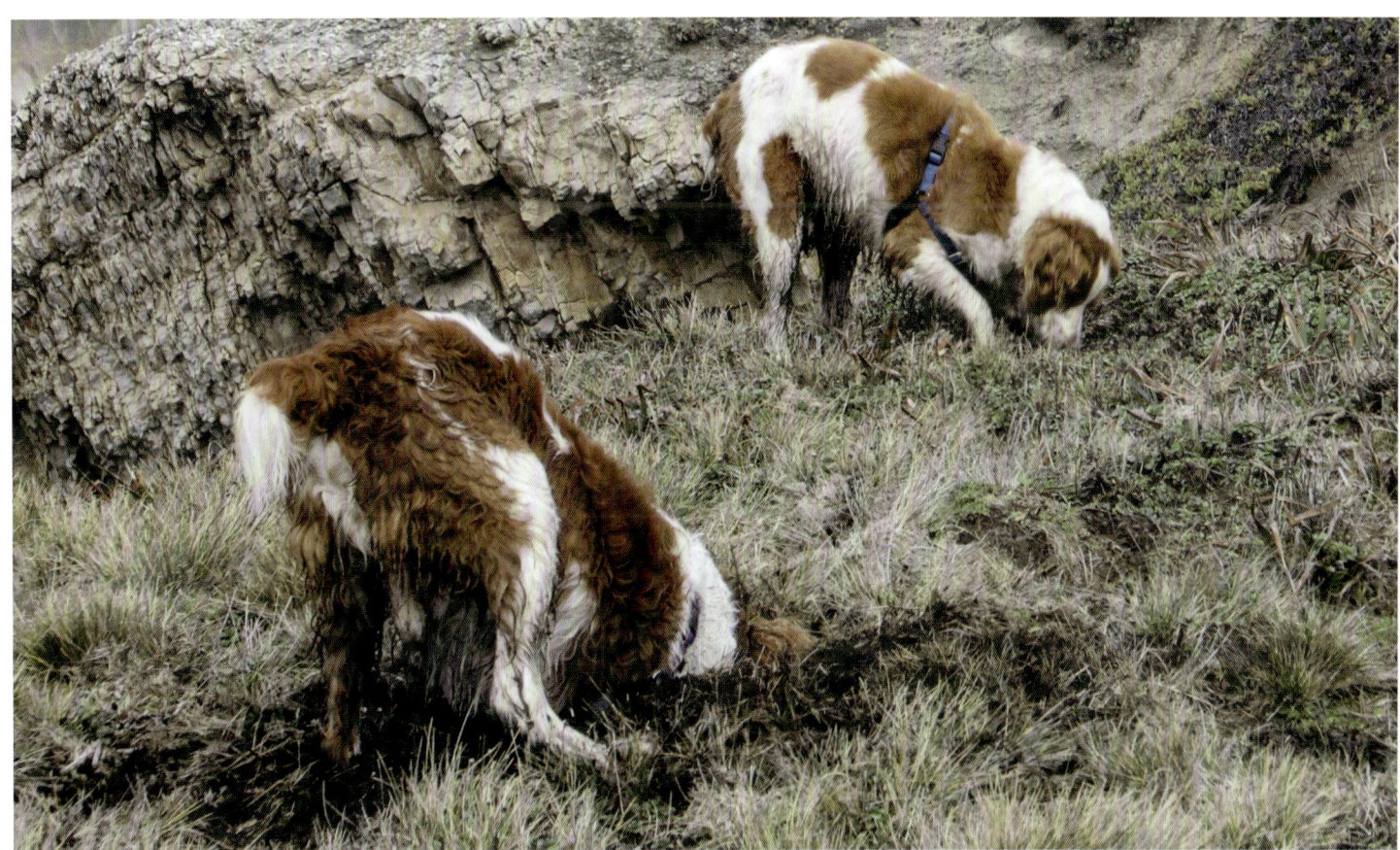

ABOVE:
Where next?
Brittany spaniels especially enjoy exploring new outdoor areas with their owners. What have these two found?

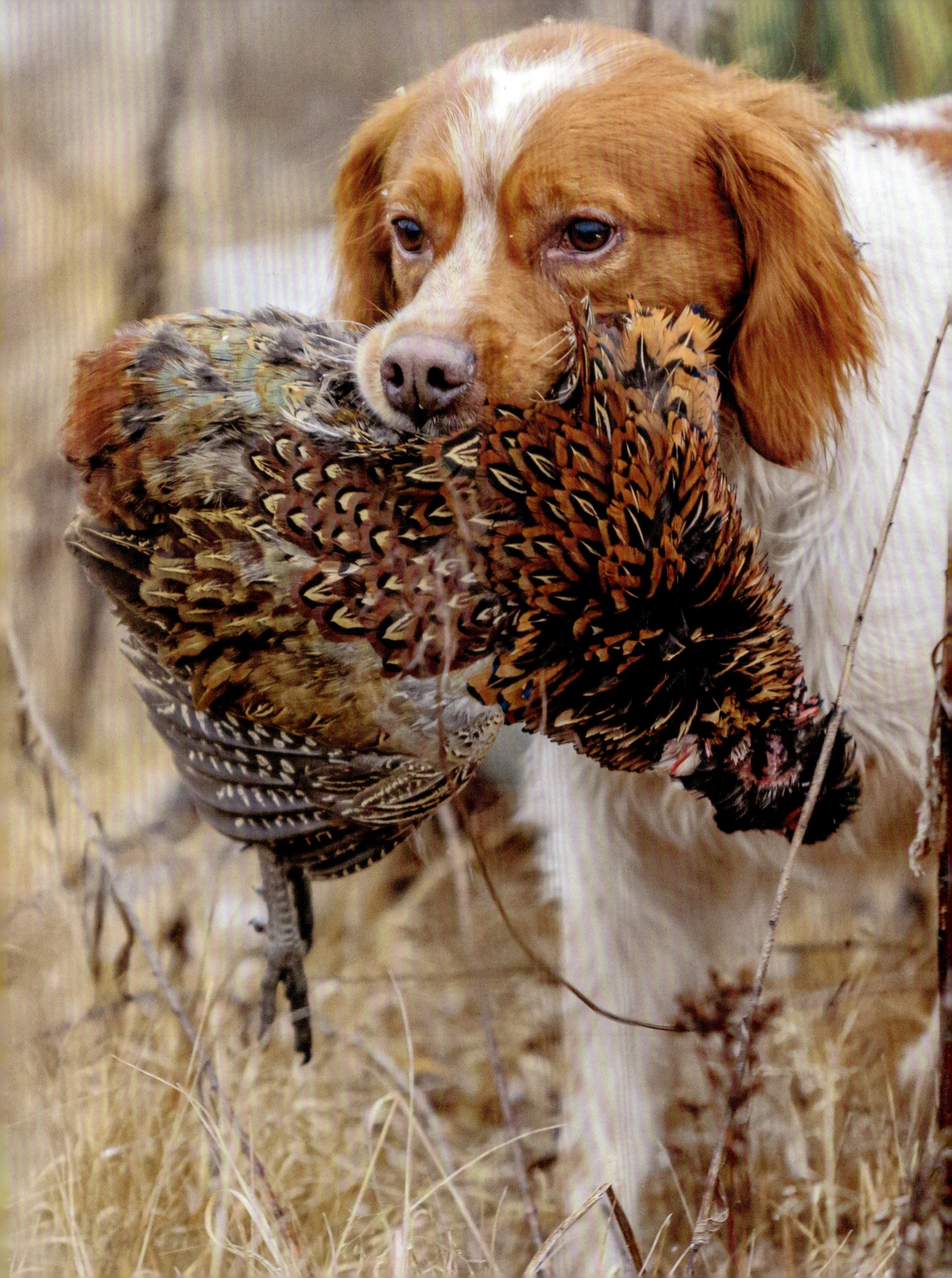

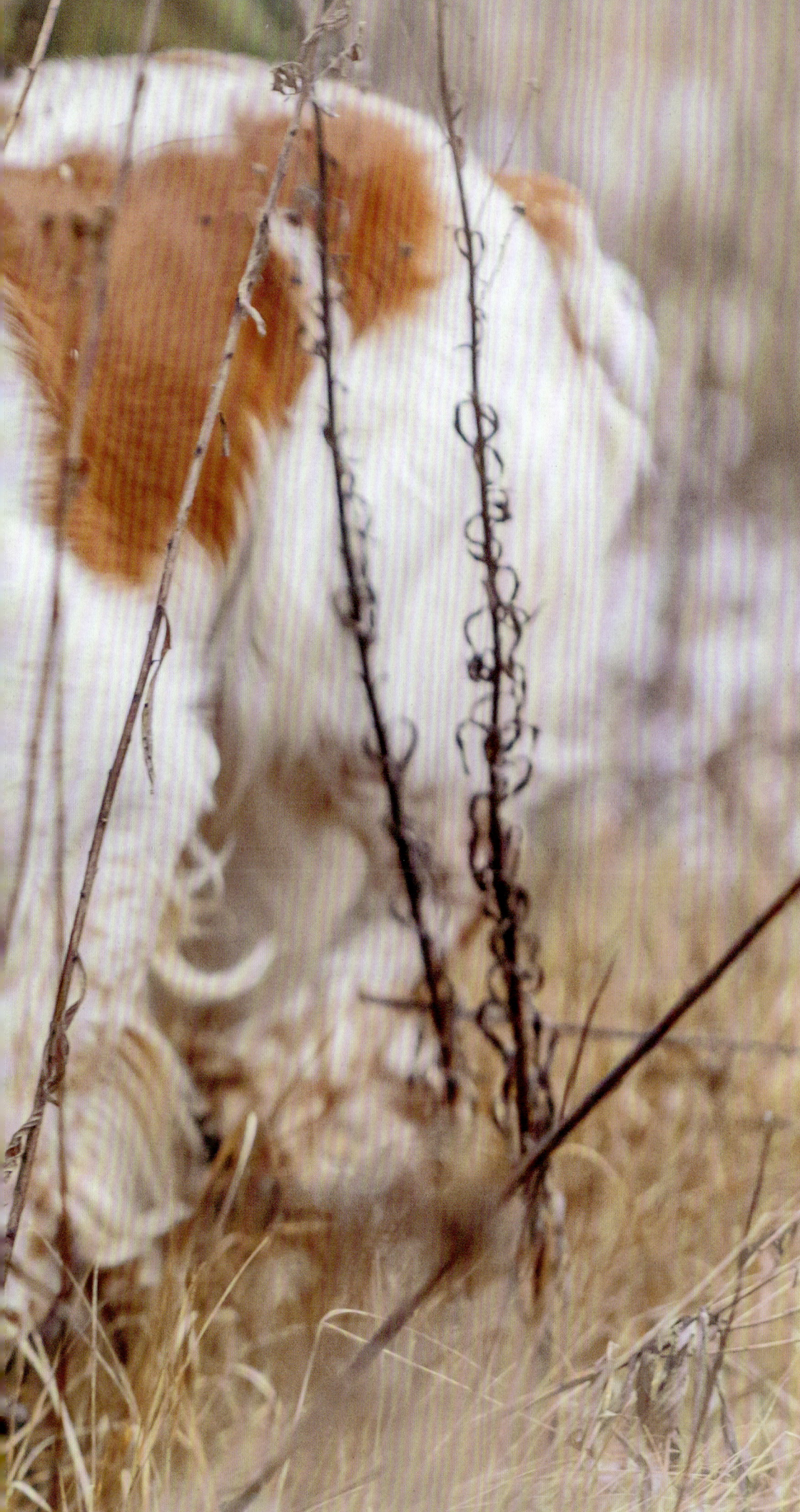

HUNTING DOGS

Soft mouths
Retrievers such as this spaniel are bred to not bite down on to killed birds and to return them to their masters without damaging them.

HUNTING DOGS

Chesapeake Bay Retriever

CHARACTERISTICS

Coat
Medium-length coat that can be brown or sedge in colour with limited white markings

Height
53–66cm (21–26in)

Weight
25–36kg (55–79lb)

Lifespan
12–13 years

Personality
Loyal and intelligent

Origin
United States

The bank of Chesapeake Bay, a large ocean inlet that penetrates into America's political and historical heartlands, is prime duck-hunting country located as it is under the Atlantic Flyway. In the 19th century, the wealthy landowners of Virginia and Maryland developed this breed as an ideal bird dog for the conditions in the bay. The waters here are mostly shallow and are still very cold in spring when the migrating birds arrive. The breeders began by crossing the Newfoundland and Irish water spaniel. Although the former is much larger than the latter both breeds are known as good retrievers. Both are also powerful swimmers with waterproof coats and webbed feet, something that the "chessie" retains. The Chesapeake Bay retriever has also inherited their tolerance of cold water. The 19th-century breeders also added various local dogs of indeterminate breeding to introduce vigour to the breed. The breed reached its current conformation in the 1880s.

The Chesapeake Bay retriever is still used as a hunting dog, and makes a loyal and obedient pet. It has a love of water and swimming should be incorporated into its exercise regimen. Away from the hunting clubs, the dog also thrives in other competitive fields, such as obedience and agility trials and tracking.

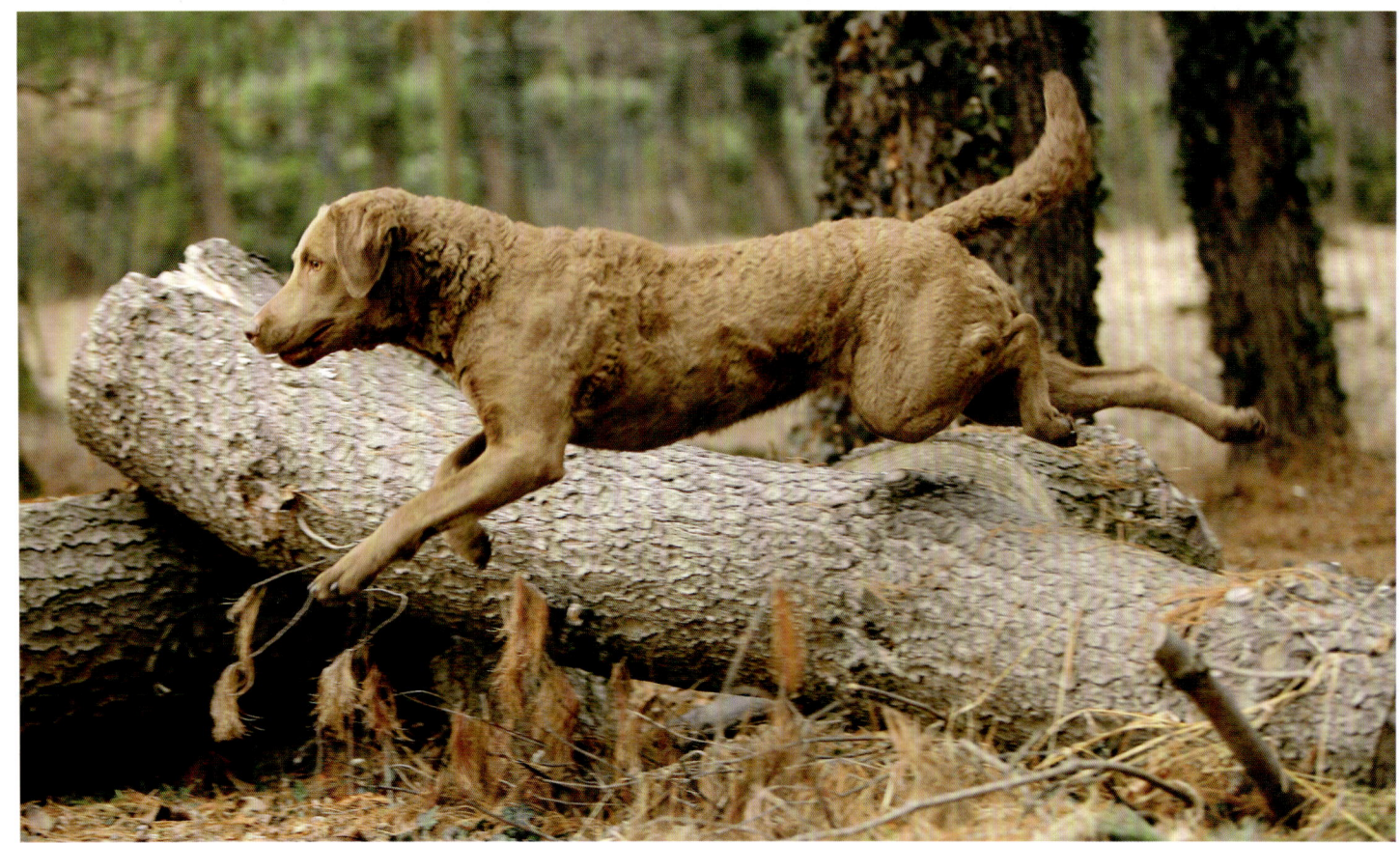

ABOVE:
Go getter
The Chesapeake Bay retriever is a superlative fetcher of downed waterbirds. It brings home the quarry among the woodland and marshes around the bay.

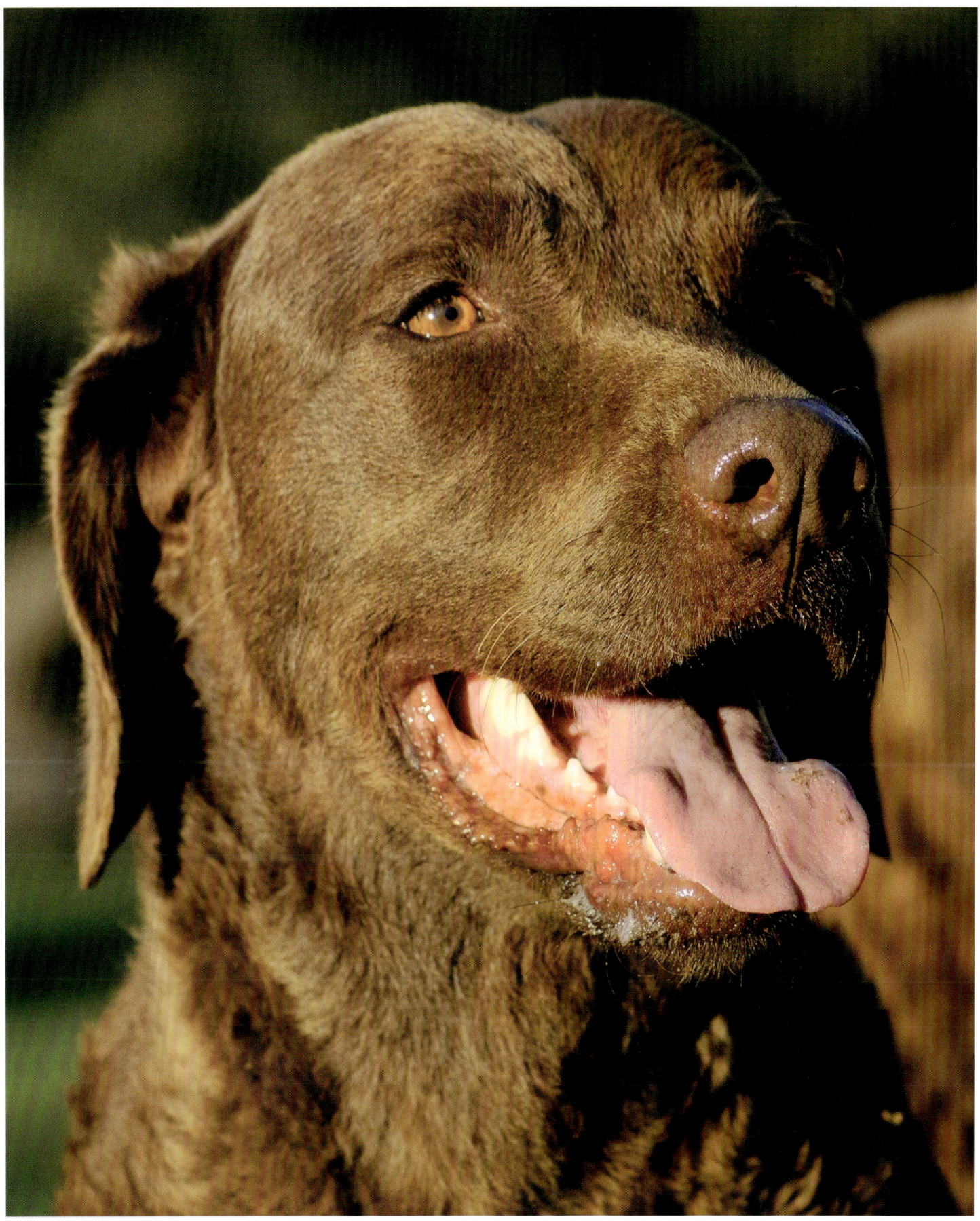

ABOVE:
Pale eyes
This breed of retriever is known for its distinctive wavy coat, which is waterproofed with oils, and its amber eyes.

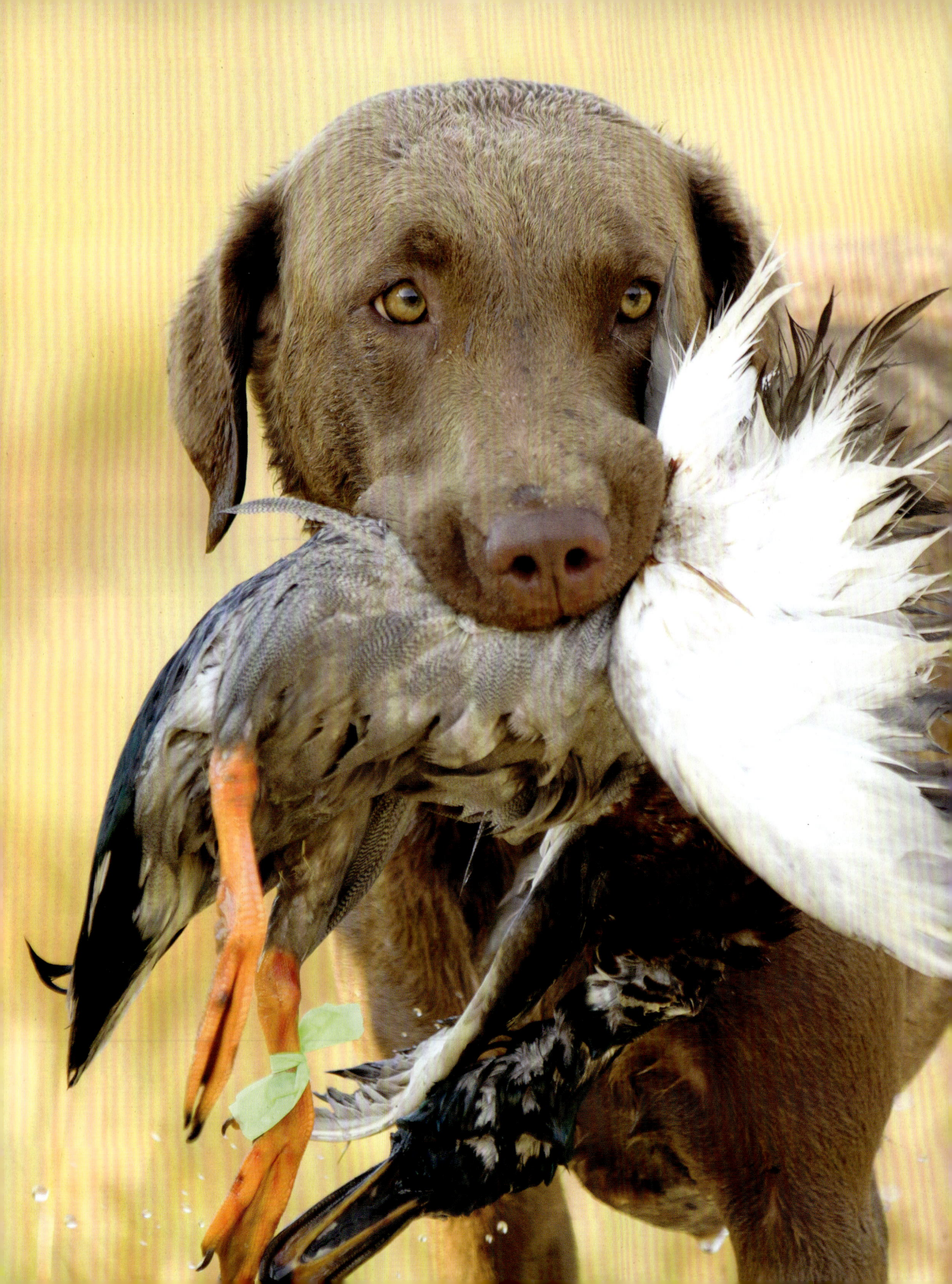

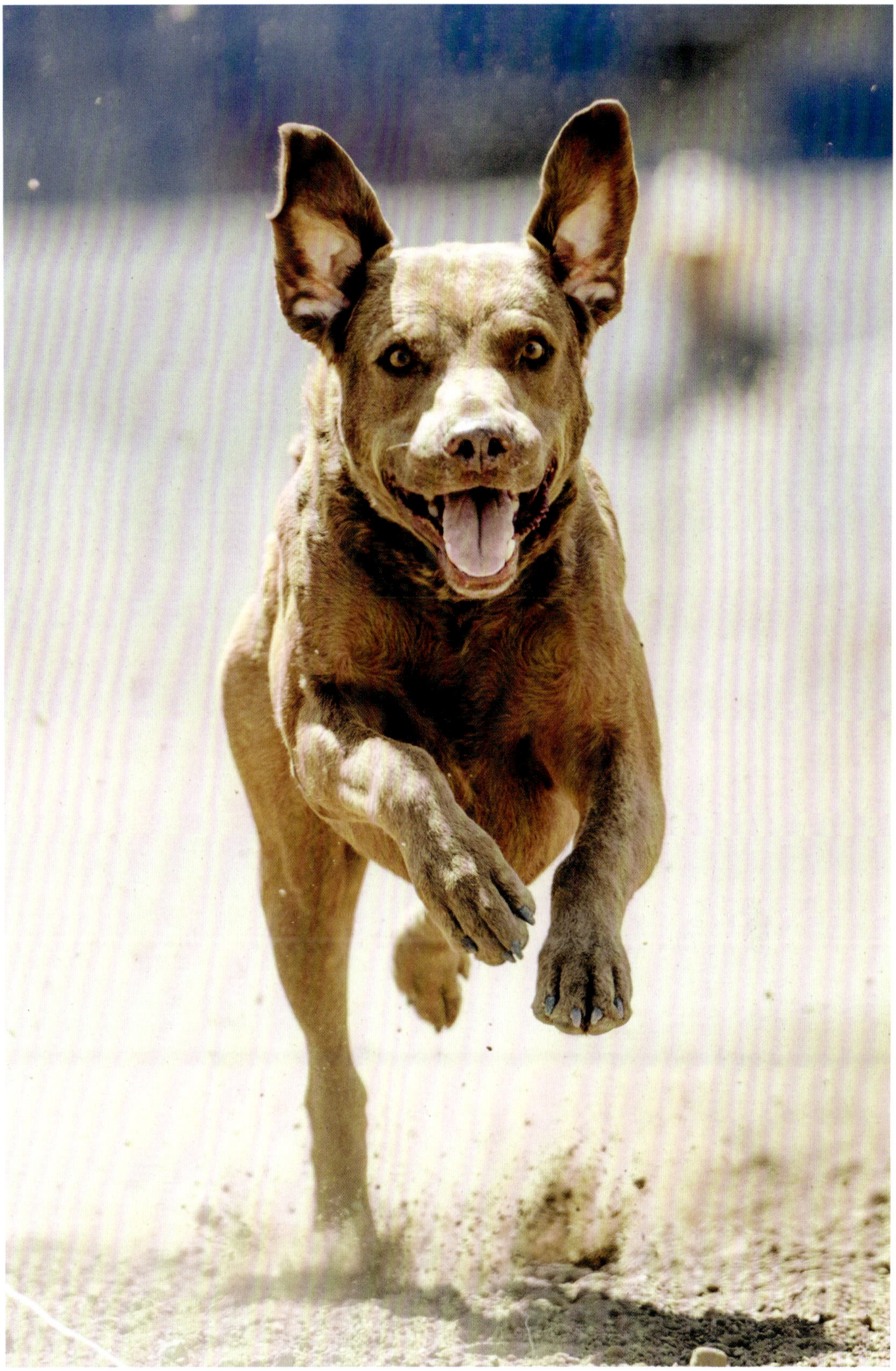

HUNTING DOGS

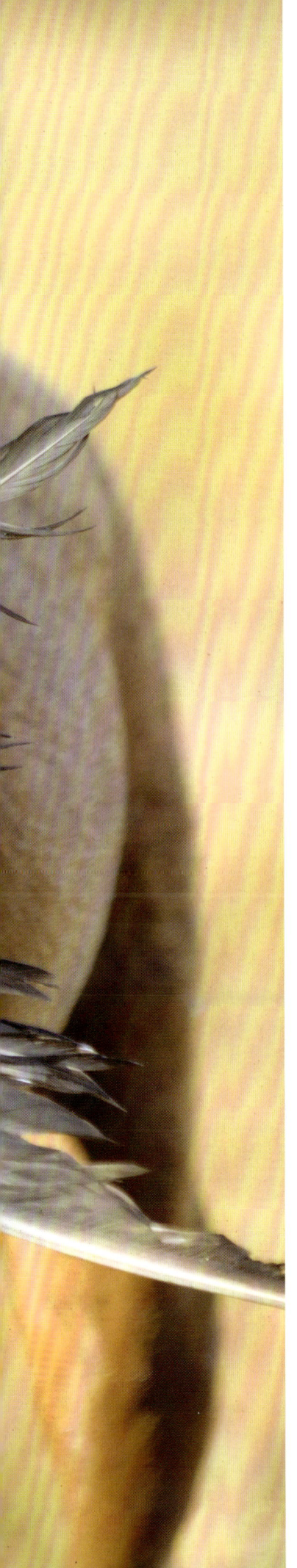

LEFT:
Hunter
This breed is a skilled swimmer with a keen sense of smell, and was bred to retrieve waterfowl for hunters.

ABOVE:
Graceful movement
When a Chesapeake Bay retriever moves they do so with a powerful smooth free and strong effortless action. As they get faster their feet converge.

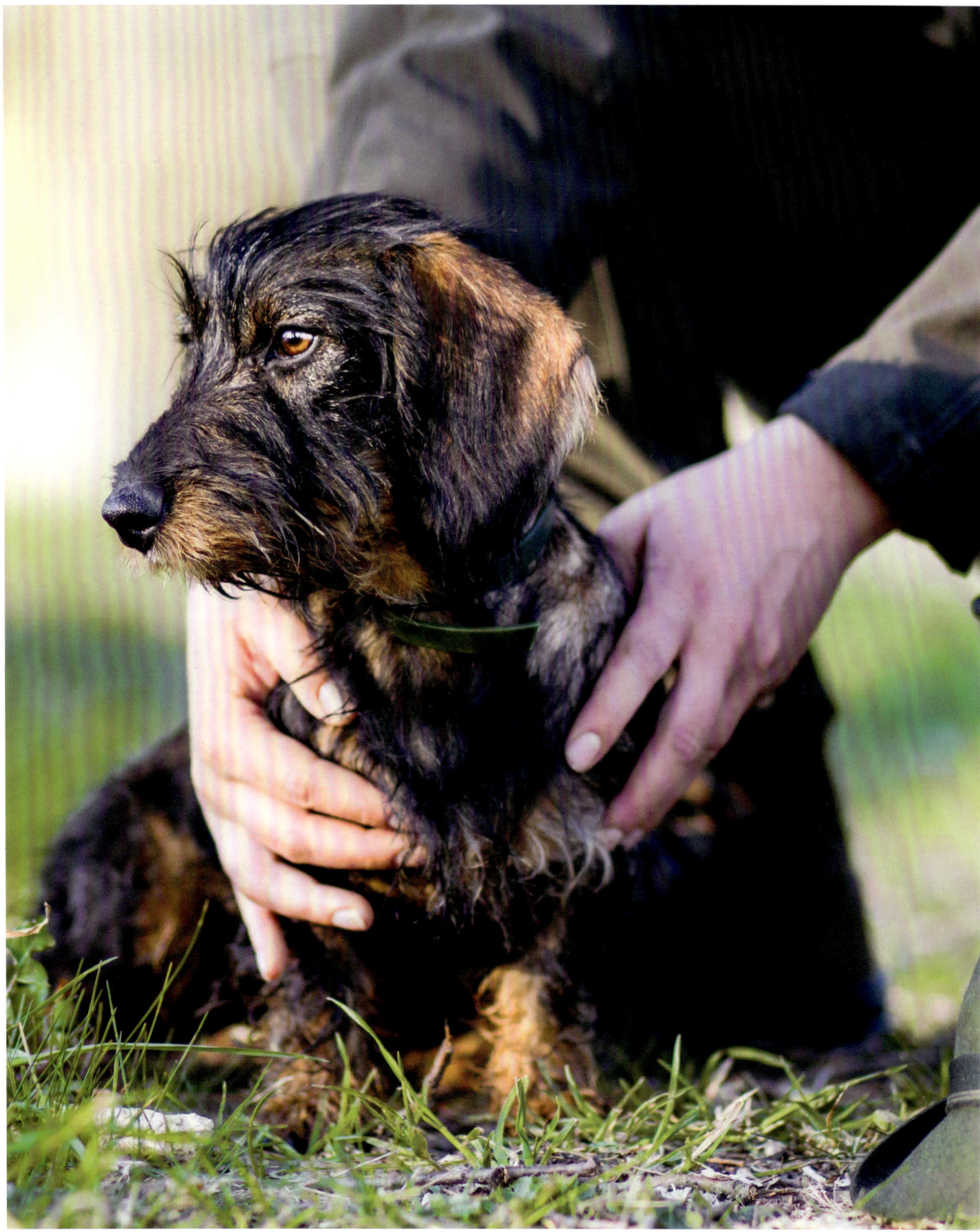

ABOVE:
Care and attention
Dachshunds have some health issues that owners should be aware of, such as spinal problems, obesity, eye diseases and dental problems. The breed is divided into two sizes: standard and miniature, depending on weight.

Dachshund (standard)

CHARACTERISTICS

Coat
Three coat types: smooth-haired, long-haired and wire-haired, and can have various colours and patterns

Height
20–23cm (8–9in)

Weight
9–12kg (20–26lb)

Lifespan
12–15 years

Personality
Loyal and intelligent

Origin
Germany

Some might call this breed a sausage dog due to the apparent mismatch between the size of its legs and cylindrical torso. However, the German name actually means "badger dog" and these low-slung hunters were bred to fit inside burrows to combat those that live underground. That included other predators like badgers and stoats. Badgers are fierce creatures, and dachshunds would be sent to attack in groups, digging down into setts from all angles. The dogs countered the gnash and slash of the British badger's teeth and claws with cunning and agility.

Dachshunds have been performing this role for at least the last 600 years. There are three coat types, with a wiry variety for working in thorny country and a long-haired type for colder regions.

Today badgers and other wild mammals are highly prized and largely protected, so dachshunds have become seen as endearing little pets. The small dogs do well in a small home but do require regular exercising nevertheless. The smart dogs enjoy playing games and like the opportunity to dig from time to time, so this should be a factor when choosing walking routes. The dachshund can be a nuisance barker and so needs consistent training and careful socialization from an early age.

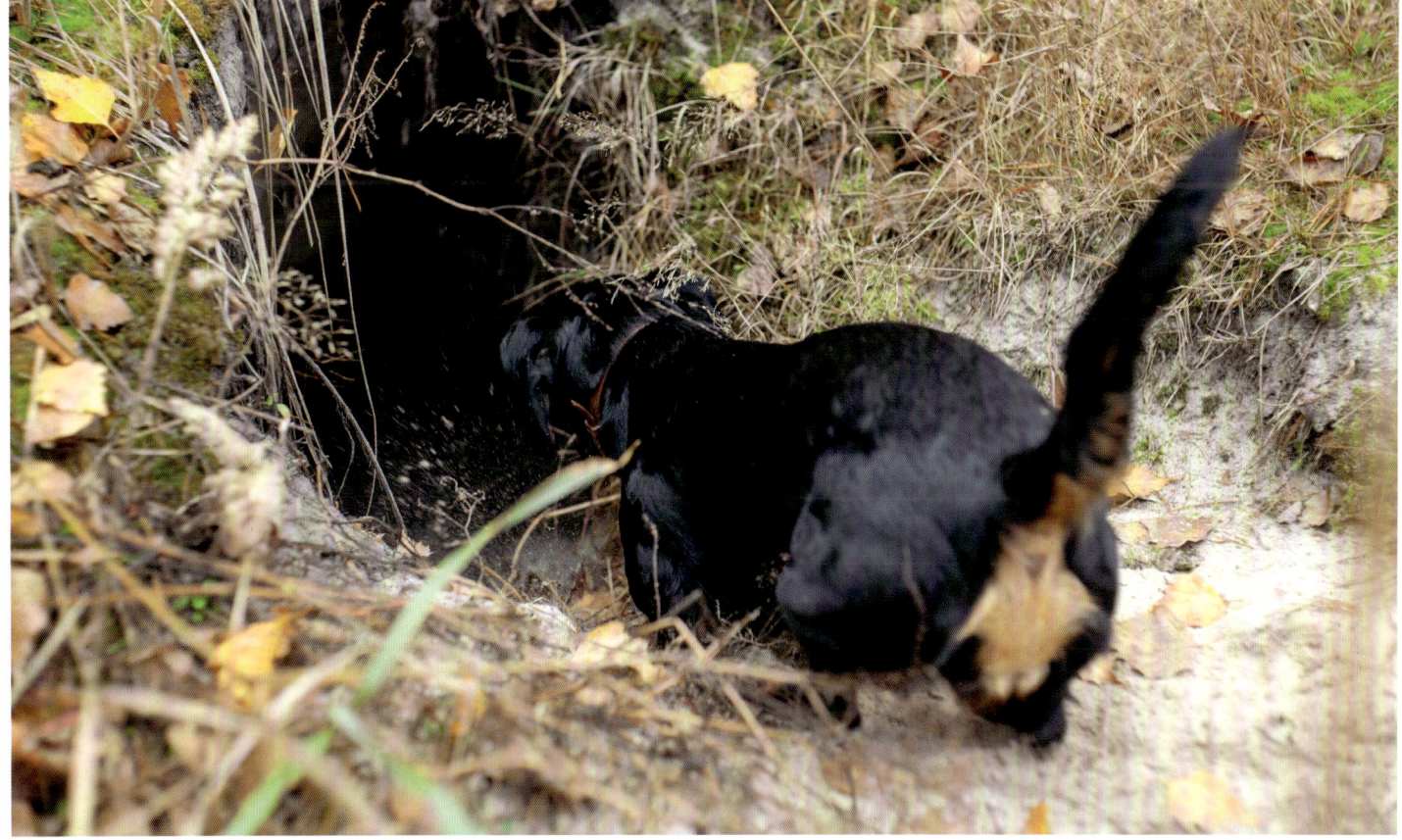

ABOVE:
Busy breed
Dachshunds are active dogs that enjoy walks, games and digging. They have a keen sense of smell, which is their primary guide.

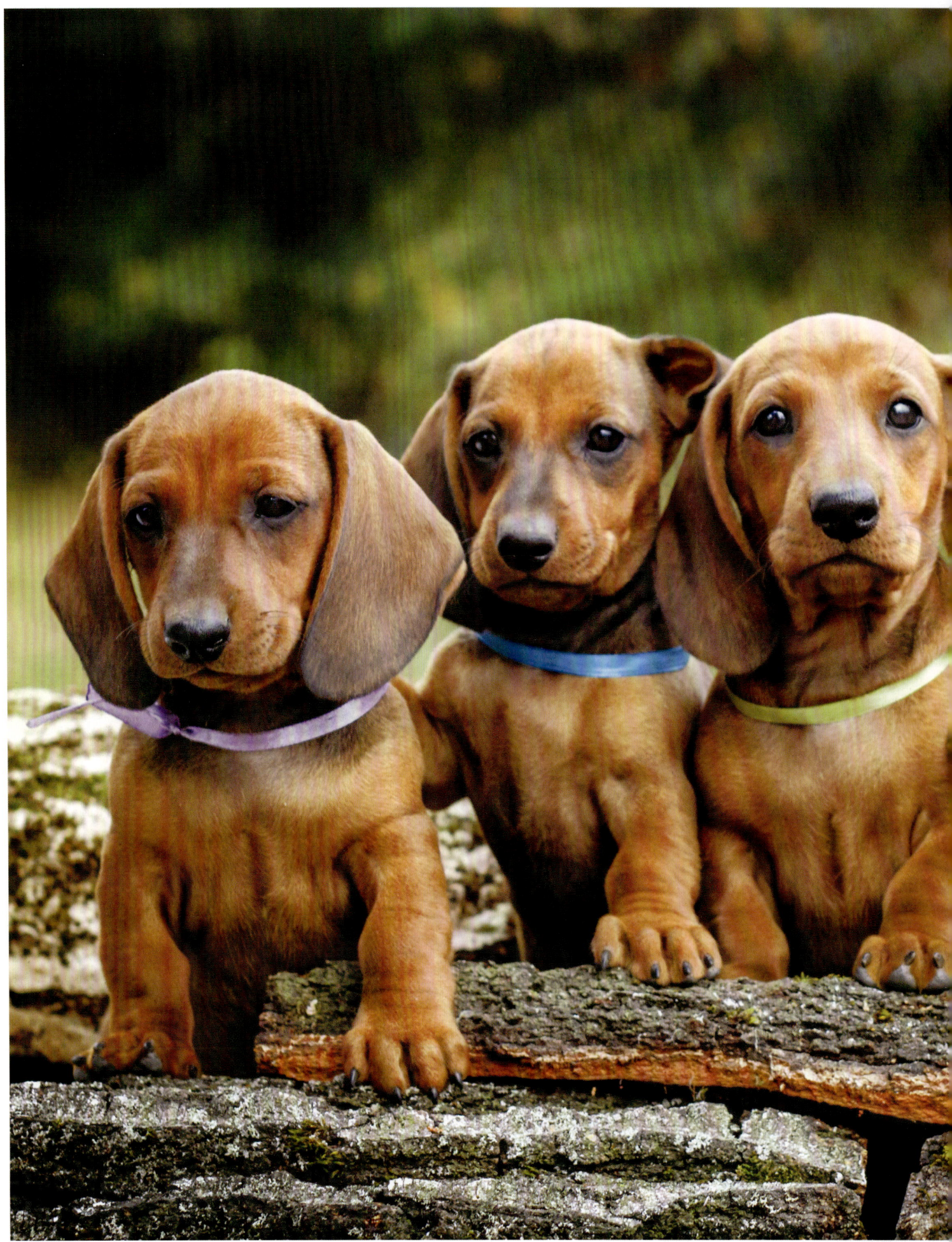

HUNTING DOGS

Pedigree puppies
With a curious nature, dachshund puppies are ready to test your boundaries and explore their new home with you.

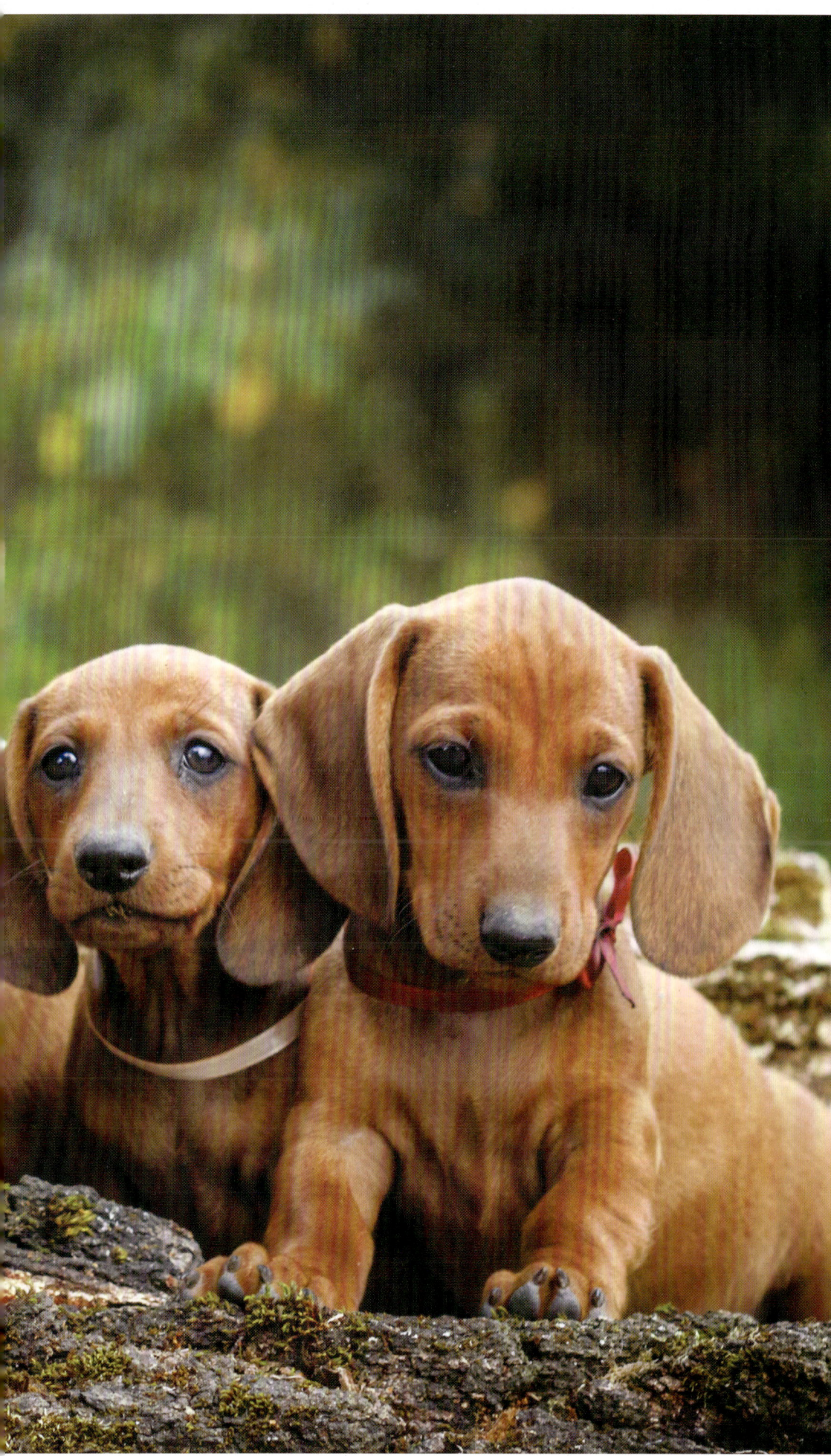

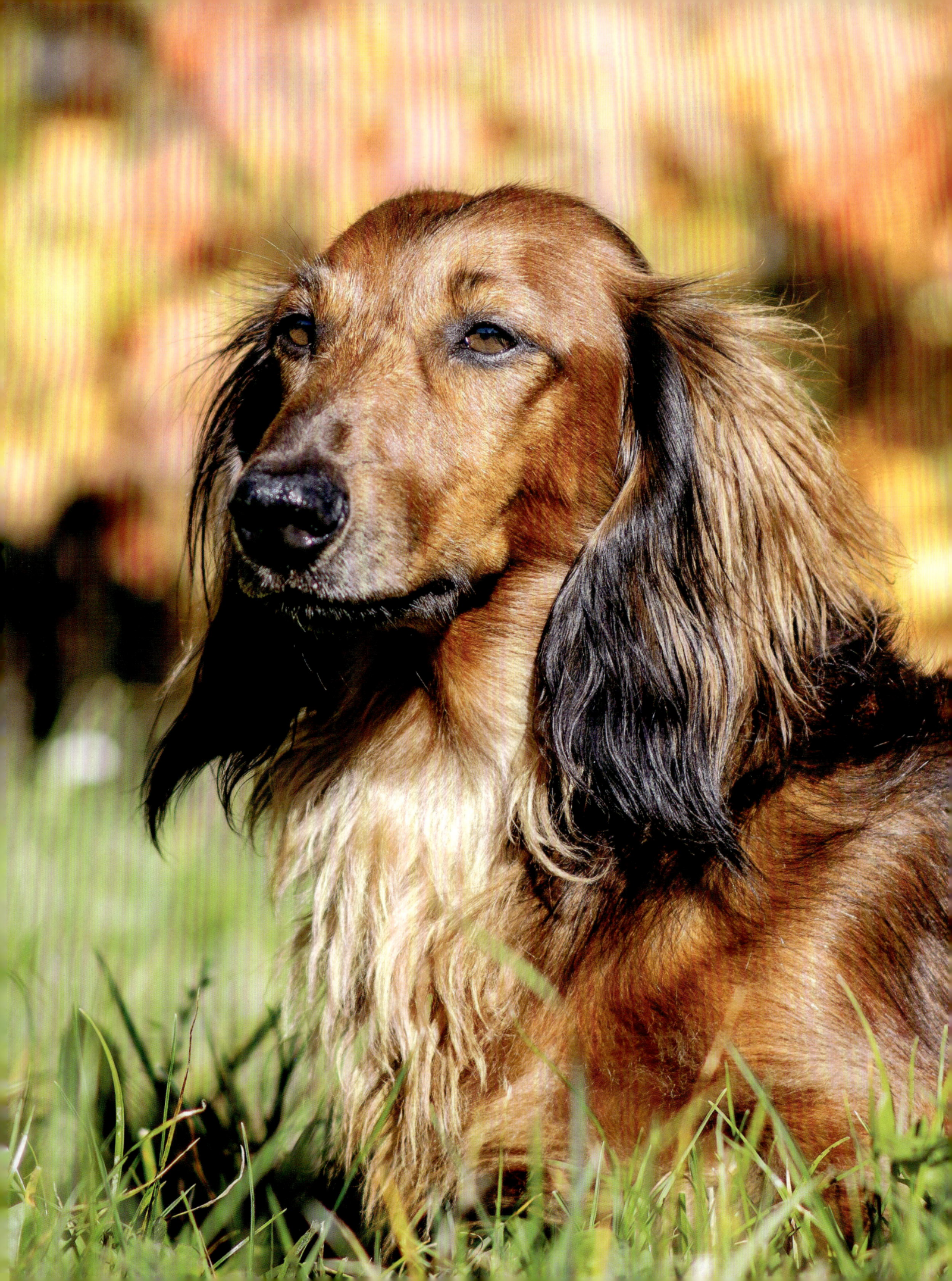

HUNTING DOGS

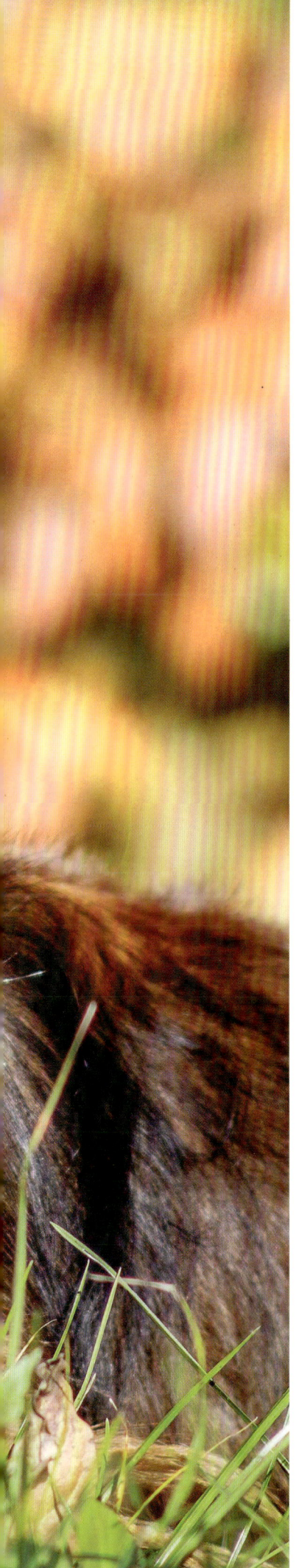
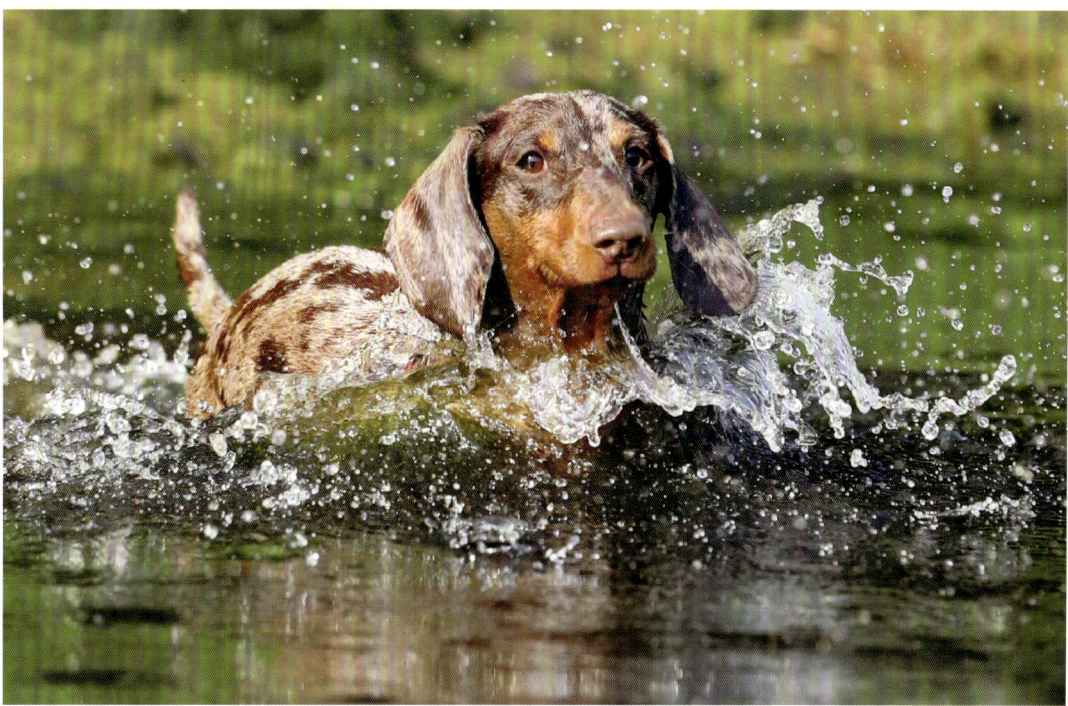
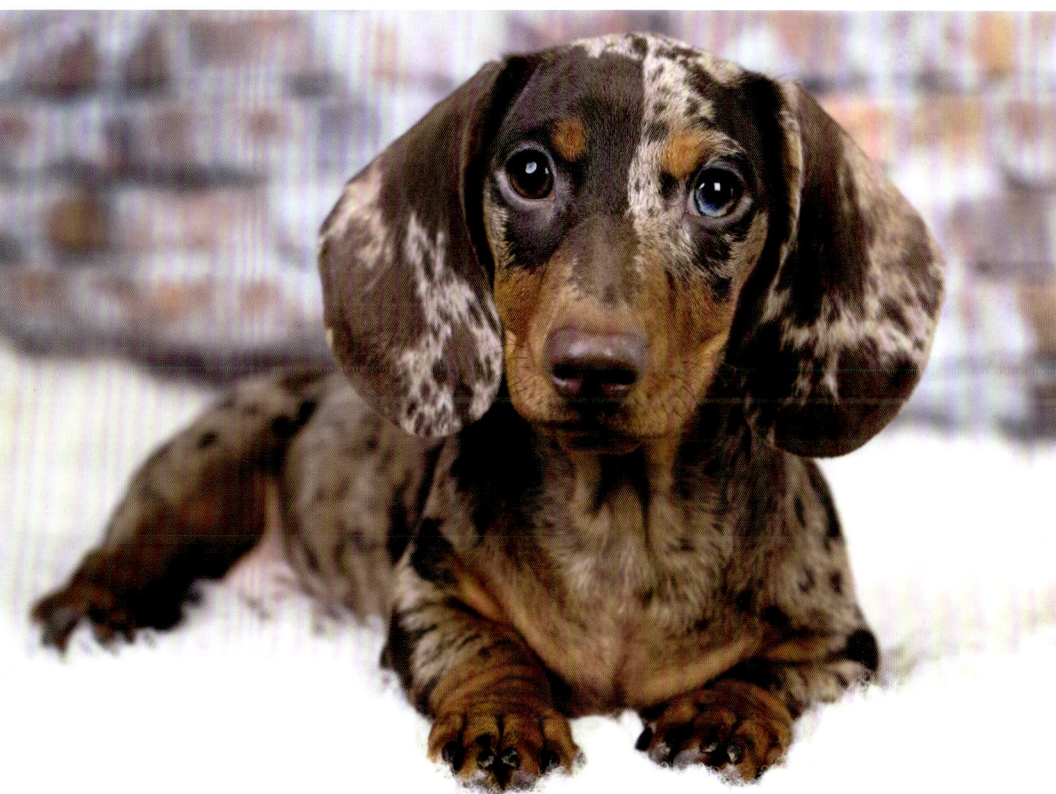

LEFT:
Sunbathing
Dachshunds are intelligent, friendly and playful and make ideal companions, even though they can be quite hard to train.

ABOVE BOTTOM:
At home
A sausage dog puppy relaxes on a comfortable rug.

ABOVE TOP:
Swimming along
With only short legs, these dogs avoid deep water, but some take pleasure in a paddle.

HUNTING DOGS
Doberman pinscher

The Doberman is the world's preeminent protection dog, being as it was created at the end of the 19th century by a breeder that had a lot of enemies. The breeder in question was a German tax collector called Louis Dobermann, who also acted as the local dog catcher in the town of Apolda. He worked in a hostile environment and wanted a dog that would deter attacks yet remain under control at all times even in often noisy or crowded situations. Dobermann crossed black and tan terriers (an English breed) with German pinschers and rottweilers. Adding in the lines of some herding dogs gave the original Doberman pinscher (the second n is generally left off) a bigger size than is typical today, but the long wedge-shaped head and sleek, muscled body were already in evidence.

The tax-collector's dog soon found other lines of work. They are very good guard dogs and are used by police and the military. Dobermans landed on Guam with the US Marines during the Pacific War, and 25 of the highly trained "devil dogs" were killed in the fighting.

Despite the reputation for brutality, Dobermans can make affectionate family pets if properly trained and socialized. They need plenty of exercise and attention to ward off destructive behaviour.

CHARACTERISTICS

Coat
A glistening coat of black, blue, red or fawn, with rust markings
Height
65–69cm (26–27in)
Weight
30–40kg (66–88lb)
Lifespan
13 years
Personality
Intelligent and alert
Origin
Germany

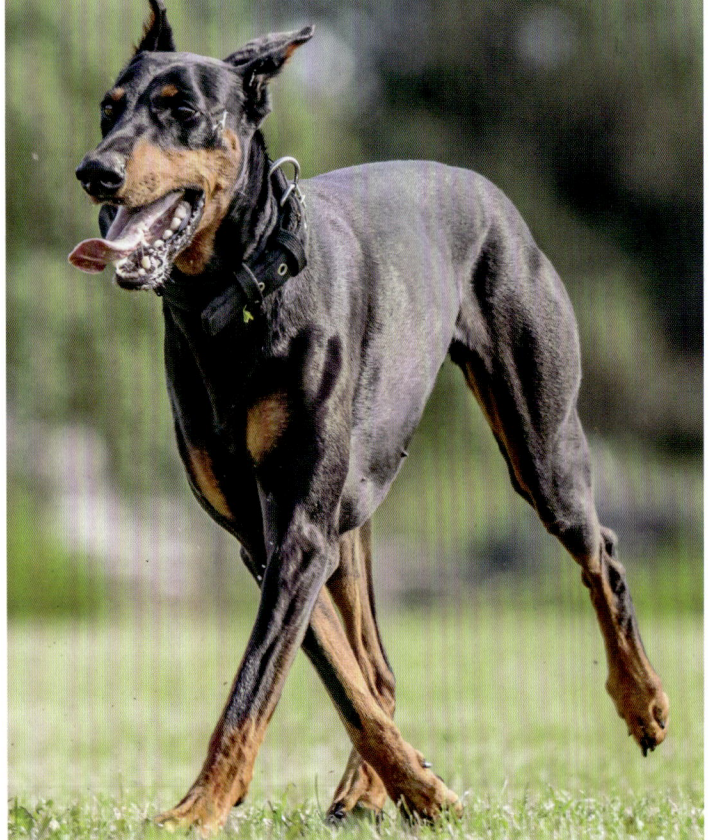

ABOVE:
Well built
Dobermans have a wedge-shaped head and a long muzzle that can produce a striking snarl when needed. It moves with a graceful gait.

RIGHT:
Eye spots
The Doberman has almond-shaped eyes with a tan spot above them.

HUNTING DOGS

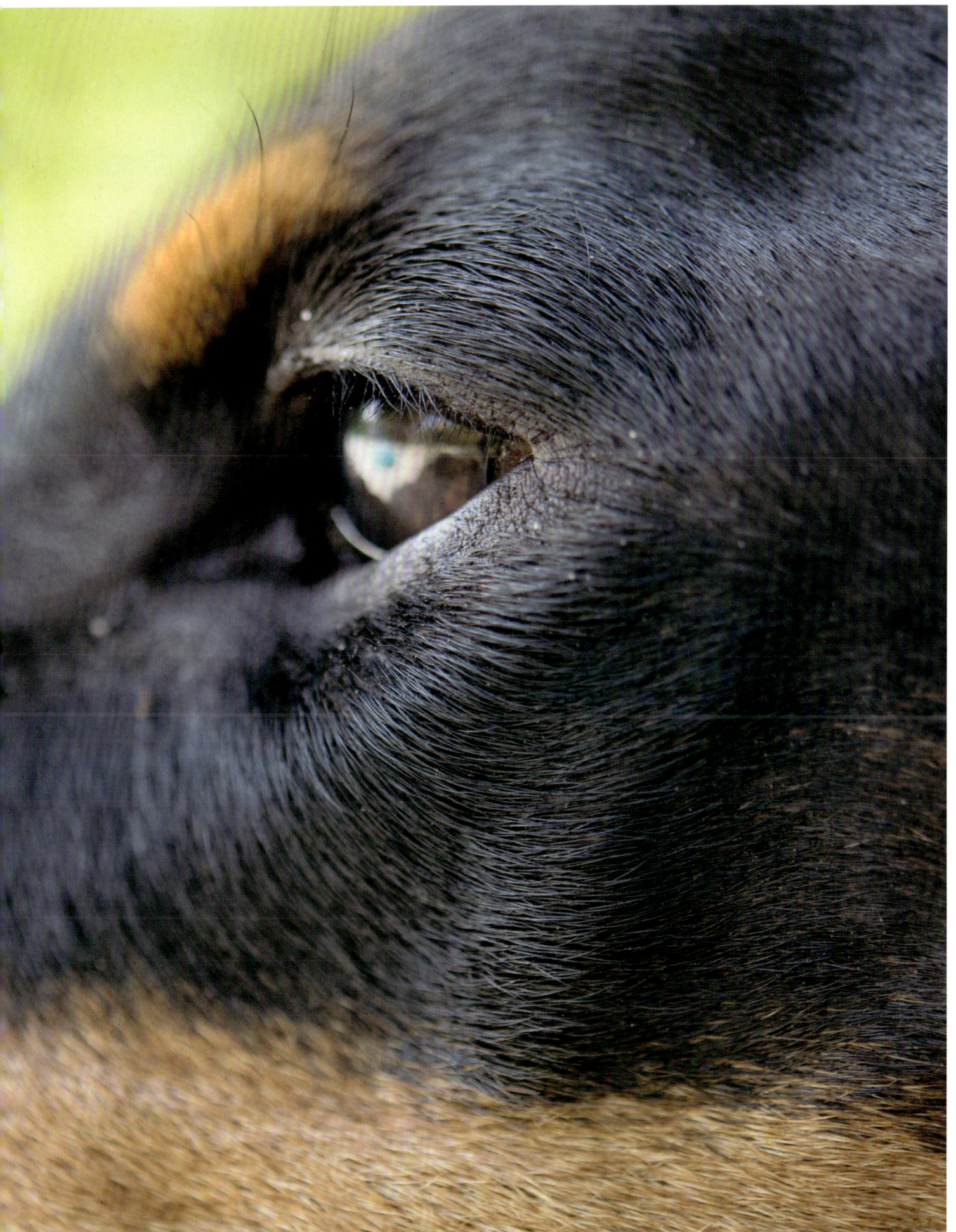

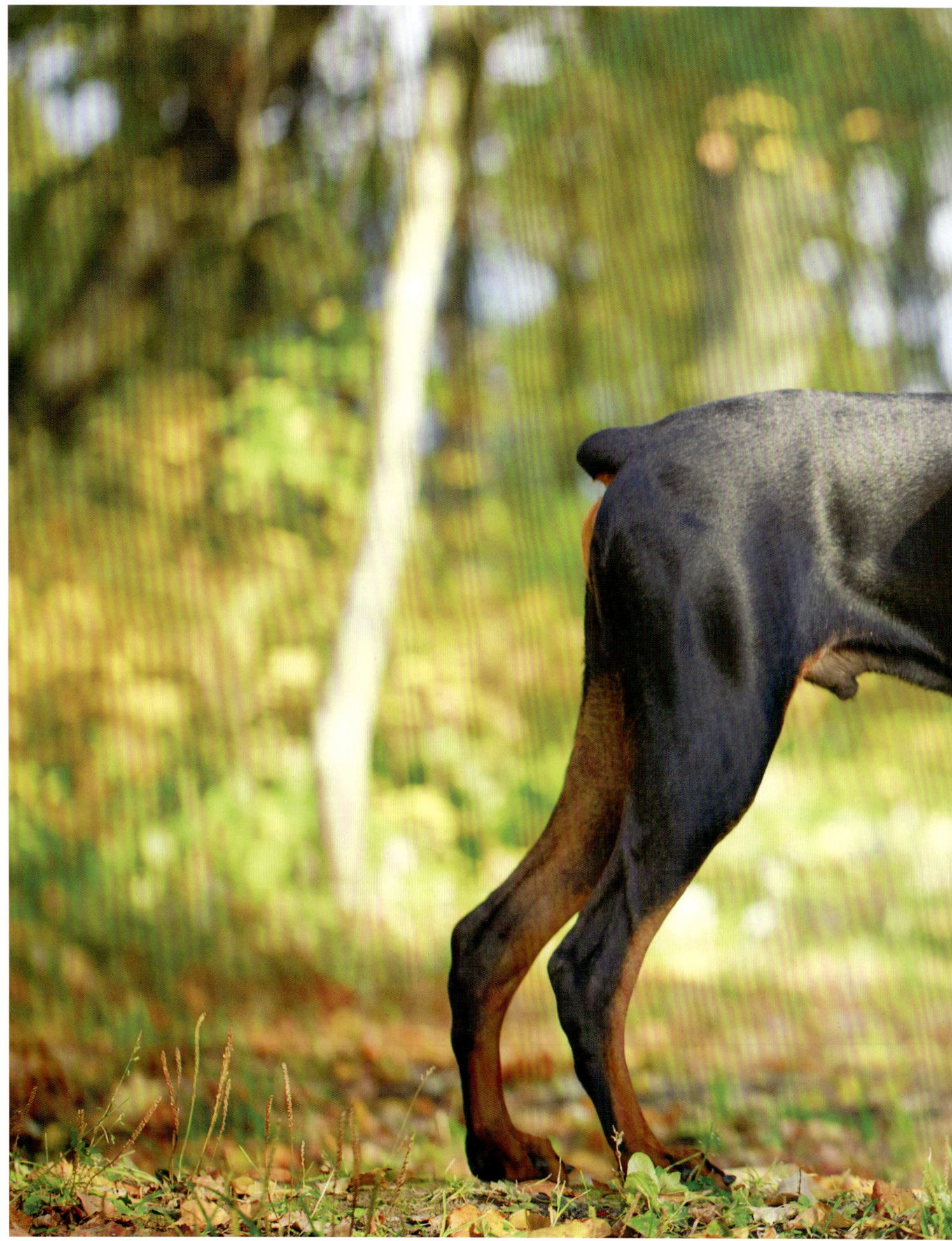

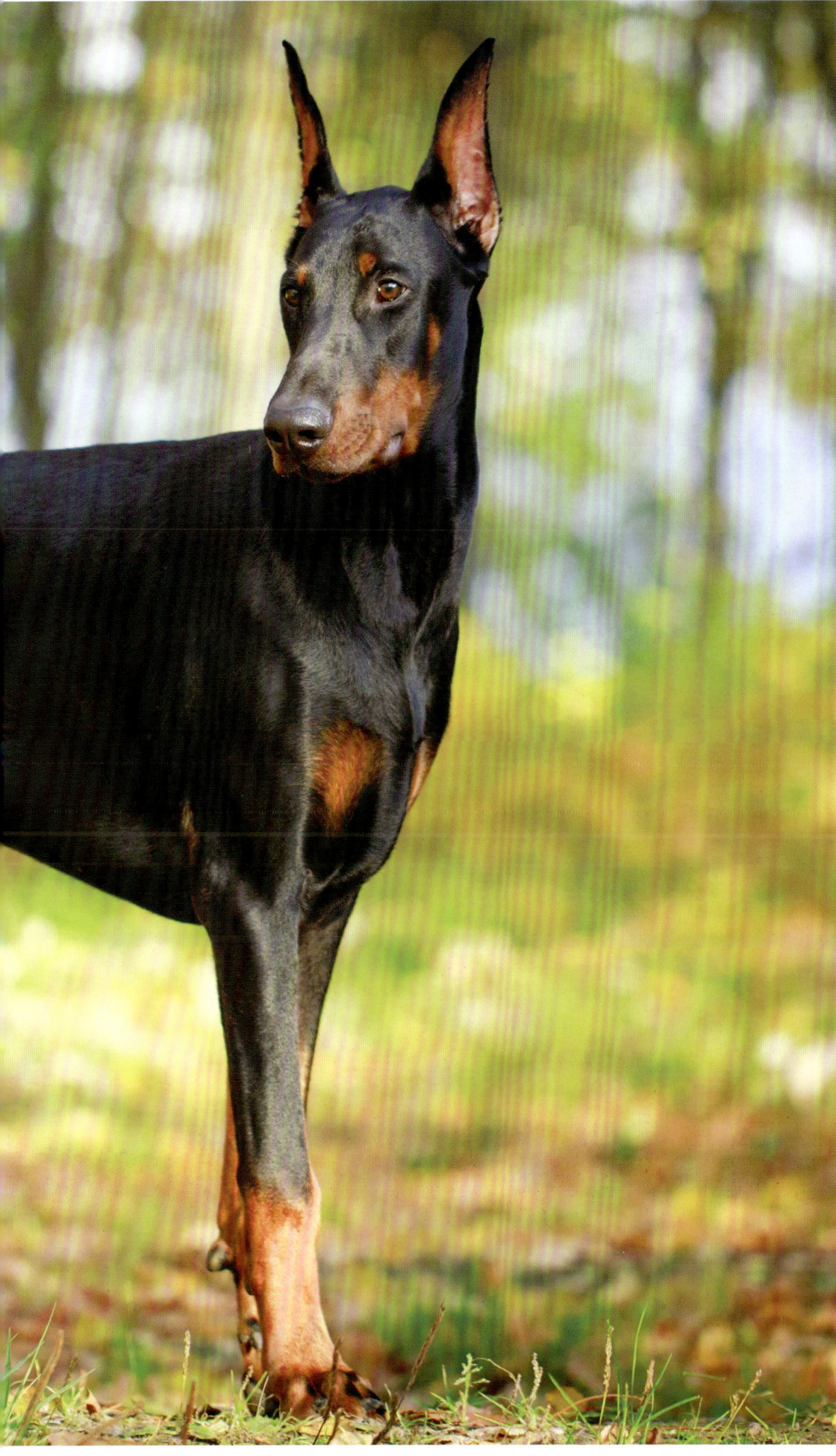

Dominant doberman
Bred as a fleet-footed scent hound for tracking fast-moving prey, this German breed now has a reputation as a particularly menacing guard dog.

HUNTING DOGS

Norwegian Elkhound

With a name like elkhound, one might expect this Norwegian dog to be a large and imposing creature. In Scandinavia, what might be termed a moose (the world's largest deer) is called an elk. (Confusingly, in the Americas elk is the name for a smaller deer.) So the proper translation of its name "elghund" is "moose dog". Nevertheless it is a medium-sized cold-weather breed, with links to the husky and other Arctic spitz-type dogs.

The elkhound features in the Norse sagas and was as important to a Viking warrior as his weapons. Skeletal remains of elkhounds have been found alongside Stone-Age tools in caves in western Norway dating back 7,000 years. The dogs were used to hunt elk (or moose). Their role was to track the scent of the giant, mostly solitary, deer. A group of dogs would surround the deer and hold it at bay until the master huntsman caught up and killed the quarry.

The elkhound is a headstrong dog that can be challenging to train. It requires a confident owner providing firm leadership. The dog is very loyal and can be an affectionate family pet but is generally wary of strangers. It makes a good watchdog, and alerts its owners to anything unusual with a piercing bark.

CHARACTERISTICS
Coat
A thick, coarse coat that is black and white in colour, giving a grey or silver appearance
Height
49–52cm (19–20in)
Weight
20–23kg (44–51lb)
Lifespan
12–16 years
Personality
Bold and energetic
Origin
Norway

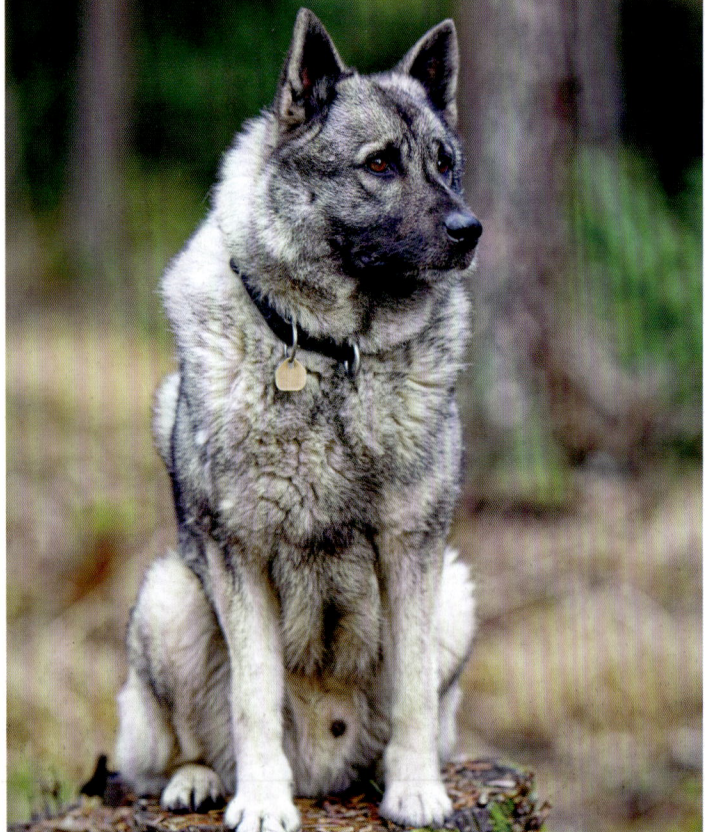

ABOVE:
Northern looks
The elkhound has a broad, wedge-shaped head with dark brown eyes and pointed, erect ears. The tail is tightly curled over the back.

RIGHT:
Out and about
This breed needs a lot of exercise and mental stimulation to keep it happy. It enjoys outdoor activities, especially in cold weather, and can excel in dog sports such as agility, obedience, tracking and rally.

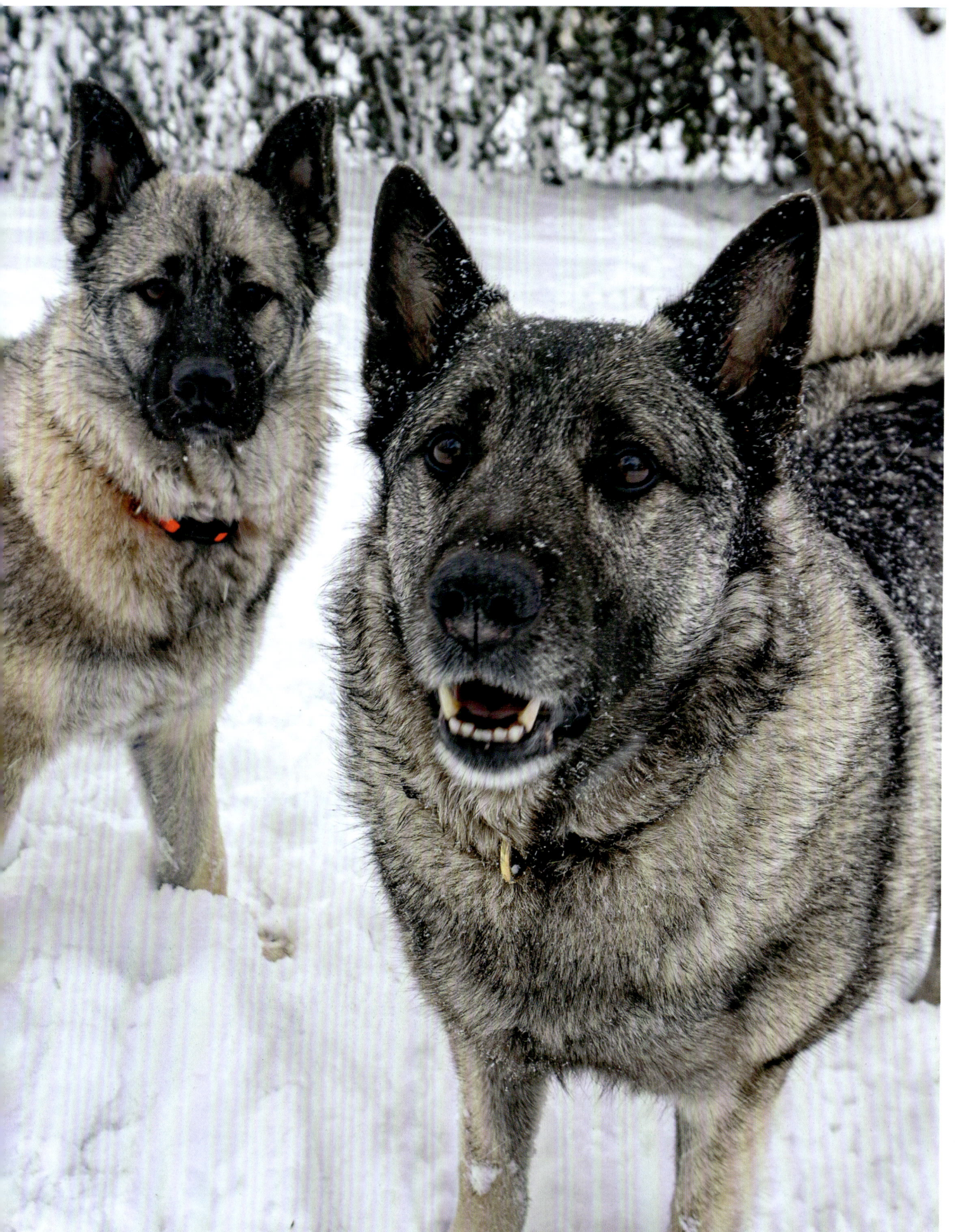

HUNTING DOGS

Adapted to the cold
From a young age, this breed is impervious to cold thanks to its thick coat.

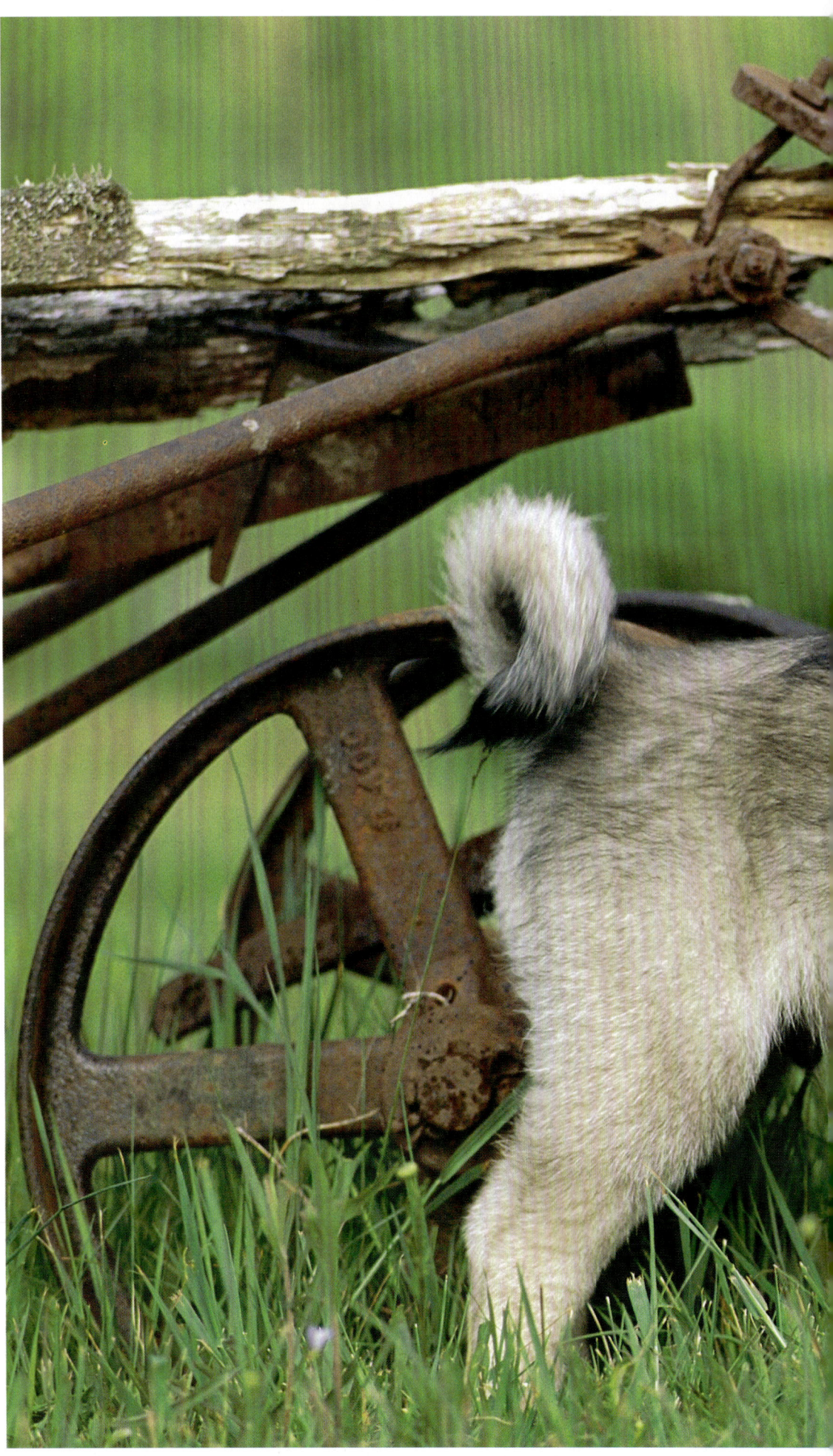

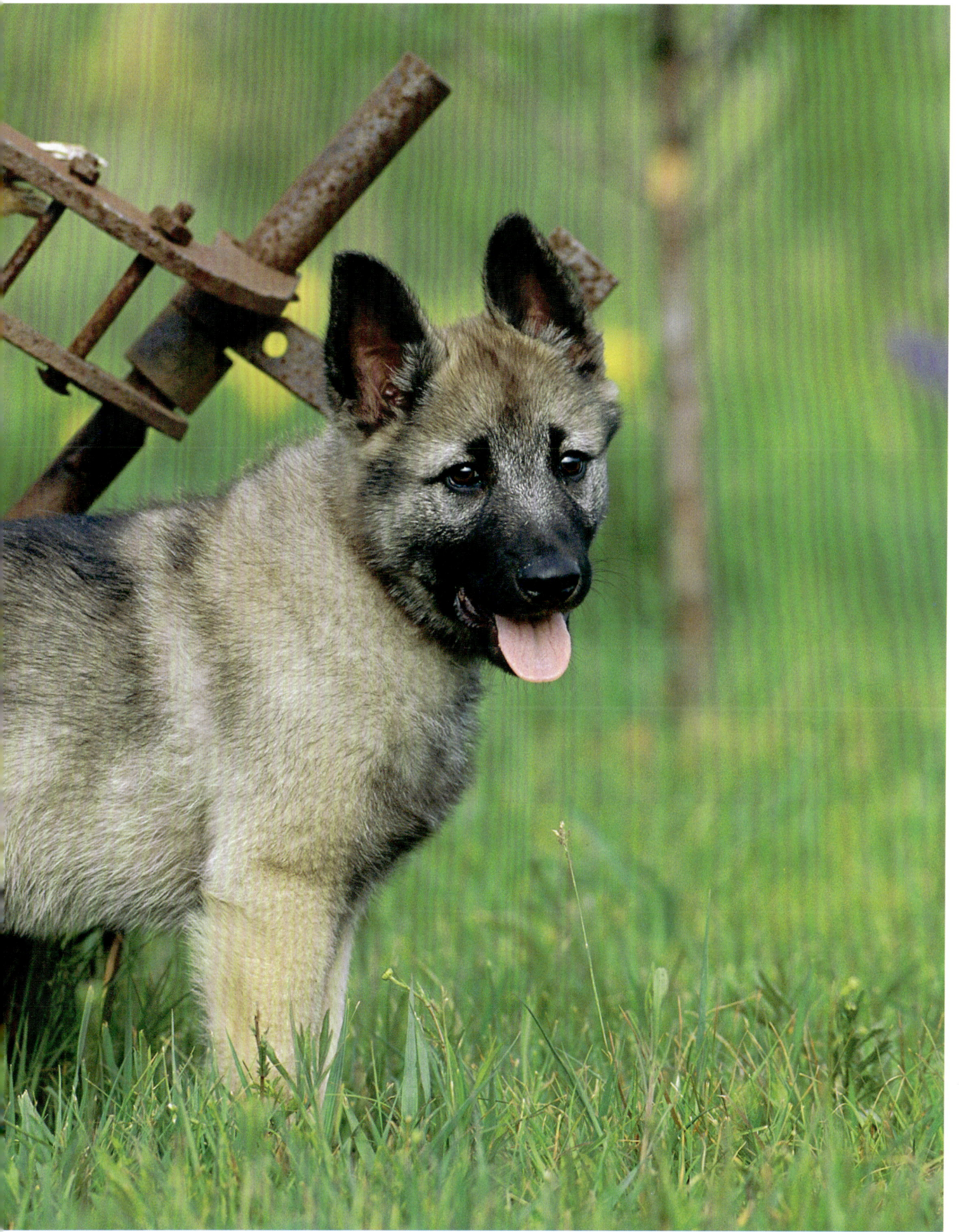

HUNTING DOGS

Swedish Elkhound

CHARACTERISTICS

Coat
A close-lying double coat that is grey with cream markings on the muzzle, underside and legs

Height
52–65cm (20–26in)

Weight
30–35kg (66–77lb)

Lifespan
12–13 years

Personality
Loyal and dominant

Origin
Sweden

The Swedish elkhound, known locally as the Jämthund, is a medium-sized dog with a wolf-like appearance. At first glance it looks very similar to its near neighbour, the Norwegian elkhound. The two breeds were only officially recognized as separate in the 1940s. However, the Swedish dogs are generally taller and less stocky. Subsequent DNA analysis of the Swedish dogs reveals that this and many other Scandinavian and Nordic breeds are descended from a male domestic dog mated with a wild female wolf around 3,000 years ago.

The current breed's Swedish name comes from its links to Jämtland, a low-lying forested region in central Sweden. Here it would have been tasked with hunting deer, bears, lynx and wolves.

The Swedish elkhound needs a lot of exercise, but has a strong prey drive so should only be let off the leash outside with care. It can be assimilated into a family if given careful training and plenty of mental stimulation. It will be an affectionate pet but will nevertheless attempt to dominate the other dogs it meets, and strangers entering the home are met with wariness.

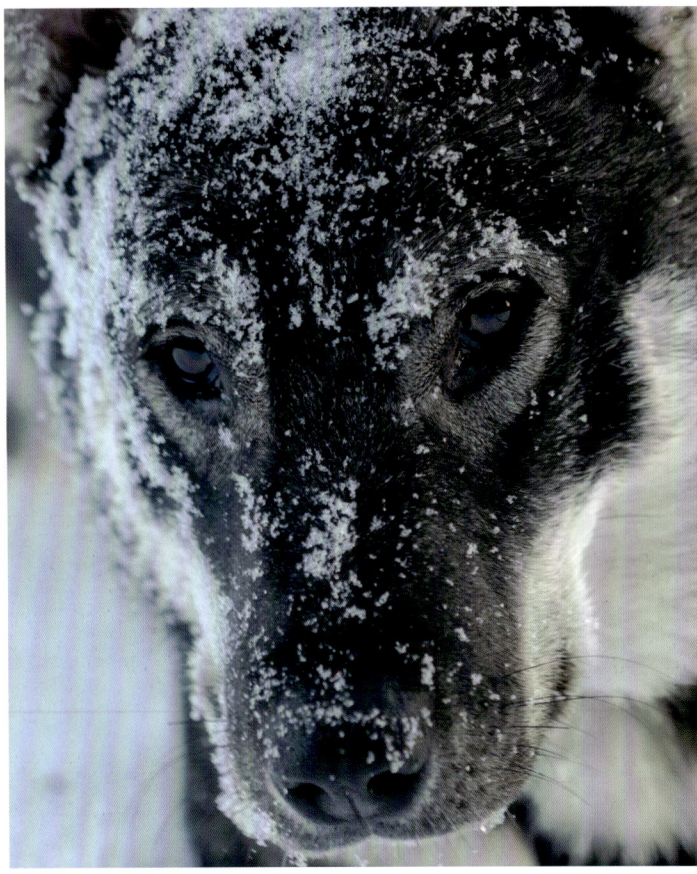

ABOVE:
National dog
Built for life in the Arctic snows, Swedish elkhound is a regular recruit to the Swedish army.

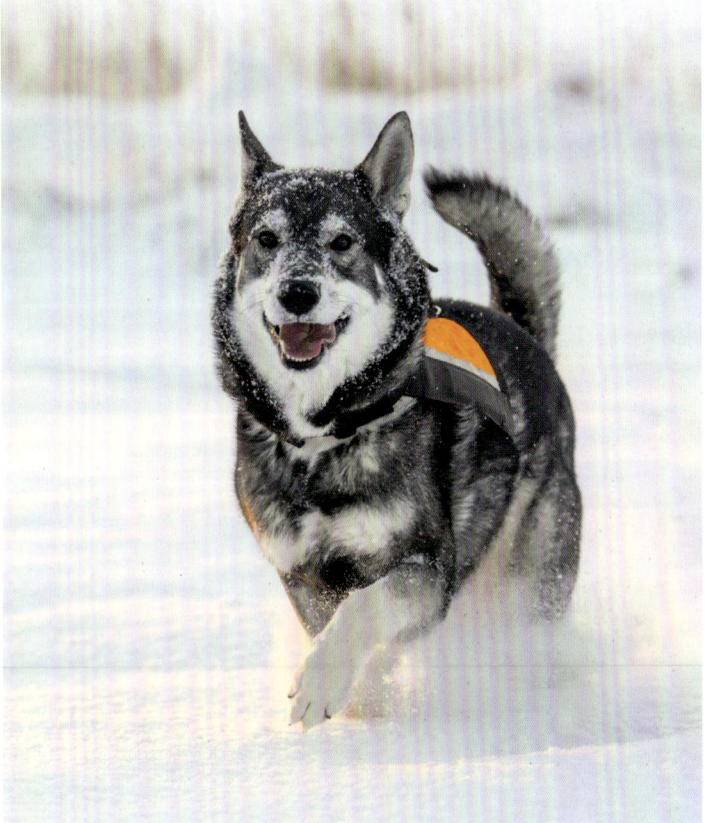

ABOVE:
Double coat
The top coat is made of dark and dense hairs. The woolier undercoat is paler.

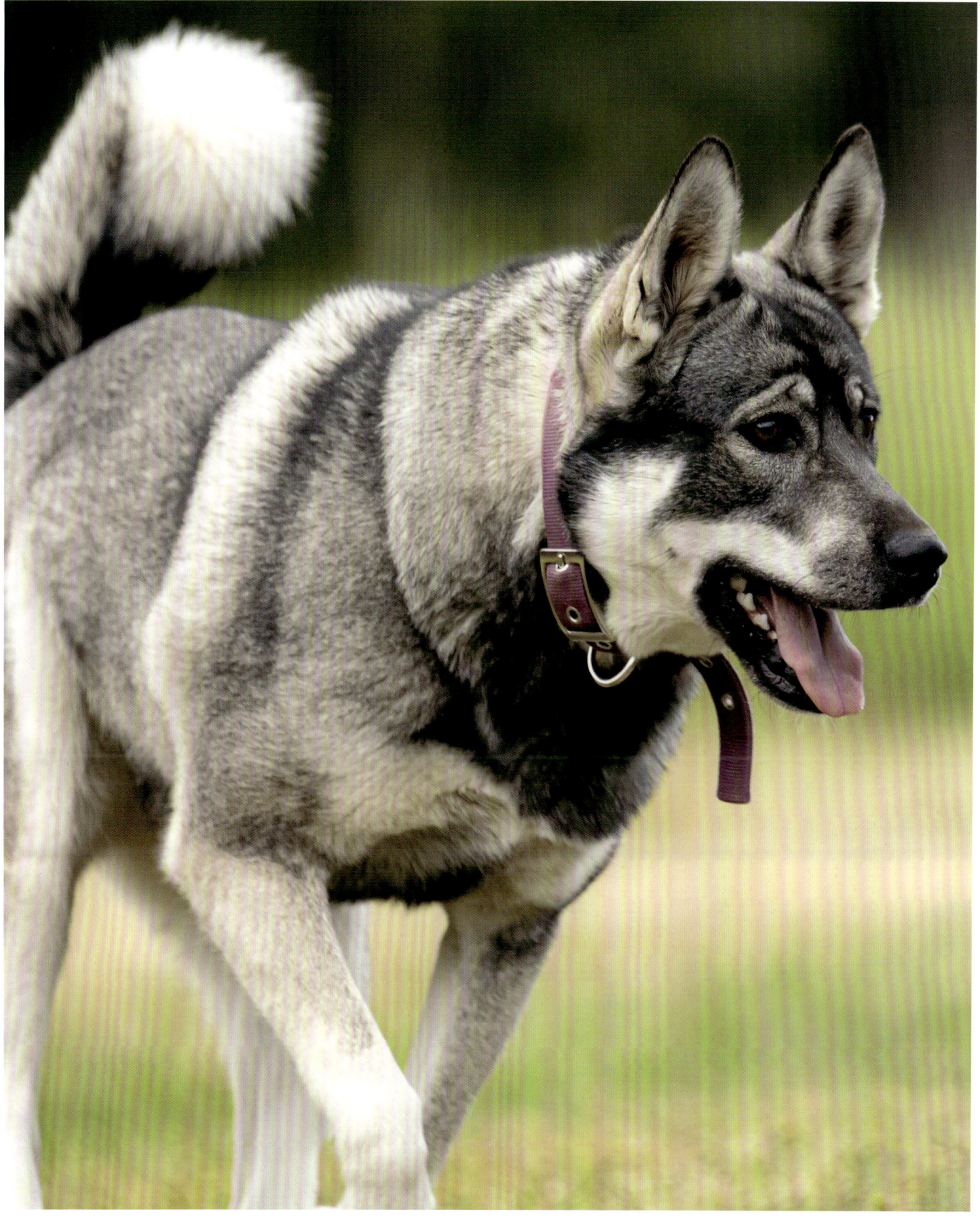

ABOVE:
Top and tail
The Swedish elkhound has erect ears lined with hairs, a curled tail and brown eyes.

HUNTING DOGS

English Pointer

These eager and athletic dogs are a bundle of fun, and have long been bred for their trainability and obedience. Originally the pointer was part of a team of hunting dogs with the job of seeking hares and other fast-running game. The pointer would then stand stock still, raise a foreleg, straighten the tail horizontally and literally point at the quarry with its muzzle. Then speedy sighthounds, such as greyhounds, or perhaps falcons would be unleashed to catch and kill the target.

The early English pointers were developed in the 17th century by mixing foxhounds, which have a strong sense of smell, with greyhounds to add some running ability. With the advent of hunting rifles, the coursing hounds were phased out, but the pointer remained an important member of the hunting party. The breed was later refined by crossing back with setters (themselves bred from pointers) to further enhance their spotting skills. Today the pointer is used as a gundog, able to point and retrieve rabbits and gamebirds.

CHARACTERISTICS
Coat
A short, smooth coat that comes in various colors, such as lemon and white, orange and white, liver and white, and black and white
Height
53–64cm (21–25in)
Weight
20–34 kg (45–75lb)
Lifespan
12–13 years
Personality
Friendly and well-behaved
Origin
England

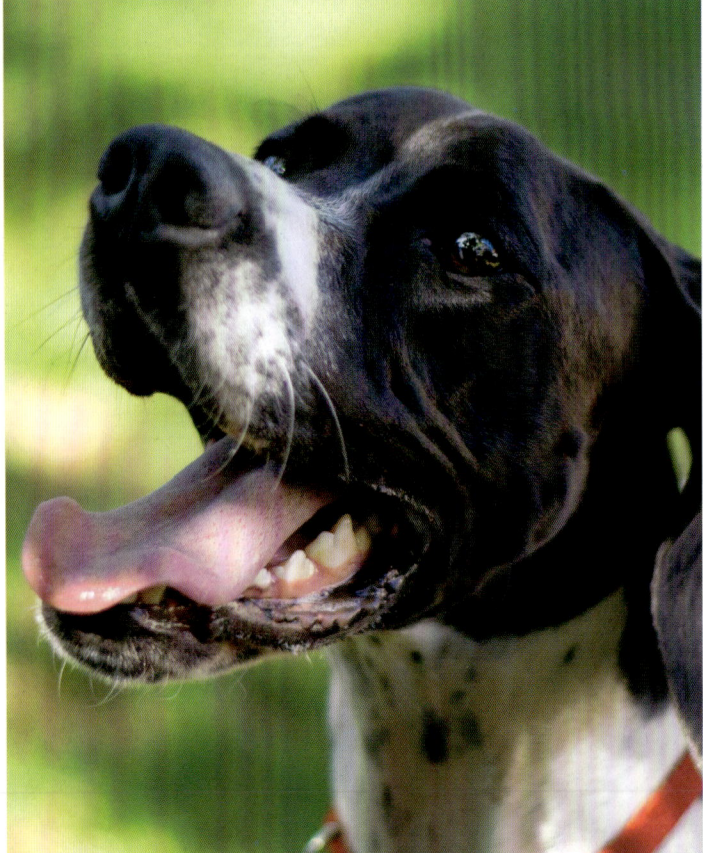

ABOVE:
Full of life
The breed is energetic, athletic and friendly, but needs a lot of exercise and training to be happy and well-behaved. It can be overly boisterous with smaller children.

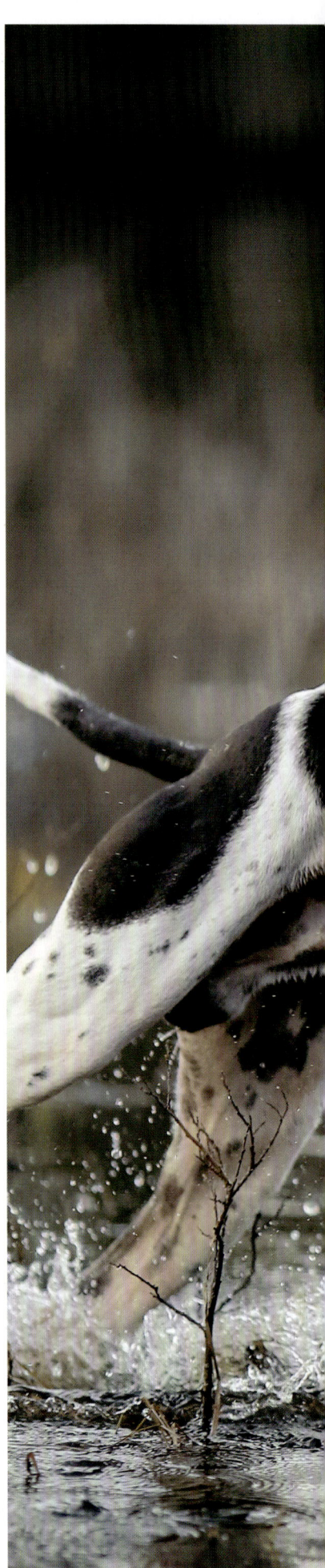

RIGHT:
Running dog
The English pointer has excellent stamina and an easy, graceful gait. This makes it a near-perfect companion for runners, which is one way for owners to stay fit and give the dog the exercise it needs.

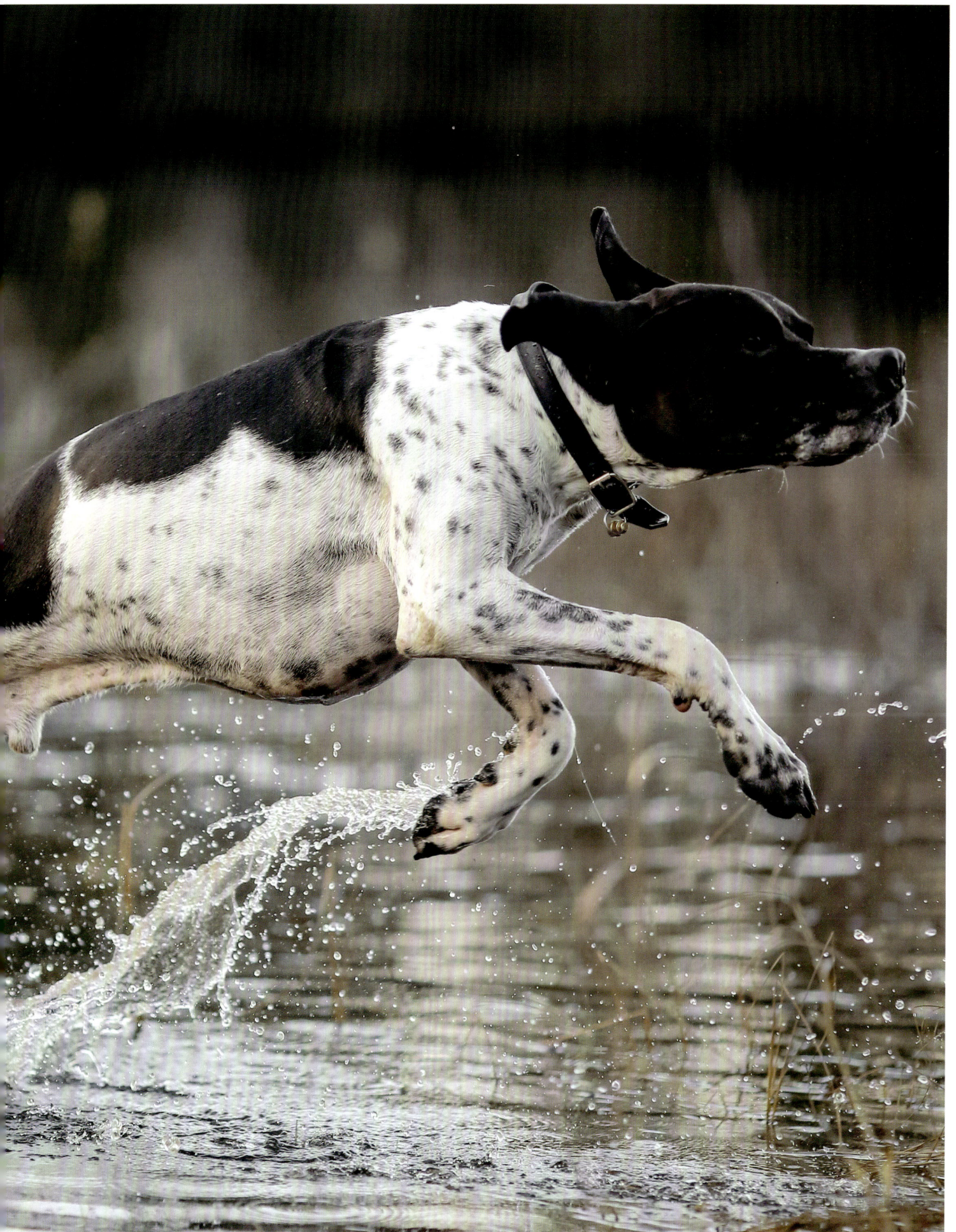

HUNTING DOGS
English Setter

CHARACTERISTICS

Coat
A silky coat that is mainly white with coloured spots or flecks that are black, orange, lemon, liver or blue in colour

Height
61–64cm (24–25in)

Weight
25–30kg (55–66lb)

Lifespan
12–13 years

Personality
Gentle and sociable

Origin
England

This is the oldest setter breed, so called because it finds gamebirds and other small, hidden prey using its powerful sense of smell and then "sets" them, or points to their location. The owner following behind then takes over, shooting at the quarry (after perhaps driving them from cover with spaniels). If that is successful, the setter is dispatched to retrieve any dead birds. With a history spread over around 400 years, this makes the English setter the first gundog breed.

The English setter was developed by crossing spaniels with pointers. Originally the dogs would sit quietly beside the birds it found, but later refinements in the mid-19th century created today's breeding standard, where, upon locating gamebirds, the setter stands tall with its tail held out straight behind it. The Victorian breeder also made the dogs rangier and more elegant, with feathered coats that have long fringes of hair dangling from the belly, chest, legs and tail. Setters bred for showing have longer coats than their workaday cousins used for hunts and field sports.

The English setter is easy going with people and other animals but also has a mischievous side. As with all gundogs, it is built to be on the move and so needs a lot of exercise. The silky coat needs frequent grooming.

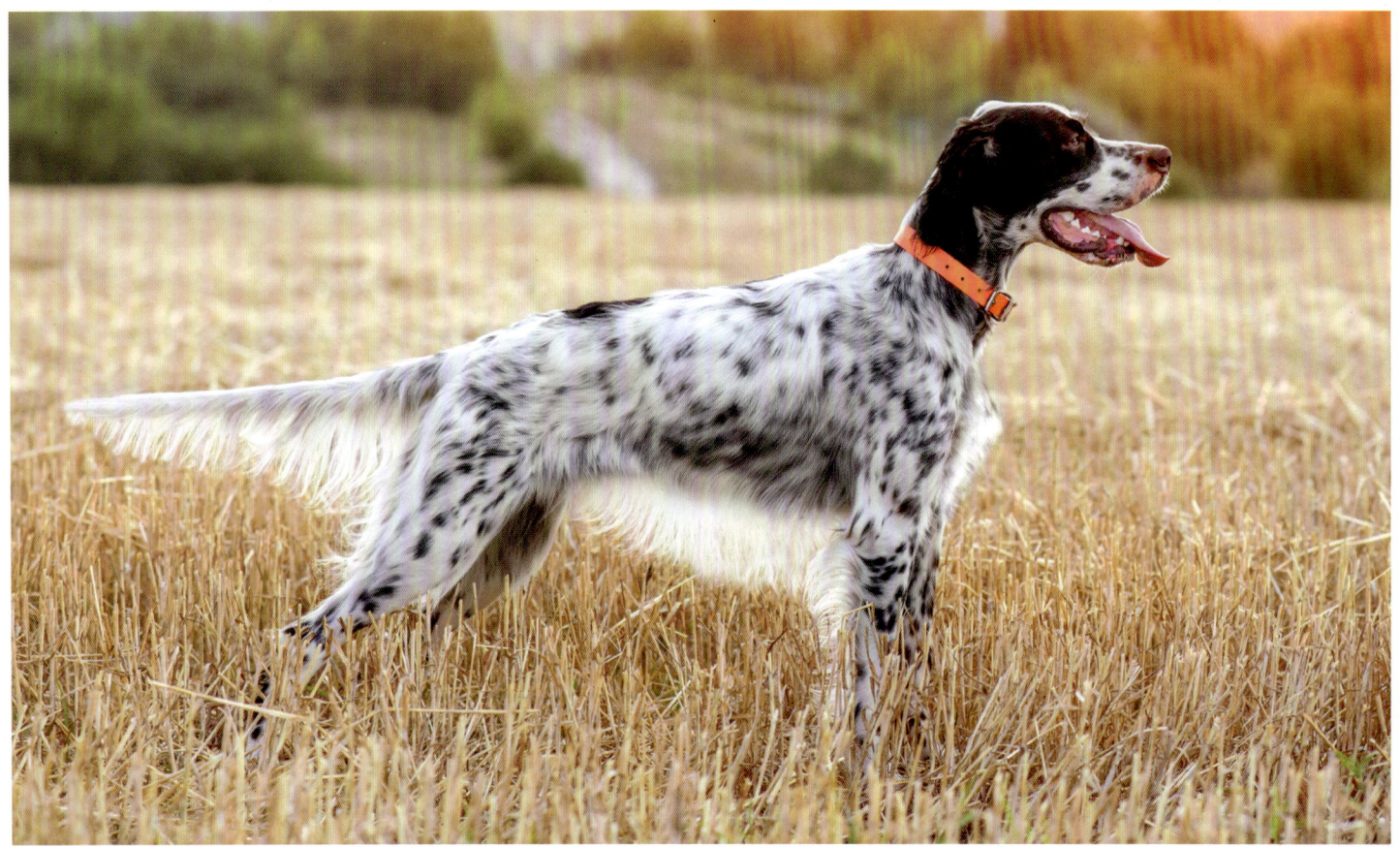

ABOVE:
That way!
The English setter is bred to point at quarry using a very upright stance. The feathered tail is easy to see when held horizontally.

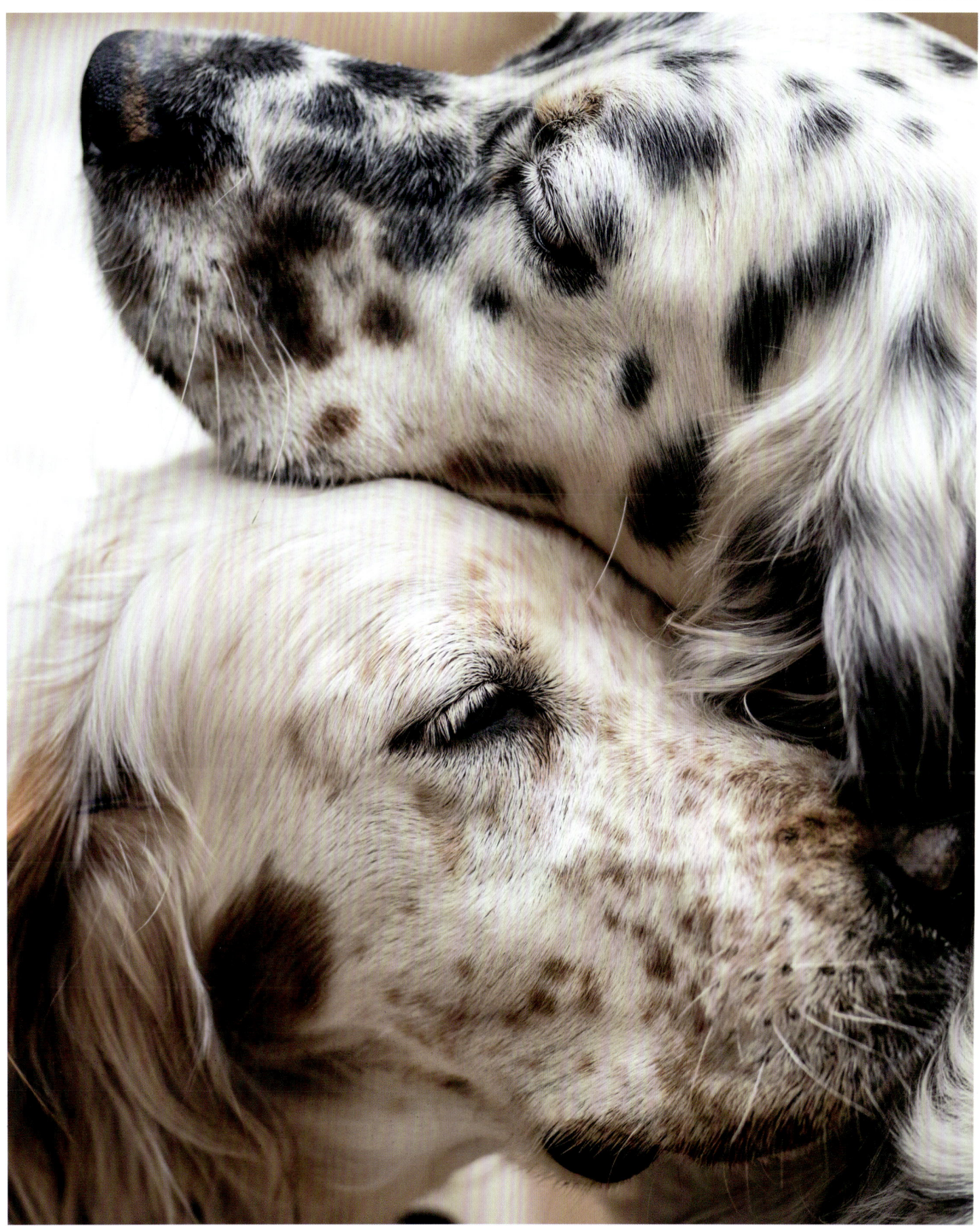

ABOVE:
Handsome looks
The English setter's coat has long fringes on the ears. The flecked coat is known as belton.

HUNTING DOGS

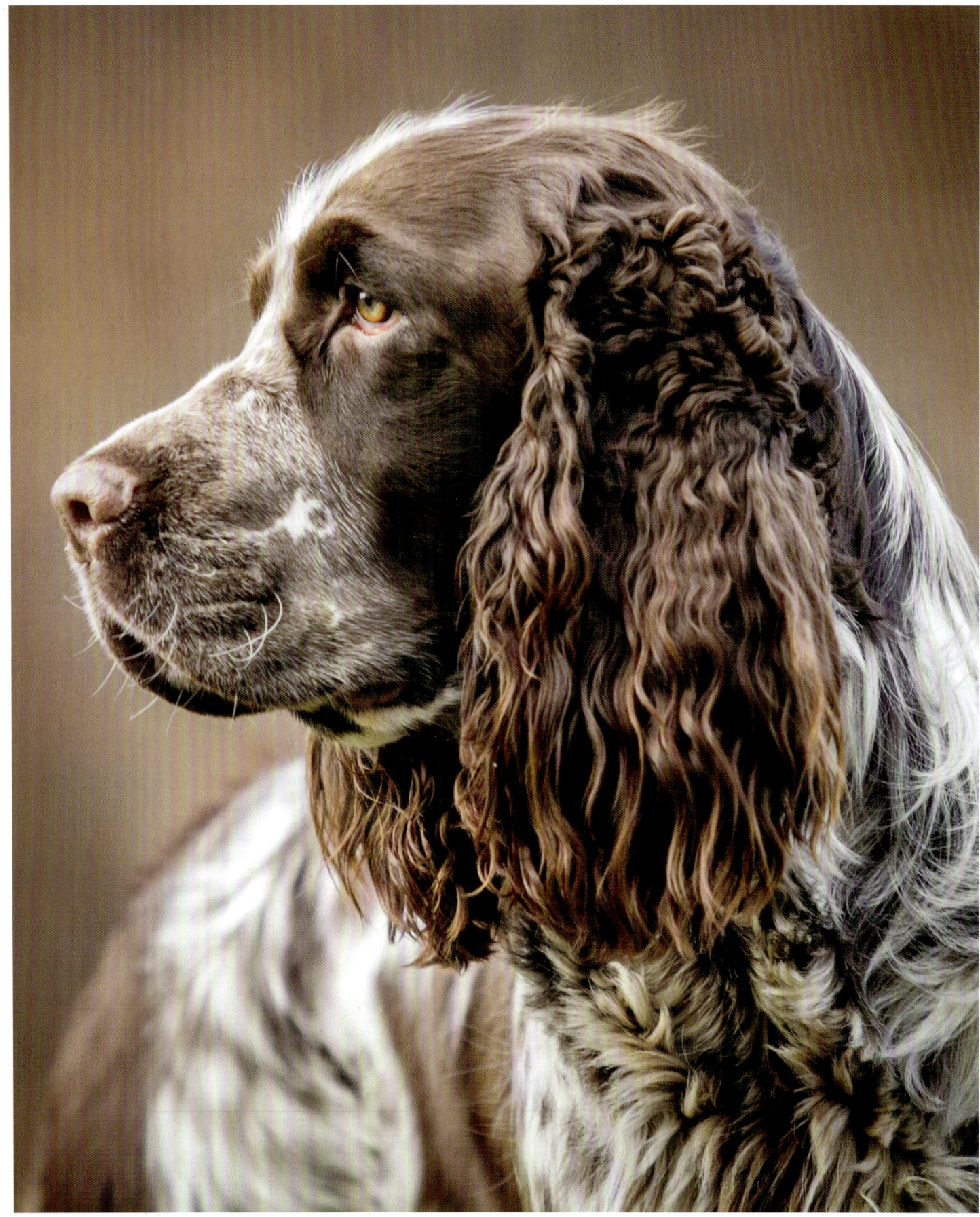

ABOVE:
Many relatives
The English springer spaniel is closely related to the cocker spaniel and the Welsh springer, but has longer legs and a longer muzzle.

English Springer Spaniel

CHARACTERISTICS

Coat
A moderate coat that has feathering on the legs and tail. The most common colour is liver and white, but black and white and tricolours also occur

Height
46–56cm (18–22in)

Weight
18–23kg (40–51lb)

Lifespan
12–14 years

Personality
Affectionate and excitable

Origin
England

The English word spaniel is ultimately derived from a term meaning "Spanish", so spaniels were known archaically as Spanish dogs. However, their origins are much more obscure than this. Small to medium-sized dogs with keen senses of smell were being used on hunts for centuries Some say they were a Roman breed derived from dogs traded from the Far East. The strongest Spanish connection is another suggestion that the first spaniels were bred by Celtic people migrating into Britain from Iberia nearly 3,000 years ago.

Whatever their origin, spaniels are hunting dogs that locate gamebirds, flush them from cover and then retrieve whatever the hunters have bagged. The springer is a larger spaniel that is so named because its role was to drive—or spring—pheasants into the air. In the days of olde, hunters would catch the birds with nets or bow, but by the 17th century, hunters were largely using guns.

Today field-bred spaniels that still work as gundogs have shorter, coarser coats, less floppy ears and more lithe, wiry frames. Pet springers tend to be show-bred dogs with longer fur, more pendulous ears and heavier bones. Highly trainable, the springer spaniel is a very companionable creature that does well in domestic settings.

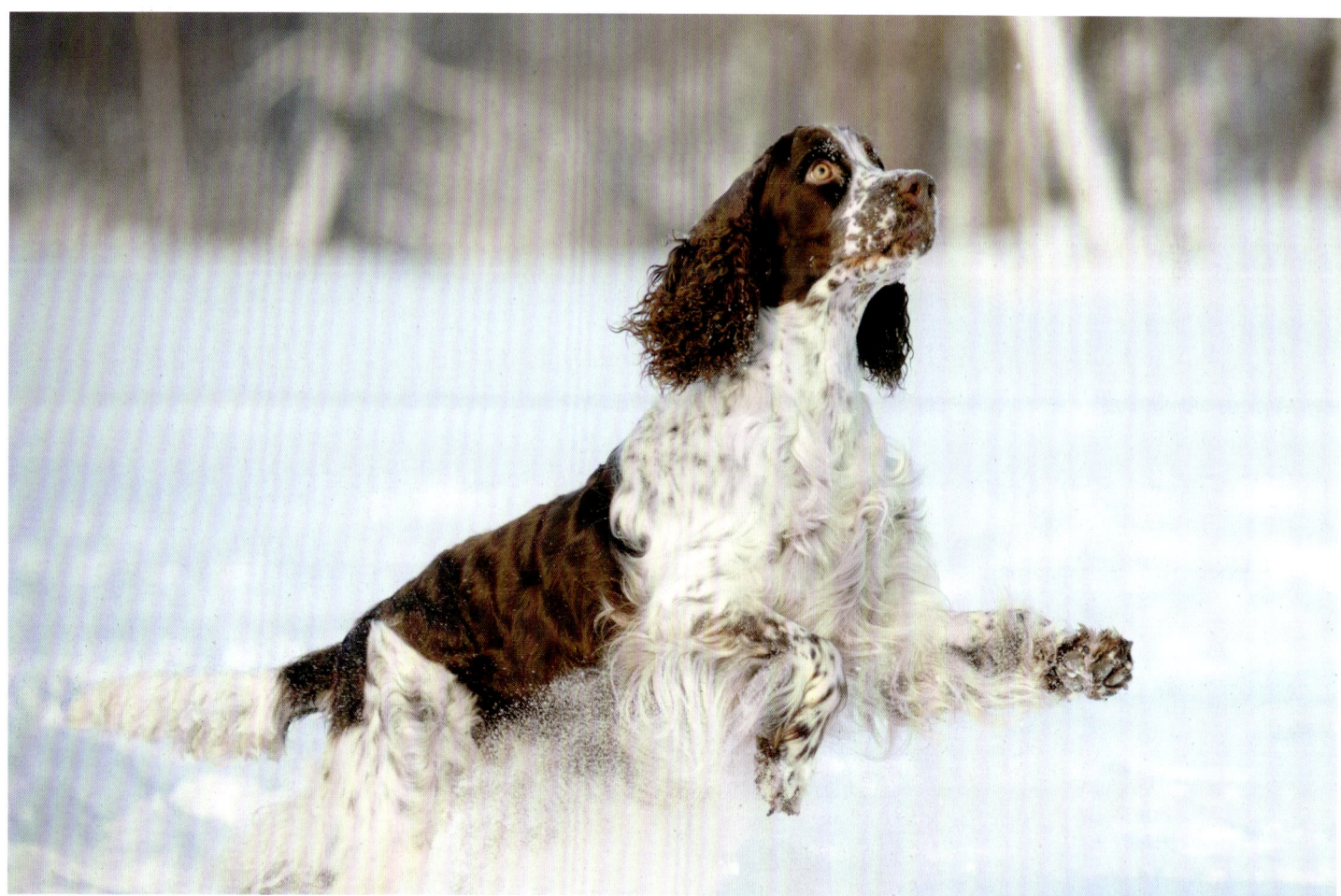

ABOVE:
Field worker
Most English springer spaniels are bred for working in the field.

HUNTING DOGS

Happy to help
Loyal and eager to please, spaniels have the job of flushing game birds into the air and into sight of the guns. It will then sniff out fallen birds and bring them back.

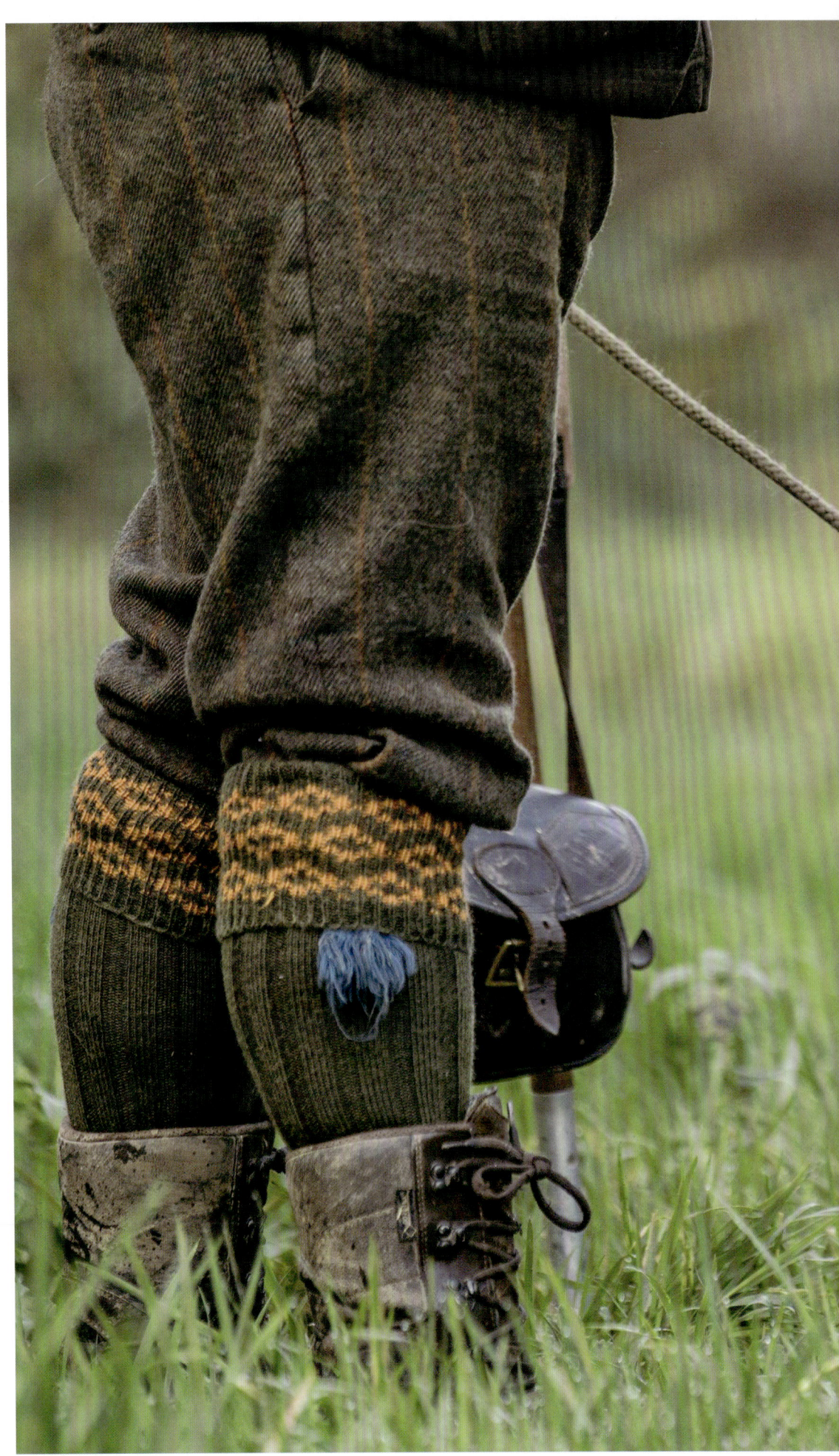

236

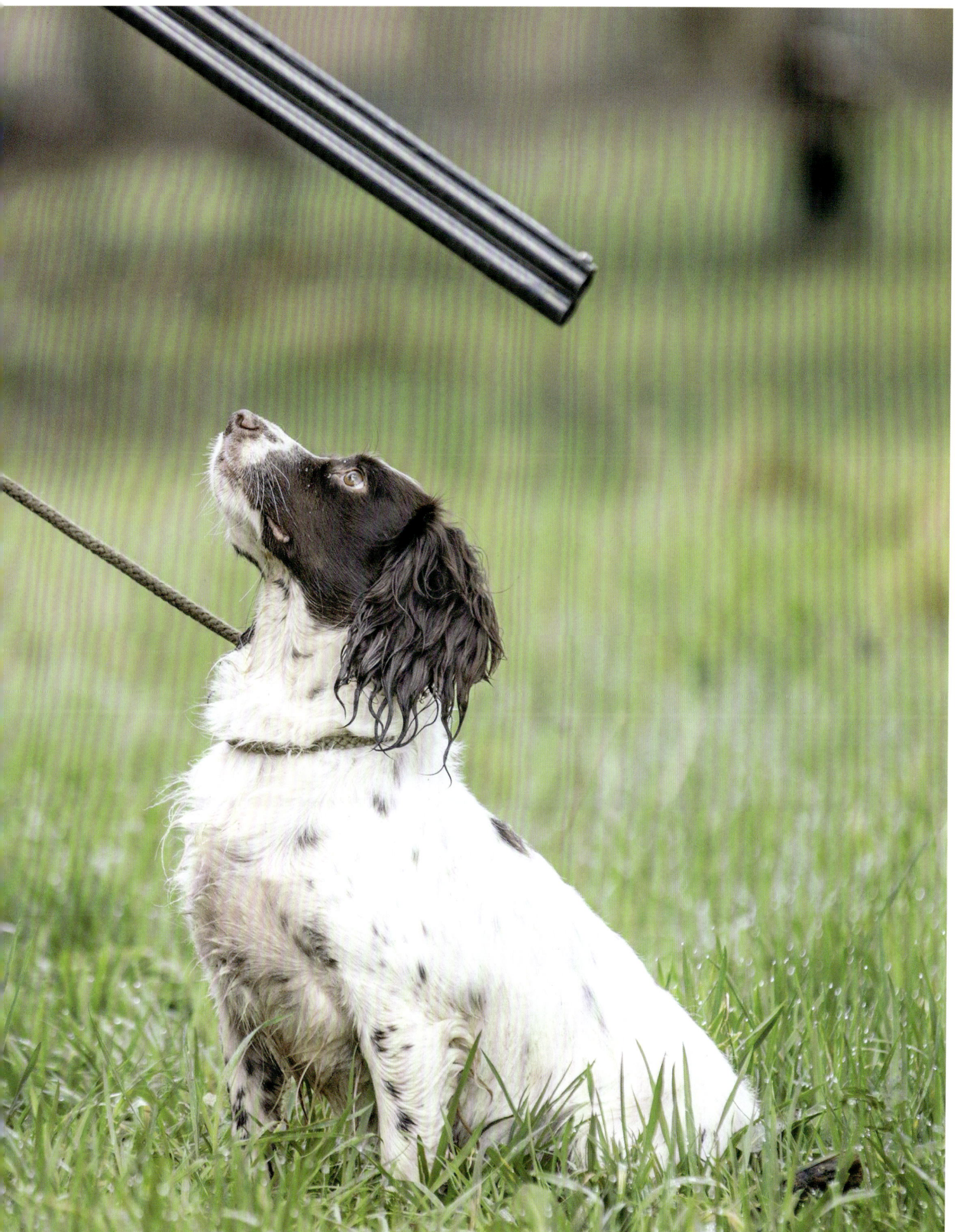

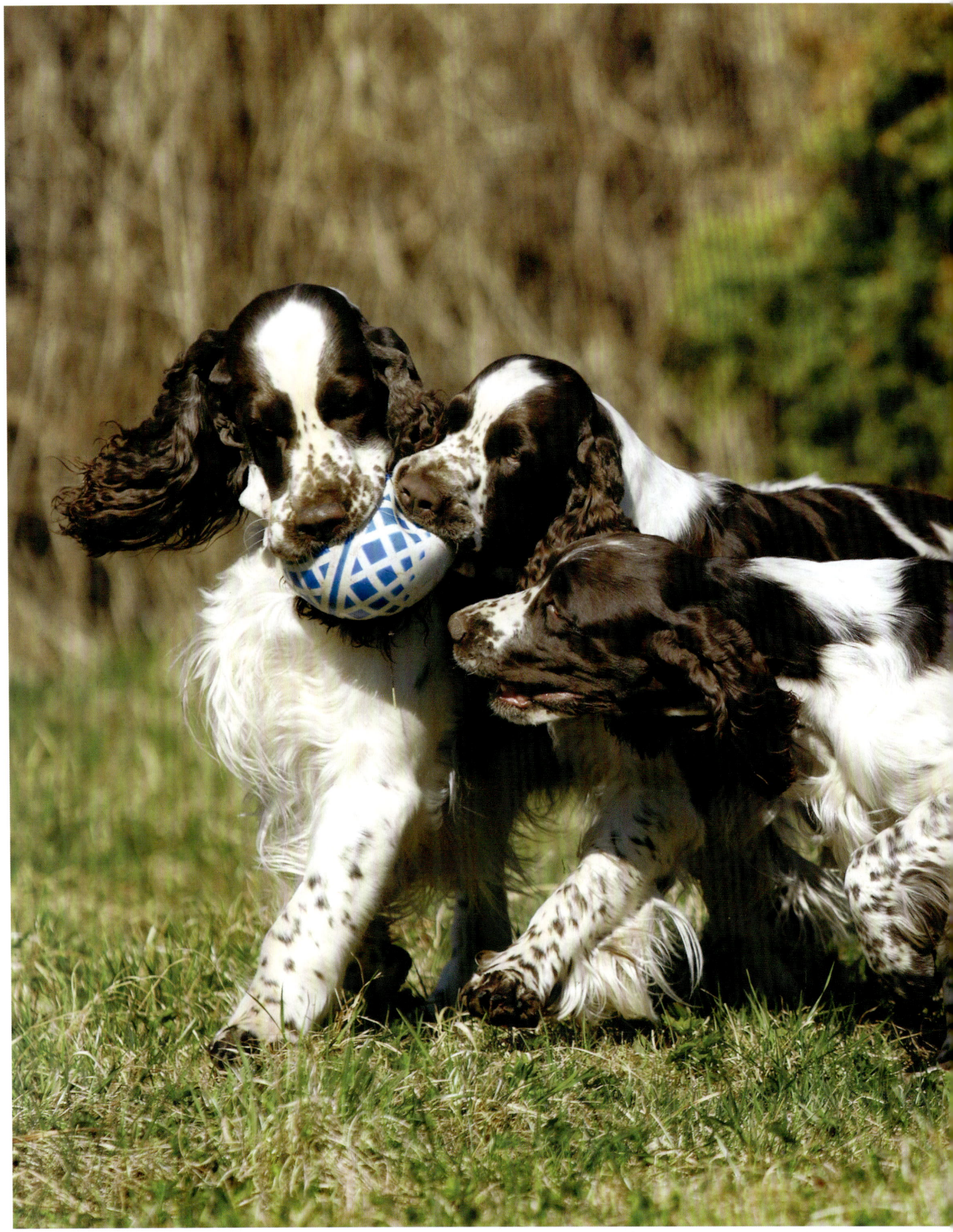

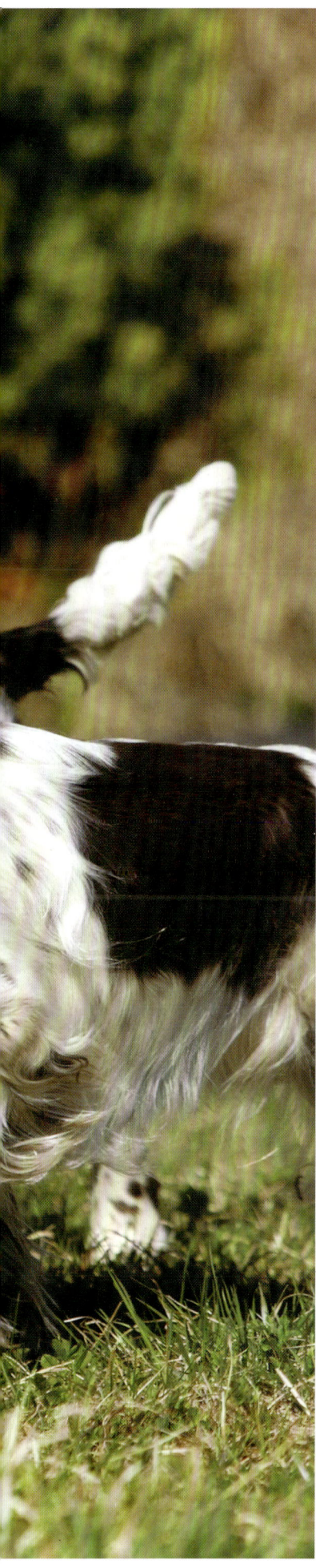

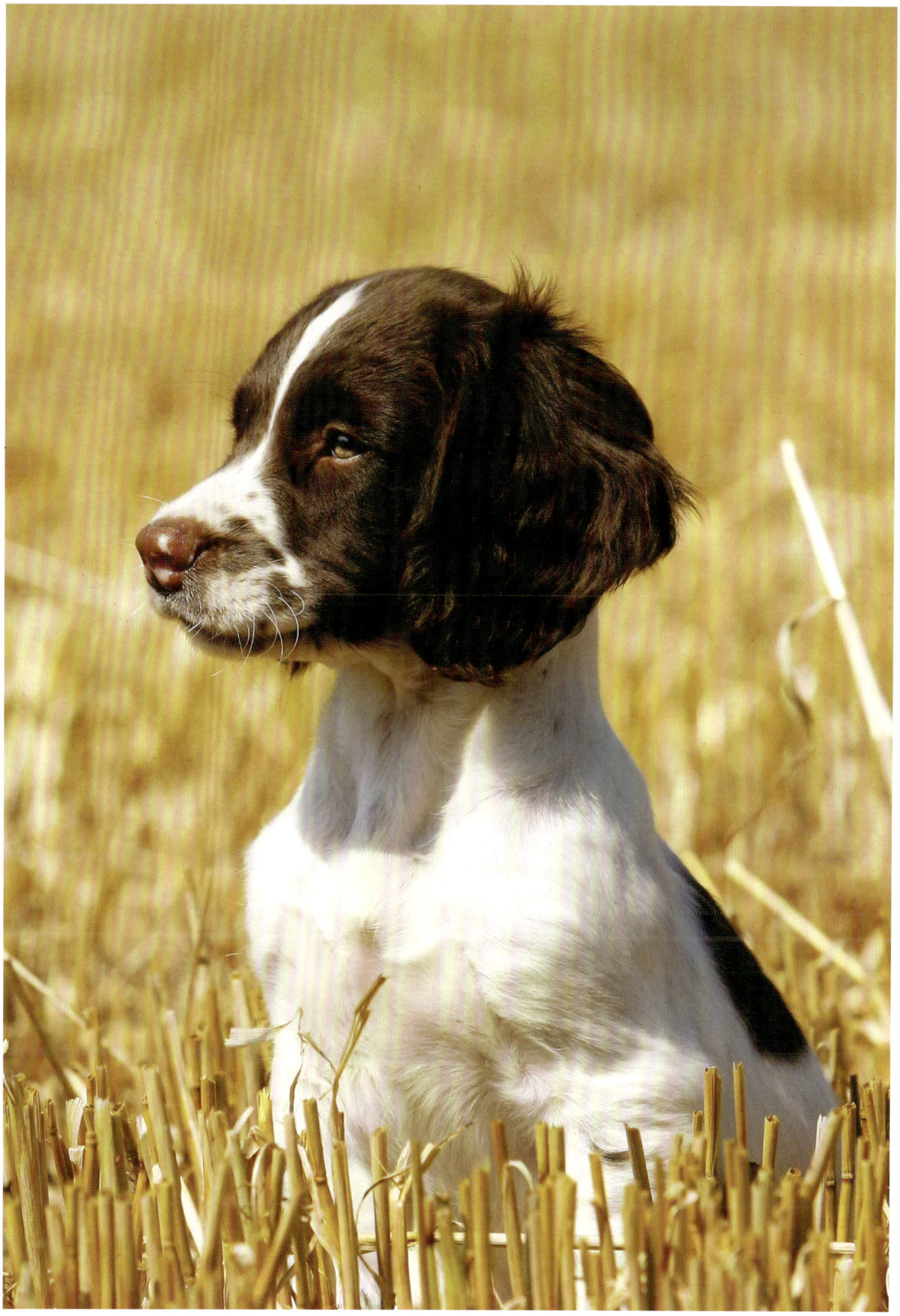

LEFT AND ABOVE:
Young spaniels
As they get older, puppies need to be exercised more frequently and for longer.

HUNTING DOGS

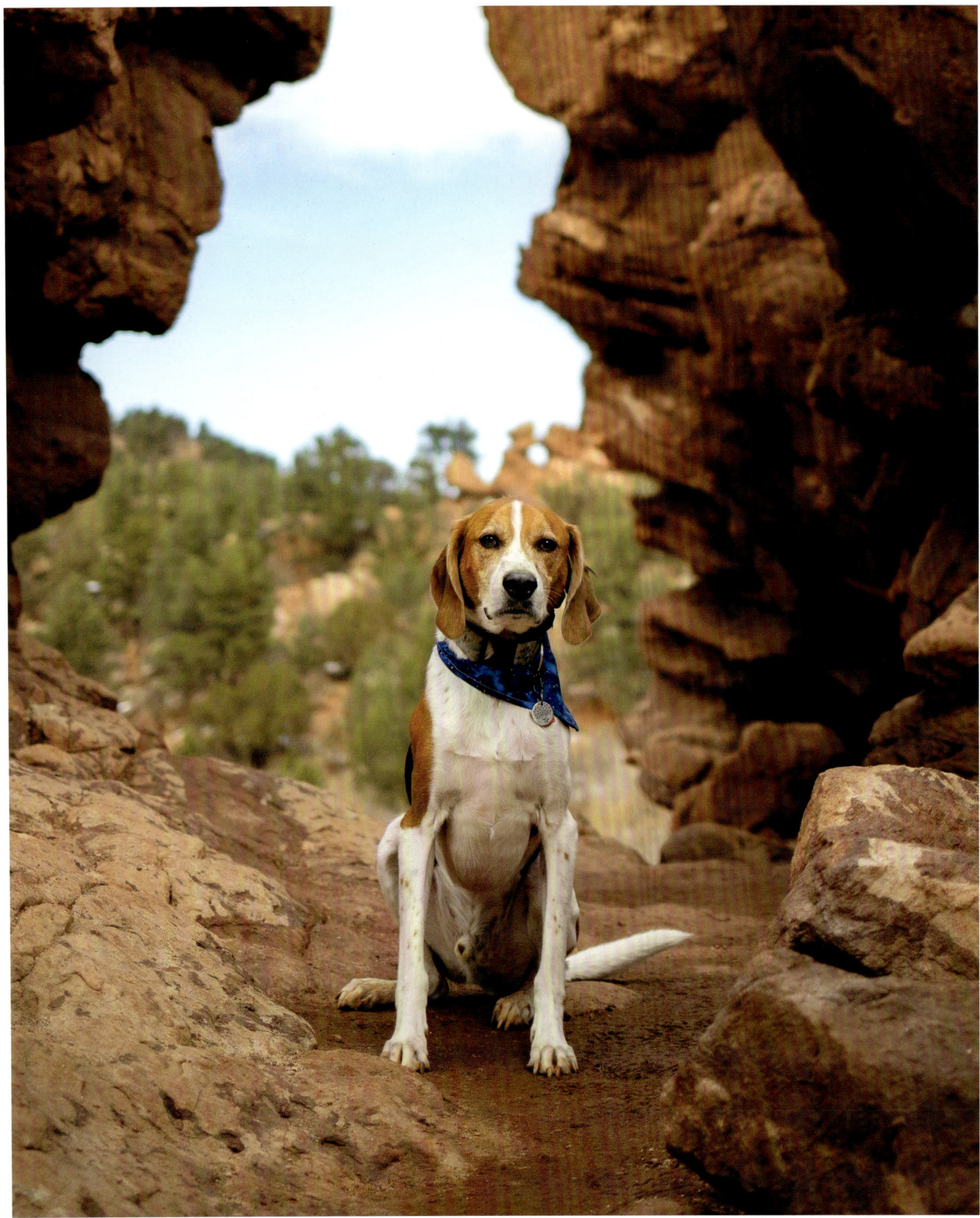

ABOVE:
All American
This foxhound is one of the oldest American breeds. It has a broader, blunter muzzle and a thicker coat than the English foxhound.

American Foxhound

CHARACTERISTICS

Coat
A short and smooth coat that is usually white, black and tan

Height
53–64cm (21–25in)

Weight
18–30kg (40–66lb)

Lifespan
12–13 years

Personality
Friendly and patient

Origin
United States

There can be few dog breeds with such strong links to the United States of America than this foxhound, but at the same time the dog's form and function come from a foreign land. One of the main breeders of the American foxhound was no less than the first U.S. president, George Washington. Although he led the Revolutionary forces to a great victory against the British, he was still deeply embedded in the customs of the old colonial master. One of Washington's favourite pastimes was fox hunting and he rode out from his home at Mount Vernon following a pack of foxhounds, just as the British elite would have done (and continue to do).

The Jeffersons and other families of the Founding Fathers, also kept foxhounds, which had originally been imported from England. Once stateside, the packs were bred with dogs of French origin. The result is a scent hound that is a little taller than the English breed and which lacks some of the original pack instinct. The American foxhound is known for its almost musical bark that can be heard from far away.

The foxhound is good with children but has an independent and stubborn streak. They need a lot of space to run and would be unsuitable for life in the city.

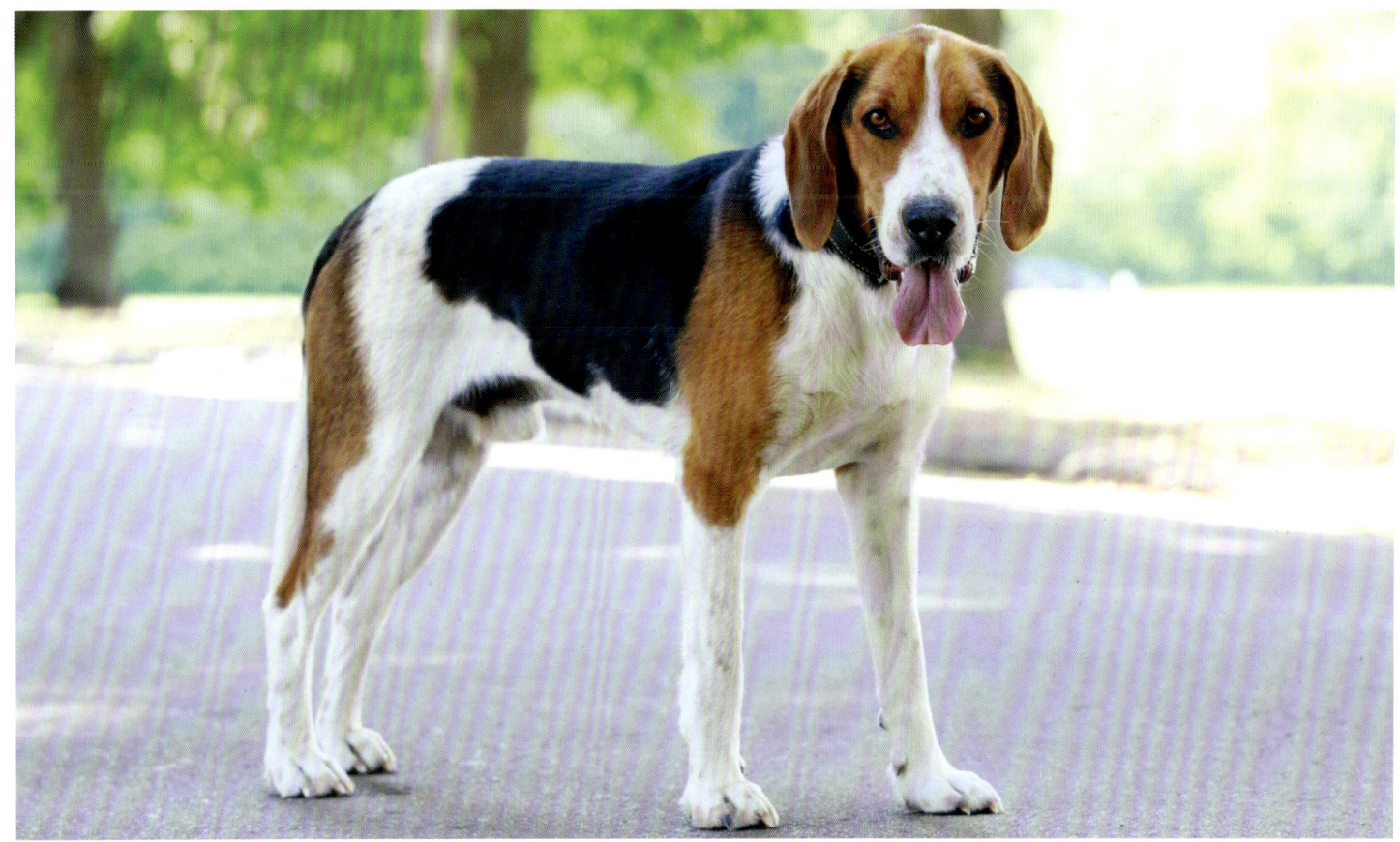

ABOVE:
Nothing but a hound dog
The American foxhound has a narrower chest than European hounds, but shares the lean and athletic body, long legs and broad floppy ears.

HUNTING DOGS
English Foxhound

CHARACTERISTICS

Coat
Usually a tricolour pattern of black, white and tan, or a lemon and white colour
Height
58–64cm (23–25in)
Weight
25–34kg (55–75lb)
Lifespan
10–11 years
Personality
Sociable and energetic
Origin
England

This medium-sized scenthound is built for the chase. It has long, sturdy legs, a strong frame and a deep chest for a big set of lungs and heart. The dog loves to run with the pack as it follows its primal instincts to chase down prey. Just as their wolf ancestors would, the dogs track a quarry over long distances, never letting it hide or take a rest. Eventually, the exhausted animal can run no further, and the pack rip it to pieces. As the name suggests, the hounds are mostly sent after foxes, which have traditionally been seen as a pest by livestock farmers, but the dogs are also traditionally used to hunt stags and will often follow the scent of rabbits and other wild animals if given the chance. There used to be hundreds of working foxhound packs kept in England (and across Britain) but those numbers have dwindled as the public mood has turned against fox hunting in that country. Today, it is illegal for the hounds to kill animals, and hunts are meant to follow artificial scent trails instead.

Nevertheless, the English foxhound is as happy in a pack of humans as it is among fellow dogs, and the breed is friendly and social. The dog needs a lot of opportunities to run and explore.

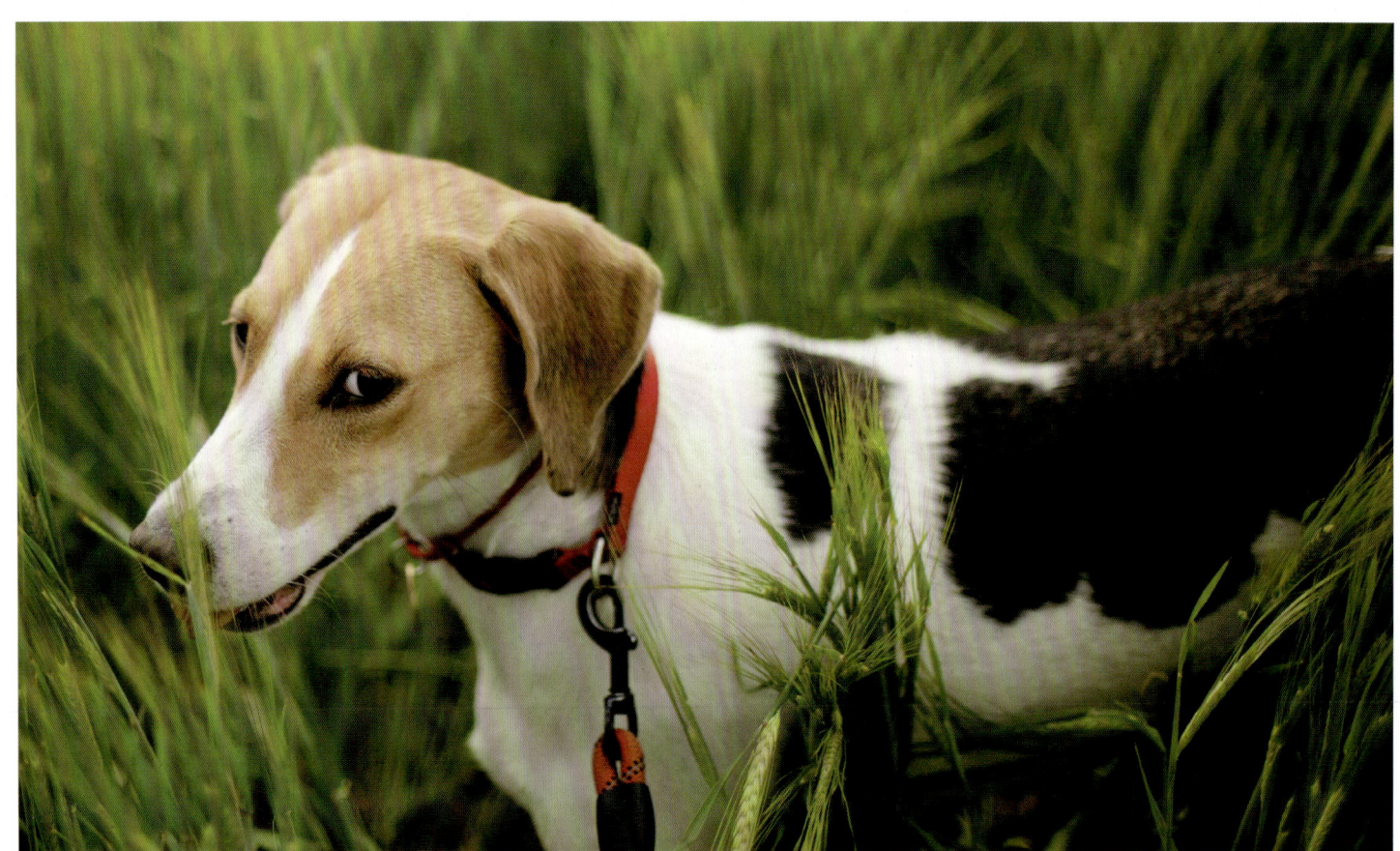

ABOVE:
Maintaining health
The short coat of every foxhound needs a brush once a week or so.

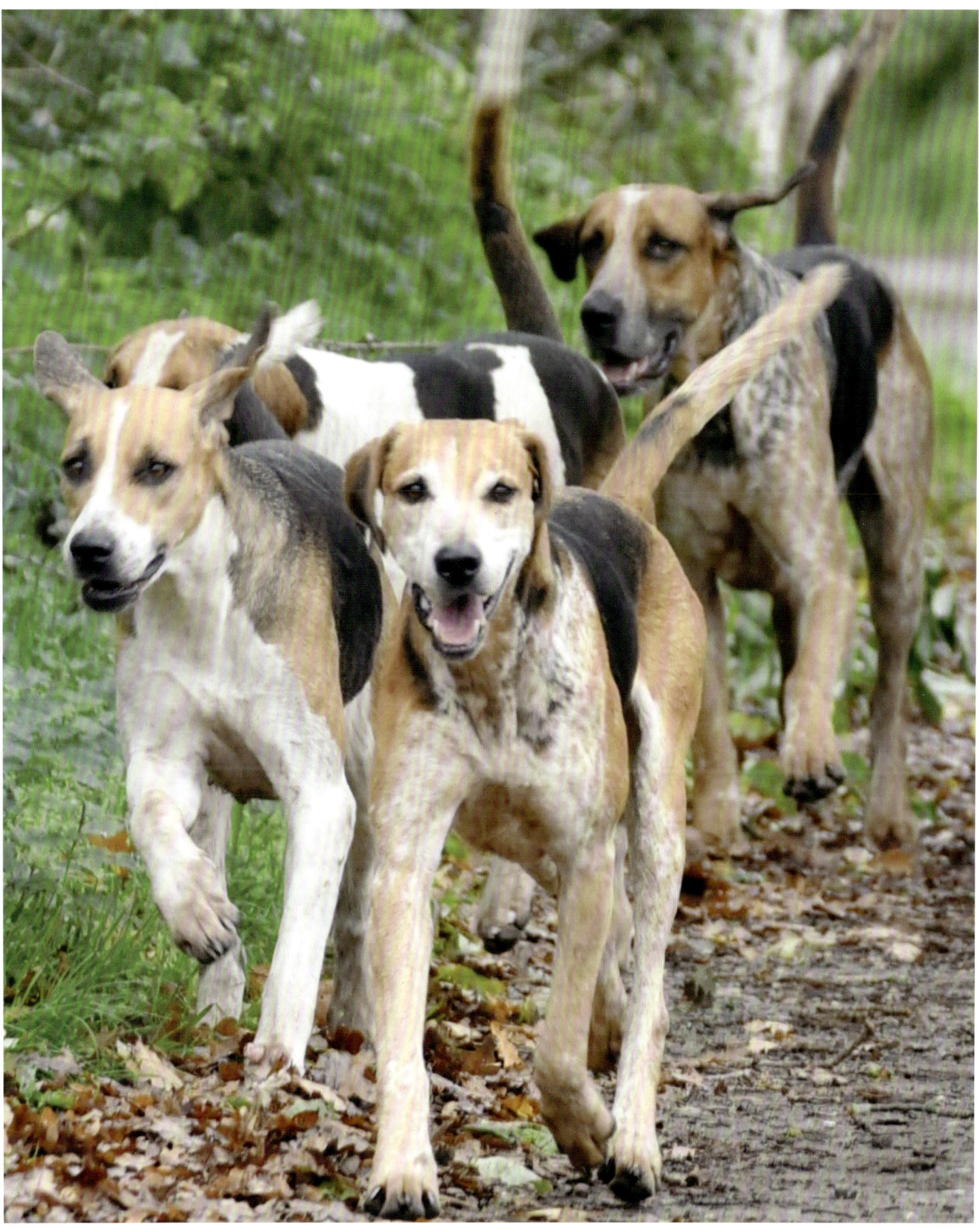

ABOVE:
Staying power
The foxhounds have a muscular body, long legs and a deep chest that allows them to run fast and endure long chases.

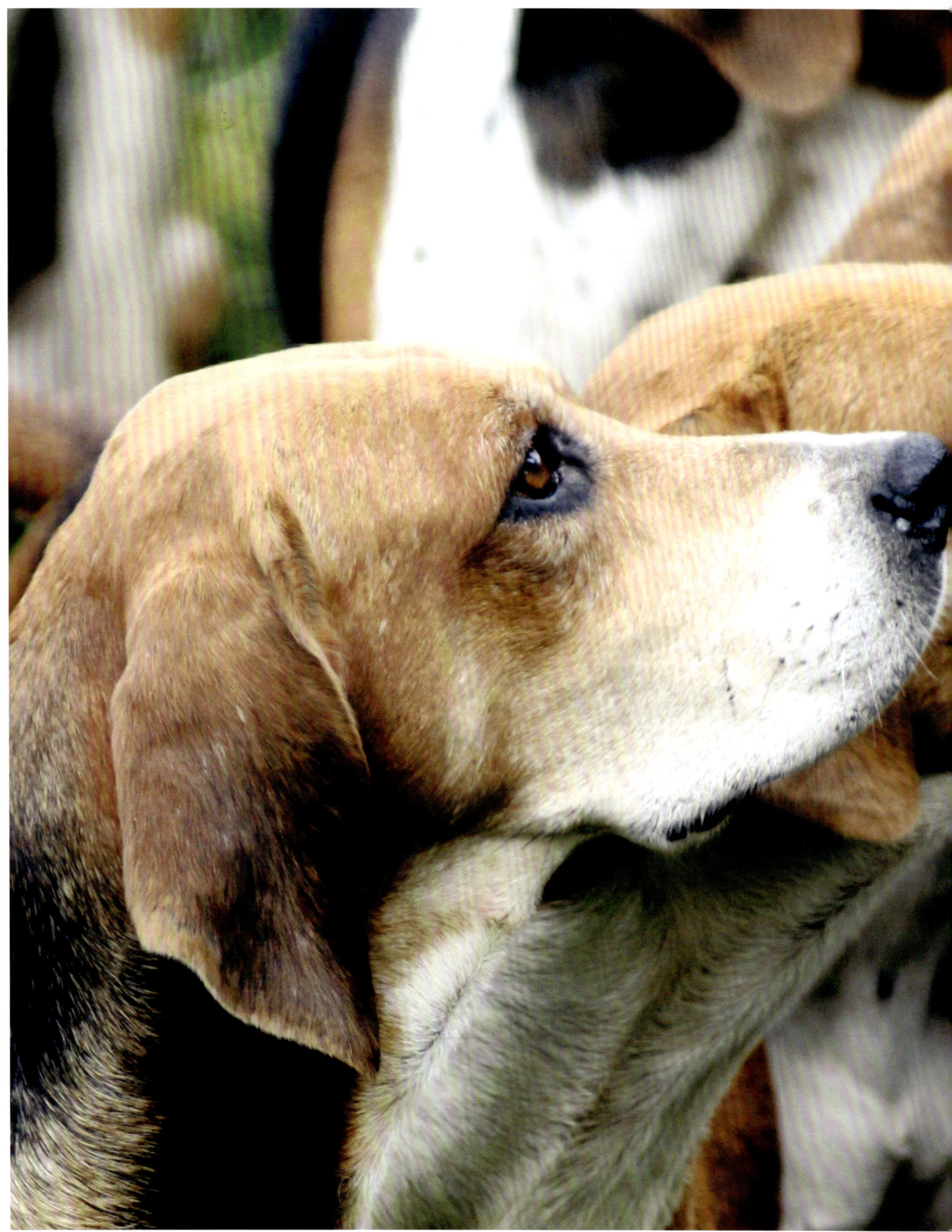

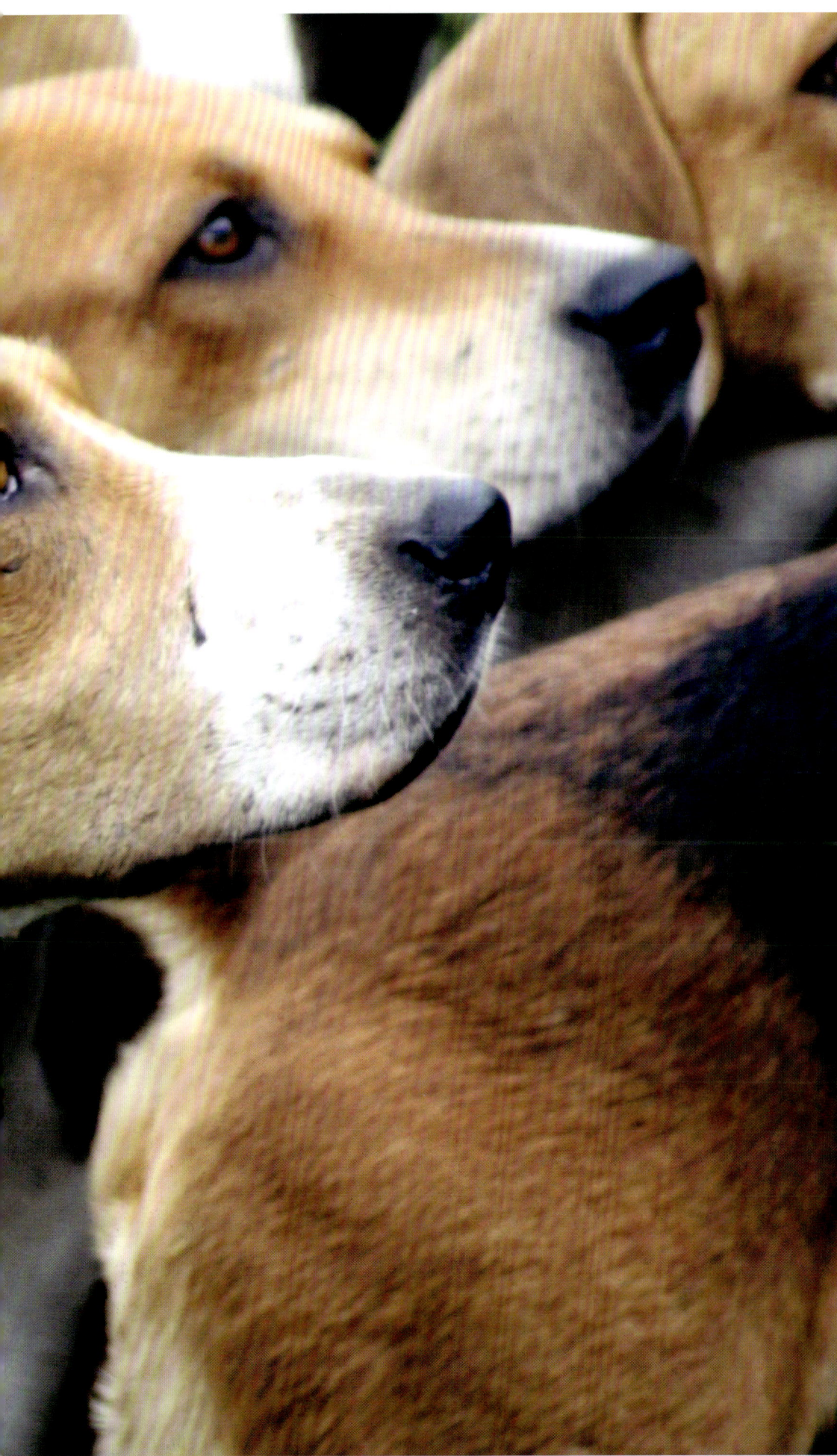

Ready to go
Foxhounds generally display a gentle and affectionate temperament despite their hunting instincts.

HUNTING DOGS

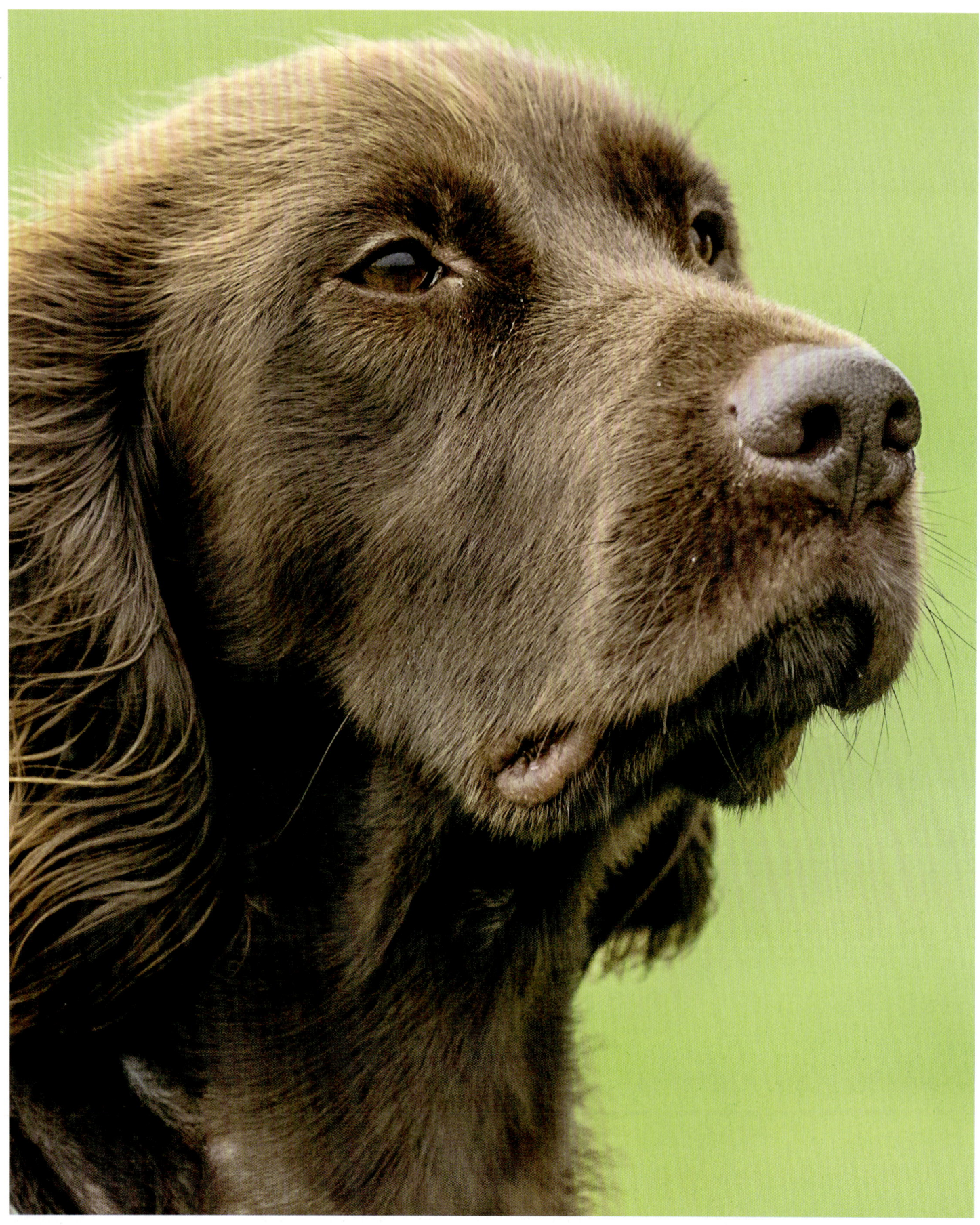

ABOVE:
Intelligent companion
The German pointer exudes intelligence and obedience. This dog will always be by your side.

German Pointer

CHARACTERISTICS

Coat
A smooth or wiry coat with solid liver, liver and white, liver roan or liver with pale speckles

Height
53–64cm (21–25in)

Weight
20–32kg (44–71lb)

Lifespan
10–14 years

Personality
Bright and gentle

Origin
Germany

This gundog was developed in Bavaria, southern Germany, by crossing several dogged German hunting and retrieving breeds with the English pointer. The pointer added grace and speed, while the other breeds maintained other hunting abilities. The result was a highly versatile all-round gundog that can track, point and retrieve well—and be a fun-loving member of the family.

There are three varieties of German pointer. The most common is the German shorthaired pointer. The wirehaired pointer has a coat better suited for moving through thorny bushes and for plunging into water to retrieve birds. The longhaired variety is less common. It was bred for colder weather in alpine regions. All varieties share the strength and endurance needed for long days out in the fields and forests. They are particularly good at tracking animals at night.

Since their creation 250 years ago German pointers have been family pets as much as working dogs. They are loyal and companionable and will thrive as long as they have plenty of exercise and mental stimulation. They are popular choices for families with older children who enjoy outdoor activities.

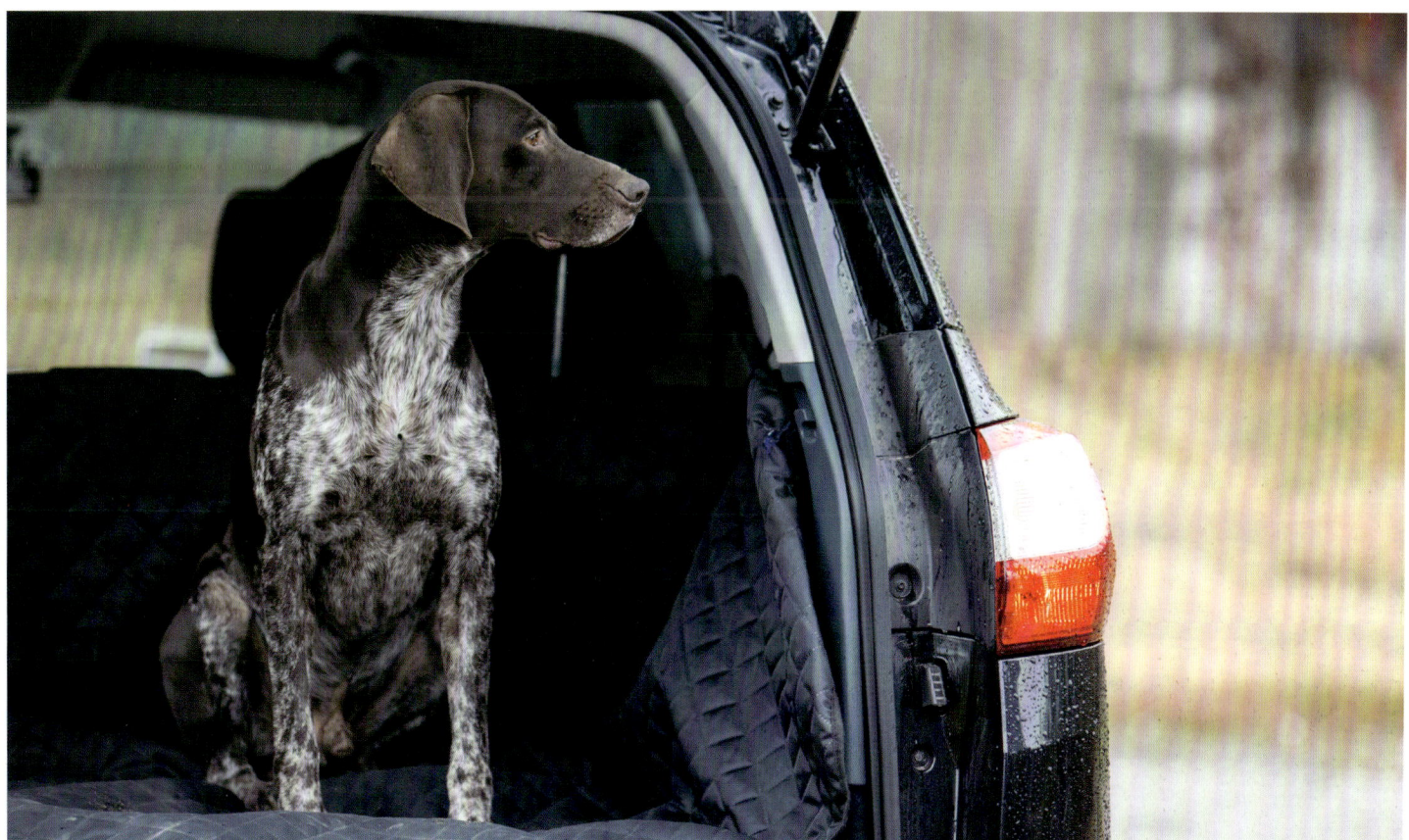

ABOVE:
Work and play
The history of the breed has meant the German pointer has been developed as a gundog and a family pet at the same time.

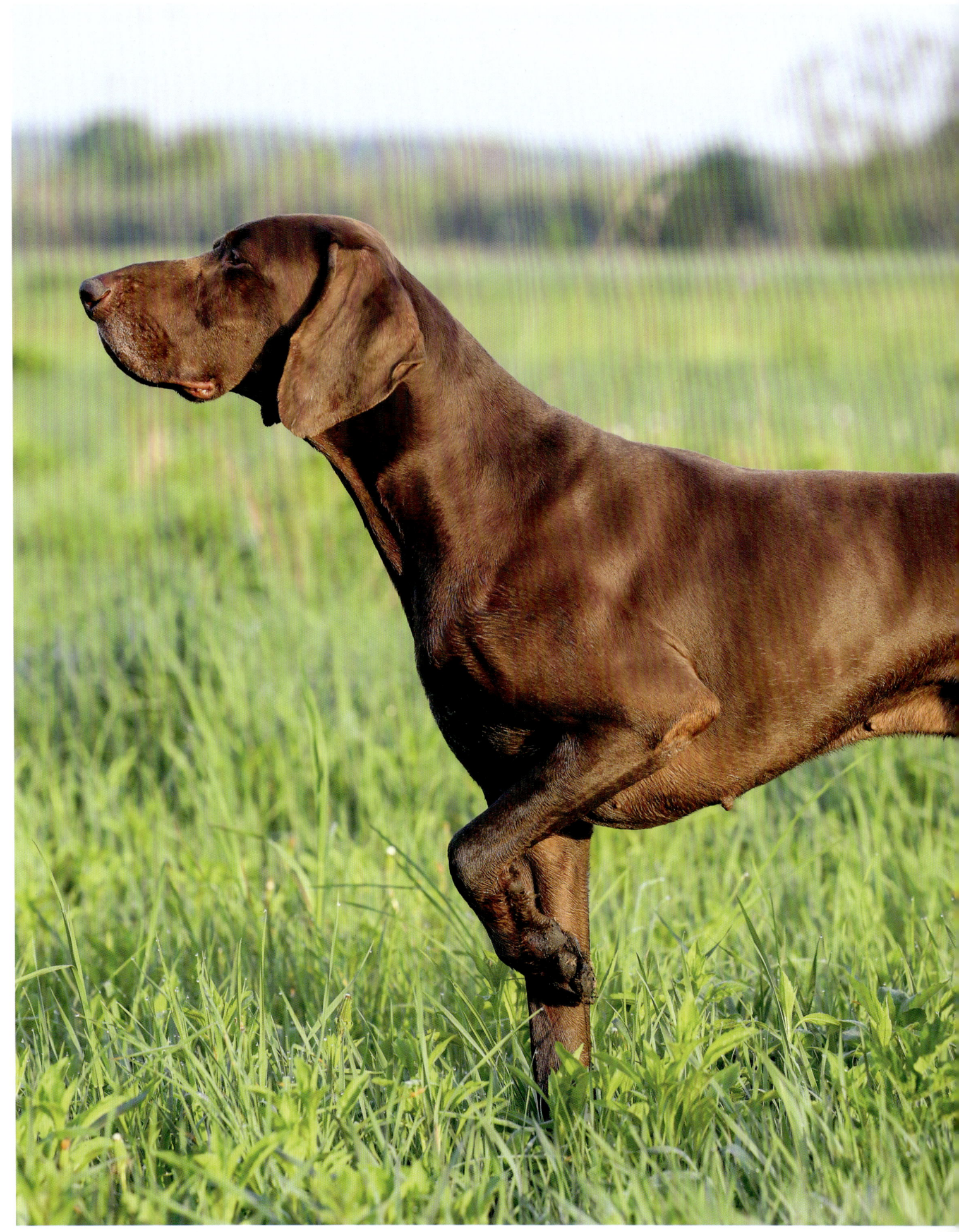

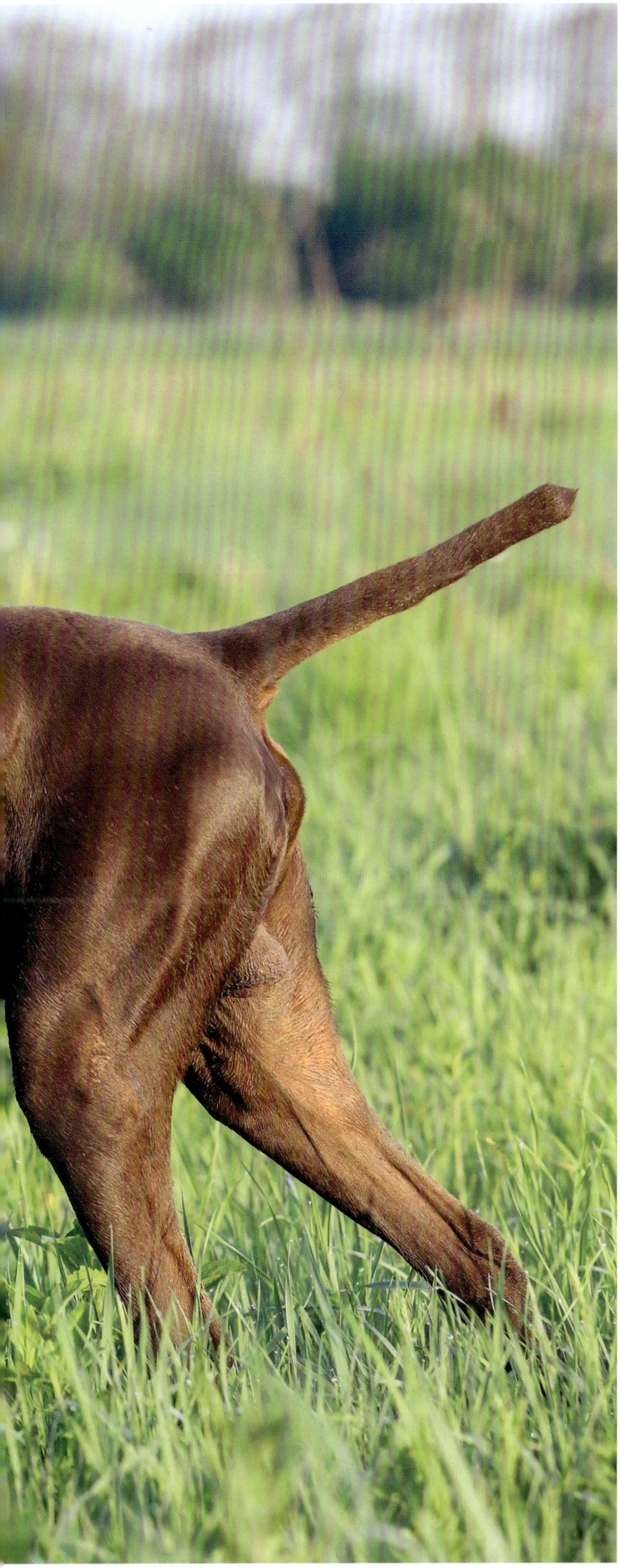

HUNTING DOGS

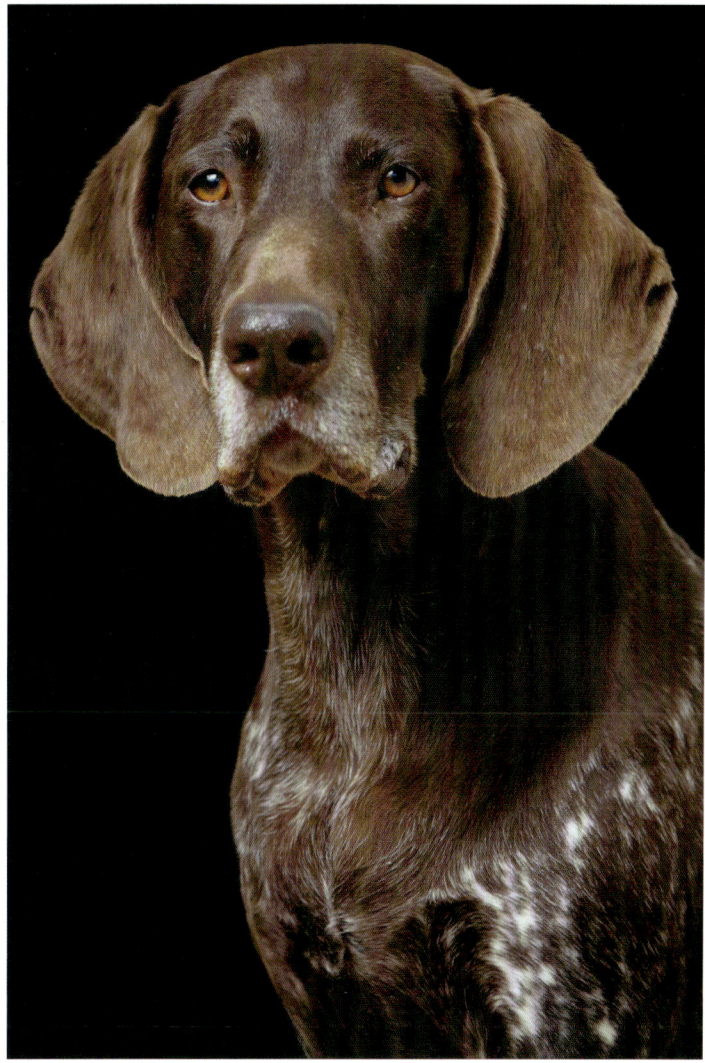

LEFT:
On the hunt
The muzzle of the pointer, as the name suggests, points directly at its target, indicating its location.

ABOVE:
Eyes on the prize
Intelligent and obedient, this breed, like all pointers, will freeze on the spot when it finds quarry.

HUNTING DOGS

Hungarian Vizsla

CHARACTERISTICS

Coat
A distinctive golden-rust coat that is short, smooth and dense. There is no undercoat

Height
53–64cm (21–25in)

Weight
20–30kg (44–66lb)

Lifespan
13–14 years

Personality
Gentle and sensitive

Origin
Hungary

A very effective hunting dog that is also a firm favourite as a pet and companion, the vizsla has it all. It has stamina and speed and is able to move as gracefully through thickets over heathland as it does along a path beside its owner out on a jog. The ancestors of this Hungarian breed were red-haired hounds that arrived with the Magyars, a horseback culture that came from the east and settled here in the 9th century. Over the ensuing centuries, the dogs were refined by wealthy landowners into the versatile vizsla.

The dog is able to track the game by scent and quietly point to it. Its Magyar creators used the vizsla alongside falcons, which would be sent in for the kill. The dog would then retrieve the quarry, splashing into water if needed, and hold the downed bird or rabbit gently in the mouth. Today, viszlas are used as gundogs, and their intelligence and eagerness to please makes them great competitors in dog sports such as obedience trials and agility courses. The breed also makes a welcoming member of the family, albeit one that needs a lot of exercise and attention to prevent boredom becoming anxiety and destructiveness.

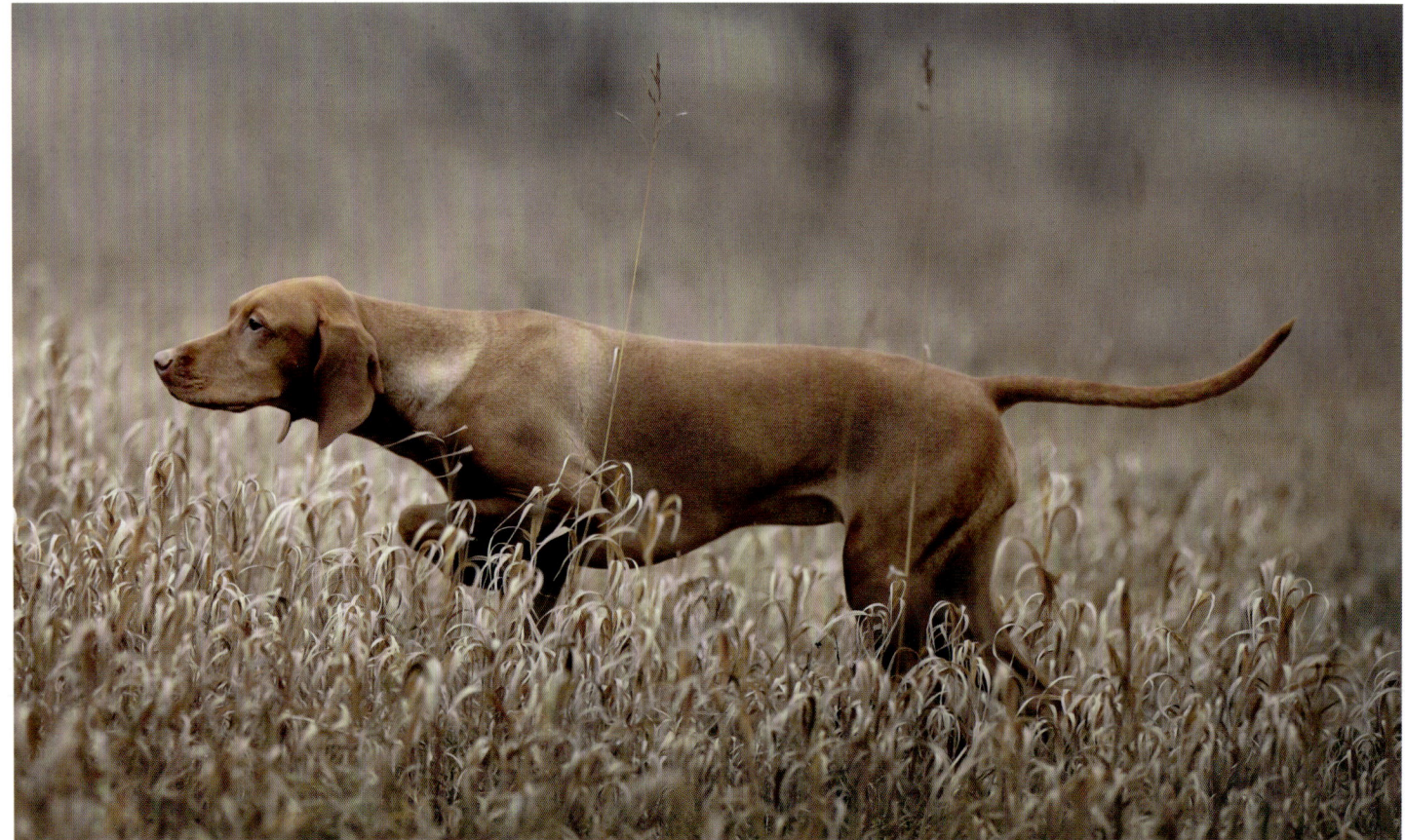

ABOVE:
Always ready
The vizsla is athletic, agile and light on its feet, with a robust body and defined muscles. It is always ready for action.

HUNTING DOGS

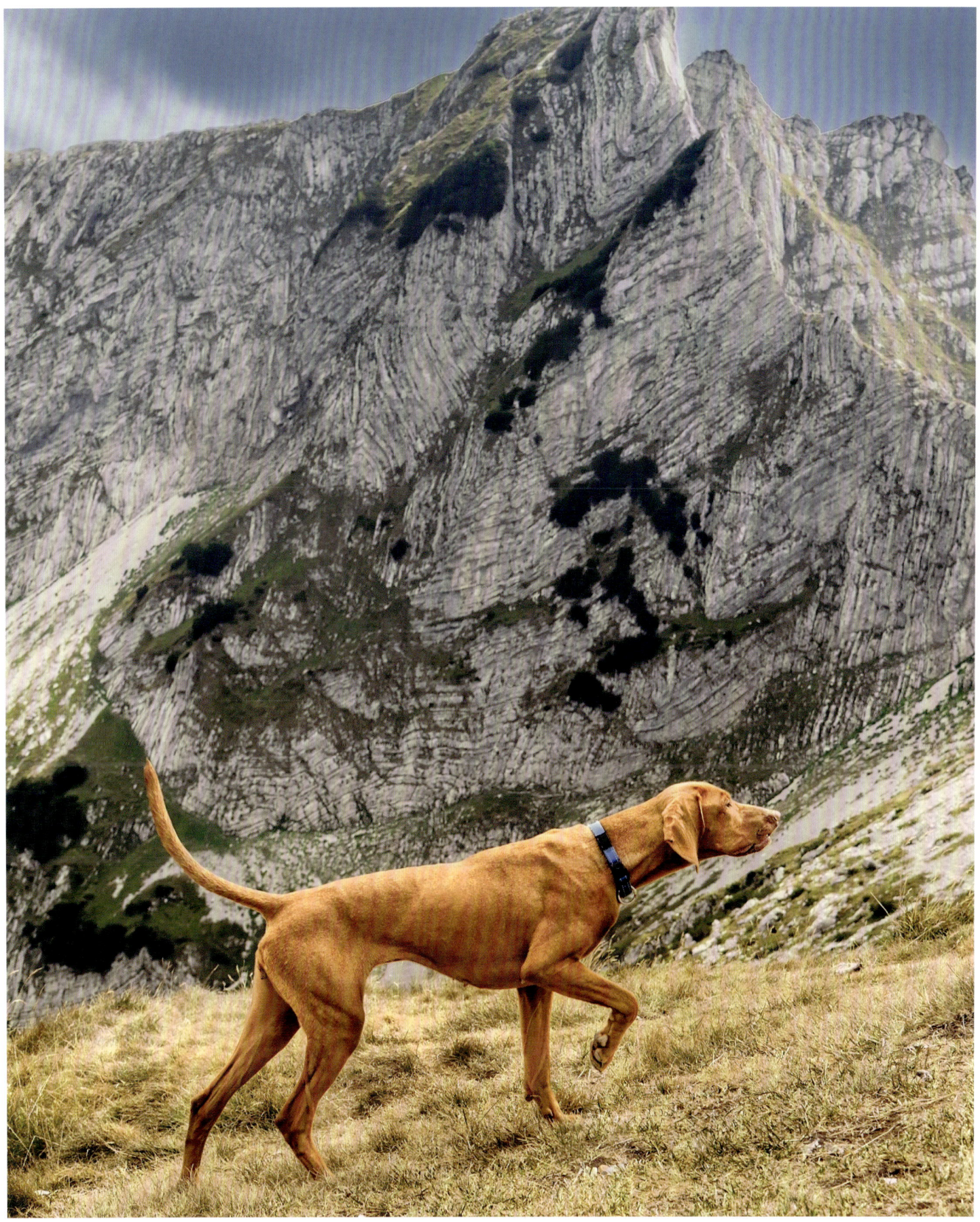

ABOVE:
Go signal
In common with many pointers, the vizsla indicates that it has located a bird or other small quarry by lifting its forepaw, raising the tail and focusing its nose intently in one direction.

HUNTING DOGS

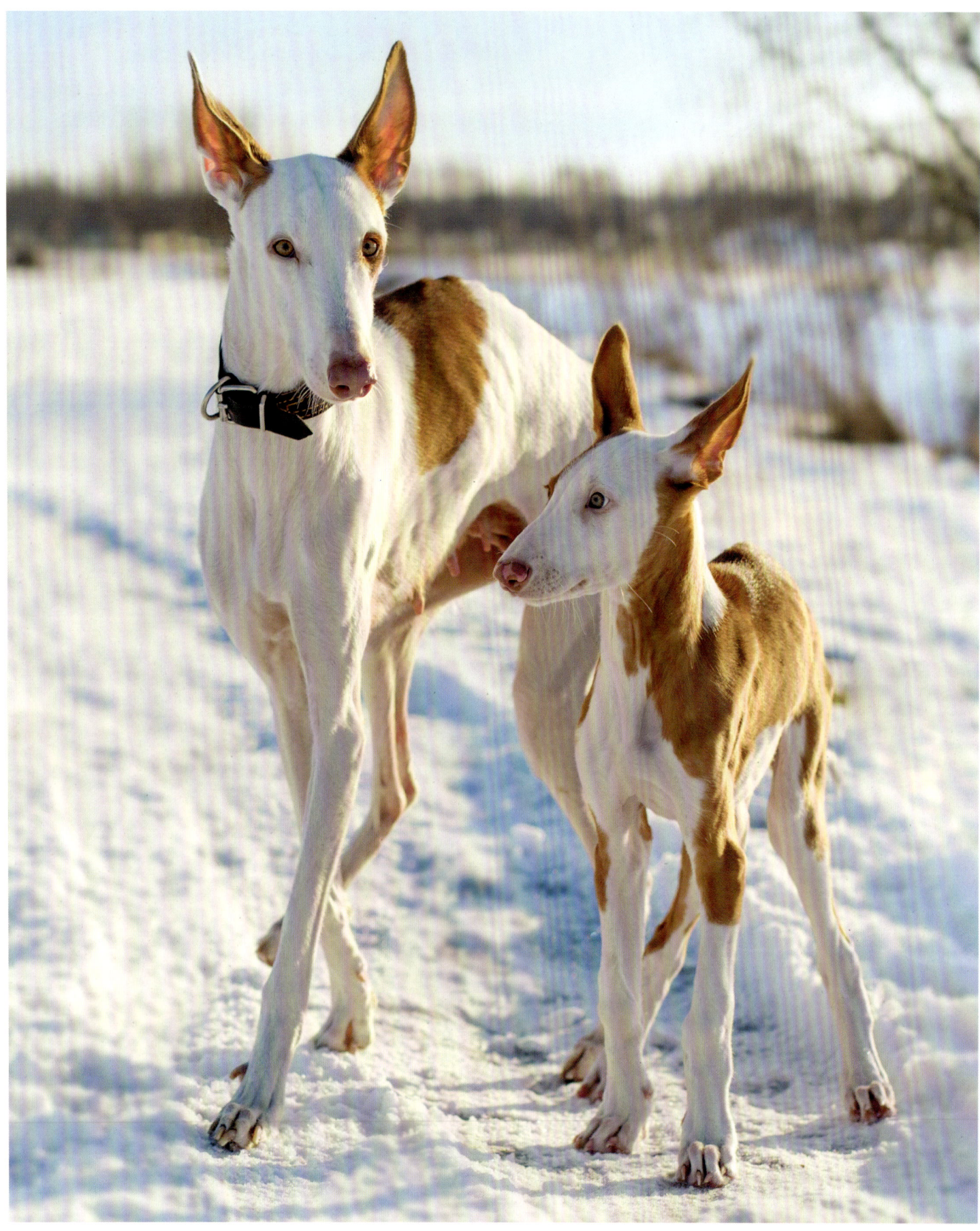

ABOVE:
Distinctive features
The Ibizan hound has a graceful and athletic appearance, with a long neck and a slender body.

Ibizan Hound

CHARACTERISTICS

Coat
The coat can be smooth or wire-haired, and the colour is usually white or red, or a combination of both

Height
56–74cm (22–29in)

Weight
20–23kg (44–51lb)

Lifespan
10–12 years

Personality
Intelligent and independent

Origin
Spain

Originating on Spain's Balearic Islands, and named after the smallest, Ibiza, this surprisingly tall breed has an ancient pedigree. It is thought that the dogs are descended from pharaoh hounds brought to the islands long ago by Phoenician merchants. It shares the lean body, pointed ears and slender snout, but unlike its African cousin, the Ibizan hound is more trainable and easier to control. Nevertheless it is rare beyond its home islands.

The dog's original job was to chase rabbits across Ibiza rocky terrain, something it has been doing for thousands of generations. The dog has an impressive turn of speed and has a "raking" or suspended trot, where the legs are held closer to the body for a fraction before putting its feet down. This gives it the appearance of making short glides as it runs, something that helps it navigate the broken ground of rock and sand.

The Ibizan hound is an active and independent dog that needs a lot of exercise and a secure fenced area to run and play. It is generally affectionate to family members but may be reserved with strangers—and will dash off in pursuit of birds and other small animals if it gets the chance.

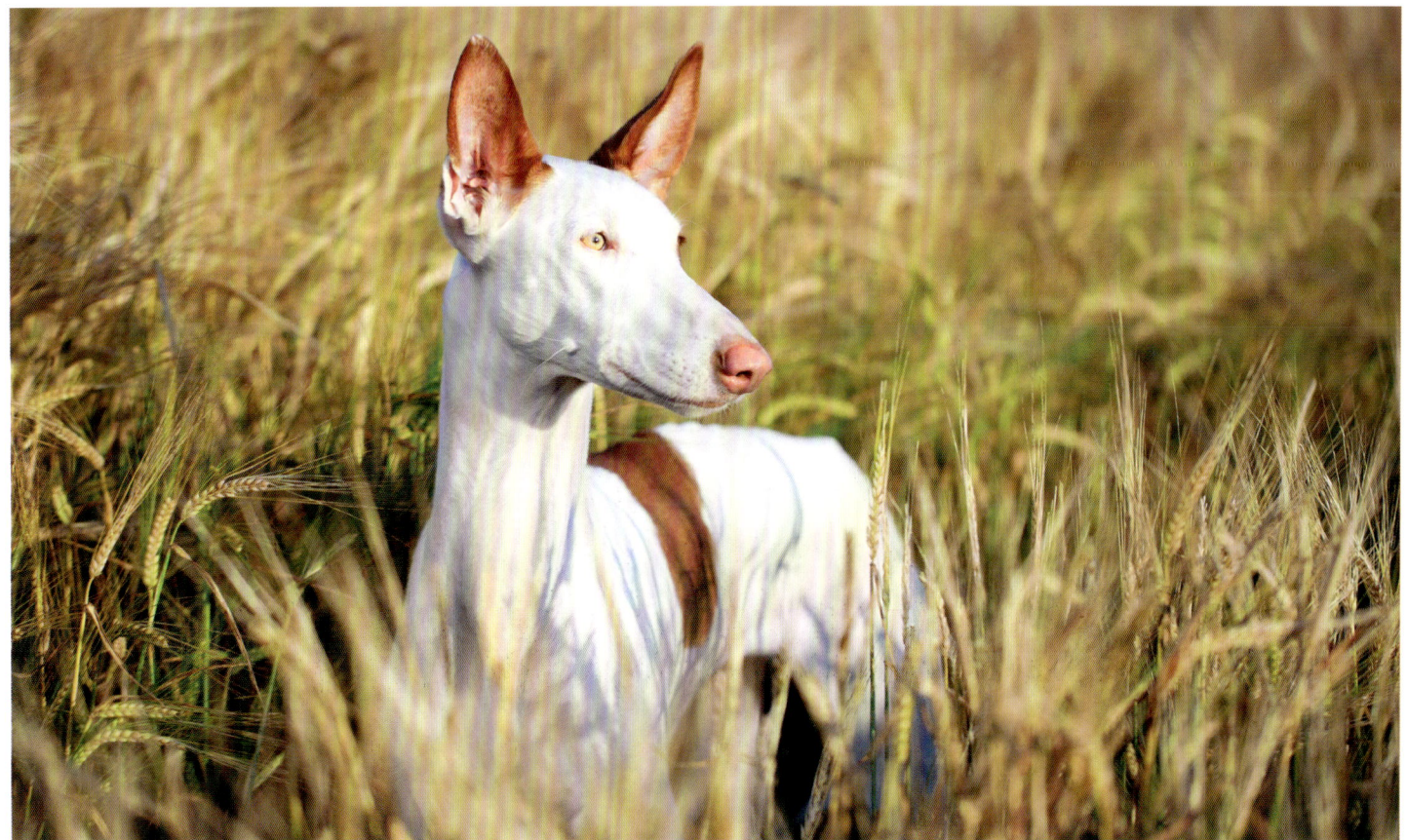

ABOVE:
Rosy skin
The rose-coloured leathers (or skin) of the nose, eye rims and lips are a defining feature of this dog, as are the amber or caramel eyes.

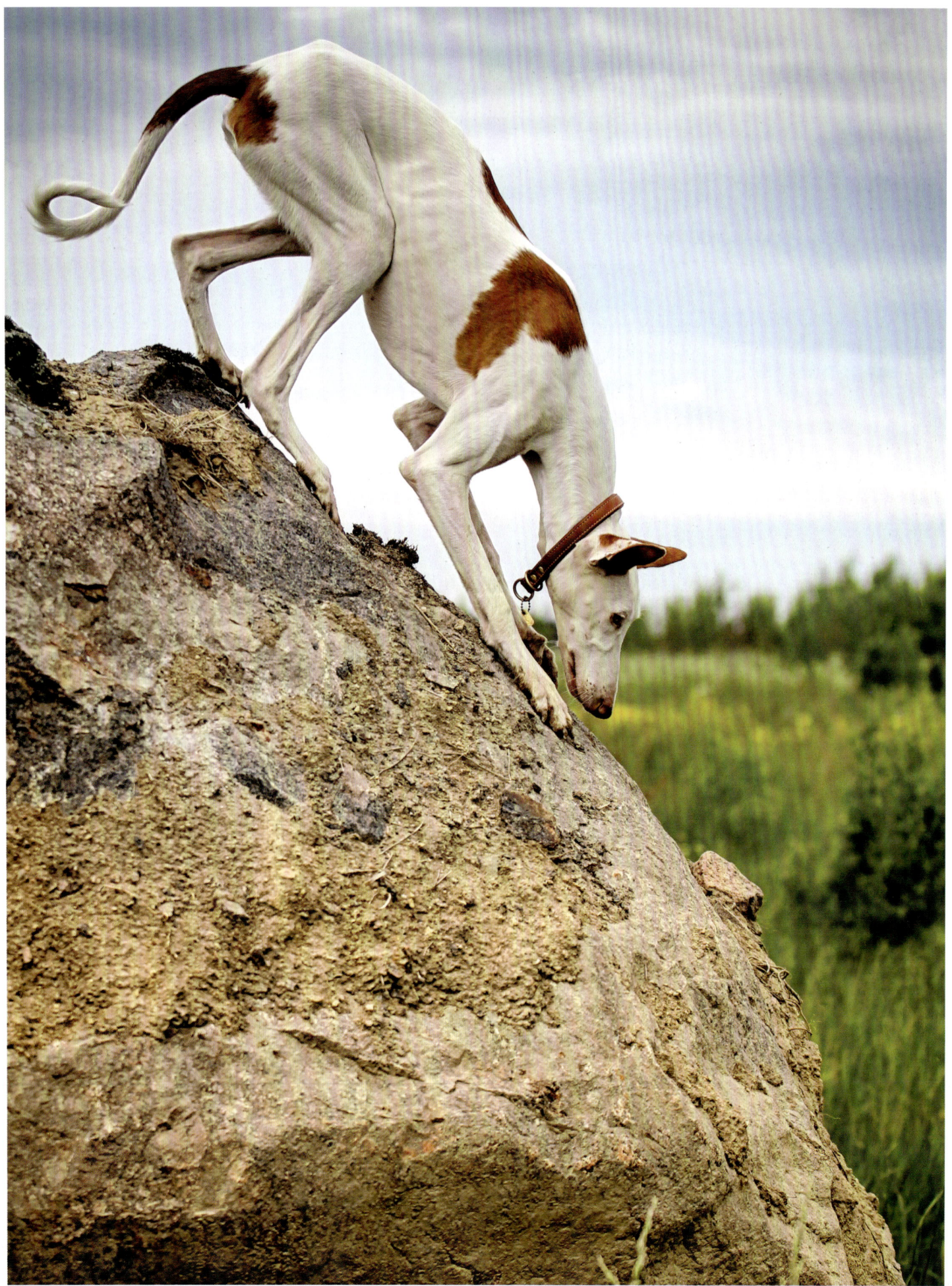

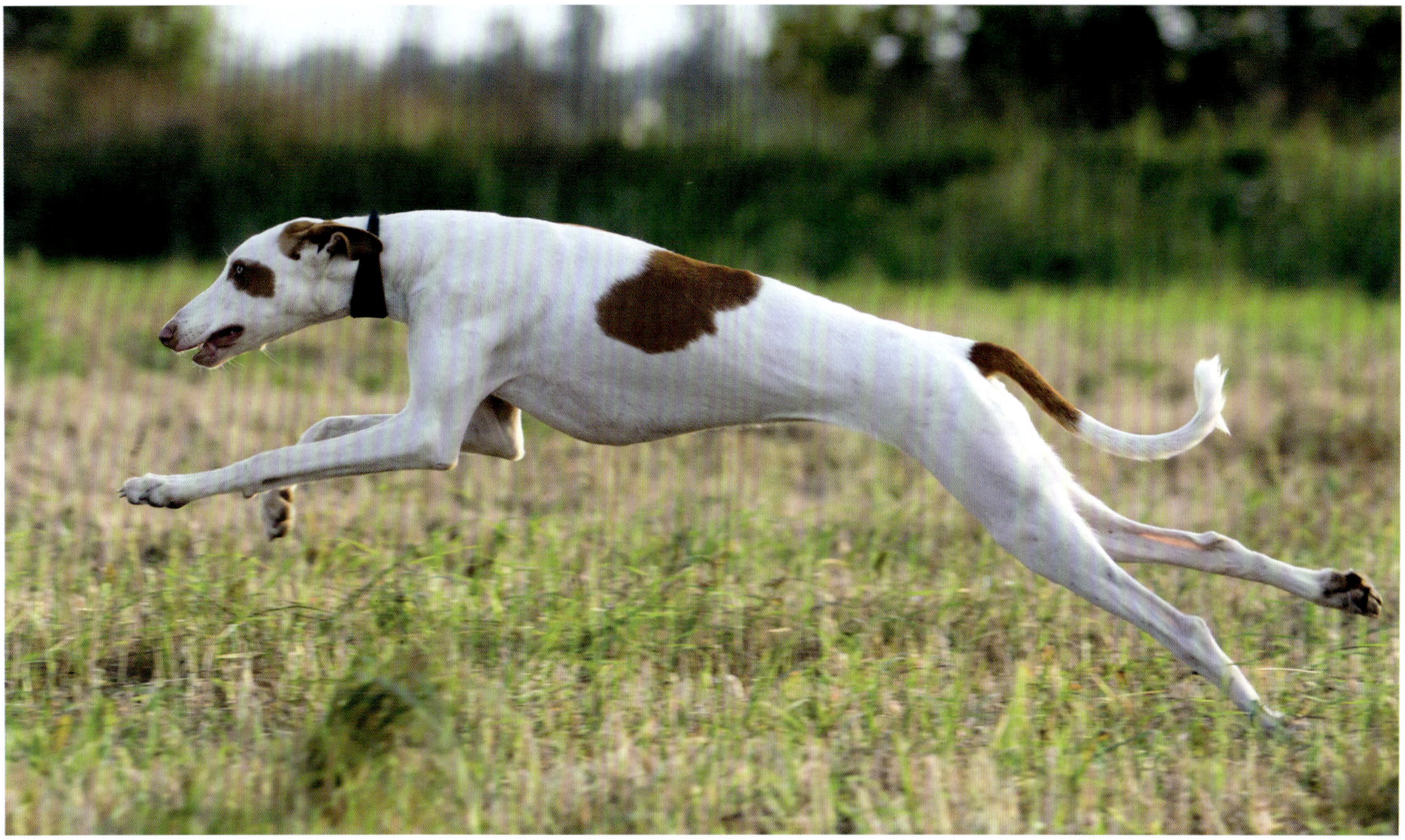

HUNTING DOGS

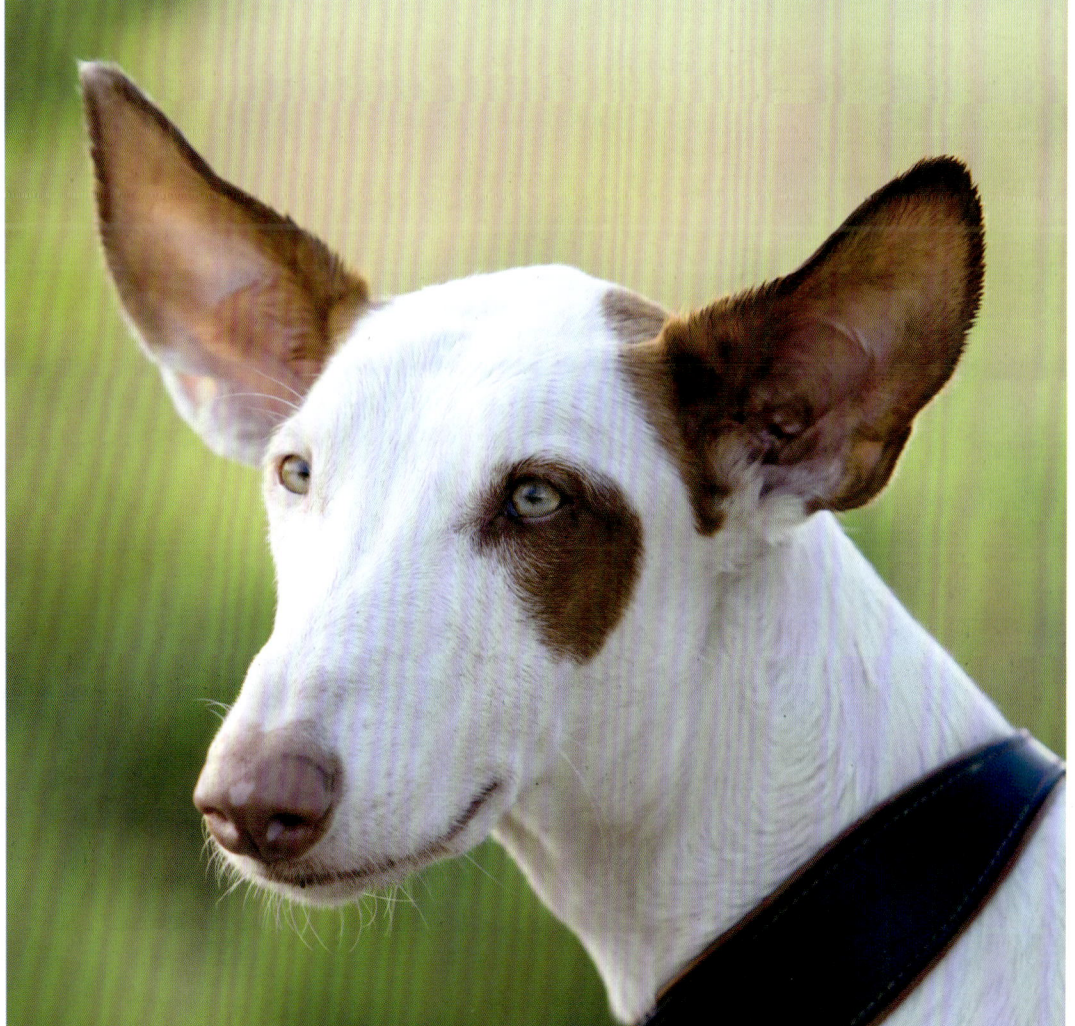

ABOVE:
Gazelle-like
Dogs of this breed are very athletic and require a lot of exercise. It is not uncommon for an Ibizan to be able to jump up to six feet from a standing position, so a tall, secure fence is the order of the day for owners.

LEFT:
Historic hound
Art history students will recognize the elongated head, with its large erect ears, as a familiar motif of ancient Egypt.

OPPOSITE:
Sniffing out prey
A popular fast-running Catalan species that is used to hunt rabbits by sight, sound and scent.

HUNTING DOGS
Irish Setter

CHARACTERISTICS

Coat
A brilliant and silky coat of mahogany or chestnut
Height
64–69cm (25–27in)
Weight
27–32kg (60–71lb)
Lifespan
12–13 years
Personality
Enthusiastic and energetic
Origin
Ireland

With its flowing red locks, this lovable gundog is one of the most recognizable of breeds. It was already a distinct variety as far back as the 16th century and was officially distinguished from the English setter in the 18th century. Its breeding saw it have a mix of English setter and Gordon setter (from Scotland) plus some spaniels including Irish water spaniels. The result is a dog that is happy to work in the exposed uplands in all weathers (often rain!) as it sniffs out birds. As with all setters, the dogs will crouch, or set, quietly nearby once they locate a suitable prey.

The dog has broad recognition far from Ireland. Its friendly and affectionate personality makes it a firm favourite for dog owners the world over, especially those living near open country, where their charge can get a lot of running and play. In North America, the Irish setter has entered local folklore as Big Red, a popular novel about the adventures of a setter and its boy owner that was made into a film in 1962. For many Americans, a pet Irish setter is a much-loved link to their ancestral homeland.

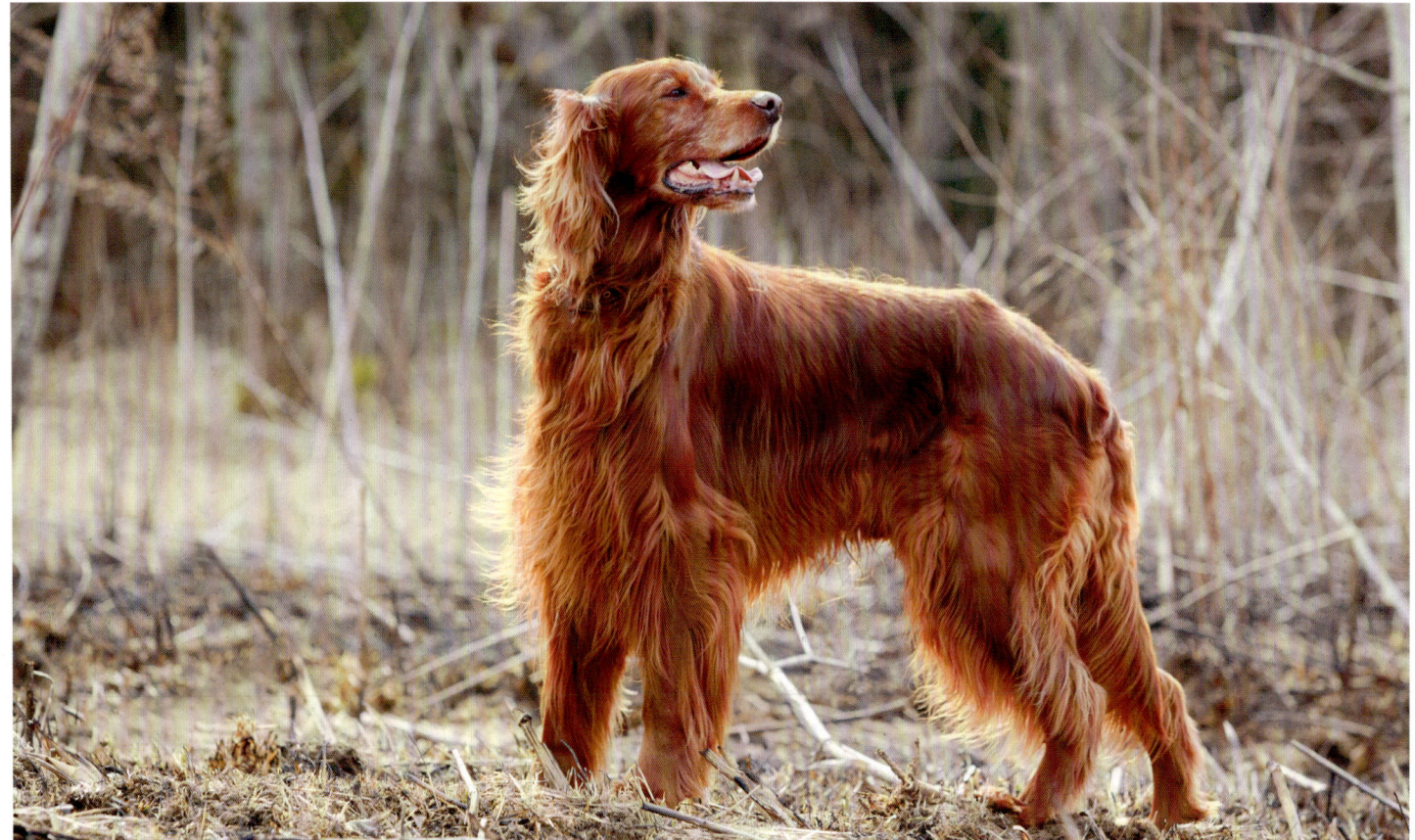

ABOVE:
Fast but not furious
Long, sinewy legs and powerful rear drive help to place the Irish among the swiftest of all sporting dogs. They need a lot of exercise and mental stimulation to keep them happy and healthy.

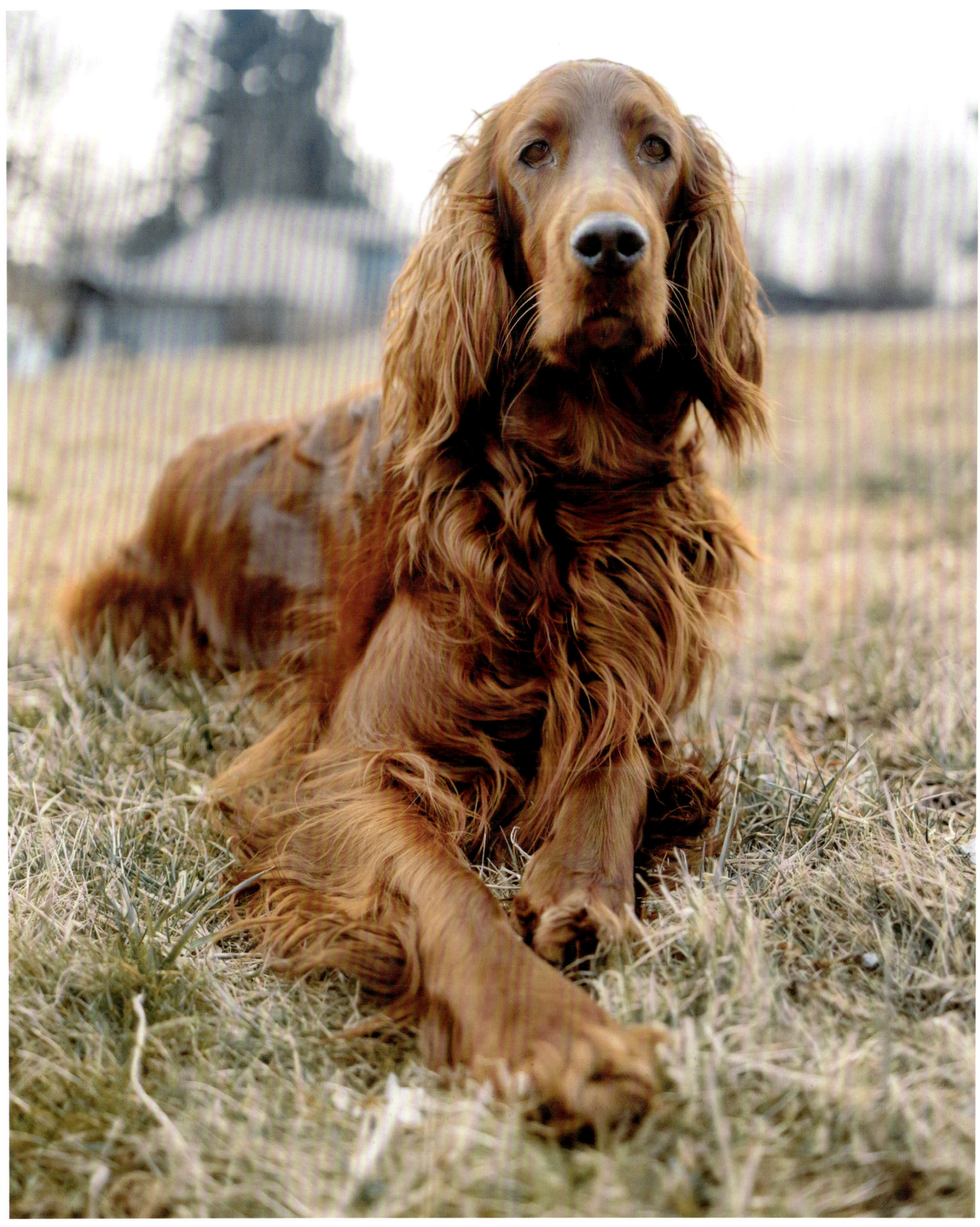

ABOVE:
Ready for fun
This is a loyal and devoted dog that thrives on human companionship and attention. They love to play with children and other dogs, but they can also be mischievous and stubborn at times.

HUNTING DOGS

Irish Wolfhound

CHARACTERISTICS

Coat
A rough and wiry coat that can be black, brindle, fawn, grey, red and white
Height
71–86cm (28–34in)
Weight
48–68kg (105–150lb)
Lifespan
6–10 years
Personality
Gentle and dignified
Origin
Ireland

This ancient sighthound holds the record as the tallest dog breed around, standing around 85cm (34in) to the shoulder. It has a storied history. Large and impressive war dogs were noted as a feature of Ireland and the other British Isles by several Roman historians.

The dogs were originally working as protection for Irish lords and also acting as deerhounds chasing down large animals like deer and boars. By the late Middle Ages, Ireland had developed a problem with wolves, and the Irish hound was refocused as a wolfhound. Within 200 years, Ireland had no wolves left—or boar, and few deer—and the wolfhound went into a steady decline. Victorian collectors took a fancy to the noble hound and assured its survival. The popularity of the breed is boosted by inclusion in a famous legend, Welsh, not Irish. Gelert the Faithful Hound is a tragic tale of how the king's bloodied wolfhound is mistakenly accused of killing a baby prince. The king destroys Gelert, only to discover in the act of doing so that the baby is safe. The blood at the scene was from a wolf that came to snatch the child, whom Gelert protected at all costs.

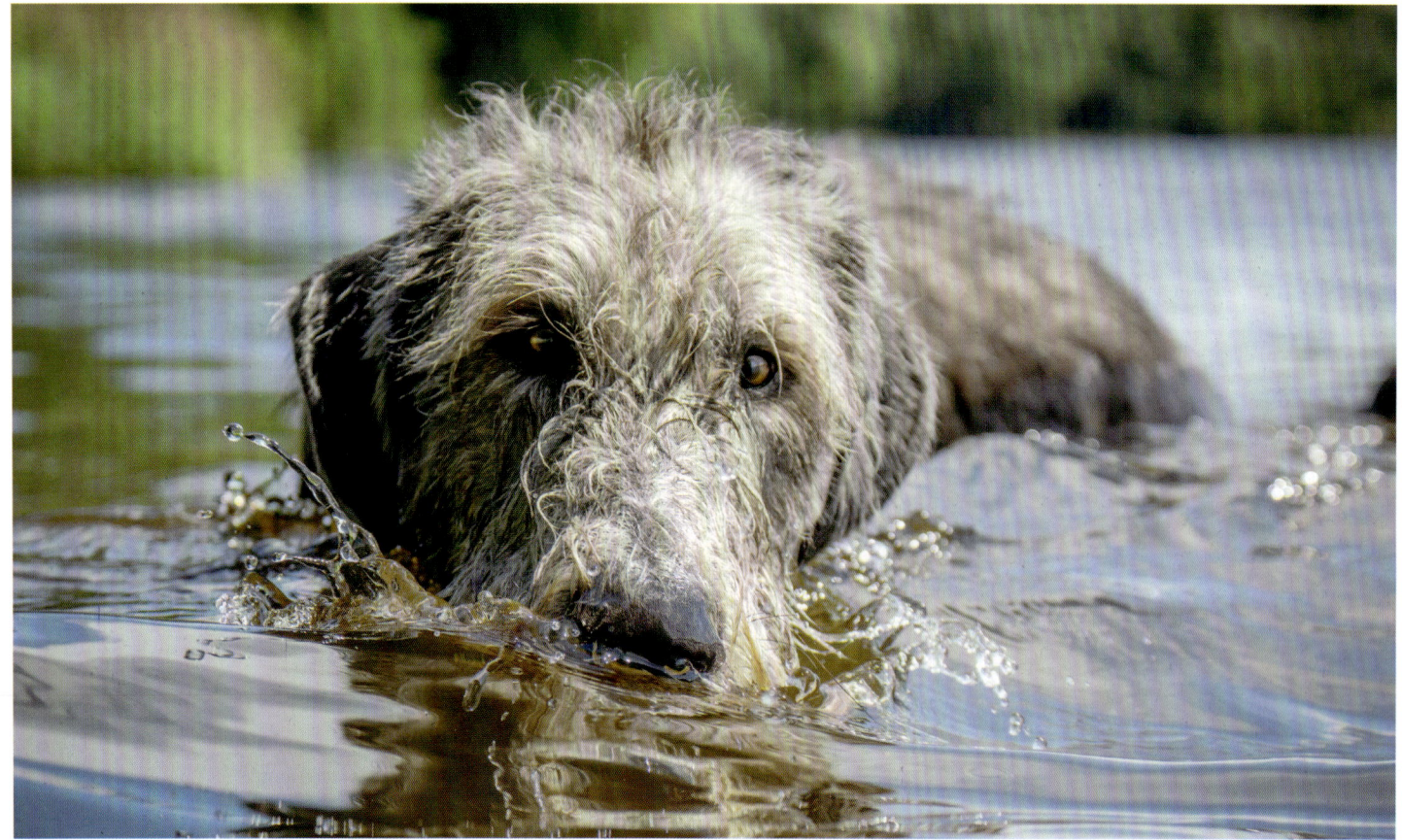

ABOVE:
Space and time
Irish wolfhounds need a lot of space to exercise and play and love companionship of people or other dogs.

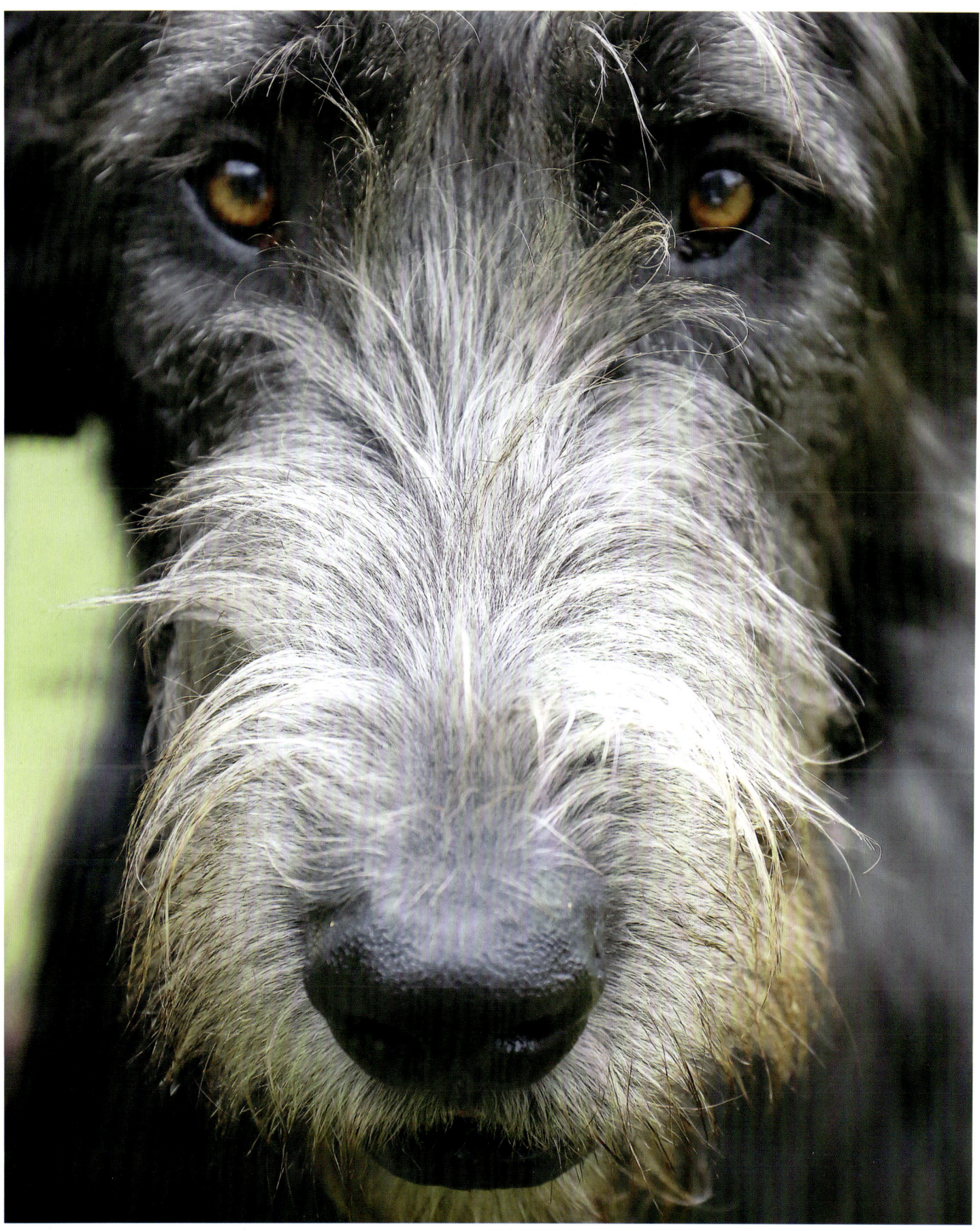

ABOVE:
Big and bouncy
The breed is known for its gentle and friendly temperament, but also for its strength and speed. It is said that these huge dogs are "gentle when stroked, fierce when provoked," and this remains a hallmark of the breed.

HUNTING DOGS

Furry friends
A pair of young wolfhounds exchange a lick. Licking is a signal of submission and trust.

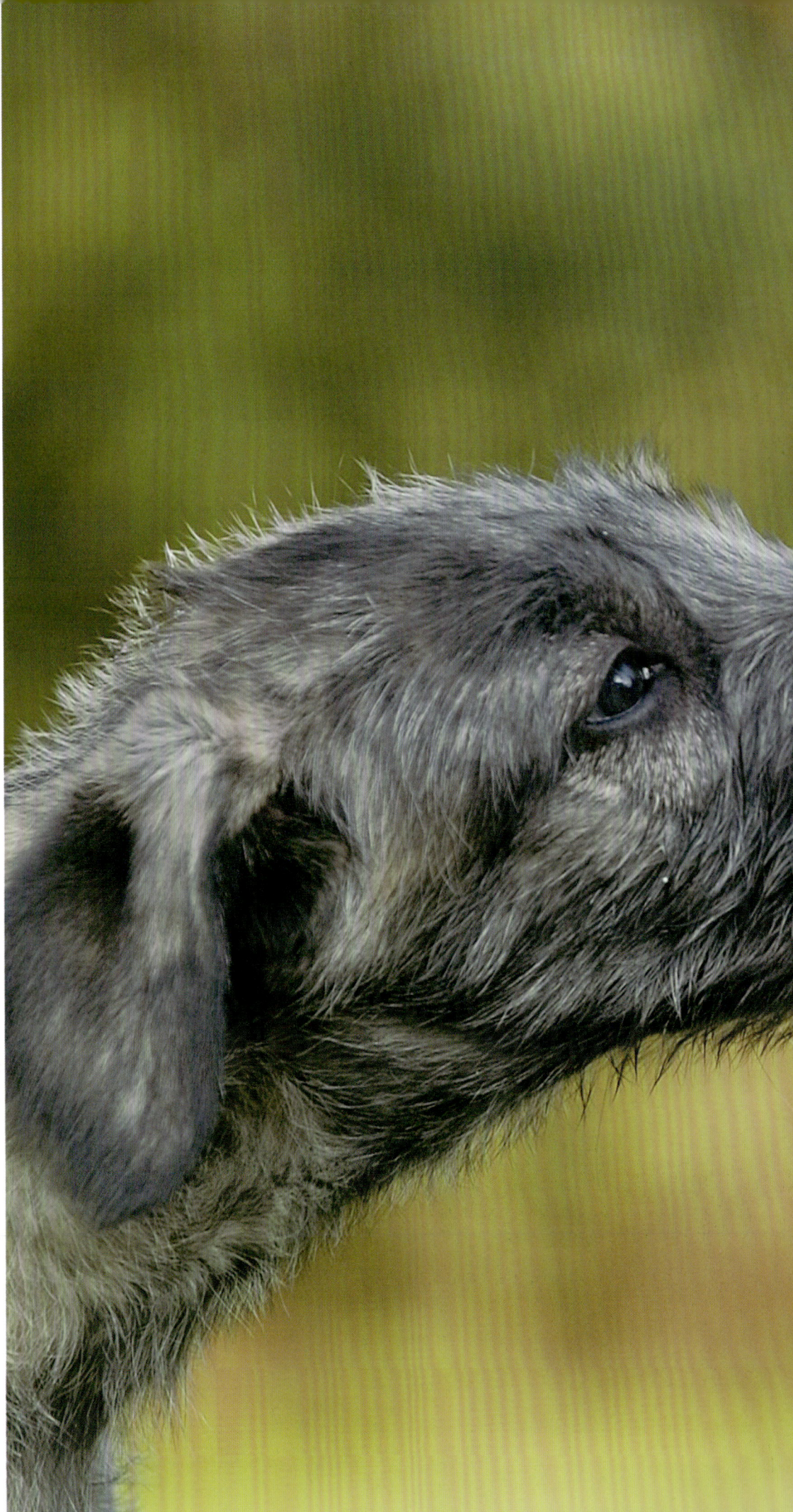

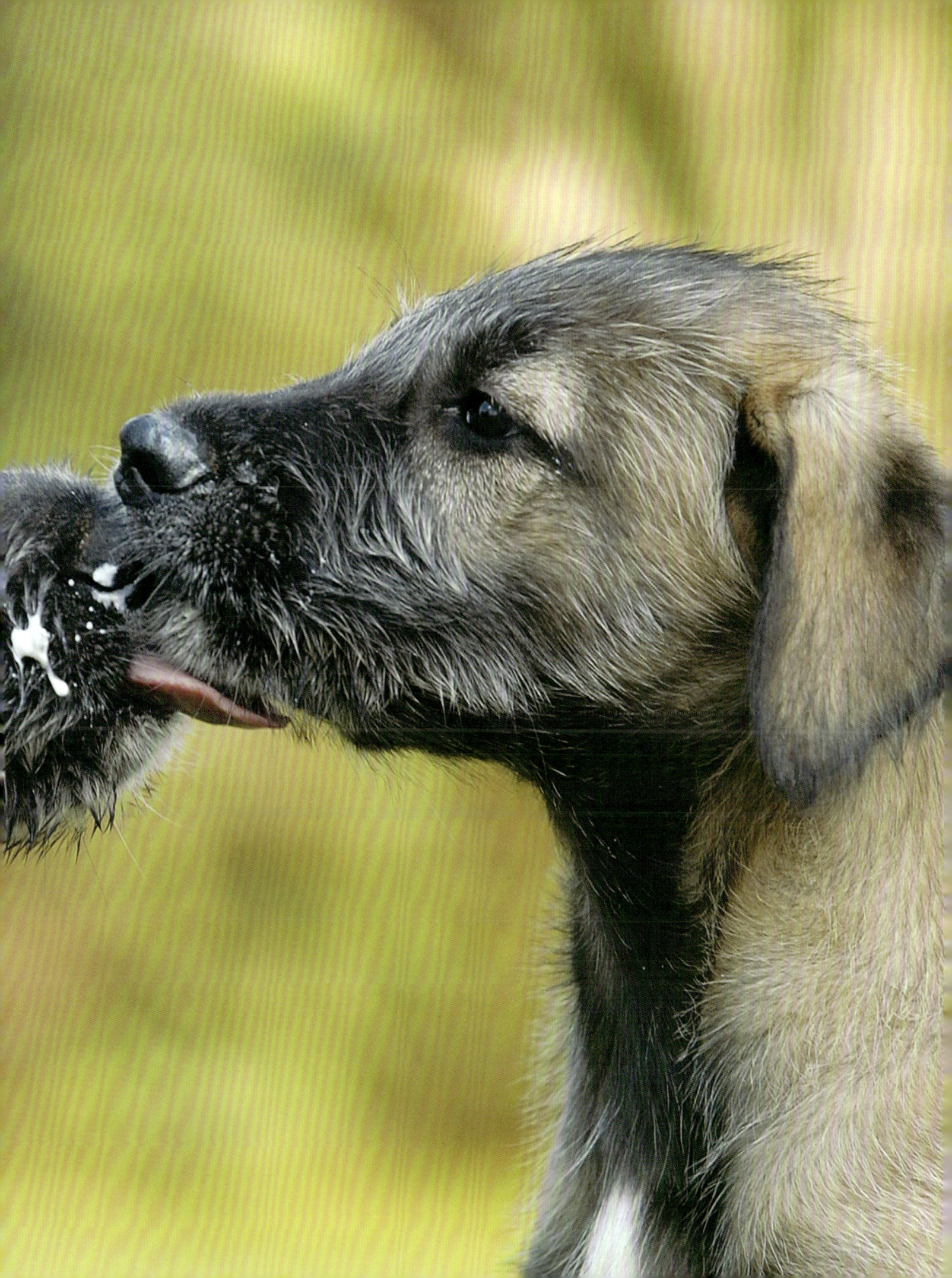

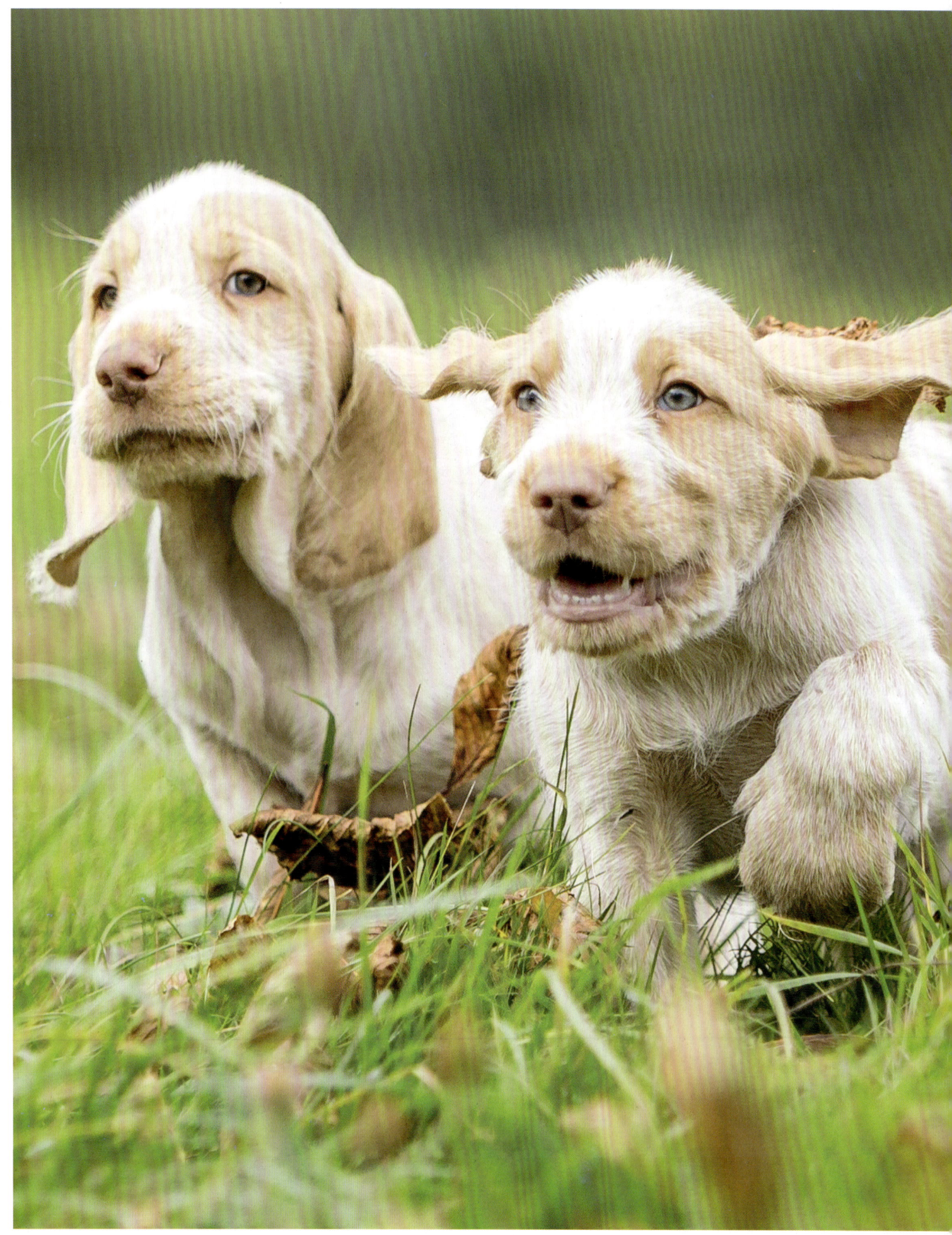

Italian Spinone

Another ancient breed with its origins dissolving into prehistory, the modern spinone is a versatile gundog with the capability to track, point and retrieve. It is most associated with the Piedmont region, in Italy's alpine north, where the weather is often cold and wet and the terrain especially rugged.

The origin of the breed's name is another small mystery. The best theory is that it comes from the Italian word for thorn or point. So the name nods to both the dog's job as a pointer and also how its thick, wiry coat offers it protection as it charges through prickly shrubs at which other dogs might baulk. When at work, the dog works closely with its owner, trotting through the area in a zig-zag path as it searches for a scent.

Despite its size, this cheerful breed makes an easy pet. It fits in well with the family and tolerates visitors well. It needs little in the way of grooming other than the occasional brush. However, its oily fur will retain a natural odour. Nevertheless Spinone owners must give their dogs a lot of attention and exercise.

CHARACTERISTICS

Coat
A wiry and dense coat that comes in various colours and patterns

Height
58–70cm (23–28in)

Weight
29–30kg (65–85lb)

Lifespan
12–13 years

Personality
Affectionate and sociable

Origin
Italy

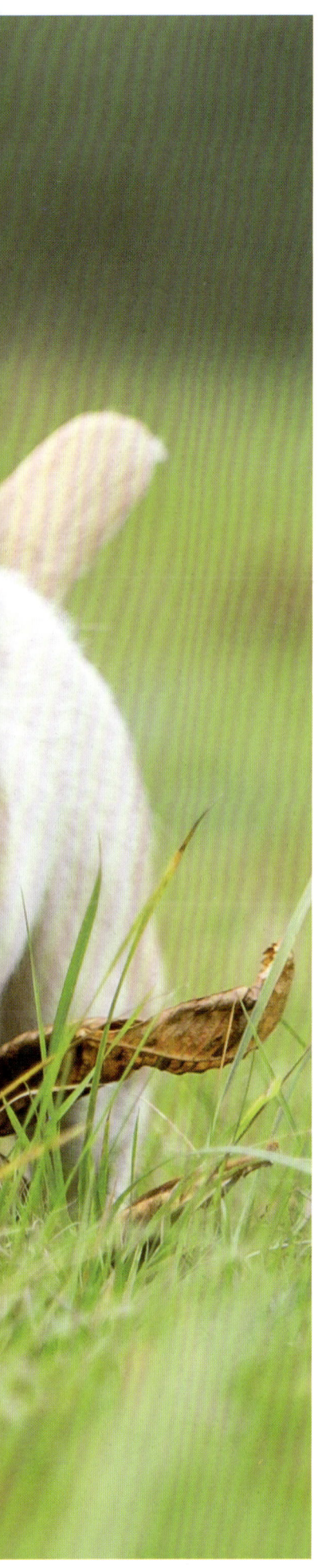

LEFT:
Making friends
The Spinone Italiano is not very common outside Italy, but it is gaining popularity as a family pet and companion.

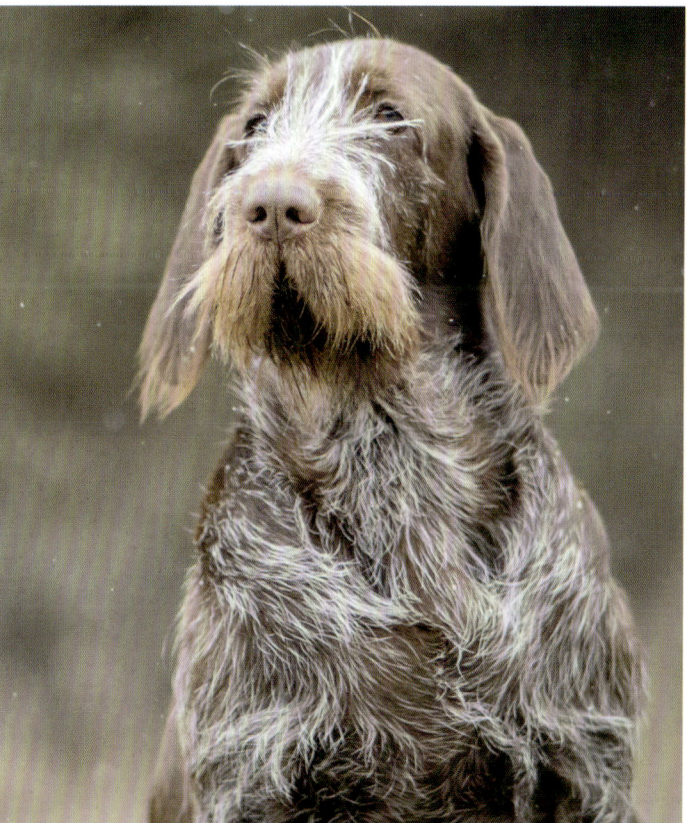

ABOVE:
Venerable appearance
The adult Italian spinone breed has a distinctive appearance.

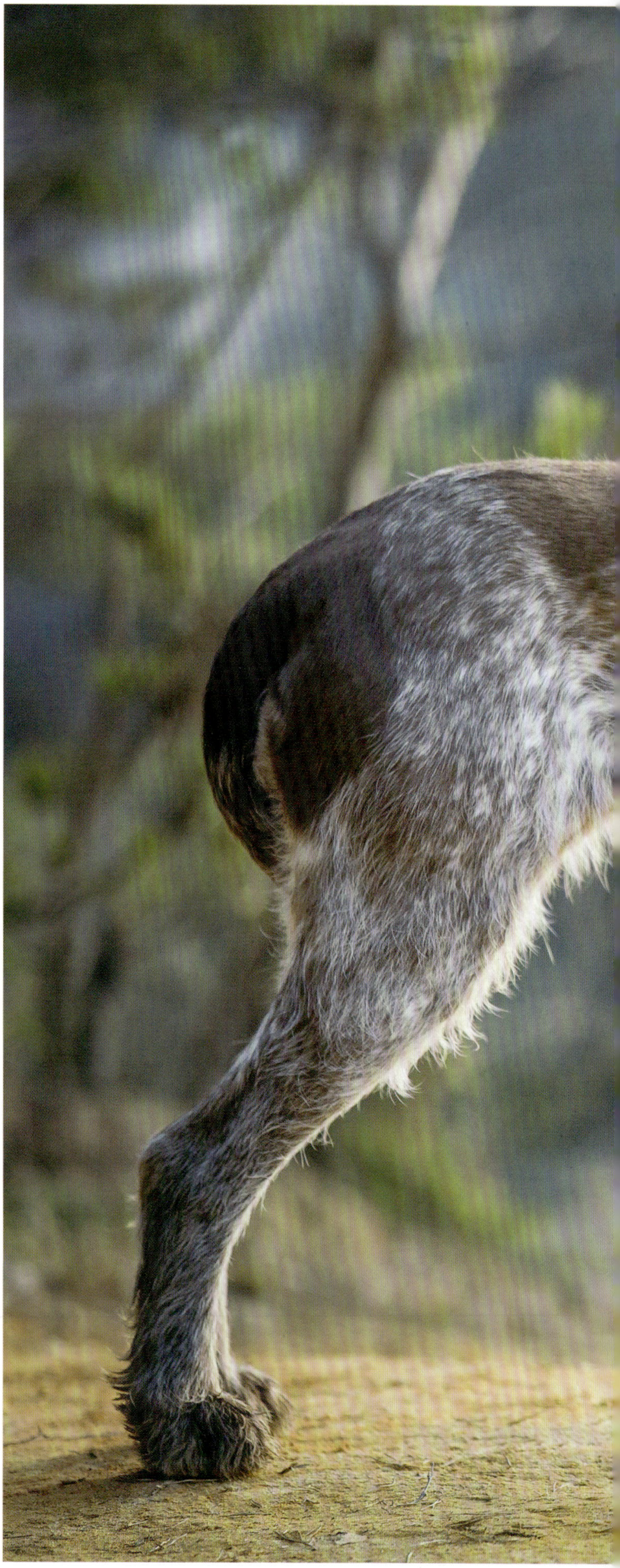

HUNTING DOGS

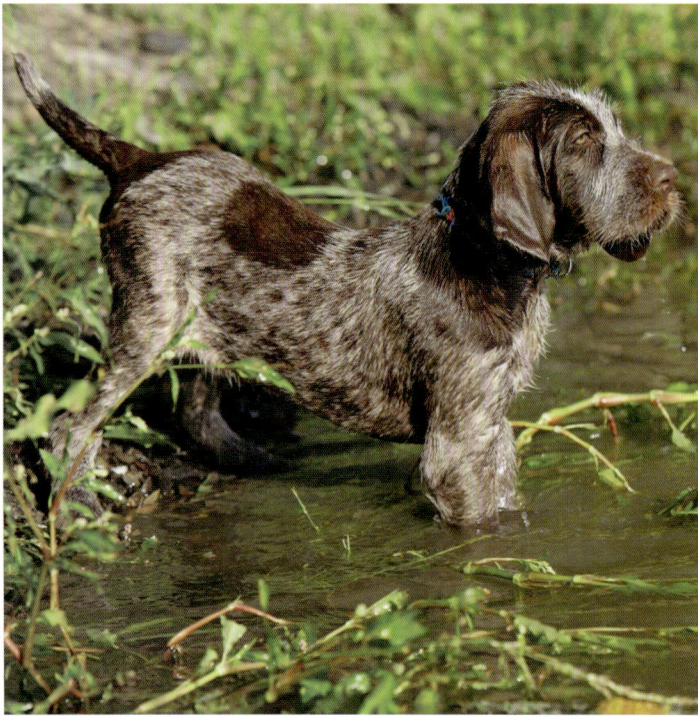

ABOVE:
Aquatic animals
Puppies are able to swim safely at the age of about ten weeks.

RIGHT:
Standing proud
With long eyebrows, a beard and moustache this gives it a human-like expression.

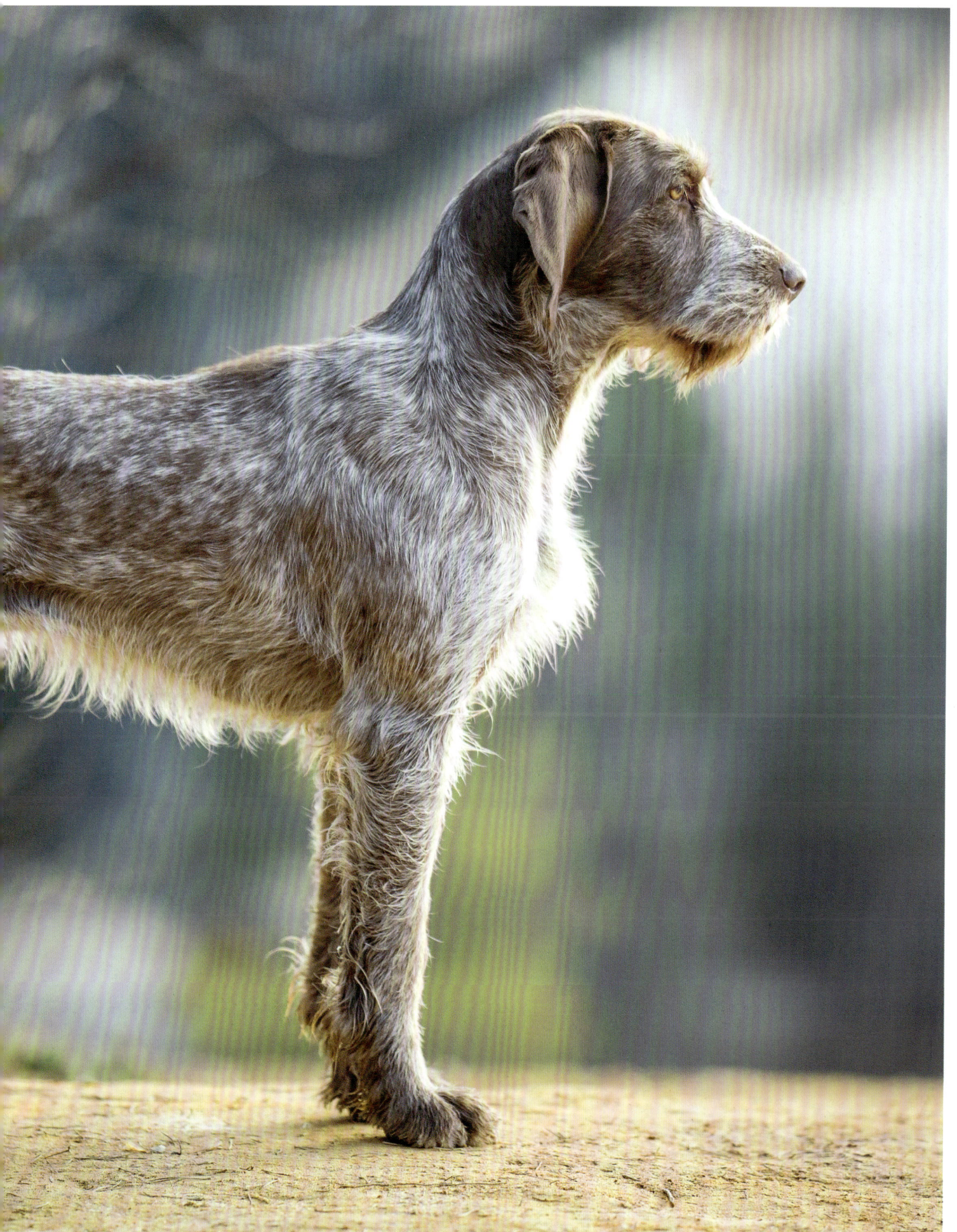

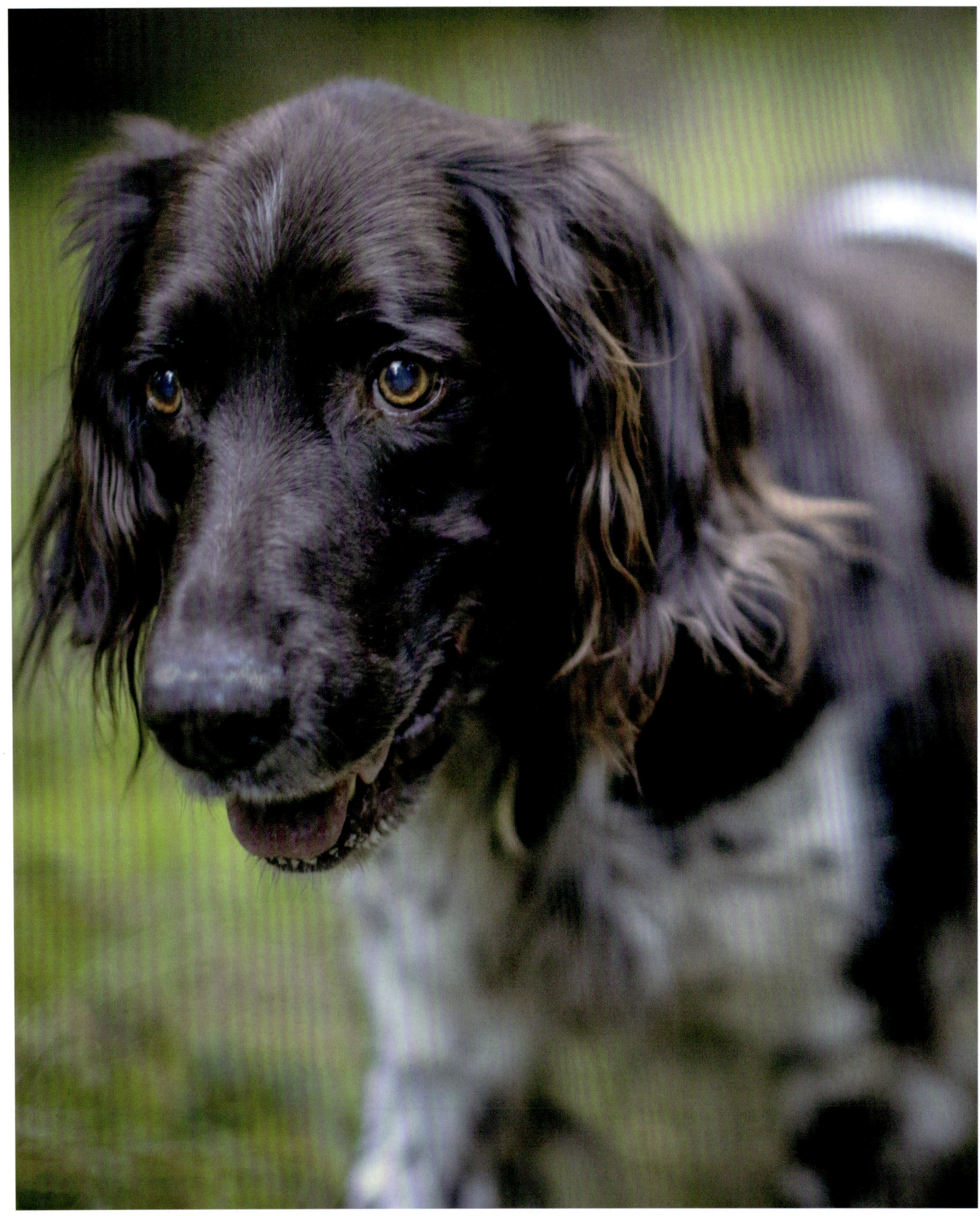

ABOVE:
Smaller breed
The small Munsterlander was recognized as a separate breed in 1912.

Munsterlander

CHARACTERISTICS

Coat
The small breed has brown and white coats, while the larger one is black and white

Height
52–65cm (20–26in)

Weight
18–31kg (40–68lb)

Lifespan
11–14 years

Personality
Loyal and affectionate

Origin
Germany

There are not one but two breeds with this name, one large, one small. They are named after a region in western Germany, once a bucolic area but now the country's industrial heartland. The Munsterlander is a breed of gundog that originated in Germany. The large Munsterlander and the small Munsterlander look quite alike but are more distantly related than their appearance suggests. Both have long dense coats, but the smaller dog's fur is silkier. The larger breed is closer to the German pointers, especially the longhair breeds, and it has the same versatility as a gundog, able to track, point, flush and retrieve game on land and in water. The small Munsterlander is derived from spaniels—known as Wachtelhunds or qual dogs in Germany—although the small breed also has blood from the larger Munsterlander in its recent heritage no doubt. The smaller dog is primarily a bird dog that is used to drive quail and other landfowl off the ground and into the path of the guns. Both dogs are loyal and fun-loving. They need a lot of exercise and stimulation to occupy them and so would be most suited to a family that enjoys a lot of outdoor activities.

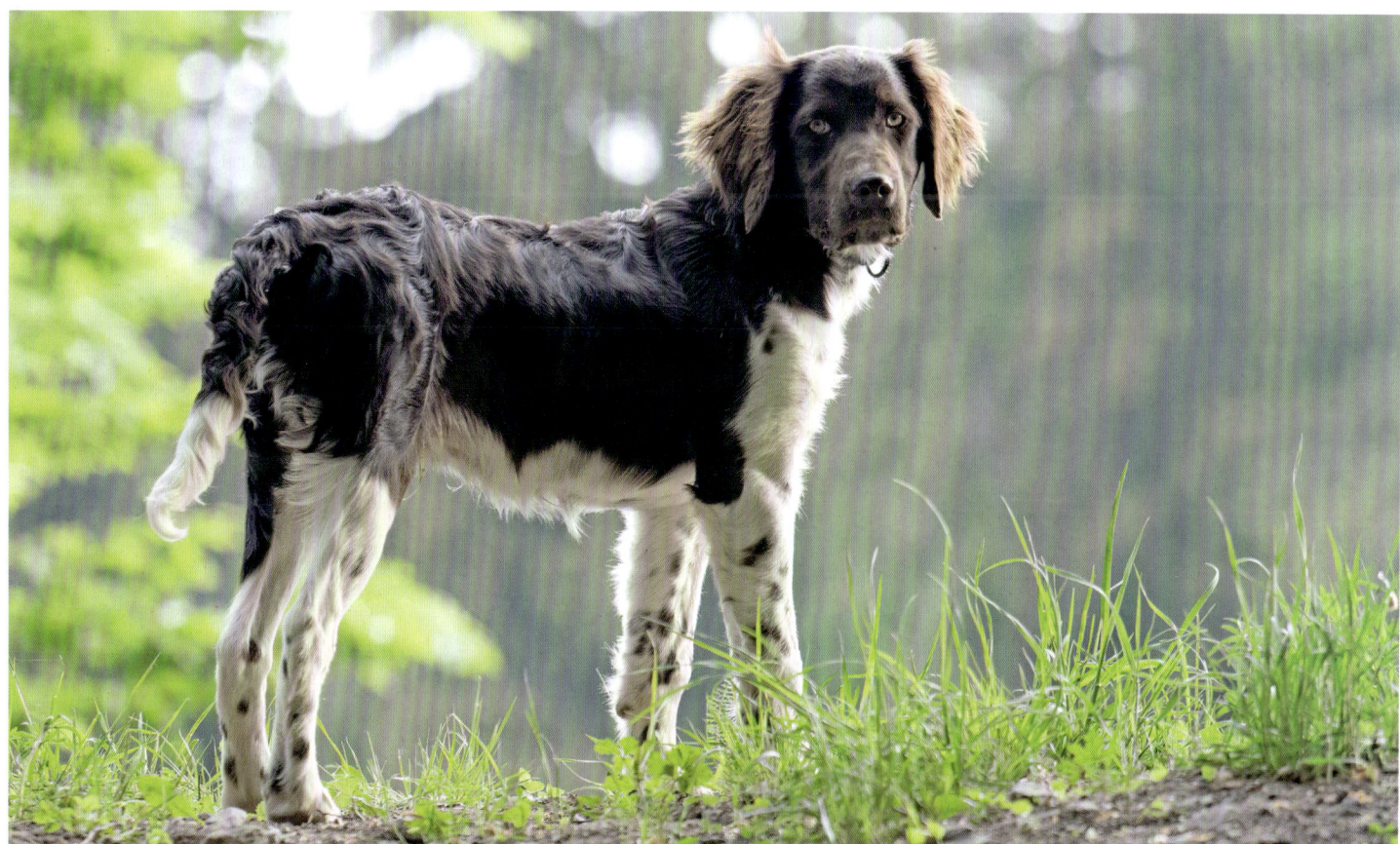

ABOVE:
Grooming needs
The large Munsterlander has a medium-length coat that requires regular grooming to prevent matting. It sheds moderately throughout the year and more heavily during seasonal changes.

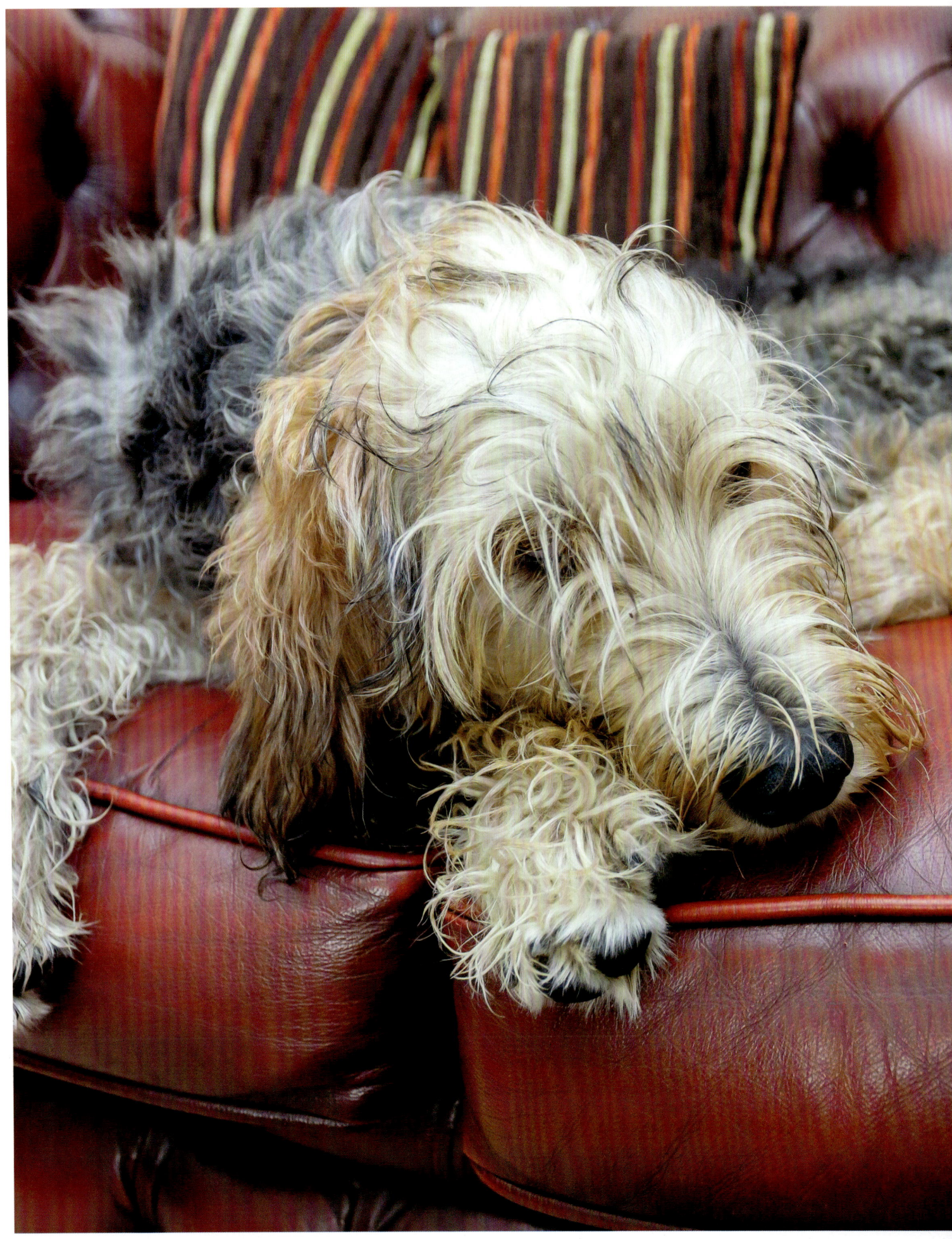

Otterhound

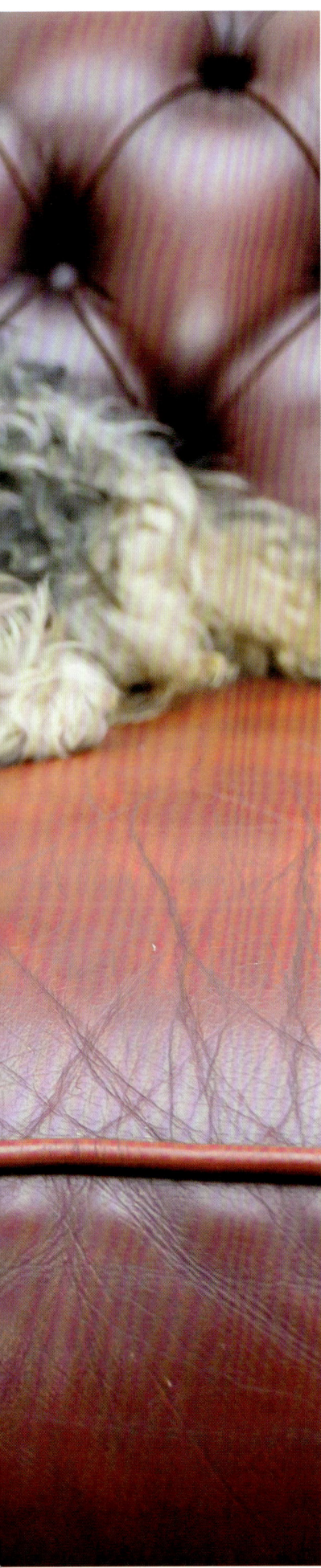

With its shaggy coat and bushy moustache, this ancient English breed has an air of old-world wisdom about it. Despite its sage looks and affectionate temperament, these big, shaggy dogs are in short supply, and some would say for good reasons. The breed was created in the Middle Ages, a time when freshwater fish stocked in ponds and rivers were a valuable source of food in England. Wild otters were a threat to that food, and the otterhound was there to protect it. The dog has webbed feet and is a skilled swimmer, diving into deep water if needed. Its sense of smell is powerful enough to follow scent through water. It seems odd from our modern viewpoint, but for centuries otters were regarded as dirty pests that did nothing but steal food, and so otter hunting morphed from a necessity, to a duty and into a sport. By the 1970s, otterhounds had almost wiped out the otter from Britain's waterways. Otters were made a protected species, and have since begun to recover, but otterhound numbers plunged. The big and bouncy dog can be a handful, and needs a lot of attention and training. They have a loud, deep bark that can carry over long distances.

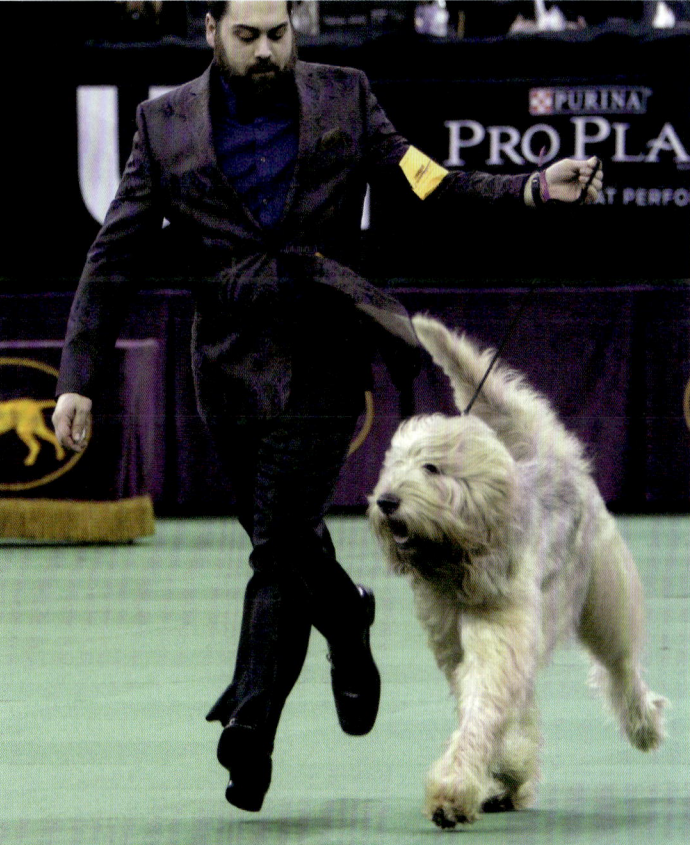

CHARACTERISTICS
Coat
A shaggy, waterproof coat of any colour
Height
61–69cm (24–27in)
Weight
30–52kg (66–115lb)
Lifespan
10–12 years
Personality
Even-tempered and amiable
Origin
England

LEFT:
Hair help
The dog's top coat needs frequent grooming, and the moustache needs a wash quite frequently.

ABOVE:
Rare creature
The otterhound is a vulnerable native breed, with only around 600 animals worldwide.

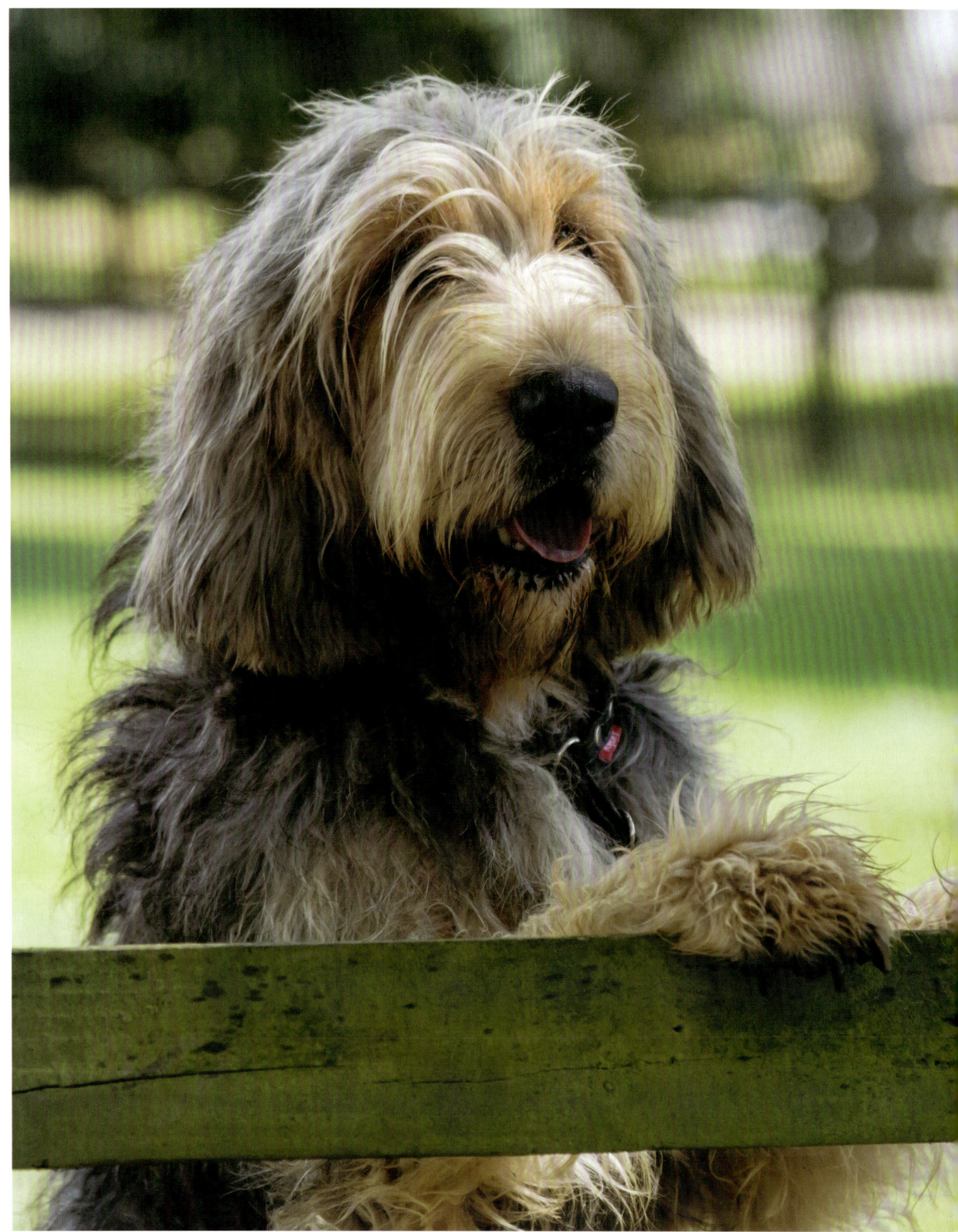

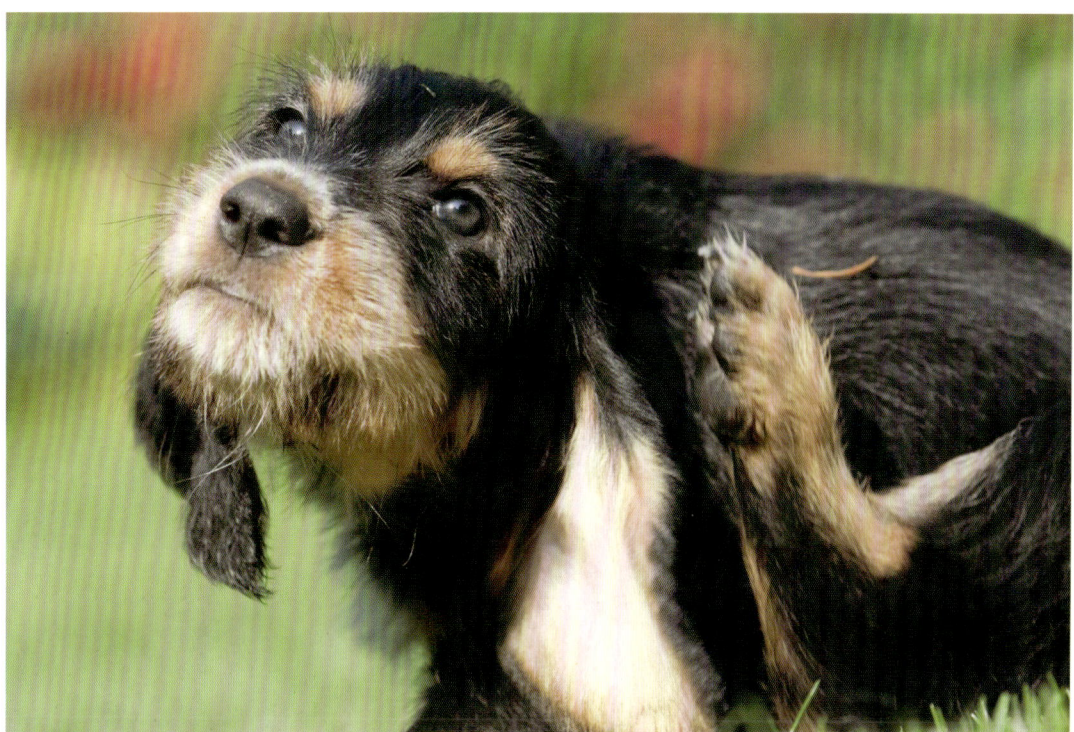
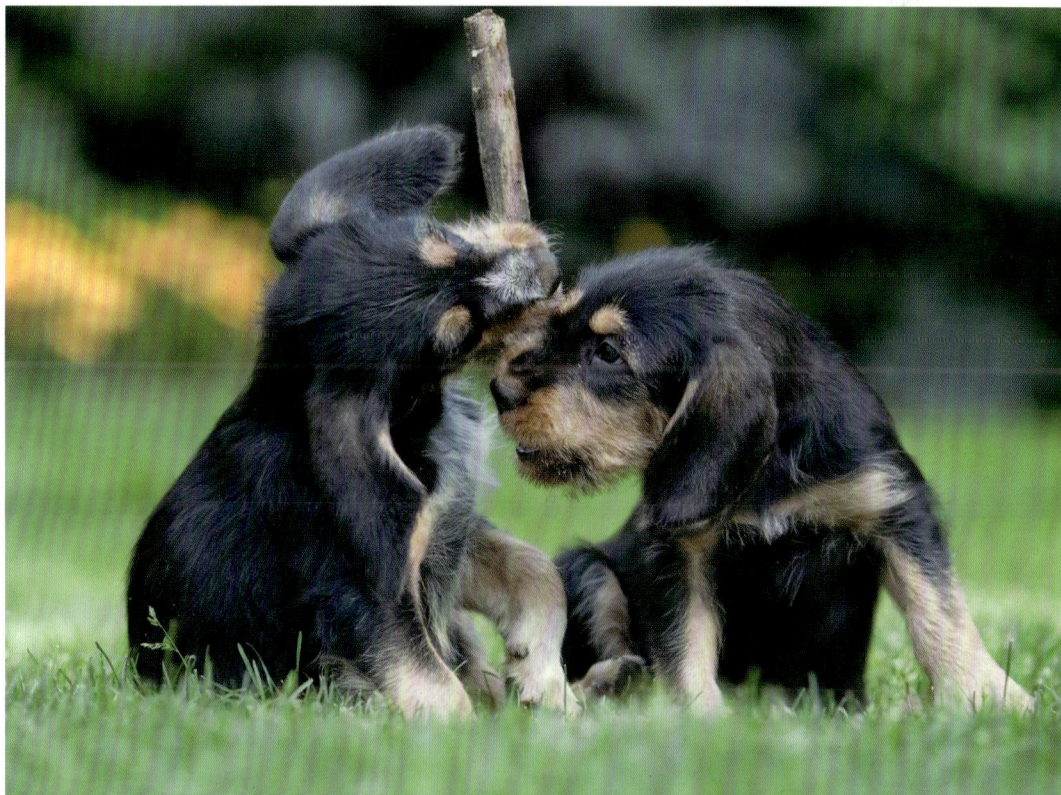

ALL PHOTOGRAPHS:
Ready to go
This English breed had the job of killing otters that threatened the fish stocks in country rivers.

HUNTING DOGS

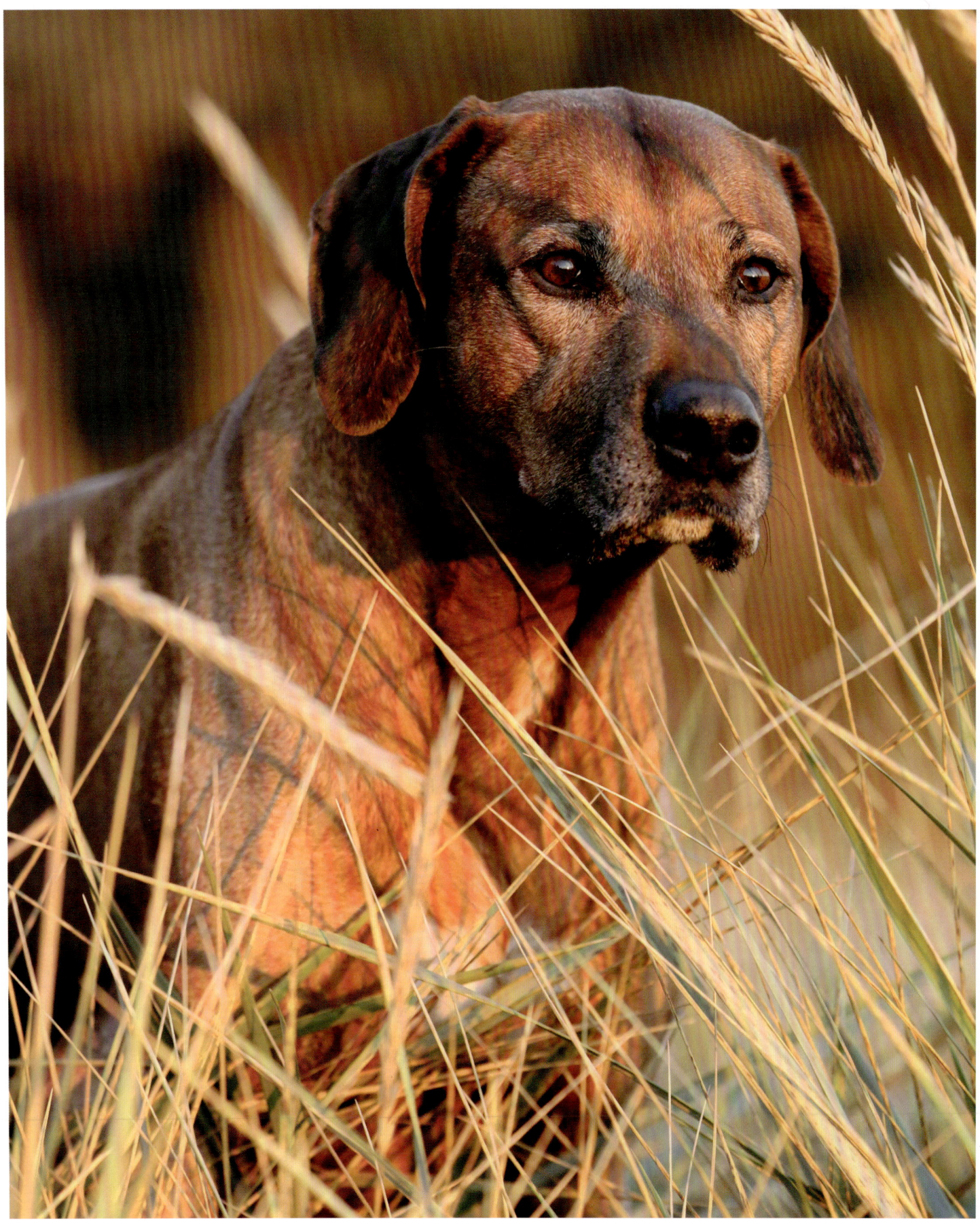

ABOVE:
Bush dog
This African breed is a versatile and powerful dog that was bred to track, chase and hold lions and other big savannah animals.

Rhodesian Ridgeback

CHARACTERISTICS

Coat
A short and dense coat ranging from light wheaten to red wheaten, with a dark muzzle and ears. There is a little white on the chest and toes

Height
61–69cm (24–27in)

Weight
29–41kg (65–90lb)

Lifespan
10–12 years

Personality
Confident and independent

Origin
Southern Africa

This southern African dog is an outlier among breeds. It was created by Dutch settlers who crossed a range of breeds brought from Europe, including greyhounds, mastiffs and bloodhounds, with the tough pack dogs of the Khoekhoe, a nomadic group living across the region. The breed retained the distinctive ridge along the back seen in the local dogs. This "ridgeback" is created by the hair along the spine growing in the opposite direction to the rest of the coat. Additionally the hybrid had a greater resilience to the hot African habitat than the European breeds, which were more prone to parasites and pests, including bites from the tsetse fly. The dog was nicknamed the lion dog—not least because packs of ridgebacks held no fear in taking on these big cats, holding them at bay until hunters could take a shot. The breed's centre of gravity moved to what is now Zimbabwe, once known as Rhodesia, where the first breed standard was drawn up in 1922.

A breed that regards a lion as an equal is not for a faint-hearted or inexperienced owner. The ridgeback has a strong guarding instinct and a very high prey drive. This makes the dog appear aloof with strangers. It is likely to impose its dominance on other dogs, especially those of the same sex.

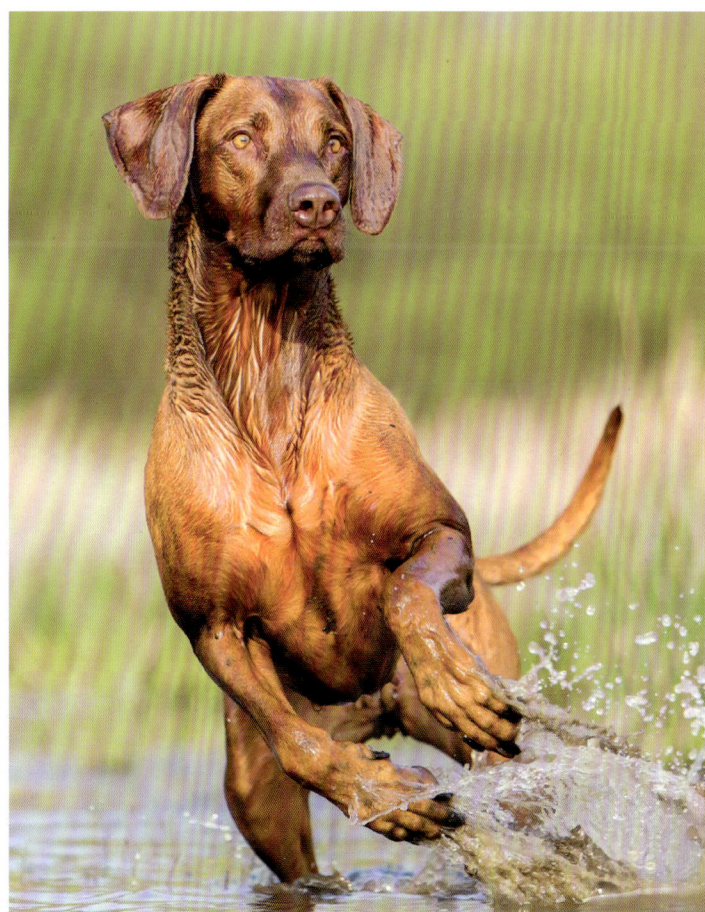

ABOVE:
Active and alert
The Rhodesian ridgeback is a muscular and athletic dog with a coat that is easy to care for.

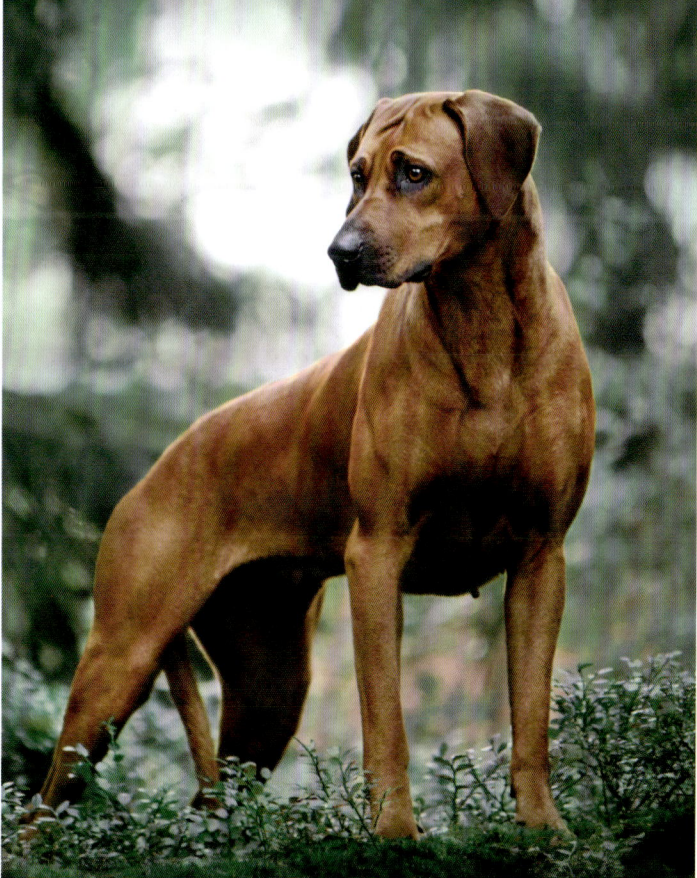

ABOVE:
Health problems
Responsible breeders should be testing these dogs for common health conditions such as hypothyroidism, dermoid sinus, deafness and bloat and provide health certificates to buyers.

HUNTING DOGS
Saluki

CHARACTERISTICS
Coat
A smooth coat that can be white, cream, fawn, red or a grizzled tan, black and tan, or tricolour
Height
58–71cm (23–28in)
Weight
16–29kg (35–65lb)
Lifespan
About 12 years
Personality
Calm and dignified
Origin
Arabia

There are pictures of this Middle-Eastern breed that were carved into walls 7,000 years ago in ancient Arabia and Egypt. That obviously makes it one of oldest breeds of all. The dogs were used by nomadic people in the Arabian Peninsula, moving across mountains and deserts between oases, and it was used for hunting gazelles and other antelopes. The dog is a sighthound that relies on its keen eyesight and speed to catch quarry.

The breed spread to the east, perhaps travelling with the invading army of Alexander the Great (who is not always known that way in Asia!). The Saluki was a favourite breed in the Tang Dynasty in the 8th and 9th centuries, a time when the Chinese nobility embraced hunting and sports of all kinds. As the breed's homeland converted to Islam, the Saluki maintained a special status. Early Muslims classed dogs as unclean animals, but the noble Saluki was given an exception. It was never bought or sold, however, but given as gifts. The Saluki came into Europe after the Crusades.

The Saluki is calm in the home but is easily excited outdoors and needs a well-fenced area to run around. The breed is not very friendly with strangers and needs a long period of training to remove its independence and stubbornness.

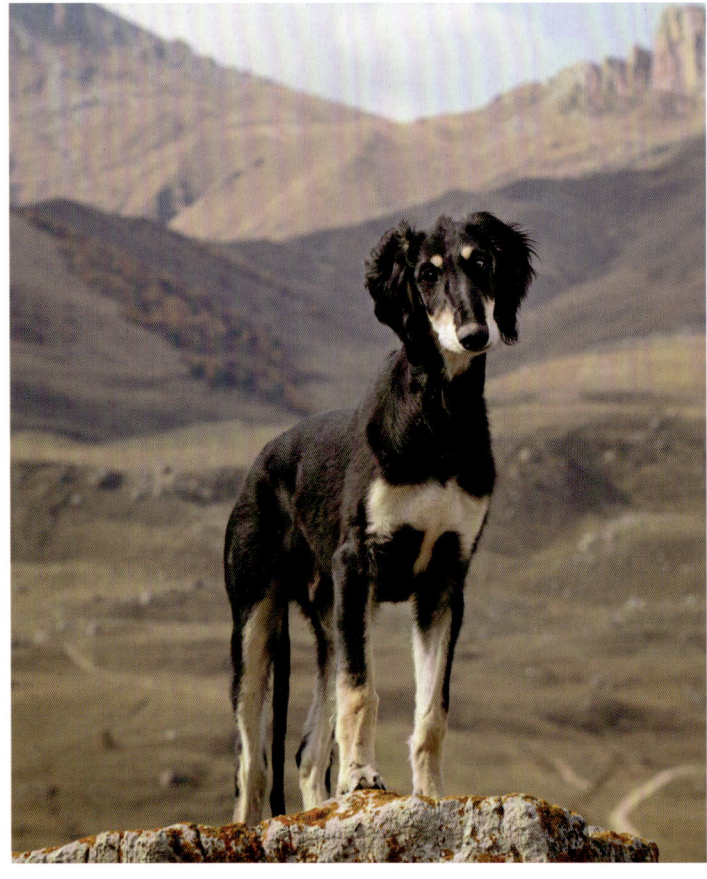

ABOVE:
Ancient breed
The Saluki is a noble dog that can be a loyal and devoted companion for the right person.

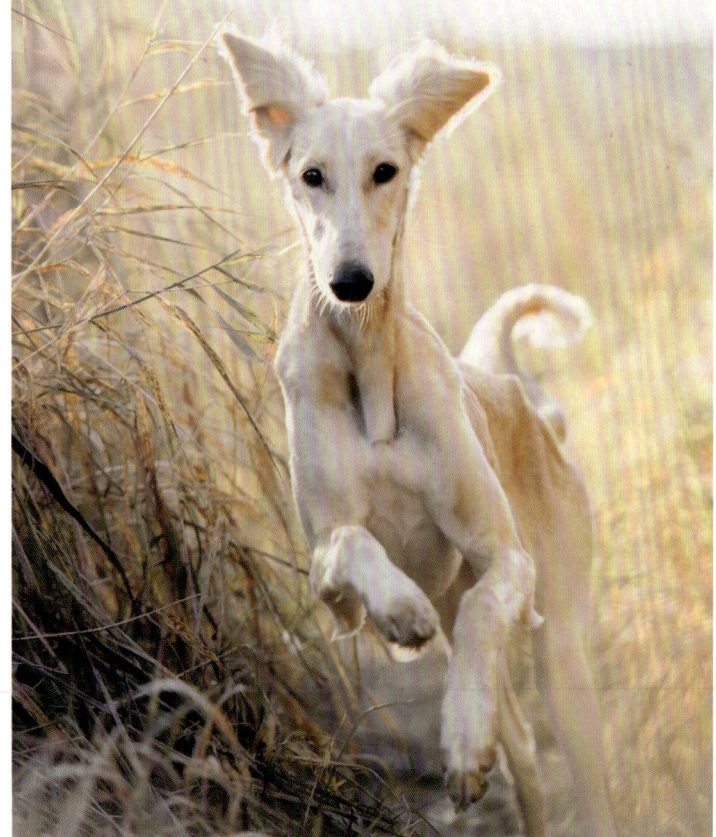

ABOVE:
Good mover
The Saluki can run up to 45 miles per hour and has a graceful and elegant appearance.

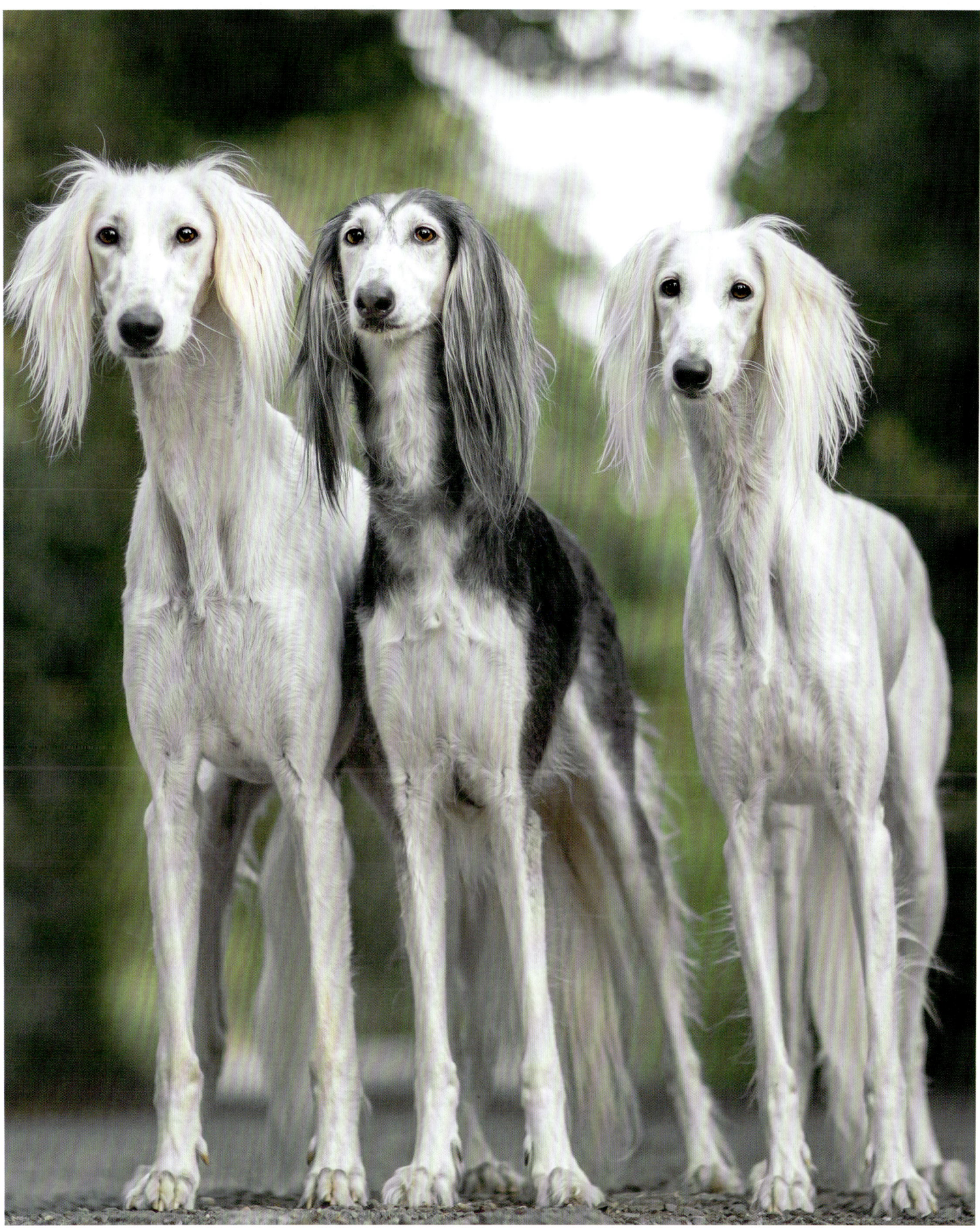

ABOVE:
Flamboyant feathers
Some Saluki dogs have long hair on their ears, tail and legs, called "feathers".

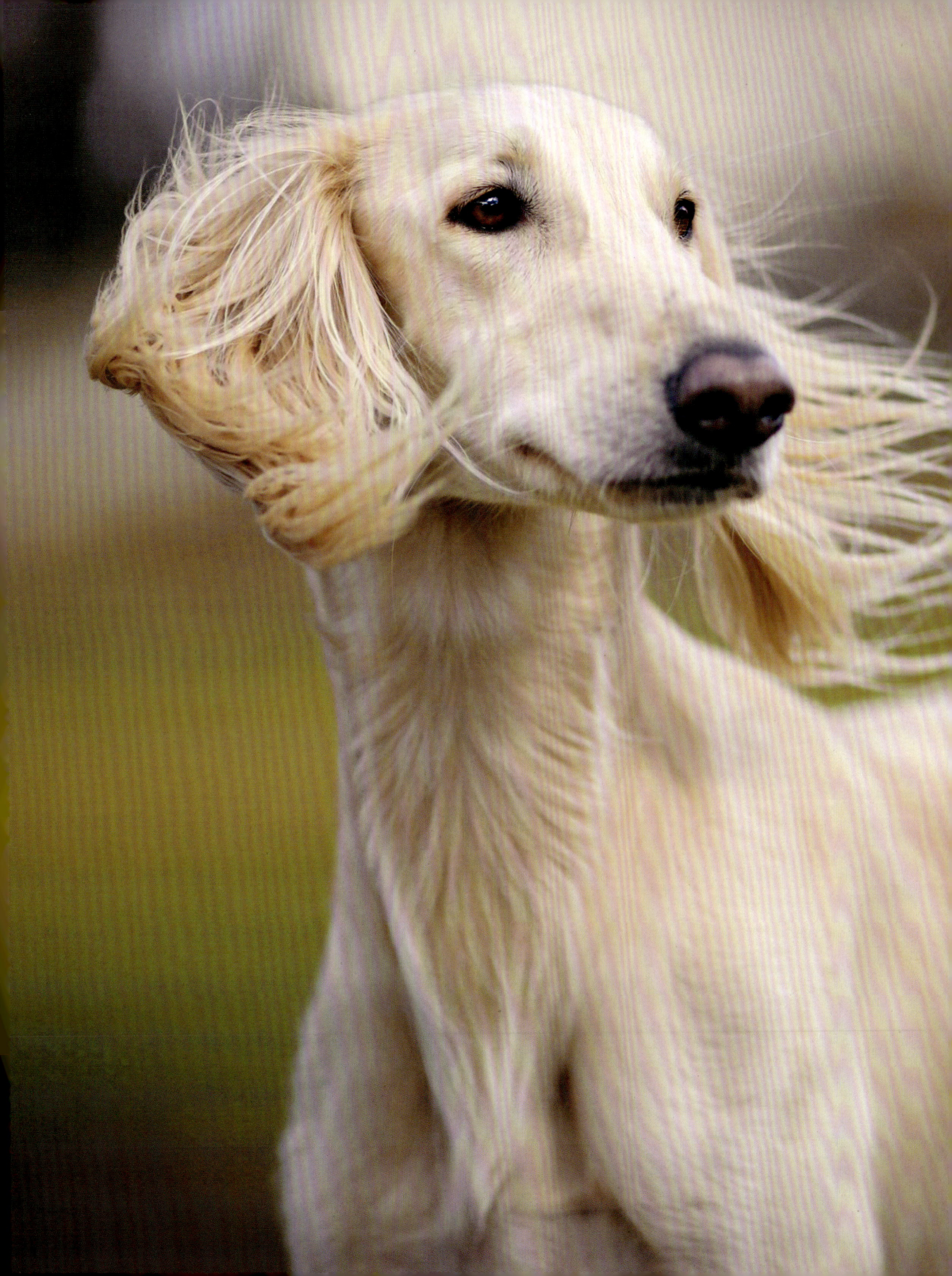

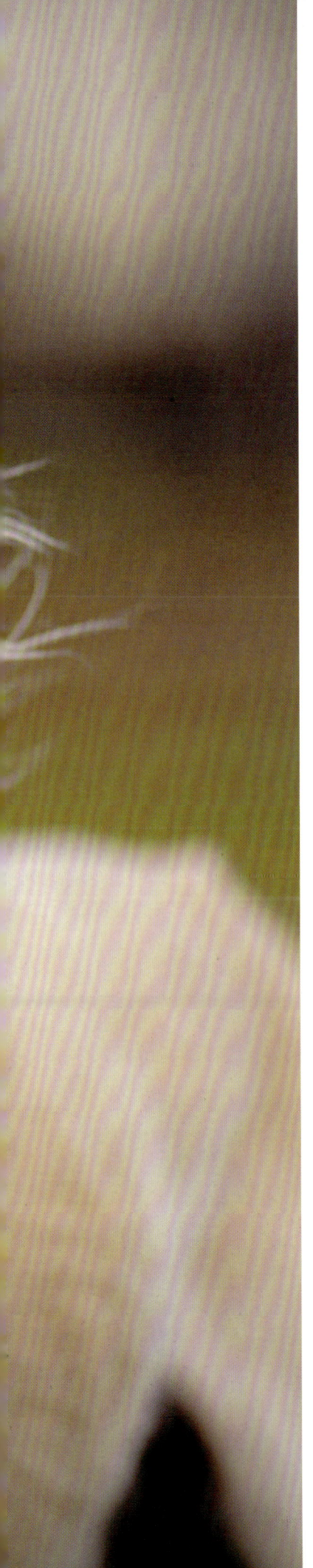
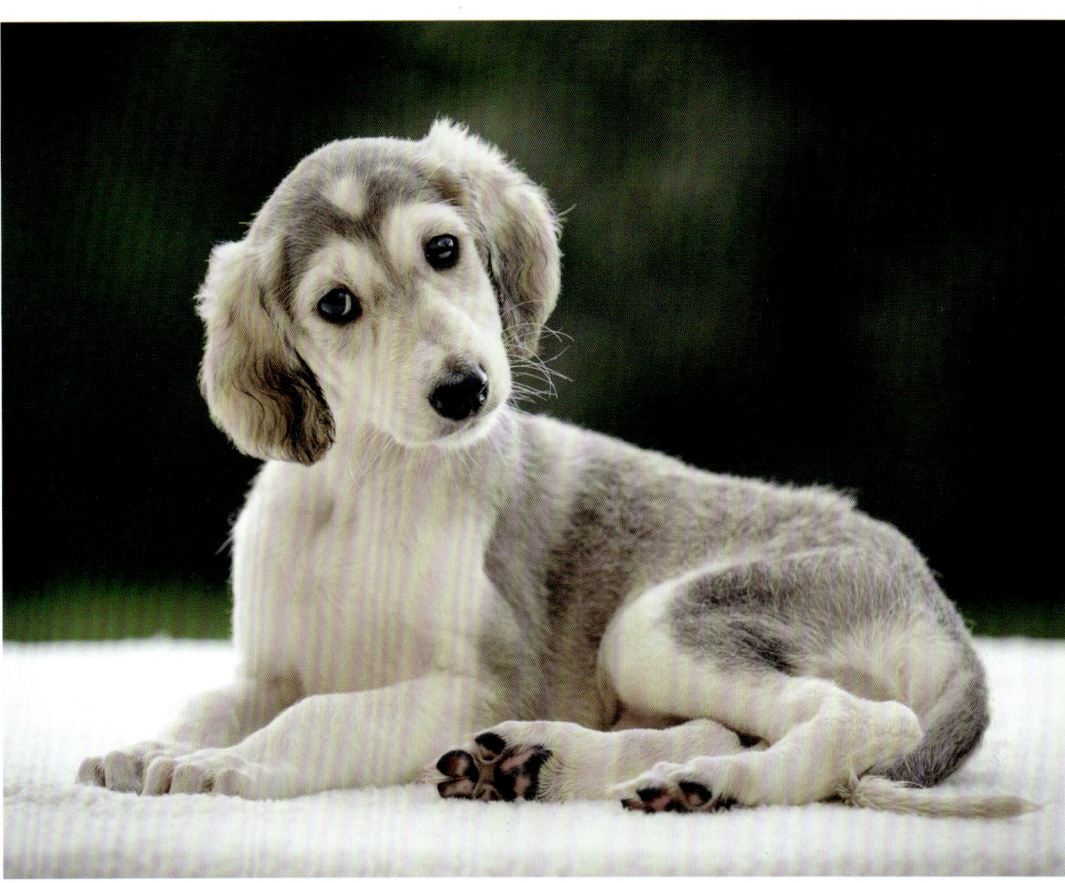
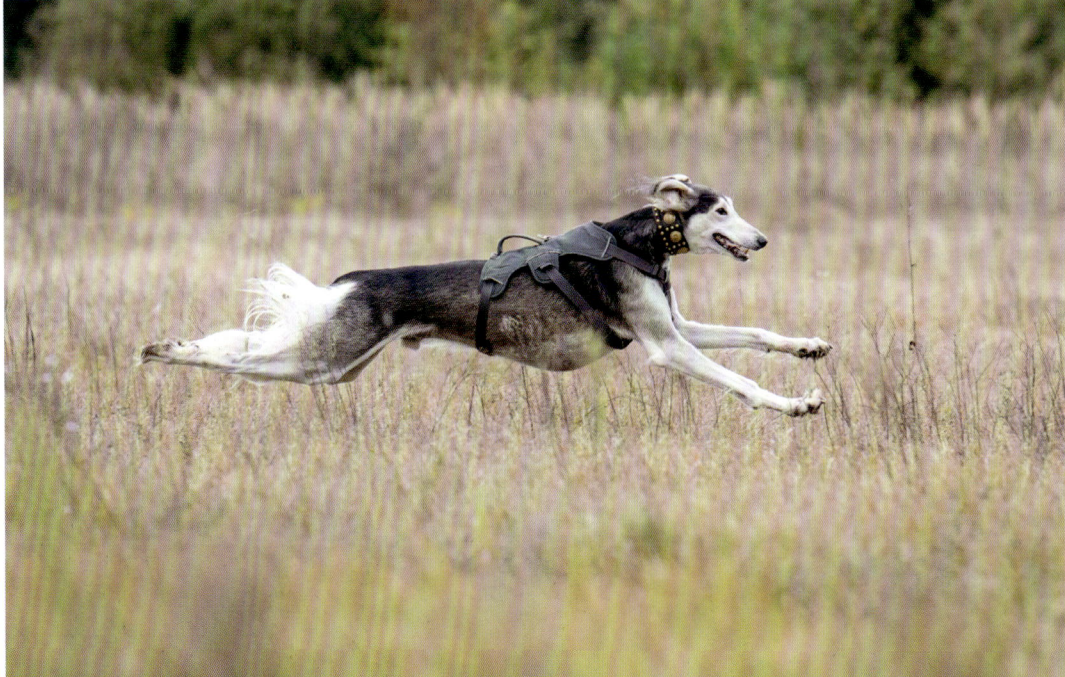

LEFT:
Ancient roots
In ancient Egypt, the Saluki was known as the Royal Dog and often hunted hare, fox and gazelle by working in small packs.

ABOVE TOP:
Saluki puppy
Salukis are quiet at home, extremely gentle with children, and good with other dogs.

ABOVE BOTTOM:
Galloping gracefully
Anyone looking to purchase a Saluki dog needs to be prepared to take them out for around one to two hours of exercise per day.

HUNTING DOGS

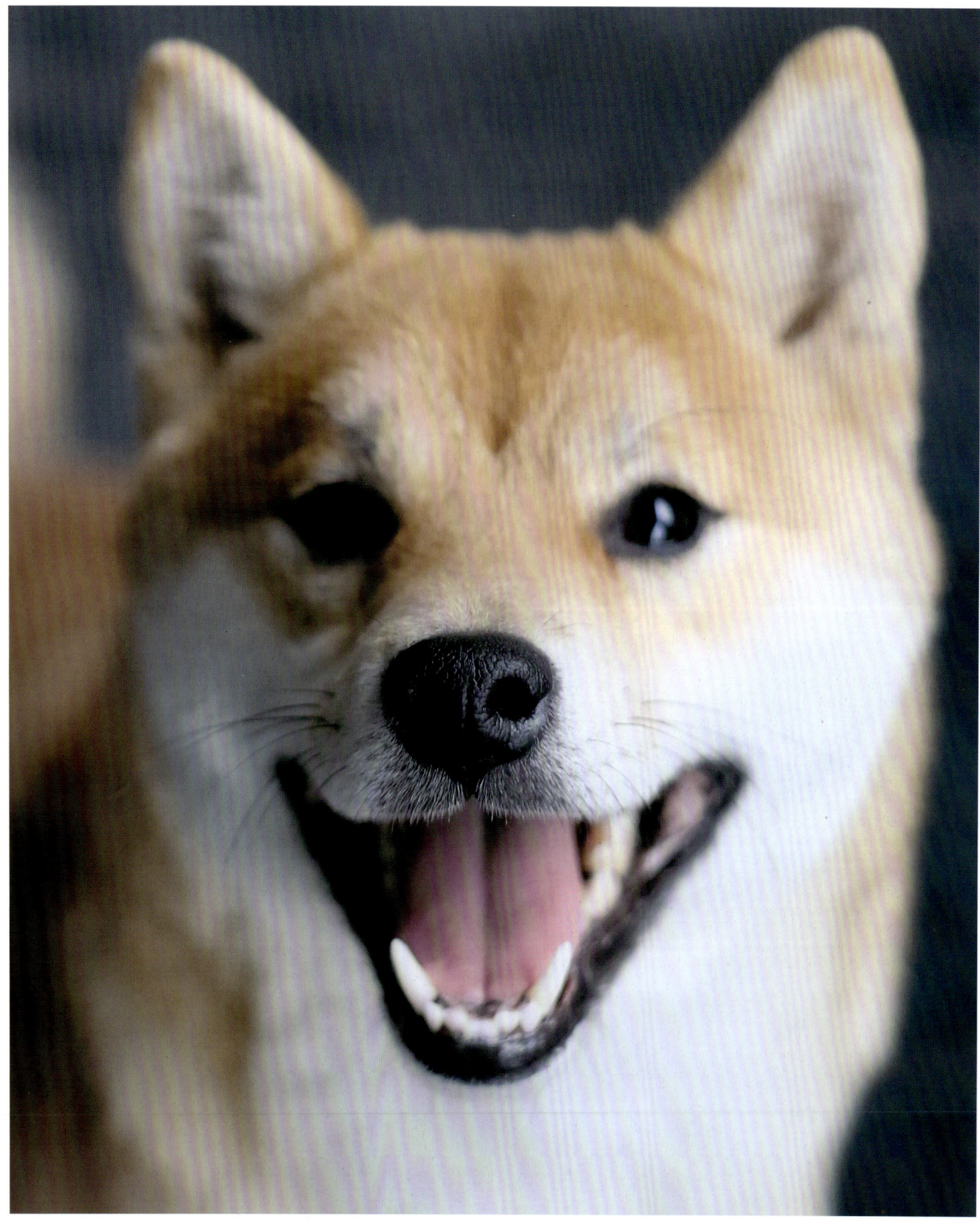

ABOVE:
Wild looks
The Japanese dog has a particularly fox-like face and colouring.

Shiba Inu

CHARACTERISTICS

Coat
The course double coat is usually red, black and tan, or sesame

Height
37–40cm (15–16in)

Weight
7–11kg (15–24lb)

Lifespan
12–15 years

Personality
Active and alert

Origin
Japan

Younger readers might recognise that Japanese breed from the Doge memes that have been shared widely for many years on social media. They show a picture of a cute Shiba Inu, originally a young female called Kabosu who looks to be almost smiling at the camera, with overlaid text written in broken English. The breed's fluffy look should not be mistaken for softness, however. The Shiba Inu is a small hunting dog that was created to hunt birds and rabbits in the cold and rugged mountains of central Japan. Its name translates into English as the "brushwood dog". This refers to both the thick vegetation on the hillsides of its homeland and the reddish tinge to its fur. That thick double coat keeps out the rain and the cold and covers a compact and muscular body. The breed's curled tail links it to the spitz-type Arctic dogs of the Asian mainland, most obviously the husky.

Shiba Inu is one of the oldest dog breeds in the world but that does not mean it is particularly suitable as a pet. They can be very stubborn and territorial and are aloof with strangers. The dogs require a lot of training and frequent socialization when young. Without this the dogs seldom behave well when confronted with other dogs.

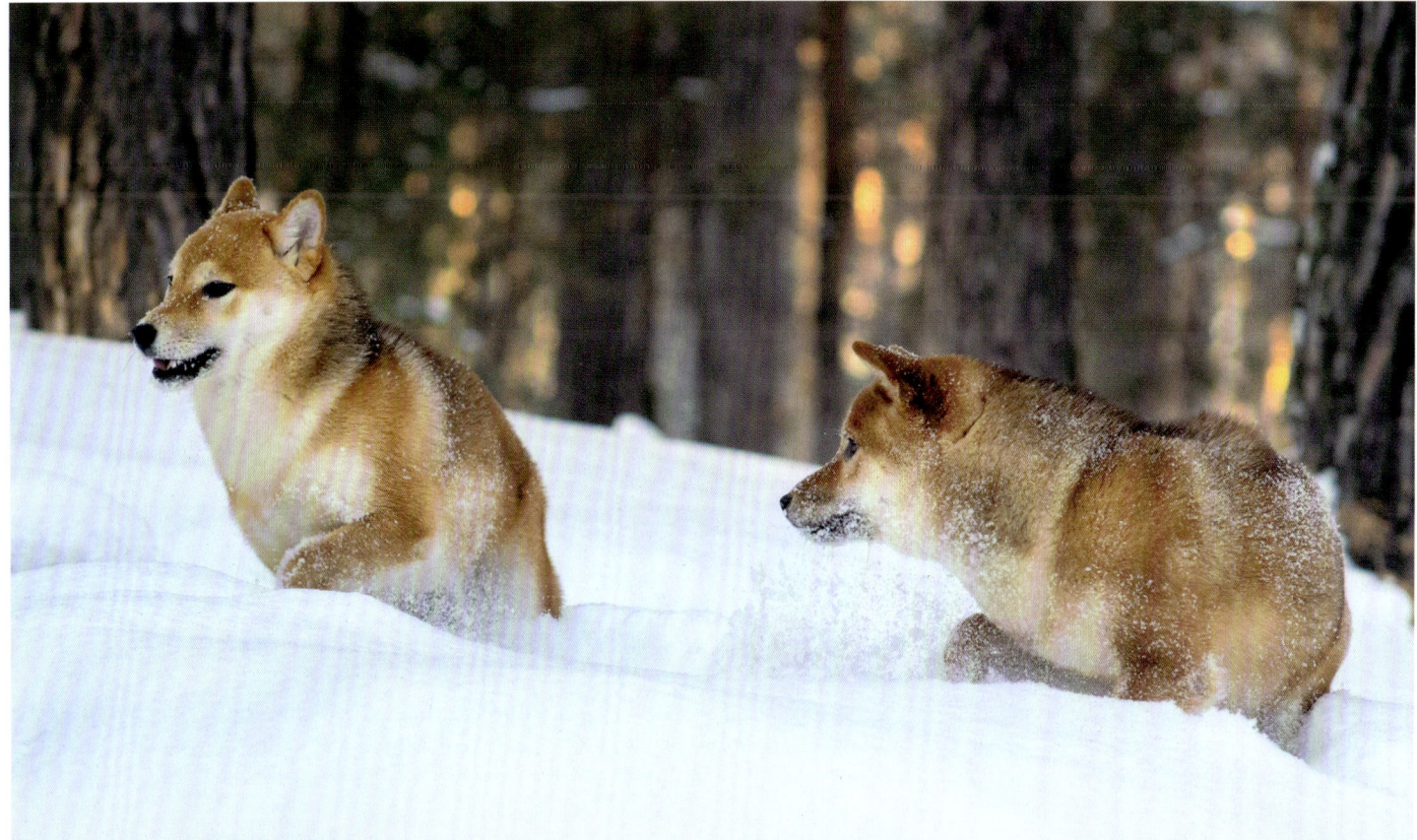

ABOVE:
Heavy weather
The Shiba Inu tends to shed a lot especially during seasonal changes.

HUNTING DOGS

Spanish Water Dog

CHARACTERISTICS

Coat
A distinctive curly coat, which is water-resistant and often forms cords when it grows long. The coat can be black, brown or white, or a combination of these colours

Height
40–50cm (16–20in)

Weight
14–22kg (31–49lb)

Lifespan
10–14 years

Personality
Cheerful and active

Origin
Spain

This woolly Iberian breed is known for being a hard worker, and it has a lot to do. Since time immemorial, the Spanish water dog has been a fixture in the fields working two jobs, if not three. Its main occupation was to be a sheep herder. It helped to move flocks along a north and south axis throughout the year as shepherds moved with the rain to find fresh grazing for their animals. When not doing this, the dogs were accompanying their handlers on hunting trips, often for waterfowl. Their job was to retrieve the birds from the water, and this is where their curly waterproof coat became important. On top of all that, the dogs have a strong protective instinct and make good guard dogs.

As pets, the water dogs are intelligent and loyal, and well-mannered enough to become a rewarding member of the family. They are very active and full of energy and will demand to play a lot and need frequent exercising, which should include swimming from time to time. Dogs hailing from the north of Spain tend to be smaller, while a larger breed lives in the rugged terrain of Andalusia in the south.

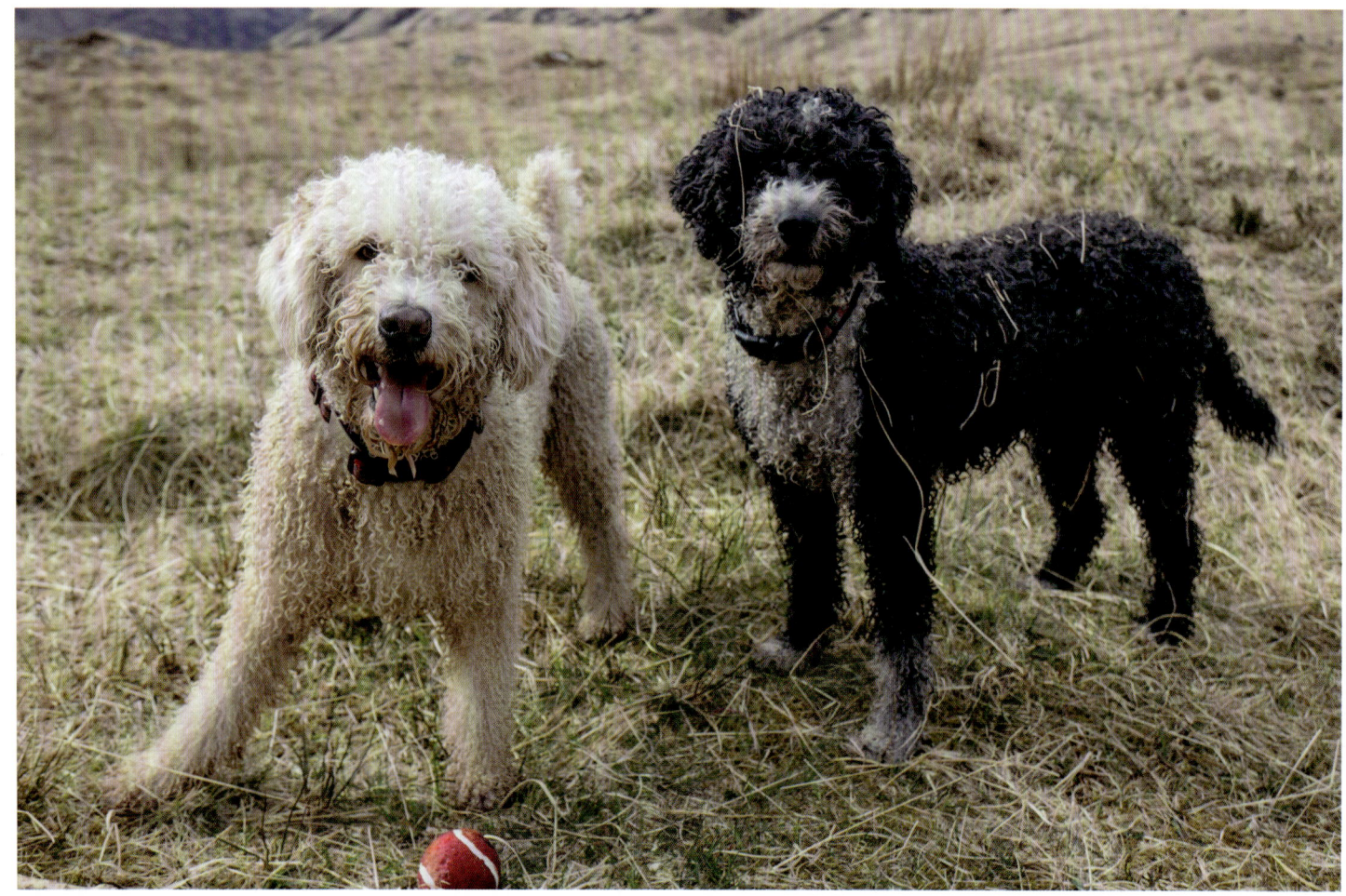

ABOVE:
Low shedding
The water dog has a hypoallergenic coat, which means it sheds very little and is suitable for people with allergies.

HUNTING DOGS

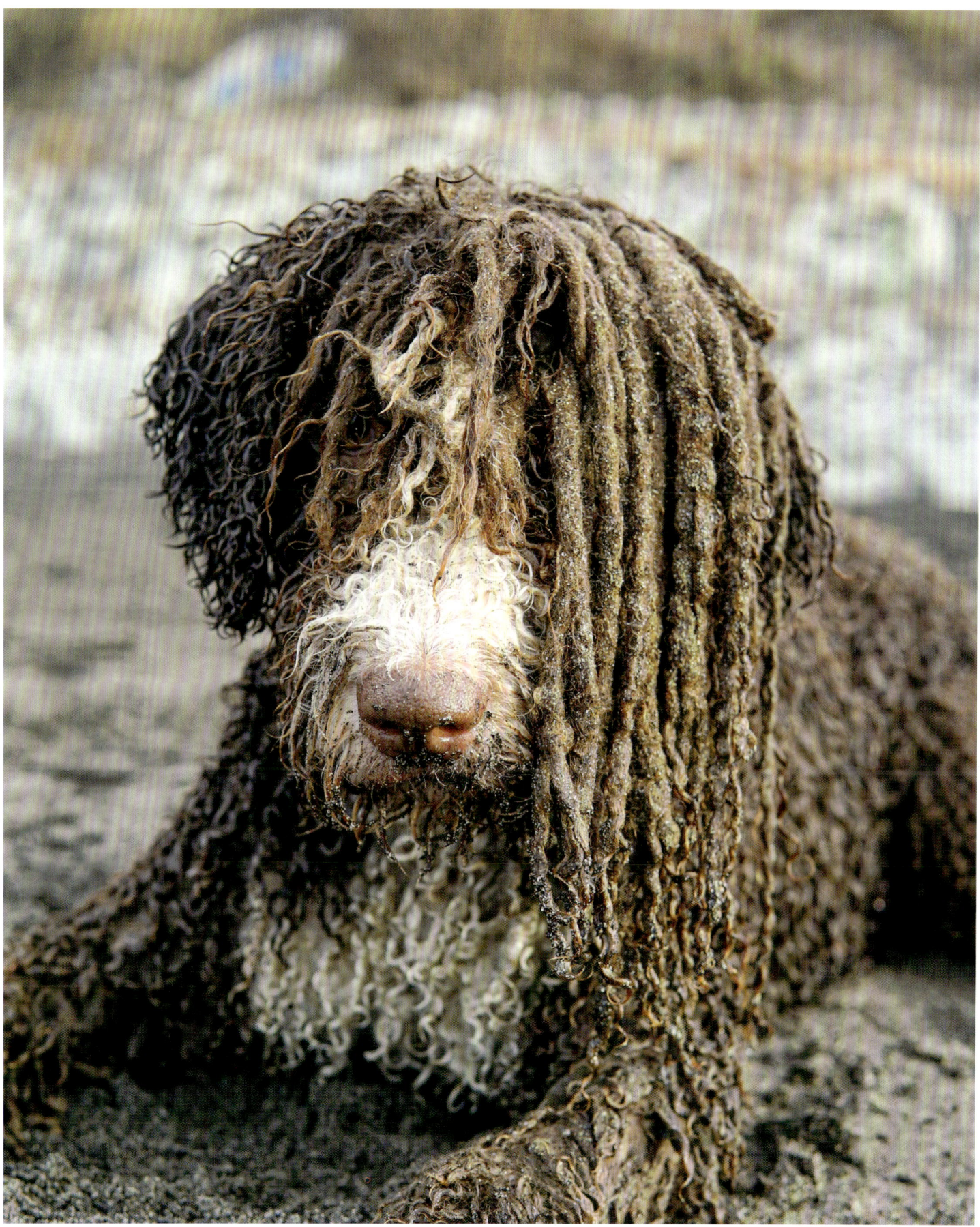

ABOVE:
Mudlark
The dogs living in the marshlands of Andalusia have a particularly long corded coat which keeps the mud off the insulatory undercoat.

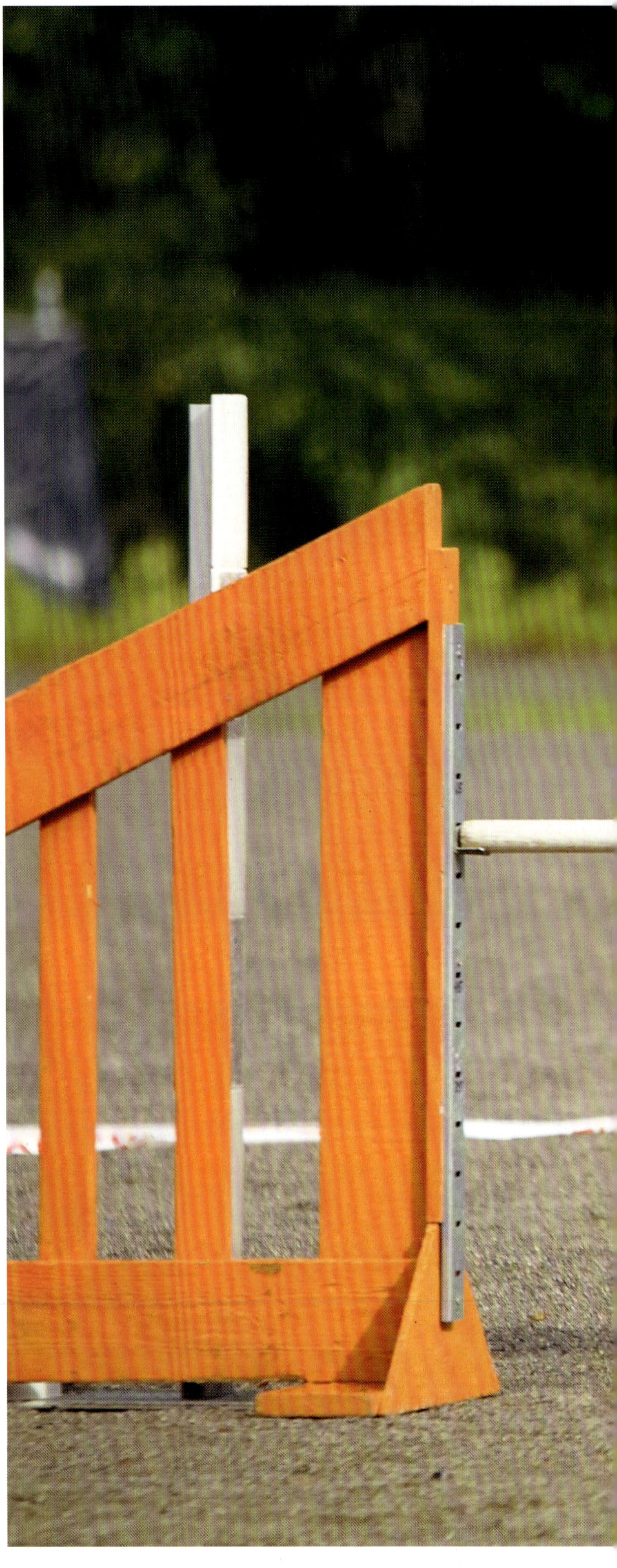

HUNTING DOGS

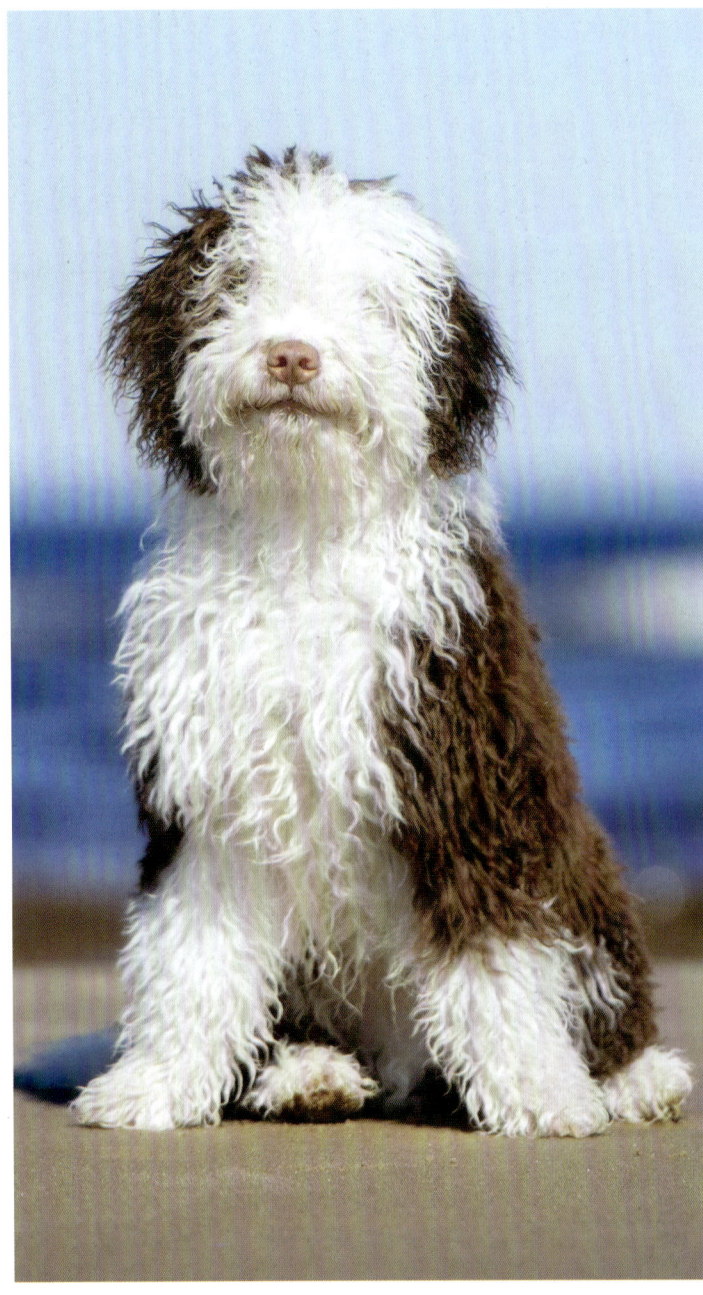

ABOVE:
Shaggy dog
Bred with a long, shaggy coat that dries quickly, this Spanish working breed has been around for more than 800 years.

RIGHT:
High jump
Although traced back many centuries, the Spanish water dog breed was only officially recognized in the 1980s.

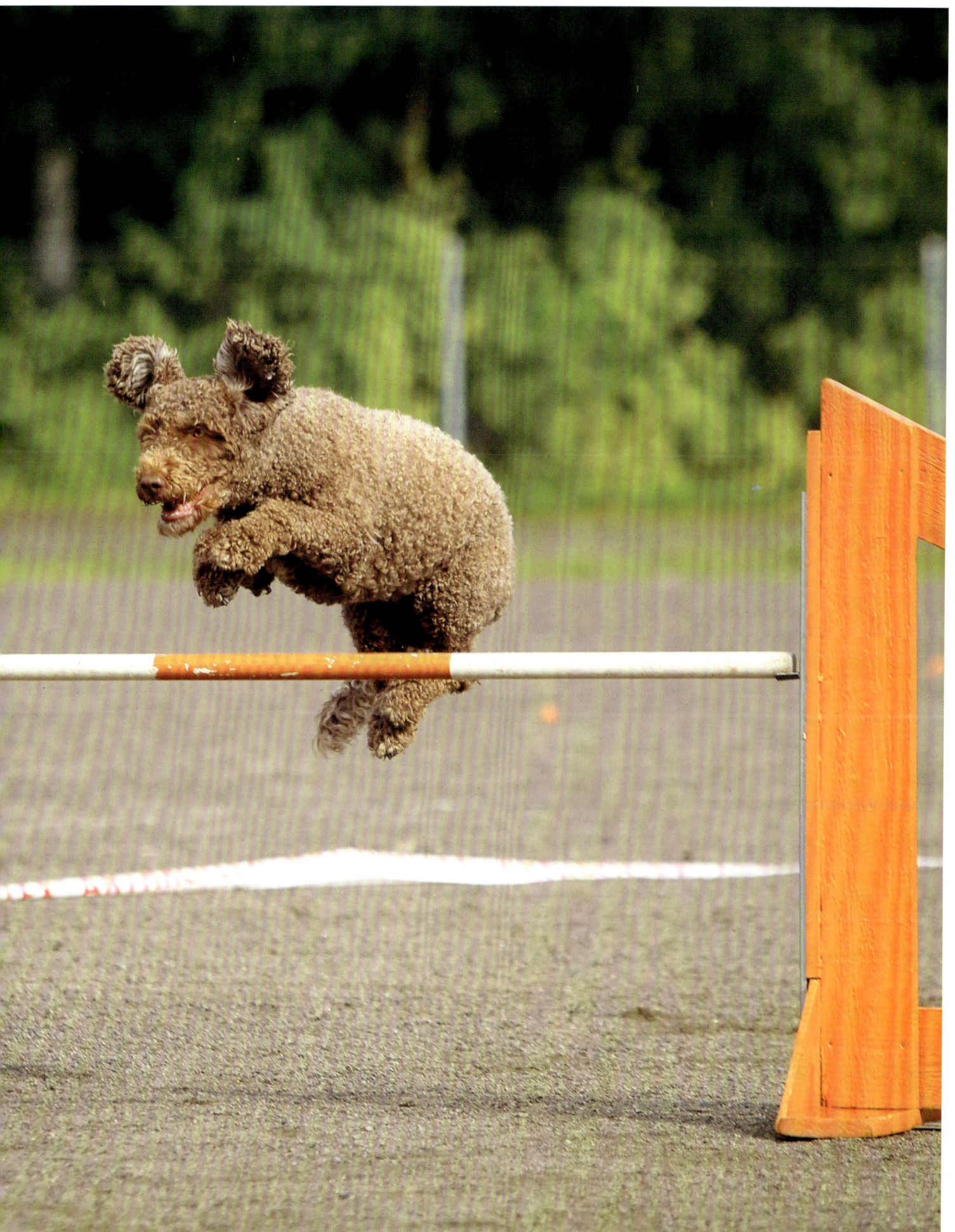

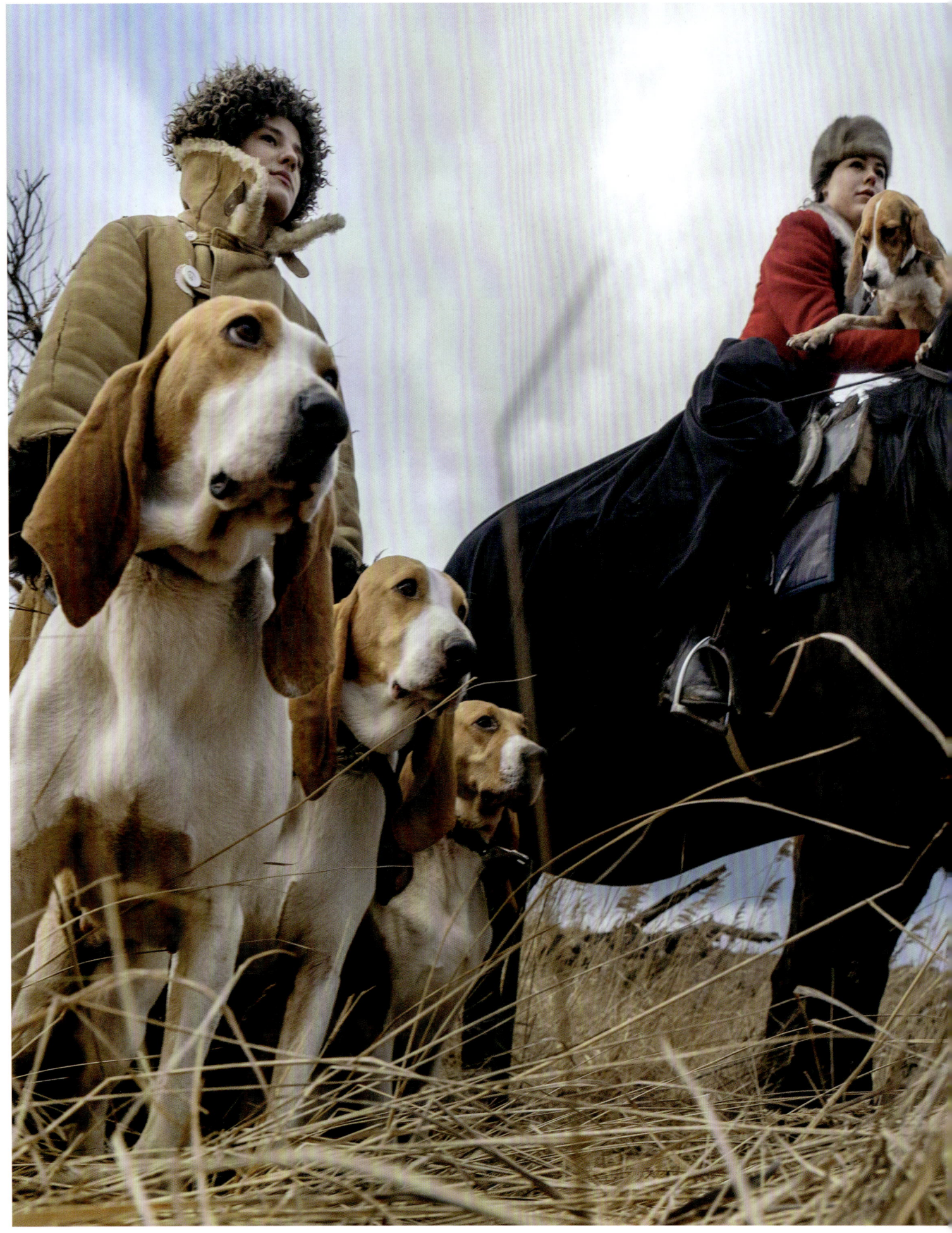

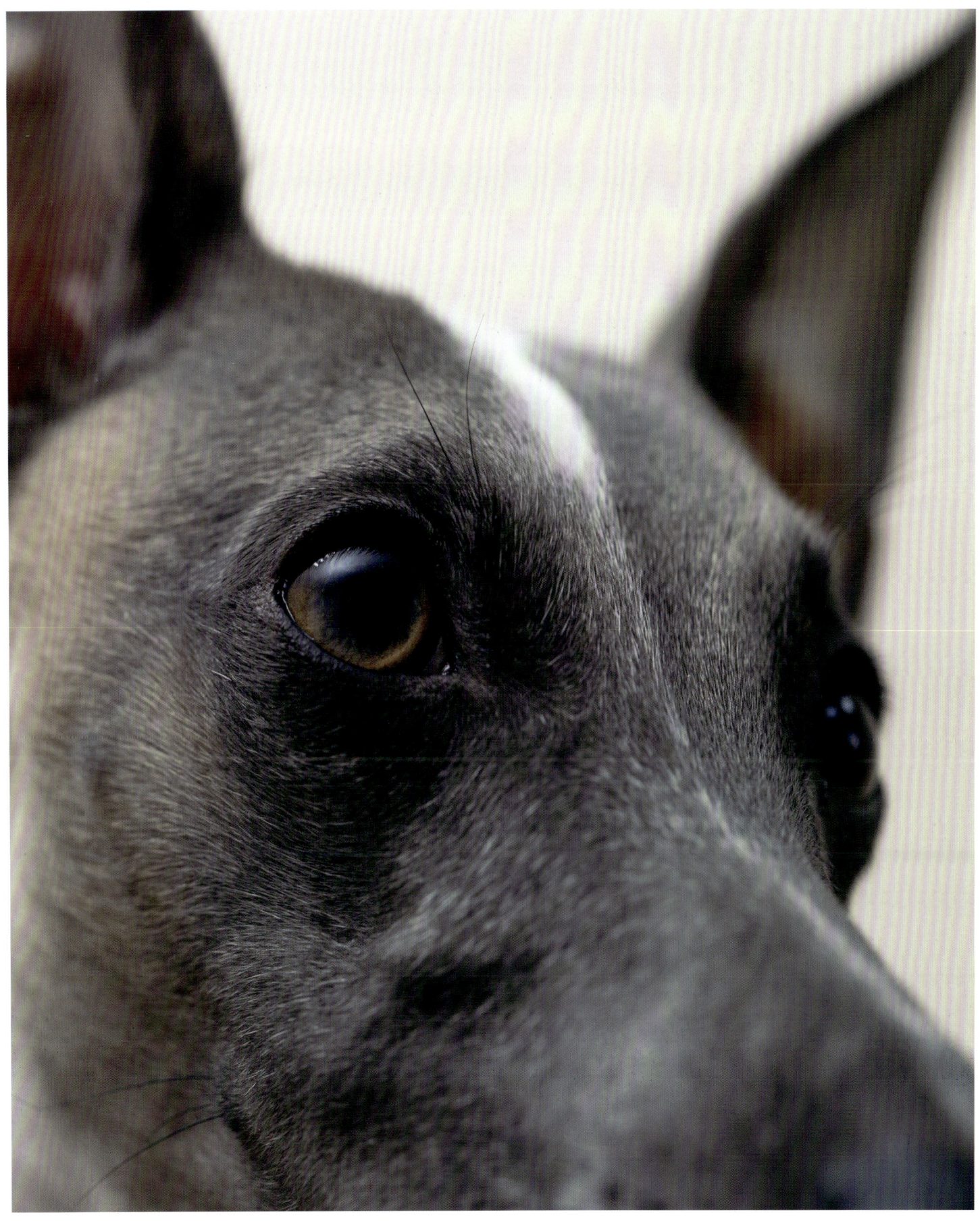

ABOVE:
Expressive features
The whippet has calm oval eyes and pointed ears, which speak volumes to the dog's closest pals.

Weimaraner

CHARACTERISTICS

Coat
A short coat with a solid silver-grey
Height
56–69cm (22–27in)
Weight
25–41kg (55–90lb)
Lifespan
12–13 years
Personality
Courageous and friendly
Origin
Germany

This elegant and unusual breed of pointer is named for the small city of Weimar in the east of Germany. The other claim to fame for this place was that the constitution of the ill-fated interwar Weimar Republic was formulated here in 1919. A century prior to all that nastiness, the area was the possession of Grand Duke Karl August, who like his peers devoted a lot of time and attention to blood sports. With that in mind he set out to develop the ultimate gundog, and the Weimaraner with its unique solid silver-grey coat is the result.

Karl August breeders crossed bloodhounds with various French and German gundogs, mostly pointers, to create the Weimaraner, an all-purpose gun dog that can point, track and retrieve almost anywhere. The breed is larger than most gundog breeds, and the Duke and his friends used it to hunt large game such as boar, bear and deer, as well as smaller animals more associated with this kind of breed.

As well as being loyal and courageous, the Weimaraner is also a friendly and affectionate companion that loves human attention. However, is needs a lot of stimulation, plenty of vigorous exercise and a large amount of training.

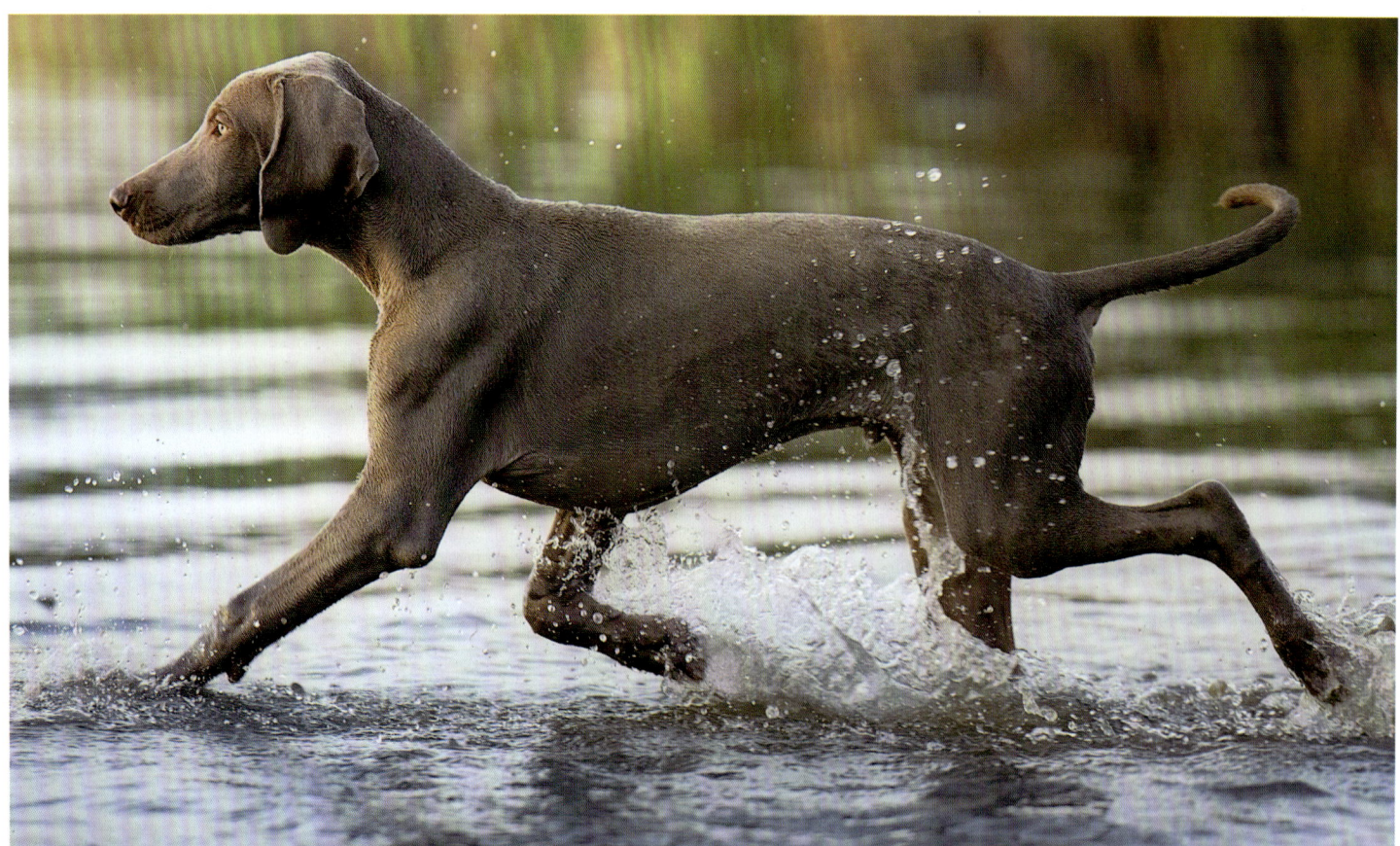

ABOVE:
Unique style
This breed is the "grey ghost" of the dog world because of its stealthy hunting style and ghostly appearance.

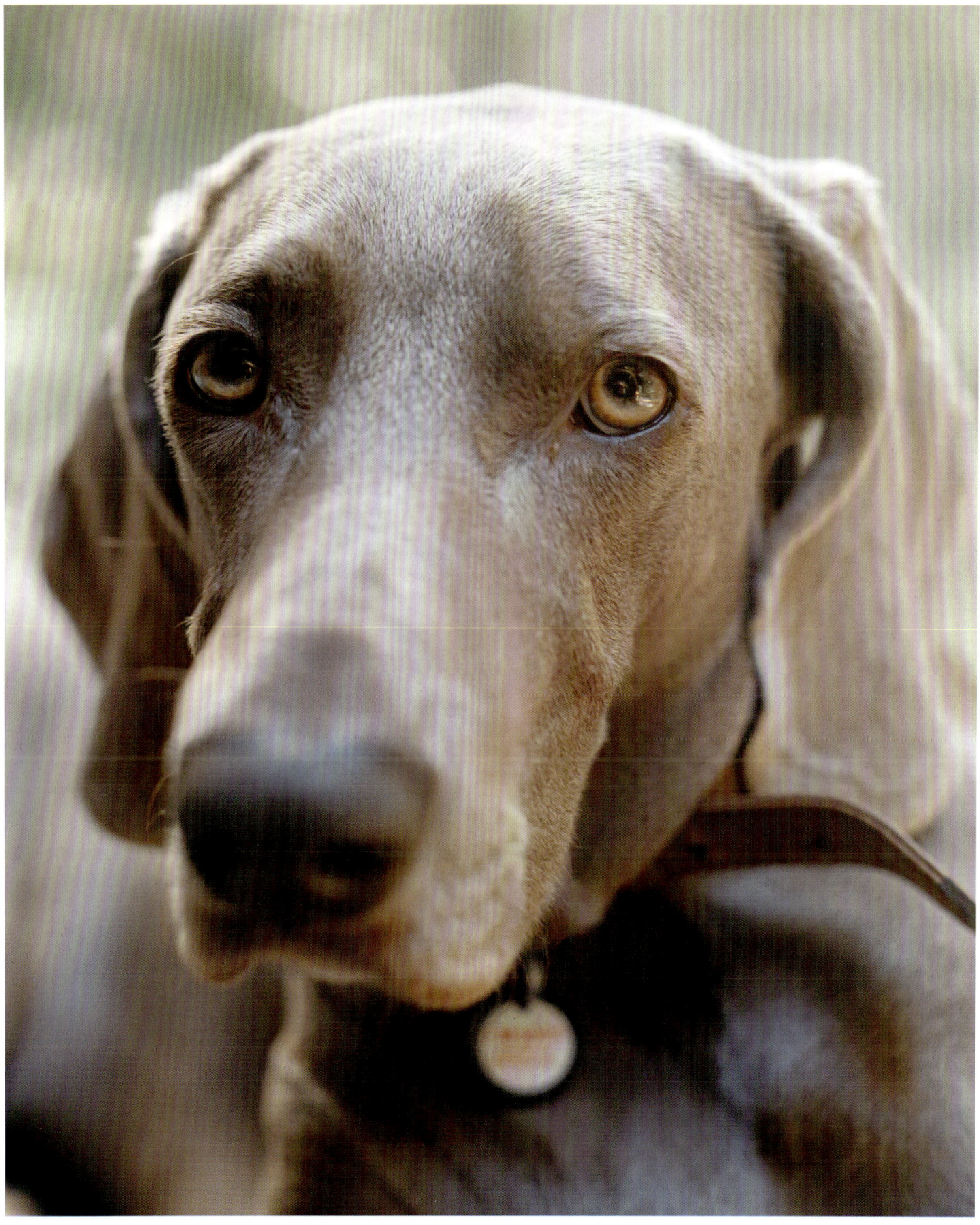

ABOVE:
Close-up
The Weimaraner has distinctive light amber, grey or blue-grey eyes.

Swiss Hound

The breed is known in its homeland as the Schweizer Laufhund, or "Swiss running dog". They have a long history in this mountainous country but have probably changed a great deal over the centuries. The running dogs are seen in Helvetian mosaics (Helvetia was the Roman province that is now known as Switzerland.) The dogs back then were scent hounds that chased hares, small deer and perhaps boars through the woodland and across the hillsides. The dogs grew famous beyond the Swiss borders as an important breeding stock for scenthounds such as foxhounds, harriers and beagles. The Swiss dogs were also influenced by foreign breeds, mostly French and Italian, that were brought home by Swiss mercenaries (a major industry for the country in the Middle Ages).

Since the 1880s, the Swiss hound was delineated into four distinct varieties, each one linked to a Swiss region, and with a distinct colouring. The Lucerne Laufhund has patches of blue fur (actually a deep black) on a paler speckled coat, the Bernese hound is mostly white with black patches, while the Schwyz variety has red patches. Finally the Bruno Jura dog has a tan coat with a black back.

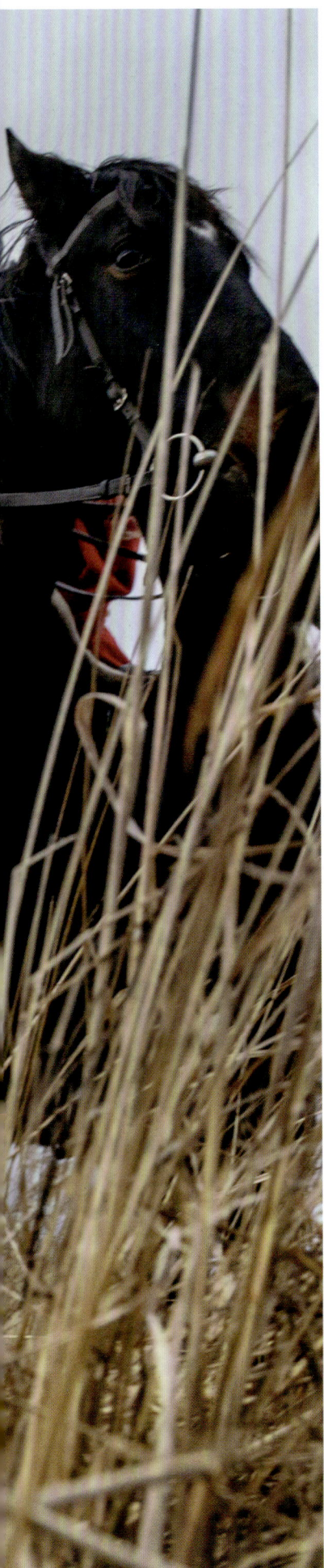

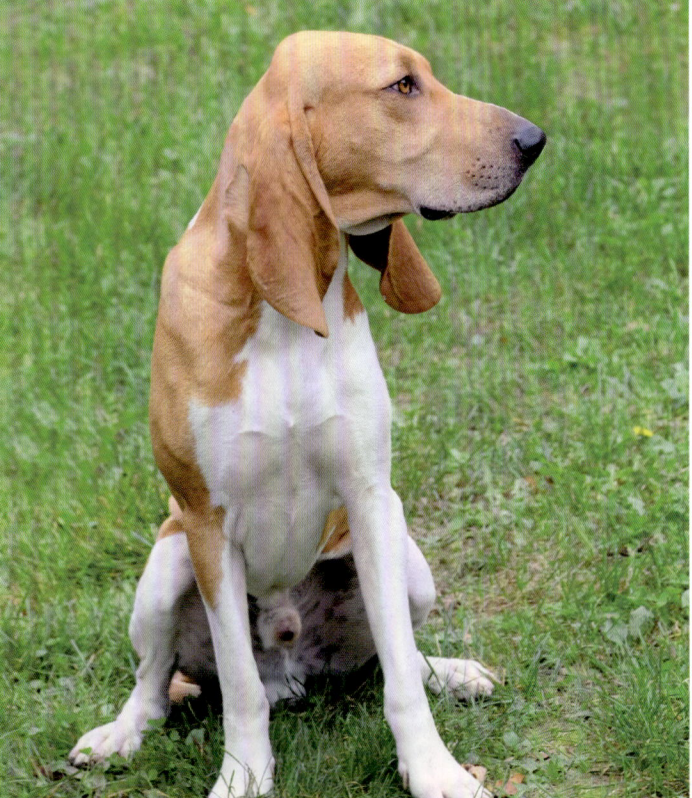

CHARACTERISTICS
Coat
A short and dense coat seen in all colours
Height
47–59cm (19–23in)
Weight
15–20kg (33–44lb)
Lifespan
12–14 years
Personality
Eager and friendly
Origin
Switzerland

LEFT:
Hunters
The hounds are pack hunters that are sent out to pursue foxes and rabbits. People follow on horse and on foot.

ABOVE:
Big nose
The Schwyz hound has an especially long muzzle.

Whippet

CHARACTERISTICS

Coat
A short, smooth coat that comes in a variety of colours and patterns

Height
44–51cm (17–20in)

Weight
11–18kg (24–40lb)

Lifespan
12–14 years

Personality
Calm and energetic

Origin
England

Compared to other sighthounds, like greyhounds or borzois, the whippet is a small dog. Nevertheless it can reach speeds of 55km/h (35mph) which, kilogram for kilogram and pound for pound, makes it the fastest dog around. (Greyhounds go a little faster but weigh twice as much.)

Whippets were bred in the mining country of northern England in the 19th century. It was created as an alternative to the greyhound for hunting rabbits and other small game. The smaller dogs were cheaper to keep and did their job just as well. The whippets also found a calling as a racing dog, which was an informal pursuit in Victorian Britain. As dog racing became professionalised, the whippets were put aside by the faster crowd-pleasing greyhounds. But whippets, mild-mannered and fun-loving, had nevertheless won the hearts of the ordinary folk. The dogs make excellent companions that are quiet and calm indoors, but love to get out and let off steam. The breed is an ideal pet for people who enjoy a long, daily walk and have access to open space for the dog to run. Whippets are highly trainable but can be shy so need positive reinforcement and socialization.

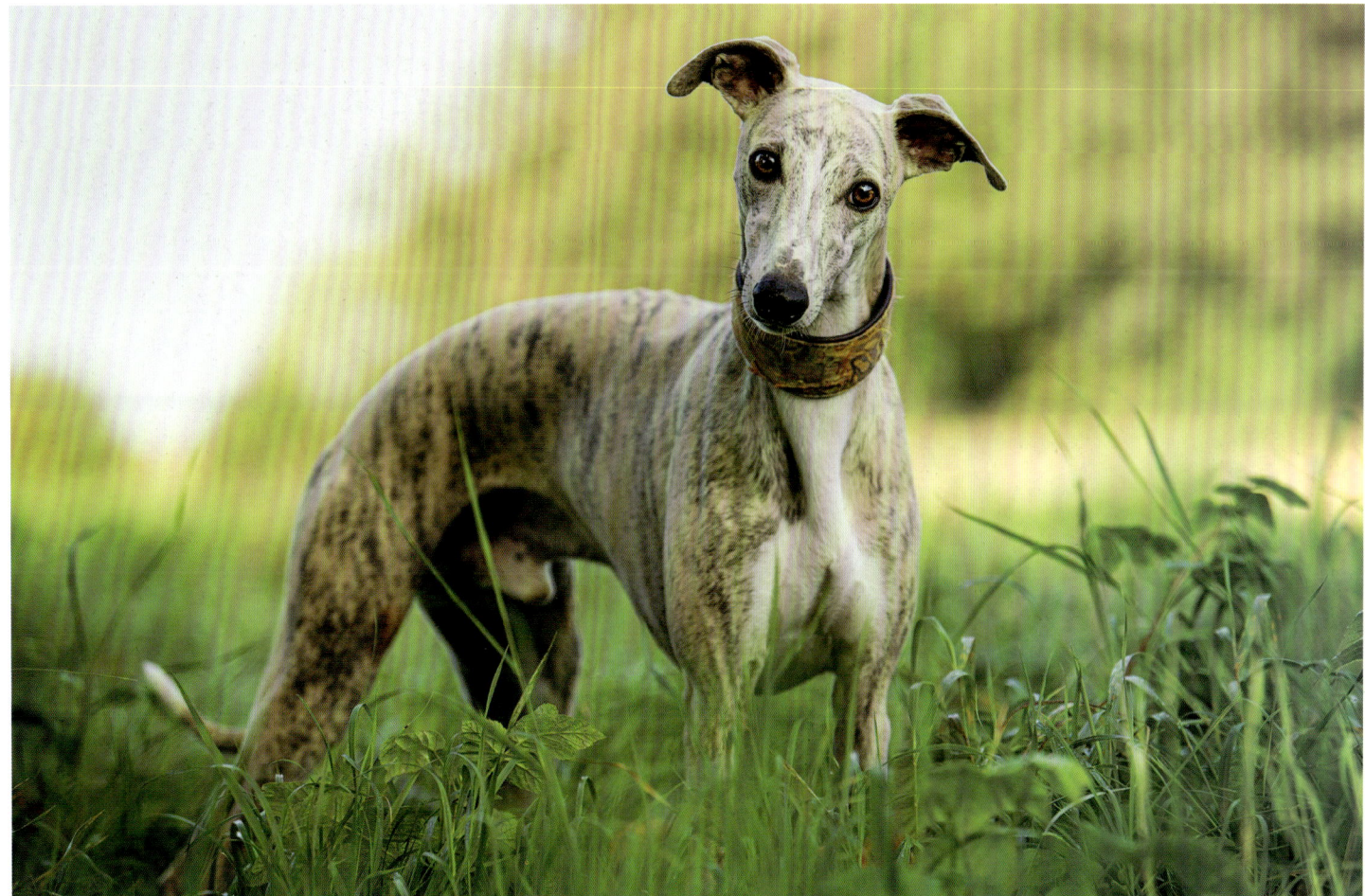

ABOVE:
Lean and not mean
The coat requires minimal grooming but is not well suited to cold weather.

HUNTING DOGS

Chasing their tails
Despite their fast moving nature, whippets feel the cold easily, when on walks the dog needs a coat in winter.

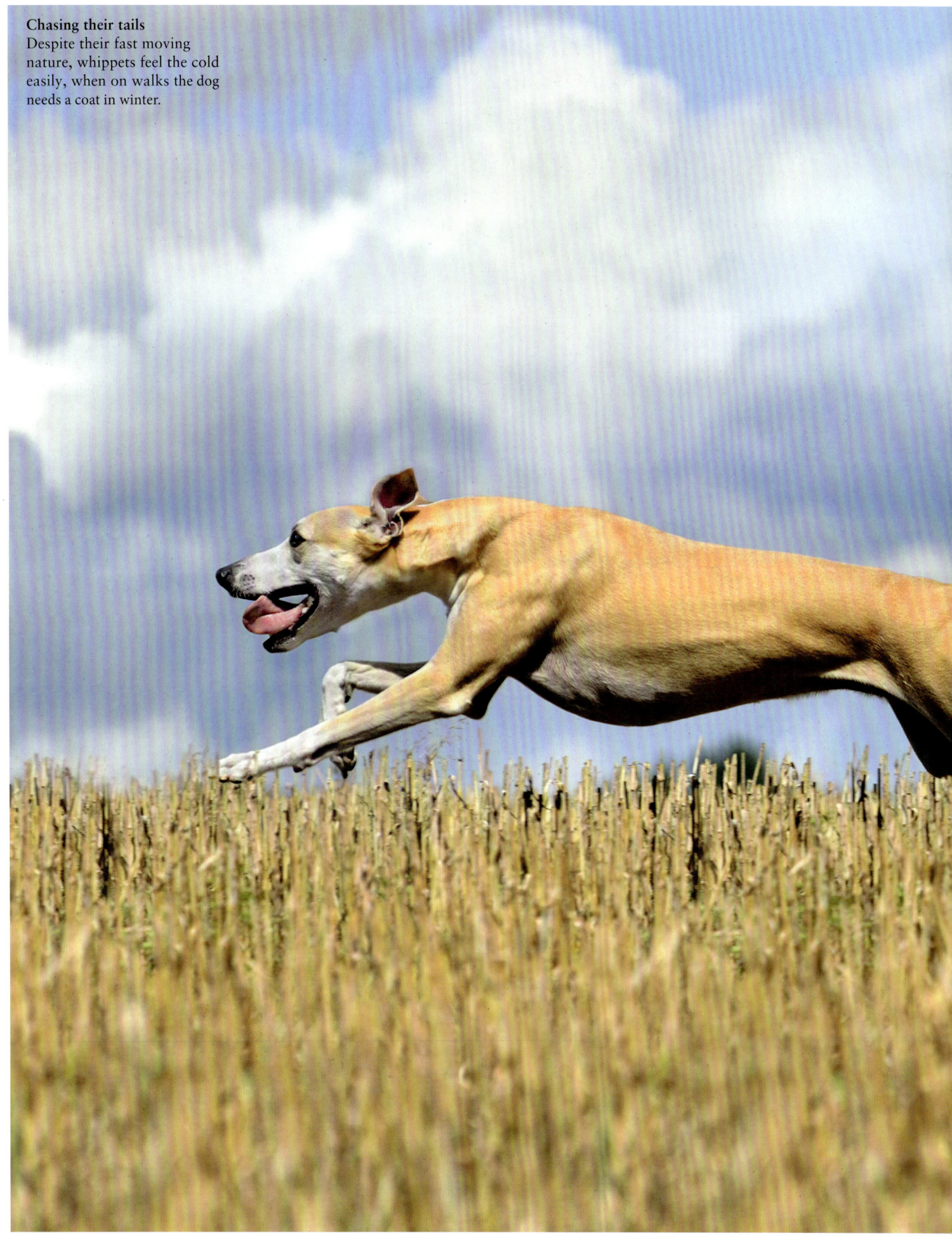

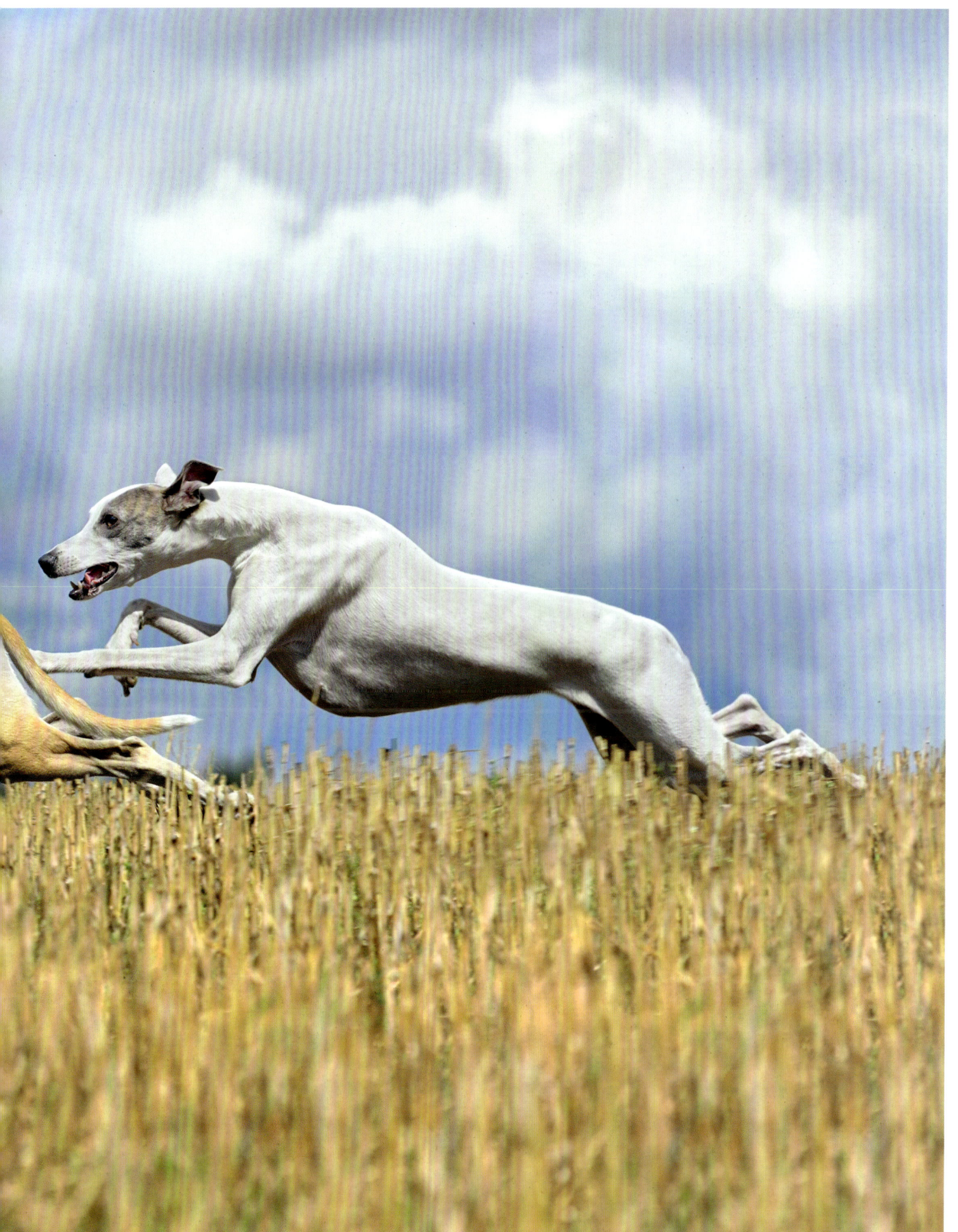

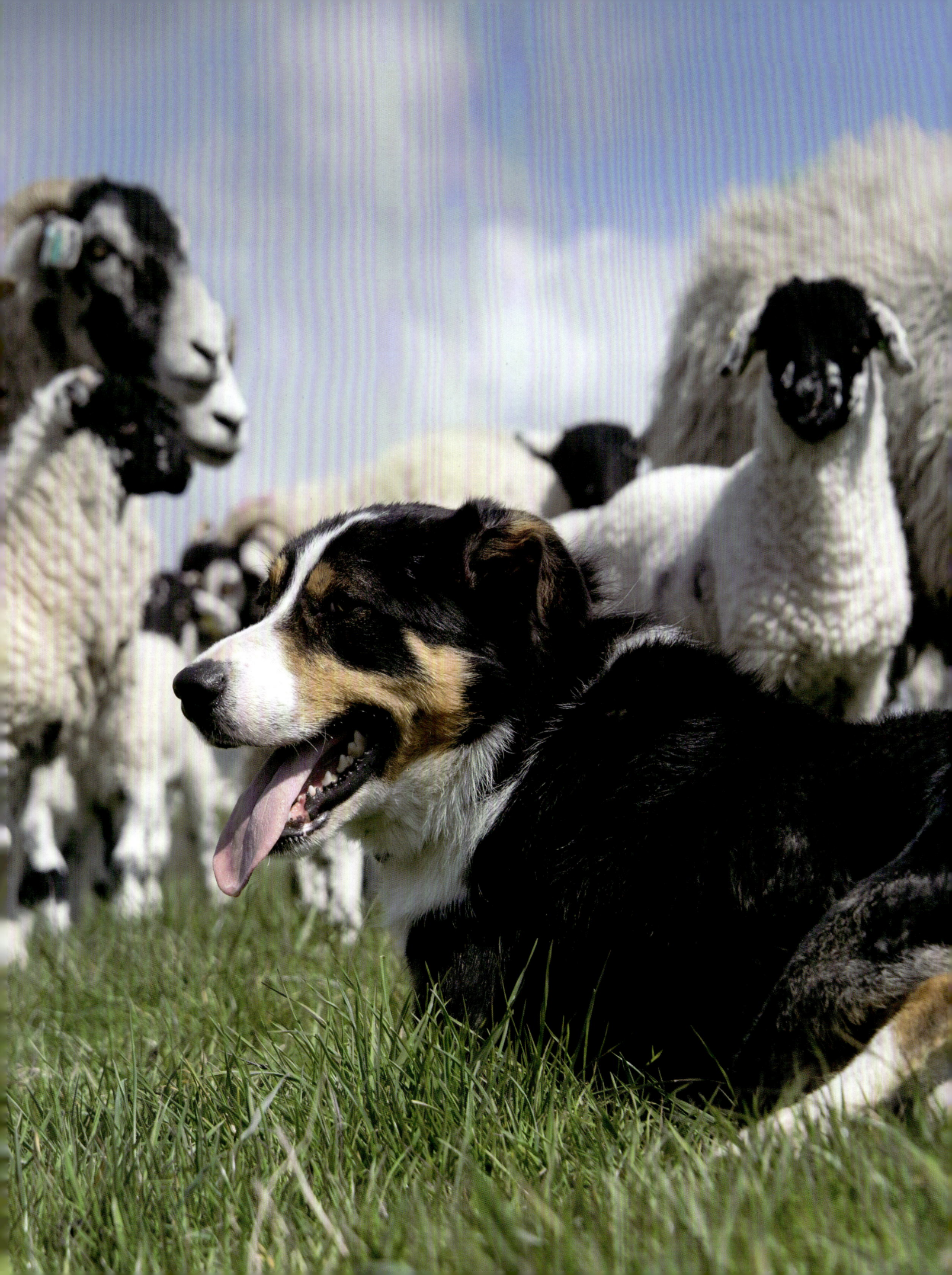

Working Dogs

A dog is a social animal driven to be part of the larger group, and pull its weight socially and physically to ensure the continued success of its family. This instinct is at the centre of the relationship between people and their dogs, and with some breeds it is used to put them to work, literally. The most common dog job is looking after livestock, keeping the herds together and moving them hither and thither. All the while the dogs protect the animals, just as a wild dog looks after the other pack members. Due to their strong guarding instinct, herding dogs also make good watchdogs and police dogs.

OPPOSITE:
Border collie
This British sheepdog breed is said to be the ultimate working dog. It works hard to please its handler and protect flocks the only way it knows how, by keeping the sheep together.

WORKING DOGS

Alaskan Malamute

CHARACTERISTICS

Coat
Very thick hairs mostly grey but with a range of colours. All dogs have white bellies

Height
58–71cm (23–28in)

Weight
38–56kg (84–123lb)

Lifespan
12–15 years

Personality
Friendly and intelligent but also strong and boisterous. Can be intolerant of strange dogs unless well socialized. Not suitable to be left with a small child or alone for long periods

Origin
Alaska and Yukon Territory

This impressive and capable breed is descended from similar spitz-type Siberian breeds that travelled into North America across the Bering Strait with human migrants around 14,000 years ago. It is named after the Mahlemut people of coastal Alaska, who used it as a beast of burden. The dogs worked in teams to pull sleds over ice and through deep snow, and were co-opted by pioneering Europeans moving into the area in the 19th century. The malamute was especially valued by prospectors during the Klondike Gold Rush in the late 1890s. Today the dog is still used to haul cargo in the most remote areas of its homeland—and further afield in expeditions to the High Arctic. Many are kept as part of dogsled racing teams.

Unsurprisingly, the malamute has a strong chasing instinct, which serves its willingness to pull loads over long distances. However, in a domestic setting this can make the breed unruly, so it should be kept on a lead unless in a large and empty area for exercise. The malamute has remarkable stamina and strength, with one dog capable of carrying half its body weight over 30km (20 miles).

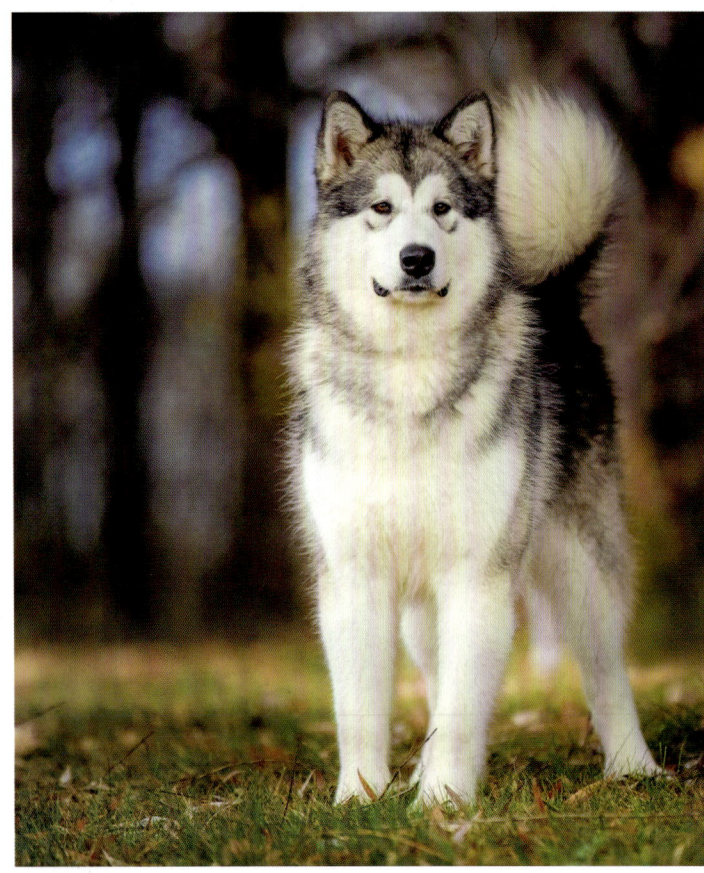

ABOVE:
Tough customer
The breed has noticeably sturdy back legs and the tail is often curled over the back.

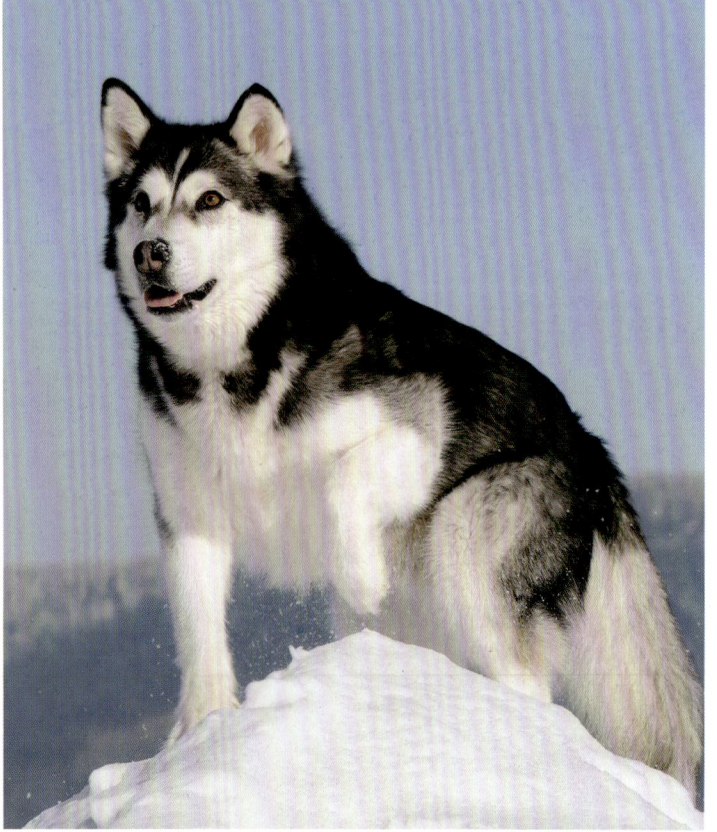

ABOVE:
Warm coat
The hair is thick and coarse, and warm enough for the dogs to sleep outside, even in the Alaskan winter—providing it has at least one companion.

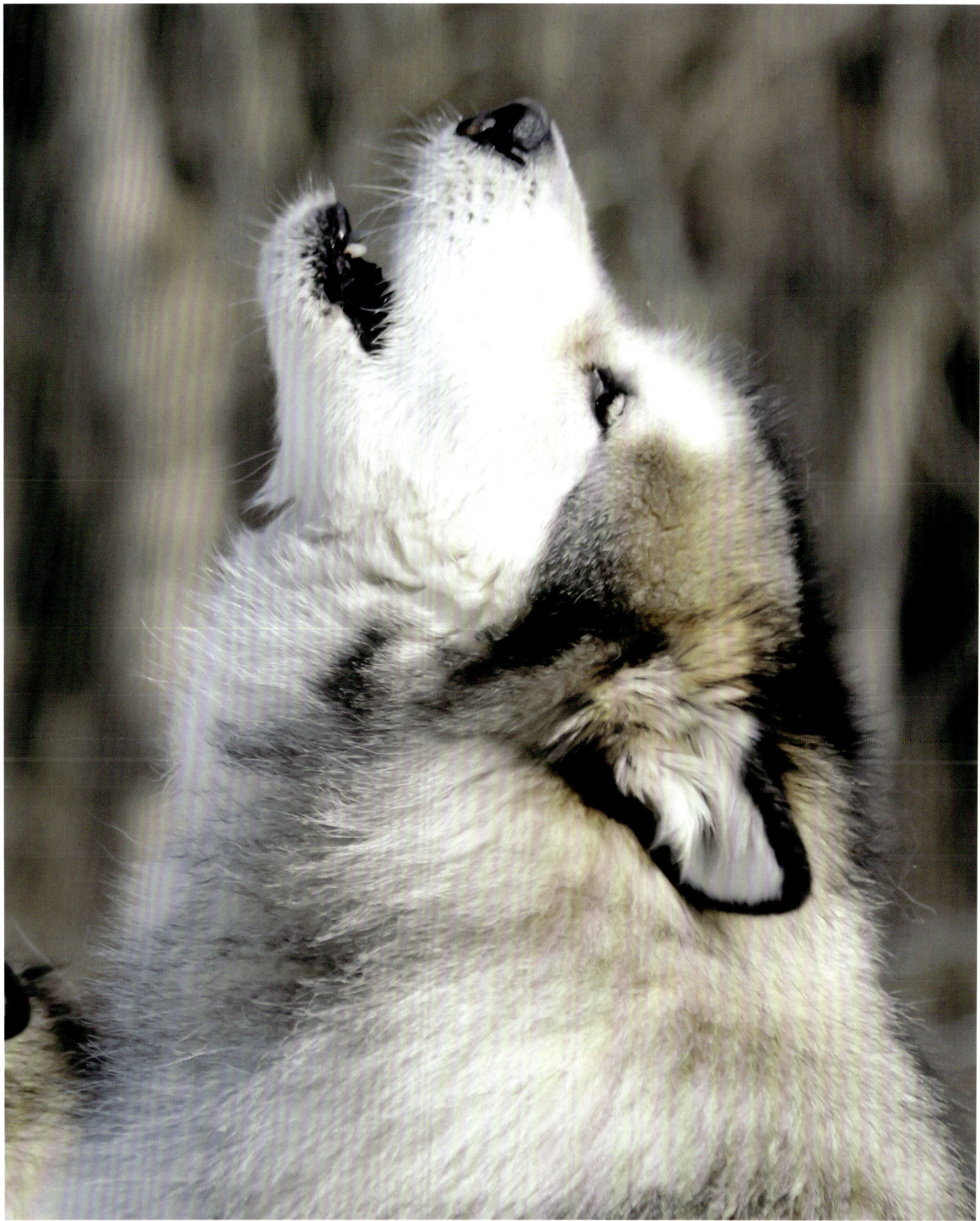

ABOVE:
Howl!
The Alaskan malamute looks rather like a wolf and behaves like them as well.

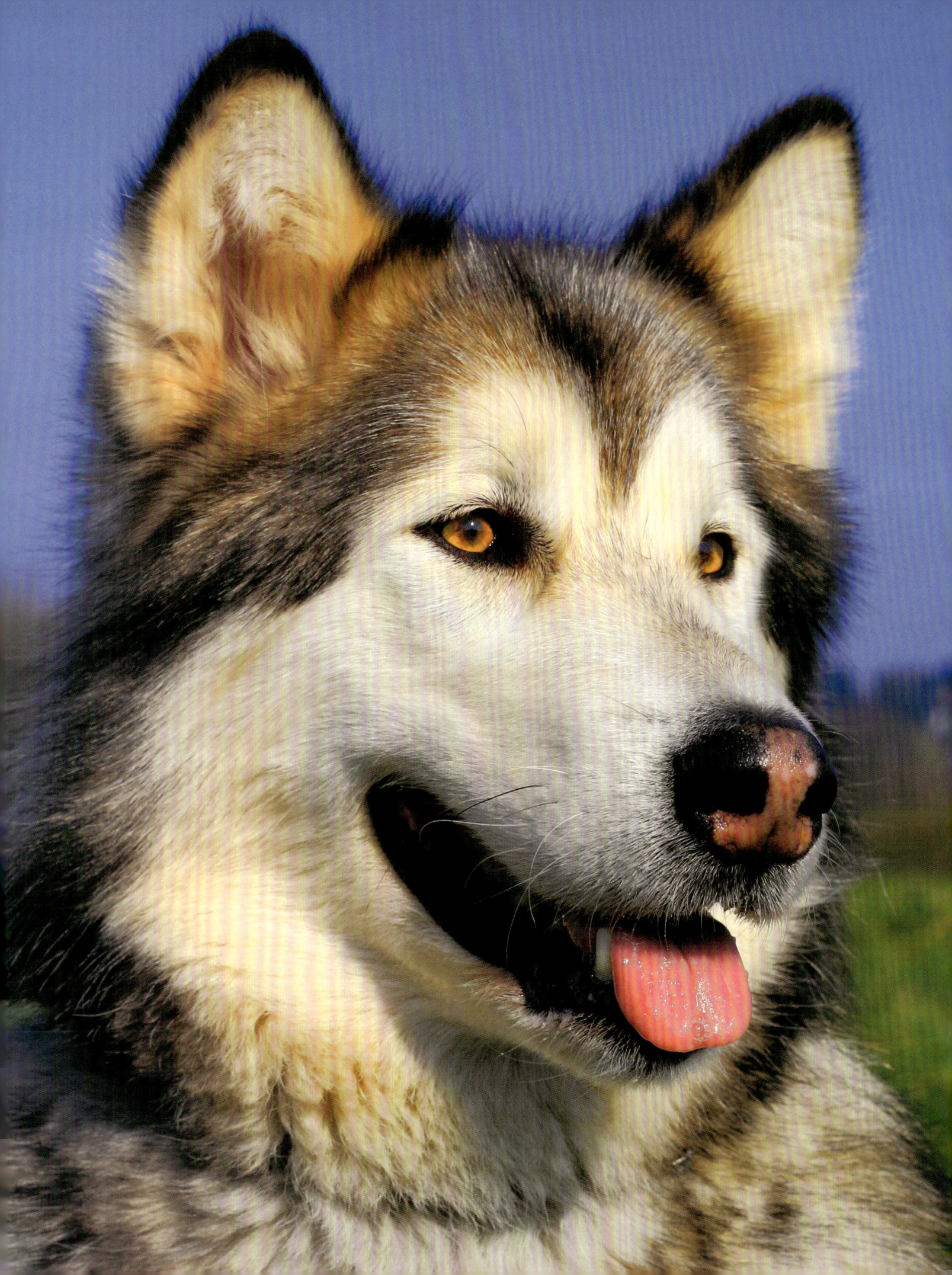

WORKING DOGS

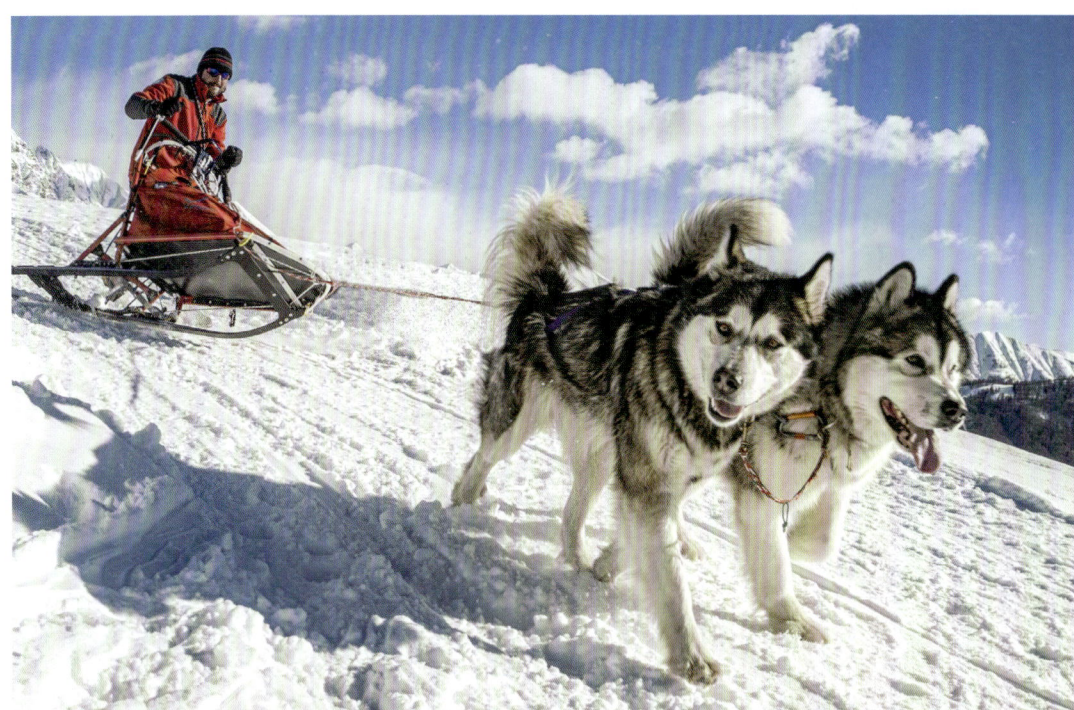

LEFT & OPPOSITE:
Snowy terrain
A pack of sled dogs will howl to each other at the end of a hard day.

BELOW:
Young pup
We are instinctively drawn to protect something as cute as this fluffy pup for the same reasons we look after our own babies.

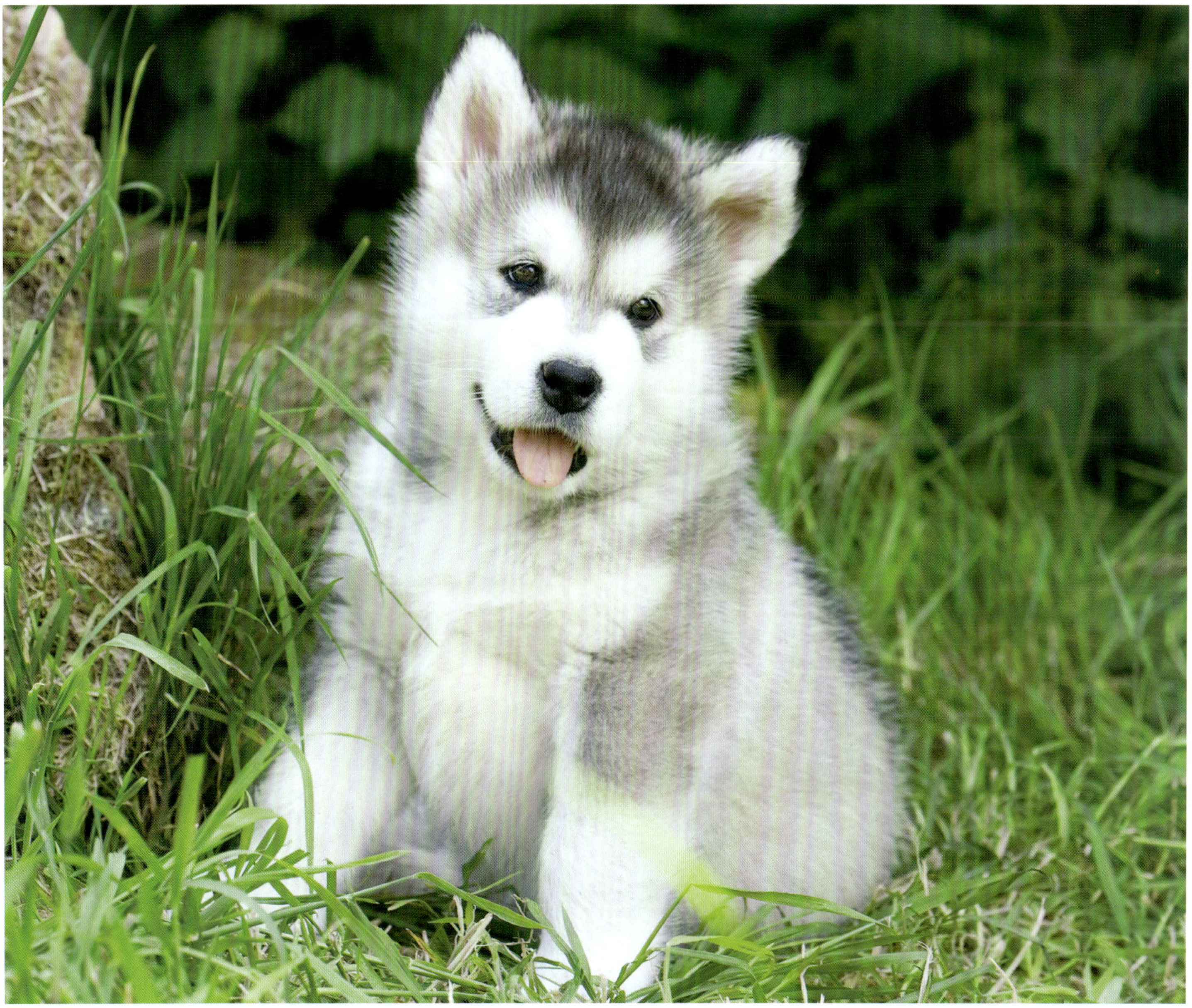

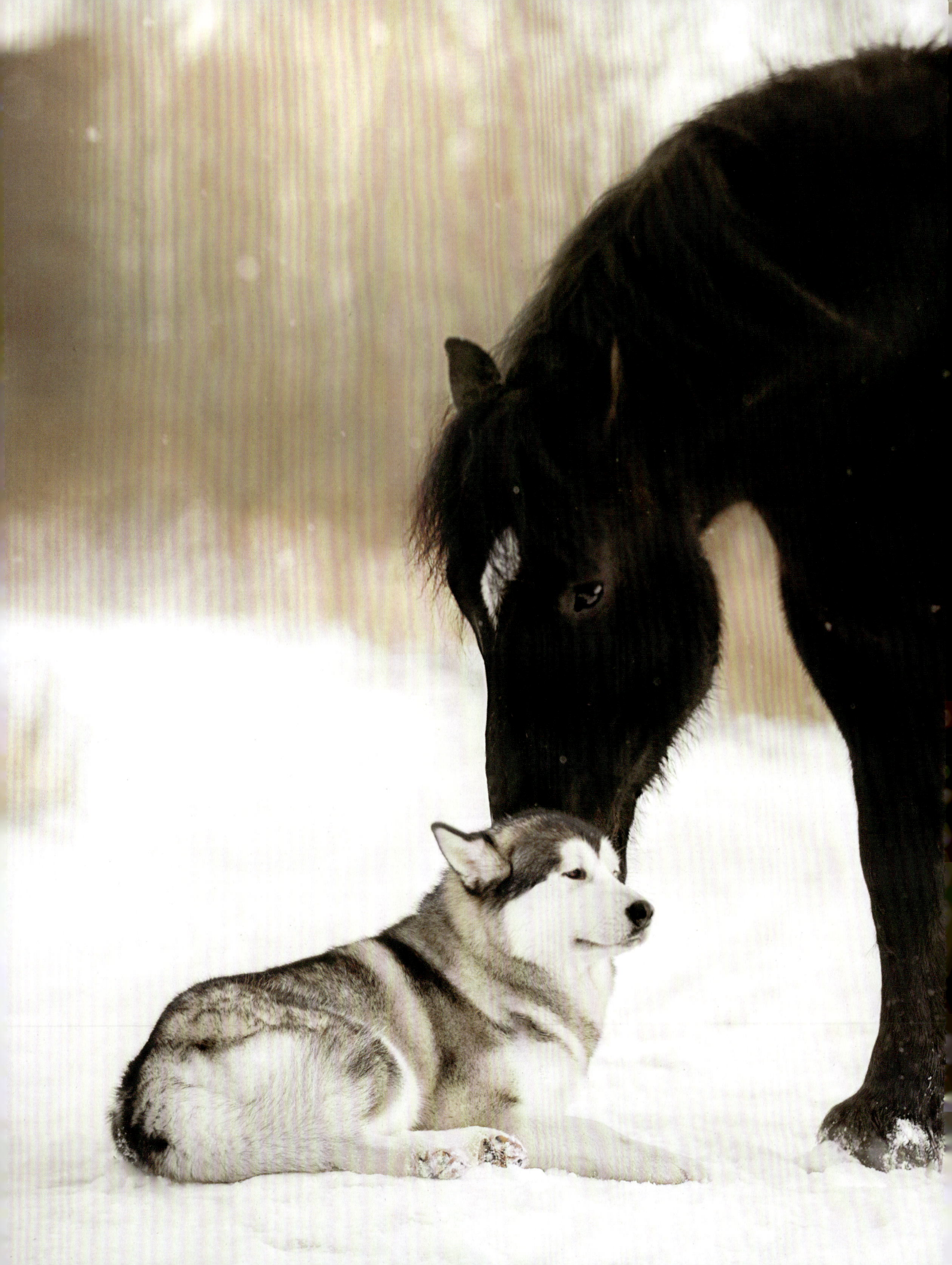

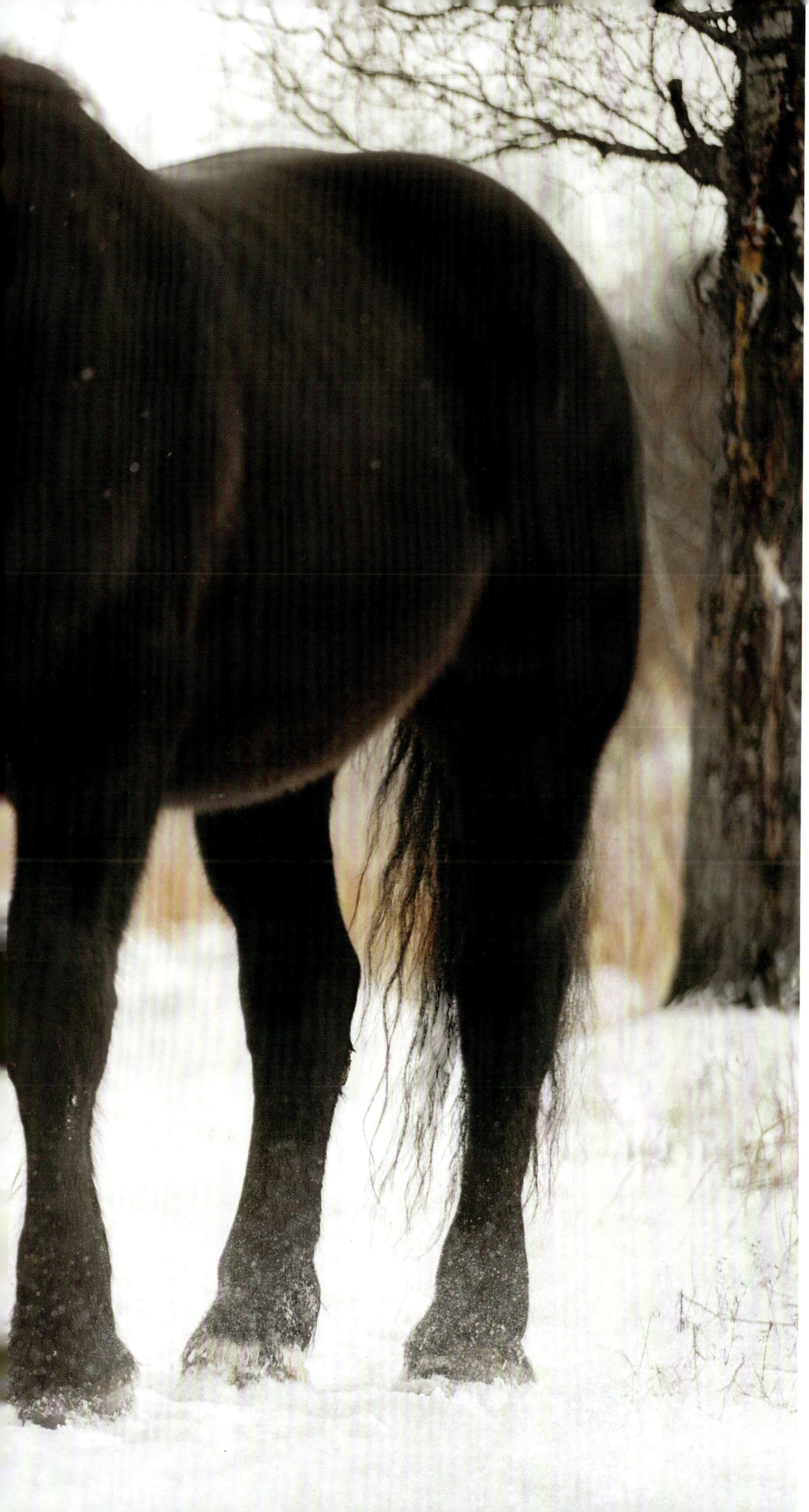

WORKING DOGS

Sociable animal
Many domestic animals – including the sometimes misunderstood and maligned house cat – are highly social animals. Here, this Malamute is perfectly at home with a horse, and visa versa.

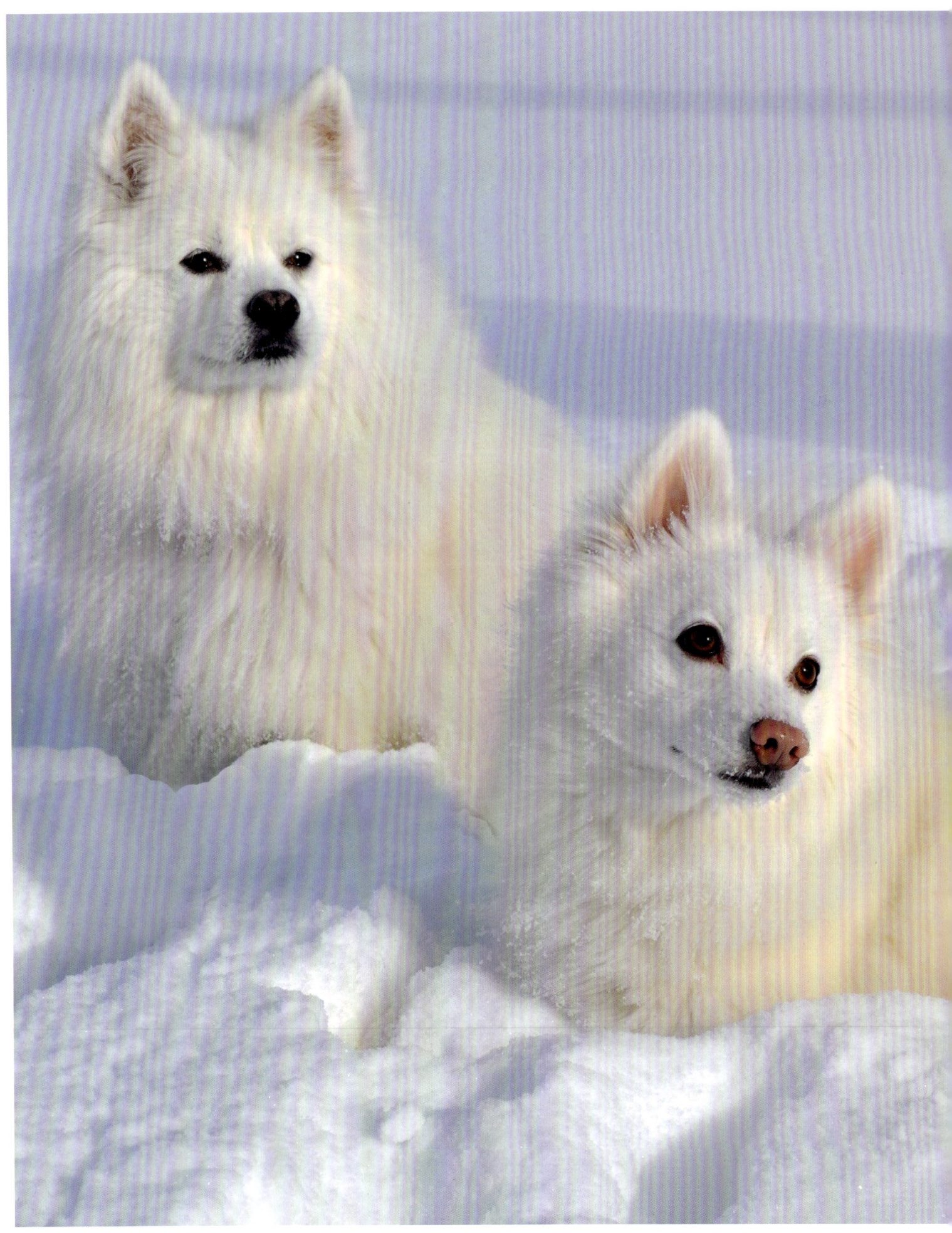

American Eskimo Dog

Despite the name this dog was created in Germany from Nordic, spitz-type stock that was imported to North America in the 19th century largely as a performing dog, thanks to its intelligence and eagerness to please. The breed only became widely recognized by officials in the 1990s and therefore is by no means linked to the Canadian eskimo dog, or Inuit dog, which is one of the oldest Arctic breeds of all. Instead it is a close relative of the German spitz, and as in that breed, its short, wispy tail is carried over the back.

The American eskimo dog is a very friendly dog that is good tempered around strangers and unlikely to be threatened by other dogs. Barking is not usually a problem and the breed is easy to train and picks up tricks and games quickly. These dogs are full of energy and can only trot but walk, but they are not likely to demand that much attention—nor are they great guard dogs!

CHARACTERISTICS

Coat
Generally white but occasionally a pale biscuit hue, medium-length fur that is thick and fluffy, especially around the neck and chest

Height
23–48cm (9–19in), comes in three sizes: toy, miniature and standard

Weight
3–18kg (7–40lb)

Lifespan
12–13 years

Personality
Eager and intelligent, a fast learner and very seldom aggressive

Origin
Germany

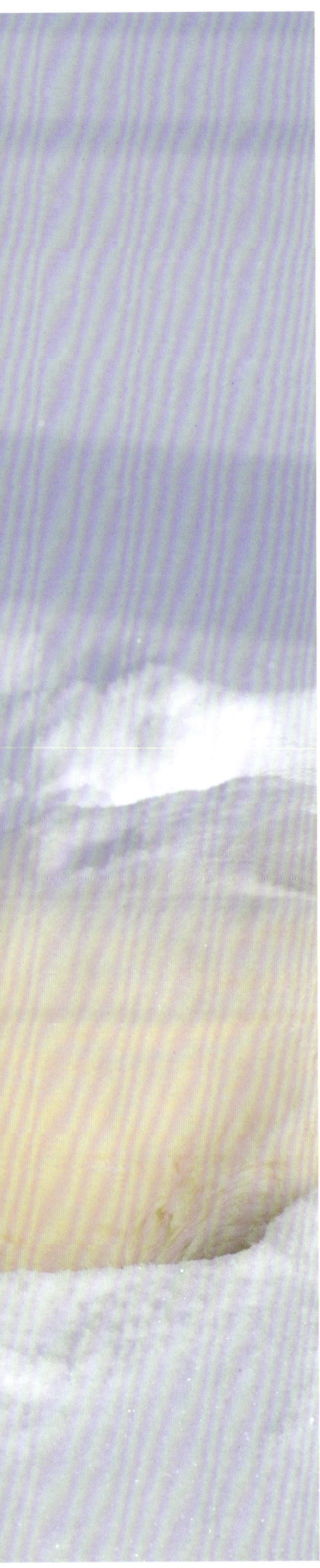

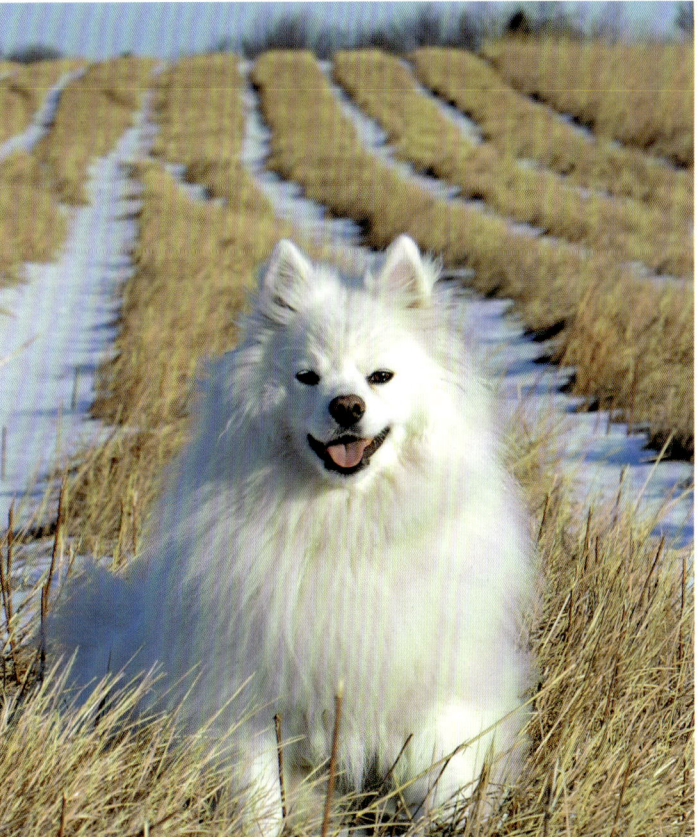

LEFT:
Built for snow
The American eskimo dog is well suited to cold weather, with a double coat, with longer wispy hairs guarding a warm woolly underfur.

ABOVE:
Easy to keep
The coat does not shed more than average and is relatively easy and economical to groom.

WORKING DOGS

Anatolian Shepherd Dog

This breed is a livestock guardian, a protector that is bred to live, day in, day out, alongside flocks of sheep and goats in the wilds of Anatolia, the rugged interior of Turkey. These big and brave dogs are easily a match for predators that threaten the flocks. Dogs like this are seen on carved reliefs made in the area 4,000 years ago. Back then shepherds were worried about attacks from lions, leopards and wolves. The breed is still performing its role today, although threats come mostly from stray feral dogs.

Anatolian shepherd dogs are highly vigilant but not welcoming to strangers, humans or animals. They are level-headed dogs that can become well-trained and obedient pets given enough attention by a strong owner. Being strong but also very fast and agile, the breed's sheer size requires that Anatolians have plenty of time to exercise and receive enough mental stimulation. The dog is easy to keep clean and healthy. Its long history means that inbred traits are uncommon.

CHARACTERISTICS
Coat
Smooth and short, mostly brown and tan but can be any colour
Height
71–81cm (28–32in)
Weight
41–64kg (90–141lb)
Lifespan
12–15 years
Personality
Aloof and wilful, this breed is a working dog through and through and needs firm control by its owner
Origin
Turkey

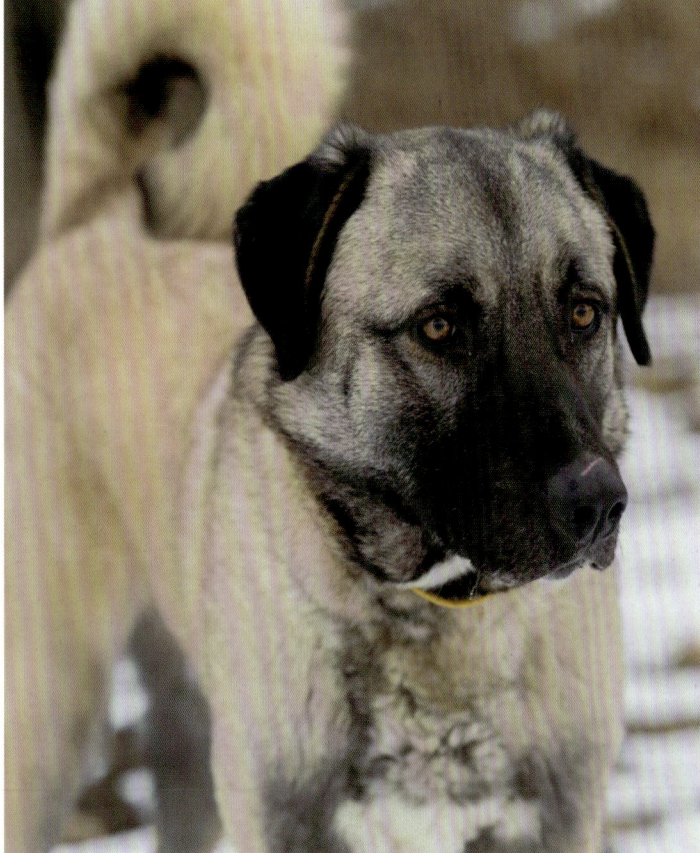

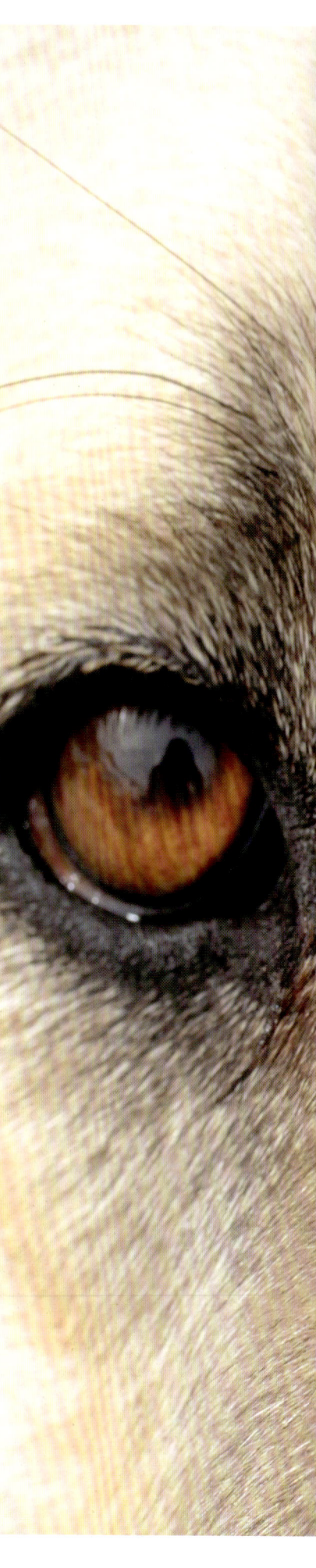

ABOVE:
Heavy shedding
Bred for a life outdoors, the coat is shed twice a year, and will need a thorough brushing during these moults.

RIGHT:
Under control
It is advised to keep the Anatolian shepherd dog on a leash when away from home.

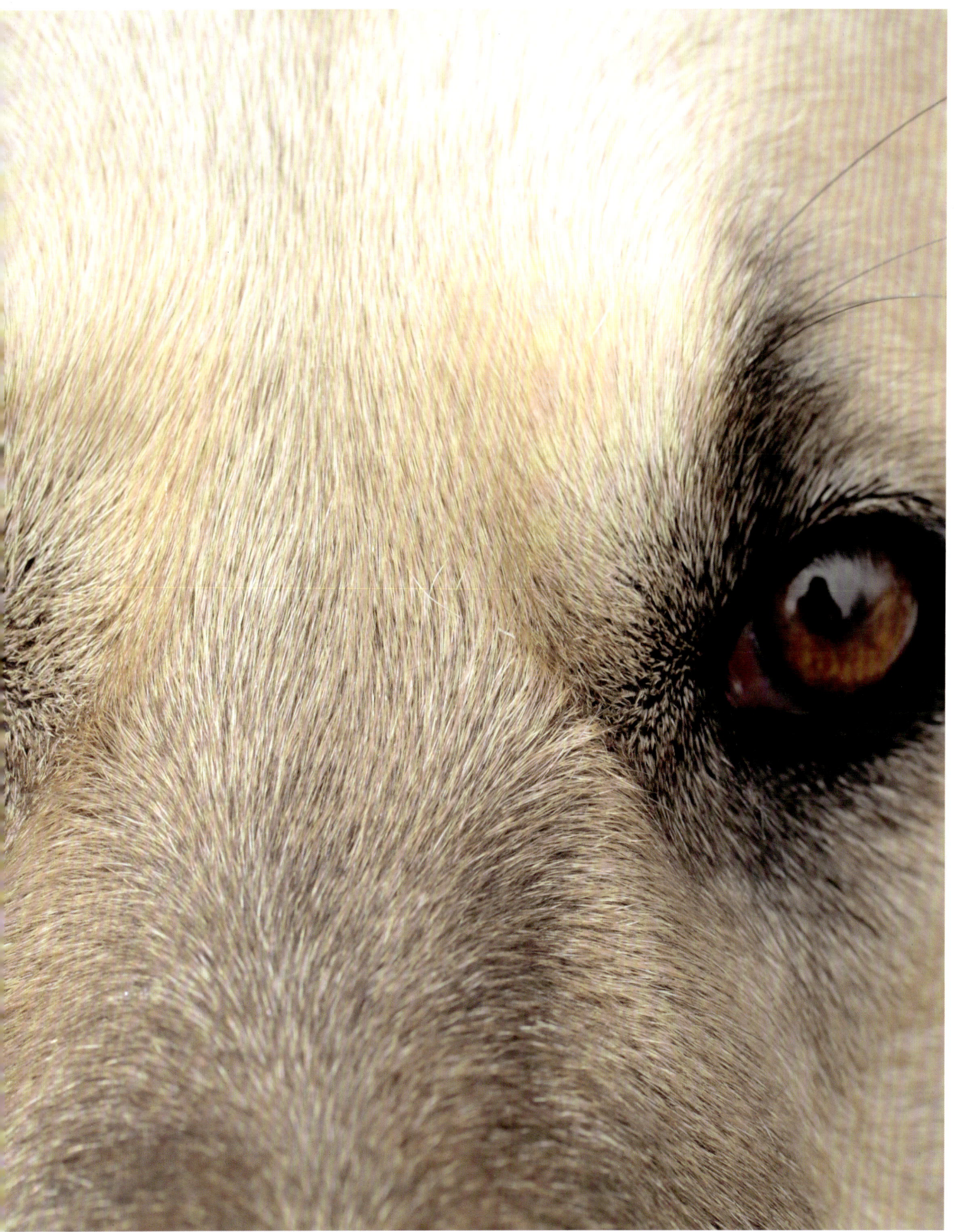

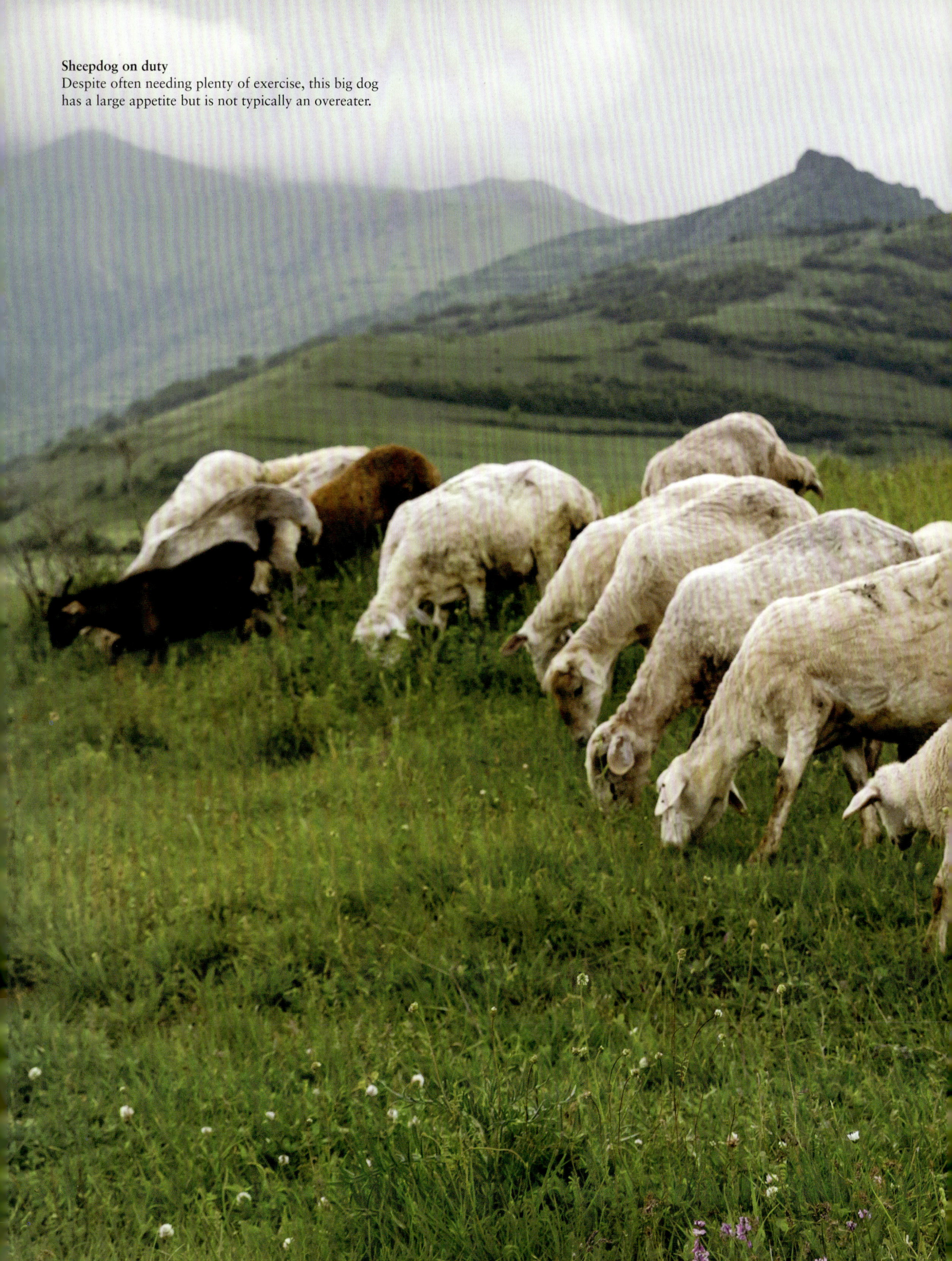

Sheepdog on duty
Despite often needing plenty of exercise, this big dog has a large appetite but is not typically an overeater.

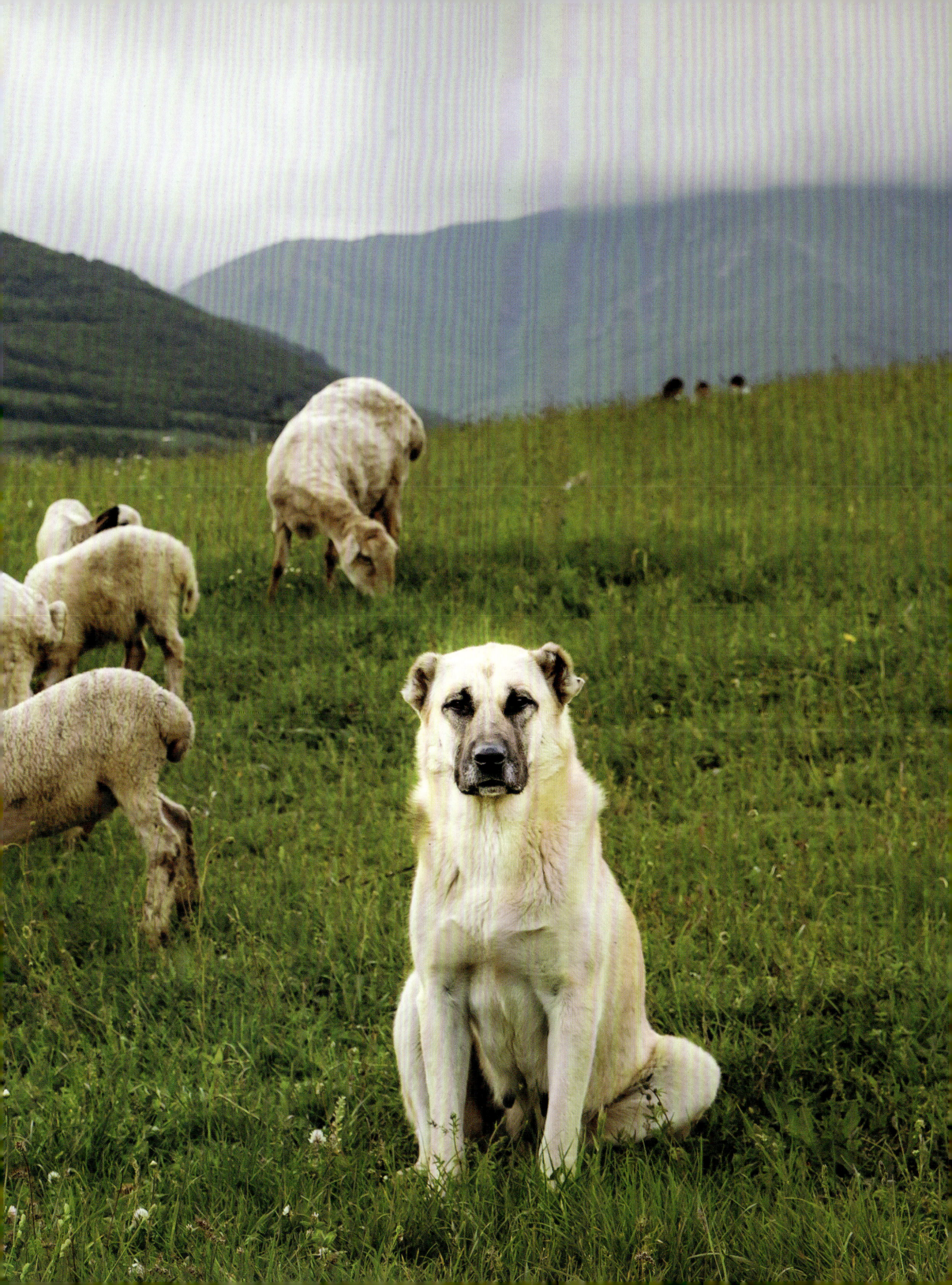

Australian Cattle Dog

As the name makes clear, this breed originated in Australia for driving large herds of cattle long distances through the rough terrain of the Queensland Outback. An alternative name for the cattle dog is "heeler"—they are generally red or blue heelers—because of their knack of biting the back legs of cattle to encourage these beasts to keep on moving.

In the early 1800s, ranchers recently arrived from Europe were clearing the bush to create vast pastures. They began to cross Highland collies with dingos. They hoped the dingo would give the working breed the ability to work at the rate needed in the heat and dry Down Under. Later Dalmatian blood was mixed in to make the Australian cattle dog less likely to harass the ranchers' horses.

In common with sheep and cattle dogs, the Australian cattle dog requires a lot of exercise and mental stimulation regularly. Without this, these faithful dogs can become unpredictable and destructive. As such the breed does not make a good pet since it needs near-constant contact with its owner. It is therefore best suited to a busy life on the land.

CHARACTERISTICS
Coat
Medium coat, longer at the neck. All colours are seen often with speckles.
Height
43–51cm (17–20in)
Weight
14–18kg (31–40lb)
Lifespan
10 years
Personality
Intelligent and willing
Origin
Australia

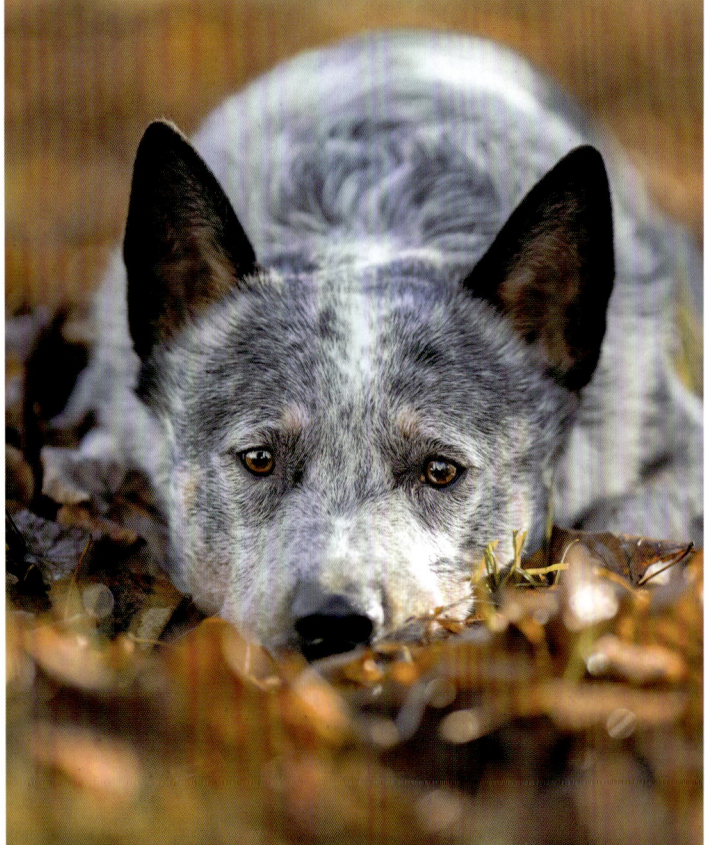

ABOVE:
Fine figure
The Australian cattle dog has long pointed ears and thick hairs around the neck and shoulders.

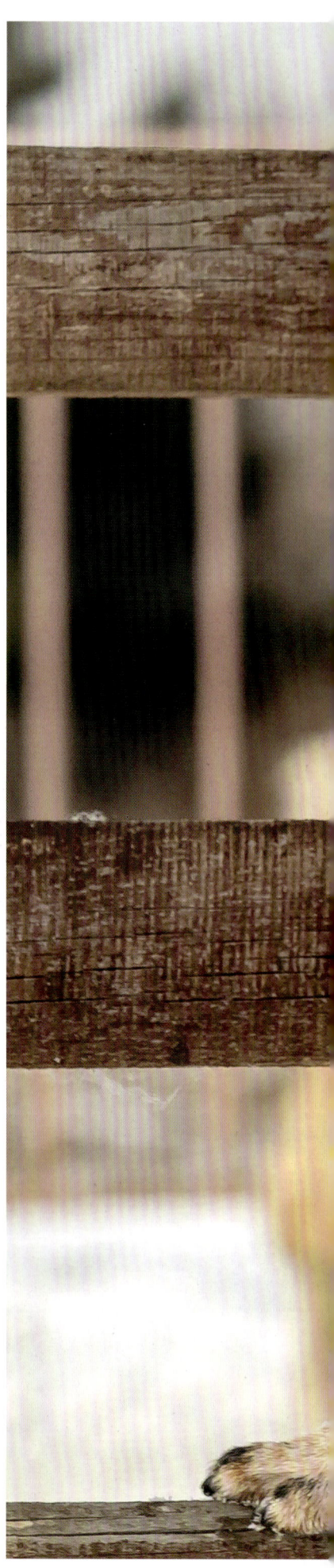

RIGHT:
Coat colours
There are two main colours, red and blue. Blue actually refers to a mid-grey, which only hints at blue, while red is the more familiar ginger or russet colouring.

WORKING DOGS

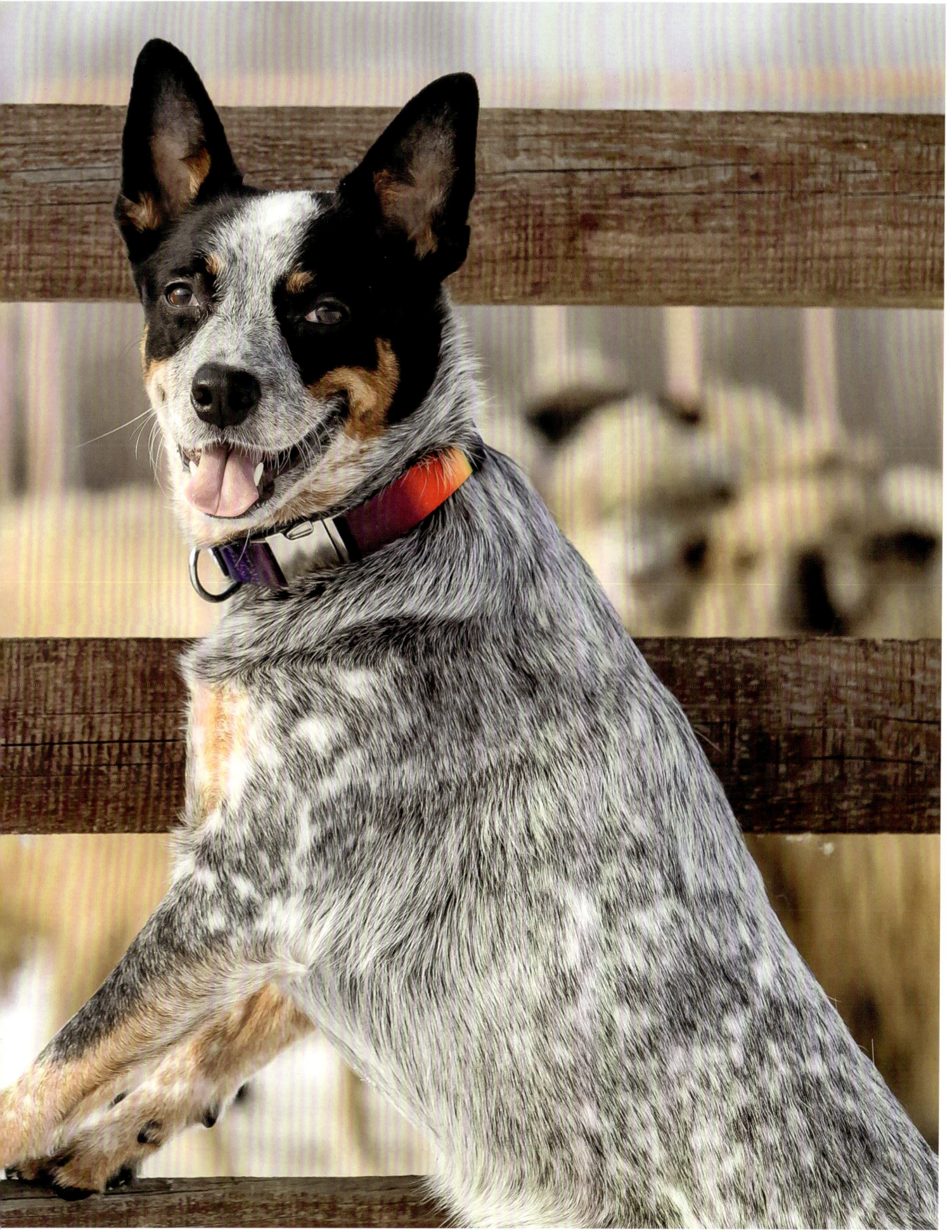

WORKING DOGS

Australian herder
Also known as the cattle dog, this is a very alert and eager breed. It drives cattle by nipping the heels of the larger animals.

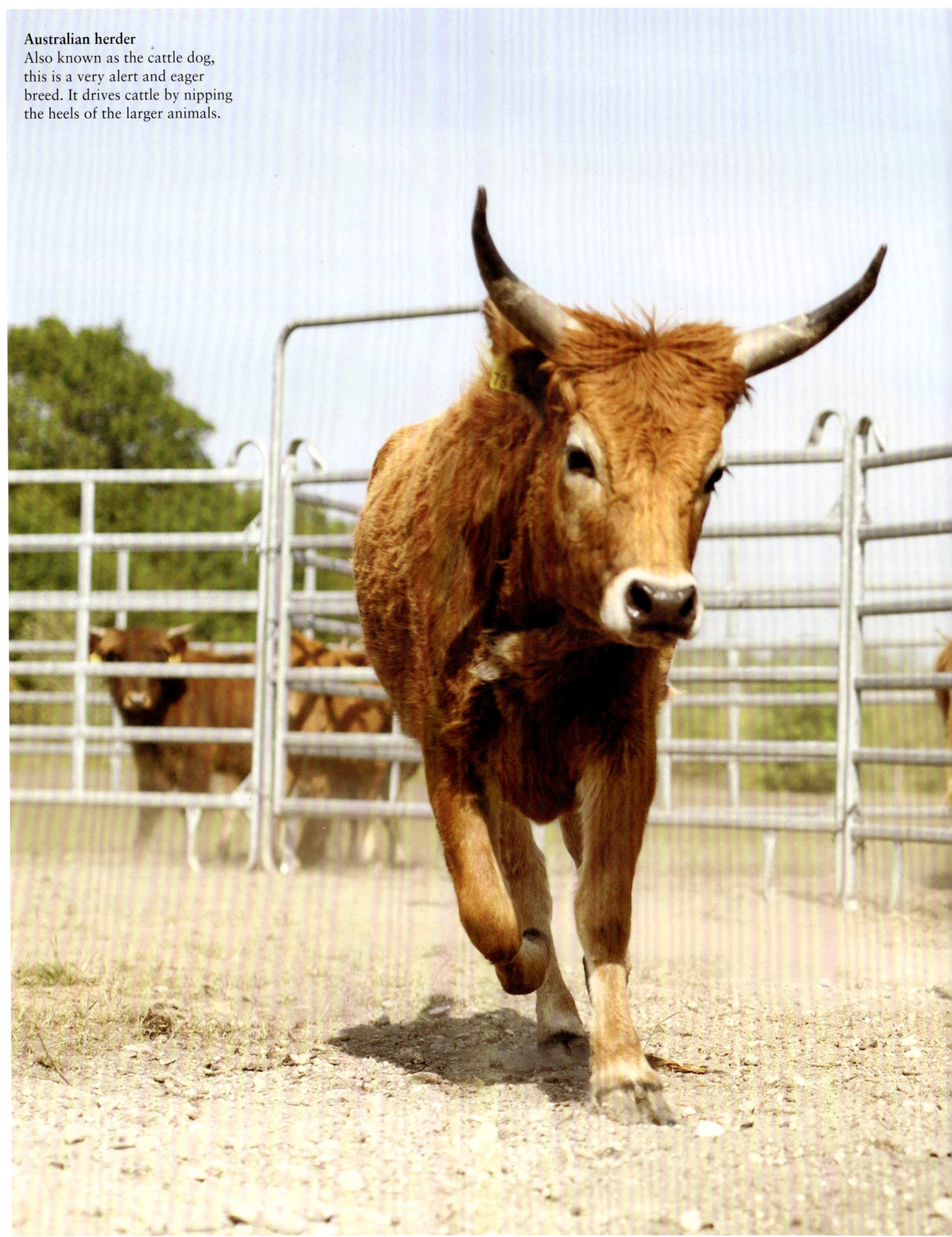

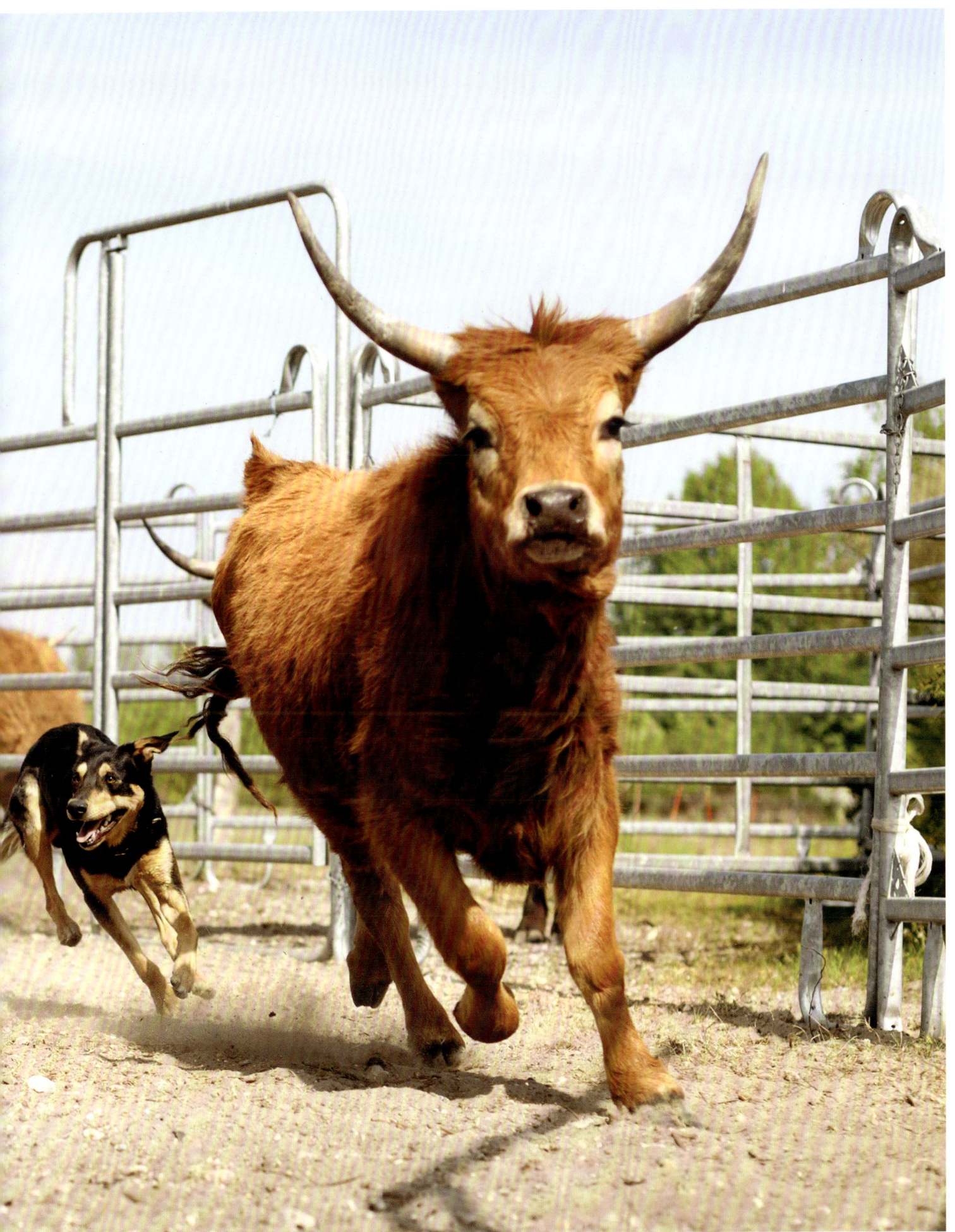

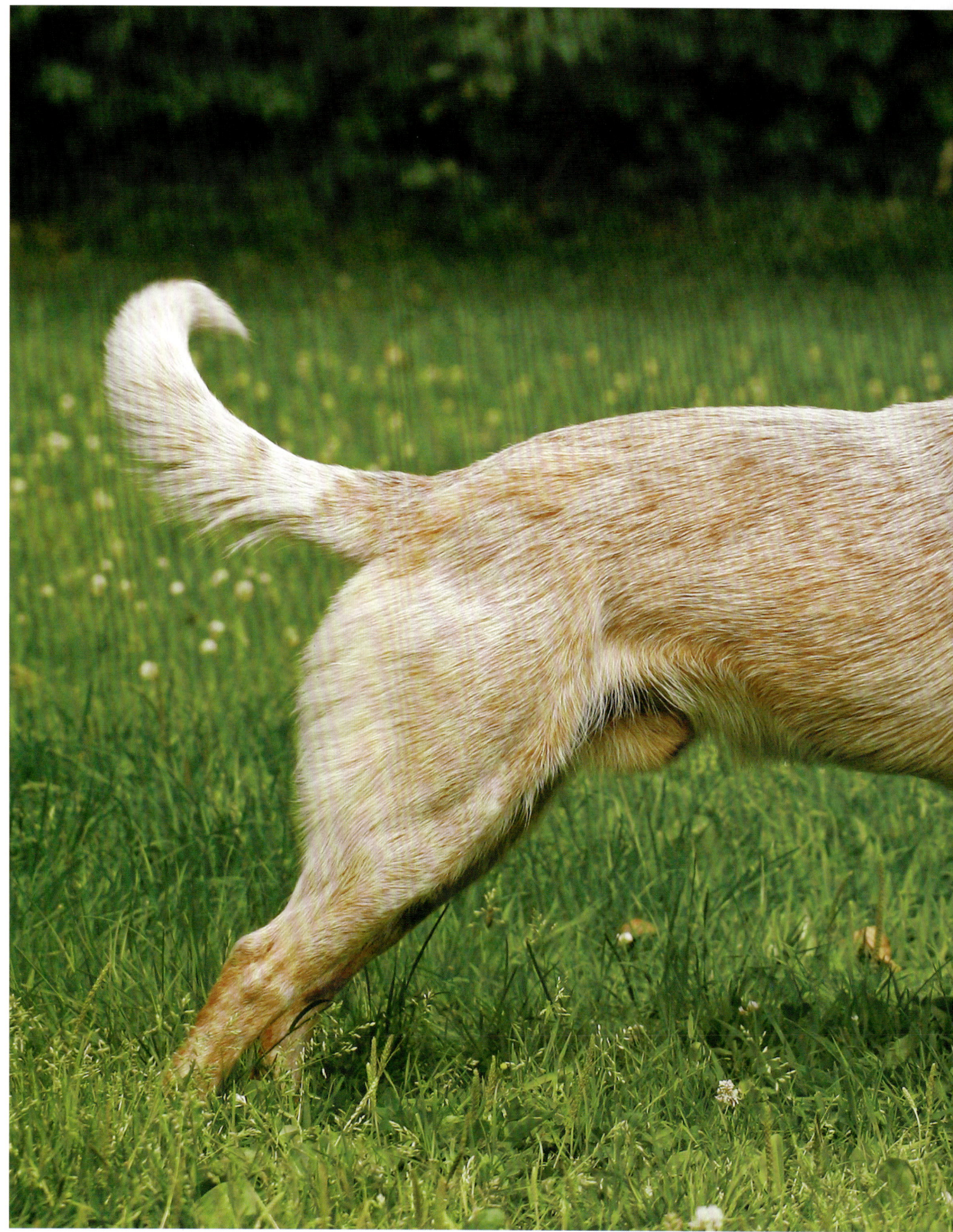

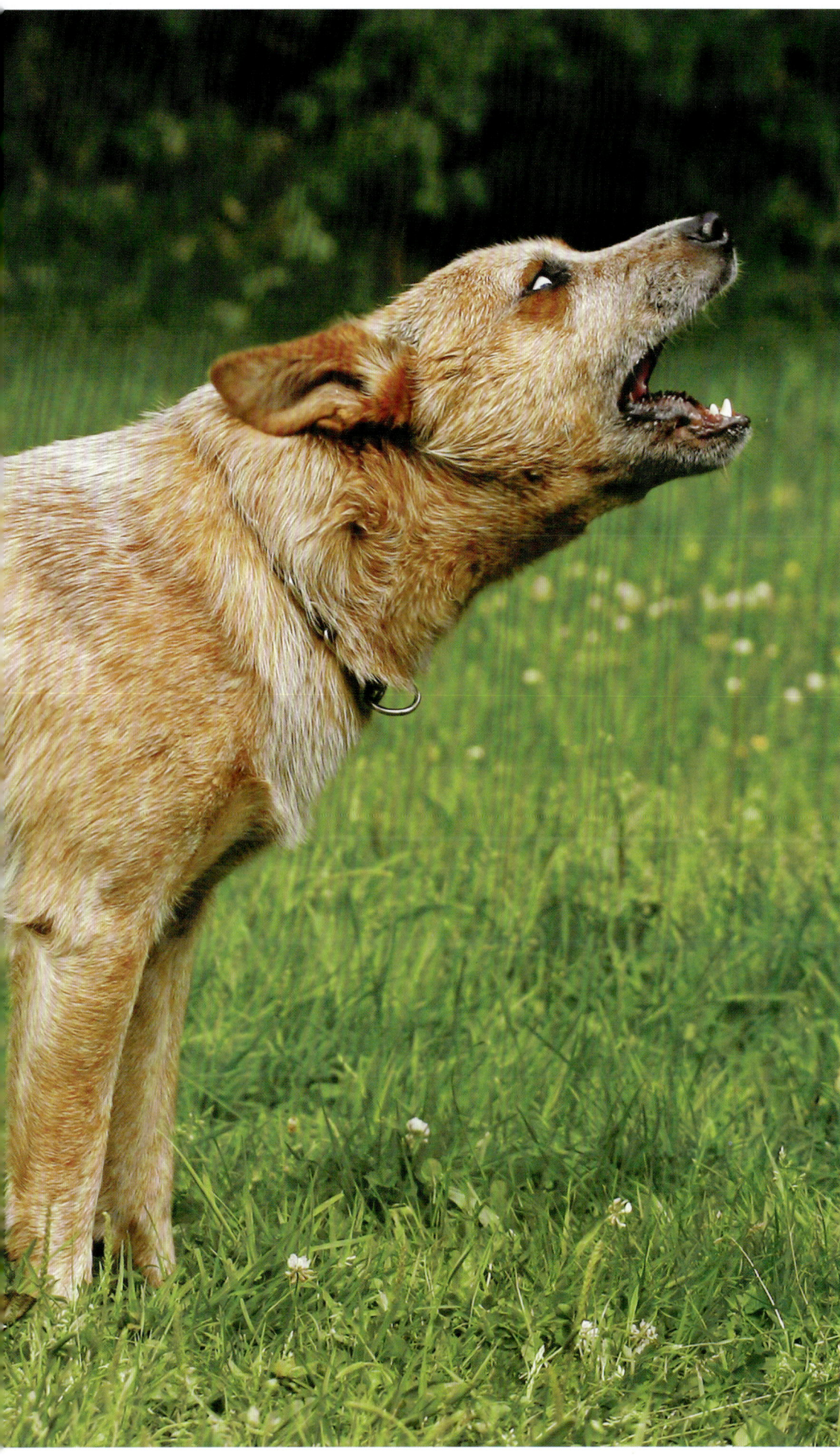

Barking

The howl is a wide-area signal, but barking is a more directing form of communication. For Australian cattle dogs it could be a call hello, or a question: "where have you gone?" It could also be an order: stay away or else.

WORKING DOGS

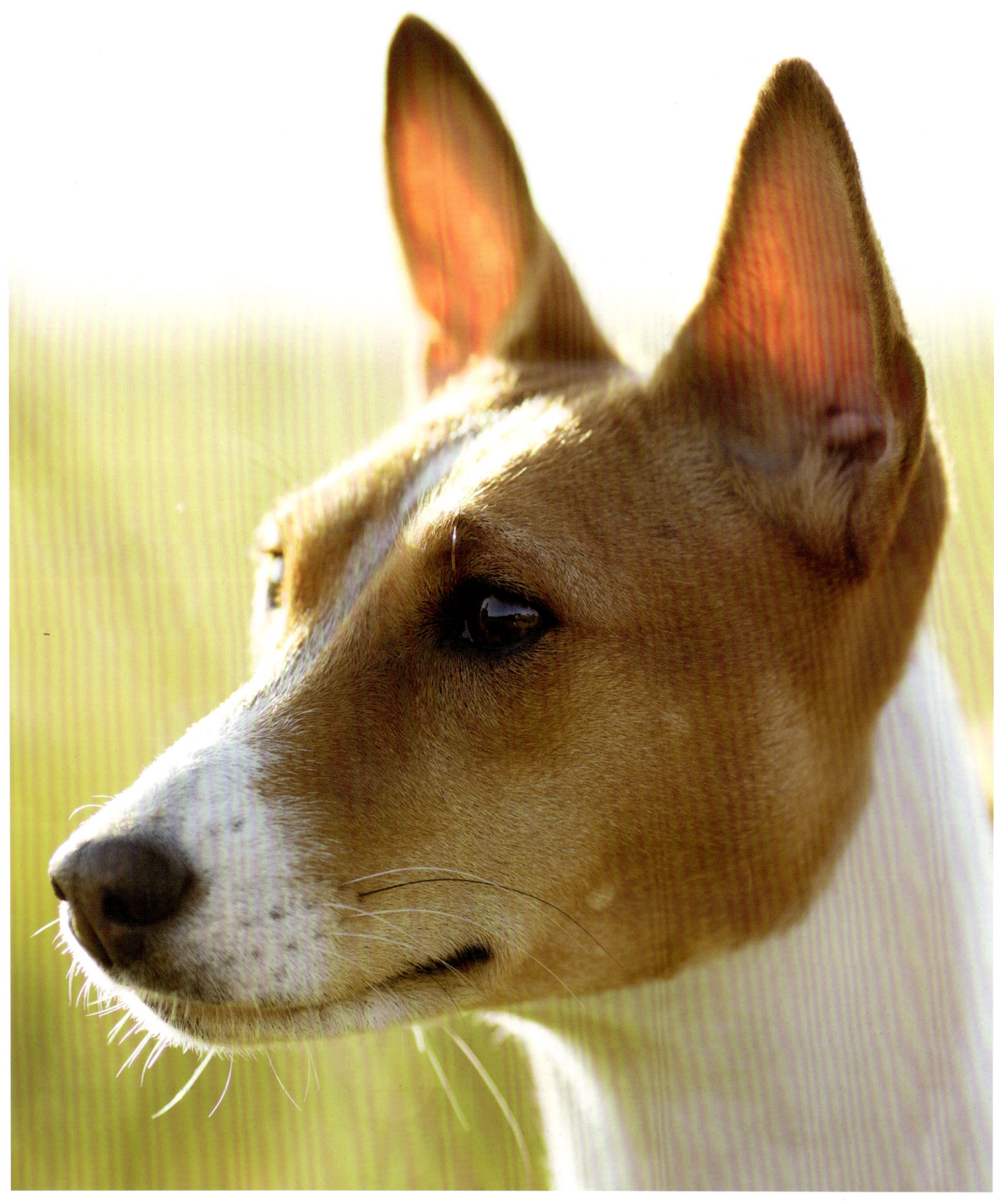

ABOVE:
Ancient profile
The dog has a long neck and narrow features that would not look out of of place on a mural in ancient Egypt.

Basenji

CHARACTERISTICS

Coat
Short and smooth with a wide variety of colours. The feet, chest and tip of the tail are often white

Height
40–43cm (16–17in)

Weight
10–11kg (22–24lb)

Lifespan
Over 10 years

Personality
Affectionate but independent

Origin
Africa

This small and smart African hunting dog is probably the most ancient breed recognized today. Its origins are lost in the midst of prehistory. The best we can muster is that the basenji was already a common breed by the days of ancient Egypt, and was living as far south as the Congo Basin in Central Africa. The name basenji means the "jumping up and down dog" and the compact breed, with their slender frames yet well-muscled hind quarters, do indeed display a remarkable ability to leap to great vertical heights.

A more memorable name for the basenji is the barkless dog. The breed is generally very quiet, and when compelled to vocalize produces a shrill whine or yodel instead of a woof. It sounds more like a cat than a dog, in fact. Additionally, the basenji grooms itself, like a cat, using its tongue to keep clean.

The basenji is an eager and friendly dog to people it knows and needs a lot of attention and exercise. Without that they can become stubbornly independent and resistant to training and instruction. This rare and interesting breed is not an easy family pet, but an obedient companion for an owner familiar with keeping dogs.

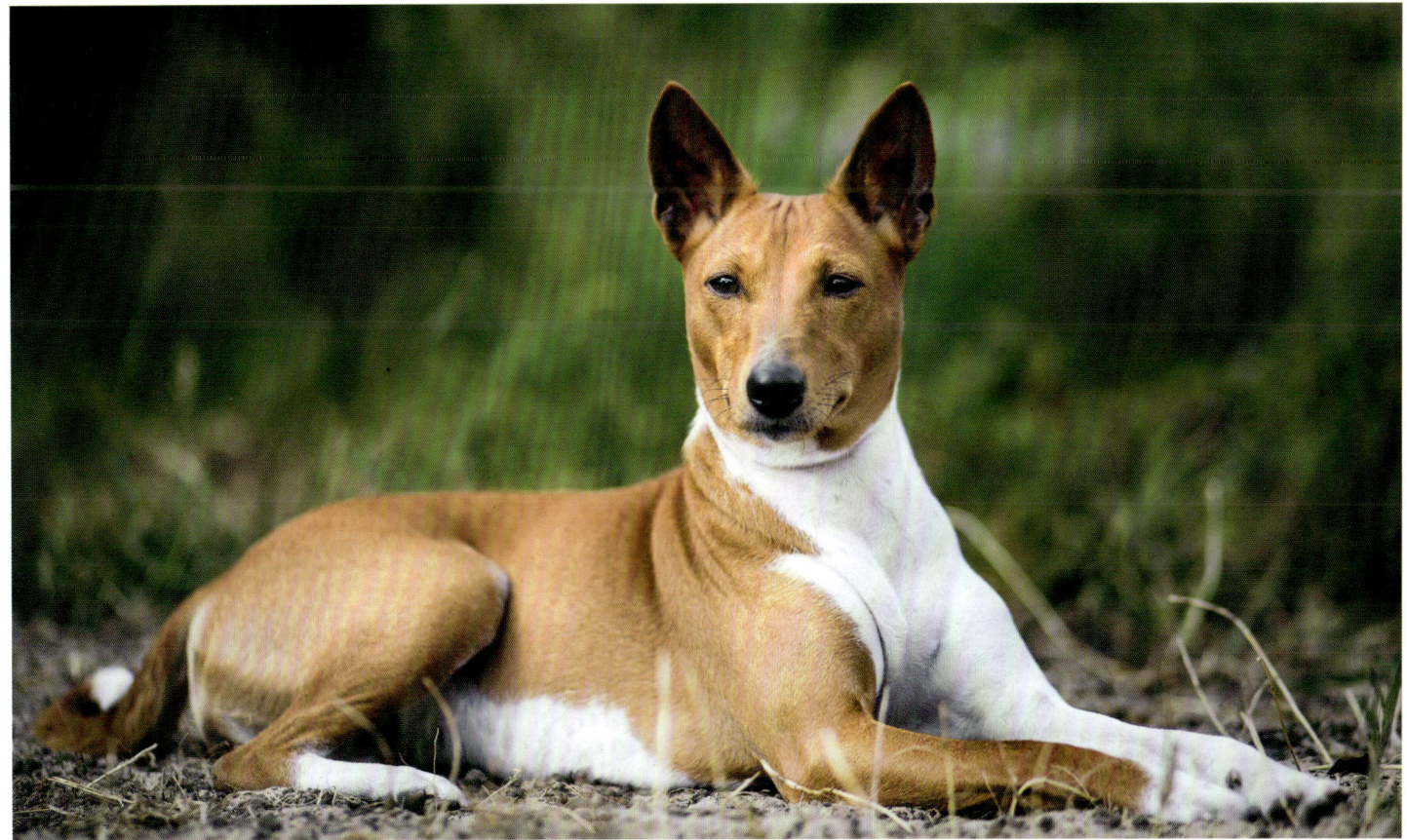

ABOVE:
Frown
The basenji's forehead indicates its mood. These wrinkles show the dog is alert and monitoring the goings on around it.

WORKING DOGS

RIGHT:
Growing up
As it gets older, this African dog will become chunkier.

OPPOSITE:
Hunter
This African hunting dog is hard to train but is a persistent and intelligent hunter.

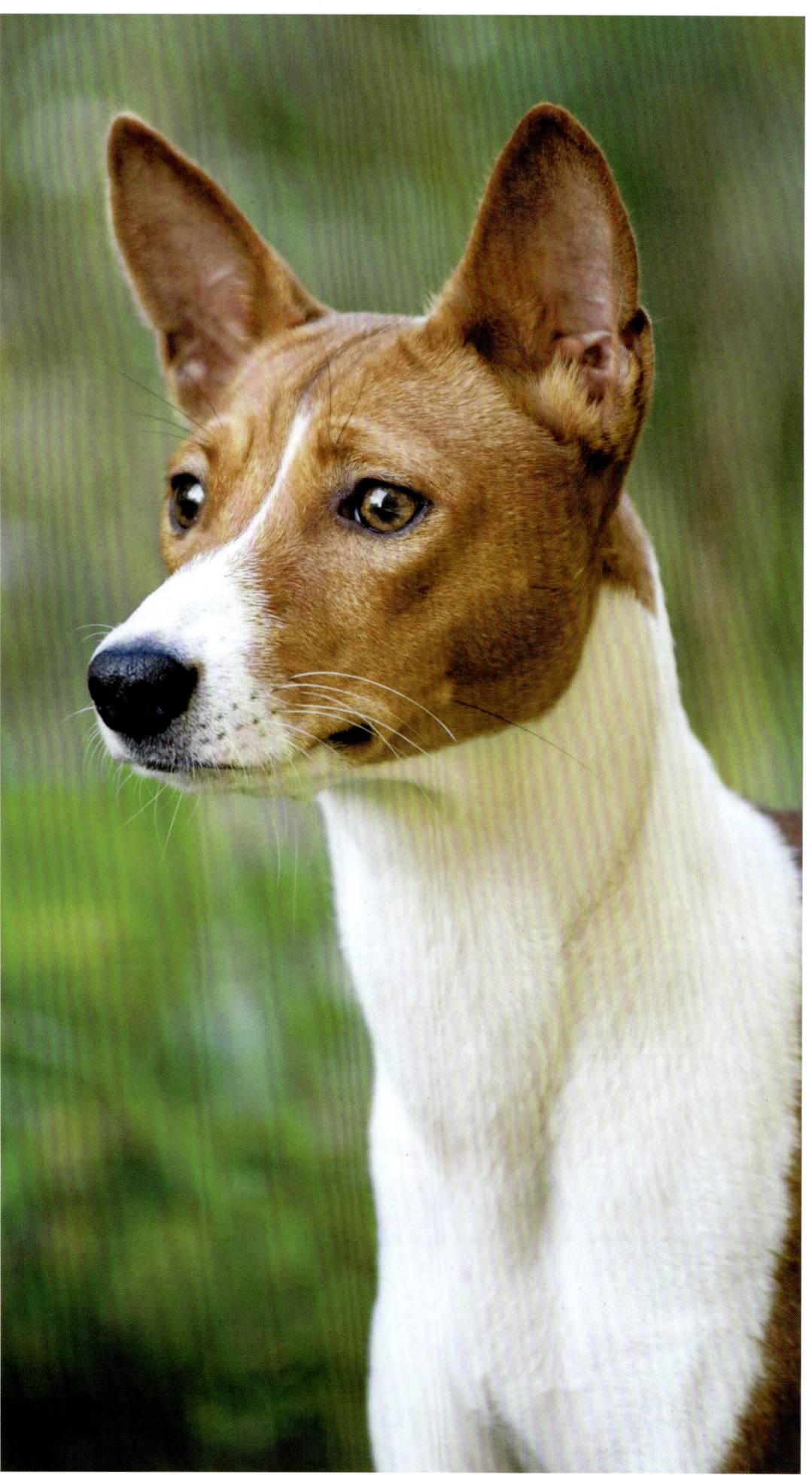

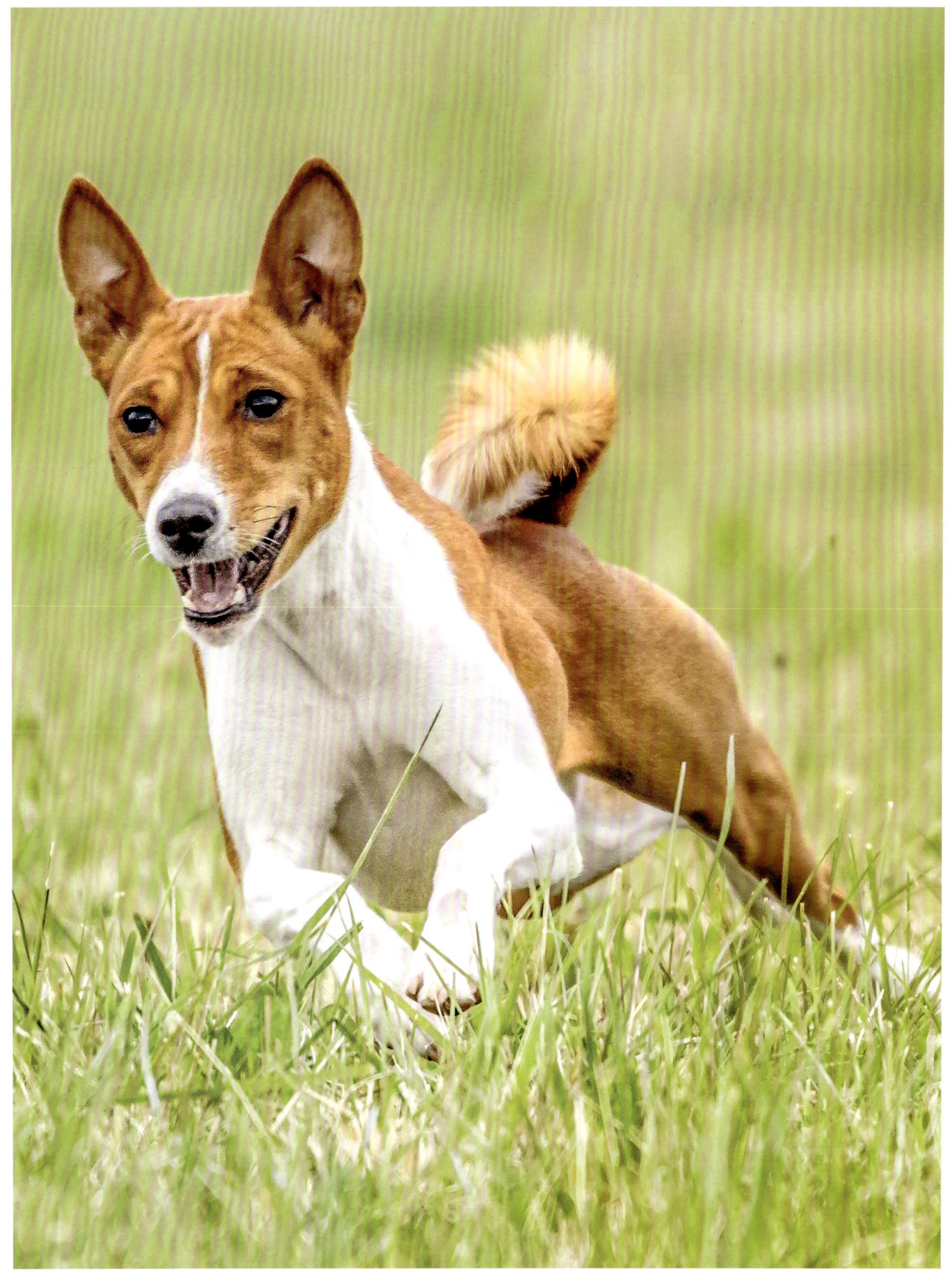

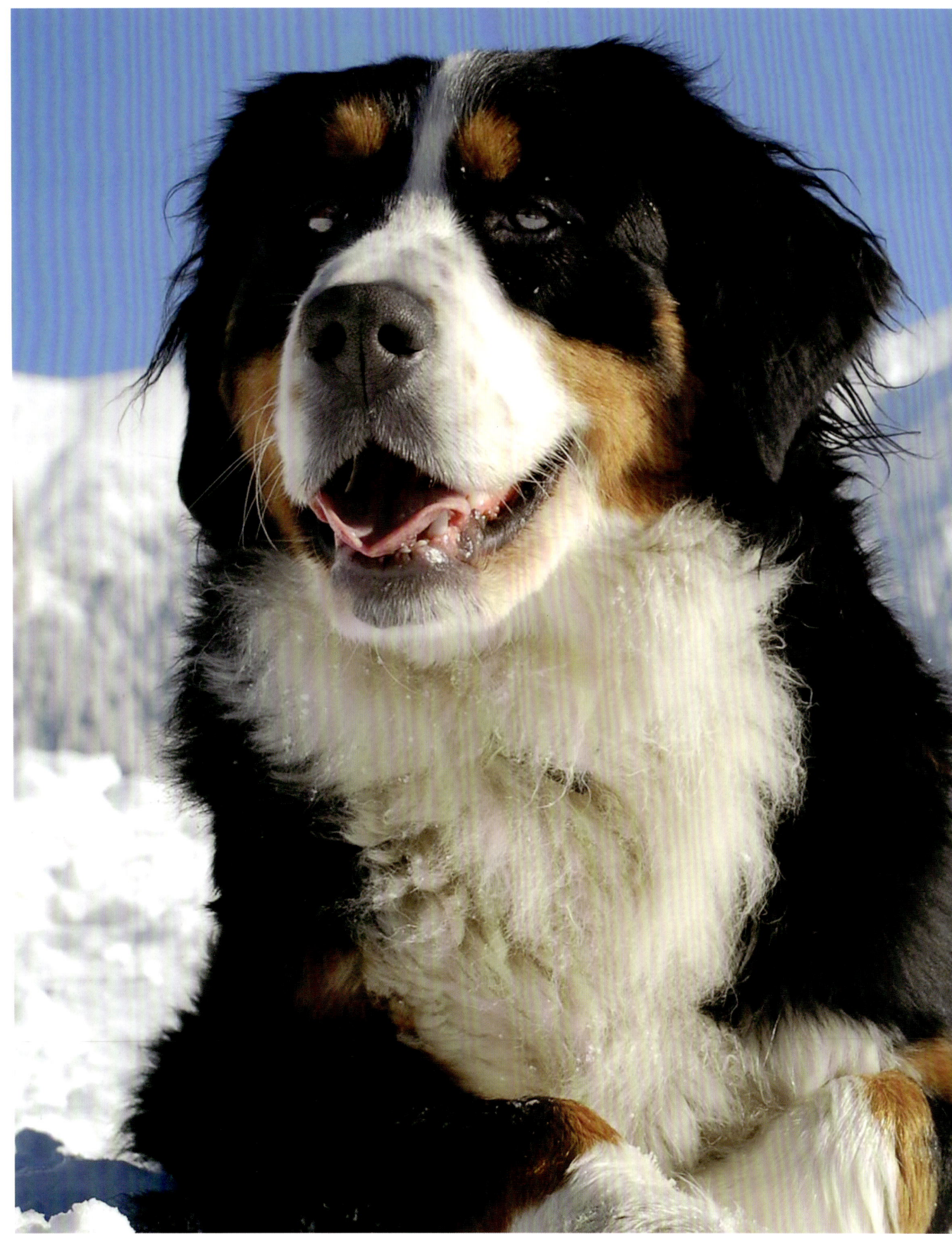

WORKING DOGS

Bernese Mountain Dog

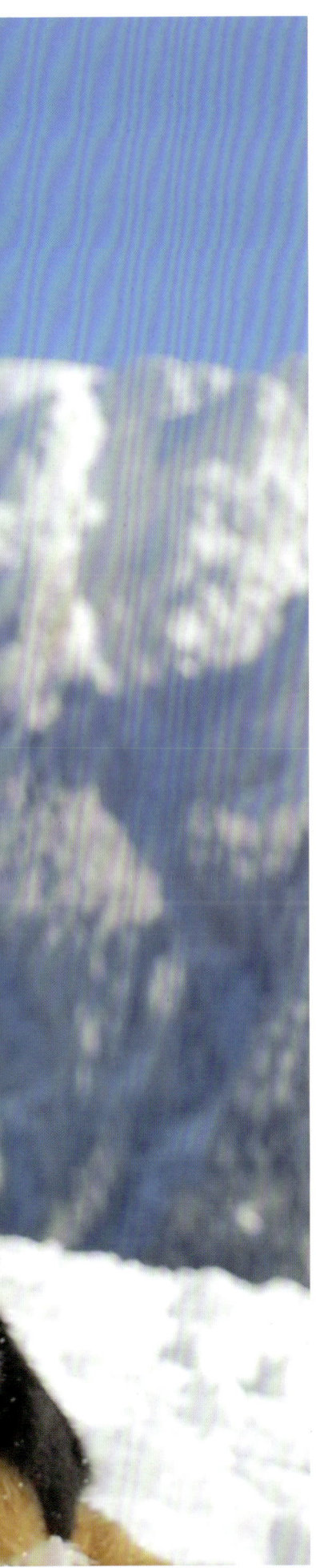

This immense, strong yet wonderfully placid working dog is named after Bern, the often overlooked capital of Switzerland. The breed was developed to work in the Swiss Alps in cattle farms and dairies. Its jobs were to drive herds, protect animals from wolves and even be harnessed to carts and haul loads of cheese and milk.

The Bernese mountain dog typically has a tricolour coat, mostly black with white and rust markings seen on the face, chest and legs. The long, glossy fur covers an insulating woolly underfur which stays warm and dry even in snow, rain and strong mountain winds. As a result the dog needs regular brushing to prevent the longer hairs matting. A pet mountain dog will shed a lot of fur, and eat a lot of food! Owners should monitor their weight. On the plus side, Bernese mountain dogs are a very playful and welcoming addition to a family, although its owners must be prepared to give it a lot of attention and exercise the dog regularly in plenty of space to emulate its mountain homeland as much as possible.

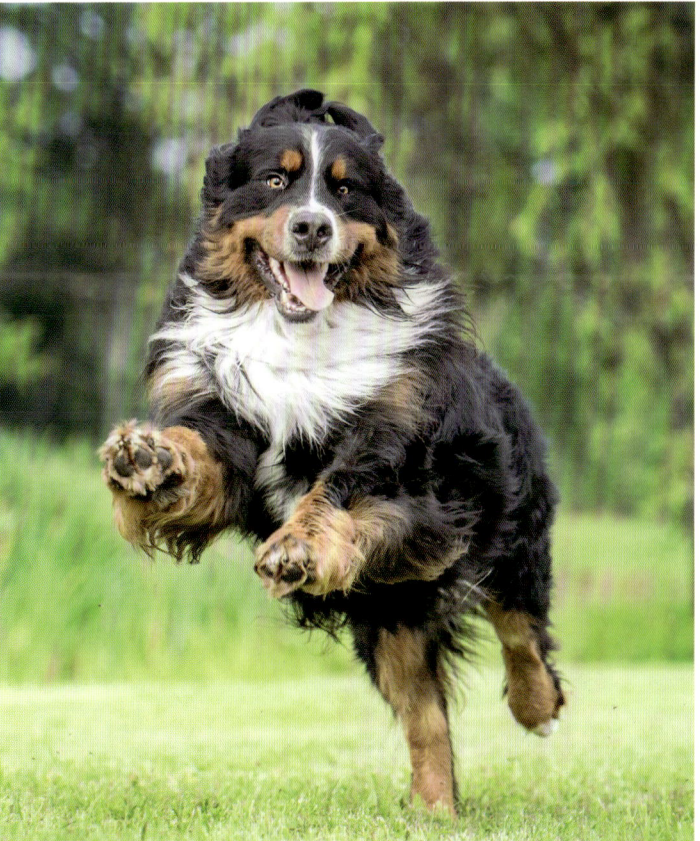

CHARACTERISTICS

Coat
Double coat is long and glossy with three colours: black on the back, reddish brown on the legs and belly, with white on the chest and muzzle

Height
58–70cm (23–28ln)

Weight
32–54kg (71–120lb)

Lifespan
Less than 10 years

Personality
Reliable and fun-loving

Origin
Switzerland

LEFT:
Alpine breeds
This is one of the mountain dog breeds, or Sennenhunds, descended from Roman mastiffs that came to this area 2,000 years ago and are much-loved companions for Alpine workers.

ABOVE:
Slobbering
The breed is a profuse drooler and is also prone to some stomach and skeletal health issues, shortening the average lifespan.

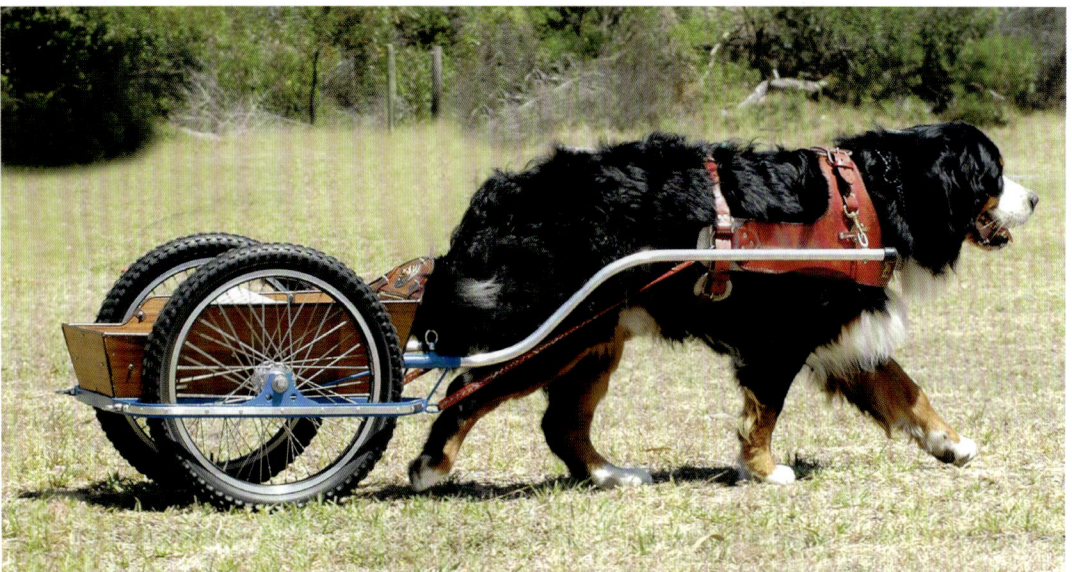

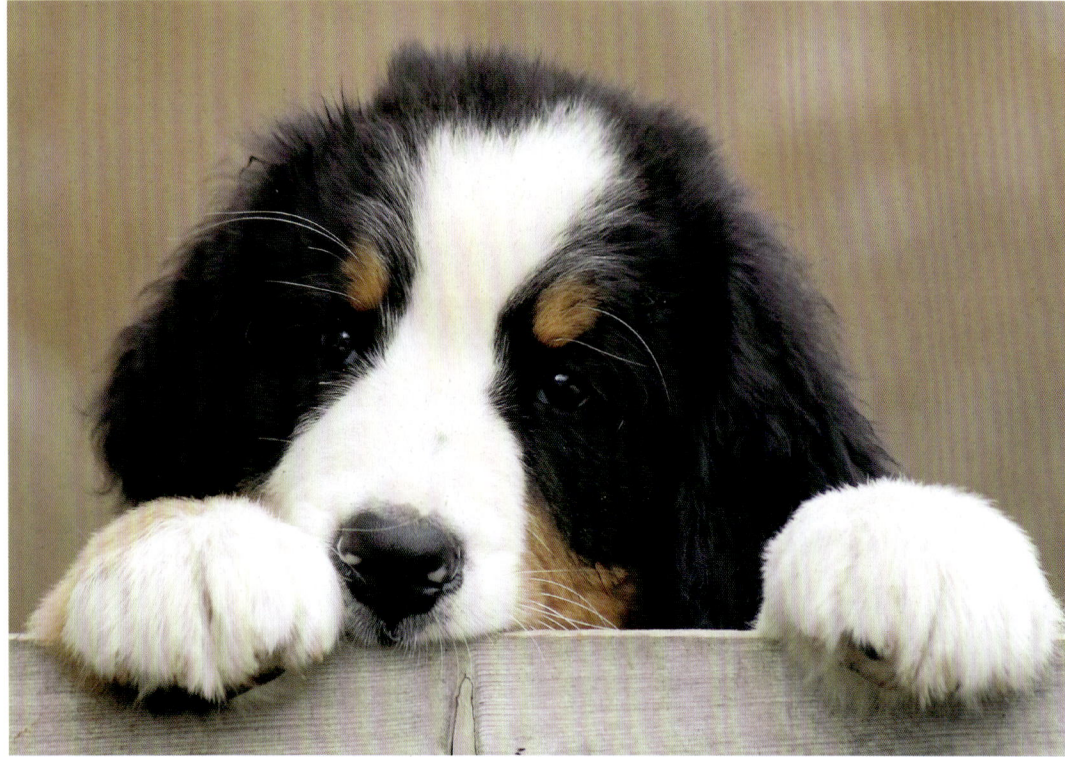

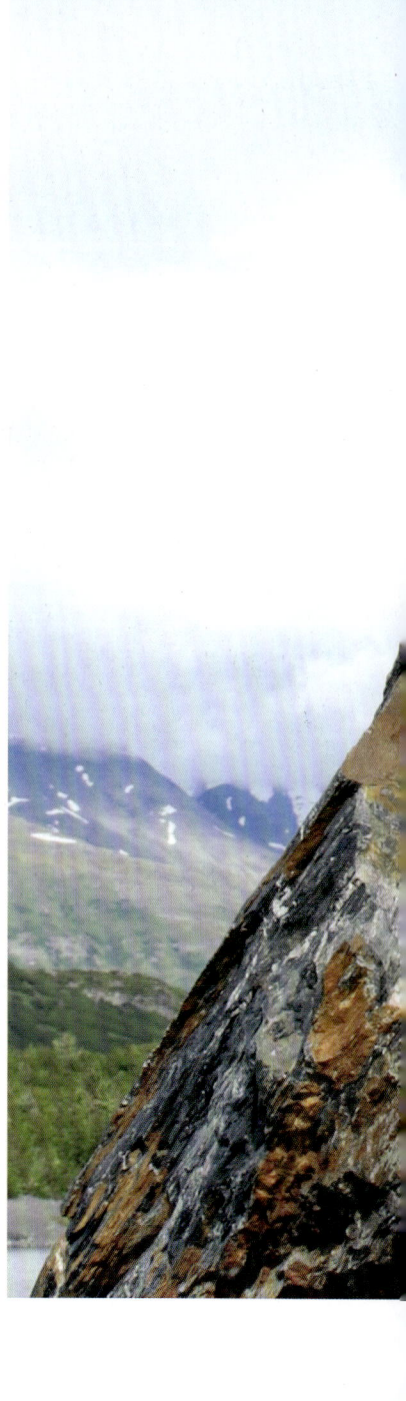

ABOVE BOTTOM:
Out and about
Once strong enough – and fully vaccinated – Bernese puppies should be allowed out and about to explore. The first 100 days of life are a critical time for the dog, when it learns so much about the world.

ABOVE TOP AND RIGHT:
Out for a hike
One of the largest breeds in the world, this Swiss dog was used as an all-round worker in alpine farms, even hauling carts laden with milk and cheese.

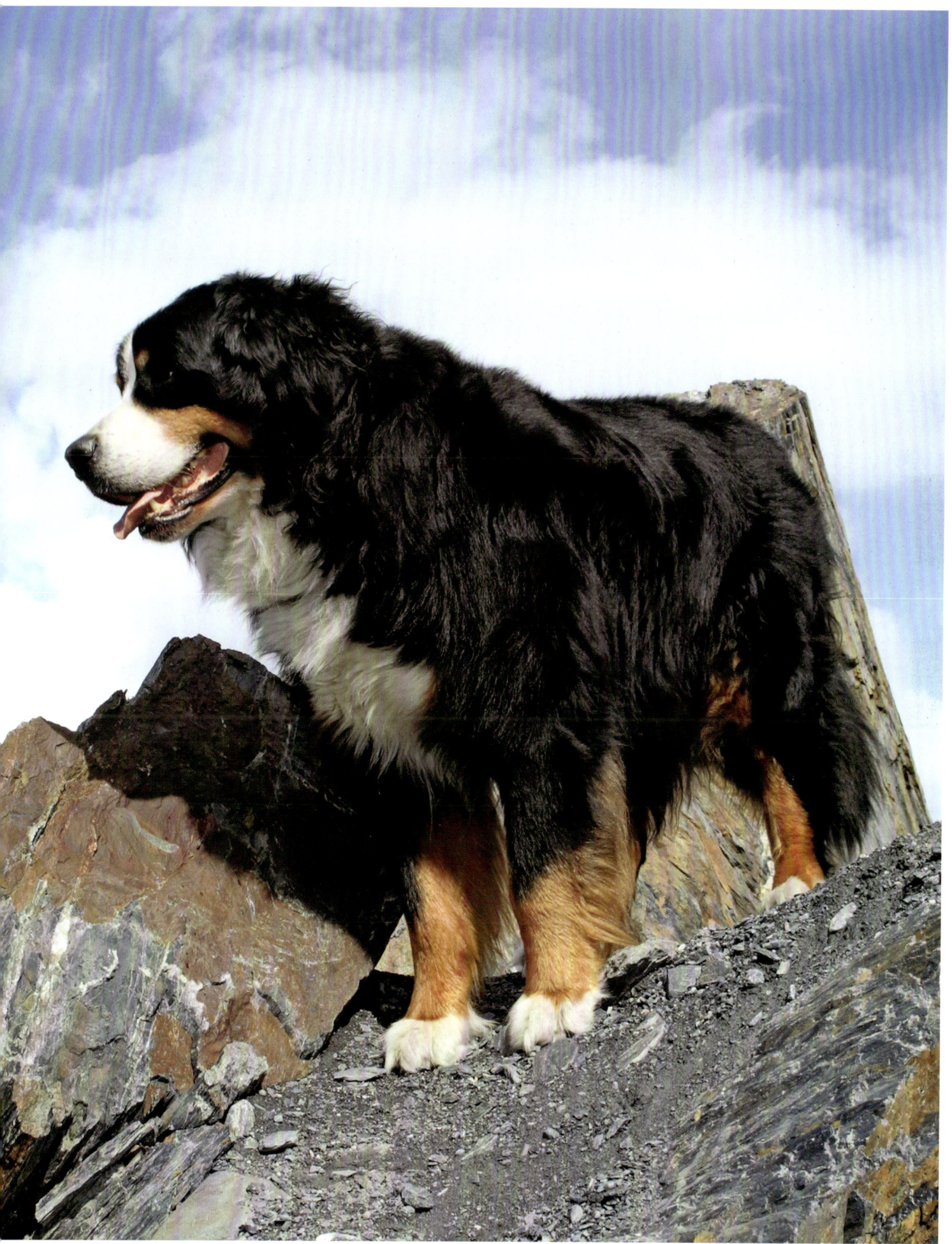

WORKING DOGS

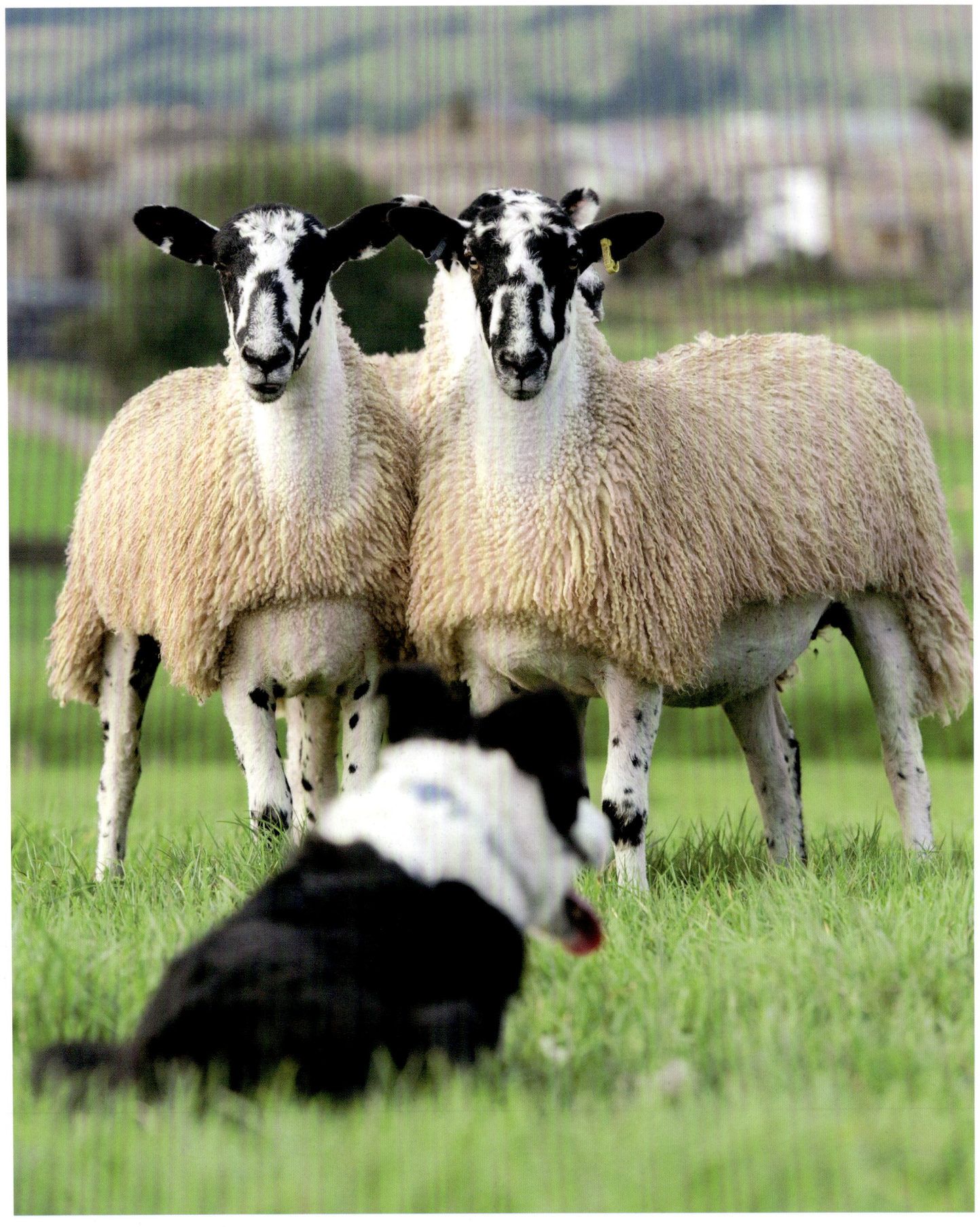

ABOVE:
At work
The border collie is most at home outside among a flock of sheep.

Border Collie

CHARACTERISTICS

Coat
Medium length and feathered, double, brush daily during shed, normally black and white but also has a variety of colours

Height
50–53cm (20–21in)

Weight
12–20kg (26–44lb)

Lifespan
Over 10 years

Personality
Intelligent and hardworking

Origin
England and Scotland

Hailing from the Scotland–England borderlands, this hardy and intelligent herding dog is the descendent of an illustrious hybrid. This region of Britain was at the edge of the Roman Empire, and the colonists brought with them heavy-set herding dogs. Centuries later, the area was the heartland of Viking invaders, who used smaller and more nimble sheepdogs. When these two working breeds were crossed they produced the border collie, which embodied their combined traits: obedience, toughness, speed and intelligence.

The border collie is often described as the world's best herding dog able to outwit and outrun livestock hour after hour. It has an intense gaze that is always taking in what is going on—the breed's so-called "herding eye". When transferred to a daily home, the dog's instincts and abilities can make it hard to handle. Owners of border collies tend to be experienced with dogs and able to put in the time needed to give their pets the attention and stimulation they need. Socialization is very important with this breed and has to be a focus for the first several months of the dog's life.

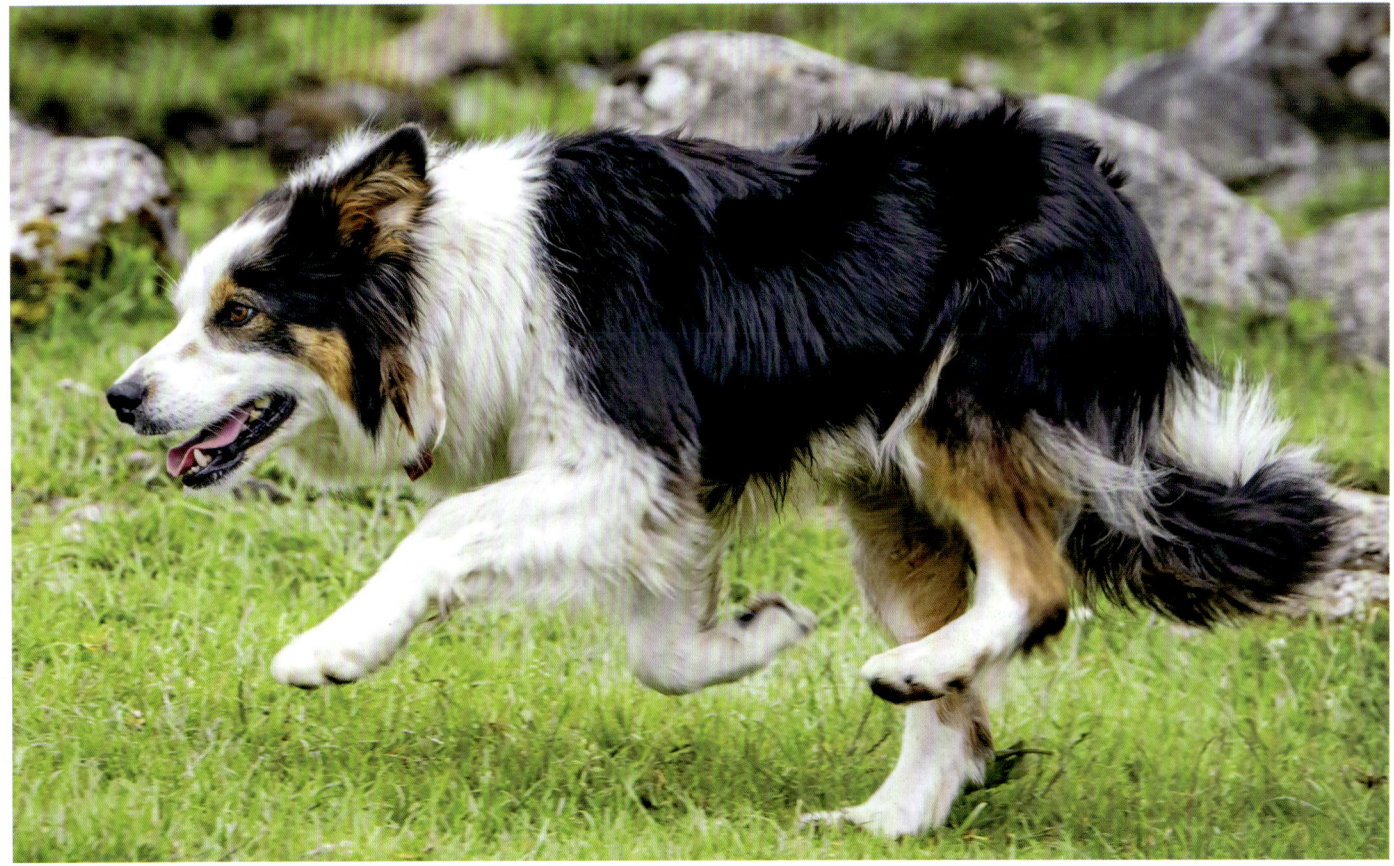

ABOVE:
Eager to please
The breed is especially disposed to agility training, learning to complete obstacle courses and perform physical feats as an outlet for its driving work ethic.

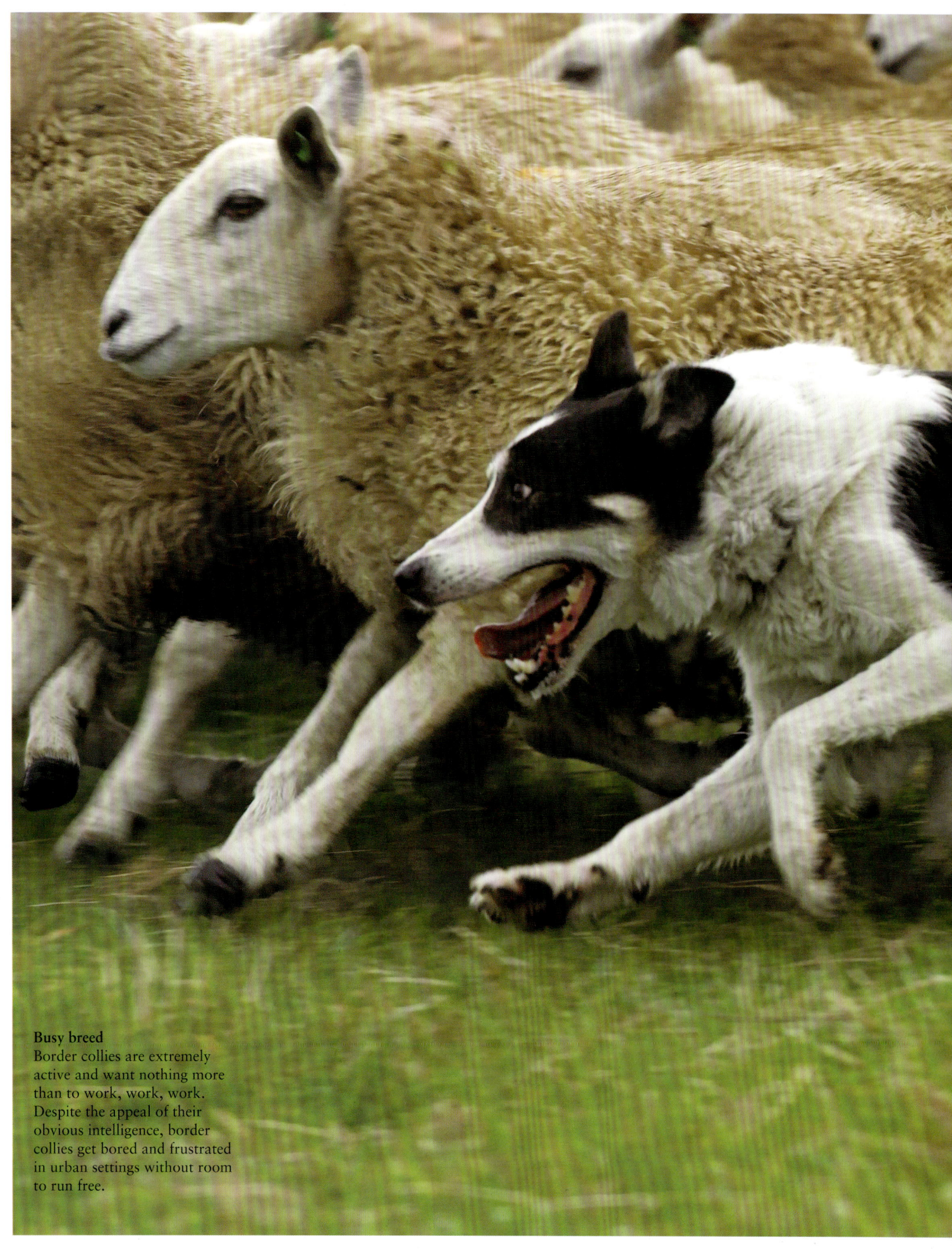

Busy breed
Border collies are extremely active and want nothing more than to work, work, work. Despite the appeal of their obvious intelligence, border collies get bored and frustrated in urban settings without room to run free.

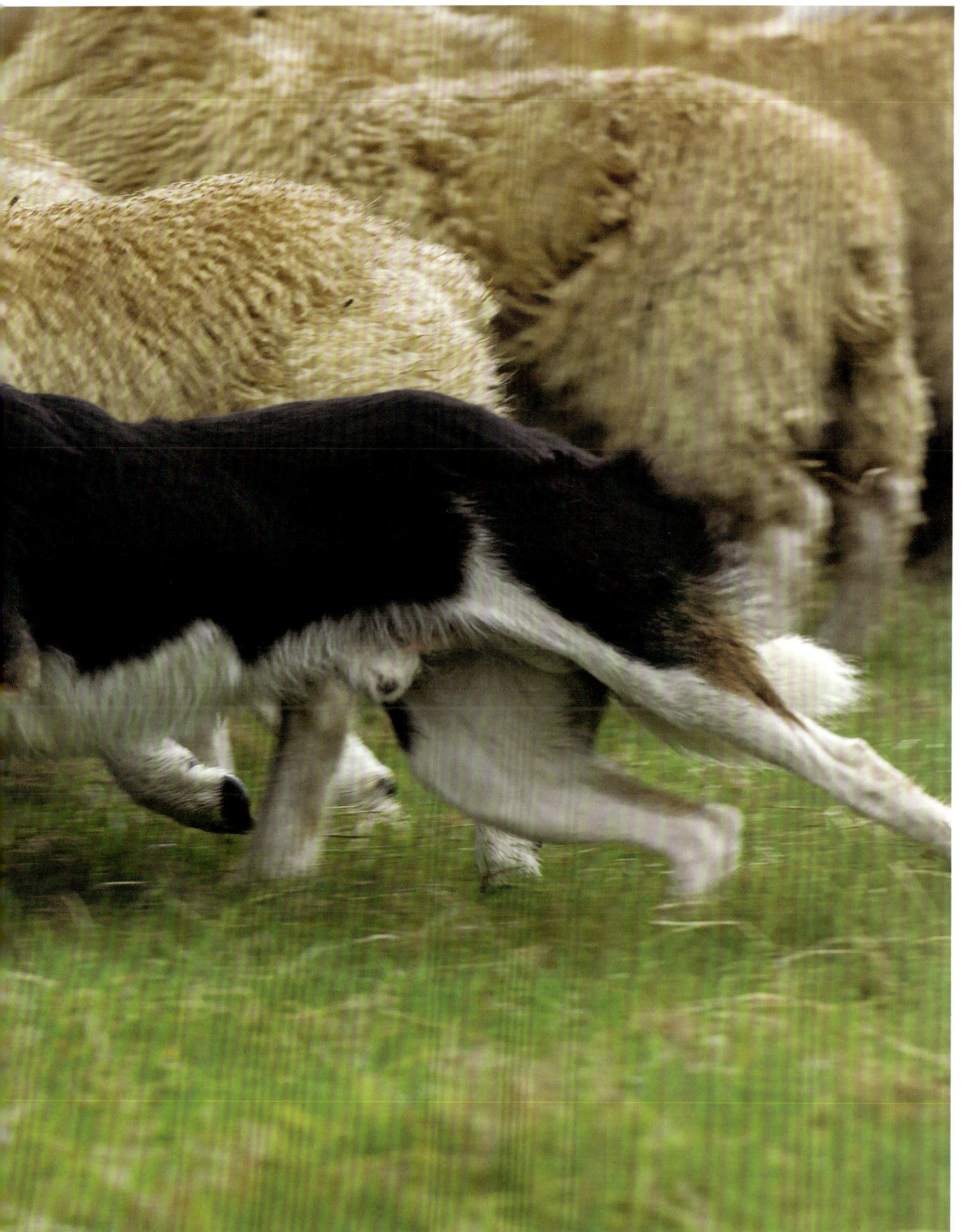

WORKING DOGS

RIGHT TOP:
Perfect puppies
Maintaining the pedigree, or quality of border collies, means careful breeding to ensure that puppies do not inherit unwanted or indeed harmful traits.

RIGHT BOTTOM:
Play time
This border collie is busy having fun. This dog needs exercise and stimulation.

OPPOSITE RIGHT BOTTOM:
Beach days
A pair of border collie puppies plays on the beach. These dogs will probably have little time for play once they are old enough to work as sheepdogs – and that is the way they like it!

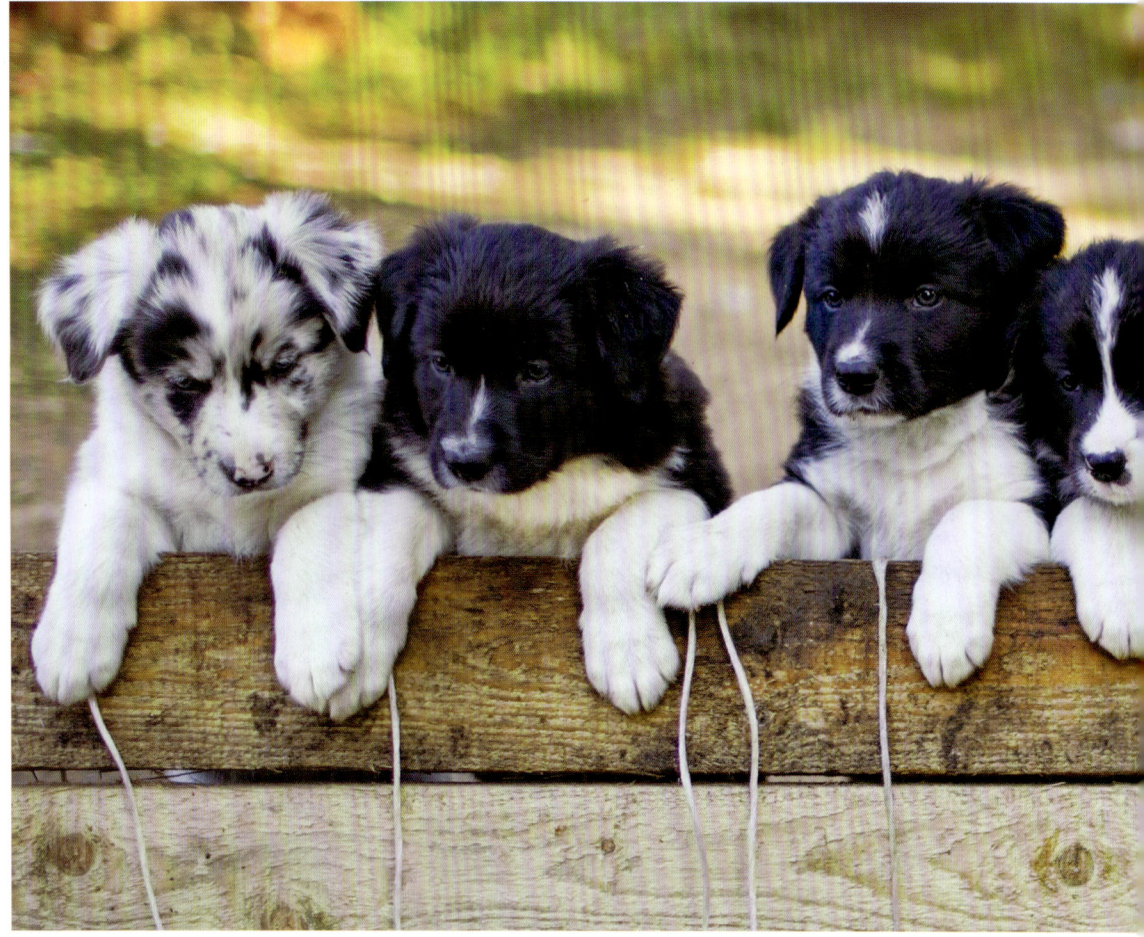

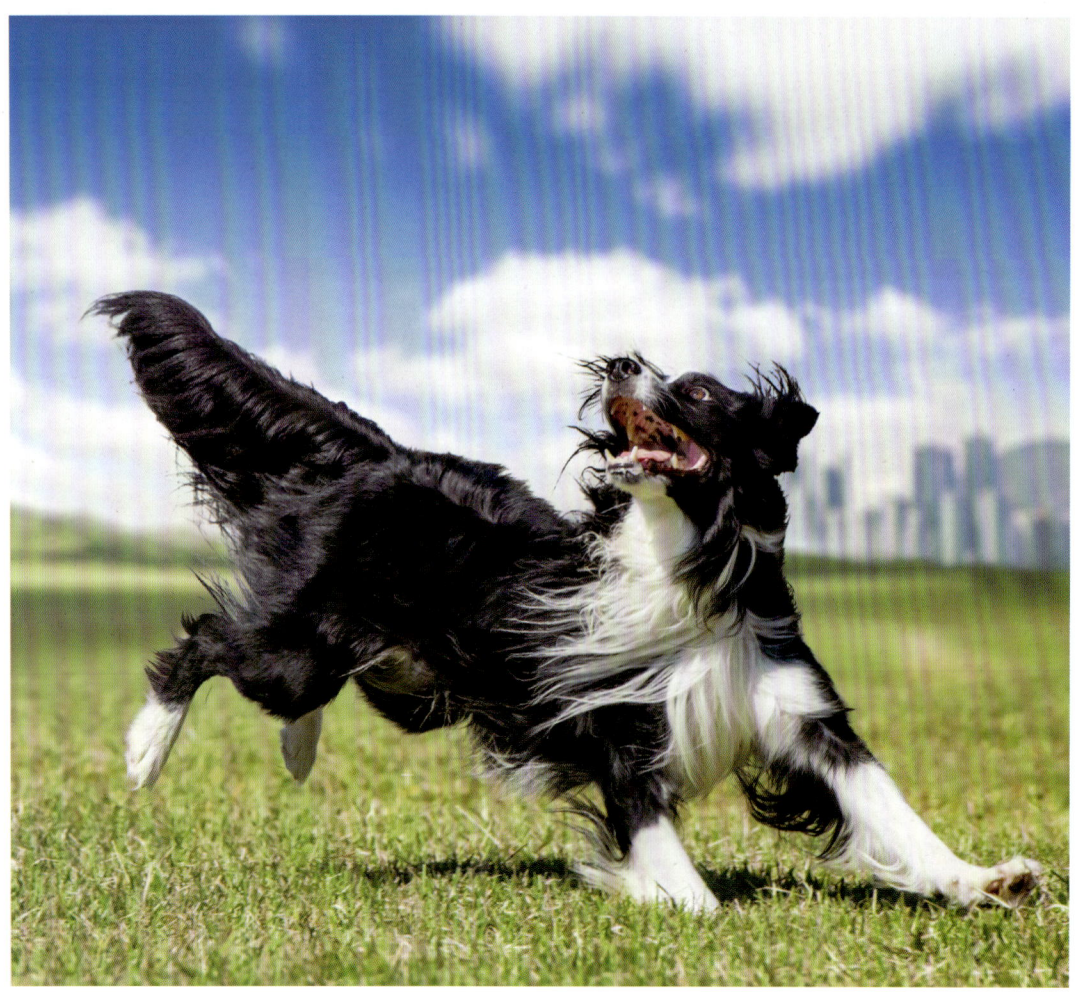

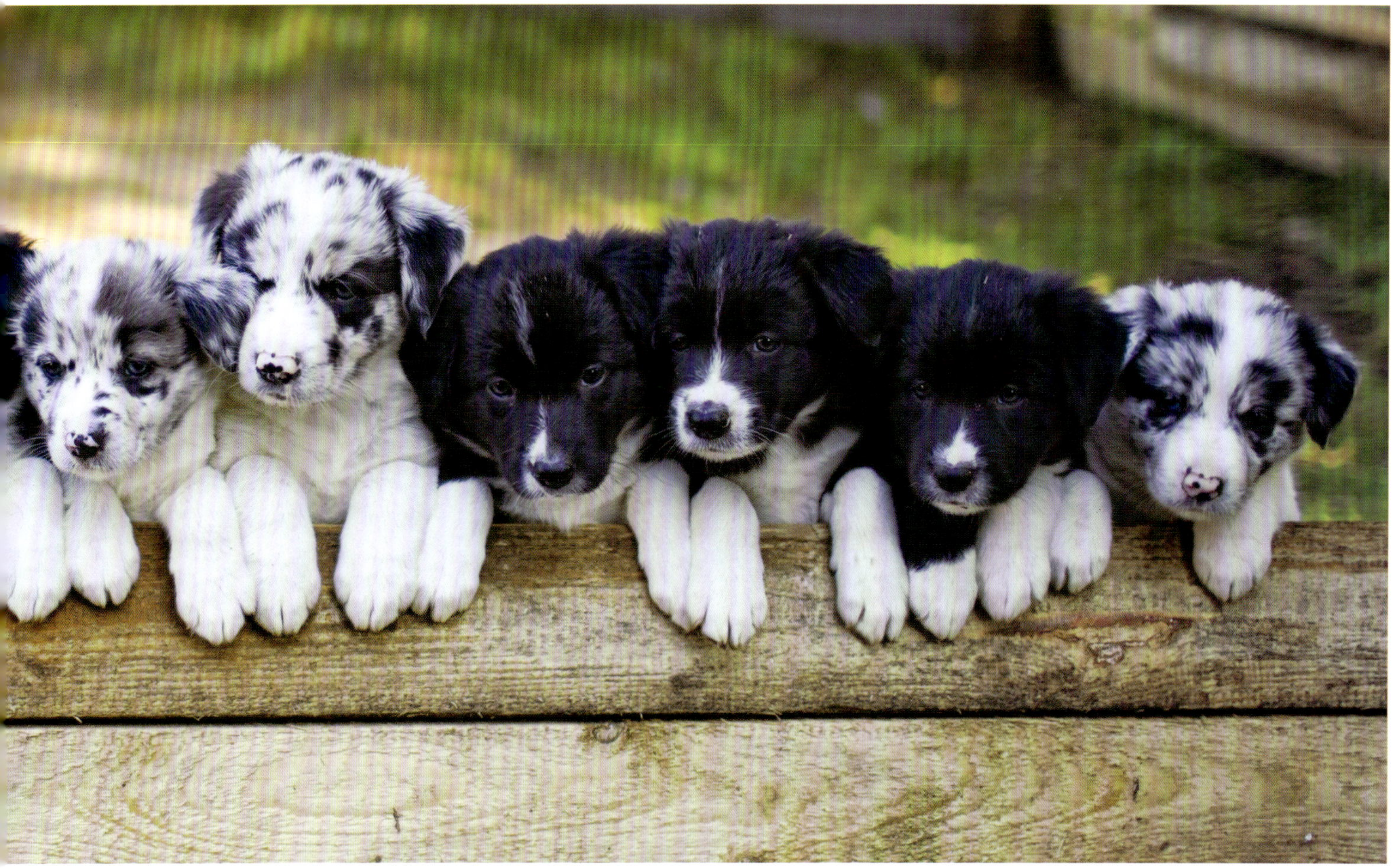

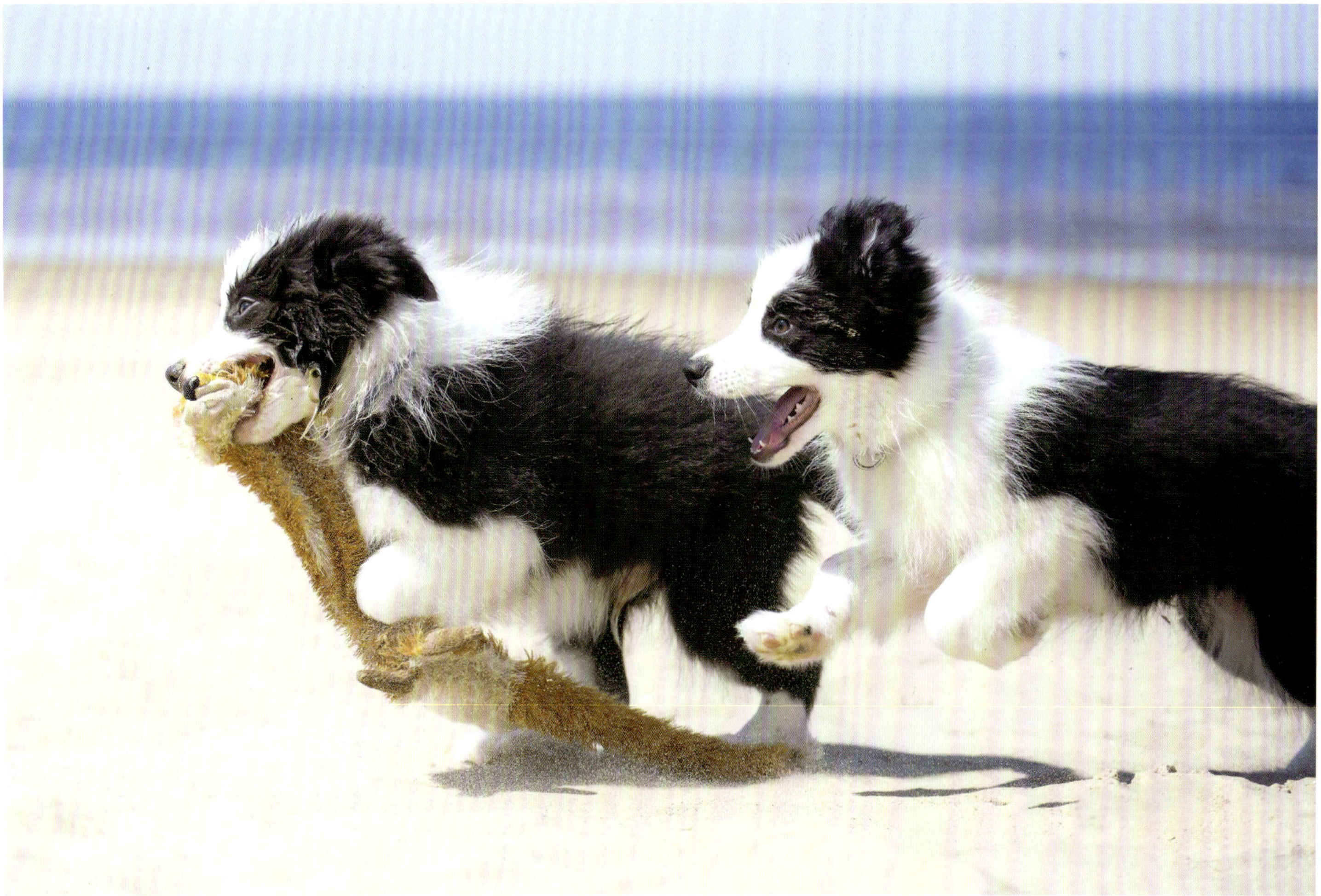

WORKING DOGS

325

WORKING DOGS

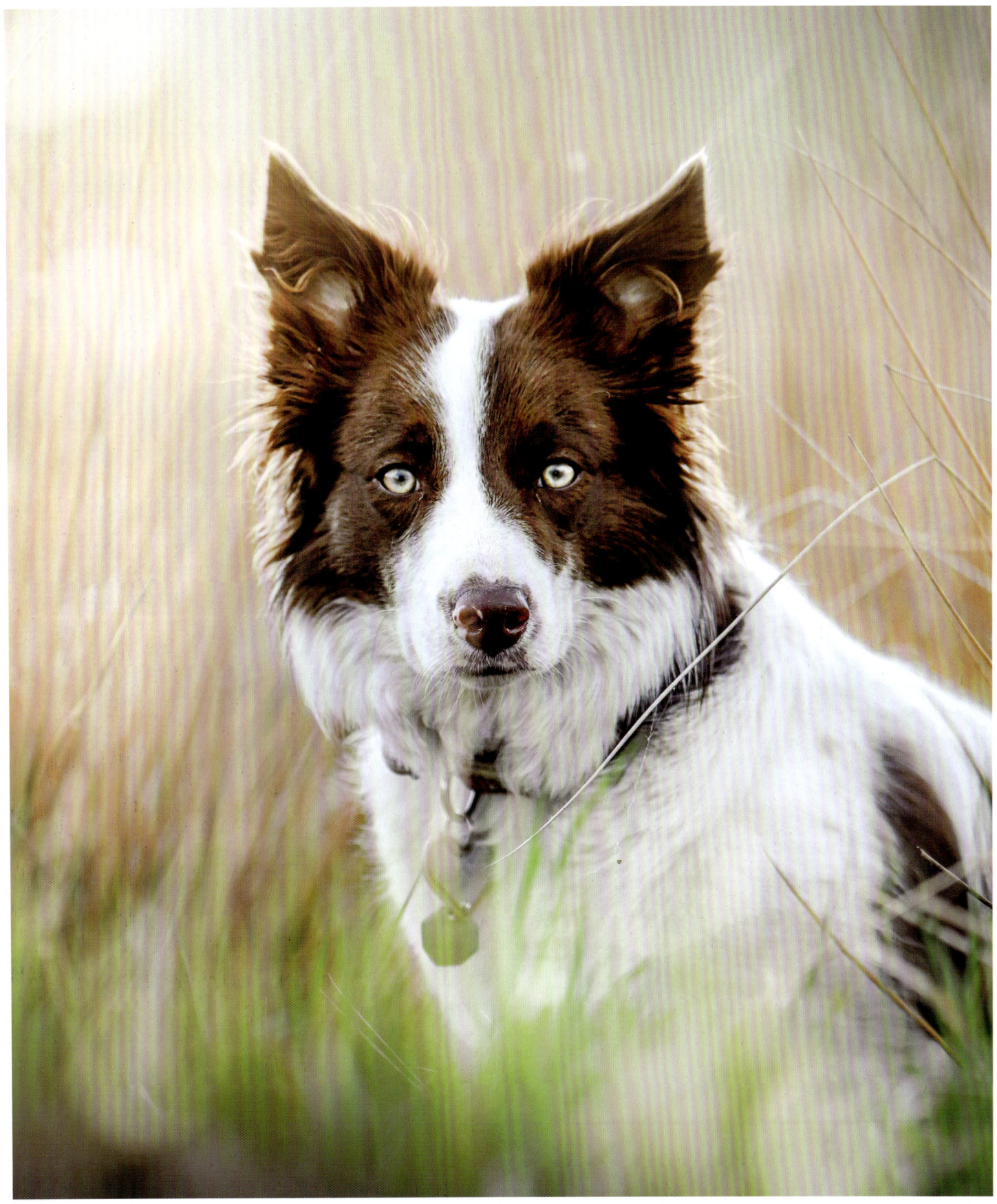

ABOVE:
Sheepdog
Radiating intelligence, this is the superlative sheepdog breed. The "border" in the name refers to the moorland region – filled with sheep farms – that forms the borderland between England and Scotland.

OPPOSITE:
Barking
Perhaps more than any other common breed, this dog requires plenty of exercise and active play to avoid frustration or excessive yowling and noise.

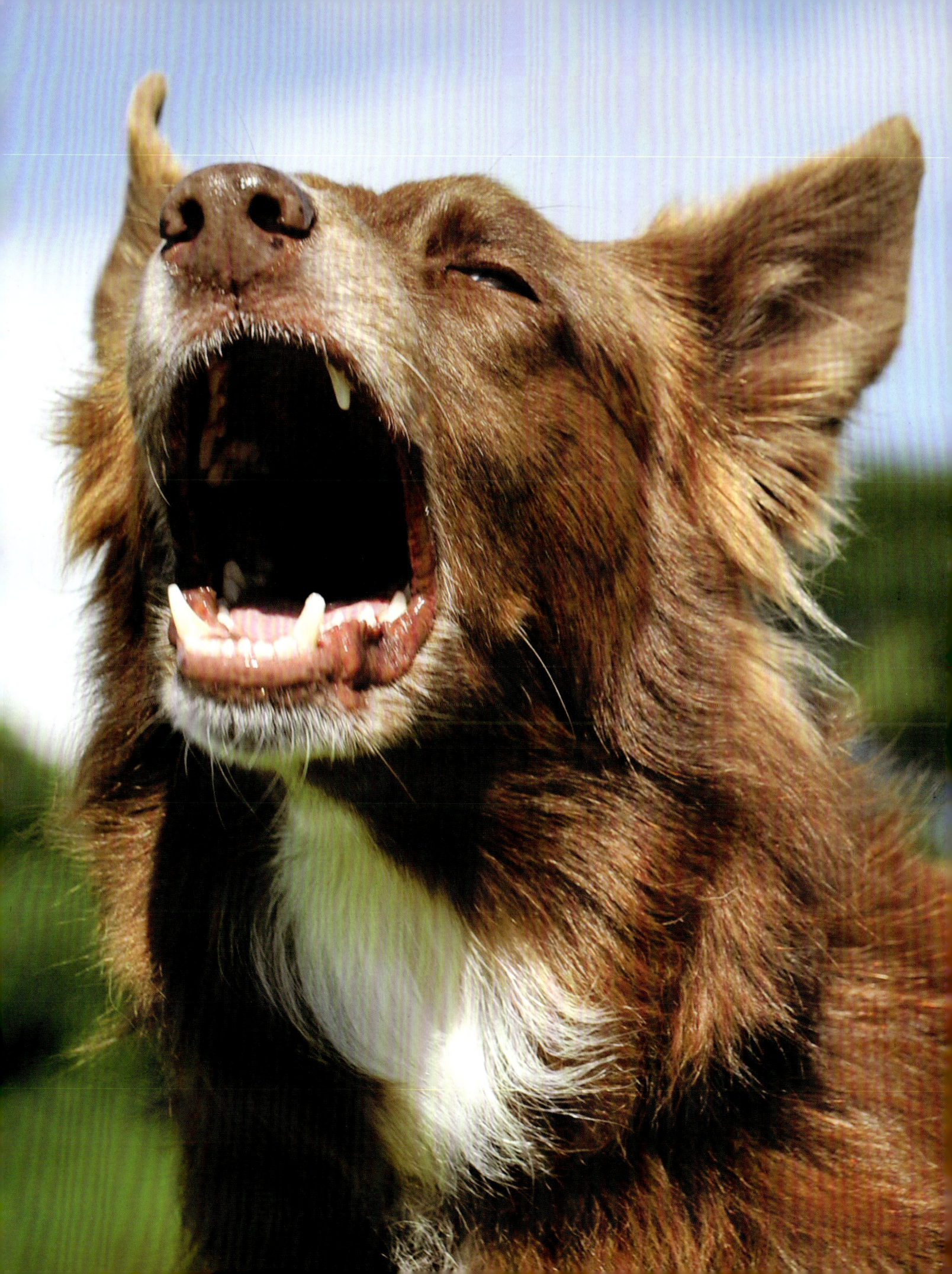

WORKING DOGS

Bouvier Des Flandres

CHARACTERISTICS

Coat
Very thick and wiry coat that has a variety of colours; there is often a white star on the chest

Height
59–68cm (23–27in)

Weight
27–40kg (60–88lb)

Lifespan
More than 10 years

Personality
Calm and obedient

Origin
Belgium and France

This big working dog is from the plains of Flanders in Belgium and northern France, and both countries claim the breed as their own. When the fighting of the First World War became stalemated in these fields, the bouvier was used to carry messages and to lead the stretcher bearers to the wounded stranded in No Man's Land. The breed's original purpose is made clear from its name. Bouvier translates roughly as "cow herder" but they were historically put to work as watchdogs, cattle guardians and also used to haul small carts. The Great War shattered this link to the land, and the bouvier faced extinction until the Belgian police chose the brave and resourceful breed as their police dogs. The bouvier is also used as a guide dog in this part of the world.

With their thick-set body, waterproof coat complete with a bushy beard and moustache, the bouvier des Flandres is no stranger to hard work. However, this urge to work comes with a strong will and, as is common for working breeds, owners that wish to keep them as family pets must have easy access to enough space to keep a bouvier well exercised and the time to do it. Plus the long, shaggy coat needs frequent grooming. This is no breed for a novice, due to its wariness of strangers and tendency to dominate other dogs. Instead the dog needs a firm and experienced owner.

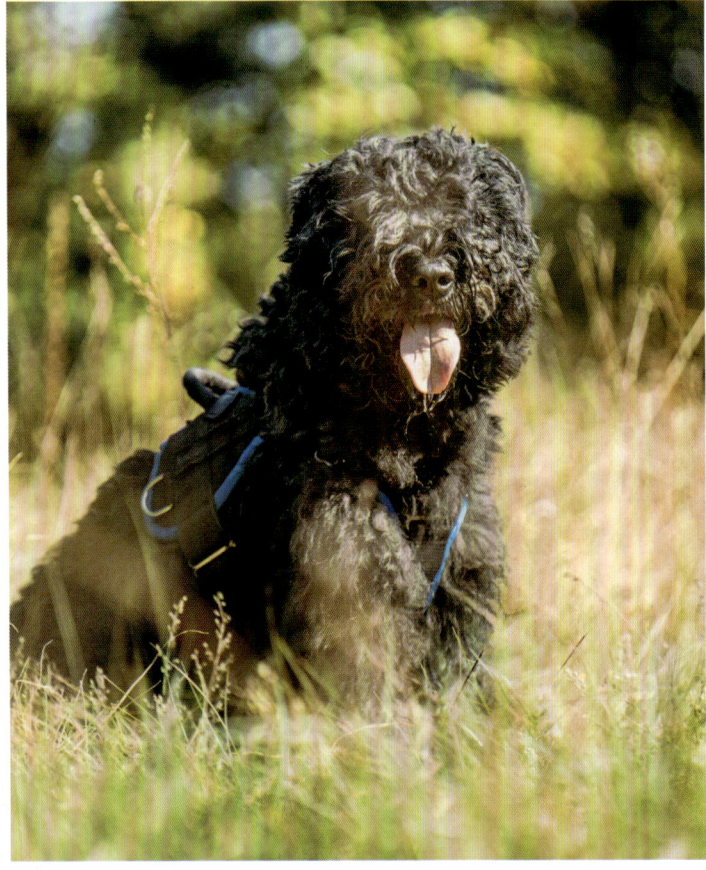

ABOVE:
Speckled coat
The most common colour is a salt and pepper fleck in the dark black-brown coat.

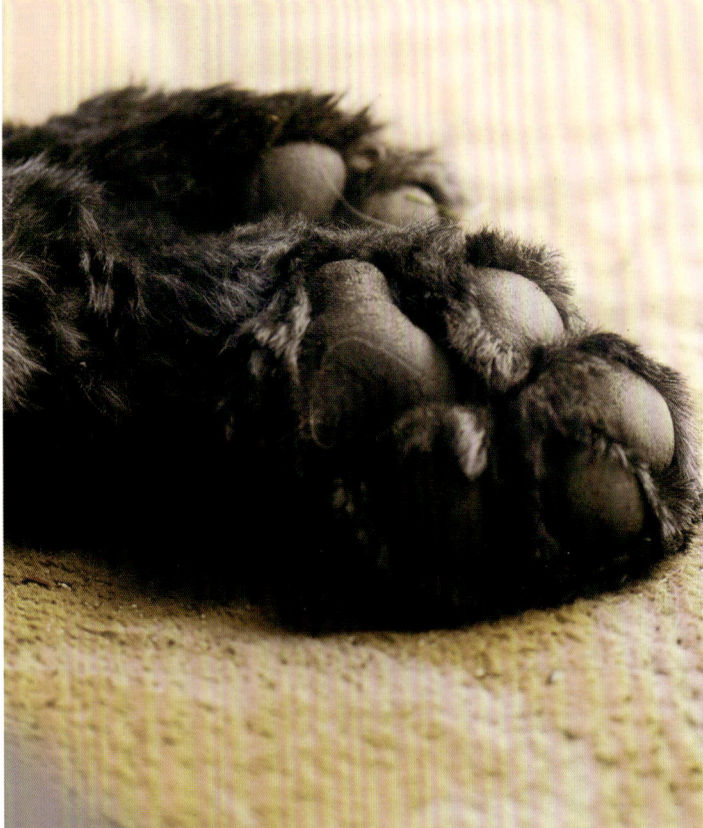

ABOVE:
Hairy creature
The soles of the paws is one of the few places where this dog is not covered in thick fur.

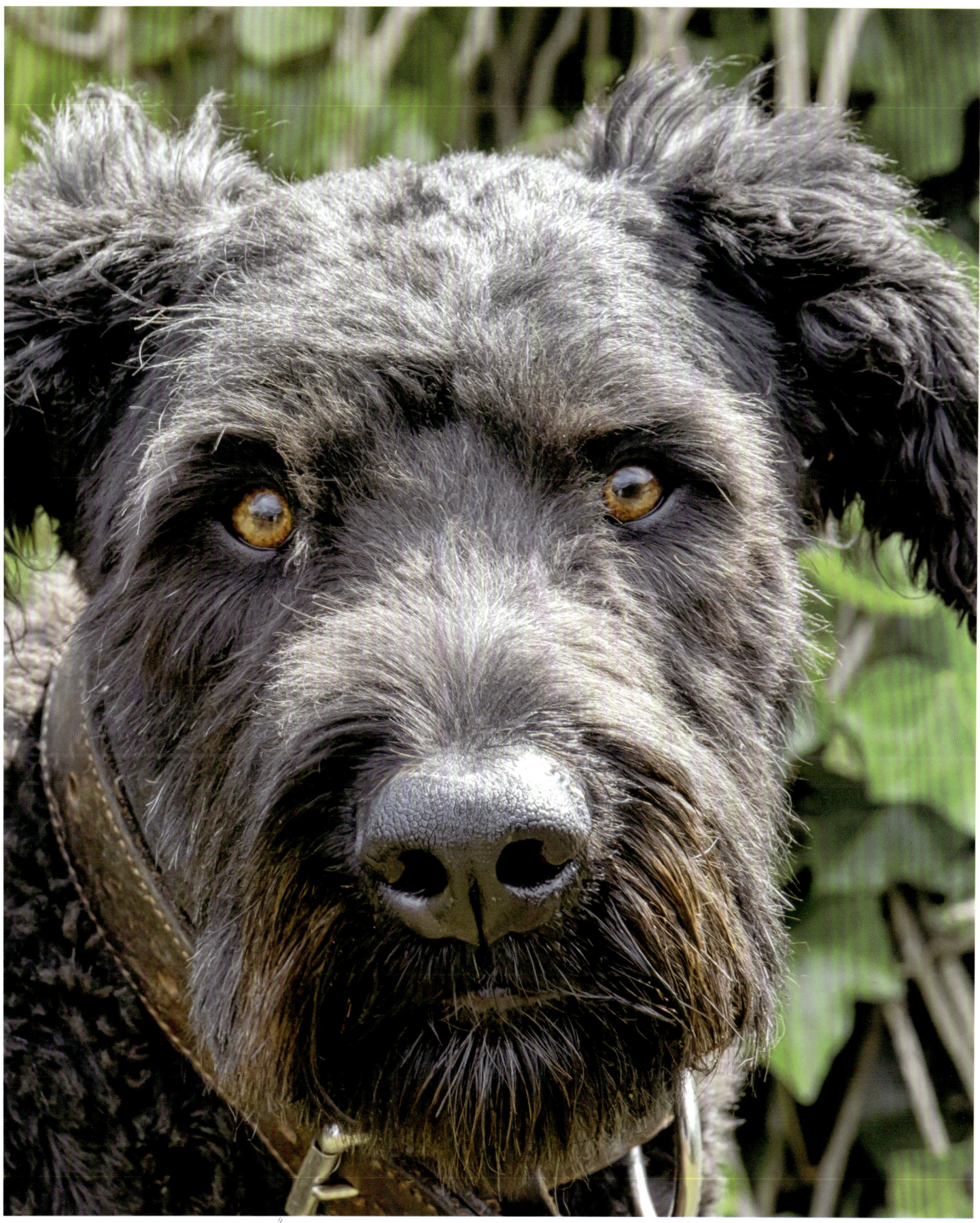

ABOVE:
Facial features
The bouvier des Flandres is known for its tousled ears and bushy eyebrows.

WORKING DOGS

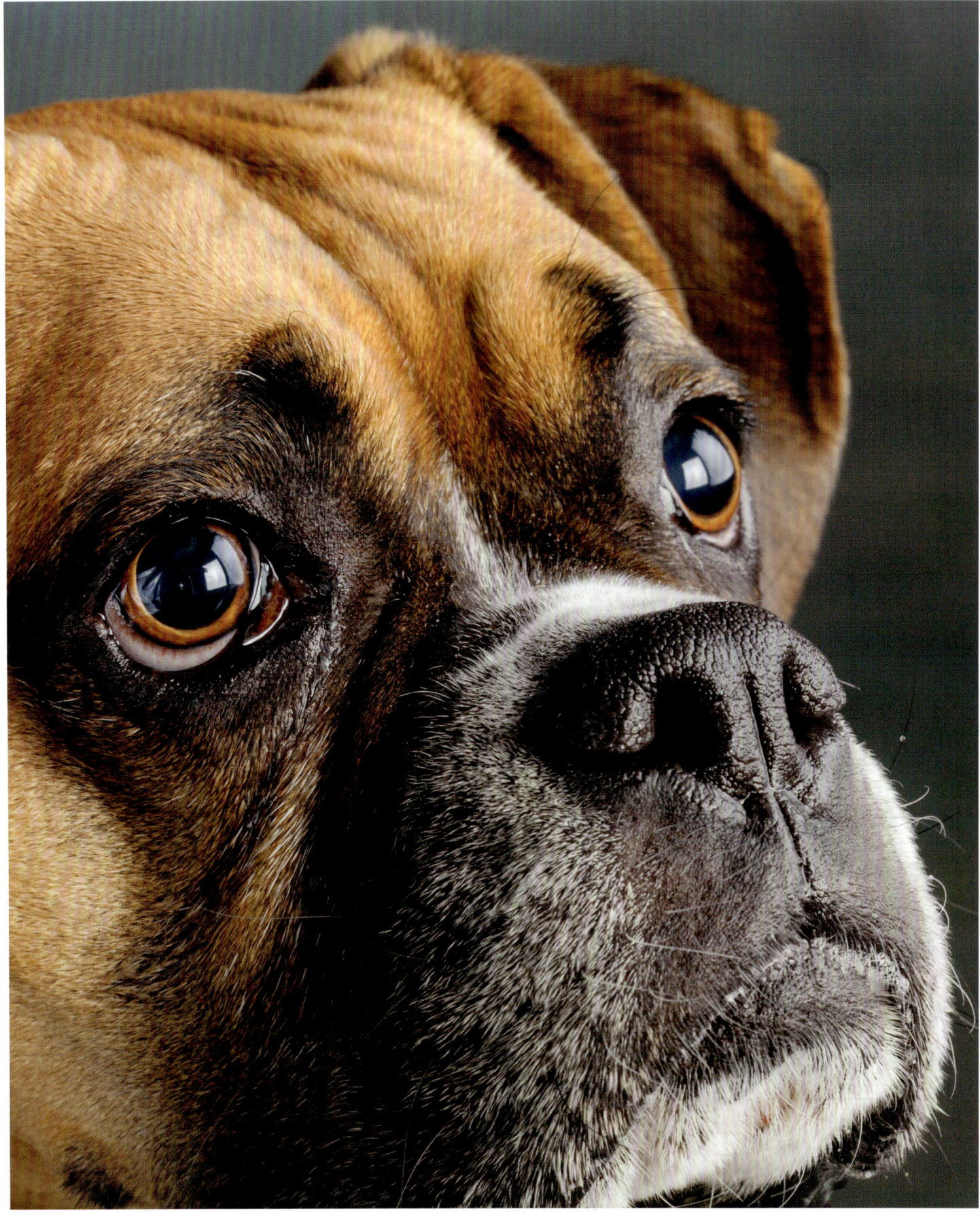

ABOVE:
Squashed face
The breed is brachycephalic, which means it has a short, stunted snout that prevents it from breathing efficiently—and losing heat from panting, so it is prone to overheating.

Boxer

CHARACTERISTICS

Coat
Short coat is mostly gold with a less common black brindle variety, small white markings are allowed

Height
53–63cm (21–25in)

Weight
25–32kg (55–71lb)

Lifespan
10–14 years

Personality
Courageous and tough

Origin
Germany

The English name for this breed refers to the way the dogs appear to punch and jab each other with their forepaws as they fight and play with each other. The heritage of this pugnacious-looking dog is mostly rooted in Germany, where it is the descendent of a much larger animal called the Bullenbeisser, or bull-biter. This now-extinct German breed was a hunting dog but in the 19th century it was then bred with English mastiffs and bulldogs to make the smaller, sleeker but still formidable working breed that we see today.

Boxers found work on cattle farms as herders, and as watchdogs, police dogs and guide dogs. Despite the belligerent looks and rippling muscles beneath the short coat, the boxer is a fun-loving and affectionate dog that makes a great family pet. They also bring patience and protectiveness, which is a good trait for any family member. However, owners must be aware of the downsides of owning boxers, most notably the breathing problems from the snubbed snout. It is important to expose boxer puppies to as many people and other animals as possible in their early months to encourage socialization and an even temper. Without this, boxers can be wary of strangers.

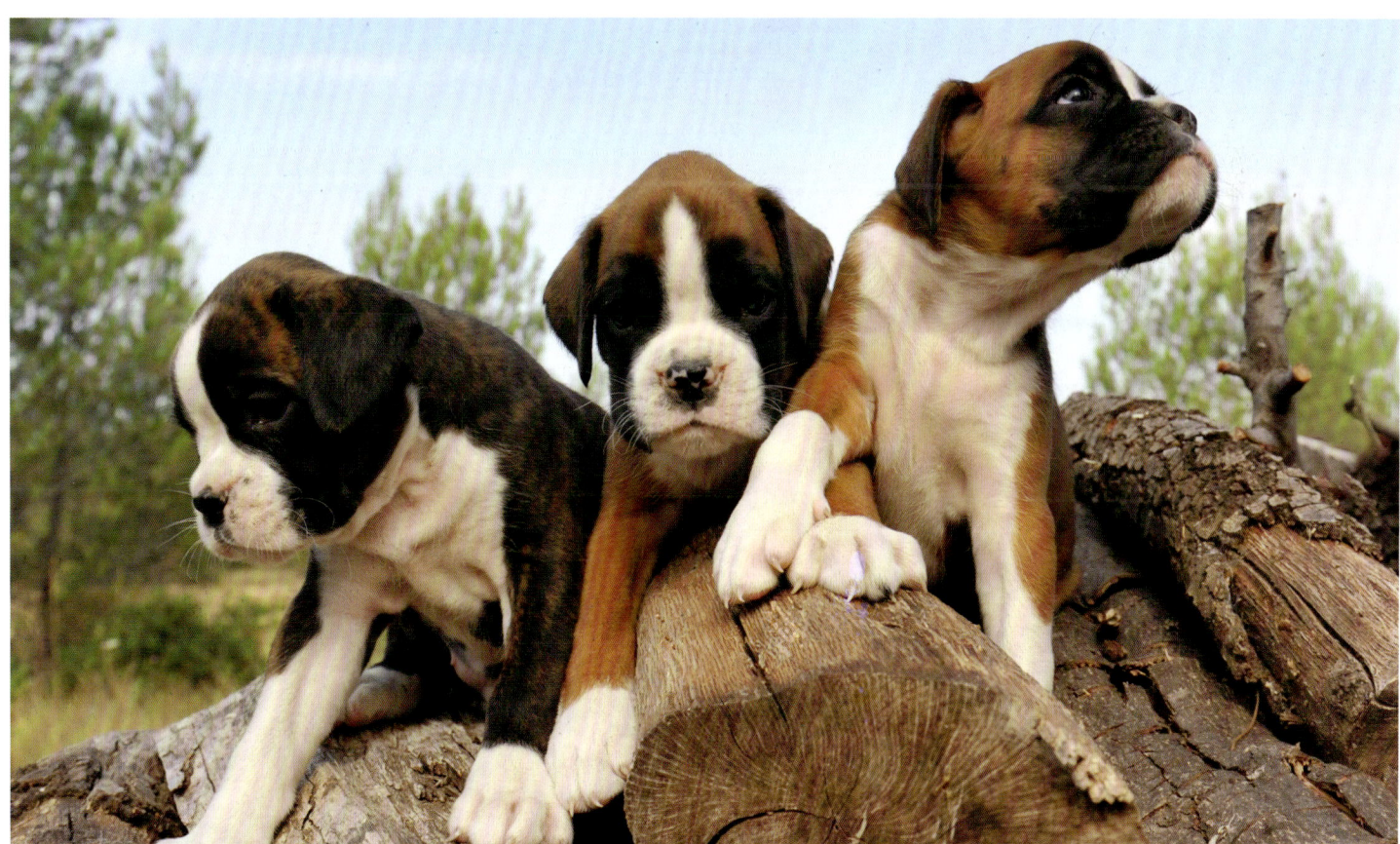

ABOVE:
High maintenance
The boxer needs regular grooming to keep its coat clean and healthy.

WORKING DOGS

RIGHT:
Serious games
A pet pooch needs its wild instincts tended to, and this boxer likes nothing more than chasing a ball. To them, it is just as important as hunting a rat or rabbit.

OPPOSITE:
Namesake
Named after the way the dogs prod each other with their front paws, this sturdy breed was developed to catch wild boar.

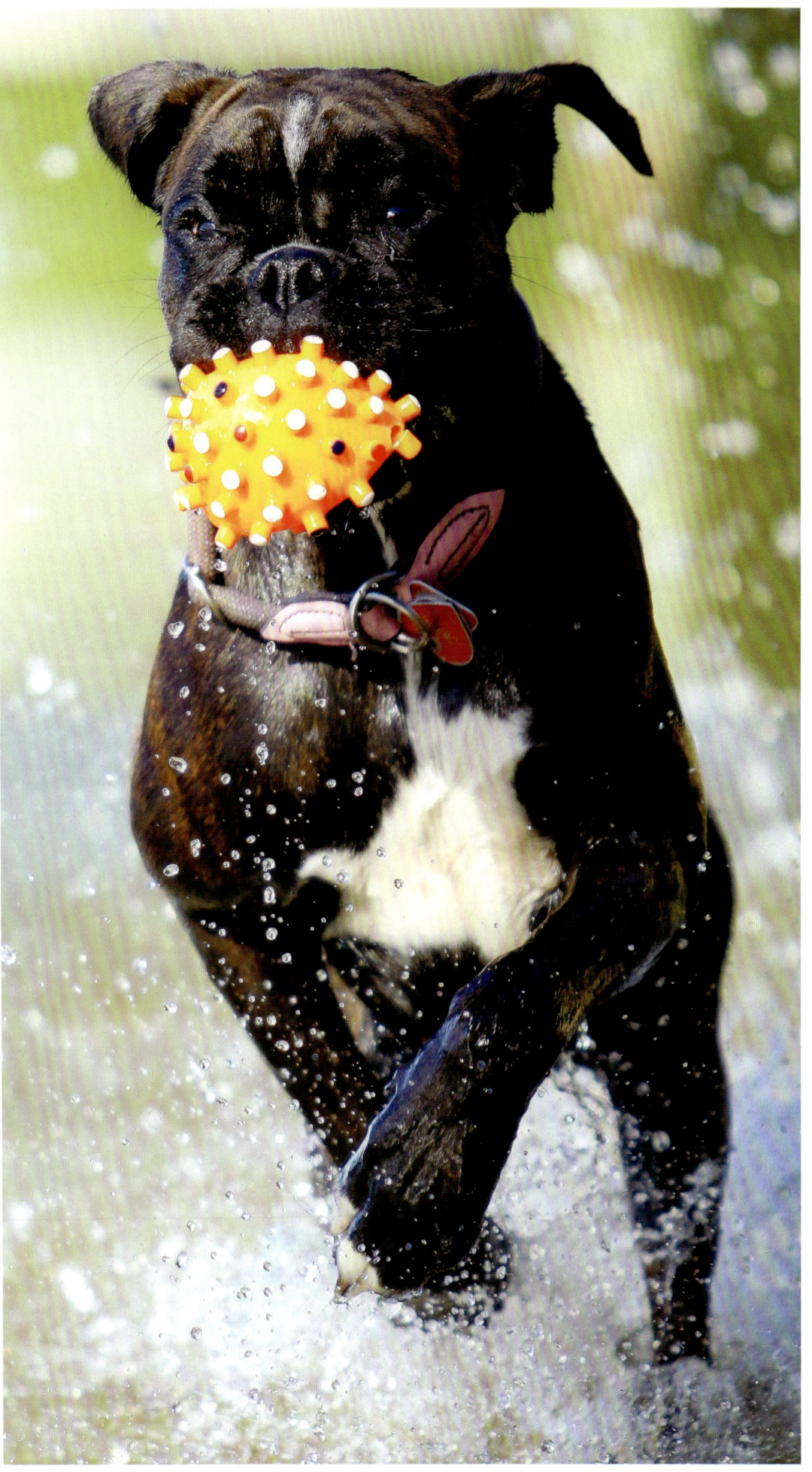

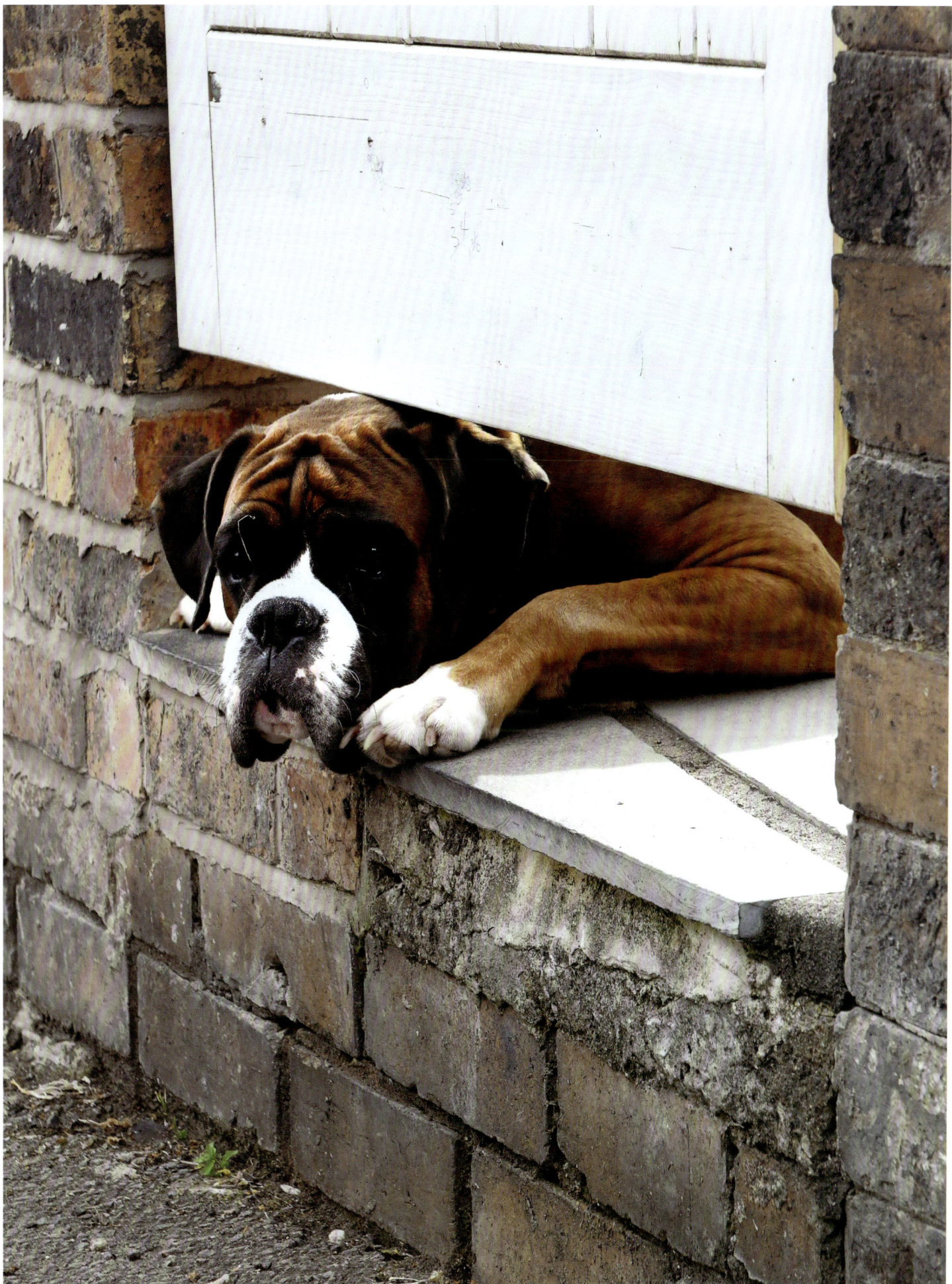

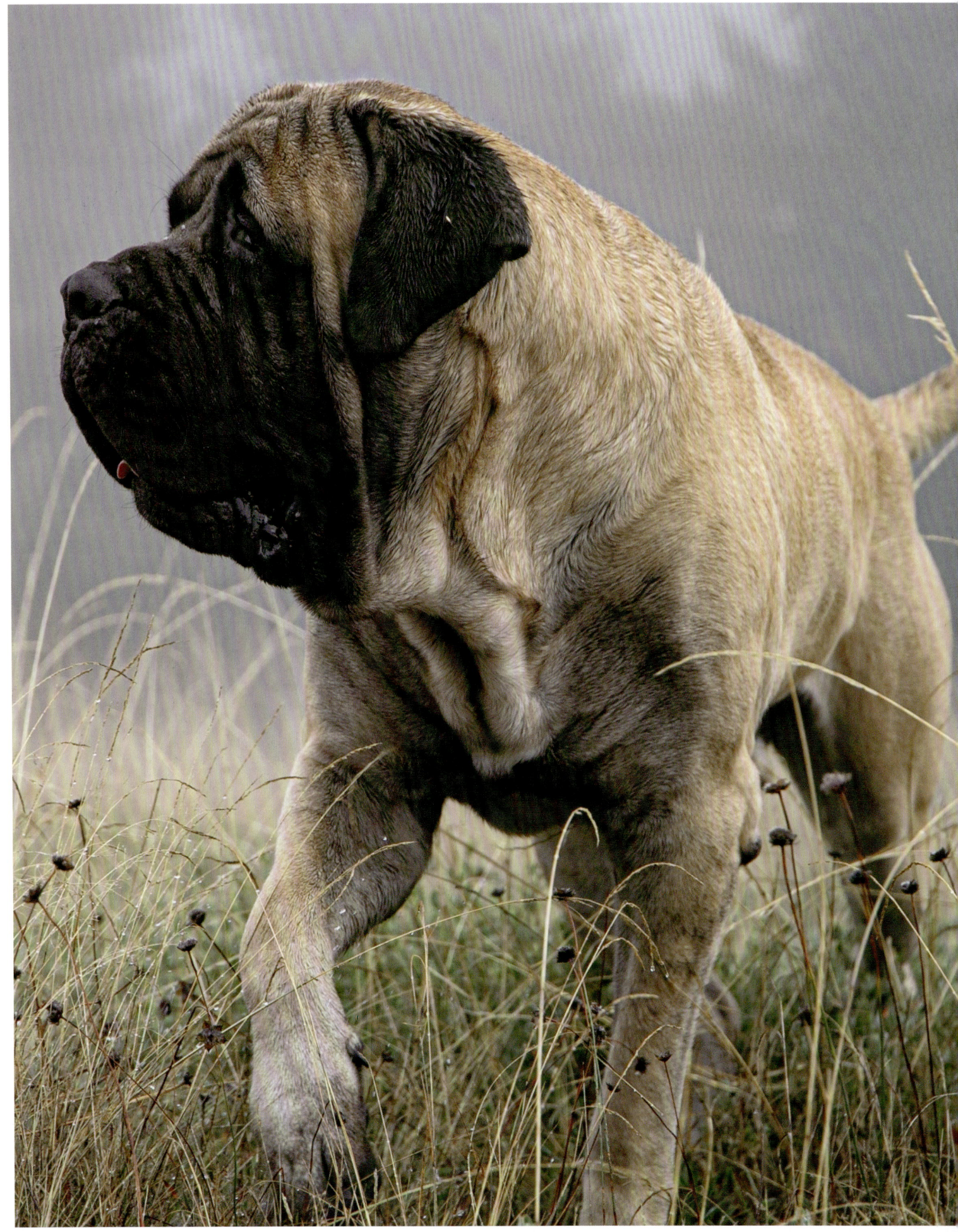

British Mastiff

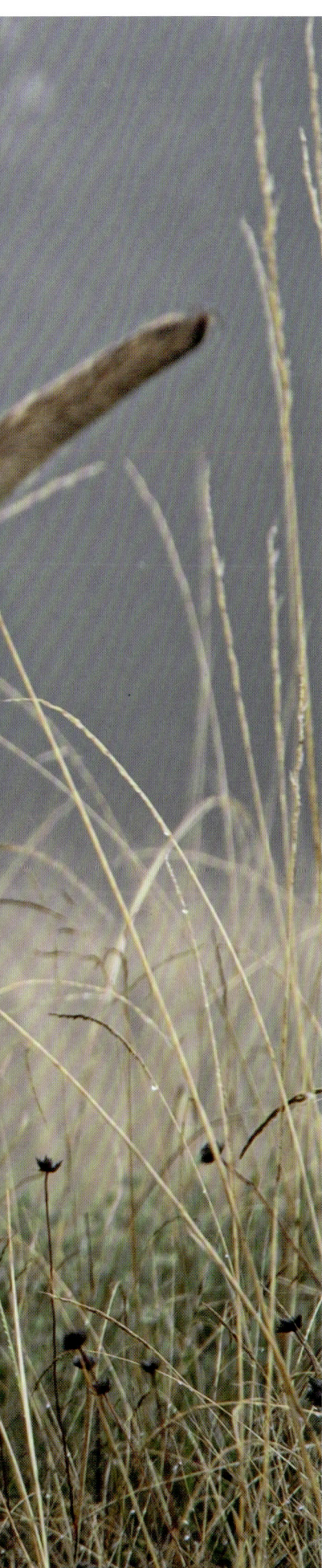

This massive dog is the traditional giant breed of Britain, and one with an ancient history. Legend has it that when Julius Caesar led an abortive invasion of Britain in 55BC he was impressed by the large and fierce dogs that fought alongside the ancient Britons—and helped to drive back his Roman legions. Caesar took several of these "Pugnaces Britanniae" dogs back to Italy.

The British mastiff is descended from these ancient giants, which had been used on the islands since the Iron Age, perhaps introduced by Phoenician traders. The later mastiff breed was developed by crossing with the molossus, another larger fighting breed originally from ancient Greece that is now extinct. By the Middle Ages they had become the literal "dogs of war" as described by William Shakespeare in *Henry V*. Pictures taken in the 19th century reveal that the British mastiff was once more slender and slight than today. Crosses with the muscled Alpine mastiff helped create the modern breed.

As a guardian breed, the mastiff is intensely loyal to its owner and is known for its stubbornness and wariness of strangers. It wrinkles its forehead into a frown when alert to threats. The dog can outweigh an adult man and so can overpower smaller people when frightened or bored.

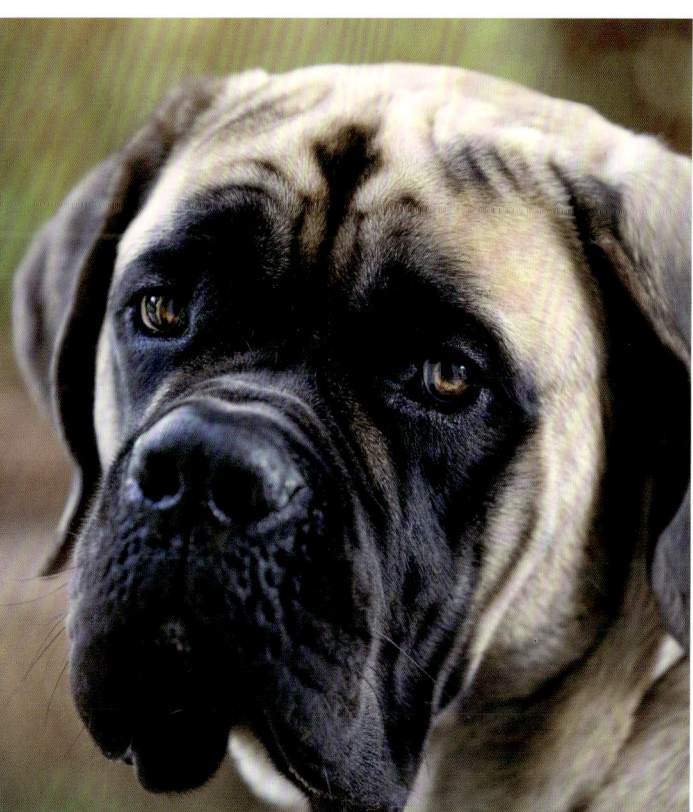

CHARACTERISTICS

Coat
Short coat can be fawn, apricot or brindle in colour. Some white patches are seen on the feet, chest and body

Height
70–77cm (28–30in)

Weight
79–86 kg (175–190lb)

Lifespan
Less than 10 years

Personality
Dignified and amiable

Origin
Britain

LEFT:
Big beast
The mastiff has a massive body, a broad head, a short coat and a distinctive black mask on its face.

ABOVE:
Health checks
The mastiff is prone to some health issues, such as hip and elbow problems, bloat and eye problems. Regular veterinary check-ups are advised.

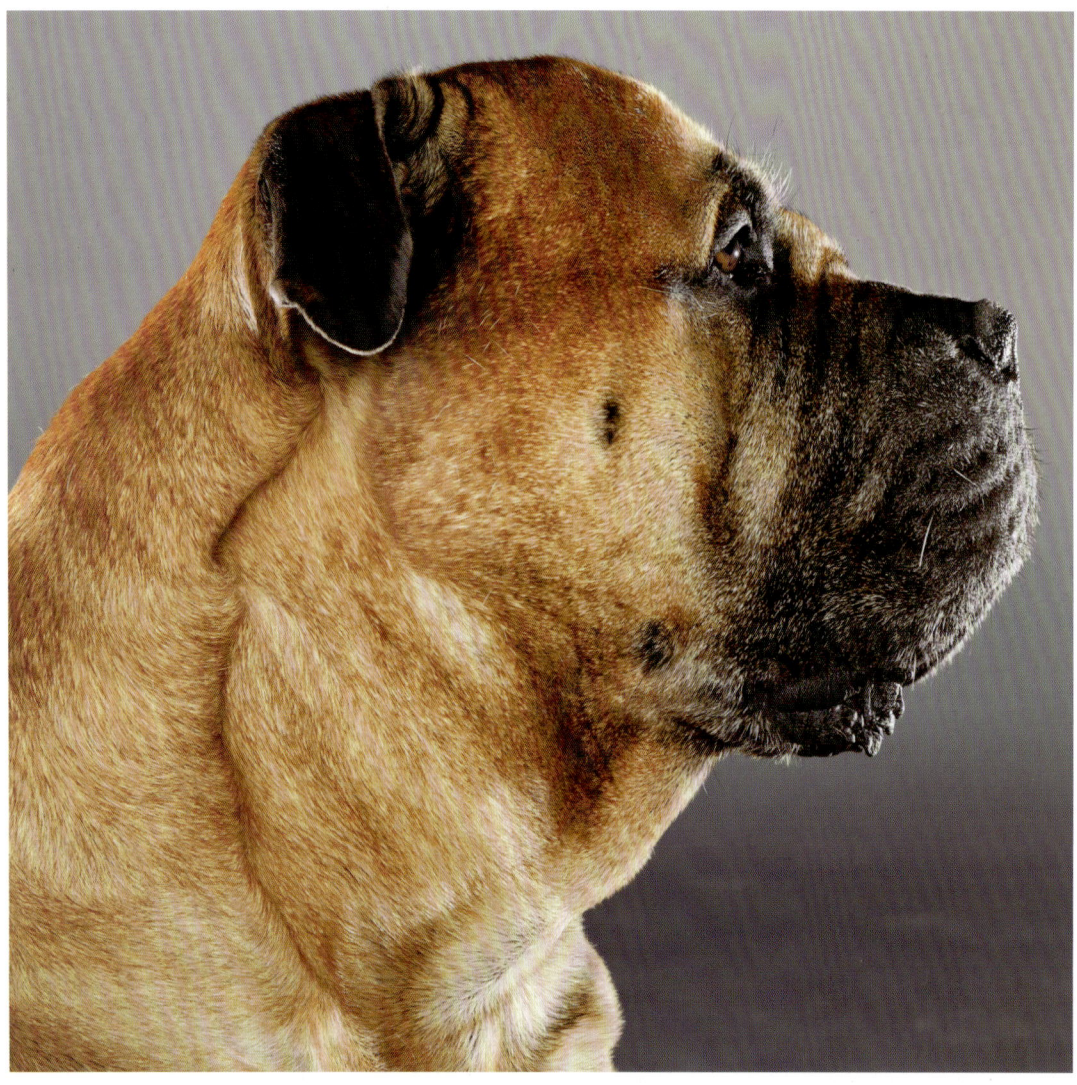
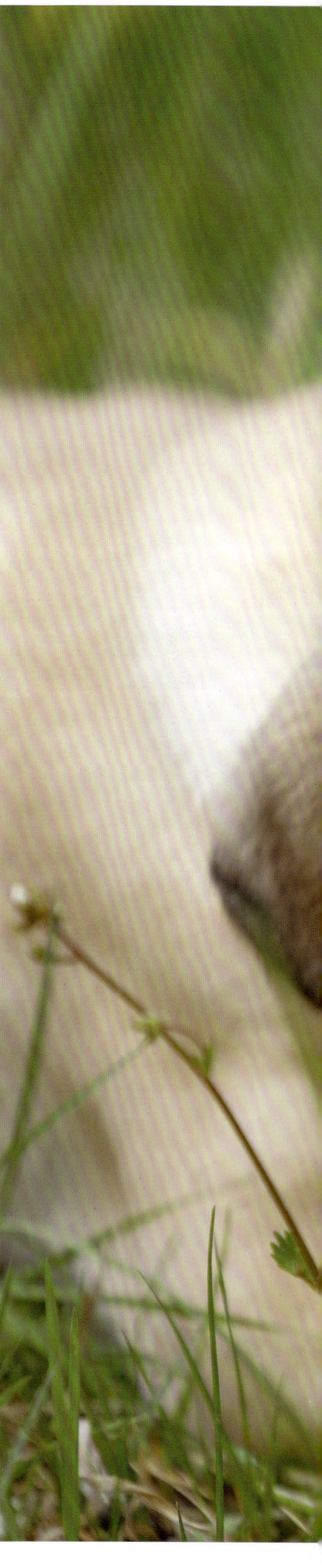

ABOVE:
Historic hound
This huge and old breed is the "dog of war" referred to in William Shakespeare's *Henry V*.

RIGHT:
Sense of smell
Smell is the main sense used by pups. They are deaf and blind at birth.

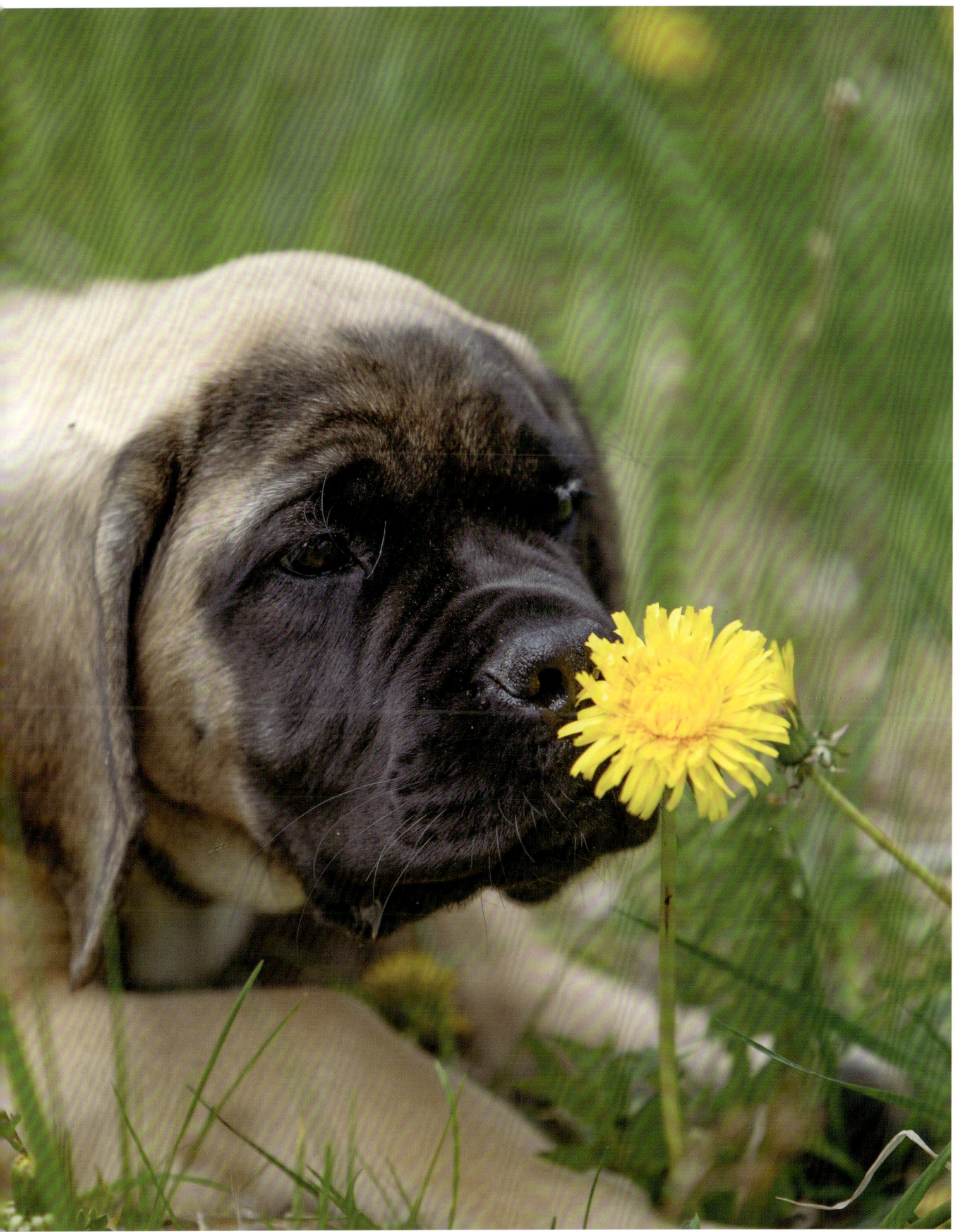

WORKING DOGS
Bullmastiff

As the name suggests this fearless English breed is the result of crosses between bulldogs (the now extinct Old English breed) and mastiffs. The result is a heavy-set breed with a broad muzzle and air of alertness. It was bred in the 19th century to combine the power and ferocity of a mastiff with the calmer nature of the bulldog. The result was a guard dog developed for gamekeepers, and one that struck fear into the heart of poachers prowling through the night. In those days, poaching was punishable by hanging, and poachers would fight to the death. The bullmastiff would be unleashed to pin them down before they knew it. The bullmastiff has the qualities required to fulfil this role. It is strong, fast and loyal, but also prone to aggression. Owners must socialize their puppies early during training to prevent long-term antipathy to strangers and other animals. If this is done right, a bullmastiff will be an obedient and striking companion. Despite its sturdy frame, this breed is a relative home body and content with only moderate exercise. The short coat is also easy to maintain. The breed is prone to some health problems, such as hip and elbow dysplasia and eye disorders.

CHARACTERISTICS
Coat
The fur is short and weather-resistant. It can be fawn, red or brindle in colour, and the muzzle is black
Height
61–69cm (24–27in)
Weight
41–59kg (90–130lb)
Lifespan
8–12 years
Personality
Faithful and courageous
Origin
England

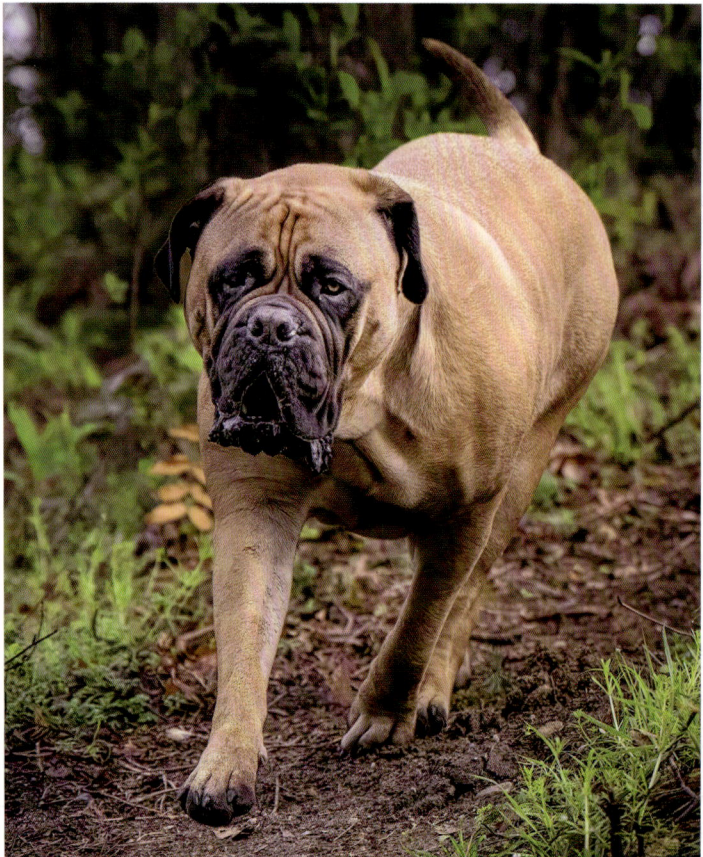

ABOVE:
High ears
The bullmastiff has V-shaped ears that are set high and droop off the head.

RIGHT:
A certain expression
The face is flat and wrinkled eyes gives the bullmastiff a beseeching look that only elevates its appeal.

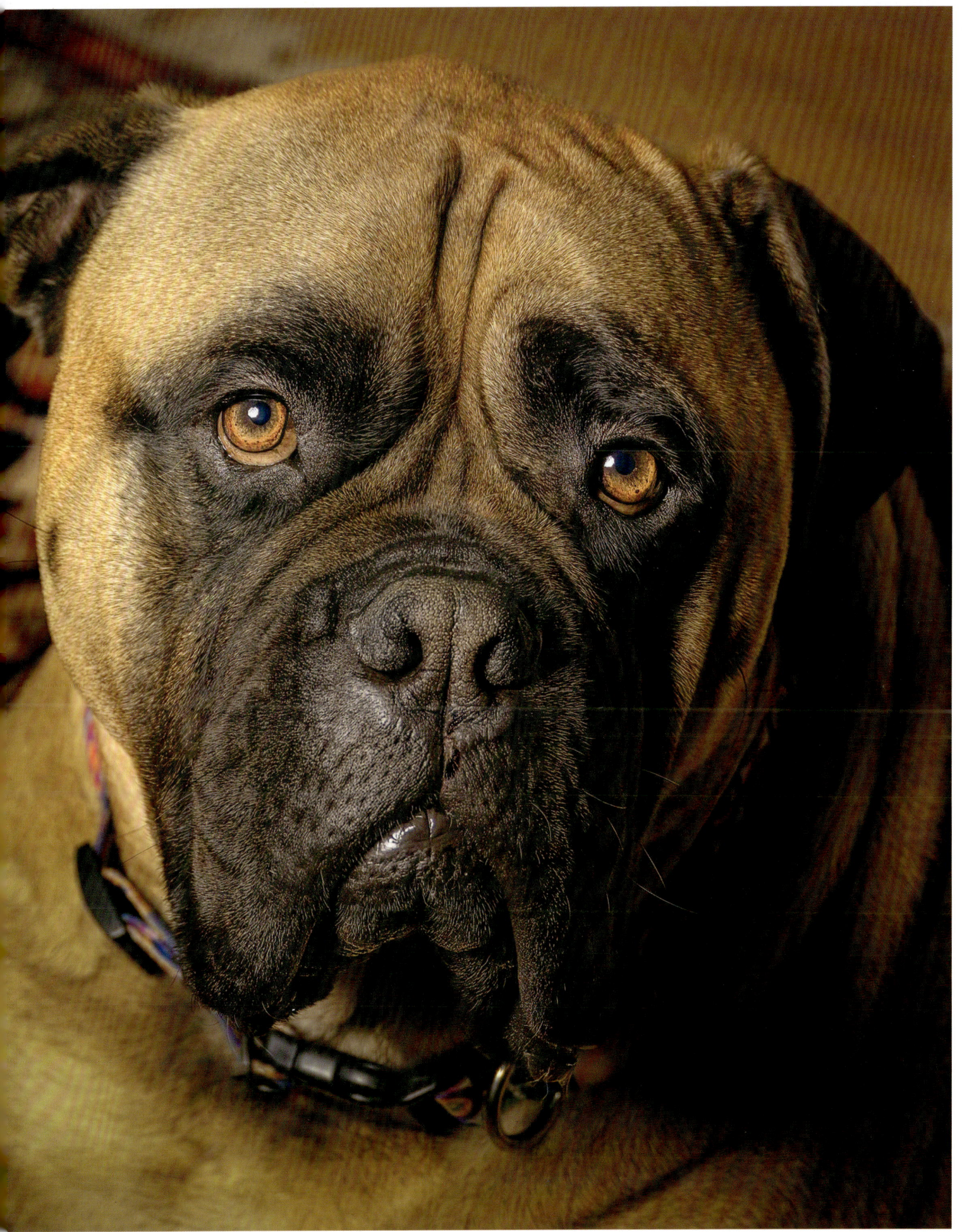

WORKING DOGS

No fear
This shepherd dog has entered into a dispute with a bull mastiff – one that it cannot win. A dog can't learn bravery but nor can it unlearn it. This kind of behaviour is purely instinctive.

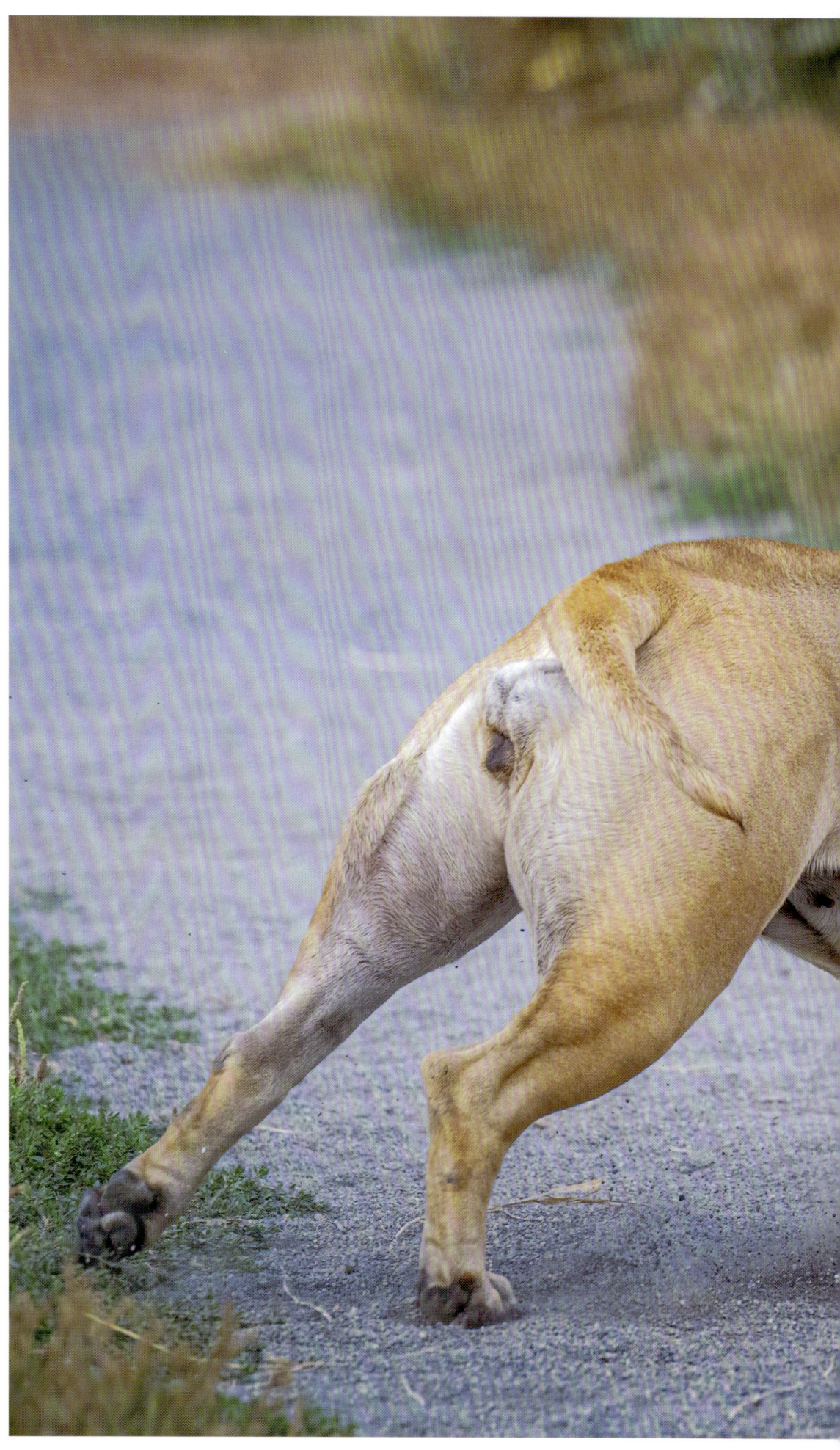

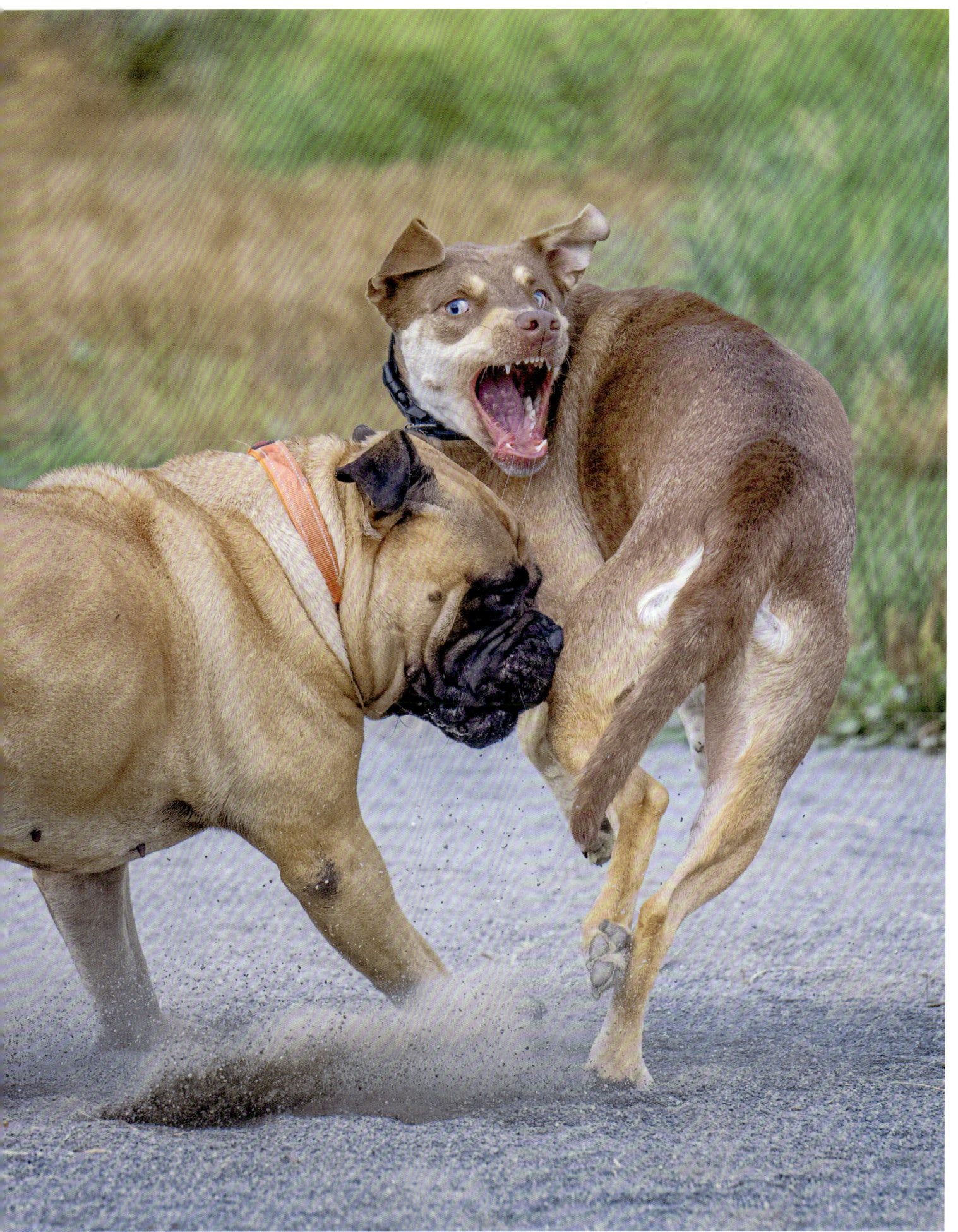

WORKING DOGS

ALL PHOTOGRAPHS:
Baby bulls
Play is a busy time for these mastiff pups. They are building mobility skills and control and also learning to interact with each other. In large sibling groups, a hierarchy is put in place through play. During training, the dog is given its place in its human family.

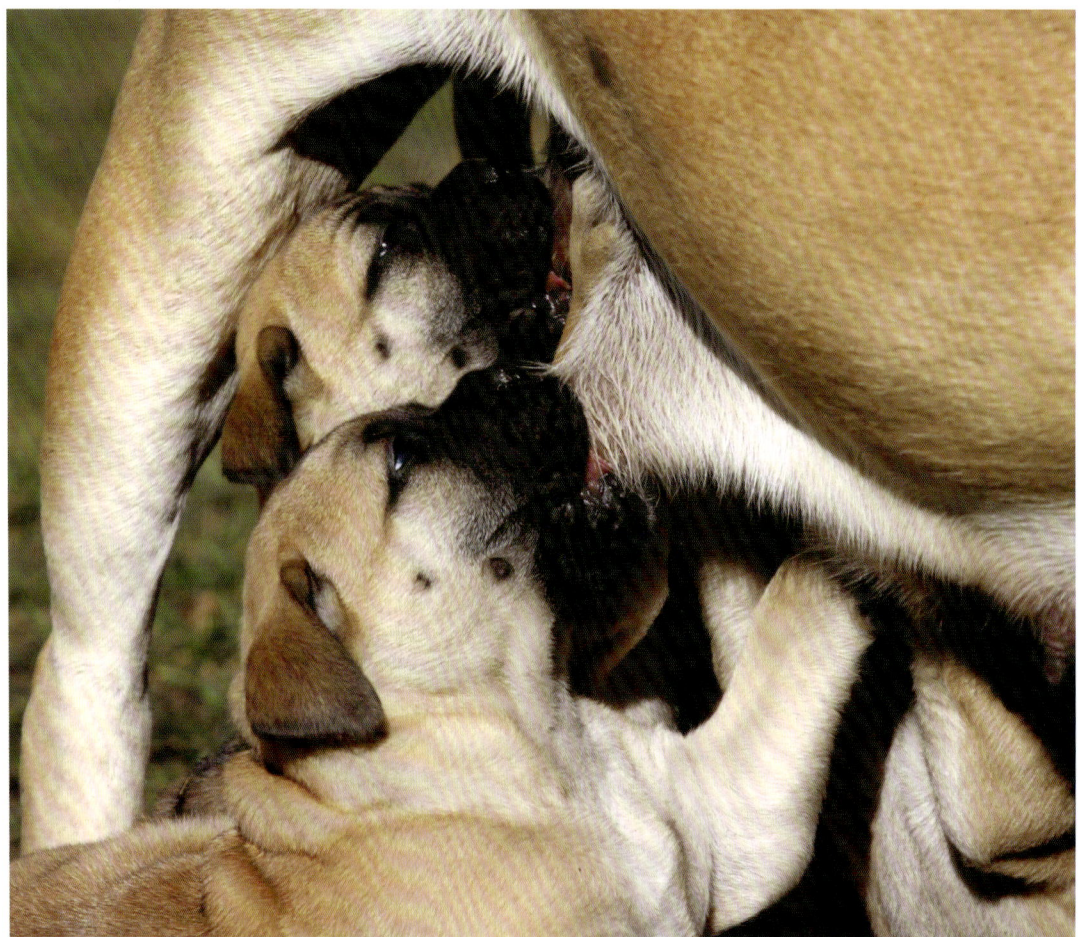

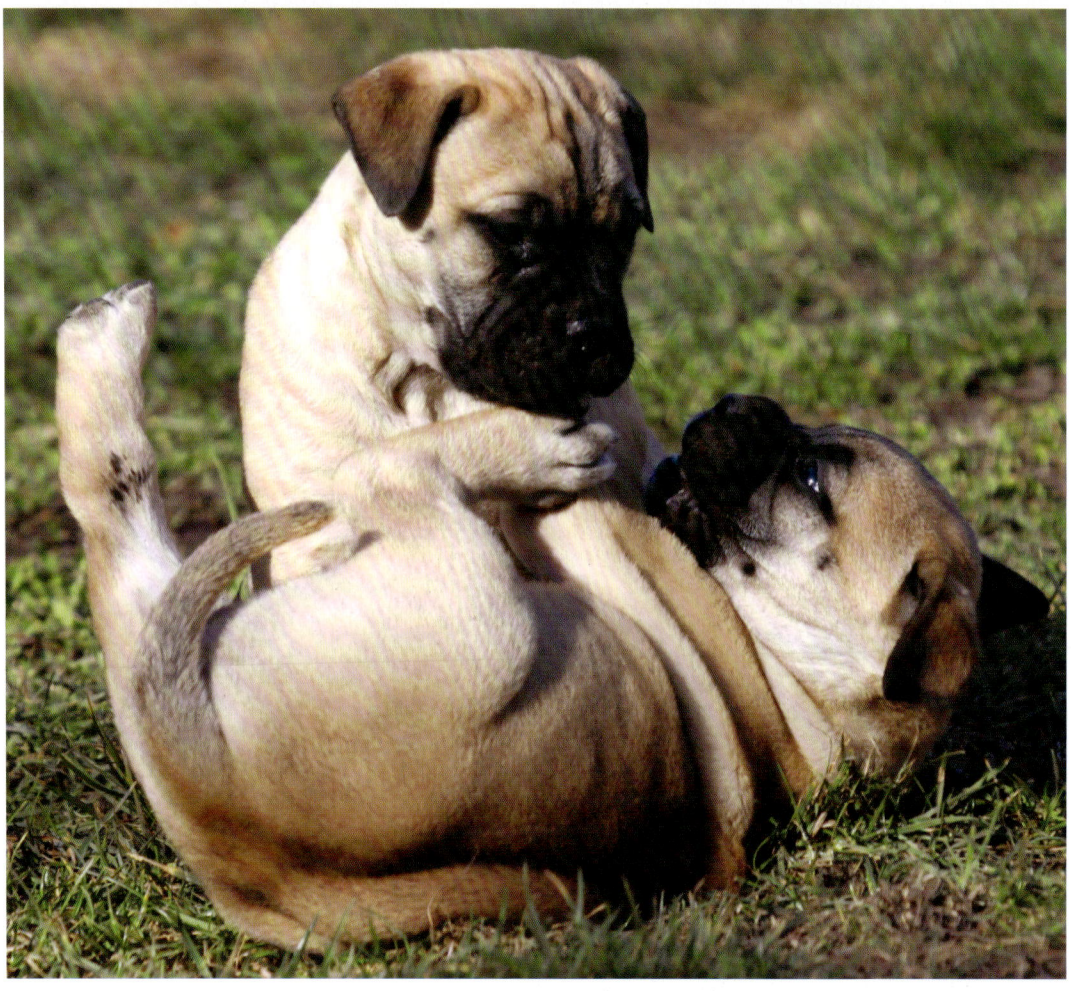

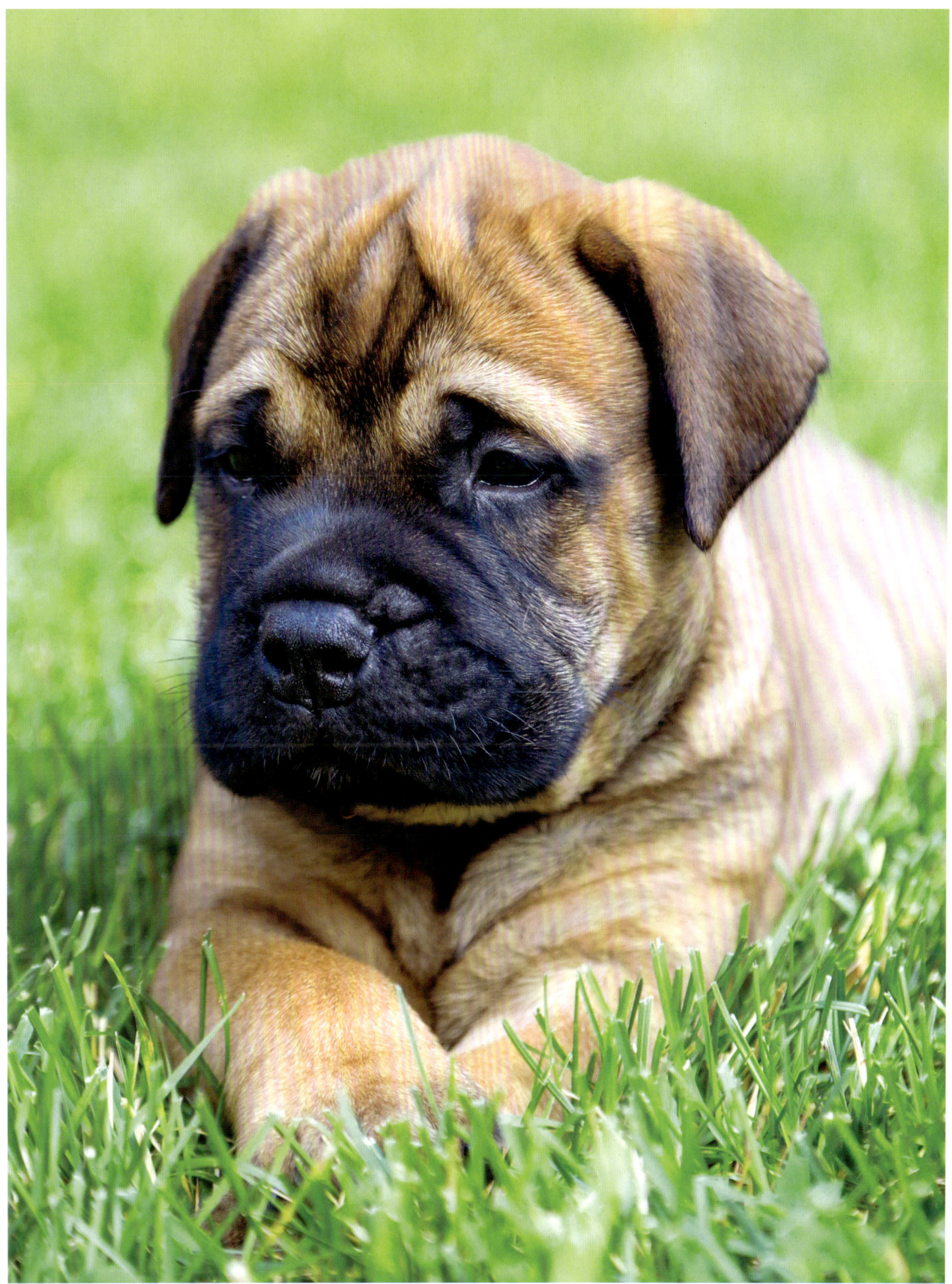

WORKING DOGS

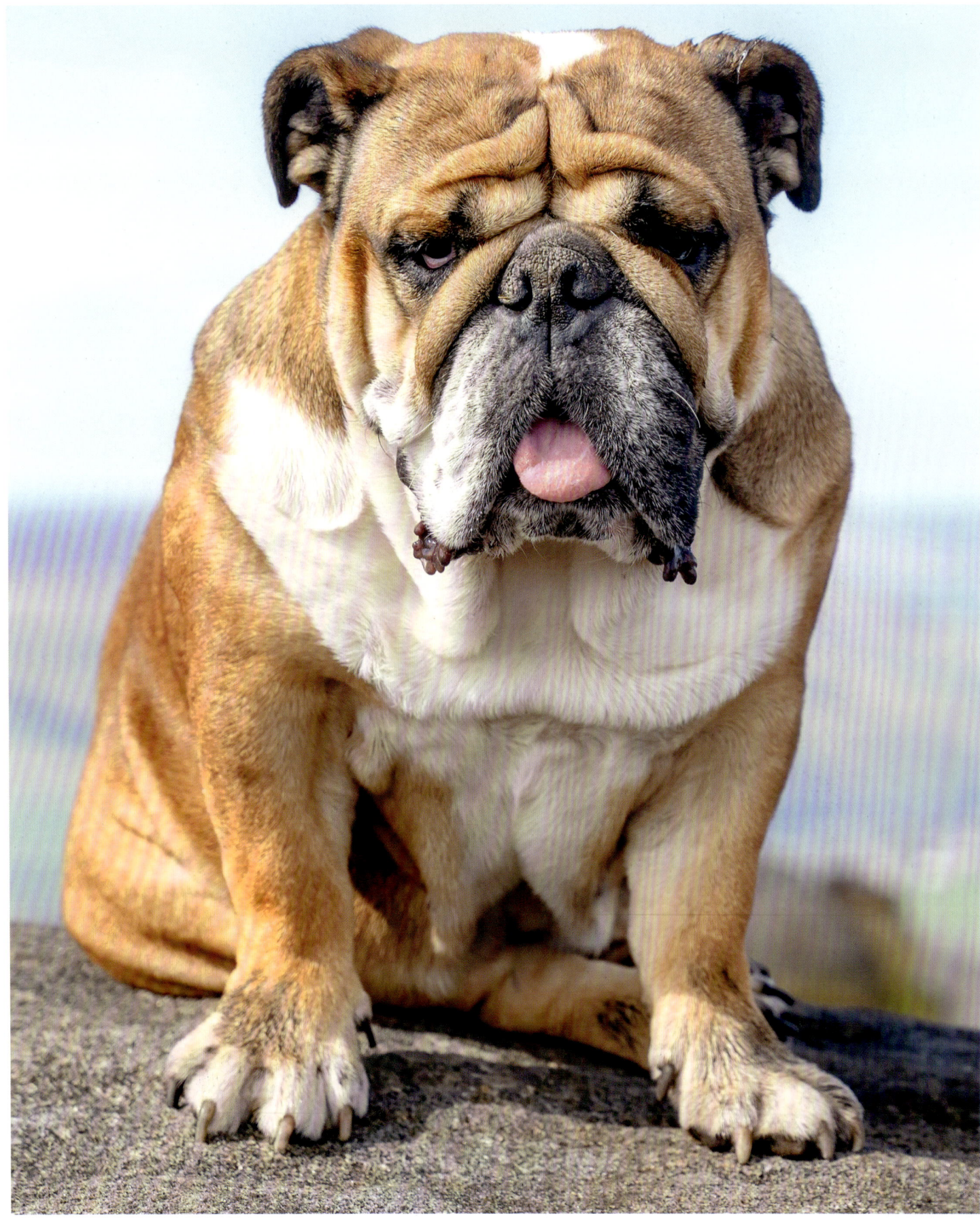

ABOVE:
Don't I know you?
The jutting lower jaw, jowls and thick lips makes this breed look like a venerable old man retired after an eventful life.

English Bulldog

CHARACTERISTICS

Coat
Smooth coat has a variety of colours
Height
38–40cm (15–16in)
Weight
23–25kg (51–55lb)
Lifespan
7–10 years
Personality
Gentle and relaxed
Origin
England

For centuries the English have identified with this stocky breed known for its tough look. It was created in the 13th century during the reign of King John. John was a cruel king and, as its name suggests, the bulldog was bred from smaller mastiffs for the cruel sport of bull baiting. This was when several dogs were pitted against a bull, biting and nipping it until it collapsed in exhaustion and was killed. A dog that was always ready for a fight and loved eating a lot of food seemed to appeal to many an Englishman's view of themselves.

However, in the 19th century, the practice of bull baiting was banned in Britain, and the bulldog was steadily transformed into a very different kind of dog. Today's bulldogs are rotund plodders that serve as affable companions. They have a steady temperament and are good around children and strangers. They need only about 30 minutes of vigorous exercise a day, and if they have a personality fault it is that they are overly protective of their food.

The big concern for bulldog owners is brachycephaly, where the nasal cavity is deformed by the short muzzle. This leads to breathing problems and overheating, which in turn makes the dogs loud snorers and prone to flatulence.

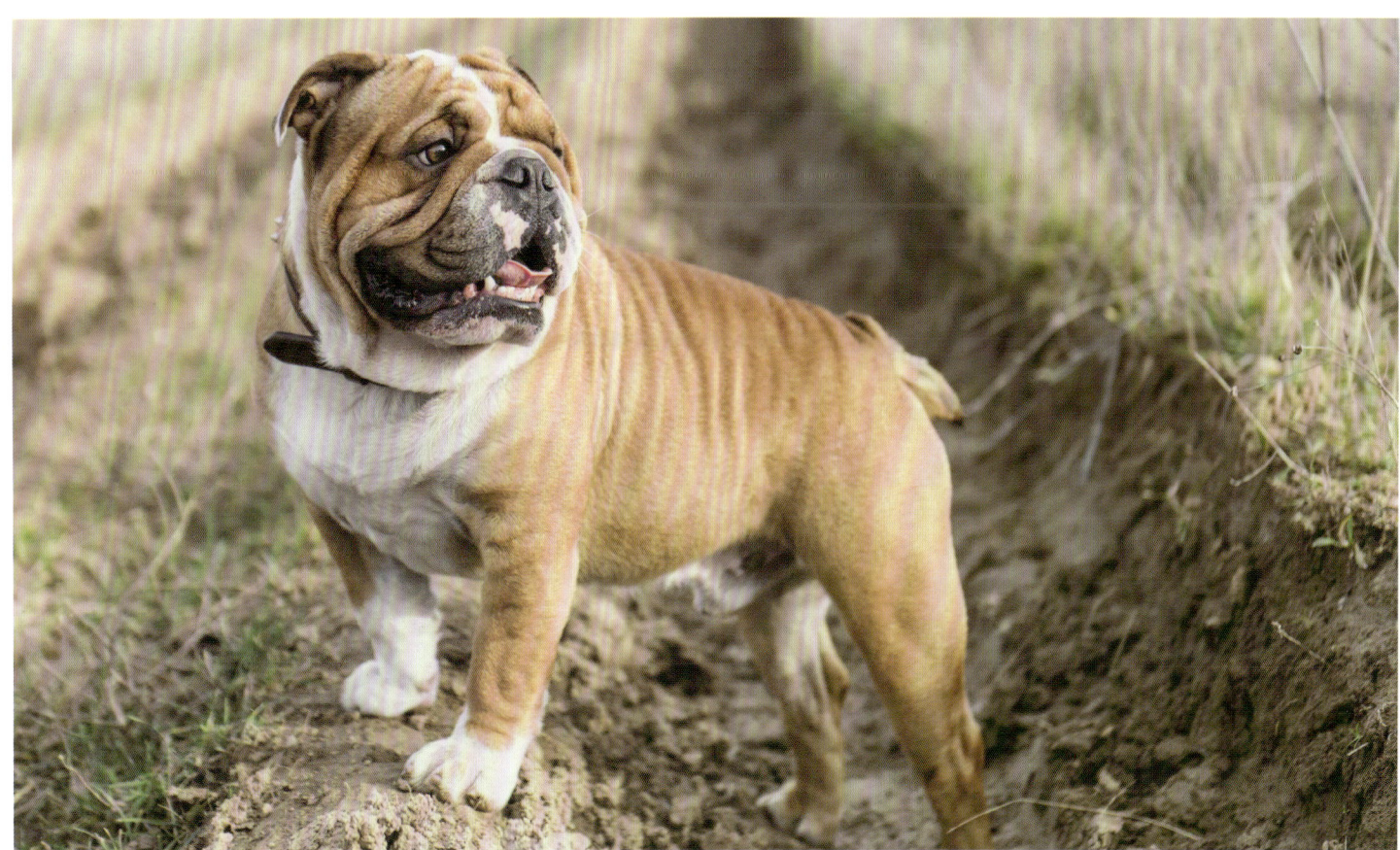

ABOVE:
Heat problem
Owners should be careful not to let their bulldogs overheat on hot days. The squashed nose makes it harder for the dog to shed heat by panting.

WORKING DOGS

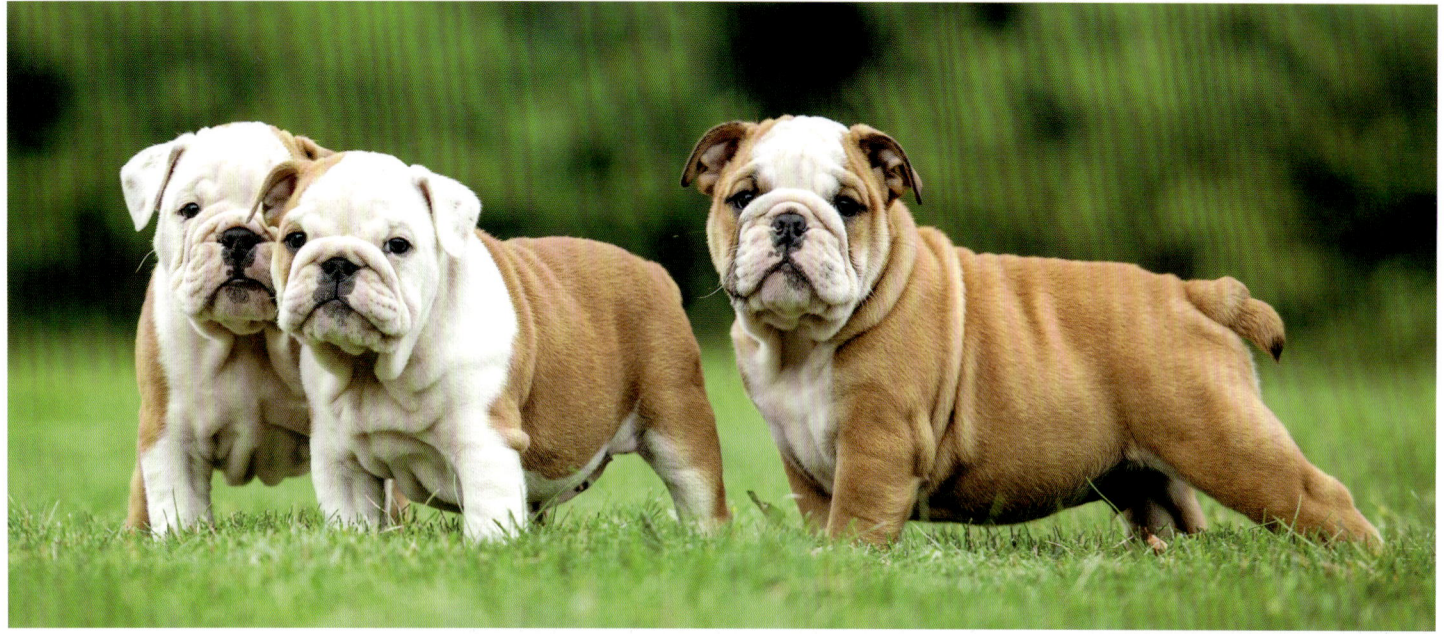

ABOVE AND RIGHT:
New generation
Despite new litters such as this one, the bulldog has long been in decline in popularity as a pet because of common health problems.

OPPOSITE:
British bulldog
This small offshoot of mastiff breeds is often used as a symbol of Britishness or Englishness because it is said to resemble a corpulent, jowly man who enjoys good living, and who is stubborn but also ready and able to fight if needed.

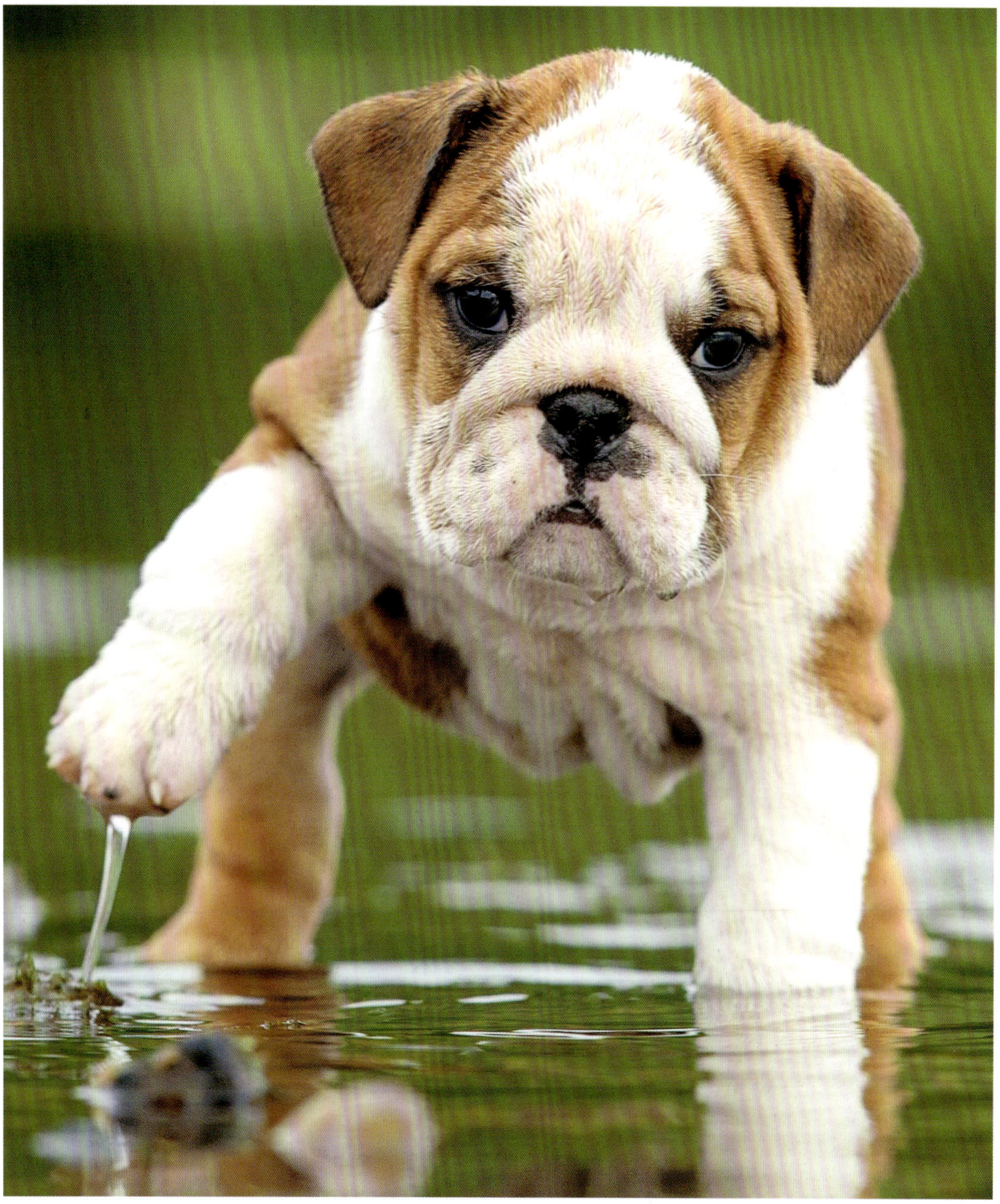

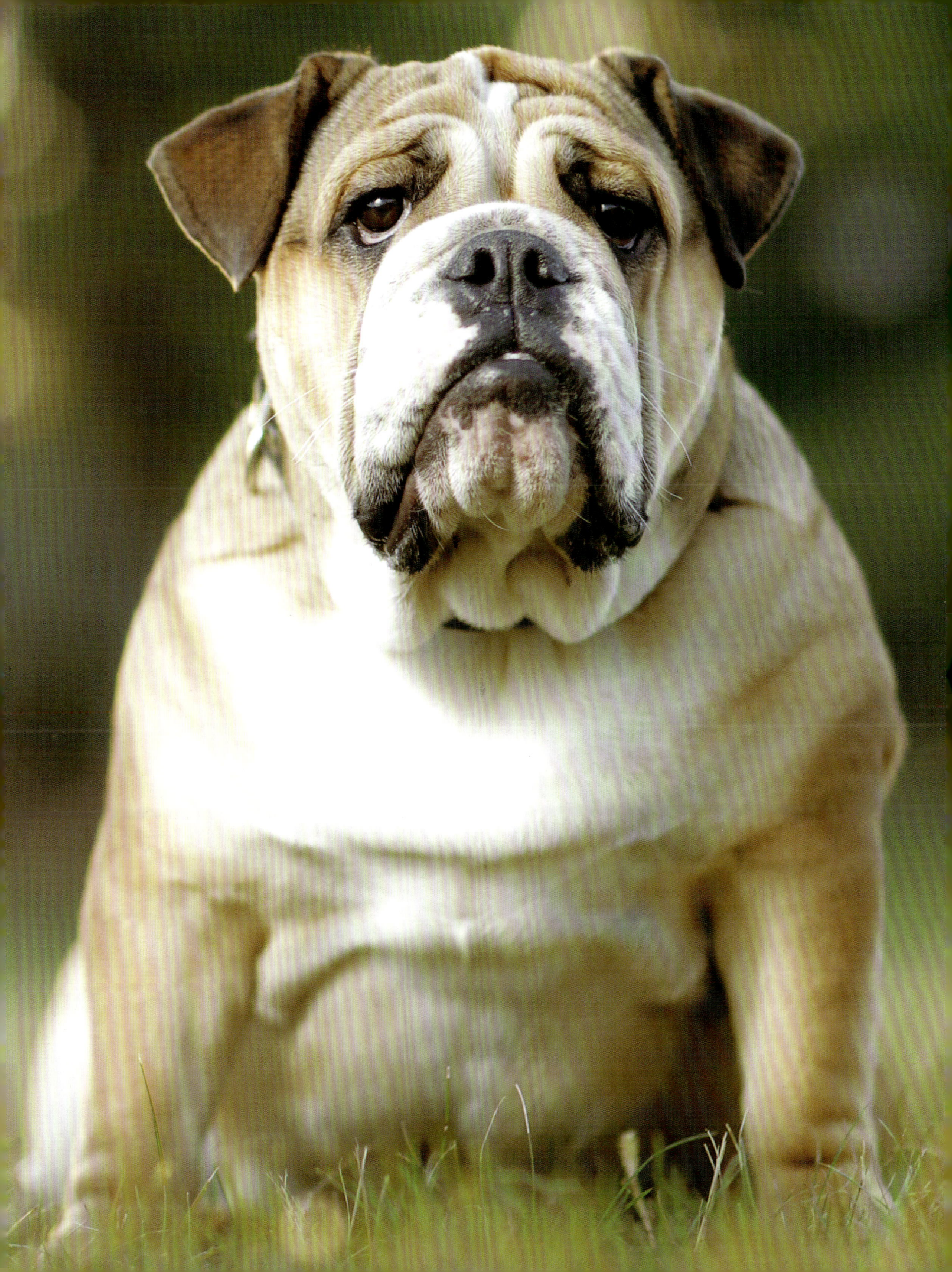

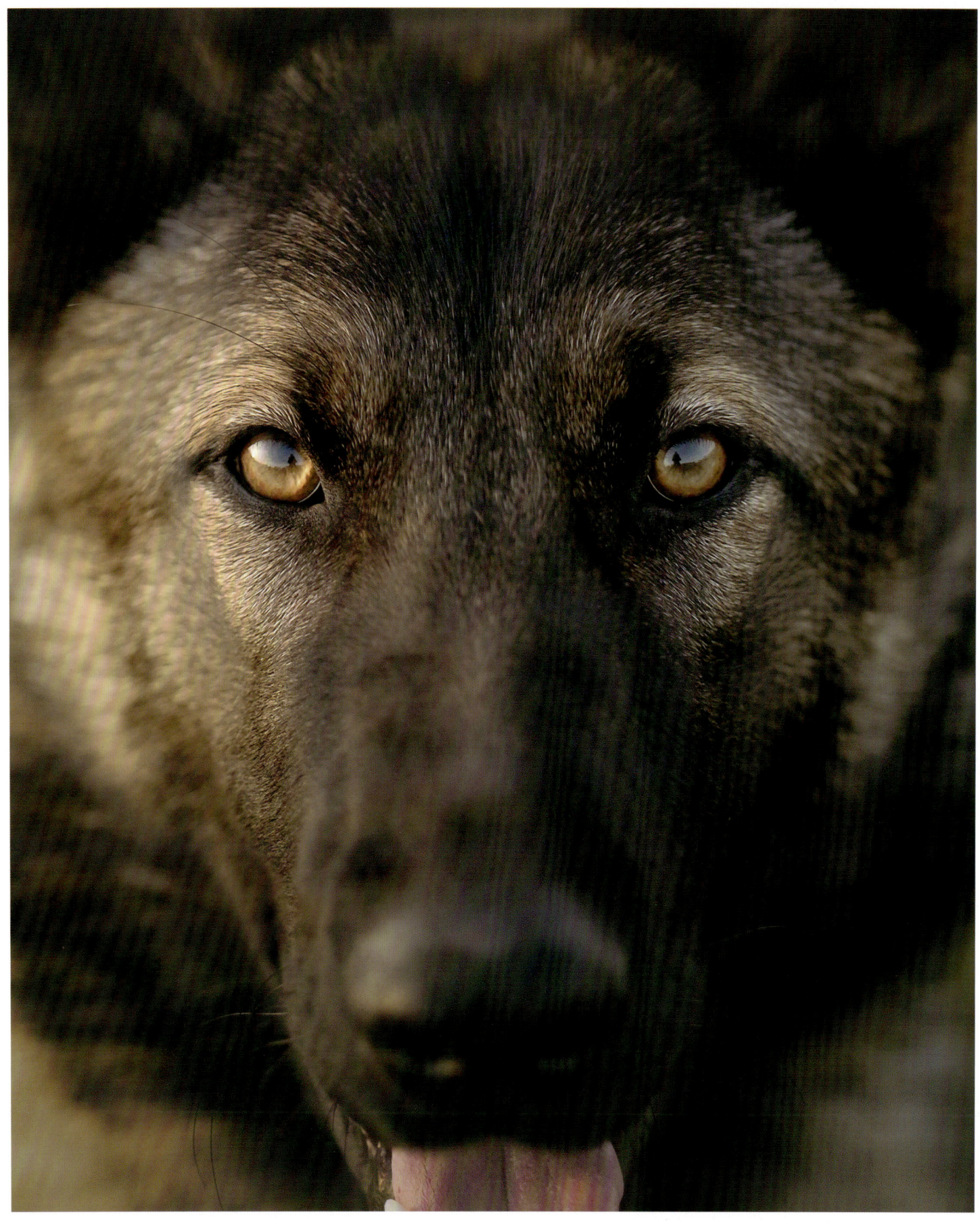

ABOVE:
Distinctive features
Retaining its wolfish looks, the German shepherd dog is regarded as the all-round working dog.

German Shepherd Dog

CHARACTERISTICS

Coat
A coarse, medium-length double coat. Hairs have various colours but black and tan is most common

Height
58–63 cm (23–25in)

Weight
22–40 kg (49–88lb)

Lifespan
More than 10 years

Personality
Alert and loyal

Origin
Germany

The German shepherd dog has strength and agility, and a fast running pace, coupled with obedience, courage and intelligence. While making a loyal and affectionate pet for a committed dog lover, the breed also has a certain aloofness. This is used to good effect when the breed is used as a police dog—they are the top breeds for this in Europe and North America—where they become a formidable tool for projecting power. Additionally, the dogs' strong work ethic and eagerness make them the breed of choice for search and rescue roles.

The medium to large breed was developed by a German cavalry officer Captain Max von Stephanitz from ancestral herding dogs in the late 19th century. The captain's aim was to create a companion to and protector of human owners, as well as working with sheep and cattle. He was very successful in that the German shepherd dog is a contented family member that responds well to voice commands, but nevertheless remains wary of outsiders. Owners must ensure the dogs are well socialized when young and given plenty of mental and physical stimulation.

In the English-speaking world, the breed was renamed to reduce the link to Germany. In Britain, for example, it is known as the Alsatian after a Germanic border region that is currently part of France.

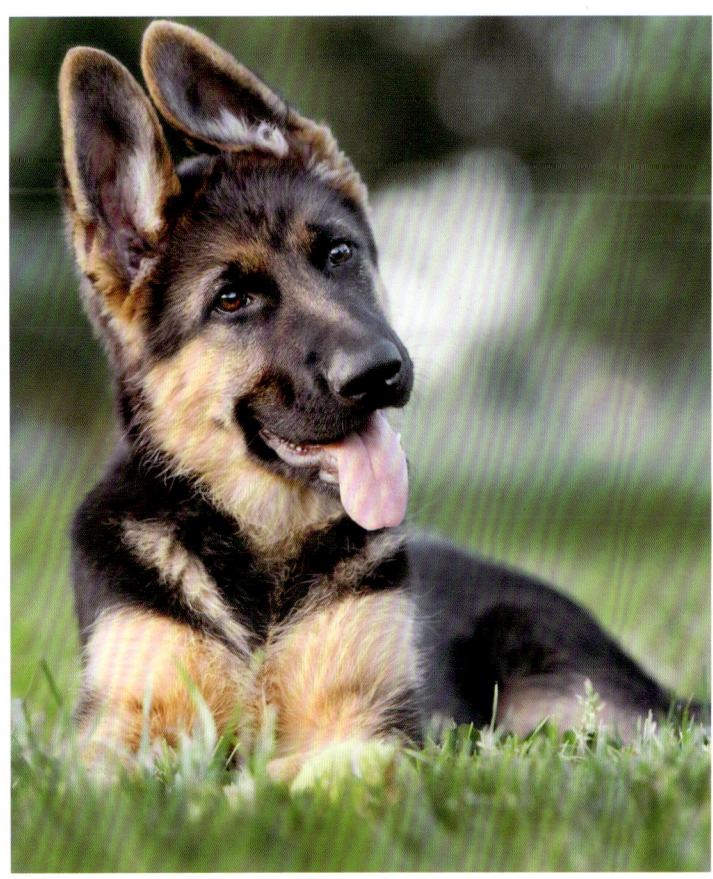
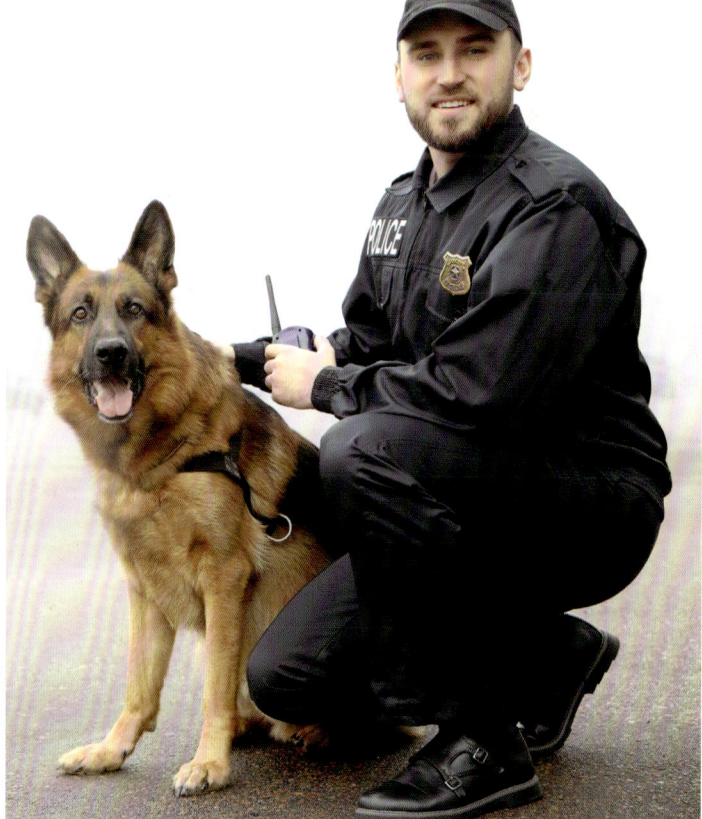

ABOVE BOTH:
Best friend
German shepherd dogs have a streamlined build, a strong work ethic and a courageous and alert temperament which makes them work well in partnerships with a human handler.

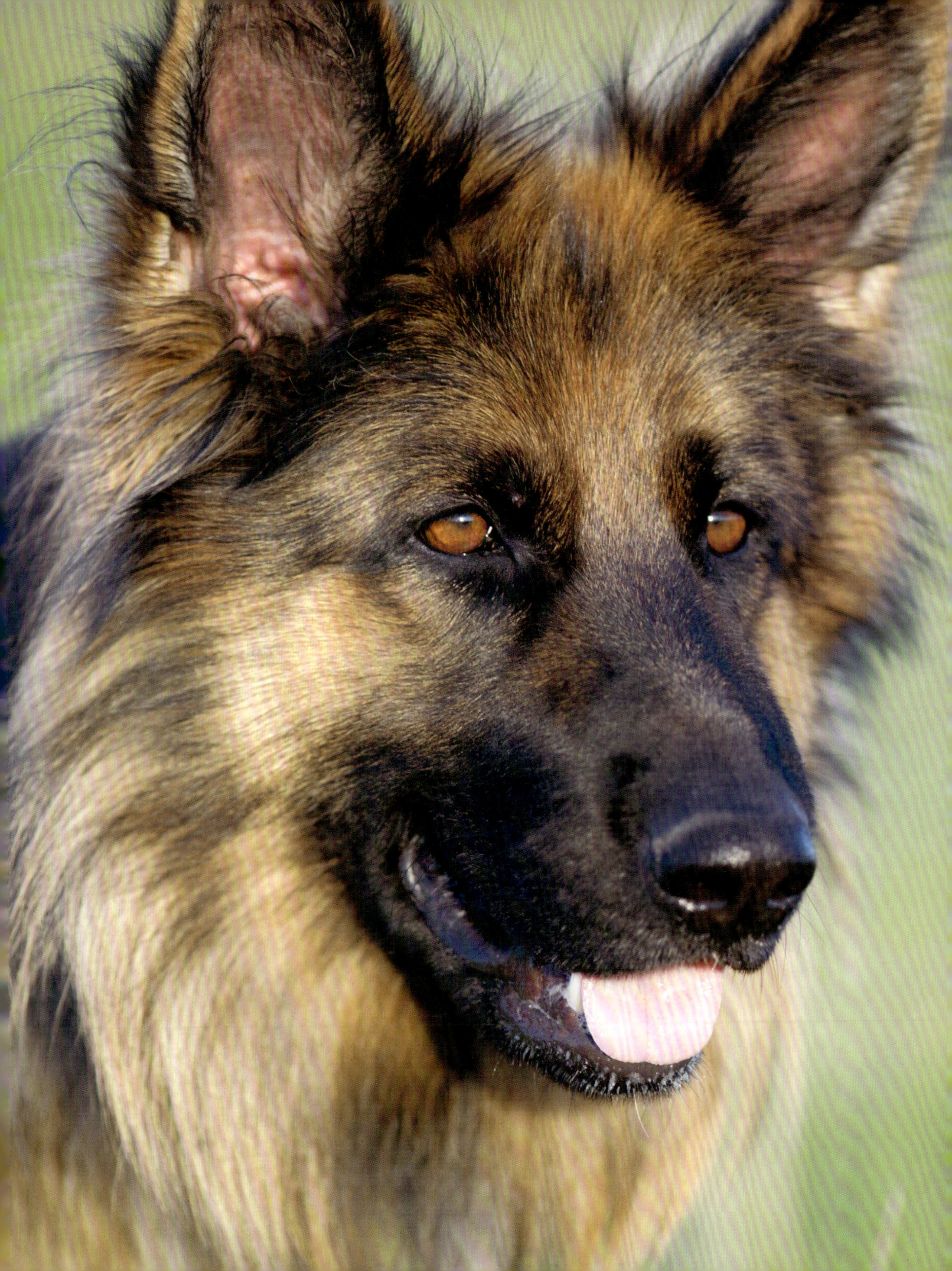

WORKING DOGS

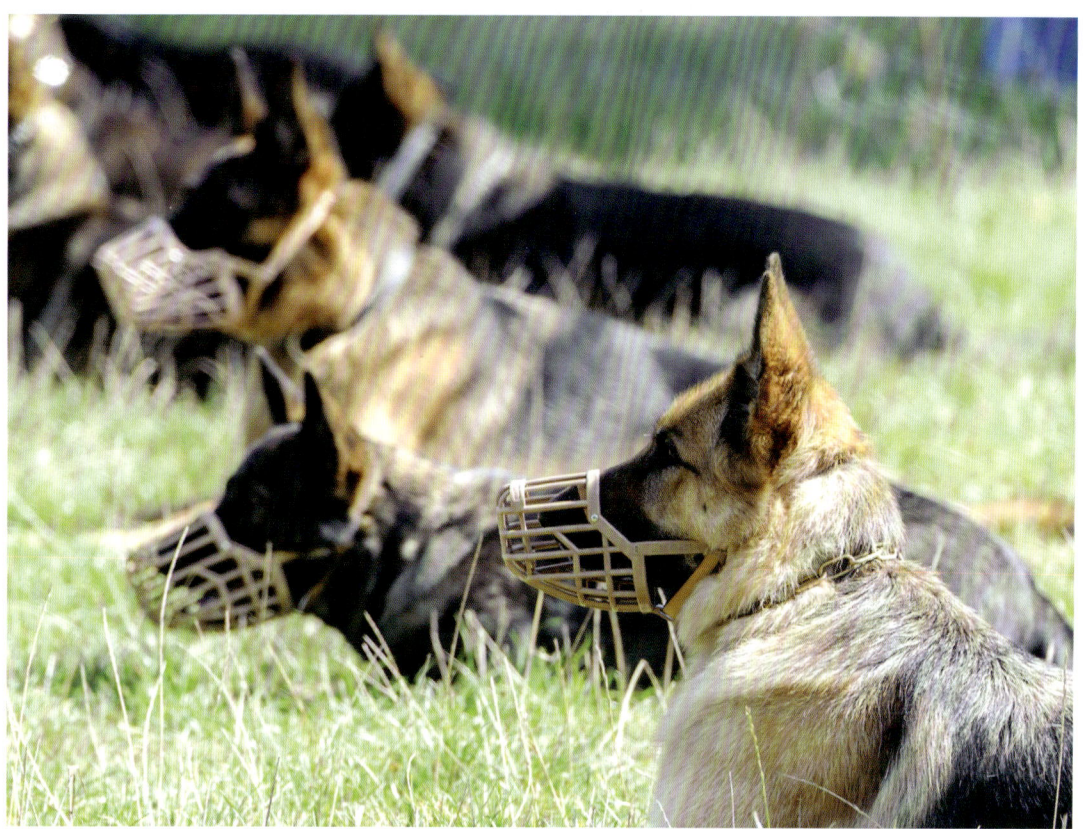

OPPOSITE:
Wartime history
This popular breed was renamed the Alsatian (a region of France) in the UK during the First World War, to distance it from Germany – the enemy at the time. The breed originates in this area, which borders Germany.

LEFT TOP:
Muzzles
Security guard dogs need to be trained to bite and so are muzzled during their obedience training until they have learned when to bite and when not to.

LEFT BELOW:
Attack dog
Police use intelligent, large dogs, such as the German shepherd dog, to find and apprehend criminals. Few people are able to outrun a police dog.

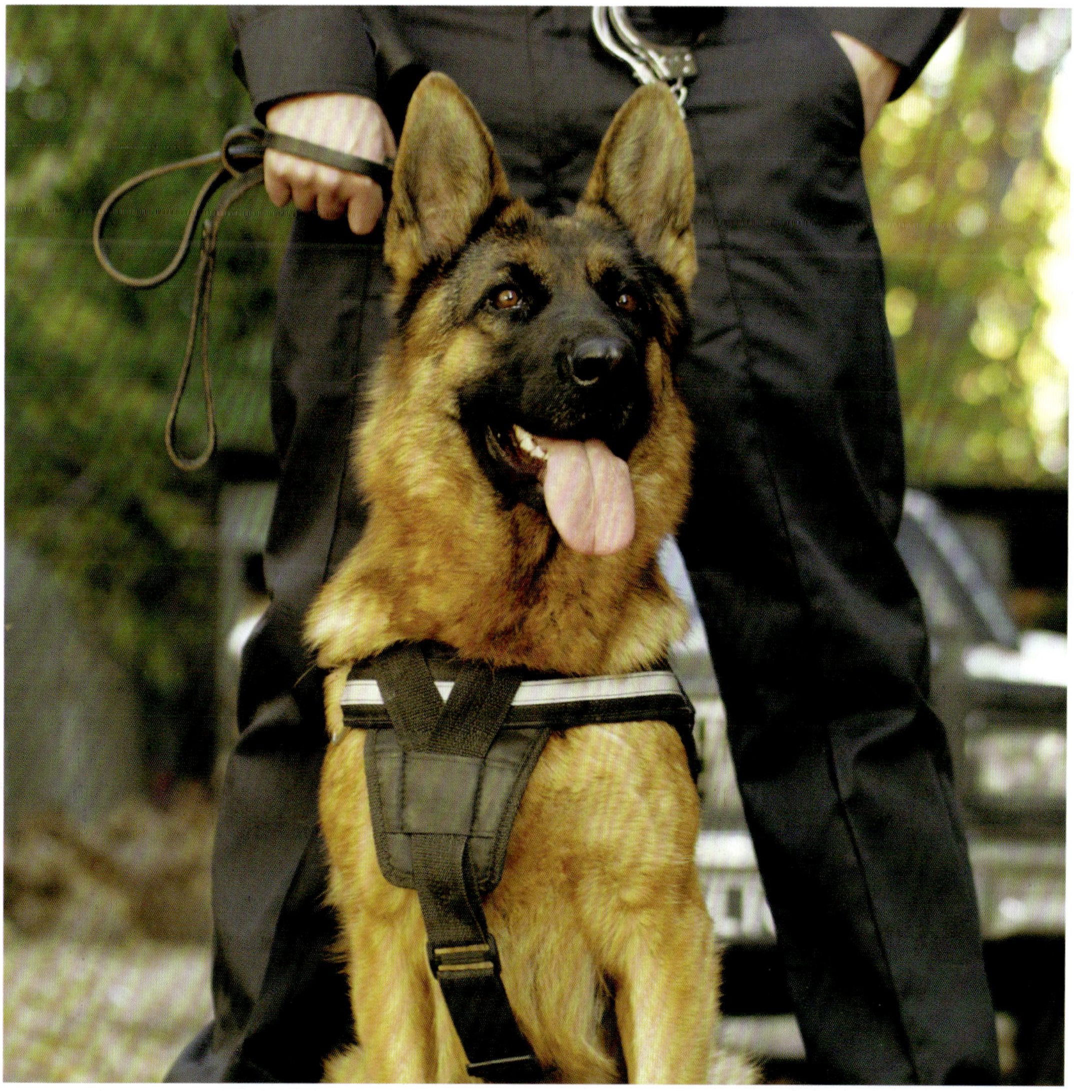

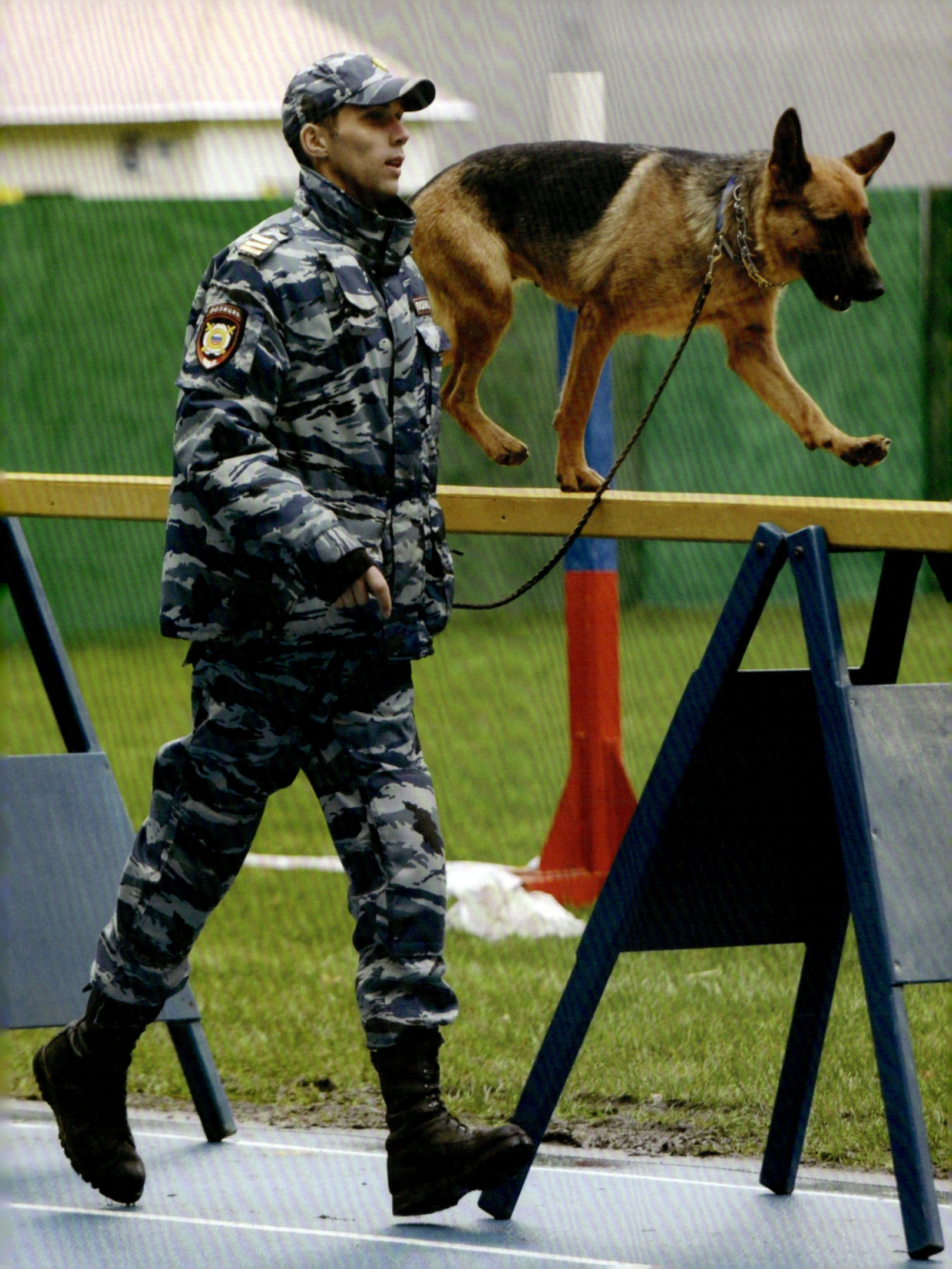

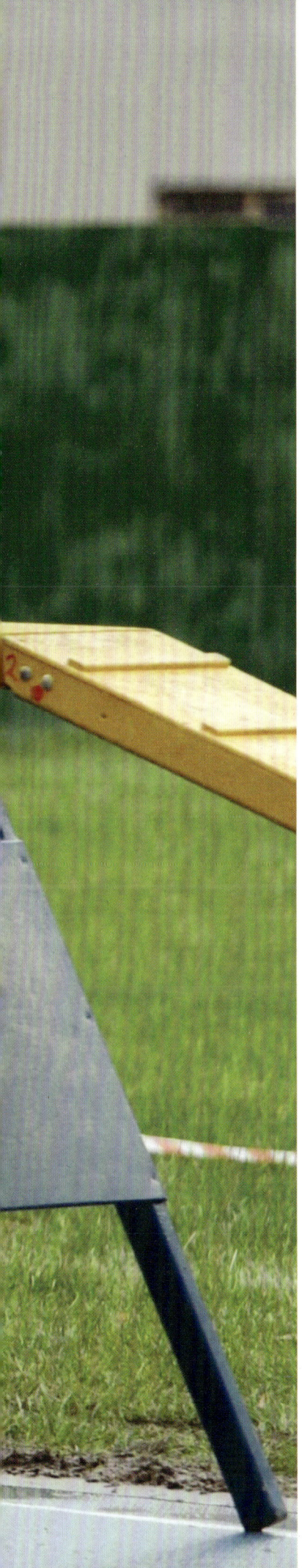

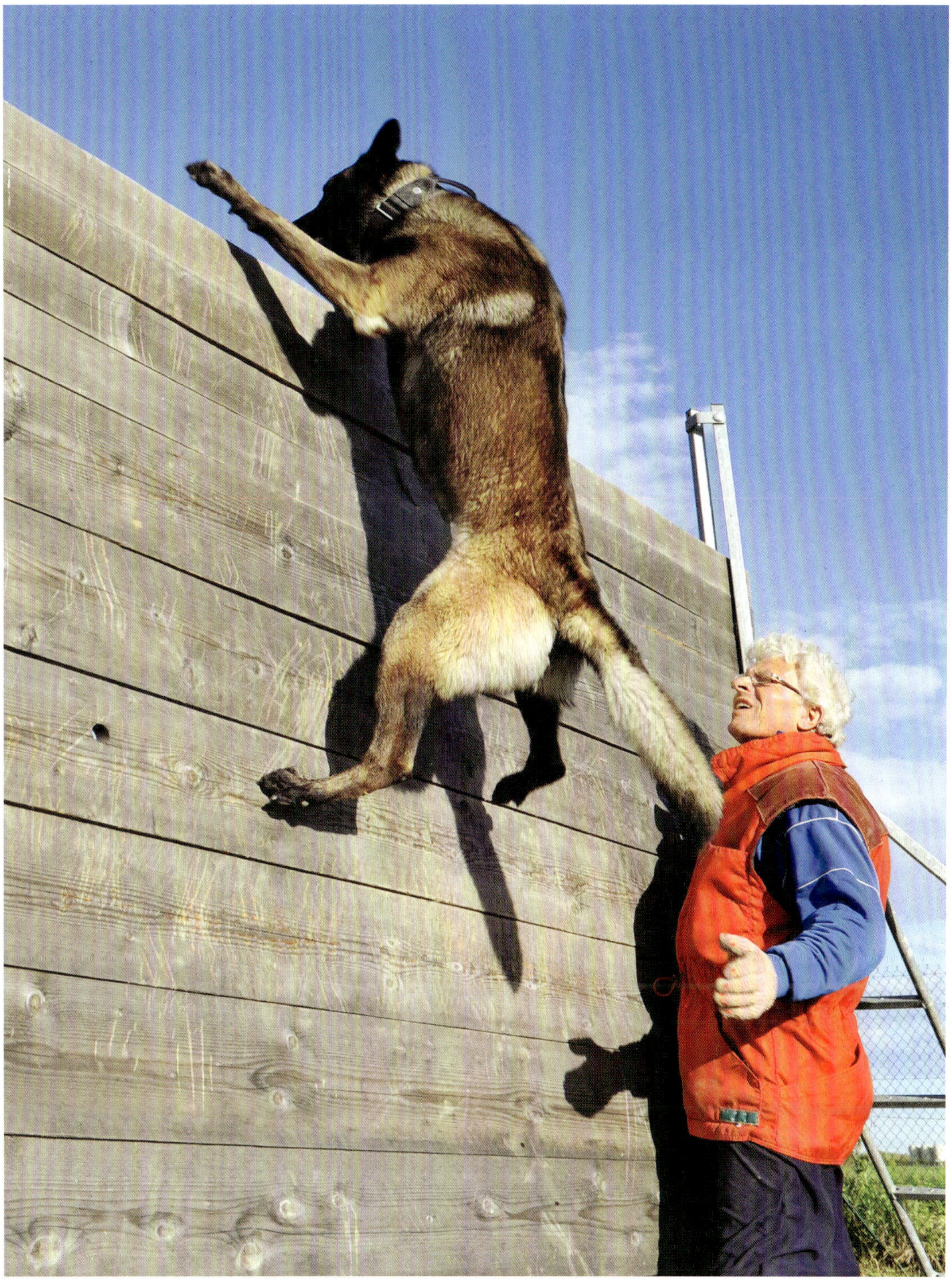

BOTH PHOTOGRAPHS:
Police dogs
Dogs are trained to use their strength, speed and intelligence to apprehend suspects. Just the presence of dogs is often enough to maintain public order.

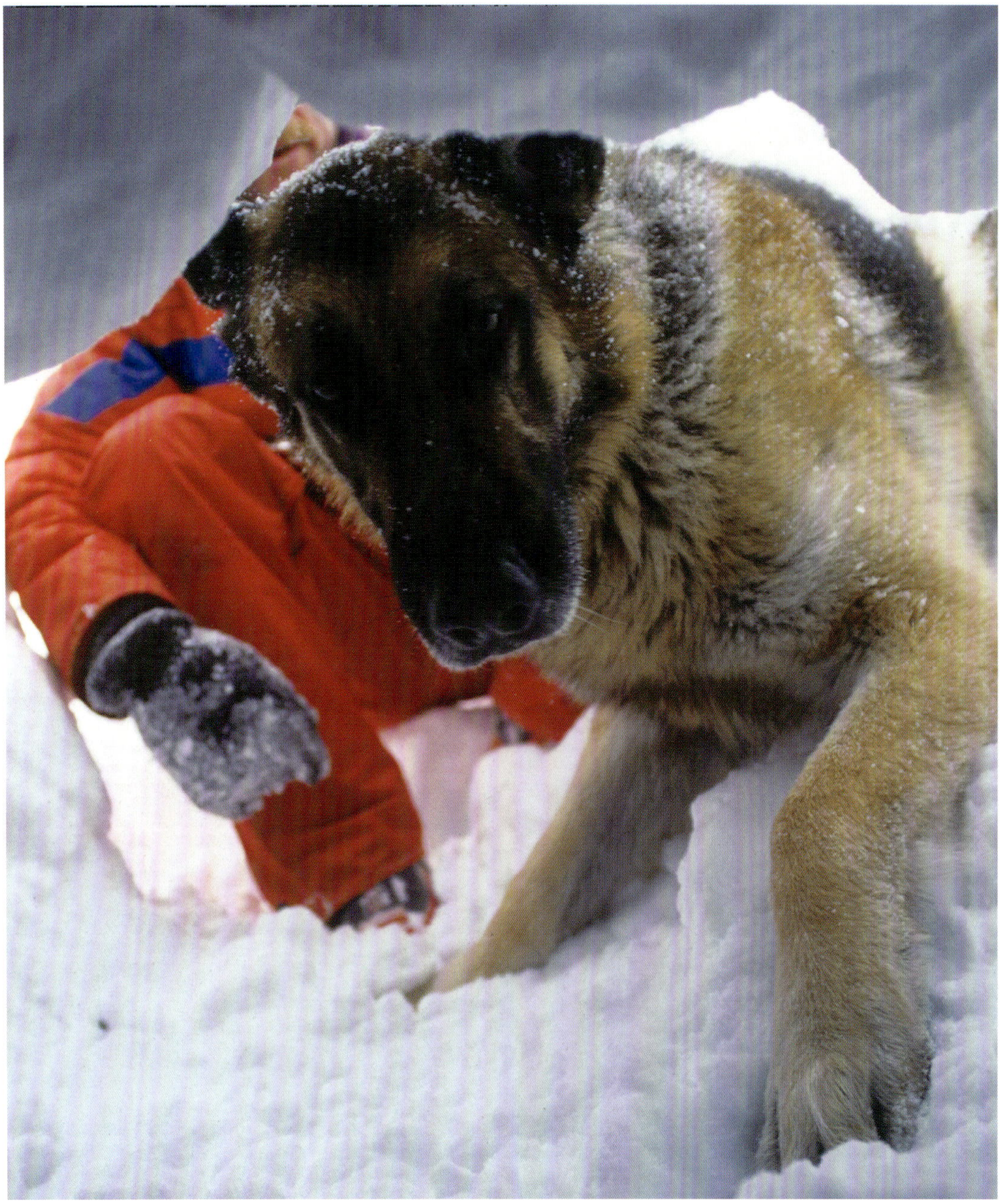

WORKING DOGS

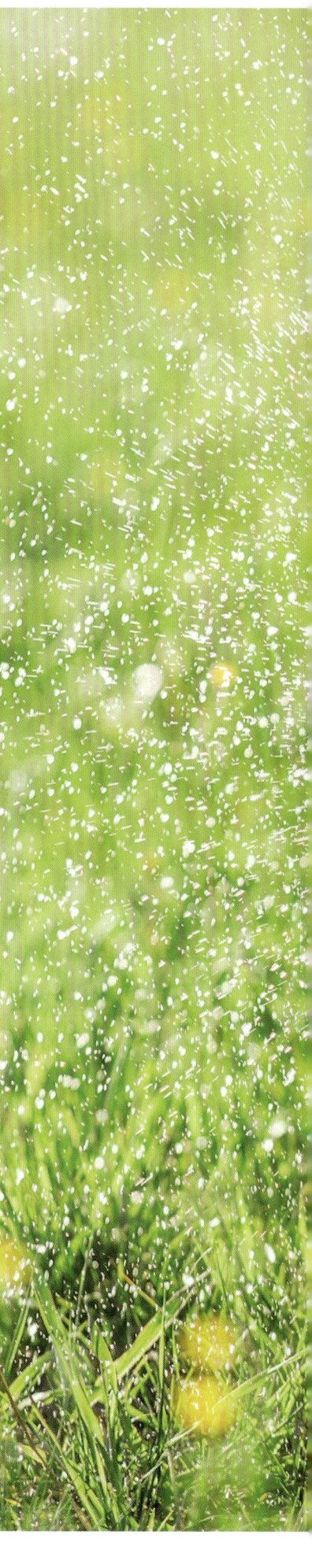

ABOVE:
Search and rescue
A German shepherd dog has been called in to find survivors buried by an avalanche. The dog can smell people under the snow and begins to dig down to them.

RIGHT:
Shake it off
A German shepherd dog shaking off water after a swim. The long outer guard hairs prevent much of the water from getting to the fluffy underfur.

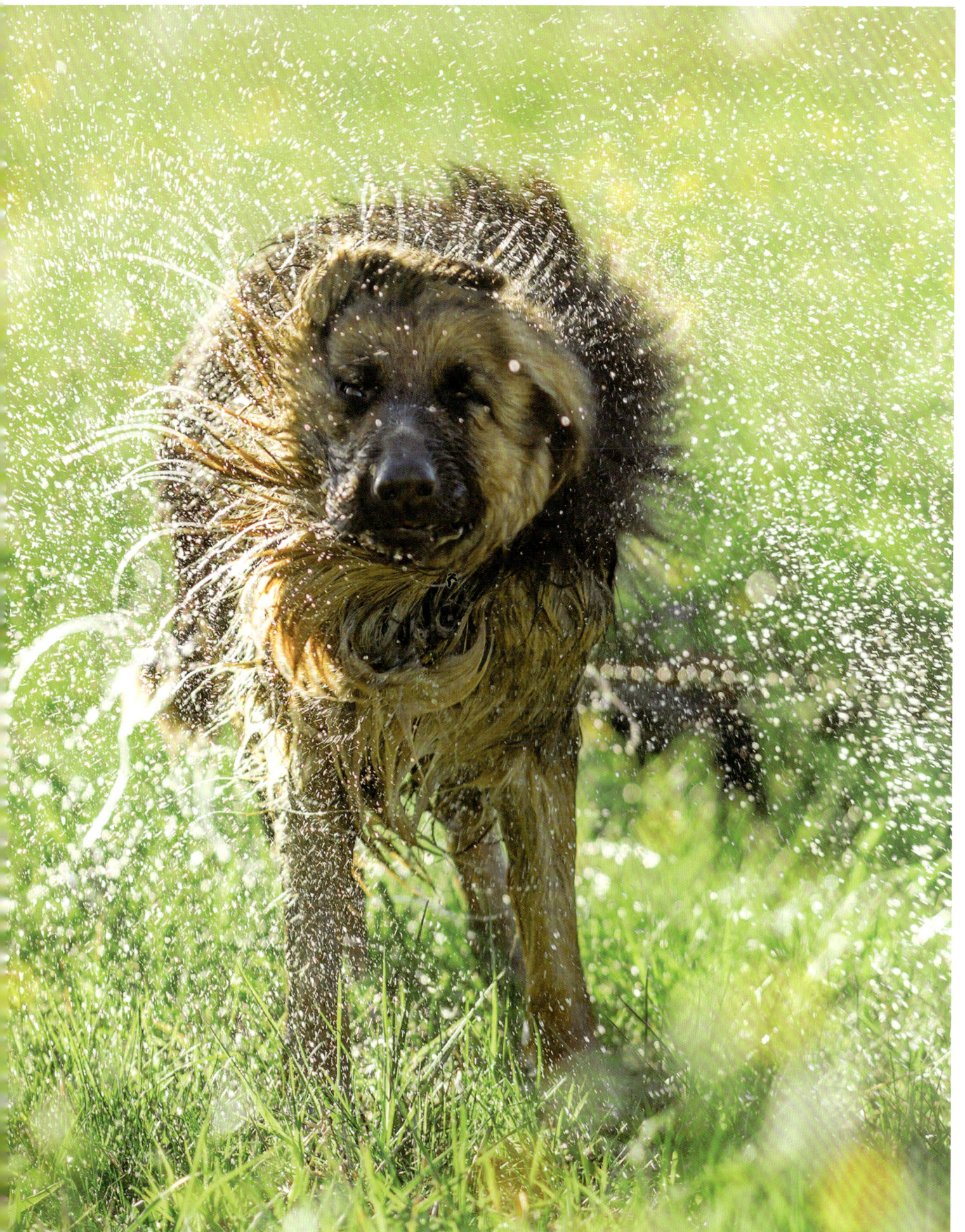

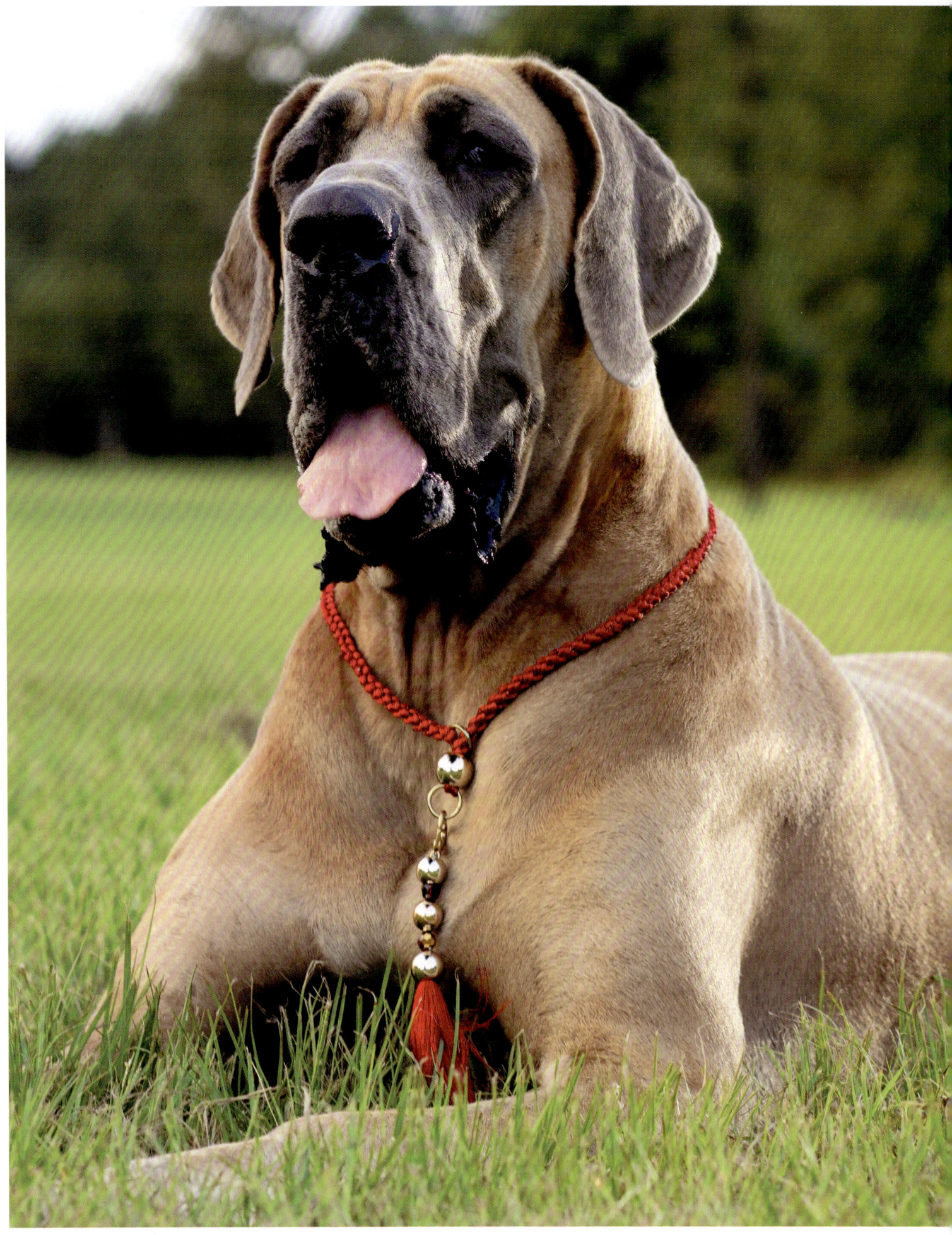

Great Dane

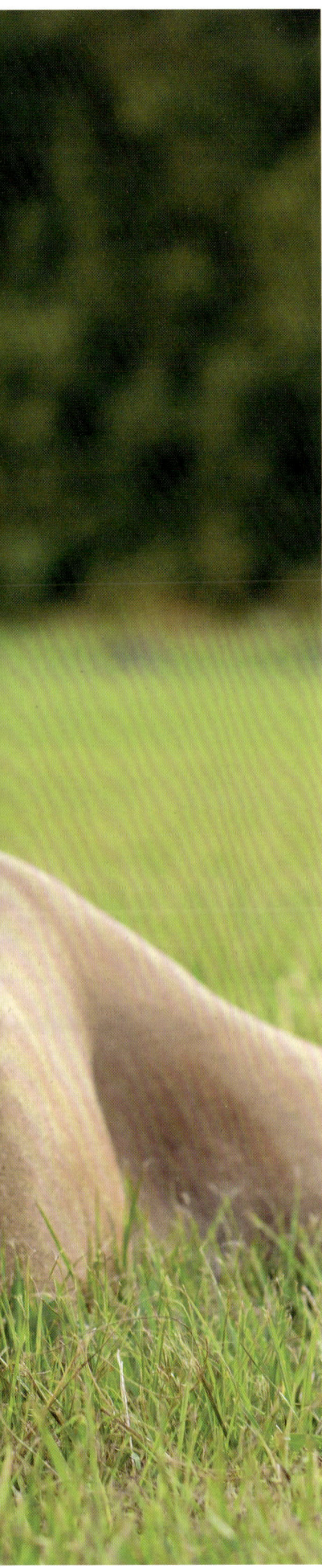

Despite the name, this immense breed is a German creation, and it is known as the Deutsche dog in that country. Why it is now associated with Denmark remains a mystery. The great Dane was by no means the first giant dog, but the modern breed is the tallest ever recorded. The record holder is an American dog called Zeus. This great Dane stands at 1.046 metres (3ft 5.18in) to the shoulder.

The breed was conceived as a boarhound able to catch fast and powerful game animals. It has a mixture of mastiff hunting dogs and wolfhounds to provide bulk and then some greyhound blood to give it speed and agility. The result was a noble dog that became a favourite status symbol—and protector—of northern European aristocrats.

A great Dane is the archetypal gentle giant. It is a loyal and affectionate pet but can be an unwieldy companion due to its great size and strength. It goes without saying that a dog this size eats a lot and requires a lot of space for all aspects of its life—exercise, play and sleep. They are prone to drooling and snoring and tend to live for less than 10 years, which belies the dog's apparent vigour.

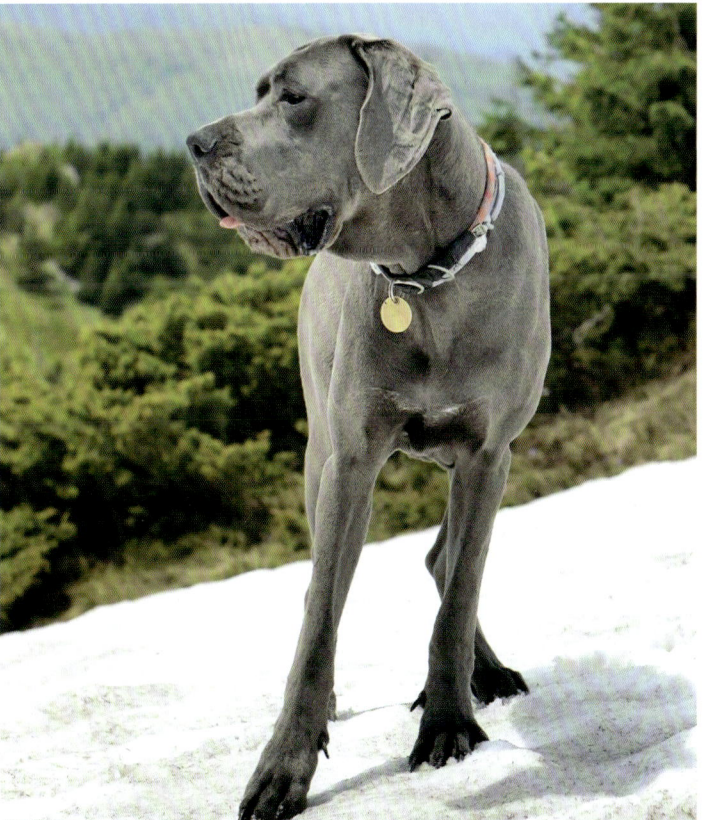

CHARACTERISTICS

Coat
A short and smooth coat that comes in various colours and patterns
Height
71–76cm (28–30in)
Weight
46–54kg (101–120lb)
Lifespan
10 years
Personality
Gentle and dignified
Origin
Germany

LEFT:
Huge hound
Great Danes have a muscular and elegant body, a massive and square head, a long and powerful muzzle.

ABOVE:
A big commitment
The great Dane is a magnificent breed that requires a lot of care and attention, but rewards its owners with unconditional love and companionship.

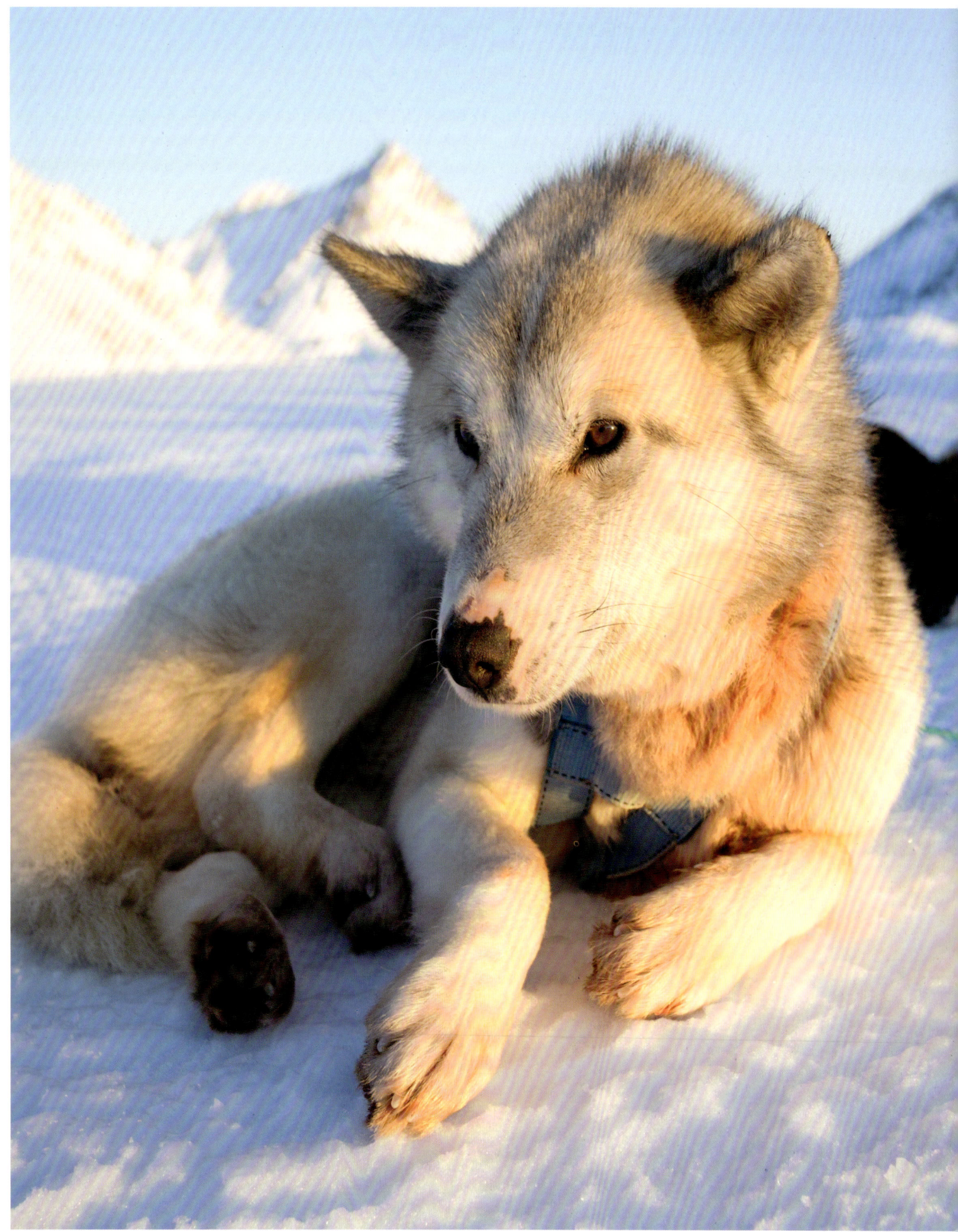

Greenland Dog

Thought by some authorities to be the ancestor of the husky and other sled dogs, this wolfish breed has been living along the coasts of the High Arctic of Asia and North America. Remains found in Siberia are 9,000 years old, and the breed had become established far to the west in Greenland by around 4,000 years ago. This makes it one of the oldest dog breeds in the world.

The Greenland dog's primitive breeding means that even when compared to the other head-strong Arctic dogs, the Greenland dog is stubborn and hard to handle. It needs to be worked hard to assuage its strong drive to chase prey. It will escape from enclosures with fencing less than 180cm (6ft) tall—and will dig under it if that is possible. If left alone for too long, the dog will become bored and begin to howl. The dog's pack instincts are still in evidence, and it will challenge the leadership of its owner from time to time, and this must be swiftly corrected. All in all, the Greenland dog is not well suited to life beyond the tundra and ice of its homeland, and very few people try to keep them as pets.

CHARACTERISTICS

Coat
A thick double coat that makes it almost impervious to freezing conditions

Height
51–68 cm (20–27in)

Weight
27–48 kg (60–106lb)

Lifespan
At least 10 years

Personality
Friendly but stubborn

Origin
Greenland

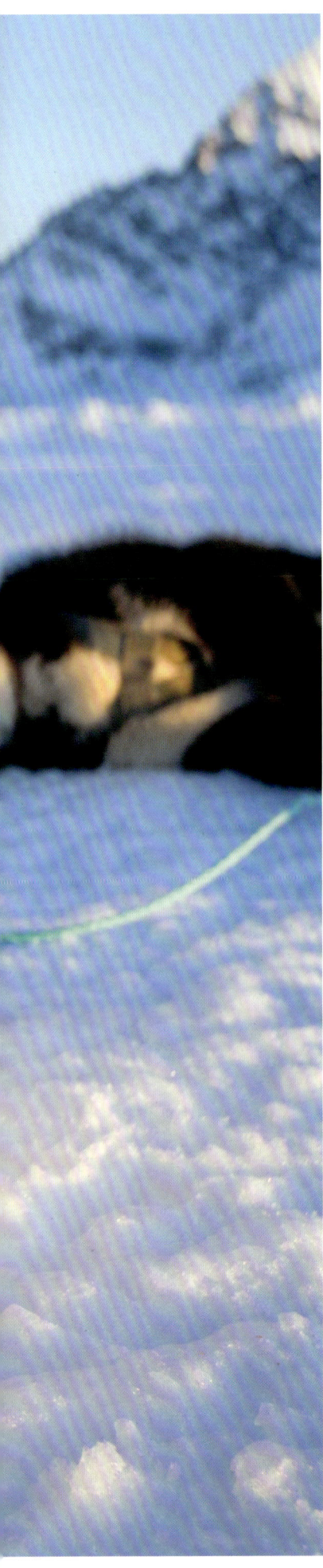

LEFT:
Polar explorer
The Greenland dog was the breed used by Roald Amundsen, the first person to reach the South Pole.

ABOVE:
National treasure
The Greenland dog is protected by law from being imported or mixed with other breeds.

WORKING DOGS

Wolf-like breed
This breed of Greenland dog is now banned from Antarctica, as are all other non-native animals, despite their history in the area.

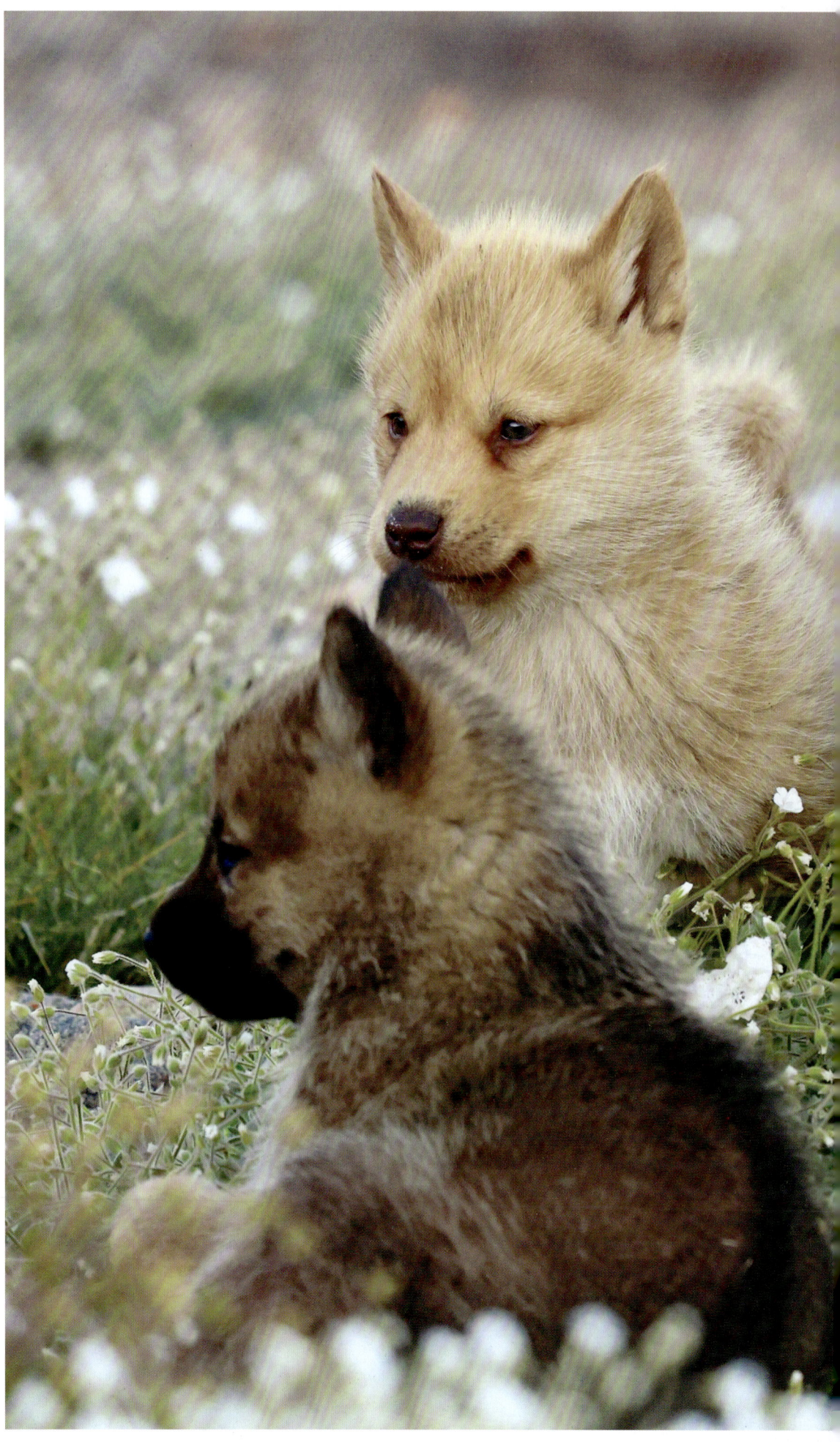

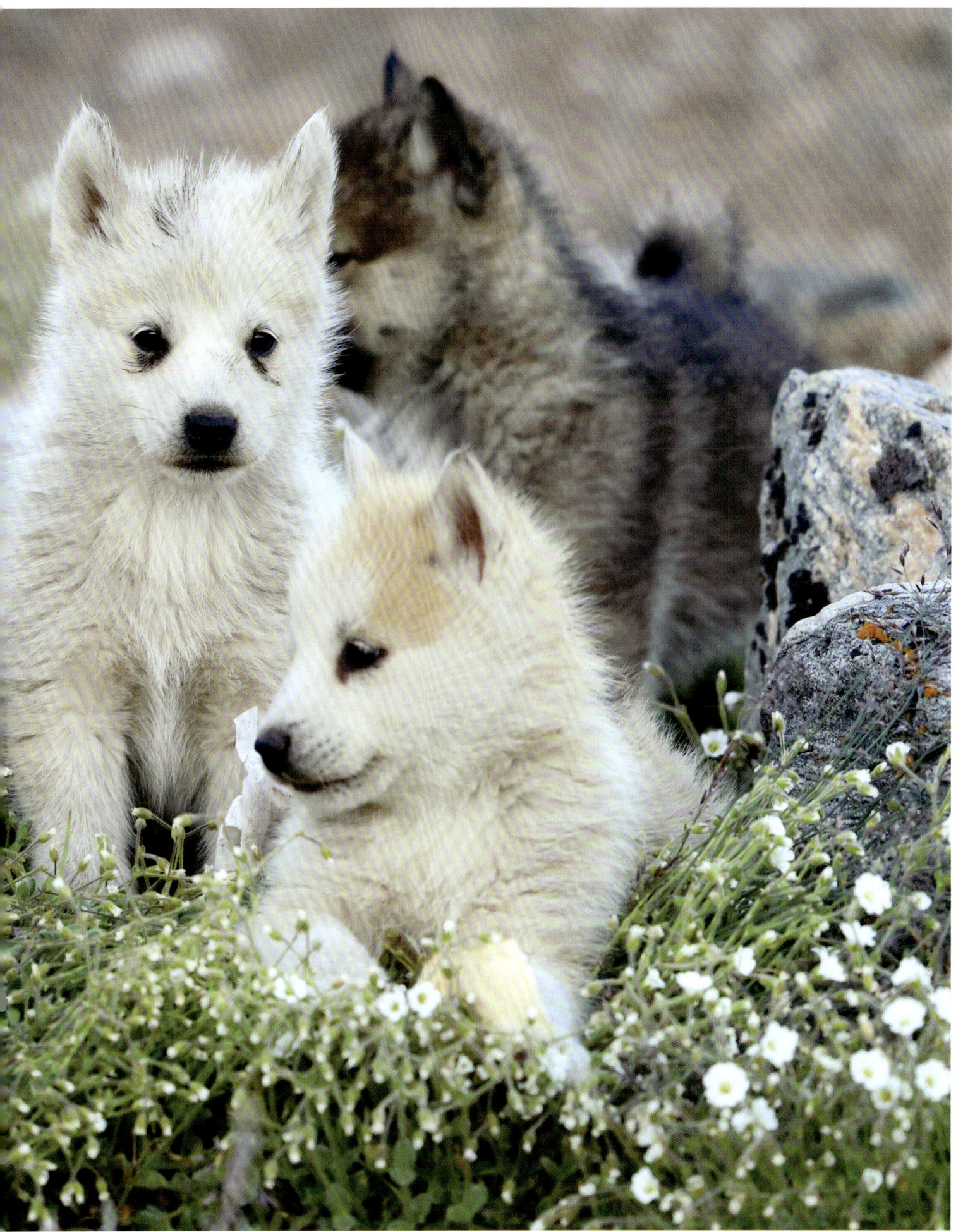

WORKING DOGS

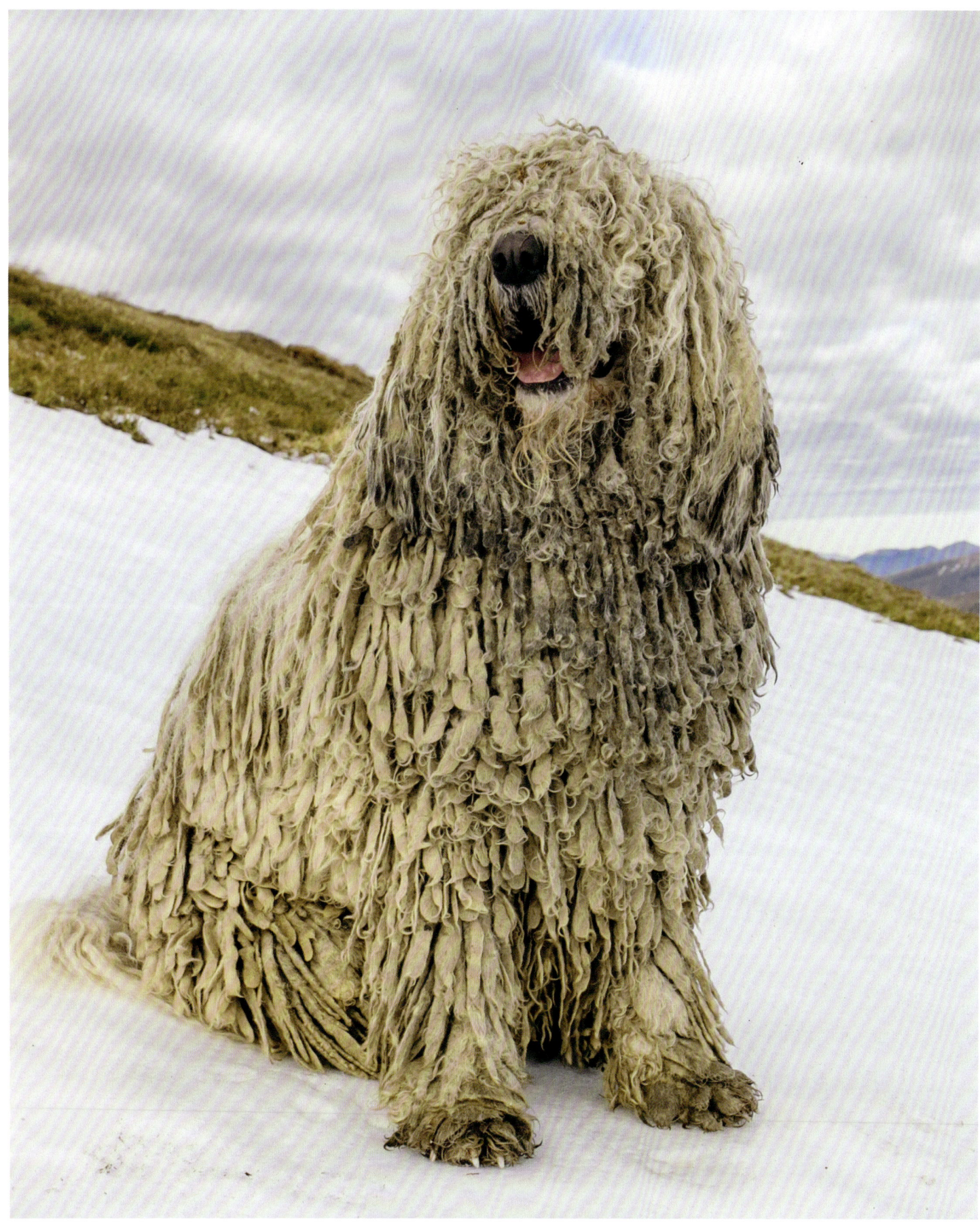

ABOVE:
Multipurpose
The distinctive locks of the Komondor keep out the cold and help it to blend in among the snow and sheep in the barren hills.

Komondor

CHARACTERISTICS
Coat
Tasselled white coat that becomes corded when long
Height
60–80cm (24–31in)
Weight
36–61kg (79–135lb)
Lifespan
Less than 10 years
Personality
Independent and alert
Origin
Hungary

Looking like an enormous mop brought to life, this Hungarian guardian dog is left to tend to a flock of sheep all by itself. The off-white tasselled coat gives the dog a cunning disguise so it can blend in among its woolly charges and catch any lynx or wolf that comes threatening by surprise. The coat also keeps the dog warm when out in the open day and night, and it also acts as a protective layer against the bites and claws of its foe.

The Komondor is big, strong and fierce when called upon, but the dog is very forgiving of its sheep neighbours. In fact the puppies are traditionally raised alongside lambs, which serves to socialize the dogs into leaving the flock animals alone, but also ensures that the sheep are not spooked by their canine companions.

Still rare outside Hungary, the dogs are thought to have been brought to the region by the Cumans, a Turkic people migrating from far to the east around 1,000 years ago. The Cumans were nomadic pastoralists, who spent their days on horseback and relied on their dogs to drive herds and flocks between pastures.

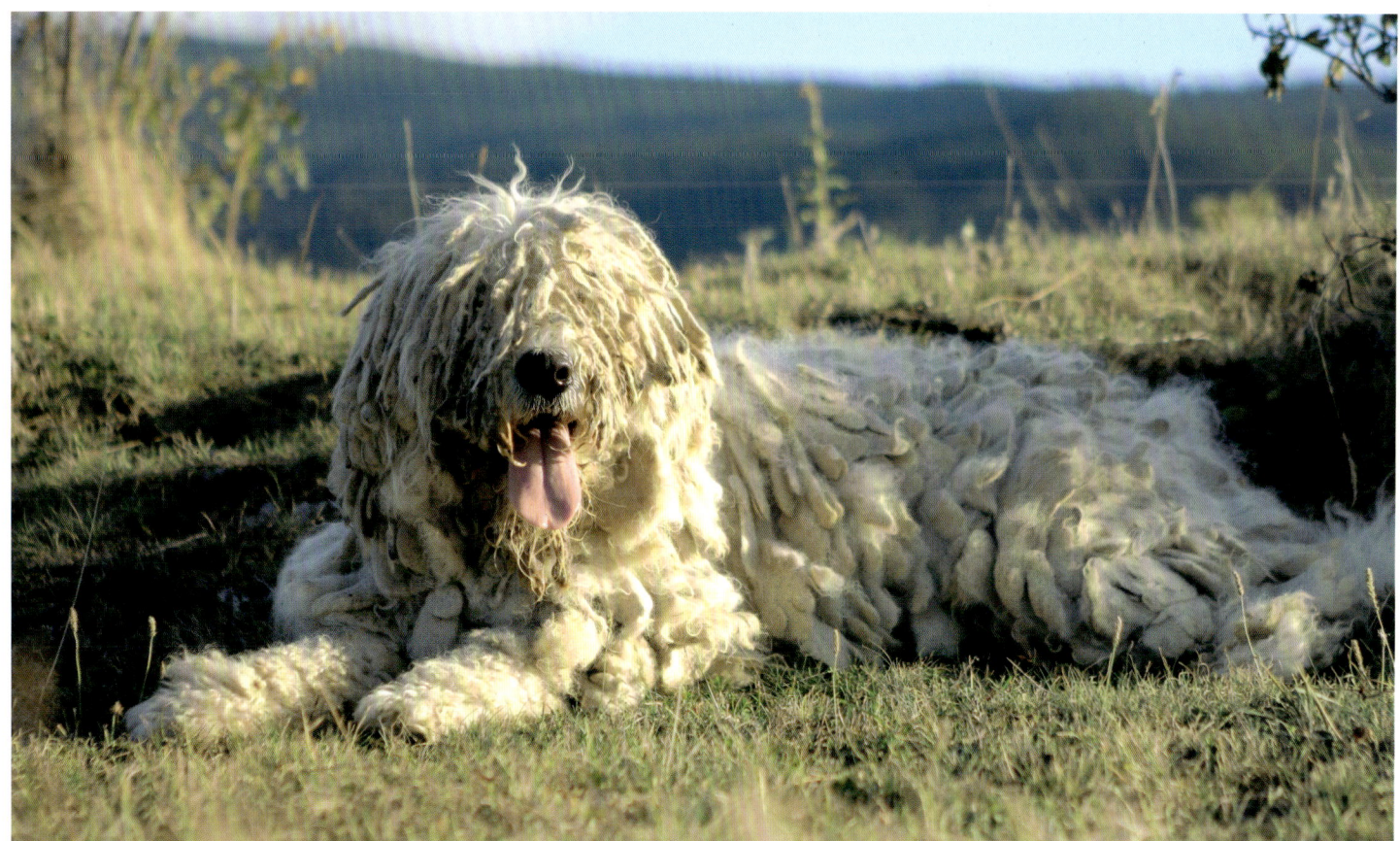

ABOVE:
Eye catching
The Komodor can find a place as a family pet, and is sure to turn a few heads, but it needs a lot of care and attention so it feels at home—not least a lot of grooming!

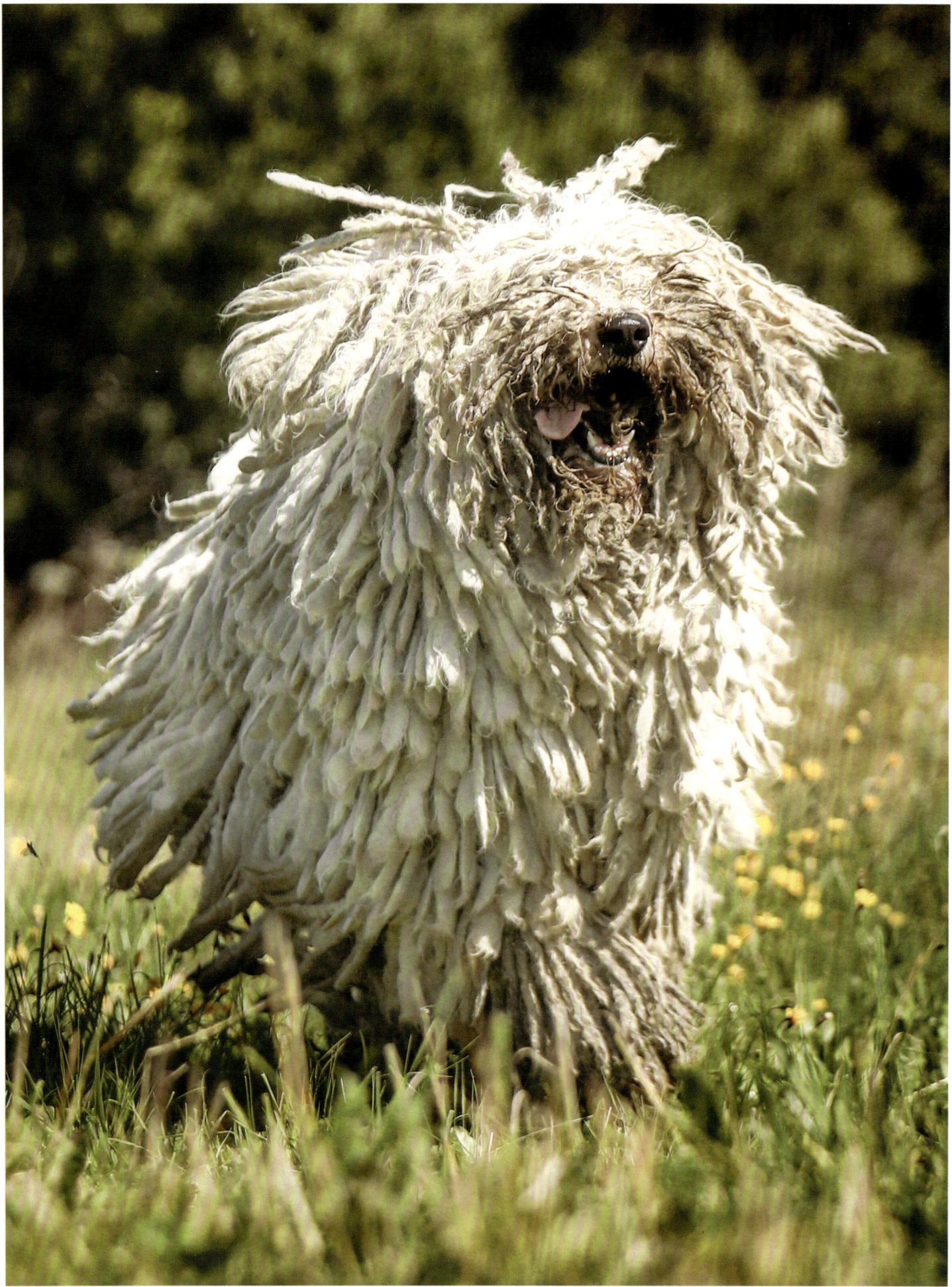

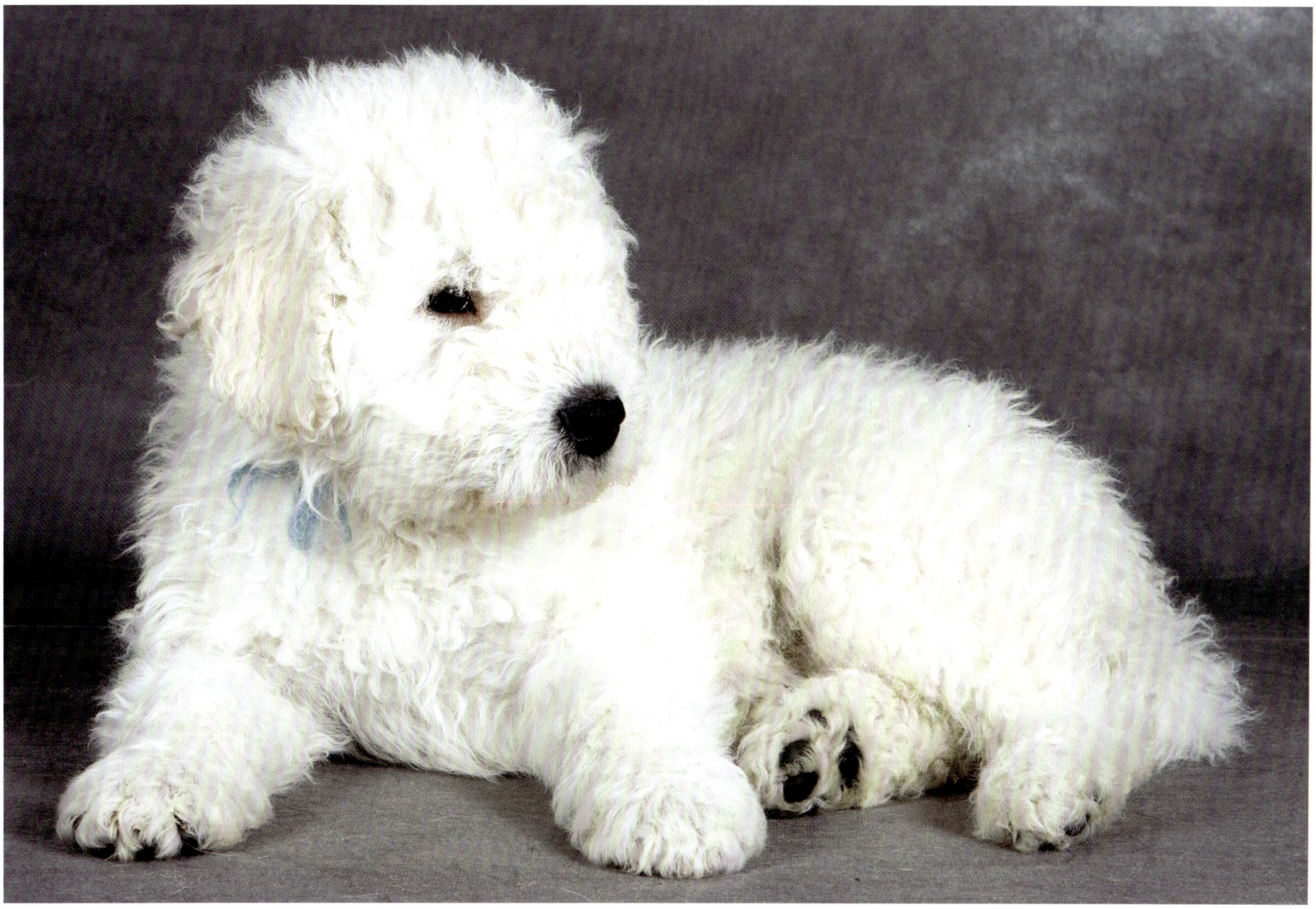

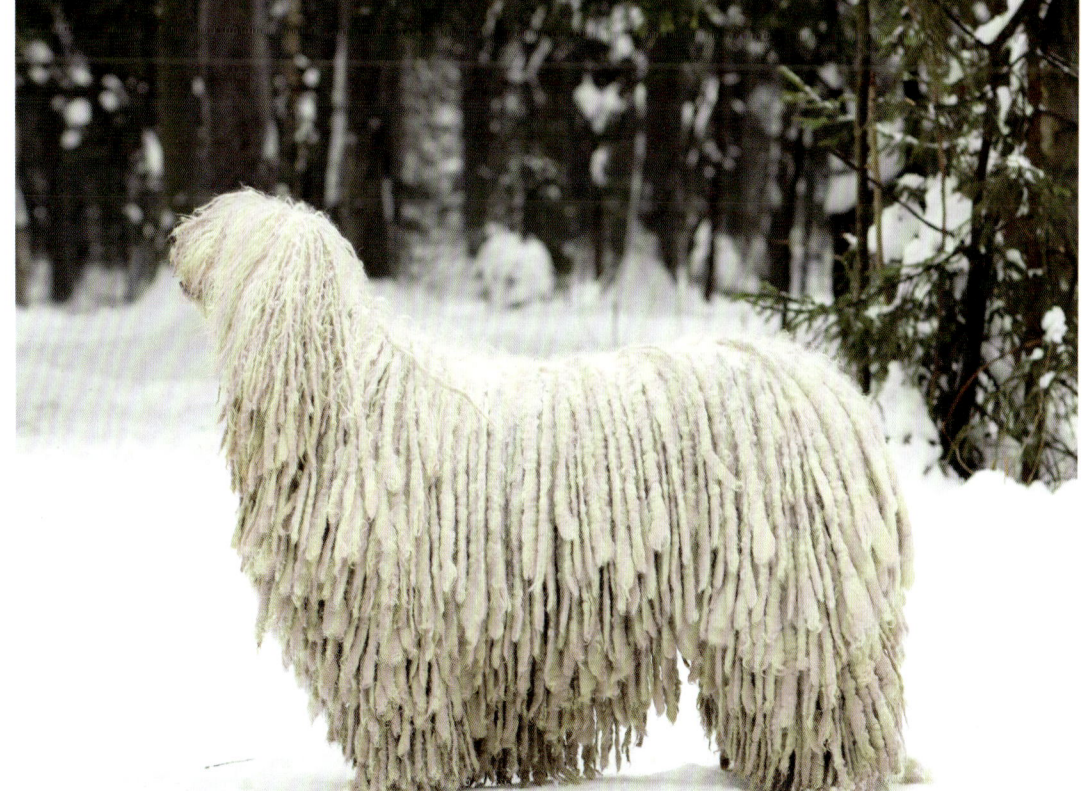

ABOVE:
Famous fur
This pup will not develop the tasselled coat for which this breed is famed for at least a year.

LEFT AND OPPOSITE:
In disguise
A shaggy Hungarian sheepdog breed that looks like it is in disguise as a sheep. This probably arrived in Eastern Europe with migrants from Asia around 1,000 years ago.

Leonberger

This 19th century German breed, named after the town of Leonberg, has the heavy-set stature of a mountain dog but the glossy good looks of a companion dog. That was the aim of its creator Heinrich Essig, a businessman and local politician who spotted a gap in the market for this kind of dog. He crossbred hefty St Bernards and Pyrenean mountain dogs with thicker-coated and good-natured Newfoundlands. The Leonberger breed proved very popular, and Essig sold around 300 a year at extravagant prices. His customers included Tsar Nicholas II of Russia, Napoleon III, Otto Von Bismark and Empress Elisabeth of Austria Hungary, to name but a few.

The Leonberger certainly has a majestic air, but it is a hard worker too. It has webbed feet and an oily coat, making it an able swimmer, and it has the size and strength to pull carts and guard livestock. However, since its creation owners have been drawn to its good nature. The Leonberger thrives as part of the family, with a well-balanced temperament, neither aggressive nor shy, although it will become protective of its family when provoked. Nevertheless, as is typical of intelligent breeds, it requires a long period of socialization to develop a sound temperament, and needs clear leadership from its owner.

CHARACTERISTICS

Coat
A double coat that is water-resistant and comes in various shades of yellow, red, brown or sandy, with a distinctive black mask on the face

Height
72–80 cm (28–31in)

Weight
45–77 kg (99–170lb)

Lifespan
More than 10 years

Personality
Good-natured

Origin
Germany

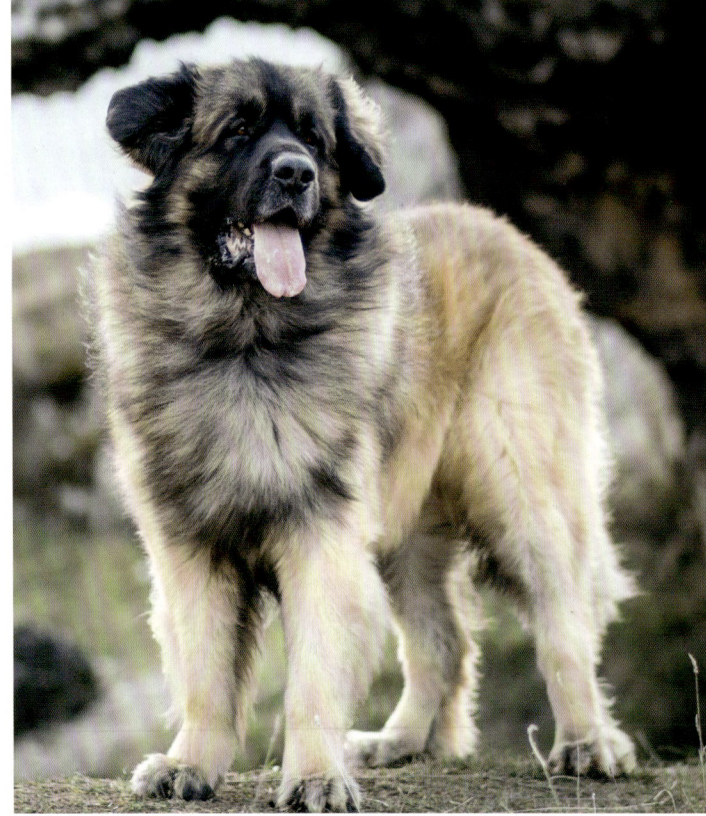

ABOVE:
Kind eyes
The Leonberger's head is deep and broad and the almond-shaped eyes express intelligence and kindness.

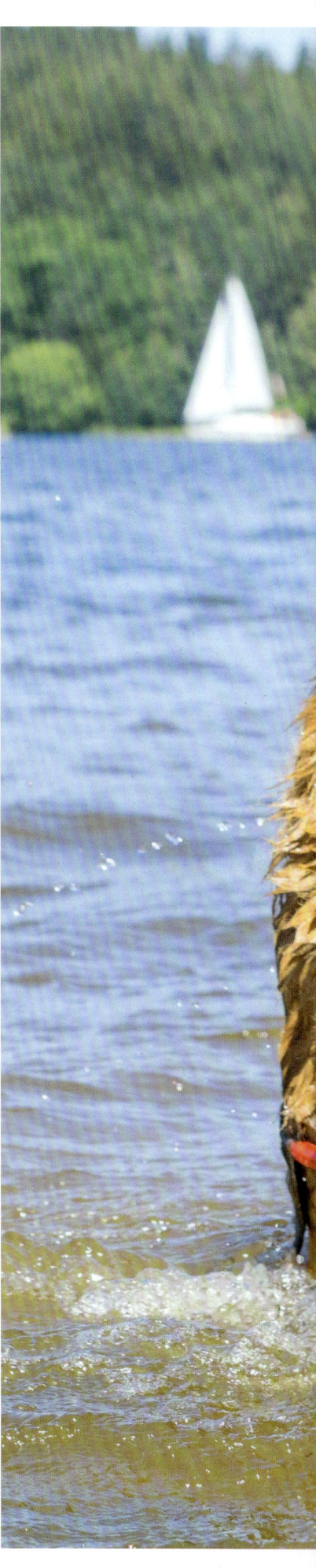

RIGHT:
Up for fun
The Leonberger enjoys outdoor activities such as hiking and swimming. It is not very interested in fetching or chasing balls.

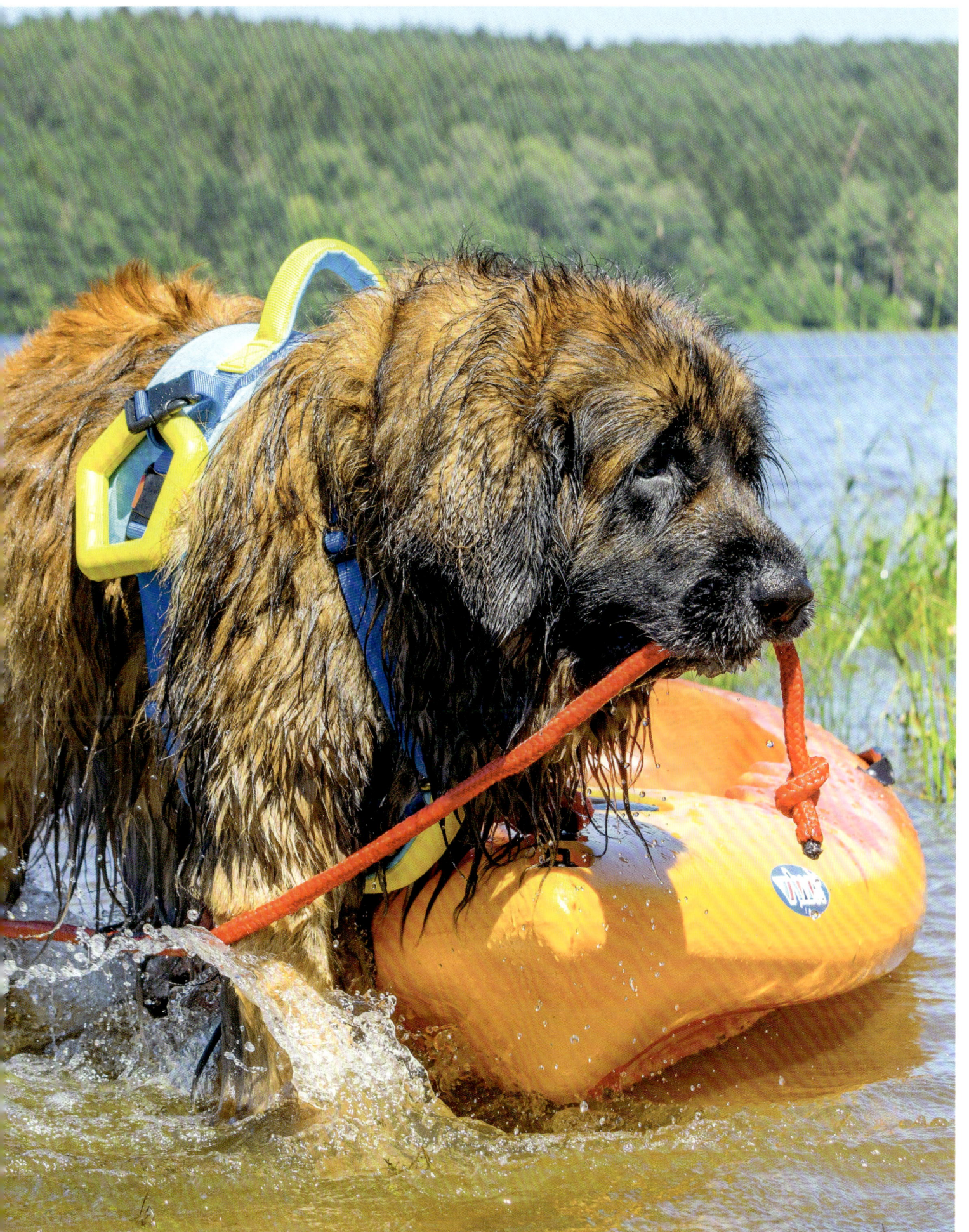

WORKING DOGS

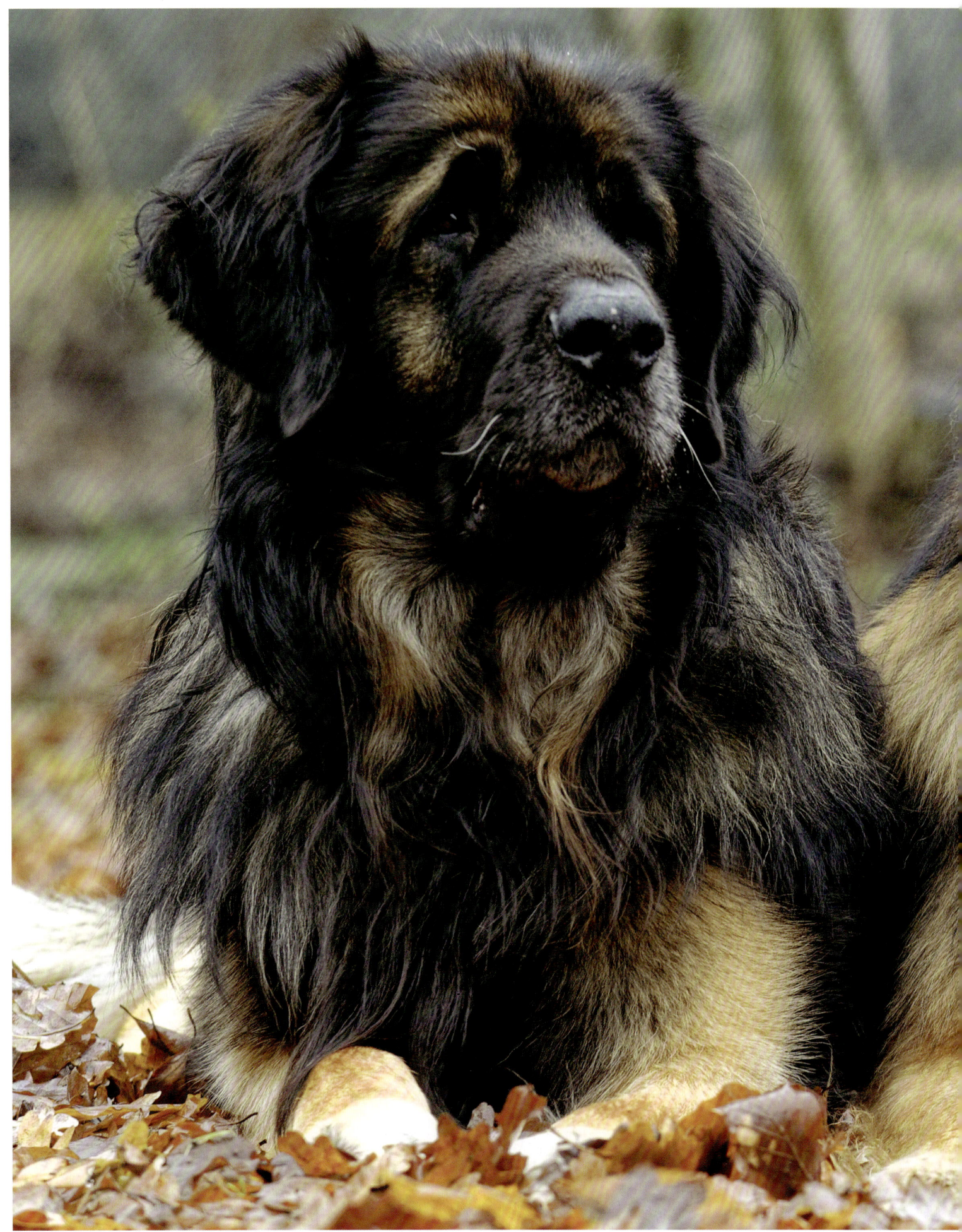

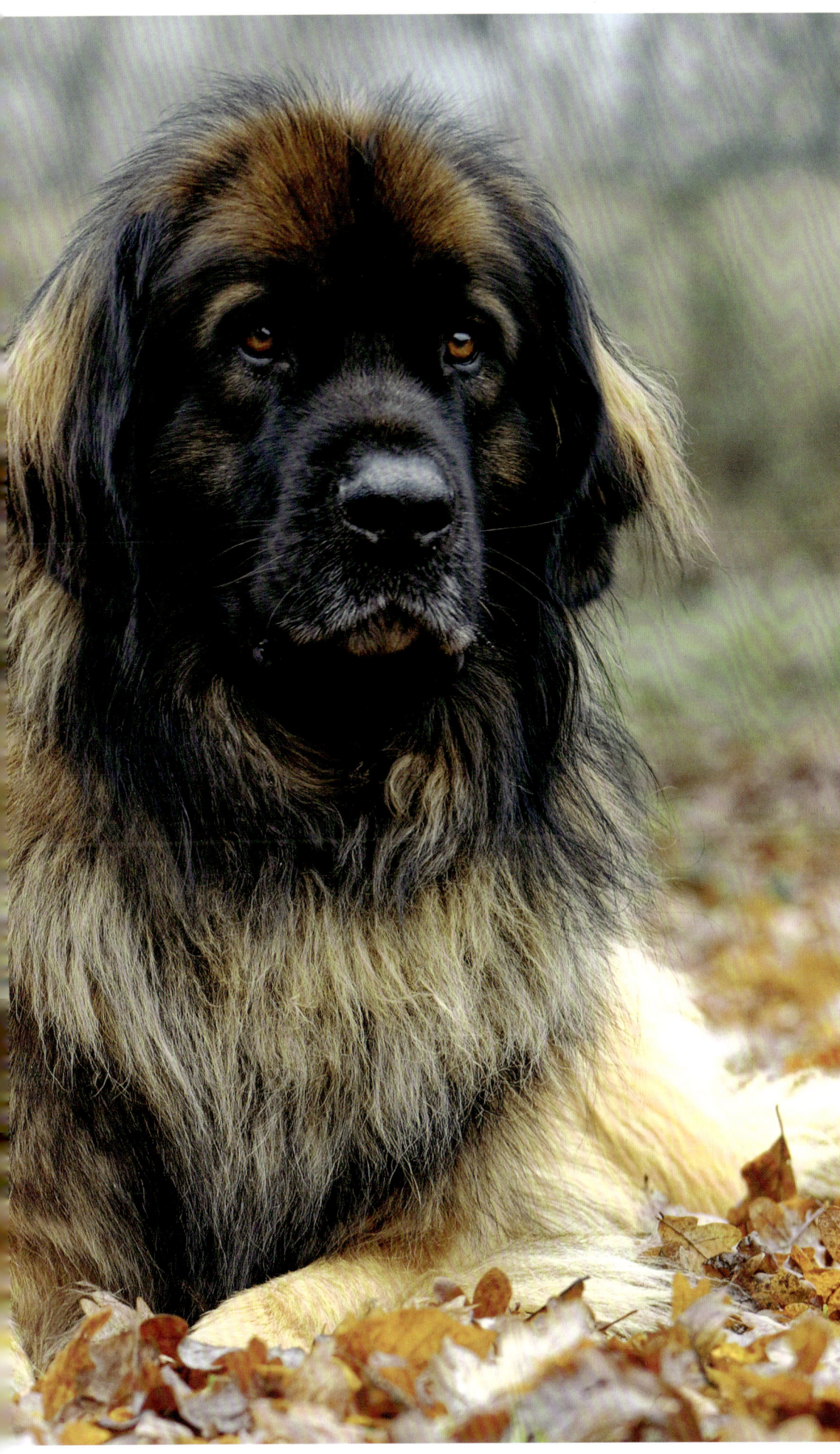

Man and wife
The dog (male) has a shaggier and wider head than the bitch (female, left). This breed are ideal family pets for those who can accommodate their giant size and cope with the hair!

WORKING DOGS

Family fun
A Leonberger mother and pup have some fun together.

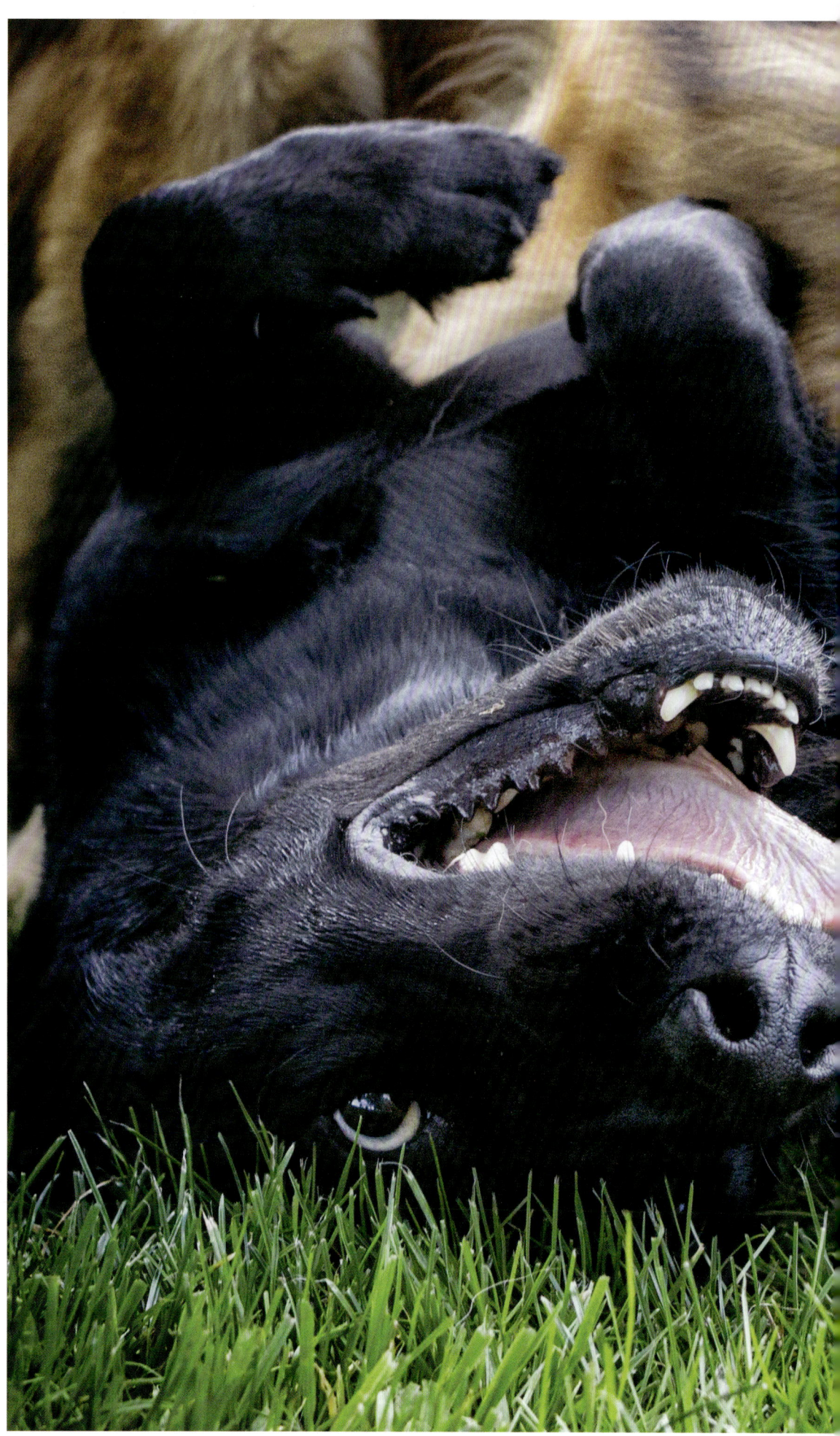

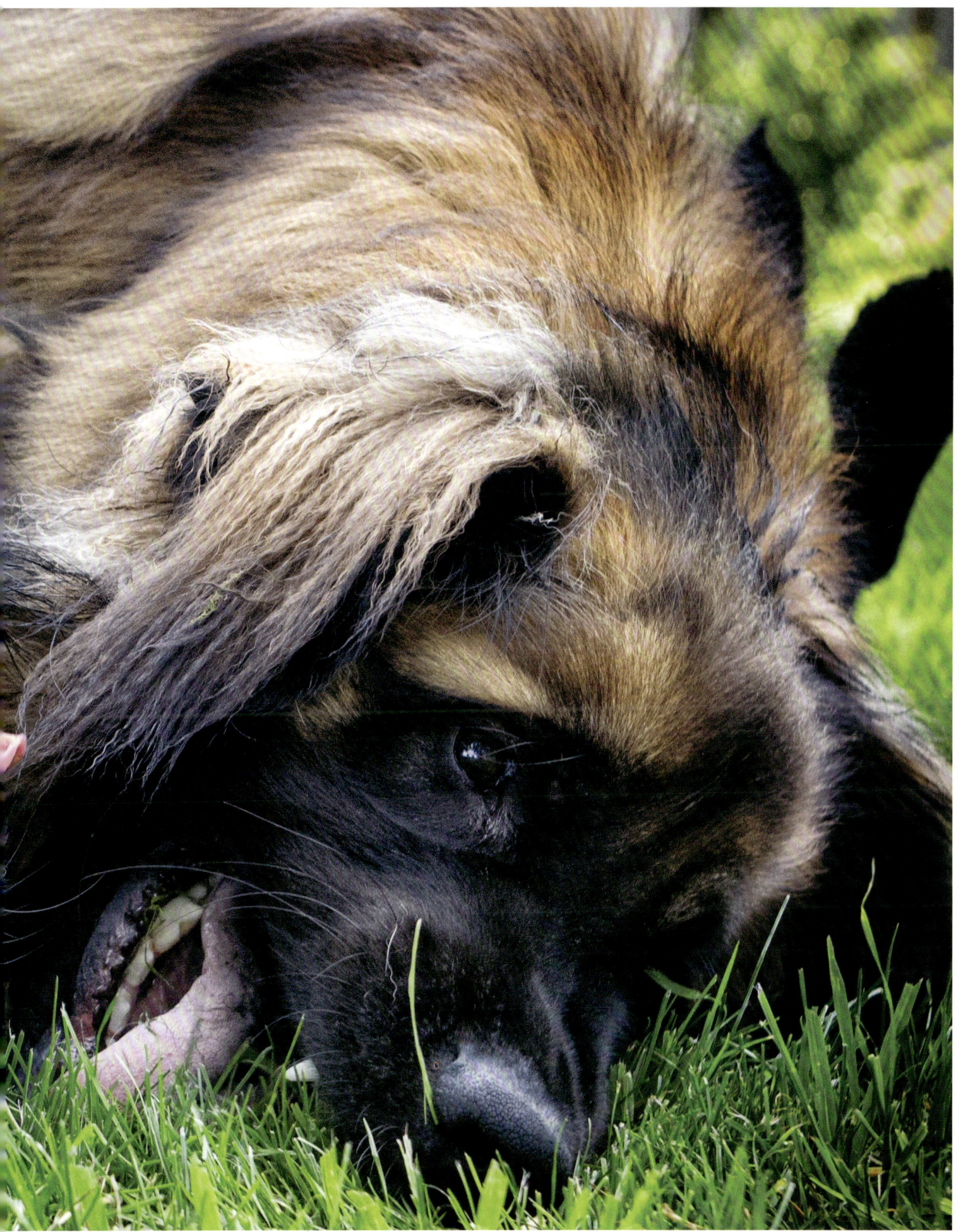

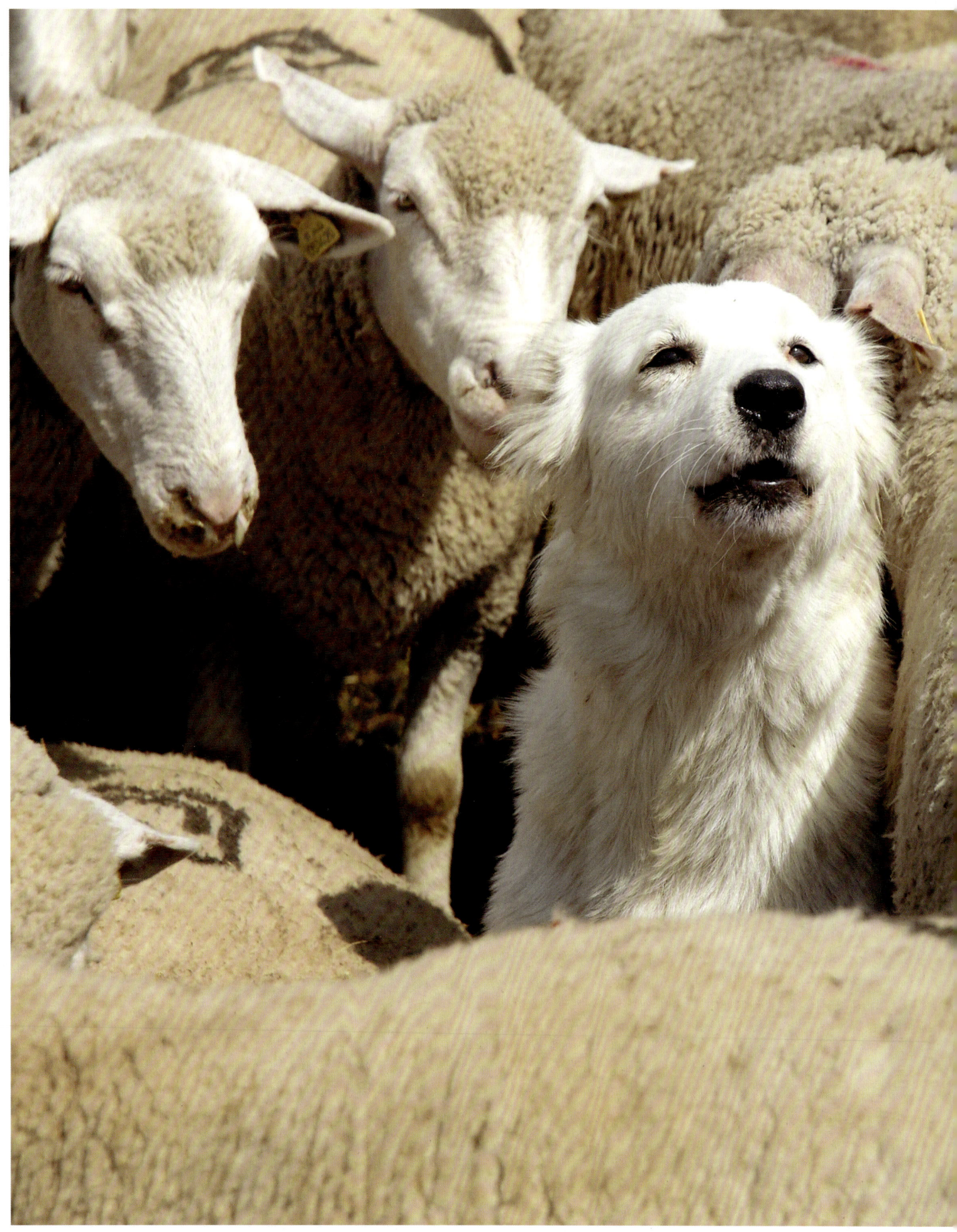

Maremma Sheepdog

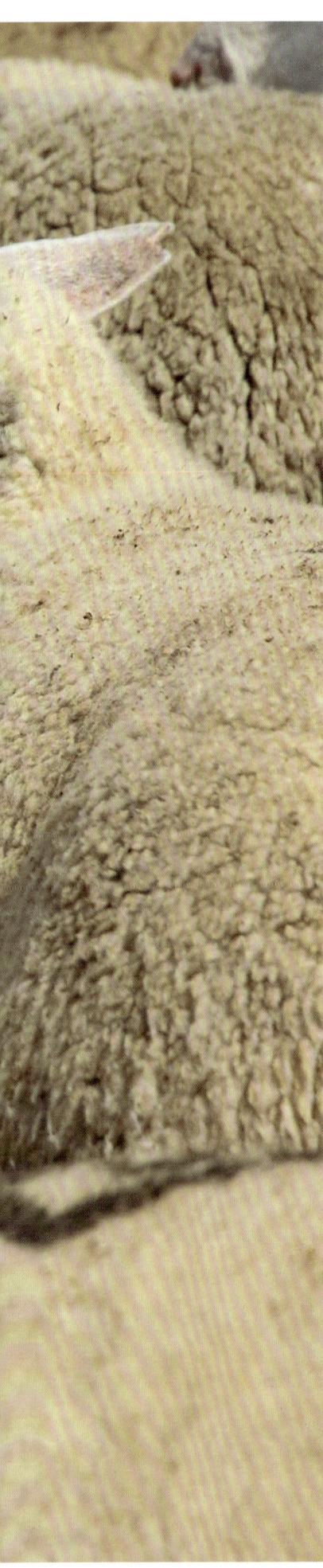

Often given the full name of the Maremmano-Abruzzese sheepdog, this breed of livestock guardian dog has strong links with both the coastal plains of Tuscany to the west and the mountainous region of Abruzzo to the south and east. These are the dogs that adorn the mosaics and painted pottery and appear in sculptures dating back to Roman Italy. It was probably widespread across the empire, so much so that it is marked as one of the ancestral lines for sheepdogs ranging from Spain to Turkey and Poland.

For more than 2,000 years these hardy white dogs with a thick coat have been out standing guard over the flocks. The dogs' chief enemy was the wolf, and as added protection shepherds would give their sheepdogs a traditional spiked iron collar. This would prove a formidable weapon to win a fight with a wolf pack, which will try to subdue the defender with bites to the neck.

The Maremma sheepdog is an impressive beast, but one used to spending long periods out in the open on constant guard against threats. Therefore a dog like this does not transfer well to living in a cramped home and urban environment. They may find a place in a rural setting but require strict training to prevent their aggressive streak from becoming dominant.

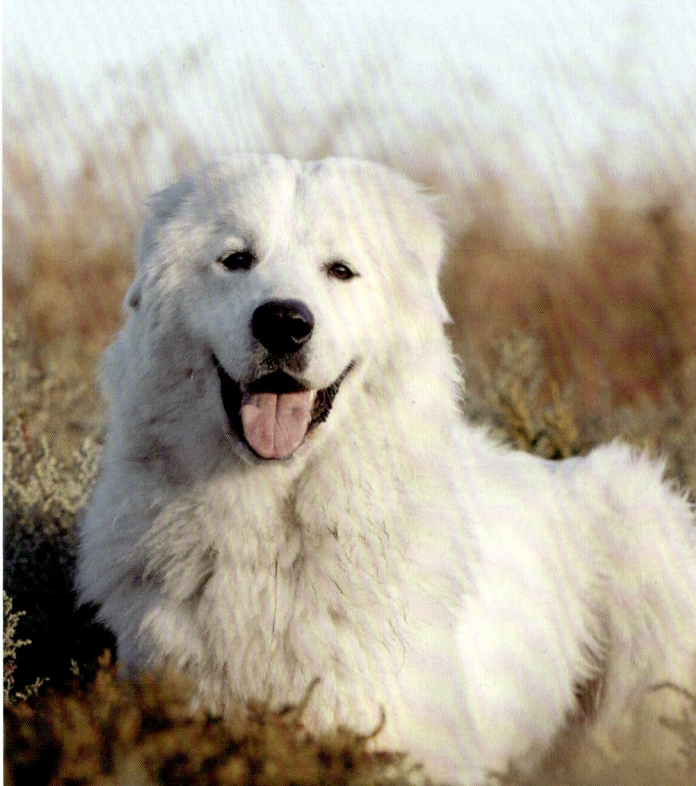

CHARACTERISTICS

Coat
Heavy coat of white wavy hairs
Height
60–73cm (24–29in)
Weight
30–45kg (66–99lb)
Lifespan
Over 10 years
Personality
Independent and brave
Origin
Italy

LEFT:
On the lookout
A Maremmano-Abruzzese sheepdog blends in with the sheep and makes sure the flock stays safe whatever the weather.

ABOVE:
Dependable
The breed is a large, strong and independent dog that is loyal to its owners and wary of strangers.

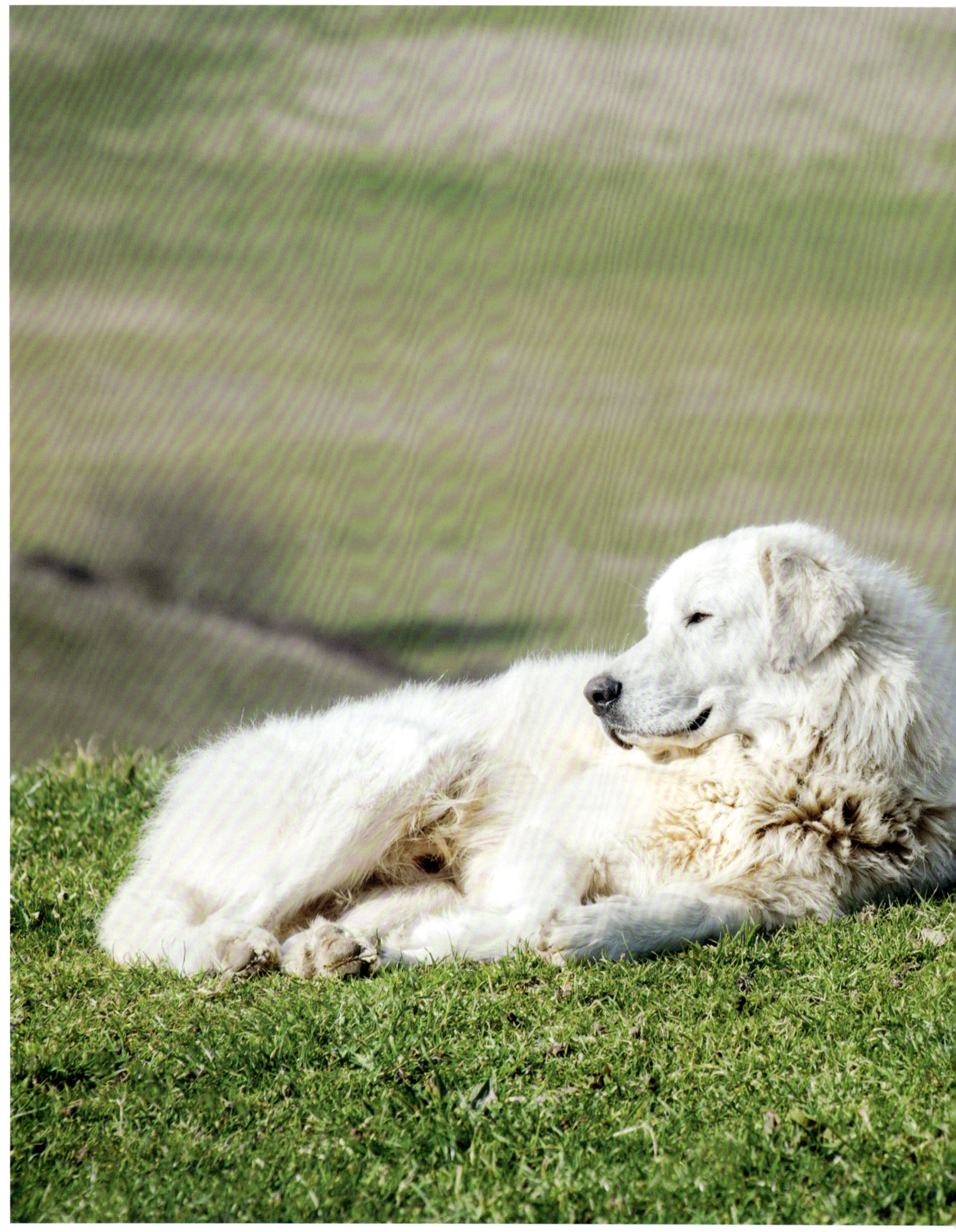

WORKING DOGS

Maremma sheepdog
This Italian sheepdog breed has a thick woolly coat rivalled only by that of their charges.

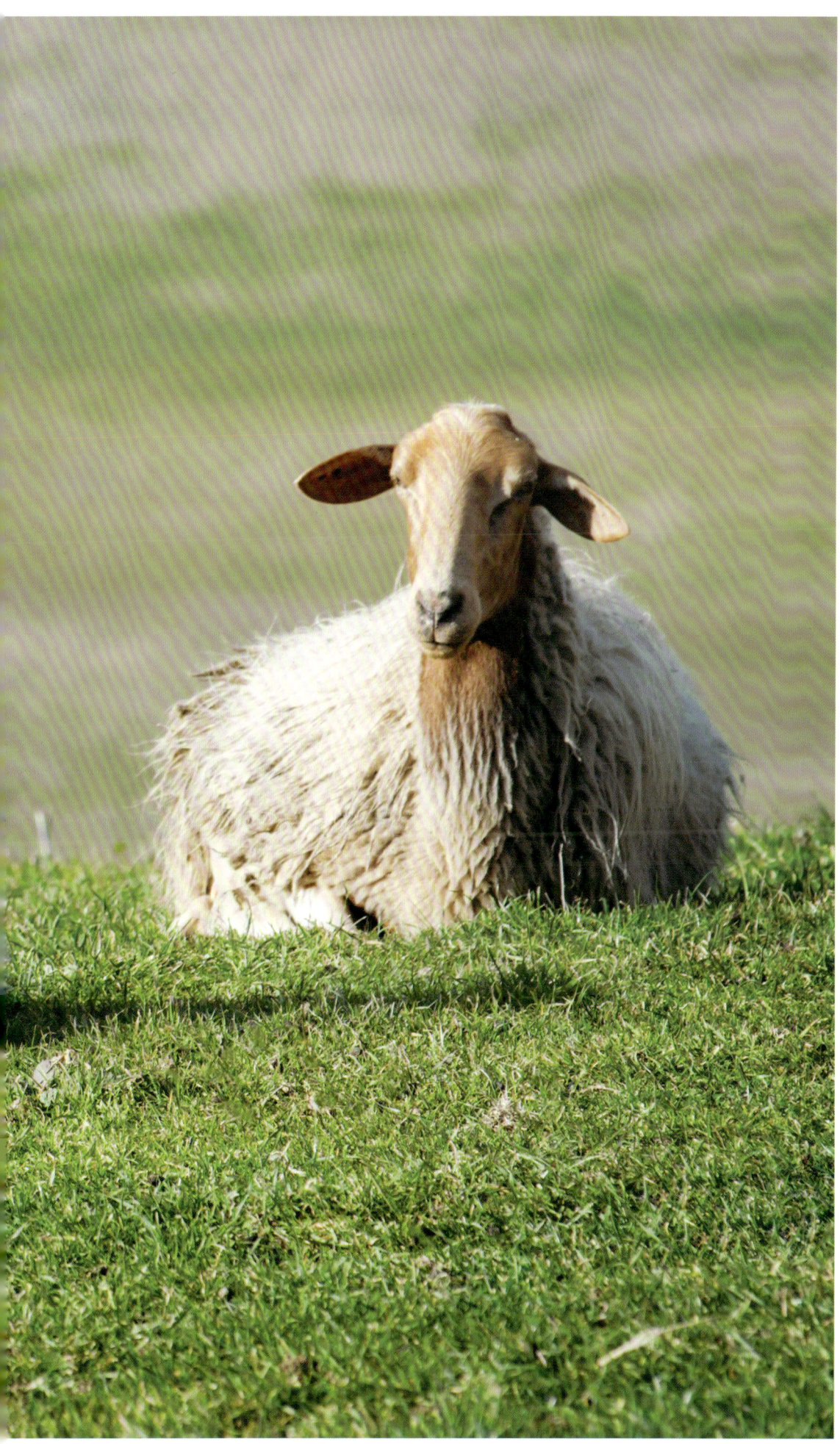

WORKING DOGS

Neapolitan Mastiff

Legend has it that this fearless heavyweight breed was bred from a Greek fighting dog called the molossus by Alexander the Great (of Macedonia). It is said that Alexander's personal favourite, Peritas, was a match for lions and elephants! In fact the breed goes further back still to Italy in the 8th century BC, when it was bred for fighting in the arena and in war. The long-established breed, also known as the mastino, only earned its link to Naples in the 1940s when the standards were first drawn up in that city.

When given proper training and plenty of stimulation, the Neapolitan mastiff is a loyal, affectionate and protective member of a family, but in line with its breeding it has little tolerance for strangers, human or animal, and so requires firm leadership with plenty of encouragement and praise. The dog can nevertheless be a handful for the first three or four years of life, but then settles into a more balanced temperament. As is often the case with big dogs, life is short for mastiffs. This breed seldom lives beyond the age of 10.

CHARACTERISTICS
Coat
A short, shiny coat that can be black, blue, mahogany, tawny, or brindle
Height
60–75cm (24–30in)
Weight
50–70kg (110–154lb)
Lifespan
7–9 years
Personality
Confident and faithful
Origin
Italy

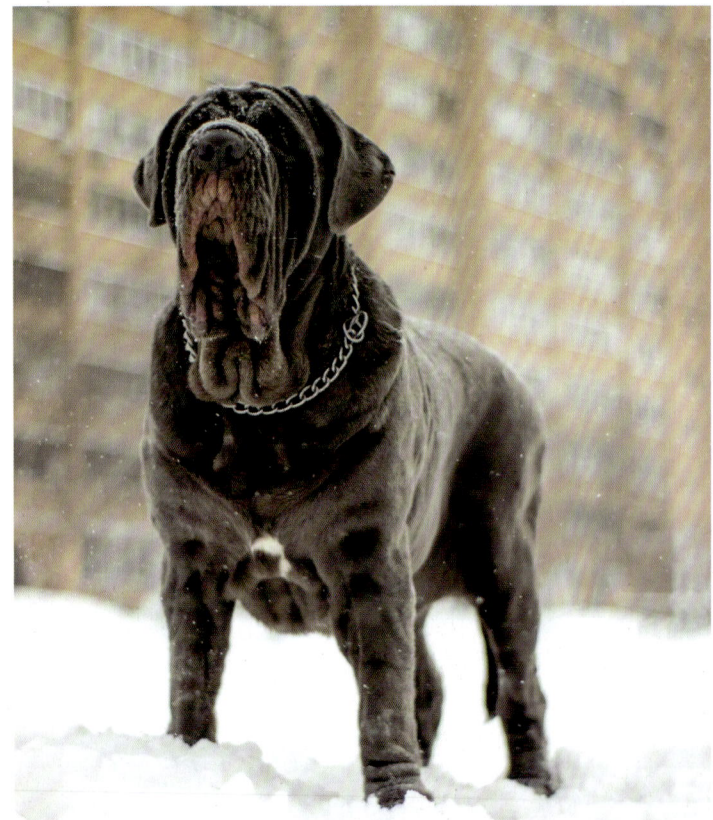

ABOVE:
Slow but steady
The mastiff has a slow and cautious gait but this should not be mistaken for faint-heartedness.

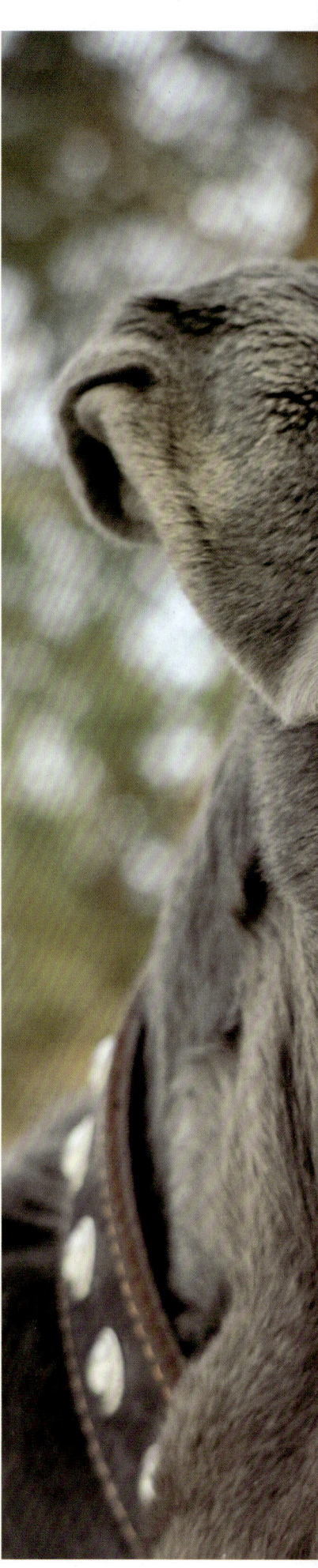

RIGHT:
Unique looks
Its size apart, the Neapolitan mastiff has a very distinctive appearance with wrinkly skin and droopy jowls that hang from its face.

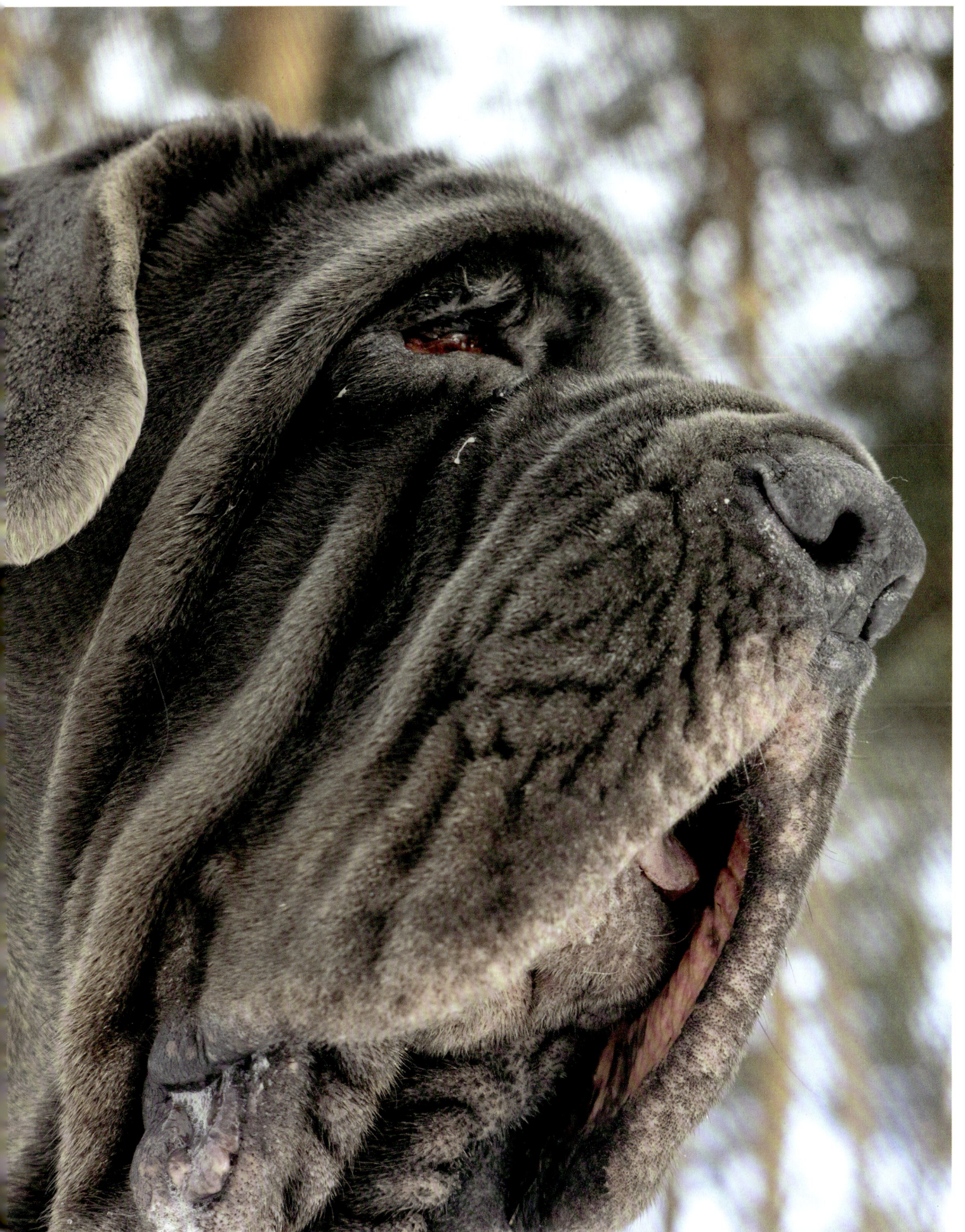

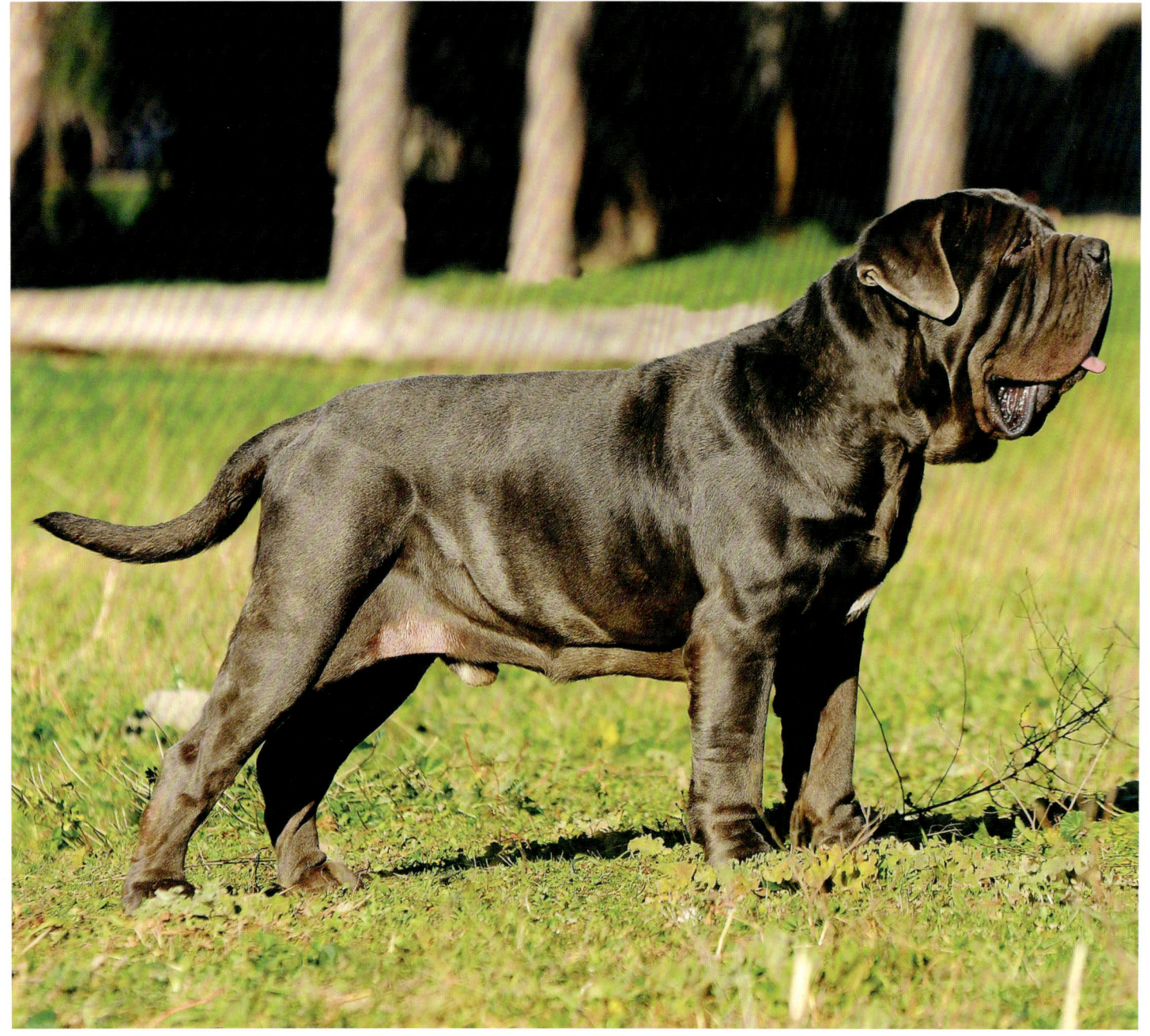

ABOVE:
Neapolitan mastiff
Descendants of fighting dogs bred to entertain in Roman arenas, this bulky breed projects immense strength as a guard dog.

OPPOSITE:
Neapolitan mastiff
The loose-fitting skin typical of this breed is apparent from a young age.

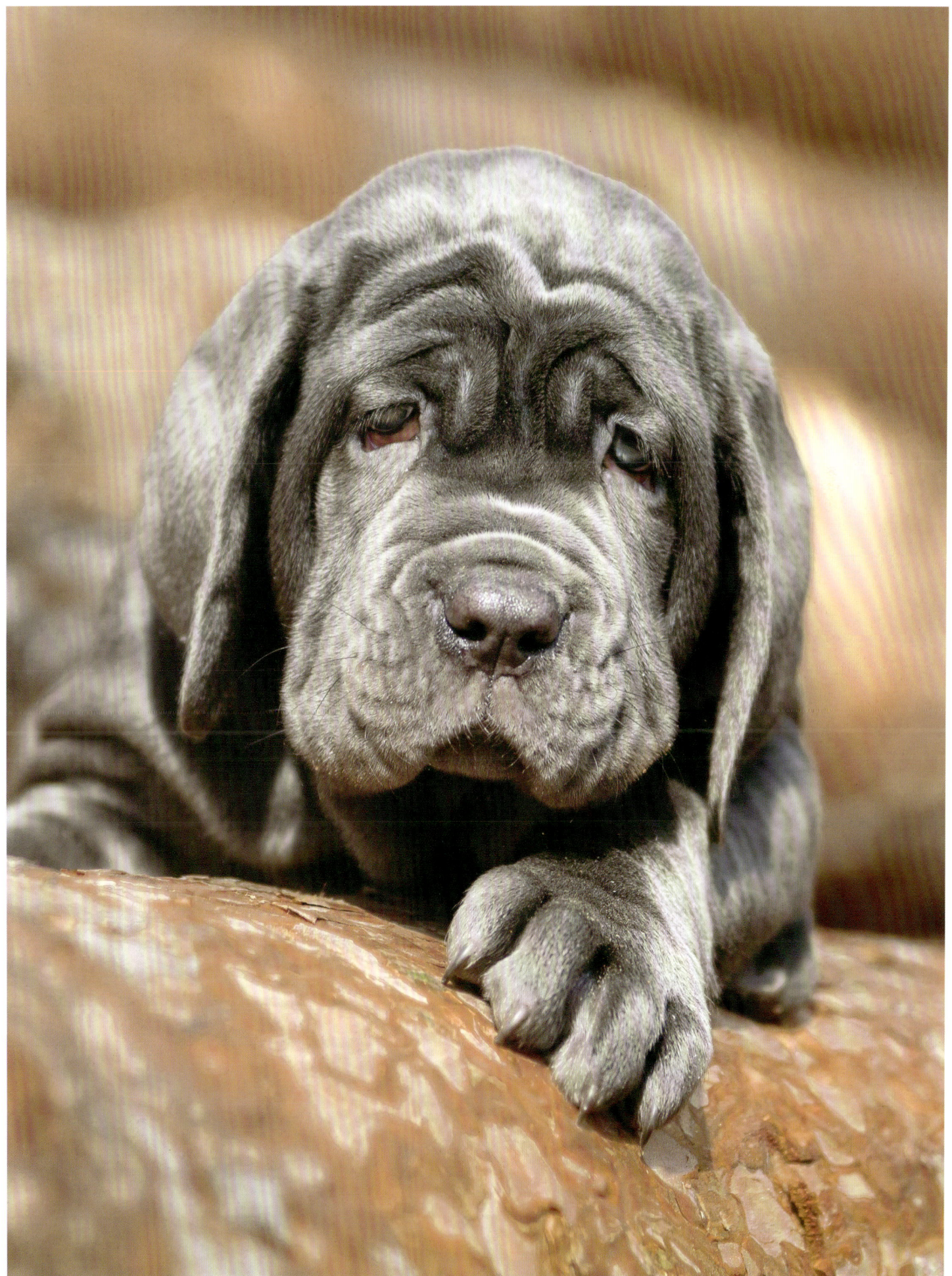

WORKING DOGS

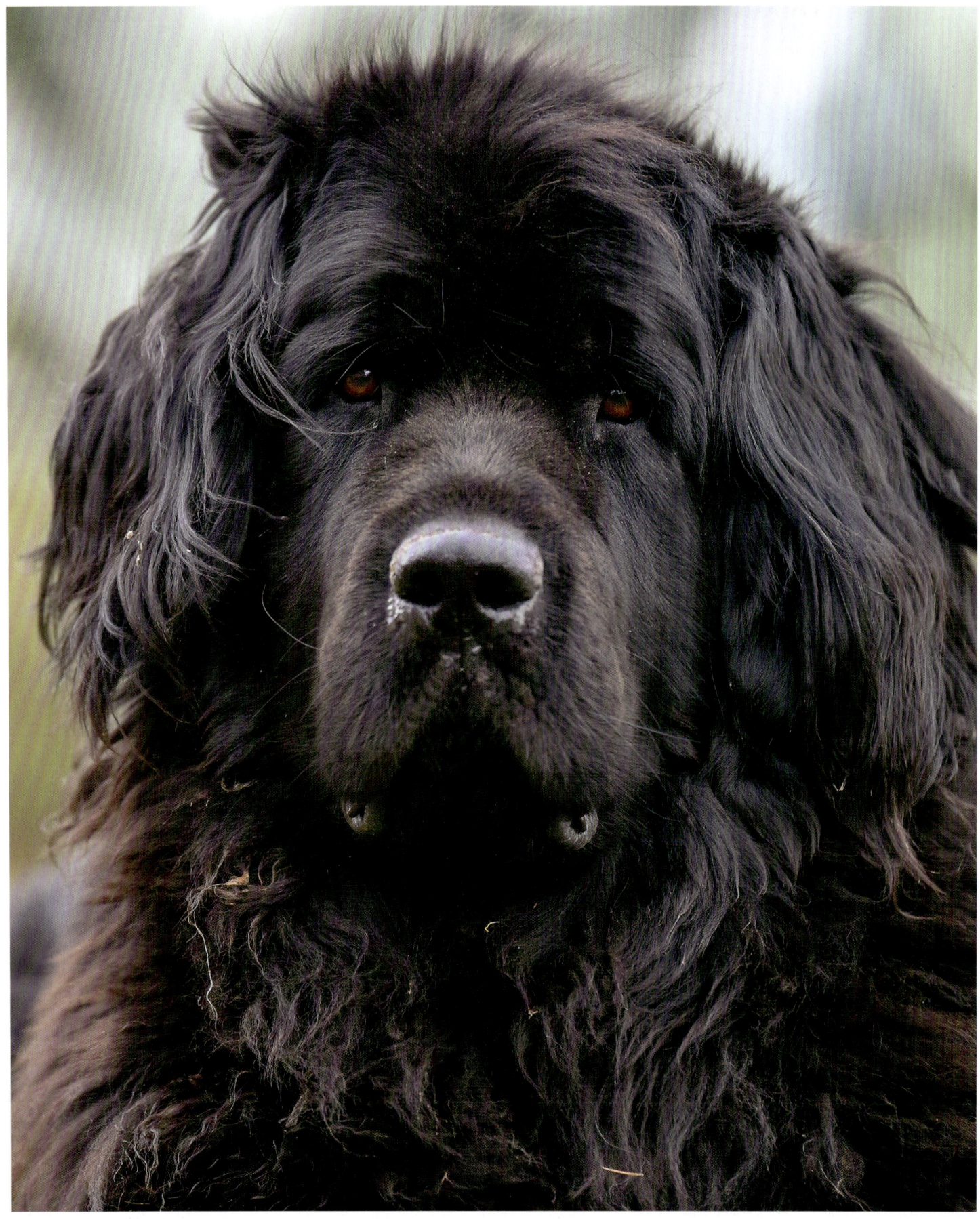

ABOVE:
Too hot!
With all that hair, a Newfoundland is best suited for life in cold climates.

Newfoundland

CHARACTERISTICS

Coat
A thick and water-resistant double coat that can be black, grey, brown or white-and-black

Height
66–71cm (26–28in)

Weight
50–69kg (110–152lb)

Lifespan
9–11 years

Personality
Gentle and protective

Origin
Canada

Tradition has it that no crew of a Canadian fishing boat was complete without a Newfoundland aboard. The dog is an excellent swimmer with webbed feet and an oily, waterproof coat. Its role was to swim out from the boat to retrieve nets and it would also dive in to rescue men overboard.

This large and powerful dog is linked to the island of Newfoundland but its precise origins are less certain. It is indeed an old and well-established breed; a Newfoundland called Seaman joined the 1802 Lewis and Clark expedition to cross America to reach the West Coast. Much of this journey was by river, and a rescue dog would have been a valuable addition to the team.

Newfoundlands make valued additions to a family as well. The poet Lord Byron was not much of a family man, but he loved his Newfoundland, Boatswain, so much that he built him a monument on his family estate. Newfoundlands are gentle and affectionate but do not like to be left alone for long. Their sheer size makes them better suited to larger homes but they only require moderate exercise. However, that should include swimming from time to time. They shed a lot and drool and so will need regular cleaning if living in a family home.

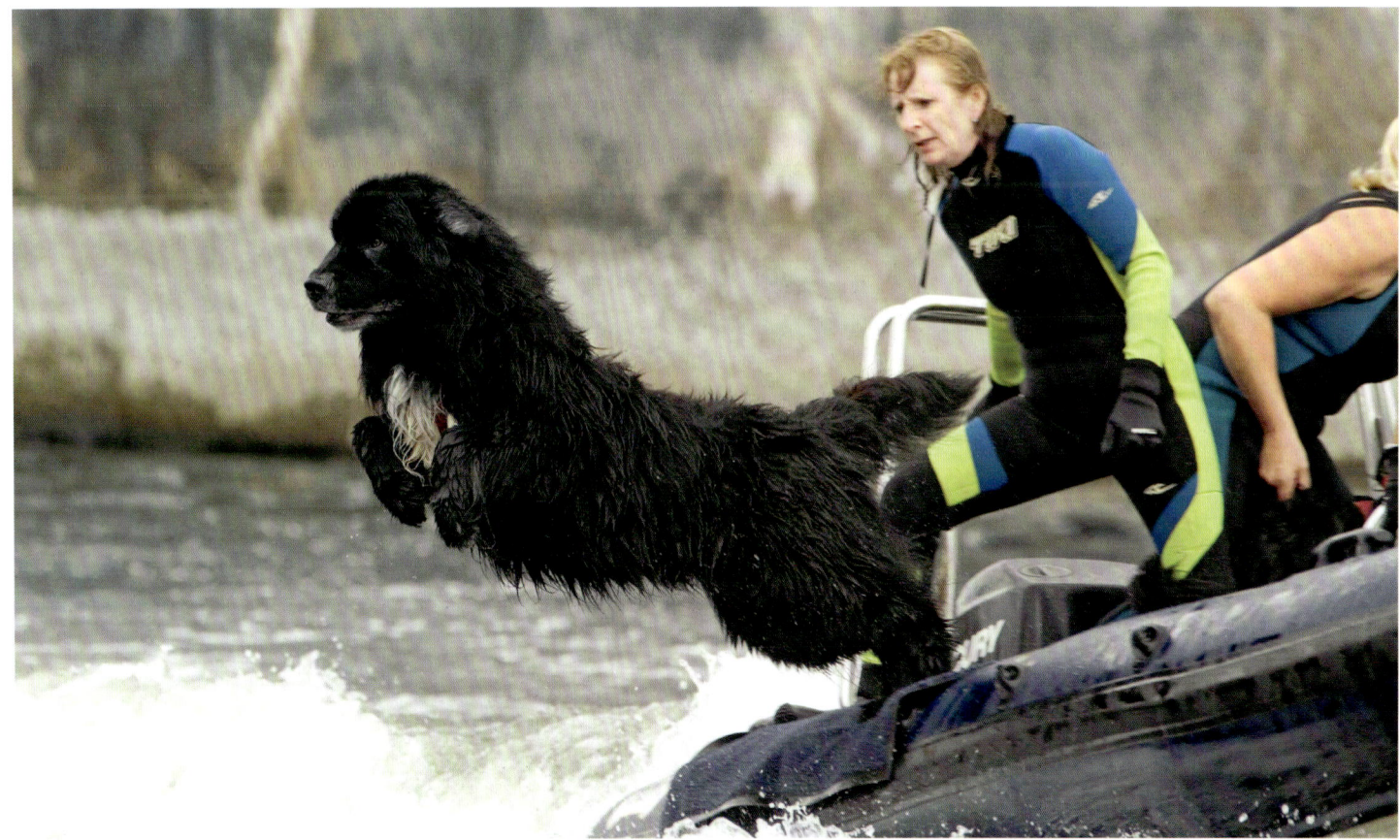

ABOVE:
Work it
In parts of Canada, Newfoundlands are still trained to rescue people who get into trouble in the water.

WORKING DOGS

Cuddly creatures
Due to their large size, this breed needs a big living space in any domestic setting. It's worth bearing this in mind when considering them as a pet.

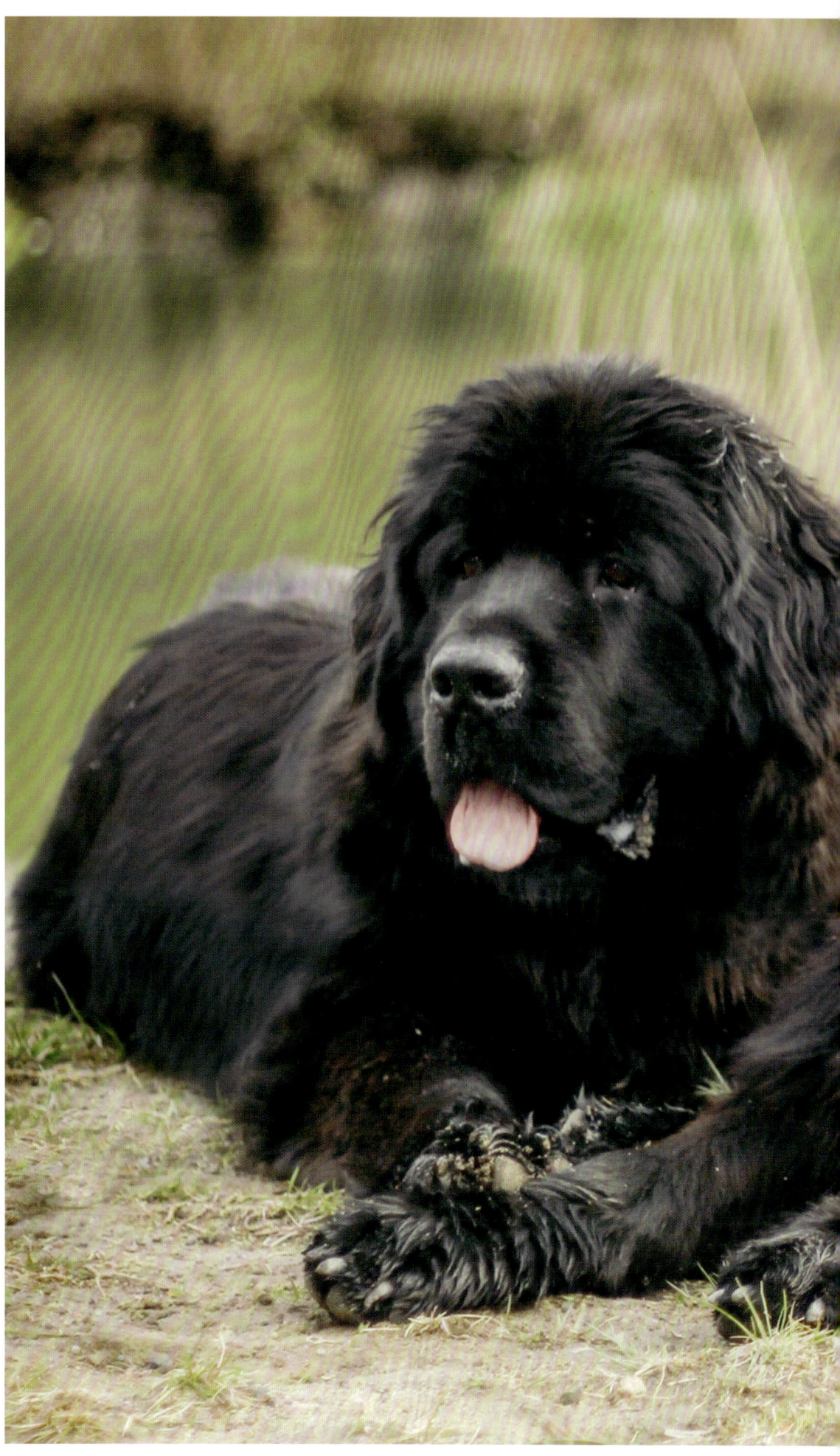

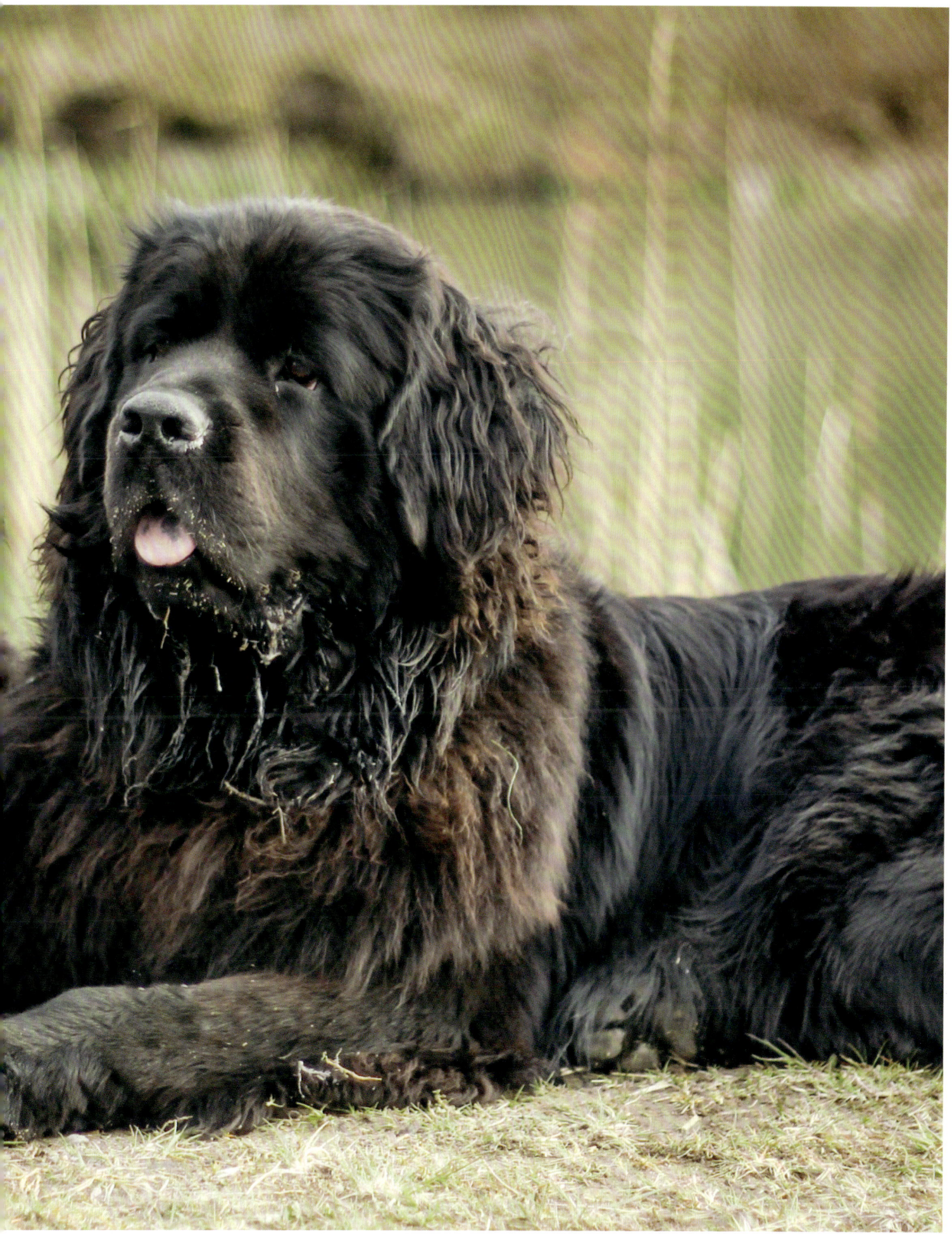

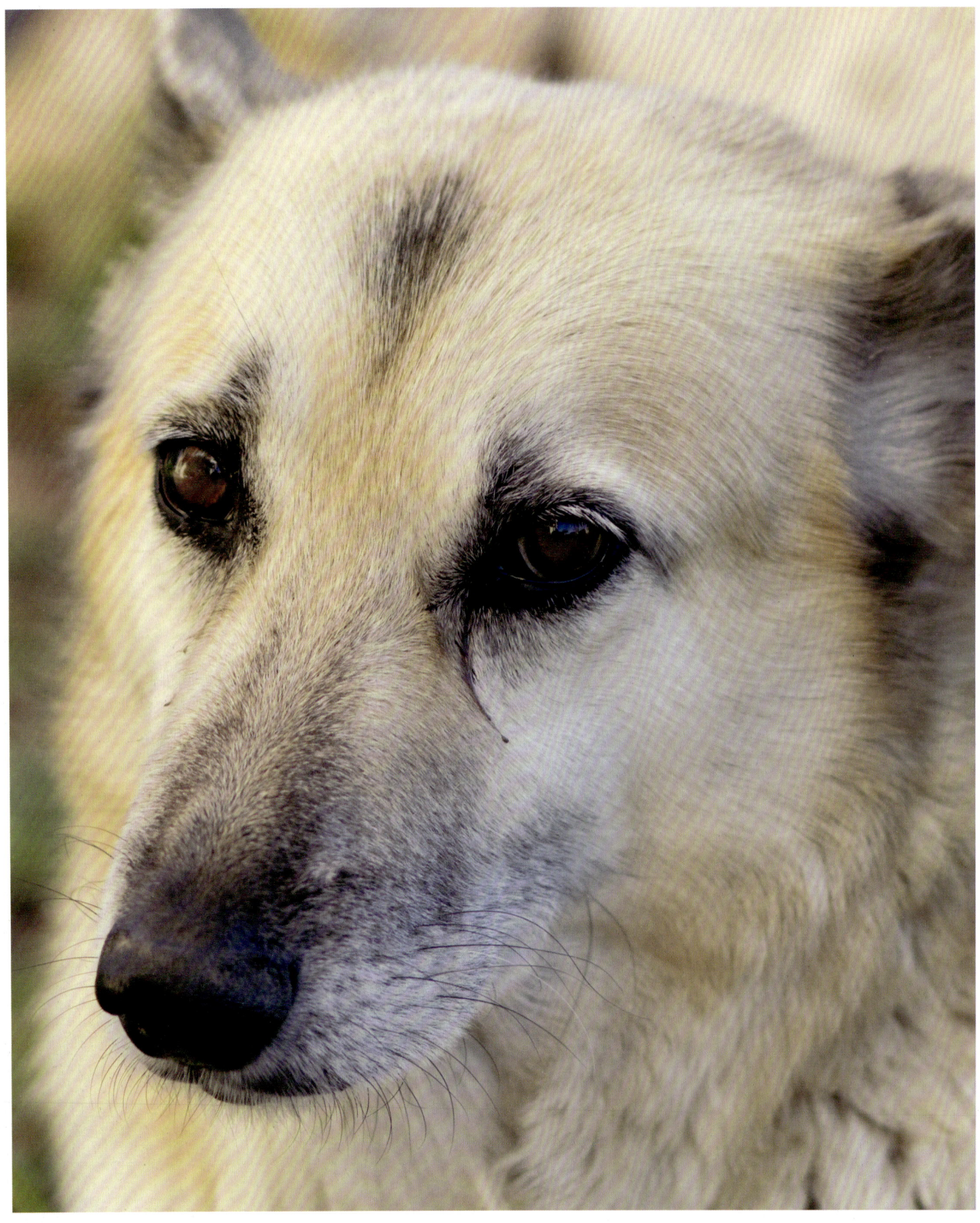

ABOVE:
Moulting
Twice a year the buhund sheds its coat to shift from a warm winter fur to a cooler summer one—and then back again.

Norwegian Buhund

CHARACTERISTICS

Coat
A thick, weather-resistant double coat either wheat coloured or black, with some white markings

Height
41–46cm (16–18in)

Weight
12–18kg (26–40lb)

Lifespan
12–15 years

Personality
Eager and brave

Origin
Norway

This small spitz-type herding dog is built for cold weather, with thick fur and small appendages. The term buhund means "farm dog" in Norwegian and for centuries they have helped out by herding livestock and performed valiant guard duties. However, they date back further, at least to the days of the Vikings, or Norsemen who sailed to distant lands to find loot, pillage and more often than not settle down. Their buhunds sailed with them, and no doubt were the first on to the beach when the longships made land.

That eagerness and energy makes the buhund a rewarding pet. The dog's confidence means it will happily accompany its owner wherever they go. However, the breed's alertness comes with a propensity to bark. That is what a watchdog should do. In a crowded urban setting, the buhund will require consistent correction and socialization to prevent it being too vocal.

Bred to work, a buhund has near boundless energy and so needs a lot of attention and exercise daily. It is a generally healthy and vigorous breed but does suffer from von Willebrand's disease, a bleeding and bruising disorder, and eye problems.

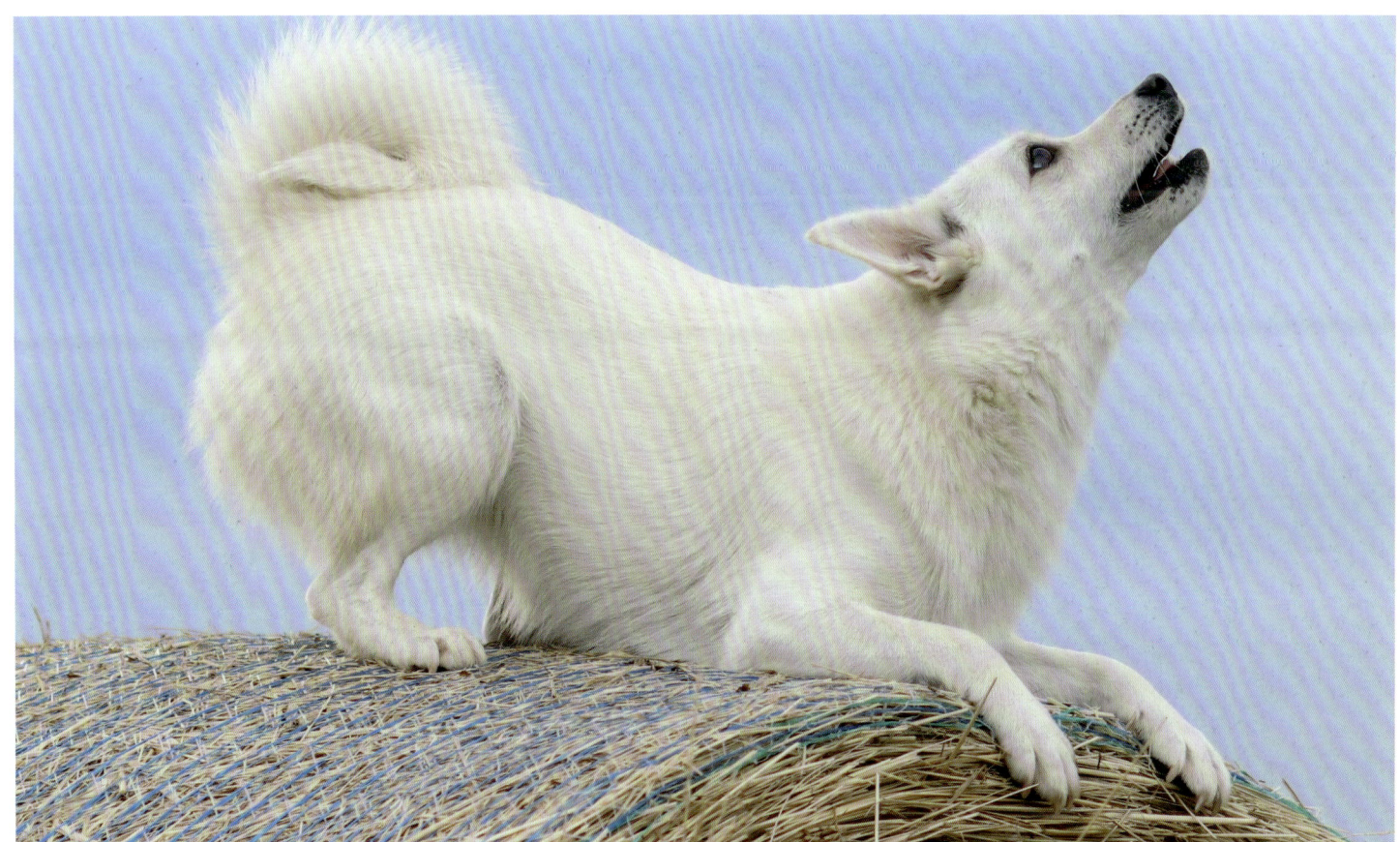

ABOVE:
Small and compact
The buhund breed has erect ears, a wedge-shaped head and a tail that curls over the back.

WORKING DOGS

Old English Sheepdog

CHARACTERISTICS

Coat
A long, thick, shaggy grey and white coat that covers its face and eyes
Height
56–61cm (22–24in)
Weight
27–45kg (60–99lb)
Lifespan
More than 10 years
Personality
Intelligent and well-mannered
Origin
England

The name of this British breed is more than a little misleading. The breed was established only around 250 years ago, which is not that old. They are also bred from ancestors from Scotland as well as England, plus some lines from Europe. And although they were developed in the west of England, they primarily worked as drovers that moved herds of cattle along the narrow lanes between pasture and dairy and market. The link with sheep is more tangential. The shaggy dogs would be clipped of their grey and white fur once a year, just as sheep are shorn of their wool, and the dog hair could be spun into yarns.

Its strong look of long tousled hairs that obscure the ears and cover the eyes (which are sometimes blue) makes the old English sheepdog one of the most recognizable breeds. The big dog is surprisingly athletic and compact under all that hair. It has a bounding gait that matches its playful and fun-loving nature. It enjoys nothing more than a good romp and will need to be indulged with regular walks. The dog fits in well with a family and is good with children. Its occasional barks have a ringing quality.

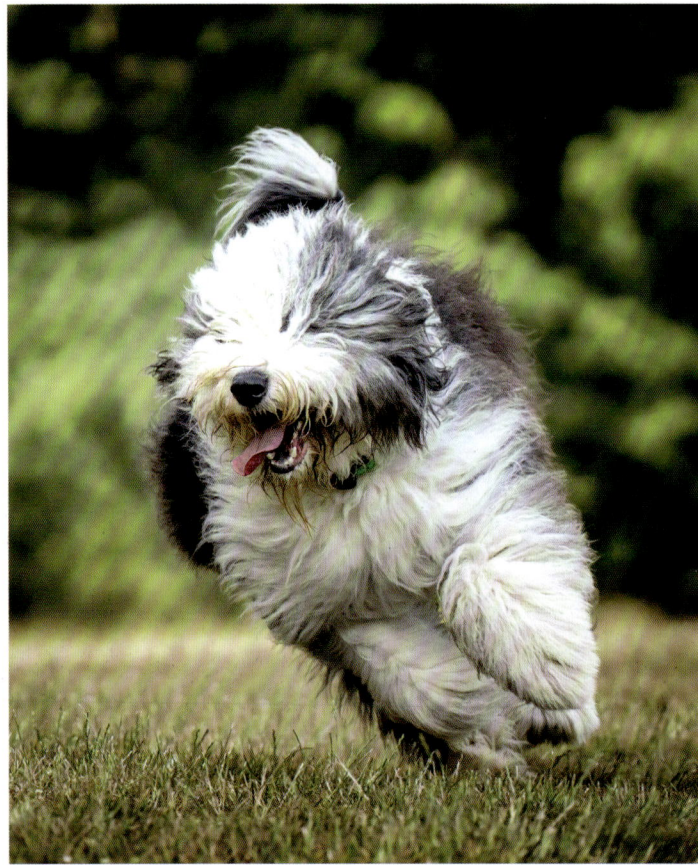

ABOVE:
Oh happy breed!
The fun-loving old sheepdog breed is also known as the shepherd's dog or bobtail.

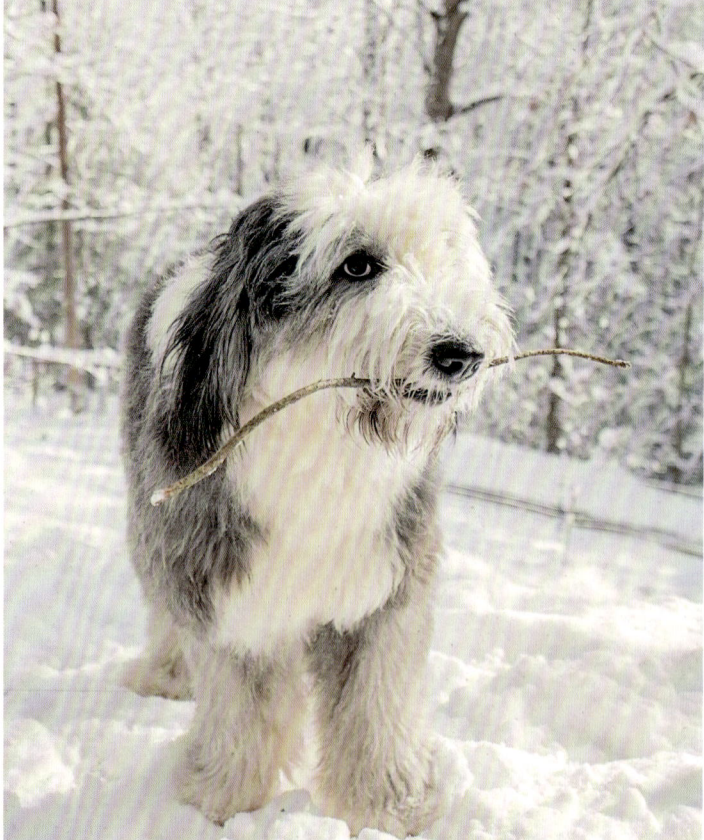

ABOVE:
Shaggy dog
The dog requires regular grooming to keep its coat healthy and free of mats.

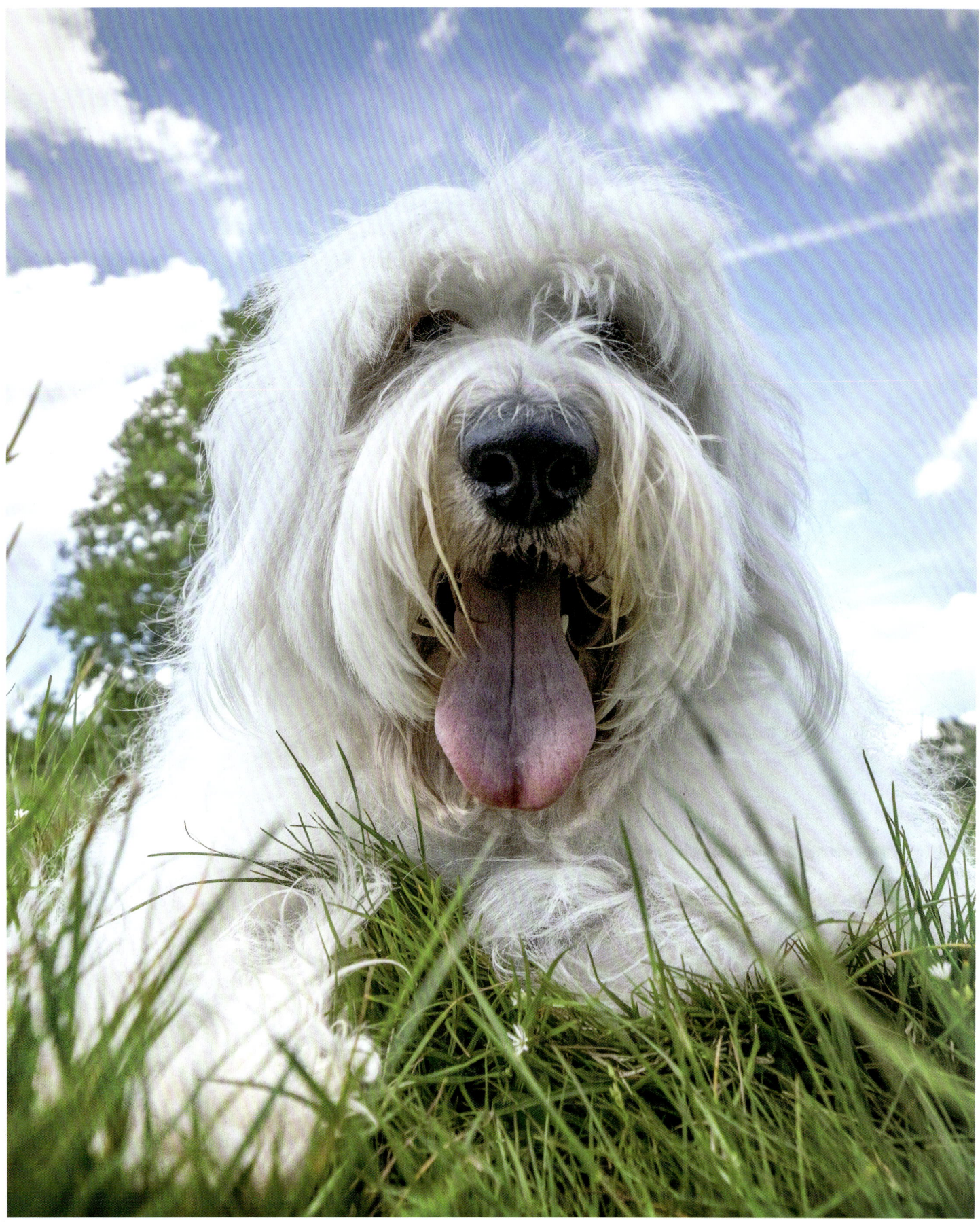

ABOVE:
Keep active
An old English sheepdog needs moderate exercise to maintain its fitness and happiness.

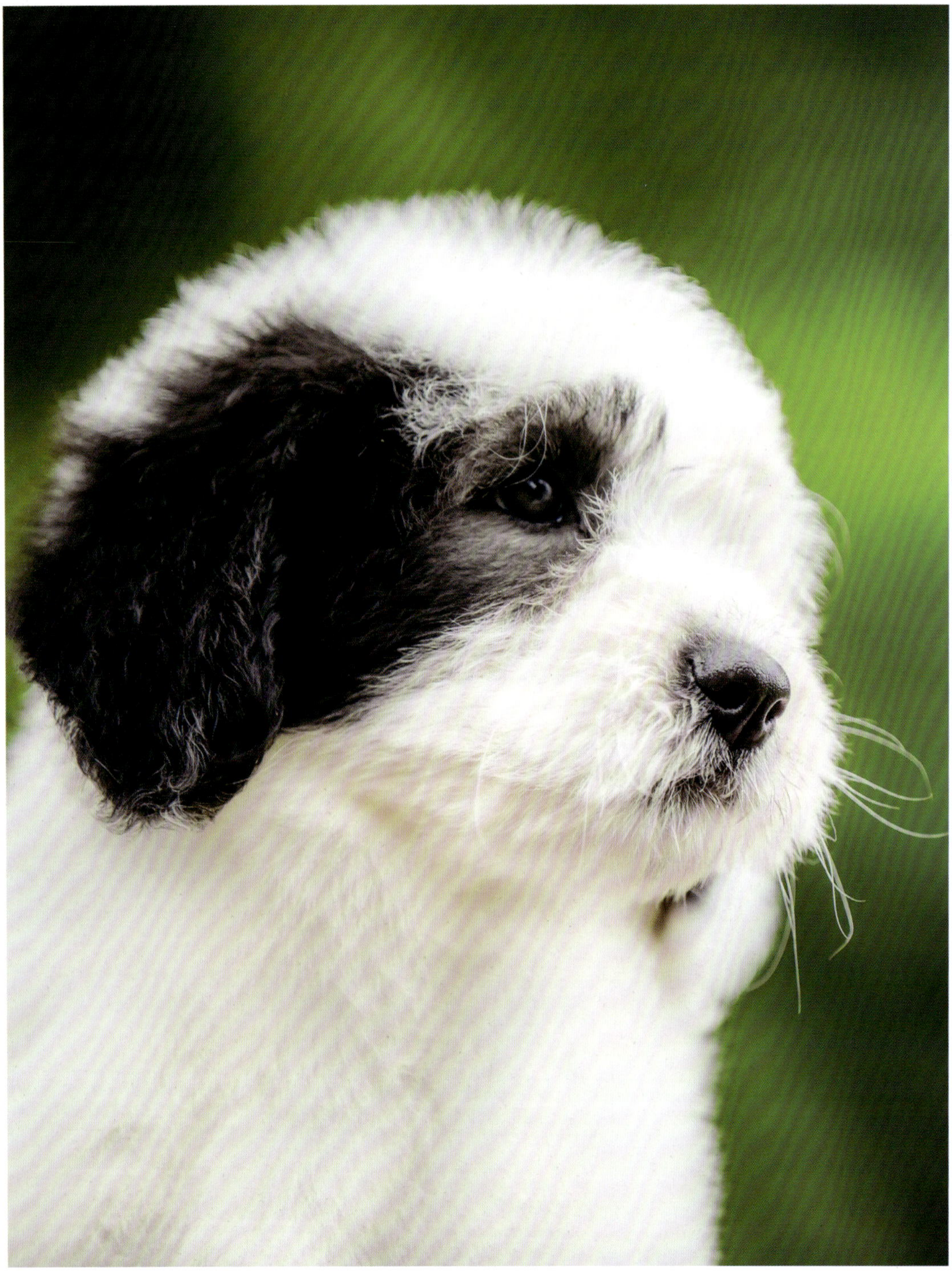

WORKING DOGS

ABOVE:
Young sheepdog
Despite their cute looks, in recent years, the breed has fallen in popularity and is now listed as endangered.

RIGHT:
Long haired
A highly distinctive breed with eyes covered by long hairs around the eyebrows. The thick, fluffy fur requires a lot of care and attention.

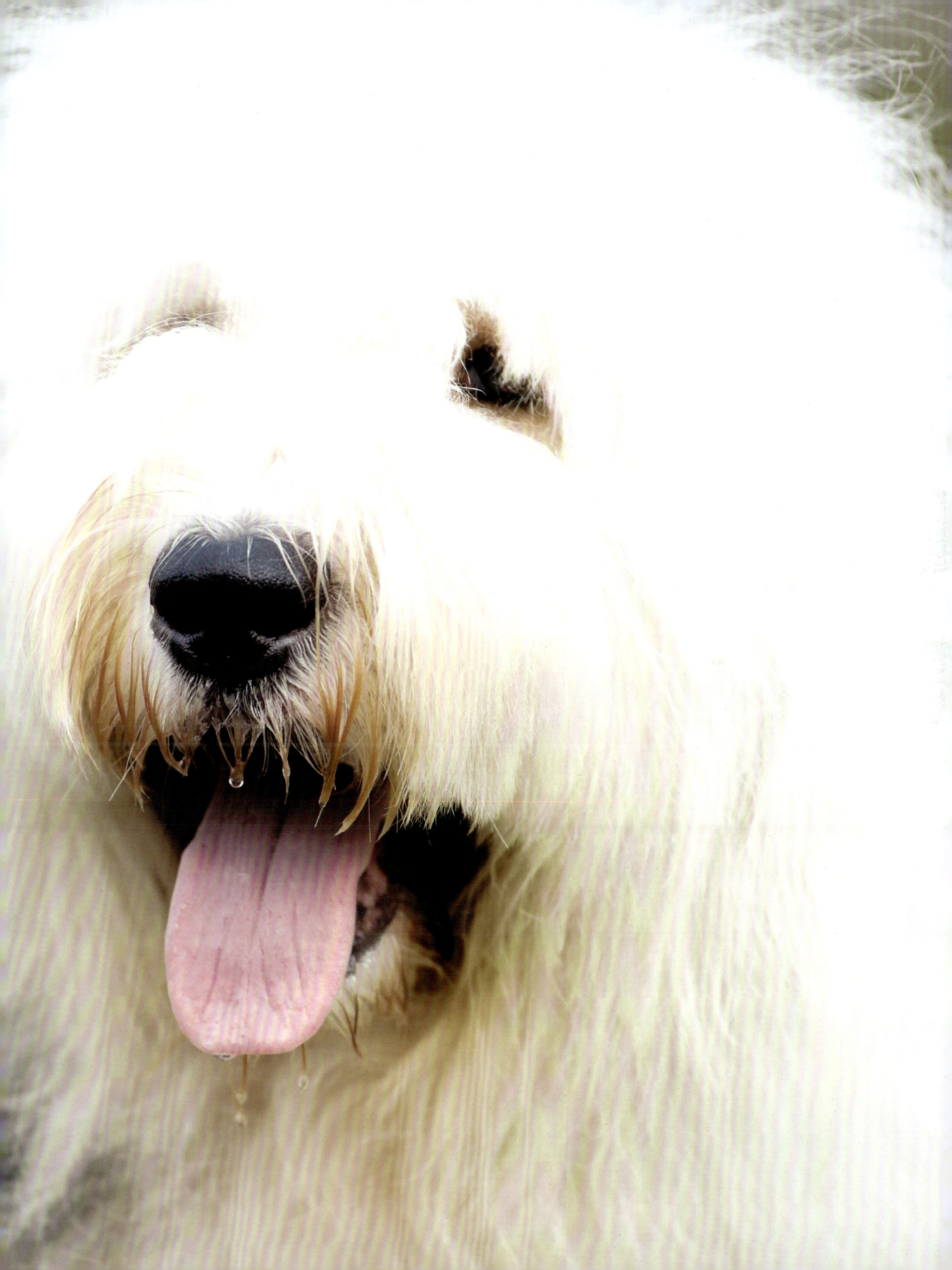

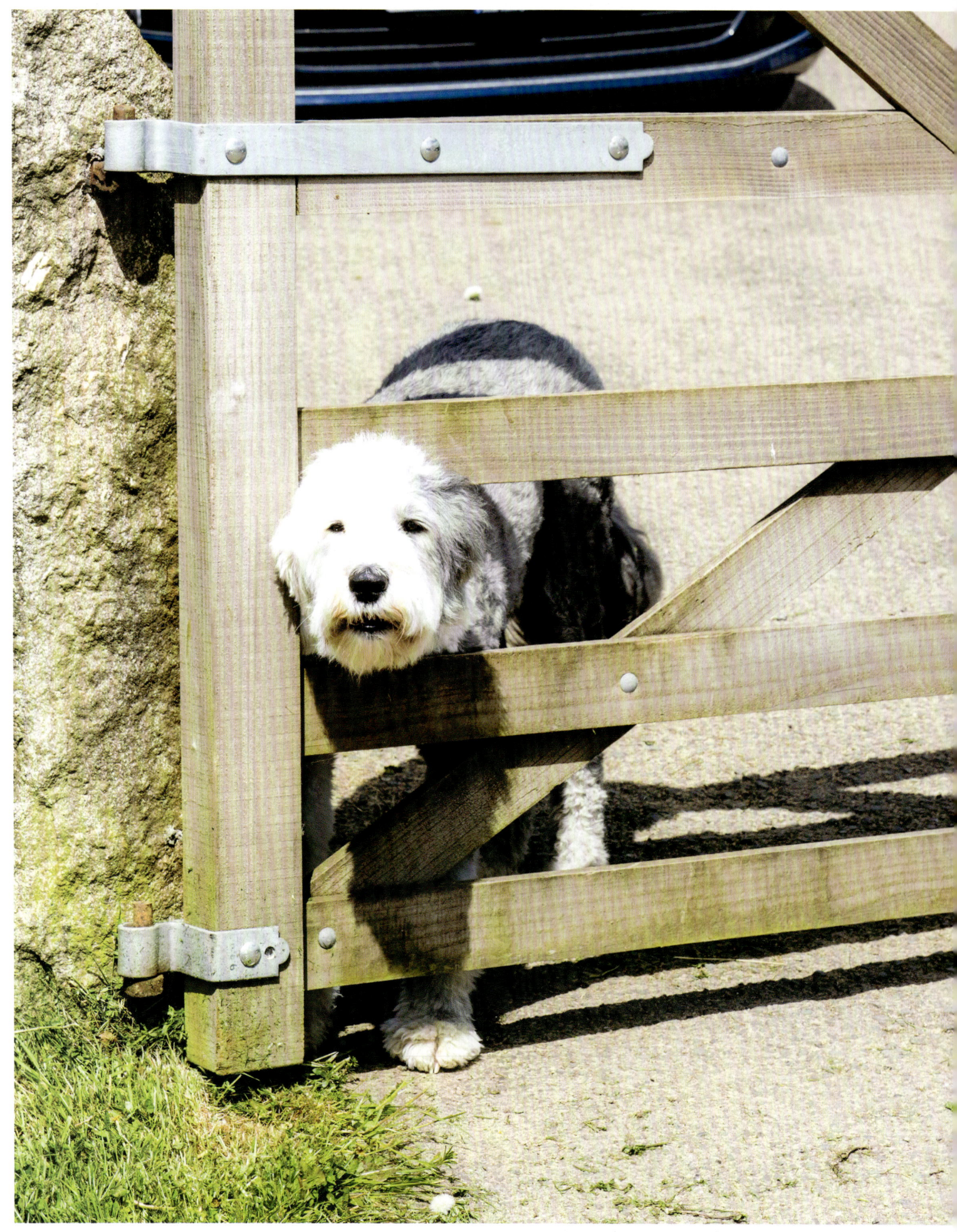

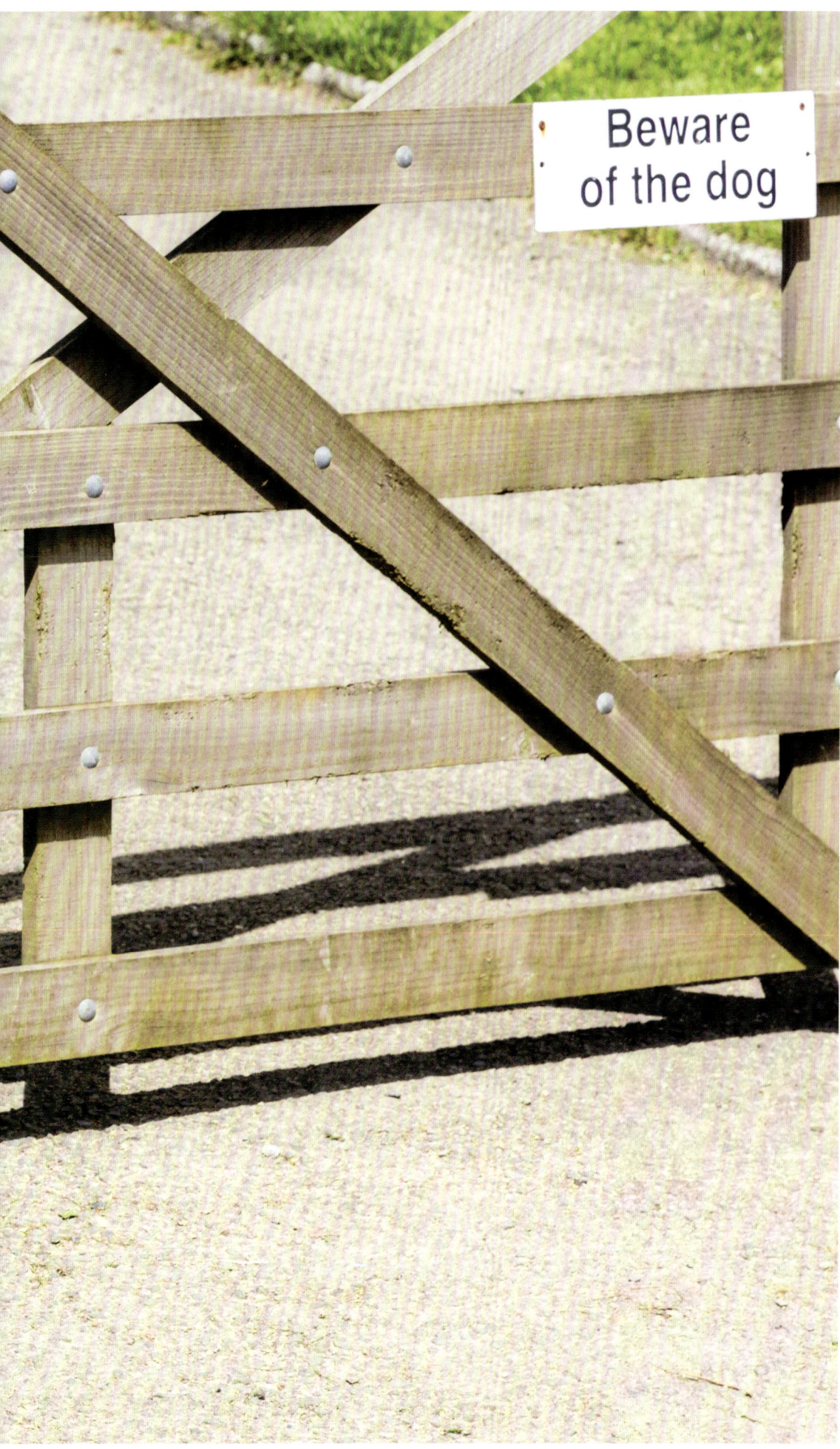

Beware of the dog
Sometimes the difference between a guard dog and an attack dog is not altogether clear. It's always best to err on the side of caution.

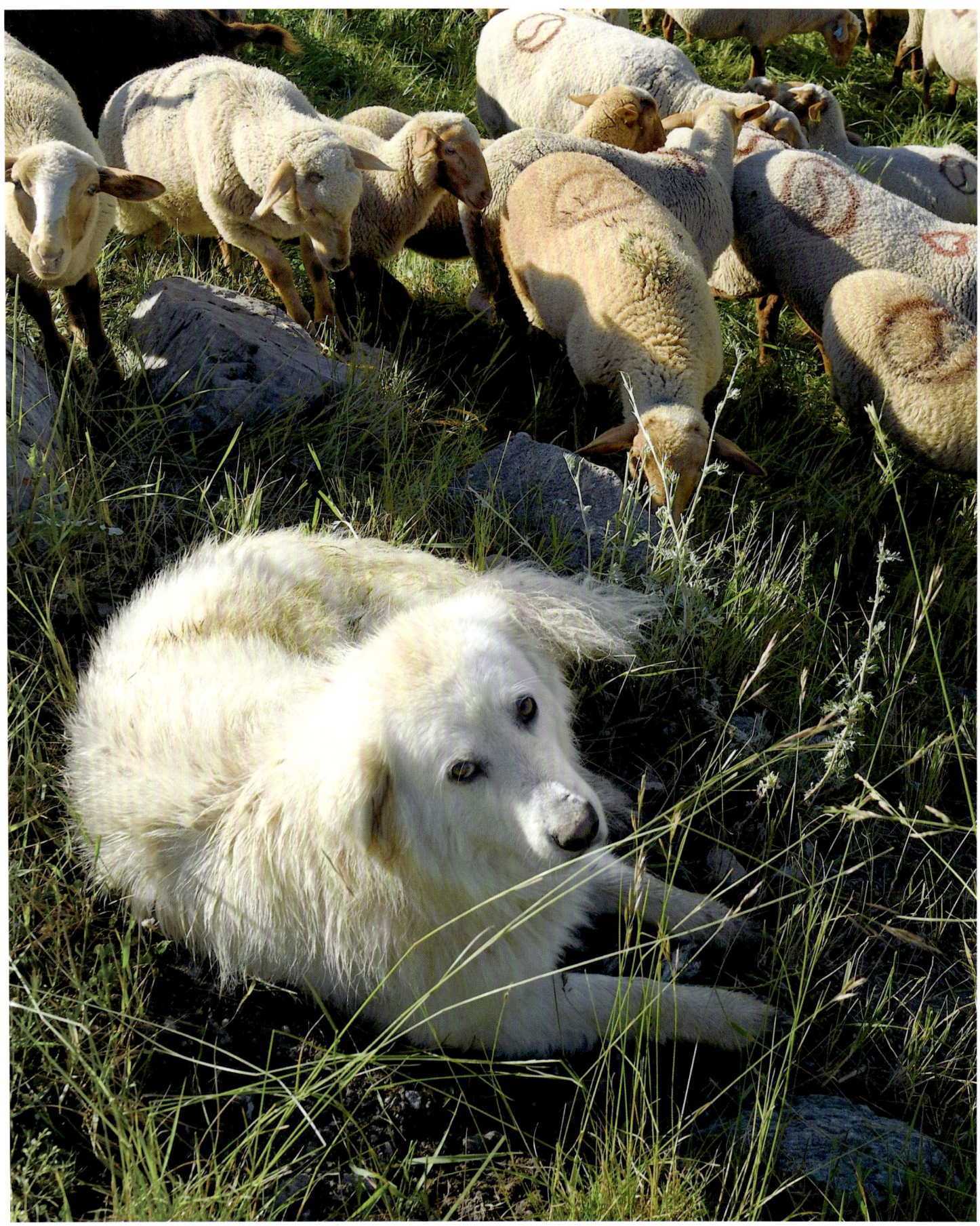

ABOVE:
Living on the edge
The dogs can spend many days and nights out in the open. Wherever the sheep go, the Pyrenean mountain dog will not be far behind.

Pyrenean Mountain Dog

CHARACTERISTICS

Coat
A pure-white thick double coat that can withstand harsh weather conditions

Height
65–70 cm (26–28in)

Weight
40–50 kg (88–110lb)

Lifespan
9–11 years

Personality
Calm and reliable

Origin
France

Named after the mountains that form a towering frontier between Spain and France, this breed is more associated with the French side, where it is known as the "patou". It is not for nothing that Louis XIV, the Sun King, appointed it as the Royal Dog. The breed was developed as a guardian dog for protecting sheep and cattle on the hillsides from marauding wolves and bears. It can be used as a pack animal and was rumoured to smuggle illicit loads over the border. Their fluffy coat keeps out the wind and snow in the harsh mountain conditions. More recently the dog was used briefly by the French army in the Second World War as a messenger dog.

Pyrenean mountain dogs are renowned for their gentle temperament and loyalty. That makes them a good fit for families, even those with small children. The dogs tolerate strangers well. However, these big dogs need a lot of exercise and like to have space to roam around as they would when working in the hills. All in all the Pyrenean mountain dog is perhaps the easiest of the giant dogs to keep as a pet but needs an engaged and experienced owner.

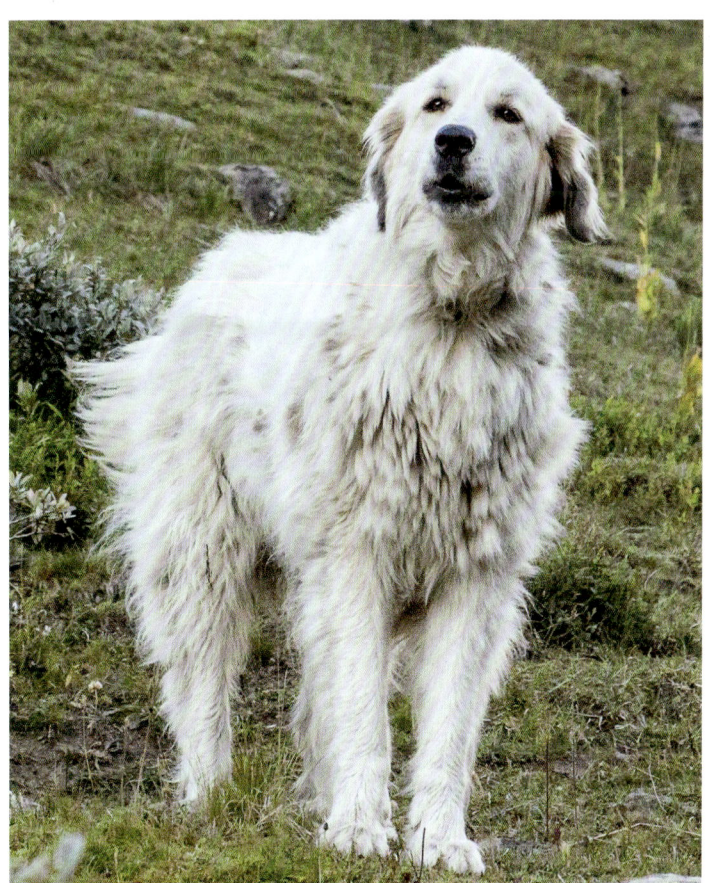
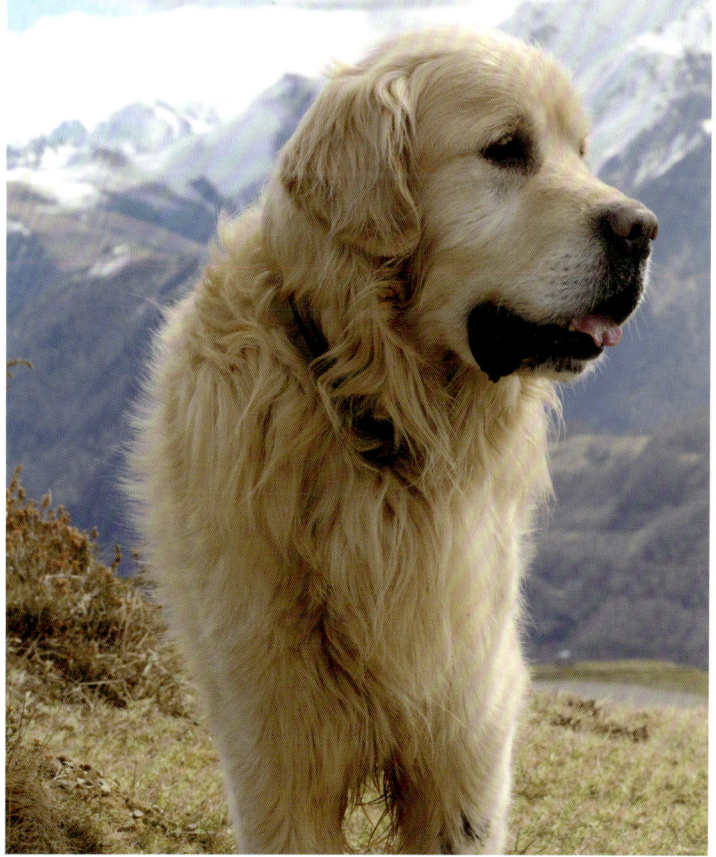

ABOVE BOTH PHOTOGRAPHS:
Built for exposure
The big dogs are equipped for the worst conditions that the mountains can hurl at them.

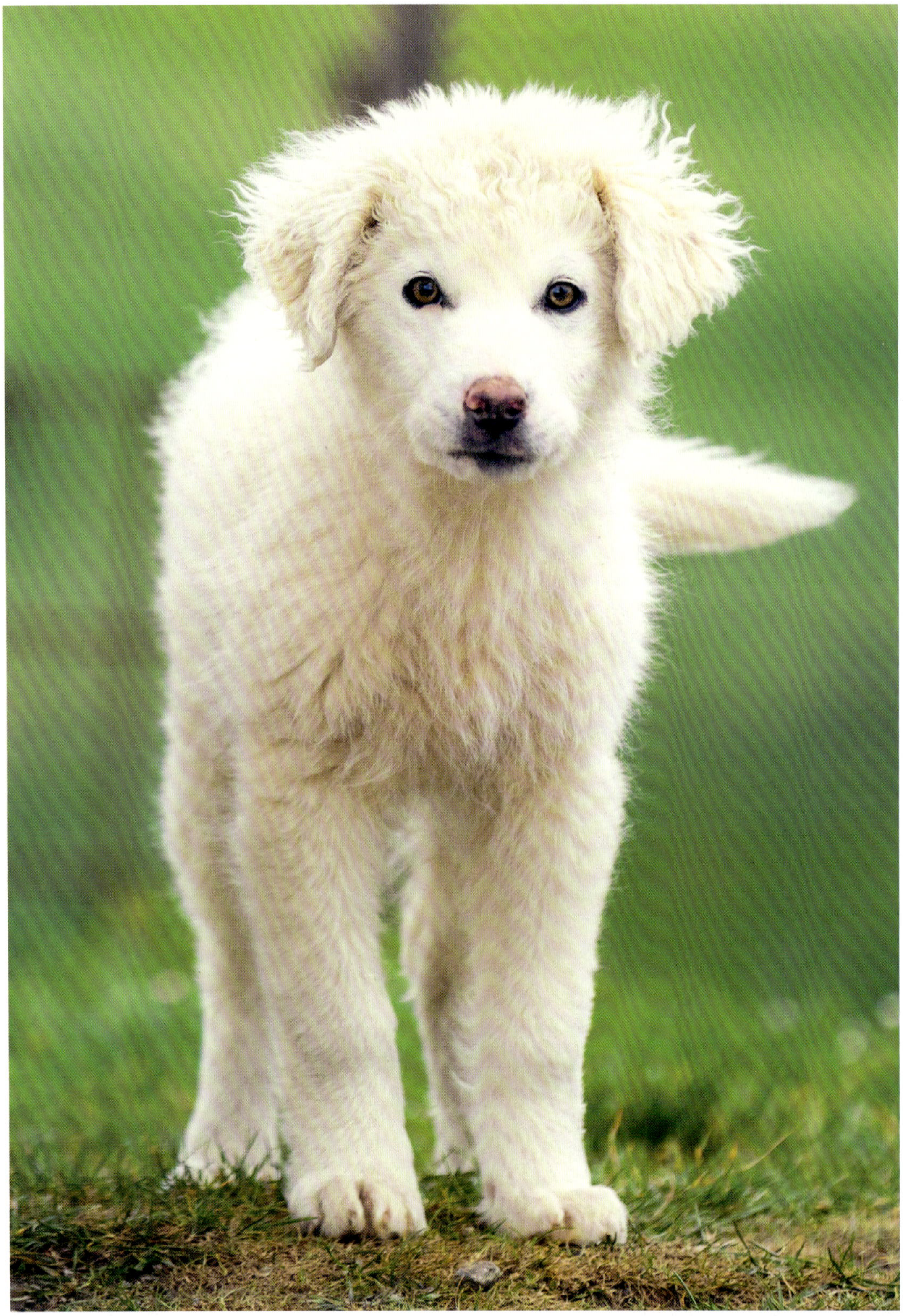

WORKING DOGS

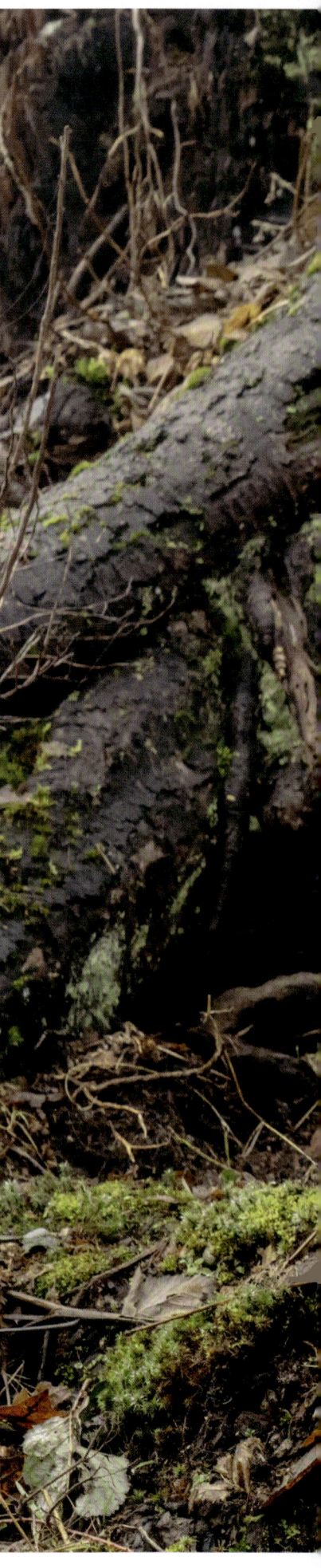

BOTH PHOTOGRAPHS:
Posing pups
The Pyrenean Mountain dogs require regular grooming to keep their coat clean and healthy—and warm!

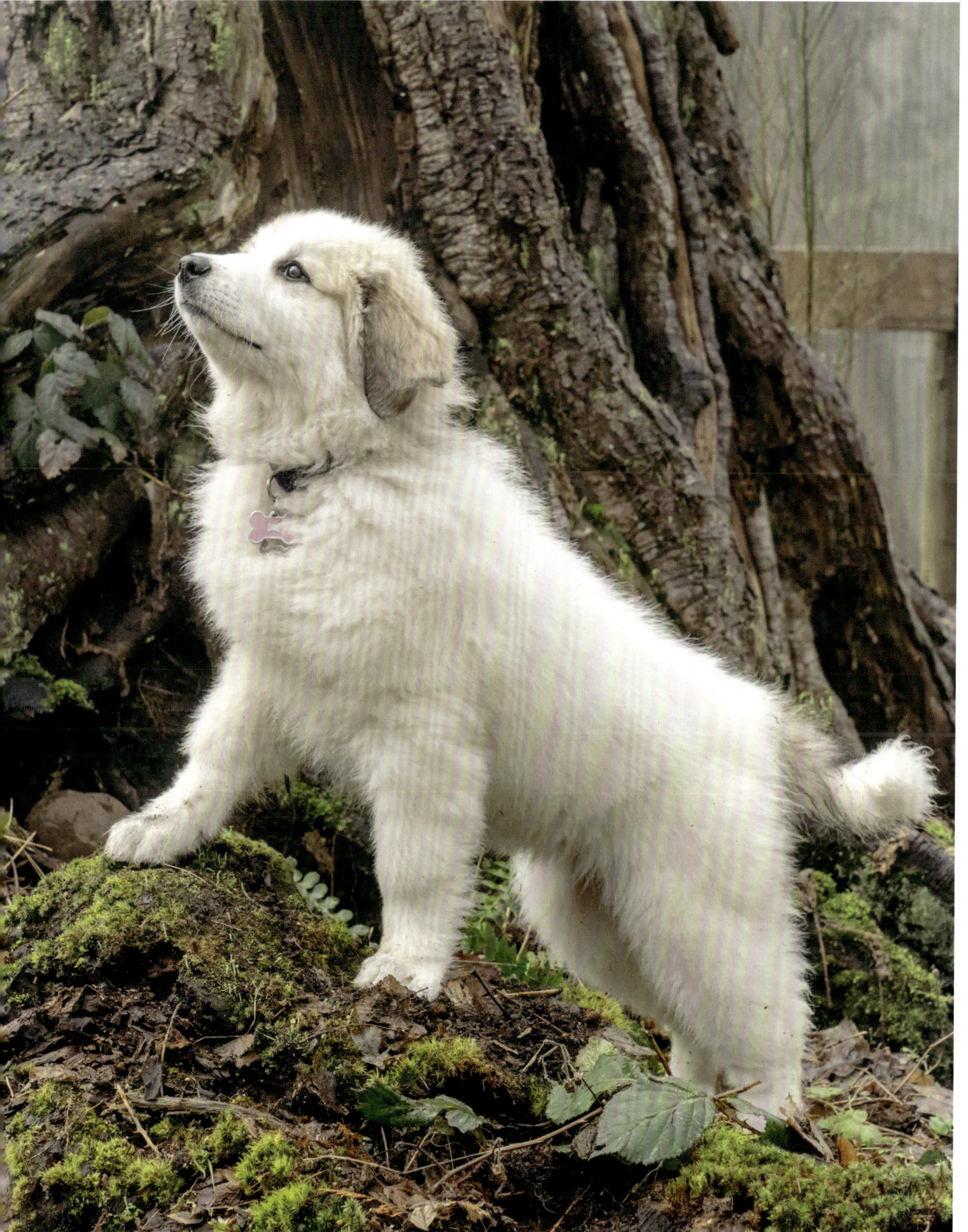

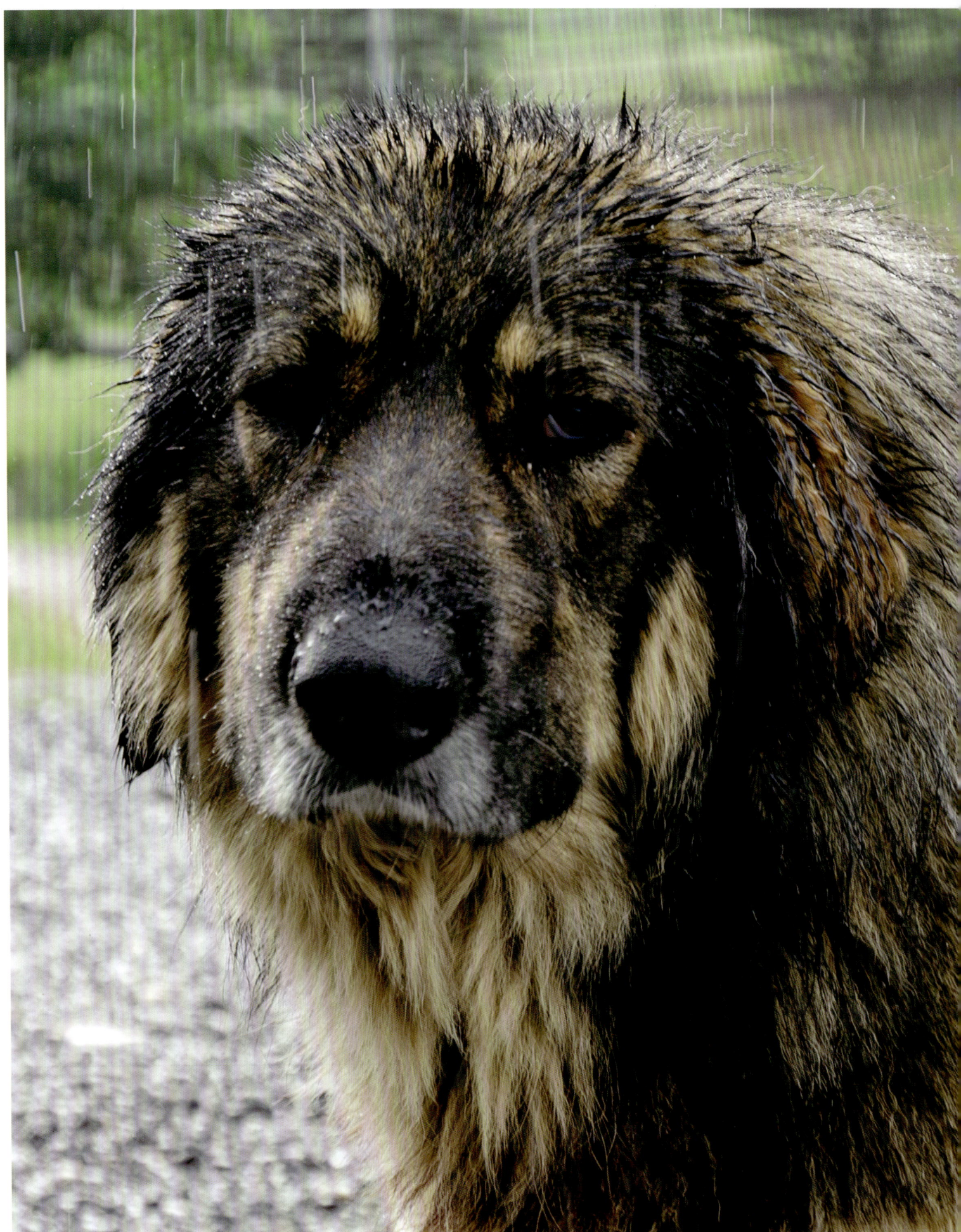

Romanian Shepherd Dog

Romania does not have one shepherd dog but three, all big beasts. The swampy flatlands of the Danube Delta in the east of the country has a wolfish shepherd dog called the Carpatin. The northeastern pastures host dairy herds and are home to a somewhat beefier dog breed that is called the Molossoid in honour of the molossus, the fighting dog from ancient Greece. The most common of the Romanian breeds is from the northern mountains. It is called the Mioritic shepherd dog. This name is derived from the Romanian for "small sheep" and relates to the breed's long, shaggy coat which blends it well with flocks and protects it from bad weather and bites from predators like wolves, lynx and bears.

The Romanian shepherd dogs are all highly independent and ever ready to challenge incomers and strangers. It does this by barking and charging, which is a behaviour that has to be trained out of the dog at a young age if they are to be a domestic pet. The dogs are highly social and will follow their fellow "pack" members, be that a flock of sheep or a human family, wherever they go. Their exercise regime needs to emulate a working life out in the open with plenty of variety.

CHARACTERISTICS

Coat
A thick and long coat that protects it from harsh weather and bites from predators. Can be white, grey or black, with a variety of markings

Height
59–78cm (23–31in)

Weight
35–70kg (77–154lb)

Lifespan
12–14 years

Personality
Alert and courageous

Origin
Romania

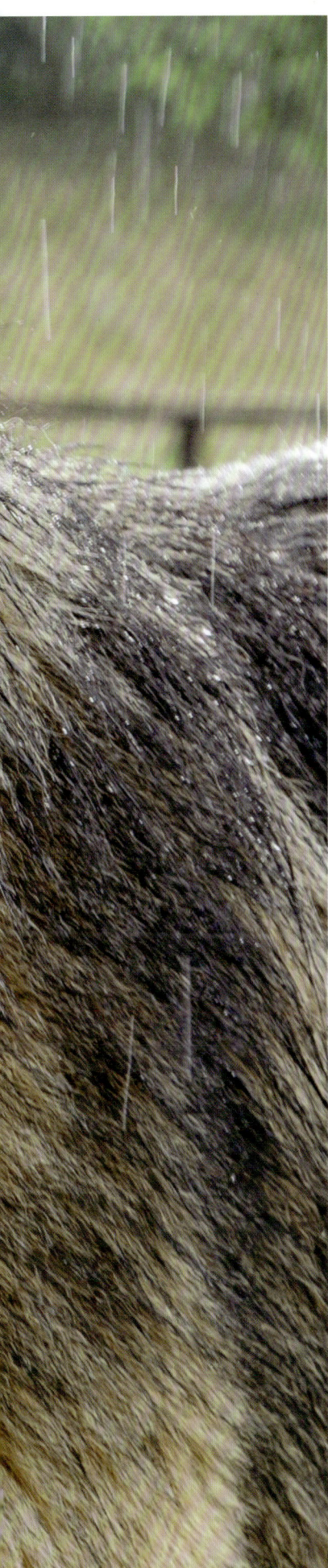

LEFT:
Weatherproof
A bit of rain does not bother the Romanian sheepdog. Its lusciously long and thick hair keeps out the water as well as any raincoat.

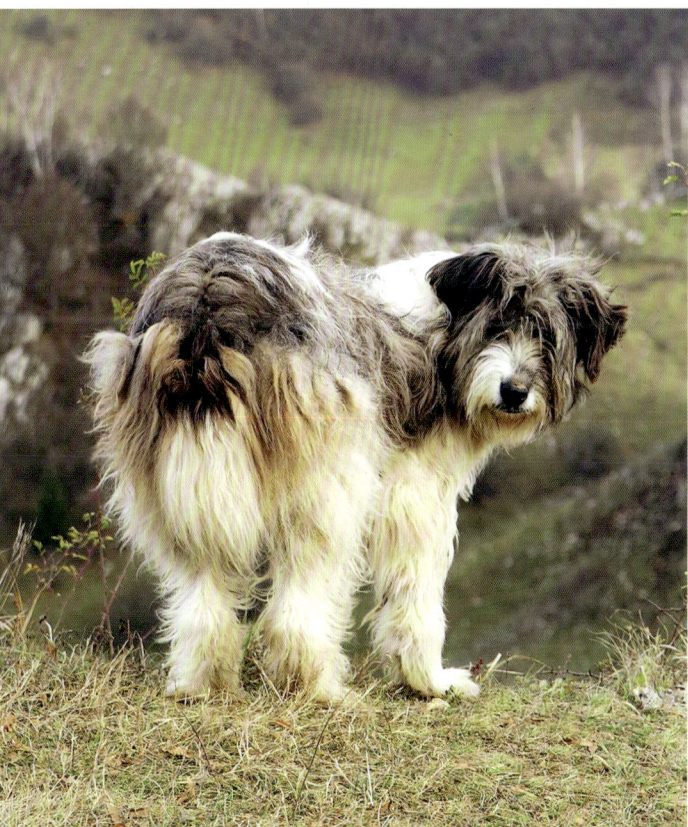

ABOVE:
Longer hair
The Mioritic shepherd dogs have longer hair than the other Romanian breeds.

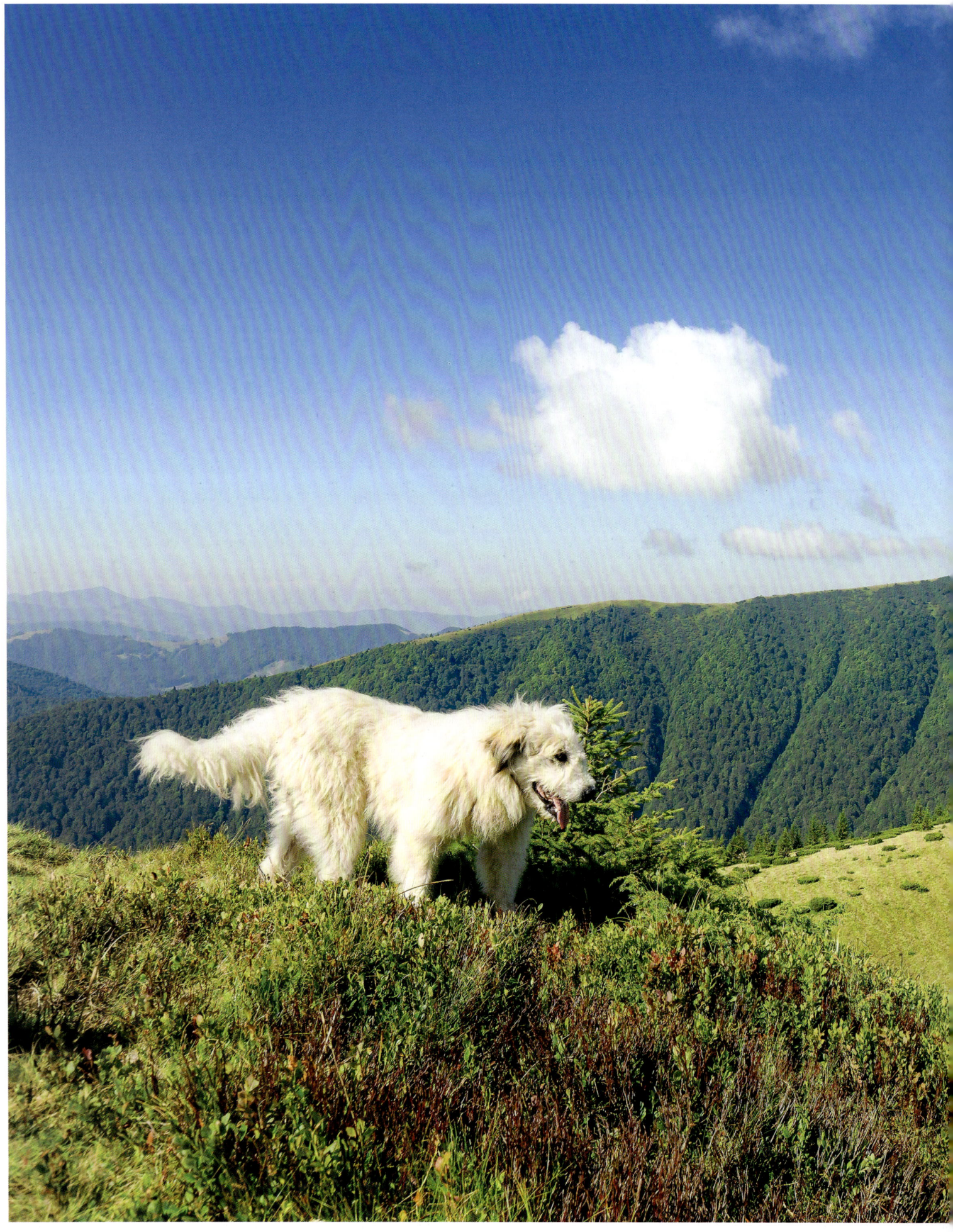

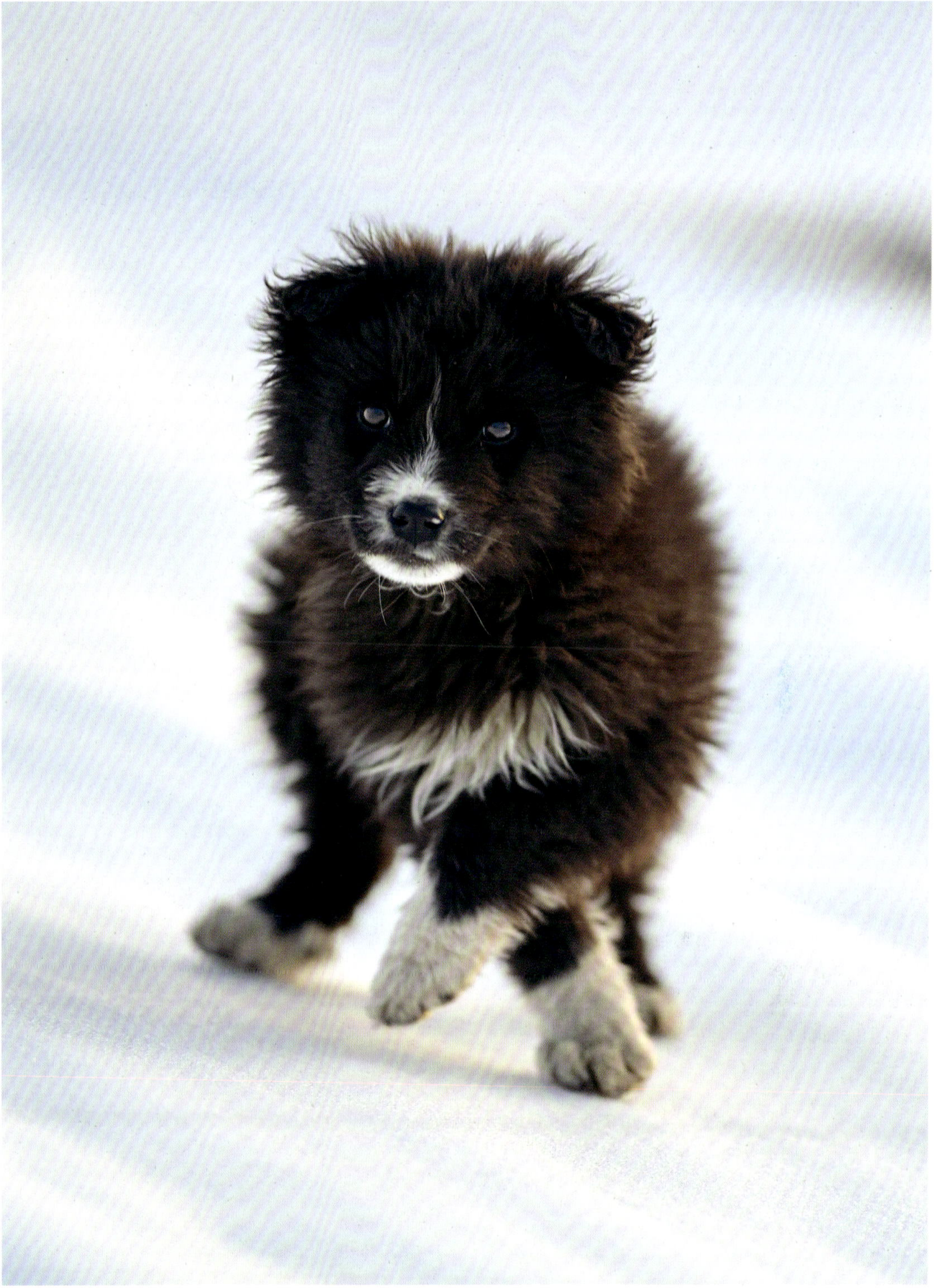

WORKING DOGS

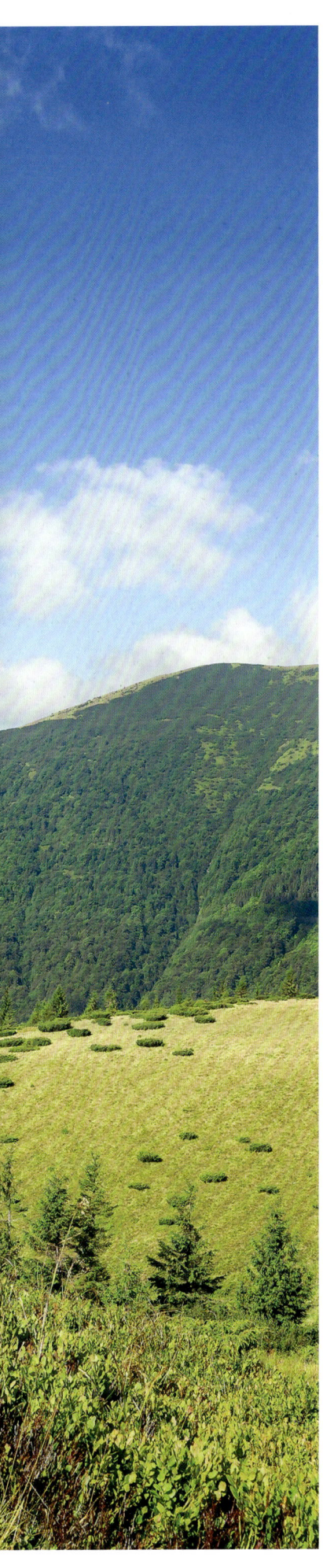

LEFT:
Thick tail
As well as their thick hair covering the body, all Romanian Shepherd dogs have a thick, bushy tail.

ABOVE:
Cold weather
The long hair and fluffy coat of this breed makes it perfectly suited to harsh cold weather such as snowy environments.

399

WORKING DOGS

Rottweiler

Named after the German town of Rottweil, this somewhat notorious breed is said to be a direct descendant of the mastiff attack dogs used by Roman legions. The dogs were introduced into Germany as the Roman armies pressed north, only to be pushed back. Even though the Romans had gone their dogs remained, and many German breeds are based on them. The herdsmen of Rottweil wanted a drover that could guide their cattle to slaughter, but found that their animals were too easily stolen by bandits. And so was born the idea for the Rottweiler breed, a cattle dog that could go on the attack. The muscle-bound dog, with an aloofness that can be read as menacing, did its job very well and became known as the "butcher's dog", protecting as it was their livelihoods as well as the cattle farmers'.

Today the breed has lost its role in the livestock industry but can be used to project menace and power in other contexts, such as police work or as guard dogs. The breed also excels as search and rescue dogs. Owners of Rottweilers maintain that their dog's tough exterior hides an affectionate and loyal pet. However, the breed needs firm training and regular exercise. They are not recommended for first-time owners.

CHARACTERISTICS
Coat
A short black coat and rust-coloured markings on its face, chest and legs
Height
58–69cm (23–27in)
Weight
38–59kg (84–130lb)
Lifespan
Around 10 years
Personality
Aloof and obedient
Origin
Germany

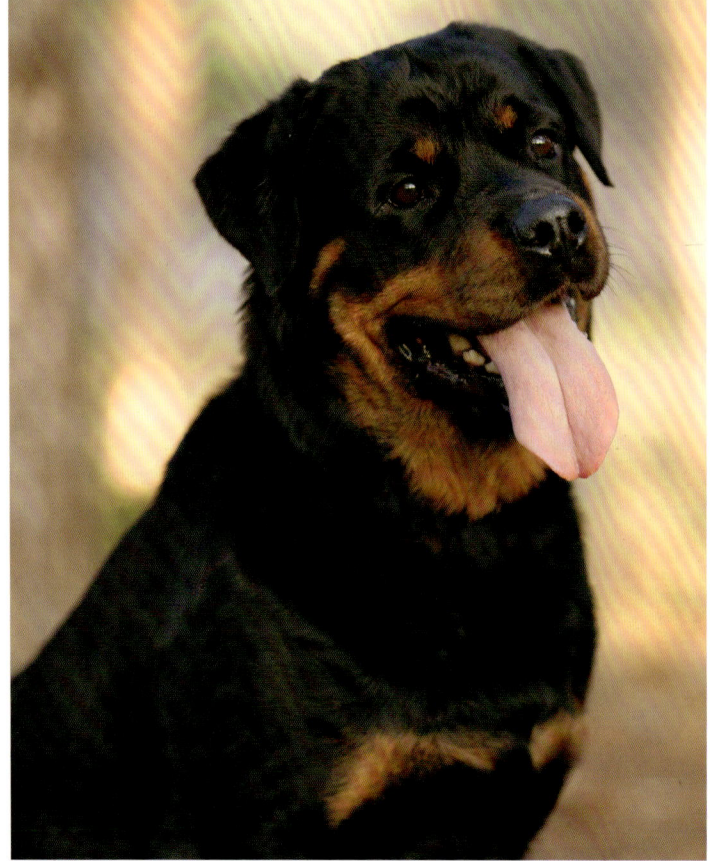

ABOVE:
A capable friend
The Rottweiler is a powerful dog with confident temperament yet it can be a gentle and devoted companion if well-trained.

RIGHT:
A happy life
The Rottweiler needs regular exercise, grooming and plenty of health checks. It is also crucial that puppies are well socialized at an early age.

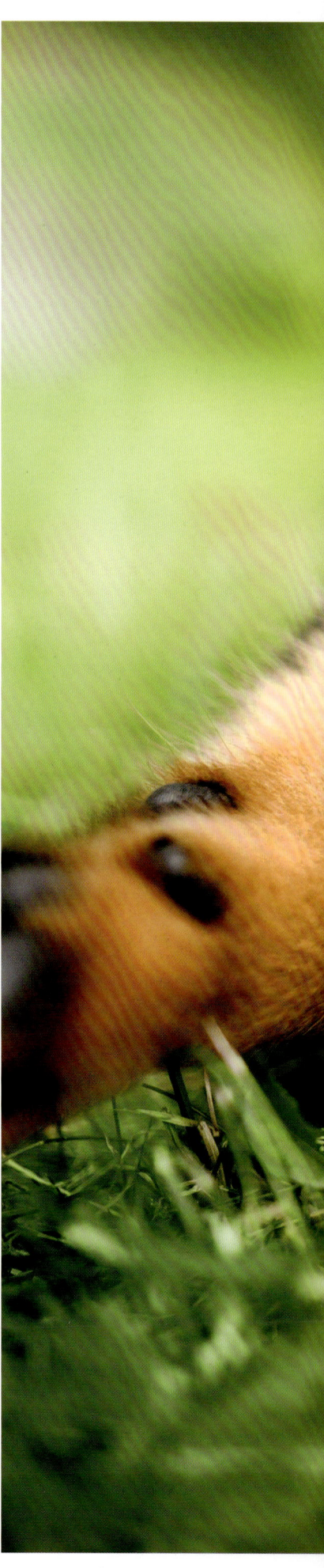

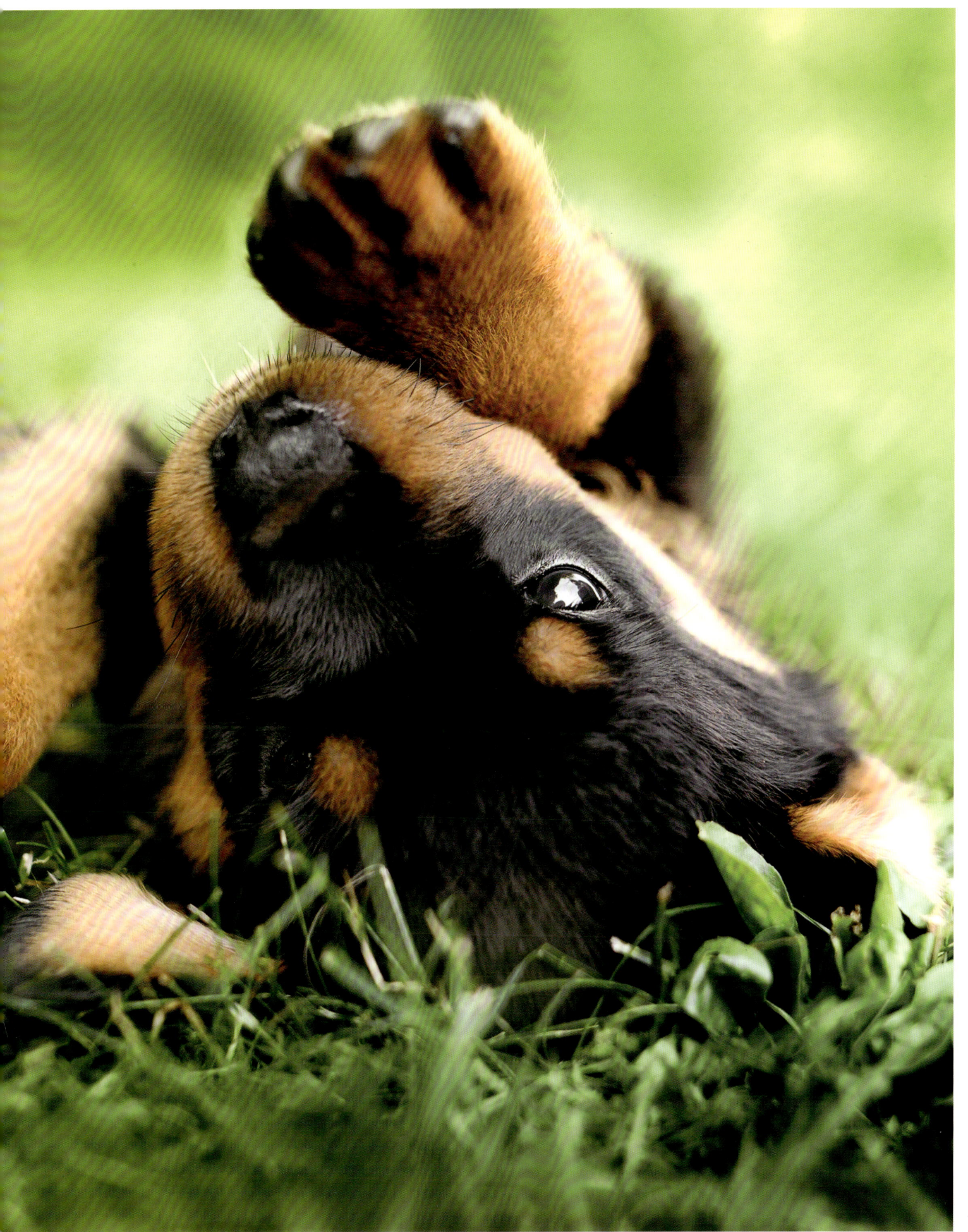

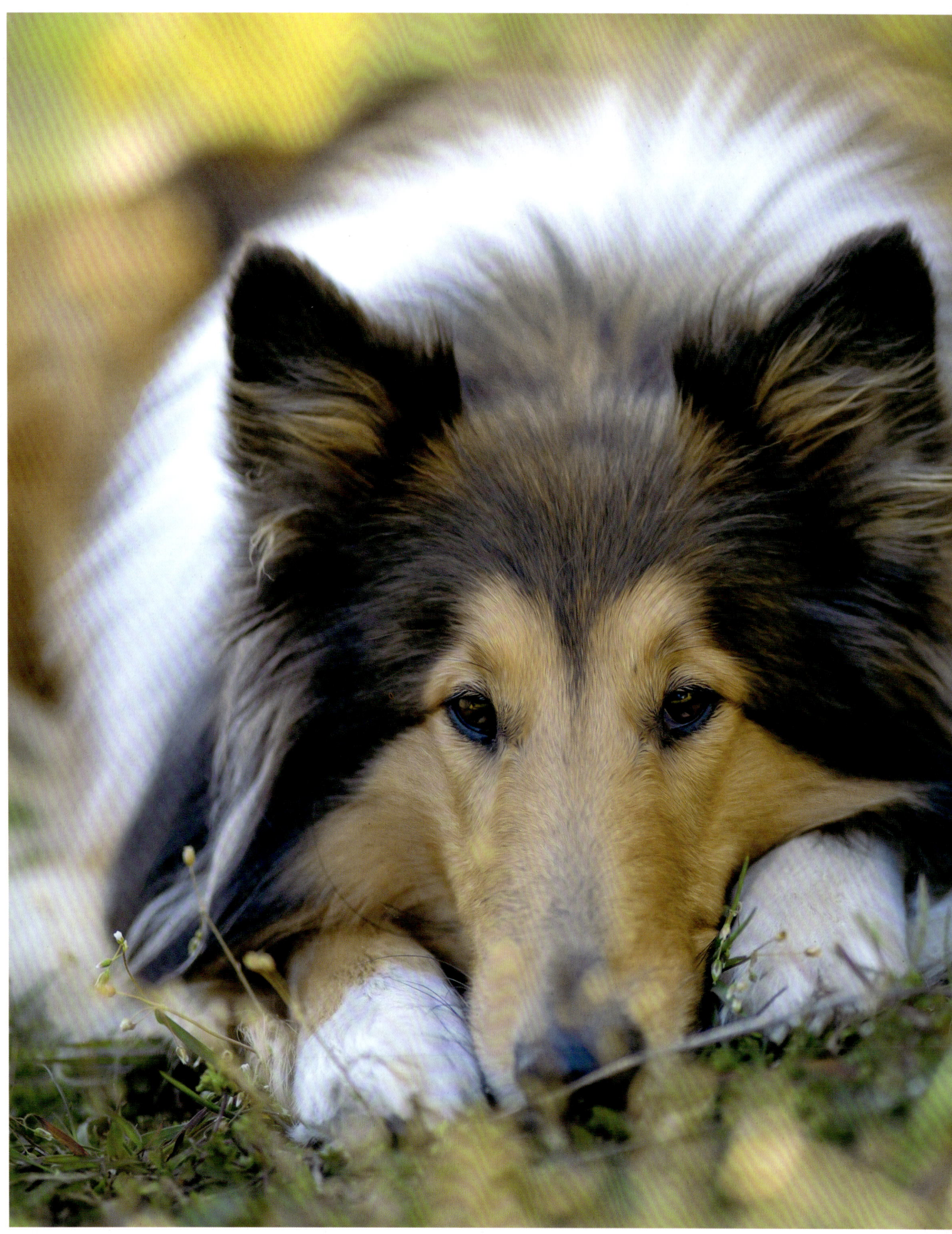

Rough Collie

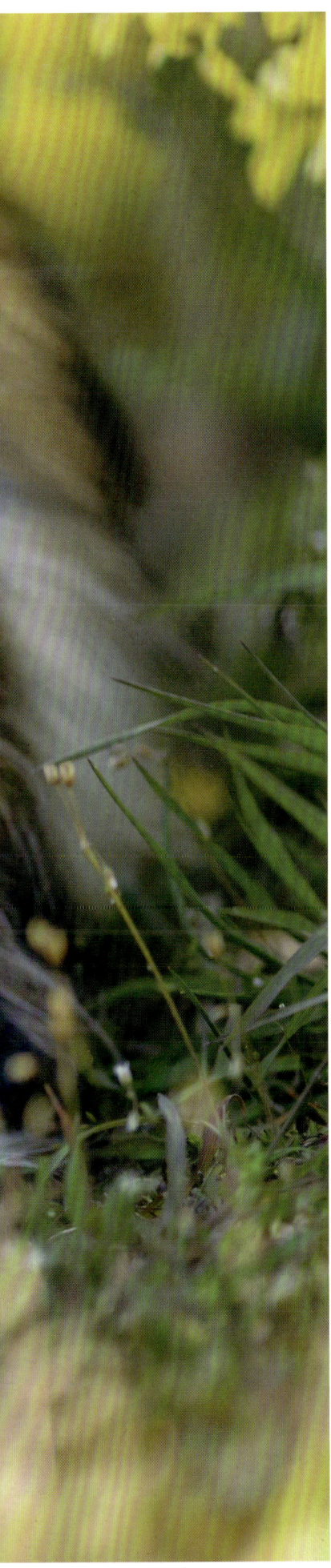

Also known as the long-haired collie, this originally Scottish breed is famous across the English-speaking world and beyond for being the leading character in the Lassie novels, TV shows and feature films. These related the story of a preternaturally intelligent rough collie with a beautiful gold and white coat as she goes about preventing crimes and averting disasters.

Like the other collies from northern Britain, the rough collie has its roots in the stock of Roman herding dogs that were introduced around 2,000 years ago. Queen Victoria, who spent much of her time in the Scottish Highlands, took an interest in the breed in the late 19th century, helping to boost the rough collie from a hard-working highland shepherd dog to a graceful possession of the glamorous rich.

The rough collie makes a better pet than other collie breeds. It shares their intelligence and loyalty but is also reportedly more friendly. As one expects with working dog breeds, it needs a lot of exercise to prevent it from becoming bored and irritable. The breed also makes a good watchdog, always alert to strangers. The collie's long coat needs regular grooming to prevent it becoming matted.

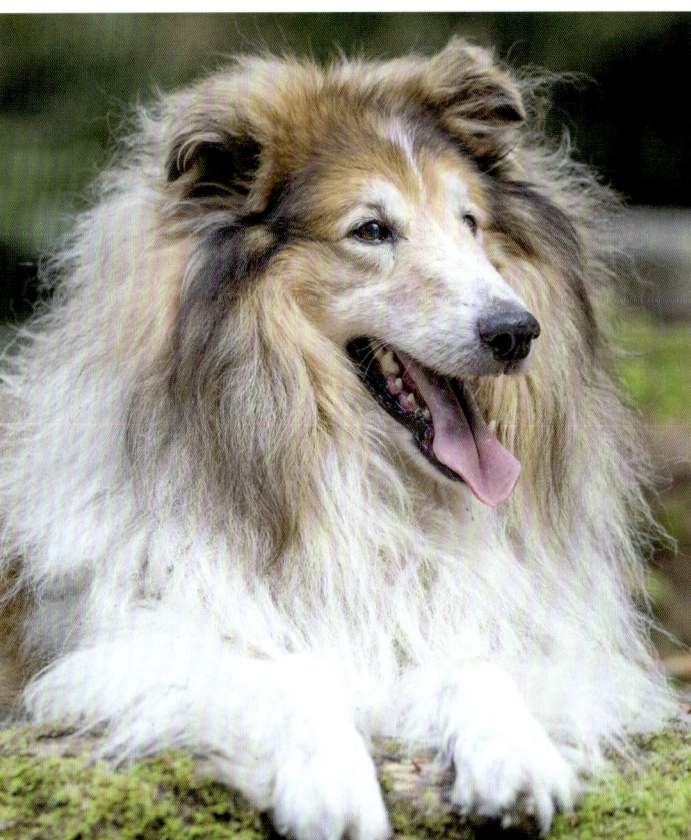

CHARACTERISTICS

Coat
A long, thick coat in various colours, such as gold, sable and white, and blue and tan

Height
51–61cm (20–24in)

Weight
23–34kg (51–75lb)

Lifespan
12–14 years

Personality
Loyal and good-natured

Origin
Scotland

LEFT:
Iconic looks
The rough collie has a graceful appearance with a wedge-shaped head, almond-shaped eyes and small pointed ears.

ABOVE:
Impressive mane
A thick mantle of hair around the shoulders and neck make the rough collie look sturdier by obscuring its sinewy frame.

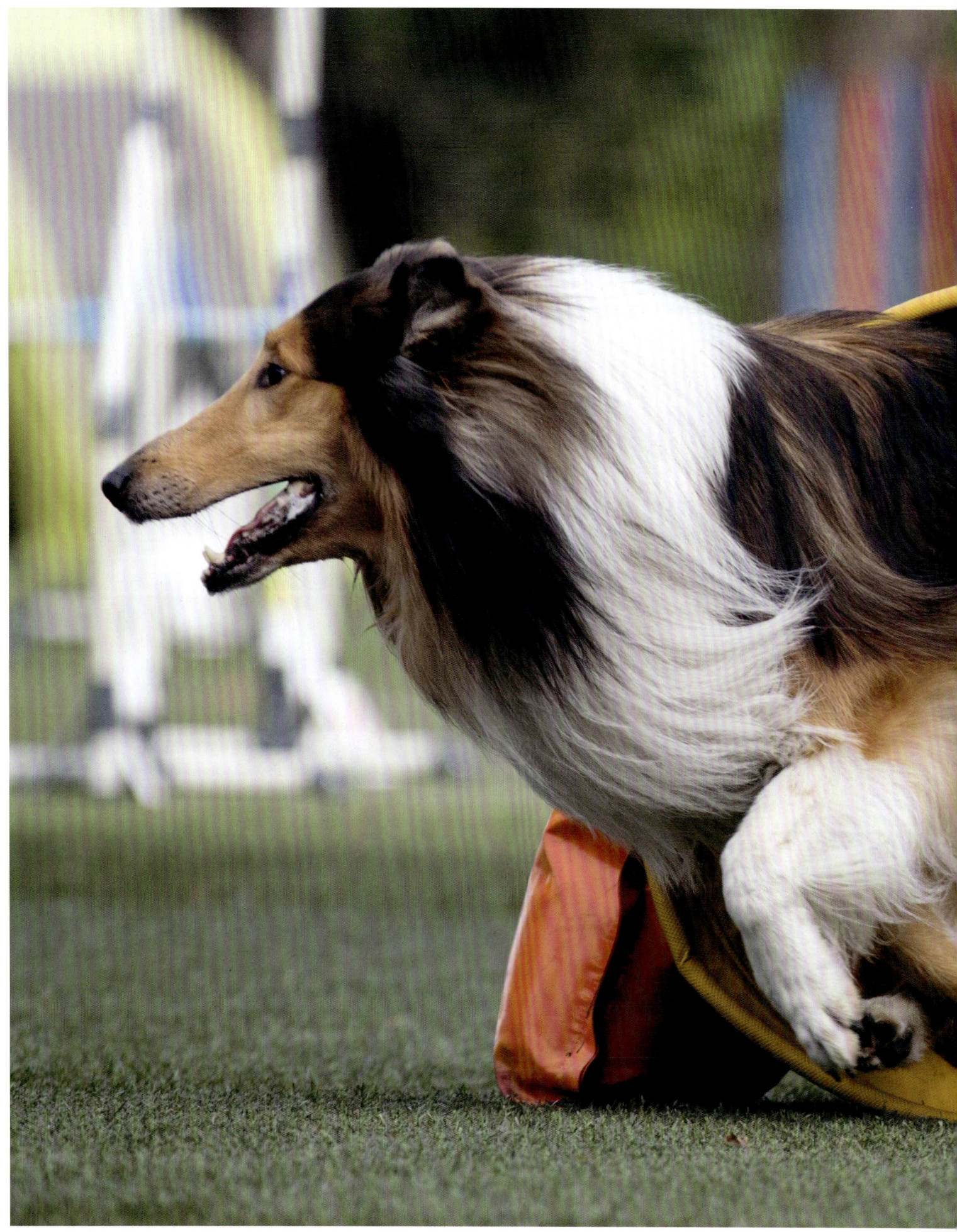

WORKING DOGS

Agility
This fast-moving collie is perfectly suited to an agility competition, with some thorough training and instruction they can perform very well.

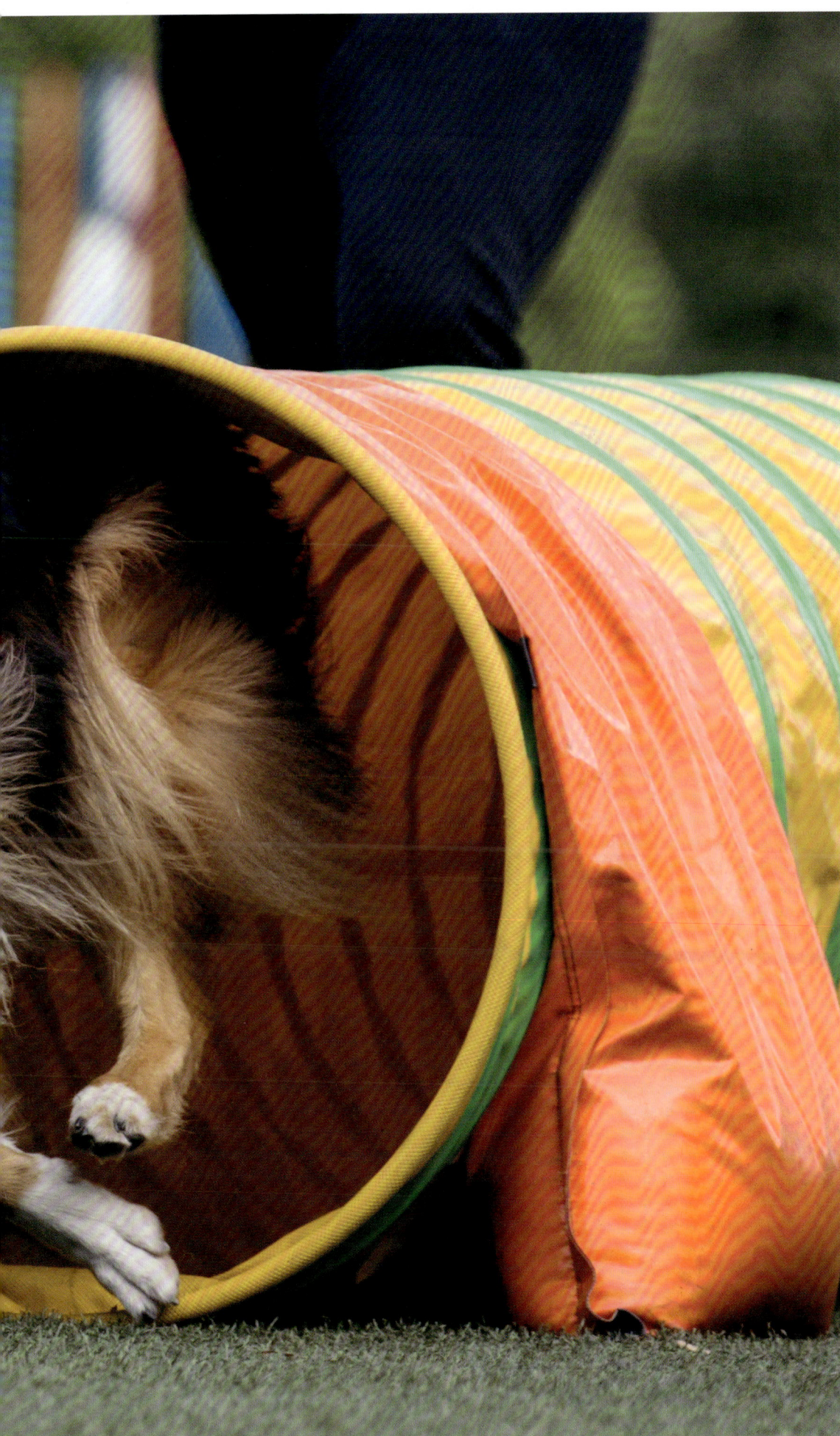

405

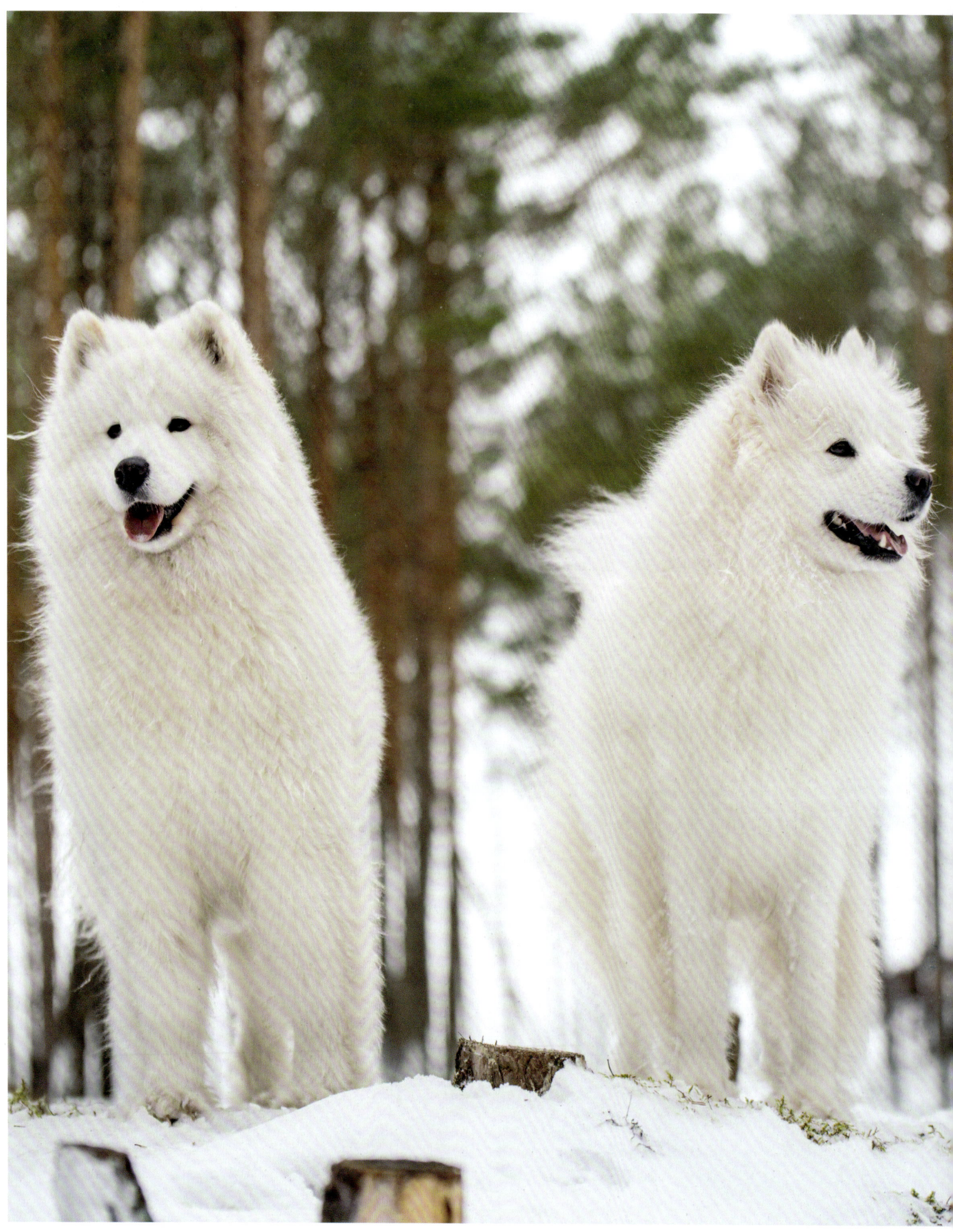

Samoyed

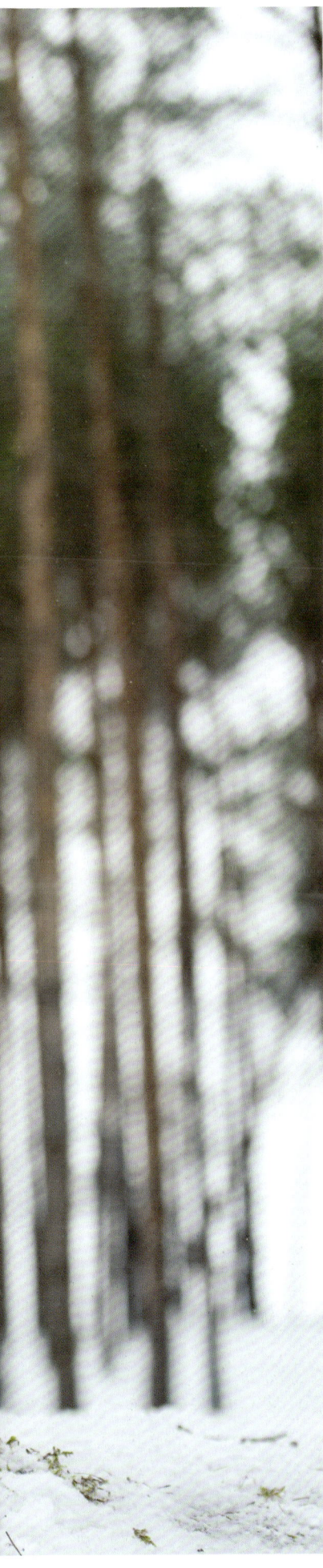

The Arctic herding dog was bred by Siberian nomads to help control reindeer on the move across the tundra. It is a spitz-type dog, similar to other cold-weather breeds from the far north of Europe and Asia, with a distinctive bushy tail, thick fur and distinctive pointed face. The eager Samoyed also accompanied its owner on hunting trips across the snow and ice, stood guard over settlements and even helped out by pulling sleds.

The white coat helps the dog stay out of sight in the snow, which helps it perform its role in protecting livestock from wolves and bears. The oiled fur is also water- and dirt-repellent but is shed twice a year during heavy moults.

In line with ancient breeds from this part of the world, the Samoyed has not been bred to be obedient and subservient. Its stubborn independence serves it much better in the harsh polar habitat. When transferred to the warmer and more predictable surroundings of a human house, the dog needs a lot of exercise and training to fend off boredom and behavioural problems. Even so, the Samoyed is very likely to bark at other people and animals, and chase them if taken off the leash, but is very seldom aggressive.

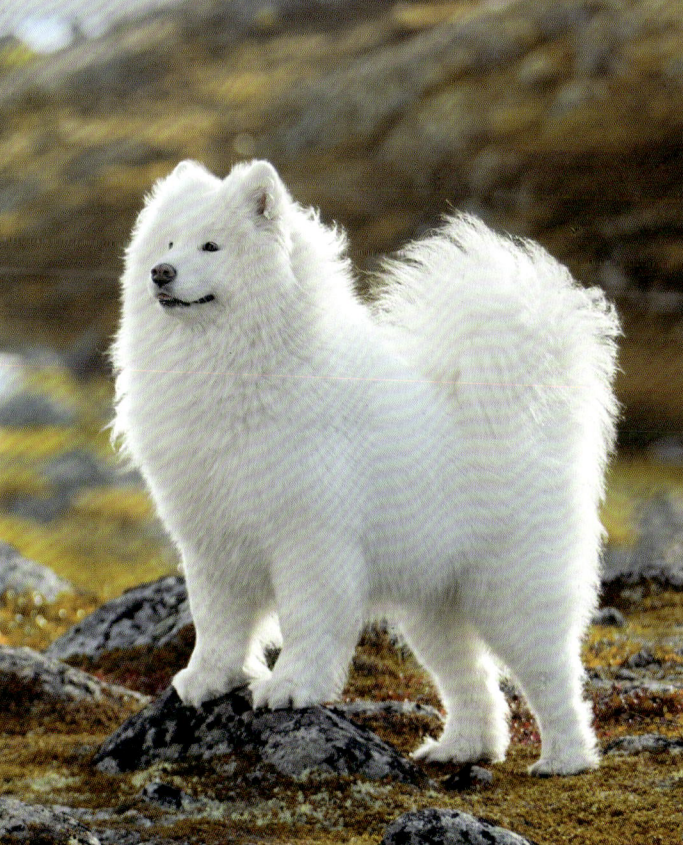

CHARACTERISTICS
Coat
A thick, white, double-layer coat that protects it from the cold weather
Height
46–56cm (18–22in)
Weight
16–30kg (35–66lb)
Lifespan
About 12 years
Personality
Spirited and self-sufficient
Origin
Russia

LEFT:
Part of the team
As working dogs in a nomadic community, Samoyeds are definite team players.

ABOVE:
Cheeky look
The Samoyed has a friendly and playful personality, and is often called the "smiling dog" because of its upturned mouth.

WORKING DOGS

Schnauzer (giant)

As the name suggests this is the bigger schnauzer breed. It was developed from the standard breed through crosses with the Great Dane and bouvier des Flandres to add size and some German pinscher lines to reinforce the intelligence and work ethic. Like its smaller cousins, the giant schnauzer was envisaged as an all-purpose farm dog but was more of use in cattle and dairy farms. They were big enough to protect the herds from bandits and predators, plus help out by hauling carts. The German military began to deploy these big dogs among their ranks, and they saw action in both world wars as guard dogs and messengers. They are now the breed of choice for some police forces.

The giant schnauzer is not recommended for novice owners or people living in small houses. Its breeding for herd protection can make it an aloof and menacing presence in crowded spaces full of strangers. This is an intelligent breed and it can be trained to be a loyal and confident pet but requires a lot of space to thrive and plenty of opportunity to socialize when young. When relaxed among family members, the big dog becomes very affectionate and playful.

CHARACTERISTICS
Coat
A dense and wiry coat that comes in two colour types, solid black or salt-and-pepper
Height
60–70cm (24–28in)
Weight
29–41kg (65–90lb)
Lifespan
10 years or more
Personality
Intelligent and calm
Origin
Germany

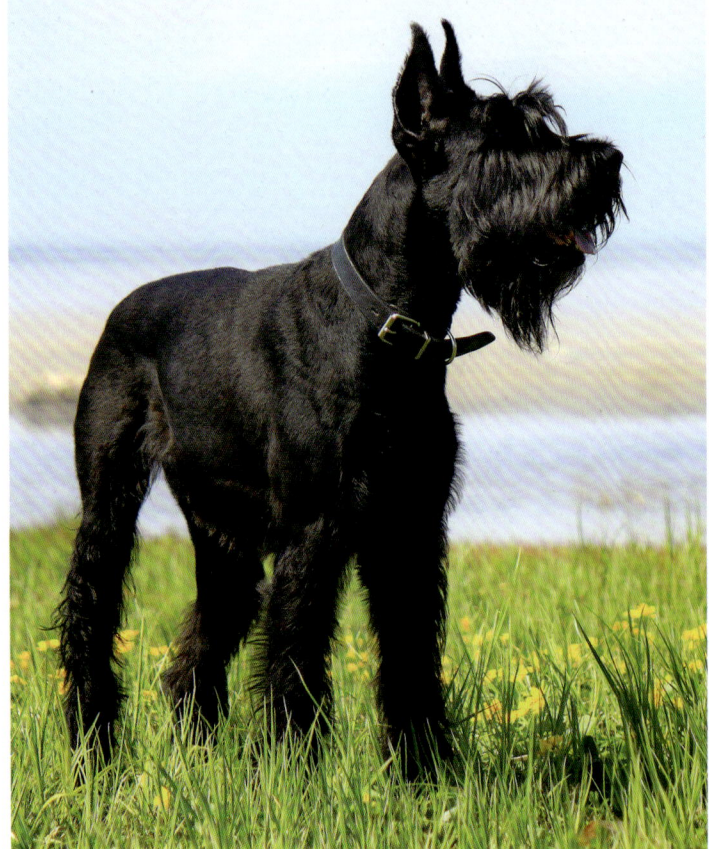

ABOVE:
Care and attention
The schnauzer's coat requires regular grooming to maintain its appearance and health.

RIGHT:
Bushy looks
The breed has distinctive facial features, such as a long muzzle, a beard and eyebrows.

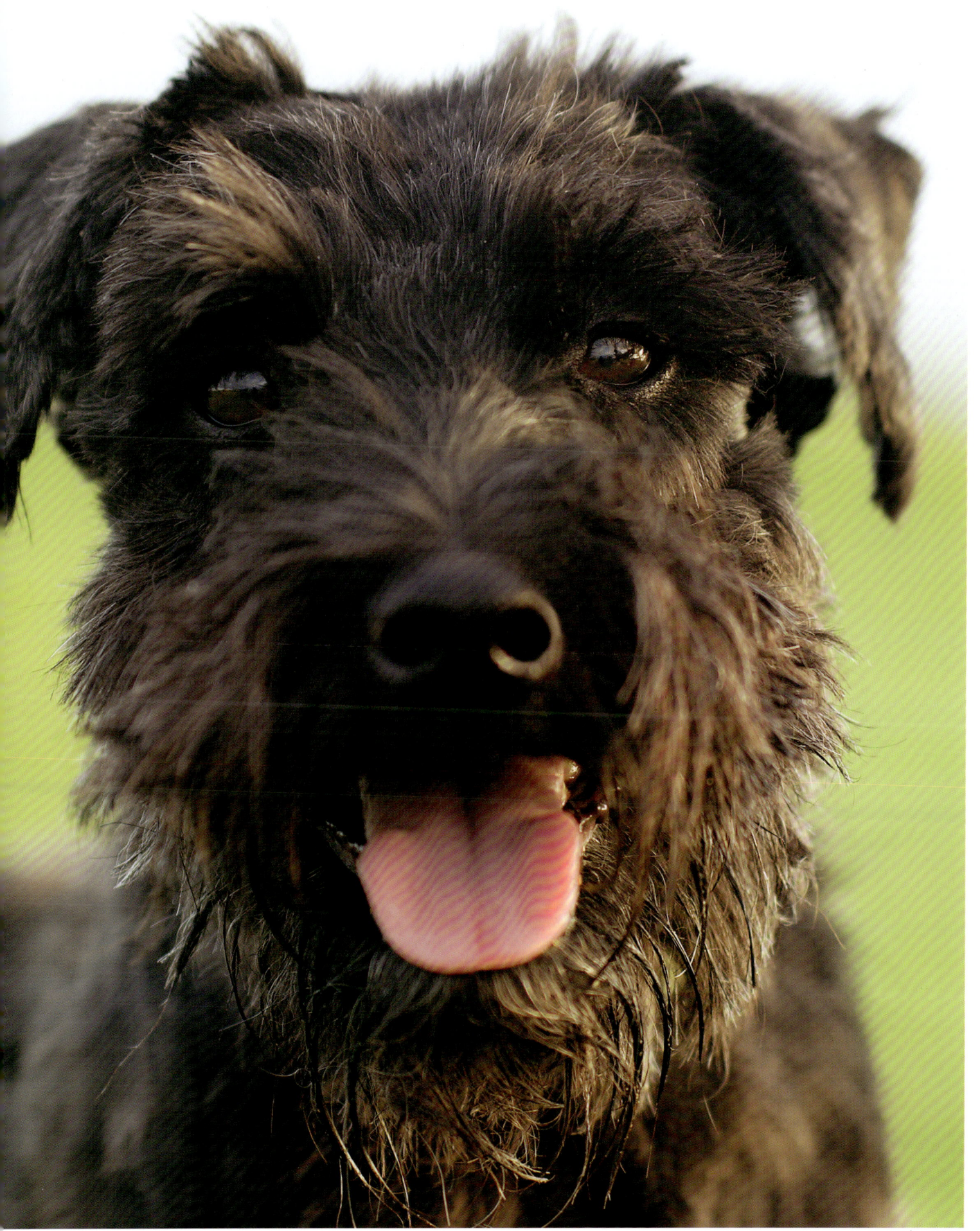

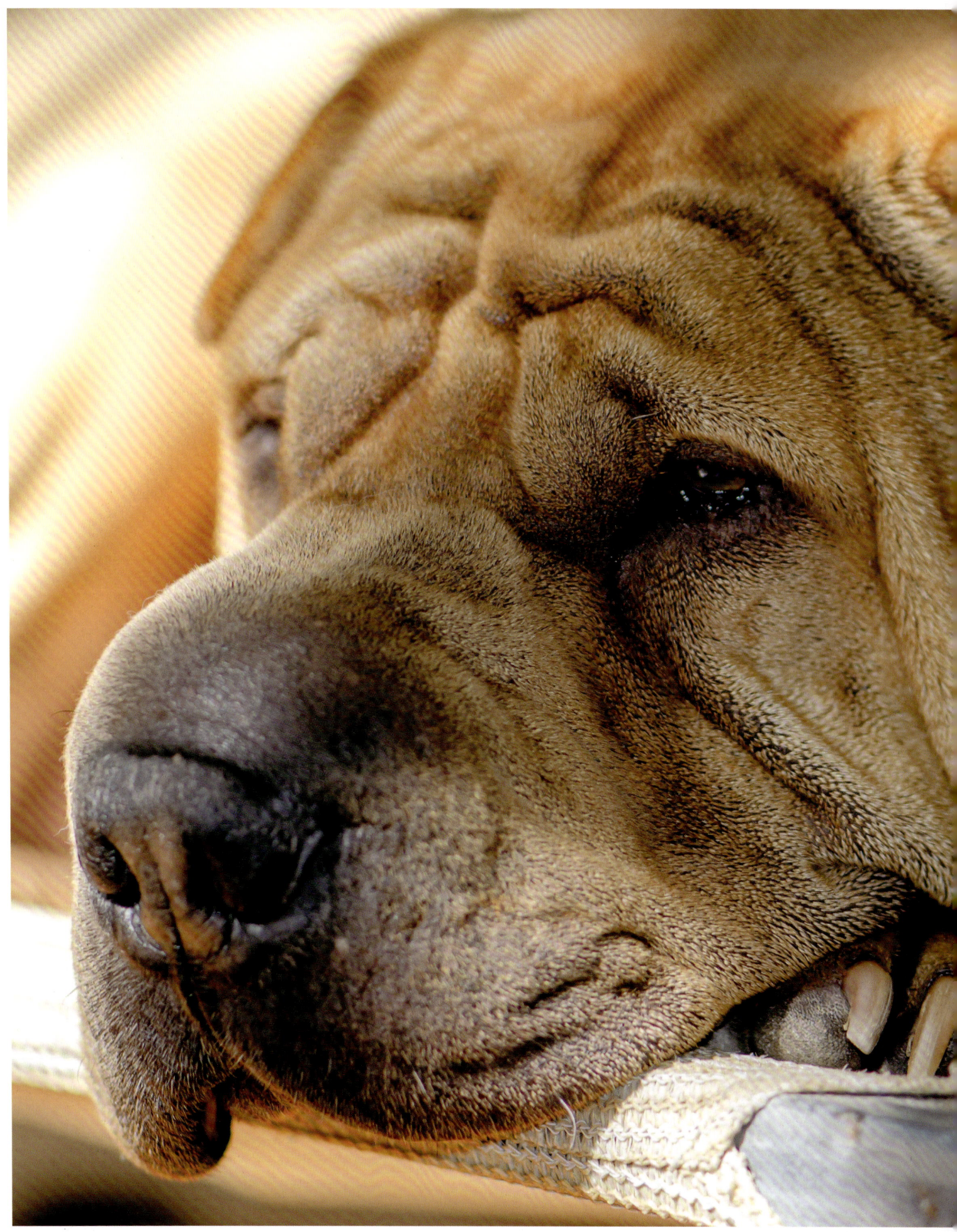

Shar Pei

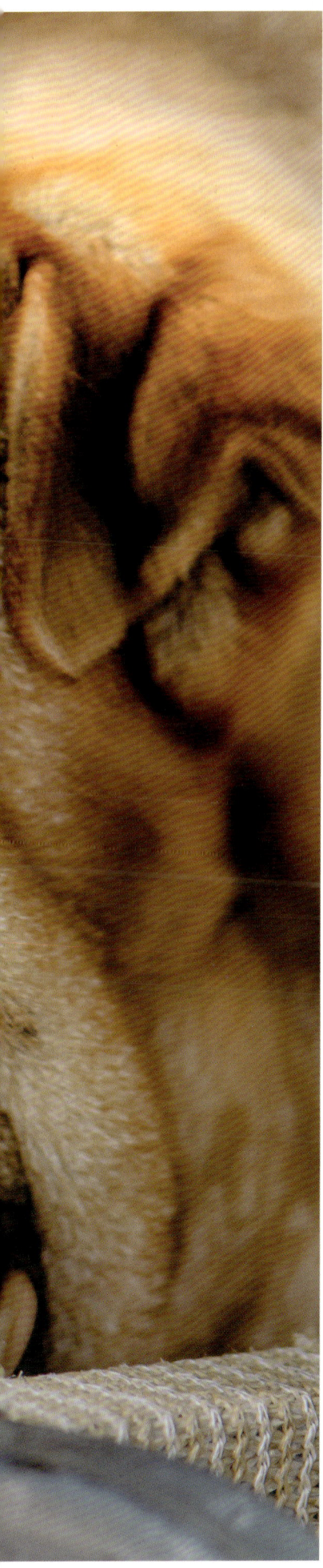

This Chinese dog breed certainly stands out among dogkind with its highly unusual wrinkled skin. The breed has a long history, being developed over many centuries in isolation from the more cosmopolitan breeds that were spreading between the continents. Its role was as a fighting dog sent to protect livestock from rustlers and poachers. The thick folds of loose skin helped to neutralize the bites of opponents. The name shar pei means "sand skin" and relates to the rough coats of short thick hairs. The eyes are protected inside sunken sockets and the ears are reduced to tiny flaps that are less vulnerable to injury. Finally, the broad muzzle supports the jaw musculature needed for a crushing bite.

The shar pei is a dog that looks dangerous, and has the ability to be so. At best it glowers with a noble calm, but at any moment it could unleash violence, on strangers and owners alike. Without expert training from the earliest stages of life, the shar pei remains an unpredictable dog particularly unsuited to domestic life.

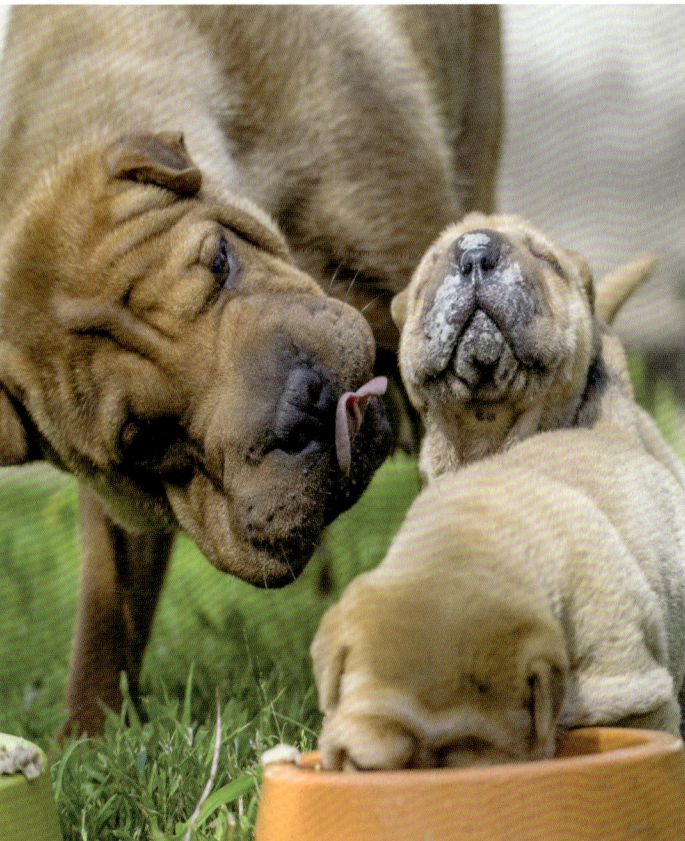

CHARACTERISTICS

Coat
A short coat in a variety of colour that is bristled and rough to the touch
Height
46–51cm (18–20in)
Weight
18–25kg (40–55lb)
Lifespan
More than 10 years
Personality
Proud and loyal
Origin
China

LEFT:
Challenging breed
The shar pei is now rare in China, where dog ownership is less common.

ABOVE:
Strange features
The shar pei has a blue tongue and in China the dog's snub snout is called a "butterfly-cookie" nose.

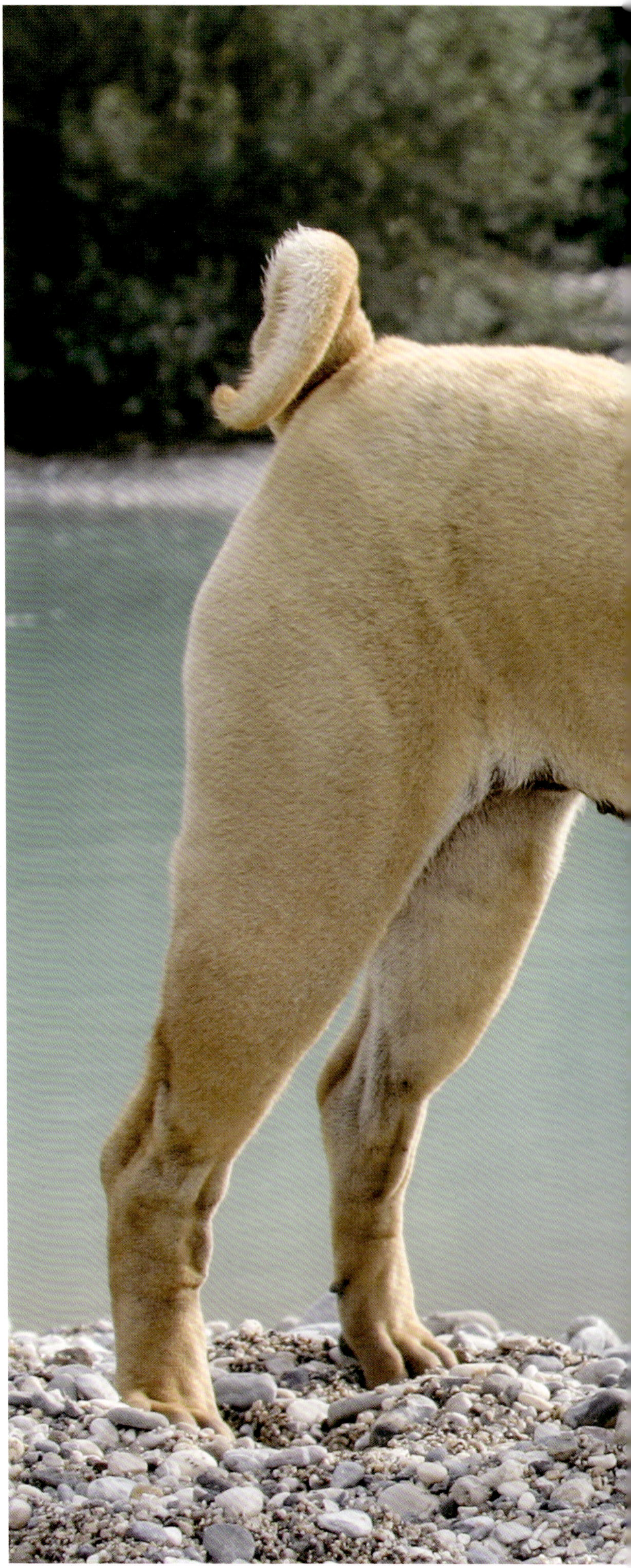

WORKING DOGS

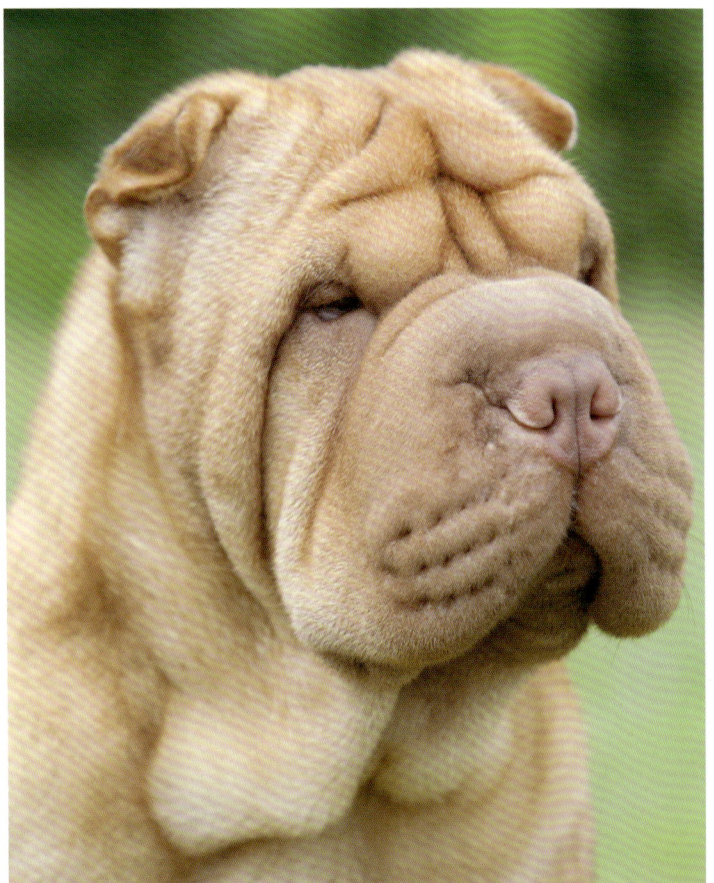

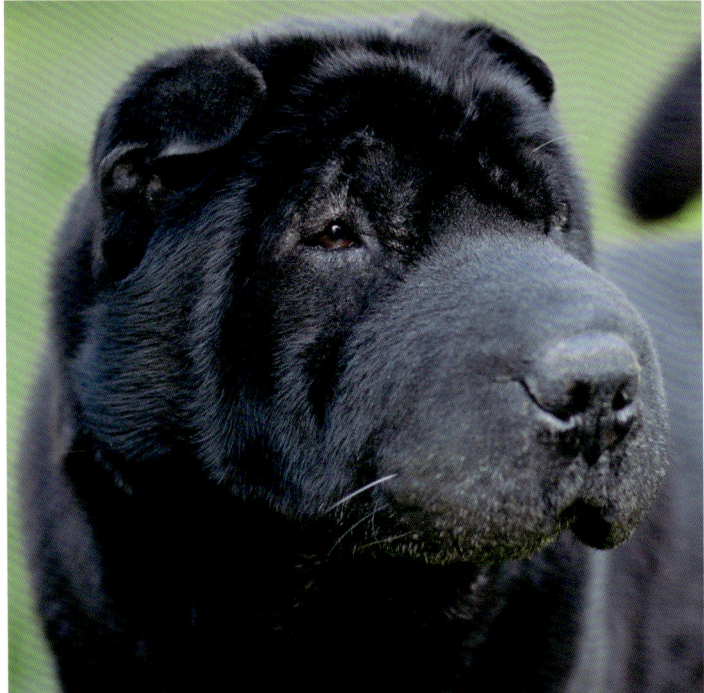

ABOVE TOP AND BOTTOM:
Strong looks
If not banned outright in other countries, most authorities will advise against owning this unusual breed.

RIGHT:
Loyal friend
This is a very loyal breed to loving owners, although can be more unfriendly and standoff-ish when faced with strange faces.

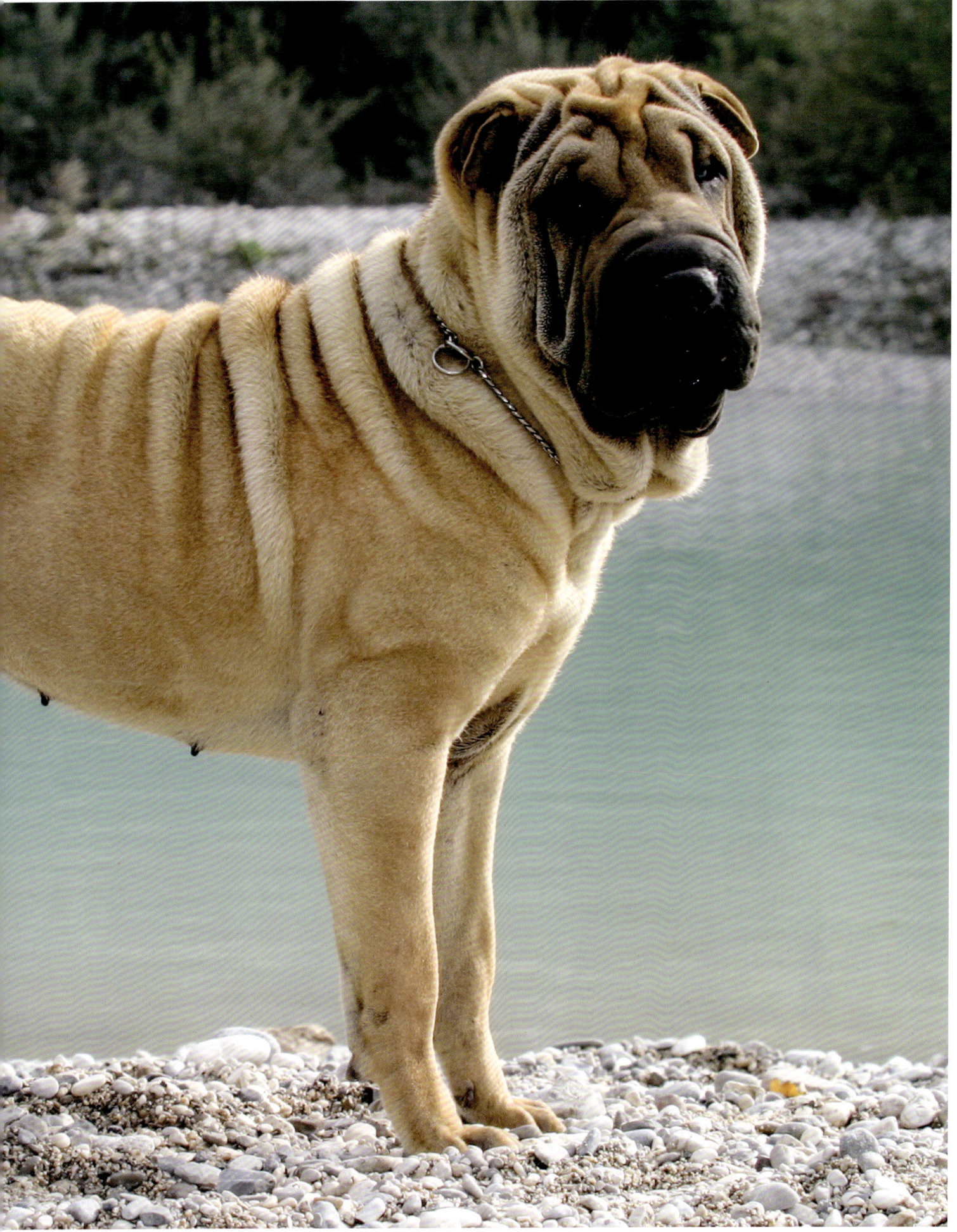

Shetland Sheepdog

Looking very much like its mainland relative, the rough collie, this island herder shares the long coat and narrow, wedge-shaped head but it is noticeably smaller. Also called the Sheltie, the long hairs obscure a deep chest that contains a formidable heart-and-lung engine that keeps the little dog active for hours on end in its windswept homeland.

Shetland is Britain's most northern territory, and the Sheltie's smaller stature may be a deliberate breeding choice or may be a product of the relative isolation of these islands. No one is quite sure. Nevertheless, the clever little herders were suited to the rocky, exposed farmland where they were expected to look after sheep, highland cattle and even poultry. The dogs were also watching over the island's famous little ponies.

Shelties are intelligent and easily trained, although are avid barkers when confronted with strangers. They can take time to relax when introduced to new people and animals. Additionally this is not a breed for the infirm (or the lazy!). The agile dog requires at least two hours of exercise a day, and will need regular grooming to maintain that impressive coat.

CHARACTERISTICS
Coat
Long, thick coat with three colours: sable, blue merle and black
Height
35–38cm (14–15in)
Weight
6–17kg (13–37lb)
Lifespan
12–14 years
Personality
Friendly and exuberant
Origin
Shetland

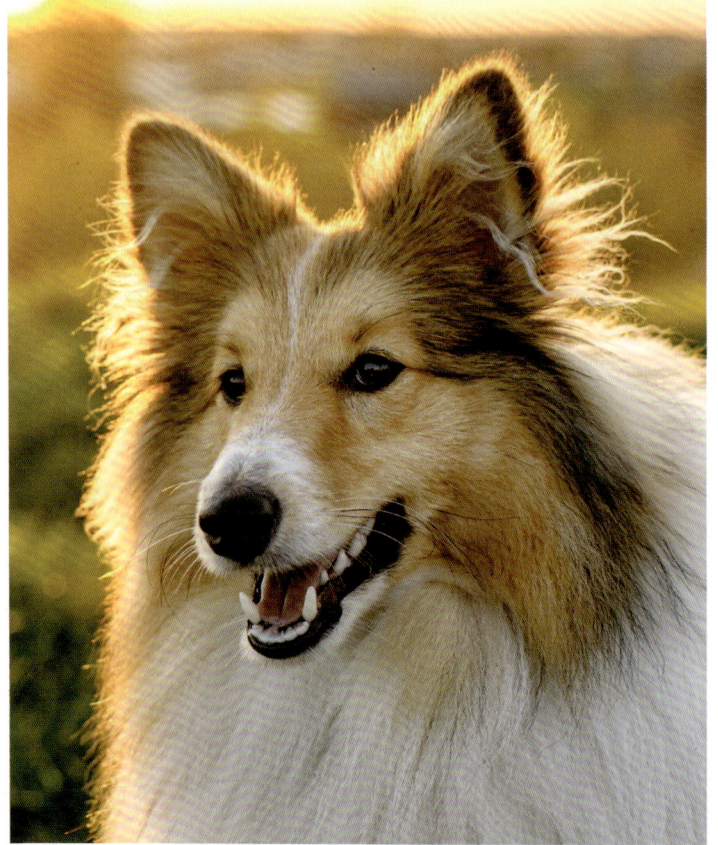

ABOVE:
Smile!
The Sheltie has an elegant wedge-shaped head and its almond-shaped eyes are normally dark brown.

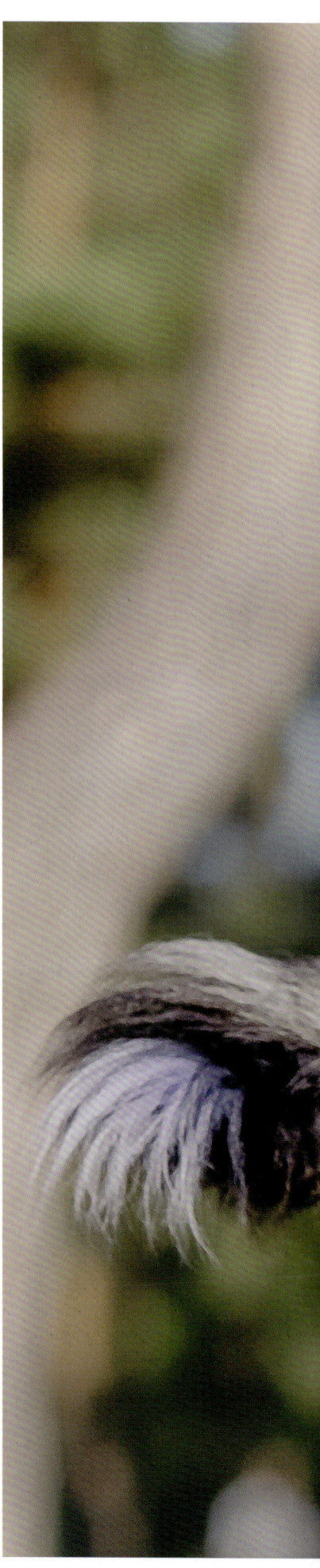

RIGHT:
A bundle of energy
Shelties make a fun and compact companion, always ready to join in the fun.

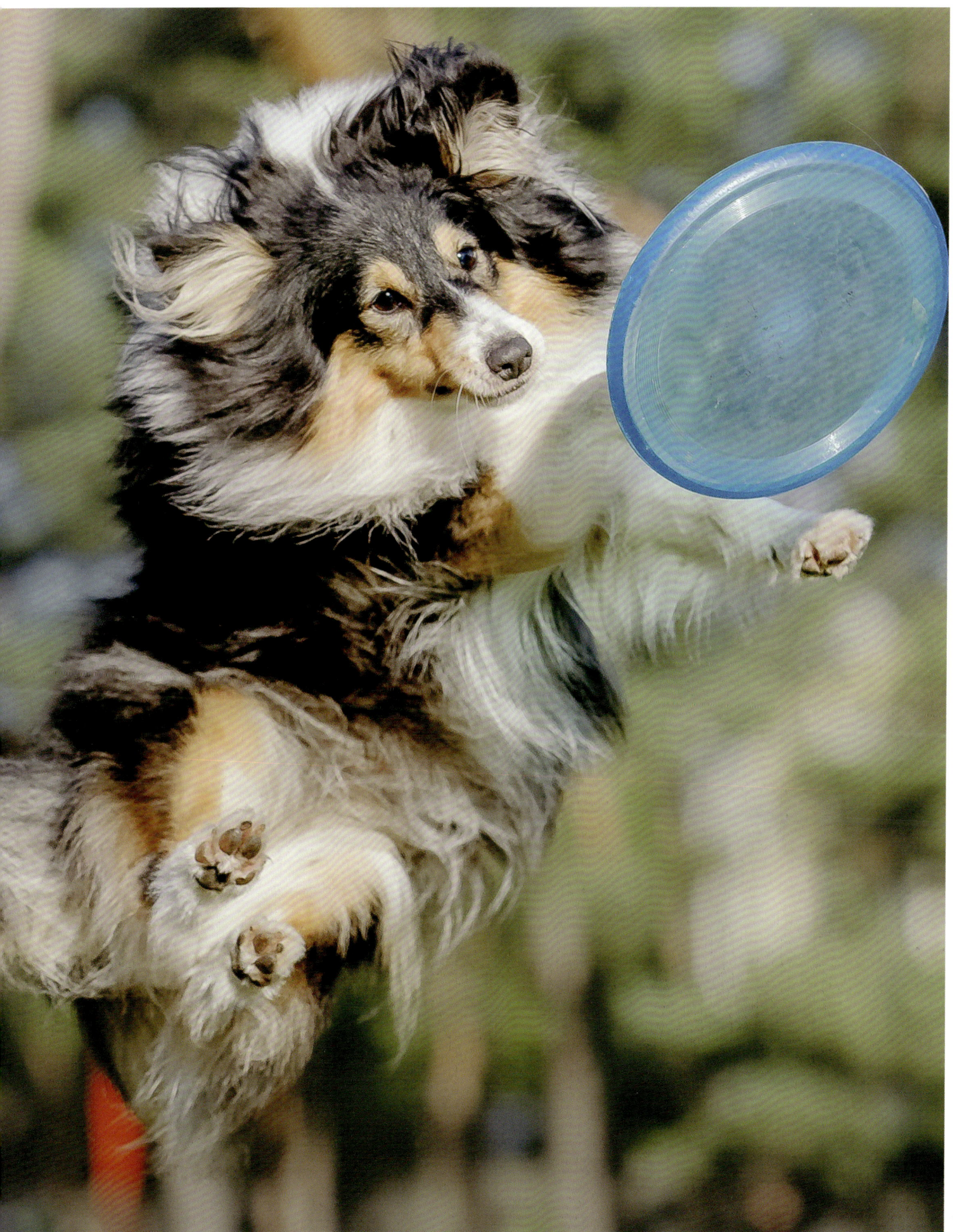

WORKING DOGS

RIGHT:
Perfectly poised
This cute, fluffy breed is also known as a Sheltie.

OPPOSITE:
Star of the small screen
The most famous Shetland sheepdog is *Lassie*, the star of a television show.

BELOW:
Shetland sheepdog
This island breed is a miniature version of the rough collie, a similar herding breed from the mainland.

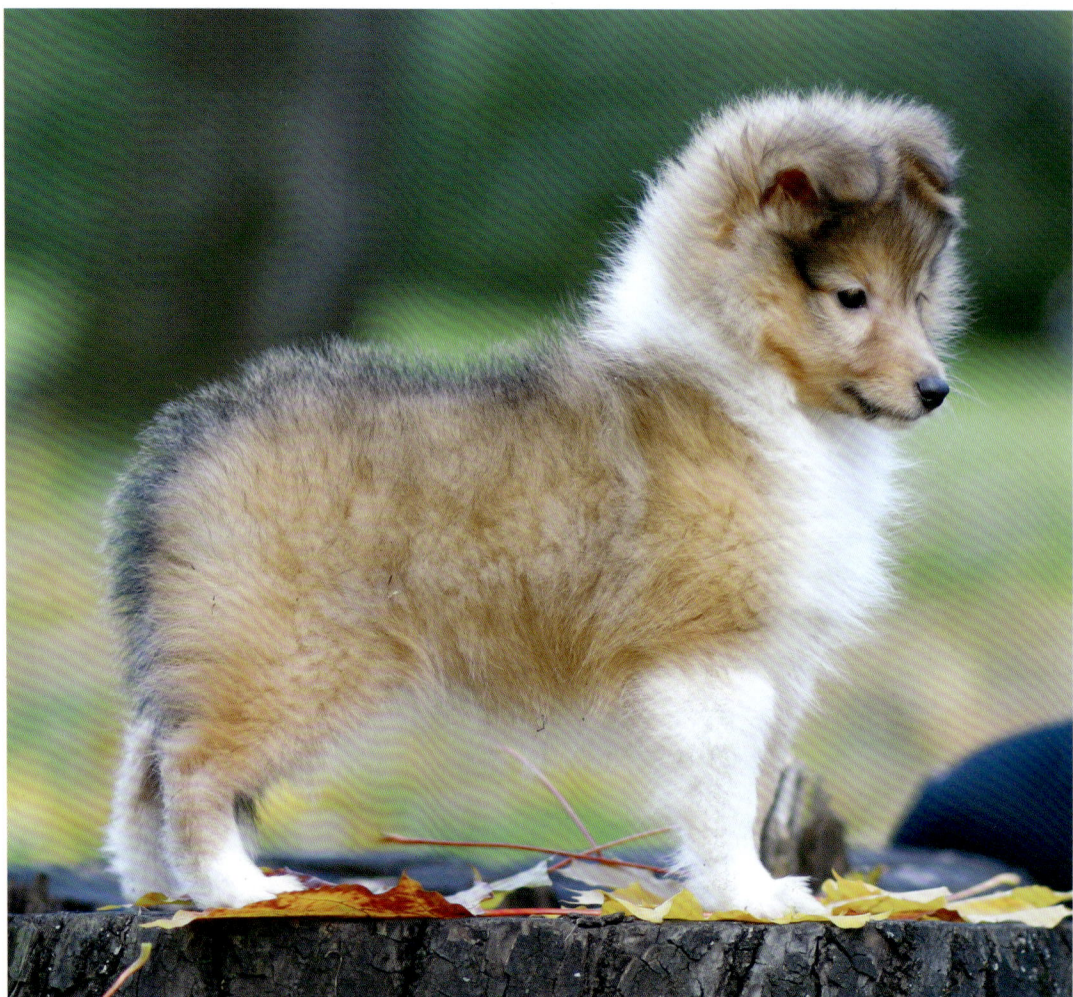

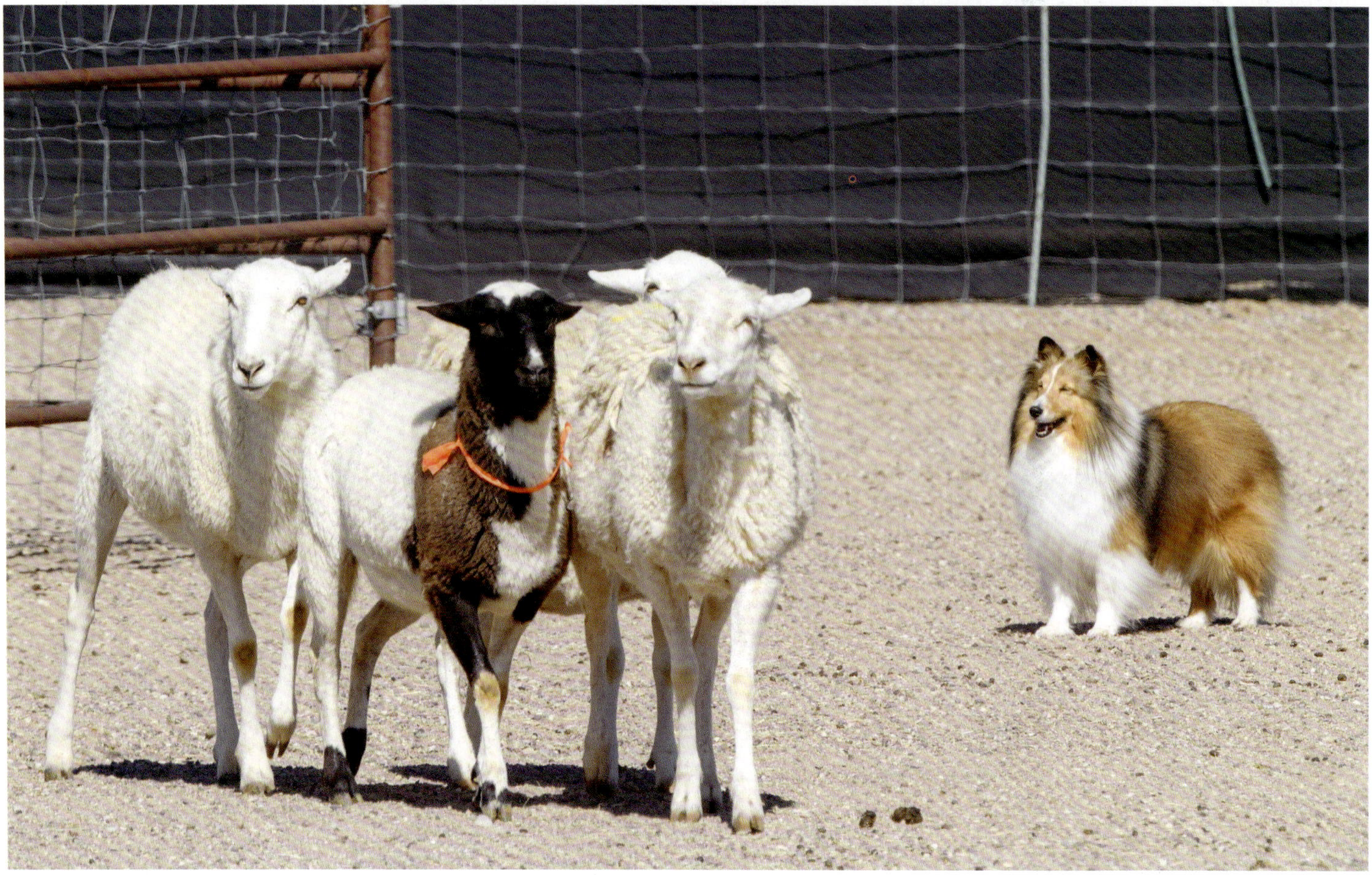

416

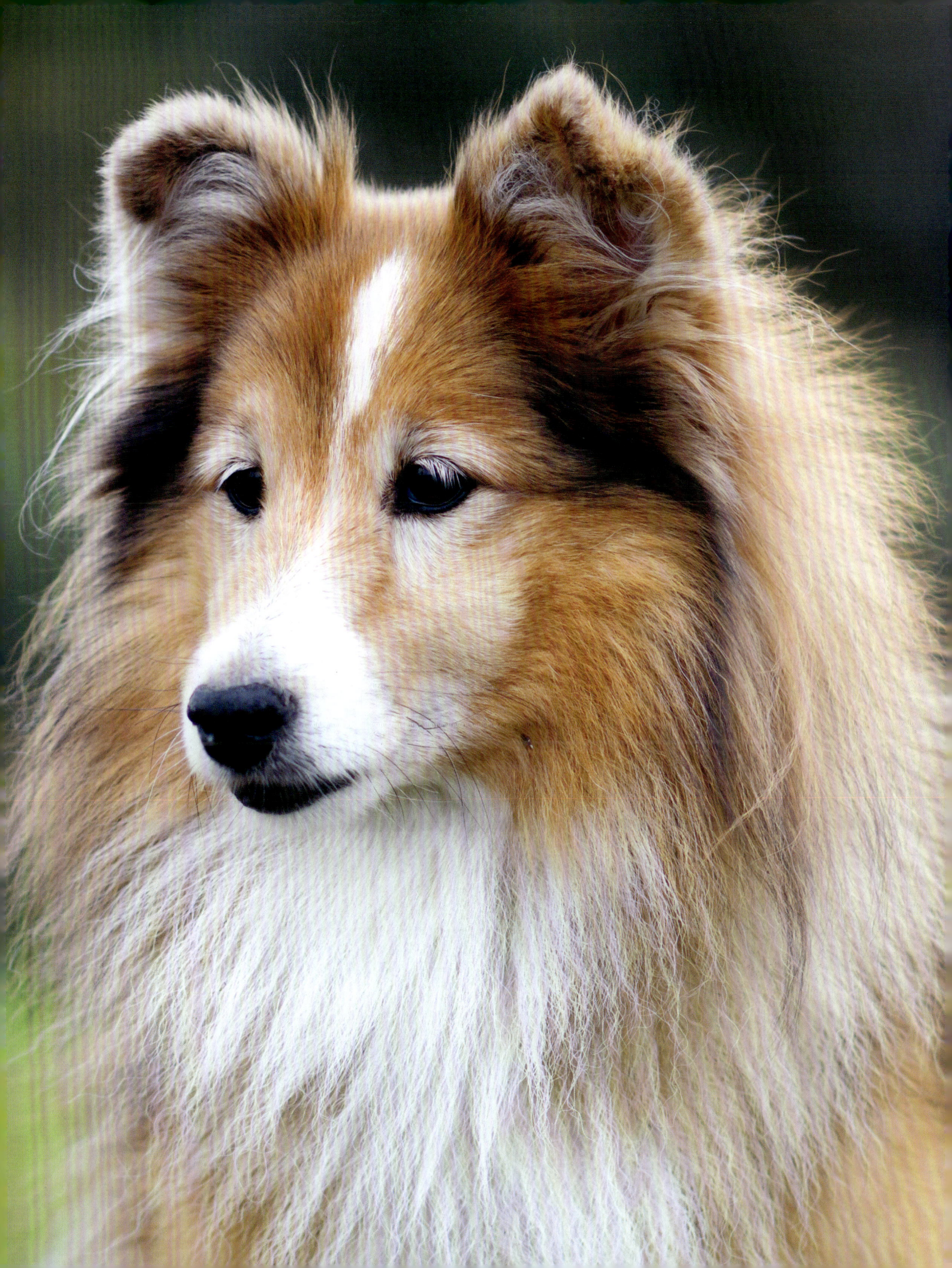

Siberian Husky

CHARACTERISTICS

Coat
A thickly furred double coat with distinctive markings on the face, legs and chest that can vary from black to pure white

Height
51–60cm (20–24in)

Weight
16–27kg (35–60lb)

Lifespan
10 years

Personality
Tough and hard working

Origin
Russia

There are few working dog breeds that have the recognition and cachet of the husky. This is a sled-dog breed supremely adapted to life in the ice and snow. It is easily confused with the larger Alaskan malamute from across the Bering Strait, but much more common, having become the Arctic working dog of choice in the 20th century. Put simply the husky needs to be fed less and can keep working in temperatures that kill other breeds! The husky is descended from cold-adapted spitz-type ancestors and is bigger than most of its brethren, although only a medium-sized breed in general.

The Siberian husky can be friendly and playful but is a social breed that was developed to work as a team to haul loads. As a result it prefers plenty of company, human or canine. Perhaps counterintuitively a husky makes a terrible watchdog because it gives a jolly welcome to everyone it meets. When in a pack, where one dog is the undisputed leader, the breed's independent streak requires a strong, experienced human master. Sled dogs are bred to want to run and huskies have an irresistible urge to chase smaller animals, something that requires firm training to control.

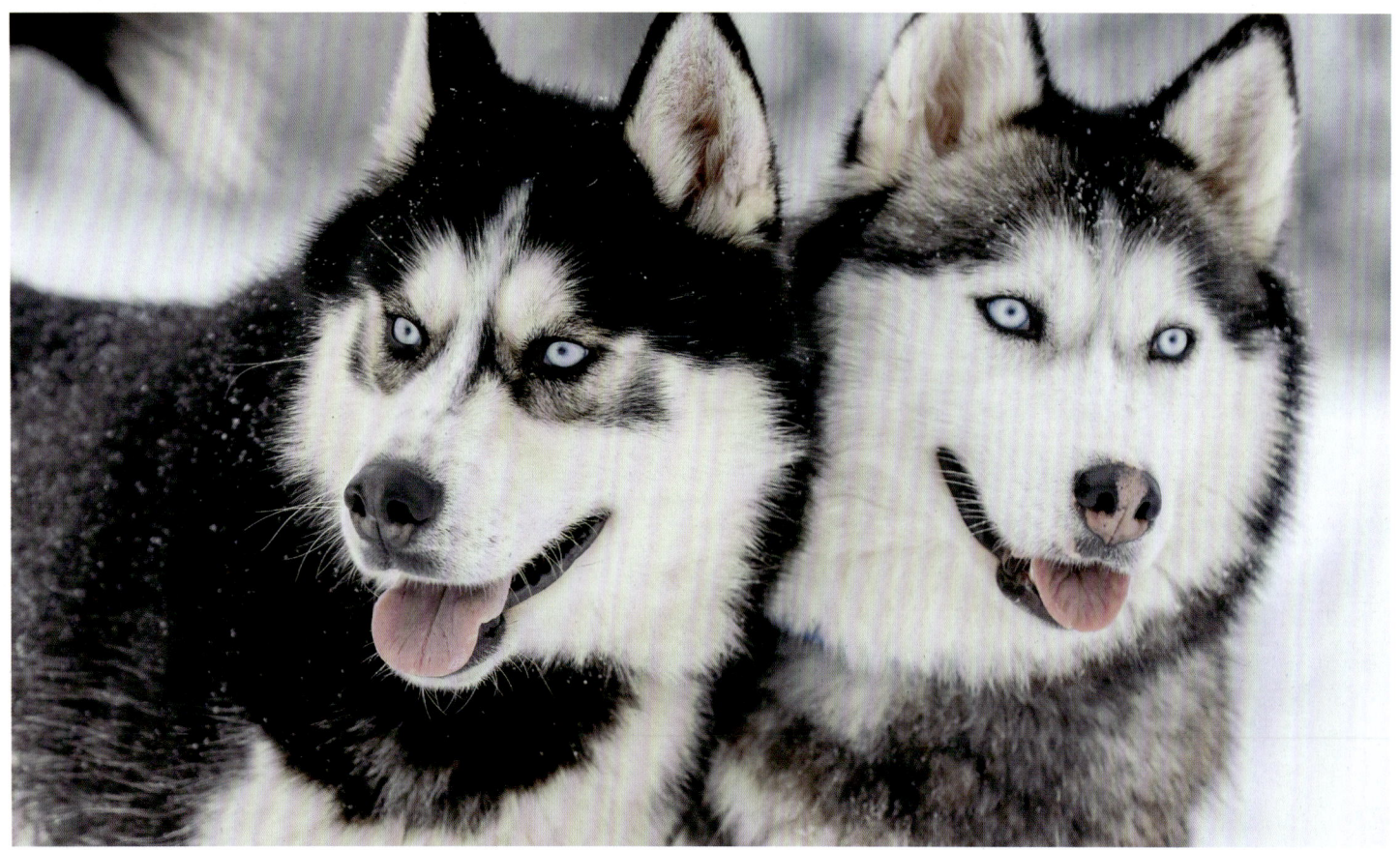

ABOVE:
Striking looks
Few dogs look as striking as the husky. Those ice-blue eyes and erect triangular ears are hard to miss.

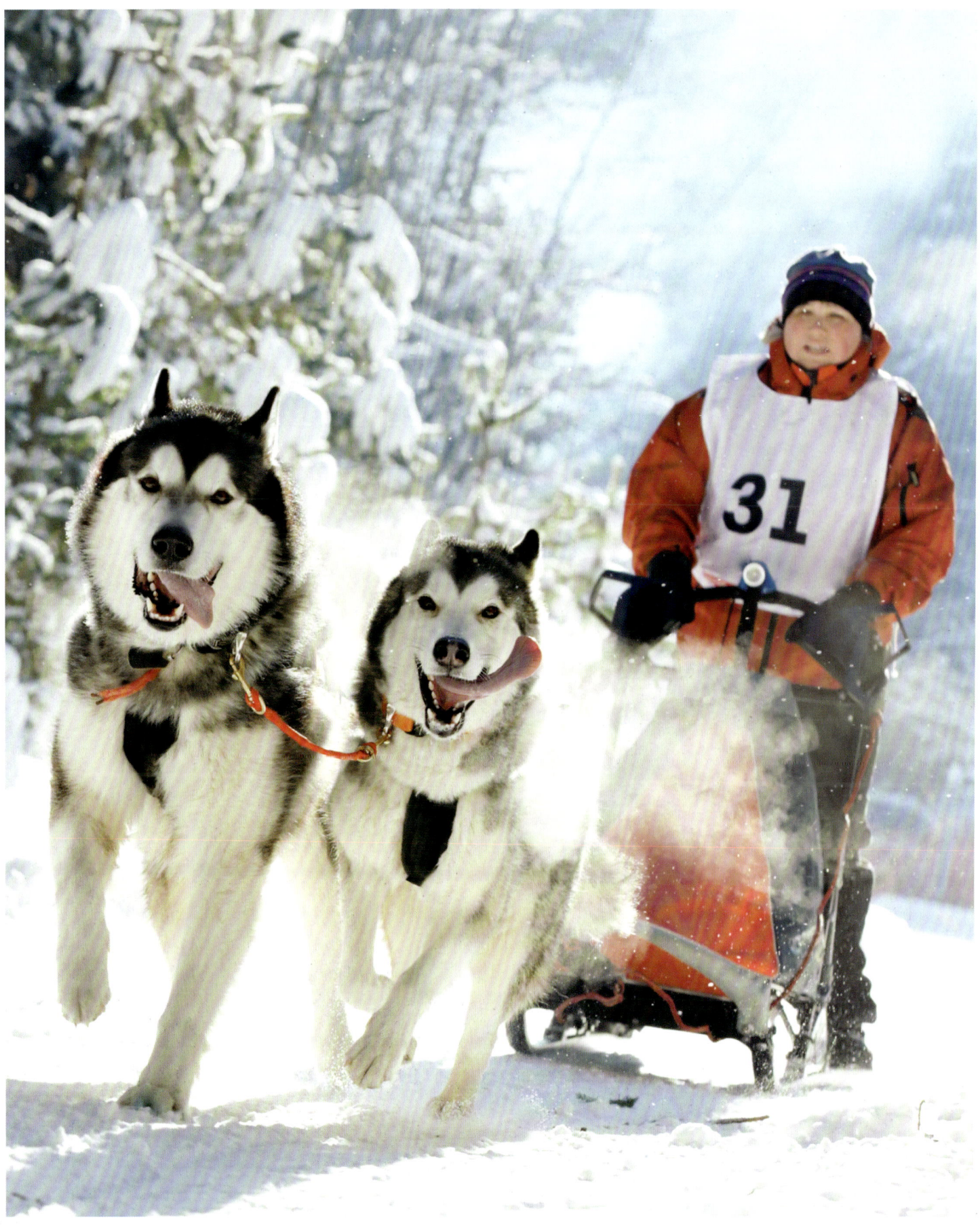

ABOVE:
Out and about
The Siberian husky needs a lot of exercise, attention and stimulation to prevent boredom and destructive behaviour, and is most at home in the cold north.

WORKING DOGS

Wolverine
This beautiful dog is the most iconic of the Spitz-type breeds, which hail from the ancient breeds of northern Asia and the Arctic. Huskies are perhaps the nearest domestic dog breed to the wild grey wolf.

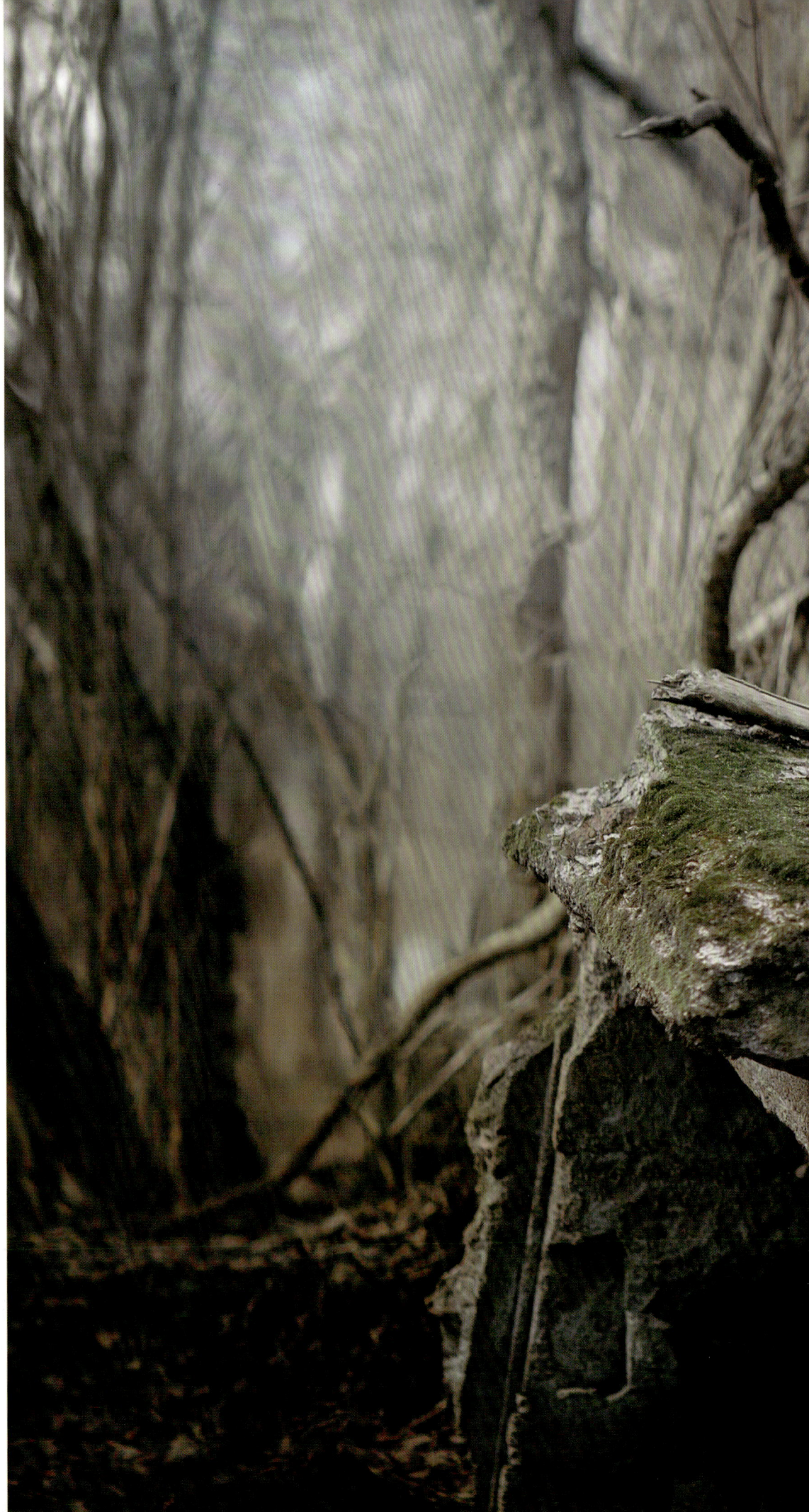

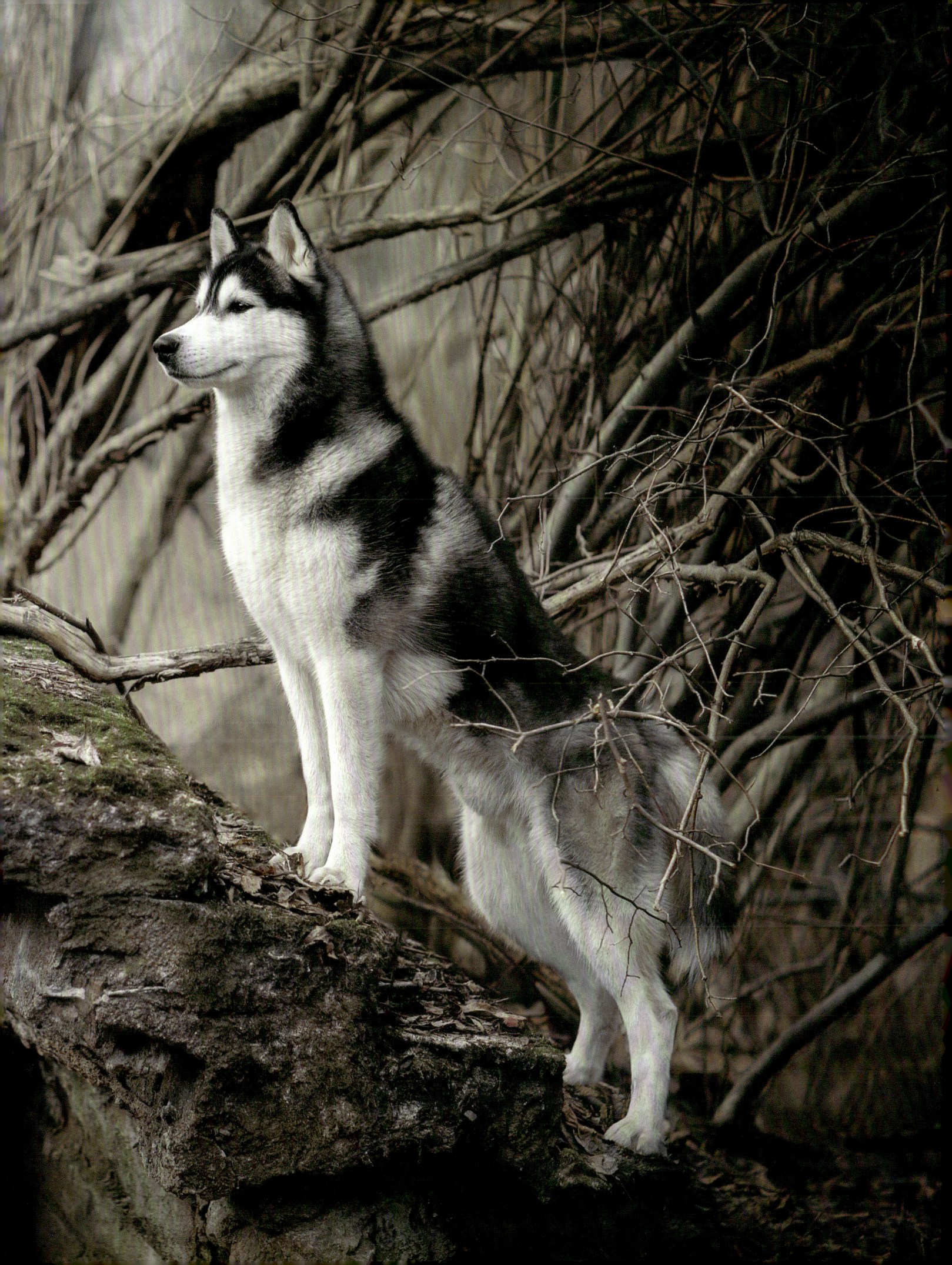

WORKING DOGS

Racing team
A sled team of huskies heads for the start of the race. The dogs wear booties to protect their paws against sharp ice and rocks.

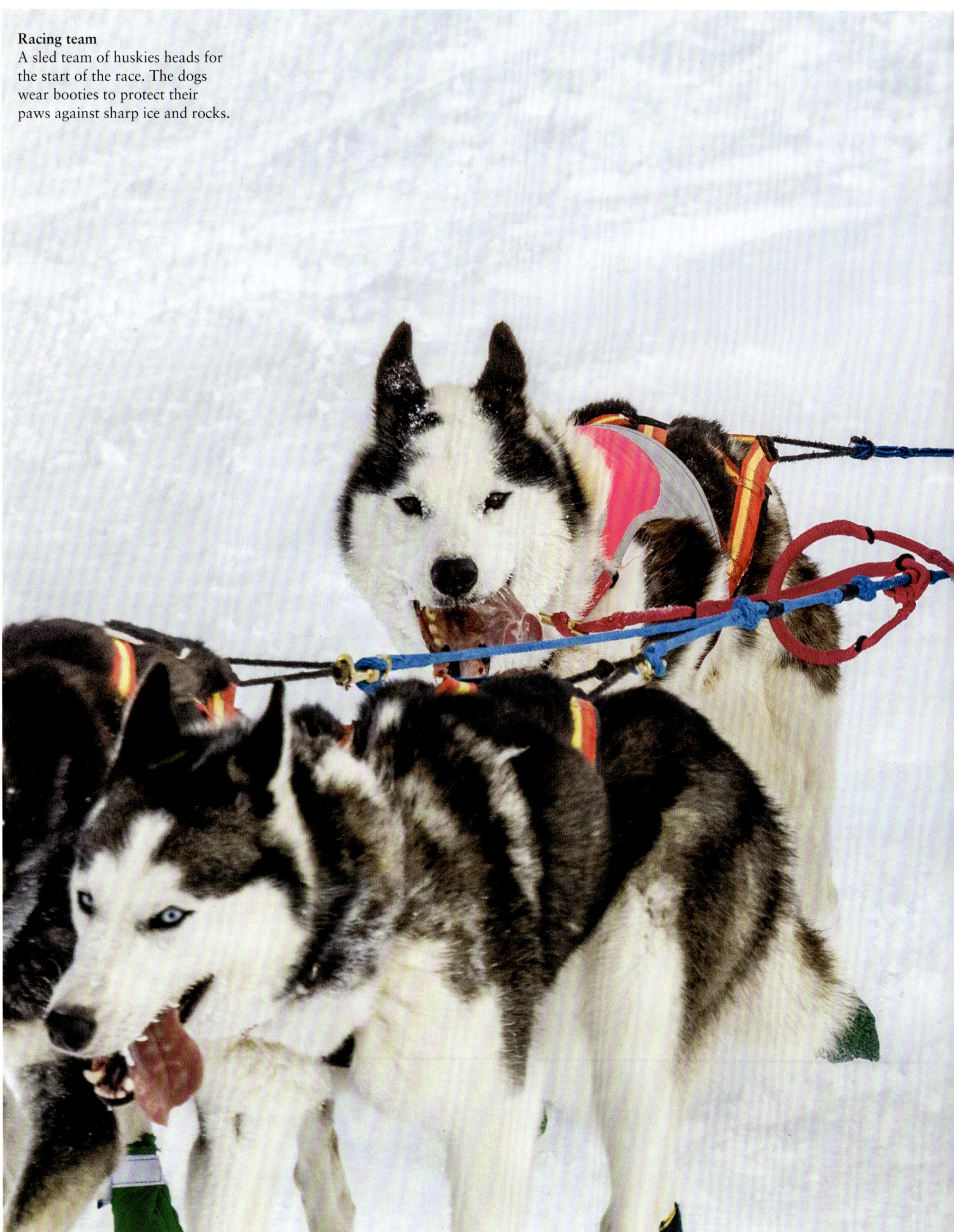

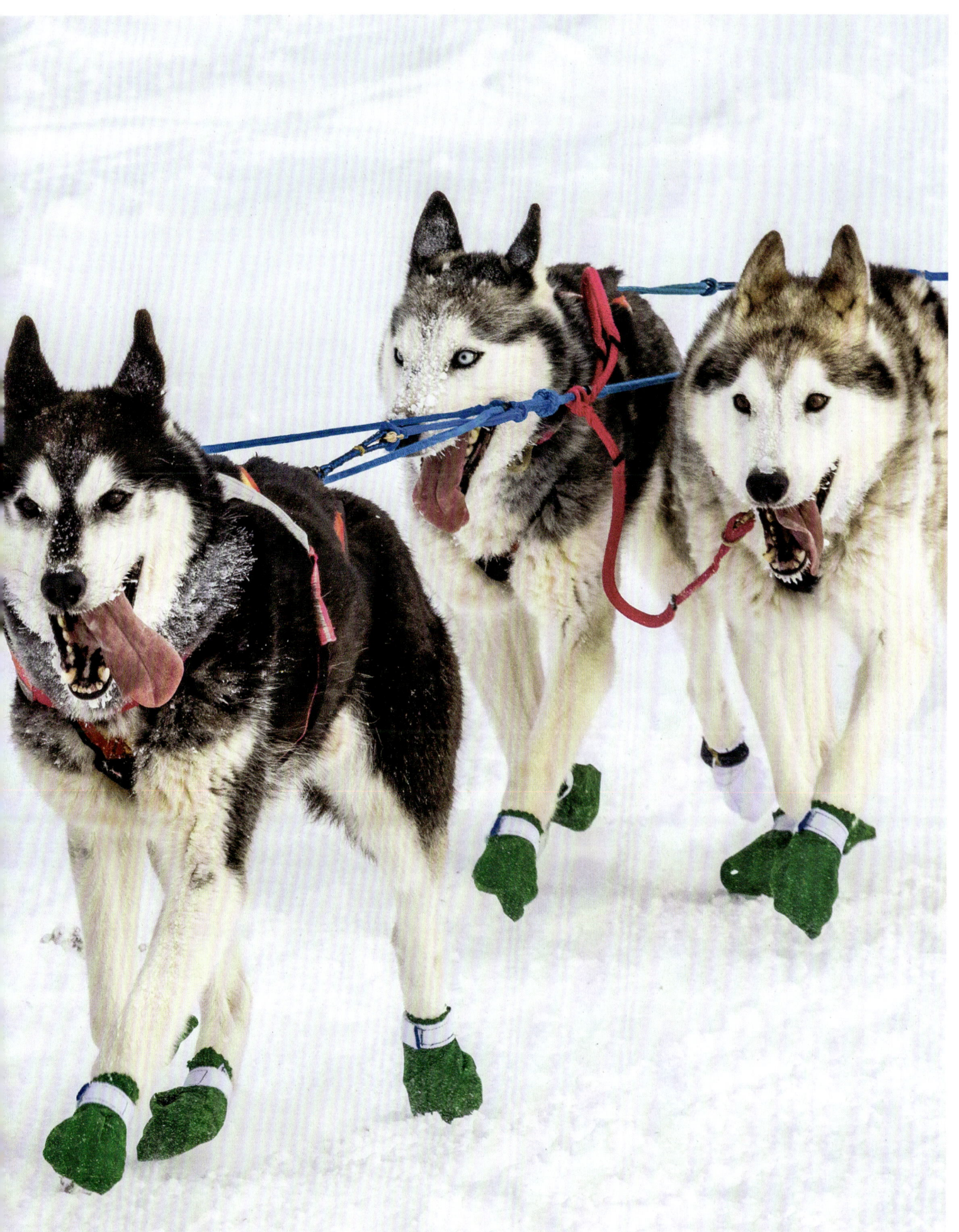

WORKING DOGS

Smooth Collie

CHARACTERISTICS

Coat
A short, dense coat in sable and white or black, tan and white

Height
51–61cm (20–24in)

Weight
18–30kg (40–66lb)

Lifespan
10 years

Personality
Loyal and adaptable

Origin
Scotland

This collie breed is much less well known than its cousins the exuberant border collie and glamourous rough. However, it is still very much a collie, probably named after the Saxon word for "useful". It is an adept and energetic herding dog. The descriptor "smooth" merely means this breed has a much shorter coat than both its relatives. Its origins are something of a mystery but probably lie in Scotland where Queen Victoria was a collie fan and kept both roughs and smooths at Balmoral Castle. Her favourite dog, a smooth collie called Sharp, travelled with her south to Windsor.

Today a smooth collie looks somewhat like a shaven rough collie. The wedge-shaped face is still there but lacks the mantle of flowing locks around it, and the legs and body have a spindly look. It is thought that the smooth collie was originally short-legged, with a similar profile to the border collie. Only in the late 19th century, when interest grew in showing these dogs, was there an effort to make them more like the rough. The breed was crossed with greyhounds to lengthen the leg and back-crossed with roughs to refine the look.

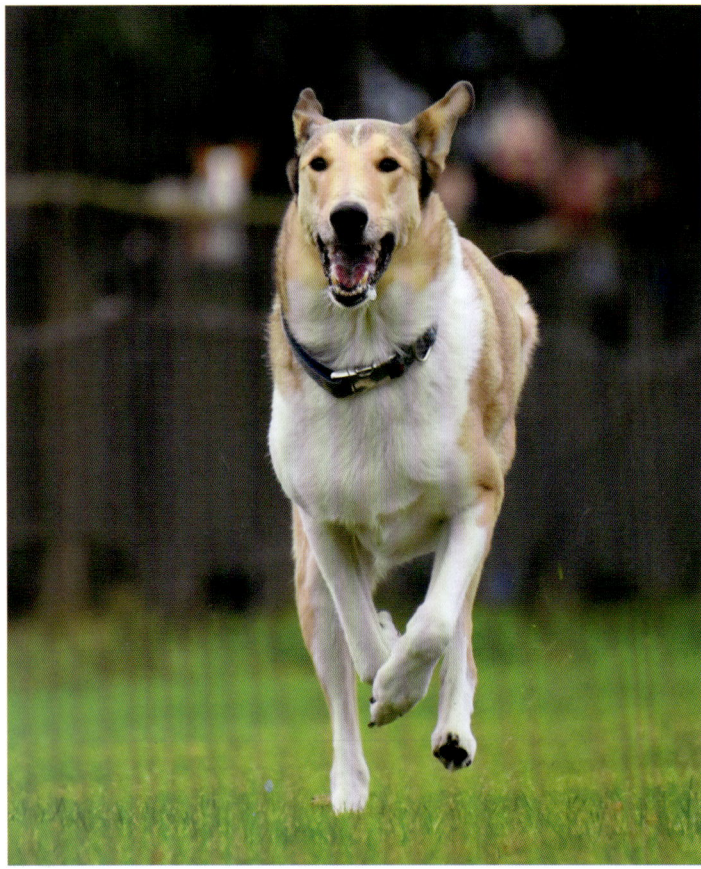

ABOVE:
Keeping busy
The smooth collie enjoys various activities such as flyball and obedience and agility trials.

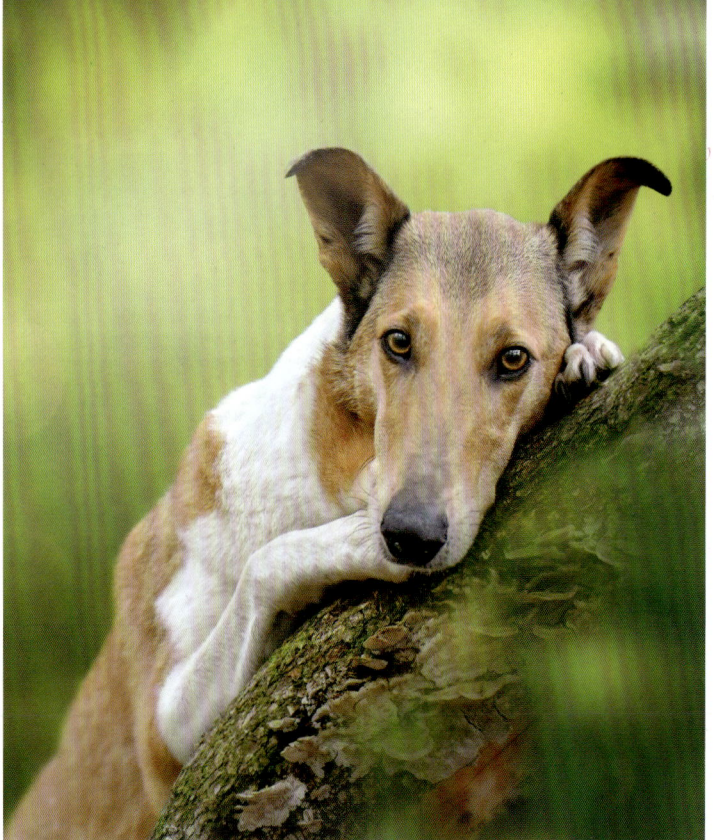

ABOVE:
Clean and tidy
The smooth collie needs regular grooming to keep its coat in good condition.

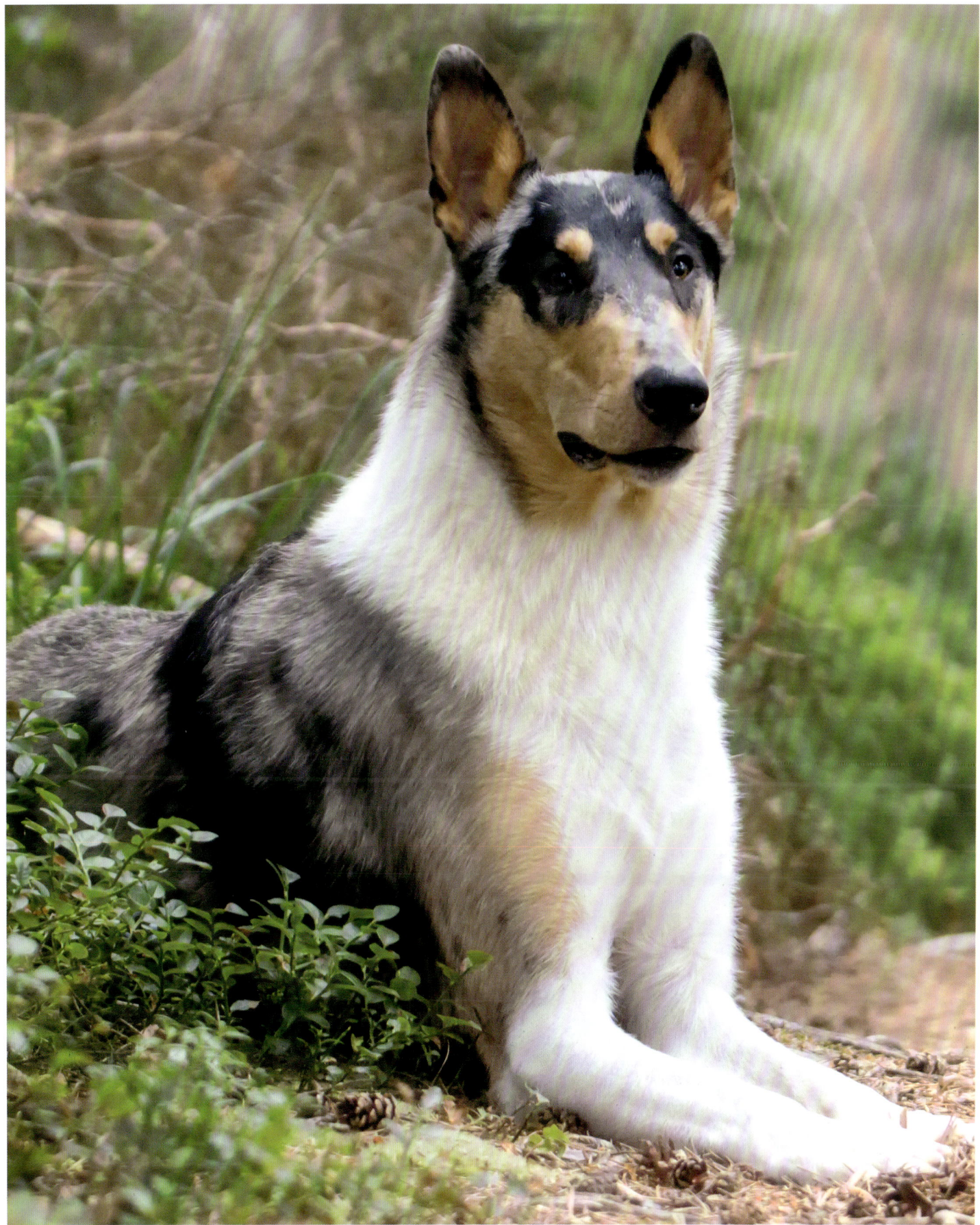

ABOVE:
Good friend
The smooth collie is intelligent and adaptable, making it a good family pet and companion.

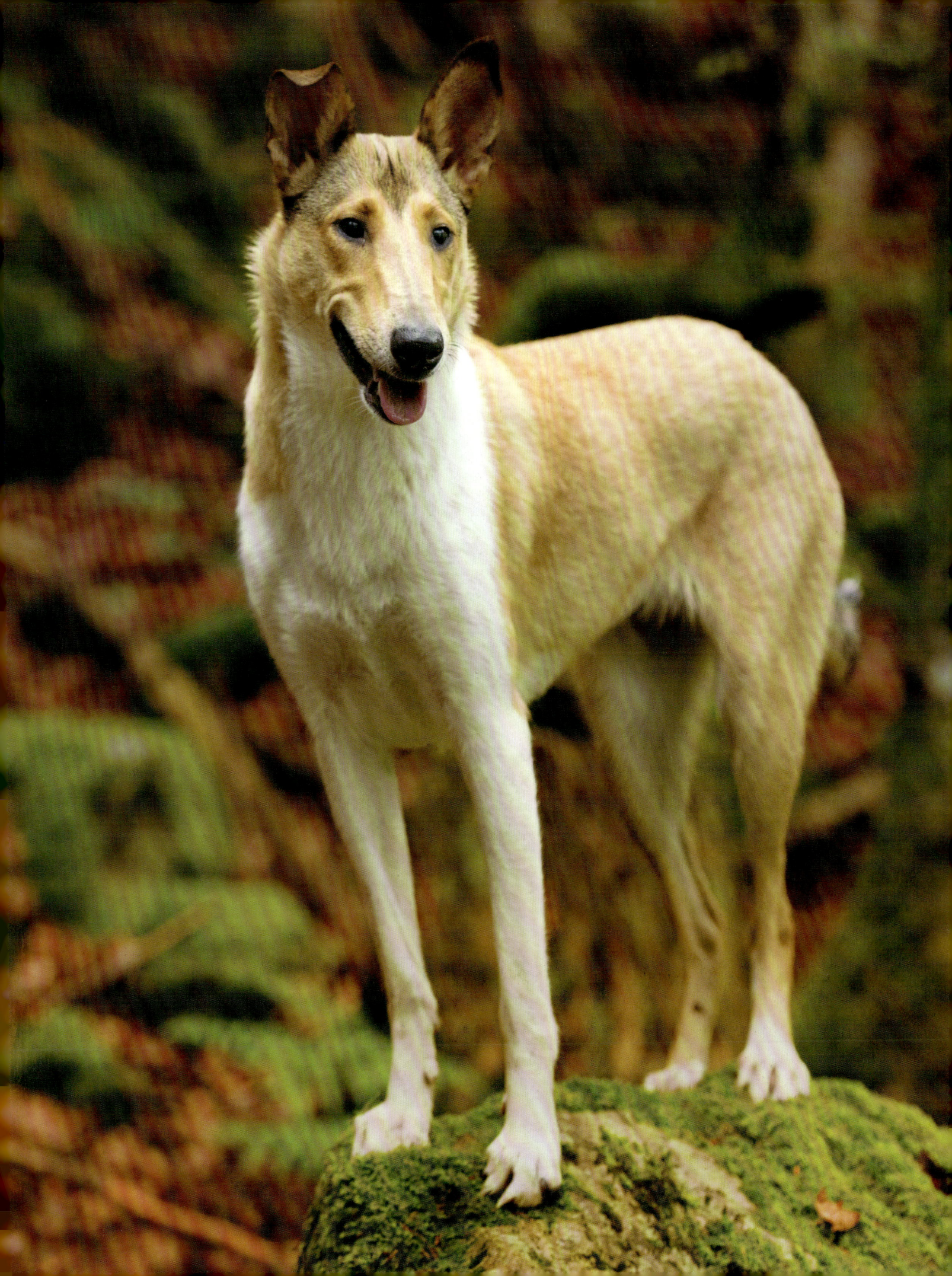

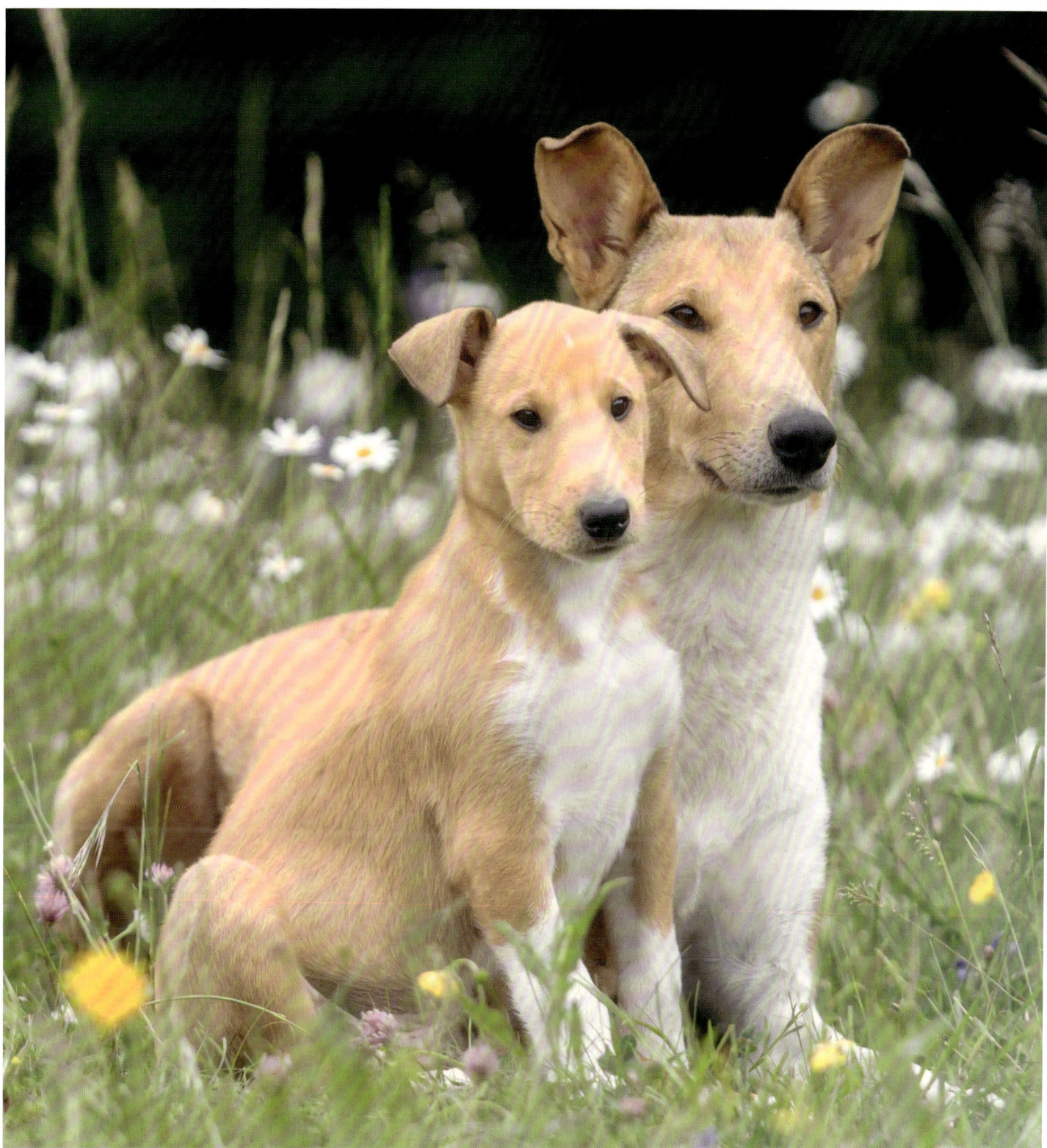

OPPOSITE:
Exploring breed
This Scottish breed makes a better pet than the border collie because it is more good-natured, though it is less refined for working as a herding dog.

ABOVE:
Ready to go
Moderate exercise is needed with this collie breed to prevent boredom and obesity.

WORKING DOGS
Saint Bernard

This Alpine breed is often depicted as a gentle giant lumbering through the snow to stranded travellers with the promise of a reviving nip of spirit from a barrel carried around their neck. Mostly this is true, but sadly the collar cask is just a myth. The breed is named for Bernard of Menthon, later canonized of course. A thousand years ago Bernard created a refuge for pilgrims heading to Rome through a high pass leading out of Switzerland. The pass was prone to deep snow and frequent avalanches, and the monks stationed up there used immense mountain dogs to sniff out and dig up stricken passersby.

With all that history behind it, the St. Bernard has become a huge but affectionate dog that makes a great family companion. It is a calm and sensible pet that is happy to be surrounded by children and other animals. However, an animal this size needs a lot of food, plus regular exercise with a walker strong enough to handle its power. The impressive mountain dog coat requires frequent grooming. Novice owners should not choose a St. Bernard as their first dog, and while highly trainable it can be stubborn if not given clear leadership.

CHARACTERISTICS
Coat
Medium to long coat of smooth hairs that are generally white and orange
Height
70–75cm (28–30in)
Weight
59–81kg (130–180lb)
Lifespan
Less than 10 years
Personality
Calm and sensible
Origin
Switzerland

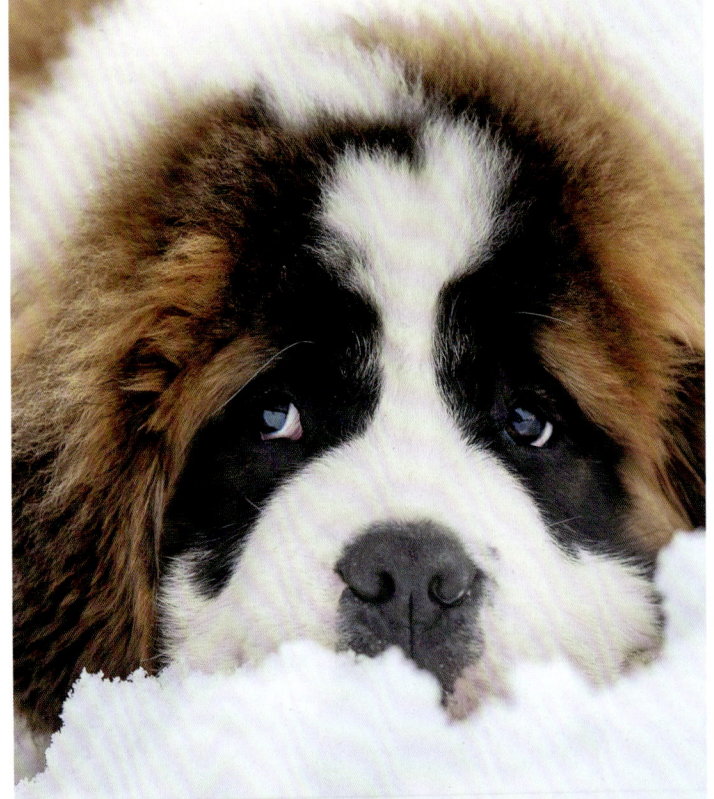

ABOVE:
In the right place
The St. Bernard is very much at home in the snowfield of the high mountains.

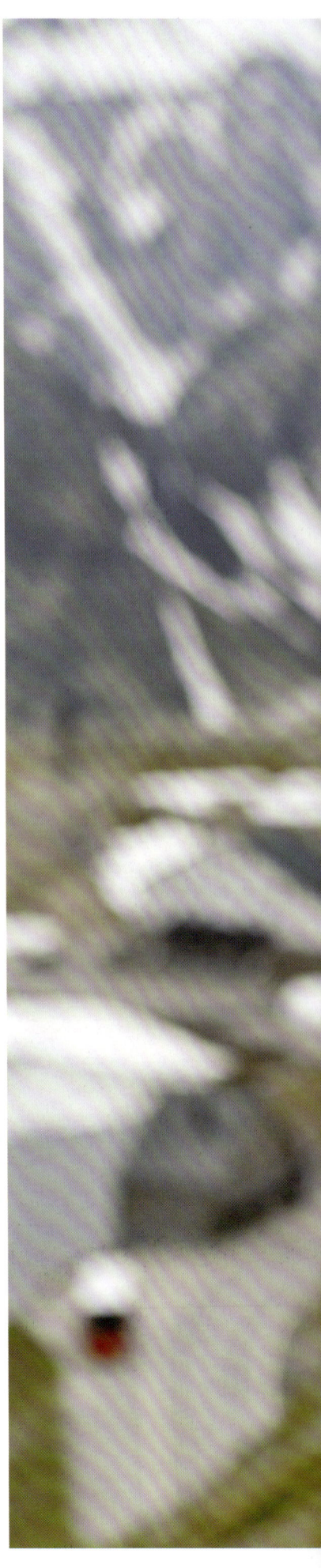

RIGHT:
Fun facts
This St. Bernard is happily reinforcing the breed's world-famous brand, which sees it carrying a brandy barrel on its collar. However, this is not a traditional piece of equipment for these Swiss rescue dogs.

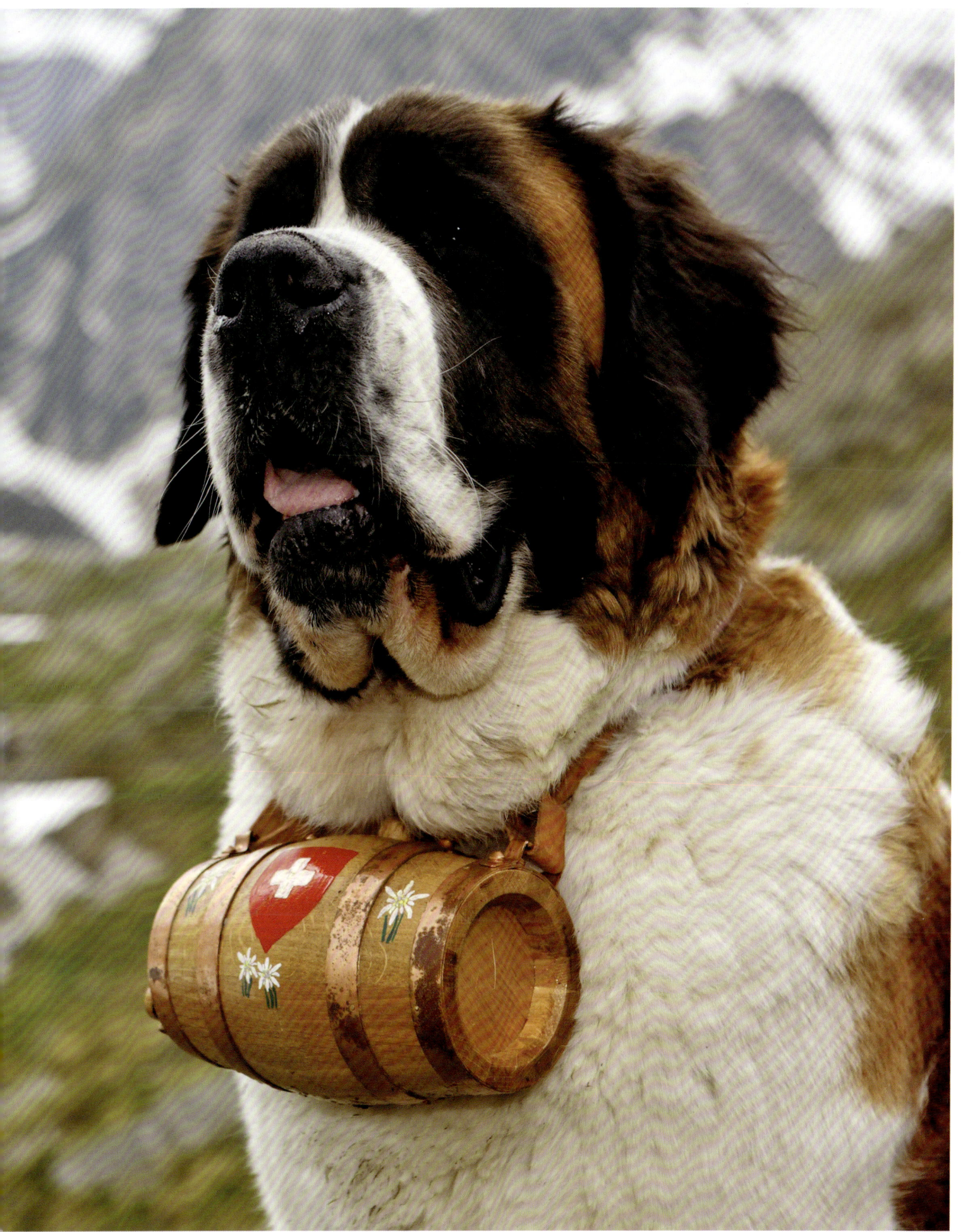

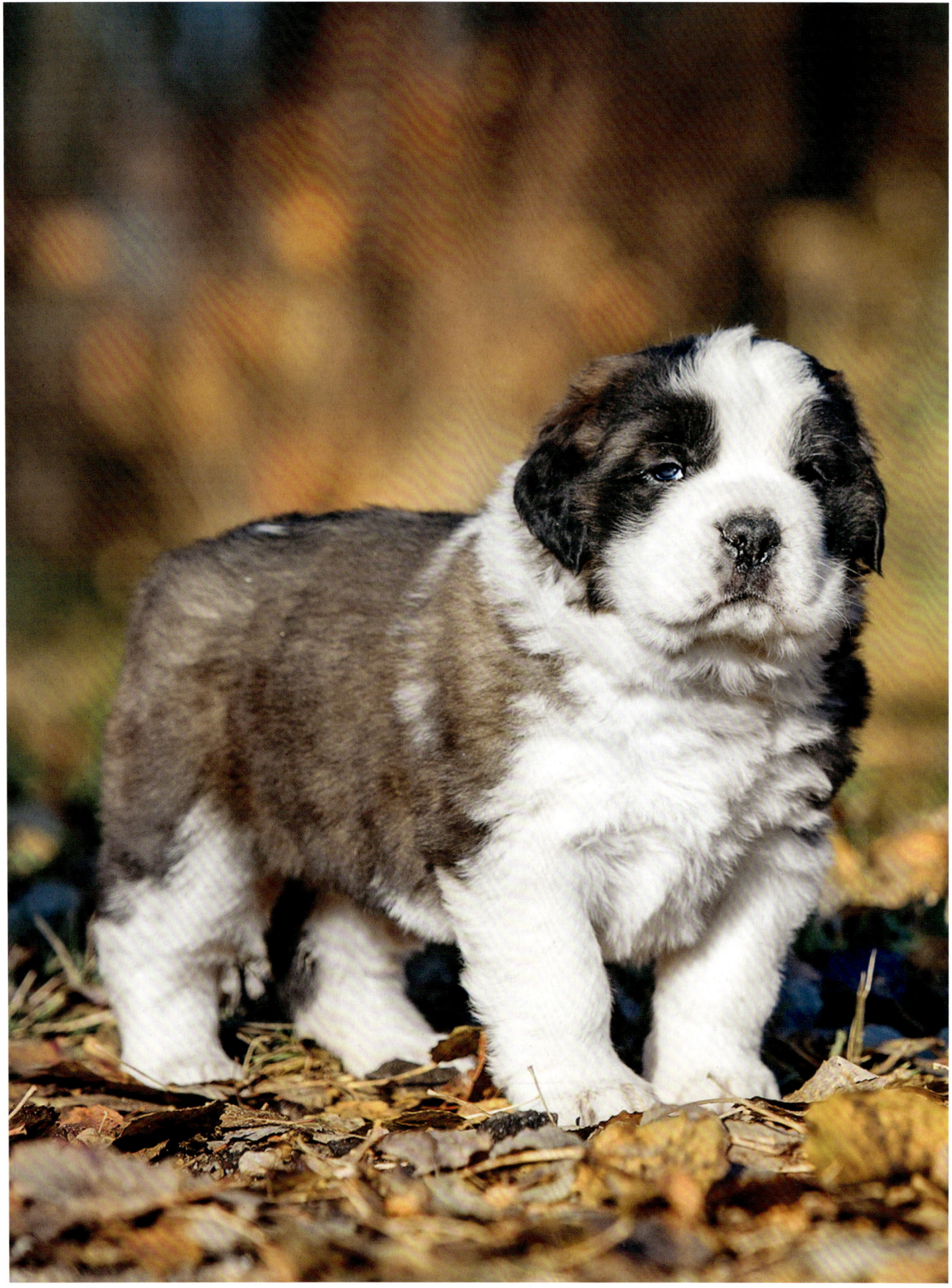

WORKING DOGS

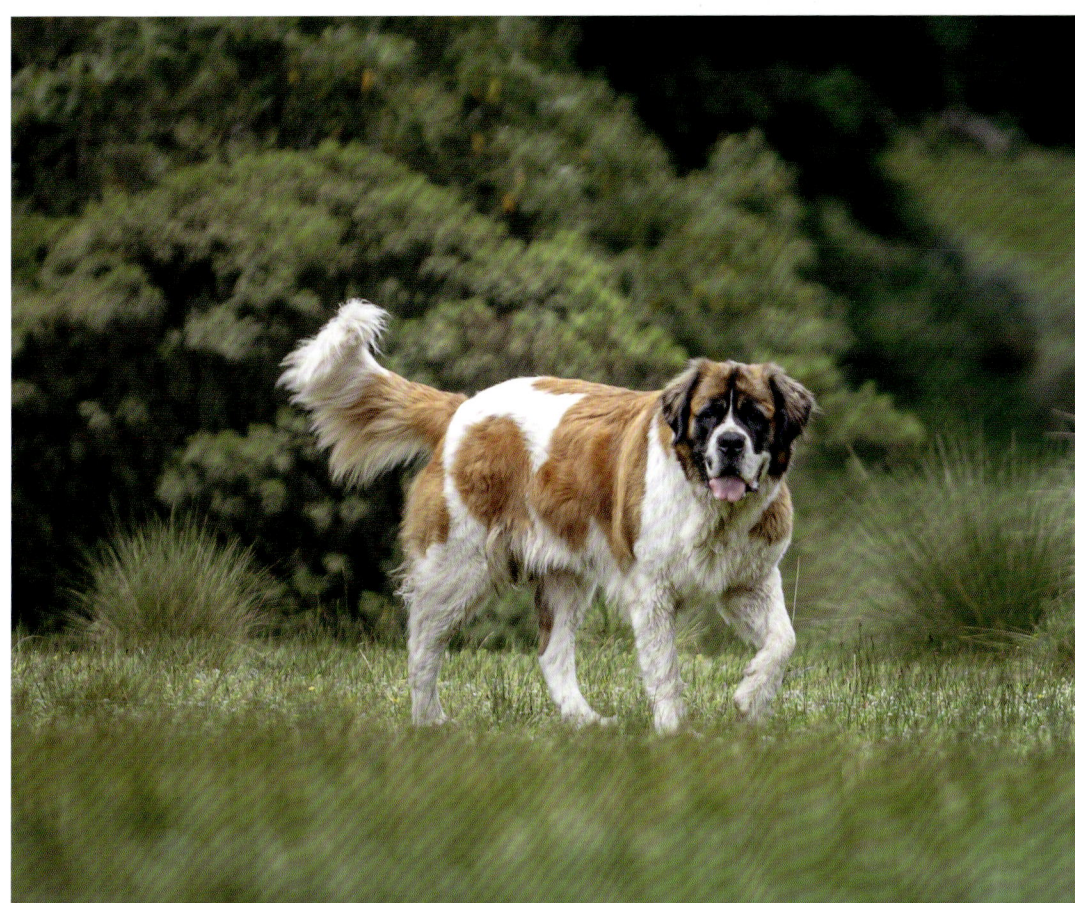

LEFT AND BELOW:
Keen helpers
This helpful breed is there to help those who are in trouble in the high mountains in need of help or rescue.

OPPOSITE:
Cute pup
Although small and fluffy now, this unassuming puppy will grow up to be a very large working dog in adulthood.

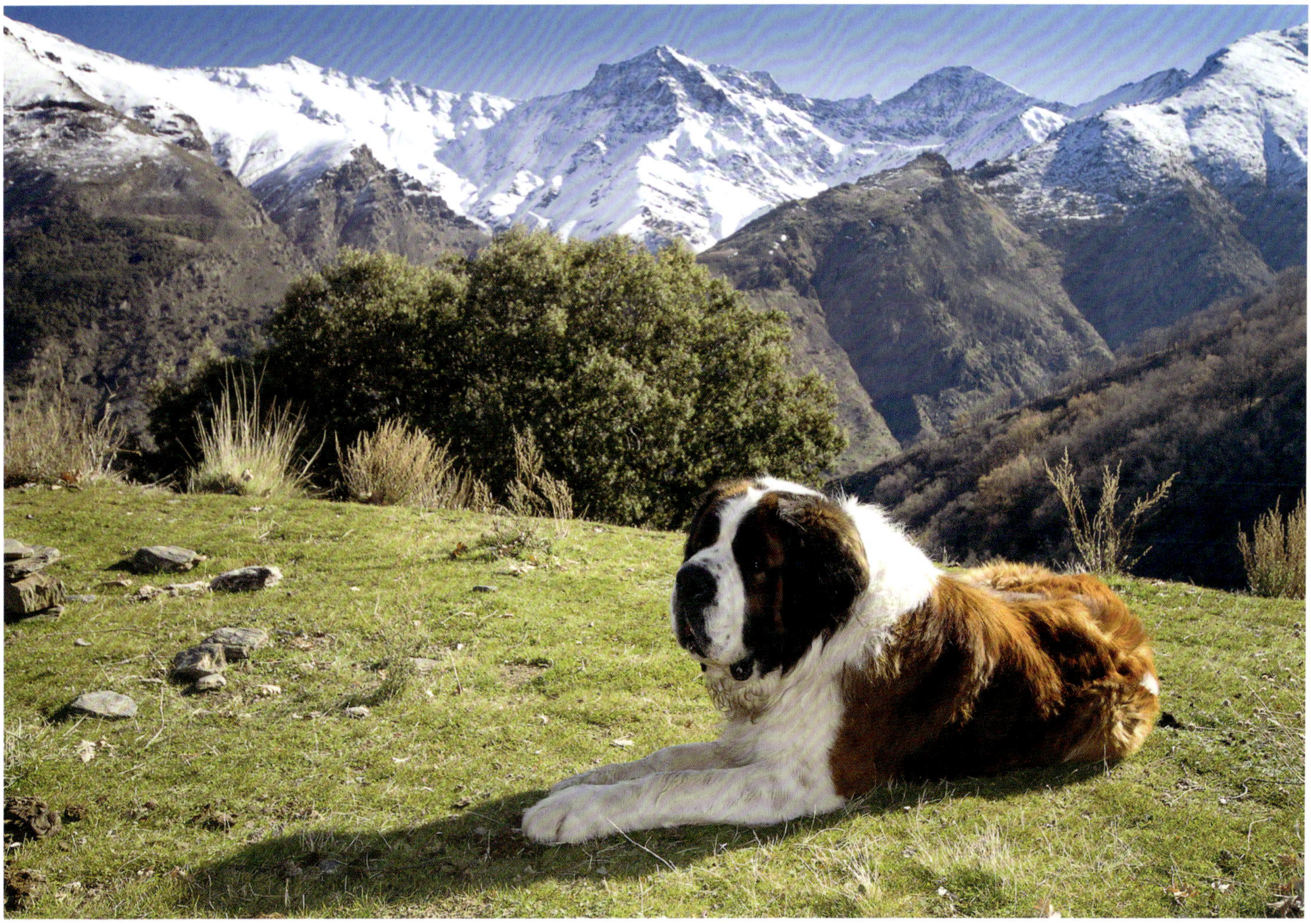

WORKING DOGS

Standard Schnauzer

CHARACTERISTICS

Coat
A wiry, harsh coat that comes in black, salt and pepper, or black and silver colours
Height
45–50cm (18–20in)
Weight
14–20kg (31–44lb)
Lifespan
Over 10 years
Personality
Lively and affectionate
Origin
Germany

This is the medium-sized schnauzer, a family of German dog breeds that have distinctive bushy whiskers that bring to mind the moustache of a distinguished Prussian officer. (The other breeds are the giant and miniature schnauzers.) The standard schnauzer is a utility dog bred for farm work during the late Middle Ages. They developed a reputation for being expert rat-catchers around the farmyard, but they were also relied upon to guard livestock, help drive them to market and be a trusty sidekick on hunting trips.

The bushy face and unusual wiry hair made this breed catch the eye of breeders as a show dog, and the features of the hard-working farm dog have since been refined into an elegant creature with a unique look.

Standard schnauzers make friendly and biddable companions. They are easy to train if the owner is consistent with a firm but gentle approach. The dogs are very alert to their surroundings and have a protective urge. Pet schnauzers need to be exercized in a large open space so they can run freely off the leash, and they will appreciate being taken to different places to explore from time to time.

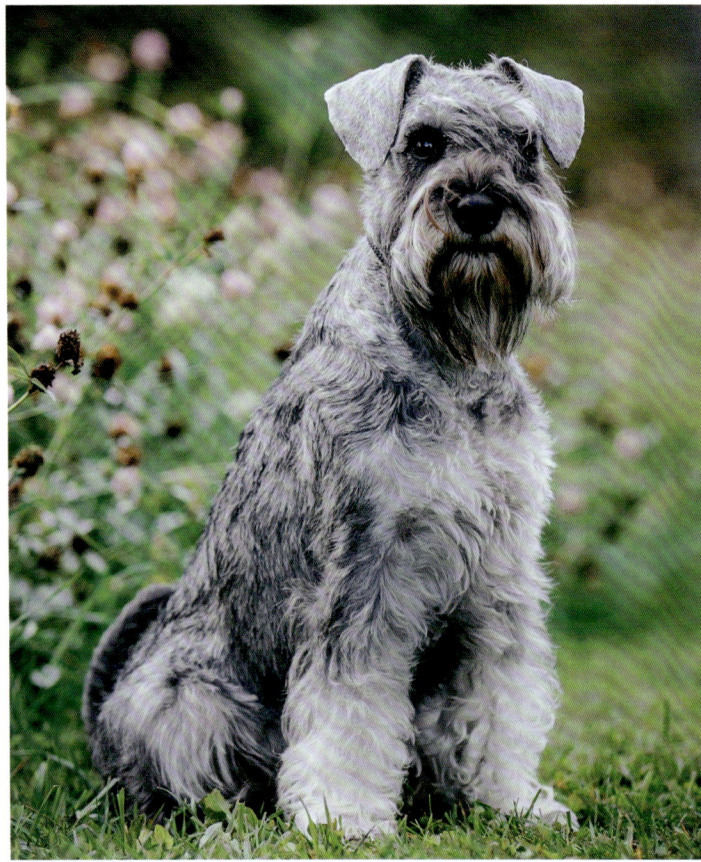

ABOVE:
Bright spark
Schnauzers are intelligent, loyal, alert and spirited dogs that make good companions and family pets.

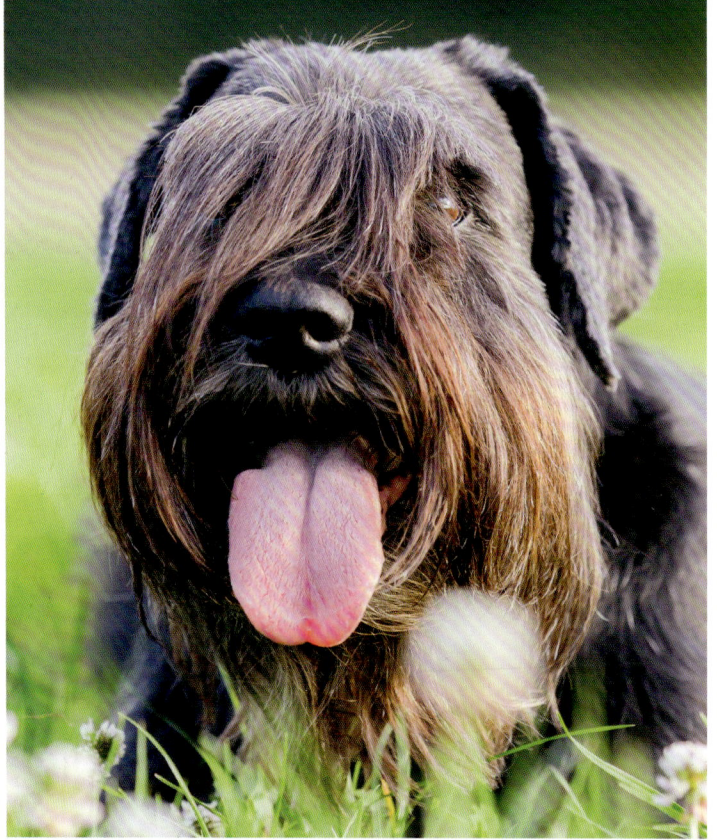

ABOVE:
Well named
The name schnauzer means "whiskered snout" in German, which refers to the distinctive beard and eyebrows of these dogs.

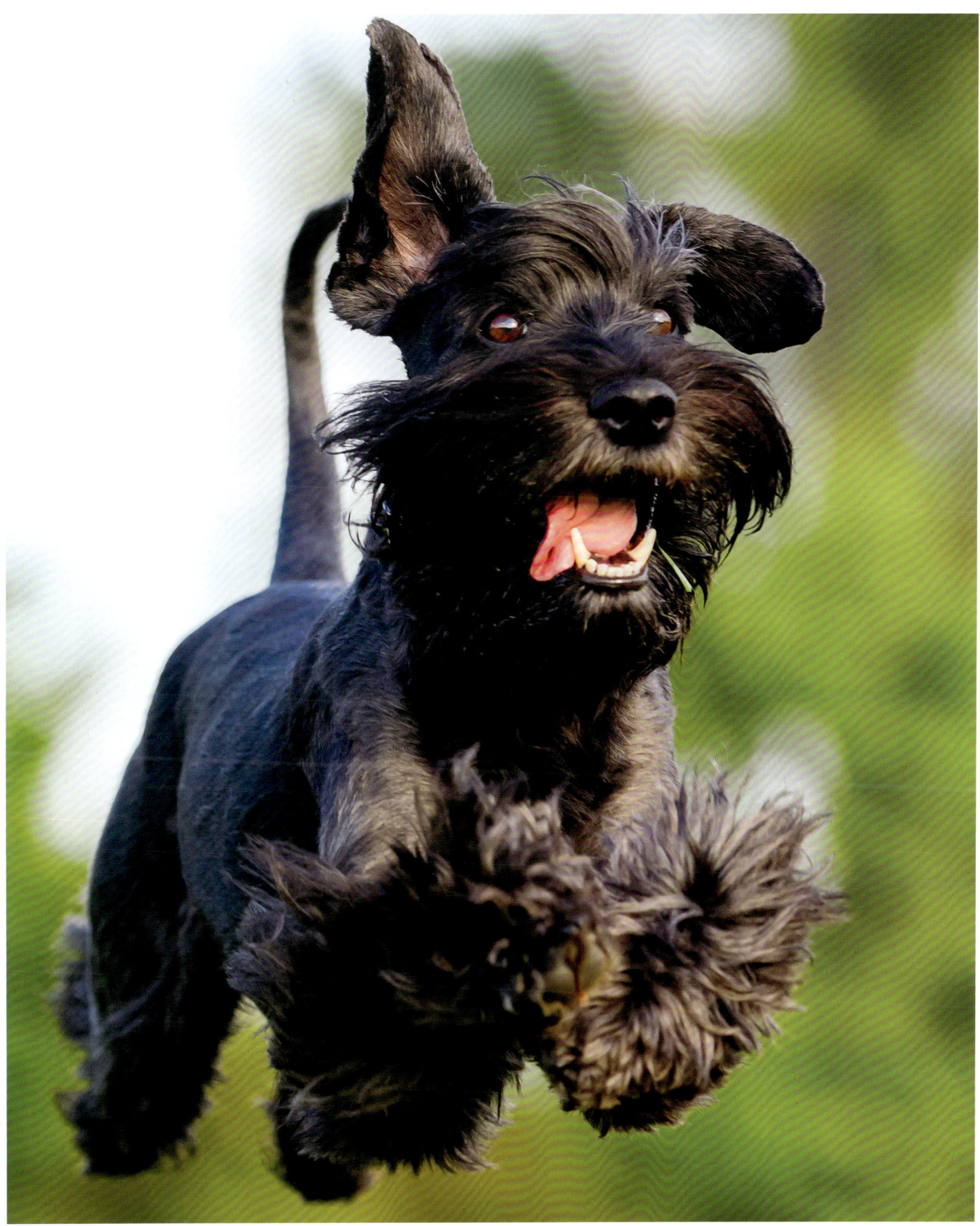

ABOVE:
Small relation
The miniature schnauzer was developed by crossing the standard breed with the toy poodles and the Affenpinscher.

WORKING DOGS

Tibetan Mastiff

One of the most ancient dog breeds in the world, the origins of this immense guardian dog are lost in the mists of time. It is thought that all mastiffs are descended from this prototypical breed which was developed in the isolation of the Himalayas. This shows that dogs were being brought west by traders and travellers many centuries ago, early enough to reach ancient Greece and Rome, even Iron-Age Britain.

They were also standing guard at temples and villages. It has a thick shaggy coat to contend with the harsh mountain weather. Many of the lions depicted in Tibetan art are not big cats at all but actually mythical versions of these dogs.

After China took over Tibet in 1950, the dogs were nearly wiped out. Only those living in the most remote villages survived and formed today's stock. The Tibetan mastiff is not suitable for living in a home without a lot of outside space and it does not do well in warm climates. Given plenty of attention and exercise, these giant dogs can be a rewarding pet for an experienced dog lover.

CHARACTERISTICS
Coat
Dense coat of straight hairs that are longer on the neck and shoulders. Often black and tan or slate-grey
Height
61–66 cm (24–26in)
Weight
39–127kg (85–280lb)
Lifespan
Over 10 years
Personality
Loyal and protective
Origin
China

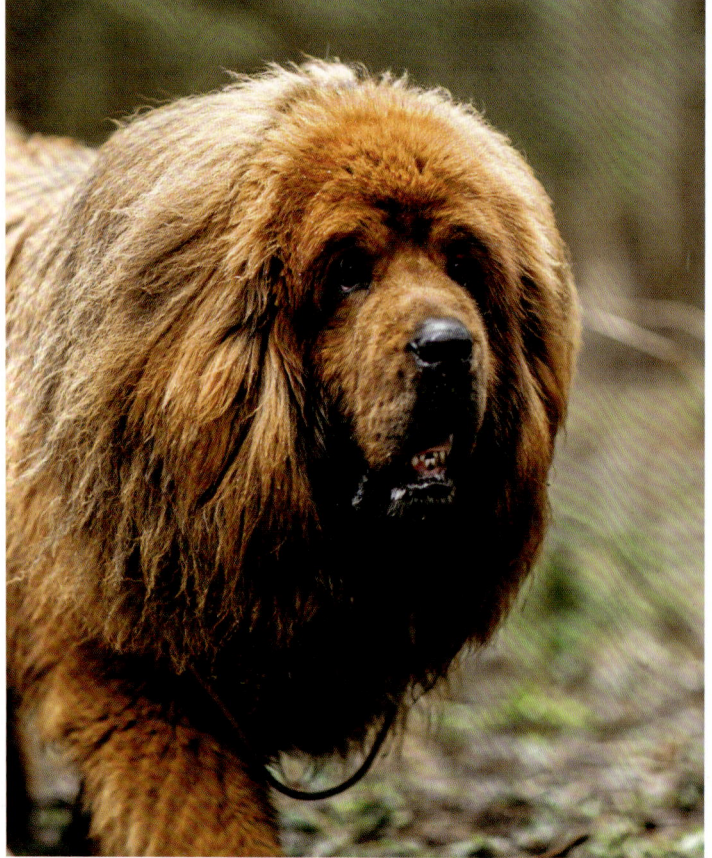

ABOVE:
Standing guard
In their homeland, Tibetan mastiffs were traditionally tethered at the entrance to mountain pastures to ward off bandits and predators.

RIGHT:
Expensive pet
The Tibetan mastiff is a rare breed, and in 2011, a puppy called Hang Dong (Big Splash) was sold for $1.5m, making the little big dog the most expensive in history.

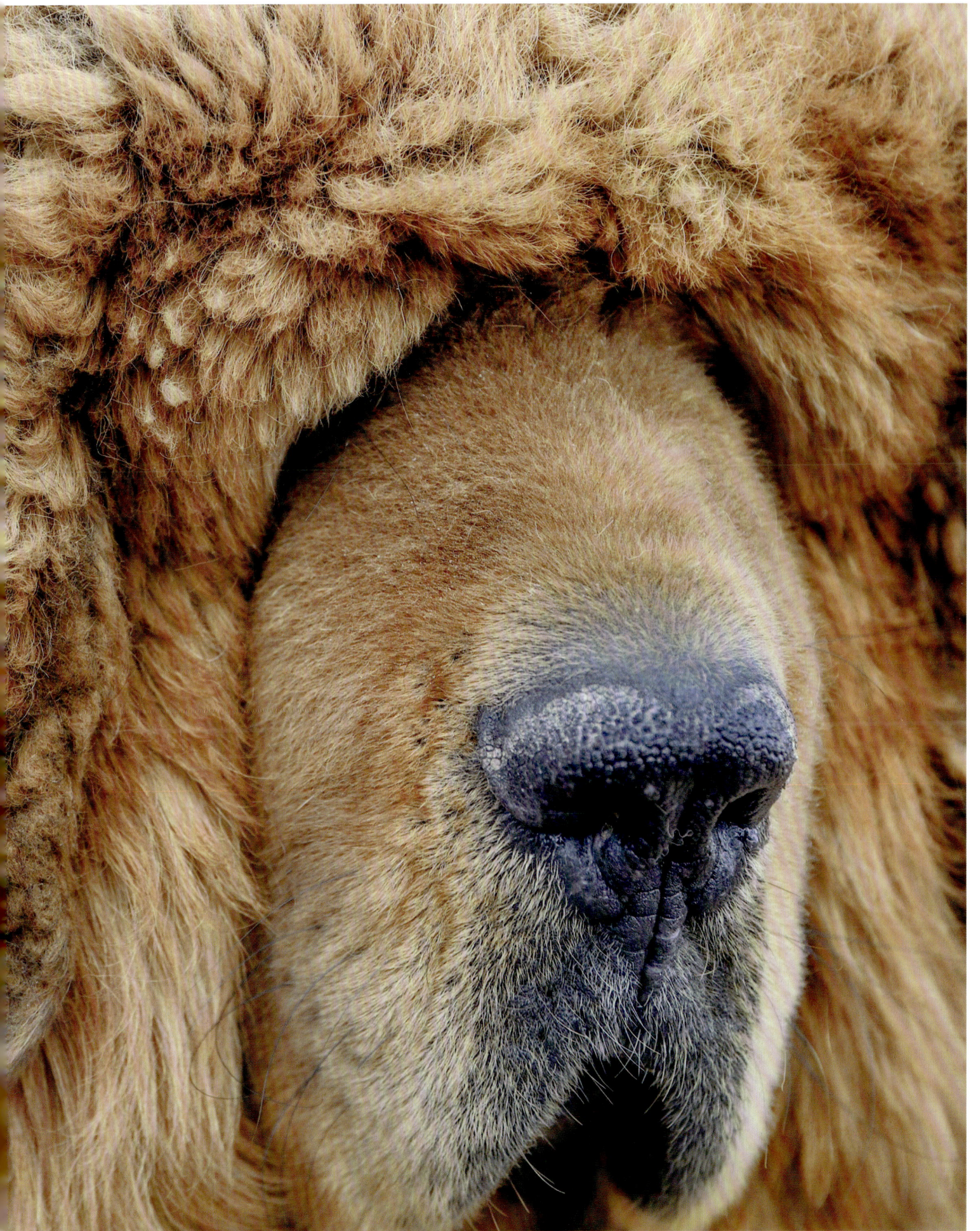

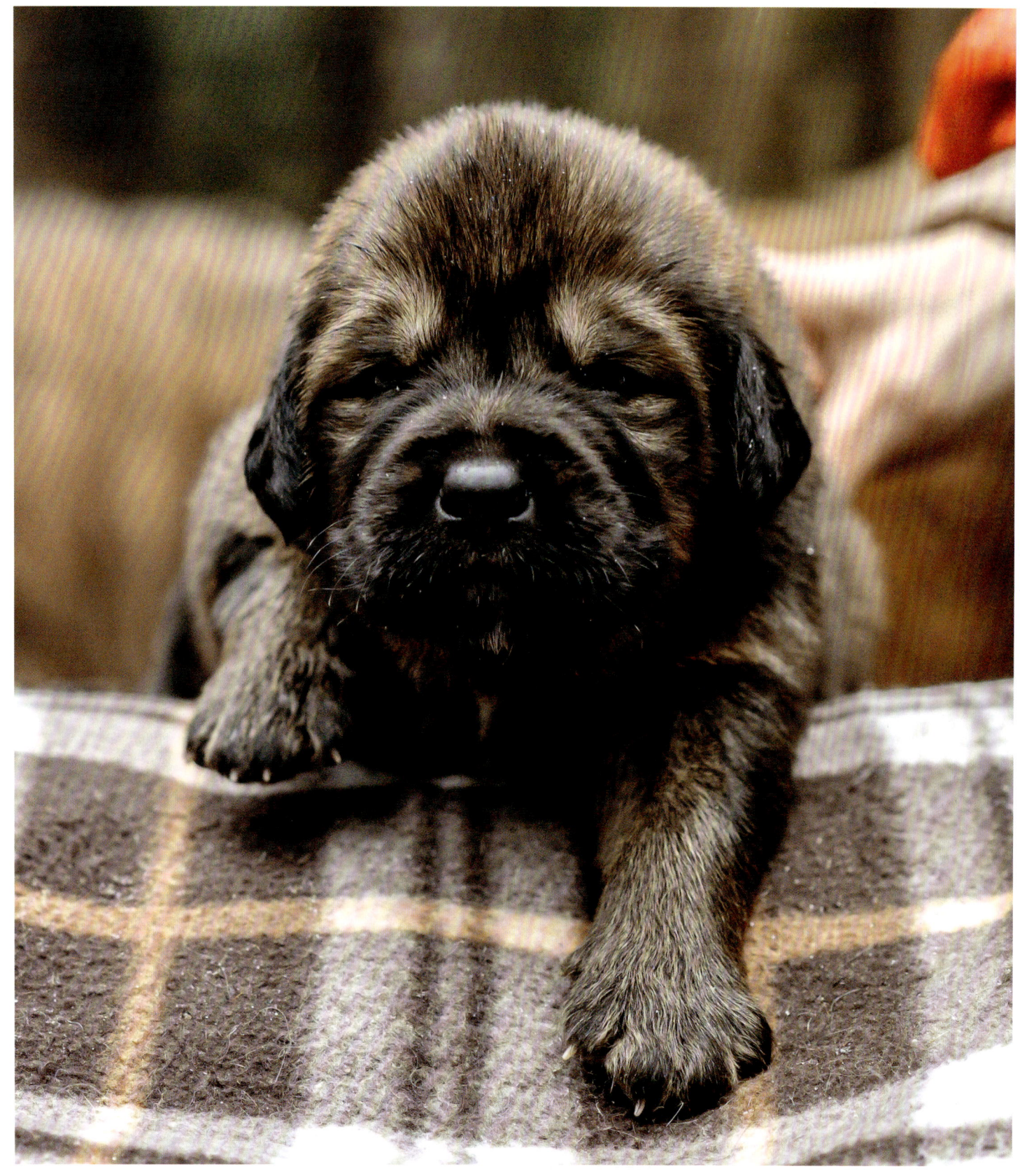

ABOVE:
Young puppy
This small Tibetan Mastiff will soon grow long, thick hair to protect themselves from harsh weathers and climates.

RIGHT:
Snowy steps
The immense double coat of this breed ensures it is comfortable in both hot and cold temperatures, making it very adaptable.

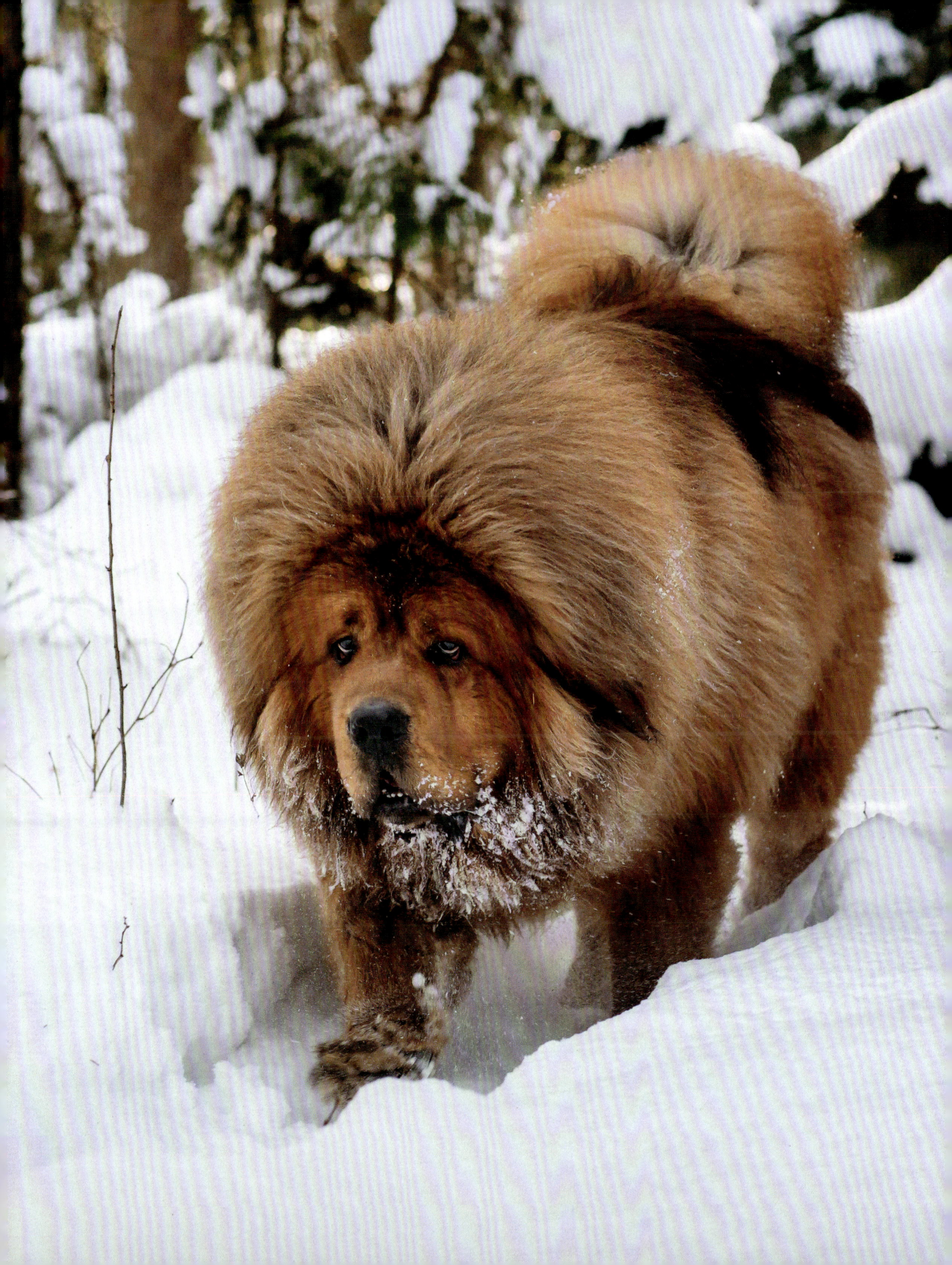

WORKING DOGS

Uruguayan Cimarron

CHARACTERISTICS

Coat
A short coat of brindle or bay and a black mask

Height
55–61cm (22–24in)

Weight
33–45kg (73–99lb)

Lifespan
10–13 years

Personality
Brave and independent

Origin
Uruguay

This breed is based on feral dogs that once lived wild in Uruguay. The term cimarron means "wild" in Spanish. Other names include the maroon dog and gaucho dog. The dogs are the descendants of the mastiff-like war dogs that were abandoned by early Spanish colonizers. For many years they were regarded as a nuisance to the burgeoning livestock industry and so the dogs were in the process of being systematically eradicated in the 18th century. Bounties were paid for every wild dig that was killed. However, the dogs persisted in the highland Cerro Lago region, where ranchers and gauchos (South American cowboys) took the dogs in and tamed them for use as guard dogs, hunters and companions. Today the Uruguayan cimarron is a national symbol and the mascot of the Uruguayan army.

The Uruguayan cimarron is only suited to a highly experienced owner. The breed is renowned for its courage, which means they must be socialized very early to prevent aggressive and destructive behaviours in later life. If well trained, the dog requires only moderate exercise. The short coat needs regular grooming.

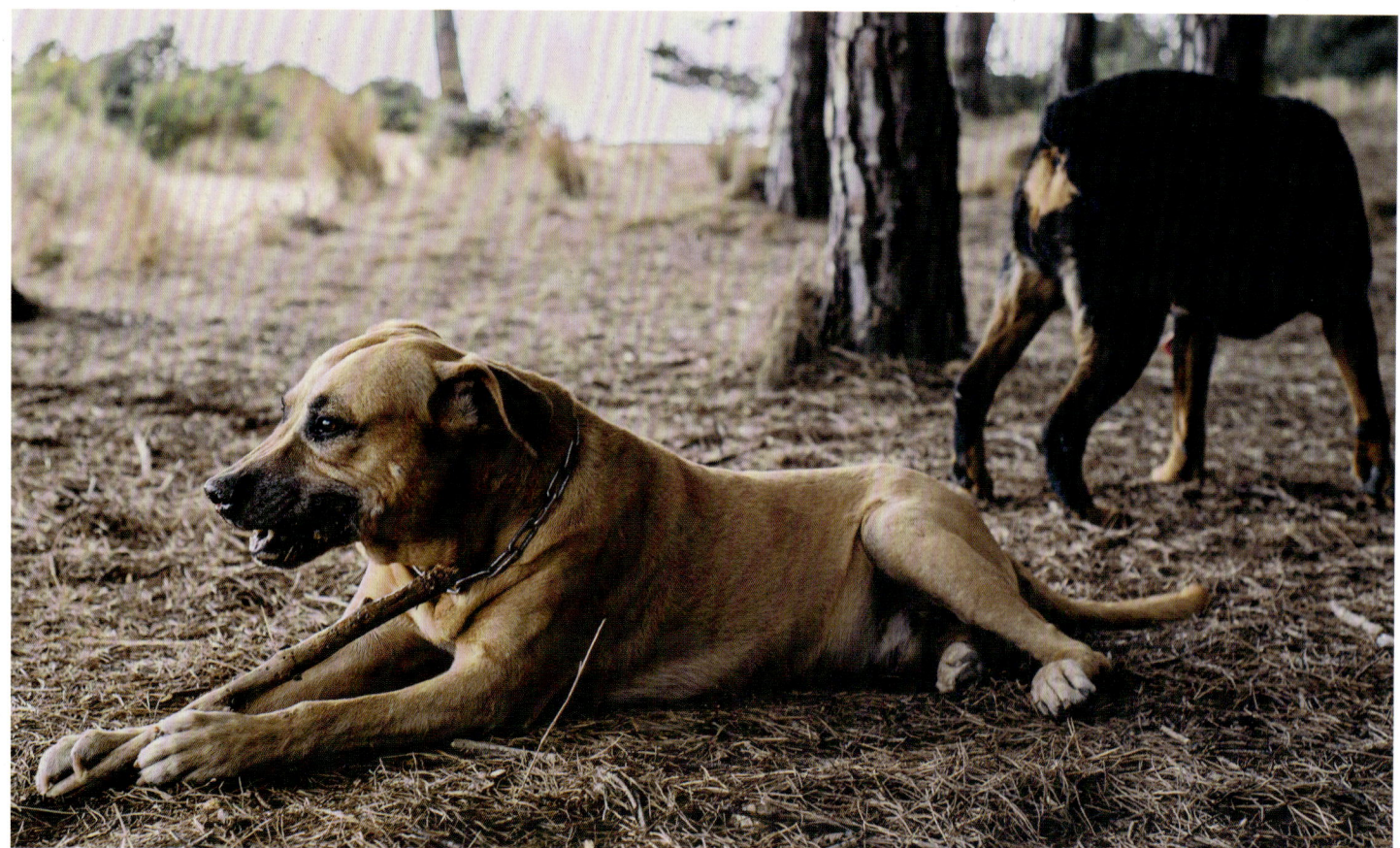

ABOVE:
Out in pampas
The cimarron comes from the grasslands and woodlands of Uruguay.

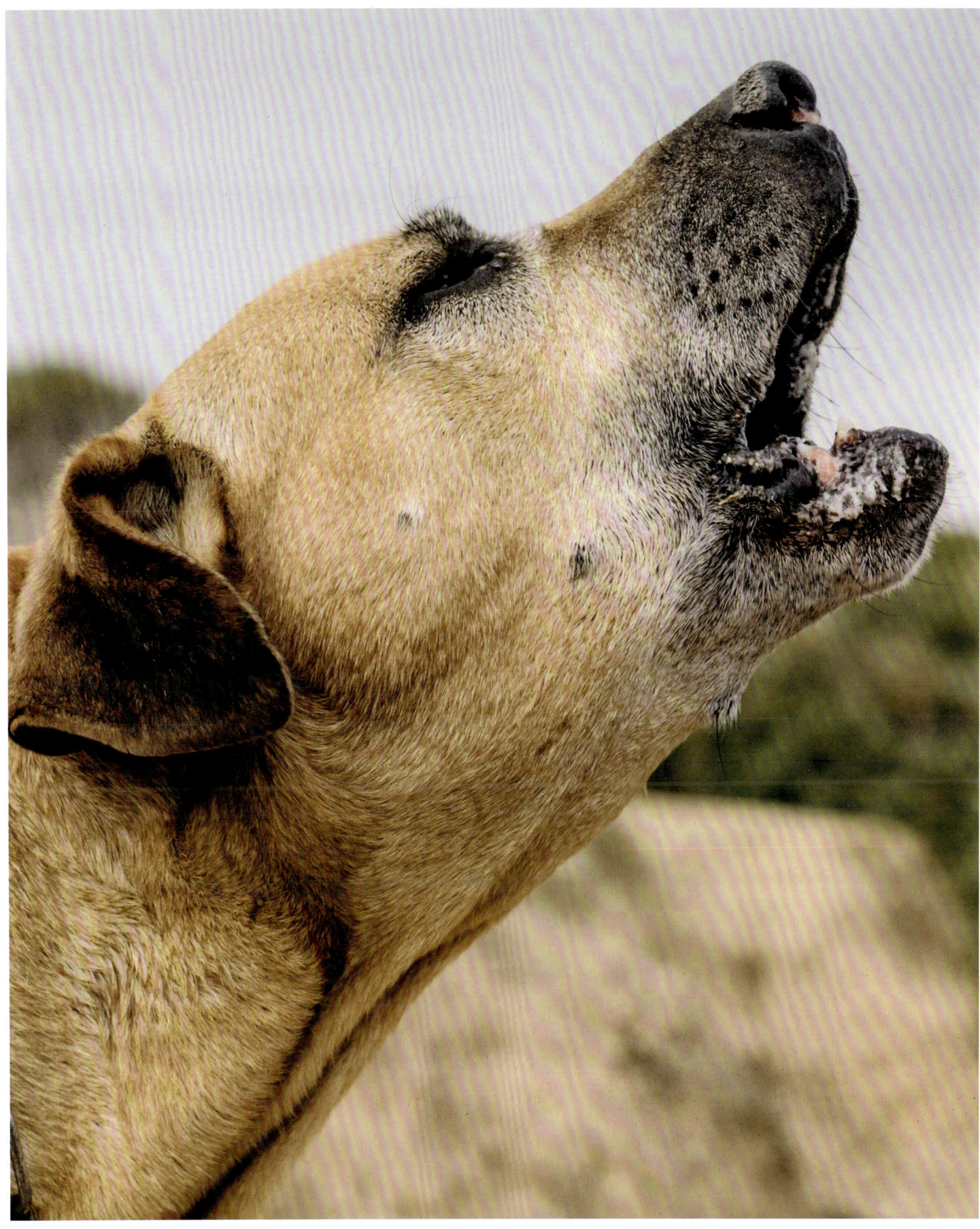

ABOVE:
Half wild
The Uruguayan cimarron has one foot in the wild world, having only recently been brought back into domesticity.

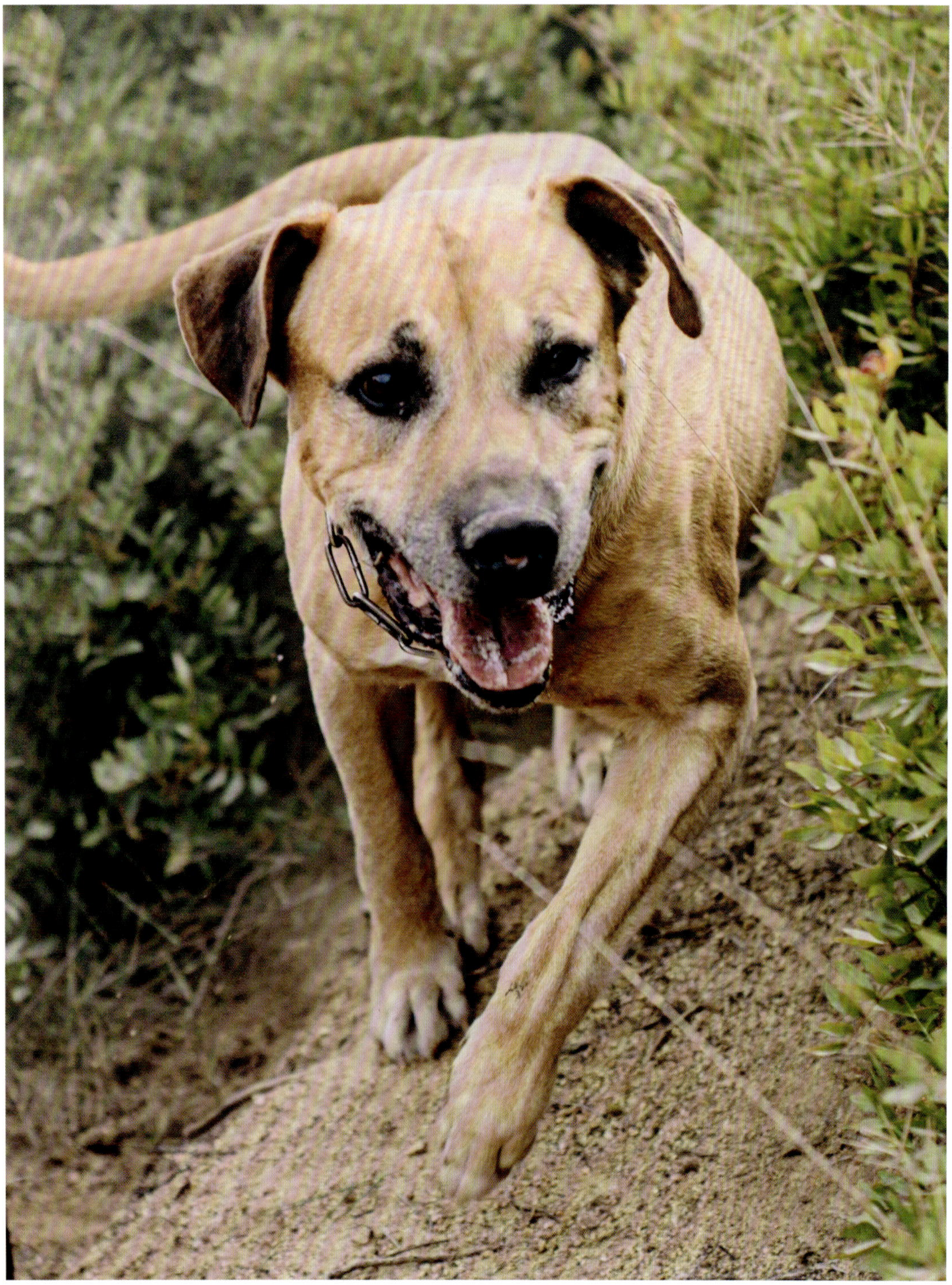

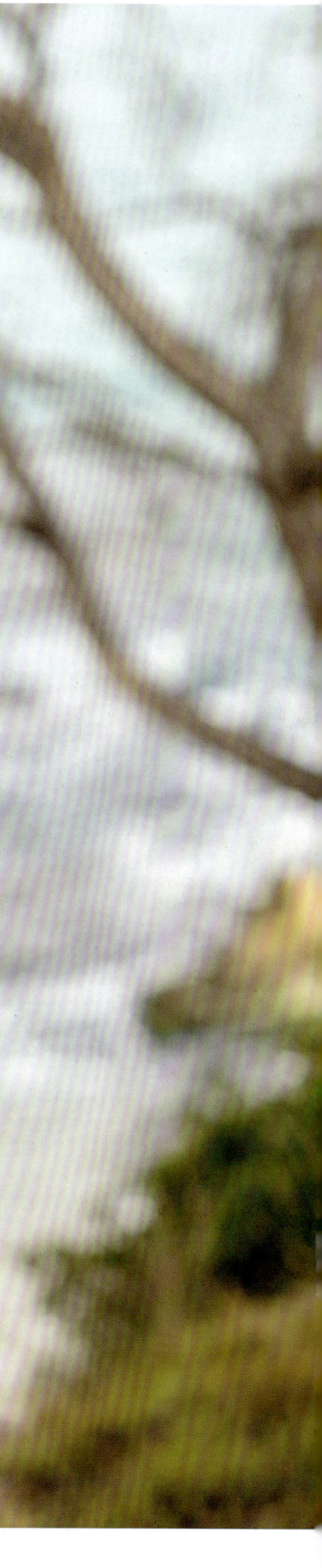

BOTH PHOTOGRAPHS:
Ready for adventure
The short coat of this breed needs regular grooming from owners to ensure proper hygiene and maintenance.

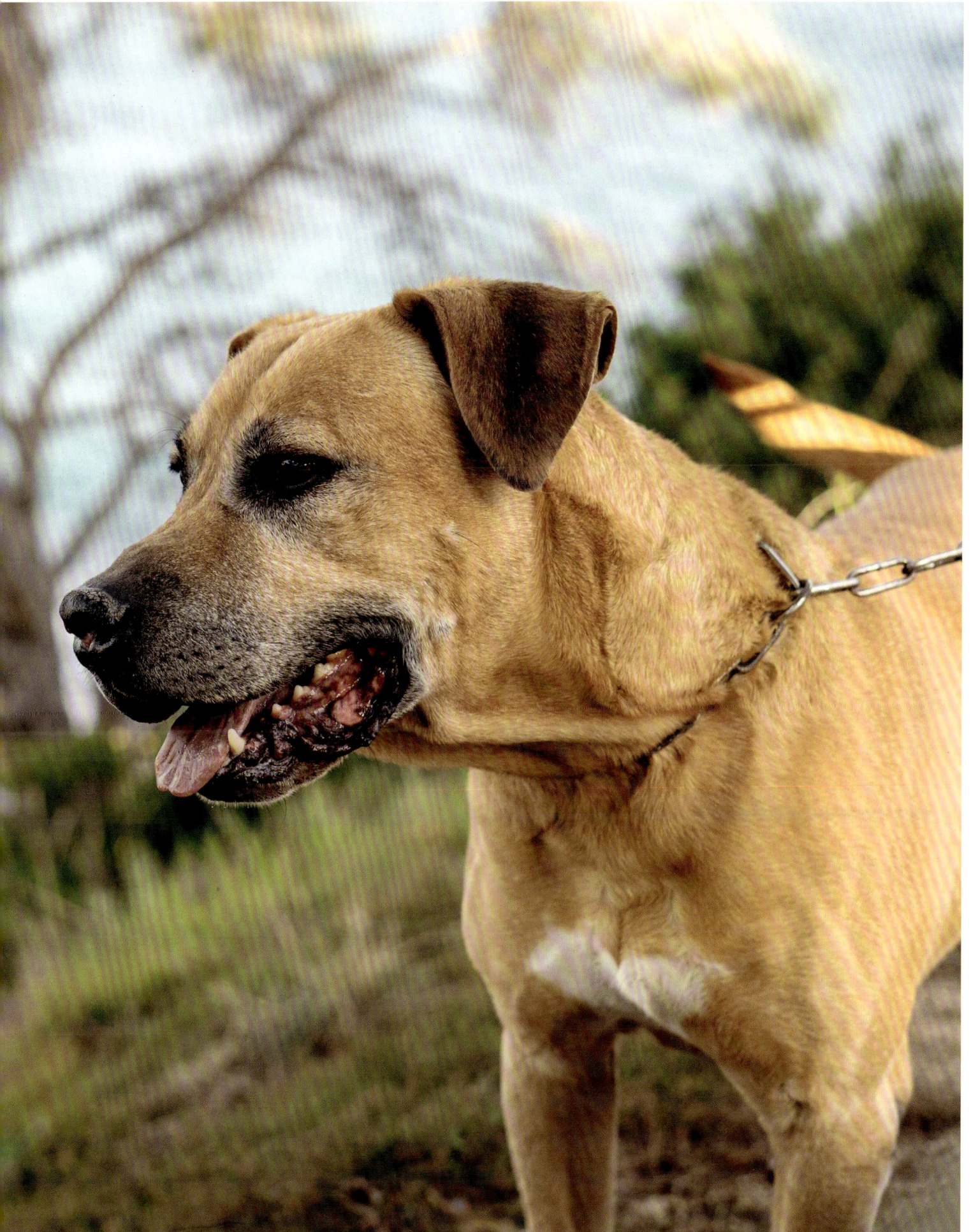

WORKING DOGS

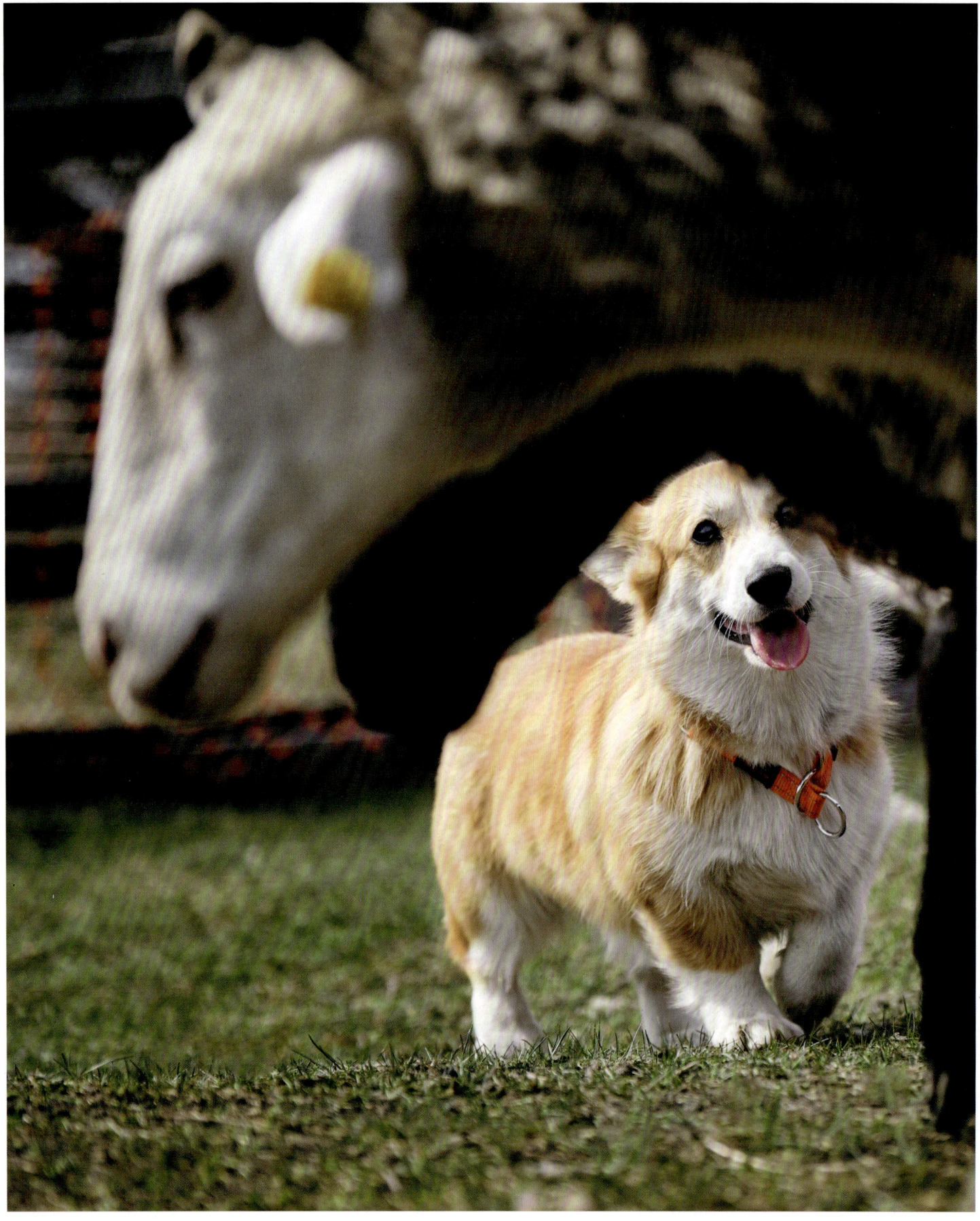

ABOVE:
Busy busy
Corgis are busy little herding dogs and they are always on the go.

Welsh Corgi

CHARACTERISTICS

Coat
Harsh, short coat that is red, sable, fawn, and black and tan, with or without white markings

Height
25–31cm (10–12in)

Weight
9–17kg (20–37lb)

Lifespan
12–15 years

Personality
Alert and confident

Origin
Wales

The corgi breed is a type of small herding dog that originated in west Wales and has found a second lease of life as popular companion dogs. There are two varieties: the Pembroke corgi and the Cardigan corgi. These two breeds have different ancestors. The Cardigan breed has rounded ears and long tails, while the Pembroke dogs have pointed ears and short tails. They both have the short-legged stature that earns them the corgi name, which means "dwarf dog" in Welsh.

The corgi has a storied history. Henry I of England set up a community of Flemish weavers in western Wales to create fine tapestries and carpets. The migrants tended sheep and cattle to create wool, leather and other raw materials and they brought herding dogs to control this livestock. The corgi breeds were developed from this original stock. More recently the Pembroke corgi had a world famous fan in Elizabeth II, another British monarch.

The little dogs can be surprisingly agile despite the small stature. The dogs drive cattle with nips to the ankle, and they can dart back and forth, all the while avoiding being trampled. Puppies will nip their owners by instinct and need to be corrected at an early age.

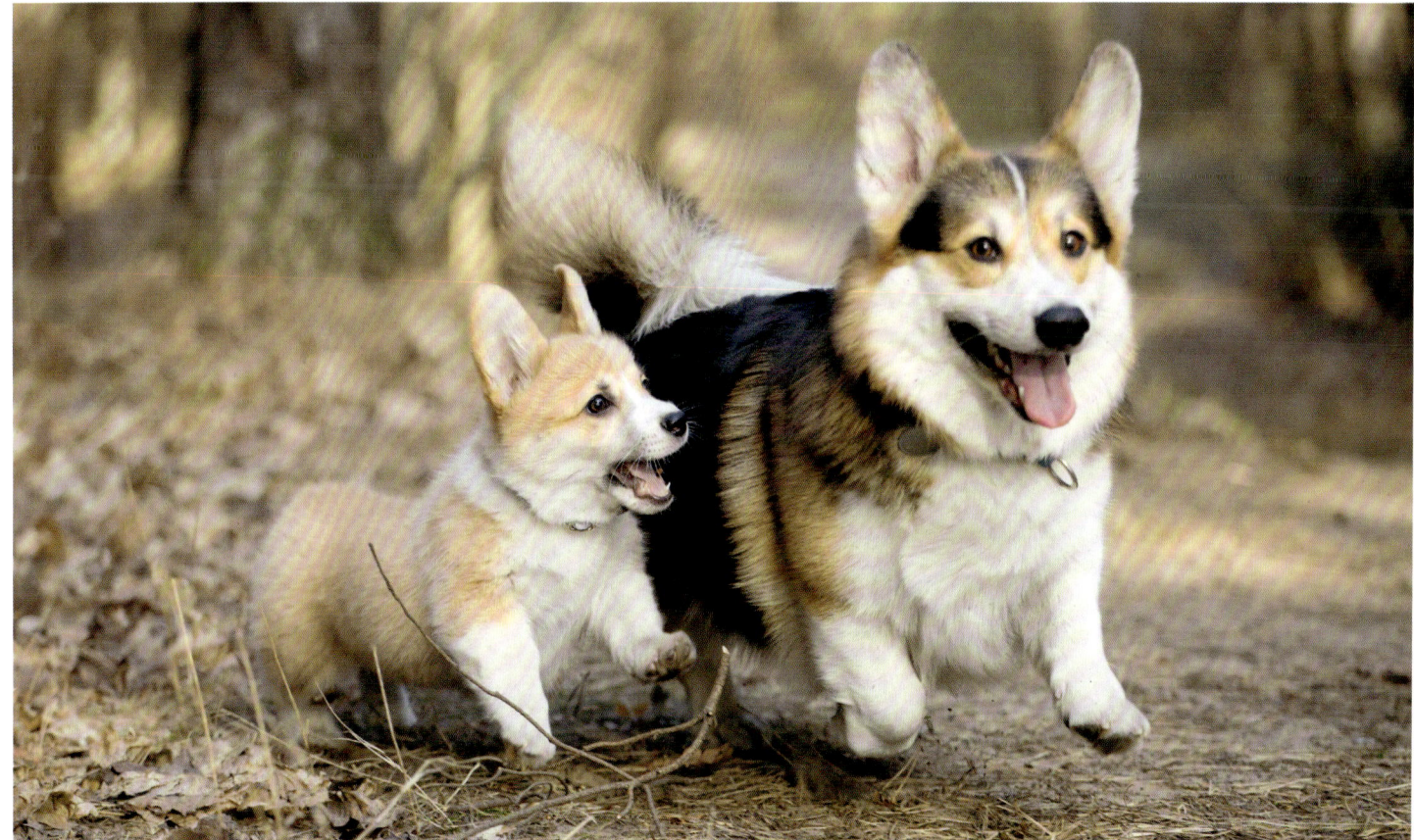

ABOVE:
Happy to be there
Welsh corgis are known for their low height and long body.

WORKING DOGS

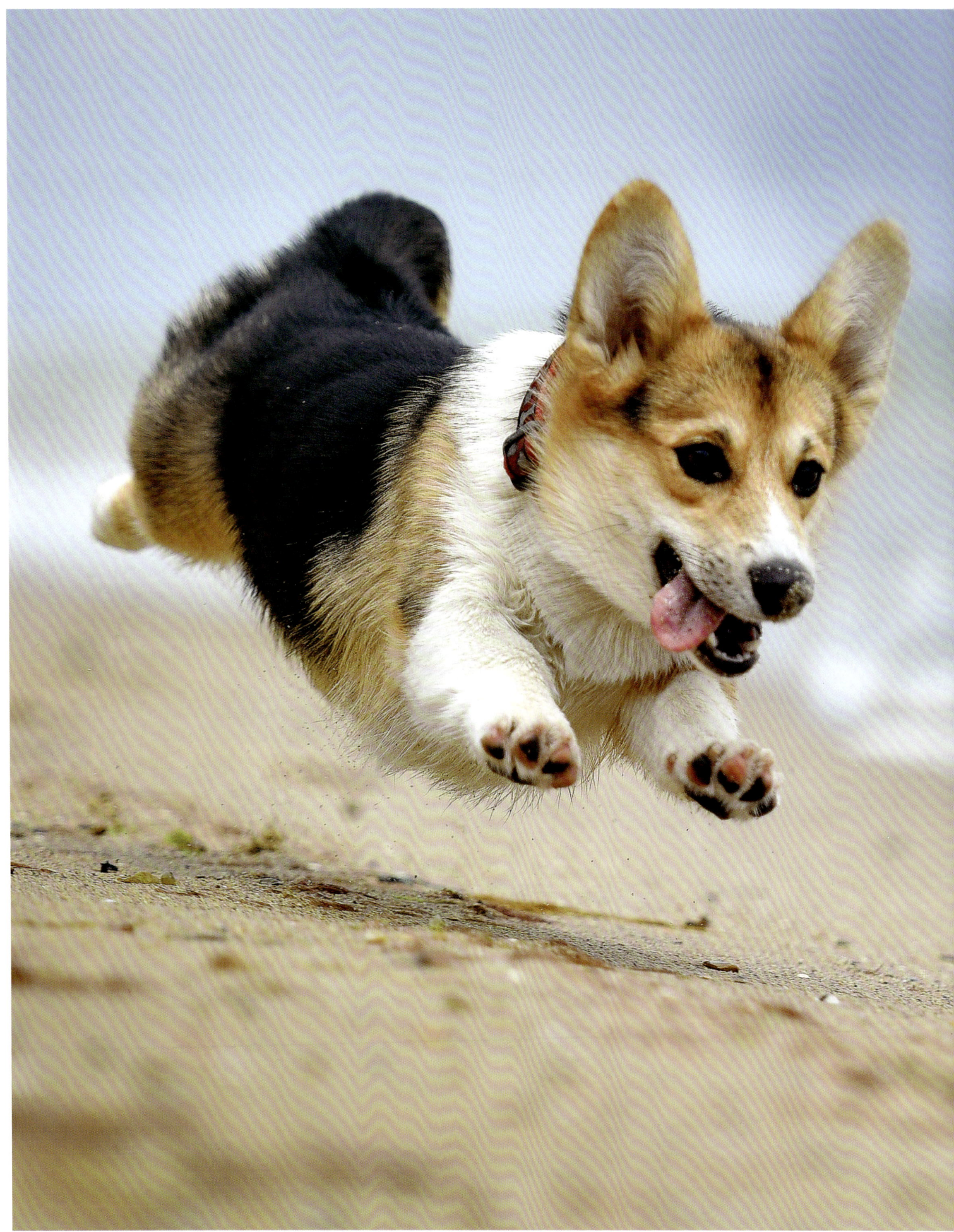

WORKING DOGS

Fun and games
Corgis tend to have upwards facing, erect ears and an intelligent expression as they bound along in enjoyment.

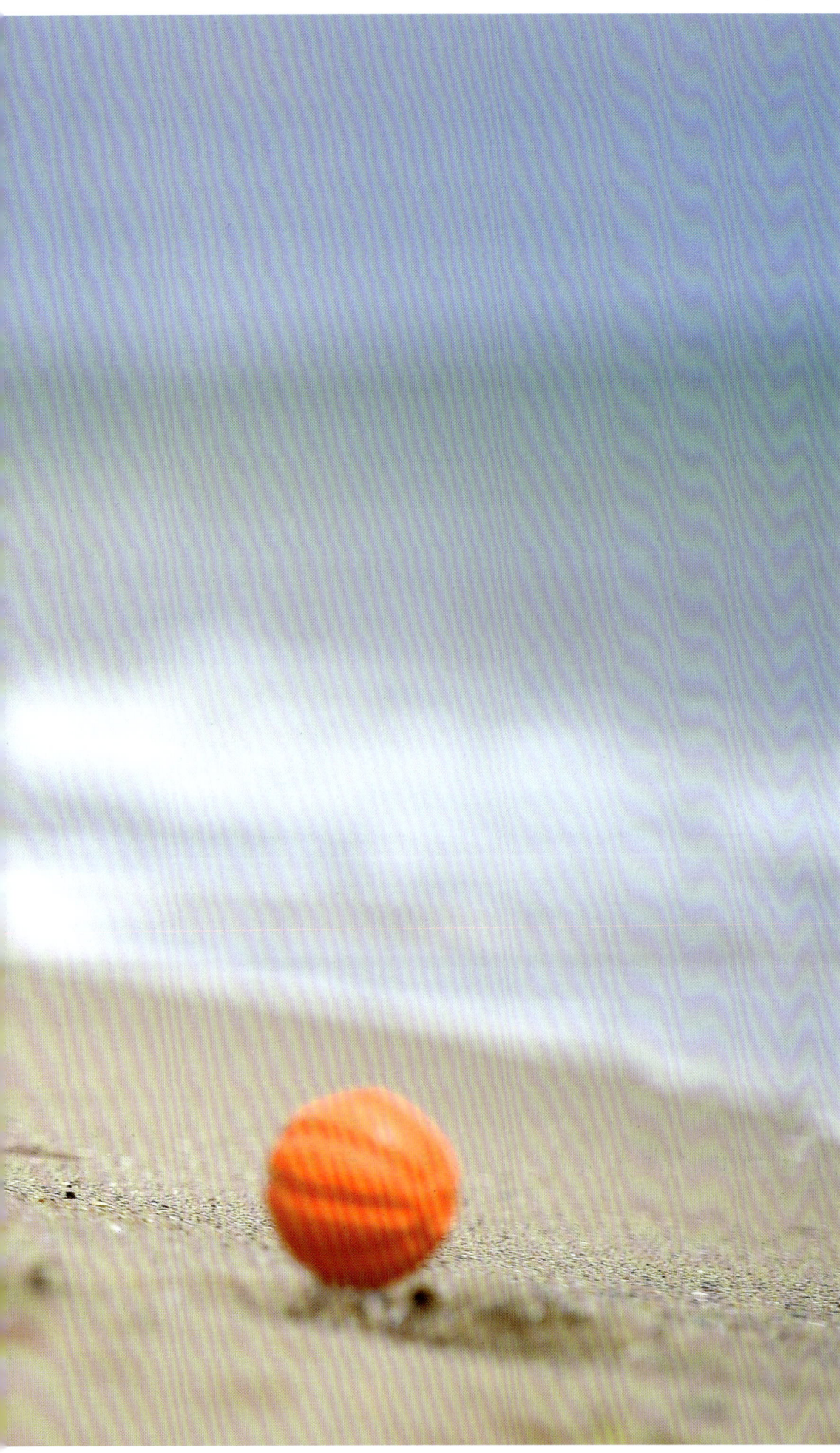

Index

Affenpinscher	10
Afghan Hound	168
Airedale	174
Akita Inu	180
Alaskan Malamute	294
American English Coonhound	186
American Eskimo Dog	300
American Foxhound	240
Anatolian Shepherd Dog	302
Australian Cattle Dog	306
Basenji	312
Basset Hound	188
Beagle	192
Bedlington Terrier	12
Bernese Mountain Dog	316
Bichon Frise	14
Bloodhound	198
Border Collie	320
Border Terrier	16
Borzoi	204
Bouvier Des Flandres	328
Boxer	330
British Mastiff	334
Brittany Spaniel	206
Brussels Griffon	20
Bullmastiff	338
Cavalier King Charles Spaniel	26
Cesky Terrier	32
Chesapeake Bay Retriever	210
Chihuahua	36
Chow Chow	40
Clumber Spaniel	42
Cocker Spaniel	46
Cockerpoo	50
Dachshund (standard)	214
Dalmatian	52
Doberman pinscher	220
English Bulldog	344
English Bull Terrier	22
English Foxhound	242
English Pointer	230
English Setter	232
English Springer Spaniel	234
French Bulldog	60
German Pointer	246
German Shepherd Dog	348
German Spitz	64
Goldendoodle	66
Golden Retriever	68
Great Dane	356
Greenland Dog	358
Hungarian Vizsla	250
Ibizan Hound	252
Irish Setter	256
Irish Terrier	72
Irish Wolfhound	258
Italian Spinone	262
Jack Russell Terrier	74
Japanese Chin	78
Komondor	362

Kooikerhondje	80
Kromfohrländer	82
Labradoodle	84
Labrador Retriever	88
Lagotto Romagnolo	96
Leonberger	366
Lhasa Apso	100
Lurcher	104
Maremma Sheepdog	372
Mexican hairless	108
Munsterlander	266
Neapolitan Mastiff	376
Newfoundland	380
Norfolk Terrier	110
Norwegian Buhund	384
Norwegian Elkhound	224
Old English Sheepdog	386
Otterhound	268
Papillon	114
Pekingese	118
Pharaoh Hound	122
Pinscher	126
Pomeranian	128
Portuguese Podengo	130
Pug	132
Puggle	136
Pyrenean Mountain Dog	392
Rhodesian Ridgeback	272
Romanian Shepherd Dog	396
Rottweiler	400
Rough Collie	402
Russian Toy	138
Saluki	274
Samoyed	406
Schnauzer (giant)	408
Scottish Terrier	140
Shar Pei	410
Shetland Sheepdog	414
Shiba Inu	278
Shih Tzu	144
Siberian Husky	418
Smooth Collie	424
Smooth Fox Terrier	56
Spanish Water Dog	280
Saint Bernard	428
Staffordshire Bull Terrier	148
Standard Schnauzer	432
Swedish Elkhound	228
Swiss Hound	284
Tibetan Mastiff	434
Tibetan Spaniel	150
Tibetan Terrier	152
Uruguayan Cimarron	438
Weimaraner	286
Welsh Corgi	442
Welsh Terrier	156
West Highland White Terrier	160
Whippet	288
Wire Fox Terrier	58
Yorkshire Terrier	162

Picture Credits

Alamy: 6 (Zoonar GmbH), 34 (Tierfotoagentur), 42 left (Phils Pet Picuters), 43 (Dempster Dogs), 76 (Veronika Gaudet), 82 (Imagebroker), 83 (Zoonar GmbH), 92 bottom (William Mullins), 112 (bob langrish), 124 (Zoonar GmbH), 131 (Stephen Chung), 142 (Tierfotoagentur), 146 top (Thierry GRUN), 147 (Tierfotoagentur), 164 (Dmytro Zinkevych), 166 (Jim Gibson), 173 top (Kelly Rann), 176/177 (Juniors Bildarchiv GmbH), 194 (Stephen Flint), 199 (Farlap), 201 (Kitti Kilian), 202 top & 203 (Farlap), 218 (Jitka Cernohorska), 226/227 (Minden Pictures), 236/237 (Farlap), 266 (Imago), 268 (Loop Images Ltd), 269 (Adam Stoltman), 284 (Nikolay Vinokurov), 292 (Wayne Hutchinson), 296 (blickwinkel), 297 bottom (Farlap), 308/309 (Juniors Bildarchiv GmbH), 310/311 (imageBroker), 314 (MariaItina), 320 & 322/323 (Wayne Hutchinson), 327 (Farlap), 328 left (agefotostock), 330 (Panoramic Images), 332 (Tierfotoagentur), 333 (David Bagnall), 350 (Andrey Kuzmin), 351 top (Alun Jenkins), 354 (Juniors Bildarchiv GmbH), 355 (Andrey Kuzmin), 358 (incamerastock), 359 (Vincent Lowe), 367 (David Bagnall), 381 (Phil Rees), 389 (Raywoo), 390/391 (Tommy Louth), 392 (Hemis), 393 left (Biosphoto), 395 (Janet Horton), 416 bottom (Gloria Anderson), 435 (Kim Hammar), 438, 439, 440 & 441 (Dolores Preciado)

Dreamstime: 11 (Samonovakovic), 12 (Jennifer59), 15 (Lu Wenzhi), 16 (Melanie Horne), 25 (Eladon), 29 (Chloe23), 30 (Lenkadan), 42 right (Volodymyr Finoshkin), 44/45 (Radomír Režný), 50 (Chrisukphoto), 54 (Tkatsai), 55 (Anke Van Wyk), 60 (Natalia Guseva), 61 (Patryk Kosmider), 68 left (Mathayward), 70/71 (Mvaligursky), 72 (Bagicat), 85 (Adamelnyk), 88 (Izadoodle), 96 left (Bakalaerozzphotography), 97 (Aerogondo), 100 (Woodygraphs), 101 (Ruthblack), 110 & 113 bottom (Robbinsbox), 116 (Cynoclub), 122 (Garosha), 128 (Iprabbitme), 130 (phoenixlabs), 136 (Kieranvyas), 149 (Ekaterina Kurakina), 165 (Saz1977), 170/171 (Anna63), 172 (Pixbilder), 173 bottom (otsphoto), 184/185 (Nkarol), 196 (Baykal11), 200 (Chinook203), 202 bottom (Sushytska), 239 (Briansedgbeer), 249 (Joopsnijder), 254 (Dragonika), 260/261 (Karinvanklaveren), 270 (Lourdesphotography), 271 both (Madrabothair), 281 (Wirestock), 283 (Ttretjak), 316 (Toryceli), 318 top (Ankevanwyk), 319 (Teekaygee), 329 (Dasya11), 342 both (Elisabethhammerschmid), 347 (Andrei51), 349 left (otsphoto), 352 (Vladgalenko), 357 (Gbelu1), 363 (Lovasz), 402 (Wirestock), 409 (Pavel1964), 419 (Kadmy), 422/423 (Troutnut), 424 left (Meinkleinesfotohaus), 424 right (TaraWilllow Photography), 442 (Kobalnova)

Getty Images: 137 (Shaw Photography Co), 198 (Cavan Images)

Shutterstock: 5 (AndyBir), 8 (Ann Lillie), 10 (Didkovska Ilona), 13 (Sue Thatcher), 14 (Lucky Business), 17 (rebeccaashworthearle), 18/19 (Colin Seddon), 20 (otsphoto), 21 (Vera Shcher), 22 (Miroshnikova Arina), 23 & 24 (Eve Photography), 26 left (Todor Rusinov), 26 right (Pautova Iuliia), 27 (Roman Milavin), 28 top (Metz Eric), 28 bottom (otsphoto), 31 (Bigandt.com), 32 (Sevostyanova Tatyana), 33 (Sue Thatcher), 35 (Sevostyanova Tatyana), 36 (Olena Tselykh), 37 (Lesia Kapinosova), 38 (otsphoto), 39 (Ratchat), 40 (Natalia Fesiun), 41 (Bigandt.com), 46 (Photobox.ks), 47 (Anna Krivitskaya), 48 (slastena), 49 (Jan Hejda), 51 (mountaintreks), 52 (Tanya Consaul Photography), 53 (Yulia YasPe), 56 (Olga Kurguzova), 57 (Gorodenkoff), 58 (TSViPhoto), 59 (Angyalosi Beata), 62 (Izergil), 63 (Eve Photography), 64 (U Photo), 65 (Lenkadan), 66 (Tara Lynn and Co), 67 (Marcello Sgarlato), 68 right (Lunja), 69 (Tatyana Vyc), 73 left (otsphoto), 73 right (Mariya Kuzema), 74 bottom left (dezy), 74 bottom right (Inna Skaldutska), 75 (Lubo Ivanko), 77 (Maryshot), 77 bottom (Dulova Olga), 78 (everydoghasastory), 79 (KaliAntye), 80 (Bigandt.com), 81 (Nordicfotos), 84 (sophiecat), 86/87 (EvgeniiAnd), 89 (My July), 90/91 (Tosha174), 92 top (fotorince), 93 (manusho), 94/95 (Africa Studio), 96 right (BarthFotografie), 98/99 (Jne Valokuvaus), 102/103 (SubertT), 104 (Kerry Ball Photography), 105 (Sue Thatcher), 106/107 (Kevin Mallon), 108 & 109 (Kalinina Maria), 111 (LukesDogPhotography), 113 top (Sue Thatcher), 114 (AndyBir), 115 (Reshetnikov art), 117 top (OlesyaNickolaeva), 117 bottom (Malivan Iuliia), 118 (Wirestock Creators), 119 (N Design), 120 top (Rita Kochmarjova), 120 bottom (Oksana Valiukevic), 121 (Kozub Vasyl), 123 (Ivanova N), 125 (Kseniya Resphoto), 126 (Dora Zett), 127 (everydoghasastory), 129 (Gucciwithfendi), 132 (gp88), 133 (studio37th), 134 (Natalia Fedosova), 135 (MVolodymyr), 138 (Alexandra Kruspe), 139 (Liudmila Bohush), 140 (Dmitri Zoubov), 141 (Robert Wedderburn), 143 (Stephen Dukelow), 144 (Sue Thatcher), 145 (Nanako Yamanaka), 146 bottom (Anna Kantowicz), 148 (Nikola Cedikova), 150 (Mikko Suhonen), 151 (Juntune), 152 (Diwali), 153 & 154 (Slavica Stajic), 155 top (Tomislav Stajduhar), 155 bottom (manfredxy), 156 & 157 (MaCross Photography), 158/159 (Thorsten Henning Photo), 160 (EMT100), 161 (OlgaOvcharenko), 162 (Zanna Pesnina), 163 (Kislitskaya Natallia), 164 top (alexkatkov), 168 (WildStrawberry), 169 (Anna Tronova), 174 (Slav Productions), 175 (Julia Siomuha), 178/179 (Lumia Studio), 180 (Lunja), 181 (Yura Devyatov), 182/183 (PardoY), 186 (richard pross), 187 (Adithya photography), 188 (Ksenia Raykova), 189 (Anna Tronova), 190/191 (Billion Photos), 192 left (Ira Bushanska), 192 right (Ignacy Sedlak), 193 (tetiana u), 195 (Lenkadan), 197 top (New Africa), 197 bottom (Igor Normann), 204 (Editos foto), 205 (George Trumpeter), 206 (Johnnie Laws), 207 (Sherry Scholl), 208/209 (Elmira N), 210 (Ricantimages), 211 (everydoghasastory), 212 (Kerrie T), 213 (Charlotte Lehman), 214 (Deniew), 215 (Denys R), 216/217 (Shedara Weinsberg), 219 both (Liliya Kulianionak), 220 (alekta), 221 (Hakase 420), 222/223 (DragoNika), 224 (Vladimir Berny), 225 (Brenton Hilbig), 228 left (Desislava Ilieva), 228 right (Robert Nyholm), 229 (Ilkka Koivula), 230 (Wirestock Creators), 231 (Jelena Safronova), 232 (zoyas2222), 233 (Lina Christa), 234 (Aneta Jungerova), 235 (otsphoto), 238 (Ivanova N), 240 (Cavan-Images), 241 (Olga Aniven), 242 (Pavel Ivashechkin), 243 (Angela Lock), 244/245 (Mick Atkins), 246 (Burry van den Brink), 247 (Goldmoon), 248 (Vitalii Mamchuk), 250 (Ivanova N), 251 (aliaksei kruhlenia), 252 (svetastar), 253, 255 both & 256 (DragoNika), 257 (Irina Shatilova), 258 (84kamila), 259 (Jolanta Beinarovica), 262 & 263 (AnetaZabranska), 264 (Zuzule), 265 (AnetaZabranska), 267 (skapuka), 272 (Ivanova N), 273 left (Christian Mueller), 273 right (olgagorovenko), 274 left (Natalia Fedosova), 274 right (Maria Ivanushkina), 275 (nik174), 276 (SubertT), 277 top (Natalia Fedosova), 277 bottom (krushelss), 278 (Robert Way), 279 (Ermolaeva Olga 84), 280 (Daz Stock), 282 (otsphoto), 285 (Radomir Rezny), 286 (Alexey Gorkiy), 287 (Callipso88), 288 (Anna List), 289 (Dora Zett), 290/291 (Natallia Yaumenenka), 294 left (Tatyana Kuznetsova), 294 right (netapics), 295 (Kate Lussier), 297 top (Colombo Nicola), 298/299 (Vivienstock), 300 & 301 (William F. Cermak), 302 (CharlitoCZ), 303 (safakcakir), 304/305 (Degtyaryov Andrey), 306 (Irina Nedikova), 307 (OlgaOvcharenko), 312 (Dimedrol68), 313 (Verbitskaya Juliya), 315 (alekta), 317 (Rita Kochmarjova), 318 bottom (Eve Photography), 321 (Photo Spirit), 324/325 (Puhach Andrei), 324 bottom (artpage), 325 bottom (Vera Reva), 326 (Krasula), 328 right (miyajima), 331 (cynoclub), 334 (Monica Arauz), 335 (Mikanah), 336 (Ysbrand Cosijn), 337 (Mikanah), 338, 339 & 340/341 (Michael J Magee), 343 (Sergey Lavrentev), 344 (Irene Miller), 345 (ltummy), 346 both (Rita Kochmarjova), 348 (Al Er), 349 right (Pixel Shot), 351 bottom (VAKS-Stock Agency), 353 (cynoclub), 356 (Guy J. Sagi), 360/361 (Chris Christophersen), 362 (devor1), 364 (Ershov Andrey), 365 top (Utekhina Anna), 365 bottom (vkysnoefoto), 366 (AnetaZabranska), 368/369 (Colin Seddon), 370/371 (Mucktin), 372 (marco branchi), 373 (Miroshnikova Arina), 374/375 (M. Rohana), 376 & 377 (wireful), 378 (Ricantimages), 379 (Evgeniia Shikhaleeva), 380 (Pandas), 382/383 (Anastasia Samuel), 384 (Wirestock Creators), 385 (Lenka Molcanyiova), 386 left (chrisukphoto), 386 right (Crystal Alba), 387 (chrisukphoto), 388 (Kate Grishakova), 393 right (PhilipImage), 394 (vvvita), 396 (Gelu Popa), 397 (Mikadun), 398 (Mike Pellinni), 399 (Slatan), 400 (Serova Ekaterina), 401 (otsphoto), 403 (Daz Stock), 404/405 (Lisjatina), 406 (Zanna Pesnina), 407 (Vivienstock), 408 (Elena Kutepova), 410 (ohqpi), 411 (Tanja Tatic), 412 top (VKarlov), 412 bottom (Svetography), 413 (Ricantimages), 414 (Piotr Piatrouski), 415 (OlgaOvcharenko), 416 top & 417 (Lisjatina), 418 (areporter), 420/421 (Vivienstock), 425 (Yps71), 426 (Harald Kreuzer), 427 (Yps71), 428 (Rita Kochmarjova), 429 (fred12), 430 (Rita Kochmarjova), 431 top (Ulrike Stein), 431 bottom (Alfaguarilla), 432 left (Eve Photography), 432 right & 433 (Christian Mueller), 434, 436 & 437 (Kat marinina), 443 (Vera Reva), 444/445 (MDavidova)